HEGARTY
ON ADVERTISING

HEGARTY
ON ADVERTISING
TURNING INTELLIGENCE INTO MAGIC

JOHN HEGARTY

105 illustrations, 84 in color

Thames & Hudson

To Anne Hegarty, for being so inspiring

For captions for the images on page 2 see page 222

First published in 2011 in hardcover in the United States
of America by Thames & Hudson Inc., 500 Fifth Avenue,
New York, New York 10110

thamesandhudsonusa.com

Library of Congress Catalog Card Number 2010936750

ISBN 978-0-500-51556-3

Printed and bound in China by Imago

Contents

Preface

What makes advertising such a fascinating industry and why does it have so much to teach us?

It is, of course, an essential component of any competitive market economy: driving growth and dynamism throughout its numerous industries.

It's also everywhere, you can't escape it. And it's unique in that you don't have to pay to see it, it's thrust upon you. And this can be a problem when so much of it is so poor. I suppose one could say the same about any creatively driven industry. How many good movies did you see last year?

But, at its best, this unique mixture of art and commerce is engaging, entertaining and informative. Look at advertising from any era and you get a unique insight into society at that time: its loves, fears, wants and needs.

It has to capture the zeitgeist. Sometimes reflecting it and sometimes, as with our Levi's advertising, helping to create it.

It's an industry that is constantly moving forward. Yesterday's idea is exactly that, yesterday's. What's new? What's next? How can one brand gain competitive advantage over another? These are the forces that drive us from one day to the next. And whatever you do in our industry, from creative, to planning, to account handling, to media thinking, you'll find exciting, funny, knowledgeable and stimulating people. It's an industry made of entrepreneurs. It's also an industry that will prepare you for almost any other business: it's fast moving, challenging, smart and inquisitive, built on the need for competitive advantage.

It's also one of the most egalitarian industries in which you can work. No one cares where you were born, where you went to school or who you do or don't know. Just think, two boys born in Baghdad to Iraqi Jewish parents became two of the most powerful people in the UK. You've all heard of Maurice and Charles Saatchi. It cares for only one thing: ideas. And have you got any?

It was Andrew Sanigar at Thames & Hudson who suggested I embark on this endeavour. Initially, I said, 'You must be joking, I'm an art director not a writer'. No problem, he said, we'll only need about 60,000 words. 60,000 words, I exclaimed, I've spent most of my life trying to make things shorter, not longer. Creativity in advertising is all about the power of reduction. Write less, say more. 60,000 words does not sound like less to me.

John Hegarty, 2008
Photographer:
Andy Paradise

As you can witness, I succumbed. I remembered some wise words from the author Frank Delaney, who, after meeting me, said, 'So, John, when are you going to write your book?' I replied with my stock answer, 'I'm an art director, I do the pictures'. Frank looked at me somewhat puzzled and said, 'But, John, writing is just describing pictures'. I was reminded of these words of wisdom as I said yes and put pen to paper. Writing is really just a series of linked-up images.

After 45 years in the business I'd seen and experienced a fair amount that might just be interesting to the odd student of advertising. And not just advertising but business. I was at the forefront of the creative revolution that swept through the boardrooms of our industry, destroying many and promoting others. A unique period of change and innovation, which broke down barriers, captured the public's imagination, creating famous brands and making and breaking governments, while also witnessing Britain emerge as a creative powerhouse in the world.

I reckoned that might be worth a comment or two.

But why write a book on advertising now?

Surely advertising is an industry that is under threat, its future in certain doubt? Belief and confidence are collapsing all around us. Headlines in the media constantly predict advertising's imminent passing as others gloat over its inability to cope with the digital age.

'Old media' is being dealt body blows as the impact of new technology sweeps all before it. The four horsemen of the apocalypse, 'digital', 'free', 'customization' and 'search', pronounce the impending doom. You can either slash your wrists now or download some Leonard Cohen. His *Bird on the Wire* might do the trick!

I think this makes it the perfect moment to comment on the advertising industry. Under threat it most certainly is, but unlike other creative industries advertising is always under threat. Innovation in both business philosophy and technology is always a challenge and advertising continuously has to rise to those challenges – that's what makes it so exciting.

Photography was supposed to put paid to painting, as television was going to kill both radio and the cinema. Now the doomsayers have it that the web is going to destroy television as it is doing with newspapers, at the hands of free news sites. And let's not even talk about the music industry.

Ironic, isn't it, that the word 'free', supposedly the most powerful word in the lexicon of advertising, could be the word that destroys it?

Well, maybe not.

But rather than debate the state of the advertising industry we should look at what is happening to the brands. And how they are having to behave in this evolving digital, social networking world. The function of advertising is simply to promote and sustain competitive advantage for brands. So, the key to the future is how the public are going to interact with them.

You could say that today we're all in the fashion business. As function fades into the background we expect things to work properly. In fact, not only expect it, but actually demand that they do. When was the last time your car broke down? These days you might hardly even have to go to the garage for a service. The function of an object is now taken for granted, so our concern shifts from function to form. We want it to look right. Just as you buy the latest fashion, so you can equip your home with the must-have gadgets. Brands such as Alessi are as much in the fashion business as they are in the appliance industry. Today, a product's emotional appeal is as important as its functional abilities.

The food we eat, the kitchens we cook in, the places we live, the holidays we take and the cars we drive have to look and feel right as much as they have to perform.

Technology and innovation play a fundamental role in all of this – digital technology has revolutionized our behaviour and it will go on doing so. But it's those brands that understand our need – our desire – to be entertained, engaged and excited by what they offer that will succeed. James Dyson has convinced many of us to pay an extraordinary amount of money for a vacuum cleaner. Until Dyson vacuum cleaners came to market I didn't have a clue which brand of vacuum cleaner I had. I never once participated in a dinner party conversation about the merits of bagless technology versus that of conventional sucking. Sucking could have been a topic of conversation during an evening out, but certainly not with regards to vacuum cleaners.

James Dyson, with his innovative technology and stylish design, has convinced us that a machine that is never put on display, spends most of its time in a dark cupboard and we probably never use is a must-have home appliance. What an achievement! Just as brown is the new black (or is it the new blue?), a Dyson is the thing to have. Dyson's customers love them because they tell themselves that it does a better job – a bagless vacuum cleaner sucks better. But really they love it because it makes them feel better. Just like the latest fashion. This is called the fickle application of logic – which is what fashion is.

So just as I believe we're increasingly in the fashion business, we're also in the entertainment industry. In fact, you could argue that advertising, from the moment it was born, was trying to entertain us.

What is interesting is how the two worlds of fashion and entertainment have now blended. Remember the days when the only ads the movie stars would appear in were those Japanese ones? The movie *Lost in*

Translation captured the absurdity of that phenomenon brilliantly. Now, however, you can't open a copy of some fashion bible without being confronted by an Oscar-laden phalanx of stars advertising everything and anything from perfume to clothes to luggage to coffee machines.

Exposure is everything. And the more fashionable that is, the better. Fashion is the new entertainment. Or is it the other way round?

For many years the fastest-growing city in the US wasn't Los Angeles, New York or Miami, it was Las Vegas. A city totally dedicated to entertainment.

Now you might not approve of gambling – it leaves me somewhat cold – but as a city Las Vegas is remarkable and it has only one function: entertainment. And it's booming.

The same is true with an increasing number of brands. One of our clients is Unilever who produce Axe, a product targeted at young, emerging males. These post-pubescent teenagers are struggling with over-productive sweat glands that can have an unfortunate side effect: they stink. They're also awash with testosterone and the desire, as they say in the US, 'to lock down some tail'. To you and me that's called dating. The brand's appeal, therefore, is very simple: you're not going to lock down that tail if you smell like a hog on heat. The brand doesn't promote itself in terms of hygiene – what's the point in that? The brand engages with its potential audience by being an aid to seduction. Smell right and you'll have a better chance of catching that girl's attention. The brand is ultimately about confidence – the one ingredient that most teenagers need help with. The real twist for Axe is to play this game and to play it with humour. I know, you know and they know that spraying Axe isn't going to turn them into George Clooney. Of course, it isn't. But this is the dating game and if the game isn't played with humour and style you'll look as though you're trying too hard. And that's not cool. Because we all know it's the cool kids who 'lock down that tail'.

It's amazing what you'll find in a can of deodorant, especially if you present that product not as a functional, practical, efficacious deodorant, but as an aid to dating.

Advertising isn't like some coat that you pull on and off depending on the weather. It has to be an integral part of a brand and stitched into the very heart of a product. It has to touch a nerve end of what makes a brand or product tick and what makes it resonate with the public.

And it doesn't matter how good your grasp is of all the new digital technology today, without understanding those fundamental facts of engaging, entertaining and exciting an audience, digitization isn't going to help you, it will in fact destroy you faster. That's the power of the net.

Technology is having a profound effect on how we communicate. This is often referred to as 'Creative Destruction': the breaking down of old structures and replacing them with new, re-vitalized, dynamic opportunities. For some this is a frightening time, but that, I feel, is misguided.

I see this as a fantastic time to be a practitioner of advertising. Of course, in the maelstrom of digital innovation it's easy to be confused about which direction to take. Or, as John Lennon said, 'How can I go forward when I don't know which way I'm facing?' Despite what Lennon thought, and despite what many futurologists are saying, our business has a stunning future. Far from destroying advertising, technology is opening up multitudes of ways we can communicate. This has to be the most exciting time to be in the communications industry.

As an industry we are one of commerce's finest examples of Darwinian theory. Survival of the smartest. The very essence of a truly creative company is innovation. So to assume we won't innovate our way into the future is nonsense.

So, before you continue, this isn't a 'how to' book. There are far too many of them for our own good. This is my story, laced with experiences, thoughts and examples of how I got to where I am. It's about how all of that moulded my attitudes and my work. Hopefully it will enlighten you and entertain you.

One of the downsides of writing a book like this is not being able to name check all the wonderful people I've had the pleasure of working with. If I were to do that it would have taken up half the book. So to all of them, thank you. You know who you are.

I've subtitled the book 'Turning Intelligence into Magic'. At its simplest this is what has defined BBH's best work and will go on doing so into its future.

Predicting the future is a dangerous business. In fact, the only true prediction about the future is you'll almost certainly be wrong. The world is littered with failed futurologists and luckily for them they're not around to answer for their mistakes. I'm not going to fall into that trap. What I am going to do is talk about the evolving trends in advertising that are going to keep on evolving and some stories, both personal and professional, that tell of what advertising is and what it can be.

If you don't believe that advertising has a future you really shouldn't go any further with this book. Just go to the last chapter on wine and read about that.

But if you want to find out what the possibilities and the adventures in advertising can be, read on…

Introduction

I've been very lucky to be in the right place at the right time enough times. The first stroke of luck in my life was being born in 1944. You might not think it so lucky to be born in London as it endured the closing months of World War II, but it was lucky in that I was born at the start of what became known as 'the baby boom' and was part of a generation that would emerge from the hardships of war and reap the rewards of change that would sweep through Western society.

The world was about to witness the rise of the 'teenager', a word first coined in the US in the late 30s, but which came of age only in the 50s when the post-war generation benefited from a period of time that combined the best of childhood irresponsibility with that of adult awareness – a unique time of freedom and of suspended responsibility. That's why I consider when I was born to be lucky: I witnessed what was certainly one of the most momentous and influential changes ever to occur within our culture – the birth of rock 'n' roll – and saw first hand the effect it had on society and how it signalled the arrival of a youth culture. We still feel those reverberations today.

Being able to experience a 'before' and 'after' gave me an understanding of the importance of the changes that occurred and hold an appreciation of them that affected my awareness forever: music changed, art changed, and fashion, film and television changed. It was a unique period of innovation and experimentation. Suddenly youth had a voice, it wanted to be in charge and it was driving the agenda. ‖ **Life was never going to be the same again.**

But such huge changes are rarely smooth – it felt at times like my rock 'n' roll heroes had appeared too fleetingly, either coming to a tragic end, like Buddy Holly, Ritchie Valens and the Big Bopper in a plane crash on 3 February 1959 (as later commemorated by Don McLean as 'the day the music died' in his hit *American Pie)* or had been subsumed into the grown-up world of responsibility as when Elvis was conscripted into the army in 1958 and finally having to learn how to use a knife and fork. The image of Elvis having his hair cut reminded all in my generation that the dead hand of authority was still able to wield power. It seemed to many of us that rock 'n' roll was over.

I began to lose interest in rock music and turned to jazz. Suddenly I was aware of this other genre of music, especially the modern jazz of Charlie Parker, Miles Davis and John Coltrane. They became my new heroes. The music was cool and so was the look: dark suits, white shirts with knitted ties and, of course, the obligatory Ray-Ban sunglasses. Miles Davis's seminal album *Kind of Blue* became the soundtrack to our lives and the Blue Note album sleeves, the graphic language.

And then, in 1963, the world changed again. The Miles Davis album came off the turntable to be replaced by *Please Please Me* by a new group, The Beatles. Rock 'n' roll was back. || The dark suits and white shirts with black knitted ties were swapped for a pair of hipster trousers and tab-collared gingham shirt from Carnaby Street – when, believe it or not, Carnaby Street was fashionable.

Don McLean was wrong – the music hadn't died, it had just crossed the Atlantic and was being played by four guys from Liverpool.

The effect was shattering: The Beatles not only changed the way we thought about rock 'n' roll, but they also changed the way we thought about rock musicians – they wrote their own music. They weren't controlled by a label telling them what to do. They decided. This was further proof that the world had changed and it wasn't going back. The corporations, the gate keepers, were beginning to lose control.

These momentous cultural changes dramatized my appreciation of creative expression and the impact it has on your psyche, especially when it exists in such stark contrast to everything else. || **The impact, the contrast, the change that was rippling through society would never again be as profound or as dramatic as in those times. These experiences infect your creativity forever.** || As I said, I was very lucky to have been born where and when I was.

The second stroke of luck was the investment of great sums of money by successive British governments in art schools. As a result, in the decades after the end of World War II, while Britain was in industrial decline with a car industry manufacturing unreliable machines that broke down, looked drab and leaked oil and a workforce that seemed to be continually on strike, creativity in art schools flourished.

British art schools of the 50s and 60s were institutions of radical thinking and experimentation – they were a hotbed of innovation. There was no way that the students at those art colleges were going to join a strike-infested British manufacturing industry. They weren't going to sign up for climbing the corporate ladder and joining the local Rotary Club. They were going to write, paint, photograph, design and film. They were going to invent modern Britain.

By 1959 my brother was at St Martin's School of Art, situated on Charing Cross Road in London. Swinging London was still a faint spark at the time but at St Martin's it was blazing red hot: Anthony Caro was teaching the sculpture department how to weld steel girders together, the fine art students were silk screening giant pop art images and the fashion students were designing and making flared trousers and stone washing their 501s. Their hair was worn long and back combed (and I'm talking about the men). Debutantes mixed with the working classes, who mixed with the aspiring middle class. Music, art and fashion mixed with everything. All of which meant that there was really only one class: the creative class. Nobody cared where you came from – they only cared what you were doing and where you were going. Art schools have always been exciting establishments, but none felt more exciting than St Martin's at that moment in time. The air was full of opportunity.

I would find every excuse I had to meet my brother in the school's common room. It felt like a place so far ahead of its time that you could hardly see across the room. || **Everything about it was 'hip' – it had a ceiling decorated with horror movie posters, there would always be someone in a corner reading Jack Kerouac's** *On the Road* **and the soundtrack would invariably be jazz, with Thelonious Monk's** *Round Midnight* **on the turntable, even though it was 2 o'clock in the afternoon.**

While I didn't go to St Martin's, I was part of that generation of art students coming of age in the right place at the right time. I ended up arriving at the London College of Printing (LCP) to study print and design, having had my creative aspirations nurtured at Hornsey Art School in London. It was at Hornsey Art School that Peter Green, one of my brilliant lecturers, encouraged me to try design. || **He realized that I wasn't going** to be the next Picasso and had spotted that I adored ideas and was better at generating them than painting. || It was Peter who pointed me in the direction of the LCP and encouraged me to learn about printing as well as design – printmaking was always at the heart of Peter's work and it was another stroke of luck that our paths crossed.

Peter's advice was excellent, but after some time at the LCP I began to realize that most of the design students there really wanted to be artists and actually feared the commercial world.

Our work typically involved us spending time on such projects as redesigning the tax form as a typographic exercise and designing record sleeves. Wonderful, but it was hardly likely to support a career in design.

A turning point during my time at the LCP came when I presented my redesign of the tax form. The brief for the project was to make the form simpler and easier to fill out. I thought the problem with the form wasn't that it was difficult to fill out, but that it was boring and people hated doing it. The solution I presented was a redesigned form, illustrated with black-and-white cartoons about money. I reasoned this would make the task of filling the form in less onerous, give the tax form some humanity and make it more engaging to the people who had to use it. However, it wasn't what my typographic lecturer wanted to see. || **I can still see his face as I showed him my work. He thought I was mad and I thought he had missed the point. He then gave up on me.** || Somehow we were not talking the same language. He saw the project as a typographic exercise using 12pt Univers Light, but I was thinking of cartoons like the ones in *Punch* magazine. I reasoned nobody laughed at 12pt Univers Light.

This illustrates the difference between art direction and design. A designer is trying to create order out of chaos, while an art director is trying to disrupt: competing for attention and empathy.

I could see expulsion from the LCP looming. Until, that is, I was res-cued by another stroke of luck and crossed paths with another brilliant teacher and an LCP legend – John Gillard. He was a passionate teacher who taught problem solving before design. He believed the first thing you needed to do was define the problem. And that ideas were fundamental to the solution before you started designing. Like Peter Green, John had recognized in me a love of ideas. || **And it was John who introduced me to the groundbreaking work of Bill Bernbach.**

Bill Bernbach had founded his own advertising agency, Doyle Dane Bernbach (DDB), in New York back in 1949 along with James Doyle and Maxwell Dane. The three of them were outsiders. Bernbach, who was the copywriter, was, like Dane, Jewish. Doyle was a hard-drinking Irishman who could sell mojitos to a devout Mormon. They were anti-establishment. They weren't WASPs (White Anglo-Saxon Protestants), as the Americans would say. || **They were definitely from the wrong side of the tracks, but it was the side where all the fun was being had.** || Their backgrounds meant that they weren't the most popular guys in the boardrooms of 1950s corporate America. Despite these supposed drawbacks, Bernbach began earning a creative reputation in New York for his thinking. Ohrbach's, a department store, and EL AL, the Israeli airline, were among the early beneficiaries of this new, maverick thinking. Then, in 1959, Bernbach got the chance to pitch for the Volkswagen account.

At the time, this might not have seemed like a gift from the gods. Selling a car designed in Nazi Germany to the citizens of the US was going to be, despite the fact that it had an air-cooled engine, a bit of an uphill struggle. And it wasn't just a problem because World War II was a recent memory – the little Beetle was reaching the American market in the late 50s, a time in American history when they really embraced 'big': it's a big country, with big ambitions, big opportunities, big food, big companies and big cars. Big in the US is a philosophical belief, not just a physical reality.

Undeterred, DDB won the account. || **Bernbach and his agency created a series of ads that are uniquely disarming and which used a breakthrough strategy: tell the truth. Alongside truth, Bernbach also used wit and charm. He helped create advertising that was not only intelligent, but also inclusive: the hardest thing to achieve. His other great skill was to instil humility into the work he produced, reminding the public that corporations are made of people like you and me.**

So, what was the <u>truth</u> about the Volkswagen Beetle?

It is a small, ugly and noisy car, but it is reliable and it is well made. It didn't pander to fashion or fads.

Bernbach created a campaign around these beliefs. With lines like 'Think small', 'Lemon' and 'After we paint the car we paint the paint'.

With wit and charm, Bernbach's work convinced a big car-loving American public to fall in love with a preposterous small car: the Beetle. It turned around the fortunes of Volkswagen and presaged a style of advertising that would influence generations of creative people.

The ads became legendary, as did Bernbach and his agency. The work showed a generation, my generation, how advertising could be witty, intelligent, smart, truthful, inclusive and, most importantly of all, successful.

Modern advertising had been born.

'Think Small' was one of the first of the seminal ads from the Volkswagen Beetle campaign. For years, all of us in the advertising industry admired it because we thought it was a comment on American consumerism, which, to an extent, it was. ‖ Some years later, Keith Reinhard, one of DDB's great writers, told me the real story: at the time IBM were running a campaign titled 'Think big' and DDB's 'Think small' ad was simply bouncing off that idea – that's what gave it its immediate energy. The real story had become lost in the mists of history. So much of what we do is related to a moment in time and, sadly, it's hard to hold on to that relevance as it marches on.

One of the other great ads from that early campaign was 'Lemon'. In the US this is slang for something that doesn't work. It was titled under a perfect picture of a Beetle and talked about the Volkswagen's quality control. Nobody had seen advertising like this before. It was honest, disarming and witty. The public lapped it up.

There is something else that is perhaps most remarkable of all about the Volkswagen Beetle campaign and the man who inspired it: Bernbach was approached to create this campaign at a time when Germany, or West Germany as it was called then, was struggling to rebuild an economy that had been shattered by war. For an economy like theirs, which is based on manufacturing and engineering, the car industry was a vital component. Success in the US, the world's single, biggest car market, was therefore essential to Volkswagen's future and that of the West German economy. ‖ **The vision and creativity of Bernbach's work helped to provide their economy with the success it so badly needed, turning the Beetle into one of the most successful cars ever produced, Volkswagen into one of the most successful car manufacturers and, in turn, re-established West Germany as an engineering giant.**

Some 15 years after the Nazis tried to exterminate the Jewish population of Europe in the Holocaust, it took a Jew – Bill Bernbach – to help

Client:
Volkswagen,
1963–1964

Titles: Lemon
and Think small

Art director:
Helmut Krone

Copywriter:
Julian Koenig

Germany re-establish its manufacturing credentials. A little lesson there in humility and the dangers of prejudice. And, of course, not forgetting the past, but not becoming a prisoner of it.

Back at the LCP, when John Gillard showed me Bernbach's work for Volkswagen it was like having a light turned on in a darkened room. Suddenly I could see what I wanted to do. || **Here was an industry that worshipped at the altar of ideas.**

Bernbach showed us that the truth is the most powerful strategy you can employ in advertising. His belief was that this style of creativity could be inclusive and inspiring as well as intelligent – it didn't have to be patronizing to succeed and it demonstrated that humour was an incredibly powerful tool.

It's amazing how you can be surrounded by advertising, but that you never really notice it until someone shows you how it can be done.

Then you understand how it can transform the fortunes of brands and how it can talk to millions without losing its integrity. I have to thank John Gillard for that insight and, of course, Bill Bernbach and his advertising agency.

Having seen the light, I now wanted a job in this industry, hopefully as an art director. I joined a renegade group of students at the LCP and gave up on most of my other tutors. || **Advertising was 'commercial',** whereas designers thought of themselves as 'artists'. Heaven forbid they should dirty their hands with commerce. Most of my design tutors practically threw their ranged left, well-ordered hands up in horror – I was going over to the dark side. As they gave up on me, I gave up on them.

I realized design was about creating order, whereas I wanted to create disorder. There was a philosophical gap here. And reason wasn't going to bridge it.

Because advertising seemed to be such a dirty word at the LCP those of us in the renegade group would leave the college each day and go across to a pub near by called the Prince Albert, which is where Gillard conducted his tutorials. There the renegade group of us worked. We'd order half a pint of lager and keep it going all day, drawing up ideas and presenting them to Gillard. God knows what the barman thought – he must have wondered what was in the lager.

I was so keen to pursue my career in advertising that I set about getting to see some good creative people in the industry to show them my portfolio. Gillard had advised me to wait until I had some really great ideas in my book, but I was impatient.

I managed to get an appointment to see a New York art director who was working at a hot agency who had just opened an office in London. The agency was called Papert, Koenig, Lois (PKL) and the art director's name was Tony Palladino. ‖ How about that for a name? At that time, most of the New York creative community working in advertising were either Jewish or Italian, the writers typically being Jewish and the art directors being Italian. No guessing what Palladino was.

My meeting with Palladino was at PKL's office, which was just off Sloane Street in Knightsbridge. Inside it was all polished parquet floors and cool Italian furniture. ‖ **His office was completely minimal: except for a white A4 layout pad and a black Pentel he had a completely clean white desk.** ‖ On the wall behind the desk was a pop art-style painting of Palladino and his writer, a then little-known scribe called Peter Mayle, who, when he left advertising, went on to write a massive bestseller: *A Year in Provence*.

I couldn't wait to show him my lager-fuelled ideas and, as I opened my portfolio, I was introduced to a young writer who had just started working at the agency and had just popped into his office. It was Alan Parker, who went on to become one of Britain's best film directors.

So out came my work. He went through it. He said nothing. He then went through it again before proceeding to throw everything in the bin apart from one piece of work. || **I was gobsmacked, disheartened and disillusioned. He held up the one remaining piece of work and said: 'Now this is good. And now I'll show you how to make it better.' He reduced an interesting headline down, cutting out words and making it succinct, punchier and to the point. He emphasized the power of reduction – a fundamental skill in advertising.**

Having done that he said, 'Come back with 10 other pieces of work as good as that, then you'll be ready for a job in this business.'

I left Palladino's office with all my work in the bin apart from one piece. The bastard. Didn't he know the price of cardboard? Sadly, I never got back to see him. Allegedly, he had to leave London in a hurry after an incident involving a very sharp Stanley knife, an account man's neck and a piece of creative work. Back at the LCP Gillard consoled me and said: 'I told you so.' || **However painful, though, the experience with Palladino was, it was a great lesson: it taught me that persistence is essential and that you must not be put off by those experiences. You just have to come back with better work.**

Not really surprising since he was Italian, there was something else that Palladino talked about in our meeting, and that was passion. || **He wanted my portfolio to be about me and to be about what I believed and the kind of work I wanted to do. He believed that those attributes were fundamental to being successful.**

It's a refrain of this book: creativity isn't an occupation, it's a pre-occupation. That was what he showed me and that was what went into making Bernbach's work so good as well.

I define creativity as an 'expression of self'. || You cannot create great work unless a little bit of you goes into it, be it your heart, your soul or your beliefs. || Whatever you create – it could be painting, writing, designing or even advertising – the work that results is an expression of you. Of course, what each of us creates may talk to different audiences and perform different functions, but, ultimately, it carries your beliefs and your thumb print. If what you create is to be successful, it has to have an integrity and humanity that touch people, and those qualities come from within. Without that, you're just going through the motions and will almost certainly produce work that won't last and won't stick. || **That's why some creative people can be so insufferable – they're not just going a job, they're expressing their beliefs.** || That's what those early advertising giants, the likes of Bernbach, showed us and that's why their work has stood the test of time and why it changed so much. || **They were more than just commercial artists, they were evangelists – they believed in what they were doing.**

They had <u>belief</u> and <u>passion</u>.

Those early days were important. Being in the right place at the right time is a matter of luck. You'll either get that or you won't, but you can manage the luck that comes your way. What I learnt from those days was it was important to have a belief – a philosophy that drives your ideas. You're not just creating work – being a hired tool of commercial enterprises – you're an individual with a story to tell who has a passion to express your ideas. || **You are someone with the chance to change the world and inspire large audiences.**

I was excited by advertising because it gave me a platform to talk to the masses. Studying painting was great, I loved it. But ultimately how many people would I have spoken to? Of course, there are compromises, there are clients and specific briefs and timetables. Everything has its downsides. But for me the upsides were exciting.

I also appreciated the value of juxtaposition – putting one culture against another, seeing radical, innovative ideas sublimate convention. That was my personal journey. || **But each of us has our own journey: the place you were born, your early memories, experiences, loves, hates – all of these things go into making you who you are. It is why you are unique and why that uniqueness must go into your creativity.** || If you remember that journey and can draw on those feelings and emotions you are part of the way to being an outstanding creative.

IDEAS

Ideas are what advertising
is built upon. We worship
them, we seek them, fight over
them, applaud them and value them
above everything else. Walk round
the floors of any agency and
the phrase you'll most hear is:
'what's the idea?'

Ideas are the most incredible thing we possess. They can change the future of brands, of countries and of the course of history. They engage, entertain and stimulate, encouraging debate, dissent and adoration. We take them for granted, but sometimes it is important to step back and marvel at their brilliance and, so often, their simplicity.

Ideas are the most egalitarian thing we do. They can be done by anyone at any time. You don't need any special qualifications to be able to do them or special equipment to conceive them: they can be created anywhere.

I believe that celebrating this unique skill is fundamentally important. The creation of ideas is the intellectual force that has driven civilization and empowered the dreams of us all. And, with ideas, the more you have them, the better you get at having them. That's one of the many reasons why advertising is such a stimulating environment in which to work.

The pressure of such creative demands can be exhausting, and one of the most relentless environments I ever worked in was the Cramer Saatchi consultancy, set up in 1967 and the forerunner of Saatchi & Saatchi, the advertising agency. It was certainly an exciting place to be, but to make it pay we had to create a major campaign a week: print, TV and posters, point of sale. Everything. We even used to redesign the packaging if we felt it needed it. This was 360° thinking before people knew what 360° thinking was. || **Most of our briefs came from agencies that had failed to crack a creative problem so they turned to us to dig them out of a hole. The problem being that as the client had run out of patience with the agency, they had also run out of time, so we were always working under extreme deadline pressure. Over night, over the weekend, over everything.**

We were working so hard and so fast that at times it was madness. We'd be presenting the ideas we'd drawn up before the ink had dried. Binning the bad ones took too much time, so we'd just chuck them over our shoulder and start on a new one. It was all slightly comic and felt a bit like a scene in the Billy Wilder movie *The Front Page*. Walter Matthau, cast as a ruthless newspaper executive, has convinced Jack Lemmon, who plays a reporter, to stay at his typewriter and cover the story of an escaped convict. Lemmon becomes so engrossed in writing the story that he can't stop. And as we all know, a journalist can't write a story without smoking. So, he simply says to Matthau, who is standing next to him, 'Cigarette me'.

As a result of working under such pressure to turn things around quickly, the consultancy would occasionally produce some work of which it wasn't really proud, typically a great piece of thinking that gradually became compromised in an attempt to get the client to buy it instead of putting it out of its misery and starting again. There is always a belief in these situations that, somehow, the compromises won't show when the finished work is produced. Sadly, this kind of wishful thinking affects us all.

At times like this we all live in hope that the fundamental brilliance of the idea, despite all the compromises, will shine through. The truth is, that hardly ever happens and you should have the courage to kill your baby before it gets really ugly.

At Cramer Saatchi one of these disasters would reach production from time to time and everyone in the office would do their best to distance themselves from that particular dog. All well and good until, with horror, we realized that on one occasion the work had been entered into the D&AD Annual – the most prestigious awards in British design and advertising. Of course, the creatives who had conceived this questionable work didn't want anything to do with it. Some glory-seeking photographer or agency had entered the abominations without telling us. As no one wanted to own up to the really bad work it was agreed we would invent a couple of fictitious characters who would go down as the creative team responsible for this drivel. We never, of course, thought any of the dreadful work we all loathed would stand a chance of being accepted, but on one occasion it was. If you look at a copy of the 1970 D&AD Annual, you will see that the entirely invented creative team of Donald Lorio and Jake Stouer made their one and only illustrious appearance in the annals of creative genius. I remember at the time Charles thought it was hilarious, saying something like even our shit work is good. And an entry into D&AD was good for business.

I digress, so let's return to my main point at its very simplest: ideas and the belief in being able to produce great ideas are everything, otherwise advertising is just information. The trick is to make the information interesting and relevant – in the world of marketing communication understanding those two words, interesting and relevant, has filled a library. But it shouldn't have. Ultimately, it's just common sense and a desire to excite people. || Always remember that all information goes in through the heart. Or, as James Stephens, in his book *The Crock of Gold*, said: 'What the heart feels today, the head will understand tomorrow.'

So how does one create that 'great idea' that turns the raw information into advertising that will engage and entertain as well as inform? || There is a fantastic book on playing tennis called *The Inner Game of Tennis* which has a very simple conclusion: relax and let your true self perform. And so it is with creativity, perhaps even more so, I would say. I have always said that I do my best thinking when I'm not thinking: that's when inspiration strikes. You've already fed all the issues, concerns, wishes and desires of the brief into your mind – then you just have to let it percolate. You can talk about it, consider the brief in terms of what you like, what you don't like, what you would like to see and what appeals. || **Out of that absurd, crazy process pops a brilliant thought: that's where the magic emerges. Of course, no one wants to believe it's so random, but it is.**

Now I can hear the corporate minds saying: 'But if it is so random and unpredictable, how can a creative business operate as a business?' This is not an unreasonable question to which my answer is: 'With great difficulty'. This is probably why wonderfully talented agencies come and go with such regularity, being brilliant, stunning and amazing one

minute, then suddenly descending into mediocrity and predictability the next.

You have to accept the creative process is completely dysfunctional. If you deny that fact, you will ultimately fail. You may get away with it for a while, but then, like paint over rust, the rust will eventually burn through. ‖ **The unpredictability is what makes what we do in advertising so exciting – you literally don't know where you're going to end up. Creativity isn't about predictability – it has to surprise and challenge, it has to be daring and yet motivating.** ‖ In a creative organization, if you understand that, then there's a good chance you'll be successful and continue being successful.

Why does Hollywood produce so many predictable, boring movies? Because they're following a formula. And there's nothing a formula-led mindset likes more than a nice, comfortable process. You can take refuge in a process. Those in business who are formula-led are always trying to find a way of processing creative thought. They want to streamline it. They want to make it more predictable. Their answer: tissue meetings.

Have you ever had to suffer a tissue meeting? All of us in advertising have at some point, haven't we? For those that don't know what I mean, count yourself lucky! A tissue meeting is a stage between the strategy having been agreed between the agency and the client and the final creative presentation. It's a meeting where the agency shares a number of creative routes with the client. The idea behind a tissue meeting is to make the client feel happy and involved with the work they're eventually going to buy. All very reasonable, you might think, but brilliance is rarely reasonable.

Everyone walks out of the meeting feeling satisfied, except the creative people – the ones who have to come up with the magic.

Whoever came up with the completely stupid idea of tissue meetings should be taken out and shot. They are the invention of a predictable mind trying to make the unpredictable predictable. Tissue meetings were created to keep clients happy and to make them feel we are in complete command of what we do, which we're not.

Creativity isn't a process, advertising is a process.

Creativity is a manic construction of absurd, unlikely irreverent thoughts and feelings that somehow, when put together, change the way we see things. That's why it's magic. If you want to be ordinary then, yes, use a process. || With a process and a series of tissue meetings you can very easily make things obvious, certain and easy to buy. And I'm not just talking about the advertising business – the world is full of predictable things: open any magazine, turn on your television and there they are. Why? Because the world wants creativity to behave like a formulaic process. You can see it happening in any creative industry.

Process is trying to make order out of chaos. Creativity is trying to make chaos to create order. They are at opposite ends of a spectrum.

You don't think Leonardo da Vinci went to a tissue meeting when he was painting the *Mona Lisa* do you? Imagine the scene: perhaps Leonardo could have her looking to the right? Maybe she could be wearing some jewelry? Bit more of a smile, maybe? Stick an apple on her head – that would get people wondering. Of course Leonardo didn't go to a bloody tissue meeting – it was a piece of inspiration. A piece of inspiration that has lasted 500 years and still has us standing back in amazement. Believe it or not, that's what any half-decent creative person is trying to do – create something that people will stand back from and look at in amazement. Creativity can change the way we feel about something and will stay with us for eternity. Is that asking for too much? Maybe, but unless we try we'll never get there. And I can guarantee one way you won't get there: in a sodding tissue meeting. By definition, a tissue meeting is trying to corral creativity. I want to set it free. Despite my rant about these meetings they'll still continue. Even I will probably have to go on enduring them. But unless we admit their limitation we won't inspire that great idea, that piece of magic that can do wonders for clients' sales figures.

But how do you know when an idea is great?
And is good the enemy of great? Does a process
that gets you to good hamper great? I think it
probably does. The more you process it, just
like food, the blander it will be.

I was once asked to present a lecture on what I looked for in a 'great idea'. My initial reaction was that it was a dysfunctional, random process and most of the time relied upon nothing more than inspiration. || But although this is what I believe, simply standing in front of an audience and saying something amounting to, 'I just buy what I like' would have made a very short speech and one, I'm sure, the organizers would not have welcomed. I therefore set about analysing how I went about my work: could I detect any formula? Was there more to it than just instinct? Like riding a bicycle, you don't really think about it. So, I had to interrogate my own beliefs. What was it about an idea that I liked? What turned me on to one thought as opposed to another? Was there a common thread that I could identify?

Now it's important to state that my intention wasn't to develop a simple formula for creating ideas. I think that's impossible. There may be a simple formula for reading a balance sheet, but certainly not one for the creative process. However, there obviously is a process of a kind that you go through as you create. Why do some ideas resonate over and above others? You have to have an understanding of the tools you use to reach a decision about when you have a 'great idea'.

When I examined my own process I realized there was a common thread that was clearly identifiable in all the work I did and in the work of others that I admired.

The common thread was irreverence.

So why do I think irreverence is so
powerful? In examining this theory
I stood back from the world of advertising
and looked at irreverence in a broader
artistic context.

If one looks at European art from before the Renaissance it was far from irreverent. It was the complete opposite and was all about control. One of art's functions was to reinforce the power of authority, be it the church, the monarchy or a despot. Reverence was the order of the day and an artist lived or died by their ability to acquire commissions – pleasing their patrons was essential for survival.

Consider artists working in Italy for the Roman Catholic Church. They had to deal with very similar problems to those designers and people in advertising face today: they had to sell the same product. In this case it was a belief in God and some pretty strange ideas about virginity, chastity and the infallibility of the Pope rather than banks or soap powder – they had to do this over and over again in a way that would still excite and interest viewers who had seen it and heard it all before. The church, just as a client today, understood the need to refresh a familiar theme continually. This, of course, was good news for the many artists. It meant lots of new and lucrative commissions. One example of refreshing a familiar theme is the ceiling of the Sistine Chapel in Rome. It's a powerful message of papal authority but, more importantly, Michelangelo's innovative and daring style ensured that the message was heard and talked about and regenerated passion and commitment in the concept of the origin of man. ‖ **So, if we accept artists working for the Roman Catholic Church had the same issues to deal with as we do today in advertising, then, in my view, Michelangelo was the first great art director – original, passionate, committed, always fighting the client, over budget and late.** But who remembers that now?

There was room for <u>wit and irreverence</u> in Michelangelo's work too.

Look down from the ceiling to the wall behind the altar in the Sistine Chapel and you will see another masterpiece: *The Last Judgment.* Michelangelo originally painted all of the figures in the fresco – Christ, the saints, angels, the lot – as nudes. Later popes and cardinals were so concerned about the nudity that they hired another artist, Daniele da Volterra, to paint drapery over breasts and genitals. Today, you will see that Jesus seems to be wearing a pink negligee. I'm not sure the great master really saw Jesus wearing underwear in his original vision. So the next time someone alters your work you'll have something in common with Michelangelo.

Client: Wallis, 1997

Art director:
Steve Hudson

Copywriter:
Victoria Fallon

Photographer:
Bob Carlos Clarke

Caravaggio used a different type of shocking image to break with decorum, or what you might call the accepted way of portraying a subject. He showed celebrated Christian figures as members of the lower classes. In his painting, *The Supper at Emmaus*, Caravaggio showed Christ as a smooth-skinned young man, to be admired for his physical beauty rather than his holiness. Shocking as that was at the time we now view the painting as a great work of art. It is thought, by some, that Caravaggio was gay, so perhaps that's why he wandered from the conventional depiction into what we now think of as homoeroticism. Who knows?

One can see the stirrings of irreverence in Michelangelo's and Caravaggio's work and sense the eventual impact those stirrings would have. ‖ **Sadly for the artists of that period, being irreverent usually meant they died in penury. And I can assure you that's not a good place to die.**

By the 19th century, art acquired a relative independence and relied less on wealthy sponsors and patrons, from which grew a questioning of the major institutions: the church, the state and the monarchy. And as society developed, becoming better educated and becoming more independent and questioning, the ability of these two massive power blocks, the church and the state, to retain their influence diminished.

Fast forward to the 20th century: economic growth brought with it greater tensions and the need for greater freedom. Competing ideas were emerging within society. ‖ **They were ideas that demanded attention and consideration. With that freedom grew the need to question and explain. What was the nature of society and authority? How did it work? Why was it changing? What was good about it? What was bad? What should be preserved and what rejected?**

The emergence of Dadaism as an art movement after the First World War was a reaction to the meaningless slaughter of millions by callous authorities who would brook no criticism or alternative views. It was this arrogance that drove writers and artists, not only those involved in Dadaism, but elsewhere too, to challenge all institutions and accepted forms of art.

The Dadaists had no fixed beliefs as such, but were driven by the need to shock and attack the established order. Marcel Duchamp's defacing of the *Mona Lisa*, by putting a moustache on her, was one way of mocking authority and the establishment. It's amazing what a simple moustache can seem to represent.

While less confrontational than the Dadaists, the artists and designers of the Bauhaus also dared to do things that broke down traditional attitudes and beliefs. In using industrial materials to design furniture, they challenged traditional crafts and, in graphic design and typography, they changed the way in which we viewed the printed word and absorbed information.

The very essence of art had changed by this time – its function became to force us to think, to reconsider, to challenge. We learned to question, and in questioning liberated our own minds. The most fundamental freedom we have is the right to ask why?

We want to challenge.
And, of course, have the choice to do so.

This need to challenge didn't apply only to fine art. Music was also affected – just look at the development of jazz, blues and rock 'n' roll. Jazz was the voice of oppressed black America and considered 'the Devil's music' by some. The blues also had a powerful, challenging sentiment driving it. It laid the foundations for rock 'n' roll, turning Elvis Presley into an iconic figure of rebellion known the world over. ‖ **Notoriously, Elvis was not allowed to be shown on American television screens below the waist because the way he gyrated his hips was considered lewd. Of course, to some extent, the censors were right – it was lewd**

Client: Choosy,
1998
Art director:
Mike Wells
Copywriter:
Tom Hudson

– but that was the whole point. || Elvis was the voice of a new generation of people the authorities didn't and couldn't understand. Within society the centre of gravity was changing. No longer did we look up to our elders, but down to a new liberated youth. A generation emboldened with wealth, a desire for change and who wanted to express themselves in their own terms with their own language.

When irreverence touches design it creates opportunities for producing genuinely innovative and lasting work: you can find lateral solutions to design problems such as Alec Issigonis's revolutionary Mini. His brief: to make the car smaller, yet create more passenger space – a seemingly impossible task. But, by throwing out the rule book – being irreverent – and turning the engine sideways, the problem was solved in one stroke: there was more space for the passengers without increasing the overall size of the car. || **I would argue that Issigonis's attitude treated design**

Client:
Robertson's, 1985
Art director:
John Hegarty
Copywriter:
Barbara Nokes

GOLDEN SHRED GETS ITS COLOUR FROM SEVILLE ORANGES.

SOME MARMALADES ADD COLOURING.

**Client: Barnardo's,
1999 and 2000**
Art director:
Adrian Rossi
Copywriter:
Alex Grieve
Photographer:
Nick Georghiou

convention with an irreverence that led to the creation of one of
the most lasting and influential products of the industrial age.

Today's practitioners of design and advertising are constantly trying to
get people to make a choice – a choice between one product and another.
Between one design and another. And not only are we trying to get people
to choose, we are also trying to get them to accept new concepts and to
'reconsider'. Irreverence is key here.

A great example of this is Cramer Saatchi's 'Pregnant man' poster for
the HEC (Health Education Council) from 1970. || **It was trying to
get men to reconsider their approach to contraception. As a piece
of communication I believe it is a lasting testament to the power of
irreverence and, as I describe later, a pivotal moment in bringing
Saatchi & Saatchi into existence as an advertising agency.**

But using irreverence for its <u>own</u> <u>sake</u> is dangerous. Do that and you risk becoming irrelevant.

The function of irreverence should be to help question and, in doing
so, offer a possible solution. If irreverence becomes purely anarchic it
eventually turns in on itself and destroys its own purpose. It just shocks
and alienates – a fate which ultimately befell the Dadaists.

I would argue that this is what happened to punk in the 1970s. In the end, it only opposed, it didn't also propose. It jolted conventional thinking, it didn't in turn put anything in its place – it created a void but failed to fill it. Elements of it remain in our culture, but as a philosophy it offered us only opposition, and history has taught us that if you're going to knock something down you have to put something in its place. Punk offered us no vision and, if your irreverence is to be constructive, you must not only get people to question, but you must also take them with you.

The infamous Benetton advertising of some years ago falls into a similar trap. Newborn babies and a man dying of AIDS: not the first things you'd think of when it comes to selling jumpers! Yes, the advertising shocked me, it gained my attention. It was, and is, profoundly irreverent, but ultimately it leaves me feeling hollow. I just think: why? What are you saying? Do you really believe in it? And with any advertising if you don't believe in what you've created, your vision becomes empty and meaningless, a sham.

I applaud anyone's desire to open my eyes, to make me look at things afresh and bring different ideas to my attention. But it _must_ be done with sincerity, integrity and with sympathy – or the danger is it can look as though it's just exploitation.

Ultimately, it is all too easy to be irreverent in order to gain attention. Here's an exercise in how irreverence works better with a little humour.

Print the word fuck in Helvetica extra bold and you have been irreverent. But, I would argue, to no purpose. What shocks today becomes boring tomorrow. Unless, that is, it has purpose. Now, if I rewrite _fuck_ in Copperplate italic I maybe, just maybe, express a sense of humour and wit. By doing that I alienate you less and begin to make you consider the purpose of my irreverence.

Humour has an important role to play in advertising. We use it because it's a way of making people relax and listen. When your audience is in that state of mind they're more likely to remember what you're saying and act upon it.

THE CREAM OF MANCHESTER.
Boddingtons Draught Bitter. Brewed at the Strangeways Brewery since 1778.

Client:
Boddingtons,
1992 (left)
Art director:
Mike Wells
Copywriter:
Tom Hudson
Photographer:
Tiff Hunter

Client:
Boddingtons,
1997 (below)
Art director:
Simon Robinson
Copywriter:
Jo Moore
Photographer:
David Gill

Client:
Boddingtons,
1992 (near
right)
Art director:
Mike Wells
Copywriter:
Tom Hudson
Photographer:
Tiff Hunter

Client:
Boddingtons,
1997 (far right)
Art director:
John Hegarty
Photographer:
David Gill

THE CREAM OF MANCHESTER.
Boddingtons Draught Bitter. Brewed at the Strangeways Brewery since 1778.

Client:
Boddingtons, 1992
Title: Face Cream
Creative director:
John Hegarty
Art director:
Mike Wells
Copywriter:
Tom Hudson
Director:
John Lloyd

Humour and irreverence are, therefore, interesting bedfellows: they feed off each other, creating opportunities to enhance each other's message. Of course, you can have one without the other – humour is the enemy of authority as much as irreverence. But, as I've already shown, when put together, they have the ability to become more persuasive.

A great example of this belief is our campaign for Boddingtons, a brand of beer originally from Manchester in England. Here was a beer that was differentiated by its creamy head. Perceived wisdom said creaminess wasn't an attribute that sold beer. We disagreed. It was and is what made it different. It was the truth of the brand. So, we created the slogan 'The cream of Manchester' and exaggerated the creamy aspect of the beer showing it as an ice cream cone, as shaving cream, as hair cream and as many more executions. We captured the consumer's imagination with irreverent images and, in doing so, turned Boddingtons into a cult brand.

You can see the lineage in this campaign all the way back to that original Volkswagen work by Doyle Dane Bernbach (DDB) in the early 60s.

So as society constantly changes and as brands and products constantly innovate it becomes the responsibility of the creative person to capture the essence of that change and the opportunity it offers. As creative people we have to strive constantly to get others to reconsider, to re-evaluate. But we must do so in a way that is constructive, not destructive. What irreverence offers us, when used intelligently, is a more stimulating way to create and to capture people's imagination and, of course, their attention.

An added value of irreverence is what it offers organizations. The companies that understand and embrace the power of irreverence are the ones who will constantly succeed. They will be the thought leaders, the ones that challenge established thinking and constantly break the mould. And it will be those companies who will stay on top and provide impetus for growth.

Irreverence is more than a tool for communication, it is an essential ingredient for corporate success and forms the core of a philosophical approach to creativity – a belief in something that helps me create challenging, persuasive thinking.

It's essential, therefore, for a creative company to have a point of view and a philosophical foundation for their work.

The greatest spur to creating ideas is confidence, specifically the confidence in your ability to make magic. That's the one truth a creative organization must hold on to. Great creative companies inject irreverence and experimentation into the system to stop the warm comforting blanket of mediocrity taking over.

It is also important to remember ideas are just energy. That's what makes them so attractive and engaging, and why people are drawn to them and why they have such power. It's perhaps why we say we 'worship ideas'. Suddenly one understands that phrase far more. Of course, we worship them because we recognize their power, their ability to transform and convert people. And when people talk about ideas they become enthusiastic. That's hardly surprising. ‖ **The origin of the word enthusiasm comes from the Greek: 'To be with God'. Now we know why ideas are so important and always will be. And why, if we constantly insert irreverence into their creation, we'll keep them fresh.**

2

BRANDS AND AUDIENCES

The best definition of a brand
I ever heard is this. A brand is the
most valuable piece of real estate
in the world: a corner of someone's
mind. I think that's about as
good as it gets when you're trying
to define what we're all talking
about and attempting to manage
when it comes to brands
and branding.

Brands were around long before the modern concept of brands and branding existed. You could argue that throughout history empires and nation states adopted brand behaviour as they flexed their muscles in their attempts to increase their influence over both their rivals and their population.

A nation's flag was a brand symbol – a device to unify and instil pride in its followers. Look at the Union Flag of Great Britain – it is not only a brilliant piece of design, but it also contains within its design the story of four nations coming together. It's not that ridiculous to think of a nation's flag as a logo. Consider it in parallel with the Audi logo, where the four rings on the bonnet of every Audi car represent the four companies that came together to become Audi. Empires and nations had slogans too: the Romans marched forward and conquered to the slogan of 'Veni, Vidi, Vici': I came, I saw, I conquered. And the French, during their revolution, got it down to 'Liberté, Egalité, Fraternité' – three words that summed up the underlying ideals, ambitions and beliefs of the French Revolution and are still emblazoned across the front of every town hall in France. ‖ **It's always amazing to me that we need so many more words than this to sell a tin of cat food. Verbosity has never been an attribute of good communication.**

Today, we are without doubt living in the age of the brand. At the time I was writing this book, Kraft Foods of the USA bought Cadbury, a British confectionery brand, for £11.5 billion. Kraft didn't pay that simply for Cadbury's factories and real estate. Oh no, Kraft paid that vast sum for the perceived value of the Cadbury name and its potential as a brand.

You could argue that we've gone <u>brand mad.</u>
Everything, from your local hospital to
ageing athletes, is being treated as 'brands',
as products that have value to be defined,
enhanced and exploited.

One of the tedious by-products of viewing everything as a brand is how slogans get slapped on everything. Personally, I'd make them subject to planning regulations. Quite why, for instance, the Metropolitan Police in London have a slogan is beyond me. On a revolving sign outside their head-quarters at New Scotland Yard, they proudly proclaim: 'Working together for a safer London'. Apart from the fact that it's really naff, what the hell else are they supposed to be doing? The slogan is a mind-numbingly obvious statement that goes in one ear and out the other. It's a statement of the obvious that is neither motivating nor memorable. I think there's no point in saying something unless it's enhancing a point. What you say has to be challenging, informative and memorable. On the other hand, if the Metropolitan Police slogan said something provocative I wouldn't mind. A slogan like 'Banging up the bastards' might stir up the debate a little. Or why not 'Giving the streets back to grannies'?

The truth is that 'everything' is not a brand. I don't think my local hospital gets any benefit from articulating its ridiculous, naïve, bland slogan of 'Connecting people to health'. It actually makes them look amateurish and so, if anything, it worries me. If you can't originate a professional, well thought-through sign-off line as your slogan, how the hell are you going to organize a complicated life-threatening operation?

Today's obsession with slogans is bringing
the whole branding debate and the value
of branding into disrepute. It has to be
remembered that brands are <u>meaningful</u>
only when the public have a choice.

I'm not in a choice-making mode when I'm being rushed to hospital after a cardiac arrest – I want to get to that hospital as fast as possible. The paramedic doesn't ask: 'Would Sir like to go the Royal Middlesex Hospital "Where health really matters" or to the Royal Free Hospital where they have "World class care and expertise"?' If it were possible to answer, I'm sure my response would be: 'Just get me to the nearest hospital, you stupid bastards.'

So, in our brand-led and slogan-saturated world, what are the key attributes that any great brand should have?

At the core of the existence of brands is trust ‖ and the history of their development is based upon it. As a consumer society grew and became more mobile and wealthy, people were no longer buying goods from their neighbours or their local community – the people they could trust – but were forced to buy from strangers instead. How could people trust those strangers and their goods? How could they know what the strangers were selling was safe, efficient and reliable? From that core issue of 'trust' grew the development of the brand.

In reality, a brand only ever exists in the minds of consumers.

Today, owing to new technology, brands are controlled by consumers more than ever. The consumer's part in a brand's success is now even more fundamental and indeed precarious. Misunderstand that relationship and a brand is doomed to failure. Great brands that continue to be successful are so because they don't think like a conventional brand owner who is obsessed only with themselves and the belief that the world revolves around them and their product.

The key to great marketing is <u>never</u> to stop thinking like your audience.

If you do this then you don't lose touch with what it feels like to be excited and entertained by a great product or service – you have to be constantly intrigued by the world around you and what it offers. I try to live by that philosophy. I work in advertising, I don't live in advertising. Understanding the role your brand plays in people's lives and knowing how to make it more relevant is crucial.

Of course, it is important to be passionate about the company you work for and to have a belief in what it produces, but not to the exclusion of all else. What makes someone who markets a brand so effective is their bringing the outside world in. Just because you work in the yellow fats market doesn't mean everyone else is obsessed with the progress and growth of this sector, God forbid.

A brand isn't only made by the people who buy it, but also by the people who know about it.

When managing and promoting your product, this is probably the most important lesson to bear in mind. Even though a person may never buy what you sell, the fact that they know about what you are selling adds value to it.

This leads to where fame comes in: || **fame is fundamentally important to a brand's success.** || Why? Because it is a form of short-hand in the decision-making process that takes place in a hugely competitive world where all manner of products and services are seeking your attention. Fame adds value and protects the brand from competitive pressure. Now, you might be thinking: 'but isn't it terrible we live in a world obsessed with fame?' No, it isn't – you're getting fame and celebrity confused. The dictionary defines fame as 'public renown – great esteem'. What brand wouldn't want that?

Fame is very difficult for a brand to build unless you broadcast a brand's values. || And by broadcast I don't just mean conventional media. An example of this is how Richard Branson has made the Virgin brand famous by being outspoken and undertaking outrageous stunts. He broadcasts Virgin's brand values in unique and memorable ways. I do have reservations, though, about him dressing as a bride for the launch of Virgin brides. But that's Branson.

Client: Glenlivet
Whisky, 1992
Art director:
Martin Galtan
Copywriter:
Will Awdry
Photographer:
Conquering Everest

They're stunts, but remember: nobody bought anything while they were asleep. The first objective of any communications plan is to get noticed.

What Branson has managed to do is to capture the attention of the public – he's occupied a corner of their mind with 'broadcast stunts' and, of course, this particular use of broadcast media he gets for free. As a result, more people know about Virgin as a brand than will ever purchase one of Virgin's products. That fame, thanks to Branson's persona and stunts, adds value to the Virgin brand.

Conquest is a fundamental part of a brand's operations. || Of course, you must not lose sight of the primary function of most advertising, which is too sell something – in effect to manage a return on an investment. But a brand must always be thinking about the future and how it goes about recruiting new users. Targeting specific audiences is a wonderful science, but unless you include broadcast in some way within your marketing strategy you'll be talking to an ever-shrinking audience. And that's not particularly good for the long-term health of any company.

According to the Bible, when Christ stood and made his Sermon on the Mount he preached to the masses. He didn't get up on that rock and say, 'I'd like to talk to 18–25-year-old ABCs, with a predisposition to change and a disposable income of X'. No, he got up and preached to as many people as possible. He was in the business of recruitment, building loyalty and getting people to change their behaviour. If I'm not mistaken that's the function of a great many brands today.

This rather neatly brings me to the question of:
what is the world's greatest brand?

This was a question I was asked while I was in the US setting up BBH in New York. I had been invited to join a panel at a marketing conference and take part in a debate centred around the question: what is the world's greatest brand? The idea behind such a debate was to see what lessons could be learned from the greatest brand each of us put forward and how those lessons could be applied to a company today. Naturally, some on the panel talked about Coca-Cola, of how it had become a global phenomenon, fuelled the expansion of American culture and had weathered competition, social change and even their own marketing mistakes. || **What made Coca-Cola even more amazing, according to its supporters, was that it really was just carbonated, sugared water with some colouring and (here's the really important ingredient) brilliant marketing. You have to admire its success and recognize it as a beacon of expertise.**

Others argued the case for the Volkswagen Beetle. A small, ugly car that took the US by storm and transformed not only the fortunes of the company that made it, but also the German economy – no mean feat for a noisy, rear-engined automobile. It was also seminal because it was a brand created with a campaign that, as I claimed earlier, invented modern advertising. || Others debated the success of Apple, or the global reach of the Marlboro cigarettes campaign 'Come to Marlboro Country', first aired in the early 70s. And, of course, some panelists said the world's greatest brand was Nike. What an amazing success, they said. It even rejuvenated basketball as a sport to help sell their shoes. 'Just do it' is known the world over.

All of these I thought were worthy candidates, but I disagreed with my fellow panelists that they were truly great and combined all the elements needed for a definitive brand.

I argued that the Catholic Church
was the greatest of all brands.

Shock, horror, gasp! The Catholic Church a brand?! How dare you! My argument was that it was a brand that had pioneered many of the beliefs and practices that modern companies still seek today. || At this point I have to say it was a bit tricky making the case – I was addressing an audience in conservative America. What I was saying could have got me stoned off the stage, but thankfully my audience, intrigued by my argument, went along with me.

It was too late for me to pull back anyway, I was going for it. The case I argued was as follows. The Catholic Church had the world's greatest logo: a simple cross. It is a logo that is easy to reproduce and is made even more powerful when you attach the company founder's son to it – demonstrating the ultimate sacrifice. Interestingly, the symbol of the cross was only introduced by the Catholic Church some 400 years after the crucifixion. They could easily have adopted the sign of a fish – the Apostles were all fisherman – or, as Christ was a carpenter, even a carpenter's plane. But no, they adopted a symbol of pain and sacrifice. Not just being satisfied with having adopted this great symbol, the Church then built its centres of worship, their churches, in the shape of the cross. That was real through-the-line, 360° thinking.

Having established the logo and places of worship, the Catholic Church very quickly became the world's first truly global brand. Taking their founder's beliefs with them, they went out to convert the world. Coca-Cola's global expansion was masterminded by one of their legendary leaders, Robert Woodruff, with his rallying cry of: 'Within an arm's reach of desire'. Well, the Catholic Church pioneered that concept 2,000 years earlier.

Seven-day opening was adopted from the word go, with the Church extending its services to weddings, funerals and christenings. Their centres of worship became the focal point of civilized life. || **If only Apple stores or branches of NikeTown could generate the same passion. Admittedly, there are those who worship at the temple of Apple, but not with quite the same fervour as the Church. And while some Nike fans make the sign of the 'swoosh', it's nowhere near as many as make the sign of the cross.**

The Catholic Church fully understood the retail mantra of 'Location, location, location' as well. They were always in the centre of a town or village and were the tallest building.

To enhance their cultural and philosophical importance, the Church worked with the best architects, painters and musicians. It employed the cream of creativity to spread the word. Michelangelo painted ceilings for them and Leonardo did his best to curry favour with the ecclesiastical hierarchy and ensure his lasting fame. When Nike launched their 'Just do it' campaign back in the 80s they used the music of The Beatles. Microsoft employed The Rolling Stones to promote one of their operating systems. Well, the church engaged Mozart, Beethoven, Handel and Bach.

Some may marvel at the dramatic new headquarters of modern corporations, but none has matched St Peter's in Rome. If power is represented in the scale of your buildings, then the Church was in a league of its own.

The greatest architects flocked to the Church, accepting commissions that they knew would immortalize their names. These iconic structures, all of them designed on the symbol of the cross, dominated the landscape – they commanded power and attention. The Catholic Church had a brand book to beat all brand books: The Bible.

And here's the best part: the Catholic Church wasn't selling a physical product – it was selling belief. You couldn't touch it, or see it, you had to believe in it. And that makes the Catholic Church, as a brand, a very modern phenomenon and one that we can learn so much from.

Here's why: increasingly in the advertising world we are selling things you cannot see. We are, as Charles Leadbeater states in his fascinating book *Living on Thin Air,* trading products that are invisible. I can't physically touch a Google product. Vodafone, my mobile phone provider, is selling vibrating air. I bank with First Direct, a UK online and telephone bank that I can't physically visit – my relationship with them is conducted entirely over the phone. || **Each of those brands therefore has to manifest itself in a way that makes me believe in them and, importantly, trust them. This the Catholic Church absolutely understands: it is selling Faith.**

Therefore, the oldest 'brand' in the world is actually the most modern. Nearly 2,000 years after its founding, it's still going strong. It's suffered competitive pressure – the Lutherans, Protestants, Episcopalians and Calvinists did their best to offer an alternative – but none of them matched the power and longevity of that 'first in market' position the Church adopted. Whatever your beliefs, I argued at the conference, you had to admire the innovation and commitment to brand building as demonstrated by this formidable institution.

I'm not sure I won the argument, but it proved a lot more entertaining than just talking about Nike vs. Coca-Cola vs. Volkswagen. I always find it challenging and interesting to look beyond the confines of your own industry. ‖ **Livening up the debate about 'the World's greatest brand' by introducing the Church of Rome made people stop and think, which is surely the primary purpose of a debate.** ‖ But more than that, it helps keep your thinking fresh. Yes, it's great reading books about advertising (please continue reading this one and recommend it to your friends – my publicist made me put that in, you just can't get away from clients), but it's also vital to embrace other creative crafts and thinkers from different professions. You can learn so much from the experience of others who are masters in their particular field or endeavour.

But what of brands now and in the future? Digital technology and the relationships brands can now build with their potential audiences are unprecedented, but only if employed with daring and distinctive thinking.

Remember:
the value of a great idea hasn't changed,
but the opportunity to exploit it has.

And, before we all get carried away with fear about all this new technology, let's just remember what it provides is simply speed and access. In other words, I can get more of what I want more easily.

Technology has accelerated people's desires, not changed them.

Just as technology has enabled and empowered creative thinking to leap forward, it has also liberated marketing from the conventional media patterns. It has created an environment in which brands can really develop their own agenda. An environment in which creative and entrepreneurial skills can be competitively deployed against the brand's needs without having to even engage with conventional media. ‖ **Technology offers brands the opportunity to occupy a greater space in the audience's mind. Surely this makes it the most exciting time to be in marketing as well as advertising? It can be, but it will be so only if brands realize the seismic shifts that are occurring in the market place.**

Suddenly a corporation no longer has the advantage. In the old world getting your message across through TV, print or posters was hugely expensive. It favoured the well-heeled, monied corporations. But in this new world that advantage diminishes. ‖ **Caution is replaced by daring. Conservatism by creativity. Now you can punch above your weight with a great idea. You can build loyalty with daring thinking and an audience to go with it.**

The issue for so many companies today is to understand how they engage with this new, liberated audience. Notice that I use the word 'audience', not 'consumers'. I purposely use this word because I want to encourage my people at BBH to think about the public in a different way. ‖ **I think the word 'consumer' is old-fashioned and almost demeaning. It assumes complacency, lethargy and a one-way, top-down means of communication. A subservient relationship: from producer to buyer.**

This doesn't mean established media outlets are wrong – they're not.

Those established outlets offer unprecedented value, but they now have to be employed in a more inventive and exciting way. Linking established media to the digital world is the Holy Grail of marketing. But unless marketing directors rethink their audiences, stop talking about compliant 'consumers' and redefine how they engage with them, success and the opportunities that now present themselves to us will be wasted.

Client: Smirnoff, 2006
Title: Tea Partay
Art director: Aimee Shah
Copywriter: Matt Ian
Director: Julien Little

In many ways it could be argued that the public do not need to consume more – they are over consuming and are, by and large, underwhelmed. More doesn't necessarily mean better – it often confuses rather than clarifies.

Many years ago, Alvin Toffler, in his book *Future Shock*, predicted that the profligation of choice was becoming bewildering and confusing for consumers and would lead to a sense of isolation. Toffler's mistake was to think of people conventionally as consumers. If, however, you change the word 'consumer' to 'audience', you begin to alter the terms of engagement. Audiences seek to be entertained – they engage, they interact, they show commitment, they enthuse. And if treated properly they return for more. What Toffler never appreciated was how fickle the public are and also their desire for entertainment.

As branding looks into the future and ponders the world that is opening up, we have to realize that a number of things are happening:

Brands are no longer just about performance and trust, though they remain fundamentally important, but the future is going to be one where brands look increasingly at how the two worlds of entertainment and fashion are merging. Brands need to become part of those worlds – where fashion sits alongside the need to be entertained.

As I said in the preface, not so long ago appearing in an advertisement would have been the kiss of death for a film actor's career. Not any more – in today's world, what a star wears to the Oscars garners almost as much attention as what they win. The red carpet does more than just guide them into the show, it is part of the show.

I could say the future is about 'fashiontainment'. I know it's a dreadful word, but I'm using it only to capture what's going on in our world.

Client: Reebok, 2000
Art director:
John Hegarty
Copywriter:
Ty Montague
Photographer:
Bert Stern

The stars of today understand the merged worlds: David Beckham is both a sportsman and a fashion icon. He played football for England and he appears as an Armani model. Jude Law is not only an international movie star, he is also a style icon. In fact, right now you can hardly open a style magazine without coming across endless stars parading their fashion credentials. For brands, this offers huge opportunities, but also presents enormous dangers.

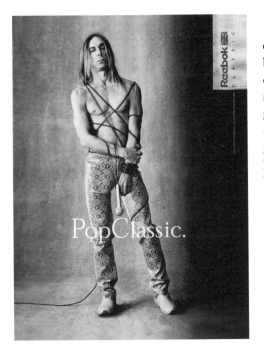

PopClassic.

So how does this relate to audiences? Our lives are increasingly driven by fashion and style, be it not just the clothes we wear, but how our homes are styled, the food we eat, the places we go and the car we drive. Performance is still important for brands, let's not forget that, and functionality is still at the heart of a product or service. But brands both today and in the future will have to employ design and style to encourage adoption and maintain loyalty.

It isn't so long ago that Volkswagen were running a powerful and memorable campaign around the thought, 'If only everything in life was as reliable as a Volkswagen'. Eventually they had to stop running the campaign because, as reliable as a Volkswagen was, it was placed around 7th in the annual reliability charts published by the Automobile Association in the UK. Technology originally provided reliability and Volkswagen's competitive edge, yet others had caught up and overtaken them, so centring their brand around reliability was no longer possible.

The issue with brands today is not about whether 'it', the product I've just bought, works – I expect 'it' to work – but what 'it' says about me. 'It' becomes a fashion statement. Brands should now be viewed through a prism of style *and* substance.

None of this is particularly new. For years we've looked to the emotional benefits a brand offers. Wishing to signal to others our place in society. Traditionally this was described as status. The paper you read, the car you drove, the place you lived, all of these reflected our wealth, knowledge and background. Top people read newspapers like *The Times* and the wealthy drove Bentleys and Rolls-Royces. Status was undoubtedly important and keeping up with the Joneses crucial.

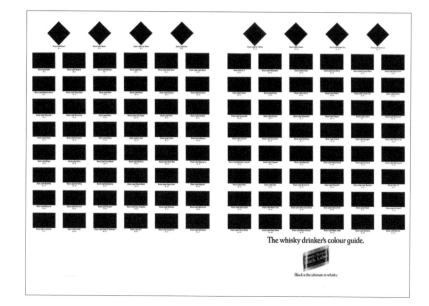

The whisky drinker's colour guide.

Black is the ultimate in whisky

Client: Johnnie
Walker, 1981
Art director:
John Hegarty
Copywriter:
Ken Mullen

But today things are different. For today's audiences it's not about status – that's class-ridden and old-fashioned – it's about staying ahead. || Vorsprung Durch Technik, Think Different, Keep Walking – these are all from brands (Audi, Apple, Johnnie Walker) that are egalitarian and inclusive. Money isn't the only measure of your success. || **Wearing the right pair of jeans in the right finish doesn't cost a fortune, but it does require an understanding of fashion.**

When we launched Häagen-Dazs in the UK in the early 90s we were in the middle of a recession. Not the best of times to be launching a luxury ice-cream brand. We positioned the brand as a sensual pleasure. We didn't compare it to other ice creams, in fact we hardly mentioned the word ice cream. But at £3 a pot it was not only accessible, it was the most stylish pleasure you could purchase. The brand took off. Häagen-Dazs weren't in the ice cream business, they were in the sensual pleasure business.

Sadly, over time, a succession of brand owners dragged it back to the ice cream sector. Now it's just one of a number of ice creams fighting for attention in the supermarket freezer. Imagine where they could have taken that brand had they realized the potential of where we had positioned it – they didn't realize we'd created a fashion brand.

The problem for many brands is that they still talk of consumers and still think of themselves in the conventional top-down world of marketing. They use the outmoded tools of FMCG (fast-moving consumer goods) brands to guide their thinking.

Client: Häagen-Dazs, 1991 (top)
Art director: Rooney Carruthers
Copywriter: Larry Barker
Photographer: Jean-Loup Sieff

Client: Häagen-Dazs, 1991 (above)
Art director: Martin Galton
Copywriter: Will Awdry
Photographer: Nadav Kander

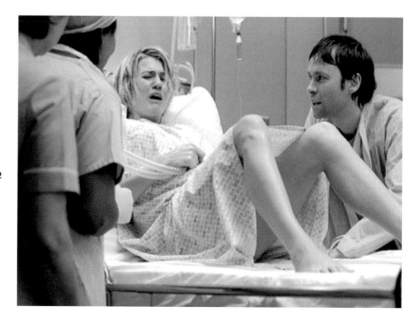

Client: X Box, 2002
Title: Champagne
Creative director:
Nick Gill
Art director:
Farid Mokart
Copywriter:
Fred Raillard
Director:
Daniel Kleinman

In the new world of fashion-driven (or perhaps
I should say style-driven) marketing, unlocking
the sales potential of your communication requires
different thinking. Increasingly, people will want
to buy the product that says the right thing about
them. Marketing directors will have to become more
like style directors. They will be making decisions
not based on consumer research but on instinct
and gut feeling.

Remember:
audiences want to be entertained, engaged, amused,
titillated. They want to interact, enthuse and be
passionate! And they want it to be constantly and
consistently new.

This new world will move too fast for the conventional marketing risk-assessment tools. Instead we will have to take our cues from the fashion world. We'll be flipping through the style as well as the business pages.

Research will move from being a measurement tool to one that is future facing.

Orange, the European mobile phone service provider, is a great example of a company thinking in a stylish way that engages its audience. When Orange launched itself as a network provider back in the mid-90s it did so with a radical name: Orange. Why Orange and not banana, or even tomato? Why not a multitude of other names? Orange, after all, doesn't seem very advanced or technologically future facing. But someone, somewhere decided it should be Orange. And out of that decision and a brilliant line – 'The future's bright, the future's Orange' – a hugely successful brand was built.

That, I would argue, was a decision based on style, taste, whatever you want to call it. One of Orange's competitors at the time in the UK was called Cellnet. Remember them? A dreary and predictable name. Well, they rebranded into O2 – another decision based on style and taste. As part of the rebranding, O2 considered the entertainment angle as well as the style one: to connect with their audience they sponsored the Millennium Dome in London, site of the disastrous, government-run Millennium Experience. It's now named 'The O2' and is a brilliant entertainment and concert venue that has almost certainly added value to O2's brand.

There is one other important point to remember when you're in the world of style and fashion: the value equation changes dramatically. Premium pricing becomes not only achievable, but also sustainable. || Consider again Mr Dyson and his remarkable, eponymous vacuum cleaner. Perhaps the most remarkable thing about it is that it's about £100 more expensive than its nearest rival. Not bad for a product that sits under the stairs and sucks up dust.

I think this is the most exciting time to be in advertising and marketing. But my fear is whether we have the people capable of grabbing this opportunity.

I recently gave a talk to a group of students studying art and design who wanted to pursue a career in advertising. I remember there was a degree of hesitation from these students about their chosen career. Despite the fact that the world is obsessed with brands, they were constantly reading headlines predicting the end of the advertising business and, in turn, the marketing one too. The digital revolution is sweeping all before it... Nothing will ever be the same... Forget everything you know... Change is the only constant.

As I stood in front of these creative students I could see fear on their faces. Was their chosen career about to disappear before they'd even graduated? I assured these students that, far from disappearing, this was the most exciting time to be in advertising. || **Yes, of course, we were being confronted by enormous change. Yes, the digital revolution was changing the way we worked. Yes, many companies would disappear, but many new companies would also be created. The world wasn't going to be less branded. If anything, it was going to be more so.**

How familiar are you with the phrase 'creative destruction'?

Creative destruction is the breaking down of old habits and practices that, in turn, create new and more powerful means of expression. The walls come down, innovation is magnified and old habits die. New avenues of expression and invention appear. In all this, opportunity and creativity are expanding exponentially. The advertising industry is experiencing creative destruction.

Technology has always been a spur to creativity and shouldn't be feared. Mozart without a piano would have been somewhat diminished as a composer. Rock 'n' roll without the electric guitar would have stayed being called folk music. And then no one would have booed Bob Dylan, calling him a Judas, when he went electric.

As I said at the start of this chapter, this is the age of the brand. But unless the long-established brands embrace the new branding and audience landscape, they'll go the way of Hoover – once a popular brand, but now swept away by the inventiveness and style of that premium-priced sucking Dyson.

3

AGENCIES

I've always felt there have been
only two great advertising agencies:
Doyle Dane Bernbach (DDB)
in New York, headed by Bill Bernbach,
and Collett Dickenson Pearce (CDP)
in London, led by another great
creative visionary, Colin Millward.
Never heard of Colin Millward?
Well, you have now.

Bernbach invented modern advertising with his legendary creative instincts and campaigns. Under Millward, CDP brought style and wit to the masses in the UK and placed British creativity at the pinnacle of the global advertising industry, making it the envy of the world. CDP's famous campaigns for brands such as Heineken beer, Hovis bread, Benson & Hedges cigarettes, Hamlet cigars and FIAT cars turned creativity into a high street phenomenon while, at the same time, winning more Cannes Grands Prix and D&AD Gold and Silver Pencils than any other agency.

Until the success of CDP in the 70s, creativity was viewed by most of the big agencies in the UK as a necessary evil – it was something the agency management had to tolerate. Millward proved that creativity and imagination could be as popular among the mass market as it was among the intelligentsia, and that creativity, if deployed properly, was an invaluable business tool. It was in their use of television that CDP proved itself most adept, creating campaigns that are still memorable today, some 40 years after they were first seen by an audience. In fact, at the time of writing this, Hovis, a brand of bread in the UK, have just launched a hugely successful campaign based on a TV commercial first broadcast in the early 70s. That's not bad value for a campaign. || **How many TV commercials can you remember from last night, never mind from 40-odd years ago?** || Sadly for the advertising business, Millward retired far too early and, today, CDP is no more, but from the start of the 70s, the cauldron of creativity that Saatchi & Saatchi launched into, through the decade that followed, CDP reigned supreme. They blazed a trail for innovative thinking, showing that it could be effective for big business with big budgets. Creativity was no longer on the fringes of advertising, but at its very core.

So what makes a great advertising agency? I believe that the function of any great agency is to help its clients stay in touch with their audience. They must ensure that their clients do not lose sight of what their advertising is trying to do – which is to engage and persuade. To an outsider this must seem absolutely ridiculous for a company to ignore this simple fact, yet it happens all the time. || Here's an example: why did General Motors have to be rescued by the US government in 2009? There is one, simple reason: GM was making cars that suited them and served their balance sheet rather than the needs of the American car driver. It really is incredible how such a company – the US's biggest car manufacturer – could find itself in such a position, but they did. The management of GM had lost sight of GM's primary purpose.

Ultimately, advertising agencies are there to generate creative solutions for their clients' problems. It's that simple. <u>Creativity is at the heart of our being.</u> When clients are asked in numerous surveys what they are looking for from their agencies, creativity is – surprise, surprise – always ranked number one.

At BBH we refer to ourselves as an 'ideas factory' – a factory that helps to manufacture brand difference. Some might think it odd to talk of an advertising agency as a manufacturing business rather than the industry norm of referring to itself as a 'service industry', but I have never liked that phrase. || It sounds so demeaning. It doesn't reflect the value we deliver. Or the kind of relationships we should be encouraging.

Creating an environment that lets ideas flourish is central to an advertising agency's success. And at the core of that success are two attributes: confidence and a belief in your ability to produce ideas that can outsmart your competitors and shape the future. Confidence and belief are elusive, though, and agencies rely on them like so many creative industries. || **But unlike a film studio or a record label, the big difference for an advertising agency is we don't own any of the software. We don't own a back catalogue. We have to come in every day and have a new idea. And that idea can't be like yesterday's. Therefore, advertising is a relentlessly creative culture where belief in the ability to produce that magical idea is everything, especially for the creative department.** || So if that sense of belief – and think of it as faith or trust as well – is ever punctured, the ability of the agency to continue is severely, one might say even fatally, damaged.

Once the damage has been done, rebuilding the confidence is close to impossible. In fact, I would say that it is impossible. I can't think of one creative agency that has pulled itself out of that nosedive once the confidence has gone. The descent might be slow, but ultimately the agency is going to crash. A smart owner will avoid the inevitable crash by selling while the craft still seems to be airworthy and the failing trajectory hasn't yet been spotted.

All too often you see agencies with a revolving door of creative directors. An agency whose creative directors come and go is an agency destined to failure. It is an agency without any real fixed view and a business without a soul. If your company is soulless, how is it supposed to inspire consumers? It can't. || If you are a creative business, as opposed to a business with a creative department, then creativity has to be at the heart of your organization. It has to be seen to be at the heart of the company, and not only to drive it, but also to attract other, equally inspiring creative thinkers. I think that's called 'a virtuous circle'. You can see companies that operate like that and the success they generate. They, of course, make it look very simple, and in many ways it is. But keeping things simple, as we all know, is very difficult. The old clichés of 'keep it simple', along with the other business maxim of 'complexity destroys profitability', are prerequisites of continuing success in business. They don't guarantee it, but you can be sure that without keeping those things in mind, you will hasten failure.

There's something else I really believe in, and this applies to clients as well as agencies: if you're genuinely going to be better than your competitors, you've got to love what you produce above everything else. That is fundamental.

So, if you are going to start a new advertising agency and you want to achieve greatness, you have to ask yourself some basic questions: what makes us different? Why choose us and not them? What are we saying that is going to add value to our clients' business and make the adoption of our offering better than the competition? || **Too many people start advertising agencies, and this applies to many other businesses as well, without any real point of difference. 'New' isn't a point of difference, it's a moment in time. Trying to be all things to all people is very tempting in a service industry, but it's impossible. Why turn good business away? Why limit your appeal? Well, you have to. It's the only way you can define yourself.**

I remember some years after BBH was established, a good friend of mine, and a highly regarded creative director, came to me for some advice. He was starting an agency with some colleagues. What advice could I give him?

I explained the need for an advertising agency to stand for something. Don't just rely on your creative reputations – have some beliefs that, when articulated, would dramatize a client benefit. In other words: work out what your 'angle' is. It's a brutal yet simple way of interrogating your value. I reminded my friend of how we started BBH, with no creative pitches from day one. We did this, perverse as it may seem, to dramatize our creative credentials – to put them on a pedestal. We reasoned you had to get the strategy right before you committed Pentel to layout pad. That's why this book is titled 'Turning intelligence into magic'. My friend explained they would like to do something similar, but they'd wait until they had some business before implementing that kind of philosophy. I realized in that moment his venture was doomed to failure. And it was.

Whatever you believe in has to be believed in from day one and implemented from day one. As you start, so shall you continue. It has a biblical sound to it, and it sounds that way because it is about fundamental beliefs. || As someone once said: don't start a business, start a revolution. How right they were. You are not going to change the world by being like everyone else. || **This always reminds me of what we used to say to each other in the early days of BBH: 'We haven't come this far to be ordinary.' No bloody way.**

It's an amazing feeling when you start an advertising agency. You really are operating with a charge of adrenalin that magnifies everything. I suppose this is why many people who do start their own agency talk about the early days and how exciting it was. || **And, of course, they're right, but it's excitement of achievement mixed with the fear of failure – they swirl around you like coalescing liquids in a glass, bitter and sweet.**

Those feelings show in your work. You are so hyped, tense and volatile, which actually doesn't help you create great work. Very often the first work a promising, new creative company produces isn't their best – they haven't learnt how to relax. They are so keen to do something amazing that they try too hard and end up producing something quite ordinary.

After overcoming opening-night fears, an agency in its early years is probably closest to its best. Holding on to that, staying true to your original principles, then becomes the important issue. Nigel Bogle, my partner at BBH, always says, 'How big can we get before we get boring?' Does size kill creativity? That is one of the great conundrums of the advertising business or in fact any creative business. As your success feeds your growth, so your growth destroys your success.

An agency can avoid that fate if they constantly elevate their creative beliefs and creative people. Like a religion they have to have a commitment to it that's unwavering. 'Sin and you shall be damned!' Well, every so often everyone in advertising has to go to confession and make amends. 'Dear God, do forgive me for that truly appalling half-page spread with a '20% off' starburst in the top right-hand corner.' An abomination. ‖ **We've all done it, we've all wandered from the creative path. And we all know what it feels like. The problem is that if it becomes a regular habit it seeps into your soul and destroys what makes you great. That's why great creative people seek the company of other like-minded creatives. We all help each other in moments of weakness.**

Money, of course, is the great temptation. I always say 'remember money has a voice, it doesn't have a soul'. When a creative company starts to elevate the status of money above everything else then it's lost. ‖ **Of course, none of us wants to die poor. 'He was buried in a pauper's grave, alongside his six D&AD Pencils and three gold lions, but, by God, you should have seen his show reel.' Bugger**

that. But if you allow mammon to drive your decisions, then you'll
most certainly end up a failure.

People constantly say, 'Money is the root of all evil'. Well, what it actually says in the Bible is, 'The love of money is the root of all evil'. And that
word 'love' is the most important part of it. Ironic that it is constantly left
out – I always try and say to my creative people money is the last reason
for doing anything. Sadly, though, the corporates with cash know how to
tempt them. And tempt them they do.

After 40 years in the advertising business, and having worked on
hundreds of businesses and brands with different clients, how would
I define success? Why do I think some businesses succeeded and others
failed? What made the difference between success and failure?

**In reality there's no single reason, but it all
relates to a <u>love of what you do</u>. For a business,
a true love of the product you're providing is,
I would say, the defining factor between success
and failure. Without a passion for what you're
producing you may well be able to manage
a business, but you'll never inspire greatness.**

Sadly, most businesses are just trying to manage what they've got. The
entrepreneurial spirit, the zeal to do better, to experiment and to try new
things has been long lost. In many ways we shouldn't be surprised – after
all we title many senior people in companies as 'managers'.

**If you were to see a long-lost friend and ask them how they were
getting on and they replied, 'Oh, I'm managing', you'd be really sorry
for them, be concerned for their well-being and try to seek ways to
help them. But in business we've elevated the 'managers' to run
things. Bizarre, isn't it? We use words without realizing sometimes
how profound they are.** || Go to the dictionary, look up 'manage' and
it describes quite succinctly why most companies are at best ordinary.
Without realizing it, we've accepted mediocrity to make our lives easier and
our work more predictable. That's why I think Dylan Thomas's words are

so important: 'Do not go gentle into that good night, but rage against the dying of the light'.

There is something else agencies, and in fact all kinds of businesses, pursue trying to achieve success: mergers.

This is something I first encountered when I was at Benton & Bowles in the mid-60s – their strategy for the future was to keep merging with other agencies as they thought that would solve their problems. In the 40 years since then I've never read a book on business management that says you can cure a sick business by merging it with a good business. Just like a virus, the sick business infects the good one and eventually destroys it.

The British car industry foundered on the belief that mergers would save them. Eventually it destroyed the whole industry. It even wounded the mighty BMW when they bought Rover, though, thankfully for the prestigious German car maker, they managed to get rid of Rover before it bled them dry by selling to a consortium that presided over its eventual demise.

The famous example here in the UK advertising business was an agency called Lintas. Every time Lintas merged with another agency to try to give it some credibility, it infected the new business with its culture of failure. Lintas even sounds like a virus, doesn't it?

> *Doctor*   I'm sorry, but our tests show you have been infected with a rare strain of Lintas.
>
> *Patient*   Oh my God! Is there a cure?
>
> *Doctor*   Sadly, no.

I think it is no coincidence that we use the word 'culture' when talking about growing viruses and company beliefs. The real lesson here is that a bad culture will always overwhelm a good one and yet mergers still continue today and I guarantee we'll continually read about good businesses being merged with bad ones in the forlorn hope that it will produce a success. Maybe more business leaders should study biology and, in particular, the behaviour of viruses. It could be good for their careers and it would certainly be better for the health of mergers.

It is no surprise then that Benton & Bowles no longer exists, which is sad for those who worked there and laboured to make it viable.

Moving on from talking about the past, where are advertising agencies going? What will they look like in the future?

At the time I'm writing this there are digital companies and advertising agencies fighting over which of them will inherit the future of advertising. || **Those kinds of debates are usually futile and somewhat barren, the simple reason being that it will be those people who are best able to come up with ideas and deploy them who will change the future of brands – they are the people who will inherit the future of advertising. And at the heart of the companies those people work for will be creativity.**

How that creative thinking is deployed will change and evolve – it will be a continually moving target. To nail your colours to any particular medium or technology will sow the seeds of your destruction.

Some people talk constantly about being 'media neutral'. It's a phrase I dislike. Neutrality isn't a position, it's an abdication of responsibility (certainly in the creative world). However, the phrase does contain a grain of truth. || As I said in chapter two, the only space worth buying is the space between someone's ears. How you get your idea there is, to a certain extent, irrelevant. Technology is a delivery system – you just have to make sure what you're delivering is memorable and motivating. || **Obsessing about one medium versus another is a waste of energy – it is the cultivation and management of ideas, and the people who generate them, that is the crucial factor.**

So, in the agency of the future, how do you manage that creative talent to extract the best value while maintaining an environment that is truly inspiring?

We are rapidly reaching a point where we have to look at the way we employ people and how our employees view work. Following the rise in digital technology, the concept of where you work and how is being questioned and challenged. Alongside this, we also see people questioning the value of their employment.

I'm going to set out a train of thought that I hope will stimulate a debate on the issue. It is radical in its construction, but possibly answers both the needs of clients and those people wishing to work in the advertising industry.

If you take a step back, you can plot a trend, which grew slowly over the last 50 years, over how we approach 'the office' and our relationship with work. Digital technology is the latest spur to that change.

The last five decades have witnessed the humanization of the work place. Before the trend began you would have found domineering, top-down organizational structures in dreary surroundings – where individuality was stamped out and uniformity imposed. These places were a throwback to how work was first industrialized. They were repetitive, boring and, in many ways, dehumanizing environments.

Over time, rigid structures in offices were gradually broken down. In an attempt to make offices more attractive Herman Miller, the office furniture and equipment manufacturer, pioneered the humanization of the office with the design of their products. The workplace began to see the addition of rubber plants, colour schemes and the deconstruction of the office layout, reaching as far today as the addition of a coffee bar where staff can socialize and take refreshment. One could say no advertising agency is now complete without the ubiquitous coffee bar.

All of those additions are and were cosmetic and, important as they may be, none of those changes answers the more fundamental question of the value of work and what individuals get from it. The old line about 'I don't live to work, I work to live' remains absolutely true, especially for creative organizations. || **How can a creative company make working more rewarding for their employees and, therefore, make those same employees more valuable to the company? People increasingly don't want to work 9 to 5 and they don't want to do so in unrewarding organizations – they want flexi-time and flexi-careers. They** want to expand their knowledge and their experiences. If creativity is at the heart of a company's offering then being creative about how that company delivers it to their employees is also essential.

Maybe we should rethink the whole organizational structure of an office and think of it as a club? A club is a place people enjoy going to and spending time in. A club is a rewarding, engaging and stimulating place to be. So why don't we think of the office as a club and learn from the way a club is run rather than an office? ‖ A club is open all hours, seven days a week. It's a place that engages people and encourages them to stay longer. There are no 'after hours' in a club – it's a place where they want to spend time and are proud to be members. If we continue the club analogy, this is how it could be for an advertising agency: you'd have a core of full-time, salaried people who would run the club. How many? Not sure, but let's say 100 out of 400. The other members would be made up of those who are paid a retainer and would be paid for the number of projects they worked on – they would decide how much they wanted to work. And there would also be associate members who were paid no retainer, but would have access to the 'club's' facilities and be paid as they worked on projects. To be an associate member, you'd have to be passed by the selection committee who would review your work credentials and see if you were eligible.

Too many people leave BBH not because they're unhappy with the agency, but because they want to spend time doing something else, broadening their experiences, their knowledge and their skills. A club structure would not stand in the way of this.

The office layout would look and feel like a club where people could drop in or spend the day to chill out or work as they chose. Like a club, the office would serve food and drink, it would organize events, talks and social outings. It would have rooms for private meetings, for thinking in and presenting. It would be an office, but it would feel like a club.

Radical though this may all sound, at BBH we are slowly evolving into this form of organization by using flexible, stimulating and radical work practices.

I know that there are lots of <u>unanswered questions</u>: how would you manage a constant relationship with a client? Who leads the organization? Who vets the work and takes responsibility for what is produced?

However, if you look at a well-run club, the full-time management ensures it runs smoothly and effectively. Clubs have managers and staff who make it happen. They deal with difficult members and organize the effective development of resources. All that is detail.

> I can't see the company of the future, especially a creative one, continuing along the path of the existing trend that has slowly developed over the last 50 years. Just as a building has to be flexible to adapt to changing patterns of work, so organizations are going to have to rethink their structures radically if they are going to attract the most interesting people in the most stimulating environment. Making an advertising agency think like a club isn't a bad place to start. And before you dismiss this completely, it would be worth taking a trip to the Google campus in California.

The communications industry should always be at the forefront of change by stimulating debate, provoking a response and, as a consequence, inevitably courting controversy. An advertising agency should not expect to reflect or revere the status quo, but to challenge it – in reality, to help re-define it. Those who grasp this reality and opportunity, be it through the work they create or the workplace they create in, are the ones who will reap the rewards on offer.

THE CREATIVE DIRECTOR

One day, if play your cards right
(or perhaps wrong), you might be a
creative director. It is the most thankless,
trying and difficult task you'll ever
undertake in your creative career.
'Surely not!' I can hear you say.
Well, let's take a moment to have
a look at the job specification.

First of all, you'll be in charge of an unruly, rebellious, egocentric, insecure and fractious bunch of lunatics who are capable of moments of genius. And that's on a good day. This should be no surprise as, let's face it, if you haven't employed people like that you're on a slow slide towards mediocrity.

All those lunatics report to you. You are now responsible for them. In fact, you have to manage them. || **'Manage' seems an odd word to employ when referring to a creative department; 'controlled mayhem' may be nearer the truth. Despite all the chaos, you also have to be reasonable, understanding, focused and sensible. You are, after all, employed by a commercial organization intent on creating competitive success for its clients.** || You are the person who has to reconcile those two opposing forces in advertising: mayhem and management.

I'm reminded of a scene in George Orwell's *Down and Out in Paris and London*. Orwell is working in a restaurant and he describes the maître d' screaming vile abuse at the various chefs attempting to get the food out on time. As the maître d' passes through the swing doors from the kitchen into the restaurant he turns into an urbane, calm, mannered host, gliding effortlessly among the diners, dispensing charm and bonhomie.

I think you get the picture.

As a creative director you have to occupy two worlds: one mad, reckless, irrational yet inspirational; the other sensible, concerned and corporate. Both are fundamentally important to the success of business. Navigating their extremes takes patience, foresight and skill.

So why do it? And how do you make sense of it all and be an effective, perhaps even great, creative director? To answer the 'why' is, in some ways, straightforward. || All of us want to control our destinies in whatever way we can. A simple human desire – even more so if you're working in a creative industry in which selling your work and persuading clients to understand what it is you're trying to achieve is fundamental to your success. You may not be very good at the selling part, but you understand its importance. ‖ **The more you can control the dialogue and have access to power, the more likely you are to get your vision implemented. That's what gets you out of your bed. And that's what gradually sucks you into the role of creative director. That's 'why'.**

'How' can you be an effective creative director? That's less straightforward, but I believe there are some things that any creative director should live by:

be the soul of your agency. <u>You are the person who defines and guides the agency's creative beliefs.</u> You are the conscience of the company and the person responsible for keeping the creative spirit burning.

Being successful at the job means accepting that responsibility alongside all the other demands the job requires. As much as some agencies try to achieve great things by transplanting a creative director into their organization, if that person doesn't or can't become the soul of the agency it will never work. You can have a heart transplant, but it doesn't work for the soul.

Always remember who has the real power. Unlike most other companies, the real power in an advertising agency doesn't lie with the person at the top – the creative director – but with the entire team of creative people within that agency. ‖ **As creative director, I'm only as good as the work I inspire. Yes, I guide, push, probe, identify promising thoughts and scribbles. But I can't do it all. I need brilliant people around me who spark magic – people who can craft a problem into a solution that dominates the airwaves and gets talked about.**

Most companies are triangular in structure. As you rise up the corporate ladder you accrue power and influence. Eventually you sit at the top dispensing decisions and directions. Steve Jobs sits at the pinnacle of Apple determining its future. Brilliant, iconoclastic and formidable, he has the final say and has probably made many of the decisions that have propelled Apple to where it is today.

In the advertising world that corporate triangle is inverted. The power lies with the people coming up with the ideas. One

brilliant piece of creativity can change the fortunes of an agency. And that brilliant idea could have come from a graduate straight out of college. ‖ The creative director has to recognize that idea and help nurture it through the corridors of compromise. A creative director must generate an atmosphere and a structure that removes barriers and hurdles to brilliant ideas, from wherever they may spring. ‖ **As well as inspiring your talent, you're also there to attract it. You're a lightening conductor, attracting the best and keeping them motivated.** ‖ Great creative departments are always on the verge of mutiny. It's their natural state. Your job is to keep them radicalized around clients' problems.

Never forget that magic is an elusive force.
Sometimes exasperating in its creation,
it is generated by confidence and certainty.
It takes swagger, madness, absurdity;
it requires encouragement, irreverence
and positivity. Magic doesn't come about
by menacing people.

Believe in your creative department and give them permission to excel. Establishing a belief in your creative people and making them confident in themselves are essential for any creative director. Permission to excel is something a creative director has to instil into them. The mantra of this book in many ways is: creativity isn't an occupation, it's a preoccupation. As creative director, you are leading people who are driven by the need to do something great. That desire to create comes from deep within their psyche, and your belief in them will energize their thinking. ‖ **Even if a team has just presented you with a bucket load of mediocrity, they have to walk out of your office believing they're on the verge of greatness. They're looking to you for direction and affirmation. Screaming, shouting and bullying them may make you feel great for a fleeting moment, but it will do nothing for the creative process.**

Earn your team's respect. ‖ **There was a time when creative directors were appointed for their organizational abilities and their skill at charming clients. But today the world is run by the 'doers', not the 'talkers'. Respect has to be earned! It can't just be** appointed. Today's creative director has to have a track record of brilliant creative work before they can inherit the title and, therefore, before they can command respect. ‖ When you turn down an idea presented to you, the dejected team responsible have to know that if they don't crack it, you can. And given half a chance you will. It's amazing how galvanizing that can be.

Always be generous with your ideas. You see a creative team struggling with a problem – they are languishing in some creative cul-de-sac getting nowhere fast. You have to rescue them. That can be achieved with an expression of belief in their potential brilliance, but, more often than not, you have to suggest an idea, a solution to the problem they're wrestling with.

And when you've done that, you have to step back and let them get on with it, taking the glory and the applause with them. For some creative directors that is hard. It may hurt your creative ego, your desire for recognition. But it is essential for your success as a creative director to accept the loss of credit. And you must not worry about not being recognized for your efforts. ‖ **If you're really good at your job, the media will begin to piece it together. Just be patient.**

Belief in yourself is essential. ‖ **But watch out for your ego. Ego is both a friend and a foe. It drives you forward, energizes your thinking, but, if left unchecked, it will destroy you.**

Work out how your creatives can deal with your clients and vice versa. While the filter of an understanding account handler, someone who understands business and business relationships, is no bad thing, as wonderful as these people are, our clients want more direct contact with the creative department. We work in an environment in which creative work is being executed over a broader media landscape, in which agility and speed of response are essential, so it is only natural that creative people are going to have to take a more active role in the client–agency relationship.

Creatives have to deal with client contact: <u>it's</u> <u>a fact of life</u>, so get on with it and work out how to help your team. It can be one of the thankless tasks, though: soothing a client's fractured ego after one of your creative people has told them, in fairly blunt terms, 'where to go' after they have wanted to change some of their work.

I recently had a client complaining to me about one of our writers being unbelievably rude. I did point out that I didn't hire the writer in question for their manners. || Creativity and politeness don't necessarily go hand in hand. It's another one of those conundrums you have to solve. A polite creative!

One of the things that you constantly hear is, 'Well, you're creative'. I always reply, 'We're all creative, it's just some of us earn our living by being so'. On a recent occasion when I made this observation I was asked what it takes to be able to earn your living being creative. I replied, 'fearlessness'.

Naturally, you have to have great ideas, but fearlessness is a prerequisite of being a great creative. Why? Because you have to present ideas that are truly fresh, distinctive and different. Ideas that break the mould of conventional thinking. Sticking by those ideas and convincing those around you takes courage. Fear of failure has to be dismissed and faith in your idea has to be paramount.

Time is the other issue you have to argue for. || **I had to explain to a client recently that if they wanted an instant response it wasn't necessarily going to be the one they wanted to hear.** || In this world of jetstream thinking, it is important that we fight for time, but you have to make sure that you and your creative team achieve a balance. Thinking on your feet is an admirable skill, but overnight reflection is still of profound importance.

Make sure your creative team stay objective. Don't over expose your creative team to your client's problems. Make them part of the solution. The fresh mind, the ability to stand back and reflect, is even more important in a harshly competitive world that moves at the click of a button. In any client–agency relationship objectivity has to be valued.

If creative people are over exposed to a client's problem they begin to lose objectivity. Once again, it is a matter of balance. Looking into a client's eyes as they talk about their brief is a fundamentally important thing for the creative team to witness. Observing the client's body language is essential. Do they lean forward or back as they brief you on the creative opportunity? When they use the word 'daring' do they blink? Is the word said with hesitancy or certainty? || **The way a client says something is as important as what they say. If you're going to work with that client's brand or product then you've got to experience that briefing in the flesh, but being constantly consumed by the brand and its problems can stifle the creative spark.**

Creative people don't want to sit in meetings with their brains going soggy as the client debates their distribution strategy and pricing policy for supermarkets, while also pondering a coherent strategy for dealing with parallel imports – they are not in the slightest bit interested, though of course they can feign interest. 'Wow! That's really fascinating! You mean we're down 3% in the North East because the distribution centre mislabelled the inventory?' At moments like this, inspiration is seeping out of every orifice.

The creative director, however, has to endure these meetings. If it means it will help sell some work, then you look interested, perhaps even concerned. It is essential that you understand the problems facing a client, but not to the extent of being overwhelmed by them. The reality is that such over exposure will dull both your creative edge and that of your creative team. It's hard enough for you, but for the people who have to find the magic it's destructive.

Learn how to occupy the dual worlds of creativity and commerce. This is the most challenging part of the job. To help you engage with the cut and thrust of commerce my recommendation is a weekly dose of the *Economist*: it will arm you with all kinds of information that will impress your clients. || All you have to do is occasionally quote a piece from the magazine and you'll have the meeting stunned into respect. || **Say something like, 'Of course, if Bill Clinton hadn't repealed the final section of the Glass-Steagall Act we might never have had the banking collapse that caused the recession' and your clients will naturally begin to see you in a different light. They'll take you more seriously and listen to your somewhat radical observations such as, 'Why not make a better product?' or perhaps something even as outlandish as, 'We should just tell the consumer the truth'.**

So sprinkling your conversation with the odd fact gleaned from the *The Economist* will do wonders for your salesmanship. It will also open you up to a different set of influences and ideas that might also benefit your creativity. Fish in different ponds and you'll catch different fish.

Remember:

the best way to sell an idea is to make the
person to whom you are selling it feel that it
is solving their problem, not feeding your ego.

In essence, that is the creative director's lot. When the team have cracked the problem, having responded to your confidence in them, you're forgotten. || **For you it's on to the next problem. And that's because the only time people want you is when there's trouble. And trouble usually appears at about 6.45 pm on a Friday as you're putting your coat on for a well-earned weekend rest.**

Still want the job?

I think the answer is still going to be 'yes'.

5

CLIENTS, BRIEFS
AND THE POWER
OF WORDS

A brief is either a friend or a foe.
It's that little piece of paper that will
be constantly referred to throughout
the whole of the creative process.
The question is: does it inspire or does
it impair? Has it been crafted, if that's
the right word, by someone who
wants to control the creative process
or liberate it? Is it a box or is it
a platform? Too often it's a box.

My view on briefs is: accept nothing and question everything. I take that view not to be an awkward bastard, but to prise open opportunity. After all, the brief is nothing but a bit of paper that has been crafted by someone who too often wants to try, and sadly, to control the process. I'm always trying to open up the process, not close it down. I don't want it to be controlled, I want it to be liberated.

The intelligent brief is the one that understands the limitations of the process and functions as a way of kick-starting the search for that simple, illusive idea that can capture the public's imagination.

That said, you cannot condone anarchy as well. When you start working on a job for a client no one knows where the answer will come from and how that idea, which may not conform to the brief's assumptions about what is required, could actually transform that client's business. The brief is an attempt to put some shape and form into a process that's looking for the unexpected.

If what you produce is predictable then everything I've just written is anathema to you, but remember that in advertising we're trying to turn intelligence into magic. The intelligence is the strategy, gained from market insights, that will hopefully liberate the execution and produce magic. Crafting a brief therefore has to walk a fine line between control and liberation.

You have to make sure the brief isn't a set piece of thinking that your client uses to reject the transformational thinking you pitch to them. || **The dreaded words 'but it doesn't answer the brief' are all too often used to destroy work that is genuinely challenging, possibly uncomfortable for the client, but is ultimately outstanding.**

I do think it's essential to get the creative people in front of the client. I find that when I'm briefed directly by the client I learn a lot more about the client's worries, concerns and expectations than can ever be transmitted through a piece of paper. || When they say they want something 'different', you can sense what they really mean by their body language. The passion with which they say those key words provides you with a powerful sense of whether they mean what they say.

Too often you're dealing with people with the power to say 'maybe'. Great work is bought by powerful people, not by the weak, the ones who say 'maybe', or the ones who hedge their bets. || When a creative person is sitting in front of the client they can sense all that. || **'I'd like something different. but I'd like to recognize it before I buy it.' I've actually had that said to me by a client. Courage is a rare quality, but when you're sitting in front of it you can generally recognize it.**

I'm much happier when a client talks about the business problem they are trying to solve. I always think getting them talking about their business, the things they understand, is more productive than their talking about the abstract business called advertising. || **Ask your client what the business problem is that you are trying to solve with your advertising? That's probably the most important thing you should have in mind when you talk to a client and, if you genuinely believe in it, you'll have them eating out of your hand (or even your layout pad).**

You must always see the problem you are trying to solve from the client's point of view. You'll be their friend for life if you do. || **It's all very well saying that in advertising 'we solve problems', of course we do, but making your client believe that what you want to do is solve *their* problem is a different matter.**

By sitting in front of a client as a creative person, you have a unique opportunity to gain their trust and their willingness to buy your work. Use it wisely.

Sadly, in this globally interconnected communications industry, it can be hard to get in front of your client. It just won't happen. You have a remote client. Then you have to reply on that piece of paper called 'the brief', the one everyone signed off.

There is no sure way of making remote clients adhere to a briefing document. They'll sign it off and, at the click of the delete button, will go back on its contents when they're confronted by a piece of work they don't like.

Client: Audi, 1989

Art director:
Dennis Lewis
Copywriter:
Steve Hooper
Photographer:
Graham Ford

A good client (no, that's not an oxymoron) will find ways of describing the problem they are trying to solve which focuses your creative energy in the right way.

I remember Brian Bowler, the marketing director at Audi who was responsible for hiring us at BBH back in 1982, saying that whatever we did, he didn't want us 'to give the pen to the car'. Now, this might seem like

MANY HAVE ASKED THE MEANING OF 'VORSPRUNG DURCH TECHNIK'. ALLOW US TO EXPLAIN.

DER AUDI 80. VORSPRUNG DURCH TECHNIK.

a strange statement, but at the time I realized absolutely what Brian meant. The brand perception of Audi in 1982 was that they made practical cars, bought by accountants and lawyers – a sensible choice.

Brian realized that Audi had to be imbued with some passion, with flair. ‖ **If the advertising focused on the clever engineering at the heart of Audis, it might make a smart ad, but all the logic in the world wasn't going to change people's perception of the brand. Unless, that is, we wrapped the logic up in emotion.**

We understood the function of the product. But what is its purpose? That's what the advertising had to capture.

Brian's ability to articulate the brand's need in a simple and evocative way helped inspire a solution that really moved the brand forward and helped create the opportunity to adopt 'Vorsprung durch Technik' as the brand's slogan.

The worst brief you can get is the one where the client says they want to win an award. Surprising as this sounds, as soon as those words are uttered you know you're in trouble. Why? First, their motivation is all wrong, and secondly, you know damn well they've already got an idea of what they want to buy because they've just seen the award winners at Cannes and they want to impress their company by having their name up in lights.

They want to buy something they've already seen.

But, as we all know, to win an award you generally have to do something different. You have to create something fresh. What your client has in mind is last year's ideas, and one thing that will certainly not please next year's Cannes jury is last year's ideas. As seductive as it sounds, a client who wants to do nothing but win awards should be avoided at all costs.

The most important word a creative person can use is 'why?' The word 'why' not only demands that we constantly challenge everything, but it also helps the creative process. It's just like that wonderful thing children do, they constantly ask: why? Why is it like that? Why do we do that? Why can't I go there? Why? Why? Why?

That's why the best creative people are those who hold on to that childhood innocence, that desire to question constantly and not to accept the status quo. The people who, if you say 'no', want to hear 'yes'.

I was once asked to speak at a conference titled 'Adopting Risk'. Now, it would seem obvious to ask a creative person to speak at such a gathering, wouldn't it? Naturally, one would assume that I was going to lambaste an audience of earnest business leaders for not adopting such an obvious course of action as 'risk'. A creative person would say that caution was not the way forward and that should be something any business person must realize. Not surprisingly, I was duly briefed to fly the flag of creativity and uphold the value of risk taking!

Now, remember what I said: always question the brief.

Never just blindly accept the brief. Challenge it, interrogate it, question its very foundation. This isn't meant to be for the sake of being awkward (well, maybe it is), but explore, probe, understand and eventually expand upon what is in the brief.

That's what I did with the conference on 'Adopting Risk'. The more I thought about the premise of the conference, the more ridiculous I thought it was.

I thought 'Adopting Risk' was an incredibly stupid thing to ask people to do. If the intention of the conference was to try to get people to behave differently and convert them to another way of thinking, then I thought the whole premise of 'Adopting Risk' was completely stupid. Who the bloody hell wants to run their lives like that? Despite the fact that every other book on business management was expounding the virtues of risk, I thought that they were all completely stupid. They were books that had obviously been written by people who'd never run a business and most certainly had no idea how human nature works. Words carry meanings for very good reasons. They inform us, warn, inspire, sooth, engage and comfort us. Yes, we constantly subvert their meaning at times to make a point, but in doing so we understand the power of our actions, our intent and, hopefully, the outcome.

Have you ever wondered how men would carry on if they had periods?

Dr White's Towels and Tampons.

The more I thought about encouraging the conference audience to adopt risk, the madder I thought I was going to sound. And pointless.

I don't worry if people think I'm mad – at times I take it as a compliment – but in this situation, if I was trying to be helpful, a half-crazed creative person extolling the virtues of risk was almost certainly going to confirm the audience's worst fears. They would think that they should stay well away from it – one of the 'long hairs' is encouraging us to adopt risk. ‖ **So I decided, I think quite rightly, to tell my audience to ignore the premise of the conference. This shocked the organizers somewhat and wasn't quite what they wanted to hear, but I was determined to try to help. I wanted to give the audience some advice that hopefully they could take away and had some practical use.**

My argument was simple: why in life would you encourage risk? That's reckless. It's fine for a stunt man, but not exactly good governance for a company with many hundreds, if not thousands, of employees with mortgages, shares and pensions to protect.

You don't get up in the morning and go: 'Oh great, another risky day. I'm looking forward to a risky meeting with a risky outcome. Maybe I'll have a risky lunch and while I'm at it book a risky holiday. That'll be fun. Wait till I get home and tell the family that we're all going on a risky holiday. I bet that'll excite them.' Like hell it will.

The other thing I love about those business books that advise on this course of action is they talk about 'risk management'. Realizing that risk is a daft piece of advice they suggest managing it. That's a bit like someone who wants to commit suicide and decides it's slightly less risky to jump out of the 30th floor rather than the 50th.

The words 'risk management' always make me think of those great rock bands in the late 60s who put together two words that didn't make sense. Bands like Curved Air, Soft Machine or Led Zeppelin. At least they knew they were absurd, they were full of contradictions and chose them for that reason. I'm surprised there wasn't one called Risk Management. Ridiculous, isn't it?

My advice to the audience was to encourage them to do something they might just enjoy doing. If they enjoy it, there's a good chance they'll keep doing it. I suggested that, instead of embracing 'risk' with all its apparent dangers, they use the word 'excitement'. Does this idea excite me? Does it excite the people around me? Am I working for an exciting company or a risky company? Would I like an exciting life or a risky one? Would I like to take my family on an exciting holiday? Replace the word risk with excitement and I said you then have a positive way forward. Let's face

Client: Dr White's, 1986 (opposite)
Art director: John Hegarty
Copywriter: Barbara Nokes
Photographer: Stak

it, the problem with so many companies today is they're just dull. Excitement attracts, risk repels. I ended the speech by saying, 'so what would you prefer, risky profits or exciting ones'?

God knows if I did any good, but I put the wind up the organizers and made the next speaker's task somewhat harder – at least I gave them something to debate. But this happened only because I questioned the brief.

When I was in the US starting up the BBH office in New York I had to learn very quickly that the word 'creative' doesn't quite mean the same in the US as it does in the UK. For many US clients the word carries all kinds of dangerous undertones. Whereas in the UK, clients actually look for creativity within their agencies, in the US that is not always the case. When you use the word with US clients it means 'edgy' to them and suggests work that will possibly upset a great many people. They think of 'creative' as potentially subversive and dangerous.

Now edgy, subversive and dangerous can be fine if you're talking to a youth audience, but if you're talking to middle America you can forget it. I thought carefully about my definition of 'creative' and it isn't founded in being edgy. It's certainly founded in being challenging, daring, breathtaking and different. Ultimately it is about being effective and memorable. So, when talking to US clients, I made sure I used words like 'memorable', 'interesting' and 'effective'. If I uttered the word 'creative' it would have been a very short meeting with an unfavourable outcome. I remember a particular company we were pitching to where the marketing chief, after seeing our showreel, turned to me and said, 'That was a very creative reel, but that went out in the 60s'. I just sat there speechless. Creativity went out in the 60s?! There's no answer to that, other than 'goodbye'.

It just goes to show how, with clients and briefs, you always have to remember the meaning and the power of words and how that changes depending on your audience. Even though we speak the same language as Americans, certain words can a carry completely different meaning in the US. How true that Oscar Wilde quotation is: 'We're two nations divided by a common language'.

PITCHES

Pitching is the life blood of the advertising business. Someone once likened an agency to a shark: if it wasn't moving forward, it was dying. You could say this is true of virtually any business – evolution is a fundamental part of business, as it is of life – but nowhere is it more true than in the adrenaline-charged, wacky world of advertising. It is a world where the business is built on confidence, both of predictions and of creative solutions. As much as clients want it to, all the research in the world cannot and will never guarantee success. For an agency, self-belief is fundamental to its success.

The truth is that, in advertising, we're in the magic business. We are constantly looking for that idea that will transform a small investment in a communications program into a bottom-line figure worth millions. Maintaining a culture that can constantly deliver these magic solutions requires an inordinate investment in the pursuit of success. Confidence is illusory – it can slip away at a moment's notice.

An advertising agency is like an addict, mainlining on success. Winning is the cocaine of the advertising industry, which is probably why the industry has so many awards schemes, and pitching is its agent. We love pitching – it brings out our competitive spirit like nothing else. We snort the energy of battle. Our best people volunteer for frontline service, committing their time, passion and creativity. || **When a 'big pitch' is on you can feel the adrenaline running through an agency. There are endless ideas, positionings, strategies and flow charts pasted on to walls, late-night meetings and discarded boxes of half-eaten pizza scattered around the building. There are cancelled social lives and late-night taxis home and then a quick shower and a clean shirt before a rapid return to the frontline. We thrive on this kind of energy. Failure is not an option.**

Pitching is more than just an advertising agency's business need: it is an opportunity for an agency to reaffirm its power. It's not only the pitch that counts, but also whom and what you're pitching for and which other agencies are pitching against you. || After all, we are judged on the company we keep. The oxygen of publicity when a big account is up for pitching adds to the drama and the adrenalin of the chase – you hear rumours of stunts being undertaken, of commercials being shot, of photographers being hired to add glamour to the final presentation – all this swirls around the process. You sometimes also hear of rival agencies blundering attempts to curry favour with potential clients. I remember an agency we were competing against blowing their chances by not realizing that the client they were pitching to was a church-going Bible-basher. The agency sent a questionnaire to his home on a Sunday, thereby demonstrating that a 24/7 work ethic can seriously backfire, especially if you haven't done your homework.

With so much at stake the big question for an agency is: how do we improve our chances of winning a pitch and increase the odds of success in what, to a certain extent, is a lottery?

Did I say something about it being a lottery? It is: I remember a pitch for Golden Wonder, a brand of British potato crisps, while I was still at TBWA. It was the very last pitch John, Nigel and I did before we left to set up BBH.

We'd arrived at 'freshness' as a strategy, with the executions being all about noise: the noisier the crisp, the fresher it was. Our final piece of creative work was a 48-sheet poster, one of those giant billboards, showing an empty Golden Wonder packet with the line: 'Silence is golden.'

When we presented the mock-up of the 48-sheet poster the chairman of Golden Wonder said that it was the finest piece of creative work he'd ever seen for his product.

I thought we've won this! It's in the bag! How wrong I was. They proceeded to give the business to JWT.

So, if it's a lottery, how do you shorten the odds?

Behave like a great brand. It's amazing how so many agencies never behave like brands despite the fact they're constantly advising their clients on brand behaviour. Great brands have a point of view – they stand for something. || And that 'something' needs to be self-selecting in terms of audience. Being all things to all people is a worthy objective, but ultimately, especially for a creative company, a disastrous positioning. It may be a perfectly sensible strategy for a nationwide retailer – from their finest to their value range the UK super-market chain Tesco can be all things to all people – but for an advertising agency? Sadly, it's not.

An obvious question to ask yourself is: <u>should we be pitching for this account?</u> In other words, has the potential client put you on their shortlist because they like your work and your beliefs? Or is it because you're conveniently located near a mainline railway station and handy for the prospective client to make a quick exit?

There's nothing worse than trying to sell a client apples when what they really want are turnips. || **So, lesson one is: are you right for them and are they right for you?**

When we started BBH our policy of not making speculative creative pitches was based on that principle. Great creative work was great only if it worked. And a vital part of that process was strategy. Get that right first and then you could start creating. It was a way of trying to find out if the potential clients really bought into our beliefs. Some people described our positioning as arrogant, but all we were trying to do was behave like a brand. If behaving like a brand was being arrogant, then we were being arrogant.

Change the rules. One of the surest ways of shortening the odds is to uncover some insight into the brand or the market that changes the rules.

Changing the rules puts you in a unique position. It gives the poten-tial client a differentiating point of view. Of course, the rule change has to be meaningful to work. A good example is when BBH pitched for Polaroid back in the early 90s. Polaroid's business was under serious threat

Client:
Polaroid, 1996
Title: Resignation
Art director:
John Gorse
Copywriter:
Nick Worthington
Director:
Michel Gondry

from the disposable camera market where the products were becoming cheaper and better quality. As a result, Polaroid's 'instant' advantage was proving less competitive. Our insight? Polaroid weren't in the camera business – they were a 'social lubricant'. Unlike a conventional photo, when you took a Polaroid people joked, had fun and let their hair down. They passed the Polaroid around. It got the party going.

We said to Polaroid: don't compare yourself to other cameras. As a social lubricant, your competition is music, alcohol and karaoke. As a result, we changed the dynamics of the market – we changed the rules – and won the business without showing a single ad. This was a perfect example of intelligence that we turned into magic with our 'Live for the moment' campaign for the brand.

It's a great shame that Polaroid never really capitalized on this positioning. Yes, it worked in terms of advertising and we have the work to show for it. But the positioning was bigger than that.

In a way it pre-dated the whole idea of file sharing, opening up a conversation with a picture you have taken. Social networking is a vital part of the internet. Polaroid could have been at the heart of it. But sadly they couldn't get away from the idea of instant film, instead of instant experiences.

It's not always possible to change the rules like that, but you'd better make sure that's not the case. If one of your competitors has unlocked a killer insight, you're dead.

Take the high ground. In the end, wherever a brand sits, they want to be the brand leader or thought of as the brand leader. No question about it. If they don't want to be that, then what are they in business for? But even if they can't realistically be the brand leader then they should think like a brand leader. ‖ A brand can own a category without dominating it – that has always been Virgin's strategy.

Therefore, making the client believe in themselves is psychologically important. They are often feeling battered and vulnerable, unsure of their competitive advantage and doubting their potential. The pitch can be about building their confidence, unlocking that potential.

I've always believed the function of a pitch is to redefine a brand's future. It's never just a pitch for the advertising account. It's a pitch for the company, and its business. || It's an opportunity to help them understand where they're going to be in five to ten years' time. || **Excite them, engage them in the opportunities that await them. But understand that will work only if they adopt the 'confident brand leader' position, if they themselves have ambitions. You'd be surprised how companies are afraid of the future, even though that's where success lies.**

Brands are no different from people: they yearn to be exciting and engaging. They want to be talked about, admired and, of course, valued. That's why, despite what some people may tell you about an ageing population, it's essential that brands remain constantly youthful. || Why? Because if you're youthful, you have a future. You own tomorrow. And owning tomorrow is where the profits, and the growth, will come from.

Remember:
nobody invests in yesterday. Unless that is, you're an undertaker or the History Channel.

Don't make your pitch just about the advertising. The greatest failing in any pitch is to keep it in the world of advertising. Fall into that trap and, ironically, you lengthen your odds rather than shortening them. By doing so you make yourself like all the others by asking prospective clients to judge something they're by and large hopeless at judging: advertising. || That's why they use research so much. Why should they make a decision when they can rely on the crutch of consumer research?

I remember one pitch in particular that captured the absurdity of this process. And how we fell into the advertising-only trap. We were asked to present for the launch of a new Sunday paper from the Daily Mail Group: the *Mail on Sunday*. They had decided there was an opportunity to compete with the ever successful *Sunday Times*. It was 1981.

They were somewhat unsure how to compete with the ever-burgeoning paper from the Murdoch stable. The only thing they were sure about was they were going to make it a tabloid. At the time that was quite daring. The *Sunday Times*, by contrast, was a broadsheet and still is.

Our strategy was to attack the tsunami of sections the *Sunday Times* was publishing: everything from news, opinions, features, sport, travel, business, pot-holing to left-arm bowling! Whatever it was, they had a section for it.

We reasoned this was becoming daunting. Readers were literally drowning in print. The *Mail on Sunday*'s position, we argued, should be about quality journalism, not quantity.

From this strategy we developed a line for the presentation: 'Depth without drowning'.

Having enthusiastically bought into our strategy we were sure we were onto a winner. How wrong we were! Having developed all kinds of ideas around quality not quantity we confidently went into the presentation. The pitch lottery then unfolded like a slow-motion car crash that it so often is.

Three main clients attended, the editor, publisher, and some bloke from distribution who kept talking about lorries and timetables! Well, he would, wouldn't he.

We diligently went over the strategy with heads nodding enthusiastically, even the man from distribution. And then I revealed the line that captured their positioning. The *Mail on Sunday*: 'Depth without drowning'.

There was stunned silence. Finally, the publisher said, 'I hate it'. Every time I read the word 'depth', I see 'death!' This is not going well, I say to myself! || No, no, no says the editor, that's absurd. That's what we do, provide news in depth. I foolishly think we're back on track. Someone with a brain is thinking about this. And then he says, but I hate the word drowning. I have a fear of swimming. Jesus, I say to myself, I really am dealing with tabloid brains here. || **There are only three words in this line, what else can go wrong. So I turn to the distribution genius and say how do you feel about the word 'without?'**

Naturally it was all over.
The pitching lottery had struck again.

They ended up giving the business to Saatchi and ran an ad with a topless woman with three tits, which is, of course, what they were. If only I'd known that's what they wanted.

Put nothing but advertising in front of them and you're asking to be judged like an advertising agency. If my business is to separate a brand from its competition then your business in a pitch is to separate you from your competitors. Are you really doing that?

Make the pitch about your people. If you can manoeuvre the process so the prospective client is not making the decision based on your work, but on your efforts to convince them that you and your creative team are interesting, intelligent, insightful people, then you'll shorten the odds again.

The pitch is also then a dummy run for how the relationship is going to develop.

Of course, you're going to show work and you're going to tempt the client by lifting the veil of creativity, but demonstrating the prospect of an evolving and stimulating relationship is more powerful then getting all your wares out in one go.

Always hold something back: intrigue is a powerful force. Use it to your advantage.

Reputation is the most powerful pitch winner. || **Of course, the ultimate pitch is not to pitch, to refuse to go through the wasteful, absurd sham of pitching and to tell a client that if they want to work with you then they just have to sign on the dotted line.** || This takes incredible courage and the most stunning showreel of success stories to make it viable. Only one agency I know of has managed this, Collett Dickenson Pearce, back in the mid-70s and then only for a short period of time.

But, even if 'not pitching' isn't realistic, great agencies have started winning the pitch before

they've pitched. The magic on their showreels has begun to seduce the client. Reputation is the most powerful pitch winner. As we say at BBH: <u>all roads lead to the work.</u>

When we opened our office in New York, introducing a British agency into the US was a real challenge. We weren't big – that was our first problem. Our other problem: clients had never heard of us. We may have had some fame among other agencies, but in the client world we were complete unknowns.

Therefore, pitching to potential clients was very difficult. Turning up and talking about BBH just sent them to sleep. It sometimes sends me to sleep! We had to do something that got the conversation off in a different way.

I had read an article by Richard Attenborough where he talked about the making of his movie *Gandhi*. He wanted the film to be successful in the US, but the problem was that most people in the US had never heard of Gandhi and didn't know the first thing about him – a movie about this skinny bloke in a loin cloth with twiglet legs was hardly going to play well. Attenborough's masterstroke was in deciding to open the film with Gandhi's funeral. Attenborough reasoned that when you see 10 million people turn out to pay their respects you have to assume that person is important, so you had better pay attention. It worked: *Gandhi* was a success in the US and went on to win eight Oscars, including best actor for Ben Kingsley, who played the great man.

So, we decided to take a leaf out of Attenborough's book. Instead of starting our meetings with our credentials in the conventional way, we introduced ourselves and said that, before the meeting starts, we'd like to play a reel of our work. We then played ten of our best ads, Levi's, Polaroid, Audi, Club Med and Unilever's Axe. All of it award-winning work. Suddenly, the tone of the conversation was entirely different. || **We began the meeting on the front foot instead of continually trying to justify our presence with charts and words. Get the magic out early.**

Our work was the finest calling card we could present. After that, clients were much more prepared to give us their time.

So it's simple really, isn't it? You want to win more pitches? Then have a <u>better showreel.</u> And play it up front.

There's one last observation about pitching. And that's the perennial debate about what order you should pitch in. When a pitch is declared agencies scramble for the last slot: to be the final agency that presents. This is seen as the killer position. The client may have asked three or four agencies to present. The last place you want to be is in the middle. The perceived wisdom is it puts you at a disadvantage. First is preferable and last is the place to be.

After we'd being going about 15 years John Bartle decided to put this theory to the test and analyse all our pitches, our wins and losses, to see if there was any relationship between where we were in the pitch process and success and failure.

Now John Bartle, as I've said before, has one of the best analytical brains in the country. He's not a man to be argued with. And do you know what he found? ‖ **There was absolutely no relationship between where we pitched and success and failure. There was, however, a relationship between quality of ideas and success. Now isn't that a surprise!**

7

STORYTELLING

Probably the most powerful form
of communication we have at our disposal
is storytelling. It has been incorporated
by virtually every civilization into
their culture. It is the simplest, most
memorable device we have for engaging,
learning, entertaining and persuading.
It's not surprising, then, that so many great
advertising campaigns are based
around this simple device.

A great author, Julian Barnes, once said: 'You could look at human beings as machines designed for storytelling. From body language to syntax, from inflection to timing, we're the perfect shape and form for utilizing this amazing art form.' We explain ourselves through this medium. Who we are, what we like, do, love, hate, our ambitions, fears and yearnings are all communicated through this device.

And, of course, when employed correctly, storytelling can make things incredibly memorable, especially for brands. || Some years ago I remember asking a friend, who was on the board of the venerable British retailer Marks & Spencer, how they managed to bind their vast company together with such a strong sense of culture. He said it was very simple: storytelling.

He then explained why Marks & Spencer had such a strong culture and such loyalty from their staff. The story he told was known by everyone who worked at the company and looked back to the very beginning of the company's life at their first store in the city of Leeds in the late 1800s. One day, Simon Marks, the company founder, was going into the basement to look for some goods. Sitting on the basement steps he found two of his salesgirls. When he asked what they were doing they explained that they were about to have their lunch. Marks looks at them both and said, 'No, you're not.' He then took the salesgirls up to his office on the first floor, cleared his desk and said, 'From now on you have your lunch sitting here'. That's why, my friend explained, over 100 years later Marks & Spencer always provide great canteen facilities for their staff.

Storytelling like that not only binds people together, but it also helps build loyalty and is incredibly memorable. || I was told that story some 15 years ago, I don't work for Marks & Spencer, and never have, yet I remember it and I'm telling you about it. I think that proves something.

It was 12th-century wandering minstrels, the troubadours, who added music to the art of storytelling and, in doing so, created an even more powerful form of communication. You could say they anticipated the jingle some 800 years before advertising developed it. ‖ **The combination of story and music has been one of advertising's most powerful tools as communication has become more emotionally based.**

At one point at BBH we thought we should define our creative approach as storytelling. We eventually backed away from the idea, reasoning it was too prescriptive. It wasn't that we didn't believe in it, but that defining our creative output via one means of expression was too limiting. ‖ Of course, the argument against this means of expression today is that technology and the need to develop a '360° platform' in advertising and branding means storytelling is outmoded. It no longer works. This kind of stupidity often raises its head as some people believe that the invention of some technological device or another will fundamentally change human nature. Well, it won't. It might change human behaviour, but not our nature. Don't get the two confused.

When the telephone was invented people genuinely believed that it would end the concept of a regional accent. They predicted that once it was possible to communicate over long distances regional accents would die out. Anyone listening to Alex Ferguson, the legendary manager of Manchester United Football Club, or indeed Dolly Parton's southern drawl will know how stupid that prediction was. Our sense of place and our sense of belonging will never be replaced by technology. It will add to it, expand it, but never replace it.

The art of storytelling in the modern age is still fundamentally important. So, how we create stories for a screen-based culture is vitally important to master.

I constantly tell creative people that if you want to learn how to write for the screen you should read William Goldman's two books: *Adventures in the Screen Trade* and *Which Lie Did I Tell?* Goldman is one of the great screenwriters, a modern-day storyteller. *Butch Cassidy and the Sundance Kid*, *Marathon Man*, *All the President's Men* and *Good Will Hunting* (which, so the rumour goes, wasn't written by Matt Damon and Ben Affleck, but was penned by Goldman) are just some of the great screenplays for which he's been responsible. Goldman has never written a commercial in his life, yet you'll learn more from his storytelling on how to write for the screen than you will from some advertising expert. And you'll learn in a memorable and entertaining way – what could be better? There is one piece of advice he offers, in particular, about writing a scene that I love. || **It's a piece of advice that could be well employed by most writers: 'Come in late, leave early'.** || And Goldman's not talking about the hours you keep. His point is that most writers leave nothing for the audience to do – the writer over explains. || **When you write a scene, and it could be a screenplay or it could be a television commercial, whatever you do, you must leave room for the audience to participate. You have to get them engaged in the process – that way you'll get them wanting more.** || With screenwriting you move from scene to scene, twisting, turning and surprising, so predictability is the death of a screenplay, as it is for those of us who write television commercials.

If I can work out what's coming why bother watching? Surprise is a fundamental factor in making something memorable.

You can also learn a bit of screenwriting magic from Pascal, the great French philosopher, who had a similar piece of advice. Naturally, it wasn't about screen writing, but Pascal wrote a series of letters, known as *The Provincial Letters*, one of which finishes with the line: 'I have only made this [letter] longer because I have not had the time to make it shorter'. Brilliant. The man was a born copywriter. Pascal totally understood the power of reduction, the skill in advertising that we're supposed to be most able to perform.

Sadly for Pascal, the television commercial wasn't going to occur for another 350 years. Bit of a bummer that. As we keep saying, timing is everything.

If you want a more recent piece of writing to study that illustrates the art of paring words down and leading your audience through a story, then it's worth reading the stageplay of Oscar Wilde's *The Importance of Being Earnest*. Every line in that play is a joke or a line leading to a joke. You literally can't alter one word without the whole construct falling apart. Genius. You've just got the joke and the next one is being set up. How often do you read scripts in our business that are sloppy, unfocused and loose. A great script is one that's absolutely complete. It's like a brilliant machine. Every word working with the other to make a story compelling. Even though that story may be just 30 or 60 seconds long it should be constructed in such a way that nothing could be added or taken away. Sadly, that's rarely the case.

When I worked in the US in the late 90s I saw how the craft of advertising in the US differs from that in Europe and specifically the UK.

Now I'm generalizing wildly here, but generalizing <u>to make a point.</u>

'Over here' I think we have been lucky, fortunate, call it what you like, to have a challenging public-service broadcast company, the BBC, producing stimulating programming. It made the competitive commercial channels work harder to engage their audiences, rather than just dumb down. But something else separated the UK from the US and it was always a conundrum to me: the US perfected the art of the screenplay. Hollywood was the one location to which the great directors and screenwriters migrated. They wanted to ply their craft in a place that had perfected the art of movies and writing for the screen. Those directors and screenwriters understood that storytelling was visual as well as verbal – non-stop words interrupt and slow the process of engaging your audience. Hollywood understood this.

Now here's the paradox: British copywriters, the best of them that is, had learnt this lesson, yet their American counterparts seemed not to have. Instead of telling a story they seemed to want to write a short lecture. They started with words and then added pictures. Watch any number of US commercials and you'll know what I mean. This is especially the case, for some peculiar reason, with life assurance companies. After a hard day's work I really don't want to sit down to a lecture. Who would?

Scripts for British commercials, when they were great (and I emphasize here, great; we're just as capable of producing rubbish), were sparse and pared down – they allowed the visuals to speak as well as the dialogue. ‖ **Virtually all of our Levi's 501 spots told stories, but none of them used words. We perfected the craft of what we called 'visual narrative'.** ‖ Storytelling is fundamental to communication, but words aren't the only way to achieve that. In fact, they can often get in the way. As Goldman points out: 'Never forget film is a visual medium'. A phrase I liked to say to my writers when they were working on a script was:

<u>Remember,</u> words are a barrier to communication.

This is a somewhat provocative statement to make to a writer – especially coming from an art director.

Sometimes, though, the desire to create something visual can go horribly wrong and some of the worst offenders are fashion ads and, in particular, fragrance commercials. || The fashionistas who've created this work have obviously looked up the word 'profundity' in the dictionary, thinking that it's spelt 'pretentious'. These commercials are invariably shot in black and white because their brains haven't quite grasped the concept of colour.

But worse than all of that are the scripts.

Now, when you are writing a script, it's best to have an idea – that small incidental phenomenon that drives communication. One dictionary definition of an idea is: 'a thought or plan formed by mental effort'.

I think the key phrase here is 'mental effort'. Gelled hair and three-day facial hair growth are not ideas. Style is an attitude not an idea. Important as they both are, confusing them can seriously impair the impact of your communication.

As I've said, profundity in the fashion world is spelt pretentious. And the scripts they shoot go something like this.

Open on a large, sparsely furnished room. A man and a woman pose at either end of the room. Tension mounts. He turns to look at her, she turns away. Man pouts. (Remember no one's being cast for their acting skills. This is about posing.) Woman exits impossibly large room. Distraught.

[Cut to billowing white gauze curtain, track back to show second, sparsely furnished room]

Woman enters the room and throws herself onto chaise longue. She raises her arm against her forehead to imply angst and drama.

[Cut to stylish container of liquid being spilt.
Note: Freudian reference for relationship in deep shit]

> Small furry animal (a cat) enters the room as a further
> Freudian reference.

[Cut to impossibly large, back-lit fragrance bottle. Solution
to relationship angst?]

[Cut to close up of woman's lips]

> Man enters the second room. The woman turns her head
> away. Acting, or should I say posing, reaches new depths
> of pretentiousness.

[Cut back to billowing gauze curtain]

> The man approaches the woman. She turns to
> face him, slaps him. He falls into her lap.

[Dissolve to back-lit fragrance bottle, packshot
and cue hysterical laughter from the audience as
voice over says]

> **Stalker.** *A new fragrance from the house of Cliché.*

Understanding the balance between words and pictures is therefore vital. Our best scripts were often no more than just a paragraph on a page. A paragraph that, when turned into celluloid, could hopefully be turned into magic. But, most importantly, within that paragraph was an idea. In the US so much TV advertising – and let's face it there is a lot – was just a wall of words. It was as though the creatives were just writing down the strategy, rather then creating something that made you feel.

The reason a script is pared down and simplified is to allow the director room to input their craft. If the idea is so jammed with words there's no room left for expression, imagination and reflection. It is often referred to as the 'audacity of simplicity'. Great writing and storytelling also has to understand the principle of input and take out. || **If I want to make you think I'm funny, I don't tell you I'm really funny, I tell you a joke.** || You laugh and think, 'Wow, that guy is really funny'. That's one example of input and take out.

One of the most important lessons to be learned by any communicator (and one of the most easily forgotten) is that you don't instruct people to do something – you inspire them.

But so much TV advertising coming out of the US is non-stop dialogue. Dialogue that tells you what it wants you to think. And this advertising is created in the country that had invented the pared-down screenplay. It's as though copywriters in the US never went to the cinema. Maybe they felt it had no relevance to what they did, which might be because cinemas in the US don't traditionally carry ads, whereas British ones always have. Perhaps, because of the competition from the BBC making commercial television raise its game, it encouraged us in British advertising to write television commercials that would be appreciated as part of an evening's entertainment. Maybe it's just because Americans like to talk more?!? Who knows? But it always seemed to me that all those words hampered their creativity. So many of their commercials were like very short instructional films rather than imaginative pieces of storytelling. We describe those commercials as 'words on wheels'.

<u>And never forget</u>: a brand is an agglomeration of stories linked together by a vision.

Perhaps the creative output of HBO, which I think is now producing some of the best television in the world, will have an effect on the creators of commercials. I hope so.

Whatever happens, as we go into this exciting future, the art of the story will remain with us. Naturally, it will change and evolve, it will employ the development of technology to enhance and underline the power of its message. But as a means of communication, it will remain with us for as long as we're interested in reacting with each other. And reacting with each other and creating work that is inventive, engaging and persuasive is at the core of what advertising is all about.

8

TRUTH AND TECHNOLOGY

The impact of new technology
is always overestimated in the short
term and underestimated in the long
term. These words are probably the most
perceptive observation one can make about
technology. Therefore, trying to see through
the blizzard of innovation that's swirling
around us and predicting its long-term
impact is ridiculously perilous.

I remember at the turn of the millennium everyone in advertising getting agitated by the appearance of the TiVo digital video recorder. The received wisdom was that TiVo was going to wipe out television advertising and change the communications industry for ever. It was all doom, doom, doom. Ripple dissolve to 10 years later and we're still making TV commercials with the great ones still making headlines and changing the futures of brands. And I can't remember the last time I read anything about TiVo.

Technology is both a friend and a fiend, energizing some parts of the economy and focusing painful change and, in some ways, fatally wounding other parts. You could see this as another example of 'creative destruction' and a vital ingredient in any dynamic economy. || **Should a brand or a company ever die? The simple answer is no. It happens only when they fail to see change coming and don't adapt to it.** || Should the makers of horse-drawn cabs have spotted the development of the internal combustion engine? If they'd have done so, they would have phased out horses and developed the motor car.

The horse-drawn cab owners were in the transport business where speed and ease of use were the constant requirements. Unfortunately, and mistakenly, they thought they were in the horse-and-cab industry and an engineer called Otto Benz put them out of business with a piece of technology that went on to revolutionize the world.

Rather than seeing technology as a challenge we should always think of it as an opportunity. If we do that then our approach to it changes. But with all these opportunities there must be a note of caution relating to an uncomfortable fact that confronts the advertising industry and its clients in this new environment. It is something to be wary of as we jump into this digitized future:

The more technology permeates society, the more it uncovers the truth.

Anyone who doubts this should refer to the wikipedia leaks during the Iraq conflict.

This, for me, is the biggest issue raised by the explosion of technology. Not how it's used, where it's used or why, but a simple thing called transparency.

Technology uncovers the truth? This is not a new concept: we can trace a historical trend leading back to Gutenberg's invention of moveable type in the 15th century when the mass publishing of books and other printed matter accelerated the spread of knowledge through society. Minds were opened up to different theories, beliefs and facts. Control by the governing authorities was weakened. I'm not suggesting for a moment that manipulation and the distortion of the truth suddenly withered in the face of this technological breakthrough – it didn't – but it very slowly began to unravel. What's the first thing a totalitarian government tries to do? Reduce people's access to technology. The command structure of medieval society was slowly undermined, and Gutenberg's invention laid the ground for an incredible period of discovery, learning and scholarship from the Renaissance onwards. || **From an advertising and branding perspective, you can think of Gutenberg as having created the questioning consumer: his innovation spread knowledge, with knowledge comes choice and with choice comes dissention.**

Fast forward to the present day. Let's look at the power of the net and its ability to subvert the conventional forms of expression: the gatekeepers, media moguls and controlling corporations are being swept aside as the power of the crowd takes over. || **Blogging, e-mailing and tweeting have unleashed both opportunity and caution. Brands can both benefit and be damned by this new force –**

the opportunity that technology provides is exciting as well as daunting – daunting because, as I've said, technology helps expose the truth.

The truth has always been a vital component of a brand's successful communication. But today, unless you embrace transparency, the chances are you'll come unstuck, especially if you've been economical with it.

The truth is not 'a narrow concept', as was claimed by Walt Price, the duplicitous film director in David Mamet's movie *State and Main*, but a fundamental building block in any marketing strategy. It is an enduring and essential ingredient in the sustainability of any relationship.

Arthur Andersen, the once highly regarded auditors and accountancy firm, was destroyed by its decision to shred documents relating to the Enron fraud. Sadly for Arthur Andersen, it was their 100-year-old reputation that was shredded. Sunny Delight, an orange soft drink marketed at children, hit a storm of protest when it had the unfortunate side effect of turning children orange when they consumed large quantities of it – a trifle upsetting, that. And with Ford and Firestone's brush with transparency when the Explorer had a tendency to roll over, both brands suffered reputational damage. And the bloggers had a field day.

In the UK, Members of Parliament have come completely unstuck in their attempt to hide their expenses. The saga of those politicians' expenses being used to pay for everything from never-used second homes to 'duck houses' and the cleaning of moats has seriously undermined the political parties in the UK. Their members failed to understand the value and necessity of transparency with the public they represent.

For the brands of today and the brands of the future, the question isn't just how they avail themselves of the opportunities technology presents, but how they ensure those same opportunities don't trip them up. || Your shareholders want profits and your consumers want honesty. Handling that little conundrum requires a new kind of management ethos. Those dark secrets locked in a company's vaults, that trail of e-mails will undo the best of intentions of a company not prepared to be open and honest.

Some believe the function of marketing is to deceive, to fool the public and to make them buy things they don't want. ‖ How many times have you heard that clichéd nonsense? This is the critic's view of our industry and usually comes from journalists with an axe to grind.

As we witness the growing power of online social communities, an honest and open dialogue between brand and audience is the conversation of the future. The real innovators of advertising and the genuinely great brands have always believed in the truth and the power of that kind of conversation. ‖ I find it bizarre that the truth, for some people, is such alien territory. Trust is the glue that holds a brand and its customers together. And, as we're increasingly buying things we can't see, trust as a component of a brand's make-up becomes ever more important. Selling a mobile phone provider is essentially selling 'vibrating air'. Getting people to buy Vodafone's vibrating air rather than Orange's, for example, demands the employment of, among other things, large quantities of trust. And trust, once lost, is difficult to rebuild. At the time I'm writing this, Toyota is spending an awful lot of money to assure the public their cars are safe after their 2010 recall. Toyota's one-time image of bullet-proof quality is now somewhat punctured.

So, when using technology to connect with an audience, be careful what you wish for. This is undoubtedly the best time to be in marketing and advertising, but it's also the most dangerous time.

It's also important to remember that our industry is in the persuasion business – the business of reaching out to as many people as possible and getting them to consider our client's products as opposed to those of our competitors. ‖ The fact that we can now do that in a multitude of different ways should be a cause for celebration, but instead the communications industry indulges itself in a sterile debate about the pluses and minuses of broadcast communication over digital, of old versus new. Get over it – they're both incredibly valuable. It's not about one or the other being better, it's about both. The question that we should be debating is: how do we link the powerful world of broadcasting to the incredibly efficient developments of digital?

Title: Vote Gail, 1999
Gail Porter projected onto the Houses of Parliament in London. It got BBH onto ITV News at Ten.

Persuasion, promotion and retention are and always will be vital ingredients of <u>any</u> communications program.

There is no question in my mind that this is the most challenging time to be guiding a brand. It's a time of enormous technological change, some would even say these changes are epoch-making. A brand can now have conversations with its potential audience in a way undreamt of 10 years ago. And, of course, audiences can have conversations with each other about a brand. More than anything, that ability for an audience to talk among itself is what makes the changes in technology incredible, but also scary.

One could also say the playing field has been levelled.

The critics of advertising have always said it's a rich man's club. The only beneficiaries of the right to advertise were the large corporations with pockets deep enough to afford entry into the game. Getting on TV, buying newspapers and poster sites all required large wedges of investment. The individual entrepreneur was excluded from this merry-go-round.

Technology has ended all that. || **Today, brands can reach out to audiences in a myriad of ways. It no longer takes vast quantities of cash to reach large groups of people, but it does require inventiveness, daring and creativity – all the attributes large companies are bad at deploying. And, if anything, those corporations are finding it difficult to deal with a medium where you have to let go and learn not to be in control.**

Bad news travels fast. And today it travels at the click of a button. The repercussions of that phenomenon are still only just being realized. Come on in baby, the water is lovely! The only trouble is, one wrong move and you'll be sucked under – the bloggers will get you. Go to a premiere of a new movie these days and the glow on people's faces isn't necessarily from the film – it's the light from their mobiles as they text the outside world their opinion.

The big question in advertising is the shape the industry will take over the coming years and what part technology will play. || There is no straightforward answer – it is, as William Goldman said about making films in Hollywood, a case of 'nobody knows anything'. Nobody really knows where it's all going to settle, if indeed it will ever settle. || **The one thing I'm certain of, however, is that we've moved from a culture of 'learn and do' to a culture of 'do and learn'.**

But you can't operate without some guiding principles. No advertising agency has operated that way and no agency ever will, if it wants to be successful.

So what are the guiding principles of working with the truth and technology?

<u>Just because something's new doesn't make it better.</u> And just because you can do something, it doesn't necessarily mean you should. We all know the advertising industry is obsessed with the word 'new', not just as a selling mechanism, but also a descriptor of its own corporate structures.

How many times have you read in advertising journals of the launch of a new agency with a new way of working? The advertising business is obsessed with the word 'new'. Of course, 'a new way of working' with technology represents an embracing of evolving technologies and their opportunities, but sometimes in advertising we can behave like a child at Christmas who just keeps opening one present after another and never stops to play. It's a case of: give me something new. New is good, old is bad. We talk about old technology as though it were bad and new as though it were virtuous. We need to have the wisdom to stand back and consider the gifts we've been given and how best to employ them.

During the campaign for the 2010 UK General Election we genuinely thought that new media, blogging, social networks and digital interactivity were going to result in a new kind of election. The truth was far from that – it was a series of three debates by the leaders of the main political parties on prime-time TV that changed the way the 2010 election was conducted.

To listen to the argument that rages between digital agencies and conventional ones makes me feel truly dismayed. Instead of bringing the old and the new disciplines together and mapping out an intelligent way forward (as much as you can in a rapidly changing world) we spend our time throwing insults at each other about our respective skills and deny ourselves what the other offers.

This makes no sense.

No wonder clients are confused and so often disillusioned with the advice offered to them.

We've been here before: the last great upheaval in the advertising industry was some 60 years ago with the introduction of commercial television, an unbelievably powerful new medium that was built on the back of new technology: television broadcasting. It was a revolution that was going to change the face of advertising. Until then the advertising business in the UK was dominated by poster artists such as Abram Games and Edward McKnight Kauffer, the creative geniuses of their age producing work for clients including Shell and British Rail. Their posters captured the imagination and developed a style of communication that was not only informative but also engaging. They ruled the advertising consciousness of the British public. Then along comes the cathode-ray tube – a piece of technology that sat in the corner of a room and drew people to it like a magnet. ‖ **Now audiences watched a flickering black-and-white picture. It was grainy and coarse, but it moved. It laughed, it told funny stories and played music. It was the future.**

And it wasn't just the poster artists who failed to understand this new order.

Many scoffed at it, claiming that it couldn't be as persuasive, or as powerful, as a well-honed piece of copy. Newspapers ran campaigns trying to persuade businesses that this new technology wouldn't be as successful as the printed word. And television, in its turn, ran commercials that talked about the persuasiveness of television. And so the debate raged on.

What none of them did was talk about how these media, old and new, worked together and how linking one with the other was the future. It was 'them and us'.

For the poster artists it was all over. They faded from view like their gouache-painted billboards, muttering into their Amontillado sherries that the world had been taken over by a bunch of neophytes in button-down shirts with mid-Atlantic accents.

The agencies that did grasp the future did so without, in reality, much understanding. Television was king and print was the past. If you could utter the words 'double-head' and 'married print' and knew how to organize 'a dub' you were a creative genius. The boffins had taken over – they could bamboozle clients with all the technical jargon of this mind-boggling new media. The fact that they didn't have the faintest notion of how you go about having an idea didn't matter.

They could talk about 12-frame dissolves.

In the land of the blind, the one-eyed producer proved to be king. And these one-eyed men – and they were all men – were the kings of advertising. Until, that is, someone said, 'We need an idea'. And then the one-eyed producers were found to be somewhat wanting.

By then, everyone else could also say 'double-head' and knew what a 'married print' was as well, so it was all over for the one-eyed producers. Eventually, everyone worked out how to make the old and new media of print and television work together.

So, lo and behold, here we are again at another great crossroads. Except this crossroads has about 20 roads intersecting it. The old versus new argument remains the same except this time we're cursed with people hankering after the past and neophytes digitally downloading the new gospel according to the net.

Start with a great idea, then choose how to use and combine media.

Over the last 10 years, while we've all been debating this brave new world, there have been two events that I think have been transformational: one of them is a cash-strapped mother sitting down in a coffee bar to start writing a book. And not just a single book, but a series of books about a character called Harry Potter. All J. K. Rowling had to create the character was a pen, a pad of paper and her imagination. The technology she chose to communicate her idea – a book – was first developed in about the 6th century AD. The Harry Potter books, as we all know, went on to be one of the publishing sensations of the last decade. And if you haven't read the books, you've probably seen one of the movies.

The other is the 2008 US Presidential election of Barack Obama. It was one of the most modern political campaigns ever conducted. It started from the ground up. With the use of digital technology it built a loyal following that became a groundswell of opinion and supporters that gave his campaign a force that his opposition just couldn't match. Of course,

Oasis
'Dig Out your Soul',
2008, New York
Creative team:
Calle Sjoenell
and Pelle Sjoenell

Members of Oasis
From left to right:
Liam Gallagher,
Gem Archer and
Andy Bell

Obama also had a powerful message, a message for those whose moment had come: 'Change. Yes we can'. What was brilliant about Obama's 2008 campaign was how its message and medium were at one with each other. Its message championed change with a medium that represented change. And the brand, Obama, embodied change.

While both of these examples began in either old or new media, what is transformational about them is how they went on to utilize and combine both: blogs about Harry Potter spread the word and debated the fate of their hero and generated excitement and anticipation of forthcoming Harry Potter books. Obama used television to amplify his ideas. In the last week of the campaign Obama's team ran a 30-minute – yes, a 30-minute – television commercial. If you're going to use a medium, be daring. I'm sure with neither of these examples people sat around debating the old and the new – they started with a powerful idea and developed that idea in the best media available to them. They had a route map of how they would or should develop.

So, as we gradually learn to live with new digital technology, we'll gradually realize it represents simply speed and access – the ability to get more of what you want faster and share it with more people. Actually, if you think about it, this is what technology has always represented to varying degrees.

Integrity and openness will be vital ingredients of a brand's make-up. Not a bolt-on, disposable luxury, but living at the very core of a brand's being.

Those are predictions I'm happy to stand by. Once all the dust has settled and the fog of technology has cleared, we'll be looking at the brilliance of ideas superbly executed.

As I've always said, the only space worth occupying is the space between someone's ears, so the important thing then is: just get there.

FROM BENTON & BOWLES TO 16 GOODGE STREET

In the introduction I talked about what led me to decide that I wanted a career in advertising. It was in June 1965 that my career in advertising really began. I had managed to get an appointment to see Dan Cromer, the head of Art at Benton & Bowles, an American agency whose London office was at 197 Knightsbridge. A place that was all sharp suits, button-down Oxford shirts and girls with Sloane Square accents and Alice bands. Or that's what I thought.

Dan was a hot art director who'd been transferred from New York to the London office to try to inject some creativity into this flagging backwater of Benton & Bowles' global network. Dan had the necessary style requirements at that time for a career in advertising: he spoke with a native Manhattan accent and he wore thin black knitted ties and penny loafers.

Dan also possessed a Gold award from the New York Art Directors Club for a print campaign he had created for Western Union, which at the time was a telegram company. These weren't bad credentials. Dan liked what he saw in my portfolio and he offered me a job as an assistant art director, probably because I had an opinion on everything including where to buy the best authentic button-down Oxford shirts. I could now say that I worked in advertising.

As a result of his efforts in trying to change things at Benton & Bowles, Dan hired some great creative minds – all of whom, in time, went on to make their mark in the advertising industry and beyond. ‖ **Charles Saatchi was one of them – you've probably heard of him – as well as Ross Cramer, Bob Brooks and Roy Carruthers.** ‖ Ross, who was a brilliant art director, and Bob went on to direct commercials and later to work together at BFCS, one of London's top film production companies. Roy was one of the best art directors I've ever worked with and, when he left Benton & Bowles, he went to Collett Dickenson Pearce, where he created the iconic 'Happiness is a cigar called Hamlet' campaign with Tim Warriner. Dan had assembled a great team, but I'm not sure the rest of the agency understood the value these creatives represented. The fact that they were continually leaving should have been a concern. Sadly, it wasn't.

Why was that? I soon found out that, while some parts of London may have been swinging – The Beatles were busily finishing their fifth album, *Help!*, at the time – **Swinging London certainly hadn't penetrated the offices at 197 Knightsbridge.** ‖ At Benton & Bowles, apart from a few Arrow-shirted American expats, it seemed that the staff consisted of public school-educated account men who were trained only to say 'yes', no matter what the question. It felt at times that the close proximity of the agency's offices to Harrods department store made life more tolerable for the 'yes' men, perhaps even civilized.

It was comfortable for them apart from when they were shown an idea.

For these so-called 'top drawer' account men creativity was a fearful occupation executed by weird, argumentative and volatile people, many of whom came from the lower classes. They saw creativity as subversive, dangerous and a <u>necessary evil</u>.

It filled them with horror.

The account men – God forbid they should have an opinion – were always trying to second guess the client. I remember being at a client meeting where a piece of work had been presented and the client, who as I recall was Courage brewery, wanted the headline to be bigger. Before I could respond, the account man, this paragon of leadership and wisdom, had agreed with the client. I was stunned. Ten minutes earlier the layout was perfect, now it was wrong. The only point of view this witless account man had was to agree with the client. Of course, I disagreed and said that I had designed the ad with a bold picture to draw the reader into it. If the headline were made bigger, the picture would have to be made smaller and, consequently, weaken the impact of the ad. This piece of brain science stopped the client in his tracks and was giving the account man a major problem. He now had two opposing opinions to deal with. I could see the slow flush of fear creeping over his collar.

The only thing the account men could really second guess was which piece of cutlery should be used for which course at dinner. It didn't matter how good the creative department was because the management, most of whom were the upper-class, public-school types, found a way of blunting their output. After about three years of this, Dan eventually realized the task he faced and he quit in defeat.

When I started at Benton & Bowles I was an assistant art director. That's how it worked back then. You couldn't come out of college and get a job as an art director straight away – you started by being an assistant. The belief was that you had to understand the craft of the job before you could properly execute it. In principle, I didn't have a problem with that, except that the 'craft' they were talking about was fading fast. I thought that learning the craft of cross-hatching 65-line screen Letterpress reproduction and the value of wood-block display type was not the future, but somehow you had to pay lip service to the craftsmen of the past. And lip service seemed to be a case of biting your lip and waiting for opportunities to appear.

The world of advertising – and this was my world now – still seemed to be stuck in the 50s and have its head stuck up the rear end of corporations. ‖ **It was afraid to challenge, question or innovate.** ‖ Looking back, apart from some bright spots such as Doyle Dane Bernbach opening their first London office on Baker Street in 1964 or Collett Dickenson Pearce showing a growing creative awareness in British advertising through their brilliant work, it was an industry without principle apart from the base principle of pleasing the client and making as much money as possible. ‖ **That principle produced advertising that was merely clichéd, dismal and trite.**

And it wasn't just the majority of agencies who were stuck in the past: the clients, many of whom were industrial behemoths, had no idea a revolution, led by the young, was fermenting from below. Their wood-panelled boardrooms were far too remote from the streets where change was fermenting.

It wasn't just the account men who were 'yes' men. Many of the existing generation of advertising writers and art directors seemed to be just passing through. They thought they were in the service industry and their skill was focused on producing work with which the client was comfortable. ‖ Those of us in the new generation were trying to produce work that would jolt people out of their complacency. We were speaking different languages founded on a different philosophy. The old guard were more interested in publishing their new novel or, if they were art directors, in daubing paint on canvas. Advertising wasn't their real occupation.

Agencies were run and owned by people who believed in the status quo, who didn't understand the needs of a mobile society. And the account handlers had the ear of the client whereas we young upstarts didn't, especially if one was creative. ‖ These fading men knew how to pour the perfect gin and tonic and laugh at the client's jokes (and God, did they know how to fawn), but beyond that they were congenitally useless. It made me wonder how they had ended up with the job they had – it almost seemed to me they had drifted into an advertising career because they had good connections, spoke with an upper-class accent and had a degree in subservience. || **For them, the 50s were a bit dangerous and pinko, never mind what was happening in the 60s – this was the world those of us in the new generation were trying to change. Of course, time was on our side, but we were impatient.**

I quickly came to three conclusions:

First of all it was clear to me that really to make a change you had to be in charge. You had to lead an agency – Bernbach had shown that. Working in big, boring agencies was like pushing a piece of string.

Secondly, if you don't believe in what you're doing, you won't be great at it.

Finally, and most importantly of all, creativity isn't a job, it's a belief. Without that belief you'll never be great.

Even though I was just starting out in my career, I wasn't slow in offering my opinion about the work Benton & Bowles was producing or the state of the business, but it felt like an uphill struggle. No matter how hard those of us in the creative department who cared about the work tried, argued and persuaded, it eventually dissipated into apathy and disbelief, voiced by our seniors. || **It was a dysfunctional business – the creative department was constantly opposed to management and management was incapable of engaging clients with the truth.**

Despite this absurd environment we did have fun, and practical jokes were a way of maintaining our sanity (or perhaps employing our under-used creativity). It was us against them: the creatives versus the management.

I remember one time we decided to get our own back on one of the chinless ones. We had a very big presentation to make to Courage, which at the time was one of the UK's largest breweries. The client team to whom we were going to be present were a group of hard-nosed male brewers – the sort of men who drank beer only in pints and never drank fewer than three at a time. The chinless account man who was tasked with presenting the work was always running late. He rushed into the creative department, all flailing arms and floppy hair, and grabbed one of the ubiquitous black art bags used to carry presentations. Now the fact that we had placed this particular art bag conveniently at the front of all the others wasn't exactly a coincidence.

All art bags were black and the same size, so, unless you carefully checked the contents, differentiating one from another was impossible.

Once the chinless one and his boss had arrived at the Courage brewery for the presentation the chinless account man's boss, who was another 'yes' man, opened the meeting by laying out the strategy and eulogizing the work the client team were about to see. When the big moment arrived the 'never on time' chinless one whips the work out of the art bag.

The hard-nosed group of clients had been primed to see ads with pictures of beefy blokes bonding with each other while sinking pints of Courage's liquid wonder. They were waiting with baited breath. They'd waited weeks for this moment and it was the culmination of much briefing and discussion. Anticipation was running high. And so the chinless one flips open the ubiquitous black art bag and extracts the first of many beer ideas carefully crafted by the creatives. Except this wasn't the Courage presentation.

The one he'd picked up was a ready-mounted presentation for the Gossard 'Cross your heart' bra, at the time a well-known British underwear brand for the woman with a fuller figure. Pandemonium and grovelling breaks out on a nuclear scale from the chinless one and his 'yes' man boss as the Courage brewers stare agog at pictures of larger ladies wearing elasticated girdles and suspenders and the new design of 'Cross your heart' bra. ‖ What would you have given to have been in that room?!

While this may have proved that sex and alcohol are a heady and dangerous mix, it did mean, sadly, that the chinless one's future in the ad business was a short one.

I didn't last long at Benton & Bowles either – after about 18 months I was told that 'our futures were not inextricably intertwined', which is a polite way of being fired. Mind you, I probably brought it on myself by continually telling them the work they were producing was patronizing and rubbish.

That's the arrogance of youth.

I'm sure I was a pain in the arse, but the truth was that Benton & Bowles wasn't responding to a changing world. For a company trying to be a leader in the field of communication this is something of a problem.

It may seem odd to say this, but where you have your offices reflects what you are. This is why, when accountants run creative businesses, they more often or not make the mistake of locating the company where it's cheap rather than where it's inspiring. With Benton & Bowles it was clear that smart offices in Knightsbridge were not where the revolution was going to take place.

There was a slightly delicious revenge for me when, about 10 years after they had decided our 'futures were not inextricably intertwined', I was asked to return to be the creative leader at Benton & Bowles. A very nice man called Bruce Rhodes was trying to dig them out of their terminal malaise. Bruce painted an honest but optimistic picture, but, as you might imagine, I politely declined to be part of it. The lesson here: never go back.

Although I didn't realize it at the time, everything about Benton & Bowles wasn't completely useless. In fact, you could argue that it had a profound impact on my future career.

After I'd been at the agency for about a month the creative director came up to me and told me that he'd found a writer for me to work with. || **The writer was also new to the business and his name was Charles Saatchi. I thought: 'Oh no! He's Italian, probably lives at home with mum and can't spell. Just my luck.'**

Well, I was wrong on only one of them: Charles did live at home with his mum, he was useless at spelling, but he wasn't Italian. He was also a brilliant writer and thinker. And the rest is history.

After my ignominious ejection from Benton & Bowles, Charles, who'd left a year earlier, asked if I would like to join a creative consultancy he had set up with Ross Cramer and to be part of their efforts to take greater control of their creative output. || **This was the start of one of the most exhilarating and exhausting periods of my career: working at the Cramer Saatchi consultancy.**

I joined Cramer Saatchi in 1967, a time when advertising in the UK was beginning to find its voice and creative confidence. The Cramer Saatchi consultancy had taken up residence in a refurbished office at 16 Goodge Street, on the corner of Goodge Street and Tottenham Court Road. Before being converted into offices, the building had been a department store called Catesby's. Now it housed one of the most remarkable groups of companies that, in their own ways, were going to revolutionize the advertising and entertainment industries. Over the next three years the people who worked in the building made it one of the most influential addresses in the advancement of British creativity.

A quick glance at the company names in the lobby would reveal the following: on the first floor was David Puttnam who had taken up residence as a photographer's agent. He represented the hottest photographers in London: David Bailey, Terence Donovan, David Montgomery, Lord Snowdon, Clive Arrowsmith and many more. David is now better known as the Oscar-winning film producer of *Chariots of Fire* and for producing *Memphis Belle, The Mission* and *The Killing Fields*. He now sits in the House of Lords.

On the second floor was a new advertising agency called Boase Massimi Pollitt (BMP), which had recently enticed a young art director called John Webster to join them. John was about to convince UK housewives of the superiority of a brand of instant mashed potatoes called 'Smash' over peeling, boiling and mashing the real thing. His 'Martians' commercial for Smash was later voted Britain's best-ever TV ad. And BMP went on to become one of the UK's hottest agencies.

The Cramer Saatchi consultancy was on the third floor and, as well as creating advertising campaigns, was also developing film scripts with David Puttnam and a brilliant writer called Alan Parker, whom, if you recall, I had first met at my interview with Tony Palladino at Papert, Koenig, Lois. Alan was a copywriter at Collett Dickenson Pearce at the time and he went on to become one of Britain's finest filmmakers, with *Bugsy Malone, Midnight Express, Fame* and *Mississippi Burning* being just some of the films he wrote and directed.

On the floor above the Cramer Saatchi consultancy was the über hot design partnership of Lou Klein and Michael Peters, though they eventually had a somewhat acrimonious split that resulted in everything in the office being divided in half, including a rubber plant in reception. Michael always claimed his half survived and thrived. After the split he went on to become one of the UK's top designers, eventually merging his business into a global design company, Michael Peters Design, which, sadly, came somewhat unstuck in the recession of the late 80s. Michael now recalls that period with great humour and amusement, though at the time it was painful. His great design work has stood the test of time somewhat better than his financial backers have. || **And, of course, Cramer Saatchi became Saatchi & Saatchi and helped change the communications industry.**

And all of that was happening on the corner of Goodge Street and Tottenham Court Road.

Client: EL AL, 1969
(opposite)
Title: Noah/Bible
Art director:
John Hegarty
Copywriter:
Linsday Dale
Illustrator:
Roy Carruthers
Photographer:
Julian Cottrell

Yes, it has been known to rain in Israel.

EL AL. The Airline of the People of Israel.

You've read a lot about us already.

EL AL. The Airline of the People of Israel.

As I said, Cramer Saatchi was one of the hardest environments in which I have ever worked. **Despite the pressure, we had some success.** || One successful campaign was for EL AL, the Israeli national airline. Their advertising at the time had been based on trying to lure people to holiday in Israel because of the guaranteed 365 days of sunshine. In rain-sodden Britain that was not an unreasonable strategy – except that Spain, which also has rather a lot of sunshine, was not only nearer but also cheaper.

Our work was based around convincing EL AL that Israel's biblical origins were slightly more compelling and would make it stand apart from other sunny holiday destinations. This, we argued, would be much more persuasive. And it was a strategy that had been successfully employed in the US. As much as the client bought the biblical strategy, they still wanted ads about sunshine. || **Clients are sometimes stunningly predictable.**

So we created one. Who could do that for us? Noah. We had a picture of the man himself holding out his hand with a drop of rain hitting it. || The headline read: 'Yes, it has been known to rain in Israel', proving we could do sunshine like no one else. The campaign we produced won a number of awards, including a D&AD Silver award, and got me a trip to the Holy Land as well. Blessed are the creative ones!

Another successful set of campaigns was for the Health Education Council (HEC). This was a UK Government agency tasked with the responsibility of kick-starting the campaign against smoking along with other health-related briefs, including food hygiene and contraception. The work we did for the anti-smoking campaign was pioneering and powerful. Until that time campaigns to stop people

Client: Health
Education Council,
1970–71
Titles: Cigarette
and Child
Art director:
John Hegarty
Copywriter:
Chris Martin
Photographers:
Ray Rathborne/
Alan Brooking

smoking had pictures of coffins and headlines that said something not very creative such as: 'Smoking kills.'

No, surely not?!!!

There was one existing ad I remember from another agency in which someone had put those two thoughts together. It was a picture of an ashtray in the shape of a coffin full of cigarette butts with, yes, you've guessed it, a line saying: 'Smoking kills'. All clever, smart and creative but, ultimately, so what? Just because you tell someone something it doesn't mean they'll react the way you want them to. Smokers would respond to such a message simply by saying: 'Yes, but it won't kill me', or 'I know someone of 85 who's still smoking.' To which my answer would be: 'Yes, and I know someone who's survived a plane crash, but I wouldn't recommend being in one.'

The problem with briefs trying to get people to stop smoking is how do you create a piece of communication that affects everyone and doesn't allow someone to say 'that won't happen to me'? ‖ **The simple breakthrough idea we had was to talk about how cigarettes work and what they do to your body. It was a matter of explaining what happens every time you light up. The disgusting reality of**

This is what happens when a fly lands on your food.

Flies can't eat solid food, so to soften it up they vomit on it.
Then they stamp the vomit in until it's a liquid, usually stamping in a few germs for good measure.
Then when it's good and runny they suck it all back again, probably dropping some excrement at the same time.
And then, when they've finished eating, it's your turn.

Cover food. Cover eating and drinking utensils. Cover dustbins.
The Health Education Council

Client: Health Education Council, 1969
Art director: John Hegarty
Copywriter: Mike Coughlan

smoking was and is alarming. It meant that the audience for the ad could not opt out. The ads nagged at their conscience.

For example, one of them said, 'What makes a cigarette so enjoyable?', underneath which was a list of all the shocking compounds that are in a cigarette. Another one, authored by Charles and Ross, showed a tray with disgusting tar being poured into it with the headline, 'No wonder smokers cough'. It produced powerful advertising that implicated every cigarette that a smoker inhaled. || **And it also gave the campaign a different, compelling look.**

We used the same approach for a number of other briefs from the HEC. One ad for food hygiene, which was aimed at getting people to cover food and protect it from flies, was particularly powerful. It used the device of dramatized reality, which, in this case, described in graphic detail what happens when a fly lands on your food, and was aimed at motivating people to take more care with public hygiene.

But the one single piece of work that ultimately stood out above all the others was the 'Pregnant man' poster. The brief from the HEC was simple: raise the issue of contraception and encourage young men to take greater responsibility.

I had been working on the project and had come up with a brilliant idea. Well, at the time I thought it was brilliant. My idea showed a picture of a 14-year-old girl, eight months' pregnant, standing in her school uniform. The headline read: 'Who taught your daughter the facts of life?' I felt really pleased with myself. || **I was about to present my idea when Jeremy Sinclair, who was a writer at the consultancy, showed me his idea: a picture** of a pregnant man. Underneath was the line: 'Would you be more careful if it was you that got pregnant?'

I took one look at it and knew Jeremy had created something that blew my idea out of the water. I sat down depressed, tore my idea out of my layout pad and chucked it in the bin. Jeremy's idea not only answered the brief brilliantly, but also became a symbol of changing sexual attitudes throughout the 70s. || **The iconic 'Pregnant man' poster has stood the test of time: it is as powerful today as it was back in 1969.** || It not only helped change attitudes to sex education, but was also the impetus for the launch of Saatchi & Saatchi as an advertising agency. Not bad for a bloke with a cushion stuffed up his jumper.

Would you be more careful if it was you that got pregnant?

Contraception is one of the facts of life.
Anyone, married or single, can get free advice on contraception from their doctor or family planning clinic.
You can find your local clinic under Family Planning in the telephone directory or Yellow Pages.

The Health Education Council
78 New Oxford Street, London WC1A 1AH

Client: Health
Education Council,
1969
Art director:
Bill Atherton
Copywriter:
Jeremy Sinclair
Photographer:
Alan Brooking

Alongside the HEC, the other direct client we worked with was Island Records. Back in 1968 Island was becoming one of – if not the most – interesting, independent and critically admired record companies. Under the charismatic guidance of its founder, Chris Blackwell, it had moved on from just being a company that represented and championed reggae and expanded its roster of musicians to include such artists as Jethro Tull, Fairport Convention, King Crimson and the enigmatic Nick Drake. Island Records was a label that promoted the artist first and worried about the money second – it was a creatively driven company that was bonded emotionally to its artists and the integrity of their music.

This was made apparent to us at our first meeting with them. David Betteridge and some of Island's top producers had come in to talk to us about Cramer Saatchi helping with their advertising. They explained that they didn't want to go to a conventional agency as that would look as though they'd joined the mainstream and gone corporate, which just didn't sit with their culture and ethos. In fact, they were so concerned with this aspect of their business that during the meeting they kept saying that they didn't believe in hype. Hype was against everything they practised. || **I remember Ross looking at Charles and then at me before saying that we certainly don't believe in hype at Cramer Saatchi. Charles looked back and said absolutely not – we don't believe in hype. I naturally concurred with both of them.** || Hype, no way, not here. We're Cramer

Saatchi. The meeting concluded and everyone seemed happy – we were going to work together and we had established that none of us believed in hype. David Betteridge and his team duly departed.

Ross, Charles and I gathered in an office and congratulated each other on a successful meeting before Charles said to Ross: || **'What do they mean they don't believe in hype? What the bloody hell is hype?' Ross said, 'I haven't the faintest idea. I thought you knew.' 'Me?', said Charles, 'I haven't a fucking clue.' They both then looked at me. I said, 'I was just agreeing with you two, I thought you knew what you were bloody talking about.' We all burst out laughing.** || We'd just agreed to work with a company on the basis we didn't believe in something we knew absolutely nothing about. We naturally established very quickly what they meant and thought to ourselves: why didn't they just say bullshit? It would have been a lot easier and possibly a lot more accurate.

Working with Island Records we had now drifted into the wacky world of the music industry. If you think advertising's bad, wait till you get into the world of music. After our appointment one of my first meetings was with Guy Stevens, one of Island's gifted producers. The phrase 'We don't believe in hype' was still ringing in my ears. At the meeting Guy told me that he'd found a new band whom he thought were really interesting, but lacked a strong vocalist, which to me seemed fairly fundamental. However, Guy was unperturbed by this little shortcoming in the band's line-up. I enquired after the band's name and he told me that they were called Mott the Hoople and asked me what I thought of the name. I sat there and said that I hadn't the faintest idea, but if the band liked it and they'd been performing with the name, why not stick to it? Guy concurred.

What was more troubling to me, however, was the lack of a vocalist. || I asked Guy how he was going to resolve this little problem, to which his answer was that he'd placed a classified ad in the weekly British music newspaper, the *New Musical Express* (*NME*), saying: 'Singer wanted'. I thought, what the bloody hell happened to the integrity of the band and all that stuff about, 'No hype here'? Here I was at my very first meeting after we'd been hired and I'm being told that one of Island Records' top producers is putting a band together through the classified columns of the *NME*. This isn't quite what I expected.

While I'm still reeling from the little disclosure about the *NME* ad, Guy continues: he's found two vocalists who have responded to the ad and who are both really good, but he's not sure which one to go with. || **They're both great singers, but one of them is always wearing sunglasses – he won't take them off. I said to Guy: that sounds interesting,**

there's nothing wrong with a bit of mystery, so why don't you go with him? || I think Guy had already reached that conclusion. This is how, according to Guy, Ian Hunter came to join Mott the Hoople: it all happened because of a classified ad in the *NME*, a great voice and a pair of sunglasses and, of course, no hype. The wacky world of music.

The last time I spoke to Guy he was working out how he could gate-crash the 1970 Dylan concert at the Isle of Wight Festival by parachuting in. He did make Mott the Hoople with Hunter and his sunglasses a great band and a huge success in the early 70s. But sadly, and despite Guy's great passion and talent for music, he died of an overdose of prescription drugs aged only 38. What a waste.

Despite how Mott the Hoople came to have their lead singer, Cramer Saatchi did actually get Island to live up to their 'no hype' mantra by getting them to run reviews of their music in the press, the placement of which had been paid for by Island, but with the reviews written by people not employed or paid by Island. The first independent reviewer was legendary British DJ and broadcaster John Peel. We ran an ad that appeared throughout the UK music press with the headline: || **'Why Island Records are going to stop telling you what they think of Island Records.' It was the sort of thing only a creative company such as Island could or would do – the idea of running a review of your own music even if you didn't like it was brave and courageous – but the ads soon petered out.** || Island Records couldn't find enough people they respected who could do it.

If you look back into the 1968 D&AD Annual you can see some of the work Cramer Saatchi created for Island Records. I still think the best of it stands out for capturing the independent spirit of the company. It's worth reflecting on how great work can last over the decades. If it has a simplicity and integrity at its core and reflects the client's beliefs then it has a chance – especially if those beliefs resonate with their audience and aren't clothed in corporate speak. I think we managed that with Island. I also think they were a company that believed in what they were doing, took risks and were prepared to back their judgment. They believed in us as we believed in them, despite the occasional lapse such as looking for a lead singer.

A great lesson for anyone in the communications industry.

10

SAATCHI & SAATCHI

By the closing months of the 60s the various occupants of 16 Goodge Street began to take separate paths. David Puttnam went entirely into film production, eventually departing for Hollywood. Boase Massimi Pollitt, having outgrown their space on the third floor, had moved to Paddington in west London. Michael Peters had split with his partner, Lou Klein, and Michael's half of the rubber plant was doing well.

And at Cramer Saatchi we were facing up to the lack of long-term viability for the creative consultancy if we continued with our existing business model. Paradoxically, the success we enjoyed as a creative consultancy had highlighted our weakness: we didn't, apart from a long-lasting client relationship with the Health Education Council (HEC), have enough connections with 'real' clients. Nearly all our work came through advertising agencies. These relationships paid well, but they produced no work beyond being used mostly to firefight an agency's client problems. It was profitable work, but not really motivating.

An example of how disappointing this could be was a brief we worked on with Jeremy Bullmore, the legendary creative director of JWT. Jeremy had asked us to create a brand campaign for RHM (Rank Hovis McDougall), which at the time was one of the UK's biggest food companies. The campaign, authored by Ross Cramer and Charles Saatchi, focused on the future danger of food shortages: could food production keep pace with an exploding population? Sounds familiar, doesn't it.

We speculated that if it didn't, we'd have to reintroduce food rationing. It was an alarming view of the future. The advertising visualized what it would be like to live in a food-rationed world with ration cards, food stamps and government-run food outlets. The only solution to this nightmare: greater investment in the production of food. Sadly, RHM ran out of money and the desire to proceed. And so another great idea bit the dust. It was situations such as the one with the RHM campaign that made it clear to many of us that we had to become a 'real' agency in which we could develop our own client relationships and have greater influence on their decisions. || **Creativity without power is too easy to subvert.**

However, at that point Ross Cramer decided he didn't want to help start an agency and wanted to direct commercials instead. Our loss was film production's gain.

Charles decided to bring his brother, Maurice, into the planned new agency and call it Saatchi & Saatchi. || **If something's good, it's always worth repeating.** || When Charles laid out his plans, offering to make me a partner in the new agency, I voiced my alarm at Maurice's youth and lack of experience, though none of us were what you might think of as 'old'. I was 26 at the time and Charles was 28. Maurice, however, was only 23 and working for Haymarket, a magazine company that published *Campaign*, the journal of the UK advertising industry.

Not only was Maurice very young, but he also didn't have any agency experience. We speculated that we'd be able to hold client meetings only after 4 o'clock because that was when Maurice would be out of school. || Actually, I think that was Tim Bell's line, but more about Tim later.

Charles's response to my concerns about Maurice was simple: if he was going to start a business he was going to do it only with someone he trusted. Maurice, his brother, was someone he trusted more than anyone else he knew. There was a deep-rooted Jewish thing going on here that working-class boys like me from north London didn't quite understand. || **In my view, family is family and business is business, but in Charles's world they were one and the same.**

To be fair to Charles, and despite my concerns about his brother, he wanted the agency to be led by creativity. Among the first people we hired were two other creative mavericks: Alan Tilby, a brilliant writer, and Ron Collins, a gifted but flawed art director from Collett Dickenson Pearce. Ron was notorious for interviewing students with a glove puppet called Sooty on one hand and would occasionally ask Sooty for his opinion on the poor student's work. This kind of 'flawed' behaviour naturally got Ron a bad reputation. Plonker would probably be a better description.

Saatchi & Saatchi opened its doors in September 1970 at 6 Golden Square, London. The offices occupied the ground floor and basement of a somewhat imposing building overlooking an elegant square in

Soho. ‖ **The tenancy of the ground floor made it look as though we had the whole building, which, of course, we didn't – it was all an illusion.** ‖ Illusion was very important to Charles, something he continued to believe in for the rest of his advertising career.

Our ambition was that the agency's reputation was to be one of unsurpassed creativity.

Charles, realizing this could also frighten clients, cut his hair short, bought shirts from Turnbull & Asser and started to wear conservative suits and club ties. Using that same 'don't frighten the client' logic, the agency's letterhead was designed to make us look like a bank rather than a creative hot shop. ‖ **It was about reassurance and, of course, maintaining the illusion.** ‖ Two decades later, Charles carried this sense of illusion through to the holding company offices Saatchi & Saatchi occupied on the south side of Berkeley Square. Although the company occupied only two floors of the building, 'Saatchi & Saatchi' was emblazoned across the front, lording it over one of the most prestigious squares in London. It was like Golden Square all over again. The poor mug of a landlord who'd let the floors to them was probably outraged and no doubt out-manoeuvred as nothing was done about it. When I saw what Charles had pulled off I laughed out loud. ‖ **He was always the great publicist, and once again he'd upstaged the establishment. I loved it.**

Making the change from being a consultancy to an agency meant we had to have a media expert as part of the team. ‖ **It's all very good having brilliant ideas but if you don't have someone who can buy the right media – who could control how and where your work ran – you were somewhat stuffed.**

Remember, we didn't want to go back to being a creative consultancy.

Charles had originally wanted Paul Green, a really smart media fixer, as our partner. Paul agreed to join, but backed out at the last moment. At the time everyone was a trifle pissed by the decision, but these things happen. With hindsight, I think it was good fortune that Paul declined as the brothers then approached Tim Bell.

At the time Tim was the rising media star at Geers Gross, an agency owned by two expat Americans, Bob Geers and Bob Gross. Their fame in the industry was founded on creating a brilliantly successful campaign in the UK for Homepride flour. The campaign was centred on animated commercials featuring little bowler-hatted men who graded the flour. They were hugely popular and memorable characters, so much so that the flour graders, as they were known, became the centre of Homepride's advertising and branding and remain so today.

The success of using animation led the two Bobs to use the same creative approach for virtually every one of their other campaigns. You certainly couldn't accuse them of a lack of consistency. However, consistency in a creative company has to relate to the quality of thinking, not to the continued use of one particular technique.

Conformity is not exactly a desired creative quality.

Tim had nothing to do with the creative work, though – he planned and bought the media.

Tim had one star quality, in particular, that became crucial to the success of Saatchi & Saatchi: he was an exceedingly bright and brilliant salesman, which is somewhat essential when you're going to help sell some pretty outrageous ideas. And he also acted as a counterbalance to Charles's creative genius and Maurice's strategic vision. He was a perfect third partner in the new agency. || **In fact, he eventually became known as the ampersand in Saatchi & Saatchi. This may seem unkind, but in fact it was a compliment.** || In reality, the agency should have been called Saatchi Bell Saatchi: that would have really reflected the power and influence in the start-up. As smart as Paul Green was, I didn't think he had the right personality to balance the brothers in the way that Tim did. Sometimes your second choice is the best choice.

Tim's legendary powers of persuasion were at work not just with clients, but also with everyone in the Saatchi & Saatchi office. Here's an example: about two years after the agency had started, things were going really well. || **The rumour was that things were going so well that Tim had bought a Ferrari. Now, the creative department, for all kinds of complicated reasons, thought this was pathetic.** || It was typical ad man behaviour – and this from the management of an agency that was trying to be unlike any other 'typical' advertising agency.

Tim was wandering through the creative department one day while I was chatting to Jeremy Sinclair. Both Jeremy and I were known for being somewhat lippy, so, as the Ferrari rumour had reached us, we couldn't help but let Tim know what we thought of his rather predictable Italian purchase. Tim confirmed the rumour. He had bought a Ferrari and it was, unsurprisingly, a red Ferrari. After we'd stopped haranguing him, Tim explained his motive for buying one.

He said, imagine it's late on a Friday and I'm visiting a client's office in Hanger Lane. Located on the western outskirts of London, it was known as Ulcer Gulch because so many multi-national client companies were located there. I think Gillette still are. Anyhow, in the scene Tim presented, he's trying to sell some spotty-faced 22-year-old assistant brand manager a brilliant, daring idea. In this imaginary meeting, Tim has to listen to the inexperienced brand manager's opinions on why the idea isn't right and how the agency should come up with some other ideas. ‖ **Tim explained that in situations such as those the only thing that keeps him sane is that, at the end of the meeting, the witless assistant brand manager gets into a Vauxhall tin can to drive home and he gets into a Ferrari.** ‖ That's why he bought one. There wasn't anything Jeremy or I could argue back to that, so we both looked at each other and went: 'fair cop'. And went sulking back to our layout pads.

Tim had expertly seeded his passion for selling ideas and how he rewarded himself for the disappointment that often followed.

At Saatchi & Saatchi selling the idea of the agency itself was incredibly important. Charles had an instinctive feel for PR and how to get a story. ‖ The launch of the agency in 1970 was a textbook case of how to go about publicizing a new business. For the launch Charles persuaded Bob Heller, the editor of *Management Today*, to write an incisive article on 'Why I think it's time for a new kind of advertising'. The article, following a brief by Maurice and Charles, with Bob Heller's byline on it, outlined the various philosophies of the agency and why it was going to be different. It was published as a full-page ad in *The Times* to coincide with all the trade publicity we were getting in the recently founded *Campaign* magazine.

However, there was a slight hitch: *Campaign* was a Haymarket publication, and so was *Management Today*, where Bob was editor. Haymarket's top brass, including the owner, Michael Heseltine, thought this was too much and might be construed by some as a conflict of interests. Heseltine banned Bob from having his byline on the piece. Charles insisted on the piece carrying a byline: it gave it greater importance and power. He couldn't persuade Haymarket to change their mind so he just used Jeremy Sinclair's name. He believed the ad carried greater authority with the 'author's' name attached – Charles wanted it, Charles got it, Bob was particularly pissed off, Haymarket was pissed off at Bob and Charles didn't give a stuff.

Charles's other great trick with the advertising trade media was to have a network of people who would feed him stories about the business. He'd then hand those stories on to the editor and various journalists at the trade magazines, therebygetting them to favour a Saatchi & Saatchi story in return when it was leaked exclusively to them. If there was a university course in media manipulation Charles would have had a PhD in it. He could have taught Citizen Kane a few tricks.

And Charles could invent stories out of nothing as well: there was an occasion when there wasn't much to report, no news stories to keep the agency at the front of the trade media's mind. New business wins are obviously the most important story an agency can release, but you can't have these tumbling out every week, so invention and spin take over. || **On this particular occasion Charles wanted to create a story that underlined the value of his creative department, so he contacted a friend in the insurance business and agreed with this associate that he'd 'insure' the Saatchi & Saatchi creative department for £1,000,000, a vast sum of money in the early 70s.** || On top of that, Charles decided he'd take a leaf out of the world of football and institute a transfer fee if any other agency wanted to poach one of his highly valuable creatives. The story was complete fiction. But a few days later there we all were, the creative department of Saatchi & Saatchi, on the back page of the *Sunday Times* business section photographed on a bench in Golden Square posing like a football team. How about that for a story? It was great PR for the agency and also underlined the value of the Saatchi & Saatchi creative department. And it was all invented from nothing, all down to Charles's conjuring skills.

Saatchi & Saatchi, Golden Square, London, 1972
Front row, from left to right: Chris Martin, Jeremy Sinclair, Charles Saatchi, John Hegarty, Bill Atherton
Back row, from left to right: John Clive, Carol Cass, Dave Woods, Melvin Redford, Nick Darke

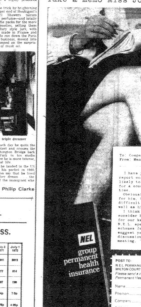
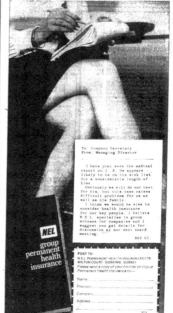

Despite the letterhead, which looked like a bank's, and Charles cutting his hair short and wearing club ties in the early 70s, it was thought in the UK advertising trade that if Collett Dickenson Pearce were The Beatles, then Saatchi & Saatchi were The Rolling Stones.

We were the young upstarts: badly behaved, irreverent, unpredictable and exciting. We were out to change not only advertising, but also the business of advertising. In its early incarnation an example of this change in the way the business worked was that Saatchi & Saatchi had no account men – the creative department dealt directly with the clients. A great piece of thinking at the time, but it was useless in execution, and in reality created an impossible situation. Creative people were hopeless at running an account. ‖ **And letting creatives loose on relationships with clients was madness. We'd argue, walk out of meetings, constantly disagree and we were hopeless at meeting deadlines.** ‖ Brilliant as we might have been at creating and making ideas, working to a strict schedule was not exactly our strong point. Taking a brief from a client is one thing, but running the account? Forget it.

Naturally, this couldn't continue, so in stepped Tim Bell, who by now had been nicknamed 'Ferrari Tim'. He moved from being our media guru to putting in place an account management team that could actually run the business. Charles was dreaming up ideas and ways to get us more and more PR, Maurice was in charge of new business and Tim was left to run the day-to-day client business and be the cement in the organization. It's all very well having brilliant ideas but they're brilliant only if you can sell those ideas to clients, and no one was better at that than Tim – he could sell condoms to a cardinal.

Shortly after the launch of the agency Charles started to develop an allergy to client contact. Not their money, mind you, just them. He was rapidly becoming the Howard Hughes of the advertising industry. This almost paranoid shyness and avoidance of clients was turned into a typical Saatchi advantage by the creation of a myth around the creative leader of the agency that was intended to make him even more intriguing. Clients were made to feel that he didn't have time to see them as he was feverishly slaving over the next piece of creative genius. Few people in those days realized Charles's illusiveness was born

The *Sunday Times*,
8 October 1972

out of necessity: he was shy. He also didn't like clients and he couldn't bear socializing with them. This was left to Maurice and Tim and the rest of us, when necessary.

Despite all the PR buzz and Charles's skill at illusion, the early days of the agency actually produced very little great advertising. The business certainly grew, but the quality of the work and the business gained were hardly mesmeric. We continued working for the HEC and produced some award-winning work that kept the agency's creative profile high, but little else that can be admired emerged from those first few years. || **It was hard back then getting big corporations to take us seriously. We were blazing a trail for off-the-wall creativity, genuine difference. But sadly, most clients were too nervous.** || Instead, Charles focused on the agency's image: it began to feel that building the mythology of Saatchi & Saatchi was taking precedent over the quality of the agency's output. || **After a couple of years a criticism in the business was that the agency was doing more to make itself famous rather than its clients. The most successful brand at Saatchi & Saatchi in those early days was...Saatchi & Saatchi.**

It also began to become apparent, to me at least, that the agency was more interested in being big rather than being better. || A number of acquisitions, and mergers with what were, in my view, some decidedly uninteresting companies, followed. The agency was trying to buy size. As important as money is, it's dangerous if it becomes a philosophical force. Money's a tool, not a philosophy. As a result, I decided I no longer wanted to be a part of an agency pursuing growth for growth's sake. Rightly or wrongly, I decided it was time to move on. In 1973 I was offered the creative directorship of a new agency opening up in London called TBWA and took that opportunity.

The rest of Saatchi & Saatchi's story is well known. It did go through a stage, towards the end of the 70s, when the agency's creative reputation was looking decidedly shaky. It took a major effort to re-establish their creative credentials, which I'm glad to say they eventually did, hiring some great creative people such as Paul Arden and producing some stunning work. || **Their groundbreaking political poster for the Conservative Party in the 1979 UK General Election, 'Labour isn't working', perhaps the best-known work from Saatchi & Saatchi, and a piece that has become part of the political history of the UK, re-engaged the agency with its creative spirit.**

The story of the founding of Saatchi & Saatchi was one of incredible achievement, but soon I was focused on the dreams of four initials: T, B, W and A.

11

TBWA: IT'S A BIT OF A MOUTHFUL

In 1973 I left Saatchi & Saatchi
to become the creative director of TBWA's
newly opened London office. TBWA was
the brainchild of Bill Tragos, the T in
TBWA. The agency's full name was Tragos,
Bonnange, Wiesendanger and Ajroldi –
trips off the tongue, doesn't it?

As you can imagine, it was quite easy to decide to suggest shortening it to TBWA, though getting my new bosses to see that this was a sensible idea was a trifle tricky – they initially put our inability to pronounce the somewhat unpronoucable full agency name down to British insularity. British insularity or not, they had to be convinced that it needed shortening, otherwise a call to a potential British client would have resulted in them hanging up the phone before we even got to 'Ajroldi'.

TBWA had been founded in Paris in 1970 by the four eponymous gentlemen. They were an intruiging mix of nationalities: Tragos was Greek-American, Bonnange was French, Wiesendanger was Swiss and Ajroldi was Italian. Talk about the Tower of Babel. When these four got together who knows which language they would speak – in reality, it was French and English.

The reason that I describe TBWA as a 'brainchild' was that the four founders had brilliantly anticipated the development of what we now call the European Union (the EU) and were creating what was the first truly pan-European agency. Now, just like everything in life, what you need in advertising is a great idea and Messrs T, B, W and A certainly had a pioneering idea. Starting in Paris in 1970, they quickly opened offices in Milan (in 1971) and Frankfurt (in 1972), a rapid expansion that under-lined their European ambitions. In 1973 it was to be London's turn. Now, as well as having a great idea, you also need to have that great idea at the right moment. The fact that TBWA had been wildly successful in France, in Italy and in Germany the following year didn't mean the same idea was

**TBWA London
launch photo, 1973**
From left to right:
Martin Denny, John
Bartle, Chris Martin,
John Hegarty, Nigel
Bogle, Clive Coates

going to leap across the English Channel – people always underestimate
the depth of that 21-mile stretch of water. In 1973, trying to convince the
British of the value of a European agency was like rolling a soggy snowball
up hill, only the hill was more like Mount Everest. In my early days at
the agency I can remember going through endless pitches to prospective
clients in which they were told how European integration was going to happen
and how taking advantage of it for their business was the future. || **The
prospective clients just looked at me as though I'd lost my mind.**

**While the concept of European unity may have been some-
thing of a reality on the continent, on the island nation of Britain
'European unity' was an oxymoron.** || As far as many people in
Britain were concerned, the only unity Europe had ever known was
those times when some of the European nations had to unite to dispense
with some dictator or another. Once you'd done that, as far as we were
concerned, it was time to retreat across the Channel and pretend nothing
else mattered. One could argue that opinion is still held by some in Britain
today, but imagine what it was like in 1973. Looking back, I'm not sure
why I joined TBWA, but something deep down said there was a good idea
behind all of it and wouldn't it be great to be in early. || **The thinking
was great, but the timing just a little out.**

Of course, it didn't help that when we started the agency the world
economy plunged into recession with the price of oil trebling overnight

and the somewhat militant unions in the UK deciding this was the moment to go on strike. Strikes back then in the UK tended to be led by the miners. Wonderful and brave as they were, they weren't slow in withdrawing their labour if their demands for better pay or better conditions weren't met. If the government of the day suggested anything they didn't approve of, that was it – they downed shovels and marched off to the working men's club for a rousing speech and a game of dominoes.

The seeds of Thatcher's economic revolution during the 80s were sown in those dark days of late '73 and early '74. The strike meant a lack of coal for power stations and, consequently, electricity cuts, so the UK was working to a three-day week to preserve energy resources. || **Imagine the scene in which we were sitting around desks on the other two days using candles. Romantic? Maybe. Dynamic? Hardly.**

Was it the right time to start a European agency in the middle of a recession when there was energy on only three days a week? Possibly not – those questions strain the logic of any new business starting up. Was it a good decision to join TBWA? <u>Absolutely.</u>

There were many positives, among which was that it was at TBWA that I really learned how to help run a business, and it was also where I met my future business partners. Along with me, as creative director, Nigel Bogle had been recruited to head up account management and John Bartle to head up planning. We had a commitment to make TBWA work, but it was also where the foundations of BBH were laid. Without the three of us getting together at that time we'd never have had the experience or, perhaps, the courage to start our own agency. So a big thank you has to go to T, B, W and A.

God and advertising move in peculiar ways.

Eventually, the British miners went back to work, having disposed of Ted Heath and his Conservative government in the General Election of February 1974. We could clear the candles off the table now that power was back on full time and continue the march of European integration. But the European angle still wasn't a vote winner with prospective clients – in fact, it was about as useful as an Aertex parachute. They were more interested and concerned about their prospective sales targets in Birmingham than the visions of a Brussels bureaucracy.

Apart from being an advocate of European Union long before it was understood, there was something else that marked TBWA out as different at that time: it had a unique financial ownership structure. Now you might think it odd for a creative person to talk about the financial structure of a company, but I think it is a fundamental factor that liberates and guides creativity within a company. My time at TBWA helped confirm this view.

In trying to mould a European agency, integrated across all the offices, TBWA had two levels of ownership – a local one and an international one. At the local level, the partners running the individual offices were given a 20% shareholding of that office. That 20% was divided up, with a small percentage of that shareholding held back for others who might join the office at a later date, among the partners of that local office. The remaining 80% shareholding of each local office was owned by a holding company in which all of the partners from all of the local offices had a small share.

This structure meant that you not only gained from your local shareholding, but also from that of the international holding company. Despite each partner's international shareholding being very small, perhaps 1–2%, the holding company was where the real value was going to be created. Or so it was believed. ‖ **The structure was also designed to encourage cross-border cooperation. If we talked of European unity then, as a business, we also had to demonstrate that we practised what we preached.**

On paper it was a smart and clever ownership concept, but, like so many ideas that are great on paper, the best intentions of a well-meaning concept were undermined by reality. The TBWA ownership structure resulted in the opposite of what the original founders wanted to achieve. ‖ Rather than breed cross-border cooperation it resulted in distrust and disillusionment. ‖ **Why? Looking back now it's obvious: it worked only if everybody toiled equally hard and was equally successful. If one of the many offices didn't do very well and failed to make any money, why should they worry?** ‖ Everyone else would be kicking profit into that international holding company, conveniently headquartered in Zug, Switzerland. The value of your global holding, where the real worth lay, would continually rise. You could go home early, sit on your arse, and cock up client relations if you wanted to. Why worry about growing your own business when others were growing your global worth for you? Bloody marvellous.

Now I'm not saying that's what people really thought. ‖ **But the danger was that breaking your back in building a hugely successful**

local office could be undermined by the failure of one of the other outposts. || The ownership structure should have been the other way round and set up so that your real road to riches would have come from building a hugely successful local office with a small bonus from the holding company.

An original, cooperative ownership structure fell foul of a set of simple human truths: self-interest and a small thing called motivation.

Those truths are as real as gravity. And you can defy gravity only for so long. In my view, the ownership structure is the reason why the company was eventually sold and is now owned by Omnicom, having first been merged with Chiat/Day.

Having said all that, we got to work with some terrific people, looked beyond the parochial shores of Britain and realized the value of cross-border cooperation. In creative terms, TBWA London didn't do too badly. Along the way it produced some outstanding work, culminating in a Cannes Grand Prix for a Lego commercial called 'Kipper', which at the time was the most awarded commercial in the world. As a result of work like this TBWA became a genuinely distinctive brand within the advertising industry, but – and this is the big shame – it fell foul of an ownership structure, put in place from the agency's inception, that was fatally flawed.

Ownership. Let the story of TBWA be a warning to anyone setting up a company, especially a creative one. If you don't understand the individual motivation of entrepreneurial people and you impose an ownership concept that doesn't reward their labour, it will all come crashing down. The structure at TBWA was a bit like socialism: a wonderful concept in theory, but sadly unworkable in reality. Unless, that is, you view low growth rates as desirable.

I certainly don't.

Marx may have been a brilliant thinker, but his ideas were born out of an era of mass production and mass exploitation. In the advertising industry talent is scarce and if it isn't properly rewarded it will just bugger off.

And that is exactly what happened. A number of us did try to convince our fellow partners of the flaw in the structure and that the ownership should have been skewed much more in favour of the individual local offices, but after months of fruitless negotiations John Bartle, Nigel Bogle and I decided we had to start our own agency. We'd done everything we could to persuade our fellow partners, but our beliefs and vision were falling on deaf ears. They believed in their view of the future and it didn't connect with ours. At the time I couldn't understand their hesitation – they thought they were building something unique and our proposition would wreck their vision. And that was their right.

It was a very hard decision for us to make the break. TBWA London was our baby. We'd built it, fought for it and struggled to create a great agency. || In 1980 it was voted *Campaign* magazine's very first 'Agency of the Year', an accolade of which we were obviously all very proud. The agency was full of people we'd hired and whom we were about to leave. It felt, in some ways, very bad. We not only respected all those people – there were some 150 in the London office – but we also liked them. || **They were colleagues and friends. Deciding to leave them was very traumatic – they trusted us and believed in our leadership. There was a genuine conflict of emotions.**

But, ultimately, we had to be true to ourselves and our beliefs. The three of us, having worked together for eight years, had built an understanding and knowledge of what was needed to create, we hoped, a great agency. We wanted to build an agency that fulfilled our beliefs and ambitions. || **Ultimately, if that couldn't be achieved at TBWA, then we owed it to ourselves to move on. That had to be the deciding factor.**

The fact that about five years after we left, T, B, W and A merged the London office with another agency called Holmes Knight Ritchie and changed the ownership structure didn't give us any satisfaction. It just seemed like a waste of time and potential. But I suppose also in some ways it was great they turned us down – if they hadn't BBH would never have been and the beliefs John, Nigel and I had about running a creative business would never have been put into practice. || **All three of us are therefore eternally grateful to Messrs T, B, W and A. Without their dogged intransigence and also, I have to say, the many lessons we learnt from them, there would have been no BBH. Sometimes 'no' is the best answer you can receive.**

Leaving a company that you're essentially running can cause some odd situations. We were directors of the company and we therefore had certain legal responsibilities. One of the most important, and most obvious, was to pursue the best interests of the company at all times. However, seeking to leave and making that decision public could be interpreted as damaging to the future of TBWA. Acting in any way that was detrimental to the well-being of the company could have been a breach of our legal responsibilities. In other words, if it had been leaked that we were leaving, the founders of the agency, Messrs T, B, W and A, could have sued us. Telling anyone that we were thinking of going could have jeopardized our departure and legal status.

In fact, so serious was this point that when I asked our legal counsel if I could tell my wife that I was leaving the agency he said: 'You ask an interesting question. If you did tell her and she mentioned it to someone else and that information got back to TBWA, you could technically be in breach of contract.' I was beginning to work out why lawyers are paid so much.

Secrecy was therefore paramount, not only because of legal requirements, but also to maximize our own chances of surprise. Controlling the release of that information was vital to our own destiny and initial success.

When we eventually resigned from TBWA we found ourselves in a weird legal hiatus. On the one hand, we were still officers of the company and duty bound to ensure the continuing success of the business, yet on the other we were planning our departure. TBWA were petrified that we were going to walk away with half the business, but, despite their fears, that wasn't our intention – we wanted to start our agency venture with a clean slate. If we took business from TBWA we'd also be taking business practices from TBWA. Paranoia comes into play at times like these. As much as we said we had no intention of enticing half the clients to come with us, they, for obvious reasons, did not believe us. We didn't want to do that and, as was proved after we left, we didn't do it.

BBH launch photo, 1982
From left to right:
Nigel Bogle, John
Hegarty, John Bartle

A number of people from TBWA did follow us – Jerry Judge, Martin Smith and the creative duo of writer Mike Cozens and art director Graham Watson were all part of the first wave of people to join us, along with the ultra efficient Sue Card, who'd been John and Nigel's PA. They formed the nucleus of the new agency.

But, first of all it was just the three of us. I remember the very first Monday after we officially left. We had no offices, no telephone number and no constituted company. <u>Nothing</u>.

12

BBH: THE AGENCY IN A SUITCASE

It's a strange sensation when you hand in your resignation. Suddenly something that has been incredibly important in your life is no longer a part of it. It feels quite weird. As I uttered my well-rehearsed words of resignation everything around me went into soft focus and started to drift away. As soon as the deed is done there's no going back.

After being involved in two start ups, Saatchi
& Saatchi and TBWA London, I didn't think
I'd find myself back in this position again:
talking to lawyers, looking for some offices
and working out who's going to change the
light bulbs.

There was a funny incident when John, Nigel and I made the final
decision to leave TBWA. We had been debating our possible departure
for some months. Having come to the end of the road of negotiations
on the restructuring of shares within TBWA, which had seemed to take
for ever, we had to make a decision. It was early in the year, around the
middle of February, and I was one of the judges for the D&AD awards that
year, which meant that I was going to be out of the office for about three
days. The decision couldn't wait any longer. || **We had to meet up, look
each other in the eye and say, 'Do we really want this? Do we want
to leave and start our own agency?'**

The nearest place we could find that was convenient for the three
of us was Euston station in London. Now for those of you who don't
know Euston station, it is the London terminus for the railway leading
to the Midlands, the north-west of England and Scotland, and it's not the
most glamorous of railway stations. Back in 1982 it was even grottier –
an underinvested, clapped-out 60s building that represented the failings
of a railway industry that was seen by many as a waste of time. However,
it was a convenient location to meet. || **We decided on a pub within
the station concourse called The Britannia. I know one thing for
sure about The Britannia – it's never going to be in a 'good pub'
guide. We therefore felt confident that we could find a quiet corner
and no one from the advertising industry would ever be in this
truly god-awful place.**

When we met we went through everything we had done in our
negotiations with TBWA and concluded there was only one thing to do:
resign. We checked that each of us was prepared for what that meant,

and that we each realized the implications, to our private lives as well as our business ones, of our decision. The decision was made. We were going to quit. As we left The Britannia and were walking down the stairs a somewhat dishevelled-looking man was standing at the bottom. He was begging and asked us to give him some money while he was singing 'Auld Lang Syne'. John, Nigel and I stopped dead and looked at each other. || **Was this a good omen or a bad one? Was this a warning? Should we reconsider? Why, in February, was this man standing there singing 'Auld Lang Syne'? Was this a message? Did he represent the past or the future?** || I think John put 50 pence into the man's hat before we all walked off.

History has judged the decision we made that day, but at the time it all felt very weird. I still can't hear 'Auld Lang Syne' without thinking of that moment. || Years later I had the pleasure of appearing on *Desert Island Discs* on BBC Radio 4 and I pondered making 'Auld Lang Syne' one of my chosen records. If only I could have found that singer.

The day after we had left TBWA we decided to meet up at my house. John turned up with a battered suitcase containing all the legal documents we needed to start our new company. || **Nigel and I looked at the knackered old suitcase and realized that it constituted our first office. We'd put our careers, our reputations and our homes on the line to start our new venture and all we had to show for it was a 40-year-old bloody suitcase. And it wasn't even leather.**

As our first meeting started that morning I offered to make coffee for us all. I went into the kitchen and, as I stood there waiting for the water to boil, I realized we had nothing as a company apart from our individual skills and enthusiasm. || **We didn't have a product, a patent or a service that was unique. We had no clients and no promises of future business. We just had our beliefs, our reputations and our energy. And a battered old suitcase.**

I suppose that is what makes starting an advertising agency incredibly exciting. It takes very little in capital investment, but a vast amount of courage. || **We'd left one of London's most successful advertising agencies to start one with nothing. Had we lost our minds completely? You might say that we were bloody mad.**

I remember confiding to a friend that I was questioning the decision all three of us had made in leaving TBWA. My friend had a perplexed look on his face as I cited all the problems we might face, including potentially losing our homes. He quite rightly brought me to my senses, saying that the worst thing that could happen in reality was that we could fail. || **If we failed with BBH it wouldn't stop me being an award-**

winning art director and I wouldn't be any worse as a creative
person because BBH hadn't succeeded. In fact, the experience of
starting a business would be incredibly energizing. Of course, he
was right. ‖ But I didn't think that as I looked at the battered old suitcase
that morning.

We eventually moved on from the old suitcase and imposed on some
friends who loaned us some space while we looked for offices. Paul
Buckley, who was an old friend at Haymarket publications, offered a spare
corner in one of their offices in Soho. We turned up, expecting to be given
a little office tucked away in the back of their building on Dean Street,
but instead found ourselves opposite some lifts in an alcove. Various
Haymarket employees would emerge from one of the lifts and be
confronted with four complete strangers – me, John, Nigel and
our PA, Sue Card, who were plotting to start a global advertising
empire. ‖ Well, maybe we didn't have the global plan at that time,
just the UK would have been nice.

We endured the lift lobby for a week before moving into
a managed office suite just off Hanover Square in Mayfair, a little more

BBH, 1982
Dean Street,
London
From left to right:
Sue Card, our first
PA, Nigel Bogle,
John Bartle, John
Hegarty

civilized. ‖ **The only problem was that our
other partners had joined by now and brought
our staff number up to eight. But the office
suite had only six chairs. We assumed that at
least two people would always be out, so it
wouldn't matter. But it did. We were all so
keen everyone was in all the time. The earlier
you got in, the more chance there was of getting a seat. You thought twice about going to the
toilet. Leaving your seat meant someone else grabbing it before you
got back.**

This was my third agency launch. I was there at the start of Saatchi
& Saatchi and then TBWA London. I should therefore have known
what to do. Watching Charles launch Saatchi & Saatchi was a textbook lesson in how to get a business into the public arena. TBWA in
1973 was exactly what you don't do. The difference? ‖ **With Saatchi
& Saatchi there was just one person in charge: Charles. He
made all the decisions. No debate, no argument, no second
parties making promises to journalists that others didn't
know about. He was single-minded, focused and determined.
The agency launch was planned and executed with precision.
The agency story and its beliefs were in the hands of the agency
from the start.** ‖ Or, should I say, in Charles's hands. The launch

of Saatchi & Saatchi wasn't a reactive process, far from it – it was relentlessly proactive.

TBWA London's launch was the exact opposite. Because so many conversations had taken place with so many journalists, and because so many promises had been made about exclusives by so many people, the agency lost control of the story. Journalists love an exclusive. If you promise them one and you don't deliver, you will be crucified.

That's exactly what happened with the launch of TBWA London. By the time we tried to engage the media it was too late: the media blew the story because they felt that the exclusives they were promised weren't going to be exclusive. We had antagonized them and lost their trust and their confidence. It took us years to recover from the flopped launch and win back the trust of a group of people that we so needed on our side.

Great publicity for the opening of your agency is crucial to getting everything off the ground successfully, so now that John, Nigel and I were in sole control we weren't going to allow the TBWA scenario to repeat itself. We took Bernard Barnett, the editor of *Campaign* magazine, into our trust, revealed our plans to him and created a week-by-week plan of exclusives. || **Instead of having a one-week 'big announcement', we created a series of stories, starting with our exit from TBWA London, which kept us on the front page of *Campaign* magazine week after week.** || Importantly, we didn't say anything in the first story about our desire to start an agency but focused on the reasons for our departure: lack of control, the ownership structure and the issue of reward. The story started a debate around those issues. In the following week we revealed our plans to start a business together. In week three the story focused on our principle of no creative pitches.

That guiding principle was Nigel's idea. He reasoned that if we really believed in the superiority of our creative product we shouldn't give it away for free, so when we pitched we would concentrate on strategy. || **Get that right first of all, then focus on the creative work, which would be directed against the most relevant strategy. Without outstanding strategic direction, creativity would be wasted.**

It was a daring business strategy to have a principle of 'no creative pitches' – some would say dangerous. In fact, great numbers of fellow advertising experts described it as business suicide. || But it made us stand out. It made us different and intrigued prospective clients. However, it also excluded us from certain pieces of business, but in a way that's what such a strategy is intended to do – to focus your skills on those potential clients that are most susceptible to your product. BBH's product was creativity. By not showing creative work in our pitches we were – perversely – emphasizing our creative credentials.

The strategy also got people talking about us. || The third week's story about BBH in *Campaign* started a debate about how agencies pitch for their business. Should agencies present creative work or not?

There's nothing the media like more than raising an issue and getting a debate going.

Our principle of 'no creative pitches' was a brave position to take and one that paid off. It did the first thing any piece of brand positioning is trying to do: made us stand out and made us interesting.

It's surprising, you might think, that an advertising agency launching itself tries to say something different and gets criticized for doing so. When these very same businesses are advising their clients to do exactly that: to dramatize a difference.

Therefore, making headlines isn't just about spin, <u>it's about substance</u>. It is about building a story out of a point of view that is challenging and interesting. It really is no different from creating a great advertising campaign – they are one and the same.

The early years of BBH were interlaced with an enormous sense of achievement and a constant fear of impending failure. Yes, we were up and running, but at the back of our minds we felt that we could just as easily fail as succeed. From the outside it may have looked like a seamless rise to success, but from the inside we were constantly dogged by the fear of failure.

I remember watching a documentary on the life of Frank Sinatra. Watching from the outside, Sinatra's career seemed like one endless chain of successes, taking him from big band singer of the 40s, to a 50s crooner, to an Academy Award-winning actor and back to being a singing sensation. An icon. The chairman of the board and leader of the Rat Pack – here was a man who had success, fun and money. But how far was that from the truth? When you look at Sinatra's career from his perspective it was forever under threat. If he hadn't got that movie break or recorded a certain song his illustrious career could have ended before it really began. So it is with a company – that's why belief in yourselves and destiny are so important and why it is so vital that you do not compromise your principles. Walking that tightrope of belief and reality is incredibly difficult, but somehow you have to do it.

This is where partnership pays off. Having partners you trust and have faith in is vital. If one waivers the others can pick up the baton. ‖ I was incredibly lucky having two partners who understood that principle – both John and Nigel, apart from being supremely talented, were brilliant at that. They trusted me with the creative work and I trusted them with the business and strategy. They made sure the creative process wasn't interfered with, was given the freedom to express itself and, most importantly, was respected. They also provided the intellectual business brains that any advertising agency needs. It was my job to make sure the creative work honoured that trust and that we used the time we were given and the opportunities that we were presented with effectively. To do that, everyone has to be united and completely focused on what they're best at doing. ‖ **It all comes down to respect – if you don't have that for each other, then you're lost. That mantra of 'none of us is as good as all of us' comes to mind.**

So we had successfully launched BBH. We had got plenty of 'ink', as the Americans say, and established our creative principles and strategies, including no creative pitches. All we needed now were some clients. It's a small detail, but somewhat important.

'Get lucky' has to be one of the strategies you need to employ. Lots of people debate how you 'get lucky', and I'm not going to go into all the theories here, but ultimately I think it comes down to doing interesting things. I don't think it's just about hard work. You know the saying that luck is 1% inspiration and 99% perspiration? Well, I think that's bullshit. If you work hard doing the same thing every day, I don't think you'll get lucky, you'll just get boring. If you work hard doing interesting things then I think your luck will change. My mantra of 'do interesting things and interesting things will happen to you' is born out of that belief.

Our first piece of luck was that, just as we were leaving TBWA, Brian Bowler, the then head of sales and marketing at Audi in the UK, was looking for a new advertising agency. I'd met Brian when we were on an award jury some years before and we seemed to hit it off. Brian remembered that I was at TBWA and called the agency asking to talk to me. Clair, the receptionist at TBWA (she always has a special place in my heart), said: 'Oh no, John's left with Nigel and John Bartle to set up their own agency, let me give you their number.' The big lesson here: always be nice to the people who sit in reception in an office. They can control your destiny.

John Bartle was the master of this. If anyone had a problem – it didn't matter what – they knew they could talk to John. It was said that he had the wettest shoulders in advertising, so many people would cry on them. Brian duly took Clair's advice and called us. Now we were pitching for Audi's business.

Audi's problem back in 1982 was that it was seen as a very worthy car bought by accountants and lawyers. It was a safe choice. || **The profile of Audi drivers was 50 years of age and older. This wasn't exactly inspiring and never looked good on the sales chart. Their cars matched their drivers: dull. Their advertising hadn't helped: it was worthy, righteous and uninspiring.** || And all this while the advertising of their major competitor, BMW, was wonderful work produced under the charismatic direction of Robin Wight.

It wasn't all bad. Things were already changing with their cars – by this time they had launched the Audi Quattro, a four-wheel-drive, high-performance car that was winning every rally it entered. The Audi Quattro represented the future of the Audi brand and its commitment to four-wheel-drive performance engineering.

Our presentation to Audi focused on the Quattro. We felt that it said everything about the future of the Audi brand: innovative, sporty and exciting.

There was one other insight we made. It seems blindingly obvious now, but then great insights usually are. || **We felt that Audi didn't seem particularly German. In fact, research revealed that a large number of drivers couldn't tell where the car was made or which country it came from. 'Audi' didn't sound particularly German and, of course, if you're marketing a piece of automotive engineering, being German is a benefit. A lot of people thought Audis came from somewhere like Belgium. It was a 'Euro car', whatever that meant.** || And let's face it, anything with the word Euro in front of it is usually a disaster.

Everyone knew Porsche, BMW and Mercedes are German, but not Audi. To us at BBH it was obvious that we had to establish the brand's heritage as German. The trick was to do it in a way that engaged people. Being German, however, was a double-edged sword – valuable in its engineering heritage, but not attractive emotionally. It really was a case of 'don't mention the war'. || **Positioning the Audi brand as youthful, sexy, exciting and German was the challenge we set for the advertising task.**

We won the pitch by simply reconnecting the brand with its heritage, innovative engineering and the promise of articulating, in a positive way, its Germanic origins.

This illustrates an interesting point: brands more often than not go wrong because they lose touch with their roots and the values and qualities that made them successful. || This doesn't mean you simply talk about the past, but it does mean that connecting a brand's audience with the positive beliefs that established the brand's original success is important.

Our first piece of work for the brand was for the launch of their new, highly aerodynamic Audi 100. It was claimed to be the most aerodynamic car in its class.

With that work, though, we made the classic mistake of being overawed by the aerodynamic positioning. We produced a TV commercial illustrating drag by using parachutes to hold the car back. The commercial connected with the head, but completely failed to win the heart. As I've said, when you start a new company your first work is rarely your best. || **You are so intent on doing something great that you try too hard. And in trying too hard, you fail to relax. You know the whole world is watching, and the work has to be great. Sadly, it rarely is.**

This was the case with our early work for Audi, and even by 1983 we were still struggling to establish the Audi's German heritage in a way that was motivating and memorable. We'd written a number of commercials that were due to air but still needed a hook to tie them together.

I remember, on one of my trips to the Audi factory in Ingolstadt, seeing the line 'Vorsprung durch Technik' on a fading piece of publicity. When I asked about it our guide dismissed it, saying it was an old line they used in the early 70s.

But it stuck in my mind. When it came to binding our different commercials together I thought, why not use this line? And, importantly, let's keep it in German. Mad as that sounds, I reasoned it would really

Client: Audi, 1987
Title: Odd couple
Art director:
John Hegarty
Copywriter:
Steve Hooper
Director:
John S. Clarke

Client: Audi, 1994
Title: No 1
Art director:
Steve Hudson
Copywriter:
Victoria Fallon
Director:
Frank Budgen

Client: Audi, 2000
Art director:
Pete Bradly
Copywriter:
Marc Hatfield
Photographer:
Simon Mooney

stand out. ‖ **Even though people wouldn't necessarily be able to translate it, it would intrigue them and, of course, the word 'technik' would make the audience understand that the line was something about technology. Back in London Barbara Nokes added the words 'as they say in Germany' and a great campaign was born.**

Of course, we had to research it. And, as you'd expect, the results of the research said, 'don't run it'. Fortunately for us, Brian Bowler at Audi said the research results were rubbish – actually, I think he said 'bollocks' – Audi was German and should be proud of it. Thank you, Brian. Another example of how much advertising research is useless.

The Audi S4 quattro. Nothing to prove.

The Audi S4 quattro with its subtle styling is not a car for those who wish to draw attention to themselves. Instead, its 2.7 litre bi-turbo engine simply offers the quiet confidence of knowing your capabilities.

Audi ⌀⌀⌀⌀
Vorsprung durch Technik

Client: Audi, 1983

Title: Glider

Art directors:
John Hegarty/
Jerry Judge

Copywriter:
Barbara Nokes

Director:
Barry Kinsman

The second pitch we made was for Whitbread which, at the time, was a famous brewery brand in the UK, though sadly not anymore. We always wanted a piece of business from them – they were brilliant clients and bought wonderful work. They were the client who had hired the agencies whose work had resulted in many of UK advertising's memorable slogans: 'Heineken refreshes the parts other beers cannot reach', 'Stella Artois: reassuringly expensive' and, with us at BBH, 'Boddingtons: the cream of Manchester'.

At the time Whitbread were looking at some of their fairly tired brands, such as Mackeson Stout, and wondering if they could be revived by some brilliant thinking and creativity. Naturally, we talked about our founding principle of 'no creative pitches' and, as with our pitch for Audi's business, hoped that would compensate for our lack of resources and back-office functions. || **At the time we were pitching for Whitbread's business, BBH was just B, B, H and Sue Card, our PA.**

When you are pitching for a piece of business and you're just starting your company, the adrenalin is coursing through your veins. You've got nothing to lose and no baggage to worry about. You are at your purest, and if you've got a point of view, then you'll make an impression, even if you lose. In those situations a prospective client will walk away from your presentation with respect for your enthusiasm and, hopefully, your opinions.

Our policy of no creative pitches played brilliantly to the people from Whitbread. They were looking for great strategic insights into their brands. They trusted our ability to come up with fantastic creative work.

We were successful with both of our first two pitches: Audi and Whitbread. Audi appointed us on a Thursday, beating Whitbread by four days. We were off. || It was a dream start. Our first two clients valued creativity and saw it as a business tool. What more could we have asked for?

In particular, Whitbread had a great tradition of buying brave, distinctive advertising. They genuinely saw advertising as an integral part of the product. It was as important to them as the barley and hops that went into their

Client: Audi, 2000

Title: Wake boarder

Art director:
Al Welsh

Copywriter:
Nick O'Bryan-Tear

Director:
Danny Kleinman

beer. Consequently, they treated their advertising with respect and employed people with that point of view. Audi also had that belief and used advertising to change the perception of the brand as dull and predictable.

Apart from the fact that we won, both pitches remain firmly in my mind for two further reasons: at the time we pitched we were in rented offices. It was one of those ghastly office suites that are decorated in a Regency style. It was what I call 'lobby architecture' and was like being in a three-star hotel that had aspirations to be a five-star one. It was the dull face of respectability. The room had framed prints all over the walls of people hunting with horses and hounds. What is it about those dreadful hunting scenes?

We decided we had to do something to stamp our personality on the conference room of our rented office, so we Blu-Tacked our work to the wall. We covered the conference room with our thinking and our creativity. || Sadly, when the Audi presentation was over we hurriedly had to take it down. We were renting the room by the hour and we had to put the hunting scenes back on the wall. || **As we were removing our work, the so-called 'no stick Blu-Tack' was turning out to be not quite so non-stick. Great chunks of wallpaper were coming off the walls as we removed our brilliance. By the time we'd finished the room looked liked some vandalized poster that someone had tried to rip from the billboard.**

I thought it was a definite improvement to what had been there. We'd taken it from dull, pretentious Regency respectability to Regency punk. It looked like the sort of thing Vivienne Westwood would do if she were an interior designer. The agents from whom we were renting the office didn't quite see it like that, so our very first piece of agency expenditure was to get the conference room redecorated. It was Bill Bernbach who said: a principle isn't a principle until it's cost you money. The money wasn't a problem. The thing that really hurt was paying good money to get the conference room redecorated in that god-awful style. || **Trying to impose our culture on that conference room certainly cost us, but winning the business was slightly more important.**

The other memorable story is about our pitching for Whitbread's business. At the time, Whitbread sponsored the London marathon. God knows why – the last thing you'd want after running 26.2 miles is a pint of lager. Later, it was sponsored by the Unilever margarine brand Flora – 'The look after your heart spread' – which seemed a better match.

Shortly before the opportunity to pitch to Whitbread came up, in a moment of madness, I had decided to run the London marathon. As if I didn't have enough to do! I was not a natural runner and found the endless training truly boring. I ran the marathon on the Sunday, in what I thought was a very respectable three and a half hours, and was still limping quite badly when we made our pitch to Whitbread the following Tuesday. The team from Whitbread had arrived – we were now back again in the newly redecorated conference room – and, unbeknown to us and the Whitbread team, their company chairman, Charles Tidbury, had decided he was going to join the presentations.

Quite why he joined the pitches no one really knew – maybe he was feeling a bit bored and fancied a bit of entertainment. ‖ **Charles arrived in our rented offices and asked me why I was limping. When I told him I'd just completed the London marathon he wouldn't stop talking about it and asked whether they should go on sponsoring it. Naturally, I said that the last thing you wanted at the end of the race was a beer – you were certainly thirsty after 26 miles, but not that kind of thirsty.**

Anyway, we made our pitch and, once it was completed, Charles and his team were off to the next agency who were pitching. This particular agency was headed by Robin Wight, who was known back then for always wearing a bow tie. In fact, so committed was he to his bow tie, he used it as his personal trademark.

BBH was one of four agencies pitching, and by the time the Whitbread team had seen all four presentations the only two Charles Tidbury could remember were ours and Robin's. So when he was asked which agency he thought should win the business he had reduced it down to 'bow tie' or 'runner'. When he was told it was to be the 'runner' he apparently said: 'Good decision, chaps, he's obviously quick on his feet.' In his mind our whole presentation – all that thinking, intelligent debate, analysis and future strategy – boiled down to a completely incidental aspect of our pitch: running a marathon.

For years Robin Wight and I used to laugh at the question of who got the business – 'bow tie' or 'runner'? Robin eventually gave up wearing his bow ties and I never ran another marathon. It was the most boring thing I ever did.

Our third pitch was even more momentous and, in many ways, amazing. It was for Levi Strauss. Our first two pitches were for clients who were UK based – a British brewer and the Audi's UK business. Obviously, Audi wasn't British, but back then the distributor in the UK was Lonrho, a British company controlled by a man called Tiny Rowland (which was a bit of a joke because he was actually over six feet tall). Levi Strauss was a global brand with its headquarters in San Francisco. This was a different league, but despite the scale of the brand, they were also a client who were renowned for their wonderful, award-winning advertising.

The first thing we knew about the possibility of pitching for Levi Strauss's business was a letter from their marketing director saying they were looking to review their business and asking if they could come and see us. || **At first we thought it was a joke, a wind-up – maybe someone had got a copy of their letterhead and they were pulling our leg. So we tentatively called Levi Strauss's office and asked for the marketing director, Miles Templeman.** || We got through to his PA and explained we'd received a letter and just wanted to establish whether it was genuine or not. Half expecting her to say, 'Letter? What letter?', to our amazement she said, 'Oh yes, we'd like to fix a meeting for the team to come in and meet you.'

We were dumbstruck – just to get asked for a credentials presentation was amazing, never mind the chance to pitch for the business. || **Levi Strauss was one of advertising's most sought-after accounts. It is a brand steeped in modern culture, in rebellion, music and fashion.** || And it's a brand whose primary target was teenagers. It offered a creative agency an incredible opportunity to shine. There were, however, a number of hurdles we had to overcome before we could consider the prospect.

The Regency-styled conference room was one of them. It was hardly the coolest of environments in which to present our credentials to one of fashion's iconic brands. || Once again, the hunting pictures had to come down. This time we decided against the Blu-Tack option and instead used framed copies of our work and casually leaned them against the wall. We thought the nonchalant, casual approach might appeal.

We still didn't know how we had been included on this long list of agencies Levi Strauss were looking at, but one thing was for sure: we were the newest. || **In fact, we were so new we didn't have our own offices.**

The credentials pitch went reasonably well. We played as hard as we could on our newness. We were the most youthful agency they would be seeing and, as Levi Strauss was a youth brand, surely they should put us on the shortlist to pitch! That was what we reasoned.

When the shortlist was announced we were on it! The only problem with the shortlist was that it was somewhat long. It had five agencies, including McCann Erickson, who were the incumbent. On a shortlist you normally expect three or four agencies at the most. Seeing five worried us as it felt like they couldn't make their minds up and perhaps were unsure themselves about what they were looking for. That is never a good sign. We've learnt over the years to be wary of a shortlist that's long. However, this was Levi Strauss and to be included on their pitch list was amazing in itself.

We later found out that we'd got onto the original list because a researcher, Judith Blundon, had joined Levi Strauss and had previously worked with us when we were at TBWA and developing work for the Ovaltine hot drink brand. She had worked closely with John Bartle and naturally rated him and the work we'd done. That's how they got to us. Luck again? Or perhaps because we did great work with Judith she had remembered us and felt that Levi Strauss should at least talk to us? Thank you, Judith.

We also found out later we made it to the final shortlist because they couldn't think of any reason to take us off. Talk about being damned with faint praise. ‖ **I also think they liked the idea of including some outsiders – people who might just come up with something wild. We had explained that we wouldn't present creative work at our pitch, but demonstrate strategically where the brand should go and the direction our work would take.** ‖ I'm not sure they quite understood what we were saying but viewed us as such mavericks that they thought that's what you had to expect.

The Levi's jeans brand at this time, 1982, was in the shit. The brand had been built on its American heritage: the open road, rock 'n' roll, chewing gum and golden sunsets. It was a very American-centric view of the world.

But sadly for Levi Strauss, the world had moved on. Punk in the mid-70s had blown fashion apart. Youth culture was now no longer one huge compliant mass – it was fragmenting into different tribes who dressed according to the bands they followed. This spelt trouble for the brand. What was also difficult for an iconic American brand at this time was that the US was no longer looked upon by youth culture as a place to be admired. It was no longer cool: Levi Strauss's target audience were no longer looking at the world through a pair of stars-and-stripes shades.

In the minds of British youth the US was Ronald Reagan, Mickey Mouse, oversized people and oversized cars. It just wasn't relevant, and in terms of music nothing new was coming out of the States that was admired. Europe had forged its own voice, especially the UK. The post-punk scene had exploded previous fashion looks – Boy George of Culture Club was dressing up in dreadlocks and dresses, the New Romantics were not only espousing a style of music, but also a fashion look that didn't include jeans. ‖ **The whole youth scene was so far removed from the blue denim look for which Levi Strauss had grown famous. How could a mass-market brand market to an audience that had stopped being a 'mass' and had spurned the origins and authenticity that had made the brand's product famous?** ‖ To make matters worse, the youth audience didn't actually consider jeans necessarily to be fashionable.

The boat wasn't just leaking, the fucking bottom was falling out.

The last piece of advertising Levi Strauss had run was truly dire. In fact, it was so bad that Peter Shilland, who was Levi Strauss's UK advertising manager at the time, said that every time they ran it sales would go down. ‖ No wonder they were holding a pitch. It's rare in advertising that, after seeing an ad, people will actually not buy the product. They may ignore the piece of communication and therefore render it less than effective, but to have an ad that actually dissuaded people from buying a product is truly a remarkable achievement. This is what the mighty McCann Erickson had done: well done, lads.

McCann Erickson's 60-second television commercial for Levi Strauss told the story of four British teenagers going to the US with their Triumph sports car and trading it for an American convertible. I think you can get where they were going! It was laden with clichés and plundered observations.

It showed a brand completely out of touch with its audience. There was one line in the ad when one of the teenagers uses a big truck driver's mirror to put on her lipstick. The creative team who'd written this ad had obviously seen the movie *Cannonball Run* and hadn't realized it was totally naff. The trucker refers to her as 'one foxy lady'. As the 'one foxy lady' line was uttered, you could sense the sales of Levi's jeans plummeting even lower. It was death by a thousand clichés. This was why the account was up for pitch.

Levi Strauss realized they had lost touch with their audience and they somehow had to reconnect. ‖ **In fact their initial brief to the agency was: do something we won't like. By definition, if they liked it, it must be wrong. You could see their logic, but to us it just didn't add up.** ‖ How could you present an idea that was going to be judged on how unacceptable it was? It would be like us pitching our strategy to them as: 'Now here's something you'll really hate. And, I mean, really hate.' To which they reply, 'Oh great then, we'll buy it.'

This was wrong. <u>This was anarchy</u>: it would never work. It was madness.

As we started working on the pitch we pointed this out. And they, too, had realized that it was an impossible, untenable position. The solution to their problem had to live in something they believed in. Their problem, however, was quite formidable. The US, the home of the brand, was culturally dead. And denim was out of fashion. Levi Strauss called this 'the Doomsday scenario' and you could see why.

It is at moments like these that some bright spark says, 'it's always darkest just before the dawn'. Now I don't know who came up with that piece of drivel, but in Levi Strauss's case it wasn't just dark, it was rapidly approaching a black hole.

It was a really daunting problem. At times like this you have to consider everything. ‖ **Some even said we should make a presentation that recommended a strategy of Levi Strauss dropping the manufacture of denim jeans and instead becoming a manufacturer of casual clothes. Accept the inevitable: jeans were a fashion phenomenon that had lasted some 30 years and their time was up.**

For an agency this sounds a very seductive strategy: it saves them having to find a solution to their problem and instead it rests with the product. It's a daring, provocative and possibly memorable approach. But, more often than not, it's useless. There are many instances of advertising doing its best to prop up a foundering brand – the advertising for the British car industry springs to mind – but somewhere, deep down in our guts, we felt Levi Strauss and its jeans had a great future. ‖ **It was a matter of unlocking the potential of the brand and their product. Crack that and you were on the path to glory, greatness and to re-establishing one of the world's most iconic brands.**

It was at about this point that we found out that some of the other agencies on the shortlist were actually making commercials. We couldn't believe it. Here we were saying we weren't even going to show them a creative solution, but instead concentrate on the brand's strategic direction. And other agencies were filming their ideas.

We considered pulling out. What was the point? Levi Strauss was a brand so overwhelmed by problems they were surely going to buy a ready-made solution from the commercials the other agencies had made – it would be just too tempting for them. Drowning men and straws come to mind. Remember we were also the complete outsiders – a brand new agency, with no established track record. We didn't even have our own office. How was a big global brand like Levi Strauss, staring at oblivion, going to buy our thinking? How would their bosses back in San Francisco respond? You did what?!? And they didn't show you any ads!

We thought we were onto a loser, no way could we win. ‖ It was Jerry Judge, who had joined us as an account man to work on the Audi business, who argued that we'd never know if we didn't try. Never give up.

We told ourselves that we were almost definitely going to lose, but we would go down fighting. We would make a virtue out of not presenting instant solutions to a formidable problem – the temptation of instant solutions lay at the heart of Levi Strauss's failure. Despite the travails of 'one foxy lady' it was crucial they stood for something. And it was that 'something' that was the key to the success of their brand.

As the day of the pitch approached our new office that we'd commissioned in Wardour Street, Soho, was still not ready and we were operating out of the offices with the Regency hunting scenes. We tried to suggest to Levi Strauss that we hold the pitch at their offices. 'Oh no,' they said, 'we want to see you in your environment, we want to get a feel for the people and the surroundings that we might be working with.' Pretentious Regency hunting scenes were hardly, I'm sure, what they had in mind. ‖ **The only solution was to have the presentation in our half-constructed offices. We didn't even have a conference table – we could hardly do the presentation with everyone sitting round as though they were at an Alcoholics Anonymous meeting.** ‖ Everyone might suddenly break out into confessions while bursting into tears.

Our solution was to get rid of the builders for the morning, create a conference room table made out of the office desks we'd purchased and hope our brand new and exceedingly cool Italian chairs with reclining backs would cover up for the lack of a finished office.

The big day arrived and about eight people from Levi Strauss turned up, stepping over half-completed office walls smelling of wet paint.

Lee Smith was one of the group. Lee was the head of Levi Strauss Europe. In the end he was the person who had to approve the appointment of the agency. Lee was about 6 feet 4 inches tall, suntanned and Californian. He looked as though he jogged everyday and had a handshake that could crack a bag of walnuts. He'd flown over from San Francisco for the pitches. As soon as I saw him I thought, 'It's all over. He's never going to buy an upstart new agency, without walls in their office. Not a chance. He's too corporate.'

In any case, we had decided that we had to tell them the unvarnished truth: the solution to their problem lay within them. They had to have confidence in who they were, where they'd come from and what they stood for. || **What made the brand famous, what gave it credibility and what was at the heart of the brand. Why did people, especially youth, adopt the brand in the past? They should not apologise for who they were, but celebrate it in a way that was relevant.**

As I've said before, and as with Audi, you don't just look to the past and stay there, but you let the past influence a brand's future. || **The future for Levi Strauss was rebuilding the brand's values by reigniting youth's love of their product.**

So what was that?

Levi Strauss originally came into being as workwear. They made tough, functional garments for gold miners, construction workers, ranch hands and the like. Their jeans were a product that helped build a nation. || **The answer for Levi Strauss was not to try to tell people that you're fashionable, but construct your communication around your enduring values of toughness, integrity and simplicity in a fresh, stylish way. By doing that you move beyond fashion and possibly make everyone else look unfashionable. And, most of all, you should execute it with confidence. If you don't believe it, why should your potential audience?**

One other thing to bear in mind is that, at the time, money was tight. The UK was in the grips of a tough recession. Although jeans weren't fashionable, people still bought them as functional garments.

The solution we pitched to Levi Strauss was to find a distinctive, dramatic way of articulating the quality of their product that surprised their audience. And, what's more, they shouldn't apologize for being American – they just shouldn't ram it down people's throats, especially with clichéd, irrelevant images. If I saw one more gnarled, old cowboy sitting on a ranch porch or a mirrored-sunglassed traffic cop I would have thrown up.

Our presentation concentrated on making Levi Strauss fall in love again with who they were. It was about how they should have pride in their great brand, expressing it from the product out. Focusing on the product's quality, durability and, yes, its American-

ness, but all in a way that captured people's imagination. ‖ I knew it had gone reasonably well because a couple of the Scandinavian managers (the brief also included northern Europe) had been secretly giving me the thumbs up, but in the end it was Lee Smith who had to say yes.

When the presentation finally finished Robin Dow, who was the President of Levi Strauss in the UK, turned to Lee and said, 'You've not said anything. Is there anything you would like to say?' Lee leaned back in one of our incredibility stylish Italian chairs and said, 'There's only one thing I want to say'. We all waited with baited breath. This was the moment he was going to say, 'You must be joking. These people haven't got any staff, they've hardly started their company and haven't even got an office.'

He didn't. He said, 'You know, these are the most comfortable chairs I've ever sat in.'

We had won the account.

At the time none of us quite realized how important those first three pieces of business – Audi, Whitbread and Levi Strauss – would prove, but it was a dream start born out of some daring and incisive thinking. And from winning all those pieces of business we eventually produced work that became defining for BBH and the clients – from 'Vorsprung durch Technik' for Audi to the 'Cream of Manchester' for Whitbread's Boddingtons brand and eventually the 501 campaigns for Levi Strauss.

There's one other story from those early successes that had a long-term influence on our business. It was this: the brief for our very first piece of work for Levi Strauss in 1982 was to launch black denim jeans. They had already booked a number of poster sites around London and quickly needed something to fill them. ‖ **Black denim was a fairly new concept and Levi Strauss had to capitalize on its fashionability. I visualized a flock of sheep going in one direction with a single black sheep going in the other. Barbara Nokes, the writer I had hired to work with me, added the line, 'When the world zigs, zag'.**

When we presented this to Levi Strauss they were somewhat taken aback. There was no picture of a pair of jeans in the execution. Surely, they reasoned, an ad for jeans has to have a picture of the product. We argued that everyone knew what of pair of jeans looked like: we had to dramatize black and its value.

In the end they reluctantly accepted our idea, probably thinking that they had just hired these lunatics, so they had better listen to what they had to say.

Client: Levi Strauss, 1982

Art director:
John Hegarty

Copywriter:
Barbara Nokes

Photographer:
Alan Brooking

The poster received great feedback from the public, and when Bob Haas, the president of Levi Strauss, saw it, he had a copy framed and put in his office, saying 'this is what Levi's the company should be about'. || **Peter Shilland, our main contact with the client, gave me a black sheep as a thank you – it stands in my office to this day. The idea also went on to underline our own agency philosophy to such an extent that we eventually adopted the black sheep as BBH's logo. You see, you can learn all sorts of things from your clients.**

Of course, winning the Levi Strauss account and the success we had with it meant all kinds of fashion brands came knocking. This is probably why, in the early days, we were known as the style agency. || **This used to upset the three of us, but in reality we should have been pleased. Better to be known for something than forgotten for nothing.**

One of my favourite campaigns from these early days was for K Shoes. It was a UK brand desperately in need of reviving. They made great shoes, but lacked style. In fact, women would buy their product but would be ashamed of admitting they owned a pair of their shoes. This made things a little tricky since they were trying to expand their market.

Client: K Shoes, 1988

Title: Creak
Art director:
Dennis Lewis
Copywriter:
Steve Hooper
Director:
Bryan Loftus

Our pitch to K Shoes was based around an emerging sector we called 'Mrs Style': women who were now in their 30s and 40s, who had families and parental responsibilities, but hadn't given up on fashion. They didn't want to dress like a teenager, but they weren't prepared to give up on style.

K produced a range of shoes of which some matched this understated stylish ambition. To appeal to the Mrs Style audience we created a series of commercials that focused on the accepted quality of the shoe, but presented it in a stylish, irreverent, tongue-in-cheek setting that would appeal to this particular market.

Our very first commercial, called 'Creak', won the top British Television Advertising Award in 1987. A brilliant example of our simple belief in product demonstration, wrapped up in an emotional delivery, and another example of turning intelligence into magic.

So we were up and running. We had some great clients, Audi, Whitbread and Levi Strauss, from our first three pitches. We felt pretty good. But, of course, once you've launched your business you've got to keep it flying. And a business like ours works on inspiration and confidence. || **Without constant injections of those two qualities you'll soon fall to earth.**

When we started we wanted to be the best agency in the UK. But as time progressed, we viewed that as somewhat parochial. || **There were agencies who'd already been rated the best in the land, so why follow them? Ridiculous. Instead, we thought, why not be the best agency in the world?**

A little far fetched, you might say. Well, why not? We reasoned that unless you have daring ambition, you'll have nothing but ordinary outcomes. And we hadn't come this far to be ordinary.

Thinking along global lines made everything we planned so much more exciting. We were going to turn BBH into a global force. Now that's something you'd get up in the morning to build.

13

FIRST LEVI'S 501s, THEN THE WORLD

The 80s were a remarkable decade
for the advertising industry. In the UK the
Conservative government led by Margaret
Thatcher had decided to privatize
large tracts of Government-owned
businesses, services and utilities. These
businesses included British Airways,
British Petroleum, British Telecom, the
water companies and the power companies.
Markets were opening up to competition
and brands needed to be created for these
companies – they had to decide how
to compete. What else could they do
apart from be a service provider?

The Conservatives were accused of selling off the nation's silver. Whatever you think of what they did, it lined the pockets of all kinds of creative companies, designers, brand thinkers and, of course, advertising agencies. It was the decade that not only adopted black as the defining colour, but also embraced the value of brands as a competitive necessity for business.

The other great development of the 80s was the emergence of global media. Established brands such as *Time*, *Newsweek* and the *Economist* had global reach, talking to a fairly niche audience. ‖ **But TV was virgin territory. It started in a very small way. MTV was one of the first truly global TV brands.** ‖ Its product – music videos – could very easily cross borders, which therefore provided the channel with a genuine advantage. Its music-based programming had a global language. They also had a clearly defined audience: youth. With the two elements, a universal language and a focused audience, it's not surprising that MTV stormed the media barricades and the 80s gave rise to the MTV generation. ‖ **While music had been a global voice for youth since the 50s, and had increasingly infected culture and fashion ever after, the music video was an added phenomenon. It allowed bands to package their looks and sounds in a unique way with MTV at hand to distribute their 'voice' to a global audience.** ‖ As well as the rise of MTV, The Live Aid concert in July 1985 was another symbol of the change in how media was being consumed and helped propel the concept of a global audience.

Held simultaneously in a number of continents, these rock concerts, the brainchild of Bob Geldof, were a phenomenon that united music, youth and a just cause, famine relief. Live Aid was estimated to have an audience of over 400 million viewers in over 50 countries. The borders had been broken down. And thanks to Geldof, the world would never be the same again.

BBH's work on Levi's meant we were at the forefront of this global audience phenomenon. We had to have an understanding of what was happening in the media and the impact it was having on youth culture. || Never before was Canadian educator, philosopher and scholar Marshall McLuhan's prediction, 'the medium is the message', more true. The emergence of global media helped us in two ways, both of which were invaluable to our future: first of all, there was the idea that advertising for brands who spoke to a youth audience could now be run from one place, or at least one region – this was obviously an advantage for a brand like Levi Strauss. Secondly, it gave us a glimpse of the future and the need for us to think beyond the borders of the UK – it showed us how advertising was going to develop.

So, with every piece of business we worked on we considered its global ambitions as well as its local ones. We argued that if music could be global, film could be global and art could be global, why couldn't advertising? It was only our imagination that was holding us back and, of course, the corporate structures of many of our clients. || How many times have we heard, 'But it won't work here!' Funny how virtually every other creative medium had managed to leap these great divides. || **One thing we knew was that imagination is limitless. Dream it and then build it.**

We were arguing the case for a new kind of global agency – one built on creativity and talent, not just on reach. Many people outside BBH laughed – they argued you had to be everywhere to understand local culture and that you had to have offices in every major city to service your client's needs.

The problem with the advertising industry is that as soon as someone comes up with a different solution to clients' needs vast swathes of our industry damn it. They criticize your beliefs and objectives. Yet these same critics spend their lives trying to convince their client to be different: don't follow the herd, stand for something and the consumer will respect you. || **Yet, when it comes to our industry, the critics shout down difference.**

At BBH, we never said that the established global networks were use-less, we just stated there could be a different approach – we were trying to bring choice into the market. Mind you, the fact that great numbers of those agencies who criticized us were rubbish did help our argument. Look back at a list of advertising agencies from 20 years ago and you'll be amazed at how many so-called great names of the industry have disappeared. It's a salutary lesson for us all:

Nothing is for ever,
especially in advertising.

Harold Wilson, a British Prime Minister, once said, 'A week is a long time in politics'. He could have been talking about advertising.

Speed is one of the aspects of the advertising business that makes it so exciting – you can literally reconfigure your business in a week. That's the pace at which we all operate. I can't think of another industry, other than perhaps the music industry, that's quite so volatile. Of course, the music industry has record labels that own back catalogues that can be re-issued, providing a financial cushion that, in the advertising business, we don't possess. Mind you, the way the music industry has dealt with the issue of downloading, it's amazing any of the major labels still exist.

In advertising we don't have back catalogues, so it's vital we constantly evolve our business propositions.

Criticizing a new agency for doing something different is madness. It's the constant evolution and the constant innovation that keep our industry fresh and relevant. The challenge for new businesses is to ensure their innovation is relevant and not just a gimmick.

There's only one way to find out:
take it to the market.

At BBH our 'take it to the market' opportunity was the launch of the Levi's 501 campaign for Europe. Our original brief from Levi Strauss only included northern Europe. The thinking that won that business had produced three memorable commercials and a poster that became part of BBH's culture: 'The black sheep'. This campaign had been success-ful at halting Levi Strauss's downward image plunge. But, in reality, Levi

Strauss still needed a flagship product that would build sales growth. They had recently reintroduced the original button-fly 501 jean in the US and, after about nine months of promotion around a campaign by FCB in San Francisco with the title 'The Original Blues', sales were beginning to respond. ‖ **But it had been a nail-biting experience. The campaign had taken time to catch on with the American consumer, though eventually, to everyone's relief, it had begun to work.** ‖ So, when they looked to Europe they considered repeating what they had achieved in the States – why not run the US work in Europe? Naturally, for an agency like BBH that would have been a bitter blow. We didn't start BBH to run other people's work. No sodding way, especially work we didn't rate.

Fortunately for us Levi Strauss tested the advertising they were running in the US and it was universally panned. Every so often I love research! It may have been great for American youth, but here in Europe it was loathed. And they weren't about to repeat the salutary lesson of 'That's one foxy lady' and see sales and brand image plummet.

That wasn't the end of the story for us, though. This was going to be a European campaign. Could BBH, operating out of London, create really effective pan-European advertising? Once again, we were in a pitch for the business and, once again, we were up against McCann Erickson, who had lost to us in the pitch for the business in 1982. This time there was no 'foxy lady', but instead they were pitching a Bruce Springsteen idea. Someone had seen Springsteen's iconic *Born in the USA* album cover, of him in jeans shot from behind with a red handkerchief stuffed into the back pocket. This amazing leap of creativity – let's use someone else's idea – was how they thought they'd win the business. Delusional, obviously.

We, on the other hand, were still this young upstart agency with everything to prove, especially our ability to come up with an idea that could cross borders and inspire European youth. Again, we agreed that the product had to be the hero, not some borrowed Springsteen association. We were in the business of selling 501s, not a rock star.

Client: Levi
Strauss, 1998
Art director:
Ed Morris
Copywriter:
James Sinclaire
Photographer:
Nadav Kander

Fortune favoured the brave once again. || Bob Rockey, the new European Chief of Levi Strauss, decided to go with us. I'm sure he was helped in his decision by Robin Dow and Peter Shilland, the previous Levi Strauss management – they had both championed our creativity and Bob had, with his own judgment as well, bought their recommendation.

It's amazing to think that if that judgment had gone the other way and McCann Erickson had won that pitch the history of BBH would have been changed.

I always love the fact that, when you look back at a piece of really successful advertising, a great piece of work looks so simple. I suppose in many ways that's its hallmark – it looks bloody obvious. || It's 'obvious' because it is so right for the brand, and that is, I suppose, the trick: making it belong. || And while it may all look simple, getting to that place takes sweat, perseverance, determination, intelligence and, of course, that thing that creativity provides: magic.

Sadly, this was one occasion when I thought the intelligence department let us down. The brief under the section, 'What must the advertising say', read, 'The right look, the only label'.

Just when you thought everyone was behind you, you realized you were standing there alone with a bit of paper and the words 'the right look, the only label', scribbled across it.

When I read that my heart sank. I thought
that says everything and nothing. I knew
it was now down to the magic department.
You think you're a great creative: prove it.
And, oh shit, not even a great brief to help
you see further.

The task we had to pull off with this new pan-European Levi Strauss campaign was to find an exciting idea that worked internationally, extol the values of the 501 jean (the original button-fly jeans) and turn the product into a must-have fashion garment with a £20 price tag. £20? Remember this was 1984, and at that time it was believed people wouldn't pay that much for a pair of mass-marketed jeans. The retail trade were very sceptical. || **In fact, Selfridges in London declined to stock 501s. Levi Strauss, however, believed consumers would pay that price. Tricky? Brave? I think you could say so.**

There was one other thing to bear in mind: when Levi Strauss had conducted some product research among the target audience the concept of a button-fly jean had gone down like Cliff Richard at a punk concert. Why have a button-fly opening? Surely that was a step backwards? || A zip was far superior, argued those who had been questioned. You can see their point. Well, the product couldn't be changed – it was what it was – so the research was quietly shelved. So we had to come up with an idea that made it not only acceptable but also desirable to own a pair of button-fly 501s. Once again, research proved distinctly fallible. Remember my story about Vorsprung durch Technik? I really don't know how research companies go on getting work when so much of what they expensively recommend is useless.

To go into the story of the creation of the campaign in detail is probably a book in itself, but it can be summarized like this: we had identified there was a growing mass fashion look – the post-punk phenomenon was beginning to wane and bands like Wham! were developing a cross-cultural following. This, we argued, gave Levi Strauss a chance to create a campaign that would touch a nerve with this new mass audience. || **So, in true BBH style, we put the brand at the centre of the advertising, made the product the hero (in fact created a product demonstration), but wrapped it in emotional power.**

I had this belief that if we went back to a time when jeans were at the heart of youth rebellion, when music was changing the world and the US was at the centre of that revolution, we could create a campaign that would be sexy, provocative and inspiring.

The essence of the idea was that Levi's 501s were at the very heart of youth culture. The idiosyncrasies of the product's button-fly and the look and feel of the stone-washed denim were the soul of what made them cool. || **In other words: don't hide your differences, but shout about them. Be proud of them.** || Out of that idea two ads, 'Laundrette' and 'Bath', were born. It wasn't all smooth running and there were many arguments and debates over the executions. Roger Lyons, the director, wanted to use Nick Kamen for the 'Bath' execution and not for 'Laundrette'. Barbara Nokes (with whom I worked on the campaign) and I disagreed. And from the moment we had mapped out the ideas for the ads I had a strong sense of the music I wanted to use and the mood that it would create. I wanted Marvin Gaye's classic *I Heard it through the Grapevine* for 'Laundrette' and for 'Bath' Sam Cooke's *Wonderful World*. Roger Lyons, along with a number of other people, thought *Grapevine* wouldn't work on 'Laundrette'. I knew it would. While he was shooting Lyons kept coming up to me with other tracks: *Grapevine* is too fast, he kept saying. I kept saying, 'Fuck off, Roger, we're using *Grapevine*.' Was it too fast? Of course, it wasn't. And when I saw the first cut of that commercial I knew we had a hit on our hands.

There's a great story about 'Laundrette' that I love to tell. When the original script was written I had the hero stripping down to a pair of Y-front underpants. No problem there, surely? The underpants look just like a pair of Speedo swimming trunks. However, the UK censorship authorities objected to the sight of a man in his 'revealing' underwear

in public. They deemed it indecent. We had hit an impasse – he had to get undressed or the script was dead. What could we do?

Client: Levi Strauss, 1985
Title: Laundrette
Art director:
John Hegarty
Copywriter:
Barbara Nokes
Director:
Roger Lyons

The censorship authority came back and said that if we were to put him in boxer shorts the script would be acceptable. 'Boxer shorts?', we thought, 'Aren't they those funny old-fashioned undergarments from the 40s?' We thought that if that's what it took to get the script through then we'd agree. ‖ **And so, in 'Laundrette', Nick Kamen strips down to a pair of boxer shorts. The result: sales of boxer shorts went through the roof and the once-ubiquitous Y-front underpants died a death.** ‖ Here's to the guiding fashion hand of authority.

The other important aspect of the idea was that by going back to a mythical time in American history we neutralized the anti-American sentiment of our current youth audience. This was somewhat vital as we couldn't hide the brand's origins: if you're selling the original jean, you have to tell people where they originally came from.

Both 'Bath' and 'Laundrette' were instant hits; 'Laundrette' was a bigger hit than 'Bath'. In fact, they were so successful that Levi Strauss had to pull the campaign after only a few weeks – they couldn't keep up with the demand. And, to top it all, Selfridges phoned Levi Strauss asking if they could stock 501s at £20 a pair.

The lesson for us at BBH was that you could create outstanding, cross-border advertising if you focused on what unites people around a brand, rather than what separates them.

Don't focus on what you can't say, but concentrate on <u>what you can</u>.

Client: Levi Strauss, 1985
Title: Airport Russia
Art director: John Hegarty
Copywriter: Chris Palmer
Director: Roger Woodburn

Client: Levi Strauss, 1992
Title: Swimmer
Art director: Rooney Carruthers
Copywriter: Larry Barker
Director: Tarsem

Sounds simple, doesn't it? But up until then the briefs for most global advertising campaigns would talk about what you can't say, rather than what you can. When you talk about opportunities in a brief, you liberate the creative process and inspire your people to create more exciting work. It becomes a positive process, not a negative one.

Armed with this belief and the stunning success of the pan-European 501s campaign we were able to build our global ambitions in a credible and distinct way. We were making advertising part of pop culture, giving the audience the chance to rediscover music and taking it into the charts. || Both *Wonderful World* and *Grapevine* got to number 1 and 2 respectively in the UK charts, higher chart positions than when they were originally released. || **We were not only selling a button-fly jean that research said wouldn't work, but also boxer shorts that were last worn by your grandfather, and making top 10 hits.**

Our third spot, which aired about ten months after 'Laundrette', was called 'Entrance' and featured black 501s. We used *Stand by Me* by Ben E. King.

At the time the BBC wanted to do a radio interview with Ben E. King, who was touring the UK on the back of his new chart success, and me.

I like them best just before they fall apart.

Client: Levi Strauss, 1990
Art director: Martin Galton
Copywriter: Will Awdry
Photographer: Richard Avedon

Of course, I would have fawned all over him. I'd have tried to sing *Stand by Me* with the great man. Now that would have been cool. The fact that I'm a crap singer wouldn't have stopped me. Just think: a duet with Ben E. King. Sadly, I had to go to Brussels to present some new work to Levi Strauss and he disappeared off on his comeback tour. That's the one regret I have from that time.

The lesson:
grab it while you can.

Looking back, this was probably the hardest piece of creativity I ever worked on.

Not only did we have to have a brilliant idea, but also that idea constantly had to reignite fashion interest in a 100-year-old product. It had to be styled in a way that surprised, and had to feature a new hero who would generate press and PR. And carry a piece of music that would chart. || Imagine all that going through

Client: Levi Strauss, 2002
Art director:
Alex Lim
Copywriter:
Tinus Strydom
Photographer:
Nadav Kander

your head as one of your creatives is spinning an idea to you that hopefully will get them a yellow pencil at D&AD.

I reckon the ratio of serious scripts pitched to one being made was about 50:1. It was exhausting. And literally as the last one was about to go on air the brief for the next one would hit your desk. Thanks, guys. It would have been nice to have basked in the glory of the new spot before being hurled back into the creative cauldron.

Would I have had it any other way? Probably not. And that's where, as an agency, I think we really delivered.

If someone was flagging under the constant pressure to come up with something brilliantly fresh, someone else would pick up the baton and run at the problem even harder. That belief – none of us is as good as all of us – comes to mind.

But in the end, however hard it was, we were making hits, winning awards and propelling the 501 to iconic status. We loved it.

And we realized that from one place we could create successful advertising of which we could be proud. The world was now our oyster.

But here I am 28 years after we won the business, helping craft a piece for *Campaign* magazine on why we've resigned Levi Strauss: a brand that helped define our agency and gave us the black sheep as our logo.

But of course all great things come to an end. We've changed, they've changed. Different people with a different perspective of what the brand needs now run the company. This is what happens in our business. || There's very little sentiment for yesterday, especially in the world of fashion.

You're only as good as your next idea. And if you can't agree on that, then it's time to walk.

Client: Levi Strauss, 1999
Title: I.D.
Creative director: John Hegarty
Art director: Tony Davidson
Copywriter: Kim Papworth
Producer: Philippa Crane
Director: Quentin Dupieux

I've always believed that clients get the advertising they deserve. It doesn't matter how good the agency, if the client wants to buy ordinary you'll never sell them extraordinary. Luckily for us we had clients at Levi Strauss who valued extraordinary. Naturally we didn't always agree on the extraordinary, but that doesn't matter. You both know what you're trying to do. Like selling Flat Eric. I had to go back three times to convince them this could be a brilliant idea. What a great way of creating a new Levi's hero, I reasoned – not one that rippled with muscles and a six pack, but a fluffy, yellow puppet. To their credit they finally bought him. The mantra 'keep zagging' comes to mind.

The question I get asked most often is which spot is your favourite? This inevitable question leads one to comparisons, which, as we all know, Oscar Wilde described as odious. But it is inevitable.

Of course, none of them would have happened without 'Laundrette'. It set the tone and style. The subtle use of humour that let everyone know we weren't taking ourselves too seriously, and the use of visual dialogue to tell a story that enabled us to run the campaign across a multi-lingual Europe.

Client: Levi Strauss, 1994
Title: Creek
Art director: John Gorse
Copywriter:
Nick Worthington
Director: Vaughn
and Anthea

But for me my favourite was 'Creek'. The opening scene, the church choir in the background, the emerging sexuality of the older sister. The music resolving into a hard rock track and then the final rug pull of humour: it's the old man's trousers she's holding. I've always said BBH is about turning intelligence into magic. For me, 'Creek' was magic.

So, for a time Levi's defied fashion, they lived beyond it: with an iconic product and communication that constantly surprised. Not only in TV, but also in print.

A campaign I particularly liked was the one shot by Richard Avedon (see page 179), which captured the relationship people have with their 501s, and the workwear campaign with Levi's made out of steel and

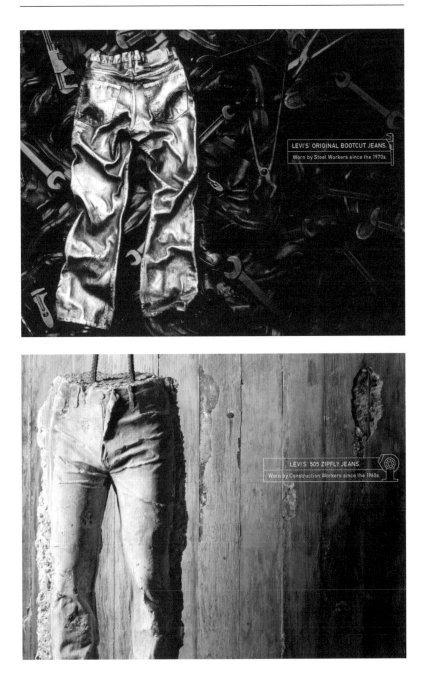

Client: Levi Strauss, 1997
Art director:
Matthew Saunby
Copywriter:
Adam Chiappe
Photographer:
Kevin Summers

**Client: Levi
Strauss, 2002**
Title: Odyssey
Art director:
Anthony Goldstein
Copywriter:
Gavin Lester
Director:
Jonathan Glazer

**Client: Levi
Strauss, 1996**
Title: Washroom
Art director:
Simon Robinson
Copywriters:
Jo Moore/
Philippa Crane
Director: Tarsem

concrete. All these helped affirm the brand's place as 'original', which is what it was.

It was a campaign that helped make an agency and promote the careers of new directors and creative people. Philippa Crane, the producer who worked on most of the spots, discovered and promoted many new directors, Tarsem and Michel Goudry being just two of them. It won every award going apart from a Cannes Grand Prix. It was said 'Drugstore' should have been awarded the title in '96 when Frank Lowe, as Chairman, decided it was a 'poor' year. Naturally, I didn't think it was a poor year! Neither did the audience at the Palais du Festival in Cannes.

I haven't mentioned the many names that helped make this one of the greatest campaigns: there are too many. I know all of them who will be reading this piece with me will be celebrating the opportunity this brand gave them to create a piece of advertising folklore. The opportunity to show how good they really all are. How brilliant their thinking and creativity is, when given the opportunity to express it.

The other thing this brand taught us: if you keep zagging you'll keep surprising. And that's what turns most of us on.

14

GOING GLOBAL
AND THE BIRTH
OF THE MICRO
NETWORK

One of the questions I get asked
most often is: 'what has been
the biggest change in advertising
over the last 40 years?'

It's easy to look at the role of technology and talk about the digital revolution, which undoubtedly is amazing, but whenever I answer this question I talk more about the globalization of the advertising business, which, of course, is a result of technology. The important issue here is that we must remember that it isn't just technology that makes a difference, but how we use it also creates change.

We all know that the phenomenon of mobile texting came about not because mobile phone operators understood its value to their subscribers – it was never viewed as a consumer product – but because subscribers recognized the value of short, sharp messages that could be responded to at the receiver's leisure. || **And, of course, it was very cost-efficient: never forget that.**

It's always important to remember that it's not the technology that matters, but what we do with it.

Remember Walkman? I bet Sony wish we would. It was a brilliant innovation based on existing technology. The genius was making taped music mobile. However, it seems Sony became obsessed with making tapes smaller instead of adopting digital technology and expanding our mobile music collection exponentially.

Technology has created the opportunity for our ideas to go global. Naturally clients have leapt upon this opportunity, which allows them to control their image and reduce costs. || **Why have 10 commercials when you could just have one?** || It's a no brainer for many big corporations. || **But in our rush towards globalization have we also lost our ability to touch people? In many cases we have. Creating work that can cross borders has too often ended up with the adoption of** some 'amazing' technique instead of an idea. **This is lazy thinking, too often born out of the difficulty of getting a number of clients from the different regions to buy in to the idea.** || It's easier selling a technique – 'Hey, we're going to get the buildings to dance!' – as opposed to a powerful idea that moves people. The often-heard reaction – that won't work here – is hard to argue against. Dancing buildings work everywhere. Or do they?

But just as Mr Bernbach showed us how to create great advertising for the masses, so today our creative challenge is to create ideas that can cross borders and yet still touch people.

I remember an interview with J. K. Rowling. She'd just finished her Harry Potter books and was asked what age child she had in mind when writing the series. Potter goes from age eight to 18. || **She said she didn't, she wrote them for herself. She created something that touched her and, in doing so, touched millions.**

That's the best advice anyone can give if you're trying to create work that talks to a global audience.

Our work at BBH for Levi Strauss showed that creativity could cross borders, yet still be acclaimed. This is a pretty basic point if you're building your agency's reputation on creativity. It was out of this experience that we developed the craft of visual narrative: telling a story without words. || **I would provocatively say to our writers: 'words are a barrier to communication'. Not because I didn't value them – I did – but all too often they were over used to explain an idea instead of enhancing it.**

In the early days of BBH our desire to create work that could cross borders opened up a number of interesting creative opportunities for us. The most unusual was a project for Pepsi.

Kevin Roberts, who now runs Saatchi & Saatchi globally, had contacted us after seeing our 501s campaign. At the time Kevin was managing director of Pepsi's business in the Middle East. It was their most profitable region outside the US. Why the Middle East? Think about it for a moment and you can see why: it's unbelievably hot, consuming alcohol may result in eternal damnation and (not least) Coca-Cola were embargoed because of their presence in Israel. I'm not sure what was more profitable at the time: just printing money or bottling Pepsi and selling it in the Middle East.

Who needs advertising, you might ask?

The reason BBH was given this brief was because of Pepsi's belief that the embargo on Coca-Cola in the Middle East was going to be lifted. Which eventually it was.

Once that happened Pepsi would have some real competition. With this in mind, Kevin decided it was time Pepsi engaged with their customers' emotions and not just their thirst. They needed to build some brand loyalty.

Now, if you think there are restrictions in creating global advertising wait until you get to a place like Saudi Arabia. I think the censors there would recoil from a blank screen. However, despite the challenges the advertising would face, he believed we could create something distinctive.

Remember:
focus on the opportunities, not on the problems.

Kevin provided BBH with one of the best briefs I've ever been issued. He explained that when he went to New York for the annual global Pepsi get-together each region from around the world presented its advertising in order of value to the company. Naturally, the US, as the biggest market, went first, followed, for the reasons I explained earlier, by the Middle East, presented by Kevin. Just to make matters worse, the US division of Pepsi had some genuinely outstanding advertising at that time. Their 'Choice of a new Generation' campaign, which used famous stars, had everyone talking. Mind you, the commercial in which Michael Jackson's hair burst into flames wasn't exactly the kind of headline they were looking for. The director of that spot, Bob Giraldi, told me how it happened: Jackson was scripted to make an entrance through two walls of fire. I know, not exactly original! Anyway, on the command 'action!', young Michael bounded through the explosions of fire. The only problem was that he had so much hair lacquer on that his head burst into flames. This is one of the sad outcomes of over-coiffured hair. Unfortunately for Michael, someone hadn't bothered to read the 'highly inflammable' warning that usually appears on the side of hair sprays.

At its heart, Kevin's brief to me was simple: when he stood up to present he didn't want egg on his face! Now that, as a brief, is brilliant. You know exactly where your client is coming from and the reaction they want from your work: it's got to stand up to scrutiny by a sophisticated but jaded marketing community in New York.

I think we delivered with a completely mad piece of advertising that got through the Saudi censors and was a hit in New York. It can be done.

We shot a two-minute spot in the Australian outback that was a cross between *Raiders of the Lost Ark* and a James Bond movie starring the refreshing taste of Pepsi. ‖ **It was so over the top it was funny. Interestingly, the more ridiculous and absurd we made it, the fewer problems the censors had. 'The thirst' became a hit.**

We had to make sure everyone held the hero can of Pepsi in their right hand. Apparently, in Saudi Arabia if you don't you're insulting everything that's sacred to Arabian culture. And that can really piss off a lot of thirsty Saudis.

While we were working on the Pepsi campaign I went to Jeddah to familiarize myself with the market. It was the weirdest place I've ever been. I remember being taken to a very smart department store by the Pepsi people, Jeddah's answer to Harvey Nichols or Bloomingdales.

Walking around the store we passed through the cosmetics department. I don't normally spend a lot of time in cosmetics departments, but the ensuing scene enthralled me.

Standing there were three veiled women, covered from head to toe, trying on Chanel lipstick. They were being served by a man as women weren't allowed to work in Saudi Arabia.

It was one of the strangest things I'd ever seen. The three women would each select a lipstick, take it up under their veil, apply some, put the lipstick down and pick up a mirror that would also then have to go up under the veil so they could check out the lipstick. I stood there mesmerized by this performance. Who knows what they could see under all that clothing or what the bearded counter assistant offered? Despite this, the end result was the purchase of several lipsticks and, therefore, an increase in Chanel's profits. Talk about a brand giving you an inner glow! What was going on underneath that veil? And the lesson here? As alien as that culture was to me, here were three women doing something as simple as buying lipstick. It could have been Bloomingdales in New York – obviously without the veils and bearded salesman.

Client: Pepsi, 1985
Title: The Thirst
Art director:
John Hegarty
Copywriter:
Barbara Nokes
Director:
Iain MacKenzie

Back at BBH it was dawning on us that you certainly could create global campaigns from one place, especially if you were talking to a relatively young audience, but time differences and the resistance of local clients to accept our business model meant that we would have to consider opening offices in other regions.

To be fair, sometimes there are genuine differences that one region finds hard to understand about another. I suppose Wieden+Kennedy have discovered this with Nike. Their office in Portland, Oregon, has produced some brilliant global work, but consider whether, from that location, they would be able to understand the relationship fans have with football, or, as Americans say, soccer? It's a very un-American sport, so they realized that they needed an office located in a football-soaked culture to help make Nike a credible player in this global sports arena. As a result, Wieden+Kennedy opened an office in Amsterdam and Nike, an American brand, are, I would argue, now a credible force in football.

It's important to have beliefs. It's also important to know how they have to evolve.

But the big question for us and our ambitions was how many offices should we open and where should we start?

It seemed to us there was no point in trying to compete with the major networks. We'd seen TBWA try to do this. || **It's not impossible, but before you know it you're spending more and more time administering a complicated network of offices. It's hard enough managing one office, but to manage 20, 30, 40? Forget it.**

If you administer a large network the passion about the work rapidly dissipates. It becomes a process rather than a principle. It does wonders for your airmiles, but nothing for your creativity.

So we started talking about the 'micro network'. A network of a few offices located in important economic centres – between seven and ten offices at the most. This made much more sense for two main reasons: one, it was manageable, and two, we sensed a desire from certain clients to be more impressed with the quality of ideas rather than dozens of pins on maps showing office locations.

The biggest problem certain clients had was finding a great idea. Delivering an idea on the ground was relatively easy: <u>a big, unifying idea was the issue.</u>

At this time, in the 90s, conventional wisdom would have said the next step in our growth would have been for BBH to take our brand to the US. We already had a number of American clients, so that would certainly have been the logical move. We would have followed a well-worn path so many agencies before us had taken. 'Go west, young man.' But by now we had our 'Black Sheep' philosophy, a philosophy born out of that very first poster we created for Levi Strauss to promote black denim: 'When the world zigs, zag'. So we decided to zag and go east and start an office in Asia: to open up our brand to a region that didn't at that time have a huge number of hot agencies. They certainly had some outstanding people, creatives who had brought their talent to the region and had produced some great work, but very few London creative agencies had gone in that direction. || **Most were looking west, so we set our eyes on Singapore.**

Starting a new office is more time-consuming than anyone ever realizes, and, I concede, more costly than they can imagine. We certainly wanted to open an office in the US (which we did, in due course), but genuinely thought we could learn a huge amount, which in due course we did, by zagging our way to Singapore.

Before we could credibly develop our global ambitions we had to have a global media partner. Without the ability to talk about media options and the reality of placing work in local markets we just wouldn't be credible. We needed media input. Of course, we could have just gone to any media player and agreed a deal to work with them. But that would have meant handing over our client relationships to a media company for nothing.

Now, as much as I've said, money is the last reason to do anything, I also don't think (and neither did John and Nigel) that our client relationships should just be handed over on a plate. They represented hard-earned business that we'd fought to help make successful. Nigel's observation was, 'I don't want my gravestone to read, "he died a pauper but you should have seen his showreel".'

It was obvious that if we were to be successful as a global agency we had to sell a stake in BBH to an agency with a respected and credible worldwide media business. We decided quite early on that there was only one option: Starcom. They were the media player we most respected and, fortunately for us, they were owned by Leo Burnett.

I say fortunately because Nigel had been a rising star at Leo Burnett in the early 70s and therefore felt an affinity with them. I think we also liked and trusted them – we very much respected what they stood for and what they had achieved. They had produced brand-building campaigns that had been globally successful and, while not exactly my kind of work, it was work that I could respect. Most of all, and this is the most important point, was this issue of trust. We weren't looking for clones of ourselves but people who had some beliefs and knew how to spell the word integrity.

As part of this journey to find a credible partner, and before we finalized the deal with Leo Burnett and Starcom, I remember having a conversation with Jay Chiat. He was trying to put together a group of like-minded agencies that, based on creative principles, would be the foundation of a network of independently owned agencies that would become a global force. He wanted us to join him in this federation of agencies.

It sounds great in <u>theory</u>, but unless you're financially bound to each other it's impossible to make it work.

Worse than that was the fact that the first agency he'd approached to set up this network was MOJO out of Australia. Now, at that time, if there was an agency that was more different from Chiat/Day it would almost certainly be one with the initials M, O, J and O. ‖ **They put jingles on just about every piece of business they worked on and obviously had a belief that singing was better than thinking. To say I hated the work they produced would probably be an understatement.**

When we expressed doubts about MOJO's creative beliefs to Jay Chiat, never mind the whole agency network concept, he talked us into having dinner at Le Caprice in London with him and MOJO's international chairman.

Out of respect for Jay, Nigel Bogle and I went and listened politely as he explained why he thought MOJO, Chiat/Day and BBH could be the start of a great business venture.

It was at this moment that Nigel went into what I call 'Bogle mode'. In no uncertain terms he explained why he thought MOJO would be the last people in advertising BBH would ever want to be in partnership with. One look at their work would have convinced you of that.

Jay took it all in his stride as the bloke from MOJO nearly choked on his steak tartare, stuttering and protesting their creative credentials. Obviously, their 'down under' definition of creative was different from ours. I recall that he wasn't singing: perhaps a quick jingle would have been better.

In the end, despite Nigel's good advice, Chiat/Day did a deal with MOJO that eventually collapsed for all the obvious reasons. In the end MOJO were bought by Publicis, where thankfully they've made them sing less and got them thinking more. I've always found it advisable to listen to Nigel. Sadly for Chiat/Day they didn't have that kind of relationship with him.

If you're going to merge two cultures, you'd better make sure they're compatible. Our part ownership with NeoGama in Brazil, now NeoGama/BBH, has been brilliantly successful because we all believe in the same things and buy the same kind of creative thinking. If the two are not compatible then what actually happens is that one organization takes over the other. It's dressed up as a merger because it's better for egos and PR.

In the advertising business most mergers don't work. Why? An agency is a collection of beliefs – you can't just package them up and merge them with someone else's. || The whole thing's a nonsense. In the end, one culture has to be dominant. You should decide, when 'merging', which of the cultures, if they're different, is going to be the dominant one and get the pain out of the way early on. We certainly weren't going to be part of a charade like that.

Our deal with Leo Burnett was certainly the best deal we've ever done and has benefited both them and us. We went into it with something to offer Leo Burnett – the chance for them and Starcom to be part of our expansion – and for us to gain access to the powerful and effective media company that was Starcom. We always went into it with a win-win philosophy – they had to gain as much as us.

It was important for us to maintain our independence and therefore our ability to operate as we saw fit. Our creativity and intelligence were built on that positioning. We were able to hire the best people because they knew they were working for us, not a holding company or another agency that might call the shots.

We sold 49% of BBH to Leo Burnett, valuing it at 100%, and held on to 51%, which had to be owned by people working within BBH.

Five years later Leo Burnett were sold to Publicis. At this point we could have bought ourselves back, as our original agreement had a clause about change of ownership. But by this time our relationship with Starcom was so well developed it would have been pointless. Our 51% ownership was there to protect us in any case, and to be fair to Publicis they have been great partners.

Remember: it's a harsh world out there, you need as many friends as you can get.

We opened our very first office abroad, in Singapore, in 1995. Simon Sherwood, our London managing director, volunteered to set it up and ran it for two years. Within two years of opening the office the so-called 'tiger economies' of Asia crashed, which is just what you want to happen as you're establishing a new office. Chris Harris, one of our board account directors, had just gone out to Singapore to take over from Simon. Literally as his plane touched the tarmac, the region was hit by an economic downturn. Actually, it was more like a bloody implosion than a downturn. Poor Chris. Of course we all blamed him. Talk about timing!

When I first went out to help recruit creative people for the new office I really didn't like Singapore. I found it sterile, oppressive and narrow. There was little I liked about the place apart from the flight home. I just couldn't understand why people like Simon and Chris wanted to go there. Culturally, I found it shallow – it was a manufactured environment, which presents a bit of a problem when you're trying to build a creative company. We wondered if we should have gone to Hong Kong instead?

But, as time's gone by, I've come to like the place more and more. It really has loosened up. It's now a vibrant, confident, cosmopolitan centre and, importantly (and something I've come to appreciate), safe. I know that might sound boring, but when you look at the region around it the success of Singapore is remarkable. It's surrounded by chaos, corruption, instability and danger, yet it is literally an island of dynamism with a cosmopolitan population who are well educated and industrious. ‖ **The true test of Singapore is if you don't like it, no one is forcing you to stay. In fact, one of the biggest problems the Singapore government has is people trying to get in illegally.**

Having weathered the Asian economic crisis, we had learnt all kinds of lessons about opening another office: make sure one of your very senior people heads it up, don't ditch your principles because you're in a different region, and play the long game. This, of course, requires steady nerves and deep pockets.

We then turned our attention to the US. The US had always been a difficult market to crack for British agencies. In fact, no UK agency had really made it in the US. Saatchi & Saatchi, through their merger with Compton, had established an office in New York, but it was a pale imitation of their head office in London. ‖ **At BBH we weren't interested in pale imitations. We wanted BBH, wherever it was, to be the same: an outstanding creative company staffed by intelligent, perceptive individuals.**

Historically, American agencies expanded on the back of their clients' growth – giant organizations such as Procter & Gamble, Kellogg's and Mars. Sadly, the days of large UK companies with a global presence have disappeared. Yes, there's Unilever and Diageo, two of our clients at BBH, but beyond that there's not much else. As a result, BBH had to expand on the back of our reputation. Of course, we had global clients Diageo, Unilever, Levi Strauss and Audi, but they never guaranteed us business beyond our London office – those global clients all had lots of other agency relationships around the world – so we had to fight to win their trust and show we could take our brand beyond the UK. Even Wieden+Kennedy, a contemporary of ours, had primarily expanded on the back of Nike's growth as a global brand. I wish we could have done the same.

However, it isn't all bad. Being in that situation does give you the advantage of deciding exactly where and what you want to be. You start with a clean slate.

When finally deciding to go to the States the first thing we had to decide was where we should locate our office. It didn't have to be New York. In fact, in the late 90s, none of the interesting creative agencies, the companies we respected, was in New York. Wieden+Kennedy were in Portland, Chiat/Day in Los Angeles, Fallon Worldwide in Minneapolis, Goodby, Silverstein in San Francisco and the emerging Crispin Porter + Bogusky in Miami.

All the big, boring agencies, yes, you've guessed it, were in New York. Bizarre, isn't it? New York is the biggest, most diverse advertising centre in the world, yet none of the challenging, interesting advertising companies is located there. ‖ Is this the case anywhere else in the world? No. It would be like coming to the UK and finding the hottest agencies were in Doncaster or Penzance or even, God forbid, Grimsby! And I can assure you, Grimsby is how it sounds.

So, the question was whether we should be in another city, or whether we should try to make a go of it in the Big Apple? Someone once said to us that, 'New York is the business of advertising, elsewhere is the craft.'

We decided on New York, not just because we loved the place, but also because we reasoned it gave us a chance to shine. None of the people we really admired were there (or if they had been, they'd pulled out): it gave us an opportunity to make a mark.

So New York it was. Once again, it was important that one of our senior people should go and set up the office, and that senior person was me. If BBH was going to make a statement about our intentions in the US and those intentions were based on our creative work, then the most senior creative person in the agency had to be there. ‖ **That's what happens when you've got your name on the door. I have to say that I didn't protest too much at having to go and live and work in New York.**

I left London in January 1999 and Cindy Gallop, our managing director who'd worked for BBH in both the London and Singapore offices, had set up a temporary office in a block owned by Robert de Niro in Tribeca. I was hoping to bump into the great man, possibly while emptying our trashcans, but sadly no luck – I think he had better things to do. We shared the office building with Harvey Weinstein's film company, Miramax, so the occasional sighting of a Hollywood star added a certain glamour to our surroundings and made sure we kept our eyes open in the elevator. After all, I'd already had the dubious honour of peeing next to Kirk Douglas at Pinewood Studios in the UK and kissing Lauren Bacall on a TV chat show.

The original plan was for me to go to New York for a year, help establish the office, having appointed a creative director, and then come home. None of that is what happened. Opening an office is a bit like warfare: the first casualty in a war is the battle plan. And so it was in New York.

After a long struggle we finally appointed Ty Montague to be our executive creative director. Then, nine months after being appointed, Ty decided to leave us and join Wieden+Kennedy, who were trying to establish their New York office. Ty eventually left Wieden+Kennedy and joined JWT and has now left to start his own business. If he sticks at it I think he will be incredibly successful.

Sticking being the operative word.

All of that delayed my departure. Not that I was upset – I loved New York, really enjoyed exploring the US and it was a wonderful experience –

but could I have stayed? Yes, I certainly could have done, but that would have cramped the style of the people running the office. They had to feel it was their responsibility and their opportunity to make a name for themselves while not being overshadowed by me.

Remember:
if the magic isn't based on intelligence
then you're in trouble.

There were a number of lessons I learned from my time in the US. One of the most important was genuinely to understand the culture. You think you do, but you come from somewhere else and are driven by all your own prejudices – you have to be aware of them. ‖ So whenever you go to another country make sure you really understand what motivates them, what drives their thinking and opinions.

One of the things about American culture is how people value 'big'. To Americans that word has a cultural importance that can easily be missed by those looking from the outside. We Europeans tend to scoff slightly at the word. For us it can mean boring, corporate and unwieldy. And, let's face it, in Europe we've done big and found it wanting: big empires, big wars, big glories and grand coalitions. We see the shortcomings of 'big' – history has taught us how the mighty can fall. For Americans, 'big' carries a different meaning. To them, 'big' is about success. The US is a big country, with big opportunities, big resources, big money and big rewards. New York is called the Big Apple, not the little apple or the average apple: it's big. Yes, Americans' cars are big, the people are big and their appetites are big, but that slightly misses the point.

The US was populated by the disadvantaged, the discriminated, the poor, the starving. These were often people who had suffered famine, persecution and loss. They landed in the US and found a land of plenty that was overflowing with opportunities. The size and scale of those opportunities seeped into their culture and psyche and today articulates itself in the word 'big'. So, when you land on the shores of the US and scoff at the word 'big', beware.

Big is important. Big isn't a problem, it's an opportunity. It's partly what made the US great.

Over here in the UK we spend most of our time convincing our European clients – those that aren't the biggest – to play off the fact that they're not big. The opportunity for them is to look small, nimble, more responsive. This is less the case in the US, where, with a potential domestic market approaching 300 million, you can run a very successful business being number two in the market or even number three. There are the exceptions with just two players going head to head – Apple versus Google, Pepsi versus Coca-Cola, for example – but they are rare. The advantage of the US is there's plenty of room. It's big. It's expansive.

Before I set off for the US I asked a fellow Brit if there was a problem being British in New York? He said, 'Absolutely not. You have to remember New York is a city populated by people from everywhere else. Virtually everyone in the city is an immigrant.' He then told me that, 'Your problem will be that when you go out to the rest of the US you'll be thought of as someone from New York. That will be your problem.' How right he was. New York is more different from the country it is part of than any other city in the world. It is a city that is viewed by the rest of Americans with deep suspicion.

I once said to a friend in New York that I was afraid I wasn't getting out enough and seeing the real America. They said that I shouldn't worry – half an hour in Duane Reade will sort that out. For those of you who have not visited New York, Duane Reade is a chain of drug stores located throughout the city that sells every kind of pill for every kind of neurosis you might possibly suffer from. Wandering around one of the stores is a uniquely American experience.

I arrived in the US at a fascinating time, January 1999. As I stepped off the flight from Heathrow it was as though I'd caught a time machine rather than British Airways flight 172 to JFK. It was absolutely incredible. I'd leapt forward 18 months in seven and a half hours and been hit by the dot-com tsunami. While the internet phenomenon was much talked about in Europe it hadn't really happened. ‖ In the US it was well under way and they were in the grip of dot-com madness. You turned on the radio or TV and virtually every ad was for a new dot-com venture. ‖ **And in a business presentation if you didn't say 'digital' in the first 30 seconds you were dead.**

We were told it was 'the new economy'. Companies proudly announced they were working on 'internet time'. What that actually meant was that they were running around in circles burning cash faster than they could fathom it all out. This was the time of the 'new new' and other such crackpot aphorisms. We had internet companies coming into BBH's offices and pleading with us to take their business – client behaviour previously unheard of in the history of advertising.

I remember one bunch of messianic digital entrepreneurs, who had raised a cool $100 million to start some dot-com nonsense, coming in to ask us to take their account. No pleading! I had to get them to explain to me three times what the actual business was apart from having digital in its name. Naturally, we turned it down.

If we couldn't understand it, how the hell were we supposed to advertise it?

The great phrase at the time was 'it's a land grab'. The thinking was that you had to get your name out there, establish a positioning for yourself and then negotiate your IPO (initial public offering). The so-called entrepeneurs following this route believed that in three years they would sell their company, make a fortune and move on. Of course, as in all these things, the very early adopters did. But by the time you're reading about the opportunities in *FastCompany* or in the business press, it's all over.

The trouble was that 99% of people didn't know it was all over, and that 99% included the money men who were throwing dollars at the so-called new economy faster than the Federal Reserve could print it.

And it all came crashing down. The problem in an environment like that is that if you try to counsel caution, if you try to point out that gravity cannot be defied for ever, you're branded a Luddite. || A collective insanity overtakes logic and God help you if you don't recite the new mantra: digital is the only future. Fast isn't fast enough. It's all about clicks, forget the bricks. You're only one click away from a disaster. We work 24/7.

Of course, those idiots did recite that mantra – they thought that within three years they would have made their fortune and be sitting on a Caribbean beach sipping a piña colada.

At BBH we were trying to build a company for the long term. A company that, hopefully, would add long-term value to our clients' balance sheets.

At the peak of the dot-com lunacy there was a moment when a really quite good digital company, which I think had been set up in about

1996, called Razorfish, had a stock market value greater than that of Omnicom. How about that? You know when someone uses that phase 'the market is always right'? Well, let me tell you the market isn't always right. Sometimes, it's disastrously wrong. And when it's wrong, by God it knows how to do it.

The ultimate example of this was how, in 2000, Time Warner decided they'd better get a grip of this digital future and merged with AOL, the then recently created on-line provider. Never has there been such disastrous and rapid failure. Here was a situation in which Time Warner, a collection of outstanding media brands built up over generations that nurtured real value and had genuine brand equity, were handing their company on a plate to a bunch of internet geeks who'd just got lucky. I remember my reaction at the time: this can't be true, surely they've made a mistake? And did they make a mistake: within about a month of this so-called merger the market crashed and took most of the new digital players with them. Two years after the merger AOL Time Warner posted a loss of $99 million. I'm not sure who in Time Warner thinks that the merger with AOL was one of their greatest triumphs, but I bet there aren't many. And I bet they're no longer working for Time Warner.

Despite the madness of the time I'm not denying the contribution and the game-changing nature of the digital revolution because it certainly was a revolution. Never before had we seen such a rapid and seismic change in how we communicate – it is going to effect so much and, if understood, create such opportunities it would be madness to deny its presence, as it seems some people want to do. || But as with all revolutions, you must be sure to embrace its values and meanings with intelligence and common sense.

So what does the dot-com crash of 2000 teach us? It showed us that companies <u>have to have</u> a business plan that's founded on genuine innovation, not the market madness of the 'new new'. It showed us that gravity is a force that will finally make itself felt on the market.

It taught me, once again, not to let go of my basic principles. It also taught me that when someone is described as 'an expert', be very wary. Over the years I've learnt not to be in awe of anyone. And I mean anyone. You can respect people, you can admire their accomplishments, but never be in awe: it's a dangerous condition to be in. || At the time of writing this book, the world is in the midst of a financial disaster. A disaster brought on us by people not understanding what was going on and being in awe of financial manipulators who assured those who should have known better that everything was all right. If someone utters a sentence to you such as, 'This is a new paradigm, it's not like it was before', run a mile (or even several).

The dot-com crash helped destroy a number of agencies that had expanded on the back of the boom. They were companies that had over committed to the lunacy that had overtaken the market. || **When the crash happened and the plug was pulled the effect was instantaneous – there was no gentle glide path back to reality. The streets were awash with casualties and I can assure you it wasn't a pretty sight.**

But, remember, I saw this all unfold during my time in the US, and in those kinds of situations the US takes the pain and moves on. Hard as that may seem, it is one of the qualities that makes the US a great country. When it comes to business it has very little sentimentality. Dead is dead to them. Mind you, in the current economic crisis, even the US is ditching some of those long-held beliefs: all I have to say is 'General Motors'.

The problem right now for Western economies is how do you balance public good with commercial reality? No one's quite worked that out yet. And I think there will be many more upsets before we understand where the equilibrium lies.

My two and a half years in the US (or rather New York) shot by. BBH established a foothold in this hugely complex market, won some great business and lost some. But we held on to our long-held belief – turning intelligence into magic – attracted some great staff and I believe have an exciting future. As I write this our current executive creative director, Kevin Roddy, has decided to leave. Life is nothing but interesting in our business. Getting the executive creative director appointment right is crucial. As I described in an earlier chapter, they represent the soul of the agency. Other people from other disciplines in the agency carry the flag of the agency, ensure that it's a well-run company, provide the strategic and business acumen that a successful company needs, but ultimately it's in the beliefs and passions of the creative director that the agency's future resides.

What that person does, the demands they make on the agency, the creative leadership they provide, the quality of work they insist on, are all fundamental to the success of the business.

Without that philosophical, intuitive leadership an agency is nothing more than a marketing consultancy. There's nothing wrong with marketing consultancies – they are stacked with intelligence – but what they don't make is magic. ‖ All the logic in the world doesn't necessarily change a thing. Changing the way people feel and behave is the ultimate brand requirement and the ultimate responsibility of a creative idea. And that will remain true wherever we open an office.

The concept of the micro network is firmly established as an alternative way of creating big, bold, global ideas. You don't need hundreds of offices with all the bureaucratic nightmares they bring. At last there's genuine competition to major networks, and clients now have a choice. And choice is something I really approve of.

15

AFTER 28 YEARS, 7 MONTHS AND 3 DAYS

Today, BBH employs about
1,000 people across the globe
with offices in Singapore,
New York, São Paulo, Shanghai,
Mumbai and London. 51% is still
owned by BBH people with
Publicis holding the other 49%.

And we do more than create great advertising: we've created a game show for Axe, set up a TV channel for Audi and a pub quiz for a soft drink, J2O, that is possibly being commissioned as a TV programme. We've made music videos for Myspace and are working with Google on a growing number of projects.

We've also created a new product division within BBH called Zag, which invents product ideas and takes them to the market. So far, Zag have launched two products: a vegetarian food range called *Pick Me*, which is available through Tesco, the UK supermarket chain, and a personal alarm for teenagers, which is named after the Hindu goddess of protection, *Ila*, and is available through another mainstay of British retailing, Marks & Spencer. As well as Zag's physical products, our digital skills are expanding too as we take on assignments for Burberry, Google and clients such as Axe. And we still work with Audi, one of our founding clients.

So what are we at BBH? Are we still an advertising agency with some extra bits

Client: Johnnie
Walker, 2002
Art directors:
Ross Ventress/
Alex Lim
Copywriter:
Steve Elrick

bolted on? Or are we a truly revolutionary communications company that puts its money where its mouth is?

You don't have to be smart to realize that I consider BBH to be the latter. Time, of course, will prove that point.

The real lesson here is to think of ways in which creative companies can evolve into multi-disciplinary organizations.

It's an obvious point to make, but I believe that if creativity is at the heart of your company and your company is not constantly evolving and expanding, then it is dying.

And I believe that applies to more than just communications companies: look at any dynamic company and you will see how they have evolved from their original positioning into very different organizations and continue to evolve today. Apple have evolved from a computer

Client: Axe, 2006
(opposite)
Art director:
John Randazzo
Copywriters:
Amir Farhang/
Matt Ian/Kash Sree/
William Gelner

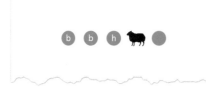

The evolution of the BBH logo, from top to bottom: 1982, 1997 and 2010

manufacturer to a supplier of entertainment via the iPhone and iPad. Another example is LG, a BBH client, which is expanding from being just being a consumer electronics company to becoming an entertainment provider as well.

How we define a brand is limited only by our imagination.

There are no facts you can consult about the future, but what is available are unlimited opportunities for a brand, but only if you stop viewing what you do in a narrow constrained way – do that and you'll open up all kinds of possibilities. Through its mantra, 'Keep walking', Johnnie Walker, another BBH client, is more than just a whisky celebrating success – it is expressing a philosophy: never give up. Keep dreaming. Success isn't a destination, it's a constant journey. With that brand philosophy, hopefully we're inspiring people to live more fulfilling lives. Whatever brand you may be working on, if that brand is not enhancing and expanding the experiences of its audience, then it is missing out on the future.

Branding and the need to promote those brands will continue to grow and be fundamentally important to the future of our economies and the creation of wealth. Always remember: a brand is the most valuable piece of real estate in the world; a corner of someone's mind.

It is also important to remember that part of advertising's role is to convert people. Brands have to get up onto that rock and preach to the masses. If a brand isn't constantly seeking new markets, broadening its appeal and building its fame, then it will slowly die. The secret of brand success is a constant restlessness.

The phrase 'brand leader' consists of only two words.

It's not hard to get this. The latter is leader.

Being a leader means you have to employ daring, vision and innovation. If you are not then you are a follower. And if you think being a follower is your future then good luck. It will also probably mean goodbye – you won't be around for too long.

One of the most exciting things about our world today is the number of ways to reach an audience, the ways we can continue a dialogue and how that can influence the market. Those who say advertising is dead are wrong. Advertising is far from dead: it is thriving in a thousand different forms.

Working out how we connect this new media landscape to potential audiences is the next big challenge. This is why we are building and thinking beyond the conventional agency structure. Creating 'big brand ideas', ideas that can help transform the bottom line for our clients, is at the heart of what we do. How we deliver those ideas will evolve and change. And while nobody can predict how, one thing is for sure: creativity will be at the heart of it.

So, we're building up and evolving what BBH does, but will we go beyond six offices? We could go to Russia, perhaps we could add another office in China – Hong Kong would be interesting. And what about the Middle East? Beirut is a creative centre for that region and is growing fast. However, at the time I write this, the answer to going beyond six offices is 'no'. We're now based in all the major continents and centres of excellence in terms of business and creativity. But that's now. The one thing I have learned is: 'never say never'.

What we don't want is to be like other global advertising groups with dozens of offices around the world. To my mind, that is just a delivery system. Fine if you want to be in that business, but it has never turned BBH on. We're continually driven by creative opportunity and focusing on the quality of our output.

At BBH, we want to 'grow different', not similar. Of course, human nature forces similarity. You have to fight that supposed inevitability to ensure that your company follows its founding principles as it grows. At BBH one founding principle is that we turn intelligence into magic. You can't be all things to all people, so you have to make choices guided by a founding philosophy.

So how are BBH's six offices getting on? Our office in Singapore was voted the 2010 Asian Agency of the Year and has more work in that

Client: Levi Strauss, 2002
Art director: Scott McClelland
Copywriter: Parag Tembulkar
Photographer: John Clang

Client: Levi Strauss, 2009
Art director: Eirma Webster
Copywriter: Angie Featherstone
Illustrator: Tye Sok Kuan

**BBH, Singapore
(below and right)**
Red is lucky
in China

**NeoGama/BBH,
São Paulo, Brazil**
The interior (above,
right) and exterior
(right) of the
joint venture with
Alexandre Gama.
On the exterior
is a picture of
everyone who
works there

BBH, New York
(below)
The photographs
behind the desk
are of everyone
who works there

BBH, London (left)
The reception area is
also used for meetings

BBH, Mumbai
You can see the letters B,
B and H in Hindi hanging
on the wall

BBH, Shanghai
The meeting rooms
have been designed
like rooms in a
home, i.e., a kitchen,
a living room
and so on

Copy Translation
Headline: Saving pandas is not our only mission.
Over 10 million hectares of forests have been protected through our forest certification program. Take a closer look at www.wwfchina.org

Client: WWF, 2009
Art directors:
Yinbo Ma/
Carol Ong
Copywriters: Carol
Ong/Leo Zhang
Illustrator: Pan
Jian Feng

Client: Bank of
the Planet, 2007
(opposite, above)
Art directors:
Marcio Ribas/
Claudia Issa
Copywriter:
Alexandre Gama
Photographer:
Paulo Vainer

Client: ADESF,
2007 (opposite,
below)
Art director:
Marcio Ribas
Copywriter:
Isabela Paulelli
Photographer:
Robert Polidori

year's prestigious D&AD Annual than any other Asian agency. It proves again that you don't have to do scam work to succeed in awards shows. I think the Singapore office's kids' Levi Strauss's campaign is one of the highlights.

The Shanghai office has just been voted China Agency of the Year by *Ad Age* magazine. I bet that gets up some corporate multinational noses. BBH New York has just been voted US Mid-size Agency of the Year, also by *Ad Age*.

The São Paulo office, which is a joint venture with Alexandre Gama's agency NeoGama, constantly amazes me. I think that Brazil is one of the most exciting countries on the planet. The energy, dynamism and possibility that exist in that part of the world have to be experienced to be believed. It is unusual for BBH to go into a joint venture – we like to do our own thing – but Alexandre's agency was so like BBH, and Alexandre, who everyone knows as Ale, is so good, we thought it worth the risk. Anyone who doubts the value of that decision should take a look at São Paulo's creative work. I think NeoGama/BBH is one of the coolest agencies on the planet.

Our Mumbai office has just moved into their own offices and are pitching like mad for business. The partners in Mumbai are refusing to do speculative creative pitches and are winning business – it's like BBH London in 1982 all over again. I describe Mumbai as madness and mayhem, out of which comes, of course, great creativity. Watch out for India as it's going to be doing exciting work. Cricket isn't the only thing they are good at.

And BBH London continues to evolve in the way I've already described. In 2010 we were beaten to *Campaign* magazine's award for the UK's Best Agency of the Decade by Mother, which I think was a fair decision – Mother have made an indelible mark on the London advertising scene and I think it right it was noted. I salute them.

As an agency you know you're doing brilliantly because of the quality of work your agency creates and, ironically, by the fact that your people keep getting lured away by other agencies. That is the price you pay for having such great people throughout the agency. Not everyone can be executive creative director and managing director. We've always been a great training ground for future stars and I'm very proud of that.

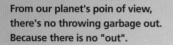

From our planet's poin of view,
there's no throwing garbage out.
Because there is no "out".

Bank of the Planet.
Investments generating
information and actions.
www.bancodoplaneta.com.br

Bank of the
Planet

Client: Umbro, 2000
Title: Grass
Art director:
Marcio Ribas
Copywriter:
Drauzio Gragnani
Photographer:
Rogerio Miranda

Our simple belief has always been to invest in better people. Those same people will produce better creativity against an expanding media landscape, so you will be investing in a better future. If you remain focused on that – invest in the best people for a better future for your company – you will always eat at the top table. Always remember that creativity is a business tool – never be ashamed of that. A creative vision will ensure your future as much as anything can.

The shape and size of that future will be determined by your enthusiasm, daring, vision and luck (so, get lucky). Technology will continue to impact on our business, but worrying about it is pointless. Technology won't be the defining difference, and eventually in the advertising business we'll all have access to the same technology. What will prove to be perennial is the quality of your thinking. BBH's future is built on the quality of our ideas – the better those ideas, the more certain our future. We never forget our 'Black sheep' logo, which is an embodiment of one of our agency's guiding principles from that very first work for Levi Strauss: 'When the world zigs, zag'.

For me, this is the most exciting time to be in advertising. There is everything to play for. As technology changes so much around us, our task is still to find ways to unite people. And the way you unite them is with ideas that capture their imagination: that's as it is, as it's always been and as it always will be.

16

HOW ADVERTISING DROVE ME TO DRINK

Eventually, possibly, one day
you might want to be in charge
of your own brand. And then put
into practice all those things
you said to your clients over the
years that they ignored.

While all of us in advertising have that fantasy, typically during a client meeting when everything you're presenting is going south, the reality is that we don't make the important decisions. In advertising we make recommendations. Our clients make important decisions. Our clients are the ones who decide to invest their money in our idea and that hard-earned cash has to make a return on the advice you're giving.

It's a salutary lesson to remember and perhaps it humbles you a little in the certainty of your views. We all think we're right and that our clients are timid and short-sighted for not adopting our invaluable advice more quickly. Well, the simple way of correcting that is to create your own brand: put your money where your advice is.

At BBH we're doing that with our own brand innovation business, Zag.

There are many lessons that have flowed from our Zag initiative. One of the most important is that developing a brand requires deep pockets and much patience alongside, of course, skill, intuition and luck.

When you create your own brand you are soon made aware that it's your precious profit on which you're going to speculate. Suddenly, that debate about how big the logo should be slides into irrelevance when it's your cash.

And in these debates, I'm told, cash is king!

I have to believe, however, that there is a space between stylishly poor and vulgarly rich, a space that brings together the best of commerce and merges it with creativity.

I've always liked that John Ruskin quotation, 'There can be no beauty without truth'. I also like to believe there can be no real profit without truth.

The important thing to remember is that money isn't a philosophy.

Style and beauty have a spiritual connection. They please us in ways that are hard to define but easy to recognize. They elevate the purpose of our endeavour, leaving us with a pleasure that inflates the initial experience.

However, if you talk like that in front of most businesses you'll be shown the door with the money men shouting, 'Get this lunatic out of my sight!' So, in advertising, we couch our creativity in competitive, commercial terms. We show we've embraced the need for fiscal reality, while holding onto the spiritual qualities that help separate one brand from another. What the heart feels today, the head will know tomorrow.

The trouble is that the head bloody well wants to know today. Especially when that head's got an accountant's brain.

Sadly, in business, logic is valued above emotion – even though it is in the emotion that a brand's true value lies. That's why so many business decisions are made on the back of research analysis.

Starting your own company and creating your own brand allows you to make those decisions. I did exactly that. I bought a vineyard. You could say advertising finally drove me to drink.

When you own a vineyard it means you've gone into partnership with God – and, let me tell you, he's bloody unreliable. Made the world in six days and took the seventh off? Believe that and you'll believe anything.

People often ask me why I did it. I tell them that it was a piece of madness and, as madness has always been something I've courted, it seemed sensible.

I know... doesn't make sense, does it?

The reality is that owning a vineyard is at the opposite end of working in advertising. The advertising business is ephemeral: here today, gone tomorrow. Viticulture couldn't be more different. You have to work to a different timetable: nature's. And you can't speed her up. You can't call her on the phone and say, 'I want it tomorrow'. Nature doesn't answer e-mails.

Appreciating that difference and working with it is incredibly enlightening. It is the ultimate ying and yang. Advertising and viticulture couldn't be more different. And I suppose it's this difference that I find so stimulating. It is what I love about being a farmer, because that's what winemaking comes down to: farming.

As a farmer, you learn how damaging chemicals are to the land. You can see how they're killing nature. Yes, you've made your farm reliable. But reliable for how long? Relying on chemical intervention isn't exactly a long-term solution for the land.

You see that when you farm organically and encourage biodiversity the land comes back to life and the birds return because you haven't killed off all the insects and plant life that are essential to healthy soil. And if you farm biodynamically, which means farming in harmony with nature and to the cycles of the moon (no, I haven't drunk too much of my own wine), you realize that you can make something very special – unique – which leaves the land in a better state than you found it.

That is very satisfying and, despite the time and devotion required, liberating.

But more than just a vineyard owner, I'm a winemaker as well, which involves a number of roles. I start as a farmer – the most important part of my job – who grows and harvests the grapes, then I become a chemist who ferments the fruit into alcohol and then, finally, I'm a marketer – I have to sell my produce.

Naturally, everyone turns to me and says that I must be an expert at the selling bit. Sadly, the thing I've learnt about wine is that it's unlike any other industry I've worked in.

Most of the clients we all work for have a limited number of competitors. The competition may even get into double figures – maybe. In the world of wine I'm pitched against thousands of competitors. There are something like 50,000-plus producing vineyards in France alone. That would make an interesting chart when analysing the competitive landscape in your annual brand review. The chart would take up the space of three buildings.

Production estimates are an interesting concept when talking of vineyards and winemaking. ‖ **Again, God is in charge of that. In August 2006 we were six weeks away from harvest and had a hailstorm that wiped out 80% of our crop in 20 minutes.**

Build that into your business plan.

A bit like creative individuals, vines, while incredibly tough, are also quite sensitive. After a hailstorm they go into a sulk that can still affect the following year's crop, so a hailstorm is really not good for business.

Then you've got a regulatory authority to deal with. That could take up another chapter, so I won't go there except to say that governments (even the French government) view alcohol as evil (or that's what they say), so they whack tax on it at every possible opportunity. And this is despite the fact that moderate drinking is good for you.

But that's enough of the bad news.
<u>This is why I still enjoy it.</u>

Wine is genuinely a gift from the gods (even if they spend most of their time somewhere else). When you open a bottle of wine, well at least a reasonable one, you're opening a time machine. Look at the year on the label and what is inside that bottle represents what happened that year. ‖ A year with a winter, spring and summer that were hot, cold, cool, long, wet, short or whatever will be represented in 75cl of liquid pleasure. A bottle of wine tells a story – it's a unique history of that place and time.

Open a bottle of our Cuvée No. 1 from 2003 and you can taste a year that produced incredible fruit with sunshine that was longer and hotter than many can remember. That story is locked into every bottle.

Some more black sheep, this time on our Hegarty Chamans No. 1, 2004, a Syrah-Carignan blend

Then there is regionality. I find this endlessly fascinating – wines reflect the places they come from. Think of a region and its people and you begin to understand their wine. With a decent bottle of wine you can delve into the culture and customs of the region you're drinking. You can find out why they make what they make and what they eat with it. That's why an 'industrial' wine with no heart and soul is just a dead product. Why bother?

There are not many other kinds of food and drink that have the diversity that wine offers. Tomato juice? No, I don't think so. This diversity is what makes wine so magical.

My first piece of wine advice to you is this: drink only good wine, drink it with respect and it will pay you back for life. It civilizes, improves the quality of food and makes conversation flow. ‖ **My second piece of advice: don't become a cork dork, one of those people who wraps wine in mystery and snobbishness and who flaunts their knowledge as though they're special. That's a big danger, so don't go there. A great wine is a wine you like, not one ordained as 'great' by others.**

Now the problem with the winemaking industry is that it is one wrapped in mystery and mystique. And this is often used to keep people confused. I once said to a wine writer, who was bemoaning the loss of mystery, that winemaking should lose the mystery but keep the magic. Wine aficionados should stop making wine difficult for people to understand and comprehend. Accessibility doesn't stop something being special – it can still be magical. I can listen to music and understand perfectly how what I'm listening to was composed and how it works: the instruments used to bring the composition to life. That knowledge doesn't impair my enjoyment, it actually enhances it.

Mystery is fine if you're writing a thriller, but not if you want to be a successful winemaker.

Simplicity and memorability along with desirability are vital ingredients to any brand's success. Wine is no different.

The wine from my vineyard needed a name – it needed branding. The question was whether I should use the name of the property I purchased – Domaine de Chamans – or whether I should use my name and utilize a symbol with which I have been associated for nearly 30 years: a black sheep?

The answer is obvious: imagine I've just bumped into an old friend. He says: 'John, I hear you're making wine, what's it called?' Now, if I say 'Domaine de Chamans', unless he's got a brain the size of Pluto, within about five minutes he'll have forgotten that catchy little label. If, on the other hand, I say 'Hegarty Chamans' he'll remember the Hegarty bit and, with luck, try to purchase a bottle.

The first lesson of branding: memorability. It's very difficult buying something you can't remember.

Our vineyard is located in the Languedoc region of southern France. I share it with Philippa Crane, my wonderful partner. She, in fact, is the person who makes it work – I just talk about it. Oh, and by the way, women have much better palates than men. So when you're in a restaurant and the waiter asks someone to taste the wine make sure it's a woman.

Above: Looking south over Domaine de Chamans towards the Pyrenees

We have dramatic views of the Pyrenees on a clear day and the property is in the foothills of the Montagne Noire, the black mountains, in Cathar country. The Cathars were a religious sect living in this part of France in the 11th and 12th centuries. Unfortunately for them their fairly benign and peaceful beliefs were seen by the Catholic Church as heretical. We all know what the Church did with heretics back then – they ordered a crusade against these peaceful, loving people and had them wiped out. The 13th-century annihilation of the Cathars is the world's first recorded genocide. I can think of some better ways of making history.

The Cathars were also often to referred to as the black sheep of France, so it seemed obvious to me to have a black sheep as our logo. It had geographic and historical relevance alongside a philosophical belief of not following the crowd.

So, now I am a brand owner, I'm seeking ways of making the product better and taking those important investment decisions myself.

As far as I'm concerned there is only one business strategy whatever you're doing – it's called quality. Now of course quality is in the eye of the beholder. Not everyone may agree. And that's fine. Especially in the world of wine.

Wine is an agricultural product subject to the whims of nature. But I believe the route to quality is working in harmony with the forces of nature. Honouring the truth of where we are and therefore producing something unique.

Someone recently said to me, 'So, John, what kind of wine do you want to make?' I replied, 'You've asked the wrong question: it's what kind of wine does our land want to make?' That's what's important. Then it's unique, and there's nothing like selling something unique. Remember, you don't just drink the wine, you drink the place.

Luckily for us, Mr Robert Parker, the legendary American wine critic, agreed. He gave our Cuvée No. 1 from our first 2003 vintage 92 points. He rates wine out of 100. As you can imagine I was pretty happy with 92. And then he gave our 2005 Black Knight, a limited edition special blend, 93 points. Samuel Berger, my brilliant winemaker, who has that wonderful French ambivalence to awards, shrugs his shoulders at such accolades, saying, but John, the wine will not be ready for drinking for another five years! Give me a break, Samuel, I say. I wouldn't mind selling the odd bottle now. And then I suddenly think to myself, oh God, I'm sounding like a client.

So, eventually you might start your own business outside the world of advertising. My advice is do it. ‖ **Find something that really** interests you, whatever, it doesn't matter, as long as you love it. And then apply all that strategic and creative thinking that advertising constantly employs.

Advertising is far more than just a communications industry. It's a problem-solving industry that also teaches you about life, how it encourages you to focus your thinking and produce something of genuine value. Why? Because that will make the advertising task so much easier. You're now equipped with a unique set of insights and experiences across a broad range of markets, allowing you to bring clarity and inspiration to anything you wish to produce.

That is the gift of our industry.
Value it and wear it well.

An enormous thank you must go to Andrew Sanigar of T&H for his encouragement and enthusiasm. Also to Ilona de Nemethy Sanigar for making sure my words made sense, to Chris Wakeling for his designer's eye and lastly to Amy Kingsbury, my long-suffering PA, who typed, re-typed and finally deciphered my appalling handwriting.

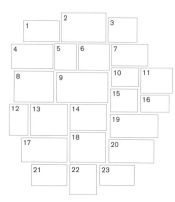

Captions for the images on page 2

1. **Client:** Google, 2010
   Title: Speed
   Art director: Steve Peck
   Copywriter: Jared Elms
   Director: Aaron Duffy

2. **Client:** Audi, 1992
   Art director: Russell Ramsey
   Copywriter: John O'Keeffe
   Photographer: Leon Steele

3. **Client:** Perfetti Van Melle –
   Vigorsol, 2002
   Title: Lotto
   Art director: Mike Wells
   Copywriter: Will Barnett
   Director: Harold Zwart

4. **Client:** Johnnie Walker, 2010
   Title: Man who walked around
   the world
   Art director: Mick Mahoney
   Copywriter: Justin Moore
   Director: Jamie Rafn

5. **Client:** Bertolli, 2003
   Art director: Adam Staples
   Copywriter: Paul Miles
   Illustrator: Syd Brak

6. **Client:** Pretty Polly, 1987
   Title: Smooth running
   Art director: Rosie Arnold
   Copywriter: Derek Payne
   Director: John Marles

7. **Client:** St John's Ambulance, 2010
   Title: Popcorn
   Art director: Adrian Rossi
   Copywriter: Alex Grieve
   Director: Jeff Labbe

8. **Client:** Levi Strauss, 1996
   Art director: Rosie Arnold
   Copywriter: Will Awdry
   Photographer: Nadav Kander

9. **Client:** Parker Pens, 2003
   Art Director: Russell Ramsey

10. **Client:** Audi, 2002
    Title: Hendrix
    Art director: Matthew Saunby
    Copywriter: Adam Chiappe
    Director: Daniel Kleinman

11. **Client:** Club Med, 1996
    Title: City
    Art director: Tony McTear
    Copywriter: Will Barnett
    Director: Jonathan Glazer

12. **Client:** Sony Walkman, 1990
    Art director: Mike Wells
    Copywriter: Tom Hudson
    Photographer: Malcolm Venville

13. **Client:** OMO – Dero, 2007
    Title: Muscle man
    Art director: Dave Monk
    Copywriter: Matt Waller
    Director: Jonty Toosey

14. **Client:** K Shoes, 1990
    Art director: Gary Denham
    Copywriter: Barbara Nokes

15. **Client:** Levi Strauss, 1995
    Title: Clayman
    Art director: Tim Ashton
    Copywriter: John McCabe
    Producer: Philippa Crane
    Directors: Michael Mort/Deiniol Morris

16. **Client:** Asda, 1987
    Writer: Nick Welch
    Art director: Billy Mawhinney
    Photographer: Stak

17. **Client:** Castlemaine XXXX, 2006
    Art director: Adrian Birkinshaw
    Copywriter: Paul Yull
    Photographer: James Day

18. **Client:** Levi Strauss, 1994
    Title: Drugstore
    Art director: John Gorse
    Copywriter: Nick Worthington
    Director: Michael Gondry

19. **Client:** Barclays, 2002
    Title: Samuel L. Jackson
    Art director: Pete Bradly
    Copywriter: Marc Hatfield
    Director: Jonathan Glazer

20. **Client:** KFC, 2008
    Art director: Kevin Stark
    Copywriter: Nick Kidney
    Illustrator: Ali Augur

21. **Client:** Barclaycard, 2009
    Title: Water slide
    Art director: Wesley Hawes
    Copywriter: Gary McCreadie
    Director: Peter Thwaites

22. **Client:** British Airways,
    2008
    Title: Bloody Mary
    Art director: Kevin Stark
    Copywriter: Nick Kidney
    Photographer: Dan Tobin Smith

23. **Client:** Axe – Lynx, 2006
    Title: Getting dressed
    Writer: Nick Gill
    Director: Ringan Ledwidge

TABLE G.2 Conversion Factors and Definitions

Fundamental Dimension	English Unit	Exact SI Value	Approximate SI Value
Length	1 in.	0.0254 m	—
Mass	1 lbm	0.453 592 37 kg	0.454 kg
Temperature	1°F	5/9 K	—

Definitions:

Acceleration of gravity: $g = 9.8066$ m/s^2 ($= 32.174$ ft/s^2)

Energy: Btu (British thermal unit) $\equiv$ amount of energy required to raise the temperature of 1 lbm of water 1°F (1 Btu $= 778.2$ ft $\cdot$ lbf)

kilocalorie $\equiv$ amount of energy required to raise the temperature of 1 kg of water 1 K (1 kcal $= 4187$ J)

Length: 1 mile $= 5280$ ft; 1 nautical mile $= 6076.1$ ft $= 1852$ m (exact)

Power: 1 horsepower $\equiv$ 550 ft $\cdot$ lbf/s

Pressure: 1 bar $\equiv 10^5$ Pa

Temperature: degree Fahrenheit, $T_F = \frac{9}{5} T_C + 32$ (where T_C is degrees Celsius)

degree Rankine, $T_R = T_F + 459.67$

Kelvin, $T_K = T_C + 273.15$ (exact)

Viscosity: 1 Poise $\equiv 0.1$ kg/(m $\cdot$ s)

1 Stoke $\equiv 0.0001$ m^2/s

Volume: 1 gal $\equiv$ 231 in.^{3} (1 ft$^3 = 7.48$ gal)

Useful Conversion Factors:

1 lbf $= 4.448$ N

1 lbf/in.$^2 = 6895$ Pa

1 Btu $= 1055$ J

1 hp $= 746$ W $= 2545$ Btu/hr

1 kW $= 3413$ Btu/hr

1 quart $= 0.000946$ m$^3 = 0.946$ liter

1 kcal $= 3.968$ Btu

Why WileyPLUS for Engineering?

WileyPLUS offers today's Engineering students the interactive and visual learning materials they need to help them grasp difficult concepts—and apply what they've learned to solve problems in a dynamic environment.

⊕ *A robust variety of examples and exercises enable students to work problems, see their results, and obtain instant feedback including hints and reading references linked directly to the online text.*

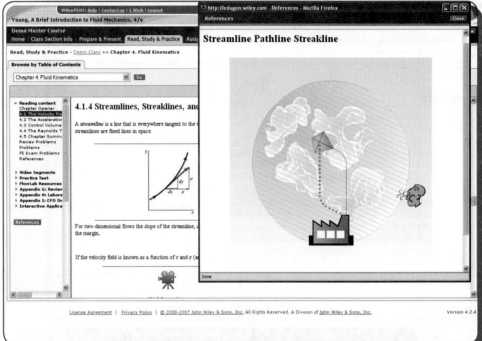

⊕ *Students can visualize concepts from the text by linking to dynamic resources such as animations, videos, and interactive LearningWare.*

www.wileyplus.com

See–and Try WileyPLUS in action!
Details and Demo: www.wileyplus.com

INTRODUCTION
TO
FLUID
MECHANICS

SEVENTH EDITION

ROBERT W. FOX
Purdue University, Emeritus

PHILIP J. PRITCHARD
Manhattan College

ALAN T. McDONALD
Purdue University, Emeritus

JOHN WILEY & SONS, INC.

The cover photograph shows a driver's eye view of a Formula 1 car in motion. All modern racing cars use aerodynamic downforce (negative lift) to improve traction without adding significant weight to the car. Using high downforce allows high cornering speeds on the twisting, turning road courses typical of Formula 1 races. The maximum downforce can exceed twice the weight of the car at 200 miles per hour straightaway speeds! Of course high downforce also causes high drag, which reduces straightaway speed, so a compromise is needed.

The photograph clearly shows some aerodynamic features. The left side of the front wing is shown. This is made as large, and placed as far forward on the chassis, as the rules allow. The rear view mirror housing is carefully streamlined, as are the suspension struts. Not shown are other aerodynamic features such as the fuselage bottom, which is designed to route the airflow carefully, using diffusers, to develop the most negative pressure, and to cause this negative pressure to act over the largest possible area under the car, to develop additional downforce.

PUBLISHER	Don Fowley
ACQUISITIONS EDITOR	Jennifer Welter
MARKETING MANAGER	Christopher Ruel
EDITORIAL ASSISTANT	Mark Owens
DESIGN DIRECTOR	Harry Nolan
SENIOR DESIGNER	Madelyn Lesure
SENIOR PHOTO EDITOR	Elle Wagner
SENIOR PRODUCTION EDITOR	Patricia McFadden
SENIOR MEDIA EDITOR	Lauren Sapira
PRODUCTION MANAGEMENT SERVICES	Ingrao Associates
COVER PHOTO	© Alan Thornton/Getty Images
TEXT DESIGNER	Lee Goldstein

This book was set in Times Roman by GGS Book Services PMG and printed and bound by RRD Willard. The cover was printed by Lehigh Press, Inc.

This book is printed on acid-free paper. ∞

To order books or for customer service, please call 1-800-CALL WILEY (225-5945).

ISBN-13   9780471742999
Printed in the United States of America

10 9 8 7 6 5 4 3 2 1

Preface

Introduction

This text was written for an introductory course in fluid mechanics. Our approach to the subject, as in previous editions, emphasizes the physical concepts of fluid mechanics and methods of analysis that begin from basic principles. The primary objective of this book is to help users develop an orderly approach to problem solving. Thus we always start from governing equations, state assumptions clearly, and try to relate mathematical results to corresponding physical behavior. We emphasize the use of control volumes to maintain a practical problem-solving approach that is also theoretically inclusive.

Examples

This approach is illustrated by using numerous Examples in each chapter. Solutions to the Examples have been prepared to illustrate good solution technique and to explain difficult points of theory. Examples are set apart in format from the text so they are easy to identify and follow. Forty-nine Examples include *Excel* workbooks, available online at the text Web site, making them useful for "What if?" analyses by students or by the instructor during class.

Additional important information about the text and our procedures is given in the "Note to Students" section on page 2 of the printed text. We urge you to study this section carefully and to integrate the suggested procedures into your problem solving and results-presentation approaches.

SI and English Units

SI units are used in about 70 percent of both Example and end-of-chapter problems. English Engineering units are retained in the remaining problems to provide experience with this traditional system and to highlight conversions among unit systems that may be derived from fundamentals.

Goals and Advantages of Using This Text

Complete explanations presented in the text, together with numerous detailed Examples, make this book understandable for students. This frees the instructor to depart from conventional lecture teaching methods. Classroom time can be used to bring in outside material, expand upon special topics (such as non-Newtonian flow, boundary-layer flow, lift and drag, or experimental methods), solve example problems, or explain difficult points of assigned homework problems. In addition, the 49 Example *Excel* workbooks are useful for presenting a variety of fluid mechanics phenomena, especially the effects produced when varying input parameters. Thus each class period can be used in the manner most appropriate to meet student needs.

When students finish the fluid mechanics course, we expect them to be able to apply the governing equations to a variety of problems, including those they have not encountered previously. We particularly emphasize physical concepts throughout to help students model the variety of phenomena that occur in real fluid flow situations. Although in this edition we collect for convenience useful equations at the end of most chapters, we stress that our philosophy is to minimize use of "magic formulas" and emphasize the systematic and fundamental approach to problem solving. By following this format, we believe students develop confidence in their ability to apply the material and find they can reason out solutions to rather challenging problems.

The book is well suited for independent study by students or practicing engineers. Its readability and clear examples help to build confidence. Answers to all the odd-numbered problems are available on the Web.

Topical Coverage

The material has been selected carefully to include a broad range of topics suitable for a one- or two-semester course at the junior or senior level. We assume a background in rigid-body dynamics and mathematics through differential equations. A background in thermodynamics is desirable for studying compressible flow.

More advanced material, not typically covered in a first course, has been moved to the Web site. There the advanced material is available to interested users of the book; available online, it does not interrupt the topic flow of the printed text.

Material in the printed text has been organized into broad topic areas:

- Introductory concepts, scope of fluid mechanics, and fluid statics (Chapters 1, 2, and 3).
- Development and application of control volume forms of basic equations (Chapter 4).
- Development and application of differential forms of basic equations (Chapters 5 and 6).
- Dimensional analysis and correlation of experimental data (Chapter 7).
- Applications for internal viscous incompressible flows (Chapter 8).
- Applications for external viscous incompressible flows (Chapter 9).
- Analysis of fluid machinery and system applications (Chapter 10).
- Analysis and applications of open-channel flows (Chapter 11).
- Analysis and applications of one- and two-dimensional compressible flows (Chapters 12 and 13).

Chapter 4 deals with analysis using both finite and differential control volumes. The Bernoulli equation is derived (in an optional subsection of Section 4-4) as an example application of the basic equations to a differential control volume. Being able to use the Bernoulli equation in Chapter 4 allows us to include more challenging problems dealing with the momentum equation for finite control volumes.

Another derivation of the Bernoulli equation is presented in Chapter 6, where it is obtained by integrating Euler's equation along a streamline. If an instructor chooses to delay introducing the Bernoulli equation, the challenging problems from Chapter 4 may be assigned during study of Chapter 6.

New to This Edition

This edition incorporates a number of significant changes.

Case Studies: At the beginning of each chapter we include a case study, chosen to illustrate interesting current applications of fluid mechanics.

Summary of Equations: At the end of most chapters we collect for the student's convenience the most used or most significant equations of the chapter. Although this is a convenience, we cannot stress enough the need for the student to ensure an understanding of the derivation and limitations of each equation before its use!

CFD: Chapter 5 now includes a brief review of some concepts of computational fluid dynamics (CFD).

Open-Channel Flow: In this edition we introduce a new chapter (Chapter 11) on open-channel flows; this will provide a sufficient background on the topic for mechanical engineers, and serve as an introduction for civil engineers.

Improvements in Clarity: We continue in this edition with our attempts to improve the clarity of the writing. For this edition there are numerous instances of rewording, and refreshing of illustrative figures in an attempt to make the material more accessible to the student.

Homework Problems: The seventh edition includes 1534 end-of-chapter problems. Many problems have been combined and contain multiple parts. Most have been structured so that all parts need not be assigned at once, and almost 25 percent of subparts have been designed to explore "What if?" questions. About 500 problems are new or modified for this edition.

Spreadsheet Problems: Many problems include a component best suited for analysis using a spreadsheet. An icon in the margin identifies these problems. Many of these problems have been designed so the computer component provides a parametric investigation of a single-point solution, to facilitate and encourage students in their attempts to perform "What if?" experimentation. The *Excel*® workbooks prepared by Professor Pritchard aid this process significantly. Appendix H, "A Brief Review of Microsoft® *Excel*," is available on the text Web site; with it the student can self-teach some "bells and whistles" of *Excel*.

We have included many open-ended problems. Some are thought-provoking questions intended to test understanding of fundamental concepts, and some require creative thought, synthesis, and/or narrative discussion. We hope these problems will inspire each instructor to develop and use more open-ended problems.

Problems in each chapter are arranged by topic, and within each topic they generally increase in complexity or difficulty. This makes it easy for the instructor to assign homework problems at the appropriate difficulty level for each section of the book.

Resources for Instructors

The following resources are available to instructors who adopt this text. Visit the website at www.wiley.com/college/fox to register for a password.

Solutions Manual for Instructors: The Solutions Manual for the seventh edition contains a complete, detailed solution for all homework problems. Each solution is prepared in the same systematic way as the Example solutions in the printed text. Each solution begins from governing equations, clearly states assumptions, reduces governing equations to computing equations, obtains an algebraic result, and finally substitutes numerical values to calculate a quantitative answer. Solutions may be reproduced for classroom or library use, eliminating the labor of problem solving for the instructor who adopts the text.

The Solutions Manual is available online after the text is adopted. Go to the text's Web site at www.wiley.com/college/fox to request access to the password-protected online version.

Problem Key: A list of all problems that are renumbered from the 6th edition of this title, to the 7th edition. There is no change to the actual solution to each of these problems.

PowerPoint Lecture Slides: Lecture slides developed by Philip Pritchard, outlining the concepts in the book, and including appropriate illustrations and equations.

Image Gallery: Illustrations from the text in a format appropriate to include in lecture presentations.

Design Problems

Where appropriate, we have used open-ended design problems in place of traditional laboratory experiments. For those who do not have complete laboratory facilities, students could be assigned to work in teams to solve these problems. Design problems encourage students to spend more time exploring applications of fluid mechanics principles to the design of devices and systems. As in the sixth edition, design problems are included with the end-of-chapter problems.

Additional Resources

A Brief Review of Microsoft Excel: Prepared by Philip Pritchard and included on the book Web site as Appendix H, this resource will coach students in setting up and solving fluid mechanics problems using *Excel* spreadsheets. Visit www.wiley.com/college/fox to access this resource.

Excel *Files*: *Excel* Files and add-ins for use with specific Example Problems from the text.

Additional Text Topics: PDF files for those topics/sections that are available only on the website. These topics are highlighted in the text's table of contents and within the chapters as being available on the website.

Answers to Selected Problems: Answers to all the odd-numbered problems are available for student self-study. Visit www.wiley.com/college/fox to access this resource.

FlowLab®: In cooperation with Wiley, Fluent, Inc. is offering to instructors who adopt this text the option to have FlowLab software installed in their department lab free of charge. (This offer is available in the Americas only. Fees vary by geographic region outside the Americas.) FlowLab is a CFD package that allows students to solve fluid dynamics problems without requiring a long training period. This software introduces CFD technology to undergraduates and uses CFD to excite students about fluid dynamics and learning more about transport phenomena of all kinds. To learn more about FlowLab, and how to have it installed in your department, visit the Instructor Companion Site at www.wiley.com/college/fox.

Videos: Many worthwhile videos are available to demonstrate and clarify basic principles of fluid mechanics. These are referenced in the text where their use would be appropriate and are also identified by supplier in Appendix C.

WileyPLUS: WileyPLUS combines the complete, dynamic online text with all of the teaching and learning resources you need, in one easy-to-use system. You assign *WileyPLUS*, but students decide how to buy it: they can buy the new, printed text packaged with a *WileyPLUS* registration code at no additional cost or choose digital delivery of *WileyPLUS*, use the online text and integrated read, study, and practice tools, and save off the cost of the new book.

WileyPLUS: WileyPLUS offers today's engineering students the interactive and visual learning materials they need to help them grasp difficult concepts—and apply what they've learned to solve problems in a dynamic environment. A robust variety of examples and exercises enable students to work problems, see their results, and obtain instant feedback including hints and reading references linked directly to the online text.

Contact your local Wiley representative, or visit www.wileyplus.com for more information about using WileyPLUS in your course.

Acknowledgments

We recognize that no single approach can satisfy all needs, and we are grateful to the many students and faculty whose comments have helped us improve upon earlier editions of this book. We especially thank our reviewers for the seventh edition, as well as those who helped with accuracy checking the Solutions Manual, and reviewers and contributors of the *WileyPLUS* course:

Nidal Al-Masoud, Central Connecticut State University;
Defne Apul, University of Toledo;
John Dietz, University of Central Florida;
Raghu Echempati, Kettering University;
Srinath Ekkad, Louisiana State University;
Drazen Fabris, Santa Clara University;
Donald Fenton, Kansas State University;
Tom Filburn, University of Hartford;
Alison R. Griffin, University of Central Florida;
Pei-feng Hsu, Florida Institute of Technology;
Nirmal Khandan, New Mexico State University;
Jay M. Khodadadi, Auburn University;
Jay Martin, University of Wisconsin-Madison;
John Mitchell, University of Wisconsin-Madison;
John Rajadas, Arizona State University Polytechnic;
Georgia Richardson, University of Alabama–Huntsville;
Dr. Messiha Saad, North Carolina A&T State University;
S.A. Sherif, University of Florida;
Troy Skinner, University of Alabama–Huntsville;
Chelakara Subramanian, Florida Institute of Technology–Melbourne;
Brian J. Swenty, University of Evansville;
Guo-Xiang Wang, University of Akron; and
Richard Wlezien, Tufts University.

In particular, we wish to thank Rajesh Bhaskaran at Cornell University and Larry Mays at Arizona State University for their contributions to the new material on computational fluid dynamics and open-channel flows, respectively. We look forward to continued interactions with these and other colleagues who use the book.

Professor Pritchard appreciates the unstinting support of his wife Penelope who is keenly aware of all the hours that went into the effort of preparing this seventh edition.

We welcome suggestions and/or criticisms from interested users of this book.

Philip J. Pritchard
Robert W. Fox
Alan T. McDonald
May 2008

Contents

An asterisk appearing in front of a section title indicates that the section can be omitted.

Chapter 1

Introduction

CASE STUDY

"Fly Like a Bird"

The airplane with various instantaneous wing shapes. (Courtesy of Dr. Rick Lind, University of Florida.)

At the beginning of each chapter, we present a case study: an interesting development in fluid mechanics chosen to illustrate that the field is constantly evolving.

No airplane, or airplane model, flies like a bird; they all have fixed wings when in flight, whereas birds are (almost) constantly flapping away! One reason for this is that airplane and model wings must support relatively significant weight and are therefore thick and stiff; another reason is that we don't yet fully understand bird flight! Engineers at the University of Florida in Gainesville, led by researcher Rick Lind, have gone back to the drawing board and have developed a small surveillance aircraft (2-foot wingspan, weight a total of 1½ lb) that can change its wing shape during flight [1]. While it is not true bird flight (the main propulsion is through a propeller), it is a radical departure from current airplane design. The airplane can change, for example, from an M shape wing configuration (very stable for gliding) to a W shape (for high maneuverability). It is amazingly dexterous: It can turn three rolls in less than a second (comparable to an F-15 fighter!), and its flight is sufficiently birdlike that it has attracted sparrows (friendly) and crows (unfriendly). Possible uses are in military surveillance, detection of biological agents in congested urban areas, and environmental studies in difficult airspaces such as forests.

We decided to title this text "Introduction to..." for the following reason: After studying the text, you will *not* be able to design the streamlining of a new car or an airplane, or design a new heart valve, or select the correct air extractors and ducting for a $100 million building; however, you *will* have developed a good understanding of the concepts behind all of these, and many other applications, and have made significant progress toward being ready to work on such state-of-the-art fluid mechanics projects.

To start toward this goal, in this chapter we cover some very basic topics: a case study, what fluid mechanics encompasses, the standard engineering definition of a fluid, and the basic equations and methods of analysis. Finally, we discuss some common engineering student pitfalls in areas such as unit systems and experimental analysis.

1-1	**NOTE TO STUDENTS**

This is a student-oriented book: We believe it is quite comprehensive for an introductory text, and a student can successfully self-teach from it. However, most students will use the text in conjunction with one or two undergraduate courses. In either case, we recommend a thorough reading of the relevant chapters. In fact, a good approach is to read a chapter quickly once, then reread more carefully a second and even a third time, so that concepts develop a context and meaning. While students often find fluid mechanics quite challenging, we believe this approach, supplemented by your instructor's lectures that will hopefully amplify and expand upon the text material (if you are taking a course), will reveal fluid mechanics to be a fascinating and varied field of study.

Other sources of information on fluid mechanics are readily available. In addition to your professor, there are many other fluid mechanics texts and journals as well as the Internet (a recent Google search for "fluid mechanics" yielded 26,400,000 links, including many with fluid mechanics calculators and animations!)

There are some prerequisites for reading this text. We assume you have already studied introductory thermodynamics, as well as statics, dynamics, and calculus; however, as needed, we will review some of this material.

It is our strong belief that one learns best by *doing*. This is true whether the subject under study is fluid mechanics, thermodynamics, or soccer. The fundamentals in any of these are few, and mastery of them comes through practice. *Thus it is extremely important that you solve problems.* The numerous problems included at the end of each chapter provide the opportunity to practice applying fundamentals to the solution of problems. Even though we provide for your convenience a summary of useful equations at the end of each chapter (except this one), you should avoid the temptation to adopt a "plug and chug" approach to solving problems. Most of the problems are such that this approach simply will not work. In solving problems we strongly recommend that you proceed using the following logical steps:

1. State briefly and concisely (in your own words) the information given.
2. State the information to be found.
3. Draw a schematic of the system or control volume to be used in the analysis. Be sure to label the boundaries of the system or control volume and label appropriate coordinate directions.
4. Give the appropriate mathematical formulation of the *basic* laws that you consider necessary to solve the problem.
5. List the simplifying assumptions that you feel are appropriate in the problem.
6. Complete the analysis algebraically before substituting numerical values.
7. Substitute numerical values (using a consistent set of units) to obtain a numerical answer.
   a. Reference the source of values for any physical properties.
   b. Be sure the significant figures in the answer are consistent with the given data.
8. Check the answer and review the assumptions made in the solution to make sure they are reasonable.
9. Label the answer.

In your initial work this problem format may seem unnecessary and even long-winded. However, it is our experience that this approach to problem solving is ultimately the most efficient; it will also prepare you to be a successful professional, for which a major prerequisite is to be able to communicate information and the results of an analysis clearly and precisely. *This format is used in all Examples presented in this text*; answers to Examples are rounded to three significant figures.

Finally, *we strongly urge you to take advantage of the many Excel tools available for this book on the text Website*, for use in solving problems. Many problems can be solved much more quickly using these tools; occasional problems can *only* be solved with the tools or with an equivalent computer application.

1-2 SCOPE OF FLUID MECHANICS

As the name implies, fluid mechanics is the study of fluids at rest or in motion. It has traditionally been applied in such areas as the design of canal, levee, and dam systems; the design of pumps, compressors, and piping and ducting used in the water and air conditioning systems of homes and businesses, as well as the piping systems needed in chemical plants; the aerodynamics of automobiles and sub- and supersonic airplanes; and the development of many different flow measurement devices such as gas pump meters.

While these are still extremely important areas (witness, for example, the current emphasis on automobile streamlining and the levee failures in New Orleans), fluid mechanics is truly a "high-tech" or "hot" discipline, and many exciting areas have developed in the last quarter-century. Some examples include environmental and energy issues (e.g., containing oil slicks, large-scale wind turbines, energy generation from ocean waves, the aerodynamics of large buildings, and the fluid mechanics of the atmosphere and ocean and of phenomena such as tornadoes, hurricanes, and tsunamis); biomechanics (e.g., artificial hearts and valves and other organs such as the liver; understanding of the fluid mechanics of blood, synovial fluid in the joints, the respiratory system, the circulatory system, and the urinary system); sport (design of bicycles and bicycle helmets, skis, and sprinting and swimming clothing, and the aerodynamics of the golf, tennis, and soccer ball); "smart fluids" (e.g., in automobile suspension systems to optimize motion under all terrain conditions, military uniforms containing a fluid layer that is "thin" until combat, when it can be "stiffened" to give the soldier strength and protection, and fluid lenses with humanlike properties for use in cameras and cell phones); and microfluids (e.g., for extremely precise administration of medications).

These are just a small sampling of the newer areas of fluid mechanics. They illustrate how the discipline is still highly relevant, and increasingly diverse, even though it may be thousands of years old.

1-3 DEFINITION OF A FLUID

We already have a common-sense idea of when we are working with a fluid, as opposed to a solid: Fluids tend to flow when we interact with them (e.g., when you stir your morning coffee); solids tend to deform or bend (e.g., when you type on a keyboard, the springs under the keys compress). Engineers need a more formal and precise definition of a fluid: A *fluid* is a substance that deforms continuously under the application of a shear (tangential) stress no matter how small the shear stress may be. Because the fluid motion continues under the application of a shear stress, we can also define a fluid as any substance that cannot sustain a shear stress when at rest.

Hence liquids and gases (or vapors) are the forms, or phases, that fluids can take. We wish to distinguish these phases from the solid phase of matter. We can see the difference between solid and fluid behavior in Fig. 1.1. If we place a specimen of

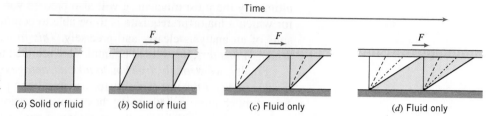

Fig. 1.1 Difference in behavior of a solid and a fluid due to a shear force.

(a) Solid or fluid   (b) Solid or fluid   (c) Fluid only   (d) Fluid only

either substance between two plates (Fig. 1.1*a*) and then apply a shearing force *F*, each will initially deform (Fig. 1.1*b*); however, whereas a solid will then be at rest (assuming the force is not large enough to go beyond its elastic limit), a fluid will *continue* to deform (Fig. 1.1*c*, Fig. 1.1*d*, etc) as long as the force is applied. Note that a fluid in contact with a solid surface does not slip—it has the same velocity as that surface because of the *no-slip* condition, an experimental fact.[1]

The amount of deformation of the solid depends on the solid's modulus of rigidity *G*; in Chapter 2 we will learn that the *rate of deformation* of the fluid depends on the fluid's viscosity μ. We refer to solids as being *elastic* and fluids as being *viscous*.

1-4   BASIC EQUATIONS

Analysis of any problem in fluid mechanics necessarily includes statement of the basic laws governing the fluid motion. The basic laws, which are applicable to any fluid, are:

1. The conservation of mass
2. Newton's second law of motion
3. The principle of angular momentum
4. The first law of thermodynamics
5. The second law of thermodynamics

Not all basic laws are always required to solve any one problem. On the other hand, in many problems it is necessary to bring into the analysis additional relations that describe the behavior of physical properties of fluids under given conditions.

For example, you probably recall studying properties of gases in basic physics or thermodynamics. The *ideal gas* equation of state

$$p = \rho RT \tag{1.1}$$

is a model that relates density to pressure and temperature for many gases under normal conditions. In Eq. 1.1, *R* is the gas constant. Values of *R* are given in Appendix A for several common gases; *p* and *T* in Eq. 1.1 are the absolute pressure and absolute temperature, respectively; ρ is density (mass per unit volume). Example 1.1 illustrates use of the ideal gas equation of state.

It is obvious that the basic laws with which we shall deal are the same as those used in mechanics and thermodynamics. Our task will be to formulate these laws in suitable forms to solve fluid flow problems and to apply them to a wide variety of situations.

We must emphasize that there are, as we shall see, many apparently simple problems in fluid mechanics that cannot be solved analytically. In such cases we must resort to more complicated numerical solutions and/or results of experimental tests.

---

[1] The no-slip condition is demonstrated in the NCFMF video *Fundamentals of Boundary Layers* (See http://web.mit.edu/fluids/www/Shapiro/ncfmf.html for free online viewing of this film; it is old but good!). A complete list of fluid mechanics video titles and sources is given in Appendix C.

1-5 METHODS OF ANALYSIS

The first step in solving a problem is to define the system that you are attempting to analyze. In basic mechanics, we made extensive use of the *free-body diagram.* We will use a *system* or a *control volume,* depending on the problem being studied. These concepts are identical to the ones you used in thermodynamics (except you may have called them *closed system* and *open system,* respectively). We can use either one to get mathematical expressions for each of the basic laws. In thermodynamics they were mostly used to obtain expressions for conservation of mass and the first and second laws of thermodynamics; in our study of fluid mechanics, we will be most interested in conservation of mass and Newton's second law of motion. In thermodynamics our focus was energy; in fluid mechanics it will mainly be forces and motion. We must always be aware of whether we are using a system or a control volume approach because each leads to different mathematical expressions of these laws. At this point we review the definitions of systems and control volumes.

System and Control Volume

A *system* is defined as a fixed, identifiable quantity of mass; the system boundaries separate the system from the surroundings. The boundaries of the system may be fixed or movable; however, no mass crosses the system boundaries.

In the familiar piston-cylinder assembly from thermodynamics, Fig. 1.2, the gas in the cylinder is the system. If the gas is heated, the piston will lift the weight; the boundary of the system thus moves. Heat and work may cross the boundaries of the system, but the quantity of matter within the system boundaries remains fixed. No mass crosses the system boundaries.

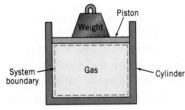

Fig. 1.2 Piston-cylinder assembly.

EXAMPLE 1.1 First Law Application to Closed System

A piston-cylinder device contains 0.95 kg of oxygen initially at a temperature of 27°C and a pressure due to the weight of 150 kPa (abs). Heat is added to the gas until it reaches a temperature of 627°C. Determine the amount of heat added during the process.

GIVEN: Piston-cylinder containing O_2, $m = 0.95$ kg.

$$T_1 = 27°C \qquad T_2 = 627°C$$

FIND: $Q_{1 \to 2}$.

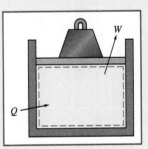

SOLUTION:

$p = \text{constant} = 150$ kPa (abs)

We are dealing with a system, $m = 0.95$ kg.

Governing equation: First law for the system, $Q_{12} - W_{12} = E_2 - E_1$

Assumptions: (1) $E = U$, since the system is stationary
(2) Ideal gas with constant specific heats

Under the above assumptions,

$$E_2 - E_1 = U_2 - U_1 = m(u_2 - u_1) = mc_v(T_2 - T_1)$$

The work done during the process is moving boundary work

$$W_{12} = \int_{V_1}^{V_2} p \, dV = p(V_2 - V_1)$$

For an ideal gas, $p\Psi = mRT$. Hence $W_{12} = mR(T_2 - T_1)$. Then from the first law equation,

$$Q_{12} = E_2 - E_1 + W_{12} = mc_v(T_2 - T_1) + mR(T_2 - T_1)$$
$$Q_{12} = m(T_2 - T_1)(c_v + R)$$
$$Q_{12} = mc_p(T_2 - T_1) \quad \{R = c_p - c_v\}$$

From the Appendix, Table A.6, for O_2, $c_p = 909.4$ J/(kg · K). Solving for Q_{12}, we obtain

$$Q_{12} = 0.95 \text{ kg} \times 909 \frac{\text{J}}{\text{kg} \cdot \text{K}} \times 600 \text{ K} = 518 \text{ kJ} \qquad \longleftarrow \qquad Q_{12}$$

This problem:
- ✓ Was solved using the nine logical steps discussed earlier.
- ✓ Reviewed use of the ideal gas equation and the first law of thermodynamics for a system.

In mechanics courses you used the free-body diagram (system approach) extensively. This was logical because you were dealing with an easily identifiable rigid body. However, in fluid mechanics we normally are concerned with the flow of fluids through devices such as compressors, turbines, pipelines, nozzles, and so on. In these cases it is difficult to focus attention on a fixed identifiable quantity of mass. It is much more convenient, for analysis, to focus attention on a volume in space through which the fluid flows. Consequently, we use the control volume approach.

A *control volume* is an arbitrary volume in space through which fluid flows. The geometric boundary of the control volume is called the control surface. The control surface may be real or imaginary; it may be at rest or in motion. Figure 1.3 shows flow through a pipe junction, with a control surface drawn on it. Note that some regions of the surface correspond to physical boundaries (the walls of the pipe) and others (at locations ①, ②, and ③) are parts of the surface that are imaginary (inlets or outlets). For the control volume defined by this surface, we could write equations for the basic laws and obtain results such as the flow rate at outlet ③ given the flow rates at inlet ① and outlet ② (similar to a problem we will analyze in Example 4.1 in Chapter 4), the force required to hold the junction in place, and so on. It is always important to take care in selecting a control volume, as the choice has a big effect on the mathematical form of the basic laws. We will illustrate the use of a control volume with an example.

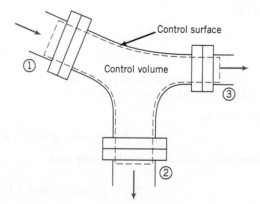

Fig. 1.3 Fluid flow through a pipe junction.

EXAMPLE 1.2   Mass Conservation Applied to Control Volume

A reducing water pipe section has an inlet diameter of 5 cm and exit diameter of 3 cm. If the steady inlet speed (averaged across the inlet area) is 2.5 m/s, find the exit speed.

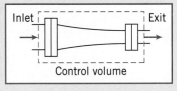

Control volume

GIVEN: Pipe, inlet D_i = 5 cm, exit D_e = 3 cm
              Inlet speed, V_i = 2.5 m/s

FIND: Exit speed, V_e

SOLUTION:

Assumption: Water is incompressible (density ρ = constant)

The physical law we use here is the conservation of mass, which you learned in thermodynamics when studying turbines, boilers, and so on. You may have seen mass flow at an inlet or outlet expressed as either $\dot{m} = VA/v$ or $\dot{m} = \rho VA$ where V, A, v, and ρ are the speed, area, specific volume, and density, respectively. We will use the density form of the equation. Hence the mass flow is:

$$\dot{m} = \rho VA$$

Applying mass conservation, from our study of thermodynamics,

$$\rho V_i A_i = \rho V_e A_e$$

(Note: $\rho_i = \rho_e = \rho$ by our first assumption)
(Note: Even though we are already familiar with this equation from thermodynamics, we will derive it in Chapter 4.)

Solving for V_e,

$$V_e = V_i \frac{A_i}{A_e} = V_i \frac{\pi D_i^2/4}{\pi D_e^2/4} = V_i \left(\frac{D_i}{D_e}\right)^2$$

$$V_e = 2.7 \frac{\text{m}}{\text{s}} \left(\frac{5}{3}\right)^2 = 7.5 \frac{\text{m}}{\text{s}} \qquad\qquad\qquad\qquad\qquad\qquad V_e$$

This problem:
  ✓ Was solved using the nine logical steps.
  ✓ Demonstrated use of a control volume and the mass conservation law.

Differential versus Integral Approach

The basic laws that we apply in our study of fluid mechanics can be formulated in terms of *infinitesimal* or *finite* systems and control volumes. As you might suspect, the equations will look different in the two cases. Both approaches are important in the study of fluid mechanics and both will be developed in the course of our work.

In the first case the resulting equations are differential equations. Solution of the differential equations of motion provides a means of determining the detailed behavior of the flow. An example might be the pressure distribution on a wing surface.

Frequently the information sought does not require a detailed knowledge of the flow. We often are interested in the gross behavior of a device; in such cases it is more appropriate to use integral formulations of the basic laws. An example might be the overall lift a wing produces. Integral formulations, using finite systems or control volumes, usually are easier to treat analytically. The basic laws of mechanics and thermodynamics, formulated in terms of finite systems, are the basis for deriving the control volume equations in Chapter 4.

Methods of Description

Mechanics deals almost exclusively with systems; you have made extensive use of the basic equations applied to a fixed, identifiable quantity of mass. On the other hand, attempting to analyze thermodynamic devices, you often found it necessary to use a control volume (open system) analysis. Clearly, the type of analysis depends on the problem.

Where it is easy to keep track of identifiable elements of mass (e.g., in particle mechanics), we use a method of description that follows the particle. This sometimes is referred to as the *Lagrangian* method of description.

Consider, for example, the application of Newton's second law to a particle of fixed mass. Mathematically, we can write Newton's second law for a system of mass m as

$$\Sigma \vec{F} = m\vec{a} = m\frac{d\vec{V}}{dt} = m\frac{d^2\vec{r}}{dt^2} \tag{1.2}$$

In Eq. 1.2, $\Sigma\vec{F}$ is the sum of all external forces acting on the system, $\vec{a}$ is the acceleration of the center of mass of the system, $\vec{V}$ is the velocity of the center of mass of the system, and $\vec{r}$ is the position vector of the center of mass of the system relative to a fixed coordinate system.

EXAMPLE 1.3 Free-Fall of Ball in Air

The air resistance (drag force) on a 200 g ball in free flight is given by $F_D = 2 \times 10^{-4} V^2$, where F_D is in newtons and V is in meters per second. If the ball is dropped from rest 500 m above the ground, determine the speed at which it hits the ground. What percentage of the terminal speed is the result? (The *terminal speed* is the steady speed a falling body eventually attains.)

GIVEN: Ball, $m = 0.2$ kg, released from rest at $y_0 = 500$ m
Air resistance, $F_D = kV^2$, where $k = 2 \times 10^{-4}$ N $\cdot$ s^2/m^2
Units: F_D(N), V(m/s)

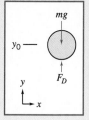

FIND: (a) Speed at which the ball hits the ground.
(b) Ratio of speed to terminal speed.

SOLUTION:

Governing equation: $\Sigma\vec{F} = m\vec{a}$

Assumption: (1) Neglect buoyancy force.

The motion of the ball is governed by the equation

$$\Sigma F_y = ma_y = m\frac{dV}{dt}$$

Since $V = V(y)$, we write $\Sigma F_y = m\dfrac{dV}{dy}\dfrac{dy}{dt} = mV\dfrac{dV}{dy}$ Then,

$$\Sigma F_y = F_D - mg = kV^2 - mg = mV\frac{dV}{dy}$$

Separating variables and integrating,

$$\int_{y_0}^{y} dy = \int_{0}^{V} \frac{mV\,dV}{kV^2 - mg}$$

$$y - y_0 = \left[\frac{m}{2k}\ln(kV^2 - mg)\right]_0^V = \frac{m}{2k}\ln\frac{kV^2 - mg}{-mg}$$

Taking antilogarithms, we obtain

$$kV^2 - mg = -mg\, e^{[(2k/m)(y - y_0)]}$$

Solving for V gives

$$V = \left\{ \frac{mg}{k} \left(1 - e^{[(2k/m)(y-y_0)]} \right) \right\}^{1/2}$$

Substituting numerical values with $y = 0$ yields

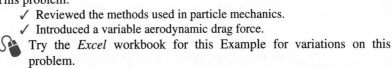

$$V = \left\{ 0.2\,\text{kg} \times 9.81\,\frac{\text{m}}{\text{s}^2} \times \frac{\text{m}^2}{2 \times 10^{-4}\,\text{N} \cdot \text{s}^2} \times \frac{\text{N} \cdot \text{s}^2}{\text{kg} \cdot \text{m}} \left(1 - e^{[(2 \times 2 \times 10^{-4}/0.2)(-500)]} \right) \right\}$$

$V = 78.7\,\text{m/s}$ $\longleftarrow$ V

At terminal speed, $a_y = 0$ and $\Sigma F_y = 0 = kV_t^2 - mg$

Then, $V_t = \left[\frac{mg}{k} \right]^{1/2} = \left[0.2\,\text{kg} \times 9.81\,\frac{\text{m}}{\text{s}^2} \times \frac{\text{m}^2}{2 \times 10^{-4}\,\text{N} \cdot \text{s}^2} \times \frac{\text{N} \cdot \text{s}^2}{\text{kg} \cdot \text{m}} \right]^{1/2} = 99.0\,\text{m/s}$

The ratio of actual speed to terminal speed is $\dfrac{V}{V_t}$

$$\frac{V}{V_t} = \frac{78.7}{99.0} = 0.795, \text{ or } 79.5\% \longleftarrow$$

This problem:
✓ Reviewed the methods used in particle mechanics.
✓ Introduced a variable aerodynamic drag force.
🖱 Try the *Excel* workbook for this Example for variations on this problem.

We could use this Lagrangian approach to analyze a fluid flow by assuming the fluid to be composed of a very large number of particles whose motion must be described. However, keeping track of the motion of each fluid particle would become a horrendous bookkeeping problem. Consequently, a particle description becomes unmanageable. Often we find it convenient to use a different type of description. Particularly with control volume analyses, it is convenient to use the field, or *Eulerian*, method of description, which focuses attention on the properties of a flow at a given point in space as a function of time. In the Eulerian method of description, the properties of a flow field are described as functions of space coordinates and time. We shall see in Chapter 2 that this method of description is a logical outgrowth of the assumption that fluids may be treated as continuous media.

1-6 DIMENSIONS AND UNITS

Engineering problems are solved to answer specific questions. It goes without saying that the answer must include units. In 1999, NASA's Mars Climate Observer crashed because the JPL engineers assumed that a measurement was in meters, but the supplying company's engineers had actually made the measurement in feet! Consequently, it is appropriate to present a brief review of dimensions and units. We say "review" because the topic is familiar from your earlier work in mechanics.

We refer to physical quantities such as length, time, mass, and temperature as *dimensions*. In terms of a particular system of dimensions, all measurable quantities are subdivided into two groups—*primary* quantities and *secondary* quantities. We refer to a small group of dimensions from which all others can be formed as primary quantities, for which we set up arbitrary scales of measure. Secondary quantities are those quantities whose dimensions are expressible in terms of the dimensions of the primary quantities.

Units are the arbitrary names (and magnitudes) assigned to the primary dimensions adopted as standards for measurement. For example, the primary dimension of length may be measured in units of meters, feet, yards, or miles. These units of length are related to each other through unit conversion factors (1 mile = 5280 feet = 1609 meters).

Systems of Dimensions

Any valid equation that relates physical quantities must be dimensionally homogeneous; each term in the equation must have the same dimensions. We recognize that Newton's second law ($\vec{F} \propto m\vec{a}$) relates the four dimensions, F, M, L, and t. Thus force and mass cannot both be selected as primary dimensions without introducing a constant of proportionality that has dimensions (and units).

Length and time are primary dimensions in all dimensional systems in common use. In some systems, mass is taken as a primary dimension. In others, force is selected as a primary dimension; a third system chooses both force and mass as primary dimensions. Thus we have three basic systems of dimensions, corresponding to the different ways of specifying the primary dimensions.

a. Mass [M], length [L], time [t], temperature [T]

b. Force [F], length [L], time [t], temperature [T]

c. Force [F], mass [M], length [L], time [t], temperature [T]

In system *a*, force [F] is a secondary dimension and the constant of proportionality in Newton's second law is dimensionless. In system *b*, mass [M] is a secondary dimension, and again the constant of proportionality in Newton's second law is dimensionless. In system *c*, both force [F] and mass [M] have been selected as primary dimensions. In this case the constant of proportionality, g_c (not to be confused with g, the acceleration of gravity!) in Newton's second law (written $\vec{F} \propto m\vec{a}/g_c$) is not dimensionless. The dimensions of g_c must in fact be [ML/Ft^2] for the equation to be dimensionally homogeneous. The numerical value of the constant of proportionality depends on the units of measure chosen for each of the primary quantities.

Systems of Units

There is more than one way to select the unit of measure for each primary dimension. We shall present only the more common engineering systems of units for each of the basic systems of dimensions. Table 1.1 shows the basic units assigned to the primary dimensions for these systems. The units in parentheses are those assigned to that unit system's secondary dimension. Following the table is a brief description of each of them.

TABLE 1.1 Common Unit Systems

System of Dimensions	Unit System	Force F	Mass M	Length L	Time t	Temperature T
a. MLtT	Système International d'Unités (SI)	(N)	kg	m	s	K
b. FLtT	British Gravitational (BG)	lbf	(slug)	ft	s	°R
c. FMLtT	English Engineering (EE)	lbf	lbm	ft	s	°R

a. MLtT

SI, which is the official abbreviation in all languages for the Système International d'Unités,[2] is an extension and refinement of the traditional metric system. More than 30 countries have declared it to be the only legally accepted system.

In the SI system of units, the unit of mass is the kilogram (kg), the unit of length is the meter (m), the unit of time is the second (s), and the unit of temperature is the kelvin (K). Force is a secondary dimension, and its unit, the newton (N), is defined from Newton's second law as

$$1\,\text{N} \equiv 1\,\text{kg} \cdot \text{m/s}^2$$

In the Absolute Metric system of units, the unit of mass is the gram, the unit of length is the centimeter, the unit of time is the second, and the unit of temperature is the kelvin. Since force is a secondary dimension, the unit of force, the dyne, is defined in terms of Newton's second law as

$$1\,\text{dyne} \equiv 1\,\text{g} \cdot \text{cm/s}^2$$

b. FLtT

In the British Gravitational system of units, the unit of force is the pound (lbf), the unit of length is the foot (ft), the unit of time is the second, and the unit of temperature is the degree Rankine (°R). Since mass is a secondary dimension, the unit of mass, the slug, is defined in terms of Newton's second law as

$$1\,\text{slug} \equiv 1\,\text{lbf} \cdot \text{s}^2/\text{ft}$$

c. FMLtT

In the English Engineering system of units, the unit of force is the pound force (lbf), the unit of mass is the pound mass (lbm), the unit of length is the foot, the unit of time is the second, and the unit of temperature is the degree Rankine. Since both force and mass are chosen as primary dimensions, Newton's second law is written as

$$\vec{F} = \frac{m\vec{a}}{g_c}$$

A force of one pound (1 lbf) is the force that gives a pound mass (1 lbm) an acceleration equal to the standard acceleration of gravity on Earth, 32.2 ft/s^2. From Newton's second law we see that

$$1\,\text{lbf} \equiv \frac{1\,\text{lbm} \times 32.2\,\text{ft/s}^2}{g_c}$$

or

$$g_c \equiv 32.2\,\text{ft} \cdot \text{lbm/(lbf} \cdot \text{s}^2)$$

The constant of proportionality, g_c, has both dimensions and units. The dimensions arose because we selected both force and mass as primary dimensions; the units (and the numerical value) are a consequence of our choices for the standards of measurement.

Since a force of 1 lbf accelerates 1 lbm at 32.2 ft/s^2, it would accelerate 32.2 lbm at 1 ft/s^2. A slug also is accelerated at 1 ft/s^2 by a force of 1 lbf. Therefore,

$$1\,\text{slug} \equiv 32.2\,\text{lbm}$$

Many textbooks and references use lb instead of lbf or lbm, leaving it up to the reader to determine from the context whether a force or mass is being referred to.

---

[2] American Society for Testing and Materials, *ASTM Standard for Metric Practice*, E380-97. Conshohocken, PA: ASTM, 1997.

Preferred Systems of Units

In this text we shall use both the *SI* and the *British Gravitational* systems of units. In either case, the constant of proportionality in Newton's second law is dimensionless and has a value of unity. Consequently, Newton's second law is written as $\vec{F} = m\vec{a}$. In these systems, it follows that the gravitational force (the "weight"[3]) on an object of mass m is given by $W = mg$.

SI units and prefixes, together with other defined units and useful conversion factors, are summarized in Appendix G.

EXAMPLE 1.4   Use of Units

The label on a jar of peanut butter states its net weight is 510 g. Express its mass and weight in SI, BG, and EE units.

GIVEN: Peanut butter "weight," $m = 510$ g

FIND: Mass and weight in SI, BG, and EE units

SOLUTION:

This problem involves unit conversions and use of the equation relating weight and mass:

$$W = mg$$

The given "weight" is actually the mass because it is expressed in units of mass:

$$m_{SI} = 0.510 \text{ kg} \qquad\qquad\longleftarrow\qquad m_{SI}$$

Using the conversions of Table G.2 (Appendix G),

$$m_{EE} = m_{SI}\left(\frac{1 \text{ lbm}}{0.454 \text{ kg}}\right) = 0.510 \text{ kg}\left(\frac{1 \text{ lbm}}{0.454 \text{ kg}}\right) = 1.12 \text{ lbm} \quad\longleftarrow\quad m_{EE}$$

Using the fact that 1 slug = 32.2 lbm,

$$m_{BG} = m_{EE}\left(\frac{1 \text{ slug}}{32.2 \text{ lbm}}\right) = 1.12 \text{ lbm}\left(\frac{1 \text{ slug}}{32.2 \text{ lbm}}\right) = 0.0349 \text{ slug} \quad\longleftarrow\quad m_{BG}$$

To find the weight, we use

$$W = mg$$

In SI units, and using the definition of a newton,

$$W_{SI} = 0.510 \text{ kg} \times 9.81\frac{\text{m}}{\text{s}^2} = 5.00\left(\frac{\text{kg}\cdot\text{m}}{\text{s}^2}\right)\left(\frac{\text{N}}{\text{kg}\cdot\text{m/s}^2}\right) = 5.00 \text{ N} \quad\longleftarrow\quad W_{SI}$$

In BG units, and using the definition of a slug,

$$W_{BG} = 0.0349 \text{ slug} \times 32.2\frac{\text{ft}}{\text{s}^2} = 1.12\frac{\text{slug}\cdot\text{ft}}{\text{s}^2} = 1.12\left(\frac{\text{slug}\cdot\text{ft}}{\text{s}^2}\right)\left(\frac{\text{s}^2\cdot\text{lbf/ft}}{\text{slug}}\right) = 1.12 \text{ lbf} \quad\longleftarrow\quad W_{BG}$$

In EE units, we use the form $W = mg/g_c$, and using the definition of g_c,

$$W_{EE} = 1.12 \text{ lbm} \times 32.2\frac{\text{ft}}{\text{s}^2} \times \frac{1}{g_c} = \frac{36.1}{g_c}\frac{\text{lbm}\cdot\text{ft}}{\text{s}^2} = 36.1\left(\frac{\text{lbm}\cdot\text{ft}}{\text{s}^2}\right)\left(\frac{\text{lbf}\cdot\text{s}^2}{32.2 \text{ ft}\cdot\text{lbm}}\right) = 1.12 \text{ lbf} \quad\longleftarrow\quad W_{EE}$$

---

[3] Note that in the English Engineering system, the weight of an object is given by $W = mg/g_c$.

This problem illustrates:
- ✓ Conversions from SI to BG and EE systems.
- ✓ Use of g_c in the EE system.

Notes: The student may feel this example involves a lot of unnecessary calculation details (e.g., a factor of 32.2 appears, then disappears), but it cannot be stressed enough that such steps should always be explicitly written out to minimize errors—if you do not write all steps and units down, it is just too easy, for example, to multiply by a conversion factor when you should be dividing by it. For the weights in SI, BG, and EE units, we could alternatively have looked up the conversion from newton to lbf.

Dimensional Consistency and "Engineering" Equations

In engineering, we strive to make equations and formulas have consistent dimensions. That is, each term in an equation, and obviously both sides of the equation, should be reducible to the same dimensions. For example, a very important equation we will derive later on is the Bernoulli equation

$$\frac{p_1}{\rho} + \frac{V_1^2}{2} + gz_1 = \frac{p_2}{\rho} + \frac{V_2^2}{2} + gz_2$$

which relates the pressure p, velocity V, and elevation z between points 1 and 2 along a streamline for a steady, frictionless incompressible flow (density ρ). This equation is dimensionally consistent because each term in the equation can be reduced to dimensions of L^2/t^2 (the pressure term dimensions are FL/M, but from Newton's law we find $F = ML/t$, so $FL/M = ML^2/Mt^2 = L^2/t^2$).

Almost all equations you are likely to encounter will be dimensionally consistent. However, you should be alert to some still commonly used equations that are not; these are often "engineering" equations derived many years ago, or are empirical (based on experiment rather than theory), or are proprietary equations used in a particular industry or company. For example, civil engineers often use the semi-empirical Manning equation

$$V = \frac{R_h^{2/3} S_0^{1/2}}{n}$$

which gives the flow speed V in an open channel (such as a canal) as a function of the hydraulic radius R_h (which is a measure of the flow cross-section and contact surface area), the channel slope S_0, and a constant n (the Manning resistance coefficient). The value of this constant depends on the surface condition of the channel. For example, for a canal made from unfinished concrete, most references give $n \approx 0.014$. Unfortunately, the equation is dimensionally inconsistent! For the right side of the equation, R_h has dimensions L, and S_0 is dimensionless, so with a dimensionless constant n, we end up with dimensions of $L^{2/3}$; for the left side of the equation the dimensions must be L/t! A user of the equation is supposed to know that the values of n, provided in most references will give correct results *only* if we ignore the dimensional inconsistency, always use R_h in meters, and interpret V to be in m/s! (The alert student will realize that this means that even though handbooks provide n values as just constants, they must have units of $s/m^{1/3}$). Because the equation is dimensionally inconsistent, using the *same* value for n with R_h in ft does *not* give the correct value for V in ft/s.

A second type of problem is one in which the dimensions of an equation are consistent but use of units is not. The commonly used *EER* of an air conditioner is

$$EER = \frac{\text{cooling rate}}{\text{electrical input}}$$

which indicates how efficiently the AC works—a higher *EER* value indicates better performance. The equation *is* dimensionally consistent, with the *EER* being dimensionless (the cooling rate and electrical input are both measured in energy/time). However, it is *used*, in a sense, incorrectly, because the *units* traditionally used in it are not consistent. For example, a good *EER* value is 10, which would appear to imply you receive, say, 10 kW of cooling for each 1 kW of electrical power. In fact, an *EER* of 10 means you receive 10 *Btu/hr* of cooling for each 1 *W* of electrical power! Manufacturers, retailers, and customers all use the *EER*, in a sense, incorrectly in that they quote an *EER* of, say, 10, rather than the correct way, of 10 Btu/hr/W. (The *EER*, as used, is an everyday, inconsistent unit version of the coefficient of performance, *COP*, studied in thermodynamics.)

The two examples above illustrate the dangers in using certain equations. Almost all the equations encountered in this text will be dimensionally consistent, but you should be aware of the occasional troublesome equation you will encounter in your engineering studies.

As a final note on units, we stated earlier that we will use SI and BG units in this text. You will become very familiar with their use through using this text but should be aware that many of the units used, although they are scientifically and engineering-wise correct, are nevertheless not units you will use in everyday activities, and vice versa; we do not recommend asking your grocer to give you, say, 22 newtons, or 0.16 slugs, of potatoes; nor should you be expected to immediately know what, say, a motor oil viscosity of 5W20 means!

SI units and prefixes, other defined units, and useful conversions are given in Appendix G.

1-7   ANALYSIS OF EXPERIMENTAL ERROR

Most consumers are unaware of it but, as with most foodstuffs, soft drink containers are filled to plus or minus a certain amount, as allowed by law. Because it is difficult to precisely measure the filling of a container in a rapid production process, a 12-fl-oz container may actually contain 12.1, or 12.7, fl oz. The manufacturer is never supposed to supply less than the specified amount; and it will reduce profits if it is unnecessarily generous. Similarly, the supplier of components for the interior of a car must satisfy minimum and maximum dimensions (each component has what are called tolerances) so that the final appearance of the interior is visually appealing. Engineers performing experiments must measure not just data but also the uncertainties in their measurements. They must also somehow determine how these uncertainties affect the uncertainty in the final result.

All of these examples illustrate the importance of *experimental uncertainty*, that is, the study of uncertainties in measurements and their effect on overall results. There is always a trade-off in experimental work or in manufacturing: We can reduce the uncertainties to a desired level, but the smaller the uncertainty (the more precise the measurement or experiment), the more expensive the procedure will be. Furthermore, in a complex manufacture or experiment, it is not always easy to see which measurement uncertainty has the biggest influence on the final outcome.

Anyone involved in manufacturing, or in experimental work, should understand experimental uncertainties. Appendix F (on the Web) has details on this topic; there is a selection of problems on this topic at the end of this chapter.

| 1-8 | SUMMARY |

In this chapter we introduced or reviewed a number of basic concepts and definitions, including:

✓ How fluids are defined, and the no-slip condition
✓ System/Control Volume concepts
✓ Lagrangian & Eulerian descriptions
✓ Units and dimensions (including SI, British Gravitational, and English Engineering systems)
✓ Experimental uncertainty

REFERENCE

1. Brown, Alan S., "Dip, Turn, and Dive," *Mechanical Engineering*, November 2005, pp. 20–22.

PROBLEMS

1.1 A number of common substances are

Tar	Sand
"Silly Putty"	Jello
Modeling clay	Toothpaste
Wax	Shaving cream

Some of these materials exhibit characteristics of both solid and fluid behavior under different conditions. Explain and give examples.

1.2 Give a word statement of each of the five basic conservation laws stated in Section 1-4, as they apply to a system.

1.3 Discuss the physics of skipping a stone across the water surface of a lake. Compare these mechanisms with a stone as it bounces after being thrown along a roadway.

1.4 The barrel of a bicycle tire pump becomes quite warm during use. Explain the mechanisms responsible for the temperature increase.

1.5 A spherical tank of inside diameter 500 cm contains compressed oxygen at 7 MPa and 25°C. What is the mass of oxygen?

1.6 Make a guess at the order of magnitude of the mass (e.g., 0.01, 0.1, 1.0, 10, 100, or 1000 lbm or kg) of standard air that is in a room 10 ft by 10 ft by 8 ft, and then compute this mass in lbm and kg to see how close your estimate was.

1.7 A cylindrical tank for containing 10 lbm of compressed nitrogen at a pressure of 200 atm (gage) and 70°F must be designed. The design constraints are that the length must be twice the diameter and the wall thickness must be $\frac{1}{4}$ in. What are the external dimensions?

1.8 Very small particles moving in fluids are known to experience a drag force proportional to speed. Consider a particle of net weight W dropped in a fluid. The particle experiences a drag force, $F_D = kV$, where V is the particle speed. Determine the time required for the particle to accelerate from rest to 95 percent of its terminal speed, V_t, in terms of k, W, and g.

1.9 Consider again the small particle of Problem 1.8. Express the distance required to reach 95 percent of its terminal speed in terms of g, k, and W.

1.10 For a small particle of styrofoam (1 lbm/ft^3) (spherical, with diameter $d = 0.3$ mm) falling in standard air at speed V, the drag is given by $F_D = 3\pi\mu Vd$, where μ is the air viscosity. Find the maximum speed starting from rest, and the time it takes to reach 95% of this speed. Plot the speed as a function of time.

1.11 In a combustion process, gasoline particles are to be dropped in air. The particles must drop at least 25 cm in 1 s. Find the diameter d of droplets required for this. (The drag on these particles is given by $F_D = 3\pi\mu Vd$, where V is the particle speed and μ is the air viscosity. To solve this problem use *Excel*'s *Goal Seek*.)

1.12 A sky diver with a mass of 70 kg jumps from an aircraft. The aerodynamic drag force acting on the sky diver is known to be $F_D = kV^2$, where $k = 0.25$ N · s^2/m^2. Determine the maximum speed of free fall for the sky diver and the speed reached after 100 m of fall. Plot the speed of the sky diver as a function of time and as a function of distance fallen.

1.13 For Problem 1.12, the initial horizontal speed of the skydiver is 70 m/s. As she falls, the k value for the vertical drag remains as before, but the value for horizontal motion is $k = 0.05$ N · s/m^2. Compute and plot the 2D trajectory of the skydiver.

1.14 In a pollution control experiment, minute solid particles (typical mass 5×10^{-11} kg) are dropped in the air. The terminal speed of the particles is measured to be 5 cm/s. The drag on these particles is given by $F_D = kV$, where V is the particle instantaneous speed. Find the value of constant k. Find the time required to reach 99 percent of terminal speed.

1.15 For Problem 1.14, find the distance the particles travel before reaching 99 percent of terminal speed. Plot the distanced traveled as a function of time.

1.16 The English perfected the longbow as a weapon after the Medieval period. In the hands of a skilled archer, the longbow was reputed to be accurate at ranges to 100 meters or more. If the maximum altitude of an arrow is less than $h = 10$ m while traveling to a target 100 m away from the archer, and neglecting air resistance, estimate the speed and angle at which the arrow must leave the bow. Plot the required release speed and angle as a function of height h.

1.17 For each quantity listed, indicate dimensions using force as a primary dimension, and give typical SI and English units:
  a. Power
  b. Pressure
  c. Modulus of elasticity
  d. Angular velocity
  e. Energy
  f. Momentum
  g. Shear stress
  h. Specific heat
  i. Thermal expansion coefficient
  j. Angular momentum

1.18 For each quantity listed, indicate dimensions using mass as a primary dimension, and give typical SI and English units:
  a. Power
  b. Pressure
  c. Modulus of elasticity
  d. Angular velocity
  e. Energy
  f. Moment of a force
  g. Momentum
  h. Shear stress
  i. Strain
  j. Angular momentum

1.19 Derive the following conversion factors:
  a. Convert a pressure of 1 psi to kPa.
  b. Convert a volume of 1 liter to gallons.
  c. Convert a viscosity of 1 lbf · s/ft^2 to N · s/m^2.

1.20 Derive the following conversion factors:
  a. Convert a viscosity of 1 m^2/s to ft^2/s.
  b. Convert a power of 100 W to horsepower.
  c. Convert a specific energy of 1 kJ/kg to Btu/lbm.

1.21 Express the following in SI units:
  a. 100 cfm (ft^3/min)
  b. 5 gal
  c. 65 mph
  d. 5.4 acres

1.22 Express the following in BG units:
  a. 50 m^2
  b. 250 cc
  c. 100 kW
  d. 5 lbf · s/ft^2

1.23 A farmer needs $1\frac{1}{2}$ in. of rain per week on his farm, with 25 acres of crops. If there is a drought, how much water (gpm) will have to be pumped in to maintain his crops?

1.24 While you're waiting for the ribs to cook, you muse about the propane tank of your barbecue. You're curious about the volume of propane versus the actual tank size. Find the liquid propane volume when full (the weight of the propane is specified on the tank). Compare this to the tank volume (take some measurements, and approximate the tank shape as a cylinder with a hemisphere on each end). Explain the discrepancy.

1.25 The density of mercury is given as 26.3 slug/ft^3. Calculate the specific gravity and the specific volume in m^3/kg of the mercury. Calculate the specific weight in lbf/ft^3 on Earth and on the moon. Acceleration of gravity on the moon is 5.47 ft/s^2.

1.26 Derive the following conversion factors:
  a. Convert a volume flow rate in in.^{3}/min to mm^3/s.
  b. Convert a volume flow rate in cubic meters per second to gpm (gallons per minute).
  c. Convert a volume flow rate in liters per minute to gpm (gallons per minute).
  d. Convert a volume flow rate of air in standard cubic feet per minute (SCFM) to cubic meters per hour. A standard cubic foot of gas occupies one cubic foot at standard temperature and pressure ($T = 15°C$ and $p = 101.3$ kPa absolute).

1.27 The kilogram force is commonly used in Europe as a unit of force. (As in the U.S. customary system, where 1 lbf is the force exerted by a mass of 1 lbm in standard gravity, 1 kgf is the force exerted by a mass of 1 kg in standard gravity.) Moderate pressures, such as those for auto or truck tires, are conveniently expressed in units of kgf/cm^2. Convert 32 psig to these units.

1.28 In Section 1-6 we learned that the Manning equation computes the flow speed V (m/s) in a canal made from unfinished concrete, given the hydraulic radius R_h (m), the channel slope S_0, and a Manning resistance coefficient constant value $n \approx 0.014$. For a canal with $R_h = 7.5$ m and a slope of 1/10, find the flow speed. Compare this result with that obtained using the same n value, but with R_h first converted to ft, with the answer assumed to be in ft/s. Finally, find the value of n if we wish to *correctly* use the equation for BG units (and compute V to check!)

1.29 The maximum theoretical flow rate (kg/s) through a supersonic nozzle is

$$\dot{m}_{max} = 0.04 \frac{A_t p_0}{\sqrt{T_0}}$$

where A_t (m^2) is the nozzle throat area, p_0 (Pa) is the tank pressure, and T_0 (K) is the tank temperature. Is this equation dimensionally correct? If not, find the units of the 0.04 term. Write the equivalent equation in BG units.

1.30 From thermodynamics, we know that the coefficient of performance of an ideal air conditioner is given by

$$COP_{Ideal} = \frac{T_L}{T_H - T_L}$$

where T_L and T_H are the room and outside temperatures (absolute). If an AC is to keep a room at 68°F when it is 95°F outside, find the COP_{Ideal}. Convert to an *EER* value, and compare this to a typical Energy Star compliant *EER* value.

1.31 In Chapter 9 we will study aerodynamics and learn that the drag force F_D on a body is given by

$$F_D = \frac{1}{2}\rho V^2 A C_D$$

Hence the drag depends on speed V, fluid density ρ, and body size (indicated by frontal area A) and shape (indicated by drag coefficient C_D). What are the dimensions of C_D?

1.32 The mean free path λ of a molecule of gas is the average distance it travels before collision with another molecule. It is given by

$$\lambda = C\frac{m}{\rho d^2}$$

where m and d are the molecule's mass and diameter, respectively, and ρ is the gas density. What are the dimensions of constant C for a dimensionally consistent equation?

1.33 An important equation in the theory of vibrations is

$$m\frac{d^2x}{dt^2} + c\frac{dx}{dt} + kx = f(t)$$

where m (kg) is the mass and x (m) is the position at time t (s). For a dimensionally consistent equation, what are the dimensions of c, k, and f? What would be suitable units for c, k, and f in the SI and BG systems?

1.34 A parameter that is often used in describing pump performance is the specific speed, $N_{S_{cu}}$, given by

$$N_{S_{cu}} = \frac{N(\text{rpm})[Q(\text{gpm})]^{1/2}}{[H(\text{ft})]^{3/4}}$$

What are the units of specific speed? A particular pump has a specific speed of 2000. What will be the specific speed in SI units (angular velocity in rad/s)?

1.35 A particular pump has an "engineering" equation form of the performance characteristic equation given by H (ft) = 1.5 − $4.5 \times 10^{-5} [Q \text{ (gpm)}]^2$, relating the head H and flow rate Q. What are the units of the coefficients 1.5 and 4.5×10^{-5}? Derive an SI version of this equation.

1.36 A container weighs 3.5 lbf when empty. When filled with water at 90°F, the mass of the container and its contents is 2.5 slug. Find the weight of water in the container, and its volume in cubic feet, using data from Appendix A.

1.37 Calculate the density of standard air in a laboratory from the ideal gas equation of state. Estimate the experimental uncertainty in the air density calculated for standard conditions (29.9 in. of mercury and 59°F) if the uncertainty in measuring the barometer height is ±0.1 in. of mercury and the uncertainty in measuring temperature is ±0.5°F. (Note that 29.9 in. of mercury corresponds to 14.7 psia.)

1.38 Repeat the calculation of uncertainty described in Problem 1.37 for air in a freezer. Assume the measured barometer height is 759 ± 1 mm of mercury and the temperature is −20 ± 0.5°C. [Note that 759 mm of mercury corresponds to 101 kPa (abs).]

1.39 The mass of the standard American golf ball is 1.62 ± 0.01 oz and its mean diameter is 1.68 ± 0.01 in. Determine the density and specific gravity of the American golf ball. Estimate the uncertainties in the calculated values.

1.40 The mass flow rate in a water flow system determined by collecting the discharge over a timed interval is 0.2 kg/s. The scales used can be read to the nearest 0.05 kg and the stopwatch is accurate to 0.2 s. Estimate the precision with which the flow rate can be calculated for time intervals of (a) 10 s and (b) 1 min.

1.41 A can of pet food has the following internal dimensions: 102 mm height and 73 mm diameter (each ±1 mm at odds of 20 to 1). The label lists the mass of the contents as 397 g. Evaluate the magnitude and estimated uncertainty of the density of the pet food if the mass value is accurate to ±1 g at the same odds.

1.42 The mass of the standard British golf ball is 45.9 ± 0.3 g and its mean diameter is 41.1 ± 0.3 mm. Determine the density and specific gravity of the British golf ball. Estimate the uncertainties in the calculated values.

1.43 The mass flow rate of water in a tube is measured using a beaker to catch water during a timed interval. The nominal mass flow rate is 100 g/s. Assume that mass is measured using a balance with a least count of 1 g and a maximum capacity of 1 kg, and that the timer has a least count of 0.1 s. Estimate the time intervals and uncertainties in measured mass flow rate that would result from using 100, 500, and 1000 mL beakers. Would there be any advantage in using the largest beaker? Assume the tare mass of the empty 1000 mL beaker is 500 g.

1.44 The estimated dimensions of a soda can are $D = 66.0 \pm 0.5$ mm and $H = 110 \pm 0.5$ mm. Measure the mass of a full can and an empty can using a kitchen scale or postal scale. Estimate the volume of soda contained in the can. From your measurements estimate the depth to which the can is filled and the uncertainty in the estimate. Assume the value of SG = 1.055, as supplied by the bottler.

1.45 From Appendix A, the viscosity $\mu(\text{N} \cdot \text{s/m}^2)$ of water at temperature T (K) can be computed from $\mu = A10^{B/(T-C)}$, where $A = 2.414 \times 10^{-5}\,\text{N} \cdot \text{s/m}^2$, $B = 247.8$ K, and $C = 140$ K. Determine the viscosity of water at 20°C, and estimate its uncertainty if the uncertainty in temperature measurement is ±0.25°C.

1.46 An enthusiast magazine publishes data from its road tests on the lateral acceleration capability of cars. The measurements are made using a 150-ft-diameter skid pad. Assume the vehicle path deviates from the circle by ±2 ft and that the vehicle speed is read from a fifth-wheel speed-measuring system to ±0.5 mph. Estimate the experimental uncertainty in a reported lateral acceleration of 0.7 g. How would you improve the experimental procedure to reduce the uncertainty?

1.47 Using the nominal dimensions of the soda can given in Problem 1.44, determine the precision with which the diameter and height must be measured to estimate the volume of the can within an uncertainty of ±0.5 percent.

1.48 An American golf ball is described in Problem 1.39 Assuming the measured mass and its uncertainty as given, determine the precision to which the diameter of the ball must be measured so the density of the ball may be estimated within an uncertainty of ±1 percent.

1.49 The height of a building may be estimated by measuring the horizontal distance to a point on the ground and the angle from this point to the top of the building. Assuming these measurements are $L = 100 \pm 0.5$ ft and $\theta = 30 \pm 0.2$ degrees, estimate the height H of the building and the uncertainty in the estimate. For the same building height and measurement uncertainties, use *Excel's Solver* to determine the angle (and the corresponding distance from the building) at which measurements should be made to minimize the uncertainty in estimated height. Evaluate and plot the optimum measurement angle as a function of building height for $50 \leq H \leq 1000$ ft.

1.50 In the design of a medical instrument it is desired to dispense 1 cubic millimeter of liquid using a piston-cylinder syringe made from molded plastic. The molding operation produces plastic parts with estimated dimensional uncertainties of ± 0.002 in. Estimate the uncertainty in dispensed volume that results from the uncertainties in the dimensions of the device. Plot on the same graph the uncertainty in length, diameter, and volume dispensed as a function of cylinder diameter D from $D = 0.5$ to 2 mm. Determine the ratio of stroke length to bore diameter that gives a design with minimum uncertainty in volume dispensed. Is the result influenced by the magnitude of the dimensional uncertainty?

Chapter 2

Fundamental Concepts

CASE STUDY

Fluid Mechanics and Your MP3 Player

The MP3 player of one of the authors.

Some people have the impression that fluid mechanics is old- or low-tech: water flow in a household pipe, the fluid forces acting on a dam, and so on. While it's true that many concepts in fluid mechanics are hundreds of years old, there are still lots of exciting new areas of research and development. Everyone has heard of the relatively high tech area of fluid mechanics called streamlining (of cars, aircraft, racing bikes, and racing swimsuits, to mention a few), but there are many others.

If you're a typical engineering student, there's a decent chance that while reading this chapter you're listening to music on your MP3 player; you can thank fluid mechanics for your ability to do this! The tiny hard disk drive (HDD) in one of these devices typically holds about 60 GB of data, so the disk platter must have a huge density (greater than 100,000 tracks per inch); in addition, the read/write head must get very close to the platter as it transfers data (typically the head is about 0.05 μm above the platter surface—a human hair is about 100 μm). The platter also spins at something greater than 500 revolutions per second! Hence the bearings in which the spindle of the platter spins must have very low friction but also have virtually no play or looseness—otherwise, at worst, the head will crash into the platter or, at best, you won't be able to read the data (it will be too closely packed). Designing such a bearing presents quite a challenge. Until a few years ago, most hard drives used ball bearings (BBs), which are essentially just like those in the wheel of a bicycle; they work on the principle that a spindle can rotate if it is held by a ring of small spheres that are supported in a cage. The problems with BBs are that they have a lot of components; they are very difficult to build to the precision needed for the HDD; they are vulnerable to shock (if you drop an HDD with such a drive, you're likely to dent one of the spheres as it hits the spindle, destroying the bearing); and they are relatively noisy.

Hard-drive makers are increasingly moving to fluid dynamic bearings (FDBs). These are mechanically much simpler than BBs; they consist basically of the spindle directly mounted in the bearing opening, with only a specially formulated viscous lubricant (such as ester oil) in the gap of only a few microns. The spindle and/or bearing surfaces have a herringbone pattern of grooves to maintain the oil in place. These bearings are extremely durable (they can often survive a shock of 500 g!) and low noise; they will also allow rotation speeds in excess of 15,000 rpm in the future, making

data access even faster than with current devices. FDBs have been used before, in devices such as gyroscopes, but making them at such a small scale is new. Some FDBs even use pressurized air as the lubrication fluid, but one of the problems with these is that they sometimes stop working when you take them on an airplane flight—the cabin pressure is insufficient to maintain the pressure the bearing needs!

It is not an overstatement to say that without these high-tech fluid bearings, your MP3 player would have to be bigger, would be more vulnerable to damage, would hold less data, and would have more extraneous noise.

In Chapter 1 we discussed in general terms what fluid mechanics is about, and described some of the approaches we will use in analyzing fluid mechanics problems. In this chapter we will be more specific in defining some important properties of fluids, and ways in which flows can be described and characterized.

2-1   FLUID AS A CONTINUUM

We are all familiar with fluids—the most common being air and water—and we experience them as being "smooth," i.e., as being a continuous medium. Unless we use specialized equipment, we are not aware of the underlying molecular nature of fluids. This molecular structure is one in which the mass is *not* continuously distributed in space, but is concentrated in molecules that are separated by relatively large regions of empty space. The sketch in Fig. 2.1a shows a schematic representation of this. A region of space "filled" by a stationary fluid (e.g., air, treated as a single gas) looks like a continuous medium, but if we zoom in on a very small cube of it, we can see that we mostly have empty space, with gas molecules scattered around, moving at high speed (indicated by the gas temperature). Note that the size of the gas molecules is greatly exaggerated (they would be almost invisible even at this scale) and that we have placed velocity vectors only on a small sample. We wish to ask: What is the minimum volume, $\delta V'$, that a "point" C must be, so that we can talk about continuous fluid properties such as the density at a point? In other words, under what circumstances can a fluid be treated as a *continuum*, for which, by definition, properties vary smoothly from point to point? This is an important question because the concept of a continuum is the basis of classical fluid mechanics.

Consider how we determine the density at a point. Density is defined as mass per unit volume; in Fig. 2.1a the mass δm will be given by the instantaneous number of

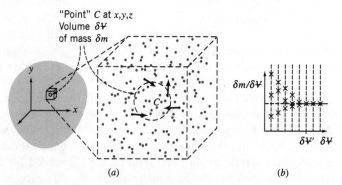

Fig. 2.1 Definition of density at a point.

molecules in δV (and the mass of each molecule), so the average density in volume δV is given by $\rho = \delta m / \delta V$. We say "average" because the number of molecules in δV, and hence the density, fluctuates. For example, if the gas in Fig. 2.1a was air at standard temperature and pressure (STP[1]) and the volume δV was a sphere of diameter 0.01 μm, there might be 15 molecules in δV (as shown), but an instant later there might be 17 (three might enter while one leaves). Hence the density at "point" C randomly fluctuates in time, as shown in Fig. 2.1b. In this figure, each vertical dashed line represents a specific chosen volume, δV, and each data point represents the measured density at an instant. For very small volumes, the density varies greatly, but above a certain volume, $\delta V'$, the density becomes stable—the volume now encloses a huge number of molecules. For example, if $\delta V = 0.001$ mm^3 (about the size of a grain of sand), there will on average be 2.5×10^{13} molecules present. Hence we can conclude that air at STP (and other gases, and liquids) can be treated as a continuous medium as long as we consider a "point" to be no larger than about this size; this is sufficiently precise for most engineering applications.

The concept of a continuum is the basis of classical fluid mechanics. The continuum assumption is valid in treating the behavior of fluids under normal conditions. It only breaks down when the mean free path of the molecules[2] becomes the same order of magnitude as the smallest significant characteristic dimension of the problem. This occurs in such specialized problems as rarefied gas flow (e.g., as encountered in flights into the upper reaches of the atmosphere). For these specialized cases (not covered in this text) we must abandon the concept of a continuum in favor of the microscopic and statistical points of view.

As a consequence of the continuum assumption, each fluid property is assumed to have a definite value at every point in space. Thus fluid properties such as density, temperature, velocity, and so on are considered to be continuous functions of position and time. For example, we now have a workable definition of density at a point,

$$\rho \equiv \lim_{\delta V \to \delta V'} \frac{\delta m}{\delta V} \tag{2.1}$$

Since point C was arbitrary, the density at any other point in the fluid could be determined in the same manner. If density was measured simultaneously at an infinite number of points in the fluid, we would obtain an expression for the density distribution as a function of the space coordinates, $\rho = \rho(x, y, z)$, at the given instant.

The density at a point may also vary with time (as a result of work done on or by the fluid and/or heat transfer to the fluid). Thus the complete representation of density (the *field* representation) is given by

$$\rho = \rho(x, y, z, t) \tag{2.2}$$

Since density is a scalar quantity, requiring only the specification of a magnitude for a complete description, the field represented by Eq. 2.2 is a scalar field.

An alternative way of expressing the density of a substance (solid or fluid) is to compare it to an accepted reference value, typically the maximum density of water, ρ_{H_2O} (1000 kg/m^3 at 4°C or 1.94 slug/ft^3 at 39°F). Thus, the *specific gravity*, SG, of a substance is expressed as

$$SG = \frac{\rho}{\rho_{H_2O}} \tag{2.3}$$

For example, the *SG* of mercury is typically 13.6—mercury is 13.6 times as dense as water. Appendix A contains specific gravity data for selected engineering materials. The specific gravity of liquids is a function of temperature; for most liquids specific gravity decreases with increasing temperature.

---

[1] STP for air are 15°C (59°F) and 101.3 kPa absolute (14.696 psia), respectively.

[2] Approximately 6×10^{-8} m at STP (Standard Temperature and Pressure) for gas molecules that show ideal gas behavior [1].

The *specific weight*, γ, of a substance is another useful material property. It is defined as the weight of a substance per unit volume and given as

$$\gamma = \frac{mg}{\forall} \rightarrow \gamma = \rho g \qquad (2.4)$$

For example, the specific weight of water is approximately 9.81 kN/m^3 (62.4 lbf/ft^3).

2-2	**VELOCITY FIELD**

In the previous section we saw that the continuum assumption led directly to the notion of the density field. Other fluid properties also may be described by fields.

A very important property defined by a field is the velocity field, given by

$$\vec{V} = \vec{V}(x, y, z, t) \qquad (2.5)$$

Velocity is a vector quantity, requiring a magnitude and direction for a complete description, so the velocity field (Eq. 2.5) is a vector field.

The velocity vector, $\vec{V}$, also can be written in terms of its three scalar components. Denoting the components in the x, y, and z directions by u, v, and w, then

$$\vec{V} = u\hat{i} + v\hat{j} + w\hat{k} \qquad (2.6)$$

In general, each component, u, v, and w, will be a function of x, y, z, and t.

We need to be clear on what $\vec{V}(x, y, z, t)$ measures: It indicates the velocity of a fluid particle that is passing through the point x, y, z at time instant t, in the Eulerian sense. We can keep measuring the velocity at the same point or choose any other point x, y, z at the next time instant; the point x, y, z is *not* the ongoing position of an *individual* particle, but a point we choose to look at. (Hence x, y, and z are independent variables. In Chapter 5 we will discuss the *material derivative* of velocity, in which we choose $x = x_p(t)$, $y = y_p(t)$, and $z = z_p(t)$, where $x_p(t)$, $y_p(t)$, $z_p(t)$ is the position of a specific particle.) We conclude that $\vec{V}(x, y, z, t)$ should be thought of as the velocity field of all particles, not just the velocity of an individual particle.

If properties at every point in a flow field do not change with time, the flow is termed *steady*. Stated mathematically, the definition of steady flow is

$$\frac{\partial \eta}{\partial t} = 0$$

where η represents any fluid property. Hence, for steady flow,

$$\frac{\partial \rho}{\partial t} = 0 \quad \text{or} \quad \rho = \rho(x, y, z)$$

and

$$\frac{\partial \vec{V}}{\partial t} = 0 \quad \text{or} \quad \vec{V} = \vec{V}(x, y, z)$$

In steady flow, any property may vary from point to point in the field, but all properties remain constant with time at every point.

One-, Two-, and Three-Dimensional Flows

A flow is classified as one-, two-, or three-dimensional depending on the number of space coordinates required to specify the velocity field.[3] Equation 2.5 indicates that the velocity field may be a function of three space coordinates and time. Such a flow

---

[3] Some authors choose to classify a flow as one-, two-, or three-dimensional on the basis of the number of space coordinates required to specify *all* fluid properties. In this text, classification of flow fields will be based on the number of space coordinates required to specify the velocity field only.

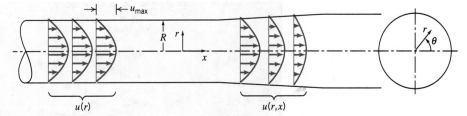

Fig. 2.2 Examples of one- and two-dimensional flows.

field is termed *three-dimensional* (it is also *unsteady*) because the velocity at any point in the flow field depends on the three coordinates required to locate the point in space.

Although most flow fields are inherently three-dimensional, analysis based on fewer dimensions is frequently meaningful. Consider, for example, the steady flow through a long straight pipe that has a divergent section, as shown in Fig. 2.2. In this example, we are using cylindrical coordinates (r, θ, x). We will learn (in Chapter 8) that under certain circumstances (e.g., far from the entrance of the pipe and from the divergent section, where the flow can be quite complicated), the velocity distribution may be described by

$$u = u_{max}\left[1 - \left(\frac{r}{R}\right)^2\right] \qquad (2.7)$$

This is shown on the left of Fig. 2.2. The velocity $u(r)$ is a function of only one coordinate, and so the flow is one-dimensional. On the other hand, in the diverging section, the velocity decreases in the x-direction, and the flow becomes two-dimensional: $u = u(r, x)$.

As you might suspect, the complexity of analysis increases considerably with the number of dimensions of the flow field. For many problems encountered in engineering, a one-dimensional analysis is adequate to provide approximate solutions of engineering accuracy.

Since all fluids satisfying the continuum assumption must have zero relative velocity at a solid surface (to satisfy the no-slip condition), most flows are inherently two- or three-dimensional. To simplify the analysis it is often convenient to use the notion of *uniform flow* at a given cross section. In a flow that is uniform at a given cross section, the velocity is constant across any section normal to the flow. Under this assumption,[4] the two-dimensional flow of Fig. 2.2 is modeled as the flow shown in Fig. 2.3. In the flow of Fig. 2.3, the velocity field is a function of x alone, and thus the flow model is one-dimensional. (Other properties, such as density or pressure, also may be assumed uniform at a section, if appropriate.)

The term *uniform flow field* (as opposed to uniform flow at a cross section) is used to describe a flow in which the velocity is constant, i.e., independent of all space coordinates, throughout the entire flow field.

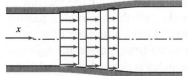

Fig. 2.3 Example of uniform flow at a section.

Timelines, Pathlines, Streaklines, and Streamlines

Airplane and auto companies and college engineering laboratories, among others, frequently use wind tunnels to visualize flow fields [2]. For example, Fig. 2.4 shows a flow pattern for flow around a car mounted in a wind tunnel, generated by releasing

---

[4] This may seem like an unrealistic simplification, but actually in many cases leads to useful results. Sweeping assumptions such as uniform flow at a cross section should always be reviewed carefully to be sure they provide a reasonable analytical model of the real flow.

Fig. 2.4 Streaklines over an automobile in a wind tunnel. (Courtesy Audi AG.)

smoke into the flow at five fixed upstream points. Flow patterns can be visualized using timelines, pathlines, streaklines, or streamlines.[5]

If a number of adjacent fluid particles in a flow field are marked at a given instant, they form a line in the fluid at that instant; this line is called a *timeline*. Subsequent observations of the line may provide information about the flow field. For example, in discussing the behavior of a fluid under the action of a constant shear force (Section 1-2) timelines were introduced to demonstrate the deformation of a fluid at successive instants.

A *pathline* is the path or trajectory traced out by a moving fluid particle. To make a pathline visible, we might identify a fluid particle at a given instant, e.g., by the use of dye or smoke, and then take a long exposure photograph of its subsequent motion. The line traced out by the particle is a pathline. This approach might be used to study, for example, the trajectory of a contaminant leaving a smokestack.

On the other hand, we might choose to focus our attention on a fixed location in space and identify, again by the use of dye or smoke, all fluid particles passing through this point. After a short period of time we would have a number of identifiable fluid particles in the flow, all of which had, at some time, passed through one fixed location in space. The line joining these fluid particles is defined as a *streakline*.

Streamlines are lines drawn in the flow field so that at a given instant they are tangent to the direction of flow at every point in the flow field. Since the streamlines are tangent to the velocity vector at every point in the flow field, there can be no flow across a streamline. Streamlines are the most commonly used visualization technique. For example, they are used to study flow over an automobile in a computer simulation. The procedure used to obtain the equation for a streamline in two-dimensional flow is illustrated in Example 2.1.

In steady flow, the velocity at each point in the flow field remains constant with time and, consequently, the streamline shapes do not vary from one instant to the next. This implies that a particle located on a given streamline will always move along the same streamline. Furthermore, consecutive particles passing through a fixed

---

[5] These are all demonstrated in the NCFMF video *Flow Visualization*. (See http://web.mit.edu/fluids/ www/Shapiro/ncfmf.html for free online viewing of the film; It is old but good!)

point in space will be on the same streamline and, subsequently, will remain on this streamline. Thus in a steady flow, pathlines, streaklines, and streamlines are identical lines in the flow field.

Figure 2.4 shows a photograph of five *streaklines* for flow over an automobile in a wind tunnel. A streakline is the line produced in a flow when all particles moving through a fixed point are marked in some way (e.g., using smoke). We can also define *streamlines*. These are lines drawn in the flow field so that *at a given instant* they are tangent to the direction of flow at every point in the flow field. Since the streamlines are tangent to the velocity vector at every point in the flow field, there is no flow across a streamline. *Pathlines* are as the name implies: They show, over time, the paths individual particles take (if you've seen time-lapse photos of nighttime traffic, you get the idea). Finally, *timelines* are created by marking a line in a flow and watching how it evolves over time.

We mentioned that Fig. 2.4 shows streaklines, but in fact the pattern shown also represents streamlines and pathlines! The steady pattern shown will exist as long as smoke is released from the five fixed points. If we were somehow to measure the velocity at all points at an instant, to generate streamlines, we'd get the same pattern; if we were instead to release only one smoke particle at each location, and video its motion over time, we'd see the particles follow the same curves. We conclude that for *steady* flow, streaklines, streamlines, and pathlines are identical.

Things are quite different for *unsteady* flow. For unsteady flow, streaklines, streamlines, and pathlines will in general have differing shapes. For example, consider holding a garden hose and swinging it side to side as water exits at high speed, as shown in Fig. 2.5. We obtain a continuous sheet of water. If we consider individual water particles, we see that each particle, once ejected, follows a straight-line path (here, for simplicity, we ignore gravity): The pathlines are straight lines, as shown. On the other hand, if we start injecting dye into the water as it exits the hose, we will generate a streakline, and this takes the shape of an expanding sine wave, as shown.

Clearly, pathlines and streaklines do not coincide for this unsteady flow (we leave determination of streamlines to an exercise).

We can use the velocity field to derive the shapes of streaklines, pathlines, and streamlines. Starting with streamlines: Because the streamlines are parallel to the velocity vector, we can write (for 2D)

$$\left.\frac{dy}{dx}\right)_{\text{streamline}} = \frac{v(x,y)}{u(x,y)} \tag{2.8}$$

Note that streamlines are obtained at an instant in time; if the flow is unsteady, time t is held constant in Eq. 2.8. Solution of this equation gives the equation $y = y(x)$, with an undetermined integration constant, the value of which determines the particular streamline.

For pathlines (again considering 2D), we let $x = x_p(t)$ and $y = y_p(t)$, where $x_p(t)$ and $y_p(t)$ are the instantaneous coordinates of a specific particle. We then get

$$\left.\frac{dx}{dt}\right)_{\text{particle}} = u(x,y,t) \qquad \left.\frac{dy}{dt}\right)_{\text{particle}} = v(x,y,t) \tag{2.9}$$

The simultaneous solution of these equations gives the path of a particle in parametric form $x_p(t)$, $y_p(t)$.

The computation of streaklines is somewhat tricky. The first step is to compute the pathline of a particle (using Eqs. 2.9) that was released from the streak source point (coordinates x_0, y_0) at time t_0, in the form

$$x_{\text{particle}}(t) = x(t, x_0, y_0, t_0) \qquad y_{\text{particle}}(t) = y(t, x_0, y_0, t_0)$$

Then, instead of interpreting this as the position of a particle over time, we rewrite these equations as

$$x_{\text{streakline}}(t_0) = x(t, x_0, y_0, t_0) \qquad y_{\text{streakline}}(t_0) = y(t, x_0, y_0, t_0) \tag{2.10}$$

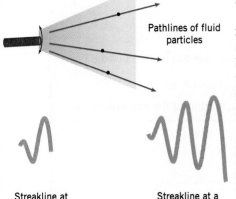

Pathlines of fluid particles

Streakline at some instant

Streakline at a later instant

Fig. 2.5 Pathlines and streaklines for flow from the exit of an oscillating garden hose.

Equations 2.10 give the line generated (by time t) from a streak source at point (x_0, y_0). In these equations, t_0 (the release times of particles) is varied from 0 to t to show the instantaneous positions of all particles released up to time t!

EXAMPLE 2.1   Streamlines and Pathlines in Two-Dimensional Flow

A velocity field is given by $\vec{V} = Ax\hat{i} - Ay\hat{j}$; the units of velocity are m/s; x and y are given in meters; $A = 0.3$ s^{-1}.
(a) Obtain an equation for the streamlines in the xy plane.
(b) Plot the streamline passing through the point (x_0, y_0) = (2, 8).
(c) Determine the velocity of a particle at the point (2, 8).
(d) If the particle passing through the point (x_0, y_0) is marked at time $t = 0$, determine the location of the particle at time $t = 6$ s.
(e) What is the velocity of this particle at time $t = 6$ s?
(f) Show that the equation of the particle path (the pathline) is the same as the equation of the streamline.

GIVEN: Velocity field, $\vec{V} = Ax\hat{i} - Ay\hat{j}$; x and y in meters; $A = 0.3$ s^{-1}

FIND: (a) Equation of the streamlines in the xy plane.
(b) Streamline plot through point (2, 8).
(c) Velocity of particle at point (2, 8).
(d) Position at $t = 6$ s of particle located at (2, 8) at $t = 0$.
(e) Velocity of particle at position found in (d).
(f) Equation of pathline of particle located at (2, 8) at $t = 0$.

SOLUTION:

(a) Streamlines are lines drawn in the flow field such that, at a given instant, they are tangent to the direction of flow at every point. Consequently,

$$\left.\frac{dy}{dx}\right)_{streamline} = \frac{v}{u} = \frac{-Ay}{Ax} = \frac{-y}{x}$$

Separating variables and integrating, we obtain

$$\int \frac{dy}{y} = -\int \frac{dx}{x}$$

or

$$\ln y = -\ln x + c_1$$

This can be written as $xy = c$ ⟵

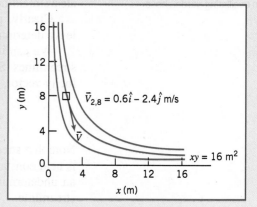

$$\vec{V}_{2,8} = 0.6\hat{i} - 2.4\hat{j} \text{ m/s}$$

$$xy = 16 \text{ m}^2$$

(b) For the streamline passing through the point (x_0, y_0) = (2, 8) the constant, c, has a value of 16 and the equation of the streamline through the point (2, 8) is

$$xy = x_0 y_0 = 16 \text{ m}^2 ⟵$$

The plot is as sketched above.

(c) The velocity field is $\vec{V} = Ax\hat{i} - Ay\hat{j}$. At the point (2, 8) the velocity is

$$\vec{V} = A(x\hat{i} - y\hat{j}) = 0.3\text{s}^{-1}(2\hat{i} - 8\hat{j})\text{m} = 0.6\hat{i} - 2.4\hat{j} \text{ m/s} ⟵$$

(d) A particle moving in the flow field will have velocity given by

$$\vec{V} = Ax\hat{i} - Ay\hat{j}$$

Thus

$$u_p = \frac{dx}{dt} = Ax \quad \text{and} \quad v_p = \frac{dy}{dt} = -Ay$$

Separating variables and integrating (in each equation) gives

$$\int_{x_0}^{x} \frac{dx}{x} = \int_{0}^{t} A\, dt \quad \text{and} \quad \int_{y_0}^{y} \frac{dy}{y} = \int_{0}^{t} -A\, dt$$

Then

$$\ln \frac{x}{x_0} = At \quad \text{and} \quad \ln \frac{y}{y_0} = -At$$

or

$$x = x_0 e^{At} \quad \text{and} \quad y = y_0 e^{-At}$$

At $t = 6$ s,

$$x = 2\,\text{m}\; e^{(0.3)6} = 12.1\,\text{m} \quad \text{and} \quad y = 8\,\text{m}\; e^{-(0.3)6} = 1.32\,\text{m}$$

At $t = 6$ s, particle is at (12.1, 1.32) m ⟵

(e) At the point (12.1, 1.32) m,

$$\vec{V} = A(x\hat{i} - y\hat{j}) = 0.3\,\text{s}^{-1}(12.1\hat{i} - 1.32\hat{j})\text{m} = 3.63\hat{i} - 0.396\hat{j}\,\text{m/s} \;\longleftarrow$$

(f) To determine the equation of the pathline, we use the parametric equations

$$x = x_0 e^{At} \quad \text{and} \quad y = y_0 e^{-At}$$

and eliminate t. Solving for e^{At} from both equations

$$e^{At} = \frac{y_0}{y} = \frac{x}{x_0}$$

Therefore $xy = x_0 y_0 = 16\,\text{m}^2$ ⟵

> **Notes:**
> ✓ This problem illustrates the method for computing streamlines and pathlines.
> ✓ Because this is a steady flow, the streamlines and pathlines have the same shape—in an unsteady flow this would not be true.
> ✓ When we follow a particle (the Lagrangian approach), its position (x, y) and velocity ($u_p = dx/dt$ and $v_p = dy/dt$) are functions of time, even though the flow is steady.

2-3 STRESS FIELD

In our study of fluid mechanics, we will need to understand what kinds of forces act on fluid particles. Each fluid particle can experience: *surface forces* (pressure, friction) that are generated by contact with other particles or a solid surface; and *body forces* (such as gravity and electromagnetic) that are experienced throughout the particle.

The gravitational body force acting on an element of volume, $d\forall$, is given by $\rho \vec{g} d\forall$, where ρ is the density (mass per unit volume) and $\vec{g}$ is the local gravitational acceleration. Thus the gravitational body force per unit volume is $\rho \vec{g}$ and the gravitational body force per unit mass is $\vec{g}$.

Surface forces on a fluid particle lead to *stresses*. The concept of stress is useful for describing how forces acting on the boundaries of a medium (fluid or solid) are transmitted throughout the medium. You have probably seen stresses discussed in solid mechanics. For example, when you stand on a diving board, stresses are generated within the board. On the other hand, when a body moves through a fluid, stresses

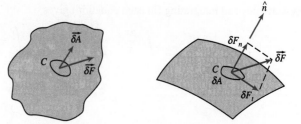

Fig. 2.6 The concept of stress in a continuum.

are developed within the fluid. The difference between a fluid and a solid is, as we've seen, that stresses in a fluid are mostly generated by motion rather than by deflection.

Imagine the surface of a fluid particle in contact with other fluid particles, and consider the contact force being generated between the particles. Consider a portion, $\delta\vec{A}$, of the surface at some point C. The orientation of $\delta\vec{A}$ is given by the unit vector, $\hat{n}$, shown in Fig. 2.6. The vector $\hat{n}$ is the outwardly drawn unit normal with respect to the particle.

The force, $\delta\vec{F}$, acting on $\delta\vec{A}$ may be resolved into two components, one normal to and the other tangent to the area. A *normal stress* σ_n and a *shear stress* τ_n are then defined as

$$\sigma_n = \lim_{\delta A_n \to 0} \frac{\delta F_n}{\delta A_n} \tag{2.11}$$

and

$$\tau_n = \lim_{\delta A_n \to 0} \frac{\delta F_t}{\delta A_n} \tag{2.12}$$

Subscript n on the stress is included as a reminder that the stresses are associated with the surface $\delta\vec{A}$ through C, having an outward normal in the $\hat{n}$ direction. The fluid is actually a continuum, so we could have imagined breaking it up any number of different ways into fluid particles around point C, and therefore obtained any number of different stresses at point C.

In dealing with vector quantities such as force, we usually consider components in an orthogonal coordinate system. In rectangular coordinates we might consider the stresses acting on planes whose outwardly drawn normals (again with respect to the material acted upon) are in the x, y, or z directions. In Fig. 2.7 we consider the stress on the element δA_x, whose outwardly drawn normal is in the x direction. The force, $\delta\vec{F}$, has been resolved into components along each of the coordinate directions. Dividing the magnitude of each force component by the area, δA_x, and taking the limit as δA_x approaches zero, we define the three stress components shown in Fig. 2.7b:

$$\sigma_{xx} = \lim_{\delta A_x \to 0} \frac{\delta F_x}{\delta A_x} \tag{2.13}$$

$$\tau_{xy} = \lim_{\delta A_x \to 0} \frac{\delta F_y}{\delta A_x} \qquad \tau_{xz} = \lim_{\delta A_x \to 0} \frac{\delta F_z}{\delta A_x}$$

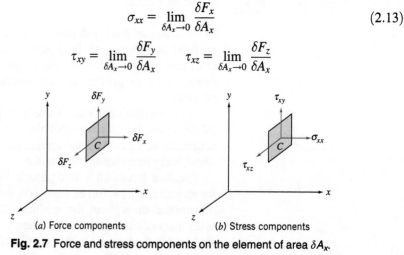

(a) Force components   (b) Stress components

Fig. 2.7 Force and stress components on the element of area δA_x.

We have used a double subscript notation to label the stresses. The *first* subscript (in this case, x) indicates the *plane* on which the stress acts (in this case, a surface perpendicular to the x axis). The *second* subscript indicates the *direction* in which the stress acts.

Consideration of area element δA_y would lead to the definitions of the stresses, σ_{yy}, τ_{yx}, and τ_{yz}; use of area element δA_z would similarly lead to the definitions of σ_{zz}, τ_{zx}, τ_{zy}.

Although we just looked at three orthogonal planes, an infinite number of planes can be passed through point C, resulting in an infinite number of stresses associated with planes through that point. Fortunately, the state of stress at a point can be described completely by specifying the stresses acting on *any* three mutually perpendicular planes through the point. The stress at a point is specified by the nine components

$$\begin{bmatrix} \sigma_{xx} & \tau_{xy} & \tau_{xz} \\ \tau_{yx} & \sigma_{yy} & \tau_{yz} \\ \tau_{zx} & \tau_{zy} & \sigma_{zz} \end{bmatrix}$$

where σ has been used to denote a normal stress, and τ to denote a shear stress. The notation for designating stress is shown in Fig. 2.8.

Referring to the infinitesimal element shown in Fig. 2.8, we see that there are six planes (two x planes, two y planes, and two z planes) on which stresses may act. In order to designate the plane of interest, we could use terms like front and back, top and bottom, or left and right. However, it is more logical to name the planes in terms of the coordinate axes. The planes are named and denoted as positive or negative according to the direction of the outwardly drawn normal to the plane. Thus the top plane, for example, is a positive y plane and the back plane is a negative z plane.

It also is necessary to adopt a sign convention for stress. A stress component is positive when the direction of the stress component and the plane on which it acts are both positive or both negative. Thus $\tau_{yx} = 5$ lbf/in.^{2} represents a shear stress on a positive y plane in the positive x direction or a shear stress on a negative y plane in the negative x direction. In Fig. 2.8 all stresses have been drawn as positive stresses.

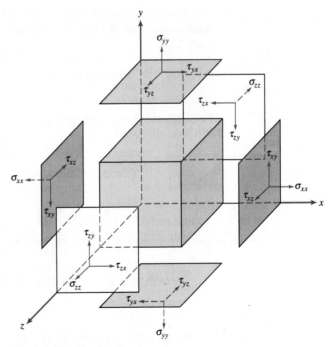

Fig. 2.8 Notation for stress.

Stress components are negative when the direction of the stress component and the plane on which it acts are of opposite sign.

| 2-4 | **VISCOSITY** |

Where do stresses come from? For a solid, stresses develop when the material is elastically deformed or strained; for a fluid, shear stresses arise due to viscous flow (we will discuss a fluid's normal stresses shortly). Hence we say solids are *elastic*, and fluids are *viscous* (and it's interesting to note that many biological tissues are *viscoelastic*, meaning they combine features of a solid and a fluid). For a fluid at rest, there will be no shear stresses. We will see that each fluid can be categorized by examining the relation between the applied shear stresses and the flow (specifically the rate of deformation) of the fluid.

Consider the behavior of a fluid element between the two infinite plates shown in Fig. 2.9*a*. The rectangular fluid element is initially at rest at time *t*. Let us now suppose a constant rightward force δF_x is applied to the upper plate so that it is dragged across the fluid at constant velocity δu. The relative shearing action of the infinite plates produces a shear stress, τ_{yx}, which acts on the fluid element and is given by

$$\tau_{yx} = \lim_{\delta A_y \to 0} \frac{\delta F_x}{\delta A_y} = \frac{dF_x}{dA_y}$$

where δA_y is the area of contact of the fluid element with the plate and δF_x is the force exerted by the plate on that element. Snapshots of the fluid element, shown in Figs. 2.9*a–c*, illustrate the deformation of the fluid element from position *MNOP* at time *t*, to *M'NOP'* at time $t + \delta t$, to *M"NOP"* at time $t + 2\delta t$, due to the imposed shear stress. As mentioned in Section 1-2, it is the fact that a fluid continually deforms in response to an applied shear stress that sets it apart from solids.

Focusing on the time interval δt (Fig. 2.9*b*), the deformation of the fluid is given by

$$deformation\ rate = \lim_{\delta t \to 0} \frac{\delta \alpha}{\delta t} = \frac{d\alpha}{dt}$$

We want to express $d\alpha/dt$ in terms of readily measurable quantities. This can be done easily. The distance, δl, between the points *M* and *M'* is given by

$$\delta l = \delta u\ \delta t$$

Alternatively, for small angles,

$$\delta l = \delta y\ \delta \alpha$$

Equating these two expressions for δl gives

$$\frac{\delta \alpha}{\delta t} = \frac{\delta u}{\delta y}$$

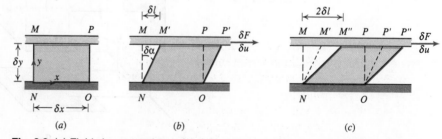

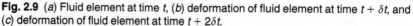

Fig. 2.9 (*a*) Fluid element at time *t*, (*b*) deformation of fluid element at time $t + \delta t$, and (*c*) deformation of fluid element at time $t + 2\delta t$.

Taking the limits of both sides of the equality, we obtain

$$\frac{d\alpha}{dt} = \frac{du}{dy}$$

Thus, the fluid element of Fig. 2.9, when subjected to shear stress, τ_{yx}, experiences a rate of deformation (*shear rate*) given by du/dy. We have established that any fluid that experiences a shear stress will flow (it will have a shear rate). What is the relation between shear stress and shear rate? Fluids in which shear stress is directly proportional to rate of deformation are *Newtonian fluids*. The term *non-Newtonian* is used to classify all fluids in which shear stress is not directly proportional to shear rate.

Newtonian Fluid

Most common fluids (the ones discussed in this text) such as water, air, and gasoline are Newtonian under normal conditions. If the fluid of Fig. 2.9 is Newtonian, then

$$\tau_{yx} \propto \frac{du}{dy} \tag{2.14}$$

We are familiar with the fact that some fluids resist motion more than others. For example, a container of SAE 30W oil is much harder to stir than one of water. Hence SAE 30W oil is much more viscous—it has a higher viscosity. (Note that a container of mercury is also harder to stir, but for a different reason!) The constant of proportionality in Eq. 2.14 is the *absolute* (or *dynamic*) viscosity, μ. Thus in terms of the coordinates of Fig. 2.9, Newton's law of viscosity is given for one-dimensional flow by

shear stress

$$\tau_{yx} = \mu \frac{du}{dy} \tag{2.15}$$

Note that, since the dimensions of τ are $[F/L^2]$ and the dimensions of du/dy are $[1/t]$, μ has dimensions $[Ft/L^2]$. Since the dimensions of force, F, mass, M, length, L, and time, t, are related by Newton's second law of motion, the dimensions of μ can also be expressed as $[M/Lt]$. In the British Gravitational system, the units of viscosity are lbf $\cdot$ s/ft^2 or slug/(ft $\cdot$ s). In the Absolute Metric system, the basic unit of viscosity is called a poise [1 poise $\equiv$ 1 g/(cm $\cdot$ s)]; in the SI system the units of viscosity are kg/(m $\cdot$ s) or Pa $\cdot$ s (1 Pa $\cdot$ s = 1 N $\cdot$ s/m^2). The calculation of viscous shear stress is illustrated in Example 2.2.

In fluid mechanics the ratio of absolute viscosity, μ, to density, ρ, often arises. This ratio is given the name *kinematic viscosity* and is represented by the symbol ν. Since density has dimensions $[M/L^3]$, the dimensions of ν are $[L^2/t]$. In the Absolute Metric system of units, the unit for ν is a stoke (1 stoke $\equiv$ 1 cm^2/s).

Viscosity data for a number of common Newtonian fluids are given in Appendix A. Note that for gases, viscosity increases with temperature, whereas for liquids, viscosity decreases with increasing temperature.

EXAMPLE 2.2 Viscosity and Shear Stress in Newtonian Fluid

An infinite plate is moved over a second plate on a layer of liquid as shown. For small gap width, d, we assume a linear velocity distribution in the liquid. The liquid viscosity is 0.65 centipoise and its specific gravity is 0.88. Determine:

(a) The absolute viscosity of the liquid, in lbf $\cdot$ s/ft^2.
(b) The kinematic viscosity of the liquid, in m^2/s.
(c) The shear stress on the upper plate, in lbf/ft^2.

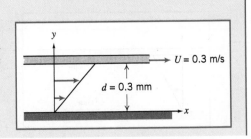

(d) The shear stress on the lower plate, in Pa.

(e) The direction of each shear stress calculated in parts (c) and (d).

GIVEN: Linear velocity profile in the liquid between infinite parallel plates as shown.

$$\mu = 0.65 \text{ cp}$$
$$SG = 0.88$$

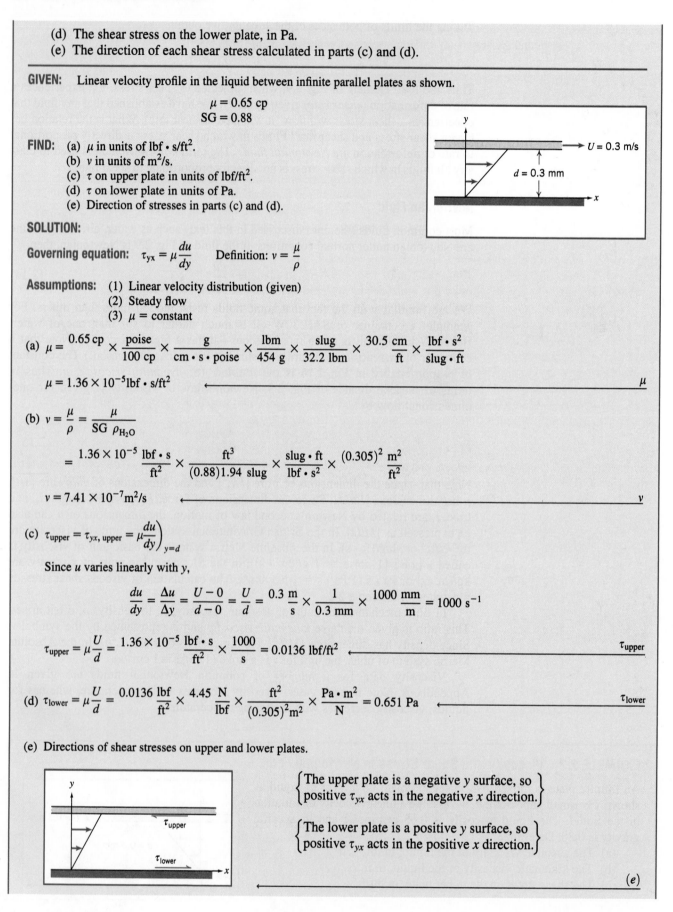

FIND:
(a) μ in units of $lbf \cdot s/ft^2$.
(b) v in units of m^2/s.
(c) τ on upper plate in units of lbf/ft^2.
(d) τ on lower plate in units of Pa.
(e) Direction of stresses in parts (c) and (d).

SOLUTION:

Governing equation: $\tau_{yx} = \mu \dfrac{du}{dy}$ **Definition:** $v = \dfrac{\mu}{\rho}$

Assumptions:
(1) Linear velocity distribution (given)
(2) Steady flow
(3) $\mu = $ constant

(a) $\mu = \dfrac{0.65\,cp}{} \times \dfrac{poise}{100\,cp} \times \dfrac{g}{cm \cdot s \cdot poise} \times \dfrac{lbm}{454\,g} \times \dfrac{slug}{32.2\,lbm} \times \dfrac{30.5\,cm}{ft} \times \dfrac{lbf \cdot s^2}{slug \cdot ft}$

$\mu = 1.36 \times 10^{-5} lbf \cdot s/ft^2$ $\longleftarrow$ _____ μ

(b) $v = \dfrac{\mu}{\rho} = \dfrac{\mu}{SG\,\rho_{H_2O}}$

$= \dfrac{1.36 \times 10^{-5}}{} \dfrac{lbf \cdot s}{ft^2} \times \dfrac{ft^3}{(0.88)1.94\,slug} \times \dfrac{slug \cdot ft}{lbf \cdot s^2} \times \dfrac{(0.305)^2\,m^2}{ft^2}$

$v = 7.41 \times 10^{-7} m^2/s$ $\longleftarrow$ _____ v

(c) $\tau_{upper} = \tau_{yx,\,upper} = \mu \dfrac{du}{dy} \biggr)_{y=d}$

Since u varies linearly with y,

$$\dfrac{du}{dy} = \dfrac{\Delta u}{\Delta y} = \dfrac{U-0}{d-0} = \dfrac{U}{d} = \dfrac{0.3\,m}{s} \times \dfrac{1}{0.3\,mm} \times \dfrac{1000\,mm}{m} = 1000\,s^{-1}$$

$\tau_{upper} = \mu \dfrac{U}{d} = 1.36 \times 10^{-5} \dfrac{lbf \cdot s}{ft^2} \times \dfrac{1000}{s} = 0.0136\,lbf/ft^2$ $\longleftarrow$ _____ τ_{upper}

(d) $\tau_{lower} = \mu \dfrac{U}{d} = 0.0136 \dfrac{lbf}{ft^2} \times 4.45 \dfrac{N}{lbf} \times \dfrac{ft^2}{(0.305)^2 m^2} \times \dfrac{Pa \cdot m^2}{N} = 0.651\,Pa$ $\longleftarrow$ ____ τ_{lower}

(e) Directions of shear stresses on upper and lower plates.

$\left\{\begin{array}{l}\text{The upper plate is a negative } y \text{ surface, so} \\ \text{positive } \tau_{yx} \text{ acts in the negative } x \text{ direction.}\end{array}\right\}$

$\left\{\begin{array}{l}\text{The lower plate is a positive } y \text{ surface, so} \\ \text{positive } \tau_{yx} \text{ acts in the positive } x \text{ direction.}\end{array}\right\}$

$\longleftarrow$ _____ (e)

Part (c) shows that the shear stress is:
- ✓ Constant across the gap for a linear velocity profile.
- ✓ Directly proportional to the speed of the upper plate (because of the linearity of Newtonian fluids).
- ✓ Inversely proportional to the gap between the plates.

Note that multiplying the shear stress by the plate area in such problems computes the force required to maintain the motion.

Non-Newtonian Fluids

Fluids in which shear stress is *not* directly proportional to deformation rate are non-Newtonian. Although we will not discuss these much in this text, many common fluids exhibit non-Newtonian behavior. Two familiar examples are toothpaste and Lucite[6] paint. The latter is very "thick" when in the can, but becomes "thin" when sheared by brushing. Toothpaste behaves as a "fluid" when squeezed from the tube. However, it does not run out by itself when the cap is removed. There is a threshold or yield stress below which toothpaste behaves as a solid. Strictly speaking, our definition of a fluid is valid only for materials that have zero yield stress. Non-Newtonian fluids commonly are classified as having time-independent or time-dependent behavior. Examples of time-independent behavior are shown in the rheological diagram of Fig. 2.10.

Numerous empirical equations have been proposed [3, 4] to model the observed relations between τ_{yx} and du/dy for time-independent fluids. They may be adequately represented for many engineering applications by the power law model, which for one-dimensional flow becomes

$$\tau_{yx} = k\left(\frac{du}{dy}\right)^n \tag{2.16}$$

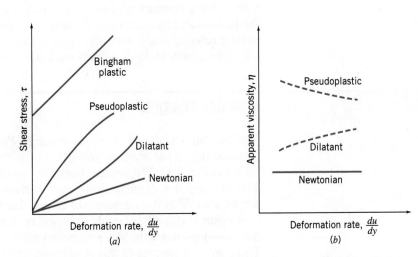

Fig. 2.10 (a) Shear stress, τ, and (b) apparent viscosity, η, as a function of deformation rate for one-dimensional flow of various non-Newtonian fluids.

---

[6] Trademark, E. I. du Pont de Nemours & Company.

where the exponent, n, is called the flow behavior index and the coefficient, k, the consistency index. This equation reduces to Newton's law of viscosity for $n = 1$ with $k = \mu$.

To ensure that τ_{yx} has the same sign as du/dy, Eq. 2.16 is rewritten in the form

$$\tau_{yx} = k \left| \frac{du}{dy} \right|^{n-1} \frac{du}{dy} = \eta \frac{du}{dy} \qquad (2.17)$$

The term $\eta = k|du/dy|^{n-1}$ is referred to as the *apparent viscosity*. The idea behind Eq. 2.17 is that we end up with a viscosity η that is used in a formula that is the same form as Eq. 2.15, in which the Newtonian viscosity μ is used. The big difference is that while μ is constant (except for temperature effects), η depends on the shear rate. Most non-Newtonian fluids have apparent viscosities that are relatively high compared with the viscosity of water.

Fluids in which the apparent viscosity decreases with increasing deformation rate ($n < 1$) are called *pseudoplastic* (or shear thinning) fluids. Most non-Newtonian fluids fall into this group; examples include polymer solutions, colloidal suspensions, and paper pulp in water. If the apparent viscosity increases with increasing deformation rate ($n > 1$) the fluid is termed *dilatant* (or shear thickening). Suspensions of starch and of sand are examples of dilatant fluids. You can get an idea of the latter when you're on the beach—if you walk slowly (and hence generate a low shear rate) on very wet sand, you sink into it, but if you jog on it (generating a high shear rate), it's very firm.

A "fluid" that behaves as a solid until a minimum yield stress, τ_y, is exceeded and subsequently exhibits a linear relation between stress and rate of deformation is referred to as an ideal or *Bingham plastic*. The corresponding shear stress model is

$$\tau_{yx} = \tau_y + \mu_p \frac{du}{dy} \qquad (2.18)$$

Clay suspensions, drilling muds, and toothpaste are examples of substances exhibiting this behavior.

The study of non-Newtonian fluids is further complicated by the fact that the apparent viscosity may be time-dependent. *Thixotropic* fluids show a decrease in η with time under a constant applied shear stress; many paints are thixotropic. *Rheopectic* fluids show an increase in η with time. After deformation some fluids partially return to their original shape when the applied stress is released; such fluids are called *viscoelastic*[7] (many biological fluids work this way).

2-5   ## SURFACE TENSION

You can tell when your car needs waxing: Water droplets tend to appear somewhat flattened out. After waxing, you get a nice "beading" effect. These two cases are shown in Fig. 2.11. We define a liquid as "wetting" a surface when the *contact angle* $\theta < 90°$. By this definition, the car's surface was wetted before waxing, and not wetted after. This is an example of effects due to *surface tension*. Whenever a liquid is in contact with other liquids or gases, or in this case a gas/solid surface, an interface develops that acts like a stretched elastic membrane, creating surface tension. There are two features to this membrane: the contact angle θ, and the magnitude of

---

[7] Examples of time-dependent and viscoelastic fluids are illustrated in the NCFMF video *Rheological Behavior of Fluids*. (See http://web.mit.edu/fluids/www/Shapiro/ncfmf.html for free online viewing of this film.)

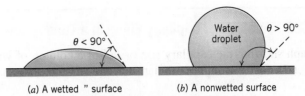

Fig. 2.11 Surface tension effects on water droplets.

the surface tension, σ (N/m or lbf/ft). Both of these depend on the type of liquid and the type of solid surface (or other liquid or gas) with which it shares an interface. In the car-waxing example, the contact angle changed from being smaller than 90°, to larger than 90°, because, in effect, the waxing changed the nature of the solid surface. Factors that affect the contact angle include the cleanliness of the surface and the purity of the liquid.

Other examples of surface tension effects arise when you are able to place a needle on a water surface and, similarly, when small water insects are able to walk on the surface of the water.[8]

Appendix A contains data for surface tension and contact angle for common liquids in the presence of air and of water.

A force balance on a segment of interface shows that there is a pressure jump across the imagined elastic membrane whenever the interface is curved. For a water droplet in air, pressure in the water is higher than ambient; the same is true for a gas bubble in liquid. For a soap bubble in air, surface tension acts on both inside and outside interfaces between the soap film and air along the curved bubble surface. Surface tension also leads to the phenomena of capillary (i.e., very small wavelength) waves on a liquid surface [5] and capillary rise or depression, discussed below.

In engineering, probably the most important effect of surface tension is the creation of a curved *meniscus* that appears in manometers or barometers, leading to a (usually unwanted) *capillary rise* (or depression), as shown in Fig. 2.12. This rise may be pronounced if the liquid is in a small-diameter tube or narrow gap, as shown in Example 2.3.

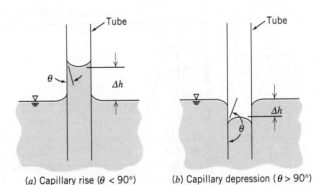

Fig. 2.12 Capillary rise and capillary depression inside and outside a circular tube.

---

[8] These and other example phenomena are illustrated in the NCFMF video *Surface Tension in Fluid Mechanics*. (See http://web.mit.edu/fluids/www/Shapiro/ncfmf.html for free online viewing of this film.)

EXAMPLE 2.3   Analysis of Capillary Effect in a Tube

Create a graph showing the capillary rise or fall of a column of water or mercury, respectively, as a function of tube diameter D. Find the minimum diameter of each column required so that the height magnitude will be less than 1 mm.

GIVEN: Tube dipped in liquid as in Fig. 2.12.

FIND: A general expression for Δh as a function of D.

SOLUTION:
Apply free-body diagram analysis, and sum vertical forces.

Governing equation:

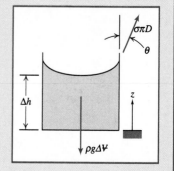

$$\sum F_z = 0$$

Assumptions: (1) Measure to middle of meniscus
(2) Neglect volume in meniscus region

Summing forces in the z direction:

$$\sum F_z = \sigma \pi D \cos \theta - \rho g \Delta \mathcal{V} = 0 \qquad (1)$$

If we neglect the volume in the meniscus region:

$$\Delta \mathcal{V} \approx \frac{\pi D^2}{4} \Delta h$$

Substituting in Eq. (1) and solving for Δh gives

$$\Delta h = \frac{4\sigma \cos \theta}{\rho g D} \qquad\qquad\qquad \Delta h$$

For water, $\sigma = 72.8$ mN/m and $\theta \approx 0°$, and for mercury $\sigma = 484$ mN/m and $\theta = 140°$ (Table A.4). Plotting,

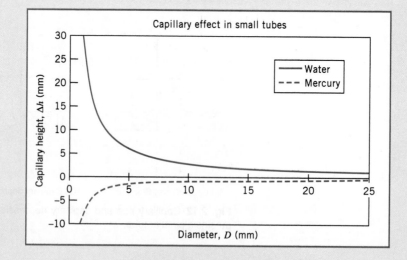

Using the above equation to compute $D_{\min}$ for $\Delta h = 1$ mm, we find for mercury and water

$$D_{M_{\min}} = 11.2 \text{ mm} \quad \text{and} \quad D_{W_{\min}} = 30 \text{ mm}$$

Notes:
  ✓ This problem reviewed use of the free-body diagram approach.
  ✓ It turns out that neglecting the volume in the meniscus region is only valid when Δh is large compared with D. However, in this problem we have the result that Δh is about 1 mm when D is 11.2 mm (or 30 mm); hence the results can only be very approximate.
  The graph and results were generated from the *Excel* workbook.

Folsom [6] shows that the simple analysis of Example 2.3 overpredicts the capillary effect and gives reasonable results only for tube diameters less than 0.1 in. (2.54 mm). Over a diameter range $0.1 < D < 1.1$ in., experimental data for the capillary rise with a water-air interface are correlated by the empirical expression $\Delta h = 0.400/e^{4.37D}$.

Manometer and barometer readings should be made at the level of the middle of the meniscus. This is away from the maximum effects of surface tension and thus nearest to the proper liquid level.

All surface tension data in Appendix A were measured for pure liquids in contact with clean vertical surfaces. Impurities in the liquid, dirt on the surface, or surface inclination can cause an indistinct meniscus; under such conditions it may be difficult to determine liquid level accurately. Liquid level is most distinct in a vertical tube. When inclined tubes are used to increase manometer sensitivity (see Section 3-3) it is important to make each reading at the same point on the meniscus and to avoid use of tubes inclined less than about 15° from horizontal.

Surfactant compounds reduce surface tension significantly (more than 40% with little change in other properties [7]) when added to water. They have wide commercial application: Most detergents contain surfactants to help water penetrate and lift soil from surfaces. Surfactants also have major industrial applications in catalysis, aerosols, and oil field recovery.

2-6 DESCRIPTION AND CLASSIFICATION OF FLUID MOTIONS

In Chapter 1 and in this chapter, we have almost completed our brief introduction to some concepts and ideas that are often needed when studying fluid mechanics. Before beginning detailed analysis of fluid mechanics in the rest of this text, we will describe some interesting examples to illustrate a broad classification of fluid mechanics on the basis of important flow characteristics. Fluid mechanics is a huge discipline: It covers everything from the aerodynamics of a supersonic transport vehicle, to the lubrication of human joints by sinovial fluid. We need to break fluid mechanics down into manageable proportions. It turns out that the two most difficult aspects of a fluid mechanics analysis to deal with are: (1) the fluid's viscous nature and (2) its compressibility. In fact, the area of fluid mechanics theory that first became highly developed (about 250 years ago!) was that dealing with a frictionless, incompressible fluid. As we will see shortly (and in more detail later on), this theory, while extremely elegant, led to the famous result called d'Alembert's paradox: All bodies experience no drag as they move through such a fluid—a result not exactly consistent with any real behavior!

Although not the only way to do so, most engineers subdivide fluid mechanics in terms of whether or not viscous effects and compressibility effects are present, as shown in Fig. 2.13. Also shown are classifications in terms of whether a flow is laminar or turbulent, and internal or external. We will now discuss each of these.

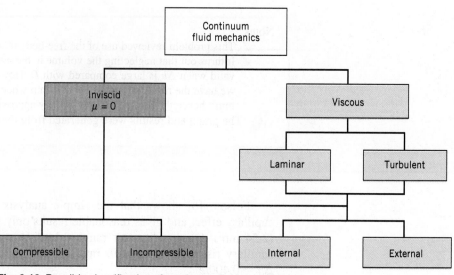

Fig. 2.13 Possible classification of continuum fluid mechanics.

Viscous and Inviscid Flows

When you send a ball flying through the air (as in a game of baseball, soccer, or any number of other sports), in addition to gravity the ball experiences the aerodynamic drag of the air. The question arises: What is the nature of the drag force of the air on the ball? At first glance, we might conclude that it's due to friction of the air as it flows over the ball; a little more reflection might lead to the conclusion that because air has such a low viscosity, friction might not contribute much to the drag, and the drag might be due to the pressure build-up in front of the ball as it pushes the air out of the way. The question arises: Can we predict ahead of time the relative importance of the viscous force, and force due to the pressure build-up in front of the ball? Can we make similar predictions for *any* object, for example, an automobile, a submarine, a red blood cell, moving through *any* fluid, for example, air, water, blood plasma? The answer (which we'll discuss in much more detail in Chapter 7) is that we can! It turns out that we can estimate whether or not viscous forces, as opposed to pressure forces, are negligible by simply computing the Reynolds number

$$Re = \rho \frac{VL}{\mu}$$

where ρ and μ are the fluid density and viscosity, respectively, and V and L are the typical or "characteristic" velocity and size scale of the flow (in this example the ball velocity and diameter), respectively. If the Reynolds number is "large," viscous effects will be negligible (but will still have important consequences, as we'll soon see), at least in most of the flow; if the Reynolds number is small, viscous effects will be dominant. Finally, if the Reynolds number is neither large nor small, no general conclusions can be drawn.

To illustrate this very powerful idea, consider two simple examples. First, the drag on your ball: Suppose you kick a soccer ball (diameter = 8.75 in.) so it moves at 60 mph. The Reynolds number (using air properties from Table A.10) for this case is about 400,000—by any measure a large number; hence the drag on the soccer ball is almost entirely due to the pressure build-up in front of it. For our second example, consider a dust particle (modeled as a sphere of diameter 1 mm) falling under gravity at a terminal velocity of 1 cm/s: In this case $Re \approx 0.7$—a quite small number; hence the drag is mostly due to the friction of the air. Of course, in both of these examples, if we wish to *determine* the drag force, we would have to do substantially more analysis.

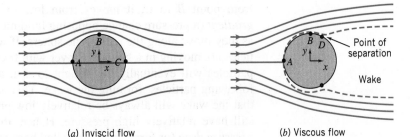

(a) Inviscid flow   *(b)* Viscous flow

Fig. 2.14 Qualitative picture of incompressible flow over a sphere.

These examples illustrate an important point: A flow is considered to be friction dominated (or not) based not just on the fluid's viscosity, but on the complete flow system. In these examples, the airflow was low friction for the soccer ball, but was high friction for the dust particle.

Let's return for a moment to the idealized notion of frictionless flow, called *inviscid flow*. This is the branch shown on the left in Fig. 2.13. This branch encompasses most aerodynamics, and among other things explains, for example, why sub- and supersonic aircraft have differing shapes, how a wing generates lift, and so forth. If this theory is applied to the ball flying through the air (a flow that is also incompressible), it predicts streamlines (in coordinates attached to the sphere) as shown in Fig. 2.14*a*.

The streamlines are symmetric front-to-back. Because the mass flow between any two streamlines is constant, wherever streamlines open up, the velocity must decrease, and vice versa. Hence we can see that the velocity in the vicinity of points *A* and *C* must be relatively low; at point *B* it will be high. In fact, the air comes to rest at points *A* and *C*: they are *stagnation points*. It turns out that (as we'll learn in Chapter 6) the pressure in this flow is high wherever the velocity is low, and vice versa. Hence, points *A* and *C* have relatively large (and equal) pressures; point *B* will be a point of low pressure. In fact, the pressure distribution on the sphere is symmetric front-to-back, and there is no net drag force due to pressure. Because we're assuming inviscid flow, there can be no drag due to friction either. Hence we have d'Alembert's paradox of 1752: The ball experiences no drag!

This is obviously unrealistic. On the other hand, everything seems logically consistent: We established that *Re* for the sphere was very large (400,000), indicating friction is negligible. We then used inviscid flow theory to obtain our no-drag result. How can we reconcile this theory with reality? It took about 150 years after the paradox first appeared for the answer, obtained by Prandtl in 1904: The no-slip condition (Section 1.2) requires that the velocity everywhere on the surface of the sphere be zero (in sphere coordinates), but inviscid theory states that it's high at point *B*. Prandtl suggested that even though friction is negligible in general for high-Reynolds number flows, there will always be a thin *boundary layer*,[9] in which friction is significant and across the width of which the velocity increases rapidly from zero (at the surface) to the value inviscid flow theory predicts (on the outer edge of the boundary layer). This is shown in Fig. 2.14*b* from point *A* to point *B*, and in more detail in Fig. 2.15.

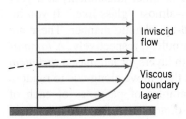

Fig. 2.15 Schematic of a boundary layer.

This boundary layer immediately allows us to reconcile theory and experiment: Once we have friction in a boundary layer we will have drag. However, this boundary layer has another important consequence: It often leads to bodies having a *wake*, as shown in Fig. 2.14*b* from point *D* onwards. Point *D* is a *separation point*, where fluid particles are pushed off the object and cause a wake to develop.[10] Consider once again the original inviscid flow (Fig. 2.14*a*): As a particle moves along the surface

[9] The formation of a boundary layer is illustrated in the NCFMF video *Fundamentals of Boundary Layers*. (See http://web.mit.edu/fluids/www/Shapiro/ncfmf.html for free online viewing of this film.)

[10] The flow over a variety of models, illustrating flow separation, is demonstrated in the University of Iowa video *Form Drag, Lift, and Propulsion*.

from point *B* to *C*, it moves from low to high pressure. This *adverse pressure gradient* (a pressure change opposing fluid motion) causes the particles to slow down as they move along the rear of the sphere. If we now add to this the fact that the particles are moving in a boundary layer with friction that also slows down the fluid, the particles will eventually be brought to rest, and then pushed off the sphere by the following particles, forming the wake. This is generally very bad news: It turns out that the wake will always be relatively low pressure, but the front of the sphere will still have relatively high pressure. Hence, the sphere will now have a quite large *pressure drag* (or *form drag*—so called because it's due to the shape of the object).

This description reconciles the inviscid flow no-drag result with the experimental result of significant drag on a sphere. It's interesting to note that although the boundary layer is necessary to explain the drag on the sphere, the drag is actually due mostly to the asymmetric pressure distribution created by the boundary layer separation—drag directly due to friction is still negligible!

We can also now begin to see how *streamlining* of a body works. The drag force in most aerodynamics is due to the low-pressure wake: If we can reduce or eliminate the wake, drag will be greatly reduced. If we consider once again why the separation occurred, we recall two features: Boundary layer friction slowed down the particles, but so did the adverse pressure gradient. The pressure increased very rapidly across the back half of the sphere in Fig. 2.14*a* because the streamlines opened up so rapidly. If we make the sphere teardrop shaped, as in Fig. 2.16, the streamlines open up gradually, and hence the pressure gradient will increase slowly, to such an extent that fluid particles are not forced to separate from the object until they almost reach the end of the object, as shown. The wake is much smaller (and it turns out the pressure will not be as low as before), leading to much less pressure drag. The only negative aspect of this streamlining is that the total surface area on which friction occurs is larger, so drag due to friction will increase a little.[11]

We should point out that none of this discussion applies to the example of a falling dust particle: This low-Reynolds number flow was viscous throughout—there is no inviscid region.

Finally, this discussion illustrates the very significant difference between inviscid flow ($\mu = 0$), and flows in which viscosity is negligible but not zero ($\mu \to 0$).

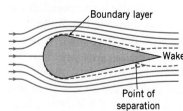

Boundary layer

Wake

Point of separation

Fig. 2.16 Flow over a streamlined object.

Laminar and Turbulent Flows

If you turn on a faucet (that doesn't have an aerator or other attachment) at a very low flow rate the water will flow out very smoothly—almost "glass-like." If you increase the flow rate, the water will exit in a churned-up, chaotic manner. These are examples of how a viscous flow can be laminar or turbulent, respectively. A *laminar* flow is one in which the fluid particles move in smooth layers, or laminas; a *turbulent* flow is one in which the fluid particles rapidly mix as they move along due to random three-dimensional velocity fluctuations. Typical examples of pathlines of each of these are illustrated in Fig. 2.17, which shows a one-dimensional flow. In most fluid

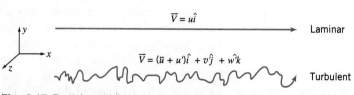

Fig. 2.17 Particle pathlines in one-dimensional laminar and turbulent flows.

[11] The effect of streamlining a body is demonstrated in the NCFMF video *Fluid Dynamics of Drag.* (See http://web.mit.edu/fluids/www/Shapiro/ncfmf.html for free online viewing of this film.)

mechanics problems—for example, flow of water in a pipe—turbulence is an unwanted but often unavoidable phenomenon, because it generates more resistance to flow; in other problems—for example, the flow of blood through blood vessels—it is desirable because the random mixing allows all of the blood cells to contact the walls of the blood vessels to exchange oxygen and other nutrients.[12]

The velocity of the laminar flow is simply u; the velocity of the turbulent flow is given by the mean velocity $\bar{u}$ plus the three components of randomly fluctuating velocity u', v', and w'.

Although many turbulent flows of interest are steady in the mean ($\bar{u}$ is not a function of time), the presence of the random, high-frequency velocity fluctuations makes the analysis of turbulent flows extremely difficult. In a one-dimensional laminar flow, the shear stress is related to the velocity gradient by the simple relation

$$\tau_{yx} = \mu \frac{du}{dy} \tag{2.15}$$

For a turbulent flow in which the mean velocity field is one-dimensional, no such simple relation is valid. Random, three-dimensional velocity fluctuations (u', v', and w') transport momentum across the mean flow streamlines, increasing the effective shear stress. (This apparent stress is discussed in more detail in Chapter 8.) Consequently, in turbulent flow there is no universal relationship between the stress field and the mean-velocity field. Thus in turbulent flows we must rely heavily on semi-empirical theories and on experimental data.

Compressible and Incompressible Flows

Flows in which variations in density are negligible are termed *incompressible*; when density variations within a flow are not negligible, the flow is called *compressible*. The most common example of compressible flow concerns the flow of gases, while the flow of liquids may frequently be treated as incompressible.

For many liquids, density is only a weak function of temperature. At modest pressures, liquids may be considered incompressible. However, at high pressures, compressibility effects in liquids can be important. Pressure and density changes in liquids are related by the *bulk compressibility modulus*, or modulus of elasticity,

$$E_v \equiv \frac{dp}{(d\rho/\rho)} \tag{2.19}$$

If the bulk modulus is independent of temperature, then density is only a function of pressure (the fluid is *barotropic*). Bulk modulus data for some common liquids are given in Appendix A.

Water hammer and cavitation[13] are examples of the importance of compressibility effects in liquid flows. *Water hammer* is caused by acoustic waves propagating and reflecting in a confined liquid, for example when a valve is closed abruptly. The resulting noise can be similar to "hammering" on the pipes, hence the term.

Cavitation occurs when vapor pockets form in a liquid flow because of local reductions in pressure (for example at the tip of a boat's propeller blades). Depending on the number and distribution of particles in the liquid to which very small pockets of undissolved gas or air may attach, the local pressure at the onset of cavitation may be at or below the vapor pressure of the liquid. These particles act as nucleation sites to initiate vaporization.

---

[12] Several examples illustrating the nature of laminar and turbulent flows are shown in the NCFMF video *Turbulence* (see http://web.mit.edu/fluids/www/Shapiro/ncfmf.html for free online viewing of this film) and in the University of Iowa video *Characteristics of Laminar and Turbulent Flow*.

[13] Examples of cavitation are illustrated in the NCFMF video *Cavitation*. (See http://web.mit.edu/fluids/www/Shapiro/ncfmf.html for free online viewing of this film.)

Vapor pressure of a liquid is the partial pressure of the vapor in contact with the saturated liquid at a given temperature. When pressure in a liquid is reduced to less than the vapor pressure, the liquid may change phase suddenly and "flash" to vapor.

The vapor pockets in a liquid flow may alter the geometry of the flow field substantially. When adjacent to a surface, the growth and collapse of vapor bubbles can cause serious damage by eroding the surface material.

Very pure liquids can sustain large negative pressures—as much as −60 atmospheres for distilled water—before the liquid "ruptures" and vaporization occurs. Undissolved air is invariably present near the free surface of water or seawater, so cavitation occurs where the local total pressure is quite close to the vapor pressure.

It turns out that gas flows with negligible heat transfer also may be considered incompressible provided that the flow speeds are small relative to the speed of sound; the ratio of the flow speed, V, to the local speed of sound, c, in the gas is defined as the Mach number,

$$M \equiv \frac{V}{c}$$

For $M < 0.3$, the maximum density variation is less than 5 percent. Thus gas flows with $M < 0.3$ can be treated as incompressible; a value of $M = 0.3$ in air at standard conditions corresponds to a speed of approximately 100 m/s. For example, although it might be a little counterintuitive, when you drive your car at 65 mph the air flowing around it has negligible change in density. As we shall see in Chapter 12, the speed of sound in an ideal gas is given by $c = \sqrt{kRT}$, where k is the ratio of specific heats, R is the gas constant, and T is the absolute temperature. For air at STP, $k = 1.40$ and $R = 286.9$ J/kg · K (53.33 ft · lbf/lbm · °R). Values of k and R are supplied in Appendix A for several selected common gases at STP. In addition, Appendix A contains some useful data on atmospheric properties, such as temperature, at various elevations.

Compressible flows occur frequently in engineering applications. Common examples include compressed air systems used to power shop tools and dental drills, transmission of gases in pipelines at high pressure, and pneumatic or fluidic control and sensing systems. Compressibility effects are very important in the design of modern high-speed aircraft and missiles, power plants, fans, and compressors.

Internal and External Flows

Flows completely bounded by solid surfaces are called *internal* or *duct flows*. Flows over bodies immersed in an unbounded fluid are termed *external flows*. Both internal and external flows may be laminar or turbulent, compressible or incompressible.

We mentioned an example of internal flow when we discussed the flow out of a faucet—the flow in the pipe leading to the faucet is an internal flow. It turns out that we have a Reynolds number for pipe flows defined as $Re = \rho \overline{V} D / \mu$, where $\overline{V}$ is the average flow velocity and D is the pipe diameter (note that we do *not* use the pipe length!). This Reynolds number indicates whether a pipe flow will be laminar or turbulent. Flow will generally be laminar for $Re \le 2300$, and turbulent for larger values: Flow in a pipe of constant diameter will be entirely laminar or entirely turbulent, depending on the value of the velocity $\overline{V}$. We will explore internal flows in detail in Chapter 8.

We already saw some examples of external flows when we discussed the flow over a sphere (Fig. 2.14*b*) and a streamlined object (Fig. 2.16). What we didn't mention was that these flows could be laminar or turbulent. In addition, we mentioned boundary layers (Fig. 2.15): It turns out these also can be laminar or turbulent. When we discuss these in detail (Chapter 9), we'll start with the simplest kind of boundary layer—that over a flat plate—and learn that just as we have a Reynolds number for the overall external flow that indicates the relative significance of viscous forces, there will also be a boundary-layer Reynolds number $Re_x = \rho U_\infty x / \mu$ where in this case the characteristic velocity U_∞ is the velocity immediately outside the boundary layer and the characteristic length x is the distance along the plate. Hence, at the leading edge of the plate $Re_x = 0$, and at the end of a plate of length L, it will be $Re_x = \rho U_\infty L/\mu$. The significance of this Reynolds number is that (as we'll learn) the boundary layer will be laminar for $Re_x \leq 5 \times 10^5$, and turbulent for larger values: A boundary layer will start out laminar, and if the plate is long enough the boundary layer will transition to become turbulent.

It is clear by now that computing a Reynolds number is often very informative for both internal and external flows. We will discuss this and other important *dimensionless groups* (such as the Mach number) in Chapter 7.

The internal flow through fluid machines is considered in Chapter 10. The principle of angular momentum is applied to develop fundamental equations for fluid machines. Pumps, fans, blowers, compressors, and propellers that add energy to fluid streams are considered, as are turbines and windmills that extract energy. The chapter features detailed discussion of operation of fluid systems.

The internal flow of liquids in which the duct does not flow full—where there is a free surface subject to a constant pressure—is termed *open-channel* flow. Common examples of open-channel flow include flow in rivers, irrigation ditches, and aqueducts. Open-channel flow will be treated in Chapter 11. Material in this chapter has been adapted with permission from Chapter 5 of *Water Resources Engineering* by Mays [8].

Both internal and external flows can be compressible or incompressible. Compressible flows can be divided into subsonic and supersonic regimes. We will study compressible flows in Chapters 12 and 13, and see among other things that *supersonic flows* ($M > 1$) will behave very differently than *subsonic flows* ($M < 1$). For example, supersonic flows can experience oblique and normal shocks, and can also behave in a counterintuitive way—e.g., a supersonic nozzle (a device to accelerate a flow) must be divergent (i.e., it has *increasing* cross-sectional area) in the direction of flow! We note here also that in a subsonic nozzle (which has a convergent cross-sectional area), the pressure of the flow at the exit plane will always be the ambient pressure; for a sonic flow, the exit pressure can be higher than ambient; and for a supersonic flow the exit pressure can be greater than, equal to, or less than the ambient pressure!

2-7 ## SUMMARY AND USEFUL EQUATIONS

In this chapter we have completed our review of some of the fundamental concepts we will utilize in our study of fluid mechanics. Some of these are:

- ✓ How to describe flows (timelines, pathlines, streamlines, streaklines).
- ✓ Forces (surface, body) and stresses (shear, normal).
- ✓ Types of fluids (Newtonian, non-Newtonian—dilatant, pseudoplastic, thixotropic, rheopectic, Bingham plastic) and viscosity (kinematic, dynamic, apparent).
- ✓ Types of flow (viscous/inviscid, laminar/turbulent, compressible/incompressible, internal/external).

We also briefly discussed some interesting phenomena, such as surface tension, boundary layers, wakes, and streamlining. Finally, we introduced two very useful dimensionless groups—the Reynolds number and the Mach number.

Note: Most of the Useful Equations in the table below have a number of constraints or limitations—*be sure to refer to their page numbers for details!*

Useful Equations			
Definition of specific gravity:	$SG = \dfrac{\rho}{\rho_{H_2O}}$	(2.3)	Page 21
Definition of specific weight:	$\gamma = \dfrac{mg}{\forall} \rightarrow \gamma = \rho g$	(2.4)	Page 22
Definition of streamlines (2D):	$\dfrac{dy}{dx}\bigg)_{\text{streamline}} = \dfrac{v(x,y)}{u(x,y)}$	(2.8)	Page 25
Definition of pathlines (2D):	$\dfrac{dx}{dt}\bigg)_{\text{particle}} = u(x,y,t) \qquad \dfrac{dy}{dt}\bigg)_{\text{particle}} = v(x,y,t)$	(2.9)	Page 25
Definition of streaklines (2D):	$x_{\text{streakline}}(t_0) = x(t, x_0, y_0, t_0) \quad y_{\text{streakline}}(t_0) = y(t, x_0, y_0, t_0)$	(2.10)	Page 25
Newton's law of viscosity (1D flow):	$\tau_{yx} = \mu \dfrac{du}{dy}$	(2.15)	Page 31
Shear stress for a non-Newtonian fluid (1D flow):	$\tau_{yx} = k \left\| \dfrac{du}{dy} \right\|^{n-1} \dfrac{du}{dy} = \eta \dfrac{du}{dy}$	(2.17)	Page 34

REFERENCES

1. Vincenti, W. G., and C. H. Kruger, Jr., *Introduction to Physical Gas Dynamics*. New York: Wiley, 1965.

2. Merzkirch, W., *Flow Visualization*, 2nd ed. New York: Academic Press, 1987.

3. Tanner, R. I., *Engineering Rheology*. Oxford: Clarendon Press, 1985.

4. Macosko, C. W., *Rheology: Principles, Measurements, and Applications*. New York: VCH Publishers, 1994.

5. Loh, W. H. T., "Theory of the Hydraulic Analogy for Steady and Unsteady Gas Dynamics," in *Modern Developments in Gas Dynamics*, W. H. T. Loh, ed. New York: Plenum, 1969.

6. Folsom, R. G., "Manometer Errors due to Capillarity," *Instruments*, 9, 1, 1937, pp. 36–37.

7. Waugh, J. G., and G. W. Stubstad, *Hydroballistics Modeling*. San Diego: Naval Undersea Center, ca. 1972.

8. Mays, L. M., *Water Resources Engineering*, 2005 Edition, New York: Wiley, 2005.

PROBLEMS

2.1 For the velocity fields given below, determine:
  a. whether the flow field is one-, two-, or three-dimensional, and why.
  b. whether the flow is steady or unsteady, and why.
  c. (The quantities a and b are constants.)
      (1) $\vec{V} = [ay^2 e^{-bt}]\hat{i}$ (2) $\vec{V} = ax^2\hat{i} + bx\hat{j} + c\hat{k}$
      (3) $\vec{V} = axy\hat{i} - byt\hat{j}$ (4) $\vec{V} = ax\hat{i} - by\hat{j} + ct\hat{k}$
      (5) $\vec{V} = [ae^{-bx}]\hat{i} + bt^2\hat{j}$ (6) $\vec{V} = a(x^2 + y^2)^{1/2}(1/z^3)\hat{k}$
      (7) $\vec{V} = (ax + t)\hat{i} - by^2\hat{j}$ (8) $\vec{V} = ax^2\hat{i} + bxz\hat{j} + cy\hat{k}$

2.2 A viscous liquid is sheared between two parallel disks; the upper disk rotates and the lower one is fixed. The velocity field between the disks is given by $\vec{V} = \hat{e}_\theta r\omega z/h$. (The origin of coordinates is located at the center of the lower disk; the upper disk is located at $z = h$.) What are the dimensions of this velocity field? Does this velocity field satisfy appropriate physical boundary conditions? What are they?

2.3 For the velocity field $\vec{V} = Ax^2\hat{j} + Bxy\hat{j}$, where $A = 1$ $m^{-1}s^{-1}$, $B = -\frac{1}{2}$ $m^{-1}s^{-1}$, and the coordinates are measured in meters, obtain an equation for the flow streamlines. Plot several streamlines for positive y.

2.4 The velocity field $\vec{V} = ax\hat{i} - by\hat{j}$, where $a = b = 1$ s^{-1}, can be interpreted to represent flow in a corner. Find an equation for the flow streamlines. Plot several streamlines in the first quadrant, including the one that passes through the point $(x, y) = (0, 0)$.

2.5 A velocity field is given by $\vec{V} = ax\hat{i} - bty\hat{j}$, where $a = 1$ s^{-1} and $b = 1$ s^{-2}. Find the equation of the streamlines at any time t. Plot several streamlines in the first quadrant at $t = 0$ s, $t = 1$ s, and $t = 20$ s.

2.6 A velocity field is specified as $\vec{V} = axy\hat{i} + by^2\hat{j}$, where $a = 2$ m^{-1}s^{-1}, $b = -6$ m^{-1}s^{-1}, and the coordinates are measured in meters. Is the flow field one-, two-, or three-dimensional? Why? Calculate the velocity components at the point $(2, \frac{1}{2})$. Develop an equation for the streamline passing through this point. Plot several streamlines in the first quadrant including the one that passes through the point $(2, \frac{1}{2})$.

2.7 A velocity field is given by $\vec{V} = ax^3\hat{i} + bxy^3\hat{j}$, where $a = 1$ m^{-2} s^{-1} and $b = 1$ m^{-3} s^{-1}. Find the equation of the streamlines. Plot several streamlines in the first quadrant.

2.8 A flow is described by the velocity field $\vec{V} = (Ax + B)\hat{i} + (-Ay)\hat{j}$, where $A = 10$ ft/s/ft and $B = 20$ ft/ s. Plot a few streamlines in the xy plane, including the one that passes through the point $(x, y) = (1, 2)$.

2.9 The velocity for a steady, incompressible flow in the xy plane is given by $\vec{V} = \hat{i}A/x + \hat{j}Ay/x^2$, where $A = 2$ m^2/s, and the coordinates are measured in meters. Obtain an equation for the streamline that passes through the point $(x, y) = (1, 3)$. Calculate the time required for a fluid particle to move from $x = 1$ m to $x = 2$ m in this flow field.

2.10 The flow field for an atmospheric flow is given by

$$\vec{V} = -\frac{Ky}{2\pi(x^2 + y^2)}\hat{i} + \frac{Kx}{2\pi(x^2 + y^2)}\hat{j}$$

where $K = 5 \times 10^4$ m^2/s and the x and y coordinates are parallel to the local latitude and longitude. Plot the velocity magnitude along the x axis, along the y axis, and along the line $y = x$. For each plot use the range -10 km $\leq x$ or $y \leq 10$ km, excluding $|x|$ or $|y| \leq 100$ m. Find the equation for the streamlines and sketch several of them. What does this flow field model?

2.11 The flow field for an atmospheric flow is given by

$$\vec{V} = -\frac{My}{2\pi}\hat{i} + \frac{Mx}{2\pi}\hat{j}$$

where $M = 0.5$ s^{-1} and the x and y coordinates are parallel to the local latitude and longitude. Plot the velocity magnitude along the x axis, along the y axis, and along the line $y = x$. For each plot use the range -10 km $\leq x$ or $y \leq 10$ km, excluding $|x|$ or $|y| \leq 100$ m. Find the equation for the streamlines and sketch several of them. What does this flow field model?

2.12 A flow field flow is given by

$$\vec{V} = -\frac{qx}{2\pi(x^2 + y^2)}\hat{i} - \frac{qy}{2\pi(x^2 + y^2)}\hat{j}$$

where $q = 2 \times 10^4$ m^2/s. Plot the velocity magnitude along the x axis, along the y axis, and along the line $y = x$. For each plot use the range -10 km $\leq x$ or $y \leq 10$ km, excluding $|x|$ or $|y| \leq 100$ m.

Find the equation for the streamlines and sketch several of them. What does this flow field model?

2.13 Beginning with the velocity field of Problem 2.4, verify that the parametric equations for particle motion are given by $x_p = c_1e^{at}$ and $y_p = c_2e^{-bt}$. Obtain the equation for the pathline of the particle located at the point $(x, y) = (1, 2)$ at the instant $t = 0$. Compare this pathline with the streamline through the same point.

2.14 A velocity field is given by $\vec{V} = ayt\hat{i} - bx\hat{j}$, where $a = 1$ s^{-2} and $b = 4$ s^{-1}. Find the equation of the streamlines at any time t. Plot several streamlines at $t = 0$ s, $t = 1$ s, and $t = 20$ s.

2.15 Verify that $x_p = -a\sin(\omega t)$, $y_p = a\cos(\omega t)$ is the equation for the pathlines of particles for the flow field of Problem 2.10. Find the frequency of motion ω as a function of the amplitude of motion, a, and K. Verify that $x_p = -a\sin(\omega t)$, $y_p = a\cos(\omega t)$ is also the equation for the pathlines of particles for the flow field of Problem 2.11, except that ω is now a function of M. Plot typical pathlines for both flow fields and discuss the difference.

2.16 Air flows downward toward an infinitely wide horizontal flat plate. The velocity field is given by $\vec{V} = (ax\hat{i} - ay\hat{j})(2 + \cos \omega t)$, where $a = 5$ s^{-1}, $\omega = 2\pi$ s^{-1}, x and y (measured in meters) are horizontal and vertically upward, respectively, and t is in s. Obtain an algebraic equation for a streamline at $t = 0$. Plot the streamline that passes through point $(x, y) = (3, 3)$ at this instant. Will the streamline change with time? Explain briefly. Show the velocity vector on your plot at the same point and time. Is the velocity vector tangent to the streamline? Explain.

2.17 Consider the flow described by the velocity field $\vec{V} = Bx(1 + At)\hat{i} + Cy\hat{j}$, with $A = 0.5$ s^{-1}, and $B = C = 1$ s^{-1}. Coordinates are measured in meters. Plot the pathline traced out by the particle that passes through the point $(1, 1)$ at time $t = 0$. Compare with the streamlines plotted through the same point at the instants $t = 0$, 1, and 2 s.

2.18 Consider the flow field given in Eulerian description by the expression $\vec{V} = A\hat{i} + Bt\hat{j}$, where $A = 2$ m/s, $B = 0.6$ m/s^2, and the coordinates are measured in meters. Derive the Lagrangian position functions for the fluid particle that was located at the point $(x, y) = (1, 1)$ at the instant $t = 0$. Obtain an algebraic expression for the pathline followed by this particle. Plot the pathline and compare with the streamlines plotted through the same point at the instants $t = 0$, 1, and 2 s.

2.19 A velocity field is given by $\vec{V} = axt\hat{i} - by\hat{j}$, where $a = 0.1$ s^{-2} and $b = 1$ s^{-1}. For the particle that passes through the point $(x, y) = (1, 1)$ at instant $t = 0$ s, plot the pathline during the interval from $t = 0$ to $t = 3$ s. Compare with the streamlines plotted through the same point at the instants $t = 0$, 1, and 2 s.

2.20 Consider the velocity field $V = ax\hat{i} + by(1 + ct)\hat{j}$, where $a = b = 2$ s^{-1}, and $c = 0.4$ s^{-1}. Coordinates are measured in meters. For the particle that passes through the point $(x, y) = (1, 1)$ at the instant $t = 0$, plot the pathline during the interval from $t = 0$ to 1.5 s. Compare this pathline with the streamlines plotted through the same point at the instants $t = 0$, 1, and 1.5 s.

2.21 Consider the flow field $\vec{V} = axt\hat{i} + b\hat{j}$, where $a = 0.1$ s^{-2} and $b = 4$ m/s. Coordinates are measured in meters. For the particle that passes through the point $(x, y) = (3, 1)$ at the instant $t = 0$, plot the pathline during the interval from $t = 0$ to 3 s. Compare this pathline with the streamlines plotted through the same point at the instants $t = 1$, 2, and 3 s.

2.22　Consider the garden hose of Fig. 2.5. Suppose the velocity field is given by $\vec{V} = u_0\hat{i} + v_0\sin[\omega(t - x/u_0)]\hat{j}$, where the x direction is horizontal and the origin is at the mean position of the hose, $u_0 = 10$ m/s, $v_0 = 2$ m/s, and $\omega = 5$ cycle/s. Find and plot on one graph the instantaneous streamlines that pass through the origin at $t = 0$ s, 0.05 s, 0.1 s, and 0.15 s. Also find and plot on one graph the pathlines of particles that left the origin at the same four times.

2.23　Using the data of Problem 2.22, find and plot the streakline shape produced after the first second of flow.

2.24　Consider the velocity field of Problem 2.17. Plot the streakline formed by particles that passed through the point $(1, 1)$ during the interval from $t = 0$ to $t = 3$ s. Compare with the streamlines plotted through the same point at the instants $t = 0$, 1, and 2 s.

2.25　Streaklines are traced out by neutrally buoyant marker fluid injected into a flow field from a fixed point in space. A particle of the marker fluid that is at point (x, y) at time t must have passed through the injection point (x_0, y_0) at some earlier instant $t = \tau$. The time history of a marker particle may be found by solving the pathline equations for the initial conditions that $x = x_0$, $y = y_0$ when $t = \tau$. The present locations of particles on the streakline are obtained by setting τ equal to values in the range $0 \leq \tau \leq t$. Consider the flow field $\vec{V} = ax(1 + bt)\hat{i} + cy\hat{j}$, where $a = c = 1$ s^{-1} and $b = 0.2$ s^{-1}. Coordinates are measured in meters. Plot the streakline that passes through the initial point $(x_0, y_0) = (1, 1)$, during the interval from $t = 0$ to $t = 3$ s. Compare with the streamline plotted through the same point at the instants $t = 0$, 1, and 2 s.

2.26　Consider the flow field $\vec{V} = axt\hat{i} + b\hat{j}$, where $a = 0.2$ s^{-2} and $b = 1$ m/s. Coordinates are measured in meters. For the particle that passes through the point $(x, y) = (1, 2)$ at the instant $t = 0$, plot the pathline during the time interval from $t = 0$ to 3 s. Compare this pathline with the streakline through the same point at the instant $t = 3$ s.

2.27　Tiny hydrogen bubbles are being used as tracers to visualize a flow. All the bubbles are generated at the origin ($x = 0$, $y = 0$). The velocity field is unsteady and obeys the equations:

$$u = 1 \text{ m/s} \qquad v = 2 \text{ m/s} \qquad 0 \leq t < 2 \text{ s}$$
$$u = 0 \qquad v = -1 \text{ m/s} \qquad 0 \leq t \leq 4 \text{ s}$$

Plot the pathlines of bubbles that leave the origin at $t = 0$, 1, 2, 3, and 4 s. Mark the locations of these five bubbles at $t = 4$ s. Use a dashed line to indicate the position of a streakline at $t = 4$ s.

2.28　A flow is described by velocity field, $\vec{V} = ay^2\hat{i} + b\hat{j}$, where $a = 1$ m^{-1} s^{-1} and $b = 2$ m/s. Coordinates are measured in meters. Obtain the equation for the streamline passing through point $(6, 6)$. At $t = 1$ s, what are the coordinates of the particle that passed through point $(1, 4)$ at $t = 0$? At $t = 3$ s, what are the coordinates of the particle that passed through point $(-3, 0)$ 2 s earlier? Show that pathlines, streamlines, and streaklines for this flow coincide.

2.29　A flow is described by velocity field, $\vec{V} = a\hat{i} + bx\hat{j}$, where $a = 2$ m/s and $b = 1$ s^{-1}. Coordinates are measured in meters. Obtain the equation for the streamline passing through point $(2, 5)$. At $t = 2$ s, what are the coordinates of the particle that

passed through point $(0, 4)$ at $t = 0$? At $t = 3$ s, what are the coordinates of the particle that passed through point $(1, 4.25)$ 2 s earlier? What conclusions can you draw about the pathline, streamline, and streakline for this flow?

2.30　A flow is described by velocity field, $\vec{V} = ay\hat{i} + bt\hat{j}$, where $a = 1$ s^{-1} and $b = 0.5$ m/s^2. At $t = 2$ s, what are the coordinates of the particle that passed through point $(1, 2)$ at $t = 0$? At $t = 3$ s, what are the coordinates of the particle that passed through point $(1, 2)$ at $t = 2$ s? Plot the pathline and streakline through point $(1, 2)$ and compare with the streamlines through the same point at the instants $t = 0$, 1, and 2 s.

2.31　A flow is described by velocity field, $\vec{V} = at\hat{i} + b\hat{j}$, where $a = 0.4$ m/s^2 and $b = 2$ m/s. At $t = 2$ s, what are the coordinates of the particle that passed through point $(2, 1)$ at $t = 0$? At $t = 3$ s, what are the coordinates of the particle that passed through point $(2, 1)$ at $t = 2$ s? Plot the pathline and streakline through point $(2, 1)$ and compare with the streamlines through the same point at the instants $t = 0$, 1, and 2 s.

2.32　The variation with temperature of the viscosity of air is correlated well by the empirical Sutherland equation

$$\mu = \frac{bT^{1/2}}{1 + S/T}$$

Best-fit values of b and S are given in Appendix A for use with SI units. Use these values to develop an equation for calculating air viscosity in British Gravitational units as a function of absolute temperature in degrees Rankine. Check your result using data from Appendix A.

2.33　The variation with temperature of the viscosity of air is represented well by the empirical Sutherland correlation

$$\mu = \frac{bT^{1/2}}{1 + S/T}$$

Best-fit values of b and S are given in Appendix A. Develop an equation in SI units for kinematic viscosity versus temperature for air at atmospheric pressure. Assume ideal gas behavior. Check using data from Appendix A.

2.34　Some experimental data for the viscosity of helium at 1 atm are

T, °C	0	100	200	300	400
μ, N · s/m^2($\times 10^5$)	1.86	2.31	2.72	3.11	3.46

Using the approach described in Appendix A-3, correlate these data to the empirical Sutherland equation

$$\mu = \frac{bT^{1/2}}{1 + S/T}$$

(where T is in kelvin) and obtain values for constants b and S.

2.35　The velocity distribution for laminar flow between parallel plates is given by

$$\frac{u}{u_{max}} = 1 - \left(\frac{2y}{h}\right)^2$$

where h is the distance separating the plates and the origin is placed midway between the plates. Consider a flow of water at 15°C, with $u_{max} = 0.10$ m/s and $h = 0.1$ mm. Calculate the shear stress on the upper plate and give its direction. Sketch the variation of shear stress across the channel.

2.36 The velocity distribution for laminar flow between parallel plates is given by

$$\frac{u}{u_{max}} = 1 - \left(\frac{2y}{h}\right)^2$$

where h is the distance separating the plates and the origin is placed midway between the plates. Consider flow of water at 15°C with maximum speed of 0.05 m/s and h = 0.1 mm. Calculate the force on a 1m^2 section of the lower plate and give its direction.

2.37 Explain how an ice skate interacts with the ice surface. What mechanism acts to reduce sliding friction between skate and ice?

2.38 Crude oil, with specific gravity SG = 0.85 and viscosity $\mu = 2.15 \times 10^{-3}$ lbf · s/ft^2, flows steadily down a surface inclined θ = 45 degrees below the horizontal in a film of thickness h = 0.1 in. The velocity profile is given by

$$u = \frac{\rho g}{\mu}\left(hy - \frac{y^2}{2}\right)\sin\theta$$

(Coordinate x is along the surface and y is normal to the surface.) Plot the velocity profile. Determine the magnitude and direction of the shear stress that acts on the surface.

2.39 A female freestyle ice skater, weighing 100 lbf, glides on one skate at speed V = 20 ft/s. Her weight is supported by a thin film of liquid water melted from the ice by the pressure of the skate blade. Assume the blade is L = 11.5 in. long and w = 0.125 in. wide, and that the water film is h = 0.0000575 in. thick. Estimate the deceleration of the skater that results from viscous shear in the water film, if end effects are neglected.

2.40 A block weighing 10 lbf and having dimensions 10 in. on each edge is pulled up an inclined surface on which there is a film of SAE 10W oil at 100°F. If the speed of the block is 2 ft/s and the oil film is 0.001 in. thick, find the force required to pull the block. Assume the velocity distribution in the oil film is linear. The surface is inclined at an angle of 25° from the horizontal.

2.41 Tape is to be coated on both sides with glue by drawing it through a narrow gap. The tape is 0.015 in. thick and 1.00 in. wide. It is centered in the gap with a clearance of 0.012 in. on each side. The glue, of viscosity μ = 0.02 slug/(ft · s), completely fills the space between the tape and gap. If the tape can withstand a maximum tensile force of 25 lbf, determine the maximum gap region through which it can be pulled at a speed of 3 ft/s.

2.42 A 73-mm-diameter aluminum (SG = 2.64) piston of 100-mm length resides in a stationary 75-mm-inner-diameter steel tube lined with SAE 10W-30 oil at 25°C. A mass m = 2 kg is suspended from the free end of the piston. The piston is set into motion by cutting a support cord. What is the terminal velocity of mass m? Assume a linear velocity profile within the oil.

2.43 The piston in Problem 2.42 is traveling at terminal speed. The mass m now disconnects from the piston. Plot the piston speed vs. time. How long does it take the piston to come within 1 percent of its new terminal speed?

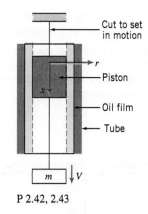

P 2.42, 2.43

2.44 A block _____ _____ oil. The film thickness is h _____ leased, mass m exerts tensi_____ _____ celerate. Neglect friction i_____ _____ an algebraic expression fo_____ _____ lock when it moves at spe_____ _____ or the block speed as a fu_____ _____ for the block speed as a fu_____ = 1 kg, A = 25 cm^2, and _____ _____ ed to reach 1 m/s, find the _____

$$W_{pist} = SG_{Al} \cdot \rho_{H_2O} \cdot g \left(\frac{\pi D^2}{4}\right) L$$

$$F_{viscous}(v) = \tau_{rz} A$$

$$= \mu \left[\frac{v}{\frac{1}{2}(D_{tube} - D_{pist})}\right](\pi D_{pis} \cdot L)$$

$$M \cdot \frac{dv}{dt} = W_{pist} - F_{vis}(v)$$

$$v(t) = \left(v_0 - \frac{g}{a}\right) \cdot e^{(-a \cdot t)} + \frac{g}{a}$$

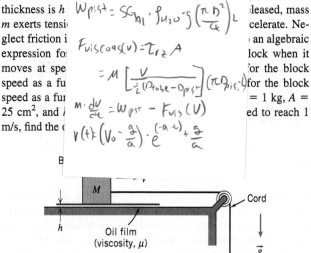

P 2.44

2.45 A block 0.1 m square, with 5 kg mass, slides down a smooth incline, 30° below the horizontal, on a film of SAE 30 oil at 20°C that is 0.20 mm thick. If the block is released from rest at t = 0, what is its initial acceleration? Derive an expression for the speed of the block as a function of time. Plot the curve for $V(t)$. Find the speed after 0.1 s. If we want the mass to instead reach a speed of 0.3 m/s at this time, find the viscosity μ of the oil we would have to use.

2.46 A block that is a mm square slides across a flat plate on a thin film of oil. The oil has viscosity μ and the film is h mm thick. The block of mass M moves at steady speed U under the influence of constant force F. Indicate the magnitude and direction of the shear stresses on the bottom of the block and the plate. If the force is removed suddenly and the block begins to slow, sketch the resulting speed versus time curve for the block. Obtain an expression for the time required for the block to lose 95 percent of its initial speed.

2.47 Magnet wire is to be coated with varnish for insulation by drawing it through a circular die of 1.0 mm diameter. The wire diameter is 0.9 mm and it is centered in the die. The varnish (μ = 20 centipoise) completely fills the space between the wire and the die for a length of 50 mm. The wire is drawn through the die at a speed of 50 m/s. Determine the force required to pull the wire.

2.48 A double-pipe heat exchanger consists of two concentric fluid-carrying pipes used to transfer heat between nonmixing fluids. The figure shown below is a full-section view of a 0.85-m length of the double-pipe apparatus.

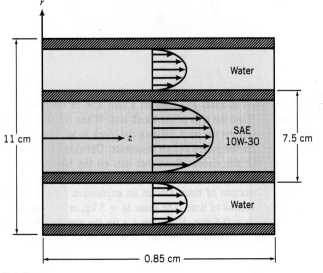

P 2.48

SAE10W-30 oil at 100°C flows through the 7.5-cm-outer-diameter inside pipe. Water at 10°C flows through the annulus between the inside pipe and the 11-cm-outer-diameter outside pipe. The wall thickness of each pipe is 3 mm. The theoretical velocity profiles for laminar flow through a pipe and annulus are:

Inner pipe: $u_z(r) = u_{max}\left[1 - \left(\dfrac{r}{R_{i,\,inside}}\right)^2\right]$

$$\text{where: } u_{max} = \frac{R_{i,\,inside}^2 \Delta P}{4\mu L}$$

Annulus: $u_z(r) = \dfrac{1}{4\mu}\left(\dfrac{\Delta P}{L}\right)$

$$\times \left[R_{i,\,outside}^2 - r^2 - \frac{R_{o,\,inside}^2 - R_{i,\,outside}^2}{\ln\left(\dfrac{R_{i,\,outside}}{R_{o,\,inside}}\right)} \cdot \ln\left(\frac{r}{R_{i,\,outside}}\right)\right]$$

Show that the no-slip condition is satisfied by these expressions. The pressure drop across the given length is 2.5 Pa and 8 Pa for the water and oil flows, respectively. If both flows are in the same direction (along the +z axis), what is the net viscous force acting on the inner pipe?

2.49 Repeat Problem 2.48 assuming a counterflow arrangement, where the oil flows in the +z direction and the water flows in the −z direction.

2.50 Fluids of viscosities $\mu_1 = 0.1$ N·s/m^2 and $\mu_2 = 0.15$ N · s/m^2 are contained between two plates (each plate is 1 m^2 in area). The thicknesses are $h_1 = 0.5$ mm and $h_2 = 0.3$ mm, respectively. Find the force F to make the upper plate move at a speed of 1 m/s. What is the fluid velocity at the interface between the two fluids?

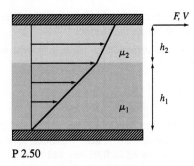

P 2.50

2.51 A concentric cylinder viscometer may be formed by rotating the inner member of a pair of closely fitting cylinders (see Fig. P2.53). For small clearances, a linear velocity profile may be assumed in the liquid filling the annular clearance gap. A viscometer has an inner cylinder of 75 mm diameter and 150 mm height, with a clearance gap width of 0.02 mm. A torque of 0.021 N · m is required to turn the inner cylinder at 100 rpm. Determine the viscosity of the liquid in the clearance gap of the viscometer.

2.52 A concentric cylinder viscometer may be formed by rotating the inner member of a pair of closely fitting cylinders (see Fig. P2.53). The annular gap is small so that a linear velocity profile will exist in the liquid sample. Consider a viscometer with an inner cylinder of 4 in. diameter and 8 in. height, and a clearance gap width of 0.001 in., filled with castor oil at 90°F. Determine the torque required to turn the inner cylinder at 400 rpm.

2.53 A concentric cylinder viscometer is driven by a falling mass M connected by a cord and pulley to the inner cylinder, as shown. The liquid to be tested fills the annular gap of width a and height H. After a brief starting transient, the mass falls at constant speed V_m. Develop an algebraic expression for the viscosity of the liquid in the device in terms of M, g, V_m, r, R, a, and H. Evaluate the viscosity of the liquid using:

$M = 0.10$ kg $r = 25$ mm
$R = 50$ mm $a = 0.20$ mm
$H = 80$ mm $V_m = 30$ mm/s

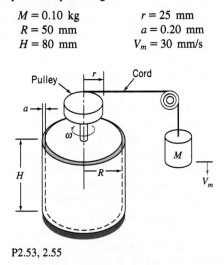

P2.53, 2.55

2.54 A shaft with outside diameter of 18 mm turns at 20 revolutions per second inside a stationary journal bearing 60 mm long. A thin film of oil 0.2 mm thick fills the concentric annulus between the shaft and journal. The torque needed to turn the shaft is 0.0036 N · m. Estimate the viscosity of the oil that fills the gap.

2.55 The viscometer of Problem 2.53 is being used to verify that the viscosity of a particular fluid is $\mu = 0.1$ N · s/m^2. Unfortunately the cord snaps during the experiment. How long will it take the cylinder to lose 99% of its speed? The moment of inertia of the cylinder/pulley system is 0.0273 kg · m².

2.56 The thin outer cylinder (mass m_2 and radius R) of a small portable concentric cylinder viscometer is driven by a falling mass, m_1, attached to a cord. The inner cylinder is stationary. The clearance between the cylinders is a. Neglect bearing friction, air resistance, and the mass of liquid in the viscometer. Obtain an algebraic expression for the torque due to viscous shear that acts on the cylinder at angular speed ω. Derive and solve a differential equation for the angular speed of the outer cylinder as a function of time. Obtain an expression for the maximum angular speed of the cylinder.

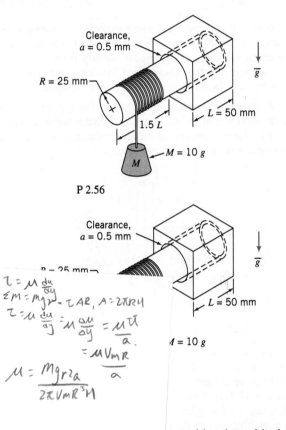

P 2.56

$\tau = \mu \frac{du}{\delta y}$

$\Sigma M = mgr - \tau AR, \quad A = 2\pi RL$

$\tau = \mu \frac{du}{dy} = \mu \frac{\partial u}{\partial y} = \mu \frac{u}{a}$

$= \mu \frac{V_m R}{a}$

$\mu = \frac{Mgr2a}{2\pi V_m R^3 L}$

...ounted in a journal is shown. ...ween the shaft and journal is filled with SAE 10W-30 oil at ... 30°C. The shaft is caused to turn by the attached mass and cord. Develop and solve a differential equation for the angular speed of the shaft as a function of time. Calculate the maximum angular speed of the shaft and the time required to reach 95 percent of this speed.

2.58 A shock-free coupling for a low-power mechanical drive is to be made from a pair of concentric cylinders. The annular space between the cylinders is to be filled with oil. The drive must transmit power, $\mathcal{P} = 10$ W. Other dimensions and properties are as shown. Neglect any bearing friction and end effects. Assume the minimum practical gap clearance δ for the device is $\delta = 0.25$ mm. Dow manufactures silicone fluids with viscosities as high as 10^6 centipoise. Determine the viscosity that should be specified to satisfy the requirement for this device.

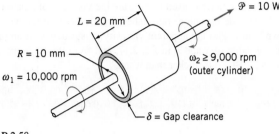

P 2.58

2.59 A proposal has been made to use a pair of parallel disks to measure the viscosity of a liquid sample. The upper disk rotates at height h above the lower disk. The viscosity of the liquid in the gap is to be calculated from measurements of the torque needed to turn the upper disk steadily. Obtain an algebraic expression for the torque needed to turn the disk. Could we use this device to measure the viscosity of a non-Newtonian fluid? Explain.

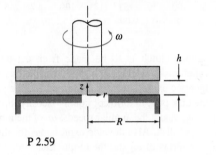

P 2.59

2.60 The cone and plate viscometer shown is an instrument used frequently to characterize non-Newtonian fluids. It consists of a flat plate and a rotating cone with a very obtuse angle (typically θ is less than 0.5 degrees). The apex of the cone just touches the plate surface and the liquid to be tested fills the narrow gap formed by the cone and plate. Derive an expression for the shear rate in the liquid that fills the gap in terms of the geometry of the system. Evaluate the torque on the driven cone in terms of the shear stress and geometry of the system.

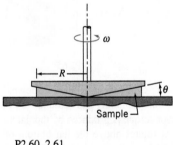

P2.60, 2.61

2.61 The viscometer of Problem 2.60 is used to measure the apparent viscosity of a fluid. The data below are obtained. What kind of non-Newtonian fluid is this? Find the values of k and n used in Eqs. 2.16 and 2.17 in defining the apparent viscosity of a fluid. (Assume θ is 0.5 degrees.) Predict the viscosity at 90 and 100 rpm.

Speed (rpm)	10	20	30	40	50	60	70	80
μ (N · s/m²)	0.121	0.139	0.153	0.159	0.172	0.172	0.183	0.185

2.62 A viscometer is used to measure the viscosity of a patient's blood. The deformation rate (shear rate)–shear stress data is shown below. Plot the apparent viscosity versus deformation rate. Find the value of k and n in Eq. 2.17, and from this examine the aphorism "Blood is thicker than water."

du/dy (s^{-1})	5	10	25	50	100	200	300	400
τ (Pa)	0.0457	0.119	0.241	0.375	0.634	1.06	1.46	1.78

2.63 An insulation company is examining a new material for extruding into cavities. The experimental data is given below for the speed U of the upper plate, which is separated from a fixed lower plate by a 1-mm-thick sample of the material, when a given shear stress is applied. Determine the type of material. If a replacement material with a minimum yield stress of 250 Pa is needed, what viscosity will the material need to have the same behavior as the current material at a shear stress of 450 Pa?

τ (Pa)	50	100	150	163	171	170	202	246	349	444
U (m/s)	0	0	0	0.005	0.01	0.025	0.05	0.1	0.2	0.3

2.64 A viscous clutch is to be made from a pair of closely spaced parallel disks enclosing a thin layer of viscous liquid. Develop algebraic expressions for the torque and the power transmitted by the disk pair, in terms of liquid viscosity, μ, disk radius, R, disk spacing, a, and the angular speeds: ω_i of the input disk and ω_o of the output disk. Also develop expressions for the slip ratio, $s = \Delta\omega/\omega_i$, in terms of ω_i and the torque transmitted. Determine the efficiency, η, in terms of the slip ratio.

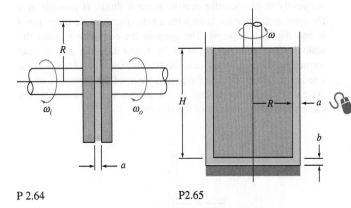

P 2.64   P2.65

2.65 A concentric-cylinder viscometer is shown. Viscous torque is produced by the annular gap around the inner cylinder. Additional viscous torque is produced by the flat bottom of the inner cylinder as it rotates above the flat bottom of the stationary outer cylinder. Obtain an algebraic expression for the viscous torque due to flow in the annular gap of width a. Obtain an algebraic expression for the viscous torque due to flow in the bottom clearance gap of height b. Prepare a plot showing the ratio, b/a, required to hold the bottom torque to 1 percent or less of the annulus torque, versus the other geometric variables. What are the design implications? What modifications to the design can you recommend?

2.66 A conical pointed shaft turns in a conical bearing. The gap between shaft and bearing is filled with heavy oil having the viscosity of SAE 30 at 30°C. Obtain an algebraic expression for the

shear stress that acts on the surface of the conical shaft. Calculate the viscous torque that acts on the shaft.

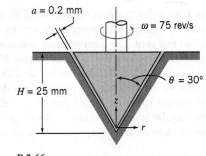

P 2.66

2.67 Design a concentric-cylinder viscometer to measure the viscosity of a liquid similar to water. The goal is to achieve a measurement accuracy of ± 1 percent. Specify the configuration and dimensions of the viscometer. Indicate what measured parameter will be used to infer the viscosity of the liquid sample.

2.68 A spherical thrust bearing is shown. The gap between the spherical member and the housing is of constant width h. Obtain and plot an algebraic expression for the nondimensional torque on the spherical member, as a function of angle α.

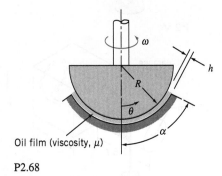

P2.68

2.69 A cross section of a rotating bearing is shown. The spherical member rotates with angular speed ω, a small distance, a, above the plane surface. The narrow gap is filled with viscous oil, having $\mu = 1250$ cp. Obtain an algebraic expression for the shear stress acting on the spherical member. Evaluate the maximum shear stress that acts on the spherical member for the conditions shown. (Is the maximum necessarily located at the maximum radius?) Develop an algebraic expression (in the form of an integral) for the total viscous shear torque that acts on the spherical member. Calculate the torque using the dimensions shown.

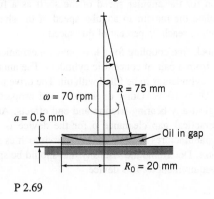

P 2.69

2.70 Small gas bubbles form in soda when a bottle or can is opened. The average bubble diameter is about 0.1 mm. Estimate the pressure difference between the inside and outside of such a bubble.

2.71 Slowly fill a glass with water to the maximum possible level. Observe the water level closely. Explain how it can be higher than the rim of the glass.

2.72 You intend to gently place several steel needles on the free surface of the water in a large tank. The needles come in two lengths: Some are 5 cm long, and some are 10 cm long. Needles of each length are available with diameters of 1 mm, 2.5 mm, and 5 mm. Make a prediction as to which needles, if any, will float.

2.73 Plan an experiment to measure the surface tension of a liquid similar to water. If necessary, review the NCFMF video *Surface Tension* for ideas. Which method would be most suitable for use in an undergraduate laboratory? What experimental precision could be expected?

2.74 Water usually is assumed to be incompressible when evaluating static pressure variations. Actually it is 100 times more compressible than steel. Assuming the bulk modulus of water is constant, compute the percentage change in density for water raised to a gage pressure of 100 atm. Plot the percentage change in water density as a function of p/p_{atm} up to a pressure of 50,000 psi, which is the approximate pressure used for high-speed cutting jets of water to cut concrete and other composite materials. Would constant density be a reasonable assumption for engineering calculations for cutting jets?

2.75 The viscous boundary layer velocity profile shown in Fig. 2.15 can be approximated by a parabolic equation,

$$u(y) = a + b\left(\frac{y}{\delta}\right) + c\left(\frac{y}{\delta}\right)^2$$

The boundary condition is $u = U$ (the free stream velocity) at the boundary edge δ (where the viscous friction becomes zero). Find the values of a, b, and c.

2.76 The viscous boundary layer velocity profile shown in Fig. 2.15 can be approximated by a cubic equation,

$$u(y) = a + b\left(\frac{y}{\delta}\right) + c\left(\frac{y}{\delta}\right)^3$$

The boundary condition is $u = U$ (the free stream velocity) at the boundary edge δ (where the viscous friction becomes zero). Find the values of a, b, and c.

2.77 At what minimum speed (in mph) would an automobile have to travel for compressibility effects to be important? Assume the local air temperature is 60°F.

2.78 Water flows through a 1-in. ID garden hose at a rate of 0.075 ft³/min. A 5-in.-long, cone-shaped nozzle is attached to the hose to accelerate the flow. If the nozzle reduces the flow area by a factor of 4, at what distance from the inlet of the nozzle does the flow become turbulent? Assume the water temperature is 60°F.

2.79 A supersonic aircraft travels at 2700 km/hr at an altitude of 27 km. What is the Mach number of the aircraft? At what approximate distance measured from the leading edge of the aircraft's wing does the boundary layer change from laminar to turbulent?

2.80 What is the Reynolds number of water at 20°C flowing at 0.25 m/s through a 5-mm-diameter tube? If the pipe is now heated, at what mean water temperature will the flow transition to turbulence? Assume the velocity of the flow remains constant.

2.81 SAE 30 oil at 100°C flows through a 12-mm-diameter stainless-steel tube. What is the specific gravity and specific weight of the oil? If the oil discharged from the tube fills a 100-mL graduated cylinder in 9 seconds, is the flow laminar or turbulent?

2.82 A seaplane is flying at 100 mph through air at 45°F. At what distance from the leading edge of the underside of the fuselage does the boundary layer transition to turbulence? How does this boundary layer transition change as the underside of the fuselage touches the water during landing? Assume the water temperature is also 45°F.

2.83 An airliner is cruising at an altitude of 5.5 km with a speed of 700 km/hr. As the airliner increases its altitude, it adjusts its speed so that the Mach number remains constant. Provide a sketch of speed vs. altitude. What is the speed of the airliner at an altitude of 8 km?

2.84 How does an airplane wing develop lift?

Chapter 3

Fluid Statics

CASE STUDY

The Falkirk Wheel

The Falkirk Wheel.

Hydrostatics, the study of fluids at rest, is an ancient discipline, so one might think there are no new or exciting applications still to be developed. The Falkirk wheel in Scotland is a dramatic demonstration that this is not the case; it is a novel replacement for a lock, a

device for moving a boat from one water level to another. The wheel, which has a diameter of 35 meters, consists of two sets of axe-shaped opposing arms (which take the shape of a Celtic-inspired, double-headed axe). Sitting in bearings in the ends of these arms are two water-filled caissons, or tanks, each with a capacity of 80,000 gallons. The hydrostatics concept of Archimedes' principle, which we will study in this chapter, states that floating objects displace their own weight of water. Hence, the boat shown entering the lower caisson displaces water from the caisson weighing exactly the same as the boat itself. This means the entire wheel remains balanced at all times (both caissons always carry the same weight, whether containing boats or not), and so, despite its enormous mass, it rotates through 180° in less than four minutes while using very little power. The electric motors used for this use 22.5 kilowatts (kW) of power, so the energy used in four minutes is about 1.5 kilowatt-hours (kWh); even at current prices, this works out to be only a few cents worth of energy.

In Chapter 1, we defined a fluid as any substance that flows (continuously deforms) when it experiences a shear stress; hence for a static fluid (or one undergoing "rigid-body" motion) only normal stress is present—in other words, pressure. We will study the topic of fluid statics (often called *hydrostatics*, even though it is not restricted to water) in this chapter.

Although fluid statics problems are the simplest kind of fluid mechanics problems, this is not the only reason we will study them. The pressure generated within a static fluid is an important phenomenon in many practical situations. Using the principles of hydrostatics, we can compute forces on submerged objects, develop instruments for measuring pressures, and deduce properties of the atmosphere and oceans. The principles of hydrostatics also may be used to determine the forces developed by hydraulic systems in applications such as industrial presses or automobile brakes.

In a static, homogeneous fluid, or in a fluid undergoing rigid-body motion, a fluid particle retains its identity for all time, and fluid elements do not deform. We may apply Newton's second law of motion to evaluate the forces acting on the particle.

3-1   THE BASIC EQUATION OF FLUID STATICS

The first objective of this chapter is to obtain an equation for computing the pressure field in a static fluid. We will deduce what we already know from everyday experience, that the pressure increases with depth. To do this, we apply Newton's second law to a differential fluid element of mass $dm = \rho\, d\forall$, with sides dx, dy, and dz, as shown in Fig. 3.1. The fluid element is stationary relative to the stationary rectangular coordinate system shown. (Fluids in rigid-body motion will be treated in Section 3-7 on the Web.)

From our previous discussion, recall that two general types of forces may be applied to a fluid: body forces and surface forces. The only body force that must be considered in most engineering problems is due to gravity. In some situations body forces caused by electric or magnetic fields might be present; they will not be considered in this text.[1]

For a differential fluid element, the body force is

$$d\vec{F}_B = \vec{g}\,dm = \vec{g}\rho\, d\forall$$

where $\vec{g}$ is the local gravity vector, ρ is the density, and $d\forall$ is the volume of the element. In Cartesian coordinates $d\forall = dx\, dy\, dz$, so

$$d\vec{F}_B = \rho\vec{g}\, dx\, dy\, dz$$

In a static fluid there are no shear stresses, so the only surface force is the pressure force. Pressure is a scalar field, $p = p(x, y, z)$; in general we expect the pressure to vary with position within the fluid. The net pressure force that results from this variation can be found by summing the forces that act on the six faces of the fluid element.

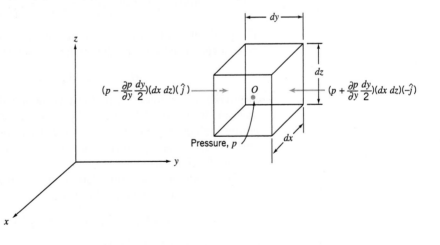

---

[1] The effect of body forces caused by magnetic fields is illustrated in the NCFMF video *Magnetohydrodynamics*. (See http://web.mit.edu/fluids/www.shapiro/ncfmf.html for free online viewing of this film; it is old but good!)

Let the pressure be p at the center, O, of the element. To determine the pressure at each of the six faces of the element, we use a Taylor series expansion of the pressure about point O. The pressure at the left face of the differential element is

$$p_L = p + \frac{\partial p}{\partial y}(y_L - y) = p + \frac{\partial p}{\partial y}\left(-\frac{dy}{2}\right) = p - \frac{\partial p}{\partial y}\frac{dy}{2}$$

(Terms of higher order are omitted because they will vanish in the subsequent limiting process.) The pressure on the right face of the differential element is

$$p_R = p + \frac{\partial p}{\partial y}(y_R - y) = p + \frac{\partial p}{\partial y}\frac{dy}{2}$$

The pressure *forces* acting on the two y surfaces of the differential element are shown in Fig. 3.1. Each pressure force is a product of three factors. The first is the magnitude of the pressure. This magnitude is multiplied by the area of the face to give the magnitude of the pressure force, and a unit vector is introduced to indicate direction. Note also in Fig. 3.1 that the pressure force on each face acts *against* the face. A positive pressure corresponds to a *compressive* normal stress.

Pressure forces on the other faces of the element are obtained in the same way. Combining all such forces gives the net surface force acting on the element. Thus

$$d\vec{F}_S = \left(p - \frac{\partial p}{\partial x}\frac{dx}{2}\right)(dy\,dz)(\hat{i}) + \left(p + \frac{\partial p}{\partial x}\frac{dx}{2}\right)(dy\,dz)(-\hat{i})$$

$$+ \left(p - \frac{\partial p}{\partial y}\frac{dy}{2}\right)(dx\,dz)(\hat{j}) + \left(p + \frac{\partial p}{\partial y}\frac{dy}{2}\right)(dx\,dz)(-\hat{j})$$

$$+ \left(p - \frac{\partial p}{\partial z}\frac{dz}{2}\right)(dx\,dy)(\hat{k}) + \left(p + \frac{\partial p}{\partial z}\frac{dz}{2}\right)(dx\,dy)(-\hat{k})$$

Collecting and canceling terms, we obtain

$$d\vec{F}_S = -\left(\frac{\partial p}{\partial x}\hat{i} + \frac{\partial p}{\partial y}\hat{j} + \frac{\partial p}{\partial z}\hat{k}\right)dx\,dy\,dz \qquad (3.1a)$$

The term in parentheses is called the gradient of the pressure or simply the pressure gradient and may be written grad p or ∇p. In rectangular coordinates

$$\text{grad } p \equiv \nabla p \equiv \left(\hat{i}\frac{\partial p}{\partial x} + \hat{j}\frac{\partial p}{\partial y} + \hat{k}\frac{\partial p}{\partial z}\right) \equiv \left(\hat{i}\frac{\partial}{\partial x} + \hat{j}\frac{\partial}{\partial y} + \hat{k}\frac{\partial}{\partial z}\right)p$$

The gradient can be viewed as a vector operator; taking the gradient of a scalar field gives a vector field. Using the gradient designation, Eq. 3.1a can be written as

$$d\vec{F}_S = -\text{grad } p\,(dx\,dy\,dz) = -\nabla p\,dx\,dy\,dz \qquad (3.1b)$$

Physically the gradient of pressure is the negative of the surface force per unit volume due to pressure. Note that the pressure magnitude itself is not relevant in computing the net pressure force; instead what counts is the rate of change of pressure with distance, the *pressure gradient*. We shall encounter this term throughout our study of fluid mechanics.

We combine the formulations for surface and body forces that we have developed to obtain the total force acting on a fluid element. Thus

$$d\vec{F} = d\vec{F}_S + d\vec{F}_B = (-\nabla p + \rho\vec{g})\,dx\,dy\,\text{dz} = (-\nabla p + \rho\vec{g})\,d\forall$$

or on a per unit volume basis

$$\frac{d\vec{F}}{d\forall} = -\nabla p + \rho\vec{g} \qquad (3.2)$$

For a fluid particle, Newton's second law gives $\vec{F} = \vec{a}\, dm = \vec{a}\rho\, d\forall$. For a static fluid, $\vec{a} = 0$. Thus

$$\frac{d\vec{F}}{d\forall} = \rho\vec{a} = 0$$

Substituting for $d\vec{F}/d\forall$ from Eq. 3.2, we obtain

$$-\nabla p + \rho\vec{g} = 0 \tag{3.3}$$

Let us review this equation briefly. The physical significance of each term is

$$\underbrace{-\nabla p}_{\substack{\text{net pressure force} \\ \text{per unit volume} \\ \text{at a point}}} + \underbrace{\rho\vec{g}}_{\substack{\text{body force per} \\ \text{unit volume} \\ \text{at a point}}} = 0$$

This is a vector equation, which means that it is equivalent to three component equations that must be satisfied individually. The component equations are

$$\left.\begin{aligned} -\frac{\partial p}{\partial x} + \rho g_x &= 0 \quad x \text{ direction} \\[2mm] -\frac{\partial p}{\partial y} + \rho g_y &= 0 \quad y \text{ direction} \\[2mm] -\frac{\partial p}{\partial z} + \rho g_z &= 0 \quad z \text{ direction} \end{aligned}\right\} \tag{3.4}$$

Equations 3.4 describe the pressure variation in each of the three coordinate directions in a static fluid. It is convenient to choose a coordinate system such that the gravity vector is aligned with one of the coordinate axes. If the coordinate system is chosen with the z axis directed vertically upward, as in Fig. 3.1, then $g_x = 0$, $g_y = 0$, and $g_z = -g$. Under these conditions, the component equations become

$$\frac{\partial p}{\partial x} = 0 \qquad \frac{\partial p}{\partial y} = 0 \qquad \frac{\partial p}{\partial z} = -\rho g \tag{3.5}$$

Equations 3.5 indicate that, under the assumptions made, the pressure is independent of coordinates x and y; it depends on z alone. Thus since p is a function of a single variable, a total derivative may be used instead of a partial derivative. With these simplifications, Eqs. 3.5 finally reduce to

$$\frac{dp}{dz} = -\rho g \equiv -\gamma \tag{3.6}$$

Restrictions: (1) Static fluid.
                (2) Gravity is the only body force.
                (3) The z axis is vertical and upward.

In Eq. 3.6, γ is the specific weight of the fluid. This equation is the basic pressure-height relation of fluid statics. It is subject to the restrictions noted. Therefore it must be applied only where these restrictions are reasonable for the physical situation. To determine the pressure distribution in a static fluid, Eq. 3.6 may be integrated and appropriate boundary conditions applied.

Before considering specific applications of this equation, it is important to remember that pressure values must be stated with respect to a reference level. If the reference level is a vacuum, pressures are termed *absolute*, as shown in Fig. 3.2.

Most pressure gages indicate a pressure *difference*—the difference between the measured pressure and the ambient level (usually atmospheric pressure). Pressure levels measured with respect to atmospheric pressure are termed *gage* pressures. Thus

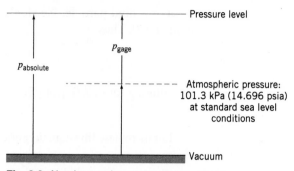

Fig. 3.2 Absolute and gage pressures, showing reference levels.

$$p_{gage} = p_{absolute} - p_{atmosphere}$$

For example, a tire gage might indicate 30 psi; the absolute pressure would be about 44.7 psi. Absolute pressures must be used in all calculations with the ideal gas equation or other equations of state.

3-2   THE STANDARD ATMOSPHERE

Scientists and engineers sometimes need a numerical or analytical model of the earth's atmosphere in order to simulate climate variations to study, for example, effects of global warming. There is no single standard model. An International Standard Atmosphere (ISA) has been defined by the International Civil Aviation Organization (ICAO); there is also a similar U.S. Standard Atmosphere.

The temperature profile of the U.S. Standard Atmosphere is shown in Fig. 3.3. Additional property values are tabulated as functions of elevation in Appendix A. Sea level conditions of the U.S. Standard Atmosphere are summarized in Table 3.1.

TABLE 3.1 Sea Level Conditions of the U.S. Standard Atmosphere

Property	Symbol	SI	English
Temperature	T	15°C	59°F
Pressure	p	101.3 kPa (abs)	14.696 psia
Density	ρ	1.225 kg/m^3	0.002377 slug/ft^3
Specific weight	γ	—	0.07651 lbf/ft^3
Viscosity	μ	1.789×10^{-5} kg/(m · s) (Pa · s)	3.737×10^{-7} lbf · s/ft^2

3-3   PRESSURE VARIATION IN A STATIC FLUID

We proved that pressure variation in any static fluid is described by the basic pressure-height relation

$$\frac{dp}{dz} = -\rho g \qquad (3.6)$$

Although ρg may be defined as the specific weight, γ, it has been written as ρg in Eq. 3.6 to emphasize that *both* ρ and g must be considered variables. In order to integrate Eq. 3.6 to find the pressure distribution, we need information about variations in both ρ and g.

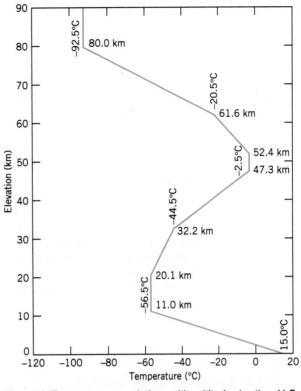

Fig. 3.3 Temperature variation with altitude in the U.S. Standard Atmosphere.

For most practical engineering situations, the variation in g is negligible. Only for a purpose such as computing very precisely the pressure change over a large elevation difference would the variation in g need to be included. Unless we state otherwise, we shall assume g to be constant with elevation at any given location.

Incompressible Liquids: Manometers

For an incompressible fluid, $\rho =$ constant. Then for constant gravity,

$$\frac{dp}{dz} = -\rho g = \text{constant}$$

To determine the pressure variation, we must integrate and apply appropriate boundary conditions. If the pressure at the reference level, z_0, is designated as p_0, then the pressure, p, at level z is found by integration:

$$\int_{p_0}^{p} dp = -\int_{z_0}^{z} \rho g \, dz$$

or

$$p - p_0 = -\rho g(z - z_0) = \rho g(z_0 - z)$$

For liquids, it is often convenient to take the origin of the coordinate system at the free surface (reference level) and to measure distances as positive downward from the free surface as in Fig. 3.4.

With h measured positive downward, we have

$$z_0 - z = h$$

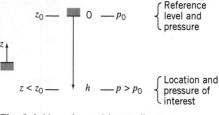

Fig. 3.4 Use of z and h coordinates.

and obtain

$$p - p_0 = \Delta p = \rho g h \qquad (3.7)$$

Equation 3.7 indicates that the pressure difference between two points in a static incompressible fluid can be determined by measuring the elevation difference between the two points. Devices used for this purpose are called *manometers*.

Use of Eq. 3.7 for a manometer is illustrated in Example 3.1.

Example 3.1   Systolic and Diastolic Pressure

Normal blood pressure for a human is 120/80 mm Hg. By modeling a sphygmomanometer pressure gage as a U-tube manometer, convert these pressures to psig.

GIVEN: Gage pressures of 120 and 80 mm Hg

FIND: The corresponding pressures in psig.

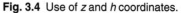

SOLUTION:
Apply hydrostatic equation to points A, A', and B.

Governing equation:

$$p - p_0 = \Delta p = \rho g h \qquad (3.7)$$

Assumptions: (1) Static fluid.
(2) Incompressible fluids.
(3) Neglect air density ($\ll$ Hg density).

Applying the governing equation between points A' and B (and p_B is atmospheric and therefore zero gage):

$$p_{A'} = p_B + \rho_{Hg} g h = SG_{Hg}\rho_{H_2O}gh$$

In addition, the pressure increases as we go downward from point A' to the bottom of the manometer, and decreases by an equal amount as we return up the left branch to point A. This means points A and A' have the same pressure, so we end up with

$$p_A = p_{A'} = SG_{Hg}\rho_{H_2O}gh$$

Substituting $SG_{Hg} = 13.6$ and $\rho_{H_2O} = 1.94$ slug/ft^3 from Appendix A-1 yields for the systolic pressure ($h = 120$ mm Hg)

$$p_{systolic} = p_A = 13.6 \times 1.94 \frac{\text{slug}}{\text{ft}^3} \times 32.2 \frac{\text{ft}}{\text{s}^2} \times 120 \text{ mm} \times \frac{\text{in.}}{25.4 \text{ mm}} \times \frac{\text{ft}}{12 \text{ in.}} \times \frac{\text{lbf} \cdot \text{s}^2}{\text{slug} \cdot \text{ft}}$$

$$p_{systolic} = 334 \text{ lbf/ft}^2 = 2.32 \text{ psi} \longleftarrow \underline{\qquad\qquad\qquad\qquad} p_{systolic}$$

By a similar process, the diastolic pressure ($h = 80$ mm Hg) is

$$p_{diastolic} = 1.55 \text{ psi} \longleftarrow \underline{\qquad\qquad\qquad\qquad} p_{diastolic}$$

Notes:
✓ Two points at the same level in a continuous single fluid have the same pressure.
✓ In manometer problems we neglect change in pressure with depth for a gas: $\rho_{gas} \ll \rho_{liquid}$.
✓ This problem shows the conversion from mm Hg to psi, using Eq. 3.7: 120 mm Hg is equivalent to about 2.32 psi. More generally, 1 atm = 14.7 psi = 101 kPa = 760 mm Hg.

Manometers are simple and inexpensive devices used frequently for pressure measurements. Because the liquid level change is small at low pressure differential, a U-tube manometer may be difficult to read accurately. The *sensitivity* of a manometer is a measure of how sensitive it is compared to a simple water-filled U-tube manometer. Specifically, it is the ratio of the deflection of the manometer to that of a water-filled U-tube manometer, due to the same applied pressure difference Δp. Sensitivity can be increased by changing the manometer design or by using two immiscible liquids of slightly different density. Analysis of an inclined manometer is illustrated in Example 3.2.

Example 3.2   Analysis of Inclined-Tube Manometer

An inclined-tube reservoir manometer is constructed as shown. Derive a general expression for the liquid deflection, L, in the inclined tube, due to the applied pressure difference, Δp. Also obtain an expression for the manometer sensitivity, and discuss the effect on sensitivity of D, d, θ, and SG.

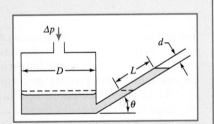

GIVEN: Inclined-tube reservoir manometer

FIND: Expression for L in terms of Δp.
General expression for manometer sensitivity.
Effect of parameter values on sensitivity.

SOLUTION:
Use the equilibrium liquid level as a reference.

Governing equations: $p - p_0 = \Delta p = \rho g h$ $SG = \dfrac{\rho}{\rho_{H_2O}}$

Assumptions: (1) Static fluid.
(2) Incompressible fluid.

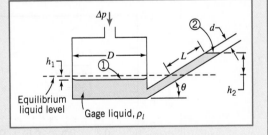

Applying the governing equation between points *1* and *2*

$$p_1 - p_2 = \Delta p = \rho_l g (h_1 + h_2) \tag{1}$$

To eliminate h_1, we recognize that the *volume* of manometer liquid remains constant; the volume displaced from the reservoir must equal the volume that rises in the tube, so

$$\frac{\pi D^2}{4} h_1 = \frac{\pi d^2}{4} L \quad \text{or} \quad h_1 = L\left(\frac{d}{D}\right)^2$$

In addition, from the geometry of the manometer, $h_2 = L \sin \theta$. Substituting into Eq. 1 gives

$$\Delta p = \rho_l g \left[L \sin \theta + L\left(\frac{d}{D}\right)^2 \right] = \rho_l g L \left[\sin \theta + \left(\frac{d}{D}\right)^2 \right]$$

Thus

$$L = \frac{\Delta p}{\rho_l g \left[\sin\theta + \left(\dfrac{d}{D}\right)^2 \right]}$$

To find the sensitivity of the manometer, we need to compare this to the deflection h a simple U-tube manometer, using water (density ρ), would experience,

$$h = \frac{\Delta p}{\rho g}$$

The sensitivity s is then

$$s = \frac{L}{h} = \frac{1}{SG_l \left[\sin\theta + \left(\dfrac{d}{D}\right)^2 \right]}$$

where we have used $SG_l = \rho_l/\rho$. This result shows that to increase sensitivity, SG_l, $\sin\theta$, and d/D each should be made as small as possible. Thus the designer must choose a gage liquid and two geometric parameters to complete a design, as discussed below.

Gage Liquid

The gage liquid should have the smallest possible specific gravity to increase sensitivity. In addition, the gage liquid must be safe (without toxic fumes or flammability), be immiscible with the fluid being gaged, suffer minimal loss from evaporation, and develop a satisfactory meniscus. Thus the gage liquid should have relatively low surface tension and should accept dye to improve its visibility.

Tables A.1, A.2, and A.4 show that hydrocarbon liquids satisfy many of these criteria. The lowest specific gravity is about 0.8, which increases manometer sensitivity by 25 percent compared to water.

Diameter Ratio

The plot shows the effect of diameter ratio on sensitivity for a vertical reservoir manometer with gage liquid of unity specific gravity. Note that $d/D = 1$ corresponds to an ordinary U-tube manometer; its sensitivity is 0.5 because for this case the total deflection will be h, and for each side it will be $h/2$, so $L = h/2$. Sensitivity doubles to 1.0 as d/D approaches zero because most of the level change occurs in the measuring tube.

The minimum tube diameter d must be larger than about 6 mm to avoid excessive capillary effect. The maximum reservoir diameter D is limited by the size of the manometer. If D is set at 60 mm, so that d/D is 0.1, then $(d/D)^2 = 0.01$, and the sensitivity increases to 0.99, very close to the maximum attainable value of 1.0.

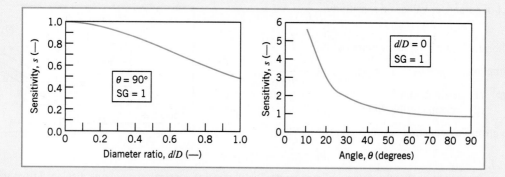

Inclination Angle

The final plot shows the effect of inclination angle on sensitivity for $d/D = 0$. Sensitivity increases sharply as inclination angle is reduced below 30 degrees. A practical limit is reached at about 10 degrees: The meniscus becomes indistinct and the level hard to read for smaller angles.

Summary

Combining the best values (SG = 0.8, $d/D = 0.1$, and $\theta = 10$ degrees) gives a manometer sensitivity of 6.81. Physically this is the ratio of observed gage liquid deflection to equivalent water column height. Thus the deflection in the inclined tube is amplified 6.81 times compared to a vertical water column. With improved sensitivity, a small pressure difference can be read more accurately than with a water manometer, or a smaller pressure difference can be read with the same accuracy.

The graphs were generated from the *Excel* workbook for this Example. This workbook has more detailed graphs, showing sensitivity curves for a range of values of d/D and θ.

Students sometimes have trouble analyzing multiple-liquid manometer situations. The following rules of thumb are useful:

1. Any two points at the same elevation in a continuous region of the same liquid are at the same pressure.
2. Pressure increases as one goes *down* a liquid column (remember the pressure change on diving into a swimming pool).

To find the pressure difference Δp between two points separated by a series of fluids, we can use the following modification of Eq. 3.7:

$$\Delta p = g \sum_i \rho_i h_i \qquad (3.8)$$

where ρ_i and h_i represent the densities and depths of the various fluids, respectively. Use care in applying signs to the depths h_i; they will be positive downwards, and negative upwards. Example 3.3 illustrates the use of a multiple-liquid manometer for measuring a pressure difference.

Example 3.3   Multiple-Liquid Manometer

Water flows through pipes A and B. Lubricating oil is in the upper portion of the inverted U. Mercury is in the bottom of the manometer bends. Determine the pressure difference, $p_A - p_B$, in units of lbf/in.²

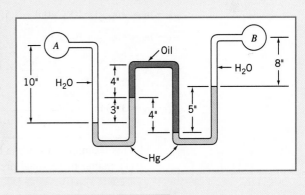

GIVEN: Multiple-liquid manometer as shown.

FIND: Pressure difference, $p_A - p_B$, in lbf/in.²

SOLUTION:

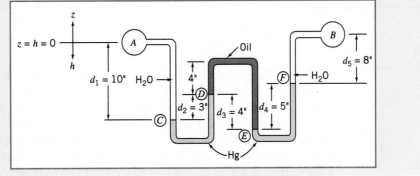

Governing equations: $\qquad \Delta p = g \sum_i \rho_i h_i \qquad SG = \dfrac{\rho}{\rho_{H_2O}}$

Assumptions: (1) Static fluid.
(2) Incompressible fluid.

Applying the governing equation, working from point B to A

$$p_A - p_B = \Delta p = g(\rho_{H_2O}d_5 + \rho_{Hg}d_4 - \rho_{oil}d_3 + \rho_{Hg}d_2 - \rho_{H_2O}d_1) \qquad (1)$$

This equation can also be derived by repeatedly using Eq. 3.7 in the following form:

$$p_2 - p_1 = \rho g(h_2 - h_1)$$

Beginning at point A and applying the equation between successive points along the manometer gives

$$p_C - p_A = +\rho_{H_2O}gd_1$$
$$p_D - p_C = -\rho_{Hg}gd_2$$
$$p_E - p_D = +\rho_{oil}gd_3$$
$$p_F - p_E = -\rho_{Hg}gd_4$$
$$p_B - p_F = -\rho_{H_2O}gd_5$$

Multiplying each equation by minus one and adding, we obtain Eq. (1)

$$p_A - p_B = (p_A - p_C) + (p_C - p_D) + (p_D - p_E) + (p_E - p_F) + (p_F - p_B)$$
$$= -\rho_{H_2O}gd_1 + \rho_{Hg}gd_2 - \rho_{oil}gd_3 + \rho_{Hg}gd_4 + \rho_{H_2O}gd_5$$

Substituting $\rho = SG\rho_{H_2O}$ with $SG_{Hg} = 13.6$ and $SG_{oil} = 0.88$ (Table A.2), yields

$$p_A - p_B = g(-\rho_{H_2O}d_1 + 13.6\rho_{H_2O}d_2 - 0.88\rho_{H_2O}d_3 + 13.6\rho_{H_2O}d_4 + \rho_{H_2O}d_5)$$
$$= g\rho_{H_2O}(-d_1 + 13.6d_2 - 0.88d_3 + 13.6d_4 + d_5)$$
$$p_A - p_B = g\rho_{H_2O}(-10 + 40.8 - 3.52 + 68 + 8) \text{ in.}$$
$$p_A - p_B = g\rho_{H_2O} \times 103.3 \text{ in.}$$
$$= 32.2 \frac{\text{ft}}{\text{s}^2} \times 1.94 \frac{\text{slug}}{\text{ft}^3} \times 103.3 \text{ in.} \times \frac{\text{ft}}{12 \text{ in.}} \times \frac{\text{ft}^2}{144 \text{ in.}^2} \times \frac{\text{lbf} \cdot \text{s}^2}{\text{slug} \cdot \text{ft}}$$
$$p_A - p_B = 3.73 \text{ lbf/in.}^2 \qquad\qquad\qquad\qquad\qquad \underleftarrow{} \quad p_A - p_B$$

> This Example shows use of both Eq. 3.7 and Eq. 3.8. Use of either equation is a matter of personal preference.

Atmospheric pressure may be obtained from a *barometer*, in which the height of a mercury column is measured. The measured height may be converted to pressure using Eq. 3.7 and the data for specific gravity of mercury given in Appendix A, as discussed in the Notes of Example 3.1. Although the vapor pressure of mercury may be neglected, for precise work, temperature and altitude corrections must be applied to the measured level and the effects of surface tension must be considered. The capillary effect in a tube caused by surface tension was illustrated in Example 2.3.

Gases

In many practical engineering problems density will vary appreciably with altitude, and accurate results will require that this variation be accounted for. Pressure variation in a compressible fluid can be evaluated by integrating Eq. 3.6 if the density can be expressed as a function of p or z. Property information or an equation of state may be used to obtain the required relation for density. Several types of property variation may be analyzed. (See Example 3.4.)

The density of gases generally depends on pressure and temperature. The ideal gas equation of state,

$$p = \rho RT \tag{1.1}$$

where R is the gas constant (see Appendix A) and T the absolute temperature, accurately models the behavior of most gases under engineering conditions. However, the use of Eq. 1.1 introduces the gas temperature as an additional variable. Therefore, an additional assumption must be made about temperature variation before Eq. 3.6 can be integrated.

In the U.S. Standard Atmosphere the temperature decreases linearly with altitude up to an elevation of 11.0 km. For a linear temperature variation with altitude given by $T = T_0 - mz$, we obtain, from Eq. 3.6,

$$dp = -\rho g \, dz = -\frac{pg}{RT} dz = -\frac{pg}{R(T_0 - mz)} dz$$

Separating variables and integrating from $z = 0$ where $p = p_0$ to elevation z where the pressure is p gives

$$\int_{p_0}^{p} \frac{dp}{p} = -\int_{0}^{z} \frac{g \, dz}{R(T_0 - mz)}$$

Then

$$\ln \frac{p}{p_0} = \frac{g}{mR} \ln \left(\frac{T_0 - mz}{T_0} \right) = \frac{g}{mR} \ln \left(1 - \frac{mz}{T_0} \right)$$

and the pressure variation, in a gas whose temperature varies linearly with elevation, is given by

$$p = p_0 \left(1 - \frac{mz}{T_0} \right)^{g/mR} = p_0 \left(\frac{T}{T_0} \right)^{g/mR} \tag{3.9}$$

Example 3.4 Pressure and Density Variation in the Atmosphere

The maximum power output capability of a gasoline or diesel engine decreases with altitude because the air density and hence the mass flow rate of air decrease. A truck leaves Denver (elevation 5280 ft) on a day when the local temperature and barometric pressure are 80°F and 24.8 in. of mercury, respectively. It travels through Vail Pass (elevation 10,600 ft), where the temperature is 62°F. Determine the local barometric pressure at Vail Pass and the percent change in density.

GIVEN: Truck travels from Denver to Vail Pass.

Denver: $z = 5280$ ft   Vail Pass: $z = 10,600$ ft
$p = 24.8$ in. Hg $T = 62°F$
$T = 80°F$

FIND: Atmospheric pressure at Vail Pass.
Percent change in air density between Denver and Vail.

SOLUTION:

Governing equations: $\dfrac{dp}{dz} = -\rho g$ $p = \rho R T$

Assumptions: (1) Static fluid.
(2) Air behaves as an ideal gas.

We shall consider four assumptions for property variations with altitude.

(a) If we assume temperature varies linearly with altitude, Eq. 3.9 gives

$$\frac{p}{p_0} = \left(\frac{T}{T_0}\right)^{g/mR}$$

Evaluating the constant m gives

$$m = \frac{T_0 - T}{z - z_0} = \frac{(80 - 62)^\circ\text{F}}{(10.6 - 5.28)10^3\text{ft}} = 3.38 \times 10^{-3}\,^\circ\text{F/ft}$$

and

$$\frac{g}{mR} = 32.2\,\frac{\text{ft}}{\text{s}^2} \times \frac{\text{ft}}{3.38 \times 10^{-3}\,^\circ\text{F}} \times \frac{\text{lbm} \cdot \,^\circ\text{R}}{53.3\,\text{ft} \cdot \text{lbf}} \times \frac{\text{slug}}{32.2\,\text{lbm}} \times \frac{\text{lbf} \cdot \text{s}^2}{\text{slug} \cdot \text{ft}} = 5.55$$

Thus

$$\frac{p}{p_0} = \left(\frac{T}{T_0}\right)^{g/mR} = \left(\frac{460 + 62}{460 + 80}\right)^{5.55} = (0.967)^{5.55} = 0.830$$

and

$$p = 0.830\,p_0 = (0.830)24.8\,\text{in. Hg} = 20.6\,\text{in. Hg} \longleftarrow \qquad\qquad p$$

Note that temperature must be expressed as an absolute temperature in the ideal gas equation of state.
The percent change in density is given by

$$\frac{\rho - \rho_0}{\rho_0} = \frac{\rho}{\rho_0} - 1 = \frac{p}{p_0}\frac{T_0}{T} - 1 = \frac{0.830}{0.967} - 1 = -0.142 \text{ or } -14.2\% \longleftarrow \qquad \frac{\Delta\rho}{\rho_0}$$

(b) For ρ assumed constant ($=\rho_0$),

$$p = p_0 - \rho_0 g(z - z_0) = p_0 - \frac{p_0 g (z - z_0)}{RT_0} = p_0\left[1 - \frac{g(z - z_0)}{RT_0}\right]$$

$$p = 20.2\,\text{in. Hg} \qquad\text{and}\qquad \frac{\Delta\rho}{\rho_0} = 0 \longleftarrow \qquad\qquad p,\frac{\Delta\rho}{\rho_0}$$

(c) If we assume the temperature is constant, then

$$dp = -\rho g\,dz = -\frac{p}{RT} g\,dz$$

and

$$\int_{p_0}^{p} \frac{dp}{p} = -\int_{z_0}^{z} \frac{g}{RT}\,dz$$

$$p = p_0 \exp\left[\frac{-g(z - z_0)}{RT}\right]$$

For T = constant = T_0,

$$p = 20.6 \text{ in. Hg} \qquad \text{and} \qquad \frac{\Delta \rho}{\rho_0} = -16.9\% \qquad \longleftarrow \qquad p, \frac{\Delta \rho}{\rho_0}$$

(d) For an adiabatic atmosphere p/ρ^k = constant,

$$p = p_0 \left(\frac{T}{T_0} \right)^{k/k-1} = 22.0 \text{ in. Hg} \qquad \text{and} \qquad \frac{\Delta \rho}{\rho_0} = -8.2\% \qquad \longleftarrow \qquad p, \frac{\Delta \rho}{\rho_0}$$

We note that over the modest change in elevation the predicted pressure is not strongly dependent on the assumed property variation; values calculated under four different assumptions vary by a maximum of approximately 9 percent. There is considerably greater variation in the predicted percent change in density. The assumption of a linear temperature variation with altitude is the most reasonable assumption.

> This Example shows use of the ideal gas equation with the basic pressure–height relation to obtain the change in pressure with height in the atmosphere under various atmospheric assumptions.

3-4   HYDRAULIC SYSTEMS

Hydraulic systems are characterized by very high pressures, so by comparison hydrostatic pressure variations often may be neglected. Automobile hydraulic brakes develop pressures up to 10 MPa (1500 psi); aircraft and machinery hydraulic actuation systems frequently are designed for pressures up to 40 MPa (6000 psi), and jacks use pressures to 70 MPa (10,000 psi). Special-purpose laboratory test equipment is commercially available for use at pressures to 1000 MPa (150,000 psi)!

Although liquids are generally considered incompressible at ordinary pressures, density changes may be appreciable at high pressures. Bulk moduli of hydraulic fluids also may vary sharply at high pressures. In problems involving unsteady flow, both compressibility of the fluid and elasticity of the boundary structure (e.g., the pipe walls) must be considered. Analysis of problems such as water hammer noise and vibration in hydraulic systems, actuators, and shock absorbers quickly becomes complex and is beyond the scope of this book.

3-5   HYDROSTATIC FORCE ON SUBMERGED SURFACES

Now that we have determined how the pressure varies in a static fluid, we can examine the force on a surface submerged in a liquid.

In order to determine completely the resultant force acting on a submerged surface, we must specify:

1. The magnitude of the force.
2. The direction of the force.
3. The line of action of the force.

We shall consider both plane and curved submerged surfaces.

Hydrostatic Force on a Plane Submerged Surface

A plane submerged surface, on whose upper face we wish to determine the resultant hydrostatic force, is shown in Fig. 3.5. The coordinates are important: They have been chosen so that the surface lies in the xy plane, and the origin O is located at the intersection of the plane surface (or its extension) and the free surface. As well as the magnitude of the force F_R, we wish to locate the point (with coordinates x', y') through which it acts on the surface.

Since there are no shear stresses in a static fluid, the hydrostatic force on any element of the surface acts normal to the surface. The pressure force acting on an element $dA = dx\, dy$ of the upper surface is given by

$$dF = p\, dA$$

The *resultant* force acting on the surface is found by summing the contributions of the infinitesimal forces over the entire area.

Usually when we sum forces we must do so in a vectorial sense. However, in this case all of the infinitesimal forces are perpendicular to the plane, and hence so is the resultant force. Its magnitude is given by

$$F_R = \int_A p\, dA \qquad (3.10a)$$

In order to evaluate the integral in Eq. 3.10a, both the pressure, p, and the element of area, dA, must be expressed in terms of the same variables.

We can use Eq. 3.7 to express the pressure p at depth h in the liquid as

$$p = p_0 + \rho g h$$

In this expression p_0 is the pressure at the free surface ($h = 0$).

In addition, we have, from the system geometry, $h = y \sin \theta$. Using this expression and the above expression for pressure in Eq. 3.10a,

$$F_R = \int_A p\, dA = \int_A (p_0 + \rho g h) dA = \int_A (p_0 + \rho g y \sin \theta) dA$$

$$F_R = p_0 \int_A dA + \rho g \sin \theta \int_A y\, dA = p_0 A + \rho g \sin \theta \int_A y\, dA$$

The integral is the first moment of the surface area about the x axis, which may be written

$$\int_A y\, dA = y_c A$$

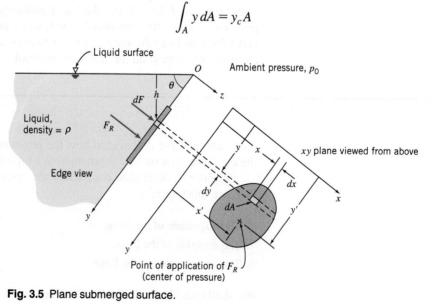

Fig. 3.5 Plane submerged surface.

where y_c is the y coordinate of the *centroid* of the area, A. Thus,

$$F_R = p_0 A + \rho g \sin \theta\, y_c A = (p_0 + \rho g h_c) A$$

or

$$F_R = p_c A \tag{3.10b}$$

where p_c is the absolute pressure in the liquid at the location of the centroid of area A. Equation 3.10b computes the resultant force due to the liquid—including the effect of the ambient pressure p_0—on one side of a submerged plane surface. It does not take into account whatever pressure or force distribution may be on the other side of the surface. However, if we have the *same* pressure, p_0, on this side as we do at the free surface of the liquid, as shown in Fig. 3.6, its effect on F_R cancels out, and if we wish to obtain the *net* force on the surface we can use Eq. 3.10b *with p_c expressed as a gage rather than absolute pressure.*

In computing F_R we can use either the integral of Eq. 3.10a or the resulting Eq. 3.10b. It is important to note that even though the force can be computed using the pressure at the center of the plate, this is *not* the point through which the force acts!

Our next task is to determine (x', y'), the location of the resultant force. Let's first obtain y' by recognizing that the moment of the resultant force about the x axis must be equal to the moment due to the distributed pressure force. Taking the sum (i.e., integral) of the moments of the infinitesimal forces dF about the x axis we obtain

$$y' F_R = \int_A yp\, dA \tag{3.11a}$$

We can integrate by expressing p as a function of y as before:

$$y' F_R = \int_A yp\, dA = \int_A y(p_0 + \rho g h)\, dA = \int_A (p_0 y + \rho g y^2 \sin \theta)\, dA$$

$$= p_0 \int_A y\, dA + \rho g \sin \theta \int_A y^2\, dA$$

The first integral is our familiar $y_c A$. The second integral, $\int_A y^2\, dA$, is the second moment of area about the x axis, I_{xx}. We can use the parallel axis theorem, $I_{xx} = I_{\hat{x}\hat{x}} + A y_c^2$, to replace I_{xx} with the standard second moment of area, about the centroidal $\hat{x}$ axis. Using all of these, we find

$$y' F_R = p_0 y_c A + \rho g \sin \theta (I_{\hat{x}\hat{x}} + A y_c^2) = y_c (p_0 + \rho g y_c \sin \theta) A + \rho g \sin \theta\, I_{\hat{x}\hat{x}}$$

$$= y_c (p_0 + \rho g h_c) A + \rho g \sin \theta\, I_{\hat{x}\hat{x}} = y_c F_R + \rho g \sin \theta\, I_{\hat{x}\hat{x}}$$

Finally, we obtain for y':

$$y' = y_c + \frac{\rho g \sin \theta\, I_{\hat{x}\hat{x}}}{F_R} \tag{3.11b}$$

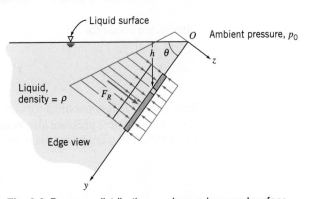

Fig. 3.6 Pressure distribution on plane submerged surface.

Equation 3.11b is convenient for computing the location y' of the force on the submerged side of the surface when we include the ambient pressure p_0. If we have the same ambient pressure acting on the other side of the surface we can use Eq. 3.10b with p_0 neglected to compute the net force,

$$F_R = p_{c_{\text{gage}}} A = \rho g h_c A = \rho g y_c \sin \theta\, A$$

and Eq. 3.11b becomes for this case

$$y' = y_c + \frac{I_{\hat{x}\hat{x}}}{A y_c} \tag{3.11c}$$

Equation 3.11a is the integral equation for computing the location y' of the resultant force; Eq. 3.11b is a useful algebraic form for computing y' when we are interested in the resultant force on the submerged side of the surface; Eq. 3.11c is for computing y' when we are interested in the net force for the case when the same p_0 acts at the free surface and on the other side of the submerged surface. For problems that have a pressure on the other side that is *not* p_0, we can either analyze each side of the surface separately or reduce the two pressure distributions to one net pressure distribution, in effect creating a system to be solved using Eq. 3.10b with p_c expressed as a gage pressure.

Note that in any event, $y' > y_c$—the location of the force is always below the level of the plate centroid. This makes sense—as Fig. 3.6 shows, the pressures will always be larger on the lower regions, moving the resultant force down the plate.

A similar analysis can be done to compute x', the x location of the force on the plate. Taking the sum of the moments of the infinitesimal forces dF about the y axis we obtain

$$x' F_R = \int_A x\, p\, dA \tag{3.12a}$$

We can express p as a function of y as before:

$$x' F_R = \int_A xp\, dA = \int_A x(p_0 + \rho g h)\, dA = \int_A (p_0 x + \rho g x y \sin \theta)\, dA$$

$$= p_0 \int_A x\, dA + \rho g \sin \theta \int_A xy\, dA$$

The first integral is $x_c A$ (where x_c is the distance of the centroid from y axis). The second integral is $\int_A xy\, dA = I_{xy}$. Using the parallel axis theorem, $I_{xy} = I_{\hat{x}\hat{y}} + A x_c y_c$, we find

$$x' F_R = p_0 x_c A + \rho g \sin \theta (I_{\hat{x}\hat{y}} + A x_c y_c) = x_c (p_0 + \rho g y_c \sin \theta) A + \rho g \sin \theta\, I_{\hat{x}\hat{y}}$$

$$= x_c (p_0 + \rho g h_c) A + \rho g \sin \theta\, I_{\hat{x}\hat{y}} = x_c F_R + \rho g \sin \theta\, I_{\hat{x}\hat{y}}$$

Finally, we obtain for x':

$$x' = x_c + \frac{\rho g \sin \theta\, I_{\hat{x}\hat{y}}}{F_R} \tag{3.12b}$$

Equation 3.12b is convenient for computing x' when we include the ambient pressure p_0. If we have ambient pressure also acting on the other side of the surface we can again use Eq. 3.10b with p_0 neglected to compute the net force and Eq. 3.12b becomes for this case

$$x' = x_c + \frac{I_{\hat{x}\hat{y}}}{A y_c} \tag{3.12c}$$

Equation 3.12a is the integral equation for computing the location x' of the resultant force; Eq. 3.12b can be used for computations when we are interested in the force on the submerged side only; Eq. 3.12c is useful when we have p_0 on the other side of the surface and we are interested in the net force.

In summary, Eqs. 3.10 through 3.12 constitute a complete set of equations for computing the magnitude and location of the force due to hydrostatic pressure on any submerged plane surface. The direction of the force will always be perpendicular to the plane.

We can now consider several examples using these equations. In Example 3.5 we use both the integral and algebraic sets of equations.

Example 3.5 Resultant Force on Inclined Plane Submerged Surface

The inclined surface shown, hinged along edge A, is 5 m wide. Determine the resultant force, F_R, of the water and the air on the inclined surface.

GIVEN: Rectangular gate, hinged along A, $w = 5$ m.

FIND: Resultant force, F_R, of the water and the air on the gate.

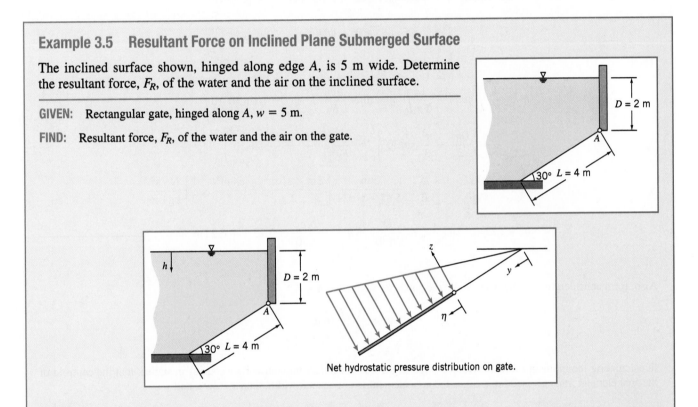

Net hydrostatic pressure distribution on gate.

SOLUTION:

In order to completely determine F_R, we need to find (a) the magnitude and (b) the line of action of the force (the direction of the force is perpendicular to the surface). We will solve this problem by using (i) direct integration and (ii) the algebraic equations.

Direct Integration

Governing equations: $\quad p = p_0 + \rho g h \quad F_R = \int_A p\, dA \quad \eta' F_R = \int_A \eta\, p\, dA \quad x' F_R = \int_A xp\, dA$

Because atmospheric pressure p_0 acts on both sides of the plate its effect cancels, and we can work in gage pressures ($p = \rho g h$). In addition, while we *could* integrate using the y variable, it will be more convenient here to define a variable η, as shown in the figure.

Using η to obtain expressions for h and dA, then

$$h = D + \eta \sin 30° \quad \text{and} \quad dA = w\, d\eta$$

Applying these to the governing equation for the resultant force,

$$F_R = \int_A p\,dA = \int_0^L \rho g(D + \eta \sin 30°)w\,d\eta$$

$$= \rho g w \left[D\eta + \frac{\eta^2}{2}\sin 30° \right]_0^L = \rho g w \left[DL + \frac{L^2}{2}\sin 30° \right]$$

$$= 999\,\frac{\text{kg}}{\text{m}^3} \times 9.81\,\frac{\text{m}}{\text{s}^2} \times 5\text{m} \left[2\text{m} \times 4\text{m} + \frac{16\,\text{m}^2}{2} \times \frac{1}{2} \right]\frac{\text{N}\cdot\text{s}^2}{\text{kg}\cdot\text{m}}$$

$$F_R = 588\,\text{kN} \qquad\longleftarrow\qquad\qquad\qquad\qquad\qquad\qquad\qquad\qquad F_R$$

For the location of the force we compute η' (the distance from the top edge of the plate),

$$\eta' F_R = \int_A \eta p\,dA$$

Then

$$\eta' = \frac{1}{F_R}\int_A \eta p\,dA = \frac{1}{F_R}\int_0^L \eta p w\,d\eta = \frac{\rho g w}{F_R}\int_0^L \eta(D + \eta \sin 30°)\,d\eta$$

$$= \frac{\rho g w}{F_R}\left[\frac{D\eta^2}{2} + \frac{\eta^3}{3}\sin 30° \right]_0^L = \frac{\rho g w}{F_R}\left[\frac{DL^2}{2} + \frac{L^3}{3}\sin 30° \right]$$

$$= 999\,\frac{\text{kg}}{\text{m}^3} \times 9.8\,\frac{\text{m}}{\text{s}^2} \times \frac{5\,\text{m}}{5.88\times 10^5\,\text{N}}\left[\frac{2\,\text{m}\times 16\,\text{m}^2}{2} + \frac{64\,\text{m}^3}{3}\times\frac{1}{2} \right]\frac{\text{N}\cdot\text{s}^2}{\text{kg}\cdot\text{m}}$$

$$\eta' = 2.22\,\text{m} \quad\text{and}\quad y' = \frac{D}{\sin 30°} + \eta' = \frac{2\,\text{m}}{\sin 30°} + 2.22\,\text{m} = 6.22\,\text{m} \qquad\longleftarrow\qquad y'$$

Also, from consideration of moments about the y axis through edge A,

$$x' = \frac{1}{F_R}\int_A xp\,dA$$

In calculating the moment of the distributed force (right side), recall, from your earlier courses in statics, that the centroid of the area element must be used for x. Since the area element is of constant width, then $x = w/2$, and

$$x' = \frac{1}{F_R}\int_A \frac{w}{2}p\,dA = \frac{w}{2F_R}\int_A p\,dA = \frac{w}{2} = 2.5\,\text{m} \qquad\longleftarrow\qquad x'$$

Algebraic Equations

In using the algebraic equations we need to take care in selecting the appropriate set. In this problem we have $p_0 = p_{\text{atm}}$ on both sides of the plate, so Eq. 3.10b with p_c as a gage pressure is used for the net force:

$$F_R = p_c A = \rho g h_c A = \rho g \left(D + \frac{L}{2}\sin 30° \right)Lw$$

$$F_R = \rho g w \left[DL + \frac{L^2}{2}\sin 30° \right]$$

This is the same expression as was obtained by direct integration.

The y coordinate of the center of pressure is given by Eq. 3.11c:

$$y' = y_c + \frac{I_{\hat{x}\hat{x}}}{A y_c} \tag{3.11c}$$

For the inclined rectangular gate

$$y_c = \frac{D}{\sin 30°} + \frac{L}{2} = \frac{2\,\text{m}}{\sin 30°} + \frac{4\,\text{m}}{2} = 6\,\text{m}$$

$$A = Lw = 4\,\text{m} \times 5\,\text{m} = 20\,\text{m}^2$$

$$I_{\hat{x}\hat{x}} = \frac{1}{12} w L^3 = \frac{1}{12} \times 5\,\text{m} \times (4\,\text{m})^3 = 26.7\,\text{m}^2$$

$$y' = y_c + \frac{I_{\hat{x}\hat{x}}}{A y_c} = 6\,\text{m} + 26.7\,\text{m}^4 \times \frac{1}{20\,\text{m}^2} \times \frac{1}{6\,\text{m}^2} = 6.22\,\text{m} \longleftarrow \underline{\qquad y'}$$

The x coordinate of the center of pressure is given by Eq. 3.12c:

$$x' = x_c + \frac{I_{\hat{x}\hat{y}}}{A y_c} \tag{3.12c}$$

For the rectangular gate $I_{\hat{x}\hat{y}} = 0$ and $x' = x_c = 2.5\,\text{m}$. $\longleftarrow \underline{\qquad x'}$

> This Example shows
> ✓ Use of integral and algebraic equations.
> ✓ Use of the algebraic equations for computing the *net* force.

Example 3.6 Force on Vertical Plane Submerged Surface with Nonzero Gage Pressure at Free Surface

The door shown in the side of the tank is hinged along its bottom edge. A pressure of 100 psfg is applied to the liquid free surface. Find the force, F_t, required to keep the door closed.

GIVEN: Door as shown in the figure.

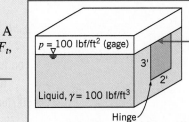

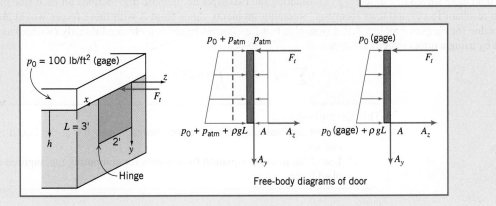

Free-body diagrams of door

FIND: Force required to keep door shut.

SOLUTION:

This problem requires a free-body diagram (FBD) of the door. The pressure distributions on the inside and outside of the door will lead to a net force (and its location) that will be included in the FBD. We need to be careful in choosing the equations for computing the resultant force and its location. We can either use absolute pressures (as on the left FBD) and compute two forces (one on each side) or gage pressures and compute one force (as on the right FBD). For simplicity we will use gage pressures. The right-hand FBD makes clear we should use Eqs. 3.10b and 3.11b, which were derived for problems in which we wish to include the effects of an ambient pressure (p_0), or in other words, for problems when we have a nonzero gage pressure at the free surface. The components of force due to the hinge are A_y and A_z. The force F_t can be found by taking moments about A (the hinge).

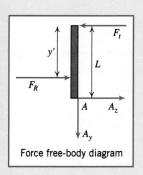

Force free-body diagram

Governing equations:

$$F_R = p_c A \qquad y' = y_c + \frac{\rho g \sin \theta \, I_{\hat{x}\hat{x}}}{F_R} \qquad \sum M_A = 0$$

The resultant force and its location are

$$F_R = (p_0 + \rho g h_c)A = \left(p_0 + \gamma \frac{L}{2}\right)bL \tag{1}$$

and

$$y' = y_c + \frac{\rho g \sin 90° \, I_{\hat{x}\hat{x}}}{F_R} = \frac{L}{2} + \frac{\gamma bL^3/12}{\left(p_0 + \gamma \frac{L}{2}\right)bL} = \frac{L}{2} + \frac{\gamma L^2/12}{\left(p_0 + \gamma \frac{L}{2}\right)} \tag{2}$$

Taking moments about point A

$$\sum M_A = F_t L - F_R(L - y') = 0 \qquad \text{or} \qquad F_t = F_R\left(1 - \frac{y'}{L}\right)$$

Using Eqs. 1 and 2 in this equation we find

$$F_t = \left(p_0 + \gamma \frac{L}{2}\right)bL\left[1 - \frac{1}{2} - \frac{\gamma L^2/12}{\left(p_0 + \gamma \frac{L}{2}\right)}\right]$$

$$F_t = \left(p_0 + \gamma \frac{L}{2}\right)\frac{bL}{2} + \gamma \frac{bL^2}{12}$$

$$= \frac{p_0 bL}{2} + \frac{\gamma bL^2}{6} \tag{3}$$

$$= \frac{100 \, \text{lbf}}{\text{ft}^2} \times 2 \, \text{ft} \times 3 \, \text{ft} \times \frac{1}{2} + \frac{100 \, \text{lbf}}{\text{ft}^3} \times 2 \, \text{ft} \times 9 \, \text{ft}^2 \times \frac{1}{6}$$

$$F_t = 600 \, \text{lbf} \qquad\qquad\qquad\qquad\qquad\qquad\qquad\qquad\qquad\qquad F_t$$

We could have solved this problem by considering the two separate pressure distributions on each side of the door, leading to two resultant forces and their locations. Summing moments about point A with these forces would also have yielded the same value for F_t. (See Problem 3.59.) Note also that Eq. 3 could have been obtained directly (without separately finding F_R and y') by using a direct integration approach:

$$\sum M_A = F_t L - \int_A y \, p \, dA = 0$$

> This Example shows:
> ✓ Use of algebraic equations for nonzero gage pressure at the liquid free surface.
> ✓ Use of the moment equation from statics for computing the required applied force.

Hydrostatic Force on a Curved Submerged Surface

For curved surfaces, we will once again derive expressions for the resultant force by integrating the pressure distribution over the surface. However, unlike for the plane surface, we have a more complicated problem—the pressure force is normal to the surface at each point, but now the infinitesimal area elements point in varying directions because of the surface curvature. This means that instead of integrating over an element dA we need to integrate over vector element $d\vec{A}$. This will initially lead to a more complicated analysis, but we will see that a simple solution technique will be developed.

Consider the curved surface shown in Fig. 3.7. The pressure force acting on the element of area, $d\vec{A}$, is given by

$$d\vec{F} = -p\,d\vec{A}$$

where the minus sign indicates that the force acts on the area, in the direction opposite to the area normal. The resultant force is given by

$$\vec{F}_R = -\int_A p\,d\vec{A} \tag{3.13}$$

We can write

$$\vec{F}_R = \hat{i}F_{R_x} + \hat{j}F_{R_y} + \hat{k}F_{R_z}$$

where F_{R_x}, F_{R_y}, and F_{R_z} are the components of $\vec{F}_R$ in the positive x, y, and z directions, respectively.

To evaluate the component of the force in a given direction, we take the dot product of the force with the unit vector in the given direction. For example, taking the dot product of each side of Eq. 3.13 with unit vector $\hat{i}$ gives

$$F_{R_x} = \vec{F}_R \cdot \hat{i} = \int d\vec{F} \cdot \hat{i} = -\int_A p\,d\vec{A} \cdot \hat{i} = -\int_{A_x} p\,dA_x$$

where dA_x is the projection of $d\vec{A}$ on a plane perpendicular to the x axis (see Fig. 3.7), and the minus sign indicates that the x component of the resultant force is in the negative x direction.

Since, in any problem, the direction of the force component can be determined by inspection, the use of vectors is not necessary. In general, the magnitude of the component of the resultant force in the l direction is given by

$$F_{R_l} = \int_{A_l} p\,dA_l \tag{3.14}$$

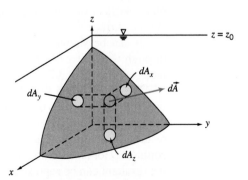

Fig. 3.7 Curved submerged surface.

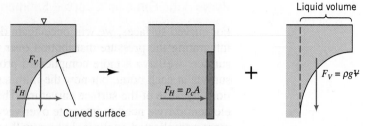

Fig. 3.8 Forces on curved submerged surface.

where dA_l is the projection of the area element dA on a plane perpendicular to the l direction. The line of action of each component of the resultant force is found by recognizing that the moment of the resultant force component about a given axis must be equal to the moment of the corresponding distributed force component about the same axis.

Equation 3.14 can be used for the horizontal forces F_{R_x} and F_{R_y}. We have the interesting result that *the horizontal force and its location are the same as for an imaginary vertical plane surface of the same projected area.* This is illustrated in Fig. 3.8, where we have called the horizontal force F_H.

Figure 3.8 also illustrates how we can compute the vertical component of force: With atmospheric pressure at the free surface and on the other side of the curved surface *the net vertical force will be equal to the weight of fluid directly above the surface.* This can be seen by applying Eq. 3.14 to determine the magnitude of the vertical component of the resultant force, obtaining

$$F_{R_z} = F_V = \int p \, dA_z$$

Since $p = \rho g h$,

$$F_V = \int \rho g h \, dA_z = \int \rho g \, d\forall$$

where $\rho g h \, dA_z = \rho g \, d\forall$ is the weight of a differential cylinder of liquid above the element of surface area, dA_z, extending a distance h from the curved surface to the free surface. The vertical component of the resultant force is obtained by integrating over the entire submerged surface. Thus

$$F_V = \int_{A_z} \rho g h \, dA_z = \int_{\forall} \rho g \, d\forall = \rho g \, \forall$$

In summary, for a curved surface we can use two simple formulas for computing the horizontal and vertical force components due to the fluid only (no ambient pressure),

$$F_H = p_c A \quad \text{and} \quad F_V = \rho g \forall \tag{3.15}$$

where p_c and A are the pressure at the center and the area, respectively, of a vertical plane surface of the same projected area, and $\forall$ is the volume of fluid above the curved surface.

It can be shown that the line of action of the vertical force component passes through the center of gravity of the volume of liquid directly above the curved surface (see Example 3.7).

We have shown that the resultant hydrostatic force on a curved submerged surface is specified in terms of its components. We recall from our study of statics that the resultant of any force system can be represented by a force-couple system, i.e., the resultant force applied at a point and a couple about that point. If the force and the couple vectors are orthogonal (as is the case for a two-dimensional curved surface), the resultant can be represented as a pure force with a unique line of action. Otherwise the resultant may be represented as a "wrench," also having a unique line of action.

Example 3.7 Force Components on a Curved Submerged Surface

The gate shown is hinged at O and has constant width, $w = 5$ m. The equation of the surface is $x = y^2/a$, where $a = 4$ m. The depth of water to the right of the gate is $D = 4$ m. Find the magnitude of the force, F_a, applied as shown, required to maintain the gate in equilibrium if the weight of the gate is neglected.

GIVEN: Gate of constant width, $w = 5$ m.
Equation of surface in xy plane is $x = y^2/a$, where $a = 4$ m.
Water stands at depth $D = 4$ m to the right of the gate.
Force F_a is applied as shown, and weight of gate is to be neglected. (Note that for simplicity we do not show the reactions at O.)

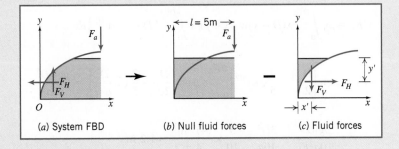

(a) System FBD (b) Null fluid forces (c) Fluid forces

FIND: Force F_a required to maintain the gate in equilibrium.

SOLUTION:
We will take moments about point O after finding the magnitudes and locations of the horizontal and vertical forces due to the water. The free body diagram (FBD) of the system is shown above in part (a). Before proceeding we need to think about how we compute F_V, the vertical component of the fluid force—we have stated that it is equal (in magnitude and location) to the weight of fluid directly above the curved surface. However, we have no fluid directly above the gate, even though it is clear that the fluid does exert a vertical force! We need to do a "thought experiment" in which we imagine having a system with water on both sides of the gate (with null effect), minus a system with water directly above the gate (which generates fluid forces). This logic is demonstrated above: the system FBD(a) = the null FBD(b) − the fluid forces FBD(c). Thus the vertical and horizontal fluid forces on the system, FBD(a), are equal and opposite to those on FBD(c). In summary, the magnitude and location of the vertical fluid force F_V are given by the weight and location of the centroid of the fluid "above" the gate; the magnitude and location of the horizontal fluid force F_H are given by the magnitude and location of the force on an equivalent vertical flat plate.

Governing equations: $F_H = p_c A$ $\quad y' = y_c + \dfrac{I_{\hat{x}\hat{x}}}{Ay_c}$ $\quad F_V = \rho g \forall$ $\quad x' = $ water center of gravity

For F_H, the centroid, area, and second moment of the equivalent vertical flat plate are, respectively, $y_c = h_c = D/2$, $A = Dw$ and $I_{\hat{x}\hat{x}} = wD^3/12$.

$$F_H = p_c A = \rho g h_c A$$

$$= \rho g \frac{D}{2} Dw = \rho g \frac{D^2}{2} w = 999 \frac{\text{kg}}{\text{m}^3} \times 9.81 \frac{\text{m}}{\text{s}^2} \times \frac{(4\,\text{m}^2)}{2} \times 5\,\text{m} \times \frac{\text{N} \cdot \text{s}^2}{\text{kg} \cdot \text{m}} \qquad (1)$$

$$F_H = 392 \text{ kN}$$

and

$$y' = y_c + \frac{I_{\hat{x}\hat{x}}}{Ay_c}$$

$$= \frac{D}{2} + \frac{wD^3/12}{wDD/2} = \frac{D}{2} + \frac{D}{6}$$

$$y' = \frac{2}{3}D = \frac{2}{3} \times 4\,\text{m} = 2.67\,\text{m} \qquad (2)$$

For F_V, we need to compute the weight of water "above" the gate. To do this we define a differential column of volume $(D - y)\, w\, dx$ and integrate

$$F_V = \rho g \cancel{V} = \rho g \int_0^{D^2/a} (D - y) w\, dx = \rho g w \int_0^{D^2/a} \left(D - \sqrt{a}x^{1/2}\right) dx$$

$$= \rho g w \left[Dx - \frac{2}{3}\sqrt{a}x^{3/2}\right]_0^{D^2/a} = \rho g w \left[\frac{D^3}{a} - \frac{2}{3}\sqrt{a}\frac{D^3}{a^{3/2}}\right] = \frac{\rho g w D^3}{3a}$$

$$F_V = \frac{999\,\text{kg}}{\text{m}^3} \times \frac{9.81\,\text{m}}{\text{s}^2} \times 5\,\text{m} \times \frac{(4)^3\,\text{m}^3}{3} \times \frac{1}{4\,\text{m}} \times \frac{\text{N} \cdot \text{s}^2}{\text{kg} \cdot \text{m}} = 261\,\text{kN} \tag{3}$$

The location x' of this force is given by the location of the center of gravity of the water "above" the gate. We recall from statics that this can be obtained by using the notion that the moment of F_V, and the moment of the sum of the differential weights about the y axis must be equal, so

$$x' F_V = \rho g \int_0^{D^2/a} x(D - y) w\, dx = \rho g w \int_0^{D^2/a} \left(D - \sqrt{a}x^{3/2}\right) dx$$

$$x' F_V = \rho g w \left[\frac{D}{2}x^2 - \frac{2}{5}\sqrt{a}x^{5/2}\right]_0^{D^2/a} = \rho g w \left[\frac{D^5}{2a^2} - \frac{2}{5}\sqrt{a}\frac{D^5}{a^{5/2}}\right] = \frac{\rho g w D^5}{10a^2}$$

$$x' = \frac{\rho g w D^5}{10a^2 F_V} = \frac{3D^2}{10a} = \frac{3}{10} \times \frac{(4)^2\,\text{m}^2}{4\,\text{m}} = 1.2\,\text{m} \tag{4}$$

Now that we have determined the fluid forces, we can finally take moments about O (taking care to use the appropriate signs), using the results of Eqs. 1 through 4

$$\sum M_O = -lF_a + x'F_V + (D - y')F_H = 0$$

$$F_a = \frac{1}{l}[x'F_V + (D - y')F_H] = \frac{1}{5\,\text{m}}[1.2\,\text{m} \times 261\,\text{kN} + (4 - 2.67)\text{m} \times 392\,\text{kN}]$$

$$F_a = 167\,\text{kN} \longleftarrow \qquad\qquad\qquad\qquad\qquad\qquad\qquad\qquad\qquad F_a$$

> This Example shows:
> ✓ Use of vertical flat plate equations for the horizontal force, and fluid weight equations for the vertical force, on a curved surface.
> ✓ The use of "thought experiments" to convert a problem with fluid below a curved surface into an equivalent problem with fluid above.

*3-6   BUOYANCY AND STABILITY

If an object is immersed in a liquid, or floating on its surface, the net vertical force acting on it due to liquid pressure is termed *buoyancy*. Consider an object totally immersed in static liquid, as shown in Fig. 3.9.

The vertical force on the body due to hydrostatic pressure may be found most easily by considering cylindrical volume elements similar to the one shown in Fig. 3.9.

We recall that we can use Eq. 3.7 for computing the pressure p at depth h in a liquid,

$$p = p_0 + \rho g h$$

---

* This section may be omitted without loss of continuity in the text material.

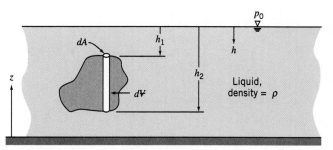

Fig. 3.9 Immersed body in static liquid.

The net vertical pressure force on the element is then

$$dF_z = (p_0 + \rho g h_2)\, dA - (p_0 + \rho g h_1)\, dA = \rho g (h_2 - h_1)\, dA$$

But $(h_2 - h_1)dA = d\Psi$, the volume of the element. Thus

$$F_z = \int dF_z = \int_\Psi \rho g\, d\Psi = \rho g \Psi$$

where Ψ is the volume of the object. Hence we conclude that for a submerged body *the buoyancy force of the fluid is equal to the weight of displaced fluid,*

$$F_{\text{buoyancy}} = \rho g \Psi \qquad (3.16)$$

This relation reportedly was used by Archimedes in 220 B.C. to determine the gold content in the crown of King Hiero II. Consequently, it is often called "Archimedes' Principle." In more current technical applications, Eq. 3.16 is used to design displacement vessels, flotation gear, and submersibles [1].

The submerged object need not be solid. Hydrogen bubbles, used to visualize streaklines and timelines in water (see Section 2-2), are positively buoyant; they rise slowly as they are swept along by the flow. Conversely, water droplets in oil are negatively bouyant and tend to sink.

Airships and balloons are termed "lighter-than-air" craft. The density of an ideal gas is proportional to molecular weight, so hydrogen and helium are less dense than air at the same temperature and pressure. Hydrogen ($M_m = 2$) is less dense than helium ($M_m = 4$), but extremely flammable, whereas helium is inert. Hydrogen has not been used commercially since the disastrous explosion of the German passenger airship *Hindenburg* in 1937. The use of buoyancy force to generate lift is illustrated in Example 3.8.

Example 3.8 Buoyancy Force in a Hot Air Balloon

A hot air balloon (approximated as a sphere of diameter 50 ft) is to lift a basket load of 600 lbf. To what temperature must the air be heated in order to achieve liftoff?

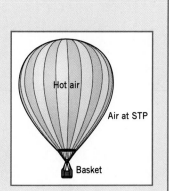

GIVEN: Atmosphere at STP, diameter of balloon $d = 50$ ft, and load $W_{\text{load}} = 600$ lbf.

FIND: The hot air temperature to attain liftoff.

SOLUTION:
Apply the buoyancy equation to determine the lift generated by atmosphere, and apply the vertical force equilibrium equation to obtain the hot air density. Then use the ideal gas equation to obtain the hot air temperature.

Governing equations:

$$F_{\text{buoyancy}} = \rho g \forall \qquad \sum F_y = 0 \qquad p = \rho RT$$

Assumptions: (1) Ideal gas.
(2) Atmospheric pressure throughout.

Summing vertical forces

$$\sum F_y = F_{\text{buoyancy}} - W_{\text{hot air}} - W_{\text{load}} = \rho_{\text{atm}} g \forall - \rho_{\text{hot air}} g \forall - W_{\text{load}} = 0$$

Rearranging and solving for $\rho_{\text{hot air}}$ (using data from Appendix A),

$$\rho_{\text{hot air}} = \rho_{\text{atm}} - \frac{W_{\text{load}}}{g \forall} = \rho_{\text{atm}} - \frac{6 W_{\text{load}}}{\pi d^3 g}$$

$$= 0.00238 \, \frac{\text{slug}}{\text{ft}^3} - 6 \times \frac{600 \, \text{lbf}}{\pi (50)^3 \text{ft}^3} \times \frac{s^2}{32.2 \, \text{ft}} \times \frac{\text{slug} \cdot \text{ft}}{s^2 \cdot \text{lbf}}$$

$$\rho_{\text{hot air}} = (0.00238 - 0.000285) \frac{\text{slug}}{\text{ft}^3} = 0.00209 \, \frac{\text{slug}}{\text{ft}^3}$$

Finally, to obtain the temperature of this hot air, we can use the ideal gas equation in the following form

$$\frac{p_{\text{hot air}}}{\rho_{\text{hot air}} RT_{\text{hot air}}} = \frac{p_{\text{atm}}}{\rho_{\text{atm}} RT_{\text{atm}}}$$

and with $p_{\text{hot air}} = p_{\text{atm}}$

$$T_{\text{hot air}} = T_{\text{atm}} \frac{\rho_{\text{atm}}}{\rho_{\text{hot air}}} = (460 + 59)°\text{R} \times \frac{0.00238}{0.00209} = 591°\text{R}$$

$$T_{\text{hot air}} = 131°\text{F} \longleftarrow \hspace{6cm} T_{\text{hot air}}$$

> **Notes:**
> ✓ Absolute pressures and temperatures are always used in the ideal gas equation.
> ✓ This problem demonstrates that for lighter-than-air vehicles the buoyancy force exceeds the vehicle weight—that is, the weight of fluid (air) displaced exceeds the vehicle weight.

Equation 3.16 predicts the net vertical pressure force on a body that is totally submerged in a single liquid. In cases of partial immersion, a floating body displaces its own weight of the liquid in which it floats.

The line of action of the buoyancy force, which may be found using the methods of Section 3-5, acts through the centroid of the displaced volume. Since floating bodies are in equilibrium under body and buoyancy forces, the location of the line of action of the buoyancy force determines stability, as shown in Fig. 3.10.

The weight of an object acts through its center of gravity, CG. In Fig. 3.10a, the lines of action of the buoyancy and the weight are offset in such a way as to produce a couple that tends to right the craft. In Fig. 3.10b, the couple tends to capsize the craft.

Ballast may be needed to achieve roll stability. Wooden warships carried stone ballast low in the hull to offset the weight of the heavy cannon on upper gun decks. Modern ships can have stability problems as well: overloaded ferry boats have capsized when passengers all gathered on one side of the upper deck, shifting the CG

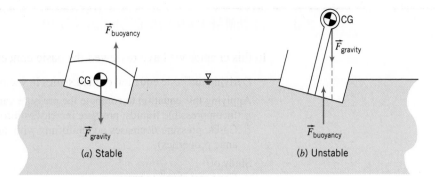

Fig. 3.10 Stability of floating bodies.

laterally. In stacking containers high on the deck of a container ship, care is needed to avoid raising the center of gravity to a level that may result in the unstable condition depicted in Fig. 3.10*b*.

For a vessel with a relatively flat bottom, as shown in Fig. 3.10*a*, the restoring moment increases as roll angle becomes larger. At some angle, typically that at which the edge of the deck goes below water level, the restoring moment peaks and starts to decrease. The moment may become zero at some large roll angle, known as the angle of vanishing stability. The vessel may capsize if the roll exceeds this angle; then, if still intact, the vessel may find a new equilibrium state upside down.

The actual shape of the restoring moment curve depends on hull shape. A broad beam gives a large lateral shift in the line of action of the buoyancy force and thus a high restoring moment. High freeboard above the water line increases the angle at which the moment curve peaks, but may make the moment drop rapidly above this angle.

Sailing vessels are subjected to large lateral forces as wind engages the sails (a boat under sail in a brisk wind typically operates at a considerable roll angle). The lateral wind force must be counteracted by a heavily weighted keel extended below the hull bottom. In small sailboats, crew members may lean far over the side to add additional restoring moment to prevent capsizing [2].

Within broad limits, the buoyancy of a surface vessel is adjusted automatically as the vessel rides higher or lower in the water. However, craft that operate fully submerged must actively adjust buoyancy and gravity forces to remain neutrally buoyant. For submarines this is accomplished using tanks which are flooded to reduce excess buoyancy or blown out with compressed air to increase buoyancy [1]. Airships may vent gas to descend or drop ballast to rise. Buoyancy of a hot-air balloon is controlled by varying the air temperature within the balloon envelope.

For deep ocean dives use of compressed air becomes impractical because of the high pressures (the Pacific Ocean is over 10 km deep; seawater pressure at this depth is greater than 1000 atmospheres!). A liquid such as gasoline, which is buoyant in seawater, may be used to provide buoyancy. However, because gasoline is more compressible than water, its buoyancy decreases as the dive gets deeper. Therefore it is necessary to carry and drop ballast to achieve positive buoyancy for the return trip to the surface.

The most structurally efficient hull shape for airships and submarines has a circular cross-section. The buoyancy force passes through the center of the circle. Therefore, for roll stability the CG must be located below the hull centerline. Thus the crew compartment of an airship is placed beneath the hull to lower the CG.

3-7   FLUIDS IN RIGID-BODY MOTION (ON THE WEB)

| 3-8 | **SUMMARY AND USEFUL EQUATIONS** |

In this chapter we have reviewed the basic concepts of fluid statics. This included:

✓ Deriving the basic equation of fluid statics in vector form.
✓ Applying this equation to compute the pressure variation in a static fluid:
  ○ Incompressible liquids: pressure increases uniformly with depth.
  ○ Gases: pressure decreases nonuniformly with elevation (dependent on other thermodynamic properties).
✓ Study of:
  ○ Gage and absolute pressure.
  ○ Use of manometers and barometers.
✓ Analysis of the fluid force magnitude and location on submerged:
  ○ Plane surfaces.
  ○ Curved surfaces.
✓ *Derivation and use of Archimedes' Principle of Buoyancy.
✓ *Analysis of rigid-body fluid motion (on the Web).

Note: Most of the Useful Equations in the table below have a number of constraints or limitations—*be sure to refer to their page numbers for details*!

Useful Equations			
Hydrostatic pressure variation:	$\dfrac{dp}{dz} = -\rho g \equiv -\gamma$	(3.6)	Page 55
Hydrostatic pressure variation (incompressible fluid):	$p - p_0 = \Delta p = \rho g h$	(3.7)	Page 58
Hydrostatic pressure variation (several incompressible fluids):	$\Delta p = g \displaystyle\sum_i \rho_i h_i$	(3.8)	Page 61
Hydrostatic force on submerged plane (integral form):	$F_R = \displaystyle\int_A p \, dA$	(3.10a)	Page 66
Hydrostatic force on submerged plane:	$F_R = p_c A$	(3.10b)	Page 67
Location y' of hydrostatic force on submerged plane (integral):	$y' F_R = \displaystyle\int_A y p \, dA$	(3.11a)	Page 67
Location y' of hydrostatic force on submerged plane (algebraic):	$y' = y_c + \dfrac{\rho g \sin\theta \, I_{\hat{x}\hat{x}}}{F_R}$	(3.11b)	Page 67
Location y' of hydrostatic force on submerged plane (p_0 neglected):	$y' = y_c + \dfrac{I_{\hat{x}\hat{x}}}{A y_c}$	(3.11c)	Page 68
Location x' of hydrostatic force on submerged plane (integral):	$x' F_R = \displaystyle\int_A x p \, dA$	(3.12a)	Page 68
Location x' of hydrostatic force on submerged plane (algebraic):	$x' = x_c + \dfrac{\rho g \sin\theta \, I_{\hat{x}\hat{y}}}{F_R}$	(3.12b)	Page 68
Location x' of hydrostatic force on submerged plane (p_0 neglected):	$x' = x_c + \dfrac{I_{\hat{x}\hat{y}}}{A y_c}$	(3.12c)	Page 68
Horizontal and vertical hydrostatic forces on curved submerged surface:	$F_H = p_c A$ and $F_V = \rho g \forall$	(3.15)	Page 74
Buoyancy force on submerged object:	$F_{\text{buoyancy}} = \rho g \forall$	(3.16)	Page 77

We have now concluded our introduction to the fundamental concepts of fluid mechanics, and the basic concepts of fluid statics. In the next chapter we will begin our study of fluids in motion.

*These topics apply to sections that may be omitted without loss of continuity in the text material.

REFERENCES

1. Burcher, R., and L. Rydill, *Concepts in Submarine Design.* Cambridge, UK: Cambridge University Press, 1994.

2. Marchaj, C. A., *Aero-Hydrodynamics of Sailing*, rev. ed. Camden, ME: International Marine Publishing, 1988.

PROBLEMS

3.1 Compressed nitrogen is stored in a spherical tank of diameter $D = 0.75$ m. The gas is at an absolute pressure of 25 MPa and a temperature of 25°C. What is the mass in the tank? If the maximum allowable wall stress in the tank is 210 MPa, find the minimum theoretical wall thickness of the tank.

3.2 Ear "popping" is an unpleasant phenomenon sometimes experienced when a change in pressure occurs, for example in a fast-moving elevator or in an airplane. If you are in a two-seater airplane at 3000 m and a descent of 100 m causes your ears to "pop," what is the pressure change that your ears "pop" at, in millimeters of mercury? If the airplane now rises to 8000 m and again begins descending, how far will the airplane descend before your ears "pop" again? Assume a U.S. Standard Atmosphere.

3.3 When you are on a mountain face and boil water, you notice that the water temperature is 195°F. What is your approximate altitude? The next day, you are at a location where it boils at 185°F. How high did you climb between the two days? Assume a U.S. Standard Atmosphere.

3.4 Because the pressure falls, water boils at a lower temperature with increasing altitude. Consequently, cake mixes and boiled eggs, among other foods, must be cooked different lengths of time. Determine the boiling temperature of water at 1000 and 2000 m elevation on a standard day, and compare with the sea-level value.

3.5 The tube shown is filled with mercury at 20°C. Calculate the force applied to the piston.

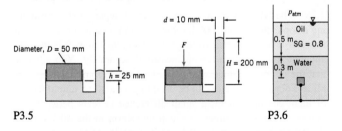

P3.5

P3.6

3.6 A 125-mL cube of solid oak is held submerged by a tether as shown. Calculate the actual force of the water on the bottom surface of the cube and the tension in the tether.

3.7 The following pressure and temperature measurements were taken by a meteorological balloon rising through the lower atmosphere:

p (in 10^3 Pa)	T (in °C)
101.4	12.0
100.8	11.1
100.2	10.5
99.6	10.2
99.0	10.1
98.4	10.0

p (in 10^3 Pa)	T (in °C)
97.8	10.3
97.2	10.8
96.6	11.6
96.0	12.2
95.4	12.1

The initial values (top of table) correspond to ground level. Using the ideal gas law ($p = \rho R T$ with R = 287 m²/(s² · K), compute and plot the variation of air density (in kg/m³) with height.

3.8 Your pressure gage indicates that the pressure in your cold tires is 0.25 MPa (gage) on a mountain at an elevation of 3500 m. What is the absolute pressure? After you drive down to sea level, your tires have warmed to 25°C. What pressure does your gage now indicate? Assume a U.S. Standard Atmosphere.

3.9 A hollow metal cube with sides 100 mm floats at the interface between a layer of water and a layer of SAE 10W oil such that 10% of the cube is exposed to the oil. What is the pressure difference between the upper and lower horizontal surfaces? What is the average density of the cube?

3.10 A cube with 6 in. sides is suspended in a fluid by a wire. The top of the cube is horizontal and 8 in. below the free surface. If the cube has a mass of 2 slugs and the tension in the wire is $T = 50.7$ lbf, compute the fluid specific gravity, and from this determine the fluid. What are the gage pressures on the upper and lower surfaces?

3.11 An air bubble, 0.3 in. in diameter, is released from the regulator of a scuba diver swimming 100 ft below the sea surface. (The water temperature is 86°F.) Estimate the diameter of the bubble just before it reaches the water surface.

3.12 Assuming the bulk modulus is constant for seawater, derive an expression for the density variation with depth, h, below the surface. Show that the result may be written

$$\rho \approx \rho_0 + bh$$

where ρ_0 is the density at the surface. Evaluate the constant b. Then using the approximation, obtain an equation for the variation of pressure with depth below the surface. Determine the percent error in pressure predicted by the approximate solution at a depth of 1000 m.

3.13 Oceanographic research vessels have descended to 10 km below sea level. At these extreme depths, the compressibility of seawater can be significant. One may model the behavior of seawater by assuming that its bulk modulus remains constant. Using this assumption, evaluate the deviations in density and pressure compared with values computed using the incompressible assumption at a depth, h, of 10 km in seawater. Express your answers in percent. Plot the results over the range $0 \leq h \leq 10$ km.

3.14 An inverted cylindrical container is lowered slowly beneath the surface of a pool of water. Air trapped in the container is compressed isothermally as the hydrostatic pressure increases. Develop an expression for the water height, y, inside the container in terms of the container height, H, and depth of submersion, h. Plot y/H versus h/H.

3.15 You close the top of your straw using your thumb and lift it out of your glass containing Coke. Holding it vertically, the total length of the straw is 17 in., but the Coke held in the straw is in the bottom 6 in. What is the pressure in the straw just below your thumb? Ignore any surface tension effects.

3.16 A water tank filled with water to a depth of 5 m has an inspection cover (2.5 cm × 2.5 cm square) at its base, held in place by a plastic bracket. The bracket can hold a load of 40 N. Is the bracket strong enough? If it is, what would the water depth have to be to cause the bracket to break?

3.17 A container with two circular vertical tubes of diameters $d_1 = 39.5$ mm and $d_2 = 12.7$ mm is partially filled with mercury. The equilibrium level of the liquid is shown in the left diagram. A cylindrical object made from solid brass is placed in the larger tube so that it floats, as shown in the right diagram. The object is $D = 37.5$ mm in diameter and $H = 76.2$ mm high. Calculate the pressure at the lower surface needed to float the object. Determine the new equilibrium level, h, of the mercury with the brass cylinder in place.

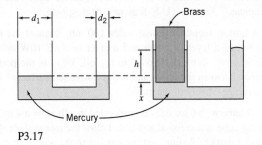

P3.17

3.18 A partitioned tank as shown contains water and mercury. What is the gage pressure in the air trapped in the left chamber? What pressure would the air on the left need to be pumped to in order to bring the water and mercury free surfaces level?

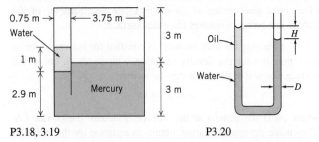

P3.18, 3.19

3.19 In the tank of Problem 3.18, if the opening to atmosphere on the right chamber is first sealed, what pressure would the air on the left now need to be pumped to in order to bring the water and mercury free surfaces level? (Assume the air trapped in the right chamber behaves isothermally.)

3.20 A manometer is formed from glass tubing with uniform inside diameter, $D = 6.35$ mm, as shown. The U-tube is partially filled with water. Then $V = 3.25$ cm^3 of Meriam red oil is added to the left side. Calculate the equilibrium height, H, when both legs of the U-tube are open to the atmosphere.

3.21 Consider the two-fluid manometer shown. Calculate the applied pressure difference.

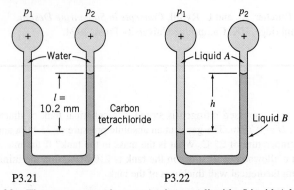

P3.21   P3.22

3.22 The manometer shown contains two liquids. Liquid A has SG = 0.88 and liquid B has SG = 2.95. Calculate the deflection, h, when the applied pressure difference is $p_1 - p_2 = 18$ lbf/ft^2.

3.23 The manometer shown contains water and kerosene. With both tubes open to the atmosphere, the free-surface elevations differ by $H_0 = 20.0$ mm. Determine the elevation difference when a pressure of 98.0 Pa (gage) is applied to the right tube.

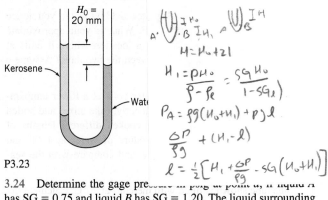

P3.23

3.24 Determine the gage pre~~ssure in psig at point a, if liquid A~~ has SG = 0.75 and liquid B has SG = 1.20. The liquid surrounding point a is water and the tank on the left is open to the atmosphere.

3.25 The NIH Corporation's engineering department is evaluating a sophisticated \$80,000 laser system to measure the difference in water level between two large water storage tanks. It is important that small differences be measured accurately. You suggest that the job can be done with a \$200 manometer arrangement. An oil less dense than water can be used to give a 10 : 1 amplification of meniscus movement; a small difference in level between the tanks will cause 10 times as much deflection in the oil levels in the manometer. Determine the specific gravity of the oil required for 10 : 1 amplification.

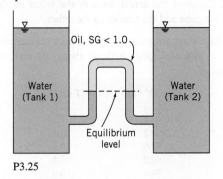

P3.25

3.26 Consider a tank containing mercury, water, benzene, and air as shown. Find the air pressure (gage). If an opening is made in the top of the tank, find the equilibrium level of the mercury in the manometer.

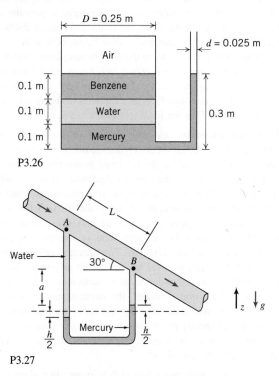

P3.26

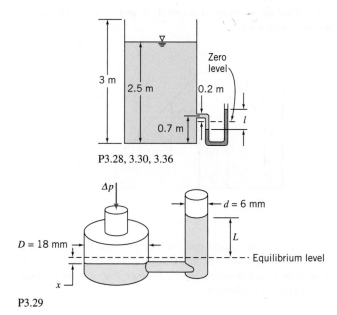

P3.27

3.27 Water flows downward along a pipe that is inclined at 30° below the horizontal, as shown. Pressure difference $p_A - p_B$ is due partly to gravity and partly to friction. Derive an algebraic expression for the pressure difference. Evaluate the pressure difference if $L = 5$ ft and $h = 6$ in.

3.28 A rectangular tank, open to the atmosphere, is filled with water to a depth of 2.5 m as shown. A U-tube manometer is connected to the tank at a location 0.7 m above the tank bottom. If the zero level of the Meriam blue manometer fluid is

P3.28, 3.30, 3.36

P3.29

0.2 m below the connection, determine the deflection l after the manometer is connected and all air has been removed from the connecting leg.

3.29 A reservoir manometer has vertical tubes of diameter $D = 18$ mm and $d = 6$ mm. The manometer liquid is Meriam red oil. Develop an algebraic expression for liquid deflection L in the small tube when gage pressure Δp is applied to the reservoir. Evaluate the liquid deflection when the applied pressure is equivalent to 25 mm of water (gage).

3.30 The manometer fluid of Problem 3.28 is replaced with mercury (same zero level). The tank is sealed and the air pressure is increased to a gage pressure of 0.5 atm. Determine the deflection l.

3.31 A reservoir manometer is calibrated for use with a liquid of specific gravity 0.827. The reservoir diameter is 5/8 in. and the (vertical) tube diameter is 3/16 in. Calculate the required distance between marks on the vertical scale for 1 in. of water pressure difference.

3.32 The inclined-tube manometer shown has $D = 76$ mm and $d = 8$ mm, and is filled with Meriam red oil. Compute the angle, θ, that will give a 15-cm oil deflection along the inclined tube for an applied pressure of 25 mm of water (gage). Determine the sensitivity of this manometer.

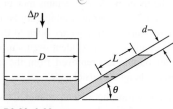

P3.32, 3.33

3.33 The inclined-tube manometer shown has $D = 96$ mm and $d = 8$ mm. Determine the angle, θ, required to provide a 5 : 1 increase in liquid deflection, L, compared with the total deflection in a regular U-tube manometer. Evaluate the sensitivity of this inclined-tube manometer.

3.34 A student wishes to design a manometer with better sensitivity than a water-filled U-tube of constant diameter. The student's concept involves using tubes with different diameters and two liquids, as shown. Evaluate the deflection h of this manometer, if the applied pressure difference is $\Delta p = 250$ N/m². Determine the sensitivity of this manometer. Plot the manometer sensitivity as a function of the diameter ratio d_2/d_1.

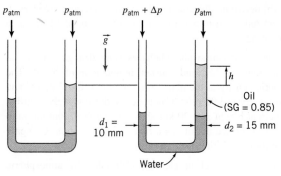

P3.34

3.35 A barometer accidentally contains 6.5 inches of water on top of the mercury column (so there is also water vapor instead of a vacuum at the top of the barometer). On a day when the temperature is 70°F, the mercury column height is 28.35 inches (corrected for thermal expansion). Determine the barometric pressure in psia. If the ambient temperature increased to 85°F and the barometric pressure did not change, would the mercury column be longer, be shorter, or remain the same length? Justify your answer.

3.36 If the tank of Problem 3.28 is sealed tightly and water drains slowly from the bottom of the tank, determine the deflection, l, after the system has attained equilibrium.

3.37 A water column stands 50 mm high in a 2.5-mm-diameter glass tube. What would be the column height if the surface tension were zero? What would be the column height in a 1.0-mm-diameter tube?

3.38 Consider a small diameter open-ended tube inserted at the interface between two immiscible fluids of different densities. Derive an expression for the height difference Δh between the interface level inside and outside the tube in terms of tube diameter D, the two fluid densities, ρ_1 and ρ_2, and the surface tension σ and angle θ for the two fluids' interface. If the two fluids are water and mercury, find the tube diameter such that $\Delta h < 10$ mm.

3.39 You have a manometer consisting of a tube that is 1.1-cm ID. On one side the manometer leg contains mercury, 10 cc of an oil (SG = 1.67), and 3 cc of air as a bubble in the oil. The other leg just contains mercury. Both legs are open to the atmosphere and are in a static condition. An accident occurs in which 3 cc of the oil and the air bubble are removed from the one leg. How much do the mercury height levels change?

3.40 Based on the atmospheric temperature data of the U.S. Standard Atmosphere of Fig. 3.3, compute and plot the pressure variation with altitude, and compare with the pressure data of Table A.3.

3.41 Two vertical glass plates 300 mm × 300 mm are placed in an open tank containing water. At one end the gap between the plates is 0.1 mm, and at the other it is 2 mm. Plot the curve of water height between the plates from one end of the pair to the other.

3.42 Compare the height due to capillary action of water exposed to air in a circular tube of diameter $D = 0.5$ mm, and between two infinite vertical parallel plates of gap $a = 0.5$ mm.

3.43 On a certain calm day, a mild inversion causes the atmospheric temperature to remain constant at 85°F between sea level and 16,000 ft altitude. Under these conditions, (a) calculate the elevation change for which a 2 percent reduction in air pressure occurs, (b) determine the change of elevation necessary to effect a 10 percent reduction in density, and (c) plot p_2/p_1 and ρ_2/ρ_1 as a function of Δz.

3.44 The Martian atmosphere behaves as an ideal gas with mean molecular mass of 32.0 and constant temperature of 200 K. The atmospheric density at the planet surface is $\rho = 0.015$ kg/m³ and Martian gravity is 3.92 m/s². Calculate the density of the Martian atmosphere at height $z = 20$ km above the surface. Plot the ratio of density to surface density as a function of elevation. Compare with that for data on the earth's atmosphere.

3.45 At ground level in Denver, Colorado, the atmospheric pressure and temperature are 83.2 kPa and 25°C. Calculate the pressure on Pike's Peak at an elevation of 2690 m above the city assuming (a) an incompressible and (b) an adiabatic atmosphere.

Plot the ratio of pressure to ground level pressure in Denver as a function of elevation for both cases.

3.46 A door 1 m wide and 1.5 m high is located in a plane vertical wall of a water tank. The door is hinged along its upper edge, which is 1 m below the water surface. Atmospheric pressure acts on the outer surface of the door. (a) If the pressure at the water surface is atmospheric, what force must be applied at the lower edge of the door in order to keep the door from opening? (b) If the water surface gage pressure is raised to 0.5 atm, what force must be applied at the lower edge of the door to keep the door from opening? (c) Find the ratio F/F_0 as a function of the surface pressure ratio p_s/p_{atm}. (F_0 is the force required when $p_s = p_{atm}$.)

3.47 A hydropneumatic elevator consists of a piston-cylinder assembly to lift the elevator cab. Hydraulic oil, stored in an accumulator tank pressurized by air, is valved to the piston as needed to lift the elevator. When the elevator descends, oil is returned to the accumulator. Design the least expensive accumulator that can satisfy the system requirements. Assume the lift is 3 floors, the maximum load is 10 passengers, and the maximum system pressure is 800 kPa (gage). For column bending strength, the piston diameter must be at least 150 mm. The elevator cab and piston have a combined mass of 3000 kg, and are to be purchased. Perform the analysis needed to define, as a function of system operating pressure, the piston diameter, the accumulator volume and diameter, and the wall thickness. Discuss safety features that your company should specify for the complete elevator system. Would it be preferable to use a completely pneumatic design or a completely hydraulic design? Why?

3.48 A door 1 m wide and 1.5 m high is located in a plane vertical wall of a water tank. The door is hinged along its upper edge, which is 1 m below the water surface. Atmospheric pressure acts on the outer surface of the door and at the water surface. (a) Determine the magnitude and line of action of the total resultant force from all fluids acting on the door. (b) If the water surface gage pressure is raised to 0.3 atm, what is the resultant force and where is its line of action? (c) Plot the ratios F/F_0 and y'/y_c for different values of the surface pressure ratio p_s/p_{atm}. (F_0 is the resultant force when $p_s = p_{atm}$.)

3.49 Find the pressures at points A, B, and C, as shown, and in the two air cavities.

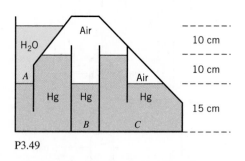

P3.49

3.50 A triangular access port must be provided in the side of a form containing liquid concrete. Using the coordinates and dimensions shown, determine the resultant force that acts on the port and its point of application.

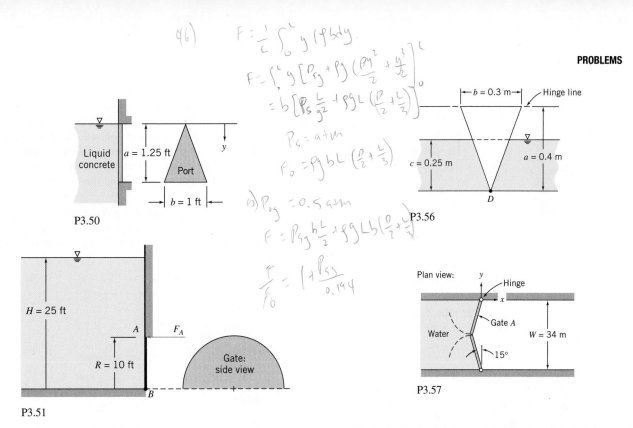

P3.50

P3.56

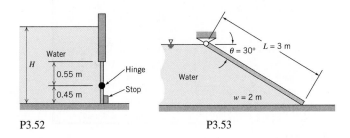

P3.51

P3.57

3.51 Semicircular plane gate *AB* is hinged along *B* and held by horizontal force F_A applied at *A*. The liquid to the left of the gate is water. Calculate the force F_A required for equilibrium.

3.52 A rectangular gate (width $w = 2$ m) is hinged as shown, with a stop on the lower edge. At what depth *H* will the gate tip?

P3.52   P3.53

3.53 A plane gate of uniform thickness holds back a depth of water as shown. Find the minimum weight needed to keep the gate closed.

3.54 Consider a semicylindrical trough of radius *R* and length *L*. Develop general expressions for the magnitude and line of action of the hydrostatic force on one end, if the trough is partially filled with water and open to atmosphere. Plot the results (in nondimensional form) over the range of water depth $0 \le d/R \le 1$.

3.55 For a mug of tea (2½ in. diameter), imagine it cut symmetrically in half by a vertical plane. Find the force that each half experiences due to a 3-in. depth of tea.

3.56 A window in the shape of an isosceles triangle and hinged at the top is placed in the vertical wall of a form that contains liquid concrete. Determine the minimum force that must be applied at point *D* to keep the window closed for the configuration of form and concrete shown. Plot the results over the range of concrete depth $0 \le c \le a$.

3.57 Gates in the Poe Lock at Sault Ste. Marie, Michigan, close a channel $W = 34$ m wide, $L = 360$ m long, and $D = 10$ m deep. The geometry of one pair of gates is shown; each gate is hinged at the channel wall. When closed, the gate edges are forced together at the center of the channel by water pressure. Evaluate the force exerted by the water on gate *A*. Determine the magnitude and direction of the force components exerted by the gate on the hinge. (Neglect the weight of the gate.)

3.58 A section of vertical wall is to be constructed from ready-mix concrete poured between forms. The wall is to be 3 m high, 0.25 m thick, and 5 m wide. Calculate the force exerted by the ready-mix concrete on each form. Determine the line of application of the force.

3.59 Solve Example 3.6 again using the first alternative method described on page 72. Consider the distributed force to be the sum of a force F_1 caused by the uniform gage pressure and a force F_2 caused by the liquid. Solve for these forces and their lines of action. Then sum moments about the hinge axis to calculate F_t.

3.60 The circular access port in the side of a water standpipe has a diameter of 0.6 m and is held in place by eight bolts evenly spaced around the circumference. If the standpipe diameter is 7 m and the center of the port is located 12 m below the free surface of the water, determine (a) the total force on the port and (b) the appropriate bolt diameter.

3.61 What holds up a car on its rubber tires? Most people would tell you that it is the air pressure inside the tires. However, the air pressure is the same all around the hub (inner wheel), and the air pressure inside the tire therefore pushes down from the top as much as it pushes up from below, having no net effect on the hub. Resolve this paradox by explaining where the force is that keeps the car off the ground.

3.62 The gate *AOC* shown is 6 ft wide and is hinged along *O*. Neglecting the weight of the gate, determine the force in bar *AB*. The gate is sealed at *C*.

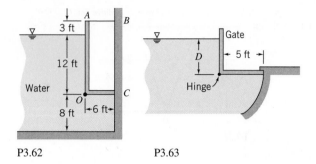

P3.62   P3.63

3.63 As water rises on the left side of the rectangular gate, the gate will open automatically. At what depth above the hinge will this occur? Neglect the mass of the gate.

3.64 The gate shown is hinged at H. The gate is 3 m wide normal to the plane of the diagram. Calculate the force required at A to hold the gate closed.

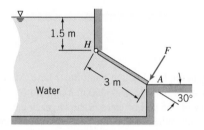

P3.64

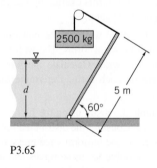

P3.65

3.65 The gate shown is 3 m wide and for analysis can be considered massless. For what depth of water will this rectangular gate be in equilibrium as shown?

3.66 A solid concrete dam is to be built to hold back a depth D of water. For ease of construction the walls of the dam must be planar. Your supervisor asks you to consider the following dam

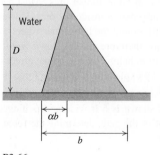

P3.66

cross-sections: a rectangle, a right triangle with the hypotenuse in contact with the water, and a right triangle with the vertical in contact with the water. She wishes you to determine which of these would require the least amount of concrete. What will your report say? You decide to look at one more possibility: a nonright triangle, as shown. Develop and plot an expression for the cross-section area A as a function of a, and find the minimum cross-sectional area.

3.67 A long, square wooden block is pivoted along one edge. The block is in equilibrium when immersed in water to the depth shown. Evaluate the specific gravity of the wood, if friction in the pivot is negligible.

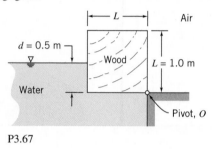

P3.67

3.68 For the geometry shown, what is the vertical force on the dam? The steps are 1 ft high, 1 ft deep, and 10 ft wide.

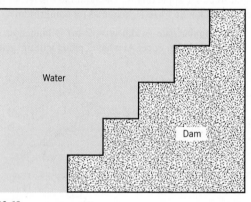

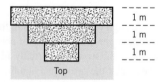

P3.68

3.69 For the dam shown, what is the vertical force of the water on the dam?

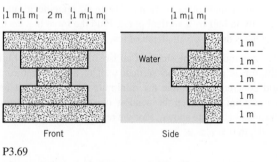

P3.69

3.70 The parabolic gate shown is 2 m wide and pivoted at O; $c = 0.25$ m^{-1}, $D = 2$ m, and $H = 3$ m. Determine (a) the magnitude and line of action of the vertical force on the gate due to the water, (b) the horizontal force applied at A required to maintain the gate in equilibrium, and (c) the vertical force applied at A required to maintain the gate in equilibrium.

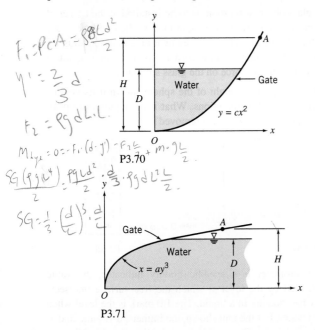

$F_1 = \rho_c A = \frac{\rho g L d^2}{2}$

$y' = \frac{2}{3} d$

$F_2 = \rho g d L \cdot L$

$M_{1_{y_2}} = 0 = -F_1 (d \cdot y') - F_2 \frac{L}{2} + m \cdot g \frac{L}{2}$

$SG (\rho g L d^2) \cdot \frac{\rho g L d^2}{2} \cdot y \frac{d}{3} \cdot \rho g d L^2 \frac{L}{2}$

$SG = \frac{1}{3} \left(\frac{d}{L}\right)^3 \cdot \frac{d}{L}$

P3.70

P3.71

3.71 The gate shown is 1.5 m wide and pivoted at O; $a = 1.0$ m^{-2}, $D = 1.20$ m, and $H = 1.40$ m. Determine (a) the magnitude and moment of the vertical component of the force about O, and (b) the horizontal force that must be applied at point A to hold the gate in position.

3.72 Liquid concrete is poured into the form shown ($R = 0.313$ m). The form is $w = 4.25$ m wide normal to the diagram. Compute the magnitude of the vertical force exerted on the form by the concrete and specify its line of action.

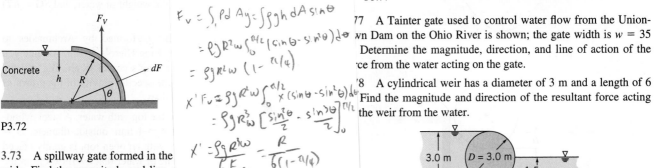

$F_v = \int_1 P \, dA_y = \int \rho g h \, dA \sin\theta$

$= \rho_J R^2 w \int_0^{\pi/2} (\sin\theta - \sin^2\theta) \, d\theta$

$= \rho g R^2 w (1 - \frac{\pi}{4})$

$x' F_v = \rho_J R^2 w \int_0^{\pi/2} x (\sin\theta - \sin^2\theta) d\theta$

$= \rho g R^3 w \left[\frac{\sin^2\theta}{2} - \frac{\sin^2\theta}{2}\right]_0^{\pi/2}$

$x' = \rho g R^3 w \cdot \frac{R}{6 F_v} = \frac{R}{6(1 - \pi/4)}$

P3.72

3.73 A spillway gate formed in the [...] wide. Find the magnitude and line [...] ponent of the force due to all fluids acting on the gate.

3.74 An open tank is filled with water to the depth indicated. Atmospheric pressure acts on all outer surfaces of the tank. Determine the magnitude and line of action of the vertical component of the force of the water on the curved part of the tank bottom.

3.75 A dam is to be constructed across the Wabash River using the cross-section shown. Assume the dam width is $w = 50$ m.

For water height $H = 2.5$ m, calculate the magnitude and line of action of the vertical force of water on the dam face. Is it possible for water forces to overturn this dam? Under what circumstances?

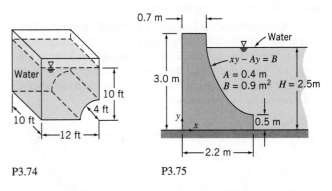

P3.74   P3.75

3.76 A gate, in the shape of a quarter-cylinder, hinged at A and sealed at B, is 3 m wide. The bottom of the gate is 4.5 m below the water surface. Determine the force on the stop at B if the gate is made of concrete; $R = 3$ m.

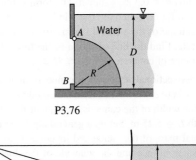

P3.76

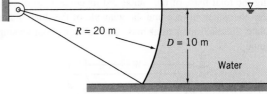

P3.77

77   A Tainter gate used to control water flow from the Union-wn Dam on the Ohio River is shown; the gate width is $w = 35$ Determine the magnitude, direction, and line of action of the ·ce from the water acting on the gate.

'8   A cylindrical weir has a diameter of 3 m and a length of 6 Find the magnitude and direction of the resultant force acting the weir from the water.

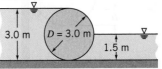

P3.78, 3.79

3.79 Consider the cylindric: m. If the fluid on the left has right has a specific gravity of of the resultant force.

$F_{x_1} = P_c A (S_1 g \frac{D}{2}) D L = \frac{1}{2} SG_1 \rho g D^2 L$

$F_{-12} = P_c \cdot A = (S_2 g \frac{D}{4})(\frac{D}{2})$

$F_{v_1} = SG_1 \rho g \frac{\pi D^2}{2} \cdot L$

$F_{v_2} = SG_2 \rho g \frac{\pi D^2}{4} \cdot L$

3.80 A cylindrical log of diameter D rests against the top of a dam. The water is level with the top of the log and the center of the log is level with the top of the dam. Obtain expressions for (a) the mass of the log per unit length and (b) the contact force per unit length between the log and dam.

3.81 A curved surface is formed as a quarter of a circular cylinder with $R = 0.750$ m as shown. The surface is $w = 3.55$ m wide. Water stands to the right of the curved surface to depth $H = 0.650$ m. Calculate the vertical hydrostatic force on the curved surface. Evaluate the line of action of this force. Find the magnitude and line of action of the horizontal force on the surface.

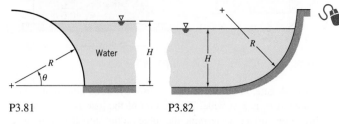

P3.81 P3.82

3.82 A curved submerged surface, in the shape of a quarter cylinder, with radius $R = 0.3$ m is shown. The form is filled to depth $H = 0.24$ m with liquid concrete. The width is $w = 1.25$ m. Calculate the magnitude of the vertical hydrostatic force on the form from the concrete. Find the line of action of the force. Plot the results over the range of concrete depth $0 \le H \le R$.

3.83 The cross-sectional shape of a canoe is modeled by the curve $y = ax^2$, where $a = 3.89$ m^{-1} and the coordinates are in meters. Assume the width of the canoe is constant at $W = 0.6$ m over its entire length $L = 5.25$ m. Set up a general algebraic expression relating the total mass of the canoe and its contents to distance d between the water surface and the gunwale of the floating canoe. Calculate the maximum total mass allowable without swamping the canoe.

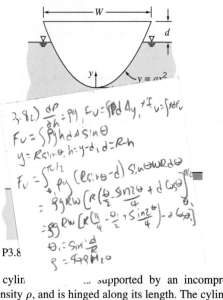

P3.8

3.84 The cylin supported by an incompressibl liquid of density ρ, and is hinged along its length. The cylinder, of mass M, length L, and radius R, is immersed in liquid to depth H. Obtain a general expression for the cylinder specific gravity versus the ratio of liquid depth to cylinder radius, $\alpha = H/R$, needed to hold the cylinder in equilibrium for $0 \le \alpha < 1$. Plot the results.

3.85 A canoe is represented by a right circular semicylinder, with $R = 0.35$ m and $L = 5.25$ m. The canoe floats in water that is $d = 0.245$ m deep. Set up a general algebraic expression for the maximum total mass (canoe and contents) that can be floated, as a function of depth. Evaluate for the given conditions. Plot the results over the range of water depth $0 \le d \le R$.

3.86 A gla observation room is to be installed at the corner of the bottom filled with seawater to a depth c here, radius 1.5 m, mounted the magnitude and directi

*3.87 Fin wn if its volume is 0.025 m equilibrium position of the

*3.88 A hydrometer is a specific gravity indicator, the value being indicated by the level at which the free surface intersects the stem when floating in a liquid. The 1.0 mark is the level when in distilled water. For the unit shown, the immersed volume in distilled water is 15 cm^3. The stem is 6 mm in diameter. Find the distance, h, from the 1.0 mark to the surface when the hydrometer is placed in a nitric acid solution of specific gravity 1.5.

*3.89 Quantify the statement, "Only the tip of an iceberg shows (in seawater)."

*3.90 The fat-to-muscle ratio of a person may be determined from a specific gravity measurement. The measurement is made by immersing the body in a tank of water and measuring the net weight. Develop an expression for the specific gravity of a person in terms of their weight in air, net weight in water, and SG $= f(T)$ for water.

*3.91 Quantify the experiment performed by Archimedes to of King Hiero's crown. Assume you ne king's crown in air, W_a, and the , the specific gravity of the crown as values.

the top with water. A steel cylind-$\delta = 1$ mm, outside diameter $D =$, with an open top, is gently placed ne of water that overflows from the must be placed in the container to ension effects.

sed to visualize water flow streak-ization. A typical hydrogen bubble diameter is $d = 0.001$ in. The bubbles tend to rise slowly in water because of buoyancy; eventually they reach terminal speed relative to the water. The drag force of the water on a bubble is given by $F_D = 3\pi\mu Vd$, where μ is the viscosity of water and V is the bubble speed relative to the water. Find the buoyancy force that

*These problems require material from sections that may be omitted without loss of continuity in the text material.

acts on a hydrogen bubble immersed in water. Estimate the terminal speed of a bubble rising in water.

*3.94 Gas bubbles are released from the regulator of a submerged scuba diver. What happens to the bubbles as they rise through the seawater? Explain.

*3.95 Hot-air ballooning is a popular sport. According to a recent article, "hot-air volumes must be large because air heated to 150°F over ambient lifts only 0.018 lbf/ft³ compared to 0.066 and 0.071 for helium and hydrogen, respectively." Check these statements for sea-level conditions. Calculate the effect of increasing the hot-air maximum temperature to 250°F above ambient.

*3.96 A hot air balloon is designed to lift a basket, two people, three gallons of fuel, a pair of binoculars, a camera, a GPS, a cell phone, a pair of blankets, twelve candy bars, and the components of the balloon itself (fabric, ropes, and torch). The total mass is estimated at 450 kg. The rides are planned in summer morning hours when the air temperature is about 9°C. The torch will warm the air inside the balloon to a temperature of 70°C. Both inside and outside pressures will be "standard" (101 kPa). What volume of hot air should the balloon hold to create neutral buoyancy? What additional volume will ensure a vertical take-off acceleration of 0.8 m/s²? For this, consider that both balloon and inside air have to be accelerated, as well as some of the surrounding air (to make way for the balloon). The rule of thumb is that the total mass subject to acceleration is the mass of the balloon, all its appurtenances, and twice its volume of air. Given that the volume of hot air is fixed during flight, what can the balloonists do when they want to go down?

*3.97 Scientific balloons operating at pressure equilibrium with the surroundings have been used to lift instrument packages to extremely high altitudes. One such balloon, constructed of polyester with a skin thickness of 0.013 mm, lifted a payload of 230 kg to an altitude of approximately 49 km, where atmospheric conditions are 0.95 mbar and −20°C. The helium gas in the balloon was at a temperature of approximately −10°C. The specific gravity of the skin material is 1.28. Determine the diameter and mass of the balloon. Assume that the balloon is spherical.

*3.98 A helium balloon is to lift a payload to an altitude of 40 km, where the atmospheric pressure and temperature are 3.0 mbar and −25°C, respectively. The balloon skin is polyester with specific gravity of 1.28 and thickness of 0.015 mm. To maintain a spherical shape, the balloon is pressurized to a gage pressure of 0.45 mbar. Determine the maximum balloon diameter if the allowable tensile stress in the skin is limited to 62 MN/m². What payload can be carried?

*3.99 A block of mass 30 kg and volume 0.025 m³ is allowed to sink in water as shown. A circular rod 5 m long and 20 cm² in cross section is attached to the weight and also to the wall. If the rod mass is 1.25 kg, what will be the angle, θ, for equilibrium?

*3.100 The stem of a glass hydrometer used to measure specific gravity is 6 mm in diameter. The distance between marks on the stem is 3 mm per 0.1 increment of specific gravity. Calculate the magnitude and direction of the error introduced by surface tension if the hydrometer floats in ethyl alcohol. (Assume the contact angle between ethanol and glass is zero degrees.)

*3.101 If the mass M in Problem 3.99 is released from the rod, at equilibrium how much of the rod will remain submerged? What will be the minimum required upward force at the tip of the rod to just lift it out of the water?

*3.102 A sphere, of radius R, is partially immersed, to depth d, in a liquid of specific gravity SG. Obtain an algebraic expression for the buoyancy force acting on the sphere as a function of submersion depth d. Plot the results over the range of water depth 0 ≤ d ≤ 2R.

*3.103 In a logging operation, timber floats downstream to a lumber mill. It is a dry year, and the river is running low, as low as 2 feet in some locations. What is the largest diameter log that may be transported in this fashion (leaving a minimum 1 in. clearance between the log and the bottom of the river)? For the wood, SG = 0.8.

*3.104 A sphere of radius R, made from material of specific gravity SG, is submerged in a tank of water. The sphere is placed over a hole, of radius a, in the tank bottom. Develop a general expression for the range of specific gravities for which the sphere will float to the surface. For the dimensions given, determine the minimum SG required for the sphere to remain in the position shown.

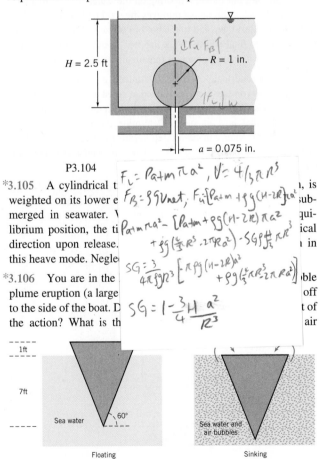

P3.104

*3.105 A cylindrical t[...] is
weighted on its lower e[...] submerged in seawater. [...] equilibrium position, the ti[...] ical
direction upon release. [...] in
this heave mode. Negle[...]

*3.106 You are in the [...] ble
plume eruption (a large [...] off
to the side of the boat. D[...] t of
the action? What is th[...] air

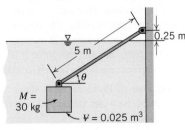

P3.99

P3.106

*These problems require material from sections that may be omitted without loss of continuity in the text material.

bubbles in the drawing on the right that will cause the boat to sink? Your boat is 10 ft long, and weight is the same in both cases.

*3.107   A bowl is inverted symmetrically and held in BXYB fluid, SG = 15.6, to a depth of 7 in. measured along the centerline of the bowl from the bowl rim. The bowl height is 3 in., and the BXYB fluid rises 1 in. inside the bowl. The bowl is unique: Its base is 4 in. inside diameter, and it is made from an old clay recipe, SG = 5.7. The volume of the bowl is about 56 in.^{3}. What is the force required to hold it in place?

*3.108   Consider a conical funnel held upside down and submerged slowly in a container of water. Discuss the force needed to submerge the funnel if the spout is open to the atmosphere. Compare with the force needed to submerge the funnel when the spout opening is blocked by a rubber stopper.

*3.109   In the "Cartesian diver" child's toy, a miniature "diver" is immersed in a column of liquid. When a diaphragm at the top of the column is pushed down, the diver sinks to the bottom. When the diaphragm is released, the diver again rises. Explain how the toy might work.

*3.110   A proposed ocean salvage scheme involves pumping air into "bags" placed within and around a wrecked vessel on the sea bottom. Comment on the practicality of this plan, supporting your conclusions with analyses.

*3.111   Three steel balls (each about half an inch in diameter) lie at the bottom of a plastic shell floating on the water surface in a partially filled bucket. Someone removes the steel balls from the shell and carefully lets them fall to the bottom of the bucket, leaving the plastic shell to float empty. What happens to the water level in the bucket? Does it rise, go down, or remain unchanged? Explain.

*3.112   A cylindrical container, similar to that analyzed in Example 3.10 (on the Web), is rotated at constant angular velocity about its axis. The cylinder is 1 ft in diameter, and initially contains water that is 4 in. deep. Determine the maximum rate at which the container can be rotated before the liquid free surface just touches the bottom of the tank. Does your answer depend on the density of the liquid? Explain.

*3.113   A crude accelerometer can be made from a liquid-filled U-tube as shown. Derive an expression for the acceleration $\vec{a}$,

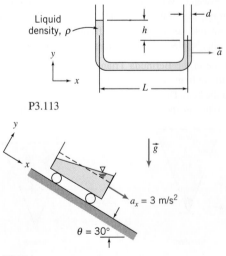

P3.113

P3.114

in terms of liquid level difference h, tube geometry, and fluid properties.

*3.114   A rectangular container of water undergoes constant acceleration down an incline as shown. Determine the slope of the free surface using the coordinate system shown.

*3.115   The U-tube shown is filled with water at $T = 68°F$. It is sealed at A and open to the atmosphere at D. The tube is rotated about vertical axis AB. For the dimensions shown, compute the maximum angular speed if there is to be no cavitation.

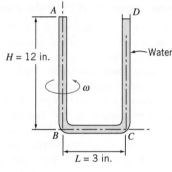

P3.115, 3.116

*3.116   If the U-tube of Problem 3.115 is spun at 200 rpm, what will be the pressure at A? If a small leak appears at A, how much water will be lost at D?

*3.117   A centrifugal micromanometer can be used to create small and accurate differential pressures in air for precise measurement work. The device consists of a pair of parallel disks that rotate to develop a radial pressure difference. There is no flow between the disks. Obtain an expression for pressure difference in terms of rotation speed, radius, and air density. Evaluate the speed of rotation required to develop a differential pressure of 8 μm of water using a device with a 50 mm radius.

*3.118   A test tube is spun in a centrifuge at $\omega = 1000$ rev/s. The tube support is mounted on a pivot so that the tube swings outward as rotation speed increases. At high speeds, the tube is nearly horizontal. Find (a) an expression for the radial component of acceleration of a liquid element located at radius r, (b) the radial pressure gradient $\partial p / \partial r$, and (c) the maximum pressure on the bottom of the test tube if it contains water. (The free surface and bottom radii are 50 and 130 mm, respectively.)

*3.119   A cubical box, 80 cm on a side, half-filled with oil (SG = 0.80), is given a constant horizontal acceleration of 0.25 g parallel to one edge. Determine the slope of the free surface and the pressure along the horizontal bottom of the box.

*3.120   A rectangular container, of base dimensions 0.4 m × 0.2 m and height 0.4 m, is filled with water to a depth of 0.2 m; the mass of the empty container is 10 kg. The container is placed on a plane inclined at 30° to the horizontal. If the coefficient of sliding friction between the container and the plane is 0.3, determine the angle of the water surface relative to the horizontal.

*3.121   If the container of Problem 3.120 slides without friction, determine the angle of the water surface relative to the horizontal. What is the slope of the free surface for the same acceleration up the plane?

*These problems require material from sections that may be omitted without loss of continuity in the text material.

*3.122 Gas centrifuges are used in one process to produce enriched uranium for nuclear fuel rods. The maximum peripheral speed of a gas centrifuge is limited by stress considerations to about 300 m/s. Assume a gas centrifuge containing uranium hexafluoride gas, with molecular mass $M_m = 352$, and ideal gas behavior. Develop an expression for the ratio of maximum pressure to pressure at the centrifuge axis. Evaluate the pressure ratio for a gas temperature of 325°C.

*3.123 A pail, 1 ft in diameter and 1 ft deep, weighs 3 lbf and contains 8 in. of water. The pail is swung in a vertical circle of 3 ft radius at a speed of 15 ft/s. Assume the water moves as a rigid body. At the instant when the pail is at the top of its trajectory, compute the tension in the string and the pressure on the bottom of the pail from the water.

*3.124 A partially full can of soft drink is placed at the outer edge of a child's merry-go-round, located $R = 1.5$ m from the axis of rotation. The can diameter and height are $D = 65$ mm and $H = 120$ mm. The can is half-full of soda, with specific gravity $SG = 1.06$. Evaluate the slope of the liquid surface in the can if the merry-go-round spins at 0.3 revolution per second. Calculate the spin rate at which the can would spill, assuming no slippage between the can bottom and the merry-go-round. Would the can most likely spill or slide off the merry-go-round?

*3.125 When a water polo ball is submerged below the surface in a swimming pool and released from rest, it is observed to pop out of the water. How would you expect the height to which it rises above the water to vary with depth of submersion below the surface? Would you expect the same results for a beach ball? For a table-tennis ball?

*3.126 Cast iron or steel molds are used in a horizontal-spindle machine to make tubular castings such as liners and tubes. A charge of molten metal is poured into the spinning mold. The radial acceleration permits nearly uniformly thick wall sections to form. A steel liner, of length $L = 2$ m, outer radius $r_o = 0.15$ m, and inner radius $r_i = 0.10$ m, is to be formed by this process. To attain nearly uniform thickness, the magnitude of the minimum radial acceleration should be $10\,g$. Determine (a) the required angular velocity and (b) the maximum and minimum pressures on the surface of the mold.

*3.127 The analysis of Problem 3.120 suggests that it may be possible to determine the coefficient of sliding friction between two surfaces by measuring the slope of the free surface in a liquid-filled container sliding down an inclined surface. Investigate the feasibility of this idea.

$$-\nabla p + \rho g = \rho a$$

$$\frac{\partial P}{\partial z} = -\rho g \qquad P_D - P_C = -\rho g H$$

$$\frac{d}{dr} p = \rho \omega^2 r$$

$$P_C - P_B = \rho \omega^2 \frac{L^2}{2}$$

$$P_B = P_{atm} + \rho g H - \rho \omega^2 \frac{L^2}{2}$$

$$P_A = P_{atm} - \rho \omega^2 \frac{L^2}{2}$$

$$\omega = \sqrt{\frac{2(P_{atm} - P_v)}{\rho \cdot L^2}}$$

---

*These problems require material from sections that may be omitted without loss of continuity in the text material.

Chapter 4

Basic Equations in Integral Form for a Control Volume

CASE STUDY

"Lab-on-a-Chip"

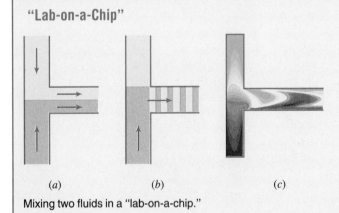

Mixing two fluids in a "lab-on-a-chip."

An exciting new area in fluid mechanics is microfluidics, applied to microelectromechanical systems (MEMS—the technology of very small devices, generally ranging in size from a micrometer to a millimeter). In particular, a lot of research is being done in "lab-on-a-chip" technology, which has many applications. An example of this is in medicine, with devices for use in the immediate point-of-care diagnosis of diseases, such as real-time detection of bacteria, viruses, and cancers in the human body. In the area of security, there are devices that continuously sample and test air or water samples for biochemical toxins and other dangerous pathogens such as those in always-on early warning systems.

Because of the extremely small geometry, flows in such devices will be very low Reynolds numbers and therefore laminar; surface tension effects will also be significant. In many common applications (for example, typical water pipes and air conditioning ducts), laminar flow would be desirable, but the flow is turbulent—it costs more to pump a turbulent as opposed to a laminar flow. In certain applications, turbulence is desirable instead because it acts as a mixing mechanism. If you couldn't generate turbulence in your coffee cup, it would take a lot of stirring before the cream and coffee were sufficiently blended; if your blood flow never became turbulent, you would not get sufficient oxygen to your organs and muscles! In the lab-on-a-chip, turbulent flow is usually desirable because the goal in these devices is often to mix minute amounts of two or more fluids.

How do we mix fluids in such devices that are inherently laminar? We could use complex geometries, or relatively long channels (relying on molecular diffusion), or some kind of MEM device with paddles. Research by professors Goullet, Glasgow, and Aubry at the New Jersey Institute of Technology instead suggests pulsing the two fluids. Part *a* of the figure shows a schematic of two fluids flowing at a constant rate (about 25 nL/s, average velocity less than 2 mm/s, in ducts about 200 μm wide) and meeting in a T junction. The two fluids do not mix because of the strongly laminar nature of the flow. Part *b* of the figure shows a schematic of an instant of a pulsed flow, and part *c* shows an instant computed using a computational fluid dynamics (CFD) model of the same flow. In this case, the interface between the two fluid samples is shown to stretch and fold, leading to good nonturbulent mixing within 2 mm downstream of the confluence (after about 1 s of contact). Such a compact mixing device would be ideal for many of the applications mentioned above.

We are now ready to study fluids in motion, so we have to decide how we are to examine a flowing fluid. There are two options available to us, discussed in Chapter 1:

1. We can study the motion of an *individual fluid particle or group of particles* as they move through space. This is the *system* approach, which has the advantage that the physical laws (e.g., Newton's second law, $\vec{F} = d\vec{P}/dt$, where $\vec{F}$ is the force and $d\vec{P}/dt$ is the rate of momentum change of the fluid) apply to matter and hence directly to the system. One disadvantage is that in practice the math associated with this approach can become somewhat complicated, usually leading to a set of partial differential equations. We will look at this approach in detail in Chapter 5. The system approach is needed if we are interested in studying the trajectory of particles over time, for example, in pollution studies.

2. We can study a *region of space* as fluid flows through it, which is the *control volume* approach. This is very often the method of choice, because it has widespread practical application; for example, in aerodynamics we are usually interested in the lift and drag on a wing (which we select as part of the control volume) rather than what happens to individual fluid particles. The disadvantage of this approach is that the physical laws apply to matter and not directly to regions of space, so we have to perform some math to convert physical laws from their system formulation to a control volume formulation.

We will examine the control volume approach in this chapter. The alert reader will notice that this chapter has the word *integral* in its title, and Chapter 5 has the word *differential*. This is an important distinction: It indicates that we will study a finite region in this chapter and the motion of a particle (an infinitesimal) in Chapter 5 (although in Section 4-4 we will look at a differential control volume to derive the famous Bernoulli equation). The agenda for this chapter is to review the physical laws as they apply to a system (Section 4-1); develop some math to convert from a system to a control volume (Section 4-2) description; and obtain formulas for the physical laws for control volume analysis by combining the results of Sections 4-1 and 4-2.

4-1   BASIC LAWS FOR A SYSTEM

The basic laws we will apply are conservation of mass, Newton's second law, the angular-momentum principle, and the first and second laws of thermodynamics. For converting these system equations to equivalent control volume formulas, it turns out we want to express each of the laws as a rate equation.

Conservation of Mass

For a system (by definition a fixed amount of matter, M, we have chosen) we have the simple result that M = constant. However, as discussed above, we wish to express each physical law as a rate equation, so we write

$$\frac{dM}{dt}\bigg)_{system} = 0 \qquad (4.1a)$$

where

$$M_{system} = \int_{M(system)} dm = \int_{\forall(system)} \rho\, d\forall \qquad (4.1b)$$

Newton's Second Law

For a system moving relative to an inertial reference frame, Newton's second law states that the sum of all external forces acting on the system is equal to the time rate of change of linear momentum of the system,

$$\vec{F} = \frac{d\vec{P}}{dt}\bigg)_{system} \qquad (4.2a)$$

where the linear momentum of the system is given by

$$\vec{P}_{system} = \int_{M(system)} \vec{V}\, dm = \int_{\forall(system)} \vec{V} \rho\, d\forall \qquad (4.2b)$$

The Angular-Momentum Principle

The angular-momentum principle for a system states that the rate of change of angular momentum is equal to the sum of all torques acting on the system,

$$\vec{T} = \frac{d\vec{H}}{dt}\bigg)_{system} \qquad (4.3a)$$

where the angular momentum of the system is given by

$$\vec{H}_{system} = \int_{M(system)} \vec{r} \times \vec{V}\, dm = \int_{\forall(system)} \vec{r} \times \vec{V} \rho\, d\forall \qquad (4.3b)$$

Torque can be produced by surface and body forces (here gravity) and also by shafts that cross the system boundary,

$$\vec{T} = \vec{r} \times \vec{F}_s + \int_{M(system)} \vec{r} \times \vec{g}\, dm + \vec{T}_{shaft} \qquad (4.3c)$$

The First Law of Thermodynamics

The first law of thermodynamics is a statement of conservation of energy for a system,

$$\delta Q - \delta W = dE$$

The equation can be written in rate form as

$$\dot{Q} - \dot{W} = \frac{dE}{dt}\bigg)_{system} \qquad (4.4a)$$

where the total energy of the system is given by

$$E_{system} = \int_{M(system)} e\, dm = \int_{\forall(system)} e \rho\, d\forall \qquad (4.4b)$$

and

$$e = u + \frac{V^2}{2} + gz \tag{4.4c}$$

In Eq. 4.4a, $\dot{Q}$ (the rate of heat transfer) is positive when heat is added to the system from the surroundings; $\dot{W}$ (the rate of work) is positive when work is done by the system on its surroundings. In Eq. 4.4c, u is the specific internal energy, V the speed, and z the height (relative to a convenient datum) of a particle of substance having mass dm.

The Second Law of Thermodynamics

If an amount of heat, δQ, is transferred to a system at temperature T, the second law of thermodynamics states that the change in entropy, dS, of the system satisfies

$$dS \geq \frac{\delta Q}{T}$$

On a rate basis we can write

$$\left. \frac{dS}{dt} \right)_{\text{system}} \geq \frac{1}{T} \dot{Q} \tag{4.5a}$$

where the total entropy of the system is given by

$$S_{\text{system}} = \int_{M(\text{system})} s \, dm = \int_{\Psi(\text{system})} s \, \rho \, d\Psi \tag{4.5b}$$

4-2   RELATION OF SYSTEM DERIVATIVES TO THE CONTROL VOLUME FORMULATION

We now have the five basic laws expressed as system rate equations. Our task in this section is to develop a general expression for converting a system rate equation into an equivalent control volume equation. Instead of converting the equations for rates of change of M, $\vec{P}$, $\vec{H}$, E, and S (Eqs. 4.1a, 4.2a, 4.3a, 4.4a, and 4.5a) one by one, we let all of them be represented by the symbol N. Hence N represents the amount of mass, or momentum, or angular momentum, or energy, or entropy of the system. Corresponding to this extensive property, we will also need the intensive (i.e., per unit mass) property η. Thus

$$N_{\text{system}} = \int_{M(\text{system})} \eta \, dm = \int_{\Psi(\text{system})} \eta \, \rho \, d\Psi \tag{4.6}$$

Comparing Eq. 4.6 with Eqs. 4.1b, 4.2b, 4.3b, 4.4b, and 4.5b, we see that if:

$$
\begin{aligned}
N &= M, & \text{then } \eta &= 1 \\
N &= \vec{P}, & \text{then } \eta &= \vec{V} \\
N &= \vec{H}, & \text{then } \eta &= \vec{r} \times \vec{V} \\
N &= E, & \text{then } \eta &= e \\
N &= S, & \text{then } \eta &= s
\end{aligned}
$$

How can we derive a control volume description from a system description of a fluid flow? Before specifically answering this question, we can describe the derivation in general terms. We imagine selecting an arbitrary piece of the flowing fluid at some time t_0, as shown in Fig. 4.1a—we could imagine dyeing this piece of fluid, say, blue. This initial shape of the fluid system is chosen as our control volume, which is fixed in space relative to coordinates xyz. After an infinitesimal time Δt the

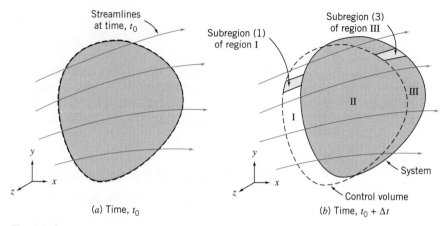

Fig. 4.1 System and control volume configuration.

system will have moved (probably changing shape as it does so) to a new location, as shown in Fig. 4.1*b*. The laws we discussed above apply to this piece of fluid—for example, its mass will be constant (Eq. 4.1a). By examining the geometry of the system/control volume pair at $t = t_0$ and at $t = t_0 + \Delta t$, we will be able to obtain control volume formulations of the basic laws.

Derivation

From Fig. 4.1 we see that the system, which was entirely within the control volume at time t_0, is partially out of the control volume at time $t_0 + \Delta t$. In fact, three regions can be identified. These are: regions I and II, which together make up the control volume, and region III, which, with region II, is the location of the system at time $t_0 + \Delta t$.

Recall that our objective is to relate the rate of change of any arbitrary extensive property, N, of the system to quantities associated with the control volume. From the definition of a derivative, the rate of change of N_{system} is given by

$$\left. \frac{dN}{dt} \right)_{\text{system}} \equiv \lim_{\Delta t \to 0} \frac{N_s)_{t_0 + \Delta t} - N_s)_{t_0}}{\Delta t} \tag{4.7}$$

For convenience, subscript s has been used to denote the system in the definition of a derivative in Eq. 4.7.

From the geometry of Fig. 4.1,

$$N_s)_{t_0 + \Delta t} = (N_{\text{II}} + N_{\text{III}})_{t_0 + \Delta t} = (N_{\text{CV}} - N_{\text{I}} + N_{\text{III}})_{t_0 + \Delta t}$$

and

$$N_s)_{t_0} = (N_{\text{CV}})_{t_0}$$

Substituting into the definition of the system derivative, Eq. 4.7, we obtain

$$\left. \frac{dN}{dt} \right)_s = \lim_{\Delta t \to 0} \frac{(N_{\text{CV}} - N_{\text{I}} + N_{\text{III}})_{t_0 + \Delta t} - N_{\text{CV}})_{t_0}}{\Delta t}$$

Since the limit of a sum is equal to the sum of the limits, we can write

$$\left. \frac{dN}{dt} \right)_s = \lim_{\Delta t \to 0} \frac{N_{\text{CV}})_{t_0 + \Delta t} - N_{\text{CV}})_{t_0}}{\Delta t} + \lim_{\Delta t \to 0} \frac{N_{\text{III}})_{t_0 + \Delta t}}{\Delta t} - \lim_{\Delta t \to 0} \frac{N_{\text{I}})_{t_0 + \Delta t}}{\Delta t} \tag{4.8}$$

$$\textcircled{1} \qquad\qquad\qquad \textcircled{2} \qquad\qquad \textcircled{3}$$

Our task now is to evaluate each of the three terms in Eq. 4.8.

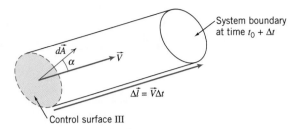

Fig. 4.2 Enlarged view of subregion (3) from Fig. 4.1.

Term ① in Eq. 4.8 simplifies to

$$\lim_{\Delta t \to 0} \frac{N_{\mathrm{CV}})_{t_0 + \Delta t} - N_{\mathrm{CV}})_{t_0}}{\Delta t} = \frac{\partial N_{\mathrm{CV}}}{\partial t} = \frac{\partial}{\partial t} \int_{\mathrm{CV}} \eta\, \rho\, d\Psi \qquad (4.9a)$$

To evaluate term ② we first develop an expression for $N_{\mathrm{III}})_{t_0 + \Delta t}$ by looking at the enlarged view of a typical subregion (subregion (3)) of region III shown in Fig. 4.2. The vector area element $d\vec{A}$ of the control surface has magnitude dA, and its direction is the *outward* normal of the area element. In general, the velocity vector $\vec{V}$ will be at some angle α with respect to $d\vec{A}$.

For this subregion we have

$$dN_{\mathrm{III}})_{t_0 + \Delta t} = (\eta\, \rho\, d\Psi)_{t_0 + \Delta t}$$

We need to obtain an expression for the volume $d\Psi$ of this cylindrical element. The vector length of the cylinder is given by $\Delta\vec{l} = \vec{V}\Delta t$. The volume of a prismatic cylinder, whose area $d\vec{A}$ is at an angle α to its length $\Delta\vec{l}$, is given by $d\Psi = \Delta l\, dA \cos\alpha = \Delta\vec{l} \cdot d\vec{A} = \vec{V} \cdot d\vec{A}\Delta t$. Hence, for subregion (3) we can write

$$dN_{\mathrm{III}})_{t_0 + \Delta t} = \eta\, \rho\, \vec{V} \cdot d\vec{A}\Delta t$$

Then, for the entire region III we can integrate and for term ② in Eq. 4.8 obtain

$$\lim_{\Delta t \to 0} \frac{N_{\mathrm{III}})_{t_0 + \Delta t}}{\Delta t} = \lim_{\Delta t \to 0} \frac{\int_{\mathrm{CS_{III}}} dN_{\mathrm{III}})_{t_0 + \Delta t}}{\Delta t} = \lim_{\Delta t \to 0} \frac{\int_{\mathrm{CS_{III}}} \eta\, \rho\, \vec{V} \cdot d\vec{A}\Delta t}{\Delta t} = \int_{\mathrm{CS_{III}}} \eta\, \rho\, \vec{V} \cdot d\vec{A}$$

$$(4.9b)$$

We can perform a similar analysis for subregion (1) of region I, and obtain for term ③ in Eq. 4.8

$$\lim_{\Delta t \to 0} \frac{N_{\mathrm{I}})_{t_0 + \Delta t}}{\Delta t} = -\int_{\mathrm{CS_1}} \eta\, \rho\, \vec{V} \cdot d\vec{A} \qquad (4.9c)$$

For subregion (1), the velocity vector acts *into* the control volume, but the area normal *always* (by convention) points outward (angle $\alpha > \pi/2$), so the scalar product in Eq. 4.9c is negative. Hence the minus sign in Eq. 4.9c is needed to cancel the negative result of the scalar product to make sure we obtain a positive result for the amount of matter that was in region I (we can't have negative matter).

This concept of the sign of the scalar product is illustrated in Fig. 4.3 for (a) the general case of an inlet or exit, (b) an exit velocity parallel to the surface normal, and (c) an inlet velocity parallel to the surface normal. Cases (b) and (c) are obviously convenient special cases of (a); the value of the cosine in case (a) automatically generates the correct sign of either an inlet or an exit.

We can finally use Eqs. 4.9a, 4.9b, and 4.9c in Eq. 4.8 to obtain

$$\frac{dN}{dt}\Big)_{\mathrm{system}} = \frac{\partial}{\partial t} \int_{\mathrm{CV}} \eta\, \rho\, d\Psi + \int_{\mathrm{CS_1}} \eta\, \rho\, \vec{V} \cdot d\vec{A} + \int_{\mathrm{CS_{III}}} \eta\, \rho\, \vec{V} \cdot d\vec{A}$$

and the two last integrals can be combined because $\mathrm{CS_I}$ and $\mathrm{CS_{III}}$ constitute the entire control surface,

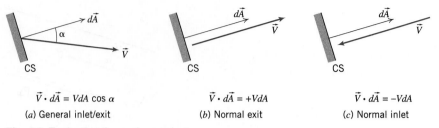

$$\vec{V} \cdot d\vec{A} = VdA \cos \alpha \qquad \vec{V} \cdot d\vec{A} = +VdA \qquad \vec{V} \cdot d\vec{A} = -VdA$$

(a) General inlet/exit   (b) Normal exit   (c) Normal inlet

Fig. 4.3 Evaluating the scalar product.

$$\left. \frac{dN}{dt} \right)_{\text{system}} = \frac{\partial}{\partial t} \int_{\text{CV}} \eta\, \rho\, d\Psi + \int_{\text{CS}} \eta\, \rho \vec{V} \cdot d\vec{A} \tag{4.10}$$

Equation 4.10 is the relation we set out to obtain. It is the fundamental relation between the rate of change of any arbitrary extensive property, N, of a system and the variations of this property associated with a control volume. Some authors refer to Eq. 4.10 as the *Reynolds Transport Theorem*.

Physical Interpretation

It took several pages, but we have reached our goal: We now have a formula (Eq. 4.10) that we can use to convert the rate of change of any extensive property N of a system to an equivalent formulation for use with a control volume. We can now use Eq. 4.10 in the various basic physical law equations (Eqs. 4.1a, 4.2a, 4.3a, 4.4a, and 4.5a) one by one, with N replaced with each of the properties M, $\vec{P}$, $\vec{H}$, E, and S (with corresponding symbols for η), to replace system derivatives with control volume expressions. Because we consider the equation itself to be "basic" we repeat it to emphasize its importance:

$$\left. \frac{dN}{dt} \right)_{\text{system}} = \frac{\partial}{\partial t} \int_{\text{CV}} \eta\, \rho\, d\Psi + \int_{\text{CS}} \eta\, \rho \vec{V} \cdot d\vec{A} \tag{4.10}$$

We need to be clear here: The system is the matter that happens to be passing through the chosen control volume, at the instant we chose. For example, if we chose as a control volume the region contained by an airplane wing and an imaginary rectangular boundary around it, the system would be the mass of the air that is instantaneously contained between the rectangle and the airfoil. Before applying Eq. 4.10 to the physical laws, let's discuss the meaning of each term of the equation:

$\left. \dfrac{dN}{dt} \right)_{\text{system}}$ is the rate of change of the system extensive property N. For example, if $N = \vec{P}$, we obtain the rate of change of momentum.

$\dfrac{\partial}{\partial t} \displaystyle\int_{\text{CV}} \eta\, \rho\, d\Psi$ is the rate of change of the amount of property N in the control volume. The term $\int_{\text{CV}} \eta\, \rho\, d\Psi$ computes the instantaneous value of N in the control volume ($\int_{\text{CV}} \rho\, d\Psi$ is the instantaneous mass in the control volume). For example, if $N = \vec{P}$, then $\eta = \vec{V}$ and $\int_{\text{CV}} \vec{V} \rho d\Psi$ computes the instantaneous amount of momentum in the control volume.

$\displaystyle\int_{\text{CS}} \eta\, \rho \vec{V} \cdot d\vec{A}$ is the rate at which property N is exiting the surface of the control volume. The term $\rho \vec{V} \cdot d\vec{A}$ computes the rate of mass transfer leaving across control surface area element $d\vec{A}$; multiplying by η computes the rate of flux of property N across the element; and integrating therefore computes the net flux of N out of the control volume. For example, if $N = \vec{P}$, then $\eta = \vec{V}$ and $\int_{\text{CS}} \vec{V} \rho \vec{V} \cdot d\vec{A}$ computes the net flux of momentum out of the control volume.

We make two comments about velocity $\vec{V}$ in Eq. 4.10. First, we reiterate the discussion for Fig. 4.3 that care should be taken in evaluating the dot product: Because $\vec{A}$ is always directed outwards, the dot product will be positive when $\vec{V}$ is outward and negative when $\vec{V}$ is inward. Second, $\vec{V}$ is measured with respect to the control volume: When the control volume coordinates xyz are stationary or moving with a constant linear velocity, the control volume will constitute an inertial frame and the physical laws (specifically Newton's second law) we have described will apply.[1]

With these comments we are ready to combine the physical laws (Eqs. 4.1a, 4.2a, 4.3a, 4.4a, and 4.5a) with Eq. 4.10 to obtain some useful control volume equations.

<table>
<tr><td>4-3</td><td>

CONSERVATION OF MASS

</td></tr>
</table>

The first physical principle to which we apply this conversion from a system to a control volume description is the mass conservation principle: The mass of the system remains constant,

$$\left. \frac{dM}{dt} \right)_{\text{system}} = 0 \tag{4.1a}$$

where

$$M_{\text{system}} = \int_{M(\text{system})} dm = \int_{\Psi(\text{system})} \rho \, d\Psi \tag{4.1b}$$

The system and control volume formulations are related by Eq. 4.10,

$$\left. \frac{dN}{dt} \right)_{\text{system}} = \frac{\partial}{\partial t} \int_{\text{CV}} \eta \, \rho \, d\Psi + \int_{\text{CS}} \eta \, \rho \vec{V} \cdot d\vec{A} \tag{4.10}$$

where

$$N_{\text{system}} = \int_{M(\text{system})} \eta \, dm = \int_{\Psi(\text{system})} \eta \, \rho \, d\Psi \tag{4.6}$$

To derive the control volume formulation of conservation of mass, we set

$$N = M \qquad \text{and} \qquad \eta = 1$$

With this substitution, we obtain

$$\left. \frac{dM}{dt} \right)_{\text{system}} = \frac{\partial}{\partial t} \int_{\text{CV}} \rho \, d\Psi + \int_{\text{CS}} \rho \vec{V} \cdot d\vec{A} \tag{4.11}$$

Comparing Eqs. 4.1a and 4.11, we arrive (after rearranging) at the control volume formulation of the conservation of mass:

$$\frac{\partial}{\partial t} \int_{\text{CV}} \rho \, d\Psi + \int_{\text{CS}} \rho \vec{V} \cdot d\vec{A} = 0 \tag{4.12}$$

In Eq. 4.12 the first term represents the rate of change of mass within the control volume; the second term represents the net rate of mass flux out through the control surface. Equation 4.12 indicates that the rate of change of mass in the control volume plus the net outflow is zero. The mass conservation equation is also called the

---

[1] For an accelerating control volume (one whose coordinates xyz are accelerating with respect to an "absolute" set of coordinates XYZ), we must modify the form of Newton's second law (Eq. 4.2a). We will do this in Sections 4-6 (linear acceleration) and 4-7 (arbitrary acceleration).

continuity equation. In common-sense terms, the rate of increase of mass in the control volume is due to the net inflow of mass:

$$\begin{array}{ccc} \text{Rate of increase} & & \text{Net influx of} \\ \text{of mass in CV} & = & \text{mass} \\ \dfrac{\partial}{\partial t}\displaystyle\int_{CV}\rho\,dV & = & -\displaystyle\int_{CS}\rho\vec{V}\cdot d\vec{A} \end{array}$$

Once again, we note that in using Eq. 4.12, care should be taken in evaluating the scalar product $\vec{V}\cdot d\vec{A} = VdA\cos\alpha$: It could be positive (outflow, $\alpha < \pi/2$), negative (inflow, $\alpha > \pi/2$), or even zero ($\alpha = \pi/2$). Recall that Fig. 4.3 illustrates the general case as well as the convenient cases $\alpha = 0$ and $\alpha = \pi$.

Special Cases

In special cases it is possible to simplify Eq. 4.12. Consider first the case of an incompressible fluid, in which density remains constant. When ρ is constant, it is not a function of space or time. Consequently, for *incompressible fluids*, Eq. 4.12 may be written as

$$\rho\frac{\partial}{\partial t}\int_{CV} dV + \rho\int_{CS}\vec{V}\cdot d\vec{A} = 0$$

The integral of dV over the control volume is simply the volume of the control volume. Thus, on dividing through by ρ, we write

$$\frac{\partial V}{\partial t} + \int_{CS}\vec{V}\cdot d\vec{A} = 0$$

For a nondeformable control volume of fixed size and shape, $V = $ constant. The conservation of mass for incompressible flow through a fixed control volume becomes

$$\int_{CS}\vec{V}\cdot d\vec{A} = 0 \tag{4.13a}$$

A useful special case is when we have (or can approximate) uniform velocity at each inlet and exit. In this case Eq. 4.13a simplifies to

$$\sum_{CS}\vec{V}\cdot\vec{A} = 0 \tag{4.13b}$$

Note that we have not assumed the flow to be steady in reducing Eq. 4.12 to the forms 4.13a and 4.13b. We have only imposed the restriction of incompressible fluid. Thus Eqs. 4.13a and 4.13b are statements of conservation of mass for flow of an incompressible fluid that may be steady or unsteady.

The dimensions of the integrand in Eq. 4.13a are L^3/t. The integral of $\vec{V}\cdot d\vec{A}$ over a section of the control surface is commonly called the *volume flow rate* or *volume rate of flow*. Thus, for incompressible flow, the volume flow rate into a fixed control volume must be equal to the volume flow rate out of the control volume. The volume flow rate Q, through a section of a control surface of area A, is given by

$$Q = \int_{A}\vec{V}\cdot d\vec{A} \tag{4.14a}$$

The average velocity magnitude, $\overline{V}$, at a section is defined as

$$\overline{V} = \frac{Q}{A} = \frac{1}{A}\int_{A}\vec{V}\cdot d\vec{A} \tag{4.14b}$$

Consider now the general case of *steady, compressible flow* through a fixed control volume. Since the flow is steady, this means that at most $\rho = \rho(x, y, z)$. By definition, no fluid property varies with time in a steady flow. Consequently, the first term of Eq. 4.12 must be zero and, hence, for steady flow, the statement of conservation of mass reduces to

$$\int_{CS} \rho \vec{V} \cdot d\vec{A} = 0 \qquad (4.15a)$$

A useful special case is when we have (or can approximate) uniform velocity at each inlet and exit. In this case, Eq. 4.15a simplifies to

$$\sum_{CS} \rho \vec{V} \cdot \vec{A} = 0 \qquad (4.15b)$$

Thus, for steady flow, the mass flow rate into a control volume must be equal to the mass flow rate out of the control volume.

We will now look at three Examples to illustrate some features of the various forms of the conservation of mass equation for a control volume. Example 4.1 involves a problem in which we have uniform flow at each section, Example 4.2 involves a problem in which we do not have uniform flow at a location, and Example 4.3 involves a problem in which we have unsteady flow.

Example 4.1 Mass Flow at a Pipe Junction

Consider the steady flow in a water pipe joint shown in the diagram. The areas are: $A_1 = 0.2 \text{ m}^2$, $A_2 = 0.2 \text{ m}^2$, and $A_3 = 0.15 \text{ m}^2$. In addition, fluid is lost out of a hole at ④, estimated at a rate of 0.1 m³/s. The average speeds at sections ① and ③ are $V_1 = 5$ m/s and $V_3 = 12$ m/s, respectively. Find the velocity at section ②.

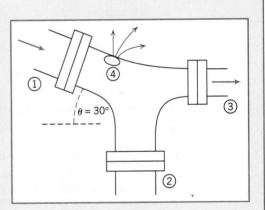

GIVEN: Steady flow of water through the device.

$A_1 = 0.2 \text{ m}^2 \qquad A_2 = 0.2 \text{ m}^2 \qquad A_3 = 0.15 \text{ m}^2$
$V_1 = 5 \text{ m/s} \qquad V_3 = 12 \text{ m/s} \qquad \rho = 999 \text{ kg/m}^3$

Volume flow rate at ④ = 0.1 m³/s

FIND: Velocity at section ②.

SOLUTION:

Choose a fixed control volume as shown. Make an assumption that the flow at section ② is outwards, and label the diagram accordingly (if this assumption is incorrect our final result will tell us).

Governing equation: The general control volume equation is Eq. 4.12, but we can go immediately to Eq. 4.13b because of assumptions (2) and (3) below,

$$\sum_{CS} \vec{V} \cdot \vec{A} = 0$$

Assumptions: (1) Steady flow (given).
(2) Incompressible flow.
(3) Uniform properties at each section.

Hence (using Eq. 4.14a for the leak)

$$\vec{V}_1 \cdot \vec{A}_1 + \vec{V}_2 \cdot \vec{A}_2 + \vec{V}_3 \cdot \vec{A}_3 + Q_4 = 0 \qquad (1)$$

where Q_4 is the flow rate out of the leak.

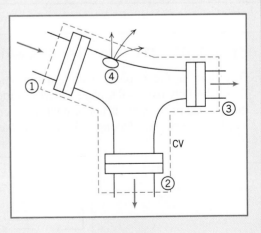

Let us examine the first three terms in Eq. 1 in light of the discussion of Fig. 4.3, and the directions of the velocity vectors:

$$\vec{V}_1 \cdot \vec{A}_1 = -V_1 A_1$$

$\left\{\begin{array}{l} \text{Sign of } \vec{V}_1 \cdot \vec{A}_1 \text{ is} \\ \text{negative at surface } ① \end{array}\right\}$

$$\vec{V}_2 \cdot \vec{A}_2 = +V_2 A_2$$

$\left\{\begin{array}{l} \text{Sign of } \vec{V}_2 \cdot \vec{A}_2 \text{ is} \\ \text{positive at surface } ② \end{array}\right\}$

$$\vec{V}_3 \cdot \vec{A}_3 = +V_3 A_3$$

$\left\{\begin{array}{l} \text{Sign of } \vec{V}_3 \cdot \vec{A}_3 \text{ is} \\ \text{positive at surface } ③ \end{array}\right\}$

Using these results in Eq. 1,

$$-V_1 A_1 + V_2 A_2 + V_3 A_3 + Q_4 = 0$$

or

$$V_2 = \frac{V_1 A_1 - V_3 A_3 - Q_4}{A_2} = \frac{5\,\dfrac{\text{m}}{\text{s}} \times 0.2\,\text{m}^2 - 12\,\dfrac{\text{m}}{\text{s}} \times 0.15\,\text{m}^2 - \dfrac{0.1\,\text{m}^3}{\text{s}}}{0.2\,\text{m}^2} = -4.5\,\text{m/s} \longleftarrow V_2$$

Recall that V_2 represents the magnitude of the velocity, which we assumed was outwards from the control volume. The fact that V_2 is negative means that in fact we have an *inflow* at location ②—our initial assumption was invalid.

This problem demonstrates use of the sign convention for evaluating $\int_A \vec{V} \cdot d\vec{A}$ or $\Sigma_{CS} \vec{V} \cdot \vec{A}$. In particular, the area normal is *always* drawn *out-wards* from the control surface.

Example 4.2   Mass Flow Rate in Boundary Layer

The fluid in direct contact with a stationary solid boundary has zero velocity; there is no slip at the boundary. Thus the flow over a flat plate adheres to the plate surface and forms a boundary layer, as depicted below. The flow ahead of the plate is uniform with velocity, $\vec{V} = U\hat{i}$; $U = 30$ m/s. The velocity distribution within the boundary layer $(0 \leq y \leq \delta)$ along cd is approximated as $u/U = 2(y/\delta) - (y/\delta)^2$.

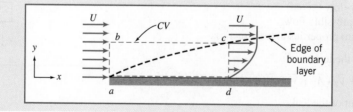

The boundary-layer thickness at location d is $\delta = 5$ mm. The fluid is air with density $\rho =$ ing the plate width perpendicular to the paper to be $w = 0.6$ m, calculate the mass flow rate control volume $abcd$.

GIVEN: Steady, incompressible flow over a flat plate, $\rho = 1.24$ kg/m³. Width of plate, $w = 0.6$ m.
Velocity ahead of plate is uniform: $\vec{V} = U\hat{i}$, $U = 30$ m/s.

At $x = x_d$:

$\delta = 5$ mm

$$\frac{u}{U} = 2\left(\frac{y}{\delta}\right) - \left(\frac{y}{\delta}\right)^2$$

FIND: Mass flow rate across surface bc.

SOLUTION:
The fixed control volume is shown by the dashed lines.

Governing equation: The general control volume equation is Eq. 4.12, but we can go immediately to Eq. 4.15a because of assumption (1) below,

$$\int_{CS} \rho \vec{V} \cdot d\vec{A} = 0$$

Assumptions: (1) Steady flow (given).
(2) Incompressible flow (given).
(3) Two-dimensional flow, given properties are independent of z.

Assuming that there is no flow in the z direction, then

$$\left(\begin{array}{c} \text{no flow} \\ \text{across } da \end{array}\right)$$

$$\int_{A_{ab}} \rho\vec{V} \cdot d\vec{A} + \int_{A_{bc}} \rho\vec{V} \cdot d\vec{A} + \int_{A_{cd}} \rho\vec{V} \cdot d\vec{A} + \int_{A_{da}} \rho\vec{V} \cdot d\vec{A} = 0$$

$$\therefore \dot{m}_{bc} = \int_{A_{bc}} \rho\vec{V} \cdot d\vec{A} = - \int_{A_{ab}} \rho\vec{V} \cdot d\vec{A} - \int_{A_{cd}} \rho\vec{V} \cdot d\vec{A} \tag{1}$$

We need to evaluate the integrals on the right side of the equation.
For depth w in the z direction, we obtain

$$\int_{A_{ab}} \rho\vec{V} \cdot d\vec{A} = -\int_{A_{ab}} \rho u\, dA = -\int_{y_a}^{y_b} \rho u w\, dy$$

$$= -\int_0^\delta \rho u w\, dy = -\int_0^\delta \rho U w\, dy$$

$\left\{\begin{array}{c} \vec{V} \cdot d\vec{A} \text{ is negative} \\ dA = w\,dy \end{array}\right\}$

$\{u = U \text{ over area } ab\}$

$$\int_{A_{ab}} \rho\vec{V} \cdot d\vec{A} = -\Big[\rho U w y\Big]_0^\delta = -\rho U w \delta$$

$$\int_{A_{cd}} \rho\vec{V} \cdot d\vec{A} = \int_{A_{cd}} \rho u\, dA = \int_{y_d}^{y_c} \rho u w\, dy$$

$$= \int_0^\delta \rho u w\, dy = \int_0^\delta \rho w U \left[2\left(\frac{y}{\delta}\right) - \left(\frac{y}{\delta}\right)^2\right] dy$$

$\left\{\begin{array}{c} \vec{V} \cdot d\vec{A} \text{ is positive} \\ dA = w\,dy \end{array}\right\}$

$$\int_{A_{cd}} \rho\vec{V} \cdot d\vec{A} = \rho w U \left[\frac{y^2}{\delta} - \frac{y^3}{3\delta^2}\right]_0^\delta = \rho w U \delta\left[1 - \frac{1}{3}\right] = \frac{2\rho U w \delta}{3}$$

bstituting into Eq. 1, we obtain

$$\therefore \dot{m}_{bc} = \rho Uw\delta - \frac{2\rho Uw\delta}{3} = \frac{\rho Uw\delta}{3}$$

$$= \frac{1}{3} \times \frac{1.24 \text{ kg}}{\text{m}^3} \times \frac{30 \text{ m}}{\text{s}} \times 0.6 \text{ m} \times 5 \text{ mm} \times \frac{\text{m}}{1000 \text{ mm}}$$

$$\left\{ \begin{array}{l} \text{Positive sign indicates flow} \\ \text{out across surface } bc. \end{array} \right\}$$

$$\dot{m}_{bc} = 0.0372 \text{ kg/s} \qquad\qquad\qquad\qquad\qquad\qquad\qquad\qquad\qquad \dot{m}_b$$

> This problem demonstrates use of the conservation of mass equation when we have nonuniform flow at a section.

Example 4.3 Density Change in Venting Tank

A tank of 0.05 m³ volume contains air at 800 kPa (absolute) and 15°C. At $t = 0$, air begins escaping from the tank through a valve with a flow area of 65 mm². The air passing through the valve has a speed of 300 m/s and a density of 6 kg/m³. Determine the instantaneous rate of change of density in the tank at $t = 0$.

GIVEN: Tank of volume $\forall = 0.05$ m³ contains air at $p = 800$ kPa (absolute), $T = 15°C$. At $t = 0$, air escapes through a valve. Air leaves with speed $V = 300$ m/s and density $\rho = 6$ kg/m³ through area $A = 65$ mm².

FIND: Rate of change of air density in the tank at $t = 0$.

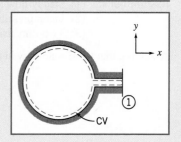

SOLUTION:
Choose a fixed control volume as shown by the dashed line.

Governing equation: $\dfrac{\partial}{\partial t} \displaystyle\int_{CV} \rho \, d\forall + \int_{CS} \rho \vec{V} \cdot d\vec{A} = 0$

Assumptions: (1) Properties in the tank are uniform, but time-dependent.
(2) Uniform flow at section ①.

Since properties are assumed uniform in the tank at any instant, we can take ρ out from within the volume integral of the first term,

$$\frac{\partial}{\partial t} \left[\rho_{CV} \int_{CV} d\forall \right] + \int_{CS} \rho \vec{V} \cdot d\vec{A} = 0$$

Now, $\int_{CV} d\forall = \forall$, and hence

$$\frac{\partial}{\partial t} (\rho\forall)_{CV} + \int_{CS} \rho \vec{V} \cdot d\vec{A} = 0$$

The only place where mass crosses the boundary of the control volume is at surface ①. Hence

$$\int_{CS} \rho \vec{V} \cdot d\vec{A} = \int_{A_1} \rho \vec{V} \cdot d\vec{A} \qquad \text{and} \qquad \frac{\partial}{\partial t}(\rho\forall) + \int_{A_1} \rho \vec{V} \cdot d\vec{A} = 0$$

At surface ① the sign of $\rho\vec{V} \cdot d\vec{A}$ is positive, so

$$\frac{\partial}{\partial t}(\rho\forall) + \int_{A_1} \rho V \, dA = 0$$

Since flow is assumed uniform over surface ①, then

$$\frac{\partial}{\partial t}(\rho\forall) + \rho_1 V_1 A_1 = 0 \qquad \text{or} \qquad \frac{\partial}{\partial t}(\rho\forall) = -\rho_1 V_1 A_1$$

Since the volume, $\forall$, of the tank is not a function of time,

$$\forall \frac{\partial \rho}{\partial t} = -\rho_1 V_1 A_1$$

and

$$\frac{\partial \rho}{\partial t} = -\frac{\rho_1 V_1 A_1}{\Psi}$$

At $t = 0$,

$$\frac{\partial \rho}{\partial t} = -6 \ \frac{\text{kg}}{\text{m}^3} \times 300 \ \frac{\text{m}}{\text{s}} \times 65 \ \text{mm}^2 \times \frac{1}{0.05 \ \text{m}^3} \times \frac{\text{m}^2}{10^6 \ \text{mm}^2}$$

$$\frac{\partial \rho}{\partial t} = -2.34 \ (\text{kg/m}^3)/\text{s} \longleftarrow \left\{\text{The density is decreasing.}\right\} \hspace{3cm} \frac{\partial \rho}{\partial t}$$

This problem demonstrates use of the conservation of mass equation for unsteady flow problems.

4-4 MOMENTUM EQUATION FOR INERTIAL CONTROL VOLUME

We now wish to obtain a control volume form of Newton's second law. We use the same procedure we just used for mass conservation, with one note of caution: the control volume coordinates (with respect to which we measure all velocities) are inertial; that is, the control volume coordinates *xyz* are either at rest or moving at constant speed with respect to an "absolute" set of coordinates *XYZ*. (Sections 4-6 and 4-7 will analyze noninertial control volumes.) We begin with the mathematical formulation for a system and then use Eq. 4.10 to go from the system to the control volume formulation.

Recall that Newton's second law for a system moving relative to an inertial coordinate system was given by Eq. 4.2a as

$$\vec{F} = \frac{d\vec{P}}{dt}\bigg)_{\text{system}} \tag{4.2a}$$

where the linear momentum of the system is given by

$$\vec{P}_{\text{system}} = \int_{M(\text{system})} \vec{V} \ dm = \int_{\Psi(\text{system})} \vec{V} \ \rho \ d\Psi \tag{4.2b}$$

and the resultant force, $\vec{F}$, includes all surface and body forces acting on the system,

$$\vec{F} = \vec{F}_S + \vec{F}_B$$

The system and control volume formulations are related using Eq. 4.10,

$$\frac{dN}{dt}\bigg)_{\text{system}} = \frac{\partial}{\partial t} \int_{\text{CV}} \eta \ \rho \ d\Psi + \int_{\text{CS}} \eta \ \rho \vec{V} \cdot d\vec{A} \tag{4.10}$$

To derive the control volume formulation of Newton's second law, we set

$$N = \vec{P} \qquad \text{and} \qquad \eta = \vec{V}$$

From Eq. 4.10, with this substitution, we obtain

$$\frac{d\vec{P}}{dt}\bigg)_{\text{system}} = \frac{\partial}{\partial t} \int_{\text{CV}} \vec{V} \ \rho \ d\Psi + \int_{\text{CS}} \vec{V} \rho \vec{V} \cdot d\vec{A} \tag{4.16}$$

From Eq. 4.2a

$$\frac{d\vec{P}}{dt}\bigg)_{\text{system}} = \vec{F})_{\text{on system}} \tag{4.2a}$$

Since, in deriving Eq. 4.10, the system and the control volume coincided at t_0, then

$$\vec{F}\big)_{\text{on system}} = \vec{F}\big)_{\text{on control volume}}$$

In light of this, Eqs. 4.2a and 4.16 may be combined to yield the control volume formulation of Newton's second law for a nonaccelerating control volume

$$\vec{F} = \vec{F}_S + \vec{F}_B = \frac{\partial}{\partial t} \int_{\text{CV}} \vec{V} \rho \, d\Psi + \int_{\text{CS}} \vec{V} \rho \vec{V} \cdot d\vec{A} \tag{4.17a}$$

For cases when we have uniform flow at each inlet and exit, we can use

$$\vec{F} = \vec{F}_S + \vec{F}_B = \frac{\partial}{\partial t} \int_{\text{CV}} \vec{V} \rho \, d\Psi + \sum_{\text{CS}} \vec{V} \rho \vec{V} \cdot \vec{A} \tag{4.17b}$$

Equations 4.17a and 4.17b are our (nonaccelerating) control volume forms of Newton's second law. It states that the total force (due to surface and body forces) acting on the control volume leads to a rate of change of momentum within the control volume (the volume integral) and/or a net rate at which momentum is leaving the control volume through the control surface.

We must be a little careful in applying Eqs. 4.17. The first step will always be to carefully choose a control volume and its control surface so that we can evaluate the volume integral and the surface integral (or summation); each inlet and exit should be carefully labeled, as should the external forces acting. In fluid mechanics the body force is usually gravity, so

$$\vec{F}_B = \int_{\text{CV}} \rho \vec{g} \, d\Psi = \vec{W}_{\text{CV}} = M\vec{g}$$

where $\vec{g}$ is the acceleration of gravity and $\vec{W}_{\text{CV}}$ is the instantaneous weight of the entire control volume. In many applications the surface force is due to pressure,

$$\vec{F}_S = \int_A -p \, d\vec{A}$$

Note that the minus sign is to ensure that we always compute pressure forces acting *onto* the control surface (recall $d\vec{A}$ was chosen to be a vector pointing *out* of the control volume). It is worth stressing that *even at points on the surface that have an outflow*, the pressure force acts *onto* the control volume.

In Eqs. 4.17 we must also be careful in evaluating $\int_{\text{CS}} \vec{V} \rho \vec{V} \cdot d\vec{A}$ or $\Sigma_{\text{CS}} \vec{V} \rho \vec{V} \cdot \vec{A}$ (this may be easier to do if we write them with the implied parentheses, $\int_{\text{CS}} \vec{V} \rho(\vec{V} \cdot d\vec{A})$ or $\Sigma_{\text{CS}} \vec{V} \rho(\vec{V} \cdot \vec{A})$). The velocity $\vec{V}$ must be measured with respect to the control volume coordinates xyz, with the appropriate signs for its vector components u, v, and w; recall also that the scalar product will be positive for outflow and negative for inflow (refer to Fig. 4.3).

The momentum equation (Eqs. 4.17) is a vector equation. We will usually write the three scalar components, as measured in the xyz coordinates of the control volume,

$$F_x = F_{S_x} + F_{B_x} = \frac{\partial}{\partial t} \int_{\text{CV}} u \rho \, d\Psi + \int_{\text{CS}} u \rho \vec{V} \cdot d\vec{A} \tag{4.18a}$$

$$F_y = F_{S_y} + F_{B_y} = \frac{\partial}{\partial t} \int_{\text{CV}} v \rho \, d\Psi + \int_{\text{CS}} v \rho \vec{V} \cdot d\vec{A} \tag{4.18b}$$

$$F_z = F_{S_z} + F_{B_z} = \frac{\partial}{\partial t} \int_{\text{CV}} w \rho \, d\Psi + \int_{\text{CS}} w \rho \vec{V} \cdot d\vec{A} \tag{4.18c}$$

or, for uniform flow at each inlet and exit,

$$F_x = F_{S_x} + F_{B_x} = \frac{\partial}{\partial t} \int_{CV} u \, \rho \, d\forall + \sum_{CS} u \, \rho \vec{V} \cdot \vec{A} \qquad (4.18d)$$

$$F_y = F_{S_y} + F_{B_y} = \frac{\partial}{\partial t} \int_{CV} v \, \rho \, d\forall + \sum_{CS} v \, \rho \vec{V} \cdot \vec{A} \qquad (4.18e)$$

$$F_z = F_{S_z} + F_{B_z} = \frac{\partial}{\partial t} \int_{CV} w \, \rho \, d\forall + \sum_{CS} w \, \rho \vec{V} \cdot \vec{A} \qquad (4.18f)$$

Note that, as we found for the mass conservation equation (Eq. 4.12), for steady flow the first term on the right in Eqs. 4.17 and 4.18 is zero.

We will now look at five Examples to illustrate some features of the various forms of the momentum equation for a control volume. Example 4.4 demonstrates how intelligent choice of the control volume can simplify analysis of a problem, Example 4.5 involves a problem in which we have significant body forces, Example 4.6 explains how to simplify surface force evaluations by working in gage pressures, Example 4.7 involves nonuniform surface forces, and Example 4.8 involves a problem in which we have unsteady flow.

Example 4.4 Choice of Control Volume for Momentum Analysis

Water from a stationary nozzle strikes a flat plate as shown. The water leaves the nozzle at 15 m/s; the nozzle area is 0.01 m². Assuming the water is directed normal to the plate, and flows along the plate, determine the horizontal force you need to resist to hold it in place.

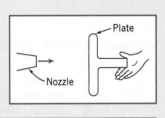

GIVEN: Water from a stationary nozzle is directed normal to the plate; subsequent flow is parallel to plate.

$$\text{Jet velocity, } \vec{V} = 15\hat{i} \text{ m/s}$$
$$\text{Nozzle area, } A_n = 0.01 \text{ m}^2$$

FIND: Horizontal force on your hand.

SOLUTION:
We chose a coordinate system in defining the problem above. We must now choose a suitable control volume. Two possible choices are shown by the dashed lines below.

In both cases, water from the nozzle crosses the control surface through area A_1 (assumed

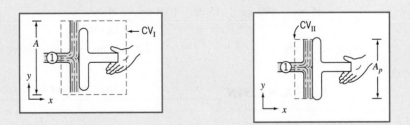

equal to the nozzle area) and is assumed to leave the control volume tangent to the plate surface in the $+y$ or $-y$ direction. Before trying to decide which is the "best" control volume to use, let us write the governing equations.

$$\vec{F} = \vec{F}_S + \vec{F}_B = \frac{\partial}{\partial t} \int_{CV} \vec{V} \rho \, d\forall + \int_{CS} \vec{V} \rho \vec{V} \cdot d\vec{A} \qquad \text{and} \qquad \frac{\partial}{\partial t} \int_{CV} \rho \, d\forall + \int_{CS} \rho \vec{V} \cdot d\vec{A} = 0$$

Assumptions: (1) Steady flow.
(2) Incompressible flow.
(3) Uniform flow at each section where fluid crosses the CV boundaries.

Regardless of our choice of control volume, assumptions (1), (2), and (3) lead to

$$\vec{F} = \vec{F}_S + \vec{F}_B = \sum_{CS} \vec{V} \rho \vec{V} \cdot \vec{A} \quad \text{and} \quad \sum_{CS} \rho \vec{V} \cdot \vec{A} = 0$$

Evaluating the momentum flux term will lead to the same result for both control volumes. We should choose the control volume that allows the most straightforward evaluation of the forces.

Remember in applying the momentum equation that the force, $\vec{F}$, represents all forces acting *on* the control volume.

Let us solve the problem using each of the control volumes.

CV$_I$

The control volume has been selected so that the area of the left surface is equal to the area of the right surface. Denote this area by A.

The control volume cuts through your hand. We denote the components of the reaction force of your hand on the control volume as R_x and R_y and assume both to be positive. (The force of the control volume on your hand is equal and opposite to R_x and R_y.)

Atmospheric pressure acts on all surfaces of the control volume. Note that *the pressure in a free jet is ambient*, i.e., in this case atmospheric. (The distributed force due to atmospheric pressure has been shown on the vertical faces only.)

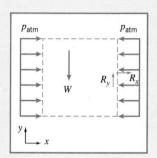

The body force on the control volume is denoted as W.

Since we are looking for the horizontal force, we write the x component of the steady flow momentum equation

$$F_{S_x} + F_{B_x} = \sum_{CS} u \rho \vec{V} \cdot \vec{A}$$

There are no body forces in the x direction, so $F_{B_x} = 0$, and

$$F_{S_x} = \sum_{CS} u \rho \vec{V} \cdot \vec{A}$$

To evaluate F_{S_x}, we must include all surface forces acting on the control volume

$$F_{S_x} = \underset{\substack{\text{force due to atmospheric} \\ \text{pressure acts to right} \\ \text{(positive direction)} \\ \text{on left surface}}}{p_{atm}A} \quad - \quad \underset{\substack{\text{force due to atmospheric} \\ \text{pressure acts to left} \\ \text{(negative direction)} \\ \text{on right surface}}}{p_{atm}A} \quad + \quad \underset{\substack{\text{force of your hand on} \\ \text{control volume} \\ \text{(assumed positive)}}}{R_x}$$

Consequently, $F_{S_x} = R_x$, and

$$R_x = \sum_{CS} u \rho \vec{V} \cdot \vec{A} = u \rho \vec{V} \cdot \vec{A}\big|_1 \qquad \{\text{For top and bottom surfaces, } u = 0\}$$

$$\{\text{At } \textcircled{1}, \rho \vec{V}_1 \cdot \vec{A}_1 = \rho(-V_1 A_1) \text{ since}$$
$$\vec{V}_1 \text{ and } \vec{A}_1 \text{ are } 180° \text{ apart.}$$

$$R_x = -u_1 \rho V_1 A_1 \qquad\qquad \text{Note that } u_1 = V_1\}$$

$$R_x = -\frac{15 \text{ m}}{\text{s}} \times 999 \frac{\text{kg}}{\text{m}^3} \times \frac{15 \text{ m}}{\text{s}} \times 0.01 \text{ m}^2 \times \frac{\text{N} \cdot \text{s}^2}{\text{kg} \cdot \text{m}} \qquad \{u_1 = 15 \text{ m/s}\}$$

$$R_x = -2.25 \text{ kN} \qquad\qquad \{R_x \text{ acts opposite to positive direction assumed.}\}$$

The horizontal force on your hand is

$$K_x = -R_x = 2.25 \text{ kN} \qquad\qquad\qquad\qquad \{\text{force on your hand acts to the right}\} \qquad K_x$$

CV$_{II}$ with Horizontal Forces Shown

The control volume has been selected so the areas of the left surface and of the right surface are equal to the area of the plate. Denote this area by A_p.

The control volume is in contact with the plate over the entire plate surface. We denote the horizontal reaction force from the plate on the control volume as B_x (and assume it to be positive).

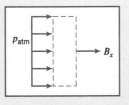

Atmospheric pressure acts on the left surface of the control volume (and on the two horizontal surfaces). The body force on this control volume has no component in the x direction.

Then the x component of the momentum equation,

$$F_{S_x} = \sum_{CS} u \, \rho \vec{V} \cdot \vec{A}$$

yields

$$F_{S_x} = p_{atm} A_p + B_x = u \, \rho \vec{V} \cdot \vec{A}|_1 = -u_1 V_1 A_1 = -2.25 \text{ kN}$$

Then

$$B_x = -p_{atm} A_p - 2.25 \text{ kN}$$

To determine the net force on the plate, we need a free-body diagram of the plate:

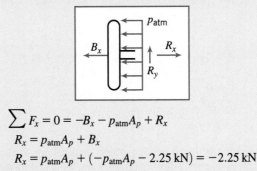

$$\sum F_x = 0 = -B_x - p_{atm} A_p + R_x$$
$$R_x = p_{atm} A_p + B_x$$
$$R_x = p_{atm} A_p + (-p_{atm} A_p - 2.25 \text{ kN}) = -2.25 \text{ kN}$$

Then the horizontal force on your hand is $K_x = -R_x = 2.25$ kN.

Note that the choice of CV_{II} meant we needed an additional free-body diagram. In general it is best to select the control volume so that the force sought acts explicitly on the control volume.

Notes:
- ✓ This problem demonstrates how thoughtful choice of the control volume can simplify use of the momentum equation.
- ✓ The analysis would have been greatly simplified if we had worked in gage pressures (see Example 4.6).
- ✓ For this problem the force generated was entirely due to the plate absorbing the jet's horizontal momentum.

Example 4.5   Tank on Scale: Body Force

A metal container 2 ft high, with an inside cross-sectional area of 1 ft², weighs 5 lbf when empty. The container is placed on a scale and water flows in through an opening in the top and out through the two equal-area openings in the sides, as shown in the diagram. Under steady flow conditions, the height of the water in the tank is $h = 1.9$ ft.

$$A_1 = 0.1 \text{ ft}^2$$
$$\vec{V}_1 = -10 \text{ ft/s}$$
$$A_2 = A_3 = 0.1 \text{ ft}^2$$

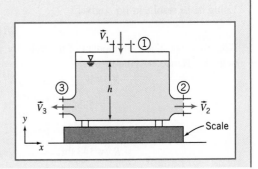

Your boss claims that the scale will read the weight of the volume of water in the tank plus the tank weight, i.e., that we can treat this as a simple statics problem. You disagree, claiming that a fluid flow analysis is required. Who is right, and what does the scale indicate?

GIVEN: Metal container, of height 2 ft and cross-sectional area $A = 1$ ft^2, weighs 5 lbf when empty. Container rests on scale. Under steady flow conditions water depth is $h = 1.9$ ft. Water enters vertically at section ① and leaves horizontally through sections ② and ③

$$A_1 = 0.1 \text{ ft}^2$$
$$\vec{V}_1 = -10\hat{j} \text{ ft/s}$$
$$A_2 = A_3 = 0.1 \text{ ft}^2$$

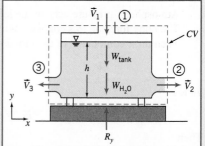

FIND: Scale reading.

SOLUTION:

Choose a control volume as shown; R_y is the force of the scale on the control volume (exerted on the control volume through the supports) and is assumed positive.

The weight of the tank is designated W_{tank}; the weight of the water in the tank is $W_{\text{H}_2\text{O}}$.

Atmospheric pressure acts uniformly on the entire control surface, and therefore has no net effect on the control volume. Because of this null effect we have not shown the pressure distribution in the diagram.

Governing equations: The general control volume momentum and mass conservation equations are Eqs. 4.17 and 4.12, respectively,

$$\vec{F}_S + \vec{F}_B = \overset{= 0(1)}{\cancel{\frac{\partial}{\partial t} \int_{CV} \vec{V} \rho \, dV}} + \int_{CS} \vec{V} \rho \vec{V} \cdot d\vec{A}$$

$$\overset{= 0(1)}{\cancel{\frac{\partial}{\partial t} \int_{CV} \rho \, dV}} + \int_{CS} \rho \vec{V} \cdot d\vec{A} = 0$$

Note that we usually start with the simplest forms (based on the problem assumptions, e.g., steady flow) of the mass conservation and momentum equations. However, in this problem, for illustration purposes, we start with the most general forms of the equations.

Assumptions: (1) Steady flow (given).
(2) Incompressible flow.
(3) Uniform flow at each section where fluid crosses the CV boundaries.

We are only interested in the y component of the momentum equation

$$F_{S_y} + F_{B_y} = \int_{CS} v \rho \vec{V} \cdot d\vec{A} \tag{1}$$

$$F_{S_y} = R_y \qquad \text{\{There is no net force due to atmosphere pressure.\}}$$

$$F_{B_y} = -W_{\text{tank}} - W_{\text{H}_2\text{O}} \qquad \text{\{Both body forces act in negative y direction.\}}$$

$$W_{\text{H}_2\text{O}} = \rho g V = \gamma A h$$

$$\int_{CS} v \rho \vec{V} \cdot d\vec{A} = \int_{A_1} v \rho \vec{V} \cdot d\vec{A} = \int_{A_1} v(-\rho V_1 dA_1) \qquad \left\{ \begin{array}{l} \vec{V} \cdot d\vec{A} \text{ is negative at } ① \\ v = 0 \text{ at sections } ② \text{ and } ③ \end{array} \right\}$$

$$\left\{ \begin{array}{l} \text{We are assuming uniform} \\ \text{properties at } ① \end{array} \right\}$$

$$= v_1(-\rho V_1 A_1)$$

Using these results in Eq. 1 gives

$$R_y - W_{\text{tank}} - \gamma A h = v_1(-\rho V_1 A_1)$$

Note that v_1 is the y component of the velocity, so that $v_1 = -V_1$, where we recall that $V_1 = 10$ ft/s is the magnitude of velocity $\vec{V}_1$. Hence, solving for R_y,

$$R_y = W_{\text{tank}} + \gamma A h + \rho V_1^2 A_1$$

$$= 5 \text{ lbf} + \frac{62.4 \text{ lbf}}{\text{ft}^3} \times 1 \text{ ft}^2 \times 1.9 \text{ ft} + \frac{1.94 \text{ slug}}{\text{ft}^3} \times \frac{100 \text{ ft}^2}{\text{s}^2} \times 0.1 \text{ ft}^2 \times \frac{\text{lbf} \cdot \text{s}^2}{\text{slug} \cdot \text{ft}}$$

$$= 5 \text{ lbf} + 118.6 \text{ lbf} + 19.4 \text{ lbf}$$

$$R_y = 143 \text{ lbf} \longleftarrow \hspace{8cm} R_y$$

Note that this is the force of the scale on the control volume; it is also the reading, on the scale. We can see that the scale reading is due to: the tank weight (5 lbf), the weight of water instantaneously in the tank (118.6 lbf), and the force involved in absorbing the downward momentum of the fluid at section ① (19.4 lbf). Hence your boss is wrong—neglecting the momentum results in an error of almost 15%.

> This problem illustrates use of the momentum equation including significant body forces.

Example 4.6 Flow through Elbow: Use of Gage Pressures

Water flows steadily through the 90° reducing elbow shown in the diagram. At the inlet to the elbow, the absolute pressure is 220 kPa and the cross-sectional area is 0.01 m². At the outlet, the cross-sectional area is 0.0025 m² and the velocity is 16 m/s. The elbow discharges to the atmosphere. Determine the force required to hold the elbow in place.

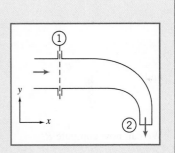

GIVEN: Steady flow of water through 90° reducing elbow.

$$p_1 = 220\,\text{kPa (abs)} \qquad A_1 = 0.01\,\text{m}^2 \qquad \vec{V}_2 = -16\,\hat{j}\,\text{m/s} \qquad A_2 = 0.0025\,\text{m}^2$$

FIND: Force required to hold elbow in place.

SOLUTION:
Choose a fixed control volume as shown. Note that we have several surface force computations: p_1 on area A_1 and p_{atm} everywhere else. The exit at section ② is to a free jet, and so at ambient (i.e., atmospheric) pressure. We can use a simplification here: If we subtract p_{atm} from the entire surface (a null effect as far as forces are concerned) we can work in gage pressures, as shown.

Note that since the elbow is anchored to the supply line, in addition to the reaction forces R_x and R_y (shown), there would also be a reaction moment (not shown).

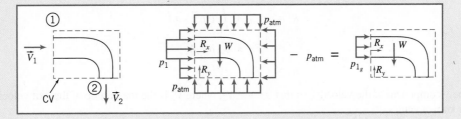

Governing equations:

$$\vec{F} = \vec{F}_s + \vec{F}_B = \overset{= 0(4)}{\cancel{\frac{\partial}{\partial t}\int_{CV} \vec{V}\rho\,dV}} + \int_{CS} \vec{V}\rho\vec{V}\cdot d\vec{A}$$

$$\overset{= 0(4)}{\cancel{\frac{\partial}{\partial t}\int_{CV}\rho\,dV}} + \int_{CS}\rho\vec{V}\cdot d\vec{A} = 0$$

Assumptions:
(1) Uniform flow at each section.
(2) Atmospheric pressure, $p_{atm} = 101\,\text{kPa (abs)}$.
(3) Incompressible flow.
(4) Steady flow (given).
(5) Neglect weight of elbow and water in elbow.

Once again (although we didn't need to) we started with the most general form of the governing equations. Writing the x component of the momentum equation results in

$$F_{S_x} = \int_{CS} u\, \rho \vec{V} \cdot d\vec{A} = \int_{A_1} u\, \rho \vec{V} \cdot d\vec{A} \qquad\qquad \{F_{B_x} = 0 \quad \text{and} \quad u_2 = 0\}$$

$$p_{1_g} A_1 + R_x = \int_{A_1} u\, \rho \vec{V} \cdot d\vec{A}$$

so

$$R_x = -p_{1_g} A_1 + \int_{A_1} u\, \rho \vec{V} \cdot d\vec{A}$$

$$= -p_{1_g} A_1 + u_1(-\rho V_1 A_1)$$

$$R_x = -p_{1_g} A_1 - \rho V_1^2 A_1$$

Note that u_1 is the x component of the velocity, so that $u_1 = V_1$. To find V_1, use the mass conservation equation:

$$\int_{CS} \rho \vec{V} \cdot d\vec{A} = \int_{A_1} \rho \vec{V} \cdot d\vec{A} + \int_{A_2} \rho \vec{V} \cdot d\vec{A} = 0$$

$$\therefore (-\rho V_1 A_1) + (\rho V_2 A_2) = 0$$

and

$$V_1 = V_2 \frac{A_2}{A_1} = \frac{16\text{ m}}{\text{s}} \times \frac{0.0025}{0.01} = 4\text{ m/s}$$

We can now compute R_x

$$R_x = -p_{1_g} A_1 - \rho V_1^2 A_1$$

$$= -1.19 \times 10^5 \frac{\text{N}}{\text{m}^2} \times 0.01\text{ m}^2 - 999 \frac{\text{kg}}{\text{m}^3} \times \frac{16\text{ m}^2}{\text{s}^2} \times 0.01\text{ m}^2 \times \frac{\text{N} \cdot \text{s}^2}{\text{kg} \cdot \text{m}}$$

$$R_x = -1.35\text{ kN} \longleftarrow\rule{4cm}{0pt} \hspace{1cm} R_x$$

Writing the y component of the momentum equation gives

$$F_{S_y} + F_{B_y} = R_y + F_{B_y} = \int_{CS} v\, \rho \vec{V} \cdot d\vec{A} = \int_{A_2} v\, \rho \vec{V} \cdot d\vec{A} \qquad\qquad \{v_1 = 0\}$$

or

$$R_y = -F_{B_y} + \int_{A_2} v\, \rho \vec{V} \cdot d\vec{A}$$

$$= -F_{B_y} + v_2(\rho V_2 A_2)$$

$$R_y = -F_{B_y} - \rho V_2^2 A_2$$

Note that v_2 is the y component of the velocity, so that $v_2 = -V_2$, where V_2 is the magnitude of the exit velocity.

Substituting known values

$$R_y = -F_{B_y} + -\rho V_2^2 A_2$$

$$= -F_{B_y} - 999 \frac{\text{kg}}{\text{m}^3} \times (16)^2 \frac{\text{m}^2}{\text{s}^2} \times 0.0025\text{ m}^2 \times \frac{\text{N} \cdot \text{s}^2}{\text{kg} \cdot \text{m}}$$

$$= -F_{B_y} - 639\text{ N} \longleftarrow\rule{4cm}{0pt} \hspace{1cm} R_y$$

Neglecting F_{B_y} gives

$$R_y = -639\text{ N} \qquad \longleftarrow\rule{4cm}{0pt} \hspace{1cm} R_y$$

> This problem illustrates how using gage pressures simplifies evaluation of the surface forces in the momentum equation.

EXAMPLE 4.7 Flow under a Sluice Gate: Hydrostatic Pressure Force

Water in an open channel is held in by a sluice gate. Compare the horizontal force of the water on the gate (a) when the gate is closed and (b) when it is open (assuming steady flow, as shown). Assume the flow at sections ① and ② is incompressible and uniform, and that (because the streamlines are straight there) the pressure distributions are hydrostatic.

GIVEN: Flow under sluice gate. Width $= w$.

FIND: Horizontal force (per unit width) on the closed and open gate.

SOLUTION:

Choose a control volume as shown for the open gate. Note that it is much simpler to work in gage pressures, as we learned in Example 4.6.

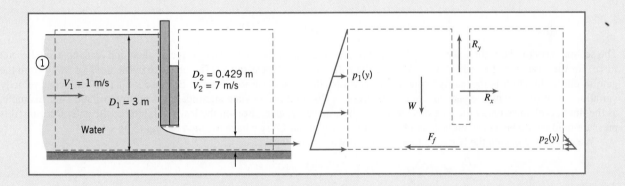

The forces acting on the control volume include:

- Force of gravity W.
- Friction force F_f.
- Components R_x and R_y of reaction force from gate.
- Hydrostatic pressure distribution on vertical surfaces, assumption (6).
- Pressure distribution $p_b(x)$ along bottom surface (not shown).

Apply the x component of the momentum equation.

Governing equation:

$$F_{S_x} + \overset{= 0(2)}{\cancel{F_{B_x}}} = \overset{= 0(3)}{\cancel{\frac{\partial}{\partial t} \int_{CV} u\, \rho\, dV}} + \int_{CS} u\, \rho \vec{V} \cdot d\vec{A}$$

Assumptions:
(1) F_f negligible (neglect friction on channel bottom).
(2) $F_{B_x} = 0$.
(3) Steady flow.
(4) Incompressible flow (given).
(5) Uniform flow at each section (given).
(6) Hydrostatic pressure distributions at ① and ② (given).

Then

$$F_{S_x} = F_{R_1} + F_{R_2} + R_x = u_1(-\rho V_1 w D_1) + u_2(\rho V_2 w D_2)$$

The surface forces acting on the CV are due to the pressure distributions and the unknown force R_x. From assumption (6), we can integrate the gage pressure distributions on each side to compute the hydrostatic forces F_{R_1} and F_{R_2},

$$F_{R_1} = \int_0^{D_1} p_1 \, dA = w \int_0^{D_1} \rho gy \, dy = \rho gw \frac{y^2}{2} \bigg|_0^{D_1} = \frac{1}{2} \rho gwD_1^2$$

where y is measured downward from the free surface of location ①, and

$$F_{R_2} = \int_0^{D_2} p_2 \, dA = w \int_0^{D_2} \rho gy \, dy = \rho gw \frac{y^2}{2} \bigg|_0^{D_2} = \frac{1}{2} \rho gwD_2^2$$

where y is measured downward from the free surface of location ②. (Note that we could have used the hydrostatic force equation, Eq. 3.10b, directly to obtain these forces.)

Evaluating F_{S_x} gives

$$F_{S_x} = R_x + \frac{\rho gw}{2} (D_1^2 - D_2^2)$$

Substituting into the momentum equation, with $u_1 = V_1$ and $u_2 = V_2$, gives

$$R_x + \frac{\rho gw}{2} (D_1^2 - D_2^2) = -\rho V_1^2 wD_1 + \rho V_2^2 wD_2$$

or

$$R_x = \rho w(V_2^2 D_2 - V_1^2 D_1) - \frac{\rho gw}{2} (D_1^2 - D_2^2)$$

The second term on the right is the net hydrostatic force on the gate; the first term "corrects" this (and leads to a smaller net force) for the case when the gate is open. What is the nature of this "correction"? The pressure in the fluid far away from the gate in either direction is indeed hydrostatic, but consider the flow close to the gate: Because we have significant velocity variations here (in magnitude and direction), the pressure distributions deviate significantly from hydrostatic—for example, as the fluid accelerates under the gate there will be a significant pressure drop on the lower left side of the gate. Deriving this pressure field would be a difficult task, but by careful choice of our CV we have avoided having to do so!

We can now compute the horizontal force per unit width,

$$\frac{R_x}{w} = \rho\left(V_2^2 D_2 - V_1^2 D_1\right) - \frac{\rho g}{2}\left(D_1^2 - D_2^2\right)$$

$$= \frac{999 \text{ kg}}{\text{m}^3} \times [(7)^2(0.429) - (1)^2(3)] \frac{\text{m}^2}{\text{s}^2} \text{m} \times \frac{\text{N} \cdot \text{s}^2}{\text{kg} \cdot \text{m}}$$

$$- \frac{1}{2} \times \frac{999 \text{ kg}}{\text{m}^3} \times \frac{9.81 \text{ m}}{\text{s}^2} \times [(3)^2 - (0.429)^2]\text{m}^2 \times \frac{\text{N} \cdot \text{s}^2}{\text{kg} \cdot \text{m}}$$

$$\frac{R_x}{w} = 18.0 \text{ kN/m} - 43.2 \text{ kN/m}$$

$$\frac{R_x}{w} = -25.2 \text{ kN/m}$$

R_x is the external force acting on the control volume, applied to the CV by the gate. Therefore, the force of the water on the gate is K_x, where $K_x = -R_x$. Thus,

$$\frac{K_x}{w} = -\frac{R_x}{w} = 25.2 \text{ kN/m} \longleftarrow \qquad \frac{K_x}{w}$$

This force can be compared to the force on the closed gate of 44.1 kN (obtained from the second term on the right in the equation above, evaluated with D_2 set to zero because for the closed gate there is no fluid on the right of the gate)—the force on the open gate is significantly less as the water accelerates out under the gate.

> This problem illustrates the application of the momentum equation to a control volume for which the pressure is not uniform on the control surface.

EXAMPLE 4.8 Conveyor Belt Filling: Rate of Change of Momentum in Control Volume

A horizontal conveyor belt moving at 3 ft/s receives sand from a hopper. The sand falls vertically from the hopper to the belt at a speed of 5 ft/s and a flow rate of 500 lbm/s (the density of sand is approximately 2700 lbm/cubic yard). The conveyor belt is initially empty but begins to fill with sand. If friction in the drive system and rollers is negligible, find the tension required to pull the belt while the conveyor is filling.

GIVEN: Conveyor and hopper shown in sketch.

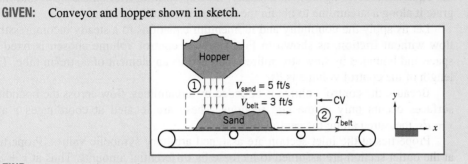

FIND: T_{belt} at the instant shown.

SOLUTION:
Use the control volume and coordinates shown. Apply the x component of the momentum equation.

Governing equations:

$$F_{S_x} + \overset{=\,0(2)}{\cancel{F_{B_x}}} = \frac{\partial}{\partial t} \int_{CV} u\,\rho\,d\forall + \int_{CS} u\,\rho\vec{V}\cdot d\vec{A} \qquad \frac{\partial}{\partial t}\int_{CV}\rho\,d\forall + \int_{CS}\rho\vec{V}\cdot d\vec{A} = 0$$

Assumptions:
(1) $F_{S_x} = T_{belt} = T$.
(2) $F_{B_x} = 0$.
(3) Uniform flow at section ①.
(4) All sand on belt moves with $V_{belt} = V_b$.

Then

$$T = \frac{\partial}{\partial t}\int_{CV} u\,\rho\,d\forall + u_1(-\rho V_1 A_1) + u_2(\rho V_2 A_2)$$

Since $u_1 = 0$, and there is no flow at section ②,

$$T = \frac{\partial}{\partial t}\int_{CV} u\,\rho\,d\forall$$

From assumption (4), inside the CV, $u = V_b$ = constant, and hence

$$T = V_b \frac{\partial}{\partial t}\int_{CV}\rho\,d\forall = V_b \frac{\partial M_s}{\partial t}$$

where M_s is the mass of sand on the belt (inside the control volume). This result is perhaps not surprising—the tension in the belt is the force required to increase the momentum inside the CV (which is increasing because even though the velocity of the mass in the CV is constant, the mass is not). From the continuity equation,

$$\frac{\partial}{\partial t}\int_{CV}\rho\,d\forall = \frac{\partial}{\partial t}M_s = -\int_{CS}\rho\vec{V}\cdot d\vec{A} = \dot{m}_s = 500\text{ lbm/s}$$

Then

$$T = V_b\dot{m}_s = \frac{3\text{ ft}}{\text{s}} \times \frac{500\text{ lbm}}{\text{s}} \times \frac{\text{slug}}{32.2\text{ lbm}} \times \frac{\text{lbf}\cdot\text{s}^2}{\text{slug}\cdot\text{ft}}$$

$$T = 46.6\text{ lbf} \qquad\qquad\qquad\qquad\qquad\qquad\qquad\qquad T$$

This problem illustrates application of the momentum equation to a control volume in which the momentum is changing.

*Differential Control Volume Analysis

The control volume approach, as we have seen in the previous examples, provides useful results when applied to a finite region.

If we apply the approach to a differential control volume, we can obtain differential equations describing a flow field. In this section, we will apply the conservation of mass and momentum equations to such a control volume to obtain a simple differential equation describing flow in a steady, incompressible, frictionless flow, and integrate it along a streamline to obtain the famous Bernoulli equation.

Let us apply the continuity and momentum equations to a steady incompressible flow without friction, as shown in Fig. 4.4. The control volume chosen is fixed in space and bounded by flow streamlines, and is thus an element of a stream tube. The length of the control volume is ds.

Because the control volume is bounded by streamlines, flow across the bounding surfaces occurs only at the end sections. These are located at coordinates s and $s + ds$, measured along the central streamline.

Properties at the inlet section are assigned arbitrary symbolic values. Properties at the outlet section are assumed to increase by differential amounts. Thus at $s + ds$, the flow speed is assumed to be $V_s + dV_s$, and so on. The differential changes, dp, dV_s, and dA, all are assumed to be positive in setting up the problem. (As in a free-body analysis in statics or dynamics, the actual algebraic sign of each differential change will be determined from the results of the analysis.)

Now let us apply the continuity equation and the s component of the momentum equation to the control volume of Fig. 4.4.

a. Continuity Equation

Basic equation:
$$\overset{\displaystyle = 0(1)}{\cancel{\frac{\partial}{\partial t}} \int_{CV} \rho \, d\Psi} + \int_{CS} \rho \vec{V} \cdot d\vec{A} = 0 \tag{4.12}$$

Assumptions: (1) Steady flow.
(2) No flow across bounding streamlines.
(3) Incompressible flow, ρ = constant.

Then

$$(-\rho V_s A) + \{\rho(V_s + dV_s)(A + dA)\} = 0$$

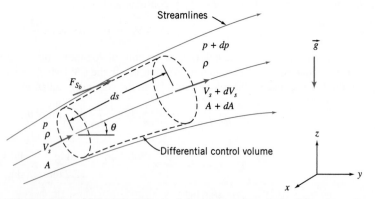

Fig. 4.4 Differential control volume for momentum analysis of flow through a stream tube.

---

*This section may be omitted without loss of continuity in the text material.

so

$$\rho(V_s + dV_s)(A + dA) = \rho V_s A \qquad (4.19a)$$

On expanding the left side and simplifying, we obtain

$$V_s \, dA + A \, dV_s + dA \, dV_s = 0$$

But $dA \, dV_s$ is a product of differentials, which may be neglected compared with $V_s \, dA$ or $A \, dV_s$. Thus

$$V_s \, dA + A \, dV_s = 0 \qquad (4.19b)$$

b. Streamwise Component of the Momentum Equation

Basic equation:
$$F_{S_s} + F_{B_s} = \overset{= \, 0(1)}{\overbrace{\frac{\partial}{\partial t} \int_{CV} u_s \, \rho \, d\forall}} + \int_{CS} u_s \, \rho \vec{V} \cdot d\vec{A} \qquad (4.20)$$

Assumption: (4) No friction, so F_{S_b} is due to pressure forces only.

The surface force (due only to pressure) will have three terms:

$$F_{S_s} = pA - (p + dp)(A + dA) + \left(p + \frac{dp}{2}\right) dA \qquad (4.21a)$$

The first and second terms in Eq. 4.21a are the pressure forces on the end faces of the control surface. The third term is F_{S_b}, the pressure force acting in the s direction on the bounding stream surface of the control volume. Its magnitude is the product of the average pressure acting on the stream surface, $p + \frac{1}{2}dp$, times the area component of the stream surface in the s direction, dA. Equation 4.21a simplifies to

$$F_{S_s} = -A \, dp - \frac{1}{2} dp \, dA \qquad (4.21b)$$

The body force component in the s direction is

$$F_{B_s} = \rho g_s \, d\forall = \rho(-g \sin \theta)\left(A + \frac{dA}{2}\right) ds$$

But $\sin \theta \, ds = dz$, so that

$$F_{B_s} = -\rho g\left(A + \frac{dA}{2}\right) dz \qquad (4.21c)$$

The momentum flux will be

$$\int_{CS} u_s \, \rho \vec{V} \cdot d\vec{A} = V_s(-\rho V_s A) + (V_s + dV_s)\{\rho(V_s + dV_s)(A + dA)\}$$

since there is no mass flux across the bounding stream surfaces. The mass flux factors in parentheses and braces are equal from continuity, Eq. 4.19a, so

$$\int_{CS} u_s \, \rho \vec{V} \cdot d\vec{A} = V_s(-\rho V_s A) + (V_s + dV_s)(\rho V_s A) = \rho V_s A \, dV_s \qquad (4.22)$$

Substituting Eqs. 4.21b, 4.21c, and 4.22 into Eq. 4.20 (the momentum equation) gives

$$-A \, dp - \frac{1}{2} dp \, dA - \rho g A \, dz - \frac{1}{2}\rho g \, dA \, dz = \rho V_s A \, dV_s$$

Dividing by ρA and noting that products of differentials are negligible compared with the remaining terms, we obtain

$$-\frac{dp}{\rho} - g\,dz = V_s\,dV_s = d\left(\frac{V_s^2}{2}\right)$$

or

$$\frac{dp}{\rho} + d\left(\frac{V_s^2}{2}\right) + g\,dz = 0 \qquad (4.23)$$

Because the flow is incompressible, this equation may be integrated to obtain

$$\frac{p}{\rho} + \frac{V_s^2}{2} + gz = \text{constant}$$

or, dropping subscript s,

$$\frac{p}{\rho} + \frac{V^2}{2} + gz = \text{constant} \qquad (4.24)$$

This equation is subject to the restrictions:

1. Steady flow.
2. No friction.
3. Flow along a streamline.
4. Incompressible flow.

We have derived one form of perhaps the most famous (and misused) equation in fluid mechanics—the Bernoulli equation. It can be used *only* when the four restrictions listed above apply, at least to reasonable accuracy! Although no real flow satisfies all these restrictions (especially the second), we can approximate the behavior of many flows with Eq. 4.24.

For example, the equation is widely used in aerodynamics to relate the pressure and velocity in a flow (e.g., it explains the lift of a subsonic wing). It could also be used to find the pressure at the inlet of the reducing elbow analyzed in Example 4.6 or to determine the velocity of water leaving the sluice gate of Example 4.7 (both of these flows approximately satisfy the four restrictions). On the other hand, Eq. 4.24 does *not* correctly describe the variation of water pressure in pipe flow. According to it, for a horizontal pipe of constant diameter, the pressure will be constant, but in fact the pressure drops significantly along the pipe—we will need most of Chapter 8 to explain this.

The Bernoulli equation, and the limits on its use, is so important we will derive it again and discuss its limitations in detail in Chapter 6.

Example 4.9   Nozzle Flow: Application of Bernoulli Equation

Water flows steadily through a horizontal nozzle, discharging to the atmosphere. At the nozzle inlet the diameter is D_1; at the nozzle outlet the diameter is D_2. Derive an expression for the minimum gage pressure required at the nozzle inlet to produce a given volume flow rate, Q. Evaluate the inlet gage pressure if $D_1 = 3.0$ in., $D_2 = 1.0$ in., and the desired flow rate is 0.7 ft³/s.

GIVEN: Steady flow of water through a horizontal nozzle, discharging to the atmosphere.

$$D_1 = 3.0 \text{ in.} \qquad D_2 = 1.0 \text{ in.} \qquad p_2 = p_{atm}$$

FIND: (a) p_{1g} as a function of volume flow rate, Q.
(b) p_{1g} for $Q = 0.7 \text{ ft}^3/s$.

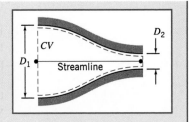

SOLUTION:

Governing equations:

$$\frac{p_1}{\rho} + \frac{V_1^2}{2} + gz_1 = \frac{p_2}{\rho} + \frac{V_2^2}{2} + gz_2$$

$$\overset{= 0(1)}{\cancel{\frac{\partial}{\partial t} \int_{CV} \rho \, dV}} + \int_{CS} \rho \vec{V} \cdot d\vec{A} = 0$$

Assumptions: (1) Steady flow (given).
(2) Incompressible flow.
(3) Frictionless flow.
(4) Flow along a streamline.
(5) $z_1 = z_2$.
(6) Uniform flow at sections ① and ②.

Apply the Bernoulli equation along a streamline between points ① and ② to evaluate p_1. Then

$$p_{1g} = p_1 - p_{atm} = p_1 - p_2 = \frac{\rho}{2}(V_2^2 - V_1^2) = \frac{\rho}{2} V_1^2 \left[\left(\frac{V_2}{V_1} \right)^2 - 1 \right]$$

Apply the continuity equation

$$(-\rho V_1 A_1) + (\rho V_2 A_2) = 0 \qquad \text{or} \qquad V_1 A_1 = V_2 A_2 = Q$$

so that

$$\frac{V_2}{V_1} = \frac{A_1}{A_2} \qquad \text{and} \qquad V_1 = \frac{Q}{A_1}$$

Then

$$p_{1g} = \frac{\rho Q^2}{2 A_1^2} \left[\left(\frac{A_1}{A_2} \right)^2 - 1 \right]$$

Since $A = \pi D^2/4$, then

$$p_{1g} = \frac{8\rho \, Q^2}{\pi^2 \, D_1^4} \left[\left(\frac{D_1}{D_2} \right)^4 - 1 \right] \qquad\qquad\qquad\qquad\qquad p_{1g}$$

(Note that for a given nozzle the pressure required is proportional to the square of the flow rate—not surprising since we have used Eq. 4.24, which shows that $p \sim V^2 \sim Q^2$.) With $D_1 = 3.0$ in., $D_2 = 1.0$ in., and $\rho = 1.94 \text{ slug/ft}^3$,

$$p_{1g} = \frac{8}{\pi^2} \times \frac{1.94 \text{ slug}}{\text{ft}^3} \times \frac{1}{(3)^4 \text{ in.}^4} \times Q^2 [(3.0)^4 - 1] \frac{\text{lbf} \cdot \text{s}^2}{\text{slug} \cdot \text{ft}} \times \frac{144 \text{ in.}^2}{\text{ft}^2}$$

$$p_{1g} = 224 \, Q^2 \frac{\text{lbf} \cdot \text{s}^2}{\text{in.}^2 \cdot \text{ft}^6}$$

With $Q = 0.7 \text{ ft}^3/s$, then $\quad p_{1g} = 110 \text{ lbf/in.}^2 \qquad\qquad\qquad\qquad\qquad\qquad p_{1g}$

> This problem illustrates application of the Bernoulli equation to a flow where the restrictions of steady, incompressible, frictionless flow along a streamline are reasonable.

Control Volume Moving with Constant Velocity

In the preceding problems, which illustrate applications of the momentum equation to inertial control volumes, we have considered only stationary control volumes. Suppose we have a control volume moving at constant speed. We can set up two coordinate systems: XYZ, "absolute", or stationary (and therefore inertial), coordinates, and the xyz coordinates attached to the control volume (also inertial because the control volume is not accelerating with respect to XYZ).

Equation 4.10, which expresses system derivatives in terms of control volume variables, is valid for any motion of the control volume coordinate system xyz, provided that all velocities are measured *relative* to the control volume. To emphasize this point, we rewrite Eq. 4.10 as

$$\frac{dN}{dt}\bigg)_{\text{system}} = \frac{\partial}{\partial t}\int_{\text{CV}} \eta\, \rho\, d\mathcal{V} + \int_{\text{CS}} \eta\, \rho\, \vec{V}_{xyz} \cdot d\vec{A} \qquad (4.25)$$

Since all velocities must be measured relative to the control volume, in using this equation to obtain the momentum equation for an inertial control volume from the system formulation, we must set

$$N = \vec{P}_{xyz} \qquad \text{and} \qquad \eta = \vec{V}_{xyz}$$

The control volume equation is then written as

$$\vec{F} = \vec{F}_S + \vec{F}_B = \frac{\partial}{\partial t}\int_{\text{CV}} \vec{V}_{xyz}\, \rho\, d\mathcal{V} + \int_{\text{CS}} \vec{V}_{xyz}\, \rho\vec{V}_{xyz} \cdot d\vec{A} \qquad (4.26)$$

Equation 4.26 is the formulation of Newton's second law applied to any inertial control volume (stationary or moving with a constant velocity). It is identical to Eq. 4.17a except that we have included subscript xyz to emphasize that velocities must be measured relative to the control volume. (It is helpful to imagine that the velocities are those that would be seen by an observer moving with the control volume.) Example 4.10 illustrates the use of Eq. 4.26 for a control volume moving at constant velocity.

Example 4.10   Vane Moving with Constant Velocity

The sketch shows a vane with a turning angle of 60°. The vane moves at constant speed, $U = 10$ m/s, and receives a jet of water that leaves a stationary nozzle with speed $V = 30$ m/s. The nozzle has an exit area of 0.003 m². Determine the force components that act on the vane.

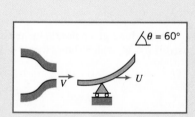

GIVEN: Vane, with turning angle $\theta = 60°$, moves with constant velocity, $\vec{U} = 10\hat{i}$ m/s. Water from a constant area nozzle, $A = 0.003$ m², with velocity $\vec{V} = 30\hat{i}$ m/s, flows over the vane as shown.

FIND: Force components acting on the vane.

SOLUTION:
Select a control volume moving with the vane at constant velocity, $\vec{U}$, as shown by the dashed lines. R_x and R_y are the components of force required to maintain the velocity of the control volume at $10\hat{i}$ m/s.

The control volume is inertial, since it is not accelerating ($U = $ constant). Remember that all velocities must be measured relative to the control volume in applying the basic equations.

Governing equations:

$$\vec{F}_S + \vec{F}_B = \frac{\partial}{\partial t}\int_{CV} \vec{V}_{xyz}\, \rho\, d\forall + \int_{CS} \vec{V}_{xyz}\, \rho \vec{V}_{xyz} \cdot d\vec{A}$$

$$\frac{\partial}{\partial t}\int_{CV} \rho\, d\forall + \int_{CS} \rho \vec{V}_{xyz} \cdot d\vec{A} = 0$$

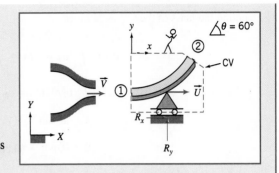

Assumptions: (1) Flow is steady relative to the vane.
(2) Magnitude of relative velocity along the vane is constant: $|\vec{V}_1| = |\vec{V}_2| = V - U$.
(3) Properties are uniform at sections ① and ②.
(4) $F_{B_x} = 0$.
(5) Incompressible flow.

The x component of the momentum equation is

$$\overset{= 0(4)\quad = 0(1)}{F_{S_x} + \cancel{F_{B_x}} = \cancel{\frac{\partial}{\partial t}\int_{CV} u_{xyz}\, \rho\, d\forall} + \int_{CS} u_{xyz}\, \rho \vec{V}_{xyz} \cdot d\vec{A}}$$

There is no net pressure force, since p_{atm} acts on all sides of the CV. Thus

$$R_x = \int_{A_1} u(-\rho V dA) + \int_{A_2} u(\rho V dA) = \; +u_1(-\rho V_1 A_1) + u_2(\rho V_2 A_2)$$

(All velocities are measured relative to xyz.) From the continuity equation

$$\int_{A_1} (-\rho V dA) + \int_{A_2} (\rho V dA) = (-\rho V_1 A_1) + (\rho V_2 A_2) = 0$$

or

$$\rho V_1 A_1 = \rho V_2 A_2$$

Therefore,

$$R_x = (u_2 - u_1)(\rho V_1 A_1)$$

All velocities must be measured relative to the CV, so we note that

$$\begin{array}{ll} V_1 = V - U & V_2 = V - U \\ u_1 = V - U & u_2 = (V - U)\cos\theta \end{array}$$

Substituting yields

$$R_x = [(V - U)\cos\theta - (V - U)](\rho(V - U)A_1) = (V - U)(\cos\theta - 1)\{\rho(V - U)A_1\}$$

$$= \frac{(30 - 10)}{s}\,\frac{m}{} \times (0.50 - 1) \times \left(999\,\frac{kg}{m^3}\,\frac{(30 - 10)}{s}\,\frac{m}{} \times 0.003\,m^2\right) \times \frac{N \cdot s^2}{kg \cdot m}$$

$$R_x = -599N \;\{\text{to the left}\}$$

Writing the y component of the momentum equation, we obtain

$$\overset{= 0(1)}{F_{S_y} + F_{B_y} = \cancel{\frac{\partial}{\partial t}\int_{CV} v_{xyz}\, \rho\, d\forall} + \int_{CS} v_{xyz}\, \rho \vec{V}_{xyz} \cdot d\vec{A}}$$

Denoting the mass of the CV as M gives

$$R_y - Mg = \int_{CS} v\,\rho\vec{V}\cdot d\vec{A} = \int_{A_2} v\rho\vec{V}\cdot d\vec{A} \qquad \{v_1 = 0\} \qquad \left\{ \begin{array}{l} \text{All velocities are} \\ \text{measured relative to} \\ xyz. \end{array} \right\}$$

$$= \int_{A_2} v(\rho V dA) = v_2(\rho V_2 A_2) = v_2(\rho V_1 A_1) \qquad \{\text{Recall } \rho V_2 A_2 = \rho V_1 A_1.\}$$

$$= (V - U)\sin\theta\{\rho(V - U)A_1\}$$

$$= \frac{(30 - 10)\,\text{m}}{\text{s}} \times (0.866) \times \left((999)\,\frac{\text{kg}}{\text{n}^3}\,\frac{(30 - 10)\,\text{m}}{\text{s}} \times 0.003\,\text{m}^2 \right) \times \frac{\text{N}\cdot\text{s}^2}{\text{kg}\cdot\text{m}}$$

$$R_y - Mg = 1.04\,\text{kN} \qquad \{\text{upward}\}$$

Thus the vertical force is

$$R_y = 1.04\,\text{kN} + Mg \qquad \{\text{upward}\}$$

Then the net force on the vane (neglecting the weight of the vane and water within the CV) is

$$\vec{R} = -0.599\hat{i} + 1.04\hat{j}\,\text{kN} \longleftarrow \hspace{5cm} \vec{R}$$

This problem illustrates how to apply the momentum equation for a control volume in constant velocity motion by evaluating all velocities relative to the control volume.

4-5   MOMENTUM EQUATION FOR CONTROL VOLUME WITH RECTILINEAR ACCELERATION

For an inertial control volume (having no acceleration relative to a stationary frame of reference), the appropriate formulation of Newton's second law is given by Eq. 4.26,

$$\vec{F} = \vec{F}_S + \vec{F}_B = \frac{\partial}{\partial t}\int_{CV} \vec{V}_{xyz}\,\rho\,d\Psi + \int_{CS} \vec{V}_{xyz}\,\rho\vec{V}_{xyz}\cdot d\vec{A} \qquad (4.26)$$

Not all control volumes are inertial; for example, a rocket must accelerate if it is to get off the ground. Since we are interested in analyzing control volumes that may accelerate relative to inertial coordinates, it is logical to ask whether Eq. 4.26 can be used for an accelerating control volume. To answer this question, let us briefly review the two major elements used in developing Eq. 4.26.

First, in relating the system derivatives to the control volume formulation (Eq. 4.25 or 4.10), the flow field, $\vec{V}(x, y, z, t)$, was specified relative to the control volume's coordinates x, y, and z. No restriction was placed on the motion of the xyz reference frame. Consequently, Eq. 4.25 (or Eq. 4.10) is valid at any instant for any arbitrary motion of the coordinates x, y, and z provided that all velocities in the equation are measured relative to the control volume.

Second, the system equation

$$\vec{F} = \frac{d\vec{P}}{dt}\bigg)_{\text{system}} \qquad (4.2a)$$

where the linear momentum of the system is given by

$$\vec{P}_{\text{system}} = \int_{M(\text{system})} \vec{V}\, dm = \int_{\Psi(\text{system})} \vec{V} \rho\, d\Psi \qquad (4.2b)$$

is valid only for velocities measured relative to an inertial reference frame. Thus, if we denote the inertial reference frame by XYZ, then Newton's second law states that

$$\vec{F} = \frac{d\vec{P}_{XYZ}}{dt}\bigg)_{\text{system}} \qquad (4.27)$$

Since the time derivatives of $\vec{P}_{XYZ}$ and $\vec{P}_{xyz}$ are not equal when the control volume reference frame xyz is accelerating relative to the inertial reference frame, Eq. 4.26 is not valid for an accelerating control volume.

To develop the momentum equation for a linearly accelerating control volume, it is necessary to relate $\vec{P}_{XYZ}$ of the system to $\vec{P}_{xyz}$ of the system. The system derivative $d\vec{P}_{xyz}/dt$ can then be related to control volume variables through Eq. 4.25. We begin by writing Newton's second law for a system, remembering that the acceleration must be measured relative to an inertial reference frame that we have designated XYZ. We write

$$\vec{F} = \frac{d\vec{P}_{XYZ}}{dt}\bigg)_{\text{system}} = \frac{d}{dt}\int_{M(\text{system})} \vec{V}_{XYZ}\, dm = \int_{M(\text{system})} \frac{d\vec{V}_{XYZ}}{dt}\, dm \qquad (4.28)$$

The velocities with respect to the inertial (XYZ) and the control volume coordinates (xyz) are related by the relative-motion equation

$$\vec{V}_{XYZ} = \vec{V}_{xyz} + \vec{V}_{rf} \qquad (4.29)$$

where $\vec{V}_{rf}$ is the velocity of the control volume coordinates xyz with respect to the "absolute" stationary coordinates XYZ.

Since we are assuming the motion of xyz is pure translation, without rotation, relative to inertial reference frame XYZ, then

$$\frac{d\vec{V}_{XYZ}}{dt} = \vec{a}_{XYZ} = \frac{d\vec{V}_{xyz}}{dt} + \frac{d\vec{V}_{rf}}{dt} = \vec{a}_{xyz} + \vec{a}_{rf} \qquad (4.30)$$

where

$\vec{a}_{XYZ}$ is the rectilinear acceleration of the system relative to inertial reference frame XYZ,

$\vec{a}_{xyz}$ is the rectilinear acceleration of the system relative to noninertial reference frame xyz (i.e., relative to the control volume), and

$\vec{a}_{rf}$ is the rectilinear acceleration of noninertial reference frame xyz (i.e., of the control volume) relative to inertial frame XYZ.

Substituting from Eq. 4.30 into Eq. 4.28 gives

$$\vec{F} = \int_{M(\text{system})} \vec{a}_{rf}\, dm + \int_{M(\text{system})} \frac{d\vec{V}_{xyz}}{dt}\, dm$$

or

$$\vec{F} - \int_{M(\text{system})} \vec{a}_{rf}\, dm = \frac{d\vec{P}_{xyz}}{dt}\bigg)_{\text{system}} \qquad (4.31a)$$

where the linear momentum of the system is given by

$$\vec{P}_{xyz}\big)_{\text{system}} = \int_{M(\text{system})} \vec{V}_{xyz}\, dm = \int_{\Psi(\text{system})} \vec{V}_{xyz} \rho\, d\Psi \qquad (4.31b)$$

and the force, $\vec{F}$, includes all surface and body forces acting on the system.

To derive the control volume formulation of Newton's second law, we set

$$N = \vec{P}_{xyz} \quad \text{and} \quad \eta = \vec{V}_{xyz}$$

From Eq. 4.25, with this substitution, we obtain

$$\frac{d\vec{P}_{xyz}}{dt}\bigg)_{\text{system}} = \frac{\partial}{\partial t}\int_{\text{CV}} \vec{V}_{xyz}\, \rho\, d\forall + \int_{\text{CS}} \vec{V}_{xyz}\, \rho\vec{V}_{xyz} \cdot d\vec{A} \qquad (4.32)$$

Combining Eq. 4.31a (the linear momentum equation for the system) and Eq. 4.32 (the system–control volume conversion), and recognizing that at time t_0 the system and control volume coincide, Newton's second law for a control volume accelerating, without rotation, relative to an inertial reference frame is

$$\vec{F} - \int_{\text{CV}} \vec{a}_{rf}\, \rho\, d\forall = \frac{\partial}{\partial t}\int_{\text{CV}} \vec{V}_{xyz}\, \rho\, d\forall + \int_{\text{CS}} \vec{V}_{xyz}\, \rho\vec{V}_{xyz} \cdot d\vec{A}$$

Since $\vec{F} = \vec{F}_S + \vec{F}_B$, this equation becomes

$$\vec{F}_S + \vec{F}_B - \int_{\text{CV}} \vec{a}_{rf}\, \rho\, d\forall = \frac{\partial}{\partial t}\int_{\text{CV}} \vec{V}_{xyz}\, \rho\, d\forall + \int_{\text{CS}} \vec{V}_{xyz}\, \rho\vec{V}_{xyz} \cdot d\vec{A} \qquad (4.33)$$

Comparing this momentum equation for a control volume with rectilinear acceleration to that for a nonaccelerating control volume, Eq. 4.26, we see that the only difference is the presence of one additional term in Eq. 4.33. When the control volume is not accelerating relative to inertial reference frame XYZ, then $\vec{a}_{rf} = 0$, and Eq. 4.33 reduces to Eq. 4.26.

The precautions concerning the use of Eq. 4.26 also apply to the use of Eq. 4.33. Before attempting to apply either equation, one must draw the boundaries of the control volume and label appropriate coordinate directions. For an accelerating control volume, one must label two coordinate systems: one (xyz) on the control volume and the other (XYZ) an inertial reference frame.

In Eq. 4.33, $\vec{F}_S$ represents all surface forces acting on the control volume. Since the mass within the control volume may vary with time, both the remaining terms on the left side of the equation may be functions of time. Furthermore, the acceleration, $\vec{a}_{rf}$, of the reference frame xyz relative to an inertial frame will in general be a function of time.

All velocities in Eq. 4.33 are measured relative to the control volume. The momentum flux, $\vec{V}_{xyz}\, \rho\vec{V}_{xyz} \cdot d\vec{A}$, through an element of the control surface area, $d\vec{A}$, is a vector. As we saw for the nonaccelerating control volume, the sign of the scalar product, $\rho\vec{V}_{xyz} \cdot d\vec{A}$, depends on the direction of the velocity vector, $\vec{V}_{xyz}$, relative to the area vector, $d\vec{A}$.

The momentum equation is a vector equation. As with all vector equations, it may be written as three scalar component equations. The scalar components of Eq. 4.33 are

$$F_{S_x} + F_{B_x} - \int_{\text{CV}} a_{rf_x}\, \rho\, d\forall = \frac{\partial}{\partial t}\int_{\text{CV}} u_{xyz}\, \rho\, d\forall + \int_{\text{CS}} u_{xyz}\, \rho\vec{V}_{xyz} \cdot d\vec{A} \qquad (4.34a)$$

$$F_{S_y} + F_{B_y} - \int_{\text{CV}} a_{rf_y}\, \rho\, d\forall = \frac{\partial}{\partial t}\int_{\text{CV}} v_{xyz}\, \rho\, d\forall + \int_{\text{CS}} v_{xyz}\, \rho\vec{V}_{xyz} \cdot d\vec{A} \qquad (4.34b)$$

$$F_{S_z} + F_{B_z} - \int_{\text{CV}} a_{rf_z}\, \rho\, d\forall = \frac{\partial}{\partial t}\int_{\text{CV}} w_{xyz}\, \rho\, d\forall + \int_{\text{CS}} w_{xyz}\, \rho\vec{V}_{xyz} \cdot d\vec{A} \qquad (4.34c)$$

We will consider two applications of the linearly accelerating control volume: Example 4.11 will analyze an accelerating control volume in which the mass contained in the control volume is constant; Example 4.12 will analyze an accelerating control volume in which the mass contained varies with time.

Example 4.11 Vane Moving with Rectilinear Acceleration

A vane, with turning angle $\theta = 60°$, is attached to a cart. The cart and vane, of mass $M = 75$ kg, roll on a level track. Friction and air resistance may be neglected. The vane receives a jet of water, which leaves a stationary nozzle horizontally at $V = 35$ m/s. The nozzle exit area is $A = 0.003$ m^2. Determine the velocity of the cart as a function of time and plot the results.

GIVEN: Vane and cart as sketched, with $M = 75$ kg.

FIND: $U(t)$ and plot results.

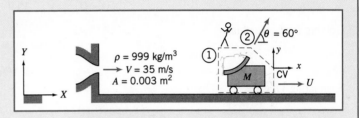

SOLUTION:
Choose the control volume and coordinate systems shown for the analysis. Note that XY is a fixed frame, while frame xy moves with the cart. Apply the x component of the momentum equation.

Governing equation:

$$\overset{=\,0(1)}{\cancel{F_{S_x}}} + \overset{=\,0(2)}{\cancel{F_{B_x}}} - \int_{CV} a_{rf_x}\, \rho\, d\cancel{V} = \overset{\simeq\,0(4)}{\cancel{\frac{\partial}{\partial t}\int_{CV} u_{xyz}\, \rho\, d\cancel{V}}} + \int_{CS} u_{xyz}\, \rho \vec{V}_{xyz} \cdot d\vec{A}$$

Assumptions:
(1) $F_{S_x} = 0$, since no resistance is present.
(2) $F_{B_x} = 0$.
(3) Neglect the mass of water in contact with the vane compared to the cart mass.
(4) Neglect rate of change of momentum of liquid inside the CV.

$$\frac{\partial}{\partial t}\int_{CV} u_{xyz}\, \rho\, d\cancel{V} \simeq 0$$

(5) Uniform flow at sections ① and ②.
(6) Speed of water stream is not slowed by friction on the vane, so $|\vec{V}_{xyz_1}| = |\vec{V}_{xyz_2}|$.
(7) $A_2 = A_1 = A$.

Then, dropping subscripts rf and xyz for clarity (but remembering that all velocities are measured relative to the moving coordinates of the control volume),

$$-\int_{CV} a_x\, \rho\, d\cancel{V} = u_1(-\rho V_1 A_1) + u_2(\rho V_2 A_2)$$
$$= (V - U)\{-\rho(V - U)A\} + (V - U)\cos\theta\{\rho(V - U)A\}$$
$$= -\rho(V - U)^2 A + \rho(V - U)^2 A \cos\theta$$

For the left side of this equation we have

$$-\int_{CV} a_x\, \rho\, d\cancel{V} = -a_x M_{CV} = -a_x M = -\frac{dU}{dt}M$$

so that

$$-M\frac{dU}{dt} = -\rho(V - U)^2 A + \rho(V - U)^2 A \cos\theta$$

or

$$M \frac{dU}{dt} = (1 - \cos \theta)\rho(V - U)^2 A$$

Separating variables, we obtain

$$\frac{dU}{(V - U)^2} = \frac{(1 - \cos \theta)\rho A}{M} dt = b\,dt \quad \text{where } b = \frac{(1 - \cos \theta)\rho A}{M}$$

Note that since V = constant, $dU = -d(V - U)$. Integrating between limits $U = 0$ at $t = 0$, and $U = U$ at $t = t$,

$$\int_0^U \frac{dU}{(V - U)^2} = \int_0^U \frac{-d(V - U)}{(V - U)^2} = \frac{1}{(V - U)} \Bigg]_0^U = \int_0^t b\,dt = bt$$

or

$$\frac{1}{(V - U)} - \frac{1}{V} = \frac{U}{V(V - U)} = bt$$

Solving for U, we obtain

$$\frac{U}{V} = \frac{Vbt}{1 + Vbt}$$

Evaluating Vb gives

$$Vb = V\frac{(1 - \cos \theta)\rho A}{M}$$

$$Vb = \frac{35 \text{ m}}{\text{s}} \times \frac{(1 - 0.5)}{75 \text{ kg}} \times \frac{999 \text{ kg}}{\text{m}^3} \times \frac{0.003 \text{ m}^2}{} = 0.699 \text{ s}^{-1}$$

Thus

$$\frac{U}{V} = \frac{0.699t}{1 + 0.699t} \qquad \qquad (t \text{ in seconds}) \qquad \qquad U(t)$$

Plot:

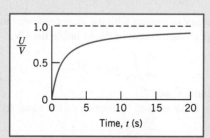

> 🖱 The graph was generated from an *Excel* workbook. This workbook is interactive: It allows one to see the effect of different values of ρ, A, M, and θ on U/V against time t, and also to determine the time taken for the cart to reach, for example, 95% of jet speed.

Example 4.12   Rocket Directed Vertically

A small rocket, with an initial mass of 400 kg, is to be launched vertically. Upon ignition the rocket consumes fuel at the rate of 5 kg/s and ejects gas at atmospheric pressure with a speed of 3500 m/s relative to the rocket. Determine the initial acceleration of the rocket and the rocket speed after 10 s, if air resistance is neglected.

GIVEN: Small rocket accelerates vertically from rest.
Initial mass, $M_0 = 400$ kg.
Air resistance may be neglected.
Rate of fuel consumption, $\dot{m}_e = 5$ kg/s.
Exhaust velocity, $V_e = 3500$ m/s, relative to rocket, leaving at atmospheric pressure.

FIND: (a) Initial acceleration of the rocket.
(b) Rocket velocity after 10 s.

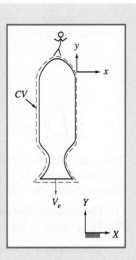

SOLUTION:

Choose a control volume as shown by dashed lines. Because the control volume is accelerating, define inertial coordinate system XY and coordinate system xy attached to the CV. Apply the y component of the momentum equation.

Governing equation: $F_{S_y} + F_{B_y} - \int_{CV} a_{rf_y}\, \rho\, d\forall = \dfrac{\partial}{\partial t}\int_{CV} v_{xyz}\,\rho\, d\forall + \int_{CS} v_{xyz}\,\rho\, \vec{V}_{xyz}\cdot d\vec{A}$

Assumptions: (1) Atmospheric pressure acts on all surfaces of the CV; since air resistance is neglected, $F_{S_y} = 0$.
(2) Gravity is the only body force; g is constant.
(3) Flow leaving the rocket is uniform, and V_e is constant.

Under these assumptions the momentum equation reduces to

$$F_{B_y} - \underbrace{\int_{CV} a_{rf_y}\, \rho\, d\forall}_{\text{(B)}} = \underbrace{\dfrac{\partial}{\partial t}\int_{CV} v_{xyz}\,\rho\, d\forall}_{\text{(C)}} + \underbrace{\int_{CS} v_{xyz}\,\rho\, \vec{V}_{xyz}\cdot d\vec{A}}_{\text{(D)}} \qquad (1)$$

$\underbrace{F_{B_y}}_{\text{(A)}}$

Let us look at the equation term by term:

(A) $F_{B_y} = -\int_{CV} g\rho\, d\forall = -g\int_{CV}\rho\, d\forall = -gM_{CV}$ {since g is constant}

The mass of the CV will be a function of time because mass is leaving the CV at rate $\dot{m}_e$. To determine M_{CV} as a function of time, we use the conservation of mass equation

$$\dfrac{\partial}{\partial t}\int_{CV}\rho\, d\forall + \int_{CS}\rho\vec{V}\cdot d\vec{A} = 0$$

Then

$$\dfrac{\partial}{\partial t}\int_{CV}\rho\, d\forall = -\int_{CS}\rho\vec{V}\cdot d\vec{A} = -\int_{CS}(\rho V_{xyz}\,dA) = -\dot{m}_e$$

The minus sign indicates that the mass of the CV is decreasing with time. Since the mass of the CV is only a function of time, we can write

$$\dfrac{dM_{CV}}{dt} = -\dot{m}_e$$

To find the mass of the CV at any time, t, we integrate

$$\int_{M_0}^{M} dM_{CV} = -\int_0^t \dot{m}_e\, dt \qquad \text{where at } t=0,\ M_{CV}=M_0,\ \text{and at } t=t,\ M_{CV}=M$$

Then, $M - M_0 = -\dot{m}_e t$, or $M = M_0 - \dot{m}_e t$.

Substituting the expression for M into term (A), we obtain

$$F_{B_y} = -\int_{CV} g\rho\, d\forall = -gM_{CV} = -g(M_0 - \dot{m}_e t)$$

(B) $-\int_{CV} a_{rf_y}\, \rho\, d\forall$

The acceleration, a_{rf_y}, of the CV is that seen by an observer in the XY coordinate system. Thus a_{rf_y} is not a function of the coordinates xyz, and

$$-\int_{CV} a_{rf_y} \rho \, d\Psi = -a_{rf_y} \int_{CV} \rho \, d\Psi = -a_{rf_y} M_{CV} = -a_{rf_y}(M_0 - \dot{m}_e t)$$

Ⓒ $\quad \dfrac{\partial}{\partial t} \displaystyle\int_{CV} v_{xyz} \rho \, d\Psi$

This is the time rate of change of the y momentum of the fluid in the control volume measured relative to the control volume.

Even though the y momentum of the fluid inside the CV, measured relative to the CV, is a large number, it does not change appreciably with time. To see this, we must recognize that:

(1) The unburned fuel and the rocket structure have zero momentum relative to the rocket.
(2) The velocity of the gas at the nozzle exit remains constant with time as does the velocity at various points in the nozzle.

Consequently, it is reasonable to assume that

$$\frac{\partial}{\partial t} \int_{CV} v_{xyz} \rho \, d\Psi \approx 0$$

Ⓓ $\quad \displaystyle\int_{CS} v_{xyz} \rho \vec{V}_{xyz} \cdot d\vec{A} = \int_{CS} v_{xyz}(\rho V_{xyz} \, dA) = -V_e \int_{CS} (\rho V_{xyz} \, dA)$

The velocity v_{xyz} (relative to the control volume) is $-V_e$ (it is in the negative y direction), and is a constant, so was taken outside the integral. The remaining integral is simply the mass flow rate at the exit (positive because flow is out of the control volume),

$$\int_{CS} (\rho V_{xyz} \, dA) = \dot{m}_e$$

and so

$$\int_{CS} v_{xyz} \rho \vec{V}_{xyz} \cdot d\vec{A} = -V_e \dot{m}_e$$

Substituting terms Ⓐ through Ⓓ into Eq. 1, we obtain

$$-g(M_0 - \dot{m}_e t) - a_{rf_y}(M_0 - \dot{m}_e t) = -V_e \dot{m}_e$$

or

$$a_{rf_y} = \frac{V_e \dot{m}_e}{M_0 - \dot{m}_e t} - g \tag{2}$$

At time $t = 0$,

$$a_{rf_y})_{t=0} = \frac{V_e \dot{m}_e}{M_0} - g = 3500 \, \frac{m}{s} \times 5 \, \frac{kg}{s} \times \frac{1}{400 \, kg} - 9.81 \, \frac{m}{s^2}$$

$$a_{rf_y})_{t=0} = 33.9 \, m/s^2 \xleftarrow{\hspace{3cm}} \qquad a_{rf_y})_{t=0}$$

The acceleration of the CV is by definition

$$a_{rf_y} = \frac{dV_{CV}}{dt}$$

Substituting from Eq. 2,

$$\frac{dV_{CV}}{dt} = \frac{V_e \dot{m}_e}{M_0 - \dot{m}_e t} - g$$

Separating variables and integrating gives

$$V_{CV} = \int_0^{V_{CV}} dV_{CV} = \int_0^t \frac{V_e \dot{m}_e \, dt}{M_0 - \dot{m}_e t} - \int_0^t g \, dt = -V_e \ln\left[\frac{M_0 - \dot{m}_e t}{M_0}\right] - gt$$

At $t = 10$ s,

$$V_{CV} = -3500 \frac{m}{s} \times \ln\left[\frac{350\,kg}{400\,kg}\right] - 9.81 \frac{m}{s^2} \times 10\,s$$

$$V_{CV} = 369\,m/s \longleftarrow \hspace{6cm} V_{CV})_{t=10\,s}$$

The velocity-time graph is shown in an *Excel* workbook. This workbook is interactive: It allows one to see the effect of different values of M_0, V_e, and $\dot{m}_e$ on V_{CV} versus time t. Also, the time at which the rocket attains a given speed, e.g., 2000 m/s, can be determined.

4-6 MOMENTUM EQUATION FOR CONTROL VOLUME WITH ARBITRARY ACCELERATION (ON THE WEB)

*4-7 THE ANGULAR-MOMENTUM PRINCIPLE

Our next task is to derive a control volume form of the angular-momentum principle. There are two obvious approaches we can use to express the angular-momentum principle: We can use an inertial (fixed) *XYZ* control volume; we can also use a rotating *xyz* control volume. For each approach we will: start with the principle in its system form (Eq. 4.3a), then write the system angular momentum in terms of *XYZ* or *xyz* coordinates, and finally use Eq. 4.10 (or its slightly different form, Eq. 4.25) to convert from a system to a control volume formulation. To verify that these two approaches are equivalent, we will use each approach to solve the same problem, in Examples 4.14 and 4.15 (on the Web), respectively.

There are two reasons for the material of this section: We wish to develop a control volume equation for each of the basic physical laws of Section 4-2; we will need the results for use in Chapter 10, where we discuss rotating machinery.

Equation for Fixed Control Volume

The angular-momentum principle for a system in an inertial frame is

$$\vec{T} = \frac{d\vec{H}}{dt}\Big)_{system} \tag{4.3a}$$

where $\vec{T}$ = total torque exerted on the system by its surroundings, and
$\vec{H}$ = angular momentum of the system.

*This section may be omitted without loss of continuity in the text material.

$$\vec{H} = \int_{M(\text{system})} \vec{r} \times \vec{V} \, dm = \int_{\Psi(\text{system})} \vec{r} \times \vec{V} \rho \, d\Psi \qquad (4.3b)$$

All quantities in the system equation must be formulated with respect to an inertial reference frame. Reference frames at rest, or translating with constant linear velocity, are inertial, and Eq. 4.3b can be used directly to develop the control volume form of the angular-momentum principle.

The position vector, $\vec{r}$, locates each mass or volume element of the system with respect to the coordinate system. The torque, $\vec{T}$, applied to a system may be written

$$\vec{T} = \vec{r} \times \vec{F}_s + \int_{M(\text{system})} \vec{r} \times \vec{g} \, dm + \vec{T}_{\text{shaft}} \qquad (4.3c)$$

where $\vec{F}_s$ is the surface force exerted on the system.

The relation between the system and fixed control volume formulations is

$$\frac{dN}{dt}\bigg)_{\text{system}} = \frac{\partial}{\partial t} \int_{\text{CV}} \eta \, \rho \, d\Psi + \int_{\text{CS}} \eta \, \rho \vec{V} \cdot d\vec{A} \qquad (4.10)$$

where

$$N_{\text{system}} = \int_{M(\text{system})} \eta \, dm$$

If we set $N = \vec{H}$, then $\eta = \vec{r} \times \vec{V}$, and

$$\frac{d\vec{H}}{dt}\bigg)_{\text{system}} = \frac{\partial}{\partial t} \int_{\text{CV}} \vec{r} \times \vec{V} \rho \, d\Psi + \int_{\text{CS}} \vec{r} \times \vec{V} \rho \vec{V} \cdot d\vec{A} \qquad (4.45)$$

Combining Eqs. 4.3a, 4.3c, and 4.45, we obtain

$$\vec{r} \times \vec{F}_s + \int_{M(\text{system})} \vec{r} \times \vec{g} \, dm + \vec{T}_{\text{shaft}} = \frac{\partial}{\partial t} \int_{\text{CV}} \vec{r} \times \vec{V} \rho \, d\Psi + \int_{\text{CS}} \vec{r} \times \vec{V} \rho \vec{V} \cdot d\vec{A}$$

Since the system and control volume coincide at time t_0,

$$\vec{T} = \vec{T}_{\text{CV}}$$

and

$$\vec{r} \times \vec{F}_s + \int_{\text{CV}} \vec{r} \times \vec{g} \, \rho \, d\Psi + \vec{T}_{\text{shaft}} = \frac{\partial}{\partial t} \int_{\text{CV}} \vec{r} \times \vec{V} \rho \, d\Psi + \int_{\text{CS}} \vec{r} \times \vec{V} \rho \vec{V} \cdot d\vec{A} \qquad (4.46)$$

Equation 4.46 is a general formulation of the angular-momentum principle for an inertial control volume. The left side of the equation is an expression for all the torques that act on the control volume. Terms on the right express the rate of change of angular momentum within the control volume and the net rate of flux of angular momentum from the control volume. All velocities in Eq. 4.46 are measured relative to the fixed control volume.

For analysis of rotating machinery, Eq. 4.46 is often used in scalar form by considering only the component directed along the axis of rotation. This application is illustrated in Chapter 10.

The application of Eq. 4.46 to the analysis of a simple lawn sprinkler is illustrated in Example 4.14. This same problem is considered in Example 4.15 (on the Web) using the angular-momentum principle expressed in terms of a *rotating* control volume.

Example 4.14 Lawn Sprinkler: Analysis Using Fixed Control Volume

A small lawn sprinkler is shown in the sketch below. At an inlet gage pressure of 20 kPa, the total volume flow rate of water through the sprinkler is 7.5 liters per minute and it rotates at 30 rpm. The diameter of each jet is 4 mm. Calculate the jet speed relative to each sprinkler nozzle. Evaluate the friction torque at the sprinkler pivot.

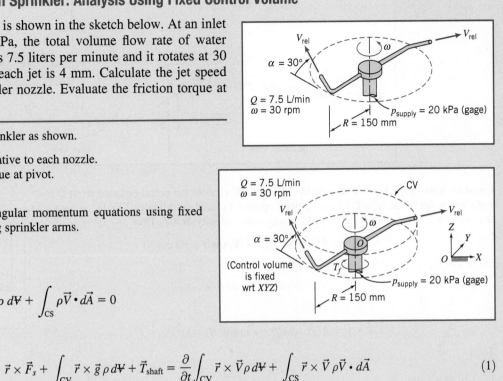

GIVEN: Small lawn sprinkler as shown.

FIND: (a) Jet speed relative to each nozzle.
(b) Friction torque at pivot.

SOLUTION:
Apply continuity and angular momentum equations using fixed control volume enclosing sprinkler arms.

Governing equations:

$$= 0(1)$$

$$\cancel{\frac{\partial}{\partial t}} \int_{CV} \rho \, d\forall + \int_{CS} \rho \vec{V} \cdot d\vec{A} = 0$$

$$\vec{r} \times \vec{F}_s + \int_{CV} \vec{r} \times \vec{g} \, \rho \, d\forall + \vec{T}_{shaft} = \frac{\partial}{\partial t} \int_{CV} \vec{r} \times \vec{V} \rho \, d\forall + \int_{CS} \vec{r} \times \vec{V} \, \rho \vec{V} \cdot d\vec{A} \tag{1}$$

where all velocities are measured relative to the inertial coordinates XYZ.

Assumptions: (1) Incompressible flow.
(2) Uniform flow at each section.
(3) $\vec{\omega} = $ constant.

From continuity, the jet speed relative to the nozzle is given by

$$V_{rel} = \frac{Q}{2A_{jet}} = \frac{Q}{2} \frac{4}{\pi D_{jet}^2}$$

$$= \frac{1}{2} \times 7.5 \frac{L}{min} \times \frac{4}{\pi (4)^2 \, mm^2} \times \frac{m^3}{1000 \, L} \times \frac{10^6 \, mm^2}{m^2} \times \frac{min}{60 \, s}$$

$$V_{rel} = 4.97 \text{ m/s} \longleftarrow \hspace{6cm} V_{rel}$$

Consider terms in the angular momentum equation separately. Since atmospheric pressure acts on the entire control surface, and the pressure force at the inlet causes no moment about O, $\vec{r} \times \vec{F}_s = 0$. The moments of the body (i.e., gravity) forces in the two arms are equal and opposite and hence the second term on the left side of the equation is zero. The only external torque acting on the CV is friction in the pivot. It opposes the motion, so

$$\vec{T}_{shaft} = -T_f \hat{K} \tag{2}$$

Our next task is to determine the two angular momentum terms on the right side of Eq. 1. Consider the unsteady term: This is the rate of change of angular momentum in the control volume. It is clear that although the position $\vec{r}$ and velocity $\vec{V}$ of fluid particles are functions of time in XYZ coordinates, because the sprinkler rotates at constant speed the control volume angular momentum *is* constant in XYZ coordinates, so this term is zero; however, as an exercise in manipulating vector quantities, let us derive this result. Before we can evaluate the control volume integral, we need to develop expressions for the instantaneous position vector, $\vec{r}$, and velocity vector, $\vec{V}$ (measured relative to the fixed coordinate system XYZ) of each element of fluid in the control volume. OA lies in the XY plane; AB is inclined at angle α to the XY plane; point B' is the projection of point B on the XY plane.

We assume that the length, L, of the tip AB is small compared with the length, R, of the horizontal arm OA. Consequently we neglect the angular momentum of the fluid in the tips compared with the angular momentum in the horizontal arms.

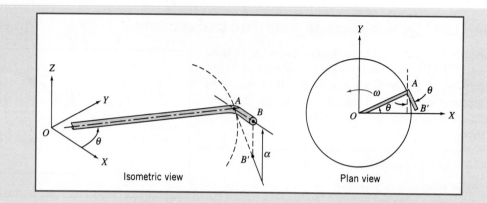

Isometric view   Plan view

Consider flow in the horizontal tube OA of length R. Denote the radial distance from O by r. At any point in the tube the fluid velocity relative to fixed coordinates XYZ is the sum of the velocity relative to the tube $\vec{V}_t$ and the tangential velocity $\vec{\omega} \times \vec{r}$. Thus

$$\vec{V} = \hat{I}(V_t \cos\theta - r\omega \sin\theta) + \hat{J}(V_t \sin\theta + r\omega \cos\theta)$$

(Note that θ is a function of time.) The position vector is

$$\vec{r} = \hat{I}r \cos\theta + \hat{J}r \sin\theta$$

and

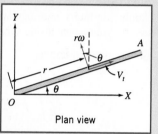

Plan view

$$\vec{r} \times \vec{V} = \hat{K}(r^2\omega \cos^2\theta + r^2\omega \sin^2\theta) = \hat{K}r^2\omega$$

Then

$$\int_{\Psi_{OA}} \vec{r} \times \vec{V} \rho \, d\Psi = \int_0^R \hat{K}r^2\omega\rho A \, dr = \hat{K}\frac{R^3\omega}{3}\rho A$$

and

$$\frac{\partial}{\partial t}\int_{\Psi_{OA}} \vec{r} \times \vec{V} \rho \, d\Psi = \frac{\partial}{\partial t}\left[\hat{K}\frac{R^3\omega}{3}\rho A\right] = 0 \tag{3}$$

where A is the cross-sectional area of the horizontal tube. Identical results are obtained for the other horizontal tube in the control volume. We have confirmed our insight that the angular momentum within the control volume does not change with time.

Now we need to evaluate the second term on the right, the flux of momentum across the control surface. There are three surfaces through which we have mass and therefore momentum flux: the supply line (for which $\vec{r} \times \vec{V} = 0$) because $\vec{r} = 0$ and the two nozzles. Consider the nozzle at the end of branch OAB. For $L \ll R$, we have

$$\vec{r}_{\text{jet}} = \vec{r}_B \approx \vec{r}|_{r=R} = (\hat{I}r \cos\theta + \hat{J}r \sin\theta)|_{r=R} = \hat{I}R \cos\theta + \hat{J}R \sin\theta$$

and for the instantaneous jet velocity $\vec{V}_j$ we have

$$\vec{V}_j = \vec{V}_{\text{rel}} + \vec{V}_{\text{tip}} = \hat{I}V_{\text{rel}} \cos\alpha \sin\theta - \hat{J}V_{\text{rel}} \cos\alpha \cos\theta + \hat{K}V_{\text{rel}} \sin\alpha - \hat{I}\omega R \sin\theta + \hat{J}\omega R \cos\theta$$

$$\vec{V}_j = \hat{I}(V_{\text{rel}} \cos\alpha - \omega R)\sin\theta - \hat{J}(V_{\text{rel}} \cos\alpha - \omega R)\cos\theta + \hat{K}V_{\text{rel}} \sin\alpha$$

$$\vec{r}_B \times \vec{V}_j = \hat{I}RV_{\text{rel}} \sin\alpha \sin\theta - \hat{J}RV_{\text{rel}} \sin\alpha \cos\theta - \hat{K}R(V_{\text{rel}} \cos\alpha - \omega R)(\sin^2\theta + \cos^2\theta)$$

$$\vec{r}_B \times \vec{V}_j = \hat{I}RV_{\text{rel}} \sin\alpha \sin\theta - \hat{J}RV_{\text{rel}} \sin\alpha \cos\theta - \hat{K}R(V_{\text{rel}} \cos\alpha - \omega R)$$

The flux integral evaluated for flow crossing the control surface at location B is then

$$\int_{\text{CS}} \vec{r} \times \vec{V}_j \rho\vec{V} \cdot d\vec{A} = \left[\hat{I}RV_{\text{rel}} \sin\alpha \sin\theta - \hat{J}RV_{\text{rel}} \sin\alpha \cos\theta - \hat{K}R(V_{\text{rel}} \cos\alpha - \omega R)\right]\rho\frac{Q}{2}$$

The velocity and radius vectors for flow in the left arm must be described in terms of the same unit vectors used for the right arm. In the left arm the $\hat{I}$ and $\hat{J}$ components of the cross product are of opposite sign, since $\sin(\theta + \pi) = -\sin(\theta)$ and $\cos(\theta + \pi) = -\cos(\theta)$. Thus for the complete CV,

$$\int_{CS} \vec{r} \times \vec{V}_j \, \rho \vec{V} \cdot d\vec{A} = -\hat{K}R(V_{\text{rel}} \cos \alpha - \omega R)\rho Q \tag{4}$$

Substituting terms (2), (3), and (4) into Eq. 1, we obtain

$$-T_f \hat{K} = -\hat{K}R(V_{\text{rel}} \cos \alpha - \omega R)\rho Q$$

or

$$T_f = R(V_{\text{rel}} \cos \alpha - \omega R)\rho Q$$

This expression indicates that when the sprinkler runs at constant speed the friction torque at the sprinkler pivot just balances the torque generated by the angular momentum of the two jets.

From the data given,

$$\omega R = \frac{30}{\min} \frac{\text{rev}}{} \times 150 \, \text{mm} \times \frac{2\pi}{\text{rev}} \frac{\text{rad}}{} \times \frac{\min}{60 \, \text{s}} \times \frac{\text{m}}{1000 \, \text{mm}} = 0.471 \, \text{m/s}$$

Substituting gives

$$T_f = 150 \, \text{mm} \times \left(4.97 \, \frac{\text{m}}{\text{s}} \times \cos 30° - 0.471 \, \frac{\text{m}}{\text{s}} \right) 999 \, \frac{\text{kg}}{\text{m}^3} \times 7.5 \, \frac{\text{L}}{\min}$$

$$\times \frac{\text{m}^3}{1000 \, \text{L}} \times \frac{\min}{60 \, \text{s}} \times \frac{\text{N} \cdot \text{s}^3}{\text{kg} \cdot \text{m}} \times \frac{\text{m}}{1000 \, \text{mm}}$$

$$T_f = 0.0718 \, \text{N} \cdot \text{m} \longleftarrow \underline{\hspace{5cm}} T_f$$

> This problem illustrates use of the angular momentum principle for an inertial control volume. Note that in this example the fluid particle position vector $\vec{r}$ and velocity vector $\vec{V}$ are time-dependent (through θ) in *XYZ* coordinates. This problem will be solved again using a noninertial (rotating) *xyz* coordinate system in Example 4.15 (on the Web).

Equation for Rotating Control Volume (on the Web)

4-8   THE FIRST LAW OF THERMODYNAMICS

The first law of thermodynamics is a statement of conservation of energy. Recall that the system formulation of the first law was

$$\dot{Q} - \dot{W} = \left. \frac{dE}{dt} \right)_{\text{system}} \tag{4.4a}$$

where the total energy of the system is given by

$$E_{\text{system}} = \int_{M(\text{system})} e \, dm = \int_{\Psi(\text{system})} e \, \rho \, d\Psi \tag{4.4b}$$

and

$$e = u + \frac{V^2}{2} + gz$$

In Eq. 4.4a, the rate of heat transfer, $\dot{Q}$, is positive when heat is added *to* the system from the surroundings; the rate of work, $\dot{W}$, is positive when work is done *by* the system on its surroundings. (Note that some texts use the opposite notation for work.)

To derive the control volume formulation of the first law of thermodynamics, we set

$$N = E \qquad \text{and} \qquad \eta = e$$

in Eq. 4.10 and obtain

$$\left. \frac{dE}{dt} \right)_{\text{system}} = \frac{\partial}{\partial t} \int_{\text{CV}} e\,\rho\,d\forall + \int_{\text{CS}} e\,\rho\vec{V} \cdot d\vec{A} \tag{4.53}$$

Since the system and the control volume coincide at t_0,

$$[\dot{Q} - \dot{W}]_{\text{system}} = [\dot{Q} - \dot{W}]_{\text{control volume}}$$

In light of this, Eqs. 4.4a and 4.53 yield the control volume form of the first law of thermodynamics,

$$\dot{Q} - \dot{W} = \frac{\partial}{\partial t} \int_{\text{CV}} e\,\rho\,d\forall + \int_{\text{CS}} e\,\rho\vec{V} \cdot d\vec{A} \tag{4.54}$$

where

$$e = u + \frac{V^2}{2} + gz$$

Note that for steady flow the first term on the right side of Eq. 4.54 is zero.

Is Eq. 4.54 the form of the first law used in thermodynamics? Even for steady flow, Eq. 4.54 is not quite the same form used in applying the first law to control volume problems. To obtain a formulation suitable and convenient for problem solutions, let us take a closer look at the work term, $\dot{W}$.

Rate of Work Done by a Control Volume

The term $\dot{W}$ in Eq. 4.54 has a positive numerical value when work is done by the control volume on the surroundings. The rate of work done *on* the control volume is of opposite sign to the work done *by* the control volume.

The rate of work done by the control volume is conveniently subdivided into four classifications,

$$\dot{W} = \dot{W}_s + \dot{W}_{\text{normal}} + \dot{W}_{\text{shear}} + \dot{W}_{\text{other}}$$

Let us consider these separately:

1. Shaft Work

We shall designate shaft work W_s and hence the rate of work transferred out through the control surface by shaft work is designated $\dot{W}_s$. Examples of shaft work are the work produced by the steam turbine (positive shaft work) of a power plant, and the work input required to run the compressor of a refrigerator (negative shaft work).

2. Work Done by Normal Stresses at the Control Surface

Recall that work requires a force to act through a distance. Thus, when a force, $\vec{F}$, acts through an infinitesimal displacement, $d\vec{s}$, the work done is given by

$$\delta W = \vec{F} \cdot d\vec{s}$$

To obtain the rate at which work is done by the force, divide by the time increment, Δt, and take the limit as $\Delta t \to 0$. Thus the rate of work done by the force, $\vec{F}$, is

$$\dot{W} = \lim_{\Delta t \to 0} \frac{\delta W}{\Delta t} = \lim_{\Delta t \to 0} \frac{\vec{F} \cdot d\vec{s}}{\Delta t} \qquad \text{or} \qquad \dot{W} = \vec{F} \cdot \vec{V}$$

We can use this to compute the rate of work done by the normal and shear stresses. Consider the segment of control surface shown in Fig. 4.6. For an elementary area $d\vec{A}$ we can write an expression for the normal stress force $d\vec{F}_{\text{normal}}$: It will be given by the normal stress σ_{nn} multiplied by the vector area element $d\vec{A}$ (normal to the control surface).

Hence the rate of work done on the area element is

$$d\vec{F}_{\text{normal}} \cdot \vec{V} = \sigma_{nn} \, d\vec{A} \cdot \vec{V}$$

Since the work out across the boundaries of the control volume is the negative of the work done on the control volume, the total rate of work out of the control volume due to normal stresses is

$$\dot{W}_{\text{normal}} = -\int_{\text{CS}} \sigma_{nn} \, d\vec{A} \cdot \vec{V} = -\int_{\text{CS}} \sigma_{nn} \vec{V} \cdot d\vec{A}$$

3. Work Done by Shear Stresses at the Control Surface

Just as work is done by the normal stresses at the boundaries of the control volume, so may work be done by the shear stresses.

As shown in Fig. 4.6, the shear force acting on an element of area of the control surface is given by

$$d\vec{F}_{\text{shear}} = \vec{\tau} \, dA$$

where the shear stress vector, $\vec{\tau}$, is the shear stress acting in some direction in the plane of dA.

The rate of work done on the entire control surface by shear stresses is given by

$$\int_{\text{CS}} \vec{\tau} \, dA \cdot \vec{V} = \int_{\text{CS}} \vec{\tau} \cdot \vec{V} dA$$

Since the work out across the boundaries of the control volume is the negative of the work done on the control volume, the rate of work out of the control volume due to shear stresses is given by

$$\dot{W}_{\text{shear}} = -\int_{\text{CS}} \vec{\tau} \cdot \vec{V} \, dA$$

This integral is better expressed as three terms

$$\dot{W}_{\text{shear}} = -\int_{\text{CS}} \vec{\tau} \cdot \vec{V} \, dA$$

$$= -\int_{A(\text{shafts})} \vec{\tau} \cdot \vec{V} \, dA - \int_{A(\text{solid surface})} \vec{\tau} \cdot \vec{V} \, dA - \int_{A(\text{ports})} \vec{\tau} \cdot \vec{V} \, dA$$

We have already accounted for the first term, since we included $\dot{W}_s$ previously. At solid surfaces, $\vec{V} = 0$, so the second term is zero (for a fixed control volume). Thus,

$$\dot{W}_{\text{shear}} = -\int_{A(\text{ports})} \vec{\tau} \cdot \vec{V} \, dA$$

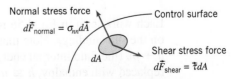

Fig. 4.6 Normal and shear stress forces.

This last term can be made zero by proper choice of control surfaces. If we choose a control surface that cuts across each port perpendicular to the flow, then $d\vec{A}$ is parallel to $\vec{V}$. Since $\vec{\tau}$ is in the plane of dA, $\vec{\tau}$ is perpendicular to $\vec{V}$. Thus, for a control surface perpendicular to $\vec{V}$,

$$\vec{\tau} \cdot \vec{V} = 0 \quad\text{and}\quad \dot{W}_{\text{shear}} = 0$$

4. Other Work

Electrical energy could be added to the control volume. Also electromagnetic energy, e.g., in radar or laser beams, could be absorbed. In most problems, such contributions will be absent, but we should note them in our general formulation.

With all of the terms in $\dot{W}$ evaluated, we obtain

$$\dot{W} = \dot{W}_s - \int_{CS} \sigma_{nn} \vec{V} \cdot d\vec{A} + \dot{W}_{\text{shear}} + \dot{W}_{\text{other}} \tag{4.55}$$

Control Volume Equation

Substituting the expression for $\dot{W}$ from Eq. 4.55 into Eq. 4.54 gives

$$\dot{Q} - \dot{W}_s + \int_{CS} \sigma_{nn} \vec{V} \cdot d\vec{A} - \dot{W}_{\text{shear}} - \dot{W}_{\text{other}} = \frac{\partial}{\partial t} \int_{CV} e \rho \, d\Psi + \int_{CS} e \rho \vec{V} \cdot d\vec{A}$$

Rearranging this equation, we obtain

$$\dot{Q} - \dot{W}_s - \dot{W}_{\text{shear}} - \dot{W}_{\text{other}} = \frac{\partial}{\partial t} \int_{CV} e \rho \, d\Psi + \int_{CS} e \rho \vec{V} \cdot d\vec{A} - \int_{CS} \sigma_{nn} \vec{V} \cdot d\vec{A}$$

Since $\rho = 1/v$, where v is *specific volume*, then

$$\int_{CS} \sigma_{nn} \vec{V} \cdot d\vec{A} = \int_{CS} \sigma_{nn} v \rho \vec{V} \cdot d\vec{A}$$

Hence

$$\dot{Q} - \dot{W}_s - \dot{W}_{\text{shear}} - \dot{W}_{\text{other}} = \frac{\partial}{\partial t} \int_{CV} e \rho \, d\Psi + \int_{CS} (e - \sigma_{nn} v) \rho \vec{V} \cdot d\vec{A}$$

Viscous effects can make the normal stress, σ_{nn}, different from the negative of the thermodynamic pressure, $-p$. However, for most flows of common engineering interest, $\sigma_{nn} \simeq -p$. Then

$$\dot{Q} - \dot{W}_s - \dot{W}_{\text{shear}} - \dot{W}_{\text{other}} = \frac{\partial}{\partial t} \int_{CV} e \rho \, d\Psi + \int_{CS} (e + pv) \rho \vec{V} \cdot d\vec{A}$$

Finally, substituting $e = u + V^2/2 + gz$ into the last term, we obtain the familiar form of the first law for a control volume,

$$\dot{Q} - \dot{W}_s - \dot{W}_{\text{shear}} - \dot{W}_{\text{other}} = \frac{\partial}{\partial t} \int_{CV} e \rho \, d\Psi + \int_{CS} \left(u + pv + \frac{V^2}{2} + gz \right) \rho \vec{V} \cdot d\vec{A} \tag{4.56}$$

Each work term in Eq. 4.56 represents the rate of work done by the control volume on the surroundings. Note that in thermodynamics, for convenience, the combination $u + pv$ (the fluid internal energy plus what is often called the "flow work") is usually replaced with enthalpy, $h \equiv u + pv$ (this is one of the reasons h was invented).

Example 4.16   Compressor: First Law Analysis

Air at 14.7 psia, 70°F, enters a compressor with negligible velocity and is discharged at 50 psia, 100°F through a pipe with 1 ft^2 area. The flow rate is 20 lbm/s. The power input to the compressor is 600 hp. Determine the rate of heat transfer.

GIVEN: Air enters a compressor at ① and leaves at ② with conditions as shown. The air flow rate is 20 lbm/s and the power input to the compressor is 600 hp.

FIND: Rate of heat transfer.

SOLUTION:

$p_1 = 14.7$ psia $p_2 = 50$ psia
① ②
$V_1 \approx 0 \longrightarrow$ $\longrightarrow A_2 = 1$ ft^2
$T_1 = 70°F$ CV $T_2 = 100°F$

Governing equations:

$$\overset{=\,0(1)}{\frac{\partial}{\partial t}\int\!\!\!\int_{CV} \rho\, d\Psi} + \int_{CS} \rho \vec{V} \cdot d\vec{A} = 0$$

$$\dot{Q} - \dot{W}_s - \cancel{\dot{W}_{shear}}^{=\,0(4)} = \overset{=\,0(1)}{\frac{\partial}{\partial t}\int\!\!\!\int_{CV} e\, \rho\, d\Psi} + \int_{CS}\left(u + pv + \frac{V^2}{2} + gz\right)\rho \vec{V} \cdot d\vec{A}$$

Assumptions: (1) Steady flow.
(2) Properties uniform over inlet and outlet sections.
(3) Treat air as an ideal gas, $p = \rho RT$.
(4) Area of CV at ① and ② perpendicular to velocity, thus $\dot{W}_{shear} = 0$.
(5) $z_1 = z_2$.
(6) Inlet kinetic energy is negligible.

Under the assumptions listed, the first law becomes

$$\dot{Q} - \dot{W}_s = \int_{CV}\left(u + pv + \frac{V^2}{2} + gz\right)\rho \vec{V} \cdot d\vec{A}$$

$$\dot{Q} - \dot{W}_s = \int_{CS}\left(h + \frac{V^2}{2} + gz\right)\rho \vec{V} \cdot d\vec{A}$$

or

$$\dot{Q} = \dot{W}_s + \int_{CS}\left(h + \frac{V^2}{2} + gz\right)\rho \vec{V} \cdot d\vec{A}$$

For uniform properties, assumption (2), we can write

$$\dot{Q} = \dot{W}_s + \left(h_1 + \cancel{\frac{V_1^2}{2}}^{\approx\,0(6)} + gz_1\right)(-\rho_1 V_1 A_1) + \left(h_2 + \frac{V_2^2}{2} + gz_2\right)(\rho_2 V_2 A_2)$$

For steady flow, from conservation of mass,

$$\int_{CS} \rho \vec{V} \cdot d\vec{A} = 0$$

Therefore, $-(\rho_1 V_1 A_1) + (\rho_2 V_2 A_2) = 0$, or $\rho_1 V_1 A_1 = \rho_2 V_2 A_2 = \dot{m}$. Hence we can write

$$\dot{Q} = \dot{W}_s + \dot{m}\left[(h_2 - h_1) + \frac{V_2^2}{2} + g(z_2 \cancel{-} z_1)^{=\,0(5)}\right]$$

Assume that air behaves as an ideal gas with constant c_p. Then $h_2 - h_1 = c_p(T_2 - T_1)$, and

$$\dot{Q} = \dot{W}_s + \dot{m}\left[c_p(T_2 - T_1) + \frac{V_2^2}{2}\right]$$

From continuity $V_2 = \dot{m}/\rho_2 A_2$. Since $p_2 = \rho_2 R T_2$,

$$V_2 = \frac{\dot{m}}{A_2}\frac{RT_2}{p_2} = \frac{20\ \text{lbm}}{\text{s}} \times \frac{1}{1\ \text{ft}^2} \times \frac{53.3}{} \frac{\text{ft} \cdot \text{lbf}}{\text{lbm} \cdot {}^\circ\text{R}} \times \frac{560{}^\circ\text{R}}{} \times \frac{\text{in.}^2}{50\ \text{lbf}} \times \frac{\text{ft}^2}{144\ \text{in.}^2}$$

$$V_2 = 82.9\ \text{ft/s}$$

$$\dot{Q} = \dot{W}_s + \dot{m}c_p\,(T_2 - T_1) + \dot{m}\,\frac{V_2^2}{2}$$

Note that power input is *to* the CV, so $\dot{W}_s = -600$ hp, and

$$\dot{Q} = -\frac{600\ \text{hp}}{} \times \frac{550\ \text{ft} \cdot \text{lbf}}{\text{hp} \cdot \text{s}} \times \frac{\text{Btu}}{778\ \text{ft} \cdot \text{lbf}} + \frac{20\ \text{lbm}}{\text{s}} \times 0.24\,\frac{\text{Btu}}{\text{lbm} \cdot {}^\circ\text{R}} \times 30{}^\circ\text{R}$$

$$+ \frac{20\ \text{lbm}}{\text{s}} \times \frac{(82.9)^2\ \text{ft}^2}{2\quad \text{s}^2} \times \frac{\text{slug}}{32.2\ \text{lbm}} \times \frac{\text{Btu}}{778\ \text{ft} \cdot \text{lbf}} \times \frac{\text{lbf} \cdot \text{s}^2}{\text{slug} \cdot \text{ft}}$$

$$\dot{Q} = -277\ \text{Btu/s} \longleftarrow \qquad\qquad\qquad\qquad \{\text{heat rejection}\}\ \dot{Q}$$

> This problem illustrates use of the first law of thermodynamics for a control volume. It is also an example of the care that must be taken with unit conversions for mass, energy, and power.

Example 4.17   Tank Filling: First Law Analysis

A tank of 0.1 m³ volume is connected to a high-pressure air line; both line and tank are initially at a uniform temperature of 20°C. The initial tank gage pressure is 100 kPa. The absolute line pressure is 2.0 MPa; the line is large enough so that its temperature and pressure may be assumed constant. The tank temperature is monitored by a fast-response thermocouple. At the instant after the valve is opened, the tank temperature rises at the rate of 0.05°C/s. Determine the instantaneous flow rate of air into the tank if heat transfer is neglected.

GIVEN: Air supply pipe and tank as shown. At $t = 0^+$, $\partial T/\partial t = 0.05{}^\circ\text{C/s}$.

FIND: $\dot{m}$ at $t = 0^+$.

SOLUTION:
Choose CV shown, apply energy equation.

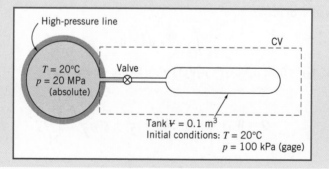

Governing equation:

$$\overset{= 0(1)}{\cancel{\dot{Q}}} - \overset{= 0(2)}{\cancel{\dot{W_s}}} - \overset{= 0(3)}{\cancel{\dot{W}_{shear}}} - \overset{= 0(4)}{\cancel{\dot{W}_{other}}} = \frac{\partial}{\partial t}\int_{CV} e\,\rho\,d\forall + \int_{CS}(e+pv)\rho\vec{V}\bullet d\vec{A}$$

$$e = u + \overset{\simeq\,0(5)}{\cancel{\frac{V^2}{2}}} + \overset{\simeq\,0(6)}{\cancel{gz}}$$

Assumptions: (1) $\dot{Q} = 0$ (given).
(2) $\dot{W_s} = 0$.
(3) $\dot{W}_{shear} = 0$.
(4) $\dot{W}_{other} = 0$.
(5) Velocities in line and tank are small.
(6) Neglect potential energy.
(7) Uniform flow at tank inlet.
(8) Properties uniform in tank.
(9) Ideal gas, $p = \rho RT$, $du = c_v\,dT$.

Then

$$\frac{\partial}{\partial t}\int_{CV} u_{tank}\,\rho\,d\forall + (u+pv)|_{line}(-\rho VA) = 0$$

This expresses the fact that the gain in energy in the tank is due to influx of fluid energy (in the form of enthalpy $h = u + pv$) from the line. We are interested in the initial instant, when T is uniform at $20°C$, so $u_{tank} = u_{line} = u$, the internal energy at T; also, $pv_{line} = RT_{line} = RT$, and

$$\frac{\partial}{\partial t}\int_{CV} u\,\rho\,d\forall + (u+RT)(-\rho VA) = 0$$

Since tank properties are uniform, $\partial/\partial t$ may be replaced by d/dt, and

$$\frac{d}{dt}(uM) = (u+RT)\dot{m}$$

(where M is the instantaneous mass in the tank and $\dot{m} = \rho VA$ is the mass flow rate), or

$$u\frac{dM}{dt} + M\frac{du}{dt} = u\dot{m} + RT\dot{m} \tag{1}$$

The term dM/dt may be evaluated from continuity:

Governing equation:

$$\frac{\partial}{\partial t}\int_{CV}\rho\,d\forall + \int_{CS}\rho\vec{V}\bullet d\vec{A} = 0$$

$$\frac{dM}{dt} + (-\rho VA) = 0 \quad \text{or} \quad \frac{dM}{dt} = \dot{m}$$

Substituting in Eq. 1 gives

$$u\dot{m} + Mc_v\frac{dT}{dt} = u\dot{m} + RT\dot{m}$$

or

$$\dot{m} = \frac{Mc_v(dT/dt)}{RT} = \frac{\rho\forall c_v(dT/dt)}{RT} \tag{2}$$

But at $t = 0$, $p_{tank} = 100$ kPa (gage), and

$$\rho = \rho_{tank} = \frac{p_{tank}}{RT} = (1.00 + 1.01)10^5\,\frac{N}{m^2} \times \frac{kg\cdot K}{287\,N\cdot m} \times \frac{1}{293\,K} = 2.39\,kg/m^3$$

Substituting into Eq. 2, we obtain

$$\dot{m} = 2.39\,\frac{kg}{m^3} \times 0.1\,m^3 \times 717\,\frac{N\cdot m}{kg\cdot K} \times 0.05\,\frac{K}{s} \times \frac{kg\cdot K}{287\,N\cdot m} \times \frac{1}{293\,K} \times 1000\,\frac{g}{kg}$$

$$\dot{m} = 0.102\,g/s \longleftarrow \underset{\dot{m}}{}$$

This problem illustrates use of the first law of thermodynamics for a control volume. It is also an example of the care that must be taken with unit conversions for mass, energy, and power.

4-9   **THE SECOND LAW OF THERMODYNAMICS**

Recall that the system formulation of the second law is

$$\left.\frac{dS}{dt}\right)_{\text{system}} \geq \frac{1}{T}\dot{Q} \tag{4.5a}$$

where the total entropy of the system is given by

$$S_{\text{system}} = \int_{M(\text{system})} s\, dm = \int_{\forall(\text{system})} s\, \rho\, d\forall \tag{4.5b}$$

To derive the control volume formulation of the second law of thermodynamics, we set

$$N = S \quad \text{and} \quad \eta = s$$

in Eq. 4.10 and obtain

$$\left.\frac{dS}{dt}\right)_{\text{system}} = \frac{\partial}{\partial t}\int_{\text{CV}} s\, \rho\, d\forall + \int_{\text{CS}} s\, \rho\vec{V} \cdot d\vec{A} \tag{4.57}$$

The system and the control volume coincide at t_0; thus in Eq. 4.5a,

$$\left.\frac{1}{T}\dot{Q}\right)_{\text{system}} = \left.\frac{1}{T}\dot{Q}\right)_{\text{CV}} = \int_{\text{CS}} \frac{1}{T}\left(\frac{\dot{Q}}{A}\right)dA$$

In light of this, Eqs. 4.5a and 4.57 yield the control volume formulation of the second law of thermodynamics

$$\frac{\partial}{\partial t}\int_{\text{CV}} s\, \rho\, d\forall + \int_{\text{CS}} s\, \rho\, \vec{V} \cdot d\vec{A} \geq \int_{\text{CS}} \frac{1}{T}\left(\frac{\dot{Q}}{A}\right)dA \tag{4.58}$$

In Eq. 4.58, the factor $(\dot{Q}/A)$ represents the heat flux per unit area into the control volume through the area element dA. To evaluate the term

$$\int_{\text{CS}} \frac{1}{T}\left(\frac{\dot{Q}}{A}\right)dA$$

both the local heat flux, $(\dot{Q}/A)$, and local temperature, T, must be known for each area element of the control surface.

4-10   **SUMMARY AND USEFUL EQUATIONS**

In this chapter we wrote the basic laws for a system: mass conservation (or continuity), Newton's second law, the angular-momentum equation, the first law of thermodynamics, and the second law of thermodynamics. We then developed an equation (sometimes called the Reynolds Transport Theorem) for relating system formulations to control volume formulations. Using this we derived control volume forms of:

✓ The mass conservation equation (sometimes called the continuity equation).
✓ Newton's second law (in other words, a momentum equation) for:
　○ An inertial control volume.
　○ A control volume with rectilinear acceleration.
　○ A control volume with arbitrary acceleration (on the Web).
✓ *The angular-momentum equation for:
　○ A fixed control volume.
　○ A rotating control volume (on the Web).
✓ The first law of thermodynamics (or energy equation).
✓ The second law of thermodynamics.

We discussed the physical meaning of each term appearing in these control volume equations, and used the equations for the solution of a variety of flow problems. In particular, we used a differential control volume* to derive a famous equation in fluid mechanics—the Bernoulli equation—and while doing so learned about the restrictions on its use in solving problems.

Note: Most of the Useful Equations in the table below have a number of constraints or limitations—*be sure to refer to their page numbers for details!*

Useful Equations			
Continuity (mass conservation), incompressible fluid:	$\int_{CS} \vec{V} \cdot d\vec{A} = 0$	(4.13a)	Page 100
Continuity (mass conservation), incompressible fluid, uniform flow:	$\sum_{CS} \vec{V} \cdot \vec{A} = 0$	(4.13b)	Page 100
Continuity (mass conservation), steady flow:	$\int_{CS} \rho \vec{V} \cdot d\vec{A} = 0$	(4.15a)	Page 101
Continuity (mass conservation), steady flow, uniform flow:	$\sum_{CS} \rho \vec{V} \cdot \vec{A} = 0$	(4.15b)	Page 101
Momentum (Newton's second law):	$\vec{F} = \vec{F}_S + \vec{F}_B = \dfrac{\partial}{\partial t} \int_{CV} \vec{V} \rho \, d\mathcal{V} + \int_{CS} \vec{V} \rho \vec{V} \cdot d\vec{A}$	(4.17a)	Page 106
Momentum (Newton's second law), uniform flow:	$\vec{F} = \vec{F}_S + \vec{F}_B = \dfrac{\partial}{\partial t} \int_{CV} \vec{V} \rho \, d\mathcal{V} + \sum_{CS} \vec{V} \rho \vec{V} \cdot \vec{A}$	(4.17b)	Page 106
Momentum (Newton's second law), scalar components:	$F_x = F_{S_x} + F_{B_x} = \dfrac{\partial}{\partial t} \int_{CV} u \rho \, d\mathcal{V} + \int_{CS} u \rho \vec{V} \cdot d\vec{A}$	(4.18a)	Page 106
	$F_y = F_{S_y} + F_{B_y} = \dfrac{\partial}{\partial t} \int_{CV} v \rho \, d\mathcal{V} + \int_{CS} v \rho \vec{V} \cdot d\vec{A}$	(4.18b)	
	$F_z = F_{S_z} + F_{B_z} = \dfrac{\partial}{\partial t} \int_{CV} w \rho \, d\mathcal{V} + \int_{CS} w \rho \vec{V} \cdot d\vec{A}$	(4.18c)	
Momentum (Newton's second law), uniform flow, scalar components:	$F_x = F_{S_x} + F_{B_x} = \dfrac{\partial}{\partial t} \int_{CV} u \rho \, d\mathcal{V} + \sum_{CS} u \rho \vec{V} \cdot \vec{A}$	(4.18d)	Page 107
	$F_y = F_{S_y} + F_{B_y} = \dfrac{\partial}{\partial t} \int_{CV} v \rho \, d\mathcal{V} + \sum_{CS} v \rho \vec{V} \cdot \vec{A}$	(4.18e)	
	$F_z = F_{S_z} + F_{B_z} = \dfrac{\partial}{\partial t} \int_{CV} w \rho \, d\mathcal{V} + \sum_{CS} w \rho \vec{V} \cdot \vec{A}$	(4.18f)	

*These topics apply to a section that may be omitted without loss of continuity in the text material.

Bernoulli equation (steady, incompressible, frictionless, flow along a streamline):	$\dfrac{p}{\rho} + \dfrac{V^2}{2} + gz = \text{constant}$ (4.24)	Page 118
Momentum (Newton's second law), inertial control volume (stationary or constant speed):	$\vec{F} = \vec{F}_S + \vec{F}_B = \dfrac{\partial}{\partial t}\displaystyle\int_{CV} \vec{V}_{xyz}\, \rho\, d\forall + \int_{CS} \vec{V}_{xyz}\, \rho \vec{V}_{xyz} \cdot d\vec{A}$ (4.26)	Page 120
Momentum (Newton's second law), rectilinear acceleration of control volume:	$\vec{F}_S + \vec{F}_B - \displaystyle\int_{CV} \vec{a}_{rf}\, \rho\, d\forall$ $= \dfrac{\partial}{\partial t}\displaystyle\int_{CV} \vec{V}_{xyz}\, \rho\, d\forall \int_{CS} \vec{V}_{xyz}\, \rho \vec{V}_{xyz} \cdot d\vec{A}$ (4.33)	Page 124
Angular-momentum principle:	$\vec{r} \times \vec{F}_s + \displaystyle\int_{CV} \vec{r} \times \vec{g}\, \rho\, d\forall + \vec{T}_{\text{shaft}}$ $= \dfrac{\partial}{\partial t}\displaystyle\int_{CV} \vec{r} \times \vec{V}\, \rho\, d\forall + \int_{CS} \vec{r} \times \vec{V}\, \rho\vec{V} \cdot d\vec{A}$ (4.46)	Page 130
First law of thermodynamics:	$\dot{Q} - \dot{W}_s - \dot{W}_{\text{shear}} - \dot{W}_{\text{other}}$ $= \dfrac{\partial}{\partial t}\displaystyle\int_{CV} e\, \rho\, d\forall + \int_{CS} \left(u + pv + \dfrac{V^2}{2} + gz \right) \rho\vec{V} \cdot d\vec{A}$ (4.56)	Page 136
Second law of thermodynamics:	$\dfrac{\partial}{\partial t}\displaystyle\int_{CV} s\, \rho\, d\forall + \int_{CS} s\, \rho\, \vec{V} \cdot d\vec{A} \geq \int_{CS} \dfrac{1}{T}\left(\dfrac{\dot{Q}}{A} \right) dA$ (4.58)	Page 140

PROBLEMS

4.1 A mass of 3 kg falls freely a distance of 5 m before contacting a spring attached to the ground. If the spring stiffness is 400 N/m, what is the maximum spring compression?

4.2 In order to cool a six-pack as quickly as possible, it is placed in a freezer for a period of 1 hr. If the room temperature is $25°C$ and the cooled beverage is at a final temperature of $5°C$, determine the change in specific entropy of the beverage.

4.3 A fully loaded Boeing 777-200 jet transport aircraft weighs 325,000 kg. The pilot brings the 2 engines to full takeoff thrust of 450 kN each before releasing the brakes. Neglecting aerodynamic and rolling resistance, estimate the minimum runway length and time needed to reach a takeoff speed of 225 kph. Assume engine thrust remains constant during ground roll.

4.4 A small steel ball of radius r, placed atop a much larger sphere of radius R, begins to roll under the influence of gravity. Rolling resistance and air resistance are negligible. As the speed of the ball increases, it leaves the surface of the sphere and becomes a projectile. Determine the location at which the ball loses contact with the sphere.

4.5 A police investigation of tire marks showed that a car traveling along a straight level street had skidded to a stop for a total distance of 50 m after the brakes were applied. The coefficient of friction between tires and pavement is estimated to be $\mu = 0.6$. What was the probable minimum speed of the car when the brakes were applied?

4.6 Air at $68°F$ and an absolute pressure of 1 atm is compressed adiabatically, without friction, to an absolute pressure of 3 atm. Determine the internal energy change.

4.7 In an experiment with a can of soda, it took 3 hr to cool from an initial temperature of $75°F$ to $50°F$ in a $40°F$ refrigerator. If the can is now taken from the refrigerator and placed in a room at $68°F$, how long will the can take to reach $60°F$? You may assume that for both processes the heat transfer is modeled by $\dot{Q} \approx k(T - T_{\text{amb}})$, where T is the can temperature, T_{amb} is the ambient temperature, and k is a heat transfer coefficient.

4.8 The average rate of heat loss from a person to the surroundings when not actively working is about 85W. Suppose that in an auditorium with volume of approximately 3.5×10^5 m³, containing 6000 people, the ventilation system fails. How much does the internal energy of the air in the auditorium increase during the first 15 min after the ventilation system fails? Considering the auditorium and people as a system, and assuming no heat transfer to the surroundings, how much does the internal energy of the system change? How do you account for the fact that the temperature of the air increases? Estimate the rate of temperature rise under these conditions.

4.9 The mass of an aluminum beverage can is 20 g. Its diameter and height are 65 and 120 mm, respectively. When full, the can contains 354 milliliters of soft drink with SG = 1.05. Evaluate the height of the center of gravity of the can as a function of liquid level. At what level would the can be least likely to tip over when subjected to a steady lateral acceleration? Calculate the minimum coefficient of static friction for which the full can would tip rather than slide on a horizontal surface. Plot the minimum coefficient of static friction for which the can would tip rather than slide on a horizontal surface as a function of beverage level in the can.

4.10 The velocity field in the region shown is given by $\vec{V} = az\hat{j} + b\hat{k}$, where $a = 10$ s^{-1} and $b = 5$ m/s. For the 1 m $\times$ 1 m triangular control volume (depth $w = 1$ m perpendicular to the diagram), an element of area ① may be represented by $w(-dz\hat{j} + dy\hat{k})$ and an element of area ② by $wdz\hat{j}$.

    a. Find an expression for $\vec{V} \cdot d\vec{A}_1$.
    b. Evaluate $\int_{A_1} \vec{V} \cdot d\vec{A}_1$.
    c. Find an expression for $\vec{V} \cdot d\vec{A}_2$.
    d. Find an expression for $\vec{V}(\vec{V} \cdot d\vec{A}_2)$.
    e. Evaluate $\int_{A_2} \vec{V}(\vec{V} \cdot d\vec{A}_2)$.

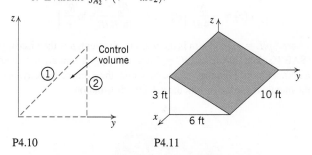

P4.10   P4.11

4.11 The shaded area shown is in a flow where the velocity field is given by $\vec{V} = ax\hat{i} - by\hat{j}$; $a = b = 1$ s^{-1}, and the coordinates are measured in meters. Evaluate the volume flow rate and the momentum flux through the shaded area.

4.12 Obtain expressions for the volume flow rate and the momentum flux through cross section ① of the control volume shown in the diagram.

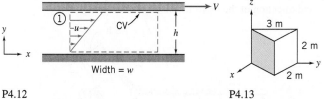

P4.12   P4.13

4.13 The area shown shaded is in a flow where the velocity field is given by $\vec{V} = -ax\hat{i} + by\hat{j} + c\hat{k}$; $a = b = 2$ s^{-1} and $c = 2.5$ m/s. Write a vector expression for an element of the shaded area. Evaluate the integrals $\int \vec{V} \cdot d\vec{A}$ and $\int \vec{V}(\vec{V} \cdot d\vec{A})$ over the shaded area.

4.14 For the flow of Problem 4.12, obtain an expression for the kinetic energy flux, $\int (V^2/2)\rho\vec{V} \cdot d\vec{A}$, through cross section ① of the control volume shown.

4.15 The velocity distribution for laminar flow in a long circular tube of radius R is given by the one-dimensional expression,

$$\vec{V} = u\hat{i} = u_{max}\left[1 - \left(\frac{r}{R}\right)^2\right]\hat{i}$$

For this profile obtain expressions for the volume flow rate and the momentum flux through a section normal to the pipe axis.

4.16 For the flow of Problem 4.15, obtain an expression for the kinetic energy flux, $\int (V^2/2)\rho\vec{V} \cdot d\vec{A}$, through a section normal to the pipe axis.

4.17 A farmer is spraying a liquid through 10 nozzles, 1/8th in. ID, at an average exit velocity of 10 ft/s. What is the average velocity in the 1-in. ID head feeder? What is the system flow rate, in gpm?

4.18 A cylindrical holding water tank has a 3 m ID, and a height of 3 m. There is one inlet of diameter 10 cm, an exit of diameter 8 cm, and a drain. The tank is initially empty when the inlet pump is turned on, producing an average inlet velocity of 5 m/s. When the level in the tank reaches 0.7 m, the exit pump turns on, causing flow out of the exit; the exit average velocity is 3 m/s. When the water level reaches 2 m the drain is opened such that the level remains at 2 m. Find (a) the time at which the exit pump is switched on, (b) the time at which the drain is opened, and (c) the flow rate into the drain (m^3/min).

4.19 A wet cooling tower cools warm water by spraying it into a forced dry-air flow. Some of the water evaporates in this air and is carried out of the tower into the atmosphere; the evaporation cools the remaining water droplets, which are collected at the exit pipe (6 in. ID) of the tower. Measurements indicate the warm water mass flow rate is 250,000 lb/hr, and the cool water (70°F) flows at an average speed of 5.55 ft/s in the exit pipe. The flow rate of the moist air is to be obtained from measurements of the velocity at four points, each representing 1/4 of the air stream cross-sectional area of 13.2 ft^2. The moist air density is 0.066 lb/ft^3. Find (a) the volume and mass flow rates of the cool water, (b) the mass flow rate of the moist air, and (c) the mass flow rate of the dry air.

4.20 A university laboratory wishes to build a wind tunnel with variable speeds. Rather than use a variable speed fan, it is proposed to build the tunnel with a sequence of three circular test sections: Section 1 will have a diameter of 5 ft, Section 2 a diameter of 3 ft, and Section 3 a diameter of 2 ft. If the average speed in Section 1 is 20 mph, what will be the speeds in the other two sections? What will be the flow rate (ft^3/min)?

4.21 Fluid with 65 lbm/ft^3 density is flowing steadily through the rectangular box shown. Given $A_1 = 0.5$ ft^2, $A_2 = 0.1$ ft^2, $A_3 = 0.6$ ft^2, $\vec{V}_1 = 10\hat{i}$ ft/s, and $\vec{V}_2 = 20\hat{j}$ ft/s, determine velocity $\vec{V}_3$.

4.22 Consider steady, incompressible flow through the device shown. Determine the magnitude and direction of the volume flow rate through port 3.

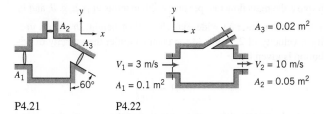

P4.21   P4.22

4.23 A rice farmer needs to fill her 5 acre field with water to a depth of 3 in. in 1 hr. How many 6 in. diameter supply pipes are needed if the average velocity in each must be less than 10 ft/s?

4.24 You are filling your car with gasoline at a rate of 5.3 gals/min. Although you can't see it, the gasoline is rising in the tank at a rate of 4.3 in. per minute. What is the horizontal cross-sectional area of your gas tank? Is this a realistic answer?

4.25 For your sink at home, the flow rate in is 5000 units/hr. Accumulation is 2500 units. What is the accumulation rate if the outflow is 60 units/min? Suddenly, the outflow becomes 13 units/min: What is the accumulation rate? At another time, the flow rate in is 5 units/sec. The accumulation is 50 units. The accumulation rate is -4 units/sec. What is the flow rate out?

4.26 You are trying to pump storm water out of your basement during a storm. The pump can extract 10 gpm. The water level in the basement is now sinking about 1 in./hr. What is the flow rate (gpm) from the storm into the basement? The basement is 25 ft by 20 ft.

4.27 In steady-state flow downstream, the density is 4 lb/ft^3, the velocity is 10 ft/sec, and the area is 1 ft^2. Upstream, the velocity is 15 ft/sec, and the area is 0.25 ft^2. What is the density upstream?

4.28 In the incompressible flow through the device shown, velocities may be considered uniform over the inlet and outlet sections. The following conditions are known: $A_1 = 0.1$ m^2, $A_2 = 0.2$ m^2, $A_3 = 0.15$ m^2, $V_1 = 10e^{-t/2}$ m/s, and $V_2 = 2\cos(2\pi t)$ m/s (t in seconds). Obtain an expression for the velocity at section ③, and plot V_3 as a function of time. At what instant does V_3 first become zero? What is the total mean volumetric flow at section ③?

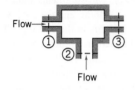

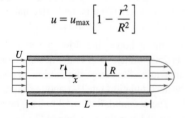

P4.28

4.29 Oil flows steadily in a thin layer down an inclined plane. The velocity profile is

$$u = \frac{\rho g \sin\theta}{\mu}\left[hy - \frac{y^2}{2}\right]$$

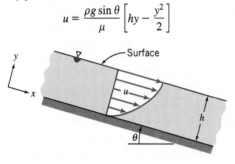

P4.29

Express the mass flow rate per unit width in terms of ρ, μ, g, θ, and h.

4.30 Water enters a wide, flat channel of height $2h$ with a uniform velocity of 2.5 m/s. At the channel outlet the velocity distribution is given by

$$\frac{u}{u_{max}} = 1 - \left(\frac{y}{h}\right)^2$$

where y is measured from the centerline of the channel. Determine the exit centerline velocity, u_{max}.

4.31 Water flows steadily through a pipe of length L and radius $R = 75$ mm. Calculate the uniform inlet velocity, U, if the velocity distribution across the outlet is given by

$$u = u_{max}\left[1 - \frac{r^2}{R^2}\right]$$

P4.31

and $u_{max} = 3$ m/s.

4.32 Incompressible fluid flows steadily through a plane diverging channel. At the inlet, of height H, the flow is uniform with magnitude V_1. At the outlet, of height $2H$, the velocity profile is

$$V_2 = V_m \cos\left(\frac{\pi y}{2H}\right)$$

where y is measured from the channel centerline. Express V_m in terms of V_1.

4.33 The velocity profile for laminar flow in an annulus is given by

$$u(r) = -\frac{\Delta p}{4\mu L}\left[R_o^2 - r^2 + \frac{R_o^2 - R_i^2}{\ln(R_i/R_o)}\ln\frac{R_o}{r}\right]$$

where $\Delta p/L = -10$ kPa/m is the pressure gradient, μ is the viscosity (SAE 10 oil at 20°C), and $R_o = 5$ mm and $R_i = 1$ mm are the outer and inner radii. Find the volume flow rate, the average velocity, and the maximum velocity. Plot the velocity distribution.

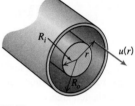

P4.33

4.34 A two-dimensional reducing bend has a linear velocity profile at section ①. The flow is uniform at sections ② and ③. The fluid is incompressible and the flow is steady. Find the magnitude and direction of the uniform velocity at section ③.

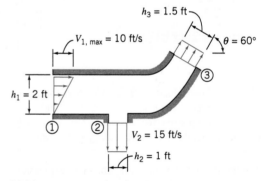

P4.34

4.35 Water enters a two-dimensional, square channel of constant width, $h = 75.5$ mm, with uniform velocity, U. The channel makes a 90° bend that distorts the flow to produce the linear velocity profile shown at the exit, with $v_{max} = 2\,v_{min}$. Evaluate v_{min}, if $U = 7.5$ m/s.

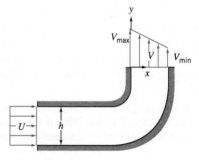

P4.35, 4.75, 4.92

4.36 A porous round tube with $D = 60$ mm carries water. The inlet velocity is uniform with $V_1 = 7.0$ m/s. Water flows radially and axisymmetrically outward through the porous walls with velocity distribution

$$v = V_0\left[1 - \left(\frac{x}{L}\right)^2\right]$$

where $V_0 = 0.03$ m/s and $L = 0.950$ m. Calculate the mass flow rate inside the tube at $x = L$.

4.37 A *hydraulic accumulator* is designed to reduce pressure pulsations in a machine tool hydraulic system. For the instant shown, determine the rate at which the accumulator gains or loses hydraulic oil.

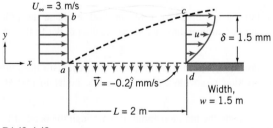

P4.37

4.38 A tank of 0.4 m^3 volume contains compressed air. A valve is opened and air escapes with a velocity of 250 m/s through an opening of 100 mm^2 area. Air temperature passing through the opening is $-20°$C and the absolute pressure is 300 kPa. Find the rate of change of density of the air in the tank at this moment.

4.39 Viscous liquid from a circular tank, $D = 300$ mm in diameter, drains through a long circular tube of radius $R = 50$ mm. The velocity profile at the tube discharge is

$$u = u_{max}\left[1 - \left(\frac{r}{R}\right)^2\right]$$

Show that the average speed of flow in the drain tube is $\bar{V} = \frac{1}{2}u_{max}$. Evaluate the rate of change of liquid level in the tank at the instant when $u_{max} = 0.155$ m/s.

4.40 Air enters a tank through an area of 0.2 ft^2 with a velocity of 15 ft/s and a density of 0.03 slug/ft^3. Air leaves with a velocity of 5 ft/s and a density equal to that in the tank. The initial density of the air in the tank is 0.02 slug/ft^3. The total tank volume is 20 ft^3 and the exit area is 0.4 ft^2. Find the initial rate of change of density in the tank.

4.41 A rectangular tank used to supply water for a Reynolds fl̶̶̶̶̶̶̶̶̶̶̶̶̶̶̶̶̶ ̶̶̶̶̶̶̶̶̶̶ ̶̶̶̶̶̶̶̶ ̶̶̶̶̶̶̶̶̶̶230 mm deep. Its width and length are $W = $

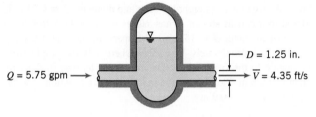

from the outlet tube (in-
olds number $Re = 2000$,
valve is closed. Find the
at this instant.

eter, drains through a hole
water depth is 0.6 m, the
be 4 kg/s. Determine the
ant.

owering Lake Shafer near
discharge through the dam
wing information for flow

Normal flow rate	290 cfs
Flow rate during draining of lake	2000 cfs

(The flow rate during draining was stated to be equivalent to $16,000$ gal/s.) The announcer also said that during draining the lake level was expected to fall at the rate of 1 ft every 8 hr. Calculate the actual flow rate during draining in gal/s. Estimate the surface area of the lake.

4.44 A cylindrical tank, of diameter $D = 50$ mm, drains through an opening, $d = 5$ mm, in the bottom of the tank. The speed of the liquid leaving the tank is approximately $V = \sqrt{2gy}$, where y is the height from the tank bottom to the free surface. If the tank is initially filled with water to $y_0 = 0.4$ m, determine the water depth at $t = 12$ s. Plot y/y_0 versus t with y_0 as a parameter for $0.1 \leq y_0 \leq 1$ m. Plot y/y_0 versus t with D/d as a parameter for $2 \leq D/d \leq 10$ and $y_0 = 0.4$ m.

4.45 For the conditions of Problem 4.44, estimate the time required to drain the tank to depth $y = 20$ mm. Plot time to drain the tank as a function of y/y_0 for $0.1 \leq y_0 \leq 1$ m with d/D as a parameter for $0.1 \leq d/D \leq 0.5$.

4.46 A conical flask contains water to height $H = 36.8$ mm, where the flask diameter is $D = 29.4$ mm. Water drains out through a smoothly rounded hole of diameter $d = 7.35$ mm at the apex of the cone. The flow speed at the exit is approximately $V = (2gy)^{1/2}$, where y is the height of the liquid free surface above the hole. A stream of water flows into the top of the flask at constant volume flow rate, $Q = 3.75 \times 10^{-7}$ m^3/hr. Find the volume flow rate from the bottom of the flask. Evaluate the direction and rate of change of water surface level in the flask at this instant.

4.47 A conical funnel of half-angle $\theta = 15°$, with maximum diameter $D = 70$ mm and height H, drains through a hole (diameter $d = 3.12$ mm) in its bottom. The speed of the liquid leaving the funnel is approximately $V = (2gy)^{1/2}$, where y is the height of the liquid free surface above the hole. Find the rate of change of surface level in the funnel at the instant when $y = H/2$.

4.48 Water flows steadily past a porous flat plate. Constant suction is applied along the porous section. The velocity profile at section cd is

$$\frac{u}{U_\infty} = 3\left[\frac{y}{\delta}\right] - 2\left[\frac{y}{\delta}\right]^{1.5}$$

Evaluate the mass flow rate across section bc.

P4.48, 4.49

4.49 Consider incompressible steady flow of standard air in a boundary layer on the length of porous surface shown. Assume the boundary layer at the downstream end of the surface has an approximately parabolic velocity profile, $u/U_\infty = 2(y/\delta) - (y/\delta)^2$. Uniform suction is applied along the porous surface, as shown. Calculate the volume flow rate across surface cd, through the porous suction surface, and across surface bc.

4.50 A tank of fixed volume contains brine with initial density, ρ_i, greater than water. Pure water enters the tank steadily and mixes thoroughly with the brine in the tank. The liquid level in the tank remains constant. Derive expressions for (a) the rate of change of density of the liquid mixture in the tank and (b) the time required for the density to reach the value ρ_f, where $\rho_i > \rho_f > \rho_{H_2O}$.

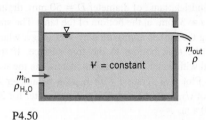

P4.50

4.51 A conical funnel of half-angle θ drains through a small hole of diameter d at the vertex. The speed of the liquid leaving the funnel is approximately $V = \sqrt{2gy}$, where y is the height of the liquid free surface above the hole. The funnel initially is filled to height y_0. Obtain an expression for the time, t, required to drain the funnel. Express the result in terms of the initial volume, V_0, of liquid in the funnel and the initial volume flow rate, $Q_0 = A\sqrt{2gy_0} = AV_0$. If the hole diameter is $d = 5$ mm, plot the time to drain the funnel as a function of y_0 over the range $0.1 \le y_0 \le 1$ m with angle θ as a parameter for $15° \le \theta \le 45°$.

4.52 Over time, air seeps through pores in the rubber of high-pressure bicycle tires. The saying is that a tire loses pressure at the rate of "a pound [1 psi] a day." The true rate of pressure loss is not constant; instead, the instantaneous leakage mass flow rate is proportional to the air density in the tire and to the gage pressure in the tire, $\dot{m} \propto \rho p$. Because the leakage rate is slow, air in the tire is nearly isothermal. Consider a tire that initially is inflated to 0.6 MPa (gage). Assume the initial rate of pressure loss is 1 psi per day. Estimate how long it will take for the pressure to drop to 500 kPa. How accurate is "a pound a day" over the entire 30 day period? Plot the pressure as a function of time over the 30 day period. Show the rule-of-thumb results for comparison.

4.53 Evaluate the net rate of flux of momentum out through the control surface of Problem 4.21.

4.54 For the conditions of Problem 4.30, evaluate the ratio of the x-direction momentum flux at the channel outlet to that at the inlet.

4.55 For the conditions of Problem 4.31, evaluate the ratio of the x-direction momentum flux at the pipe outlet to that at the inlet.

4.56 Evaluate the net momentum flux through the bend of Problem 4.34, if the depth normal to the diagram is $w = 3$ ft.

4.57 Evaluate the net momentum flux through the channel of Problem 4.35. Would you expect the outlet pressure to be higher, lower, or the same as the inlet pressure? Why?

4.58 What force (lbf) will a horizontal 2-in.-diameter stream of water moving at 20 ft/s generate upon hitting a vertical flat plate?

4.59 Considering that in the fully developed region of a pipe, the integral of the axial momentum is the same at all cross sections, explain the reason for the pressure drop along the pipe.

4.60 Find the force required to hold the plug in place at the exit of the water pipe. The flow rate is 1.5 m³/s, and the upstream pressure is 3.5 MPa.

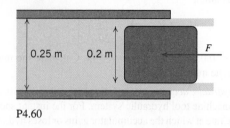

P4.60

4.61 A large tank of height $h = 1$ m and diameter $D = 0.75$ m is affixed to a cart as shown. Water issues from the tank through a nozzle of diameter $d = 15$ mm. The speed of the liquid leaving the tank is approximately $V = \sqrt{2gy}$ where y is the height from the nozzle to the free surface. Determine the tension in the wire when $y = 0.9$ m. Plot the tension in the wire as a function of water depth for $0 \le y \le 0.9$ m.

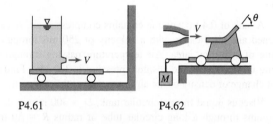

P4.61   P4.62

4.62 A jet of water issuing from a stationary nozzle at 10 m/s ($A_j = 0.1$ m²) strikes a turning vane mounted on a cart as shown. The vane turns the jet through angle $\theta = 40°$. Determine the value of M required to hold the cart stationary. If the vane angle θ is adjustable, plot the mass, M, needed to hold the cart stationary versus θ for $0 \le \theta \le 180°$.

4.63 A vertical plate has a sharp-edged orifice at its center. A water jet of speed V strikes the plate concentrically. Obtain an expression for the external force needed to hold the plate in place, if the jet leaving the orifice also has speed V. Evaluate the force for $V = 15$ ft/s, $D = 4$ in., and $d = 1$ in. Plot the required force as a function of diameter ratio for a suitable range of diameter d.

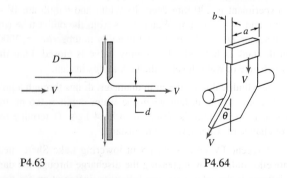

P4.63   P4.64

4.64 A circular cylinder inserted across a stream of flowing water deflects the stream through angle θ, as shown. (This is termed the "Coanda effect.") For $a = 12.5$ mm, $b = 2.5$ mm, $V = 3$ m/s, and $\theta = 20°$, determine the horizontal component of the force on the cylinder caused by the flowing water.

4.65 In a laboratory experiment, the water flow rate is to be measured catching the water as it vertically exits a pipe into an empty open cylindrical (3-ft diameter) tank that is on a zeroed balance. The tank bottom is 5 ft directly below the pipe exit, and the pipe diameter is 2 in. One student obtains a flow rate by noting that after 30 seconds the volume of water (at 50°F) in the tank was 15 ft^3. Another student obtains a flow rate by reading the instantaneous weight of 960 lb indicated at the 30-second point. Find the mass flow rate each student computes. Why do they disagree? Which one is more accurate? Show that the magnitude of the discrepancy can be explained by any concept you may have.

4.66 A tank of water sits on a cart with frictionless wheels as shown. The cart is attached using a cable to a 9 kg mass, and the coefficient of static friction of the mass with the ground is 0.5. At time $t = 0$, a second cable is used to remove a gate blocking the tank exit. Will the resulting exit flow be sufficient to start the tank moving? (Assume the water flow is frictionless.)

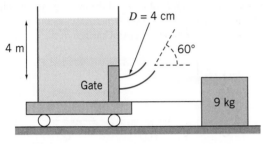

P4.66

4.67 A gate is 0.5 m wide and 0.6 m tall, and is hinged at the bottom. On one side the gate holds back a 0.5-m deep body of water. On the other side, a 10-cm diameter water jet hits the gate at a height of 0.5 m. What jet speed V is required to hold the gate vertical? What will the speed be if the body of water is lowered to 0.25 m? What will the speed be if the water level is at the top of the gate?

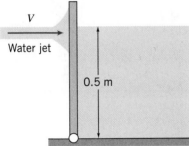

P4.67

4.68 A farmer purchases
The grain is loaded into hi
let diameter of 0.3 m. The
by observing the indicatec
time. The grain flow from
when the indicated scale r
the grain density is 600 kg.

4.69 Water flows steadi
hose is 75 mm inside dia
water gage pressure in the
the nozzle is uniform. The
atmospheric, respectively

coupling between the nozzle and hose. Indicate whether the coupling is in tension or compression.

4.70 Obtain expressions for the rate of change in mass of the control volume shown, as well as the horizontal and vertical forces required to hold it in place, in terms of $p_1, A_1, V_1, p_2, A_2, V_2, p_3, A_3, V_3, p_4, A_4, V_4$, and the constant density ρ.

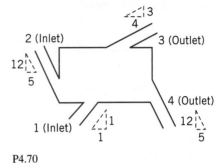

P4.70

4.71 A shallow circular dish has a sharp-edged orifice at its center. A water jet, of speed V, strikes the dish concentrically. Obtain an expression for the external force needed to hold the dish in place if the jet issuing from the orifice also has speed V. Evaluate the force for $V = 5$ m/s, $D = 100$ mm, and $d = 25$ mm. Plot the required force as a function of the angle θ ($0 \le \theta \le 90°$) with diameter ratio as a parameter for a suitable range of diameter d.

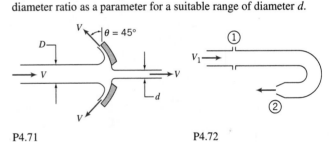

P4.71   P4.72

4.72 Water is flowing steadily through the 180° elbow shown. At the inlet to the elbow the gage pressure is 15 psi. The water discharges to atmospheric pressure. Assume properties are uniform over the inlet and outlet areas: $A_1 = 4$ in.^{2}, $A_2 = 1$ in.^{2}, and $V_1 = 10$ ft/s. Find the horizontal component of force required to hold the elbow in place.

4.73 A 180° elbow takes in water at an average velocity of 0.8 m/s and a pressure of 350 kPa (gage) at the inlet, where the diameter is 0.2 m. The exit pressure is 75 kPa, and the diameter is 0.04 m. What is the force required to hold the elbow in place?

4.74 Water flows steadily through the nozzle shown, discharging to atmosphere. Calculate the horizontal component of force ... the joint is in tension or

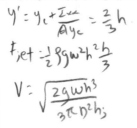

.35 is a segment of a larger
ane. The inlet pressure is

(handwritten notes):

$F_x = f_{s+} f_{Bx} = \frac{\partial}{\partial t}\int u\, \rho\, dV$
$+ \int_{cs} u\, \rho\, \vec{V} \cdot dA$

$F_R = p_c \cdot A$ $\frac{\partial}{\partial t}\eta_c + \frac{I_{xx}}{A \cdot y_c}$

$R_x = V \cdot \rho \,(-V \cdot A_{jet}) = -\rho V^2 \frac{\pi D^2}{4}$

$F_{jet} = -R_x = \rho V^2 \frac{\pi D^2}{4}$

$F_R = p_c A = \frac{1}{2}\rho g\, w h^2$

$y' = y_c + \frac{I_{xx}}{A y_c} = \frac{2}{3}h$

$f_{jet} = \frac{1}{2}\rho g w^2 h^2 \frac{2h}{3}$

$V = \sqrt{\frac{2 g w h^3}{3\pi D^2 h_j}}$

170 kPa (abs), and the outlet pressure is 130 kPa (abs). Find the force required to hold the bend in place.

4.76 A flat plate orifice of 2 in. diameter is located at the end of a 4-in. diameter pipe. Water flows through the pipe and orifice at 20 ft³/s. The diameter of the water jet downstream from the orifice is 1.5 in. Calculate the external force required to hold the orifice in place. Neglect friction on the pipe wall.

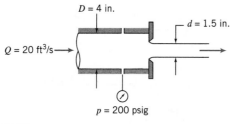

P4.76

4.77 A spray system is shown in the diagram. Water is supplied at $p = 1.45$ psig, through the flanged opening of area $A = 3$ in.² The water leaves in a steady free jet at atmospheric pressure. The jet area and speed are $a = 1.0$ in.² and $V = 15$ ft/s. The mass of the spray system is 0.2 lbm and it contains $\Psi = 12$ in.³ of water. Find the force exerted on the supply pipe by the spray system.

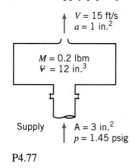

P4.77

4.78 The nozzle shown discharges a sheet of water through a 180° arc. The water speed is 15 m/s and the jet thickness is 30 mm at a radial distance of 0.3 m from the centerline of the supply pipe. Find (a) the volume flow rate of water in the jet sheet and (b) the y component of force required to hold the nozzle in place.

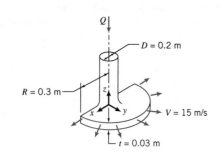

P4.78

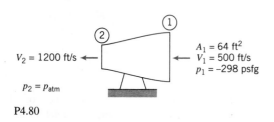

P4.80

4.79 At rated thrust, a liquid-fueled rocket motor consumes 80 kg/s of nitric acid as oxidizer and 32 kg/s of aniline as fuel. Flow leaves axially at 180 m/s relative to the nozzle and at 110 kPa. The nozzle exit diameter is $D = 0.6$ m. Calculate the thrust produced by the motor on a test stand at standard sea-level pressure.

4.80 A typical jet engine test stand installation is shown, together with some test data. Fuel enters the top of the engine vertically at a rate equal to 2 percent of the mass flow rate of the inlet air. For the given conditions, compute the air flow rate through the engine and estimate the thrust.

4.81 Consider flow through the sudden expansion shown. If the flow is incompressible and friction is neglected, show that the pressure rise, $\Delta p = p_2 - p_1$, is given by

$$\frac{\Delta p}{\frac{1}{2}\rho \overline{V}_1^2} = 2\left(\frac{d}{D}\right)^2\left[1 - \left(\frac{d}{D}\right)^2\right]$$

Plot the nondimensional pressure rise versus diameter ratio to determine the optimum value of d/D and the corresponding value of the nondimensional pressure rise. *Hint:* Assume the pressure is uniform and equal to p_1 on the vertical surface of the expansion.

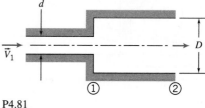

P4.81

4.82 A free jet of water with constant cross-section area 0.005 m² is deflected by a hinged plate of length 2 m supported by a spring with spring constant $k = 1$ N/m and uncompressed length $x_0 = 1$ m. Find and plot the deflection angle θ as a function of jet speed V. What jet speed has a deflection of 10°?

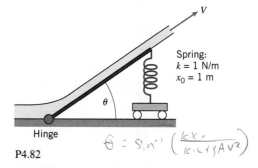

$$\theta = \sin^{-1}\left(\frac{kx_0}{k \cdot x + \rho A V^2}\right)$$

P4.82

4.83 A conical spray head is shown. The fluid is water and the exit stream is uniform. Evaluate (a) the thickness of the spray sheet at 400 mm radius and (b) the axial force exerted by the spray head on the supply pipe.

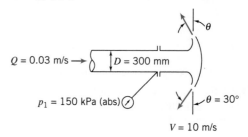

P4.83

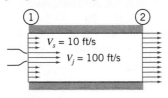

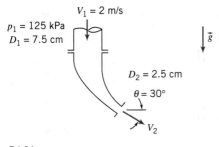

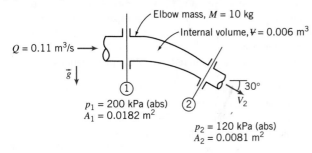

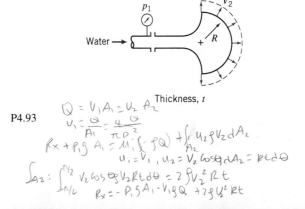

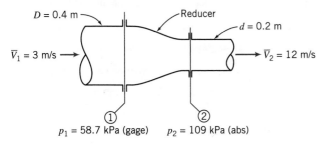

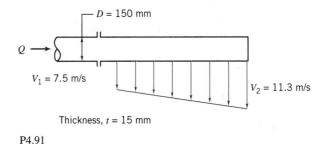

4.84   A curved nozzle assembly that discharges to the atmosphere is shown. The nozzle mass is 4.5 kg and its internal volume is 0.002 m³. The fluid is water. Determine the reaction force exerted by the nozzle on the coupling to the inlet pipe.

$V_1 = 2$ m/s
$p_1 = 125$ kPa
$D_1 = 7.5$ cm

$\vec{g}$

$D_2 = 2.5$ cm
$\theta = 30°$
V_2

P4.84

4.85   A reducer in a piping system is shown. The internal volume of the reducer is 0.2 m³ and its mass is 25 kg. Evaluate the total force that must be provided by the surrounding pipes to support the reducer. The fluid is gasoline.

$D = 0.4$ m   Reducer
                        $d = 0.2$ m
$\overline{V}_1 = 3$ m/s $\overline{V}_2 = 12$ m/s

①   ②
$p_1 = 58.7$ kPa (gage) $p_2 = 109$ kPa (abs)

P4.85

4.86   A water jet pump has jet area 0.1 ft² and jet speed 100 ft/s. The jet is within a secondary stream of water having speed $V_s =$ 10 ft/s. The total area of the duct (the sum of the jet and secondary stream areas) is 0.75 ft². The water is thoroughly mixed and leaves the jet pump in a uniform stream. The pressures of the jet and secondary stream are the same at the pump inlet. Determine the speed at the pump exit and the pressure rise, $p_2 - p_1$.

①   ②
$V_s = 10$ ft/s
$V_j = 100$ ft/s

P4.86

4.87   A 30° reducing elbow is shown. The fluid is water. Evaluate the components of force that must be provided by the adjacent pipes to keep the elbow from moving.

Elbow mass, $M = 10$ kg
Internal volume, $\forall = 0.006$ m³
$Q = 0.11$ m³/s
$\vec{g}$
①
$p_1 = 200$ kPa (abs)   ②
$A_1 = 0.0182$ m² $30°$
                              V_2
                  $p_2 = 120$ kPa (abs)
                  $A_2 = 0.0081$ m²

P4.87

4.88   A monotube boiler consists of a 20 ft length of tubing with 0.375 in. inside diameter. Water enters at the rate of 0.3 lbm/s at 500 psia. Steam leaves at 400 psig with 0.024 slug/ft³ density. Find the magnitude and direction of the force exerted by the flowing fluid on the tube.

4.89   Consider the steady adiabatic flow of air through a long straight pipe with 0.05 m² cross-sectional area. At the inlet, the air is at 200 kPa (gage), 60°C and has a velocity of 150 m/s. At the exit, the air is at 80 kPa and has a velocity of 300 m/s. Calculate the axial force of the air on the pipe. (Be sure to make the direction clear.)

4.90   A gas flows steadily through a heated porous pipe of constant 0.15 m² cross-sectional area. At the pipe inlet, the absolute pressure is 400 kPa, the density is 6 kg/m³, and the mean velocity is 170 m/s. The fluid passing through the porous wall leaves in a direction normal to the pipe axis, and the total flow rate through the porous wall is 20 kg/s. At the pipe outlet, the absolute pressure is 300 kPa and the density is 2.75 kg/m³. Determine the axial force of the fluid on the pipe.

4.91   Water is discharged from a narrow slot in a 150-mm diameter pipe. The resulting horizontal two-dimensional jet is 1 m long and 15 mm thick, but of nonuniform velocity. The pressure at the inlet section is 30 kPa (gage). Calculate (a) the volume flow rate at the inlet section and (b) the forces required at the coupling to hold the spray pipe in place. Neglect the mass of the pipe and the water it contains.

$D = 150$ mm
Q
$V_1 = 7.5$ m/s $V_2 = 11.3$ m/s

Thickness, $t = 15$ mm

P4.91

4.92   Water flows steadily through the square bend of Problem 4.35. Flow at the inlet is at $p_1 = 185$ kPa (abs). Flow at the exit is nonuniform, vertical, and at atmospheric pressure. The mass of the channel structure is $M_c = 2.05$ kg; the internal volume of the channel is $\forall = 0.00355$ m³. Evaluate the force exerted by the channel assembly on the supply duct.

4.93   A nozzle for a spray system is designed to produce a flat radial sheet of water. The sheet leaves the nozzle at $V_2 = 10$ m/s, covers 180° of arc, and has thickness $t = 1.5$ mm. The nozzle discharge radius is $R = 50$ mm. The water supply pipe is 35 mm in diameter and inlet pressure is $p_1 = 150$ kPa (abs). Evaluate the axial force exerted by the spray nozzle on the coupling.

p_1
            V_2
Water → $+$ R

Thickness, t

P4.93

$Q = V_1 A_1 = V_2 A_2$
$u_1 = \frac{Q}{A_1} = \frac{4Q}{\pi D^2}$
$R_x + p_1 g A_1 = u_1 \{-\rho Q\} + \int_{A_2} u_2 \rho V_2 dA_2$
$u_1 = V_1, \quad u_2 = V_2 \cos\theta \, dA_2 = R t \, d\theta$
$\int_{A_2} = \int_{-\pi/2}^{\pi/2} V_2 \cos\theta \rho V_2 R t \, d\theta = 2 \rho V_2^2 R t$
$R_x = -p_1 g A_1 - V_1 g Q + 2 \rho V_2^2 R t$

4.94 A small round object is tested in a 0.75-m diameter wind tunnel. The pressure is uniform across sections ① and ②. The upstream pressure is 30 mm H_2O (gage), the downstream pressure is 15 mm H_2O (gage), and the mean air speed is 12.5 m/s. The velocity profile at section ② is linear; it varies from zero at the tunnel centerline to a maximum at the tunnel wall. Calculate (a) the mass flow rate in the wind tunnel, (b) the maximum velocity at section ②, and (c) the drag of the object and its supporting vane. Neglect viscous resistance at the tunnel wall.

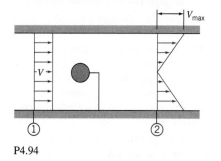

P4.94

4.95 The horizontal velocity in the wake behind an object in an air stream of velocity U is given by

$$u(r) = U\left[1 - \cos^2\left(\frac{\pi r}{2}\right)\right] \quad |r| \le 1$$

$$u(r) = U \quad |r| > 1$$

where r is the non-dimensional radial coordinate, measured perpendicular to the flow. Find an expression for the drag on the object.

4.96 An incompressible fluid flows steadily in the entrance region of a two-dimensional channel of height $2h$. The uniform velocity at the channel entrance is $U_1 = 7.5$ m/s. The velocity distribution at a section downstream is

$$\frac{u}{u_{max}} = 1 - \left[\frac{y}{h}\right]^2$$

Evaluate the maximum velocity at the downstream section. Calculate the pressure drop that would exist in the channel if viscous friction at the walls could be neglected.

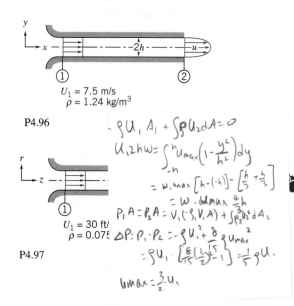

P4.96

$U_1 = 7.5$ m/s
$\rho = 1.24$ kg/m³

P4.97

$U_1 = 30$ ft/
$\rho = 0.075$

4.97 An incompressible fluid flows steadily in the entrance region of a circular tube of radius R. The uniform velocity at the tube entrance is $U_1 = 30$ ft/s. The velocity distribution at a section downstream is

$$\frac{u}{u_{max}} = 1 - \left[\frac{r}{R}\right]^2$$

Evaluate the maximum velocity at the downstream section. Calculate the pressure drop that would exist in the tube if viscous friction at the walls could be neglected.

4.98 Air enters a duct, of diameter $D = 25.0$ mm, through a well-rounded inlet with uniform speed, $U_1 = 0.870$ m/s. At a downstream section where $L = 2.25$ m, the fully developed velocity profile is

$$\frac{u(r)}{U_c} = 1 - \left(\frac{r}{R}\right)^2$$

The pressure drop between these sections is $p_1 - p_2 = 1.92$ N/m². Find the total force of friction exerted by the tube on the air.

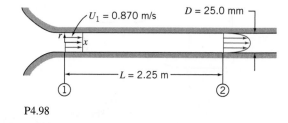

P4.98

4.99 Consider the incompressible flow of fluid in a boundary layer as depicted in Example 4.2. Show that the friction drag force of the fluid on the surface is given by

$$F_f = \int_0^\delta \rho u(U - u) w \, dy$$

Evaluate the drag force for the conditions of Example 4.2.

4.100 Air at standard conditions flows along a flat plate. The undisturbed freestream speed is $U_0 = 30$ ft/s. At $L = 6$ in. downstream from the leading edge of the plate, the boundary-layer thickness is $\delta = 0.1$ in. The velocity profile at this location is

$$\frac{u}{U_0} = \frac{3}{2}\frac{y}{\delta} - \frac{1}{2}\left[\frac{y}{\delta}\right]^3$$

Calculate the horizontal component of force per unit width required to hold the plate stationary.

4.101 Air at standard conditions flows along a flat plate. The undisturbed freestream speed is $U_0 = 20$ m/s. At $L = 0.4$ m downstream from the leading edge of the plate, the boundary-layer thickness is $\delta = 2$ mm. The velocity profile at this location is approximated as $u/U_0 = y/\delta$. Calculate the horizontal component of force per unit width required to hold the plate stationary.

4.102 A sharp-edged splitter plate inserted part way into a flat stream of flowing water produces the flow pattern shown. Analyze the situation to evaluate θ as a function of α, where $0 \le \alpha < 0.5$. Evaluate the force needed to hold the splitter plate in place. (Neglect any friction force between the water stream and the splitter plate.) Plot both θ and R_x as functions of α.

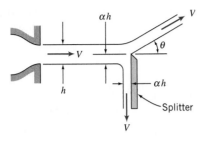

P4.102

4.103 When a plane liquid jet strikes an inclined flat plate, it splits into two streams of equal speed but unequal thickness. For frictionless flow there can be no tangential force on the plate surface. Use this assumption to develop an expression for h_2/h as a function of plate angle, θ. Plot your results and comment on the limiting cases, $\theta = 0$ and $\theta = 90°$.

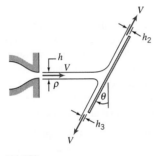

P4.103

4.104 Gases leaving the propulsion nozzle of a rocket are modeled as flowing radially outward from a point upstream from the nozzle throat. Assume the speed of the exit flow, V_e, has constant magnitude. Develop an expression for the axial thrust, T_a, developed by flow leaving the nozzle exit plane. Compare your result to the one-dimensional approximation, $T = \dot{m}V_e$. Evaluate the percent error for $\alpha = 15°$. Plot the percent error versus α for $0 \le \alpha \le 22.5°$.

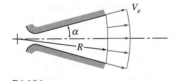

P4.104

*4.105 Two large tanks containing water have small smoothly contoured orifices of equal area. A jet of liquid issues from the left tank. Assume the flow is uniform and unaffected by friction. The jet impinges on a vertical flat plate covering the opening of the right tank. Determine the minimum value for the height, h, required to keep the plate in place over the opening of the right tank.

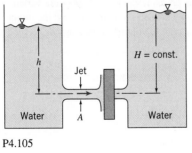

P4.105

*4.106 A horizontal axisymmetric jet of air with 0.5 in. diameter strikes a stationary vertical disk of 8 in. diameter. The jet speed is 225 ft/s at the nozzle exit. A manometer is connected to the center of the disk. Calculate (a) the deflection, h, if the manometer liquid has SG = 1.75 and (b) the force exerted by the jet on the disk.

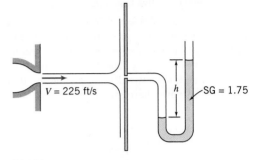

P4.106

*4.107 Students are planning a mock battle with water hoses on a campus lawn. The engineering students know that in order to have a greater impact on the adversary, it is advantageous to adjust the hose nozzle to create a narrower jet. How do they know this? Explain in terms of the force generated by a horizontal water jet impacting on a fixed vertical plane.

If 650 N is the maximum force that human skin can tolerate over a small area without damage, what is the maximum safe water flow (in liters per minute) that can be supplied to each hose when the minimum exit diameter of the nozzles is 6 mm?

*4.108 A uniform jet of water leaves a 15-mm diameter nozzle and flows directly downward. The jet speed at the nozzle exit plane is 2.5 m/s. The jet impinges on a horizontal disk and flows radially outward in a flat sheet. Obtain a general expression for the velocity the liquid stream would reach at the level of the disk. Develop an expression for the force required to hold the disk stationary, neglecting the mass of the disk and water sheet. Evaluate for $h = 3$ m.

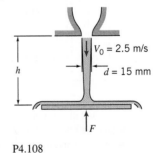

P4.108

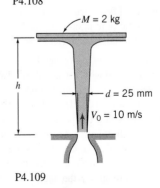

P4.109

*These problems require material from sections that may be omitted without loss of continuity in the text material.

*4.109   A 2-kg disk is constrained horizontally but is free to move vertically. The disk is struck from below by a vertical jet of water. The speed and diameter of the water jet are 10 m/s and 25 mm at the nozzle exit. Obtain a general expression for the speed of the water jet as a function of height, h. Find the height to which the disk will rise and remain stationary.

*4.110   Water from a jet of diameter D is used to support the cone-shaped object shown. Derive an expression for the combined mass of the cone and water, M, that can be supported by the jet, in terms of parameters associated with a suitably chosen control volume. Use your expression to calculate M when $V_0 = 10$ m/s, $H = 1$ m, $h = 0.8$ m, $D = 50$ mm, and $\theta = 30°$. Estimate the mass of water in the control volume.

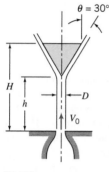

P4.110

*4.111   A stream of air at standard conditions from a 2-in. diameter nozzle strikes a curved vane as shown. A stagnation tube connected to a water-filled U-tube manometer is located in the nozzle exit plane. Calculate the speed of the air leaving the nozzle. Estimate the horizontal component of force exerted on the vane by the jet. Comment on each assumption used to solve this problem.

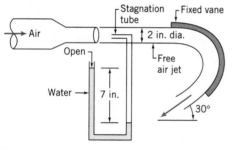

P4.111

*4.112   A Venturi meter installed along a water pipe consists of a convergent section, a constant-area throat, and a divergent section. The pipe diameter is $D = 100$ mm and the throat diameter is $d = 40$ mm. Find the net fluid force acting on the convergent section if the water pressure in the pipe is 600 kPa (gage) and the average velocity is 5 m/s. For this analysis neglect viscous effects.

*4.113   A plane nozzle discharges vertically downward to atmosphere. The nozzle is supplied with a steady flow of water. A stationary, inclined, flat plate, located beneath the nozzle, is struck by the water stream. The water stream divides and flows along the inclined plate; the two streams leaving the plate are of *unequal* thickness. Frictional effects are negligible in the nozzle and in the flow along the plate surface. Evaluate the minimum gage pressure required at the nozzle inlet. Calculate the magnitude and direction of the force exerted by the water stream on the inclined plate. Sketch the

pressure distribution along the surface of the plate. Explain why the pressure distribution is shaped the way you sketched it.

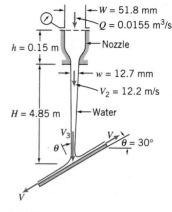

P4.113

*4.114   In ancient Egypt, circular vessels filled with water sometimes were used as crude clocks. The vessels were shaped in such a way that, as water drained from the bottom, the surface level dropped at constant rate, s. Assume that water drains from a small hole of area A. Find an expression for the radius of the vessel, r, as a function of the water level, h. Obtain an expression for the volume of water needed so that the clock will operate for n hours.

*4.115   A stream of incompressible liquid moving at low speed leaves a nozzle pointed directly upward. Assume the speed at any cross section is uniform and neglect viscous effects. The speed and area of the jet at the nozzle exit are V_0 and A_0, respectively. Apply conservation of mass and the momentum equation to a differential control volume of length dz in the flow direction. Derive expressions for the variations of jet speed and area as functions of z. Evaluate the vertical distance required to reduce the jet speed to zero. (Take the origin of coordinates at the nozzle exit.)

*4.116   A stream of incompressible liquid moving at low speed leaves a nozzle pointed directly downward. Assume the speed at any cross section is uniform and neglect viscous effects. The speed and area of the jet at the nozzle exit are V_0 and A_0, respectively. Apply conservation of mass and the momentum equation to a differential control volume of length dz in the flow direction. Derive expressions for the variations of jet speed and area as functions of z. Evaluate the distance at which the jet area is half its original value. (Take the origin of coordinates at the nozzle exit.)

*4.117   Incompressible fluid of negligible viscosity is pumped, at total volume flow rate Q, through a porous surface into the small gap between closely spaced parallel plates as shown. The fluid has only horizontal motion in the gap. Assume uniform flow across any vertical section. Obtain an expression for the pressure variation as a function of x. *Hint:* Apply conservation of mass and the momentum equation to a differential control volume of thickness dx, located at position x.

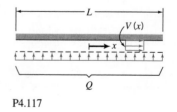

P4.117

*These problems require material from sections that may be omitted without loss of continuity in the text material.

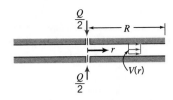

P4.118

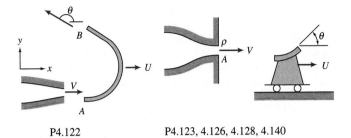

P4.122   P4.123, 4.126, 4.128, 4.140

*4.118 Incompressible liquid of negligible viscosity is pumped, at total volume flow rate Q, through two small holes into the narrow gap between closely spaced parallel disks as shown. The liquid flowing away from the holes has only radial motion. Assume uniform flow across any vertical section and discharge to atmospheric pressure at $r = R$. Obtain an expression for the pressure variation and plot as a function of radius. *Hint:* Apply conservation of mass and the momentum equation to a differential control volume of thickness dr located at radius r.

*4.119 The narrow gap between two closely spaced circular plates initially is filled with incompressible liquid. At $t = 0$ the upper plate begins to move downward toward the lower plate with constant speed, V_0, causing the liquid to be squeezed from the narrow gap. Neglecting viscous effects and assuming uniform flow in the radial direction, develop an expression for the velocity field between the parallel plates. *Hint:* Apply conservation of mass to a control volume with outer surface located at radius r. Note that even though the speed of the upper plate is constant, the flow is unsteady.

*4.120 Liquid falls vertically into a short horizontal rectangular open channel of width b. The total volume flow rate, Q, is distributed uniformly over area bL. Neglect viscous effects. Obtain an expression for h_1 in terms of h_2, Q, and b. *Hint:* Choose a control volume with outer boundary located at $x = L$. Sketch the surface profile, $h(x)$. *Hint:* Use a differential control volume of width dx.

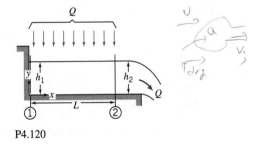

P4.120

*4.121 Design a clepsydra (Egyptian water clock)—a vessel from which water drains by gravity through a hole in the bottom and which indicates time by the level of the remaining water. Specify the dimensions of the vessel and the size of the drain hole; indicate the amount of water needed to fill the vessel and the interval at which it must be filled. Plot the vessel radius as a function of elevation.

4.122 A jet of water is directed against a vane, which could be a blade in a turbine or in any other piece of hydraulic machinery. The water leaves the stationary 40-mm diameter nozzle with a speed of 25 m/s and enters the vane tangent to the surface at A. The inside surface of the vane at B makes angle $\theta = 150°$ with the x direction. Compute the force that must be applied to maintain the vane speed constant at $U = 5$ m/s.

4.123 Water from a stationary nozzle impinges on a moving vane with turning angle $\theta = 120°$. The vane moves away from the nozzle with constant speed, $U = 10$ m/s, and receives a jet that leaves the nozzle with speed $V = 30$ m/s. The nozzle has an exit area of 0.004 m². Find the force that must be applied to maintain the vane speed constant.

4.124 The circular dish, whose cross section is shown, has an outside diameter of 0.20 m. A water jet with speed of 35 m/s strikes the dish concentrically. The dish moves to the left at 15 m/s. The jet diameter is 20 mm. The dish has a hole at its center that allows a stream of water 10 mm in diameter to pass through without resistance. The remainder of the jet is deflected and flows along the dish. Calculate the force required to maintain the dish motion.

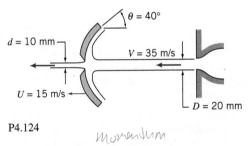

P4.124   Momentum

4.125 A jet boat takes in water at a constant volumetric rate Q through side vents and ejects it at a high jet speed V_j at the rear. A variable-area exit orifice controls the jet speed. The drag on the boat is given by $F_{drag} \approx kV^2$, where V is the boat speed. Find an expression for the steady speed V. If a jet speed $V_j = 25$ m/s produces a boat speed of 10 m/s, what jet speed will be required to double the boat speed?

4.126 $F_{drg} = V \cdot (-\rho Q) + V_j (\rho Q)$ rved blade that turns the flu $kV^2 + \rho Q V - \rho Q V_j = 0$ is 1200 mm² and its speed $V = -\frac{\rho Q}{2k} + \sqrt{(\frac{\rho Q}{2k})^2 + \frac{\rho Q V_j}{k}}$ /s. The blade moves towar $\alpha = \frac{\rho Q}{2k}$ orce that must be applied t $V = -\alpha + \sqrt{\alpha^2 + 2\alpha V_j}$

4.127 $V = 0$ aircraft is specially design $0 = -\alpha + \sqrt{\alpha^2 + 2.25\alpha}$ tion aircraft that can scoop from any lake, river, or oce $V = 0$ l during water scooping, a reasonable range of speeds

4.128 _____ ingle θ, moving horizontally at constant speed, U, under the influence of an impinging jet as in Problem 4.123. The absolute speed of the jet is V. Obtain general expressions for the resultant force and power that the vane could produce. Show that the power is maximized when $U = V/3$.

*These problems require material from sections that may be omitted without loss of continuity in the text material.

4.129   The circular dish, whose cross section is shown, has an outside diameter of 0.15 m. A water jet strikes the dish concentrically and then flows outward along the surface of the dish. The jet speed is 45 m/s and the dish moves to the left at 10 m/s. Find the thickness of the jet sheet at a radius of 75 mm from the jet axis. What horizontal force on the dish is required to maintain this motion?

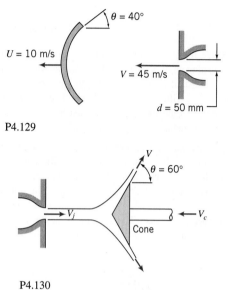

P4.129

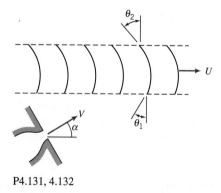

P4.130

4.130   Water, in a 4-in. diameter jet with speed of 100 ft/s to the right, is deflected by a cone that moves to the left at 45 ft/s. Determine (a) the thickness of the jet sheet at a radius of 9 in. and (b) the external horizontal force needed to move the cone.

4.131   Consider a series of turning vanes struck by a continuous jet of water that leaves a 50-mm diameter nozzle at constant speed, $V = 86.6$ m/s. The vanes move with constant speed, $U = 50$ m/s. Note that all the mass flow leaving the jet crosses the vanes. The curvature of the vanes is described by angles $\theta_1 = 30°$ and $\theta_2 = 45°$, as shown. Evaluate the nozzle angle, α, required to ensure that the jet enters tangent to the leading edge of each vane. Calculate the force that must be applied to maintain the vane speed constant.

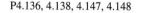

P4.131, 4.132

4.132   Consider again the moving multiple-vane system described in Problem 4.131. Assuming that a way could be found to make α nearly zero (and thus, θ_1 nearly 90°), evaluate the vane speed, U, that would result in maximum power output from the moving vane system.

4.133   A steady jet of water is used to propel a small cart along a horizontal track as shown. Total resistance to motion of the cart assembly is given by $F_D = kU^2$, where $k = 0.92$ N $\cdot$ s²/m². Evaluate the acceleration of the cart at the instant when its speed is $U = 10$ m/s.

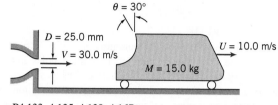

P4.133, 4.135, 4.139, 4.167

4.134   A plane jet of water strikes a splitter vane and divides into two flat streams as shown. Find the mass flow rate ratio, $\dot{m}_2/\dot{m}_3$, required to produce zero net vertical force on the splitter vane. Determine the horizontal force that must be applied under these conditions to maintain the vane motion at steady speed.

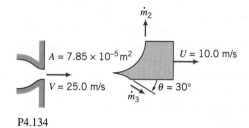

P4.134

4.135   The hydraulic catapult of Problem 4.133 is accelerated by a jet of water that strikes the curved vane. The cart moves along a level track with negligible resistance. At any time its speed is U. Calculate the time required to accelerate the cart from rest to $U = V/2$.

4.136   A vane/slider assembly moves under the influence of a liquid jet as shown. The coefficient of kinetic friction for motion of the slider along the surface is $\mu_k = 0.30$. Calculate the terminal speed of the slider.

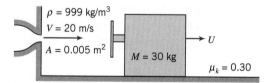

P4.136, 4.138, 4.147, 4.148

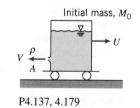

P4.137, 4.179

4.137   A cart is propelled by a liquid jet issuing horizontally from a tank as shown. The track is horizontal; resistance to motion may be neglected. The tank is pressurized so that the jet speed may be considered constant. Obtain a general expression for the speed of the cart as it accelerates from rest. If $M_0 = 100$ kg, $\rho = 999$ kg/m³, and $A = 0.005$ m², find the jet speed V required for the cart to reach a speed of 1.5 m/s after 30 seconds. For this condition, plot the cart speed U as a function of time. Plot the cart speed after 30 seconds as a function of jet speed.

4.138 For the vane/slider problem of Problem 4.136, find and plot expressions for the acceleration, speed, and position of the slider as a function of time.

4.139 If the cart of Problem 4.133 is released at $t = 0$, when would you expect the acceleration to be maximum? Sketch what you would expect for the curve of acceleration versus time. What value of θ would maximize the acceleration at any time? Why? Will the cart speed ever equal the jet speed? Explain briefly.

4.140 The acceleration of the vane/cart assembly of Problem 4.123 is to be controlled as it accelerates from rest by changing the vane angle, θ. A constant acceleration, $a = 1.5$ m/s², is desired. The water jet leaves the nozzle of area $A = 0.025$ m², with speed $V = 15$ m/s. The vane/cart assembly has a mass of 55 kg; neglect friction. Determine θ at $t = 5$ s. Plot $\theta(t)$ for the given constant acceleration over a suitable range of t.

4.141 The wheeled cart shown rolls with negligible resistance. The cart is to accelerate to the right at a constant rate of 2 m/s². This is to be accomplished by "programming" the water jet area, $A(t)$, that reaches the cart. The jet speed remains constant at 10 m/s. Obtain an expression for $A(t)$ required to produce the motion. Sketch the area variation for $t \leq 4$ s. Evaluate the jet area at $t = 2$ s.

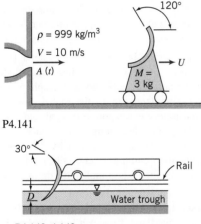

P4.141

P4.142, 4.143

4.142 A rocket sled, weighing 10,000 lbf and traveling 600 mph, is to be braked by lowering a scoop into a water trough. The scoop is 6 in. wide. Determine the time required (after lowering the scoop to a depth of 3 in. into the water) to bring the sled to a speed of 20 mph. Plot the sled speed as a function of time.

4.143 A rocket sled is to be slowed from an initial speed of 300 m/s by lowering a scoop into a water trough. The scoop is 0.3 m wide; it deflects the water through 150°. The trough is 800 m long. The mass of the sled is 8000 kg. At the initial speed it experiences an aerodynamic drag force of 90 kN. The aerodynamic force is proportional to the square of the sled speed. It is desired to slow the sled to 100 m/s. Determine the depth D to which the scoop must be lowered into the water.

4.144 Starting from rest, the cart shown is propelled by a hydraulic catapult (liquid jet). The jet strikes the curved surface and makes a 180° turn, leaving horizontally. Air and rolling resistance

may be neglected. If the mass of the cart is 100 kg and the jet of water leaves the nozzle (of area 0.001 m²) with a speed of 35 m/s, determine the speed of the cart 5 s after the jet is directed against the cart. Plot the cart speed as a function of time.

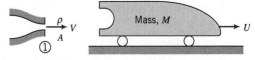

P4.144, 4.145, 4.168

4.145 Consider the jet and cart of Problem 4.144 again, but include an aerodynamic drag force proportional to the square of cart speed, $F_D = kU^2$, with $k = 2.0$ N · s²/m². Derive an expression for the cart acceleration as a function of cart speed and other given parameters. Evaluate the acceleration of the cart at $U = 10$ m/s. What fraction is this speed of the terminal speed of the cart?

4.146 A small cart that carries a single turning vane rolls on a level track. The cart mass is $M = 10.5$ kg and its initial speed is $U_0 = 12.5$ m/s. At $t = 0$, the vane is struck by an opposing jet of water, as shown. Neglect any external forces due to air or rolling resistance. Determine the time and distance needed for the liquid jet to bring the cart to rest. Plot the cart speed (nondimensionalized on U_0) and the distance traveled as functions of time.

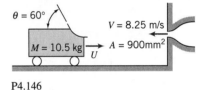

P4.146

4.147 Solve Problem 4.136 if the vane and slider ride on a film of oil instead of sliding in contact with the surface. Assume motion resistance is proportional to speed, $F_R = kU$, with $k = 7.5$ N · s/m.

4.148 For the vane/slider problem of Problem 4.147, find and plot expressions for the acceleration, speed, and position of the slider as functions of time. (Consider numerical integration.)

4.149 A rectangular block of mass M, with vertical faces, rolls without resistance along a smooth horizontal plane as shown. The block travels initially at speed U_0. At $t = 0$ the block is struck by a liquid jet and its speed begins to slow. Obtain an algebraic expression for the acceleration of the block for $t > 0$. Solve the equation to determine the time at which $U = 0$.

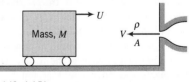

P4.149, 4.151

4.150 A rectangular block of mass M, with vertical faces, rolls on a horizontal surface between two opposing jets as shown. At $t = 0$ the block is set into motion at speed U_0. Subsequently, it moves without friction parallel to the jet axes with speed $U(t)$. Neglect the mass of any liquid adhering to the block compared with M. Obtain general expressions for the acceleration of the block, $a(t)$, and the block speed, $U(t)$.

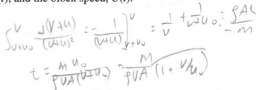

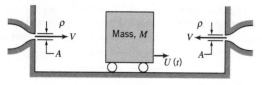

P4.150, 4.152

4.151 Consider the diagram of Problem 4.149. If $M = 100$ kg, $\rho = 999$ kg/m^3, and $A = 0.01$ m^2, find the jet speed V required for the cart to be brought to rest after one second if the initial speed of the cart is $U_0 = 5$ m/s. For this condition, plot the speed U and position x of the cart as functions of time. What is the maximum value of x, and how long does the cart take to return to its initial position?

4.152 Consider the statement and diagram of Problem 4.150. Assume that at $t = 0$, when the block is at $x = 0$, it is set into motion at speed $U_0 = 10$ m/s, to the right. Calculate the time required to reduce the block speed to $U = 0.5$ m/s, and the block position at that instant.

*4.153 A vertical jet of water impinges on a horizontal disk as shown. The disk assembly mass is 30 kg. When the disk is 3 m above the nozzle exit, it is moving upward at $U = 5$ m/s. Compute the vertical acceleration of the disk at this instant.

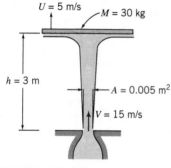

P4.153, 4.154, 4.175

*4.154 A vertical jet of water leaves a 75-mm diameter nozzle. The jet impinges on a horizontal disk (see Problem 4.153). The disk is constrained horizontally but is free to move vertically. The mass of the disk is 35 kg. Plot disk mass versus flow rate to determine the water flow rate required to suspend the disk 3 m above the jet exit plane.

4.155 A rocket sled traveling on a horizontal track is slowed by a retro-rocket fired in the direction of travel. The initial speed of the sled is $U_0 = 500$ m/s. The initial mass of the sled is $M_0 = 1500$ kg. The retro-rocket consumes fuel at the rate of 7.75 kg/s, and the exhaust gases leave the nozzle at atmospheric pressure and a speed of 2500 m/s relative to the rocket. The retro-rocket fires for 20 s. Neglect aerodynamic drag and rolling resistance. Obtain and plot an algebraic expression for sled speed U as a function of firing time. Calculate the sled speed at the end of retro-rocket firing.

4.156 A manned space capsule travels in level flight above the Earth's atmosphere at initial speed $U_0 = 8.00$ km/s. The capsule is to be slowed by a retro-rocket to $U = 5.00$ km/s in preparation for a reentry maneuver. The initial mass of the capsule is $M_0 = 1600$ kg. The rocket consumes fuel at $\dot{m} = 8.0$ kg/s, and exhaust

gases leave at $V_e = 3000$ m/s relative to the capsule and at negligible pressure. Evaluate the duration of the retro-rocket firing needed to accomplish this. Plot the final speed as a function of firing duration for a time range $\pm 10\%$ of this firing time.

4.157 A rocket sled accelerates from rest on a level track with negligible air and rolling resistances. The initial mass of the sled is $M_0 = 600$ kg. The rocket initially contains 150 kg of fuel. The rocket motor burns fuel at constant rate $\dot{m} = 15$ kg/s. Exhaust gases leave the rocket nozzle uniformly and axially at $V_e = 2900$ m/s relative to the nozzle, and the pressure is atmospheric. Find the maximum speed reached by the rocket sled. Calculate the maximum acceleration of the sled during the run.

4.158 A rocket sled has an initial mass of 4 metric tons, including 1 ton of fuel. The motion resistance in the track on which the sled rides and that of the air total kU, where k is 75 N $\cdot$ s/m, and U is the speed of the sled in m/s. The exit speed of the exhaust gas relative to the rocket is 1500 m/s, and the exit pressure is atmospheric. The rocket burns fuel at the rate of 75 kg/s. Compute the speed of the sled after 10 s. Plot the sled speed and acceleration as functions of time. Find the maximum speed.

4.159 A rocket sled with initial mass of 900 kg is to be accelerated on a level track. The rocket motor burns fuel at constant rate $\dot{m} = 13.5$ kg/s. The rocket exhaust flow is uniform and axial. Gases leave the nozzle at 2750 m/s relative to the nozzle, and the pressure is atmospheric. Determine the minimum mass of rocket fuel needed to propel the sled to a speed of 265 m/s before burnout occurs. As a first approximation, neglect resistance forces.

4.160 A rocket motor is used to accelerate a kinetic energy weapon to a speed of 3500 mph in horizontal flight. The exit stream leaves the nozzle axially and at atmospheric pressure with a speed of 6000 mph relative to the rocket. The rocket motor ignites upon release of the weapon from an aircraft flying horizontally at $U_0 = 600$ mph. Neglecting air resistance, obtain an algebraic expression for the speed reached by the weapon in level flight. Determine the minimum fraction of the initial mass of the weapon that must be fuel to accomplish the desired acceleration.

4.161 A rocket sled with initial mass of 3 metric tons, including 1 ton of fuel, rests on a level section of track. At $t = 0$, the solid fuel of the rocket is ignited and the rocket burns fuel at the rate of 75 kg/s. The exit speed of the exhaust gas relative to the rocket is 2500 m/s, and the pressure is atmospheric. Neglecting friction and air resistance, calculate the acceleration and speed of the sled at $t = 10$ s.

4.162 A daredevil considering a record attempt—for the world's longest motorcycle jump—asks for your consulting help: He must reach 875 km/hr (from a standing start on horizontal ground) to make the jump, so he needs rocket propulsion. The total mass of the motorcycle, the rocket motor without fuel, and the rider is 375 kg. Gases leave the rocket nozzle horizontally, at atmospheric pressure, with a speed of 2510 m/s. Evaluate the minimum amount of rocket fuel needed to accelerate the motorcycle and rider to the required speed.

4.163 A "home-made" solid propellant rocket has an initial mass of 20 lbm; 15 lbm of this is fuel. The rocket is directed vertically upward from rest, burns fuel at a constant rate of 0.5 lbm/s, and ejects exhaust gas at a speed of 6500 ft/s relative to the rocket. Assume that the pressure at the exit is atmospheric and that air

---

*These problems require material from sections that may be omitted without loss of continuity in the text material.

resistance may be neglected. Calculate the rocket speed after 20 s and the distance traveled by the rocket in 20 s. Plot the rocket speed and the distance traveled as functions of time.

4.164 A large two-stage liquid rocket with mass of 30,000 kg is to be launched from a sea-level launch pad. The main engine burns liquid hydrogen and liquid oxygen in a stoichiometric mixture at 2450 kg/s. The thrust nozzle has an exit diameter of 2.6 m. The exhaust gases exit the nozzle at 2270 m/s and an exit plane pressure of 66 kPa absolute. Calculate the acceleration of the rocket at liftoff. Obtain an expression for speed as a function of time, neglecting air resistance.

4.165 Neglecting air resistance, what speed would a vertically directed rocket attain in 8 s if it starts from rest, has initial mass of 300 kg, burns 8 kg/s, and ejects gas at atmospheric pressure with a speed of 3000 m/s relative to the rocket? Plot the rocket speed as a function of time.

4.166 Inflate a toy balloon with air and release it. Watch as the balloon darts about the room. Explain what causes the phenomenon you see.

4.167 The vane/cart assembly of mass $M = 30$ kg, shown in Problem 4.123, is driven by a water jet. The water leaves the stationary nozzle of area $A = 0.02$ m^2, with a speed of 20 m/s. The coefficient of kinetic friction between the assembly and the surface is 0.10. Plot the terminal speed of the assembly as a function of vane turning angle, θ, for $0 \le \theta \le \pi/2$. At what angle does the assembly begin to move if the coefficient of static friction is 0.15?

4.168 Consider the vehicle shown in Problem 4.144. Starting from rest, it is propelled by a hydraulic catapult (liquid jet). The jet strikes the curved surface and makes a 180° turn, leaving horizontally. Air and rolling resistance may be neglected. Using the notation shown, obtain an equation for the acceleration of the vehicle at any time and determine the time required for the vehicle to reach $U = V/2$.

4.169 The moving tank shown is to be slowed by lowering a scoop to pick up water from a trough. The initial mass and speed of the tank and its contents are M_0 and U_0, respectively. Neglect external forces due to pressure or friction and assume that the track is horizontal. Apply the continuity and momentum equations to show that at any instant $U = U_0 M_0/M$. Obtain a general expression for U/U_0 as a function of time.

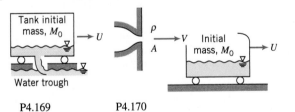

P4.169   P4.170

4.170 The tank shown rolls with negligible resistance along a horizontal track. It is to be accelerated from rest by a liquid jet that strikes the vane and is deflected into the tank. The initial mass of the tank is M_0. Use the continuity and momentum equations to show that at any instant the mass of the vehicle and liquid contents is $M = M_0 V/(V - U)$. Obtain a general expression for U/V as a function of time.

4.171 A model solid propellant rocket has a mass of 69.6 g, of which 12.5 g is fuel. The rocket produces 5.75 N of thrust for a duration of 1.7 s. For these conditions, calculate the maximum speed and height attainable in the absence of air resistance. Plot the rocket speed and the distance traveled as functions of time.

4.172 A small rocket motor is used to power a "jet pack" device to lift a single astronaut above the Earth's surface. The rocket motor produces a uniform exhaust jet with constant speed, $V_e = 2940$ m/s. The total initial mass of the astronaut and the jet pack is $M_0 = 130$ kg. Of this, 40 kg is fuel for the rocket motor. Develop an algebraic expression for the variable fuel mass flow rate required to keep the jet pack and astronaut hovering in a fixed position above the ground. Calculate the maximum hover time aloft before the fuel supply is expended.

*4.173 Several toy manufacturers sell water "rockets" that consist of plastic tanks to be partially filled with water and then pressurized with air. Upon release, the compressed air forces water out of the nozzle rapidly, propelling the rocket. You are asked to help specify optimum conditions for this water-jet propulsion system. To simplify the analysis, consider horizontal motion only. Perform the analysis and design needed to define the acceleration performance of the compressed air/water-propelled rocket. Identify the fraction of tank volume that initially should be filled with compressed air to achieve optimum performance (i.e., maximum speed from the water charge). Describe the effect of varying the initial air pressure in the tank.

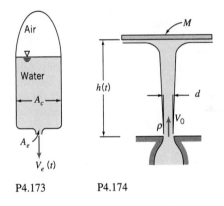

P4.173   P4.174

*4.174 A disk, of mass M, is constrained horizontally but is free to move vertically. A jet of water strikes the disk from below. The jet leaves the nozzle at initial speed V_0. Obtain a differential equation for the disk height, $h(t)$, above the jet exit plane if the disk is released from large height, H. Assume that when the disk reaches equilibrium, its height above the jet exit plane is h_0. Sketch $h(t)$ for the disk released at $t = 0$ from $H > h_0$. Explain why the sketch is as you show it.

*4.175 Consider the configuration of the vertical jet impinging on a horizontal disk shown in Problem 4.153. Assume the disk is released from rest at an initial height of 2 m above the jet exit plane. Solve for the subsequent motion of this disk. Identify the steady-state height of the disk.

4.176 A small solid-fuel rocket motor is fired on a test stand. The combustion chamber is circular, with 100 mm diameter. Fuel,

*These problems require material from sections that may be omitted without loss of continuity in the text material.

of density 1660 kg/m³, burns uniformly at the rate of 12.7 mm/s. Measurements show that the exhaust gases leave the rocket at ambient pressure, at a speed of 2750 m/s. The absolute pressure and temperature in the combustion chamber are 7.0 MPa and 3610 K, respectively. Treat the combustion products as an ideal gas with molecular mass of 25.8. Evaluate the rate of change of mass and of linear momentum within the rocket motor. Express the rate of change of linear momentum within the motor as a percentage of the motor thrust.

*4.177   The capability of the Aircraft Landing Loads and Traction Facility at NASA's Langley Research Center is to be upgraded. The facility consists of a rail-mounted carriage propelled by a jet of water issuing from a pressurized tank. (The setup is identical in concept to the hydraulic catapult of Problem 4.133.) Specifications require accelerating the carriage with 49,000 kg mass to a speed of 220 knots in a distance of 122 m. (The vane turning angle is 170°.) Identify a range of water jet sizes and speeds needed to accomplish this performance. Specify the recommended operating pressure for the water-jet system and determine the shape and estimated size of tankage to contain the pressurized water.

*4.178   A classroom demonstration of linear momentum is planned, using a water-jet propulsion system for a cart traveling on a horizontal linear air track. The track is 5 m long, and the cart mass is 155 g. The objective of the design is to obtain the best performance for the cart, using 1 L of water contained in an open cylindrical tank made from plastic sheet with density of 0.0819 g/cm². For stability, the maximum height of the water tank cannot exceed 0.5 m. The diameter of the smoothly rounded water jet may not exceed 10 percent of the tank diameter. Determine the best dimensions for the tank and the water jet by modeling the system performance. Plot acceleration, velocity, and distance as functions of time. Find the optimum dimensions of the water tank and jet opening from the tank. Discuss the limitations on your analysis. Discuss how the assumptions affect the predicted performance of the cart. Would the actual performance of the cart be better or worse than predicted? Why? What factors account for the difference(s)?

*4.179   Analyze the design and optimize the performance of a cart propelled along a horizontal track by a water jet that issues under gravity from an open cylindrical tank carried on board the cart. (A water-jet-propelled cart is shown in the diagram for Problem 4.137.) Neglect any change in slope of the liquid free surface in the tank during acceleration. Analyze the motion of the cart along a horizontal track, assuming it starts from rest and begins to accelerate when water starts to flow from the jet. Derive algebraic equations or solve numerically for the acceleration and speed of the cart as functions of time. Present results as plots of acceleration and speed versus time, neglecting the mass of the tank. Determine the dimensions of a tank of minimum mass required to accelerate the cart from rest along a horizontal track to a specified speed in a specified time interval.

*4.180   A large irrigation sprinkler unit, mounted on a cart, discharges water with a speed of 40 m/s at an angle of 30° to the horizontal. The 50 mm diameter nozzle is 3 m above the ground. The mass of the sprinkler and cart is $M = 350$ kg. Calculate the magnitude of the moment that tends to overturn the cart. What value of V will cause impending motion? What will be the nature

of the impending motion? What is the effect of the angle of jet inclination on the results? For the case of impending motion, plot the jet velocity as a function of the angle of jet inclination over an appropriate range of the angles.

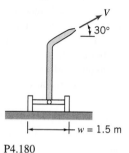

P4.180

*4.181   The 90° reducing elbow of Example 4.6 discharges to atmosphere. Section ② is located 0.3 m to the right of Section ①. Estimate the moment exerted by the flange on the elbow.

*4.182   Crude oil (SG = 0.95) from a tanker dock flows through a pipe of 0.25 m diameter in the configuration shown. The flow rate is 0.58 m³/s, and the gage pressures are shown in the diagram. Determine the force and torque that are exerted by the pipe assembly on its supports.

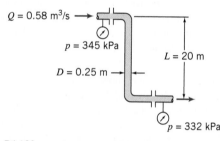

P4.182

*4.183   The simplified lawn sprinkler shown rotates in the horizontal plane. At the center pivot, $Q = 4.5$ gpm of water enters vertically. Water discharges in the horizontal plane from each jet. If the pivot is frictionless, calculate the torque needed to keep the sprinkler from rotating. Neglecting the inertia of the sprinkler itself, calculate the angular acceleration that results when the torque is removed.

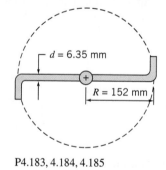

P4.183, 4.184, 4.185

*4.184   Consider the sprinkler of Problem 4.183 again. Derive a differential equation for the angular speed of the sprinkler as a function of time. Evaluate its steady-state speed of rotation if there is no friction in the pivot.

*4.185   Repeat Problem 4.184, but assume a constant retarding torque in the pivot of 0.045 ft · lbf.

*These problems require material from sections that may be omitted without loss of continuity in the text material.

*4.186 Water flows in a uniform flow out of the 5 mm slots of the rotating spray system as shown. The flow rate is 15 kg/s. Find the torque required to hold the system stationary, and the steady-state speed of rotation after it is released.

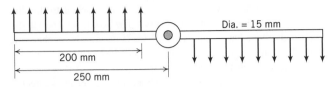

Dia. = 15 mm

200 mm

250 mm

P4.186, 4.187

4.187 If the same flow rate in the rotating spray system of Problem 4.186 is not uniform but instead varies linearly from a maximum at the outer radius to zero at a point 50 mm from the axis, find the torque required to hold it stationary, and the steady-state speed of rotation.

*4.188 A single tube carrying water rotates at constant angular speed, as shown. Water is pumped through the tube at volume flow rate $Q = 13.8$ L/min. Find the torque that must be applied to maintain the steady rotation of the tube using two methods of analysis: (a) a rotating control volume and (b) a fixed control volume.

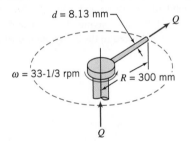

$d = 8.13$ mm

Q

$\omega = 33\text{-}1/3$ rpm

$R = 300$ mm

Q

P4.188

*4.189 The lawn sprinkler shown is supplied with water at a rate of 68 L/min. Neglecting friction in the pivot, determine the steady-state angular speed for $\theta = 30°$. Plot the steady-state angular speed of the sprinkler for $0 \leq \theta \leq 90°$.

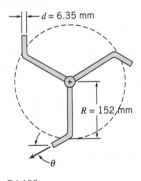

$d = 6.35$ mm

$R = 152$ mm

θ

P4.189

*4.190 A small lawn sprinkler is shown. The sprinkler operates at a gage pressure of 140 kPa. The total flow rate of water through the sprinkler is 4 L/min. Each jet discharges at 17 m/s (relative to the sprinkler arm) in a direction inclined 30° above the horizontal. The sprinkler rotates about a vertical axis. Friction in the bearing causes a torque of 0.18 N · m opposing rotation. Evaluate the torque required to hold the sprinkler stationary.

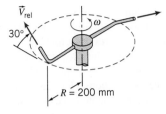

$\vec{V}_{rel}$

ω

30°

$R = 200$ mm

P4.190, 4.191, 4.192

*4.191 In Problem 4.190, calculate the initial acceleration of the sprinkler from rest if no external torque is applied and the moment of inertia of the sprinkler head is 0.1 kg · m² when filled with water.

*4.192 A small lawn sprinkler is shown (Problem 4.190). The sprinkler operates at an inlet gage pressure of 140 kPa. The total flow rate of water through the sprinkler is 4.0 L/min. Each jet discharges at 17 m/s (relative to the sprinkler arm) in a direction inclined 30° above the horizontal. The sprinkler rotates about a vertical axis. Friction in the bearing causes a torque of 0.18 N · m opposing rotation. Determine the steady speed of rotation of the sprinkler and the approximate area covered by the spray.

*4.193 When a garden hose is used to fill a bucket, water in the bucket may develop a swirling motion. Why does this happen? How could the amount of swirl be calculated approximately?

*4.194 Water flows at the rate of 0.15 m³/s through a nozzle assembly that rotates steadily at 30 rpm. The arm and nozzle masses are negligible compared with the water inside. Determine the torque required to drive the device and the reaction torques at the flange.

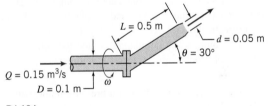

$L = 0.5$ m

$d = 0.05$ m

$\theta = 30°$

$Q = 0.15$ m³/s

ω

$D = 0.1$ m

P4.194

*4.195 A pipe branches symmetrically into two legs of length L, and the whole system rotates with angular speed ω around its axis of symmetry. Each branch is inclined at angle α to the axis of rotation. Liquid enters the pipe steadily, with zero angular momentum, at volume flow rate Q. The pipe diameter, D, is much smaller than L. Obtain an expression for the external torque required to turn the pipe. What additional torque would be required to impart angular acceleration $\dot{\omega}$?

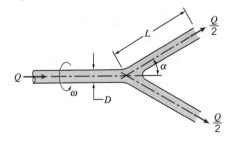

L

$\frac{Q}{2}$

α

Q

ω

D

$\frac{Q}{2}$

P4.195

*These problems require material from sections that may be omitted without loss of continuity in the text material.

*4.196 Liquid in a thin sheet, of width w and thickness h, flows from a slot and strikes a stationary inclined flat plate, as shown. Experiments show that the resultant force of the liquid jet on the plate does not act through point O, where the jet centerline intersects the plate. Determine the magnitude and line of application of the resultant force as functions of θ. Evaluate the equilibrium angle of the plate if the resultant force is applied at point O. Neglect any viscous effects.

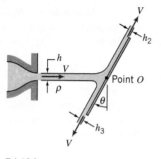

P4.196

 *4.197 For the rotating sprinkler of Example 4.14, what value of α will produce the maximum rotational speed? What angle will provide the maximum area of coverage by the spray? Draw a velocity diagram (using an r, θ, z coordinate system) to indicate the absolute velocity of the water jet leaving the nozzle. What governs the steady rotational speed of the sprinkler? Does the rotational speed of the sprinkler affect the area covered by the spray? How would you estimate the area? For fixed α, what might be done to increase or decrease the area covered by the spray?

4.198 Air at standard conditions enters a compressor at 75 m/s and leaves at an absolute pressure and temperature of 200 kPa and 345 K, respectively, and speed $V = 125$ m/s. The flow rate is 1 kg/s. The cooling water circulating around the compressor casing removes 18 kJ/kg of air. Determine the power required by the compressor.

4.199 Compressed air is stored in a pressure bottle with a volume of 0.5 m³, at 20 MPa and 60°C. At a certain instant a valve is opened and mass flows from the bottle at $\dot{m} = 0.05$ kg/s. Find the rate of change of temperature in the bottle at this instant.

4.200 A centrifugal water pump with a 0.1-m diameter inlet and a 0.1-m diameter discharge pipe has a flow rate of 0.02 m³/s. The inlet pressure is 0.2 m Hg vacuum and the exit pressure is 240 kPa. The inlet and outlet sections are located at the same elevation. The measured power input is 6.75 kW. Determine pump efficiency.

4.201 A turbine is supplied with 0.6 m³/s of water from a 0.3-m diameter pipe; the discharge pipe has a 0.4 m diameter. Determine the pressure drop across the turbine if it delivers 60 kW.

4.202 Air enters a compressor at 14 psia, 80°F with negligible speed and is discharged at 70 psia, 500°F with a speed of 500 ft/s. If the power input is 3200 hp and the flow rate is 20 lbm/s, determine the rate of heat transfer.

4.203 Air is drawn from the atmosphere into a turbomachine. At the exit, conditions are 500 kPa (gage) and 130°C. The exit speed is 100 m/s and the mass flow rate is 0.8 kg/s. Flow is steady and there is no heat transfer. Compute the shaft work interaction with the surroundings.

4.204 All major harbors are equipped with fire boats for extinguishing ship fires. A 3-in. diameter hose is attached to the discharge of a 15-hp pump on such a boat. The nozzle attached to the end of the hose has a diameter of 1 in. If the nozzle discharge is held 10 ft above the surface of the water, determine the volume flow rate through the nozzle, the maximum height to which the water will rise, and the force on the boat if the water jet is directed horizontally over the stern.

4.205 A pump draws water from a reservoir through a 150-mm diameter suction pipe and delivers it to a 75-mm diameter discharge pipe. The end of the suction pipe is 2 m below the free surface of the reservoir. The pressure gage on the discharge pipe (2 m above the reservoir surface) reads 170 kPa. The average speed in the discharge pipe is 3 m/s. If the pump efficiency is 75 percent, determine the power required to drive it.

*4.206 The total mass of the helicopter-type craft shown is 1500 kg. The pressure of the air is atmospheric at the outlet. Assume the flow is steady and one-dimensional. Treat the air as incompressible at standard conditions and calculate, for a hovering position, the speed of the air leaving the craft and the minimum power that must be delivered to the air by the propeller.

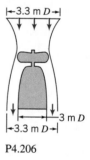

P4.206

4.207 Liquid flowing at high speed in a wide, horizontal open channel under some conditions can undergo a hydraulic jump, as shown. For a suitably chosen control volume, the flows entering and leaving the jump may be considered uniform with hydrostatic pressure distributions (see Example 4.7). Consider a channel of width w, with water flow at $D_1 = 0.6$ m and $V_1 = 5$ m/s. Show that in general, $D_2 = D_1[\sqrt{1 + 8V_1^2/gD_1} - 1]/2$. Evaluate the change in mechanical energy through the hydraulic jump. If heat transfer to the surroundings is negligible, determine the change in water temperature through the jump.

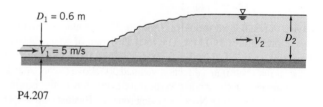

P4.207

*These problems require material from sections that may be omitted without loss of continuity in the text material.

Chapter 5

Introduction to Differential Analysis of Fluid Motion

5-1 CONSERVATION OF MASS

5-2 STREAM FUNCTION FOR TWO-DIMENSIONAL INCOMPRESSIBLE FLOW

5-3 MOTION OF A FLUID PARTICLE (KINEMATICS)

5-4 MOMENTUM EQUATION

5-5 INTRODUCTION TO COMPUTATIONAL FLUID DYNAMICS

5-6 SUMMARY AND USEFUL EQUATIONS

CASE STUDY

Olympic Swimming and Bobsledding

CFD simulation of water flow over typical female elite swimmer in the glide position showing contours of shear stress. (Courtesy of Speedo and Fluent Inc.)

Athletes in many competitive sports are using technology to gain an advantage. In recent years, Fastskin® fabric has been developed by Speedo. This material allows the lowest-drag racing swimwear in the world to be developed. The fabric mimics the rough denticles of sharks' skin to reduce drag in key areas of the body. (Shark scales are tiny compared with those of most fishes and have a toothlike structure, called dermal denticles—literally, "tiny skin teeth." These denticles are nature's way of reducing drag on the shark.) Detailed design of swimsuits was based on tests in a water flume and on computational fluid dynamics (CFD) analyses. The figure shows an example of the results obtained. To optimize the suits, the results were used to guide the position of the seams; gripper panels on the underside of the forearms; and "vortex" riblets on the chest, shoulders, and back of the suit—as well as the positioning of different patches of fabric and fabric coatings.

The same technology is now being used to make outfits for athletes in the bobsled and luge events in the winter Olympics. The fabric has been modified, based on wind tunnel tests, to reduce drag based on the airflow direction unique to sledding sports. The new outfits also eliminate most of the fabric vibration (a major source of drag) found in other speed suits.

For both summer and winter sports, the ability to perform experimental and theoretical fluid dynamics analysis and make design changes based on these can make the difference in speed of several percent—the difference between silver and gold!

In Chapter 4, we developed the basic equations in integral form for a control volume. Integral equations are useful when we are interested in the gross behavior of a flow field and its effect on various devices. However, the integral approach does not enable us to obtain detailed point-by-point knowledge of the flow field. For example, the integral approach could provide information on the lift generated by a wing; it could not be used to determine the pressure distribution that produced the lift on the wing.

To see what is happening in a flow in detail, we need differential forms of the equations of motion. In this chapter we shall develop differential equations for the conservation of mass and Newton's second law of motion. Since we are interested in developing differential equations, we will need to analyze infinitesimal systems and control volumes.

5-1   ## CONSERVATION OF MASS

In Chapter 2, we developed the field representation of fluid properties. The property fields are defined by continuous functions of the space coordinates and time. The density and velocity fields were related through conservation of mass in integral form in Chapter 4 (Eq. 4.12). In this chapter we shall derive the differential equation for conservation of mass in rectangular and in cylindrical coordinates. In both cases the derivation is carried out by applying conservation of mass to a differential control volume.

Rectangular Coordinate System

In rectangular coordinates, the control volume chosen is an infinitesimal cube with sides of length dx, dy, dz as shown in Fig. 5.1. The density at the center, O, of the control volume is assumed to be ρ and the velocity there is assumed to be $\vec{V} = \hat{i}u + \hat{j}v + \hat{k}w$.

To evaluate the properties at each of the six faces of the control surface, we use a Taylor series expansion about point O. For example, at the right face,

$$\rho)_{x+dx/2} = \rho + \left(\frac{\partial \rho}{\partial x}\right)\frac{dx}{2} + \left(\frac{\partial^2 \rho}{\partial x^2}\right)\frac{1}{2!}\left(\frac{dx}{2}\right)^2 + \cdots$$

Neglecting higher-order terms, we can write

$$\rho)_{x+dx/2} = \rho + \left(\frac{\partial \rho}{\partial x}\right)\frac{dx}{2}$$

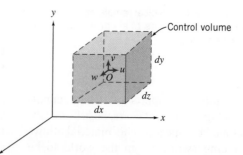

Fig. 5.1 Differential control volume in rectangular coordinates.

and

$$u)_{x+dx/2} = u + \left(\frac{\partial u}{\partial x}\right)\frac{dx}{2}$$

where ρ, u, $\partial\rho/\partial x$, and $\partial u/\partial x$ are all evaluated at point O. The corresponding terms at the left face are

$$\rho)_{x-dx/2} = \rho + \left(\frac{\partial \rho}{\partial x}\right)\left(-\frac{dx}{2}\right) = \rho - \left(\frac{\partial \rho}{\partial x}\right)\frac{dx}{2}$$

$$u)_{x-dx/2} = u + \left(\frac{\partial u}{\partial x}\right)\left(-\frac{dx}{2}\right) = u - \left(\frac{\partial u}{\partial x}\right)\frac{dx}{2}$$

We can write similar expressions involving ρ and v for the front and back faces and ρ and w for the top and bottom faces of the infinitesimal cube $dx\,dy\,dz$. These can then be used to evaluate the surface integral in Eq. 4.12 (recall that $\int_{CS} \rho\vec{V} \cdot d\vec{A}$ is the net flux of mass out of the control volume):

$$\frac{\partial}{\partial t}\int_{CV} \rho d\mathcal{V} + \int_{CS} \rho\vec{V} \cdot d\vec{A} = 0 \qquad (4.12)$$

Table 5.1 shows the details of this evaluation. Note: We assume that the velocity components u, v, and w are positive in the x, y, and z directions, respectively; the area normal is by convention positive out of the cube; and higher-order terms [e.g., $(dx)^2$] are neglected in the limit as dx, dy, and $dz \to 0$.

The result of all this work is

$$\left[\frac{\partial \rho u}{\partial x} + \frac{\partial \rho v}{\partial x} + \frac{\partial \rho w}{\partial x}\right] dx\,dy\,dz$$

This expression is the surface integral evaluation for our differential cube. To complete Eq. 4.12, we need to evaluate the volume integral (recall that $\partial/\partial t\int_{CV} \rho d\mathcal{V}$ is the rate of change of mass in the control volume):

$$\frac{\partial}{\partial t}\int_{CV} \rho d\mathcal{V} \to \frac{\partial}{\partial t}\left[\rho dx\,dy\,dz\right] = \frac{\partial \rho}{\partial t} dx\,dy\,dz$$

Hence, we obtain (after canceling $dx\,dy\,dz$) from Eq. 4.12 a differential form of the mass conservation law

$$\frac{\partial \rho u}{\partial x} + \frac{\partial \rho v}{\partial y} + \frac{\partial \rho w}{\partial z} + \frac{\partial \rho}{\partial t} = 0 \qquad (5.1a)$$

Equation 5.1a is frequently called the *continuity equation*.

Since the vector operator, ∇, in rectangular coordinates, is given by

$$\nabla = \hat{i}\frac{\partial}{\partial x} + \hat{j}\frac{\partial}{\partial y} + \hat{k}\frac{\partial}{\partial z}$$

then

$$\frac{\partial \rho u}{\partial x} + \frac{\partial \rho v}{\partial y} + \frac{\partial \rho w}{\partial z} = \nabla \cdot \rho\vec{V}$$

Note that the del operator ∇ acts on ρ *and* $\vec{V}$. Think of it as $\nabla \cdot (\rho\vec{V})$. The conservation of mass may be written as

$$\nabla \cdot \rho\vec{V} + \frac{\partial \rho}{\partial t} = 0 \qquad (5.1b)$$

TABLE 5.1 Mass Flux through the Control Surface of a Rectangular Differential Control Volume

Surface	Evaluation of $\int \rho \vec{V} \cdot d\vec{A}$

Left
$(-x)$
$$= -\left[\rho - \left(\frac{\partial \rho}{\partial x}\right)\frac{dx}{2}\right]\left[u - \left(\frac{\partial u}{\partial x}\right)\frac{dx}{2}\right] dy\,dz = -\rho u\,dy\,dz + \frac{1}{2}\left[u\left(\frac{\partial \rho}{\partial x}\right) + \rho\left(\frac{\partial u}{\partial x}\right)\right] dx\,dy\,dz$$

Right
$(+x)$
$$= \left[\rho + \left(\frac{\partial \rho}{\partial x}\right)\frac{dx}{2}\right]\left[u + \left(\frac{\partial u}{\partial x}\right)\frac{dx}{2}\right] dy\,dz = \rho u\,dy\,dz + \frac{1}{2}\left[u\left(\frac{\partial \rho}{\partial x}\right) + \rho\left(\frac{\partial u}{\partial x}\right)\right] dx\,dy\,dz$$

Bottom
$(-y)$
$$= -\left[\rho - \left(\frac{\partial \rho}{\partial y}\right)\frac{dy}{2}\right]\left[v - \left(\frac{\partial v}{\partial y}\right)\frac{dy}{2}\right] dx\,dz = -\rho v\,dx\,dz + \frac{1}{2}\left[v\left(\frac{\partial \rho}{\partial y}\right) + \rho\left(\frac{\partial v}{\partial y}\right)\right] dx\,dy\,dz$$

Top
$(+y)$
$$= \left[\rho + \left(\frac{\partial \rho}{\partial y}\right)\frac{dy}{2}\right]\left[v + \left(\frac{\partial v}{\partial y}\right)\frac{dy}{2}\right] dx\,dz = \rho v\,dx\,dz + \frac{1}{2}\left[v\left(\frac{\partial \rho}{\partial y}\right) + \rho\left(\frac{\partial v}{\partial y}\right)\right] dx\,dy\,dz$$

Back
$(-z)$
$$= -\left[\rho - \left(\frac{\partial \rho}{\partial z}\right)\frac{dz}{2}\right]\left[w - \left(\frac{\partial w}{\partial z}\right)\frac{dz}{2}\right] dx\,dy = -\rho w\,dx\,dy + \frac{1}{2}\left[w\left(\frac{\partial \rho}{\partial z}\right) + \rho\left(\frac{\partial w}{\partial z}\right)\right] dx\,dy\,dz$$

Front
$(+z)$
$$= \left[\rho + \left(\frac{\partial \rho}{\partial z}\right)\frac{dz}{2}\right]\left[w + \left(\frac{\partial w}{\partial z}\right)\frac{dz}{2}\right] dx\,dy = \rho w\,dx\,dy + \frac{1}{2}\left[w\left(\frac{\partial \rho}{\partial z}\right) + \rho\left(\frac{\partial w}{\partial z}\right)\right] dx\,dy\,dz$$

Adding the results for all six faces,

$$\int_{CS} \rho \vec{V} \cdot d\vec{A} = \left[\left\{u\left(\frac{\partial \rho}{\partial x}\right) + \rho\left(\frac{\partial u}{\partial x}\right)\right\} + \left\{v\left(\frac{\partial \rho}{\partial y}\right) + \rho\left(\frac{\partial v}{\partial y}\right)\right\} + \left\{w\left(\frac{\partial \rho}{\partial z}\right) + \rho\left(\frac{\partial w}{\partial z}\right)\right\}\right] dx\,dy\,dz$$

or

$$\int_{CS} \rho \vec{V} \cdot d\vec{A} = \left[\frac{\partial \rho u}{\partial x} + \frac{\partial \rho v}{\partial y} + \frac{\partial \rho w}{\partial z}\right] dx\,dy\,dz$$

Two flow cases for which the differential continuity equation may be simplified are worthy of note.

For an *incompressible* fluid, ρ = constant; density is neither a function of space coordinates nor a function of time. For an incompressible fluid, the continuity equation simplifies to

$$\frac{\partial u}{\partial x} + \frac{\partial v}{\partial y} + \frac{\partial w}{\partial z} = \nabla \cdot \vec{V} = 0 \qquad (5.1c)$$

Thus the velocity field, $\vec{V}(x, y, z, t)$, for incompressible flow must satisfy $\nabla \cdot \vec{V} = 0$.

For *steady* flow, all fluid properties are, by definition, independent of time. Thus $\partial \rho/\partial t = 0$ and at most $\rho = \rho(x, y, z)$. For steady flow, the continuity equation can be written as

$$\frac{\partial \rho u}{\partial x} + \frac{\partial \rho v}{\partial y} + \frac{\partial \rho w}{\partial z} = \nabla \cdot \rho \vec{V} = 0 \qquad (5.1d)$$

(and remember that the del operator ∇ acts on ρ *and* $\vec{V}$).

Example 5.1 Integration of Two-Dimensional Differential Continuity Equation

For a two-dimensional flow in the xy plane, the x component of velocity is given by $u = Ax$. Determine a possible y component for incompressible flow. How many y components are possible?

GIVEN: Two-dimensional flow in the xy plane for which $u = Ax$.

FIND: (a) Possible y component for incompressible flow.
(b) Number of possible y components.

SOLUTION:

Governing equation: $\nabla \cdot \rho \vec{V} + \dfrac{\partial \rho}{\partial t} = 0$

For incompressible flow this simplifies to $\nabla \cdot \vec{V} = 0$. In rectangular coordinates

$$\frac{\partial u}{\partial x} + \frac{\partial v}{\partial y} + \frac{\partial w}{\partial z} = 0$$

For two-dimensional flow in the xy plane, $\vec{V} = \vec{V}(x, y)$. Then partial derivatives with respect to z are zero, and

$$\frac{\partial u}{\partial x} + \frac{\partial v}{\partial y} = 0$$

Then

$$\frac{\partial v}{\partial y} = -\frac{\partial u}{\partial x} = -A$$

which gives an expression for the rate of change of v holding x constant. This equation can be integrated to obtain an expression for v. The result is

$$v = \int \frac{\partial v}{\partial y} dy + f(x, t) = -Ay + f(x, t) \underline{\hspace{6cm}} v$$

{The function of x and t appears because we had a partial derivative of v with respect to y.}

Any function $f(x, t)$ is allowable, since $\partial/\partial y \, f(x, t) = 0$. Thus any number of expressions for v could satisfy the differential continuity equation under the given conditions. The simplest expression for v would be obtained by setting $f(x, t) = 0$. Then $v = -Ay$, and

$$\vec{V} = Ax\hat{i} - Ay\hat{j} \underline{\hspace{6cm}} \vec{V}$$

This problem:
✓ Shows use of the differential continuity equation for obtaining information on a flow field.
✓ Demonstrates integration of a partial derivative.
✓ Proves that the flow originally discussed in Example 2.1 is indeed incompressible.

Example 5.2 Unsteady Differential Continuity Equation

A gas-filled pneumatic strut in an automobile suspension system behaves like a piston-cylinder apparatus. At one instant when the piston is $L = 0.15$ m away from the closed end of the cylinder, the gas density is uniform at $\rho = 18$ kg/m^3 and the piston begins to move away from the closed end at $V = 12$ m/s. Assume as a simple model that the gas velocity is one-dimensional and proportional to distance from the closed end; it varies linearly from zero at the end to $u = V$ at the piston. Find the rate of change of gas density at this instant. Obtain an expression for the average density as a function of time.

GIVEN: Piston-cylinder as shown.

FIND: (a) Rate of change of density.
(b) $\rho(t)$.

SOLUTION:

Governing equation: $\nabla \cdot \rho \vec{V} + \dfrac{\partial \rho}{\partial t} = 0$

In rectangular coordinates, $\dfrac{\partial \rho u}{\partial x} + \dfrac{\partial \rho v}{\partial y} + \dfrac{\partial \rho w}{\partial z} + \dfrac{\partial \rho}{\partial t} = 0$

Since $u = u(x)$, partial derivatives with respect to y and z are zero, and

$$\frac{\partial \rho u}{\partial x} + \frac{\partial \rho}{\partial t} = 0$$

Then

$$\frac{\partial \rho}{\partial t} = -\frac{\partial \rho u}{\partial x} = -\rho \frac{\partial u}{\partial x} - u \frac{\partial \rho}{\partial x}$$

Since ρ is assumed uniform in the volume, $\dfrac{\partial \rho}{\partial x} = 0$, and $\dfrac{\partial \rho}{\partial t} = \dfrac{d\rho}{dt} = -\rho \dfrac{\partial u}{\partial x}$.

Since $u = V\dfrac{x}{L}$, $\dfrac{\partial u}{\partial x} = \dfrac{V}{L}$, then $\dfrac{d\rho}{dt} = -\rho \dfrac{V}{L}$. However, note that $L = L_0 + Vt$.

Separate variables and integrate,

$$\int_{\rho_0}^{\rho} \frac{d\rho}{\rho} = -\int_0^t \frac{V}{L} dt = -\int_0^t \frac{V\,dt}{L_0 + Vt}$$

$$\ln \frac{\rho}{\rho_0} = \ln \frac{L_0}{L_0 + Vt} \qquad \text{and} \qquad \rho(t) = \rho_0 \left[\frac{1}{1 + Vt/L_0} \right] \underline{\hspace{3cm}} \rho(t)$$

At $t = 0$,

$$\frac{\partial \rho}{\partial t} = -\rho_0 \frac{V}{L} = -18 \frac{\text{kg}}{\text{m}^3} \times 12 \frac{\text{m}}{\text{s}} \times \frac{1}{0.15\,\text{m}} = -1440 \text{ kg/(m}^3 \cdot \text{s)} \underleftarrow{\hspace{2cm}} \frac{\partial \rho}{\partial t}$$

This problem demonstrates use of the differential continuity equation for obtaining the density variation with time for an unsteady flow.

 The density-time graph is shown in an *Excel* workbook. This workbook is interactive: It allows one to see the effect of different values of ρ_0, L, and V on ρ versus t. Also, the time at which the density falls to any prescribed value can be determined.

Cylindrical Coordinate System

A suitable differential control volume for cylindrical coordinates is shown in Fig. 5.2. The density at the center, O, of the control volume is assumed to be ρ and the velocity there is assumed to be $\vec{V} = \hat{e}_r V_r + \hat{e}_\theta V_\theta + \hat{k} V_z$, where $\hat{e}_r$, $\hat{e}_\theta$, and $\hat{k}$ are unit vectors in the r, θ, and z directions, respectively, and V_r, V_θ, and V_z are the velocity components in the r, θ, and z directions, respectively. To evaluate $\int_{CS} \rho \vec{V} \cdot d\vec{A}$, we must consider the mass flux through each of the six faces of the control surface. The properties at each of the six faces of the control surface are obtained from a Taylor series expansion about point O. The details of the mass flux evaluation are shown in Table 5.2. Velocity components V_r, V_θ, and V_z are all assumed to be in the positive coordinate directions and we have again used the convention that the area normal is positive outwards on each face, and higher-order terms have been neglected.

We see that the net rate of mass flux out through the control surface (the term $\int_{CS} \rho \vec{V} \cdot d\vec{A}$ in Eq. 4.12) is given by

$$\left[\rho V_r + r \frac{\partial \rho V_r}{\partial r} + \frac{\partial \rho V_\theta}{\partial \theta} + r \frac{\partial \rho V_z}{\partial z} \right] dr \, d\theta \, dz$$

The mass inside the control volume at any instant is the product of the mass per unit volume, ρ, and the volume, $r \, d\theta \, dr \, dz$. Thus the rate of change of mass inside the control volume (the term $\partial/\partial t \int_{CV} \rho \, d\Psi$ in Eq. 4.12) is given by

$$\frac{\partial \rho}{\partial t} r \, d\theta \, dr \, dz$$

In cylindrical coordinates the differential equation for conservation of mass is then

$$\rho V_r + r \frac{\partial \rho V_r}{\partial r} + \frac{\partial \rho V_\theta}{\partial \theta} + r \frac{\partial \rho V_z}{\partial z} + r \frac{\partial \rho}{\partial t} = 0$$

or

$$\frac{\partial(r\rho V_r)}{\partial r} + \frac{\partial \rho V_\theta}{\partial \theta} + r \frac{\partial \rho V_z}{\partial z} + r \frac{\partial \rho}{\partial t} = 0$$

Dividing by r gives

$$\frac{1}{r} \frac{\partial(r\rho V_r)}{\partial r} + \frac{1}{r} \frac{\partial(\rho V_\theta)}{\partial \theta} + \frac{\partial(\rho V_z)}{\partial z} + \frac{\partial \rho}{\partial t} = 0 \qquad (5.2a)$$

In cylindrical coordinates the vector operator ∇ is given by

$$\nabla = \hat{e}_r \frac{\partial}{\partial r} + \hat{e}_\theta \frac{1}{r} \frac{\partial}{\partial \theta} + \hat{k} \frac{\partial}{\partial z} \qquad (3.19)$$

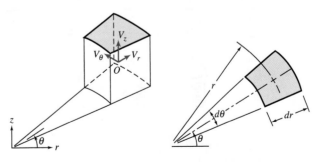

(a) Isometric view   (b) Projection on $r\theta$ plane

Fig. 5.2 Differential control volume in cylindrical coordinates.

TABLE 5.2 Mass Flux through the Control Surface of a Cylindrical Differential Control Volume

Surface	Evaluation of $\int \rho\vec{V}\cdot d\vec{A}$
Inside $(-r)$	$= -\left[\rho - \left(\dfrac{\partial \rho}{\partial r}\right)\dfrac{dr}{2}\right]\left[V_r - \left(\dfrac{\partial V_r}{\partial r}\right)\dfrac{dr}{2}\right]\left(r - \dfrac{dr}{2}\right)d\theta\,dz = -\rho V_r\,rd\theta\,dz + \rho V_r\dfrac{dr}{2}d\theta\,dz + \rho\left(\dfrac{\partial V_r}{\partial r}\right)r\dfrac{dr}{2}d\theta\,dz + V_r\left(\dfrac{\partial \rho}{\partial r}\right)r\dfrac{dr}{2}d\theta\,dz$
Outside $(+r)$	$= \left[\rho + \left(\dfrac{\partial \rho}{\partial r}\right)\dfrac{dr}{2}\right]\left[V_r + \left(\dfrac{\partial V_r}{\partial r}\right)\dfrac{dr}{2}\right]\left(r + \dfrac{dr}{2}\right)d\theta\,dz = \rho V_r\,rd\theta\,dz + \rho V_r\dfrac{dr}{2}d\theta\,dz + \rho\left(\dfrac{\partial V_r}{\partial r}\right)r\dfrac{dr}{2}d\theta\,dz + V_r\left(\dfrac{\partial \rho}{\partial r}\right)r\dfrac{dr}{2}d\theta\,dz$
Front $(-\theta)$	$= -\left[\rho - \left(\dfrac{\partial \rho}{\partial \theta}\right)\dfrac{d\theta}{2}\right]\left[V_\theta - \left(\dfrac{\partial V_\theta}{\partial \theta}\right)\dfrac{d\theta}{2}\right]dr\,dz = -\rho V_\theta\,dr\,dz + \rho\left(\dfrac{\partial V_\theta}{\partial \theta}\right)\dfrac{d\theta}{2}dr\,dz + V_\theta\left(\dfrac{\partial \rho}{\partial \theta}\right)\dfrac{d\theta}{2}dr\,dz$
Back $(+\theta)$	$= \left[\rho + \left(\dfrac{\partial \rho}{\partial \theta}\right)\dfrac{d\theta}{2}\right]\left[V_\theta + \left(\dfrac{\partial V_\theta}{\partial \theta}\right)\dfrac{d\theta}{2}\right]dr\,dz = \rho V_\theta\,dr\,dz + \rho\left(\dfrac{\partial V_\theta}{\partial \theta}\right)\dfrac{d\theta}{2}dr\,dz + V_\theta\left(\dfrac{\partial \rho}{\partial \theta}\right)\dfrac{d\theta}{2}dr\,dz$
Bottom $(-z)$	$= -\left[\rho - \left(\dfrac{\partial \rho}{\partial z}\right)\dfrac{dz}{2}\right]\left[V_z - \left(\dfrac{\partial V_z}{\partial z}\right)\dfrac{dz}{2}\right]rd\theta\,dr = -\rho V_z\,rd\theta\,dr + \rho\left(\dfrac{\partial V_z}{\partial z}\right)\dfrac{dz}{2}rd\theta\,dr + V_z\left(\dfrac{\partial \rho}{\partial z}\right)\dfrac{dz}{2}rd\theta\,dr$
Top $(+z)$	$= \left[\rho + \left(\dfrac{\partial \rho}{\partial z}\right)\dfrac{dz}{2}\right]\left[V_z + \left(\dfrac{\partial V_z}{\partial z}\right)\dfrac{dz}{2}\right]rd\theta\,dr = \rho V_z\,rd\theta\,dr + \rho\left(\dfrac{\partial V_z}{\partial z}\right)\dfrac{dz}{2}rd\theta\,dr + V_z\left(\dfrac{\partial \rho}{\partial z}\right)\dfrac{dz}{2}rd\theta\,dr$

Adding the results for all six faces,

$$\int_{CS} \rho\vec{V}\cdot d\vec{A} = \left[\rho V_r + r\left\{\rho\left(\frac{\partial V_r}{\partial r}\right) + V_r\left(\frac{\partial \rho}{\partial r}\right)\right\} + \left\{\rho\left(\frac{\partial V_\theta}{\partial \theta}\right) + V_\theta\left(\frac{\partial \rho}{\partial \theta}\right)\right\} + r\left\{\rho\left(\frac{\partial V_z}{\partial z}\right) + V_z\left(\frac{\partial \rho}{\partial z}\right)\right\}\right]dr\,d\theta\,dz$$

or

$$\int_{CS} \rho\vec{V}\cdot d\vec{A} = \left[\rho V_r + r\frac{\partial \rho V_r}{\partial r} + \frac{\partial \rho V_\theta}{\partial \theta} + r\frac{\partial \rho V_z}{\partial z}\right]dr\,d\theta\,dz$$

Equation 5.2a also may be written[1] in vector notation as

$$\nabla \cdot \rho\vec{V} + \frac{\partial \rho}{\partial t} = 0 \tag{5.1b}$$

For an *incompressible* fluid, ρ = constant, and Eq. 5.2a reduces to

$$\frac{1}{r}\frac{\partial(rV_r)}{\partial r} + \frac{1}{r}\frac{\partial V_\theta}{\partial \theta} + \frac{\partial V_z}{\partial z} = \nabla \cdot \vec{V} = 0 \tag{5.2b}$$

Thus the velocity field, $\vec{V}(x, y, z, t)$, for incompressible flow must satisfy $\nabla \cdot \vec{V} = 0$. For *steady* flow, Eq. 5.2a reduces to

$$\frac{1}{r}\frac{\partial(r\rho V_r)}{\partial r} + \frac{1}{r}\frac{\partial(\rho V_\theta)}{\partial \theta} + \frac{\partial(\rho V_z)}{\partial z} = \nabla \cdot \rho\vec{V} = 0 \tag{5.2c}$$

(and remember once again that the del operator ∇ acts on ρ *and* $\vec{V}$).

When written in vector form, the differential continuity equation (the mathematical statement of conservation of mass), Eq. 5.1b, may be applied in any coordinate system. We simply substitute the appropriate expression for the vector operator ∇. In retrospect, this result is not surprising since mass must be conserved regardless of our choice of coordinate system.

Example 5.3   Differential Continuity Equation in Cylindrical Coordinates

Consider a one-dimensional radial flow in the $r\theta$ plane, given by $V_r = f(r)$ and $V_\theta = 0$. Determine the conditions on $f(r)$ required for the flow to be incompressible.

GIVEN: One-dimensional radial flow in the $r\theta$ plane: $V_r = f(r)$ and $V_\theta = 0$.

FIND: Requirements on $f(r)$ for incompressible flow.

SOLUTION:

Governing equation: $\nabla \cdot \rho\vec{V} + \dfrac{\partial \rho}{\partial t} = 0$

For incompressible flow in cylindrical coordinates this reduces to Eq. 5.2b,

$$\frac{1}{r}\frac{\partial}{\partial r}(rV_r) + \frac{1}{r}\frac{\partial}{\partial \theta}V_\theta + \frac{\partial V_z}{\partial z} = 0$$

For the given velocity field, $\vec{V} = \vec{V}(r)$. $V_\theta = 0$ and partial derivatives with respect to z are zero, so

$$\frac{1}{r}\frac{\partial}{\partial r}(rV_r) = 0$$

Integrating with respect to r gives

$$rV_r = \text{constant}$$

Thus the continuity equation shows that the radial velocity must be $V_r = f(r) = C/r$ for one-dimensional radial flow of an incompressible fluid. This is not a surprising result: As the fluid moves outwards from the center, the volume flow rate (per unit depth in the z direction) $Q = 2\pi rV$ at any radius r is constant.

---

[1] To evaluate $\nabla \cdot \rho\vec{V}$ in cylindrical coordinates, we must remember that

$$\frac{\partial \hat{e}_r}{\partial \theta} = \hat{e}_\theta \quad \text{and} \quad \frac{\partial \hat{e}_\theta}{\partial \theta} = -\hat{e}_r$$

*5.2 STREAM FUNCTION FOR TWO-DIMENSIONAL INCOMPRESSIBLE FLOW

We already briefly discussed streamlines in Chapter 2, where we stated that they were lines tangent to the velocity vectors in a flow at an instant

$$\left.\frac{dy}{dx}\right|_{\text{streamline}} = \frac{v}{u} \tag{2.8}$$

We can now develop a more formal definition of streamlines by introducing the *stream function*, ψ. This will allow us to represent two entities—the velocity components $u(x, y, t)$ and $v(x, y, t)$ of a two-dimensional incompressible flow—with a single function $\psi(x, y, t)$.

There are various ways to define the stream function. We start with the two-dimensional version of the continuity equation for incompressible flow (Eq. 5.1c):

$$\frac{\partial u}{\partial x} + \frac{\partial v}{\partial y} = 0 \tag{5.3}$$

We use what looks at first like a purely mathematical exercise (we will see a physical basis for it later) and define the stream function by

$$u \equiv \frac{\partial \psi}{\partial y} \quad \text{and} \quad v \equiv -\frac{\partial \psi}{\partial x} \tag{5.4}$$

so that Eq. 5.3 is *automatically* satisfied for *any* $\psi(x, y, t)$ we choose! To see this, use Eq. 5.4 in Eq. 5.3:

$$\frac{\partial u}{\partial x} + \frac{\partial v}{\partial y} = \frac{\partial^2 \psi}{\partial x \partial y} - \frac{\partial^2 \psi}{\partial y \partial x} = 0$$

Using Eq. 2.8, we can obtain an equation valid only *along* a streamline

$$u\,dy - v\,dx = 0$$

or, using the definition of our stream function,

$$\frac{\partial \psi}{\partial x} dx + \frac{\partial \psi}{\partial y} dy = 0 \tag{5.5}$$

On the other hand, from a strictly mathematical point of view, at any instant in time t the variation in a function $\psi(x, y, t)$ in space (x, y) is given by

$$d\psi = \frac{\partial \psi}{\partial x} dx + \frac{\partial \psi}{\partial y} dy \tag{5.6}$$

Comparing Eqs. 5.5 and 5.6, we see that along an instantaneous streamline, $d\psi = 0$; in other words, ψ *is a constant along a streamline*. Hence we can specify individual streamlines by their stream function values: $\psi = 0, 1, 2$, etc. What is the significance of the ψ values? The answer is that they can be used to obtain the volume flow rate between any two streamlines. Consider the streamlines shown in Fig. 5.3. We can compute the volume flow rate between streamlines ψ_1 and ψ_2 by using line AB, BC, DE, or EF (recall that there is no flow *across* a streamline).

Let us compute the flow rate by using line AB, and also by using line BC—they should be the same!

---

* This section may be omitted without loss of continuity in the text material.

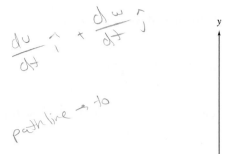

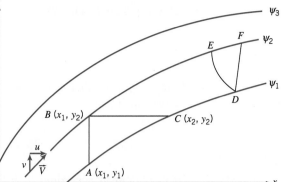

Fig. 5.3 Instantaneous streamlines in a two-dimensional flow.

For a unit depth (dimension perpendicular to the xy plane), the flow rate across AB is

$$Q = \int_{y_1}^{y_2} u\,dy = \int_{y_1}^{y_2} \frac{\partial \psi}{\partial y}\,dy$$

But along AB, x = constant, and (from Eq. 5.6) $d\psi = \partial\psi/\partial y\,dy$. Therefore,

$$Q = \int_{y_1}^{y_2} \frac{\partial \psi}{\partial y}\,dy = \int_{\psi_1}^{\psi_2} d\psi = \psi_2 - \psi_1$$

For a unit depth, the flow rate across BC is

$$Q = \int_{x_1}^{x_2} v\,dx = -\int_{x_1}^{x_2} \frac{\partial \psi}{\partial x}\,dx$$

Along BC, y = constant, and (from Eq. 5.6) $d\psi = \partial\psi/\partial x\,dx$. Therefore,

$$Q = -\int_{x_1}^{x_2} \frac{\partial \psi}{\partial x}\,dx = -\int_{\psi_2}^{\psi_1} d\psi = \psi_2 - \psi_1$$

Hence, whether we use line AB or line BC (or for that matter lines DE or DF), we find that *the volume flow rate (per unit depth) between two streamlines is given by the difference between the two stream function values.*[2] (The derivations for lines AB and BC are the justification for using the stream function definition of Eq. 5.4.) If the streamline through the origin is designated $\psi = 0$, then the ψ value for any other streamline represents the flow between the origin and that streamline. [We are free to select any streamline as the zero streamline because the stream function is defined as a differential (Eq. 5.3); also, the flow rate will always be given by a *difference* of ψ values.] Note that because the volume flow between any two streamlines is constant, *the velocity will be relatively high wherever the streamlines are close together, and relatively low wherever the streamlines are far apart*—a very useful concept for "eyeballing" velocity fields to see where we have regions of high or low velocity.

---

[2] For two-dimensional steady compressible flow in the xy plane, the stream function, ψ, can be defined such that

$$\rho u \equiv \frac{\partial \psi}{\partial y} \quad \text{and} \quad \rho v \equiv -\frac{\partial \psi}{\partial x}$$

The difference between the constant values of ψ defining two streamlines is then the mass flow rate (per unit depth) between the two streamlines.

For a two-dimensional, incompressible flow in the $r\theta$ plane, conservation of mass, Eq. 5.2b, can be written as

$$\frac{\partial(rV_r)}{\partial r} + \frac{\partial V_\theta}{\partial \theta} = 0 \tag{5.7}$$

Using a logic similar to that used for Eq. 5.4, the stream function, $\psi(r, \theta, t)$, then is defined such that

$$V_r \equiv \frac{1}{r}\frac{\partial \psi}{\partial \theta} \quad \text{and} \quad V_\theta \equiv -\frac{\partial \psi}{\partial r} \tag{5.8}$$

With ψ defined according to Eq. 5.8, the continuity equation, Eq. 5.7, is satisfied exactly.

Example 5.4   Stream Function for Flow in a Corner

Given the velocity field for steady, incompressible flow in a corner (Example 2.1), $\vec{V} = Ax\hat{i} - Ay\hat{j}$, with $A = 0.3\,\text{s}^{-1}$, determine the stream function that will yield this velocity field. Plot and interpret the streamline pattern in the first and second quadrants of the xy plane.

GIVEN: Velocity field, $\vec{V} = Ax\hat{i} - Ay\hat{j}$, with $A = 0.3\,\text{s}^{-1}$.

FIND: Stream function ψ and plot in first and second quadrants; interpret the results.

SOLUTION:

The flow is incompressible, so the stream function satisfies Eq. 5.4.

From Eq. 5.4, $u = \dfrac{\partial \psi}{\partial y}$ and $v = -\dfrac{\partial \psi}{\partial y}$. From the given velocity field,

$$u = Ax = \frac{\partial \psi}{\partial y}$$

Integrating with respect to y gives

$$\psi = \int \frac{\partial \psi}{\partial y}\,dy + f(x) = Axy + f(x) \tag{1}$$

where $f(x)$ is arbitrary. The function $f(x)$ may be evaluated using the equation for v. Thus, from Eq. 1,

$$v = -\frac{\partial \psi}{\partial x} = -Ay - \frac{df}{dx} \tag{2}$$

From the given velocity field, $v = -Ay$. Comparing this with Eq. 2 shows that $\dfrac{df}{dx} = 0$, or $f(x) = \text{constant}$. Therefore, Eq. 1 becomes

$$\psi = Axy + c \longleftarrow \hspace{3cm} \psi$$

Lines of constant ψ represent streamlines in the flow field. The constant c may be chosen as any convenient value for plotting purposes. The constant is chosen as zero in order that the streamline through the origin be designated as $\psi = \psi_1 = 0$. Then the value for any other streamline represents the flow between the origin and that streamline. With $c = 0$ and $A = 0.3\,\text{s}^{-1}$, then

$$\psi = 0.3xy \quad (\text{m}^3/\text{s/m})$$

{This equation of a streamline is identical to the result ($xy = \text{constant}$) obtained in Example 2.1.}

Separate plots of the streamlines in the first and second quadrants are presented below. Note that in quadrant 1, $u > 0$, so ψ values are positive. In quadrant 2, $u < 0$, so ψ values are negative.

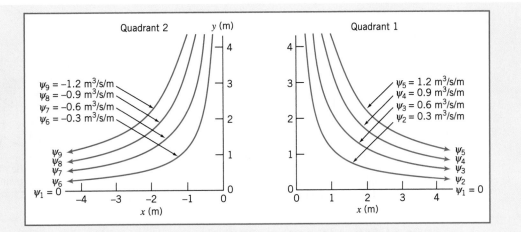

In the first quadrant, since $u > 0$ and $v < 0$, the flow is from left to right and down. The volume flow rate between the streamline $\psi = \psi_1$ through the origin and the streamline $\psi = \psi_2$ is

$$Q_{12} = \psi_2 - \psi_1 = 0.3 \text{ m}^3/\text{s/m}$$

In the second quadrant, since $u < 0$ and $v < 0$, the flow is from right to left and down. The volume flow rate between streamlines ψ_7 and ψ_9 is

$$Q_{79} = \psi_9 - \psi_7 = [-1.2 - (-0.6)] \text{ m}^3/\text{s/m} = -0.6 \text{ m}^3/\text{s/m}$$

The negative sign is consistent with flow having $u < 0$.

As both the streamline spacing in the graphs and the equation for $\vec{V}$ indicate, the velocity is smallest near the origin (a "corner").

There is an *Excel* workbook for this problem that can be used to generate streamlines for this and many other stream functions.

5-3 MOTION OF A FLUID PARTICLE (KINEMATICS)

Figure 5.4 shows a typical finite fluid element, within which we have selected an infinitesimal particle of mass dm and initial volume $dx\,dy\,dz$, at time t, and as it (and the infinitesimal particle) may appear after a time interval dt. The finite element has moved and changed its shape and orientation. Note that while the finite element has quite severe distortion, the infinitesimal particle has changes in shape limited to stretching/shrinking and rotation of the element's sides—this is because we are considering both an infinitesimal time step and particle, so that the sides remain straight. We will examine the infinitesimal particle so that we will eventually obtain results applicable to a point. We can decompose this particle's motion into four components: *translation*, in which the particle moves from one point to another; *rotation* of the particle, which can occur about any or all of the x, y or z axes; *linear deformation*, in which the particle's sides stretch or contract; and *angular deformation*, in which the angles (which were initially 90° for our particle) between the sides change.

It may seem difficult by looking at Fig. 5.4 to distinguish between rotation and angular deformation of the infinitesimal fluid particle. It is important to do so, because pure rotation involves no deformation but angular deformation does and, as we learned in Chapter 2, fluid deformation generates shear stresses. Figure 5.5 shows a

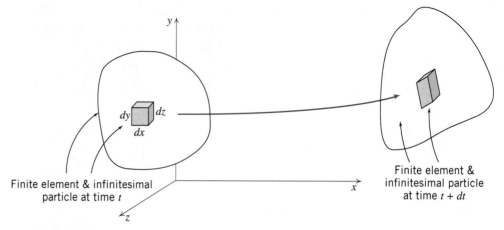

Fig. 5.4 Finite fluid element and infinitesimal particle at times t and $t + dt$.

typical xy plane motion decomposed into the four components described above, and as we examine each of these four components in turn we will see that we *can* distinguish between rotation and angular deformation.

Fluid Translation: Acceleration of a Fluid Particle in a Velocity Field

The translation of a fluid particle is obviously connected with the velocity field $\vec{V} = \vec{V}(x, y, z, t)$ that we previously discussed in Section 2-2. We will need the acceleration of a fluid particle for use in Newton's second law. It might seem that we could simply compute this as $\vec{a} = \partial \vec{V}/\partial t$. This is incorrect, because $\vec{V}$ is a *field*, i.e., it describes the whole flow and not just the motion of an individual particle. (We can see that this way of computing is incorrect by examining Example 5.4, in which particles are clearly accelerating and decelerating so $\vec{a} \neq 0$, but $\partial \vec{V}/\partial t = 0$.)

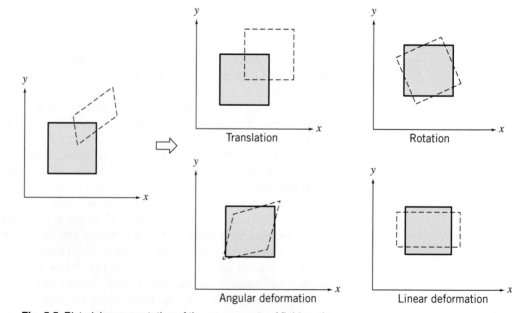

Fig. 5.5 Pictorial representation of the components of fluid motion.

The problem, then, is to retain the field description for fluid properties and obtain an expression for the acceleration of a fluid particle as it moves in a flow field. Stated simply, the problem is:

Given the velocity field, $\vec{V} = \vec{V}(x, y, z, t)$, find the acceleration of a fluid particle, $\vec{a}_p$.

Consider a particle moving in a velocity field. At time t, the particle is at the position x, y, z and has a velocity corresponding to the velocity at that point in space at time t,

$$\vec{V}_p]_t = \vec{V}(x, y, z, t)$$

At $t + dt$, the particle has moved to a new position, with coordinates $x + dx$, $y + dy$, $z + dz$, and has a velocity given by

$$\vec{V}_p]_{t+dt} = \vec{V}(x + dx, y + dy, z + dz, t + dt)$$

This is shown pictorially in Fig. 5.6.

The particle velocity at time t (position $\vec{r}$) is given by $\vec{V}_p = \vec{V}(x, y, z, t)$. Then $d\vec{V}_p$, the change in the velocity of the particle, in moving from location $\vec{r}$ to $\vec{r} + d\vec{r}$, in time dt, is given by the chain rule,

$$d\vec{V}_p = \frac{\partial \vec{V}}{\partial x} dx_p + \frac{\partial \vec{V}}{\partial y} dy_p + \frac{\partial \vec{V}}{\partial z} dz_p + \frac{\partial \vec{V}}{\partial t} dt$$

The total acceleration of the particle is given by

$$\vec{a}_p = \frac{d\vec{V}_p}{dt} = \frac{\partial \vec{V}}{\partial x} \frac{dx_p}{dt} + \frac{\partial \vec{V}}{\partial y} \frac{dy_p}{dt} + \frac{\partial \vec{V}}{\partial z} \frac{dz_p}{dt} + \frac{\partial \vec{V}}{\partial t}$$

Since

$$\frac{dx_p}{dt} = u, \qquad \frac{dy_p}{dt} = v, \qquad \text{and} \qquad \frac{dz_p}{dt} = w,$$

we have

$$\vec{a}_p = \frac{d\vec{V}_p}{dt} = u\frac{\partial \vec{V}}{\partial x} + v\frac{\partial \vec{V}}{\partial y} + w\frac{\partial \vec{V}}{\partial z} + \frac{\partial \vec{V}}{\partial t}$$

To remind us that calculation of the acceleration of a fluid particle in a velocity field requires a special derivative, it is given the symbol $D\vec{V}/Dt$. Thus

$$\frac{D\vec{V}}{Dt} \equiv \vec{a}_p = u\frac{\partial \vec{V}}{\partial x} + v\frac{\partial \vec{V}}{\partial y} + w\frac{\partial \vec{V}}{\partial z} + \frac{\partial \vec{V}}{\partial t} \qquad (5.9)$$

The derivative, D/Dt, defined by Eq. 5.9, is commonly called the *substantial derivative* to remind us that it is computed for a particle of "substance." It often is called the *material derivative* or *particle derivative*.

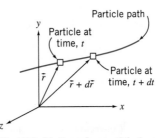

Fig. 5.6 Motion of a particle in a flow field.

The physical significance of the terms in Eq. 5.9 is

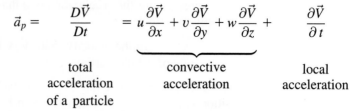

$$\vec{a}_p = \underbrace{\frac{D\vec{V}}{Dt}}_{\substack{\text{total} \\ \text{acceleration} \\ \text{of a particle}}} = \underbrace{u\frac{\partial \vec{V}}{\partial x} + v\frac{\partial \vec{V}}{\partial y} + w\frac{\partial \vec{V}}{\partial z}}_{\substack{\text{convective} \\ \text{acceleration}}} + \underbrace{\frac{\partial \vec{V}}{\partial t}}_{\substack{\text{local} \\ \text{acceleration}}}$$

From Eq. 5.9 we recognize that a fluid particle moving in a flow field may undergo acceleration for either of two reasons. As an illustration, refer to Example 5.4. This is a steady flow in which particles are *convected* toward the low-velocity region (near the "corner"), and then away to a high-velocity region.[3] If a flow field is unsteady a fluid particle will undergo an additional *local* acceleration, because the velocity field is a function of time.

The convective acceleration may be written as a single vector expression using the gradient operator ∇. Thus

$$u\frac{\partial \vec{V}}{\partial x} + v\frac{\partial \vec{V}}{\partial y} + w\frac{\partial \vec{V}}{\partial z} = (\vec{V} \cdot \nabla)\vec{V}$$

(We suggest that you check this equality by expanding the right side of the equation using the familiar dot product operation.) Thus Eq. 5.9 may be written as

$$\frac{D\vec{V}}{Dt} \equiv \vec{a}_p = (\vec{V} \cdot \nabla)\vec{V} + \frac{\partial \vec{V}}{\partial t} \qquad (5.10)$$

For a *two-dimensional flow*, say $\vec{V} = \vec{V}(x, y, t)$, Eq. 5.9 reduces to

$$\frac{D\vec{V}}{Dt} = u\frac{\partial \vec{V}}{\partial x} + v\frac{\partial \vec{V}}{\partial y} + \frac{\partial \vec{V}}{\partial t}$$

For a *one-dimensional flow*, say $\vec{V} = \vec{V}(x, t)$, Eq. 5.9 becomes

$$\frac{D\vec{V}}{Dt} = u\frac{\partial \vec{V}}{\partial x} + \frac{\partial \vec{V}}{\partial t}$$

Finally, for a *steady flow in three dimensions*, Eq. 5.9 becomes

$$\frac{D\vec{V}}{Dt} = u\frac{\partial \vec{V}}{\partial x} + v\frac{\partial \vec{V}}{\partial y} + w\frac{\partial \vec{V}}{\partial z}$$

which, as we have seen, is not necessarily zero even though the flow is steady. Thus a fluid particle may undergo a convective acceleration due to its motion, even in a steady velocity field.

Equation 5.9 is a vector equation. As with all vector equations, it may be written in scalar component equations. Relative to an *xyz* coordinate system, the scalar components of Eq. 5.9 are written

$$a_{x_p} = \frac{Du}{Dt} = u\frac{\partial u}{\partial x} + v\frac{\partial u}{\partial y} + w\frac{\partial u}{\partial z} + \frac{\partial u}{\partial t} \qquad (5.11a)$$

$$a_{y_p} = \frac{Dv}{Dt} = u\frac{\partial v}{\partial x} + v\frac{\partial v}{\partial y} + w\frac{\partial v}{\partial z} + \frac{\partial v}{\partial t} \qquad (5.11b)$$

$$a_{z_p} = \frac{Dw}{Dt} = u\frac{\partial w}{\partial x} + v\frac{\partial w}{\partial y} + w\frac{\partial w}{\partial z} + \frac{\partial w}{\partial t} \qquad (5.11c)$$

[3]Convective accelerations are demonstrated and calculation of total acceleration of a fluid particle is illustrated in the NCFMF video *Eulerian and Lagrangian Descriptions in Fluid Mechanics*. (See http://web.mit.edu/fluids/www/Shapiro/ncfmf.html for free online viewing of this film; it is old but good!)

The components of acceleration in cylindrical coordinates may be obtained from Eq. 5.10 by expressing the velocity, $\vec{V}$, in cylindrical coordinates (Section 5-1) and utilizing the appropriate expression (Eq. 3.19, on the Web) for the vector operator ∇. Thus,[4]

$$a_{r_p} = V_r \frac{\partial V_r}{\partial r} + \frac{V_\theta}{r} \frac{\partial V_r}{\partial \theta} - \frac{V_\theta^2}{r} + V_z \frac{\partial V_r}{\partial z} + \frac{\partial V_r}{\partial t} \qquad (5.12a)$$

$$a_{\theta_p} = V_r \frac{\partial V_\theta}{\partial r} + \frac{V_\theta}{r} \frac{\partial V_\theta}{\partial \theta} + \frac{V_r V_\theta}{r} + V_z \frac{\partial V_\theta}{\partial z} + \frac{\partial V_\theta}{\partial t} \qquad (5.12b)$$

$$a_{z_p} = V_r \frac{\partial V_z}{\partial r} + \frac{V_\theta}{r} \frac{\partial V_z}{\partial \theta} + V_z \frac{\partial V_z}{\partial z} + \frac{\partial V_z}{\partial t} \qquad (5.12c)$$

Equations 5.9, 5.11, and 5.12 are useful for computing the acceleration of a fluid particle anywhere in a flow from the velocity field (a function of x, y, z, and t); this is the *Eulerian* method of description, the most-used approach in fluid mechanics.

As an alternative (e.g., if we wish to track an individual particle's motion in, for example, pollution studies) we sometimes use the *Lagrangian* description of particle motion, in which the acceleration, position, and velocity of a particle are specified as a function of time only. Both descriptions are illustrated in Example 5.5.

Example 5.5   Particle Acceleration in Eulerian and Lagrangian Descriptions

Consider two-dimensional, steady, incompressible flow through the plane converging channel shown. The velocity on the horizontal centerline (x axis) is given by $\vec{V} = V_1[1 + (x/L)]\hat{i}$. Find an expression for the acceleration of a particle moving along the centerline using (a) the Eulerian approach and (b) the Lagrangian approach. Evaluate the acceleration when the particle is at the beginning and at the end of the channel.

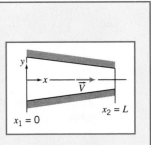

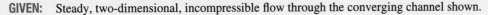

GIVEN: Steady, two-dimensional, incompressible flow through the converging channel shown.

$$\vec{V} = V_1\left(1 + \frac{x}{L}\right)\hat{i} \quad \text{on } x \text{ axis}$$

FIND: (a) The acceleration of a particle moving along the centerline using the Eulerian approach.
  (b) The acceleration of a particle moving along the centerline using the Lagrangian approach.
  (c) Evaluate the acceleration when the particle is at the beginning and at the end of the channel.

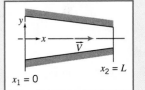

SOLUTION:

(a) The Eulerian approach

The governing equation for acceleration of a fluid particle is Eq. 5.9:

$$\vec{a}_p(x,y,z,t) = \frac{D\vec{V}}{Dt} = u \frac{\partial \vec{V}}{\partial x} + v \frac{\partial \vec{V}}{\partial y} + w \frac{\partial \vec{V}}{\partial z} + \frac{\partial \vec{V}}{\partial t} \qquad (5.9)$$

In this case we are interested in the x component of velocity (Eq. 5.11a):

$$a_{x_p}(x,y,z,t) = \frac{Du}{Dt} = u \frac{\partial u}{\partial x} + v \frac{\partial u}{\partial y} + w \frac{\partial u}{\partial z} + \frac{\partial u}{\partial t} \qquad (5.11a)$$

On the x axis, $v = w = 0$ and $u = V_1\left(1 + \frac{x}{L}\right)$, so for steady flow we obtain

$$a_{x_p}(x) = \frac{Du}{Dt} = u \frac{\partial u}{\partial x} = V_1\left(1 + \frac{x}{L}\right)\frac{V_1}{L}$$

---

[4] In evaluating $(\vec{V} \cdot \nabla)\vec{V}$, recall that $\hat{e}_r$ and $\hat{e}_\theta$ are functions of θ (see footnote 1 on p. 169).

or

$$a_{x_p}(x) = \frac{V_1^2}{L}\left(1 + \frac{x}{L}\right) \longleftarrow \qquad\qquad a_{x_p}(x)$$

This expression gives the acceleration of *any* particle that is at point *x* at an instant.

(b) The Lagrangian approach

In this approach we need to obtain the motion of a fluid particle as we would in particle mechanics; that is, we need the position $\vec{x}_p(t)$, and then we can obtain the velocity $\vec{V}_p(t) = d\vec{x}_p/dt$ and acceleration $\vec{a}_p(t) = d\vec{V}_p/dt$. Actually, we are considering motion along the *x* axis, so we want $x_p(t)$, $u_p(t) = dx_p/dt$, and $a_{x_p}(t) = du_p/dt$. We are not given $x_p(t)$, but we do have

$$u_p = \frac{dx_p}{dt} = V_1\left(1 + \frac{x_p}{L}\right)$$

Separating variables, and using limits $x_p(t = 0) = 0$ and $x_p(t = t) = x_p$,

$$\int_0^{x_p} \frac{dx_p}{\left(1 + \frac{x_p}{L}\right)} = \int_0^t V_1 dt \qquad \text{and} \qquad L\ln\left(1 + \frac{x_p}{L}\right) = V_1 t \qquad (1)$$

We can then solve for $x_p(t)$:

$$x_p(t) = L(e^{V_1 t/L} - 1)$$

The velocity and acceleration are then

$$u_p(t) = \frac{dx_p}{dt} = V_1 e^{V_1 t/L}$$

and

$$a_{z_p}(t) = \frac{du_p}{dt} = \frac{V_1^2}{L} e^{V_1 t/L} \longleftarrow \qquad\qquad (2) \quad a_{x_p}(t)$$

This expression gives the acceleration at any time *t* of the particle that was initially at *x* = 0.

(c) We wish to evaluate the acceleration when the particle is at *x* = 0 and *x* = *L*. For the Eulerian approach this is straightforward:

$$a_{z_p}(x = 0) = \frac{V_1^2}{L}, \qquad a_{x_p}(x = L) = 2\frac{V_1^2}{L} \longleftarrow \qquad\qquad a_{x_p}$$

For the Lagrangian approach, we need to find the times at which *x* = 0 and *x* = *L*. Using Eq. 1, these are

$$t(x_p = 0) = \frac{L}{V_1} \qquad t(x_p = L) = \frac{L}{V_1}\ln(2)$$

Then, from Eq. 2,

$$a_{z_p}(t = 0) = \frac{V_1^2}{L}, \qquad \text{and} \qquad a_{x_p}\left(t = \frac{L}{V_1}\ln(2)\right) = \frac{V_1^2}{L}e^{\ln(2)} = 2\frac{V_1^2}{L} \longleftarrow \qquad a_{x_p}$$

Note that both approaches yield the same results for particle acceleration, as they should.

> This problem illustrates use of the Eulerian and Lagrangian descriptions of the motion of a fluid particle.

Fluid Rotation

A fluid particle moving in a general three-dimensional flow field may rotate about all three coordinate axes. Thus particle rotation is a vector quantity and, in general,

$$\vec{\omega} = \hat{i}\omega_x + \hat{j}\omega_y + \hat{k}\omega_z$$

where ω_x is the rotation about the *x* axis, ω_y is the rotation about the *y* axis, and ω_z is the rotation about the *z* axis. The positive sense of rotation is given by the right-hand rule.

We now see how we can extract the rotation component of the particle motion. Consider the xy plane view of the particle at time t. The left and lower sides of the particle are given by the two perpendicular line segments oa and ob of lengths Δx and Δy, respectively, shown in Fig. 5.7a. In general, after an interval Δt the particle will have translated to some new position, and also have rotated and deformed. A possible instantaneous orientation of the lines at time $t + \Delta t$ is shown in Fig. 5.7b.

We need to be careful here with our signs for angles. Following the right-hand rule, *counterclockwise rotation is positive*, and we have shown side oa rotating counterclockwise through angle $\Delta \alpha$, but be aware that we have shown edge ob rotating at a *clockwise* angle $\Delta \beta$. Both angles are obviously arbitrary, but it will help visualize the discussion if we assign values to these angles, e.g., let $\Delta \alpha = 6°$ and $\Delta \beta = 4°$.

How do we extract from $\Delta \alpha$ and $\Delta \beta$ a measure of the particle's rotation? The answer is that we take an average of the rotations $\Delta \alpha$ and $\Delta \beta$, so that the particle's rigid body counterclockwise rotation is $\frac{1}{2}(\Delta \alpha - \Delta \beta)$, as shown in Fig. 5.7c. The minus sign is needed because the *counterclockwise* rotation of ob is $-\Delta \beta$. Using the assigned values, the rotation of the particle is then $\frac{1}{2}(6° - 4°) = 1°$. (Given the two rotations, taking the average is the only way we can measure the particle's rotation, because any other approach would favor one side's rotation over the other, which doesn't make sense.)

Now we can determine from $\Delta \alpha$ and $\Delta \beta$ a measure of the particle's angular deformation, as shown in Fig. 5.7d. To obtain the deformation of side oa in Fig. 5.7d, we use Fig. 5.7b and 5.7c: If we subtract the particle rotation $\frac{1}{2}(\Delta \alpha - \Delta \beta)$, in Fig. 5.7c, from the actual rotation of oa, $\Delta \alpha$, in Fig. 5.7b, what remains must be pure deformation $[\Delta \alpha - \frac{1}{2}(\Delta \alpha - \Delta \beta) = \frac{1}{2}(\Delta \alpha + \Delta \beta)$, in Fig. 5.7d]. Using the assigned values, the deformation of side oa is $6° - \frac{1}{2}(6° - 4°) = 5°$. By a similar process, for side ob we end with $\Delta \beta - \frac{1}{2}(\Delta \alpha - \Delta \beta) = -\frac{1}{2}(\Delta \alpha + \Delta \beta)$, or a *clockwise* deformation $\frac{1}{2}(\Delta \alpha + \Delta \beta)$, as shown in Fig. 5.7d. The total deformation of the particle is the sum of the deformations of the sides, or $(\Delta \alpha + \Delta \beta)$ (with our example values, 10°). We verify that this leaves us with the correct value for the particle's deformation: Recall that in Section 2-4 we saw that deformation is measured by the change in a 90° angle. In Fig. 5.7a we see this is angle aob, and in Fig. 5.7d we see the total change of this angle is indeed $\frac{1}{2}(\Delta \alpha + \Delta \beta) + \frac{1}{2}(\Delta \alpha + \Delta \beta) = (\Delta \alpha + \Delta \beta)$.

We need to convert these angular measures to quantities obtainable from the flow field. To do this, we recognize that (for small angles) $\Delta \alpha = \Delta \eta / \Delta x$, and $\Delta \beta = \Delta \xi / \Delta y$. But $\Delta \xi$ arises because, if in interval Δt point o moves horizontally distance $u \Delta t$, then point b will have moved distance $(u + [\partial u / \partial y]\Delta y)\Delta t$ (using a Taylor series expansion). Likewise, $\Delta \eta$ arises because, if in interval Δt point o moves vertically distance $v \Delta t$, then point a will have moved distance $(v + [\partial v / \partial x]\Delta x)\Delta t$. Hence,

$$\Delta \xi = \left(u + \frac{\partial u}{\partial y} \Delta y \right) \Delta t - u \Delta t = \frac{\partial u}{\partial y} \Delta y \Delta t$$

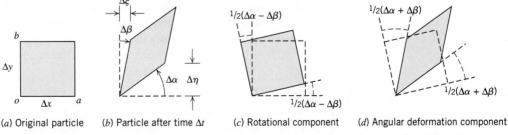

(a) Original particle   (b) Particle after time Δt (c) Rotational component   (d) Angular deformation component

Fig. 5.7 Rotation and angular deformation of perpendicular line segments in a two-dimensional flow.

and

$$\Delta\eta = \left(v + \frac{\partial v}{\partial x}\Delta x\right)\Delta t - v\Delta t = \frac{\partial v}{\partial x}\Delta x\Delta t$$

We can now compute the angular velocity of the particle about the z axis, ω_z, by combining all these results:

$$\omega_z = \lim_{\Delta t \to 0}\frac{\frac{1}{2}(\Delta\alpha - \Delta\beta)}{\Delta t} = \lim_{\Delta t \to 0}\frac{\frac{1}{2}\left(\frac{\Delta\eta}{\Delta x} - \frac{\Delta\xi}{\Delta y}\right)}{\Delta t} = \lim_{\Delta t \to 0}\frac{\frac{1}{2}\left(\frac{\partial v}{\partial x}\frac{\Delta x}{\Delta x}\Delta t - \frac{\partial u}{\partial y}\frac{\Delta y}{\Delta y}\Delta t\right)}{\Delta t}$$

$$\omega_z = \frac{1}{2}\left(\frac{\partial v}{\partial x} - \frac{\partial u}{\partial y}\right)$$

By considering the rotation of pairs of perpendicular line segments in the yz and xz planes, one can show similarly that

$$\omega_x = \frac{1}{2}\left(\frac{\partial w}{\partial y} - \frac{\partial v}{\partial z}\right) \qquad \text{and} \qquad \omega_y = \frac{1}{2}\left(\frac{\partial u}{\partial z} - \frac{\partial w}{\partial x}\right)$$

Then $\vec{\omega} = \hat{i}\omega_x + \hat{j}\omega_y + \hat{k}\omega_z$ becomes

$$\vec{\omega} = \frac{1}{2}\left[\hat{i}\left(\frac{\partial w}{\partial y} - \frac{\partial v}{\partial z}\right) + \hat{j}\left(\frac{\partial u}{\partial z} - \frac{\partial w}{\partial x}\right) + \hat{k}\left(\frac{\partial v}{\partial x} - \frac{\partial u}{\partial y}\right)\right] \qquad (5.13)$$

We recognize the term in the square brackets as

$$\text{curl } \vec{V} = \nabla \times \vec{V}$$

Then, in vector notation, we can write

$$\vec{\omega} = \frac{1}{2}\nabla \times \vec{V} \qquad (5.14)$$

It is worth noting here that we should not confuse rotation of a fluid particle with flow consisting of circular streamlines, or *vortex* flow. As we will see in Example 5.6, in such a flow the particles *could* rotate as they move in a circular motion, but they do not have to!

When might we expect to have a flow in which the particles rotate as they move ($\vec{\omega} \neq 0$)? One possibility is that we start out with a flow in which (for whatever reason) the particles already have rotation. On the other hand, if we assumed the particles are not initially rotating, particles will only begin to rotate if they experience a torque caused by surface shear stresses; the particle body forces and normal (pressure) forces may accelerate and deform the particle, but cannot generate a torque. We can conclude that rotation of fluid particles will *always* occur for flows in which we have shear stresses. We have already learned in Chapter 2 that shear stresses are present whenever we have a viscous fluid that is experiencing angular deformation (shearing). Hence we conclude that rotation of fluid particles only occurs in viscous flows[5] (unless the particles are initially rotating, as in Example 3.10).

Flows for which no particle rotation occurs are called *irrotational* flows. Although no real flow is truly irrotational (all fluids have viscosity), it turns out that many flows can be successfully studied by assuming they are inviscid and irrotational, because viscous effects are often negligible.[6] As we discussed in Chapter 1, and will again in Chapter 6, much of aerodynamics theory assumes inviscid flow. We just need to be aware that in any flow there will always be regions (e.g., the boundary layer for flow over a wing) in which viscous effects cannot be ignored.

---

[5] A rigorous proof using the complete equations of motion for a fluid particle is given in [1], pp. 142–145.
[6] Examples of rotational and irrotational motion are shown in the NCFMF video *Vorticity*. (See http://web.mit.edu/fluids/www/Shapiro/ncfmf.html for free online viewing of this film.)

The factor of $\frac{1}{2}$ can be eliminated from Eq. 5.14 by defining the *vorticity*, $\vec{\zeta}$, to be twice the rotation,

$$\vec{\zeta} \equiv 2\vec{\omega} = \nabla \times \vec{V} \tag{5.15}$$

The vorticity is a measure of the rotation of a fluid element as it moves in the flow field. In cylindrical coordinates the vorticity is[7]

$$\nabla \times \vec{V} = \hat{e}_r \left(\frac{1}{r} \frac{\partial V_z}{\partial \theta} - \frac{\partial V_\theta}{\partial z} \right) + \hat{e}_\theta \left(\frac{\partial V_r}{\partial z} - \frac{\partial V_z}{\partial r} \right) + \hat{k} \left(\frac{1}{r} \frac{\partial_r V_\theta}{\partial r} - \frac{1}{r} \frac{\partial V_r}{\partial \theta} \right) \tag{5.16}$$

The *circulation*, Γ (which we will revisit in Example 6.12), is defined as the line integral of the tangential velocity component about any closed curve fixed in the flow,

$$\Gamma = \oint_c \vec{V} \cdot d\vec{s} \tag{5.17}$$

where $d\vec{s}$ is an elemental vector tangent to the curve and having length ds of the element of arc; a positive sense corresponds to a counterclockwise path of integration around the curve. We can develop a relationship between circulation and vorticity by considering the rectangular circuit shown in Fig. 5.8, where the velocity components at o are assumed to be (u, v), and the velocities along segments bc and ac can be derived using Taylor series approximations.

For the closed curve $oacb$,

$$\Delta\Gamma = u\Delta x + \left(v + \frac{\partial v}{\partial x}\Delta x \right)\Delta y - \left(u + \frac{\partial u}{\partial y}\Delta y \right)\Delta x - v\,\Delta y$$

$$\Delta\Gamma = \left(\frac{\partial v}{\partial x} - \frac{\partial u}{\partial y} \right)\Delta x \Delta y$$

$$\Delta\Gamma = 2\omega_z \Delta x \Delta y$$

Then,

$$\Gamma = \oint_c \vec{V} \cdot d\vec{s} = \int_A 2\omega_z\, dA = \int_A (\nabla \times \vec{V})_z\, dA \tag{5.18}$$

Equation 5.18 is a statement of the Stokes Theorem in two dimensions. Thus the circulation around a closed contour is equal to the total vorticity enclosed within it.

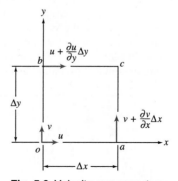

Fig. 5.8 Velocity components on the boundaries of a fluid element.

---

[7] In carrying out the curl operation, recall that $\hat{e}_r$ and $\hat{e}_\theta$ are functions of θ (see footnote 1 on p. 169).

Example 5.6   Free and Forced Vortex Flows

Consider flow fields with purely tangential motion (circular streamlines): $V_r = 0$ and $V_\theta = f(r)$. Evaluate the rotation, vorticity, and circulation for rigid-body rotation, a *forced vortex*. Show that it is possible to choose $f(r)$ so that flow is irrotational, i.e., to produce a *free vortex*.

GIVEN: Flow fields with tangential motion, $V_r = 0$ and $V_\theta = f(r)$.

FIND: (a) Rotation, vorticity, and circulation for rigid-body motion (a *forced vortex*).
(b) $V_\theta = f(r)$ for irrotational motion (a *free vortex*).

SOLUTION:

Governing equation: $\vec{\zeta} = 2\vec{\omega} = \nabla \times \vec{V}$ (5.15)

For motion in the $r\theta$ plane, the only components of rotation and vorticity are in the z direction,

$$\zeta_z = 2\omega_z = \frac{1}{r}\frac{\partial rV_\theta}{\partial r} - \frac{1}{r}\frac{\partial V_r}{\partial \theta}$$

Because $V_r = 0$ everywhere in these fields, this reduces to $\zeta_z = 2\omega_z = \dfrac{1}{r}\dfrac{\partial rV_\theta}{\partial r}$.

(a) For rigid-body rotation, $V_\theta = \omega r$.

Then $\omega_z = \dfrac{1}{2}\dfrac{1}{r}\dfrac{\partial rV_\theta}{\partial r} = \dfrac{1}{2}\dfrac{1}{r}\dfrac{\partial}{\partial r}\omega r^2 = \dfrac{1}{2r}(2\omega r) = \omega$ and $\zeta_z = 2\omega$.

The circulation is $\Gamma = \oint_c \vec{V} \cdot d\vec{s} = \int_A 2\omega_z\, dA$.   (5.18)

Since $\omega_z = \omega = $ constant, the circulation about any closed contour is given by $\Gamma = 2\omega A$, where A is the area enclosed by the contour. Thus for rigid-body motion (a forced vortex), the rotation and vorticity are constants; the circulation depends on the area enclosed by the contour.

(b) For irrotational flow, $\omega_z = \dfrac{1}{r}\dfrac{\partial}{\partial r}rV_\theta = 0$. Integrating, we find

$$rV_\theta = \text{constant} \qquad \text{or} \qquad V_\theta = f(r) = \frac{C}{r}$$

For this flow, the origin is a singular point where $V_\theta \to \infty$. The circulation for any contour enclosing the origin is

$$\Gamma = \oint_c \vec{V} \cdot d\vec{s} = \int_0^{2\pi} \frac{C}{r} r\, d\theta = 2\pi C$$

It turns out that the circulation around any contour *not* enclosing the singular point at the origin is zero. Streamlines for the two vortex flows are shown below, along with the location and orientation at different instants of a cross marked in the fluid that was initially at the 12 o'clock position. For the rigid-body motion (which occurs, for example, at the eye of a tornado, creating the "dead" region at the very center), the cross rotates as it moves in a circular motion; also, the streamlines are closer together as we move away from the origin. For the irrotational motion (which occurs, for example, outside the eye of a tornado—in such a large region viscous effects are negligible), the cross does not rotate as it moves in a circular motion; also, the streamlines are farther apart as we move away from the origin.

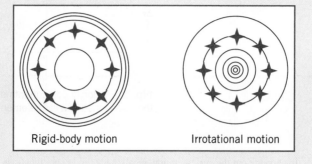

Rigid-body motion   Irrotational motion

Fluid Deformation

a. Angular Deformation

As we discussed earlier (and as shown in Fig. 5.7d), the *angular deformation* of a particle is given by the sum of the two angular deformations, or in other words by $(\Delta\alpha + \Delta\beta)$.

We also recall that $\Delta\alpha = \Delta\eta/\Delta x$, $\Delta\beta = \Delta\xi/\Delta y$, and $\Delta\xi$ and $\Delta\eta$ are given by

$$\Delta\xi = \left(u + \frac{\partial u}{\partial y}\Delta y\right)\Delta t - u\Delta t = \frac{\partial u}{\partial y}\Delta y\Delta t$$

and

$$\Delta\eta = \left(v + \frac{\partial v}{\partial x}\Delta x\right)\Delta t - v\Delta t = \frac{\partial v}{\partial x}\Delta x\Delta t$$

We can now compute the rate of angular deformation of the particle in the *xy* plane by combining these results,

$$\begin{array}{l} \text{Rate of angular} \\ \text{deformation} \\ \text{in } xy \text{ plane} \end{array} = \lim_{\Delta t \to 0} \frac{(\Delta\alpha + \Delta\beta)}{\Delta t} = \lim_{\Delta t \to 0} \frac{\left(\dfrac{\Delta\eta}{\Delta x} + \dfrac{\Delta\xi}{\Delta y}\right)}{\Delta t}$$

$$\begin{array}{l} \text{Rate of angular} \\ \text{deformation} \\ \text{in } xy \text{ plane} \end{array} = \lim_{\Delta t \to 0} \frac{\left(\dfrac{\partial v}{\partial x}\dfrac{\Delta x}{\Delta x}\Delta t + \dfrac{\partial u}{\partial y}\dfrac{\Delta y}{\Delta y}\Delta t\right)}{\Delta t} = \left(\frac{\partial v}{\partial x} + \frac{\partial u}{\partial y}\right) \qquad (5.19a)$$

Similar expressions can be written for the rate of angular deformation of the particle in the *yz* and *zx* planes,

$$\text{Rate of angular deformation in } yz \text{ plane} = \left(\frac{\partial w}{\partial y} + \frac{\partial v}{\partial z}\right) \qquad (5.19b)$$

$$\text{Rate of angular deformation in } zx \text{ plane} = \left(\frac{\partial w}{\partial x} + \frac{\partial u}{\partial z}\right) \qquad (5.19c)$$

We saw in Chapter 2 that for one-dimensional laminar Newtonian flow the shear stress is given by the rate of deformation (du/dy) of the fluid particle,

$$\tau_{yx} = \mu\frac{du}{dy} \qquad (2.15)$$

We will see shortly that we can generalize Eq. 2.15 to the case of three-dimensional laminar flow; this will lead to expressions for three-dimensional shear stresses involving the three rates of angular deformation given above. (Eq. 2.15 is a special case of Eq. 5.19a.)

The concepts of rotation and deformation are treated at length in the NCFMF video *Deformation of Continuous Media* (see http://web.mit.edu/fluids/www/Shapiro/ncfmf.html for free online viewing of this film.) Calculation of angular deformation is illustrated for a simple flow field in Example 5.7.

Example 5.7 Rotation in Viscometric Flow

A viscometric flow in the narrow gap between large parallel plates is shown. The velocity field in the narrow gap is given by $\vec{V} = U(y/h)\hat{i}$, where $U = 4$ mm/s and $h = 4$ mm. At $t = 0$ line segments *ac* and *bd* are marked in the fluid to form a cross as shown. Evaluate the positions of the marked points at $t = 1.5$ s and sketch for comparison.

Calculate the rate of angular deformation and the rate of rotation of a fluid particle in this velocity field. Comment on your results.

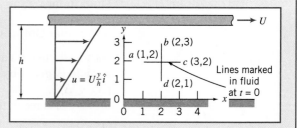

GIVEN: Velocity field, $\vec{V} = U(y/h)\hat{i}$; $U = 4$ mm/s, and $h = 4$ mm. Fluid particles marked at $t = 0$ to form cross as shown.

FIND: (a) Positions of points a', b', c', and d' at $t = 1.5$ s; plot.
  (b) Rate of angular deformation.
  (c) Rate of rotation of a fluid particle.
  (d) Significance of these results.

SOLUTION:

For the given flow field $v = 0$, so there is no vertical motion. The velocity of each point stays constant, so $\Delta x = u\Delta t$ for each point. At point b, $u = 3$ mm/s, so

$$\Delta x_b = \frac{3 \text{ mm}}{\text{s}} \times 1.5 \text{ s} = 4.5 \text{ mm}$$

Similarly, points a and c each move 3 mm, and point d moves 1.5 mm. Hence the plot at $t = 1.5$ s is

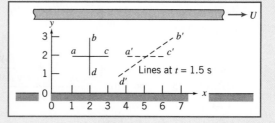

The rate of angular deformation is

$$\frac{\partial u}{\partial y} + \frac{\partial v}{\partial x} = U\frac{1}{h} + 0 = \frac{U}{h} = \frac{4 \text{ mm}}{\text{s}} \times \frac{1}{4 \text{ mm}} = 1 \text{ s}^{-1} \qquad \longleftarrow$$

The rate of rotation is

$$\omega_z = \frac{1}{2}\left(\frac{\partial v}{\partial x} - \frac{\partial u}{\partial y}\right) = \frac{1}{2}\left(0 - \frac{U}{h}\right) = -\frac{1}{2} \times \frac{4 \text{ mm}}{\text{s}} \times \frac{1}{4 \text{ mm}} = -0.5 \text{ s}^{-1} \qquad \longleftarrow \qquad \omega_z$$

> In this problem we have a viscous flow, and hence should have expected both angular deformation and particle rotation.

b. Linear Deformation

During linear deformation, the shape of the fluid element, described by the angles at its vertices, remains unchanged, since all right angles continue to be right angles (see Fig. 5.5). The element will change length in the x direction only if $\partial u/\partial x$ is other than zero. Similarly, a change in the y dimension requires a nonzero value of $\partial v/\partial y$ and a change in the z dimension requires a nonzero value of $\partial w/\partial z$. These quantities represent the components of longitudinal rates of strain in the x, y, and z directions, respectively.

Changes in length of the sides may produce changes in volume of the element. The rate of local instantaneous *volume dilation* is given by

$$\text{Volume dilation rate} = \frac{\partial u}{\partial x} + \frac{\partial v}{\partial y} + \frac{\partial w}{\partial z} = \nabla \cdot \vec{V} \qquad (5.20)$$

For incompressible flow, the rate of volume dilation is zero (Eq. 5.1c).

Example 5.8   Deformation Rates for Flow in a Corner

The velocity field $\vec{V} = Ax\hat{i} - Ay\hat{j}$ represents flow in a "corner," as shown in Example 5.4, where $A = 0.3\ \text{s}^{-1}$ and the coordinates are measured in meters. A square is marked in the fluid as shown at $t = 0$. Evaluate the new positions of the four corner points when point a has moved to $x = \frac{3}{2}$ m after τ seconds. Evaluate the rates of linear deformation in the x and y directions. Compare area $a'b'c'd'$ at $t = \tau$ with area $abcd$ at $t = 0$. Comment on the significance of this result.

GIVEN: $\vec{V} = Ax\hat{i} - Ay\hat{j}$; $A = 0.3\ \text{s}^{-1}$, x and y in meters.

FIND: (a) Position of square at $t = \tau$ when a is at

a' at $x = \frac{3}{2}$ m.

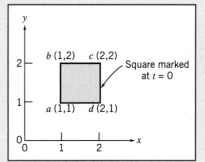

(b) Rates of linear deformation.
(c) Area $a'b'c'd'$ compared with area $abcd$.
(d) Significance of the results.

SOLUTION:

First we must find τ, so we must follow a fluid particle using a Lagrangian description. Thus

$$u = \frac{dx_p}{dt} = Ax_p, \quad \frac{dx}{x} = A\,dt, \text{ so} \quad \int_{x_0}^{x} \frac{dx}{x} = \int_{0}^{\tau} A\,dt \quad \text{and} \quad \ln\frac{x}{x_0} = A\tau$$

$$\tau = \frac{\ln x/x_0}{A} = \frac{\ln\left(\dfrac{3}{2}\right)}{0.3\ \text{s}^{-1}} = 1.35\ \text{s}$$

In the y direction

$$v = \frac{dy_p}{dt} = -Ay_p \qquad \frac{dy}{y} = -A\,dt \qquad \frac{y}{y_0} = e^{-A\tau}$$

The point coordinates at τ are:

The plot is:

Point	$t = 0$	$t = \tau$
a	$(1, 1)$	$\left(\dfrac{3}{2}, \dfrac{2}{3}\right)$
b	$(1, 2)$	$\left(\dfrac{3}{2}, \dfrac{4}{3}\right)$
c	$(2, 2)$	$\left(3, \dfrac{4}{3}\right)$
d	$(2, 1)$	$\left(3, \dfrac{2}{3}\right)$

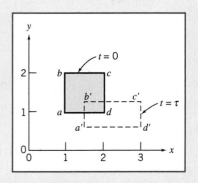

The rates of linear deformation are:

$$\frac{\partial u}{\partial x} = \frac{\partial}{\partial x}Ax = A = 0.3\ \text{s}^{-1} \qquad \text{in the } x \text{ direction}$$

$$\frac{\partial v}{\partial y} = \frac{\partial}{\partial y}(-Ay) = -A = -0.3\ \text{s}^{-1} \qquad \text{in the } y \text{ direction}$$

The rate of volume dilation is

$$\nabla \cdot \vec{V} = \frac{\partial u}{\partial x} + \frac{\partial v}{\partial y} = A - A = 0$$

Area $abcd = 1\ \text{m}^2$ and area $a'b'c'd' = (3 - \frac{3}{2})(\frac{4}{3} - \frac{2}{3}) = 1\ \text{m}^2$.

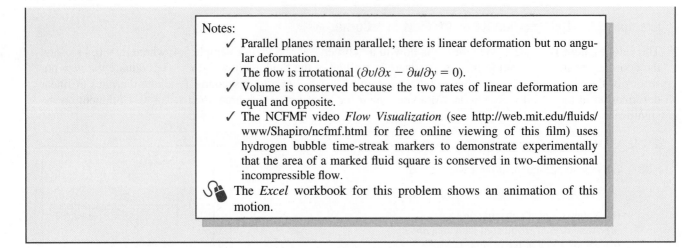

Notes:
- ✓ Parallel planes remain parallel; there is linear deformation but no angular deformation.
- ✓ The flow is irrotational ($\partial v/\partial x - \partial u/\partial y = 0$).
- ✓ Volume is conserved because the two rates of linear deformation are equal and opposite.
- ✓ The NCFMF video *Flow Visualization* (see http://web.mit.edu/fluids/www/Shapiro/ncfmf.html for free online viewing of this film) uses hydrogen bubble time-streak markers to demonstrate experimentally that the area of a marked fluid square is conserved in two-dimensional incompressible flow.
- The *Excel* workbook for this problem shows an animation of this motion.

We have shown in this section that the velocity field can be used to find the acceleration, rotation, angular deformation, and linear deformation of a fluid particle in a flow field.

5-4   MOMENTUM EQUATION

A dynamic equation describing fluid motion may be obtained by applying Newton's second law to a particle. To derive the differential form of the momentum equation, we shall apply Newton's second law to an infinitesimal fluid particle of mass dm.

Recall that Newton's second law for a finite system is given by

$$\vec{F} = \frac{d\vec{P}}{dt}\bigg)_{\text{system}} \tag{4.2a}$$

where the linear momentum, $\vec{P}$, of the system is given by

$$\vec{P}_{\text{system}} = \int_{\text{mass (system)}} \vec{V}\, dm \tag{4.2b}$$

Then, for an infinitesimal system of mass dm, Newton's second law can be written

$$d\vec{F} = dm \frac{d\vec{V}}{dt}\bigg)_{\text{system}} \tag{5.21}$$

Having obtained an expression for the acceleration of a fluid element of mass dm, moving in a velocity field (Eq. 5.9), we can write Newton's second law as the vector equation

$$d\vec{F} = dm \frac{D\vec{V}}{Dt} = dm \left[u\frac{\partial \vec{V}}{\partial x} + v\frac{\partial \vec{V}}{\partial y} + w\frac{\partial \vec{V}}{\partial z} + \frac{\partial \vec{V}}{\partial t} \right] \tag{5.22}$$

We now need to obtain a suitable formulation for the force, $d\vec{F}$, or its components, dF_x, dF_y, and dF_z, acting on the element.

Forces Acting on a Fluid Particle

Recall that the forces acting on a fluid element may be classified as body forces and surface forces; surface forces include both normal forces and tangential (shear) forces.

We shall consider the x component of the force acting on a differential element of mass dm and volume $d\mathbf{V} = dx\,dy\,dz$. Only those stresses that act in the x direction will give rise to surface forces in the x direction. If the stresses at the center of the differential element are taken to be σ_{xx}, τ_{yx}, and τ_{zx}, then the stresses acting in the x direction on all faces of the element (obtained by a Taylor series expansion about the center of the element) are as shown in Fig. 5.9.

To obtain the net surface force in the x direction, dF_{S_x}, we must sum the forces in the x direction. Thus,

$$dF_{S_x} = \left(\sigma_{xx} + \frac{\partial \sigma_{xx}}{\partial x}\frac{dx}{2}\right)dy\,dz - \left(\sigma_{xx} - \frac{\partial \sigma_{xx}}{\partial x}\frac{dx}{2}\right)dy\,dz$$

$$+ \left(\tau_{yx} + \frac{\partial \tau_{yx}}{\partial y}\frac{dy}{2}\right)dx\,dz - \left(\tau_{yx} - \frac{\partial \tau_{yx}}{\partial y}\frac{dy}{2}\right)dx\,dz$$

$$+ \left(\tau_{zx} + \frac{\partial \tau_{zx}}{\partial z}\frac{dz}{2}\right)dx\,dy - \left(\tau_{zx} - \frac{\partial \tau_{zx}}{\partial z}\frac{dz}{2}\right)dx\,dy$$

On simplifying, we obtain

$$dF_{S_x} = \left(\frac{\partial \sigma_{xx}}{\partial x} + \frac{\partial \tau_{yx}}{\partial y} + \frac{\partial \tau_{zx}}{\partial z}\right)dx\,dy\,dz$$

When the force of gravity is the only body force acting, then the body force per unit mass is $\vec{g}$. The net force in the x direction, dF_x, is given by

$$dF_x = dF_{B_x} + dF_{S_x} = \left(\rho g_x + \frac{\partial \sigma_{xx}}{\partial x} + \frac{\partial \tau_{yx}}{\partial y} + \frac{\partial \tau_{zx}}{\partial z}\right)dx\,dy\,dz \qquad (5.23a)$$

We can derive similar expressions for the force components in the y and z directions:

$$dF_y = dF_{B_y} + dF_{S_y} = \left(\rho g_y + \frac{\partial \tau_{xy}}{\partial x} + \frac{\partial \sigma_{yy}}{\partial y} + \frac{\partial \tau_{zy}}{\partial z}\right)dx\,dy\,dz \qquad (5.23b)$$

$$dF_z = dF_{B_z} + dF_{S_z} = \left(\rho g_z + \frac{\partial \tau_{xz}}{\partial x} + \frac{\partial \tau_{yz}}{\partial y} + \frac{\partial \sigma_{zz}}{\partial z}\right)dx\,dy\,dz \qquad (5.23c)$$

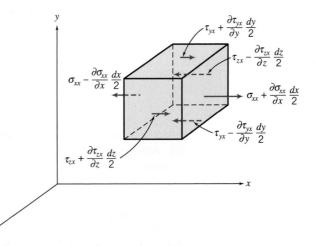

Fig. 5.9 Stresses in the x direction on an element of fluid.

Differential Momentum Equation

We have now formulated expressions for the components, dF_x, dF_y, and dF_z, of the force, $d\vec{F}$, acting on the element of mass dm. If we substitute these expressions (Eqs. 5.23) for the force components into the x, y, and z components of Eq. 5.22, we obtain the differential equations of motion,

$$\rho g_x + \frac{\partial \sigma_{xx}}{\partial x} + \frac{\partial \tau_{yx}}{\partial y} + \frac{\partial \tau_{zx}}{\partial z} = \rho \left(\frac{\partial u}{\partial t} + u \frac{\partial u}{\partial x} + v \frac{\partial u}{\partial y} + w \frac{\partial u}{\partial z} \right) \tag{5.24a}$$

$$\rho g_y + \frac{\partial \tau_{xy}}{\partial x} + \frac{\partial \sigma_{yy}}{\partial y} + \frac{\partial \tau_{zy}}{\partial z} = \rho \left(\frac{\partial v}{\partial t} + u \frac{\partial v}{\partial x} + v \frac{\partial v}{\partial y} + w \frac{\partial v}{\partial z} \right) \tag{5.24b}$$

$$\rho g_z + \frac{\partial \tau_{xz}}{\partial x} + \frac{\partial \tau_{yz}}{\partial y} + \frac{\partial \sigma_{zz}}{\partial z} = \rho \left(\frac{\partial w}{\partial t} + u \frac{\partial w}{\partial x} + v \frac{\partial w}{\partial y} + w \frac{\partial w}{\partial z} \right) \tag{5.24c}$$

Equations 5.24 are the differential equations of motion for any fluid satisfying the continuum assumption. Before the equations can be used to solve for u, v, and w, suitable expressions for the stresses must be obtained in terms of the velocity and pressure fields.

Newtonian Fluid: Navier–Stokes Equations

For a Newtonian fluid the viscous stress is directly proportional to the rate of shearing strain (angular deformation rate). We saw in Chapter 2 that for one-dimensional laminar Newtonian flow the shear stress is proportional to the rate of angular deformation: $\tau_{yx} = du/dy$ (Eq. 2.15). For a three-dimensional flow the situation is a bit more complicated (among other things we need to use the more complicated expressions for rate of angular deformation, Eq. 5.19). The stresses may be expressed in terms of velocity gradients and fluid properties in rectangular coordinates as follows:[8]

$$\tau_{xy} = \tau_{yx} = \mu \left(\frac{\partial v}{\partial x} + \frac{\partial u}{\partial y} \right) \tag{5.25a}$$

$$\tau_{yz} = \tau_{zy} = \mu \left(\frac{\partial w}{\partial y} + \frac{\partial v}{\partial z} \right) \tag{5.25b}$$

$$\tau_{zx} = \tau_{xz} = \mu \left(\frac{\partial u}{\partial z} + \frac{\partial w}{\partial x} \right) \tag{5.25c}$$

$$\sigma_{xx} = -p - \frac{2}{3} \mu \nabla \cdot \vec{V} + 2\mu \frac{\partial u}{\partial x} \tag{5.25d}$$

$$\sigma_{yy} = -p - \frac{2}{3} \mu \nabla \cdot \vec{V} + 2\mu \frac{\partial v}{\partial y} \tag{5.25e}$$

$$\sigma_{zz} = -p - \frac{2}{3} \mu \nabla \cdot \vec{V} + 2\mu \frac{\partial w}{\partial z} \tag{5.25f}$$

where p is the local thermodynamic pressure.[9] Thermodynamic pressure is related to the density and temperature by the thermodynamic relation usually called the equation of state.

---

[8] The derivation of these results is beyond the scope of this book. Detailed derivations may be found in References 2, 3, and 4.

[9] Reference 5 discusses the relation between the thermodynamic pressure and the average pressure defined as $p = -(\sigma_{xx} + \sigma_{yy} + \sigma_{zz})/3$.

If these expressions for the stresses are introduced into the differential equations of motion (Eqs. 5.24), we obtain

$$\rho \frac{Du}{Dt} = \rho g_x - \frac{\partial p}{\partial x} + \frac{\partial}{\partial x}\left[\mu\left(2\frac{\partial u}{\partial x} - \frac{2}{3}\nabla \cdot \vec{V}\right)\right] + \frac{\partial}{\partial y}\left[\mu\left(\frac{\partial u}{\partial y} + \frac{\partial v}{\partial x}\right)\right]$$
$$+ \frac{\partial}{\partial z}\left[\mu\left(\frac{\partial w}{\partial x} + \frac{\partial u}{\partial z}\right)\right] \tag{5.26a}$$

$$\rho \frac{Dv}{Dt} = \rho g_y - \frac{\partial p}{\partial y} + \frac{\partial}{\partial x}\left[\mu\left(\frac{\partial u}{\partial y} + \frac{\partial v}{\partial x}\right)\right] + \frac{\partial}{\partial y}\left[\mu\left(2\frac{\partial v}{\partial y} - \frac{2}{3}\nabla \cdot \vec{V}\right)\right]$$
$$+ \frac{\partial}{\partial z}\left[\mu\left(\frac{\partial v}{\partial z} + \frac{\partial w}{\partial y}\right)\right] \tag{5.26b}$$

$$\rho \frac{Dw}{Dt} = \rho g_z - \frac{\partial p}{\partial z} + \frac{\partial}{\partial x}\left[\mu\left(\frac{\partial w}{\partial x} + \frac{\partial u}{\partial z}\right)\right] + \frac{\partial}{\partial y}\left[\mu\left(\frac{\partial w}{\partial z} + \frac{\partial w}{\partial y}\right)\right]$$
$$+ \frac{\partial}{\partial z}\left[\mu\left(2\frac{\partial w}{\partial z} - \frac{2}{3}\nabla \cdot \vec{V}\right)\right] \tag{5.26c}$$

These equations of motion are called the *Navier–Stokes* equations. The equations are greatly simplified when applied to *incompressible flow* with *constant viscosity*. Under these conditions the equations reduce to

$$\rho\left(\frac{\partial u}{\partial t} + u\frac{\partial u}{\partial x} + v\frac{\partial u}{\partial y} + w\frac{\partial u}{\partial z}\right) = \rho g_x - \frac{\partial p}{\partial x} + \mu\left(\frac{\partial^2 u}{\partial x^2} + \frac{\partial^2 u}{\partial y^2} + \frac{\partial^2 u}{\partial z^2}\right) \tag{5.27a}$$

$$\rho\left(\frac{\partial v}{\partial t} + u\frac{\partial v}{\partial x} + v\frac{\partial v}{\partial y} + w\frac{\partial v}{\partial z}\right) = \rho g_y - \frac{\partial p}{\partial y} + \mu\left(\frac{\partial^2 v}{\partial x^2} + \frac{\partial^2 v}{\partial y^2} + \frac{\partial^2 v}{\partial z^2}\right) \tag{5.27b}$$

$$\rho\left(\frac{\partial w}{\partial t} + u\frac{\partial w}{\partial x} + v\frac{\partial w}{\partial y} + w\frac{\partial w}{\partial z}\right) = \rho g_z - \frac{\partial p}{\partial z} + \mu\left(\frac{\partial^2 w}{\partial x^2} + \frac{\partial^2 w}{\partial y^2} + \frac{\partial^2 w}{\partial z^2}\right) \tag{5.27c}$$

This form of the Navier–Stokes equations is probably (next to the Bernoulli equation) the most famous set of equations in fluid mechanics, and has been widely studied. These equations, with the continuity equation (Eq. 5.1c), form a set of four coupled nonlinear partial differential equations for u, v, w, and p. In principle, these four equations describe many common flows; the only restrictions are that the fluid be Newtonian (with a constant viscosity) and incompressible. For example, lubrication theory (describing the behavior of machine bearings), pipe flows, and even the motion of your coffee as you stir it are explained by these equations. Unfortunately, they are impossible to solve analytically, except for the most basic cases [3], in which we have simple boundaries and initial or boundary conditions! We will solve the equations for such a simple problem in Example 5.9.

The Navier–Stokes equations for constant density and viscosity are given in cylindrical coordinates in Appendix B; they have also been derived for spherical coordinates [3]. We will apply the cylindrical coordinate form in solving Example 5.10.

In recent years computational fluid dynamics (CFD) computer applications (such as *Fluent* [6] and *STAR-CD* [7]) have been developed for analyzing the Navier–Stokes equations for more complicated, real-world problems. Although a detailed treatment of the topic is beyond the scope of this text, we shall have a brief introduction to CFD in the next section.

For the case of frictionless flow ($\mu = 0$) the equations of motion (Eqs. 5.26 or Eqs. 5.27) reduce to *Euler's equation*,

$$\rho \frac{D\vec{V}}{Dt} = \rho\vec{g} - \nabla p$$

We shall consider the case of frictionless flow in Chapter 6.

Example 5.9   Analysis of Fully Developed Laminar Flow down an Inclined Plane Surface

A liquid flows down an inclined plane surface in a steady, fully developed laminar film of thickness h. Simplify the continuity and Navier–Stokes equations to model this flow field. Obtain expressions for the liquid velocity profile, the shear stress distribution, the volume flow rate, and the average velocity. Relate the liquid film thickness to the volume flow rate per unit depth of surface normal to the flow. Calculate the volume flow rate in a film of water $h = 1$ mm thick, flowing on a surface $b = 1$ m wide, inclined at $\theta = 15°$ to the horizontal.

GIVEN: Liquid flow down an inclined plane surface in a steady, fully developed laminar film of thickness h.

FIND: (a) Continuity and Navier–Stokes equations simplified to model this flow field.
(b) Velocity profile.
(c) Shear stress distribution.
(d) Volume flow rate per unit depth of surface normal to diagram.
(e) Average flow velocity.
(f) Film thickness in terms of volume flow rate per unit depth of surface normal to diagram.
(g) Volume flow rate in a film of water 1 mm thick on a surface 1 m wide, inclined at 15° to the horizontal.

SOLUTION:
The geometry and coordinate system used to model the flow field are shown. (It is convenient to align one coordinate with the flow down the plane surface.)

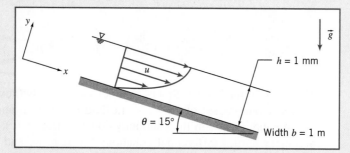

The Governing equations written for incompressible flow with constant viscosity are

$$\frac{\partial u}{\partial x}^{\,4} + \frac{\partial v}{\partial y} + \frac{\partial w}{\partial z}^{\,3} = 0 \tag{5.1c}$$

$$\rho\left(\frac{\partial u}{\partial t}^{\,1} + u\frac{\partial u}{\partial x}^{\,4} + v\frac{\partial u}{\partial y}^{\,5} + w\frac{\partial u}{\partial z}^{\,3}\right) = \rho g_x - \frac{\partial p}{\partial x}^{\,4} + \mu\left(\frac{\partial^2 u}{\partial x^2}^{\,4} + \frac{\partial^2 u}{\partial y^2} + \frac{\partial^2 u}{\partial z^2}^{\,3}\right) \tag{5.27a}$$

$$\rho\left(\frac{\partial v}{\partial t}^{\,1} + u\frac{\partial v}{\partial x}^{\,4} + v\frac{\partial v}{\partial y}^{\,5} + w\frac{\partial v}{\partial z}^{\,3}\right) = \rho g_y - \frac{\partial p}{\partial y} + \mu\left(\frac{\partial^2 v}{\partial x^2}^{\,4} + \frac{\partial^2 v}{\partial y^2}^{\,5} + \frac{\partial^2 v}{\partial z^2}^{\,3}\right) \tag{5.27b}$$

$$\rho\left(\frac{\partial w}{\partial t}^{\,1} + u\frac{\partial w}{\partial x}^{\,3} + v\frac{\partial w}{\partial y}^{\,3} + w\frac{\partial w}{\partial z}^{\,3}\right) = \rho g_z^{\,3} - \frac{\partial p}{\partial z}^{\,3} + \mu\left(\frac{\partial^2 w}{\partial x^2}^{\,3} + \frac{\partial^2 w}{\partial y^2}^{\,3} + \frac{\partial^2 w}{\partial z^2}^{\,3}\right) \tag{5.27c}$$

The terms canceled to simplify the basic equations are keyed by number to the assumptions listed below. The assumptions are discussed in the order in which they are applied to simplify the equations.

Assumptions: (1) Steady flow (given).
(2) Incompressible flow; ρ = constant.
(3) No flow or variation of properties in the z direction; $w = 0$ and $\partial/\partial z = 0$.
(4) Fully developed flow, so no properties vary in the x direction; $\partial/\partial x = 0$.

Assumption (1) eliminates time variations in any fluid property.

Assumption (2) eliminates space variations in density.

Assumption (3) states that there is no z component of velocity and no property variations in the z direction. All terms in the z component of the Navier–Stokes equation cancel.

After assumption (4) is applied, the continuity equation reduces to $\partial v/\partial y = 0$. Assumptions (3) and (4) also indicate that $\partial v/\partial z = 0$ and $\partial v/\partial x = 0$. Therefore v must be constant. Since v is zero at the solid surface, then v must be zero everywhere.

The fact that $v = 0$ reduces the Navier–Stokes equations further, as indicated by (5) in Eqs 5.27a and 5.27b. The final simplified equations are

$$0 = \rho g_x + \mu \frac{\partial^2 u}{\partial y^2} \tag{1}$$

$$0 = \rho g_y - \frac{\partial p}{\partial y} \tag{2}$$

Since $\partial u/\partial z = 0$ (assumption 3) and $\partial u/\partial x = 0$ (assumption 4), then u is at most a function of y, and $\partial^2 u/\partial y^2 = d^2 u/dy^2$, and from Eq. 1, then

$$\frac{d^2 u}{dy^2} = -\frac{\rho g_x}{\mu} = -\rho g \frac{\sin \theta}{\mu}$$

Integrating,

$$\frac{du}{dy} = -\rho g \frac{\sin \theta}{\mu} y + c_1 \tag{3}$$

and integrating again,

$$u = -\rho g \frac{\sin \theta}{\mu} \frac{y^2}{2} + c_1 y + c_2 \tag{4}$$

The boundary conditions needed to evaluate the constants are the no-slip condition at the solid surface ($u = 0$ at $y = 0$) and the zero-shear-stress condition at the liquid free surface ($du/dy = 0$ at $y = h$).

Evaluating Eq. 4 at $y = 0$ gives $c_2 = 0$. From Eq. 3 at $y = h$,

$$0 = -\rho g \frac{\sin \theta}{\mu} h + c_1$$

or

$$c_1 = \rho g \frac{\sin \theta}{\mu} h$$

Substituting into Eq. 4 we obtain the velocity profile

$$u = -\rho g \frac{\sin \theta}{\mu} \frac{y^2}{2} + \rho g \frac{\sin \theta}{\mu} hy$$

or

$$u = \rho g \frac{\sin \theta}{\mu} \left(hy - \frac{y^2}{2} \right) \qquad\qquad u(y)$$

The shear stress distribution is (from Eq. 5.25a after setting $\partial v/\partial x$ to zero, or alternatively, for one-dimensional flow, from Eq. 2.15)

$$\tau_{yx} = \mu \frac{du}{dy} = \rho g \sin \theta \, (h - y) \qquad\qquad \tau_{yx}(y)$$

The shear stress in the fluid reaches its maximum value at the wall ($y = 0$); as we expect, it is zero at the free surface ($y = h$). At the wall the shear stress τ_{yx} is positive but the surface normal *for the fluid* is in the negative y direction; hence the shear force acts in the negative x direction, and just balances the x component of the body force acting on the fluid. The volume flow rate is

$$Q = \int_A u \, dA = \int_0^h u \, b \, dy$$

where b is the surface width in the z direction. Substituting,

$$Q = \int_0^h \frac{\rho g \sin\theta}{\mu}\left(hy - \frac{y^2}{2}\right) b \, dy = \rho g \frac{\sin\theta \, b}{\mu}\left[\frac{hy^2}{2} - \frac{y^3}{6}\right]_0^h$$

$$Q = \frac{\rho g \sin\theta \, b}{\mu}\frac{h^3}{3} \qquad\qquad\qquad\qquad\qquad\qquad\qquad\qquad (5)\,Q$$

The average flow velocity is $\vec{V} = Q/A = Q/bh$. Thus

$$\vec{V} = \frac{Q}{bh} = \frac{\rho g \sin\theta \, h^2}{\mu}\frac{}{3} \qquad\qquad\qquad\qquad\qquad\qquad \overline{V}$$

Solving for film thickness gives

$$h = \left[\frac{3\mu Q}{\rho g \sin\theta \, b}\right]^{1/3} \qquad\qquad\qquad\qquad\qquad\qquad\qquad (6)\,h$$

A film of water $h = 1$ mm thick on a plane $b = 1$ m wide, inclined at $\theta = 15°$, would carry

$$Q = \frac{999 \text{ kg}}{\text{m}^3} \times \frac{9.81 \text{ m}}{\text{s}^2} \times \sin(15°) \times 1 \text{ m} \times \frac{\text{m} \cdot \text{s}}{1.00 \times 10^{-3} \text{ kg}} \times \frac{(0.001)^3 \text{ m}^3}{3} \times \frac{1000 \text{ L}}{\text{m}^3}$$

$$Q = 0.846 \text{ L/s} \qquad\qquad\qquad\qquad\qquad\qquad\qquad\qquad\qquad\qquad\qquad Q$$

Notes:

✓ This problem illustrates how the full Navier–Stokes equations (Eqs. 5.27) can sometimes be reduced to a set of solvable equations (Eqs. 1 and 2 in this problem).

✓ After integration of the simplified equations, boundary (or initial) conditions are used to complete the solution.

✓ Once the velocity field is obtained, other useful quantities (e.g., shear stress, volume flow rate) can be found.

✓ Equations (5) and (6) show that even for fairly simple problems the results can be quite complicated: The depth of the flow depends in a nonlinear way on flow rate ($h \propto Q^{1/3}$).

Example 5.10   Analysis of Laminar Viscometric Flow between Coaxial Cylinders

A viscous liquid fills the annular gap between vertical concentric cylinders. The inner cylinder is stationary, and the outer cylinder rotates at constant speed. The flow is laminar. Simplify the continuity, Navier–Stokes, and tangential shear stress equations to model this flow field. Obtain expressions for the liquid velocity profile and the shear stress distribution. Compare the shear stress at the surface of the inner cylinder with that computed from a planar approximation obtained by "unwrapping" the annulus into a plane and assuming a linear velocity profile across the gap. Determine the ratio of cylinder radii for which the planar approximation predicts the correct shear stress at the surface of the inner cylinder within 1 percent.

GIVEN: Laminar viscometric flow of liquid in annular gap between vertical concentric cylinders. The inner cylinder is stationary, and the outer cylinder rotates at constant speed.

FIND: (a) Continuity and Navier–Stokes equations simplified to model this flow field.
(b) Velocity profile in the annular gap.
(c) Shear stress distribution in the annular gap.
(d) Shear stress at the surface of the inner cylinder.
(e) Comparison with "planar" approximation for constant shear stress in the narrow gap between cylinders.
(f) Ratio of cylinder radii for which the planar approximation predicts shear stress within 1 percent of the correct value.

SOLUTION:

The geometry and coordinate system used to model the flow field are shown. (The z coordinate is directed vertically upward; as a consequence, $g_r = g_\theta = 0$ and $g_z = -g$.)

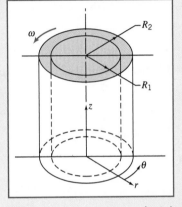

The continuity, Navier–Stokes, and tangential shear stress equations (from Appendix B) written for incompressible flow with constant viscosity are

$$\frac{1}{r}\frac{\partial}{\partial r}(rv_r) + \frac{1}{r}\frac{\partial}{\partial \theta}(v_\theta)^4 + \frac{\partial}{\partial z}(v_z)^3 = 0 \qquad \text{(B.1)}$$

r component:

$$\rho\left(\frac{\partial v_r}{\partial t}^1 + v_r\frac{\partial v_r}{\partial r}^5 + \frac{v_\theta}{r}\frac{\partial v_r}{\partial \theta}^4 - \frac{v_\theta^2}{r} + v_z\frac{\partial v_r}{\partial z}^3\right)$$

$$= \rho g_r^0 - \frac{\partial p}{\partial r} + \mu\left\{\frac{\partial}{\partial r}\left(\frac{1}{r}\frac{\partial}{\partial r}[rv_r]\right) + \frac{1}{r^2}\frac{\partial^2 v_r}{\partial \theta^2}^4 - \frac{2}{r^2}\frac{\partial v_\theta}{\partial \theta}^4 + \frac{\partial^2 v_r}{\partial z^2}^3\right\} \qquad \text{(B.3a)}$$

θ component:

$$\rho\left(\frac{\partial v_\theta}{\partial t}^1 + v_r\frac{\partial v_\theta}{\partial r}^5 + \frac{v_\theta}{r}\frac{\partial v_\theta}{\partial \theta}^4 + \frac{v_r v_\theta}{r}^5 + v_z\frac{\partial v_\theta}{\partial z}^3\right)$$

$$= \rho g_\theta^0 - \frac{1}{r}\frac{\partial p}{\partial \theta}^4 + \mu\left\{\frac{\partial}{\partial r}\left(\frac{1}{r}\frac{\partial}{\partial r}[rv_\theta]\right) + \frac{1}{r^2}\frac{\partial^2 v_\theta}{\partial \theta^2}^4 + \frac{2}{r^2}\frac{\partial v_r}{\partial \theta}^4 + \frac{\partial^2 v_\theta}{\partial z^2}^3\right\} \qquad \text{(B.3b)}$$

z component:

$$\rho\left(\frac{\partial v_z}{\partial t}^1 + v_r\frac{\partial v_z}{\partial r}^5 + \frac{v_\theta}{r}\frac{\partial v_z}{\partial \theta}^4 + v_z\frac{\partial v_z}{\partial z}^3\right) = \rho g_z - \frac{\partial p}{\partial z} + \mu\left\{\frac{1}{r}\frac{\partial}{\partial r}\left(r\frac{\partial v_z}{\partial r}^3\right) + \frac{1}{r^2}\frac{\partial^2 v_z}{\partial \theta^2}^3 + \frac{\partial^2 v_z}{\partial z^2}^3\right\} \qquad \text{(B.3c)}$$

$$\tau_{r\theta} = \mu\left[r\frac{\partial}{\partial r}\left(\frac{v_\theta}{r}\right) + \frac{1}{r}\frac{\partial v_r}{\partial \theta}^4\right] \qquad \text{(B.2)}$$

The terms canceled to simplify the basic equations are keyed by number to the assumptions listed below. The assumptions are discussed in the order in which they are applied to simplify the equations.

Assumptions: (1) Steady flow; angular speed of outer cylinder is constant.
(2) Incompressible flow; ρ = constant.
(3) No flow or variation of properties in the z direction; $v_z = 0$ and $\partial/\partial z = 0$.
(4) Circumferentially symmetric flow, so properties do not vary with θ, so $\partial/\partial \theta = 0$.

Assumption (1) eliminates time variations in fluid properties.

Assumption (2) eliminates space variations in density.

Assumption (3) causes all terms in the z component of the Navier–Stokes equation (Eq. B.3c) to cancel, except for the hydrostatic pressure distribution.

After assumptions (3) and (4) are applied, the continuity equation (Eq. B.1) reduces to

$$\frac{1}{r}\frac{\partial}{\partial r}(r v_r) = 0$$

Because $\partial/\partial\theta = 0$ and $\partial/\partial z = 0$ by assumptions (3) and (4), then $\frac{\partial}{\partial r} \rightarrow \frac{d}{dr}$, so integrating gives

$$r v_r = \text{constant}$$

Since v_r is zero at the solid surface of each cylinder, then v_r must be zero everywhere.

The fact that $v_r = 0$ reduces the Navier–Stokes equations further, as indicated by cancellations (5). The final equations (Eqs. B.3a and B.3b) reduce to

$$-\rho\frac{v_\theta^2}{r} = -\frac{\partial p}{\partial r}$$

$$0 = \mu\left\{\frac{\partial}{\partial r}\left(\frac{1}{r}\frac{\partial}{\partial r}[r v_\theta]\right)\right\} \underline{\hspace{4cm}}$$

But since $\partial/\partial\theta = 0$ and $\partial/\partial z = 0$ by assumptions (3) and (4), then v_θ is a function of radius only, and

$$\frac{d}{dr}\left(\frac{1}{r}\frac{d}{dr}[r v_\theta]\right) = 0$$

Integrating once,

$$\frac{1}{r}\frac{d}{dr}[r v_\theta] = c_1$$

or

$$\frac{d}{dr}[r v_\theta] = c_1 r$$

Integrating again,

$$r v_\theta = c_1\frac{r^2}{2} + c_2 \qquad \text{or} \qquad v_\theta = c_1\frac{r}{2} + c_2\frac{1}{r}$$

Two boundary conditions are needed to evaluate constants c_1 and c_2. The boundary conditions are

$$
\begin{aligned}
v_\theta &= \omega R_2 && \text{at} && r = R_2 && \text{and}\\
v_\theta &= 0 && \text{at} && r = R_1
\end{aligned}
$$

Substituting

$$\omega R_2 = c_1\frac{R_2}{2} + c_2\frac{1}{R_2}$$

$$0 = c_1\frac{R_1}{2} + c_2\frac{1}{R_1}$$

After considerable algebra

$$c_1 = \frac{2\omega}{1 - \left(\dfrac{R_1}{R_2}\right)^2} \qquad \text{and} \qquad c_2 = \frac{-\omega R_1^2}{1 - \left(\dfrac{R_1}{R_2}\right)^2}$$

Substituting into the expression for v_θ,

$$v_\theta = \frac{\omega r}{1 - \left(\dfrac{R_1}{R_2}\right)^2} - \frac{\omega R_1^2/r}{1 - \left(\dfrac{R_1}{R_2}\right)^2} = \frac{\omega R_1}{1 - \left(\dfrac{R_1}{R_2}\right)^2}\left[\frac{r}{R_1} - \frac{R_1}{r}\right] \qquad\qquad \overset{\longleftarrow}{} v_\theta(r)$$

The shear stress distribution is obtained from Eq.B.2 after using assumption (4):

$$\tau_{r\theta} = \mu r \frac{d}{dr}\left(\frac{v_\theta}{r}\right) = \mu r \frac{d}{dr}\left\{\frac{\omega R_1}{1-\left(\frac{R_1}{R_2}\right)^2}\left[\frac{1}{R_1}-\frac{R_1}{r^2}\right]\right\} = \mu r \frac{\omega R_1}{1-\left(\frac{R_1}{R_2}\right)^2}(-2)\left(-\frac{R_1}{r^3}\right)$$

$$\tau_{r\theta} = \mu\frac{2\omega R_1^2}{1-\left(\frac{R_1}{R_2}\right)^2}\frac{1}{r^2} \qquad\qquad\qquad \tau_{r\theta}$$

At the surface of the inner cylinder, $r = R_1$, so

$$\tau_{\text{surface}} = \mu\frac{2\omega}{1-\left(\frac{R_1}{R_2}\right)^2} \qquad\qquad\qquad \tau_{\text{surface}}$$

For a "planar" gap

$$\tau_{\text{planar}} = \mu\frac{\Delta v}{\Delta y} = \mu\frac{\omega R_2}{R_2-R_1}$$

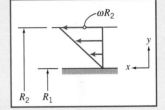

or

$$\tau_{\text{planar}} = \mu\frac{\omega}{1-\frac{R_1}{R_2}} \qquad\qquad\qquad \tau_{\text{planar}}$$

Factoring the denominator of the exact expression for shear stress at the surface gives

$$\tau_{\text{surface}} = \mu\frac{2\omega}{\left(1-\frac{R_1}{R_2}\right)\left(1+\frac{R_1}{R_2}\right)} = \mu\frac{\omega}{1-\frac{R_1}{R_2}}\cdot\frac{2}{1+\frac{R_1}{R_2}}$$

Thus

$$\frac{\tau_{\text{surface}}}{\tau_{\text{planar}}} = \frac{2}{1+\frac{R_1}{R_2}}$$

For 1 percent accuracy,

$$1.01 = \frac{2}{1+\frac{R_1}{R_2}}$$

or

$$\frac{R_1}{R_2} = \frac{1}{1.01}(2-1.01) = 0.980 \qquad\qquad\qquad \frac{R_1}{R_2}$$

The accuracy criterion is met when the gap width is less than 2 percent of the cylinder radius.

Notes:
  ✓ This problem illustrates how the full Navier–Stokes equations in cylindrical coordinates (Eqs. B1 to B.3) can sometimes be reduced to a set of solvable equations.
  ✓ As in Example 5.9, after integration of the simplified equations, boundary (or initial) conditions are used to complete the solution.
  ✓ Once the velocity field is obtained, other useful quantities (in this problem, shear stress) can be found. The *Excel* workbook for this problem compares the viscometer and linear velocity profiles. It also allows one to derive the appropriate value of the viscometer outer radius to meet a prescribed accuracy of the planar approximation. We will discuss the concentric cylinder–infinite parallel plates approximation again in Chapter 8.

*5-5   INTRODUCTION TO COMPUTATIONAL FLUID DYNAMICS

In this section we will discuss in a very basic manner the ideas behind *computational fluid dynamics* (CFD). We will review some numerical methods concepts by applying them only to a simple 1D model, but these concepts are so fundamental that they are applicable to almost any CFD calculation. As we apply the CFD solution procedure to the model, we'll comment on the extension to the general case. The goal is to enable the reader to apply the CFD solution procedure to simple nonlinear equations.

The Need for CFD

As discussed in Section 5-4, the equations describing fluid flow can be a bit intimidating. For example, even though we may limit ourselves to incompressible flows for which the viscosity is constant, we still end up with the following equations:

$$\frac{\partial u}{\partial x} + \frac{\partial v}{\partial y} + \frac{\partial w}{\partial z} = 0 \tag{5.1c}$$

$$\rho\left(\frac{\partial u}{\partial t} + u\frac{\partial u}{\partial x} + v\frac{\partial u}{\partial y} + w\frac{\partial u}{\partial z}\right) = \rho g_x - \frac{\partial p}{\partial x} + \mu\left(\frac{\partial^2 u}{\partial x^2} + \frac{\partial^2 u}{\partial y^2} + \frac{\partial^2 u}{\partial z^2}\right) \tag{5.27a}$$

$$\rho\left(\frac{\partial v}{\partial t} + u\frac{\partial v}{\partial x} + v\frac{\partial v}{\partial y} + w\frac{\partial v}{\partial z}\right) = \rho g_y - \frac{\partial p}{\partial y} + \mu\left(\frac{\partial^2 v}{\partial x^2} + \frac{\partial^2 v}{\partial y^2} + \frac{\partial^2 v}{\partial z^2}\right) \tag{5.27b}$$

$$\rho\left(\frac{\partial w}{\partial t} + u\frac{\partial w}{\partial x} + v\frac{\partial w}{\partial y} + w\frac{\partial w}{\partial z}\right) = \rho g_z - \frac{\partial p}{\partial z} + \mu\left(\frac{\partial^2 w}{\partial x^2} + \frac{\partial^2 w}{\partial y^2} + \frac{\partial^2 w}{\partial z^2}\right) \tag{5.27c}$$

Equation 5.1c is the continuity equation (mass conservation) and Eqs. 5.27 are the Navier–Stokes equations (momentum), expressed in Cartesian coordinates. In principle, we can solve these equations for the velocity field $\vec{V} = \hat{i}u + \hat{j}v + \hat{k}w$ and pressure field p, given sufficient initial and boundary conditions. Note that in general, u, v, w, and p all depend on x, y, z, and t. In practice, there is no general analytic solution to these equations, for the combined effect of a number of reasons (none of which is insurmountable by itself):

1. They are coupled. The unknowns, u, v, w, and p, appear in all the equations (p is not in Eq. 5.1c) and we cannot manipulate the equations to end up with a single equation for any one of the unknowns. Hence we must solve for all unknowns simultaneously.

2. They are nonlinear. For example, in Eq. 5.27a, the convective acceleration term, $u\,\partial u/\partial x + v\,\partial u/\partial y + w\,\partial u/\partial z$, has products of u with itself as well as with v and w. The consequence of this is that we cannot take one solution to the equations and combine it with a second solution to obtain a third solution. We will see in Chapter 6 that if we can limit ourselves to frictionless flow, we *can* derive linear equations, which will allow us to do this combining procedure (you may wish to look at Table 6.3 for some beautiful examples of this).

3. They are second-order partial differential equations. For example, in Eq. 5.27a, the viscous term, $\mu(\partial^2 u/\partial x^2 + \partial^2 u/\partial y^2 + \partial^2 u/\partial z^2)$, is second-order in u. These are obviously of a different order of complexity (no pun intended) than, say, a first-order ordinary differential equation.

These difficulties have led engineers, scientists, and mathematicians to adopt several approaches to the solution of fluid mechanics problems.

For relatively simple physical geometries and boundary or initial conditions, the equations can often be reduced to a solvable form. We saw two examples of this in Examples 5.9 and 5.10 (for cylindrical forms of the equations).

If we can neglect the viscous terms, the resulting incompressible, inviscid flow can often be successfully analyzed. This is the entire topic of Chapter 6.

---

*This section may be omitted without loss of continuity in the text material.

Of course, most incompressible flows of interest do not have simple geometries and are not inviscid; for these, we are stuck with Eqs. 5.1c and 5.27. The only option remaining is to use numerical methods to analyze problems. It is possible to obtain approximate computer-based solutions to the equations for a variety of engineering problems. This is the main subject matter of CFD.

Applications of CFD

CFD is employed in a variety of applications and is now widely used in various industries. To illustrate the industrial applications of CFD, we present below some examples developed using FLUENT, a CFD software package from ANSYS, Inc. CFD is used to study the flow field around vehicles including cars, trucks, airplanes, helicopters, and ships. Figure 5.10 shows the paths taken by selected fluid particles around a Formula 1 car. By studying such pathlines and other flow attributes, engineers gain insights into how to design the car so as to reduce drag and enhance performance. The flow through a catalytic converter, a device used to clean automotive exhaust gases so that we can all breathe easier, is shown in Figure 5.11. This image shows path lines colored by velocity magnitude. CFD helps engineers develop more effective catalytic converters by allowing them to study how different chemical species mix and react in the device. Figure 5.12 presents contours of static pressure in a backward-inclined centrifugal fan used in ventilation applications. Fan performance characteristics obtained from the CFD simulations compared well with results from physical tests.

Fig. 5.10 Pathlines around a Formula1 Car (image courtesy of ANSYS, Inc. © 2008).

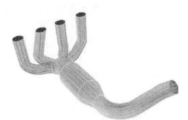

Fig. 5.11 Flow through a catalytic converter (image courtesy of ANSYS, Inc. © 2008).

Fig. 5.12 Static pressure contours for flow through a centrifugal fan (image courtesy of ANSYS, Inc. © 2008).

CFD is attractive to industry since it is more cost-effective than physical testing. However, we must note that complex flow simulations are challenging and error-prone, and it takes a lot of engineering expertise to obtain realistic solutions.

The Strategy of CFD

Broadly, the strategy of CFD is to replace the continuous problem domain with a discrete domain using a "grid" or "mesh." In the continuous domain, each flow variable is defined at every point in the domain. For instance, the pressure p in the continuous 1D domain shown in Fig. 5.13 would be given as

$$p = p(x), \qquad 0 \leq x \leq 1$$

In the discrete domain, each flow variable is defined only at the grid points. So, in the discrete domain in Fig. 5.13, the pressure would be defined only at the N grid points,

$$p_i = p(x_i), \quad i = 1, 2, \ldots, N$$

We can extend this continuous-to-discrete conversion to two or three dimensions. Figure 5.14 shows a 2D grid used for solving the flow over an airfoil. The grid points are the locations where the grid lines cross. In a CFD solution, we would directly solve for the relevant flow variables only at the grid points. The values at other locations are determined by interpolating the values at the grid points. The governing partial differential equations and boundary conditions are defined in terms of the continuous variables p, $\vec{V}$, and so on. We can approximate these in the discrete domain in terms of the discrete variables p_i, $\vec{V}_i$, and so on. Using this procedure, we end up with a discrete system that consists of a large set of coupled, algebraic equations in the

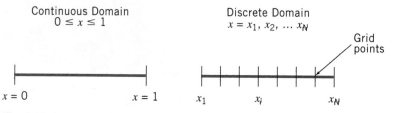

Fig. 5.13 Continuous and discrete domains for a one-dimensional problem.

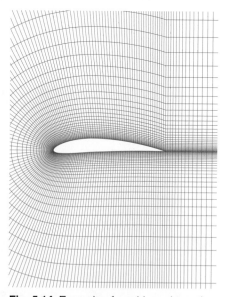

Fig. 5.14 Example of a grid used to solve for the flow around an airfoil.

discrete variables. Setting up the discrete system and solving it (which is a matrix inversion problem) involves a very large number of repetitive calculations, a task made possible only with the advent of modern computers.

Discretization Using the Finite-Difference Method

To keep the details simple, we will illustrate the process of going from the continuous domain to the discrete domain by applying it to the following simple 1D equation:

$$\frac{du}{dx} + u^m = 0; \qquad 0 \le x \le 1; \qquad u(0) = 1 \tag{5.28}$$

We'll first consider the case where $m = 1$, which is the case when the equation is linear. We'll later consider the nonlinear case $m = 2$. Keep in mind that the above problem is an initial-value problem, while the numerical solution procedure below is more suitable for boundary-value problems. Most CFD problems are boundary-value problems.

We'll derive a discrete representation of Eq. 5.28 with $m = 1$ on the rudimentary grid shown in Fig. 5.15. This grid has four equally spaced grid points, with $\Delta x = \frac{1}{3}$ being the spacing between successive points. Since the governing equation is valid at any grid point, we have

$$\left(\frac{du}{dx}\right)_i + u_i = 0 \tag{5.29}$$

where the subscript i represents the value at grid point x_i. In order to get an expression for $(du/dx)_i$ in terms of u values at the grid points, we expand u_{i-1} in a Taylor series:

$$u_{i-1} = u_i - \left(\frac{du}{dx}\right)_i \Delta x + \left(\frac{d^2u}{dx^2}\right)_i \frac{\Delta x^2}{2} - \left(\frac{d^3u}{dx^3}\right)_i \frac{\Delta x^3}{6} + \cdots$$

Rearranging this gives

$$\left(\frac{du}{dx}\right)_i = \frac{u_i - u_{i-1}}{\Delta x} + \left(\frac{d^2u}{dx^2}\right)_i \frac{\Delta x}{2} - \left(\frac{d^3u}{dx^3}\right)_i \frac{\Delta x^2}{6} + \cdots \tag{5.30}$$

We'll neglect the second-, third-, and higher-order terms on the right. Thus, the first term on the right is the finite-difference representation for $(du/dx)_i$ we are seeking. The error in $(du/dx)_i$ due to the neglected terms in the Taylor series is called the *truncation error*. In general, the truncation error is the difference between the differential equation and its finite-difference representation. The leading-order term in the truncation error in Eq. 5.30 is proportional to Δx. Equation 5.30 is rewritten as

$$\left(\frac{du}{dx}\right)_i = \frac{u_i - u_{i-1}}{\Delta x} + O(\Delta x) \tag{5.31}$$

where the last term is pronounced "order of delta x." The notation $O(\Delta x)$ has a precise mathematical meaning, which we will not go into here. Instead, in the interest of brevity, we'll return to it briefly later when we discuss the topic of grid convergence. Since the truncation error is proportional to the first power of Δx, this discrete representation is termed *first-order accurate*.

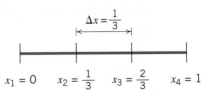

Fig. 5.15 A simple 1D grid with four grid points.

Using Eq. 5.31 in Eq. 5.29, we get the following discrete representation for our model equation:

$$\frac{u_i - u_{i-1}}{\Delta x} + u_i = 0 \tag{5.32}$$

Note that we have gone from a differential equation to an algebraic equation! Though we have not written it out explicitly, don't forget that the error in this representation is $O(\Delta x)$.

This method of deriving the discrete equation using Taylor's series expansions is called the *finite-difference method*. Keep in mind that most industrial CFD software packages use the *finite-volume* or *finite-element* discretization methods since they are better suited to modeling flow past complex geometries. We will stick with the finite-difference method in this text since it is the easiest to understand; the concepts discussed also apply to the other discretization methods.

Assembly of Discrete System and Application of Boundary Conditions

Rearranging the discrete equation, Eq. 5.32, we get

$$-u_{i-1} + (1 + \Delta x)u_i = 0$$

Applying this equation at grid points $i = 2, 3, 4$ for the 1D grid in Fig. 5.15 gives

$$-u_1 + (1 + \Delta x)u_2 = 0 \tag{5.33a}$$

$$-u_2 + (1 + \Delta x)u_3 = 0 \tag{5.33b}$$

$$-u_3 + (1 + \Delta x)u_4 = 0 \tag{5.33c}$$

The discrete equation cannot be applied at the left boundary ($i = 1$) since $u_{i-1} = u_0$ is not defined. Instead, we use the boundary condition to get

$$u_1 = 1 \tag{5.33d}$$

Equations 5.33 form a system of four simultaneous algebraic equations in the four unknowns u_1, u_2, u_3, and u_4. It's convenient to write this system in matrix form:

$$\begin{bmatrix} 1 & 0 & 0 & 0 \\ -1 & 1+\Delta x & 0 & 0 \\ 0 & -1 & 1+\Delta x & 0 \\ 0 & 0 & -1 & 1+\Delta x \end{bmatrix} \begin{bmatrix} u_1 \\ u_2 \\ u_3 \\ u_4 \end{bmatrix} = \begin{bmatrix} 1 \\ 0 \\ 0 \\ 0 \end{bmatrix} \tag{5.34}$$

In a general situation (e.g., 2D or 3D domains), we would apply the discrete equations to the grid points in the interior of the domain. For grid points at or near the boundary, we would apply a combination of the discrete equations and boundary conditions. In the end, one would obtain a system of simultaneous algebraic equations similar to Eqs. 5.33 and a matrix equation similar to Eq. 5.34, with the number of equations being equal to the number of independent discrete variables. The process is essentially the same as for the model equation above, with the details obviously being much more complex.

Solution of Discrete System

The discrete system (Eq. 5.34) for our own simple 1D example can be easily inverted, using any number of techniques of linear algebra, to obtain the unknowns at the grid points. For $\Delta x = \frac{1}{3}$, the solution is

$$u_1 = 1 \quad u_2 = \frac{3}{4} \quad u_3 = \frac{9}{16} \quad u_4 = \frac{27}{64}$$

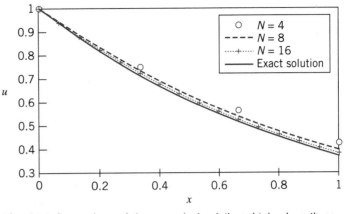

Fig. 5.16 Comparison of the numerical solution obtained on three different grids with the exact solution.

The exact solution for Eq. 5.28 with $m = 1$ is easily shown to be

$$u_{\text{exact}} = e^{-x}$$

Figure 5.16 shows the comparison of the discrete solution obtained on the four-point grid with the exact solution, using *Excel*. The error is largest at the right boundary, where it is equal to 14.7 percent. [It also shows the results using eight points ($N = 8$, $\Delta x = \frac{1}{7}$) and sixteen points ($N = 16$, $\Delta x = \frac{1}{15}$), which we discuss below.]

In a practical CFD application, we would have thousands, even millions, of unknowns in the discrete system; if one were to use, say, a Gaussian elimination procedure to invert the calculations, it would be extremely time-consuming even with a fast computer. Hence a lot of work has gone into optimizing the matrix inversion in order to minimize the CPU time and memory required. The matrix to be inverted is sparse; that is, most of the entries in it are zeros. The nonzero entries are clustered around the diagonal since the discrete equation at a grid point contains only quantities at the neighboring grid points, as shown in Eq. 5.34. A CFD code would store only the nonzero values to minimize memory usage. It would also generally use an iterative procedure to invert the matrix; the longer one iterates, the closer one gets to the true solution for the matrix inversion. We'll return to this idea a little later.

Grid Convergence

While developing the finite-difference approximation for the 1D model problem (Eq. 5.34), we saw that the truncation error in our discrete system is $O(\Delta x)$. Hence we expect that as the number of grid points is increased and Δx is reduced, the error in the numerical solution would decrease and the agreement between the numerical and exact solutions would get better.

Let's consider the effect of increasing the number of grid points N on the numerical solution of the 1D problem. We'll consider $N = 8$ and $N = 16$ in addition to the $N = 4$ case solved previously. We repeat the above assembly and solution steps on each of these additional grids; instead of the 4×4 problem of Eq. 5.34, we end up with an 8×8 and a 16×16 problem, respectively. Figure 5.16 compares the results obtained (using *Excel*) on the three grids with the exact solution. As expected, the numerical error decreases as the number of grid points is increased (but this only goes so far—if we make Δx too small, we start to get round-off errors accumulating to make the results get worse!). When the numerical solutions obtained on different grids agree to within a level of tolerance specified by the user, they are referred to as "grid-converged" solutions. It is very important to investigate the effect of grid resolution on the solution in all CFD problems. We should never trust a CFD solution unless we are convinced that the solution is grid-converged to an acceptance level of tolerance (which will be problem dependent).

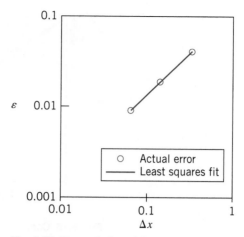

Fig. 5.17 The variation of the aggregate error ε with Δx.

Let ε be some aggregate measure of the error in the numerical solution obtained on a specific grid. For the numerical solutions in Fig. 5.17, ε is, for instance, estimated as the RMS of the difference between the numerical and exact solutions:

$$\varepsilon = \sqrt{\frac{\sum_{i=1}^{N} \left(u_i - u_{i_{\text{exact}}}\right)^2}{N}}$$

It's reasonable to expect that

$$\varepsilon \propto \Delta x^n$$

Since the truncation error is $O(\Delta x)$ for our discretization scheme, we expect $n = 1$ (or more precisely, $n \to 1$ as $\Delta x \to 0$). The ε values for the three grids are plotted on a logarithmic scale in Fig. 5.17. The slope of the least squares fit gives the value of n. For Fig. 5.17, we get $n = 0.92$, which is quite close to 1. We expect that as the grid is refined further and Δx becomes progressively smaller, the value of n will approach 1. For a second-order scheme, we would expect $n \sim 2$; this means the discretization error will decrease twice as fast on refining the grid.

Dealing with Nonlinearity

The Navier–Stokes equations (Eqs. 5.27) contain nonlinear convection terms; for example, in Eq. 5.27a, the convective acceleration term, $u\,\partial u/\partial x + v\,\partial u/\partial y + w\,\partial u/\partial z$, has products of u with itself as well as with v and w. Phenomena such as turbulence and chemical reaction introduce additional nonlinearities. The highly nonlinear nature of the governing equations for a fluid makes it challenging to obtain accurate numerical solutions for complex flows of practical interest.

We will demonstrate the effect of nonlinearity by setting $m = 2$ in our simple 1D example, Eq. 5.28:

$$\frac{du}{dx} + u^2 = 0; \quad 0 \le x \le 1; \quad u(0) = 1$$

A first-order finite-difference approximation to this equation, analogous to that in Eq. 5.32 for $m = 1$, is

$$\frac{u_i - u_{i-1}}{\Delta x} + u_i^2 = 0 \tag{5.35}$$

This is a nonlinear algebraic equation with the u_i^2 term being the source of the nonlinearity.

The strategy that is adopted to deal with nonlinearity is to linearize the equations around a *guess value* of the solution and to iterate until the guess agrees with the solution to a specified tolerance level. We'll illustrate this on the above example. Let u_{g_i} be the guess for u_i. Define

$$\Delta u_i = u_i - u_{g_i}$$

Rearranging and squaring this equation gives

$$u_i^2 = u_{g_i}^2 + 2u_{g_i}\Delta u_i + (\Delta u_i)^2$$

Assuming that $\Delta u_i \ll u_{g_i}$, we can neglect the $(\Delta u_i)^2$ term to get

$$u_i^2 \approx u_{g_i}^2 + 2u_{g_i}\Delta u_i = u_{g_i}^2 + 2u_{g_i}(u_i - u_{g_i})$$

Thus

$$u_i^2 \approx 2u_{g_i}u_i - u_{g_i}^2 \tag{5.36}$$

The finite-difference approximation, Eq. 5.35, after linearization in u_i, becomes

$$\frac{u_i - u_{i-1}}{\Delta x} + 2u_{g_i}u_i - u_{g_i}^2 = 0 \tag{5.37}$$

Since the error due to linearization is $O(\Delta u^2)$, it tends to zero as $u_g \to u$.

In order to calculate the finite-difference approximation, Eq. 5.37, we need guess values u_g at the grid points. We start with an initial guess value in the first iteration. For each subsequent iteration, the u value obtained in the previous iteration is used as the guess value. We continue the iterations until they converge. We'll defer the discussion on how to evaluate convergence until a little later.

This is essentially the process used in CFD codes to linearize the nonlinear terms in the conservation equations, with the details varying depending on the code. The important points to remember are that the linearization is performed about a guess and that it is necessary to iterate through successive approximations until the iterations converge.

Direct and Iterative Solvers

We saw that we need to perform iterations to deal with the nonlinear terms in the governing equations. We next discuss another factor that makes it necessary to carry out iterations in practical CFD problems.

As an exercise, you can verify that the discrete equation system resulting from the finite-difference approximation of Eq. 5.37, on our four-point grid, is

$$\begin{bmatrix} 1 & 0 & 0 & 0 \\ -1 & 1 + 2\Delta x u_{g_2} & 0 & 0 \\ 0 & -1 & 1 + 2\Delta x u_{g_3} & 0 \\ 0 & 0 & -1 & 1 + 2\Delta x u_{g_4} \end{bmatrix} \begin{bmatrix} u_1 \\ u_2 \\ u_3 \\ u_4 \end{bmatrix} = \begin{bmatrix} 1 \\ \Delta x u_{g_2}^2 \\ \Delta x u_{g_3}^2 \\ \Delta x u_{g_4}^2 \end{bmatrix} \tag{5.38}$$

In a practical problem, one would usually have thousands to millions of grid points or cells so that each dimension of the above matrix would be of the order of a million (with most of the elements being zeros). Inverting such a matrix directly would take a prohibitively large amount of memory, so instead the matrix is inverted using an iterative scheme as discussed below.

Rearrange the finite-difference approximation, Eq. 5.37, at grid point i so that u_i is expressed in terms of the values at the neighboring grid points and the guess values:

$$u_i = \frac{u_{i-1} + \Delta x\, u_{g_i}^2}{1 + 2\Delta x\, u_{g_i}}$$

If a neighboring value at the current iteration level is not available, we use the guess value for it. Let's say that we sweep from right to left on our grid; that is, we update u_4, then u_3, and finally u_2 in each iteration. In any iteration, u_{i-1} is not available while updating u_i and so we use the guess value $u_{g_{i-1}}$ for it instead:

$$u_i = \frac{u_{g_{i-1}} + \Delta x\, u_{g_i}^2}{1 + 2\Delta x\, u_{g_i}} \tag{5.39}$$

Since we are using the guess values at neighboring points, we are effectively obtaining only an approximate solution for the matrix inversion in Eq. 5.38 during each iteration, but in the process we have greatly reduced the memory required for the inversion. This trade-off is a good strategy since it doesn't make sense to expend a great deal of resources to do an exact matrix inversion when the matrix elements depend on guess values that are continuously being refined. We have in effect combined the iteration to handle nonlinear terms with the iteration for matrix inversion into a single iteration process. Most importantly, as the iterations converge and $u_g \rightarrow u$, the approximate solution for the matrix inversion tends towards the exact solution for the inversion, since the error introduced by using u_g instead of u in Eq. 5.39 also tends to zero. We arrive at the solution without explicitly forming the matrix system (Eq. 5.38), which greatly simplifies the computer implementation.

Thus, iteration serves two purposes:

1. It allows for efficient matrix inversion with greatly reduced memory requirements.

2. It enables us to solve nonlinear equations.

In steady problems, a common and effective strategy used in CFD codes is to solve the unsteady form of the governing equations and "march" the solution in time until the solution converges to a steady value. In this case, each time step is effectively an iteration, with the the guess value at any time level being given by the solution at the previous time level.

Iterative Convergence

Recall that as $u_g \rightarrow u$, the linearization and matrix inversion errors tend to zero. Hence we continue the iteration process until some selected measure of the difference between u_g and u, referred to as the residual, is "small enough." We could, for instance, define the residual R as the RMS value of the difference between u and u_g on the grid:

$$R \equiv \sqrt{\frac{\sum\limits_{i=1}^{N} (u_i - u_{g_i})^2}{N}}$$

It's useful to scale this residual with the average value of u in the domain. Scaling ensures that the residual is a *relative* rather than an *absolute* measure. Scaling the above residual by dividing by the average value of u gives

$$R = \left(\sqrt{\frac{\sum\limits_{i=1}^{N} (u_i - u_{g_i})^2}{N}} \right) \left(\frac{N}{\sum\limits_{i=1}^{N} u_i} \right) = \frac{\sqrt{N \sum\limits_{i=1}^{N} (u_i - u_{g_i})^2}}{\sum\limits_{i=1}^{N} u_i} \tag{5.40}$$

In our nonlinear 1D example, we'll take the initial guess at all grid points to be equal to the value at the left boundary, that is, $u_g^{(1)} = 1$ (where $^{(1)}$ signifies the first iteration). In each iteration, we update u_g, sweep from right to left on the grid updating, in turn, u_4, u_3, and u_2 using Eq. 5.39, and calculate the residual using Eq. 5.40. We'll terminate the iterations when the residual falls below 10^{-9} (this is referred to as the *convergence criterion*). The variation of the residual with iterations is shown in Fig. 5.18. Note that a logarithmic scale is used for the ordinate. The iterative process

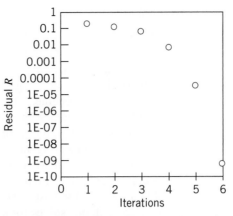

Fig. 5.18 Convergence history for the model nonlinear problem.

converges to a level smaller than 10^{-9} in only six iterations. In more complex problems, many more iterations would be necessary for achieving convergence.

The solution after two, four, and six iterations and the exact solution are shown in Fig. 5.19. It can easily be verified that the exact solution is given by

$$u_{\text{exact}} = \frac{1}{x+1}$$

The solutions for four and six iterations are indistinguishable on the graph. This is another indication that the solution has converged. The converged solution doesn't agree well with the exact solution because we are using a coarse grid for which the truncation error is relatively large (we will repeat this problem with finer grids as problems at the end of the chapter). The iterative convergence error, which is of order 10^{-9}, is swamped by the truncation error, which is of order 10^{-1}. So driving the residual down to 10^{-9} when the truncation error is of order 10^{-1} is obviously a waste of computing resources. In an efficient calculation, both errors would be set at comparable levels, and less than a tolerance level that was chosen by the user. The agreement between the numerical and exact solutions should get much better on refining the grid, as was the linear case (for $m = 1$). Different CFD codes use slightly different definitions for the residual. You should always read the documentation from the application to understand how the residual is calculated.

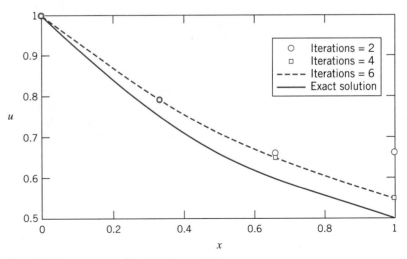

Fig. 5.19 Progression of the iterative solution.

Concluding Remarks

In our simple 1D example, the iterations converged very rapidly. In practice, one encounters many instances when the iterative process doesn't converge or converges lethargically. Hence, it's useful to know *a priori* the conditions under which a given numerical scheme converges. This is determined by performing a stability analysis of the numerical scheme. Stability analysis of numerical schemes and the various stabilization strategies used to overcome nonconvergence are very important topics and necessary for you to explore if you decide to delve further into the topic of CFD.

Many engineering flows are turbulent, characterized by large, nearly random fluctuations in velocity and pressure in both space and time. Turbulent flows often occur in the limit of high Reynolds numbers. For most turbulent flows, it is not possible to resolve the vast range of time and length scales, even with powerful computers. Instead, one solves for a statistical average of the flow properties. In order to do this, it is necessary to augment the governing equations with a turbulence model. Unfortunately, there is no single turbulence model that is uniformly valid for all flows, so most CFD packages allow you to choose from among several models. Before you use a turbulence model, you need to understand its possibilities and limitations for the type of flow being considered.

In this brief introduction we have tried to explain some of the concepts behind CFD. Because it is so difficult and time consuming to develop CFD code, most engineers use commercial packages such as *Fluent* [6] and *STAR-CD* [7]. This introduction will have hopefully indicated for you the complexity behind those applications, so that they are not completely a "black box" of magic tricks.

5-6 **SUMMARY AND USEFUL EQUATIONS**

In this chapter we have:

✓ Derived the differential form of the conservation of mass (continuity) equation in vector form as well as in rectangular and cylindrical coordinates.

✓ *Defined the stream function ψ for a two-dimensional incompressible flow and learned how to derive the velocity components from it, as well as to find ψ from the velocity field.

✓ Learned how to obtain the total, local, and convective accelerations of a fluid particle from the velocity field.

✓ Presented examples of fluid particle translation and rotation, and both linear and angular deformation.

✓ Defined vorticity and circulation of a flow.

✓ Derived, and solved for simple cases, the Navier–Stokes equations, and discussed the physical meaning of each term.

✓ *Been introduced to some basis ideas behind computational fluid dynamics.

We have also explored such ideas as how to determine whether a flow is incompressible by using the velocity field and, given one velocity component of a two-dimensional incompressible flow field, how to derive the other velocity component.

In this chapter we studied the effects of viscous stresses on fluid particle deformation and rotation; in the next chapter we examine flows for which viscous effects are negligible.

---

*This topic applies to a section that may be omitted without loss of continuity in the text material.

Note: Most of the Useful Equations in the table below have a number of constraints or limitations—*be sure to refer to their page numbers for details!*

	Useful Equations		
Continuity equation (general, rectangular coordinates):	$$\frac{\partial \rho u}{\partial x} + \frac{\partial \rho v}{\partial y} + \frac{\partial \rho w}{\partial z} + \frac{\partial \rho}{\partial t} = 0$$ $$\nabla \cdot \rho \vec{V} + \frac{\partial \rho}{\partial t} = 0$$	(5.1a) (5.1b)	Page 163
Continuity equation (incompressible, rectangular coordinates):	$$\frac{\partial u}{\partial x} + \frac{\partial v}{\partial y} + \frac{\partial w}{\partial z} = \nabla \cdot \vec{V} = 0$$	(5.1c)	Page 164
Continuity equation (steady, rectangular coordinates):	$$\frac{\partial \rho u}{\partial x} + \frac{\partial \rho v}{\partial y} + \frac{\partial \rho w}{\partial z} = \nabla \cdot \rho \vec{V} = 0$$	(5.1d)	Page 165
Continuity equation (general, cylindrical coordinates):	$$\frac{1}{r}\frac{\partial (r\rho V_r)}{\partial r} + \frac{1}{r}\frac{\partial (\rho V_\theta)}{\partial \theta} + \frac{\partial (\rho V_z)}{\partial z} + \frac{\partial \rho}{\partial t} = 0$$ $$\nabla \cdot \rho \vec{V} + \frac{\partial \rho}{\partial t} = 0$$	(5.2a) (5.1b)	Pages 167
Continuity equation (incompressible, cylindrical coordinates):	$$\frac{1}{r}\frac{\partial (rV_r)}{\partial r} + \frac{1}{r}\frac{\partial V_\theta}{\partial \theta} + \frac{\partial V_z}{\partial z} = \nabla \cdot \vec{V} = 0$$	(5.2b)	Page 169
Continuity equation (steady, cylindrical coordinates):	$$\frac{1}{r}\frac{\partial (r\rho V_r)}{\partial r} + \frac{1}{r}\frac{\partial (\rho V_\theta)}{\partial \theta} + \frac{\partial (\rho V_z)}{\partial z} = \nabla \cdot \rho \vec{V} = 0$$	(5.2c)	Page 169
Continuity equation (2D, incompressible, rectangular coordinates):	$$\frac{\partial u}{\partial x} + \frac{\partial v}{\partial y} = 0$$	(5.3)	Page 170
Stream function (2D, incompressible, rectangular coordinates):	$$u \equiv \frac{\partial \psi}{\partial y} \quad \text{and} \quad v \equiv -\frac{\partial \psi}{\partial x}$$	(5.4)	Page 170
Continuity equation (2D, incompressible, cylindrical coordinates):	$$\frac{\partial (rV_r)}{\partial r} + \frac{\partial V_\theta}{\partial \theta} = 0$$	(5.7)	Page 172
Stream function (2D, incompressible, cylindrical coordinates):	$$V_r \equiv \frac{1}{r}\frac{\partial \psi}{\partial \theta} \quad \text{and} \quad V_\theta \equiv -\frac{\partial \psi}{\partial r}$$	(5.8)	Page 172
Particle acceleration (rectangular coordinates):	$$\frac{D\vec{V}}{Dt} \equiv \vec{a}_p = u\frac{\partial \vec{V}}{\partial x} + v\frac{\partial \vec{V}}{\partial y} + w\frac{\partial \vec{V}}{\partial z} + \frac{\partial \vec{V}}{\partial t}$$	(5.9)	Page 175
Particle acceleration components in rectangular coordinates:	$$a_{x_p} = \frac{Du}{Dt} = u\frac{\partial u}{\partial x} + v\frac{\partial u}{\partial y} + w\frac{\partial u}{\partial z} + \frac{\partial u}{\partial t}$$ $$a_{y_p} = \frac{Dv}{Dt} = u\frac{\partial v}{\partial x} + v\frac{\partial v}{\partial y} + w\frac{\partial v}{\partial z} + \frac{\partial v}{\partial t}$$ $$a_{z_p} = \frac{Dw}{Dt} = u\frac{\partial w}{\partial x} + v\frac{\partial w}{\partial y} + w\frac{\partial w}{\partial z} + \frac{\partial w}{\partial t}$$	(5.11a) (5.11b) (5.11c)	Page 176

Particle acceleration components in cylindrical coordinates:	$a_{r_p} = V_r \dfrac{\partial V_r}{\partial r} + \dfrac{V_\theta}{r}\dfrac{\partial V_r}{\partial \theta} - \dfrac{V_\theta^2}{r} + V_z\dfrac{\partial V_r}{\partial z} + \dfrac{\partial V_r}{\partial t}$	(5.12a)	Page 177
	$a_{\theta_p} = V_r \dfrac{\partial V_\theta}{\partial r} + \dfrac{V_\theta}{r}\dfrac{\partial V_\theta}{\partial \theta} + \dfrac{V_r V_\theta}{r} + V_z\dfrac{\partial V_\theta}{\partial z}$		
	$\qquad + \dfrac{\partial V_\theta}{\partial t}$	(5.12b)	
	$a_{z_p} = V_r \dfrac{\partial V_z}{\partial r} + \dfrac{V_\theta}{r}\dfrac{\partial V_z}{\partial \theta} + V_z\dfrac{\partial V_z}{\partial z} + \dfrac{\partial V_z}{\partial t}$	(5.12c)	
Navier–Stokes equations (incompressible, constant viscosity):	$\rho\left(\dfrac{\partial u}{\partial t} + u\dfrac{\partial u}{\partial x} + v\dfrac{\partial u}{\partial y} + w\dfrac{\partial u}{\partial z}\right)$		Page 189
	$\qquad = \rho g_x - \dfrac{\partial p}{\partial x} + \mu\left(\dfrac{\partial^2 u}{\partial x^2} + \dfrac{\partial^2 u}{\partial y^2} + \dfrac{\partial^2 u}{\partial z^2}\right)$	(5.27a)	
	$\rho\left(\dfrac{\partial v}{\partial t} + u\dfrac{\partial v}{\partial x} + v\dfrac{\partial v}{\partial y} + w\dfrac{\partial v}{\partial z}\right)$		
	$\qquad = \rho g_y - \dfrac{\partial p}{\partial y} + \mu\left(\dfrac{\partial^2 v}{\partial x^2} + \dfrac{\partial^2 v}{\partial y^2} + \dfrac{\partial^2 v}{\partial z^2}\right)$	(5.27b)	
	$\rho\left(\dfrac{\partial w}{\partial t} + u\dfrac{\partial w}{\partial x} + v\dfrac{\partial w}{\partial y} + w\dfrac{\partial w}{\partial z}\right)$		
	$\qquad = \rho g_z - \dfrac{\partial p}{\partial z} + \mu\left(\dfrac{\partial^2 w}{\partial x^2} + \dfrac{\partial^2 w}{\partial y^2} + \dfrac{\partial^2 w}{\partial z^2}\right)$	(5.27c)	

REFERENCES

1. Li, W. H., and S. H. Lam, *Principles of Fluid Mechanics.* Reading, MA: Addison-Wesley, 1964.

2. Daily, J. W., and D. R. F. Harleman, *Fluid Dynamics.* Reading, MA: Addison-Wesley, 1966.

3. Schlichting, H., *Boundary-Layer Theory*, 7th ed. New York: McGraw-Hill, 1979.

4. White, F. M., *Viscous Fluid Flow*, 3rd ed. New York: McGraw-Hill, 2000.

5. Sabersky, R. H., A. J. Acosta, E. G. Hauptmann, and E. M. Gates, *Fluid Flow—A First Course in Fluid Mechanics*, 4th ed. New Jersey: Prentice Hall, 1999.

6. *Fluent.* Fluent Incorporated, Centerra Resources Park, 10 Cavendish Court, Lebanon, NH 03766 (www.fluent.com).

7. *STAR-CD.* Adapco, 60 Broadhollow Road, Melville, NY 11747 (www.cd-adapco.com).

PROBLEMS

5.1 Which of the following sets of equations represent possible two-dimensional incompressible flow cases?
   a. $u = 2x^2 + y^2 - x^2y$; $v = x^3 + x(y^2 - 2y)$
   b. $u = 2xy - x^2 + y$; $v = 2xy - y^2 + x^2$
   c. $u = xt + 2y$; $v = xt^2 - yt$
   d. $u = (x + 2y)xt$; $v = -(2x + y)yt$

5.2 Which of the following sets of equations represent possible three-dimensional incompressible flow cases?
   a. $u = y^2 + 2xz$; $v = -2yz + x^2yz$; $w = \frac{1}{2}x^2z^2 + x^3y^4$
   b. $u = xyzt$; $v = -xyzt^2$; $w = (z^2/2)(xt^2 - yt)$
   c. $u = x^2 + y + z^2$; $v = x - y + z$; $w = -2xz + y^2 + z$

5.3 The three components of velocity in a velocity field are given by $u = Ax + By + Cz$, $v = Dx + Ey + Fz$, and $w = Gx + Hy + Jz$. Determine the relationship among the coefficients A through J that is necessary if this is to be a possible incompressible flow field.

5.4 For a flow in the xy plane, the x component of velocity is given by $u = Ax(y - B)$, where $A = 1\ \text{ft}^{-1}\cdot\text{s}^{-1}$, $B = 6$ ft, and x and y are measured in feet. Find a possible y component for steady, incompressible flow. Is it also valid for unsteady, incompressible flow? Why? How many y components are possible?

5.5 For a flow in the xy plane, the x component of velocity is given by $u = x^3 - 3xy^2$. Determine a possible y component for steady, incompressible flow. Is it also valid for unsteady, incompressible flow? Why? How many possible y components are there?

5.6 The x component of velocity in a steady, incompressible flow field in the xy plane is $u = A/x$, where $A = 2\ \text{m}^2/\text{s}$, and x is measured in meters. Find the simplest y component of velocity for this flow field.

5.7 The y component of velocity in a steady, incompressible flow field in the xy plane is $v = Axy(y^2 - x^2)$, where $A = 2$

$m^{-3} \cdot s^{-1}$ and x and y are measured in meters. Find the simplest x component of velocity for this flow field.

5.8 The x component of velocity in a steady incompressible flow field in the xy plane is $u = Ae^{x/b} \cos(y/b)$, where $A = 10$ m/s, $b = 5$ m, and x and y are measured in meters. Find the simplest y component of velocity for this flow field.

5.9 The y component of velocity in a steady incompressible flow field in the xy plane is

$$v = \frac{2xy}{(x^2 + y^2)^2}$$

Show that the simplest expression for the x component of velocity is

$$u = \frac{1}{(x^2 + y^2)} - \frac{2y^2}{(x^2 + y^2)^2}$$

5.10 A crude approximation for the x component of velocity in an incompressible laminar boundary layer is a linear variation from $u = 0$ at the surface ($y = 0$) to the freestream velocity, U, at the boundary-layer edge ($y = \delta$). The equation for the profile is $u = Uy/\delta$, where $\delta = cx^{1/2}$ and c is a constant. Show that the simplest expression for the y component of velocity is $v = uy/4x$. Evaluate the maximum value of the ratio v/U, at a location where $x = 0.5$ m and $\delta = 5$ mm.

5.11 A useful approximation for the x component of velocity in an incompressible laminar boundary layer is a parabolic variation from $u = 0$ at the surface ($y = 0$) to the freestream velocity, U, at the edge of the boundary layer ($y = \delta$). The equation for the profile is $u/U = 2(y/\delta) - (y/\delta)^2$, where $\delta = cx^{1/2}$ and c is a constant. Show that the simplest expression for the y component of velocity is

$$\frac{v}{U} = \frac{\delta}{x}\left[\frac{1}{2}\left(\frac{y}{\delta}\right)^2 - \frac{1}{3}\left(\frac{y}{\delta}\right)^3\right]$$

Plot v/U versus y/δ to find the location of the maximum value of the ratio v/U. Evaluate the ratio where $\delta = 5$ mm and $x = 0.5$ m.

5.12 A useful approximation for the x component of velocity in an incompressible laminar boundary layer is a sinusoidal variation from $u = 0$ at the surface ($y = 0$) to the freestream velocity, U, at the edge of the boundary layer ($y = \delta$). The equation for the profile is $u = U \sin(\pi y/2\delta)$, where $\delta = cx^{1/2}$ and c is a constant. Show that the simplest expression for the y component of velocity is

$$\frac{v}{U} = \frac{1}{\pi}\frac{\delta}{\chi}\left[\cos\left(\frac{\pi}{2}\frac{y}{\delta}\right) + \left(\frac{\pi}{2}\frac{y}{\delta}\right)\sin\left(\frac{\pi}{2}\frac{y}{\delta}\right) - 1\right]$$

Plot u/U and v/U versus y/δ, and find the location of the maximum value of the ratio v/U. Evaluate the ratio where $x = 0.5$ m and $\delta = 5$ mm.

5.13 A useful approximation for the x component of velocity in an incompressible laminar boundary layer is a cubic variation from $u = 0$ at the surface ($y = 0$) to the freestream velocity, U, at the edge of the boundary layer ($y = \delta$). The equation for the profile is $u/U = \frac{3}{2}(y/\delta) - \frac{1}{2}(y/\delta)^3$, where $\delta = cx^{1/2}$ and c is a constant. Derive the simplest expression for v/U, the y component of velocity ratio. Plot u/U and v/U versus y/δ, and find the location of the maximum value of the ratio v/U. Evaluate the ratio where $\delta = 5$ mm and $x = 0.5$ m.

5.14 The y component of velocity in a steady, incompressible flow field in the xy plane is $v = -Bxy^3$, where $B = 0.2$ m$^{-3} \cdot$s^{-1}, and x and y are measured in meters. Find the simplest x component of velocity for this flow field. Find the equation of the streamlines for this flow. Plot the streamlines through points (1, 4) and (2, 4).

5.15 For a flow in the xy plane, the x component of velocity is given by $u = Ax^2y^2$, where $A = 0.3$ m$^{-3} \cdot$s^{-1}, and x and y are measured in meters. Find a possible y component for steady, incompressible flow. Is it also valid for unsteady, incompressible flow? Why? How many possible y components are there? Determine the equation of the streamline for the simplest y component of velocity. Plot the streamlines through points (1, 4) and (2, 4).

5.16 Derive the differential form of conservation of mass in rectangular coordinates by expanding the *products* of density and the velocity components, ρu, ρv, and ρw, in a Taylor series about a point O. Show that the result is identical to Eq. 5.1a.

5.17 Consider a water stream from a jet of an oscillating lawn sprinkler. Describe the corresponding pathline and streakline.

5.18 Which of the following sets of equations represent possible incompressible flow cases?
 a. $V_r = U \cos \theta$; $V_\theta = -U \sin \theta$
 b. $V_r = -q/2\pi r$; $V_\theta = K/2\pi r$
 c. $V_r = U \cos \theta [1 - (a/r)^2]$; $V_\theta = -U \sin \theta[1 + (a/r)^2]$

5.19 For an incompressible flow in the $r\theta$ plane, the r component of velocity is given as $V_r = -\Lambda \cos \theta/r^2$. Determine a possible θ component of velocity. How many possible θ components are there?

5.20 A viscous liquid is sheared between two parallel disks of radius R, one of which rotates while the other is fixed. The velocity field is purely tangential, and the velocity varies linearly with z from $V_\theta = 0$ at $z = 0$ (the fixed disk) to the velocity of the rotating disk at its surface ($z = h$). Derive an expression for the velocity field between the disks.

5.21 Evaluate $\nabla \cdot \rho \vec{V}$ in cylindrical coordinates. Use the definition of ∇ in cylindrical coordinates. Substitute the velocity vector and perform the indicated operations, using the hint in footnote 1 on page 169. Collect terms and simplify; show that the result is identical to Eq. 5.2c.

5.22 A velocity field in cylindrical coordinates is given as $\vec{V} = \hat{e}_r A/r + \hat{e}_\theta B/r$, where A and B are constants with dimensions of m^2/s. Does this represent a possible incompressible flow? Sketch the streamline that passes through the point $r_0 = 1$ m, $\theta = 90°$ if $A = B = 1$ m^2/s, if $A = 1$ m^2/s and $B = 0$, and if $B = 1$ m^2/s and $A = 0$.

*5.23 The velocity field for the viscometric flow of Example 5.7 is $\vec{V} = U(y/h)\hat{i}$. Find the stream function for this flow. Locate the streamline that divides the total flow rate into two equal parts.

*5.24 Determine the family of stream functions ψ that will yield the velocity field $\vec{V} = y(2x + 1)\hat{i} + [x(x + 1) - y^2]\hat{j}$.

*5.25 The stream function for a certain incompressible flow field is given by the expression $\psi = -Ur \sin \theta + q\theta/2\pi$. Obtain an expression for the velocity field. Find the stagnation point(s) where $|\vec{V}| = 0$, and show that $\psi = 0$ there.

---

*These problems require material from sections that may be omitted without loss of continuity in the text material.

*5.26 Does the velocity field of Problem 5.22 represent a possible incompressible flow case? If so, evaluate and sketch the stream function for the flow. If not, evaluate the rate of change of density in the flow field.

*5.27 Consider a flow with velocity components $u = 0$, $v = y(y^2 - 3z^2)$, and $w = z(z^2 - 3y^2)$.

    a. Is this a one-, two-, or three-dimensional flow?

    b. Demonstrate whether this is an incompressible or compressible flow.

    c. If possible, derive a stream function for this flow.

*5.28 An incompressible frictionless flow field is specified by the stream function $\psi = -2Ax - 5Ay$, where $A = 1$ m/s, and x and y are coordinates in meters. Sketch the streamlines $\psi = 0$ and $\psi = 5$. Indicate the direction of the velocity vector at the point $(0, 0)$ on the sketch. Determine the magnitude of the flow rate between the streamlines passing through the points $(2, 2)$ and $(4, 1)$.

*5.29 In a parallel one-dimensional flow in the positive x direction, the velocity varies linearly from zero at $y = 0$ to 30 m/s at $y = 1.5$ m. Determine an expression for the stream function, ψ. Also determine the y coordinate above which the volume flow rate is half the total between $y = 0$ and $y = 1.5$ m.

*5.30 A linear velocity profile was used to model flow in a laminar incompressible boundary layer in Problem 5.10. Derive the stream function for this flow field. Locate streamlines at one-quarter and one-half the total volume flow rate in the boundary layer.

*5.31 A parabolic velocity profile was used to model flow in a laminar incompressible boundary layer in Problem 5.11. Derive the stream function for this flow field. Locate streamlines at one-quarter and one-half the total volume flow rate in the boundary layer.

*5.32 Derive the stream function that represents the sinusoidal approximation used to model the x component of velocity for the boundary layer of Problem 5.12. Locate streamlines at one-quarter and one-half the total volume flow rate in the boundary layer.

*5.33 A cubic velocity profile was used to model flow in a laminar incompressible boundary layer in Problem 5.13. Derive the stream function for this flow field. Locate streamlines at one-quarter and one-half the total volume flow rate in the boundary layer.

*5.34 A rigid-body motion was modeled in Example 5.6 by the velocity field $\vec{V} = r\omega\hat{e}_\theta$. Find the stream function for this flow. Evaluate the volume flow rate per unit depth between $r_1 = 0.10$ m and $r_2 = 0.12$ m, if $\omega = 0.5$ rad/s. Sketch the velocity profile along a line of constant θ. Check the flow rate calculated from the stream function by integrating the velocity profile along this line.

*5.35 Example 5.6 showed that the velocity field for a free vortex in the $r\theta$ plane is $\vec{V} = \hat{e}_\theta C/r$. Find the stream function for this flow. Evaluate the volume flow rate per unit depth between $r_1 = 0.10$ m and $r_2 = 0.12$ m, if $C = 0.5$ m²/s. Sketch the velocity profile along a line of constant θ. Check the flow rate calculated from the stream function by integrating the velocity profile along this line.

5.36 Consider the velocity field $\vec{V} = A(x^4 - 6x^2y^2 + y^4)\hat{i} + A(4xy^3 - 4x^3y)\hat{j}$ in the xy plane, where $A = 0.25$ m⁻³·s⁻¹, and the coordinates are measured in meters. Is this a possible incompressible flow field? Calculate the acceleration of a fluid particle at point $(x, y) = (2, 1)$.

5.37 Consider the flow field given by $\vec{V} = xy^2\hat{i} - \frac{1}{3}y^3\hat{j} + xy\hat{k}$. Determine (a) the number of dimensions of the flow, (b) if it is a possible incompressible flow, and (c) the acceleration of a fluid particle at point $(x, y, z) = (1, 2, 3)$.

5.38 Consider the flow field given by $\vec{V} = ax^2y\hat{i} - by\hat{j} + cz^2\hat{k}$, where $a = 1$ m⁻²·s⁻¹, $b = 3$ s⁻¹, and $c = 2$ m⁻¹·s⁻¹. Determine (a) the number of dimensions of the flow, (b) if it is a possible incompressible flow, and (c) the acceleration of a fluid particle at point $(x, y, z) = (3, 1, 2)$.

5.39 The velocity field within a laminar boundary layer is approximated by the expression

$$\vec{V} = \frac{AUy}{x^{1/2}}\hat{i} + \frac{AUy^2}{4x^{3/2}}\hat{j}$$

In this expression, $A = 141$ m⁻¹ᐟ², and $U = 0.240$ m/s is the free-stream velocity. Show that this velocity field represents a possible incompressible flow. Calculate the acceleration of a fluid particle at point $(x, y) = (0.5$ m, 5 mm$)$. Determine the slope of the streamline through the point.

5.40 The x component of velocity in a steady, incompressible flow field in the xy plane is $u = A(x^5 - 10x^3y^2 + 5xy^4)$, where $A = 2$ m⁻⁴·s⁻¹ and x is measured in meters. Find the simplest y component of velocity for this flow field. Evaluate the acceleration of a fluid particle at point $(x, y) = (1, 3)$.

5.41 Consider the velocity field $\vec{V} = Ax/(x^2 + y^2)\hat{i} + Ay/(x^2 + y^2)\hat{j}$ in the xy plane, where $A = 10$ m²/s, and x and y are measured in meters. Is this an incompressible flow field? Derive an expression for the fluid acceleration. Evaluate the velocity and acceleration along the x axis, the y axis, and along a line defined by $y = x$. What can you conclude about this flow field?

5.42 The y component of velocity in a two-dimensional, incompressible flow field is given by $v = -Axy$, where v is in m/s, x and y are in meters, and A is a dimensional constant. There is no velocity component or variation in the z direction. Determine the dimensions of the constant, A. Find the simplest x component of velocity in this flow field. Calculate the acceleration of a fluid particle at point $(x, y) = (1, 2)$.

5.43 An incompressible liquid with negligible viscosity flows steadily through a horizontal pipe of constant diameter. In a porous section of length $L = 0.3$ m, liquid is removed at a constant rate per unit length, so the uniform axial velocity in the pipe is $u(x) = U(1 - x/2L)$, where $U = 5$ m/s. Develop an expression for the acceleration of a fluid particle along the centerline of the porous section.

5.44 An incompressible liquid with negligible viscosity flows steadily through a horizontal pipe. The pipe diameter linearly varies from a diameter of 10 cm to a diameter of 2.5 cm over a length of 2 m. Develop an expression for the acceleration of a fluid particle along the pipe centerline. Plot the centerline velocity and acceleration versus position along the pipe, if the inlet centerline velocity is 1 m/s.

5.45 Solve Problem 4.118 to show that the radial velocity in the narrow gap is $V_r = Q/2\pi rh$. Derive an expression for the acceleration of a fluid particle in the gap.

5.46 Consider the low-speed flow of air between parallel disks as shown. Assume that the flow is incompressible and inviscid,

---

*These problems require material from sections that may be omitted without loss of continuity in the text material.

$apx = u\frac{du}{dx} + v\frac{dv}{dy} + w\frac{dy}{dz} + \frac{\partial u}{\partial t}$

$apx = u\frac{du}{dx} = U(1 - \frac{x}{2L})U(\frac{-1}{2L}) = \frac{-U^2}{2L}(1 - \frac{x}{2L})$

and that the velocity is purely radial and uniform at any section. The flow speed is $V = 15$ m/s at $R = 75$ mm. Simplify the continuity equation to a form applicable to this flow field. Show that a general expression for the velocity field is $\vec{V} = V(R/r)\hat{e}_r$ for $r_i \leq r \leq R$. Calculate the acceleration of a fluid particle at the locations $r = r_i$ and $r = R$.

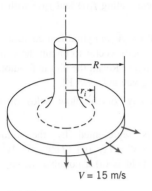

$$V = 15 \text{ m/s}$$

P5.46

5.47 As part of a pollution study, a model concentration c as a function of position x has been developed,

$$c(x) = A(e^{-x/a} - e^{-x/2a})$$

where $A = 10^{-5}$ ppm (parts per million) and $a = 1$ m. Plot this concentration from $x = 0$ to $x = 10$ m. If a vehicle with a pollution sensor travels through this atmosphere at $u = U(U = 20$ m/s), develop an expression for the measured concentration rate of change of c with time, and plot using given data. At what location will the sensor indicate the most rapid rate of change, and what is the value of this rate of change?

5.48 An aircraft flies due North at 300 mph ground speed. Its rate of climb is 3000 ft/min. The vertical temperature gradient is $-3°F$ per 1000 ft of altitude. The ground temperature varies with position through a cold front, falling at the rate of $1°F$ per mile. Compute the rate of temperature change shown by a recorder on board the aircraft.

5.49 As an aircraft flies through a cold front, an on-board instrument indicates that ambient temperature drops at the rate of $0.5°F$ per minute. Other instruments show an air speed of 300 knots and a 3500 ft/min rate of climb. The front is stationary and vertically uniform. Compute the rate of change of temperature with respect to horizontal distance through the cold front.

5.50 After a rainfall the sediment concentration at a certain point in a river increases at the rate of 100 parts per million (ppm) per hour. In addition, the sediment concentration increases with distance downstream as a result of influx from tributary streams; this rate of increase is 50 ppm per mile. At this point the stream flows at 0.5 mph. A boat is used to survey the sediment concentration. The operator is amazed to find three different apparent rates of change of sediment concentration when the boat travels upstream, drifts with the current, or travels downstream. Explain physically why the different rates are observed. If the speed of the boat is 2.5 mph, compute the three rates of change.

5.51 Expand $(\vec{V} \cdot \nabla)\vec{V}$ in rectangular coordinates by direct substitution of the velocity vector to obtain the convective acceleration of a fluid particle. Verify the results given in Eqs. 5.11.

5.52 A velocity field is represented by the expression $\vec{V} = (Ax - B)\hat{i} + Cy\hat{j} + Dt\hat{k}$, where $A = 2$ s^{-1}, $B = 4$ m·s^{-1},

$D = 5$ m·s^{-2}, and the coordinates are measured in meters. Determine the proper value for C if the flow field is to be incompressible. Calculate the acceleration of a fluid particle located at point $(x, y) = (3, 2)$. Plot a few flow streamlines in the xy plane.

5.53 A steady, two-dimensional velocity field is given by $\vec{V} = Ax\hat{i} - Ay\hat{j}$, where $A = 1$ s^{-1}. Show that the streamlines for this flow are rectangular hyperbolas, $xy = C$. Obtain a general expression for the acceleration of a fluid particle in this velocity field. Calculate the acceleration of fluid particles at the points $(x, y) = (\frac{1}{2}, 2)$, $(1, 1)$, and $(2, \frac{1}{2})$, where x and y are measured in meters. Plot streamlines that correspond to $C = 0$, 1, and 2 m^2 and show the acceleration vectors on the streamline plot.

5.54 A velocity field is represented by the expression $\vec{V} = (Ax - B)\hat{i} - Ay\hat{j}$, where $A = 0.2$ s^{-1}, $B = 0.6$ m·s^{-1}, and the coordinates are expressed in meters. Obtain a general expression for the acceleration of a fluid particle in this velocity field. Calculate the acceleration of fluid particles at points $(x, y) = (0, \frac{4}{3})$, $(1, 2)$, and $(2, 4)$. Plot a few streamlines in the xy plane. Show the acceleration vectors on the streamline plot.

5.55 Show that the velocity field of Problem 2.16 represents a possible incompressible flow field. Determine and plot the streamline passing through point $(x, y) = (2, 4)$ at $t = 1.5$ s. For the particle at the same point and time, show on the plot the velocity vector and the vectors representing the local, convective, and total accelerations.

5.56 A linear approximate velocity profile was used in Problem 5.10 to model a laminar incompressible boundary layer on a flat plate. For this profile, obtain expressions for the x and y components of acceleration of a fluid particle in the boundary layer. Locate the maximum magnitudes of the x and y accelerations. Compute the ratio of the maximum x magnitude to the maximum y magnitude for the flow conditions of Problem 5.10.

5.57 A parabolic approximate velocity profile was used in Problem 5.11 to model flow in a laminar incompressible boundary layer on a flat plate. For this profile, find the x component of acceleration, a_x, of a fluid particle within the boundary layer. Plot a_x at location $x = 0.8$ m, where $\delta = 1.2$ mm, for a flow with $U = 6$ m/s. Find the maximum value of a_x at this x location.

5.58 A sinusoidal approximate velocity profile was used in Problem 5.12 to model flow in a laminar incompressible boundary layer on a flat plate. For this profile, obtain an expression for the x and y components of acceleration of a fluid particle in the boundary layer. Plot a_x and a_y at location $x = 1$ m, where $\delta = 1$ mm, for a flow with $U = 5$ m/s. Find the maxima of a_x and a_y at this x location.

5.59 Air flows into the narrow gap, of height h, between closely spaced parallel plates through a porous surface as shown. Use a control volume, with outer surface located at position x, to show that the uniform velocity in the x direction is $u = v_0 x/h$. Find an expression for the velocity component in the y direction. Evaluate the acceleration of a fluid particle in the gap.

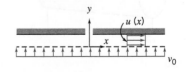

P5.59

5.60 Air flows into the narrow gap, of height h, between closely spaced parallel disks through a porous surface as shown. Use a control volume, with outer surface located at position r, to show that the uniform velocity in the r direction is $V = v_0 r/2h$. Find an expression for the velocity component in the z direction ($v_0 \ll V$). Evaluate the components of acceleration for a fluid particle in the gap.

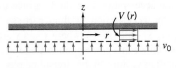

P5.60

5.61 The velocity field for steady inviscid flow from left to right over a circular cylinder, of radius R, is given by

$$\vec{V} = U \cos\theta \left[1 - \left(\frac{R}{r} \right)^2 \right] \hat{e}_r - U \sin\theta \left[1 + \left(\frac{R}{r} \right)^2 \right] \hat{e}_\theta$$

Obtain expressions for the acceleration of a fluid particle moving along the stagnation streamline ($\theta = \pi$) and for the acceleration along the cylinder surface ($r = R$). Plot a_r as a function of r/R for $\theta = \pi$, and as a function of θ for $r = R$; plot a_θ as a function of θ for $r = R$. Comment on the plots. Determine the locations at which these accelerations reach maximum and minimum values.

5.62 Consider the incompressible flow of a fluid through a nozzle as shown. The area of the nozzle is given by $A = A_0(1 - bx)$ and the inlet velocity varies according to $U = U_0(1 - e^{-\lambda t})$, where $A_0 = 0.5$ m^2, $L = 5$ m, $b = 0.1$ m^{-1}, $\lambda = 0.2$ s^{-1}, and $U_0 = 5$ m/s. Find and plot the acceleration on the centerline, with time as a parameter.

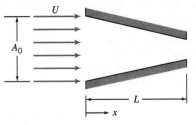

P5.62

5.63 Consider the one-dimensional, incompressible flow through the circular channel shown. The velocity at section ① is given by $U = U_0 + U_1 \sin\omega t$, where $U_0 = 20$ m/s, $U_1 = 2$ m/s, and $\omega = 0.3$ rad/s. The channel dimensions are $L = 1$ m, $R_1 = 0.2$ m, and $R_2 = 0.1$ m. Determine the particle acceleration at the channel exit. Plot the results as a function of time over a complete cycle. On the same plot, show the acceleration at the channel exit if the channel is constant area, rather than convergent, and explain the difference between the curves.

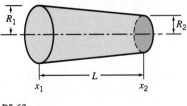

P5.63

5.64 Consider again the steady, two-dimensional velocity field of Problem 5.53. Obtain expressions for the particle coordinates, $x_p = f_1(t)$ and $y_p = f_2(t)$, as functions of time and the initial particle position, (x_0, y_0) at $t = 0$. Determine the time required for a particle to travel from initial position, $(x_0, y_0) = (\frac{1}{2}, 2)$ to positions $(x, y) = (1, 1)$ and $(2, \frac{1}{2})$. Compare the particle accelerations determined by differentiating $f_1(t)$ and $f_2(t)$ with those obtained in Problem 5.53.

5.65 Expand $(\vec{V} \cdot \nabla)\vec{V}$ in cylindrical coordinates by direct substitution of the velocity vector to obtain the convective acceleration of a fluid particle. (Recall the hint in footnote 1 on page 169.) Verify the results given in Eqs. 5.12.

5.66 Which, if any, of the flow fields of Problem 5.1 are irrotational?

5.67 A flow is represented by the velocity field $\vec{V} = (x^7 - 21x^5y^2 + 35x^3y^4 - 7xy^6)\hat{i} + (7x^6y - 35x^4y^3 + 21x^2y^5 - y^7)\hat{j}$. Determine if the field is (a) a possible incompressible flow and (b) irrotational.

5.68 Consider again the sinusoidal velocity profile used to model the x component of velocity for a boundary layer in Problem 5.12. Neglect the vertical component of velocity. Evaluate the circulation around the contour bounded by $x = 0.4$ m, $x = 0.6$ m, $y = 0$, and $y = 8$ mm. What would be the results of this evaluation if it were performed 0.2 m further downstream? Assume $U = 0.5$ m/s.

5.69 Consider the velocity field for flow in a rectangular "corner," $\vec{V} = Ax\hat{i} - Ay\hat{j}$, with $A = 0.3$ s^{-1}, as in Example 5.8. Evaluate the circulation about the unit square of Example 5.8.

5.70 Consider the two-dimensional flow field in which $u = Axy$ and $v = By^2$, where $A = 1$ m$^{-1} \cdot$ s^{-1}, $B = -\frac{1}{2}$m$^{-1} \cdot$ s^{-1}, and the coordinates are measured in meters. Show that the velocity field represents a possible incompressible flow. Determine the rotation at point $(x, y) = (1, 1)$. Evaluate the circulation about the "curve" bounded by $y = 0$, $x = 1$, $y = 1$, and $x = 0$.

*5.71 Consider the flow field represented by the stream function $\psi = x^6 - 15x^4y^2 + 15x^2y^4 - y^6$. Is this a possible two-dimensional, incompressible flow? Is the flow irrotational?

*5.72 Consider a flow field represented by the stream function $\psi = 3x^5y - 10x^3y^3 + 3xy^5$. Is this a possible two-dimensional incompressible flow? Is the flow irrotational?

*5.73 Consider a flow field represented by the stream function $\psi = -A/2(x^2 + y^2)$, where $A =$ constant. Is this a possible two-dimensional incompressible flow? Is the flow irrotational?

*5.74 Consider a velocity field for motion parallel to the x axis with constant shear. The shear rate is $du/dy = A$, where $A = 0.1$ s^{-1}. Obtain an expression for the velocity field, $\vec{V}$. Calculate the rate of rotation. Evaluate the stream function for this flow field.

*5.75 A flow field is represented by the stream function $\psi = x^2 - y^2$. Find the corresponding velocity field. Show that this flow field is irrotational. Plot several streamlines and illustrate the velocity field.

*5.76 Consider the velocity field given by $\vec{V} = Axy\hat{i} + By^2\hat{j}$, where $A = 4$ m$^{-1} \cdot$ s^{-1}, $B = -2$ m$^{-1} \cdot$ s^{-1}, and the coordinates are measured in meters. Determine the fluid rotation. Evaluate the circulation about the "curve" bounded by $y = 0$, $x = 1$, $y = 1$, and x

*These problems require material from sections that may be omitted without loss of continuity in the text material.

= 0. Obtain an expression for the stream function. Plot several streamlines in the first quadrant.

*5.77 Consider the flow field represented by the stream function $\psi = Axy + Ay^2$, where $A = 1 \text{ s}^{-1}$. Show that this represents a possible incompressible flow field. Evaluate the rotation of the flow. Plot a few streamlines in the upper half plane.

*5.78 Consider the flow represented by the velocity field $\vec{V} = (Ay + B)\hat{i} + Ax\hat{j}$, where $A = 6 \text{ s}^{-1}$, $B = 3 \text{ m} \cdot \text{s}^{-1}$, and the coordinates are measured in meters. Obtain an expression for the stream function. Plot several streamlines (including the stagnation streamline) in the first quadrant. Evaluate the circulation about the "curve" bounded by $y = 0$, $x = 1$, $y = 1$, and $x = 0$.

5.79 Consider again the viscometric flow of Example 5.7. Evaluate the average rate of rotation of a pair of perpendicular line segments oriented at $\pm 45°$ from the x axis. Show that this is the same as in the example.

*5.80 The velocity field near the core of a tornado can be approximated as

$$\vec{V} = -\frac{q}{2\pi r}\hat{e}_r + \frac{K}{2\pi r}\hat{e}_\theta$$

Is this an irrotational flow field? Obtain the stream function for this flow.

5.81 Consider the pressure-driven flow between stationary parallel plates separated by distance b. Coordinate y is measured from the bottom plate. The velocity field is given by $u = U(y/b)[1 - (y/b)]$. Obtain an expression for the circulation about a closed contour of height h and length L. Evaluate when $h = b/2$ and when $h = b$. Show that the same result is obtained from the area integral of the Stokes Theorem (Eq. 5.18).

5.82 The velocity profile for fully developed flow in a circular tube is $V_z = V_{max}[1 - (r/R)^2]$. Evaluate the rates of linear and angular deformation for this flow. Obtain an expression for the vorticity vector, $\vec{\zeta}$.

5.83 Consider the pressure-driven flow between stationary parallel plates separated by distance $2b$. Coordinate y is measured from the channel centerline. The velocity field is given by $u = u_{max}[1 - (y/b)^2]$. Evaluate the rates of linear and angular deformation. Obtain an expression for the vorticity vector, $\vec{\zeta}$. Find the location where the vorticity is a maximum.

5.84 A linear velocity profile was used to model flow in a laminar incompressible boundary layer in Problem 5.10. Express the rotation of a fluid particle. Locate the maximum rate of rotation. Express the rate of angular deformation for a fluid particle. Locate the maximum rate of angular deformation. Express the rates of linear deformation for a fluid particle. Locate the maximum rates of linear deformation. Express the shear force per unit volume in the x direction. Locate the maximum shear force per unit volume; interpret this result.

5.85 The x component of velocity in a laminar boundary layer in water is approximated as $u = U \sin(\pi y/2\delta)$, where $U = 3$ m/s and $\delta = 2$ mm. The y component of velocity is much smaller than u. Obtain an expression for the net shear force per unit volume in the x direction on a fluid element. Calculate its maximum value for this flow.

5.86 Problem 4.31 gave the velocity profile for fully developed laminar flow in a circular tube as $u = u_{max}[1 - (r/R)^2]$. Obtain an expression for the shear force per unit volume in the x direction for this flow. Evaluate its maximum value for the conditions of Problem 4.31.

5.87 Use *Excel* to generate the solution of Eq. 5.28 for $m = 1$ shown in Fig. 5.16. To do so, you need to learn how to perform linear algebra in Excel. For example, for $N = 4$ you will end up with the matrix equation of Eq. 5.34. To solve this equation for the u values, you will have to compute the inverse of the 4×4 matrix, and then multiply this inverse into the 4×1 matrix on the right of the equation. In *Excel*, to do *array operations*, you must use the following rules: Pre-select the cells that will contain the result; use the appropriate *Excel array function* (look at *Excel's* Help for details); press Ctrl+Shift+Enter, not just Enter. For example, to invert the 4×4 matrix you would: Pre-select a blank 4×4 array that will contain the inverse matrix; type = *minverse*([array containing matrix to be inverted]); press Ctrl+Shift+Enter. To multiply a 4×4 matrix into a 4×1 matrix you would: Pre-select a blank 4×1 array that will contain the result; type = *mmult*([array containing 4×4 matrix], [array containing 4×1 matrix]); press Ctrl+Shift+Enter.

5.88 Following the steps to convert the differential equation Eq. 5.28 (for $m = 1$) into a difference equation (for example, Eq. 5.34 for $N = 4$), solve

$$\frac{du}{dx} + u = 2\sin(x) \qquad 0 \leq x \leq 1 \qquad u(0) = 0$$

for $N = 4$, 8, and 16 and compare to the exact solution

$$u_{exact} = \sin(x) - \cos(x) + e^{-x}$$

Hints: Follow the rules for *Excel* array operations as described in Problem 5.87. Only the right side of the difference equations will change, compared to the solution method of Eq. 5.28 (for example, only the right side of Eq. 5.34 needs modifying).

5.89 Following the steps to convert the differential equation Eq. 5.28 (for $m = 1$) into a difference equation (for example, Eq. 5.34 for $N = 4$), solve

$$\frac{du}{dx} + u = x^2 \qquad 0 \leq x \leq 1 \qquad u(0) = 2$$

For $N = 4$, 8, and 16 and compare to the extract solution

$$u_{exact} = x^2 - 2x + 2$$

Hint: Follow the hints provided in Problem 5.88.

5.90 A 10-cm cube of mass $M = 5$ kg is sliding across an oiled surface. The oil viscosity is $\mu = 0.4$ N $\cdot$ s/m^2, and the thickness of the oil between the cube and surface is $\delta = 0.25$ mm. If the initial speed of the block is $u_0 = 1$ m/s, use the numerical method that was applied to the linear form of Eq. 5.28 to predict the cube motion for the first second of motion, Use $N = 4$, 8, and 16 and compare to the exact solution

$$u_{exact} = u_0 e^{-(A\mu/M\delta)t}$$

where A is the area of contact. Hint: Follow the hints provided in Problem 5.87.

5.91 Use *Excel* to generate the solutions of Eq. 5.28 for $m = 2$ shown in Fig. 5.19.

*These problems require material from sections that may be omitted without loss of continuity in the text material.

5.92   Use *Excel* to generate the solutions of Eq. 5.28 for $m = 2$, as shown in Fig. 5.19, except use 16 points and as many iterations as necessary to obtain reasonable convergence.

5.93   Use *Excel* to generate the solutions of Eq. 5.28 for $m = -1$, with $u(0) = 2$, using four and 16 points, with sufficient iterations, and compare to the exact solution

$$u_{\text{exact}} = \sqrt{4 - 2x}$$

To do so, follow the steps described in "Dealing with Nonlinearity" section.

5.94   You (someone whose mass is $M = 70$ kg) fall into a fast moving river (the speed of the water is $U = 7.5$ m/s). The equation of motion for your speed u is

$$M\frac{du}{dt} = k(U - u)^2$$

where $k = 10$ N $\cdot$ s^2/m^2 is a constant indicating the drag of the water. Use *Excel* to generate and plot your speed versus time (for the first 10 s) using the same approach as the solutions of Eq. 5.28 for $m = 2$, as shown in Fig. 5.19, except use 16 points and as many iterations as necessary to obtain reasonable convergence. Compare your results to the exact solution

$$u_{\text{exact}} = \frac{kU^2t}{M + kUt}$$

Hint: Use a substitution for $(U - u)$ so the equation of motion looks similar to Eq. 5.28.

Chapter 6

Incompressible Inviscid Flow

CASE STUDY

The Humpback Whale Flipper

Humpback whale flipper and new airfoil design.

Although the Navier–Stokes equations, developed in Chapter 5, and the Euler equation, which we will discuss in this chapter, describe many phenomena in fluid mechanics, we still have a lot to learn about lots of different flow problems. For example, it is conventional knowledge that airfoils and hydrofoils should have leading edges that are smooth and streamlined—even insect debris stuck to the leading edge of a wind turbine rotor, for example, can reduce performance. However,

Dr. Frank E. Fish at West Chester University, Pennsylvania, and research colleagues at Duke University and the U.S. Naval Academy have studied the fluid mechanics of the flippers of the humpback whale, which are anything but smooth, as shown in the figure. The researchers were curious that even allowing for the natural variability that any animal's profile would have, the whale seems to have evolved flippers that have a unique row of bumps, or tubercles, along their leading edges that produce a serrated look.

What are the bumps doing on those flippers? Testing and analysis (using many of the ideas behind incompressible, inviscid flow, which is the topic of this chapter) have been done comparing airfoils with tubercles to similar airfoils with a traditional smooth leading edge. This research showed that the stall angle (the angle of attack at which serious loss of lift occurs as the flow loses its streamlined nature and becomes chaotic) was greatly increased and that when stall occurs, it does so gradually, not suddenly as in most traditional airfoils. In addition, the tubercles airfoil was more efficient: It had significantly less drag and more lift.

It's believed that this occurs because the tubercles channel the wind as it hits the leading edge of the airfoil, causing vortices to develop as the flow moves along the air-foil surface, stabilizing the flow and, among other things, preventing secondary flow from moving across the span of the airfoil to its tip, which causes noise and loss of lift.

Possible future uses of tubercles airfoil sections in-clude virtually any application that needs efficient, quiet performance, with excellent stall behavior: wind tur-bines, airplane wings, ship propellers and rudders, household fans, and so on. It is even possible that exist-ing devices such as large-scale wind turbines may be ret-rofitted with tubercles to improve their performance and reduce their noise.

In Chapter 5 we devoted a great deal of effort to deriving the differential equations (Eqs. 5.24) that describe the behavior of any fluid satisfying the continuum assumption. We also saw how these equations reduced to various particular forms—the most well known being the Navier–Stokes equations for an incompressible, constant viscosity fluid (Eqs. 5.27). Although Eqs. 5.27 describe the behavior of common fluids (e.g., water, air, lubricating oil) for a wide range of problems, as we discussed in Chapter 5, they are unsolvable analytically except for the simplest of geometries and flows. For example, even using the equations to predict the motion of your coffee as you slowly stir it would require the use of an advanced computational fluid dynamics computer application, and the prediction would take a lot longer to compute than the actual stirring! In this chapter, instead of the Navier–Stokes equations, we will study Euler's equation, which applies to an inviscid fluid. Although truly inviscid fluids do not exist, many flow problems (especially in aerodynamics) can be successfully ana-lyzed with the approximation that $\mu = 0$.

6-1   MOMENTUM EQUATION FOR FRICTIONLESS FLOW: EULER'S EQUATION

Euler's equation (obtained from Eqs. 5.27 after neglecting the viscous terms) is

$$\rho \frac{D\vec{V}}{Dt} = \rho\vec{g} - \nabla p \tag{6.1}$$

This equation states that for an inviscid fluid the change in momentum of a fluid par-ticle is caused by the body force (assumed to be gravity only) and the net pressure force. For convenience we recall that the particle acceleration is

$$\frac{D\vec{V}}{Dt} = \frac{\partial\vec{V}}{\partial t} + (\vec{V}\cdot\nabla)\vec{V} \tag{5.10}$$

In this chapter we will apply Eq. 6.1 to the solution of incompressible, inviscid flow problems. In addition to Eq. 6.1 we have the incompressible form of the mass conser-vation equation,

$$\nabla\cdot\vec{V} = 0 \tag{5.1c}$$

Equation 6.1 expressed in rectangular coordinates is

$$\rho\left(\frac{\partial u}{\partial t} + u\frac{\partial u}{\partial x} + v\frac{\partial u}{\partial y} + w\frac{\partial u}{\partial z}\right) = \rho g_x - \frac{\partial p}{\partial x} \tag{6.2a}$$

$$\rho\left(\frac{\partial v}{\partial t} + u\frac{\partial v}{\partial x} + v\frac{\partial v}{\partial y} + w\frac{\partial v}{\partial z}\right) = \rho g_y - \frac{\partial p}{\partial y} \tag{6.2b}$$

$$\rho\left(\frac{\partial w}{\partial t} + u\frac{\partial w}{\partial x} + v\frac{\partial w}{\partial y} + w\frac{\partial w}{\partial z}\right) = \rho g_z - \frac{\partial p}{\partial z} \tag{6.2c}$$

If the z axis is assumed vertical, then $g_x = 0$, $g_y = 0$, and $g_z = -g$, so $\vec{g} = -g\hat{k}$.

In cylindrical coordinates, the equations in component form, with gravity the only body force, are

$$\rho a_r = \rho \left(\frac{\partial V_r}{\partial t} + V_r \frac{\partial V_r}{\partial r} + \frac{V_\theta}{r} \frac{\partial V_r}{\partial \theta} + V_z \frac{\partial V_r}{\partial z} - \frac{V_\theta^2}{r} \right) = \rho g_r - \frac{\partial p}{\partial r} \qquad (6.3a)$$

$$\rho a_\theta = \rho \left(\frac{\partial V_\theta}{\partial t} + V_r \frac{\partial V_\theta}{\partial r} + \frac{V_\theta}{r} \frac{\partial V_\theta}{\partial \theta} + V_z \frac{\partial V_\theta}{\partial z} + \frac{V_r V_\theta}{r} \right) = \rho g_\theta - \frac{1}{r} \frac{\partial p}{\partial \theta} \qquad (6.3b)$$

$$\rho a_z = \rho \left(\frac{\partial V_z}{\partial t} + V_r \frac{\partial V_z}{\partial r} + \frac{V_\theta}{r} \frac{\partial V_z}{\partial \theta} + V_z \frac{\partial V_z}{\partial z} \right) = \rho g_z - \frac{\partial p}{\partial z} \qquad (6.3c)$$

If the z axis is directed vertically upward, then $g_r = g_\theta = 0$ and $g_z = -g$.

Equations 6.1, 6.2, and 6.3 apply to problems in which there are no viscous stresses. Before continuing with the main topic of this chapter (inviscid flow), let's consider for a moment when we have no viscous stresses, other than when $\mu = 0$. We recall from previous discussions that, in general, viscous stresses are present when we have fluid deformation (in fact this is how we initially defined a fluid); when we have no fluid deformation, i.e., when we have *rigid-body* motion, no viscous stresses will be present, even if $\mu \neq 0$. Hence Euler's equations apply to rigid-body motions as well as to inviscid flows. We discussed rigid-body motion in detail in Section 3-7 as a special case of fluid statics. As an exercise, you can show that Euler's equations can be used to solve Examples 3.9 and 3.10.

6-2 EULER'S EQUATIONS IN STREAMLINE COORDINATES

In Chapters 2 and 5 we pointed out that streamlines, drawn tangent to the velocity vectors at every point in the flow field, provide a convenient graphical representation. In steady flow a fluid particle will move along a streamline because, for steady flow, pathlines and streamlines coincide. Thus, in describing the motion of a fluid particle in a steady flow, in addition to using orthogonal coordinates x, y, z, the distance along a streamline is a logical coordinate to use in writing the equations of motion. "Streamline coordinates" also may be used to describe unsteady flow. Streamlines in unsteady flow give a graphical representation of the instantaneous velocity field.

For simplicity, consider the flow in the yz plane shown in Fig. 6.1. We wish to write the equations of motion in terms of the coordinate s, distance along a streamline, and the coordinate n, distance normal to the streamline. The pressure at the center of the fluid element is p. If we apply Newton's second law in the direction s of the

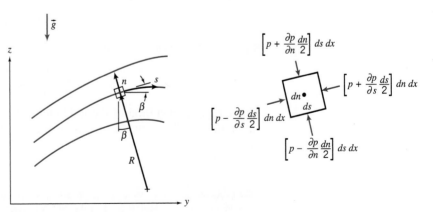

Fig. 6.1 Fluid particle moving along a streamline.

streamline, to the fluid element of volume $ds\,dn\,dx$, then neglecting viscous forces we obtain

$$\left(p - \frac{\partial p}{\partial s}\frac{ds}{2}\right)dn\,dx - \left(p + \frac{\partial p}{\partial s}\frac{ds}{2}\right)dn\,dx - \rho g \sin\beta\,ds\,dn\,dx = \rho a_s\,ds\,dn\,dx$$

where β is the angle between the tangent to the streamline and the horizontal, and a_s is the acceleration of the fluid particle along the streamline. Simplifying the equation, we obtain

$$-\frac{\partial p}{\partial s} - \rho g \sin\beta = \rho a_s$$

Since $\sin\beta = \partial z/\partial s$, we can write

$$-\frac{1}{\rho}\frac{\partial p}{\partial s} - g\frac{\partial z}{\partial s} = a_s$$

Along any streamline $V = V(s, t)$, and the material or total acceleration of a fluid particle in the streamwise direction is given by

$$a_s = \frac{DV}{Dt} = \frac{\partial V}{\partial t} + V\frac{\partial V}{\partial s}$$

Euler's equation in the streamwise direction with the z axis directed vertically upward is then

$$-\frac{1}{\rho}\frac{\partial p}{\partial s} - g\frac{\partial z}{\partial s} = \frac{\partial V}{\partial t} + V\frac{\partial V}{\partial s} \tag{6.4a}$$

For steady flow, and neglecting body forces, Euler's equation in the streamwise direction reduces to

$$\frac{1}{\rho}\frac{\partial p}{\partial s} = -V\frac{\partial V}{\partial s} \tag{6.4b}$$

which indicates that (for an incompressible, inviscid flow) *a decrease in velocity is accompanied by an increase in pressure* and conversely.[1] This makes sense: The only force experienced by the particle is the net pressure force, so the particle accelerates toward low-pressure regions and decelerates when approaching high-pressure regions.

To obtain Euler's equation in a direction normal to the streamlines, we apply Newton's second law in the n direction to the fluid element. Again, neglecting viscous forces, we obtain

$$\left(p - \frac{\partial p}{\partial n}\frac{dn}{2}\right)ds\,dx - \left(p + \frac{\partial p}{\partial n}\frac{dn}{2}\right)ds\,dx - \rho g \cos\beta\,dn\,dx\,ds = \rho a_n\,dn\,dx\,ds$$

where β is the angle between the n direction and the vertical, and a_n is the acceleration of the fluid particle in the n direction. Simplifying the equation, we obtain

$$-\frac{\partial p}{\partial n} - \rho g \cos\beta = \rho a_n$$

Since $\cos\beta = \partial z/\partial n$, we write

$$-\frac{1}{\rho}\frac{\partial p}{\partial n} - g\frac{\partial z}{\partial n} = a_n$$

The normal acceleration of the fluid element is toward the center of curvature of the streamline, in the minus n direction; thus in the coordinate system of Fig. 6.1, the

---

[1] The relationship between variations in pressure and velocity in the streamwise direction for steady incompressible inviscid flow is illustrated in the NCFMF video *Pressure Fields and Fluid Acceleration*. (See http://web.mit.edu/fluids/www/Shapiro/ncfmf.html for free online viewing of this film; it is old but good!)

familiar centripetal acceleration is written

$$a_n = \frac{-V^2}{R}$$

for steady flow, where R is the radius of curvature of the streamline at the point chosen. Then, Euler's equation normal to the streamline is written for steady flow as

$$\frac{1}{\rho}\frac{\partial p}{\partial n} + g\frac{\partial z}{\partial n} = \frac{V^2}{R} \qquad (6.5a)$$

For steady flow in a horizontal plane, Euler's equation normal to a streamline becomes

$$\frac{1}{\rho}\frac{\partial p}{\partial n} = \frac{V^2}{R} \qquad (6.5b)$$

Equation 6.5b indicates that *pressure increases in the direction outward from the center of curvature of the streamlines.*[2] This also makes sense: Because the only force experienced by the particle is the net pressure force, the pressure field creates the centripetal acceleration. In regions where the streamlines are straight, the radius of curvature, R, is infinite so *there is no pressure variation normal to straight streamlines.*

Example 6.1   Flow in a Bend

The flow rate of air at standard conditions in a flat duct is to be determined by installing pressure taps across a bend. The duct is 0.3 m deep and 0.1 m wide. The inner radius of the bend is 0.25 m. If the measured pressure difference between the taps is 40 mm of water, compute the approximate flow rate.

GIVEN: Flow through duct bend as shown.

$$p_2 - p_1 = \rho_{H_2O}\, g\, \Delta h$$

where $\Delta h = 40$ mm H_2O. Air is at STP.

FIND: Volume flow rate, Q.

SOLUTION:
Apply Euler's n component equation across flow streamlines.

Governing equation: $\dfrac{\partial p}{\partial r} = \dfrac{\rho V^2}{r}$

Assumptions: (1) Frictionless flow.
(2) Incompressible flow.
(3) Uniform flow at measurement section.

For this flow, $p = p(r)$, so

$$\frac{\partial p}{\partial r} = \frac{dp}{dr} = \frac{\rho V^2}{r}$$

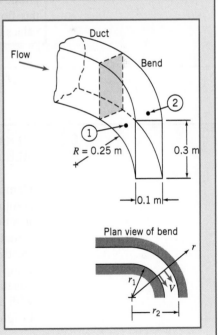

---

[2] The effect of streamline curvature on the pressure gradient normal to a streamline is illustrated in the NCFMF video *Pressure Fields and Fluid Acceleration.* (See http://web.mit.edu/fluids/www/Shapiro/ncfmf.html for free online viewing of this film.)

or

$$dp = \rho V^2 \frac{dr}{r}$$

Integrating gives

$$p_2 - p_1 = \rho V^2 \ln r \,]_{r_1}^{r_2} = \rho V^2 \ln \frac{r_2}{r_1}$$

and hence

$$V = \left[\frac{p_2 - p_1}{\rho \ln(r_2/r_1)} \right]^{1/2}$$

But

$$\Delta p = p_2 - p_1 = \rho_{H_2O}\, g\, \Delta h, \text{ so } V = \left[\frac{\rho_{H_2O}\, g\, \Delta h}{\rho \ln(r_2/r_1)} \right]^{1/2}$$

Substituting numerical values,

$$V = \left[999\, \frac{kg}{m^3} \times 9.81\, \frac{m}{s^2} \times 0.04\, m \times \frac{m^3}{1.23\, kg} \times \frac{1}{\ln(0.35\, m/0.25\, m)} \right]^{1/2} = 30.8\ m/s$$

For uniform flow

$$Q = VA = 30.8\, \frac{m}{s} \times 0.1\, m \times 0.3 m$$

$$Q = 0.924\ m^3/s \qquad\qquad\qquad\qquad\qquad\qquad Q$$

In this problem we assumed that the velocity is uniform across the section. In fact, the velocity in the bend approximates a free vortex (irrotational) profile in which $V \propto 1/r$ (where r is the radius) instead of $V =$ const. Hence, this flow-measurement device could only be used to obtain approximate values of the flow rate (see Problem 6.28).

6-3   ## BERNOULLI EQUATION—INTEGRATION OF EULER'S EQUATION ALONG A STREAMLINE FOR STEADY FLOW

Compared to the viscous-flow equivalents, the momentum or Euler's equation for incompressible, inviscid flow (Eq. 6.1) is simpler mathematically, but solution (in conjunction with the mass conservation equation, Eq. 5.1c) still presents formidable difficulties in all but the most basic flow problems. One convenient approach for a steady flow is to integrate Euler's equation along a streamline. We will do this below using two different mathematical approaches, and each will result in the Bernoulli equation. Recall that in Section 4-4 we derived the Bernoulli equation by starting with a differential control volume; these two additional derivations will give us more insight into the restrictions inherent in use of the Bernoulli equation.

Derivation Using Streamline Coordinates

Euler's equation for steady flow along a streamline (from Eq. 6.4a) is

$$-\frac{1}{\rho}\frac{\partial p}{\partial s} - g\frac{\partial z}{\partial s} = V\frac{\partial V}{\partial s} \tag{6.6}$$

If a fluid particle moves a distance, ds, along a streamline, then

$$\frac{\partial p}{\partial s} ds = dp \qquad \text{(the change in pressure along } s)$$

$$\frac{\partial z}{\partial s} ds = dz \qquad \text{(the change in elevation along } s)$$

$$\frac{\partial V}{\partial s} ds = dV \qquad \text{(the change in speed along } s)$$

Thus, after multiplying Eq. 6.6 by ds, we can write

$$-\frac{dp}{\rho} - g\,dz = V\,dV \qquad \text{or} \qquad \frac{dp}{\rho} + V\,dV + g\,dz = 0 \qquad \text{(along } s)$$

Integration of this equation gives

$$\int \frac{dp}{\rho} + \frac{V^2}{2} + gz = \text{constant} \quad \text{(along } s) \tag{6.7}$$

Before Eq. 6.7 can be applied, we must specify the relation between pressure and density. For the special case of incompressible flow, ρ = constant, and Eq. 6.7 becomes the Bernoulli equation,

$$\frac{p}{\rho} + \frac{V^2}{2} + gz = \text{constant} \tag{6.8}$$

Restrictions: (1) Steady flow.
(2) Incompressible flow.
(3) Frictionless flow.
(4) Flow along a streamline.

The Bernoulli equation is probably the most famous, and abused, equation in all of fluid mechanics. It is always tempting to use because it is a simple algebraic equation for relating the pressure, velocity, and elevation in a fluid. For example, it is used to explain the lift of a wing: In aerodynamics the gravity term is usually negligible, so Eq. 6.8 indicates that wherever the velocity is relatively high (e.g., on the upper surface of a wing), the pressure must be relatively low, and wherever the velocity is relatively low (e.g., on the lower surface of a wing), the pressure must be relatively high, generating substantial lift. On the other hand, it cannot be used to explain the pressure drop in a horizontal constant diameter pipe flow: according to it, for z = constant and V = constant, p = constant! Equation 6.8 indicates that, in general (if the flow is not constrained in some way), if a particle increases its elevation ($z \uparrow$) or moves into a higher pressure region ($p \uparrow$), it will tend to decelerate ($V \downarrow$); this makes sense from a momentum point of view (recall that the equation was derived from momentum considerations). These comments *only* apply if the four restrictions listed are reasonable. We cannot stress enough that you should *keep the restrictions firmly in mind whenever you consider using the Bernoulli equation!* (In general, the Bernoulli constant in Eq. 6.8 has different values along different streamlines.[3])

*Derivation Using Rectangular Coordinates

The vector form of Euler's equation, Eq. 6.1, also can be integrated along a streamline. We shall restrict the derivation to steady flow; thus, the end result of our effort should be Eq. 6.7.

---

[3] For the case of irrotational flow, the constant has a single value throughout the entire flow field (Section 6-7).
*This section may be omitted without loss of continuity in the text material.

For steady flow, Euler's equation in rectangular coordinates can be expressed as

$$\frac{D\vec{V}}{Dt} = u\frac{\partial \vec{V}}{\partial x} + v\frac{\partial \vec{V}}{\partial y} + w\frac{\partial \vec{V}}{\partial z} = (\vec{V} \cdot \nabla)\vec{V} = -\frac{1}{\rho}\nabla p - g\hat{k} \tag{6.9}$$

For steady flow the velocity field is given by $\vec{V} = \vec{V}(x, y, z)$. The streamlines are lines drawn in the flow field tangent to the velocity vector at every point. Recall again that for steady flow, streamlines, pathlines, and streaklines coincide. The motion of a particle along a streamline is governed by Eq. 6.9. During time interval dt the particle has vector displacement $d\vec{s}$ along the streamline.

If we take the dot product of the terms in Eq. 6.9 with displacement $d\vec{s}$ along the streamline, we obtain a scalar equation relating pressure, speed, and elevation along the streamline. Taking the dot product of $d\vec{s}$ with Eq. 6.9 gives

$$(\vec{V} \cdot \nabla)\vec{V} \cdot d\vec{s} = -\frac{1}{\rho}\nabla p \cdot d\vec{s} - g\hat{k} \cdot d\vec{s} \tag{6.10}$$

where

$$d\vec{s} = dx\hat{i} + dy\hat{j} + dz\hat{k} \quad \text{(along } s\text{)}$$

Now we evaluate each of the three terms in Eq. 6.10, starting on the right,

$$-\frac{1}{\rho}\nabla p \cdot d\vec{s} = -\frac{1}{\rho}\left[\hat{i}\frac{\partial p}{\partial x} + \hat{j}\frac{\partial p}{\partial y} + \hat{k}\frac{\partial p}{\partial z}\right] \cdot [dx\hat{i} + dy\hat{j} + dz\hat{k}]$$

$$= -\frac{1}{\rho}\left[\frac{\partial p}{\partial x}dx + \frac{\partial p}{\partial y}dy + \frac{\partial p}{\partial z}dz\right] \quad \text{(along } s\text{)}$$

$$-\frac{1}{\rho}\nabla p \cdot d\vec{s} = -\frac{1}{\rho}dp \quad \text{(along } s\text{)}$$

and

$$-g\hat{k} \cdot d\vec{s} = -g\hat{k} \cdot [dx\hat{i} + dy\hat{j} + dz\hat{k}]$$

$$= -g\,dz \quad \text{(along } s\text{)}$$

Using a vector identity,[4] we can write the third term as

$$(\vec{V} \cdot \nabla)\vec{V} \cdot d\vec{s} = \left[\frac{1}{2}\nabla(\vec{V} \cdot \vec{V}) - \vec{V} \times (\nabla \times \vec{V})\right] \cdot d\vec{s}$$

$$= \left\{\frac{1}{2}\nabla(\vec{V} \cdot \vec{V})\right\} \cdot d\vec{s} - \{\vec{V} \times (\nabla \times \vec{V})\} \cdot d\vec{s}$$

The last term on the right side of this equation is zero, since $\vec{V}$ is parallel to $d\vec{s}$ [recall from vector math that $\vec{V} \times (\nabla \times \vec{V}) \cdot d\vec{s} = -(\nabla \times \vec{V}) \times \vec{V} \cdot d\vec{s} = -(\nabla \times \vec{V}) \cdot \vec{V} \times d\vec{s}$]. Consequently,

$$(\vec{V} \cdot \nabla)\vec{V} \cdot d\vec{s} = \frac{1}{2}\nabla(\vec{V} \cdot \vec{V}) \cdot d\vec{s} = \frac{1}{2}\nabla(V^2) \cdot d\vec{s} \quad \text{(along } s\text{)}$$

$$= \frac{1}{2}\left[\hat{i}\frac{\partial V^2}{\partial x} + \hat{j}\frac{\partial V^2}{\partial y} + \hat{k}\frac{\partial V^2}{\partial z}\right] \cdot [dx\hat{i} + dy\hat{j} + dz\hat{k}]$$

---

[4] The vector identity

$$(\vec{V} \cdot \nabla)\vec{V} = \frac{1}{2}\nabla(\vec{V} \cdot \vec{V}) - \vec{V} \times (\nabla \times \vec{V})$$

may be verified by expanding each side into components.

$$= \frac{1}{2} \left[\frac{\partial V^2}{\partial x} dx + \frac{\partial V^2}{\partial y} dy + \frac{\partial V^2}{\partial z} dz \right]$$

$$(\vec{V} \cdot \nabla)\vec{V} \cdot d\vec{s} = \frac{1}{2} d(V^2) \quad \text{(along } s\text{)}$$

Substituting these three terms into Eq. 6.10 yields

$$\frac{dp}{\rho} + \frac{1}{2} d(V^2) + g \, dz = 0 \quad \text{(along } s\text{)}$$

Integrating this equation, we obtain

$$\int \frac{dp}{\rho} + \frac{V^2}{2} + gz = \text{constant} \quad \text{(along } s\text{)}$$

If the density is constant, we obtain the Bernoulli equation

$$\frac{p}{\rho} + \frac{V^2}{2} + gz = \text{constant}$$

As expected, we see that the last two equations are identical to Eqs. 6.7 and 6.8 derived previously using streamline coordinates. The Bernoulli equation, derived using rectangular coordinates, is still subject to the restrictions: (1) steady flow, (2) incompressible flow, (3) frictionless flow, and (4) flow along a streamline.

Static, Stagnation, and Dynamic Pressures

The pressure, p, which we have used in deriving the Bernoulli equation, Eq. 6.8, is the thermodynamic pressure; it is commonly called the *static pressure*. The static pressure is the pressure experienced by the fluid particle as it moves (so it is something of a misnomer!)—we also have the stagnation and dynamic pressures, which we will define shortly. How do we measure the pressure in a fluid in motion?

In Section 6-2 we showed that there is no pressure variation normal to straight streamlines. This fact makes it possible to measure the static pressure in a flowing fluid using a wall pressure "tap," placed in a region where the flow streamlines are straight, as shown in Fig. 6.2a. The pressure tap is a small hole, drilled carefully in the wall, with its axis perpendicular to the surface. If the hole is perpendicular to the duct wall and free from burrs, accurate measurements of static pressure can be made by connecting the tap to a suitable pressure-measuring instrument [1].

In a fluid stream far from a wall, or where streamlines are curved, accurate static pressure measurements can be made by careful use of a static pressure probe, shown in Fig. 6.2b. Such probes must be designed so that the measuring holes are placed correctly with respect to the probe tip and stem to avoid erroneous results [2]. In use, the measuring section must be aligned with the local flow direction. (In these figures, it may appear that the pressure tap and small holes would allow flow to enter or leave or otherwise be entrained by the main flow, but each of these is ultimately attached to

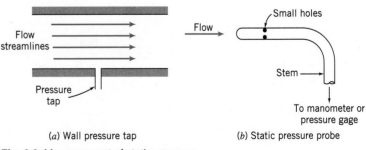

(a) Wall pressure tap   (b) Static pressure probe

Fig. 6.2 Measurement of static pressure.

a pressure sensor or manometer and is therefore a dead-end, leading to no flow being possible—see Example 6.2.)

Static pressure probes, such as that shown in Fig 6.2*b*, and in a variety of other forms, are available commercially in sizes as small as 1.5 mm ($\frac{1}{16}$ in.) in diameter [3].

The *stagnation pressure* is obtained when a flowing fluid is decelerated to zero speed by a frictionless process. For incompressible flow, the Bernoulli equation can be used to relate changes in speed and pressure along a streamline for such a process. Neglecting elevation differences, Eq. 6.8 becomes

$$\frac{p}{\rho} + \frac{V^2}{2} = \text{constant}$$

If the static pressure is p at a point in the flow where the speed is V, then the stagnation pressure, p_0, where the stagnation speed, V_0, is zero, may be computed from

$$\frac{p_0}{\rho} + \overset{=\,0}{\cancel{\frac{V_0^2}{2}}} = \frac{p}{\rho} + \frac{V^2}{2}$$

or

$$p_0 = p + \frac{1}{2}\rho V^2 \tag{6.11}$$

Equation 6.11 is a mathematical statement of the definition of stagnation pressure, valid for incompressible flow. The term $\frac{1}{2}\rho V^2$ generally is called the *dynamic pressure*. Equation 6.11 states that the stagnation (or *total*) pressure equals the static pressure plus the dynamic pressure. One way to picture the three pressures is to imagine you are standing in a steady wind holding up your hand: The static pressure will be atmospheric pressure; the larger pressure you feel at the center of your hand will be the stagnation pressure; and the buildup of pressure (the difference between the stagnation and static pressures) will be the dynamic pressure. Solving Eq. 6.11 for the speed,

$$V = \sqrt{\frac{2(p_0 - p)}{\rho}} \tag{6.12}$$

Thus, if the stagnation pressure and the static pressure could be measured at a point, Eq. 6.12 would give the local flow speed.

Stagnation pressure is measured in the laboratory using a probe with a hole that faces directly upstream as shown in Fig. 6.3. Such a probe is called a stagnation pressure probe, or pitot (pronounced *pea-toe*) tube. Again, the measuring section must be aligned with the local flow direction.

We have seen that static pressure at a point can be measured with a static pressure tap or probe (Fig. 6.2). If we knew the stagnation pressure at the same point, then the flow speed could be computed from Eq. 6.12. Two possible experimental setups are shown in Fig. 6.4.

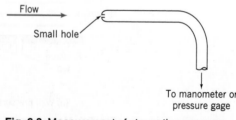

Fig. 6.3 Measurement of stagnation pressure.

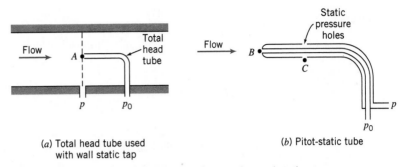

(a) Total head tube used
with wall static tap

(b) Pitot-static tube

Fig. 6.4 Simultaneous measurement of stagnation and static pressures.

In Fig. 6.4a, the static pressure corresponding to point A is read from the wall static pressure tap. The stagnation pressure is measured directly at A by the total head tube, as shown. (The stem of the total head tube is placed downstream from the measurement location to minimize disturbance of the local flow.)

Two probes often are combined, as in the pitot-static tube shown in Fig. 6.4b. The inner tube is used to measure the stagnation pressure at point B, while the static pressure at C is sensed using the small holes in the outer tube. In flow fields where the static pressure variation in the streamwise direction is small, the pitot-static tube may be used to infer the speed at point B in the flow by assuming $p_B = p_C$ and using Eq. 6.12. (Note that when $p_B \neq p_C$, this procedure will give erroneous results.)

Remember that the Bernoulli equation applies only for incompressible flow (Mach number $M \leq 0.3$). The definition and calculation of the stagnation pressure for compressible flow will be discussed in Section 12-3.

Example 6.2   Pitot Tube

A pitot tube is inserted in an air flow (at STP) to measure the flow speed. The tube is inserted so that it points up-stream into the flow and the pressure sensed by the tube is the stagnation pressure. The static pressure is measured at the same location in the flow, using a wall pressure tap. If the pressure difference is 30 mm of mercury, determine the flow speed.

GIVEN: A pitot tube inserted in a flow as shown. The flowing fluid is air and the manometer liquid is mercury.

FIND: The flow speed.

SOLUTION:

Governing equation: $\dfrac{p}{\rho} + \dfrac{V^2}{2} + gz = \text{constant}$

Assumptions: (1) Steady flow.
(2) Incompressible flow.
(3) Flow along a streamline.
(4) Frictionless deceleration along stagnation streamline.

Writing Bernoulli's equation along the stagnation streamline (with $\Delta z = 0$) yields

$$\frac{p_0}{\rho} = \frac{p}{\rho} + \frac{V^2}{2}$$

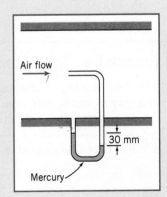

p_0 is the stagnation pressure at the tube opening where the speed has been reduced, without friction, to zero. Solving for V gives

$$V = \sqrt{\frac{2(p_0 - p)}{\rho_{\text{air}}}}$$

From the diagram,

$$p_0 - p = \rho_{Hg}\, gh = \rho_{H_2O}\, gh(SG_{Hg})$$

and

$$V = \sqrt{\frac{2\rho_{H_2O}\, gh(SG_{Hg})}{\rho_{air}}}$$

$$= \sqrt{2 \times 1000\,\frac{kg}{m^3} \times 9.81\,\frac{m}{s^2} \times 30\ mm \times 13.6 \times \frac{m^3}{1.23\ kg} \times \frac{1\ m}{1000\ mm}}$$

$$V = 80.8\ m/s \longleftarrow \hspace{9cm} V$$

At $T = 20°C$, the speed of sound in air is 343 m/s. Hence, $M = 0.236$ and the assumption of incompressible flow is valid.

> This problem illustrates use of a pitot tube to determine flow speed. Pitot (or pitot-static) tubes are often placed on the exterior of aircraft to indicate air speed relative to the aircraft, and hence aircraft speed relative to the air.

Applications

The Bernoulli equation can be applied between any two points on a streamline provided that the other three restrictions are satisfied. The result is

$$\frac{p_1}{\rho} + \frac{V_1^2}{2} + gz_1 = \frac{p_2}{\rho} + \frac{V_2^2}{2} + gz_2 \tag{6.13}$$

where subscripts 1 and 2 represent any two points on a streamline. Applications of Eqs. 6.8 and 6.13 to typical flow problems are illustrated in Examples 6.3 through 6.5.

In some situations, the flow appears unsteady from one reference frame, but steady from another, which translates with the flow. Since the Bernoulli equation was derived by integrating Newton's second law for a fluid particle, it can be applied in any inertial reference frame (see the discussion of translating frames in Section 4-4). The procedure is illustrated in Example 6.6.

Example 6.3   Nozzle Flow

Air flows steadily at low speed through a horizontal *nozzle* (by definition a device for accelerating a flow), discharging to atmosphere. The area at the nozzle inlet is 0.1 m². At the nozzle exit, the area is 0.02 m². Determine the gage pressure required at the nozzle inlet to produce an outlet speed of 50 m/s.

GIVEN: Flow through a nozzle, as shown.

FIND: $p_1 - p_{atm}$.

SOLUTION:

Governing equations:

$$\frac{p_1}{\rho} + \frac{V_1^2}{2} + gz_1 = \frac{p_2}{\rho} + \frac{V_2^2}{2} + gz_2 \tag{6.13}$$

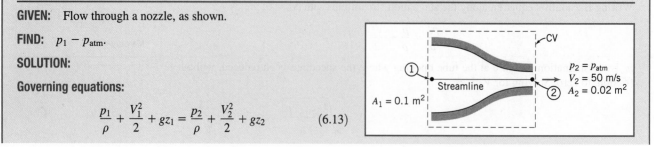

Continuity for incompressible and uniform flow:

$$\sum_{CS} \vec{V} \cdot \vec{A} = 0 \qquad (4.13b)$$

Assumptions: (1) Steady flow.
(2) Incompressible flow.
(3) Frictionless flow.
(4) Flow along a streamline.
(5) $z_1 = z_2$.
(6) Uniform flow at sections ① and ②.

The maximum speed of 50 m/s is well below 100 m/s, which corresponds to Mach number $M \approx 0.3$ in standard air. Hence, the flow may be treated as incompressible.

Apply the Bernoulli equation along a streamline between points ① and ② to evaluate p_1. Then

$$p_1 - p_{\text{atm}} = p_1 - p_2 = \frac{\rho}{2}(V_2^2 - V_1^2)$$

Apply the continuity equation to determine V_1,

$$(-\rho V_1 A_1) + (\rho V_2 A_2) = 0 \qquad \text{or} \qquad V_1 A_1 = V_2 A_2$$

so that

$$V_1 = V_2 \frac{A_2}{A_1} = \frac{50 \text{ m}}{\text{s}} \times \frac{0.02 \text{ m}^2}{0.1 \text{ m}^2} = 10 \text{ m/s}$$

For air at standard conditions, $\rho = 1.23 \text{ kg/m}^3$. Then

$$p_1 - p_{\text{atm}} = \frac{\rho}{2}(V_2^2 - V_1^2)$$

$$= \frac{1}{2} \times 1.23 \frac{\text{kg}}{\text{m}^3} \left[(50)^2 \frac{\text{m}^2}{\text{s}^2} - (10)^2 \frac{\text{m}^2}{\text{s}^2} \right] \frac{\text{N} \cdot \text{s}^2}{\text{kg} \cdot \text{m}}$$

$$p_1 - p_{\text{atm}} = 1.48 \text{ kPa} \quad\longleftarrow\qquad\qquad\qquad\qquad \underline{\quad p_1 - p_{\text{atm}} \quad}$$

> **Notes:**
> ✓ This problem illustrates a typical application of the Bernoulli equation.
> ✓ The streamlines must be straight at the inlet and exit in order to have uniform pressures at those locations.

Example 6.4   Flow through a Siphon

A U-tube acts as a water siphon. The bend in the tube is 1 m above the water surface; the tube outlet is 7 m below the water surface. The water issues from the bottom of the siphon as a free jet at atmospheric pressure. Determine (after listing the necessary assumptions) the speed of the free jet and the minimum absolute pressure of the water in the bend.

GIVEN: Water flowing through a siphon as shown.

FIND: (a) Speed of water leaving as a free jet.
(b) Pressure at point Ⓐ (the minimum pressure point) in the flow.

SOLUTION:

Governing equation: $\dfrac{p}{\rho} + \dfrac{V^2}{2} + gz = \text{constant}$

Assumptions: (1) Neglect friction.
(2) Steady flow.
(3) Incompressible flow.
(4) Flow along a streamline.
(5) Reservoir is large compared with pipe.

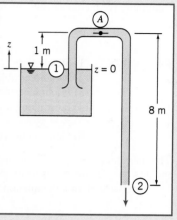

Apply the Bernoulli equation between points ① and ②.

$$\frac{p_1}{\rho} + \frac{V_1^2}{2} + gz_1 = \frac{p_2}{\rho} + \frac{V_2^2}{2} + gz_2$$

Since area$_{\text{reservoir}} \gg$ area$_{\text{pipe}}$, then $V_1 \approx 0$. Also $p_1 = p_2 = p_{\text{atm}}$, so

$$gz_1 = \frac{V_2^2}{2} + gz_2 \qquad \text{and} \qquad V_2^2 = 2g(z_1 - z_2)$$

$$V_2 = \sqrt{2g(z_1 - z_2)} = \sqrt{2 \times 9.81\ \frac{\text{m}}{\text{s}^2} \times 7\ \text{m}} = 11.7\ \text{m/s} \quad\longleftarrow \hspace{3cm} V_2$$

To determine the pressure at location Ⓐ, we write the Bernoulli equation between ① and Ⓐ.

$$\frac{p_1}{\rho} + \frac{V_1^2}{2} + gz_1 = \frac{p_A}{\rho} + \frac{V_A^2}{2} + gz_A$$

Again $V_1 \approx 0$ and from conservation of mass $V_A = V_2$. Hence

$$\frac{p_A}{\rho} = \frac{p_1}{\rho} + gz_1 - \frac{V_2^2}{2} - gz_A = \frac{p_1}{\rho} + g(z_1 - z_A) - \frac{V_2^2}{2}$$

$$p_A = p_1 + \rho g(z_1 - z_A) - \rho \frac{V_2^2}{2}$$

$$= 1.01 \times 10^5\ \frac{\text{N}}{\text{m}^3} + 999\ \frac{\text{kg}}{\text{m}^3} \times 9.81\ \frac{\text{m}}{\text{s}^2} \times (-1\ \text{m})\ \frac{\text{N} \cdot \text{s}^2}{\text{kg} \cdot \text{m}}$$

$$- \frac{1}{2} \times 999\ \frac{\text{kg}}{\text{m}^3} \times (11.7)^2\ \frac{\text{m}^2}{\text{s}^2} \times \frac{\text{N} \cdot \text{s}^2}{\text{kg} \cdot \text{m}}$$

$$p_A = 22.8\ \text{kPa (abs) or } -78.5\ \text{kPa (gage)} \quad\longleftarrow \hspace{3cm} p_A$$

Notes:
  ✓ This problem illustrates an application of the Bernoulli equation that in-
    cludes elevation changes.
  ✓ It is interesting to note that when the Bernoulli equation applies be-
    tween a reservoir and a free jet that it feeds at a location h below the re-
    servoir surface, the jet speed will be $V = \sqrt{2\,gh}$; this is the same
    velocity a droplet (or stone) falling without friction from the reservoir
    level would attain if it fell a distance h. Can you explain why?
  ✓ Always take care when neglecting friction in any internal flow. In this
    problem, neglecting friction is reasonable if the pipe is smooth-surfaced
    and is relatively short. In Chapter 8 we will study frictional effects in
    internal flows.

Example 6.5   Flow under a Sluice Gate

Water flows under a sluice gate on a horizontal bed at the inlet to a flume. Upstream from the gate, the water depth is 1.5 ft and the speed is negligible. At the vena contracta downstream from the gate, the flow streamlines are straight and the depth is 2 in. Determine the flow speed downstream from the gate and the discharge in cubic feet per second per foot of width.

GIVEN: Flow of water under a sluice gate.

FIND: (a) V_2.
(b) Q in $ft^3/s/ft$ of width.

SOLUTION:
Under the assumptions listed below, the flow satisfies all conditions necessary to apply the Bernoulli equation. The question is, what streamline do we use?

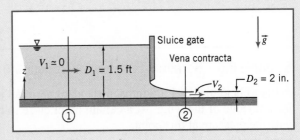

Governing equation: $\dfrac{p_1}{\rho} + \dfrac{V_1^2}{2} + gz_1 = \dfrac{p_2}{\rho} + \dfrac{V_2^2}{2} + gz_2$

Assumptions: (1) Steady flow.
(2) Incompressible flow.
(3) Frictionless flow.
(4) Flow along a streamline.
(5) Uniform flow at each section.
(6) Hydrostatic pressure distribution (at each location, pressure increases linearly with depth).

If we consider the streamline that runs along the bottom of the channel ($z = 0$), because of assumption 6 the pressures at ① and ② are

$$p_1 = p_{atm} + \rho g D_1 \qquad \text{and} \qquad p_2 = p_{atm} + \rho g D_2$$

so that the Bernoulli equation for this streamline is

$$\frac{(p_{atm} + \rho g D_1)}{\rho} + \frac{V_1^2}{2} = \frac{(p_{atm} + \rho g D_2)}{\rho} + \frac{V_2^2}{2}$$

or

$$\frac{V_1^2}{2} + gD_1 = \frac{V_2^2}{2} + gD_2 \tag{1}$$

On the other hand, consider the streamline that runs along the free surface on both sides and down the inner surface of the gate. For this streamline

$$\frac{p_{atm}}{\rho} + \frac{V_1^2}{2} + gD_1 = \frac{p_{atm}}{\rho} + \frac{V_2^2}{2} + gD_2$$

or

$$\frac{V_1^2}{2} + gD_1 = \frac{V_2^2}{2} + gD_2 \tag{1}$$

We have arrived at the same equation (Eq. 1) for the streamline at the bottom and the streamline at the free surface, implying the Bernoulli constant is the same for both streamlines. We will see in Section 6-6 that this flow is one of a family of flows for which this is the case. Solving for V_2 yields

$$V_2 = \sqrt{2g(D_1 - D_2) + V_1^2}$$

But $V_1^2 \approx 0$, so

$$V_2 = \sqrt{2g(D_1 - D_2)} = \sqrt{2 \times 32.2 \ \frac{ft}{s^2} \times \left(1.5 \ ft - 2 \ in. \times \frac{ft}{12 \ in.}\right)}$$

$$V_2 \qquad$$

$$V_2 = 9.27 \ ft/s \quad \longleftarrow$$

For uniform flow, $Q = VA = VDw$, or

$$\frac{Q}{w} = VD = V_2 D_2 = \frac{9.27 \text{ ft}}{\text{s}} + 2 \text{ in.} \times \frac{\text{ft}}{12 \text{ in.}} = 1.55 \text{ ft}^2/\text{s}$$

$$\frac{Q}{w} = 1.55 \text{ ft}^3/\text{s/foot of width} \longleftarrow \qquad\qquad \frac{Q}{w}$$

Example 6.6   Bernoulli Equation in Translating Reference Frame

A light plane flies at 150 km/hr in standard air at an altitude of 1000 m. Determine the stagnation pressure at the leading edge of the wing. At a certain point close to the wing, the air speed *relative* to the wing is 60 m/s. Compute the pressure at this point.

GIVEN: Aircraft in flight at 150 km/hr at 1000 m altitude in standard air.

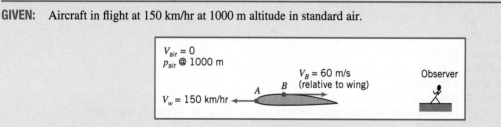

FIND: Stagnation pressure, p_{0_A}, at point A and static pressure, p_B, at point B.

SOLUTION:

Flow is unsteady when observed from a fixed frame, that is, by an observer on the ground. However, an observer *on* the wing sees the following steady flow:

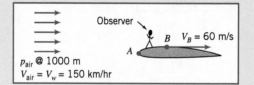

At $z = 1000$ m in standard air, the temperature is 281 K and the speed of sound is 336 m/s. Hence at point B, $M_B = V_B/c = 0.178$. This is less than 0.3, so the flow may be treated as incompressible. Thus the Bernoulli equation can be applied along a streamline in the moving observer's inertial reference frame.

Governing equation: $\dfrac{p_{\text{air}}}{\rho} + \dfrac{V_{\text{air}}^2}{2} + gz_{\text{air}} = \dfrac{p_A}{\rho} + \dfrac{V_A^2}{2} + gz_A = \dfrac{p_B}{\rho} + \dfrac{V_B^2}{2} + gz_B$

Assumptions: (1) Steady flow.
(2) Incompressible flow ($V < 100$ m/s).
(3) Frictionless flow.
(4) Flow along a streamline.
(5) Neglect Δz.

Values for pressure and density may be found from Table A.3. Thus, at 1000 m, $p/p_{SL} = 0.8870$ and $\rho/\rho_{SL} = 0.9075$. Consequently,

$$p = 0.8870 p_{SL} = 0.8870 \times 1.01 \times 10^5 \ \frac{\text{N}}{\text{m}^2} = 8.96 \times 10^4 \ \text{N/m}^2$$

and

$$\rho = 0.9075 \rho_{SL} = 0.9075 \times 1.23 \ \frac{\text{kg}}{\text{m}^3} = 1.12 \ \text{kg/m}^3$$

Since the speed is $V_A = 0$ at the stagnation point,

$$p_{0_A} = p_{\text{air}} + \frac{1}{2} \rho V_{\text{air}}^2$$

$$= 8.96 \times 10^4 \ \frac{\text{N}}{\text{m}^2} + \frac{1}{2} \times 1.12 \ \frac{\text{kg}}{\text{m}^3} \left(150 \ \frac{\text{km}}{\text{hr}} \times 1000 \ \frac{\text{m}}{\text{km}} \times \frac{\text{hr}}{3600 \ \text{s}} \right)^2 \times \frac{\text{N} \cdot \text{s}^2}{\text{kg} \cdot \text{m}}$$

$$p_{0_A} = 90.6 \ \text{kPa(abs)} \longleftarrow \qquad\qquad\qquad p_{0_A}$$

Solving for the static pressure at B, we obtain

$$p_B = p_{\text{air}} + \frac{1}{2} \rho (V_{\text{air}}^2 - V_B^2)$$

$$p_B = 8.96 \times 10^4 \ \frac{\text{N}}{\text{m}^2} + \frac{1}{2} \times 1.12 \ \frac{\text{kg}}{\text{m}^3} \left[\left(150 \ \frac{\text{km}}{\text{hr}} \times 1000 \ \frac{\text{m}}{\text{km}} \times \frac{\text{hr}}{3600 \ \text{s}} \right)^2 - (60)^2 \ \frac{\text{m}^2}{\text{s}^2} \right] \frac{\text{N} \cdot \text{s}^2}{\text{kg} \cdot \text{m}}$$

$$p_B = 88.6 \ \text{kPa (abs)} \longleftarrow \qquad\qquad\qquad p_B$$

> This problem gives a hint as to how a wing generates lift. The incoming air has a velocity $V_{\text{air}} = 150 \ \text{km/hr} = 41.7 \ \text{m/s}$ and *accelerates* to 60 m/s on the upper surface. This leads, through the Bernoulli equation, to a pressure *drop* of 1 kPa (from 89.6 kPa to 88.6 kPa). It turns out that the flow *decelerates* on the lower surface, leading to a pressure *rise* of about 1 kPa. Hence, the wing experiences a net upward pressure difference of about 2 kPa, a significant effect.

Cautions on Use of the Bernoulli Equation

In Examples 6.3 through 6.6, we have seen several situations where the Bernoulli equation may be applied because the restrictions on its use led to a reasonable flow model. However, in some situations you might be tempted to apply the Bernoulli equation where the restrictions are not satisfied. Some subtle cases that violate the restrictions are discussed briefly in this section.

Example 6.3 examined flow in a nozzle. In a *subsonic nozzle* (a converging section) the pressure drops, accelerating a flow. Because the pressure drops and the walls of the nozzle converge, there is no flow separation from the walls and the boundary layer remains thin. In addition, a nozzle is usually relatively short so frictional effects are not significant. All of this leads to the conclusion that the Bernoulli equation is suitable for use for subsonic nozzles.

Sometimes we need to decelerate a flow. This can be accomplished using a *subsonic diffuser* (a diverging section), or by using a sudden expansion (e.g., from a pipe into a reservoir). In these devices the flow decelerates because of an adverse pressure gradient. As we discussed in Section 2-6, an adverse pressure gradient tends to lead to rapid growth of the boundary layer and its separation.[5] Hence, we should be careful in applying the Bernoulli equation in such devices—at best, it will be an approximation. Because of area blockage caused by boundary-layer growth, pressure rise in actual diffusers always is less than that predicted for inviscid one-dimensional flow.

The Bernoulli equation was a reasonable model for the siphon of Example 6.4 because the entrance was well rounded, the bends were gentle, and the overall length was short. Flow separation, which can occur at inlets with sharp corners and in abrupt bends, causes the flow to depart from that predicted by a one-dimensional model and the Bernoulli equation. Frictional effects would not be negligible if the tube were long.

---

[5] See the NCFMF video *Flow Visualization*. (See http://web.mit.edu/fluids/www/Shapiro/ncfmf.html for free online viewing of this film.)

Example 6.5 presented an open-channel flow analogous to that in a nozzle, for which the Bernoulli equation is a good flow model. The hydraulic jump[6] is an example of an open-channel flow with adverse pressure gradient. Flow through a hydraulic jump is mixed violently, making it impossible to identify streamlines. Thus the Bernoulli equation cannot be used to model flow through a hydraulic jump. We will see a more detailed presentation of open channel flows in Chapter 11.

The Bernoulli equation cannot be applied *through* a machine such as a propeller, pump, turbine, or windmill. The equation was derived by integrating along a stream tube (Section 4-4) or a streamline (Section 6-3) in the absence of moving surfaces such as blades or vanes. It is impossible to have locally steady flow or to identify streamlines during flow through a machine. Hence, while the Bernoulli equation may be applied between points *before* a machine, or between points *after* a machine (assuming its restrictions are satisfied), it cannot be applied *through* the machine. (In effect, a machine will change the value of the Bernoulli constant.)

Finally, compressibility must be considered for flow of gases. Density changes caused by dynamic compression due to motion may be neglected for engineering purposes if the local Mach number remains below about $M \approx 0.3$, as noted in Examples 6.3 and 6.6. Temperature changes can cause significant changes in density of a gas, even for low-speed flow. Thus the Bernoulli equation could not be applied to air flow through a heating element (e.g., of a hand-held hair dryer) where temperature changes are significant.

6-4   THE BERNOULLI EQUATION INTERPRETED AS AN ENERGY EQUATION

The Bernoulli equation, Eq. 6.8, was obtained by integrating Euler's equation along a streamline for steady, incompressible, frictionless flow. Thus Eq. 6.8 was derived from the momentum equation for a fluid particle.

An equation identical in form to Eq. 6.8 (although requiring very different restrictions) may be obtained from the first law of thermodynamics. Our objective in this section is to reduce the energy equation to the form of the Bernoulli equation given by Eq. 6.8. Having arrived at this form, we then compare the restrictions on the two equations to help us understand more clearly the restrictions on the use of Eq. 6.8.

Consider steady flow in the absence of shear forces. We choose a control volume bounded by streamlines along its periphery. Such a boundary, shown in Fig. 6.5, often is called a *stream tube*.

Basic equation:

$$\overset{= 0(1)}{\dot{Q}} - \overset{= 0(2)}{\dot{W}_s} - \overset{= 0(3)}{\dot{W}_{shear}} - \overset{= 0(4)}{\dot{W}_{other}} = \frac{\partial}{\partial t} \int_{CV} e\,\rho\,d\forall + \int_{CS} (e + pv)\,\rho\vec{V}\cdot d\vec{A} \qquad (4.56)$$

$$e = u + \frac{V^2}{2} + gz$$

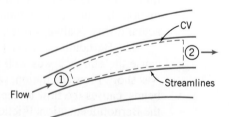

Fig. 6.5 Flow through a stream tube.

[6] See the NCFMF videos *Waves in Fluids* and *Stratified Flow* for examples of this behavior. (See http://web.mit.edu/fluids/www/Shapiro/ncfmf.html for free online viewing of this film.)

Restrictions: (1) $\dot{W}_s = 0$.
         (2) $\dot{W}_{shear} = 0$.
         (3) $\dot{W}_{other} = 0$.
         (4) Steady flow.
         (5) Uniform flow and properties at each section.

(Remember that here v represents the specific volume, and u represents the specific internal energy, not velocity!) Under these restrictions, Eq. 4.56 becomes

$$\left(u_1 + p_1 v_1 + \frac{V_1^2}{2} + gz_1\right)(-\rho_1 V_1 A_1) + \left(u_2 + p_2 v_2 + \frac{V_2^2}{2} + gz_2\right)(\rho_2 V_2 A_2) - \dot{Q} = 0$$

From continuity, with restrictions (4) and (5):

$$\sum_{CS} \rho\vec{V} \cdot \vec{A} = 0 \qquad (4.15b)$$

or

$$(-\rho_1 V_1 A_1) + (\rho_2 V_2 A_2) = 0$$

That is,

$$\dot{m} = \rho_1 V_1 A_1 = \rho_2 V_2 A_2$$

Also

$$\dot{Q} = \frac{\delta Q}{dt} = \frac{\delta Q}{dm}\frac{dm}{dt} = \frac{\delta Q}{dm}\dot{m}$$

Thus, from the energy equation, after rearranging

$$\left[\left(p_2 v_2 + \frac{V_2^2}{2} + gz_2\right) - \left(p_1 v_1 + \frac{V_1^2}{2} + gz_1\right)\right]\dot{m} + \left(u_2 - u_1 - \frac{\delta Q}{dm}\right)\dot{m} = 0$$

or

$$p_1 v_1 + \frac{V_1^2}{2} + gz_1 = p_2 v_2 + \frac{V_2^2}{2} + gz_2 + \left(u_2 - u_1 - \frac{\delta Q}{dm}\right)$$

Under the additional assumption (6) of incompressible flow, $v_1 = v_2 = 1/\rho$ and hence

$$\frac{p_1}{\rho} + \frac{V_1^2}{2} + gz_1 = \frac{p_2}{\rho} + \frac{V_2^2}{2} + gz_2 + \left(u_2 - u_1 - \frac{\delta Q}{dm}\right) \qquad (6.14)$$

Equation 6.14 would reduce to the Bernoulli equation if the term in parentheses were zero. Thus, under the further restriction,

$$(7) \quad \left(u_2 - u_1 - \frac{\delta Q}{dm}\right) = 0$$

the energy equation reduces to

$$\frac{p_1}{\rho} + \frac{V_1^2}{2} + gz_1 = \frac{p_2}{\rho} + \frac{V_2^2}{2} + gz_2$$

or

$$\frac{p}{\rho} + \frac{V^2}{2} + gz = \text{constant} \qquad (6.15)$$

Equation 6.15 is identical in form to the Bernoulli equation, Eq. 6.8. The Bernoulli equation was derived from momentum considerations (Newton's second law), and is valid for steady, incompressible, frictionless flow along a streamline. Equation 6.15 was obtained by applying the first law of thermodynamics to a stream tube control volume, subject to restrictions 1 through 7 above. Thus the Bernoulli equation (Eq. 6.8) and the identical form of the energy equation (Eq. 6.15) were developed from entirely different models, coming from entirely different basic concepts, and involving different restrictions.

It looks like we needed restriction (7) to finally transform the energy equation into the Bernoulli equation. In fact, we didn't! It turns out that for an incompressible and frictionless flow [restriction (6), and the fact we are looking only at flows with no shear forces], restriction (7) is automatically satisfied, as we will demonstrate in Example 6.7.

Example 6.7   Internal Energy and Heat Transfer in Frictionless Incompressible Flow

Consider frictionless, incompressible flow with heat transfer. Show that

$$u_2 - u_1 = \frac{\delta Q}{dm}$$

GIVEN: Frictionless, incompressible flow with heat transfer.

SHOW: $u_2 - u_1 = \dfrac{\delta Q}{dm}$.

SOLUTION:

In general, internal energy can be expressed as $u = u(T, v)$. For incompressible flow, $v = $ constant, and $u = u(T)$. Thus the thermodynamic state of the fluid is determined by the single thermodynamic property, T. For any process, the internal energy change, $u_2 - u_1$, depends only on the temperatures at the end states.

From the Gibbs equation, $T ds = du + \rho \, dv$, valid for a pure substance undergoing any process, we obtain

$$T ds = du$$

for incompressible flow, since $dv = 0$. Since the internal energy change, du, between specified end states, is independent of the process, we take a reversible process, for which $T ds = d(\delta Q/dm) = du$. Therefore,

$$u_2 - u_1 = \frac{\delta Q}{dm} \quad \longleftarrow$$

For the steady, frictionless, and incompressible flow considered in this section, it is true that the first law of thermodynamics reduces to the Bernoulli equation. Each term in Eq. 6.15 has dimensions of energy per unit mass (we sometimes refer to the three terms in the equation as the "pressure" energy, kinetic energy, and potential energy per unit mass of the fluid). It is not surprising that Eq. 6.15 contains energy terms—after all, we used the first law of thermodynamics in deriving it. How did we end up with the same energy-like terms in the Bernoulli equation, which we derived from the momentum equation? The answer is because we integrated the momentum equation (which involves force terms) along a streamline (which involves distance), and by doing so ended up with work or energy terms (work being defined as force times distance): The work of gravity and pressure forces leads to a kinetic energy change (which came from integrating momentum over distance). In this context, we can think of the Bernoulli equation as a *mechanical energy balance*—the mechanical energy ("pressure" plus potential plus kinetic) will be constant. We must always bear in mind that for the Bernoulli equation to be valid along a streamline requires an incompressible inviscid flow, in addition to steady flow. It's interesting that these two properties of the flow—its compressibility and friction—are what "link" thermodynamic and mechanical energies. If a fluid is compressible, any flow-induced pressure changes will compress or expand the fluid, thereby doing work and changing the particle thermal energy; and friction, as we know from everyday experience, always converts mechanical to thermal energy. Their absence, therefore, breaks the link between the mechanical and thermal energies, and they are independent—it's as if they're in parallel universes!

In summary, when the conditions are satisfied for the Bernoulli equation to be valid, we can consider separately the mechanical energy and the internal thermal energy of a fluid particle (this is illustrated in Example 6.8); when they are not satisfied, there will be an interaction between these energies, the Bernoulli equation becomes invalid, and we must use the full first law of thermodynamics.

Example 6.8   Frictionless Flow with Heat Transfer

Water flows steadily from a large open reservoir through a short length of pipe and a nozzle with cross-sectional area $A = 0.864$ in.^{2} A well-insulated 10 kW heater surrounds the pipe. Find the temperature rise of the water.

GIVEN: Water flows from a large reservoir through the system shown and discharges to atmospheric pressure. The heater is 10 kW; $A_4 = 0.864$ in.^{2}

FIND: The temperature rise of the water between points ① and ②.

SOLUTION:

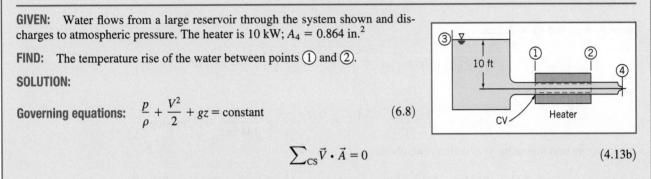

Governing equations:
$$\frac{p}{\rho} + \frac{V^2}{2} + gz = \text{constant} \qquad (6.8)$$

$$\sum_{CS} \vec{V} \cdot \vec{A} = 0 \qquad (4.13b)$$

$$\overset{= 0(4)}{\dot{Q}} - \overset{= 0(4)}{\dot{W}_s} - \overset{= 0(1)}{\dot{W}_{shear}} = \frac{\partial}{\partial t}\int_{CV} e\,\rho\,dV + \int_{CS}\left(u + pv + \frac{V^2}{2} + gz\right)\rho\vec{V}\cdot d\vec{A} \qquad (4.56)$$

Assumptions:
(1) Steady flow.
(2) Frictionless flow.
(3) Incompressible flow.
(4) No shaft work, no shear work.
(5) Flow along a streamline.
(6) Uniform flow at each section [a consequence of assumption (2)].

Under the assumptions listed, the first law of thermodynamics for the CV shown becomes

$$\dot{Q} = \int_{CS}\left(u + pv + \frac{V^2}{2} + gz\right)\rho\vec{V}\cdot d\vec{A}$$

$$= \int_{A_1}\left(u + pv + \frac{V^2}{2} + gz\right)\rho\vec{V}\cdot d\vec{A} + \int_{A_2}\left(u + pv + \frac{V^2}{2} + gz\right)\rho\vec{V}\cdot d\vec{A}$$

For uniform properties at ① and ②

$$\dot{Q} = -(\rho V_1 A_1)\left(u_1 + p_1 v + \frac{V_1^2}{2} + gz_1\right) + (\rho V_2 A_2)\left(u_2 + p_2 v + \frac{V_2^2}{2} + gz_2\right)$$

From conservation of mass, $\rho V_1 A_1 = \rho V_2 A_2 = \dot{m}$, so

$$\dot{Q} = \dot{m}\left[u_2 - u_1 + \left(\frac{p_2}{\rho} + \frac{V_2^2}{2} + gz_2\right) - \left(\frac{p_1}{\rho} + \frac{V_1^2}{2} + gz_1\right)\right]$$

For frictionless, incompressible, steady flow, along a streamline,

$$\frac{p}{\rho} + \frac{V^2}{2} + gz = \text{constant}$$

Therefore,

$$\dot{Q} = \dot{m}\,(u_2 - u_1)$$

Since, for an incompressible fluid, $u_2 - u_1 = c(T_2 - T_1)$, then

$$T_2 - T_1 = \frac{\dot{Q}}{\dot{m}c}$$

From continuity,

$$\dot{m} = \rho V_4 A_4$$

To find V_4, write the Bernoulli equation between the free surface at ③ and point ④.

$$\frac{p_3}{\rho} + \frac{V_3^2}{2} + gz_3 = \frac{p_4}{\rho} + \frac{V_4^2}{2} + gz_4$$

Since $p_3 = p_4$ and $V_3 \approx 0$, then

$$V_4 = \sqrt{2g(z_3 - z_4)} = \sqrt{2 \times 32.2 \, \frac{\text{ft}}{\text{s}^2} \times 10 \, \text{ft}} = 25.4 \, \text{ft/s}$$

and

$$\dot{m} = \rho V_4 A_4 = 1.94 \, \frac{\text{slug}}{\text{ft}^3} \times 25.4 \, \frac{\text{ft}}{\text{s}} \times 0.864 \, \text{in.}^2 \times \frac{\text{ft}^2}{144 \, \text{in.}^2} = 0.296 \, \text{slug/s}$$

Assuming no heat loss to the surroundings, we obtain

$$T_2 - T_1 = \frac{\dot{Q}}{\dot{m}c} = 10 \, \text{kW} \times 3413 \, \frac{\text{Btu}}{\text{kW} \cdot \text{hr}} \times \frac{\text{hr}}{3600 \, \text{s}} \times \frac{\text{s}}{0.296 \, \text{slug}} \times \frac{\text{slug}}{32.2 \, \text{lbm}} \times \frac{\text{lbm} \cdot °\text{R}}{1 \, \text{Btu}}$$

$$T_2 - T_1 = 0.995 \, °\text{R} \longleftarrow \hspace{3cm} T_2 - T_1$$

This problem illustrates that:

✓ In general, the first law of thermodynamics and the Bernoulli equation are independent equations.

✓ For an incompressible, inviscid flow the internal thermal energy is only changed by a heat transfer process, and is independent of the fluid mechanics.

6-5   **ENERGY GRADE LINE AND HYDRAULIC GRADE LINE**

We have learned that for a steady, incompressible, frictionless flow, we may use the Bernoulli equation (Eq. 6.8), derived from the momentum equation, and also Eq. 6.15, derived from the energy equation:

$$\frac{p}{\rho} + \frac{V^2}{2} + gz = \text{constant} \tag{6.15}$$

We also interpreted the three terms comprised of "pressure," kinetic, and potential energies to make up the total mechanical energy, per unit mass, of the fluid. If we divide Eq. 6.15 by g, we obtain another form,

$$\frac{p}{\rho g} + \frac{V^2}{2g} + z = H \tag{6.16a}$$

Here H is the *total head* of the flow; it measures the total mechanical energy in units of meters or feet. We will learn in Chapter 8 that in a real fluid (one with friction) this head will *not* be constant but will continuously decrease in value as mechanical energy is converted to thermal; in this chapter H is constant. We can go one step further here and get a very useful graphical approach if we also define this to be the *energy grade line* (EGL),

$$EGL = \frac{p}{\rho g} + \frac{V^2}{2g} + z \tag{6.16b}$$

This can be measured using the pitot (total head) tube (shown in Fig. 6.3). Placing such a tube in a flow measures the total pressure, $p_0 = p + \frac{1}{2}\rho V^2$, so this will cause the height of a column *of the same fluid* to rise to a height $h = p_0/\rho g = p/\rho g + V^2/2g$. If the vertical location of the pitot tube is z, measured from some datum (e.g., the ground), the height of column of fluid *measured from the datum* will then be $h + z = p/\rho g + V^2/2g + z = EGL = H$. In summary, the height of the column, measured from the datum, attached to a pitot tube directly indicates the EGL.

We can also define the *hydraulic grade line* (HGL),

$$HGL = \frac{p}{\rho g} + z \tag{6.16c}$$

This can be measured using the static pressure tap (shown in Fig. 6.2*a*). Placing such a tube in a flow measures the static pressure, p, so this will cause the height of a column *of the same fluid* to rise to a height $h = p/\rho g$. If the vertical location of the tap is also at z, measured from some datum, the height of column of fluid *measured from the datum* will then be $h + z = p/\rho g + z = HGL$. The height of the column attached to a static pressure tap thus directly indicates the HGL.

From Eqs. 6.16b and 6.16c we obtain

$$EGL - HGL = \frac{V^2}{2g} \tag{6.16d}$$

which shows that the difference between the EGL and HGL is always the dynamic pressure term.

To see a graphical interpretation of the EGL and HGL, refer to the example shown in Fig. 6.6, which shows frictionless flow from a reservoir, through a pipe reducer.

At all locations the EGL is the same because there is no loss of mechanical energy. Station ① is at the reservoir, and here the EGL and HGL coincide with the free surface: in Eqs. 6.16b and 6.16c $p = 0$ (gage), $V = 0$, and $z = z_1$, so $EGL_1 = HGL_1 = H = z_1$; all of the mechanical energy is potential. (If we were to place a pitot tube in the fluid at station ①, the fluid would of course just rise to the free surface level.)

At station ② we have a pitot (total head) tube and a static head tap. The pitot tube's column indicates the correct value of the EGL ($EGL_1 = EGL_2 = H$), but *something* changed between the two stations: The fluid now has significant kinetic energy and has lost some potential energy (can you determine from the figure what happened to the pressure?). From Eq. 6.16d, we can see that the HGL is lower than the EGL by $V_2^2/2g$; the HGL at station ② shows this.

From station ② to station ③ there is a reduction in diameter, so continuity requires that $V_3 > V_2$; hence the gap between the EGL and HGL increases further, as shown.

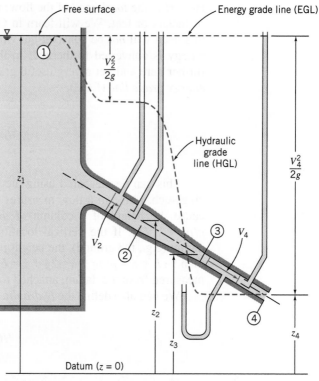

Fig. 6.6 Energy and hydraulic grade lines for frictionless flow.

Station ④ is at the exit (to the atmosphere). Here the pressure is zero (gage), so the EGL consists entirely of kinetic and potential energy terms, and $HGL_4 = HGL_3$. We can summarize two important ideas when sketching EGL and HGL curves:

1. The EGL is constant for incompressible, inviscid flow (in the absence of work devices). We will see in Chapter 8 that work devices may increase or decrease the EGL, and friction will always lead to a fall in the EGL.
2. The HGL is always lower than the EGL by distance $V^2/2g$. Note that the value of velocity V depends on the overall system (e.g., reservoir height, pipe diameter, etc.), but *changes* in velocity *only* occur when the diameter changes.

6-6   **UNSTEADY BERNOULLI EQUATION—INTEGRATION OF EULER'S EQUATION ALONG A STREAMLINE   (ON THE WEB)**

---

*6-7   **IRROTATIONAL FLOW**

We have already discussed irrotational flows in Section 5-3. These are flows in which the fluid particles do not rotate ($\vec{\omega} = 0$). We recall that the only stresses that can generate particle rotation are shear stresses; hence, inviscid flows (i.e., those with zero

---

* This section may be omitted without loss of continuity in the text material. (Note that Section 5-2 contains background material needed for study of this section.)

shear stresses) will be irrotational, unless the particles were initially rotating. Using Eq. 5.14, we obtain the irrotationality condition

$$\nabla \times \vec{V} = 0 \qquad (6.22)$$

leading to

$$\frac{\partial w}{\partial y} - \frac{\partial v}{\partial z} = \frac{\partial u}{\partial z} - \frac{\partial w}{\partial x} = \frac{\partial v}{\partial x} - \frac{\partial u}{\partial y} = 0 \qquad (6.23)$$

In cylindrical coordinates, from Eq. 5.16, the irrotationality condition requires that

$$\frac{1}{r}\frac{\partial V_z}{\partial \theta} - \frac{\partial V_\theta}{\partial z} = \frac{\partial V_r}{\partial z} - \frac{\partial V_z}{\partial r} = \frac{1}{r}\frac{\partial r V_\theta}{\partial r} - \frac{1}{r}\frac{\partial V_r}{\partial \theta} = 0 \qquad (6.24)$$

Bernoulli Equation Applied to Irrotational Flow

In Section 6-3, we integrated Euler's equation along a streamline for steady, incompressible, inviscid flow to obtain the Bernoulli equation

$$\frac{p}{\rho} + \frac{V^2}{2} + gz = \text{constant} \qquad (6.8)$$

Equation 6.8 can be applied between any two points on the *same* streamline. In general, the value of the constant will vary from streamline to streamline.

If, in addition to being inviscid, steady, and incompressible, the flow field is also irrotational (i.e., the particles had no initial rotation), so that $\nabla \times \vec{V} = 0$ (Eq. 6.22), we can show that Bernoulli's equation can be applied between any and all points in the flow. Then the value of the constant in Eq. 6.8 is the same for all streamlines. To illustrate this, we start with Euler's equation in vector form,

$$(\vec{V} \cdot \nabla)\vec{V} = -\frac{1}{\rho}\nabla p - g\hat{k} \qquad (6.9)$$

Using the vector identity

$$(\vec{V} \cdot \nabla)\vec{V} = \frac{1}{2}\nabla(\vec{V} \cdot \vec{V}) - \vec{V} \times (\nabla \times \vec{V})$$

we see for irrotational flow, where $\nabla \times \vec{V} = 0$, that

$$(\vec{V} \cdot \nabla)\vec{V} = \frac{1}{2}\nabla(\vec{V} \cdot \vec{V})$$

and Euler's equation for irrotational flow can be written as

$$\frac{1}{2}\nabla(\vec{V} \cdot \vec{V}) = \frac{1}{2}\nabla(V^2) = -\frac{1}{\rho}\nabla p - g\hat{k} \qquad (6.25)$$

Consider a displacement in the flow field from position $\vec{r}$ to position $\vec{r} + d\vec{r}$; the displacement $d\vec{r}$ is an *arbitrary* infinitesimal displacement in *any* direction, not necessarily along a streamline. Taking the dot product of $d\vec{r} = dx\hat{i} + dy\hat{j} + dz\hat{k}$ with each of the terms in Eq. 6.25, we have

$$\frac{1}{2}\nabla(V^2) \cdot d\vec{r} = -\frac{1}{\rho}\nabla p \cdot d\vec{r} - g\hat{k} \cdot d\vec{r}$$

and hence

$$\frac{1}{2} d(V^2) = -\frac{dp}{\rho} - gdz$$

or

$$\frac{dp}{\rho} + \frac{1}{2} d(V^2) + gdz = 0$$

Integrating this equation for incompressible flow gives

$$\frac{p}{\rho} + \frac{V^2}{2} + gz = \text{constant} \tag{6.26}$$

Since $d\vec{r}$ was an arbitrary displacement, Eq. 6.26 is valid between *any* two points (i.e., not just along a streamline) in a steady, incompressible, inviscid flow that is also irrotational (see Example 6.5).

Velocity Potential

We were introduced in Section 5-2 to the notion of the stream function ψ for a two-dimensional incompressible flow.

For irrotational flow we can introduce a companion function, the *potential function* ϕ, defined by

$$\vec{V} = -\nabla\phi \tag{6.27}$$

Why this definition? Because it guarantees that *any* continuous scalar function $\phi(x, y, z, t)$ *automatically* satisfies the irrotationality condition (Eq. 6.22) because of a fundamental indentity[7]:

$$\nabla \times \vec{V} = -\nabla \times \nabla\phi = -\text{curl}(\text{grad }\phi) \equiv 0 \tag{6.28}$$

The minus sign (used in most textbooks) is inserted simply so that ϕ decreases in the flow direction (analogous to the temperature decreasing in the direction of heat flow in heat conduction). Thus,

$$u = -\frac{\partial\phi}{\partial x}, \quad v = -\frac{\partial\phi}{\partial y}, \quad \text{and} \quad w = -\frac{\partial\phi}{\partial z} \tag{6.29}$$

(You can check that the irrotationality condition, Eq. 6.22, is satisfied identically.)

In cylindrical coordinates,

$$\nabla = \hat{e}_r \frac{\partial}{\partial r} + \hat{e}_\theta \frac{1}{r}\frac{\partial}{\partial \theta} + \hat{k}\frac{\partial}{\partial z} \tag{3.19}$$

---

[7] That $\nabla \times \nabla(\ ) \equiv 0$ can easily be demonstrated by expanding into components.

From Eq. 6.27, then, in cylindrical coordinates

$$V_r = -\frac{\partial \phi}{\partial r} \qquad V_\theta = -\frac{1}{r}\frac{\partial \phi}{\partial \theta} \qquad V_z = -\frac{\partial \phi}{\partial z} \qquad (6.30)$$

Because $\nabla \times \nabla \phi \equiv 0$ for all ϕ, the velocity potential exists only for irrotational flow.

Irrotationality may be a valid assumption for those regions of a flow in which viscous forces are negligible.[8] (For example, such a region exists outside the boundary layer in the flow over a wing surface, and can be analyzed to find the lift produced by the wing.) The theory for irrotational flow is developed in terms of an imaginary ideal fluid whose viscosity is identically zero. Since, in an irrotational flow, the velocity field may be defined by the potential function ϕ, the theory is often referred to as potential flow theory.

All real fluids possess viscosity, but there are many situations in which the assumption of inviscid flow considerably simplifies the analysis and, at the same time, gives meaningful results. Because of its relative simplicity and mathematical beauty, potential flow has been studied extensively.[9]

Stream Function and Velocity Potential for Two-Dimensional, Irrotational, Incompressible Flow: Laplace's Equation

For a two-dimensional, incompressible, irrotational flow we have expressions for the velocity components, u and v, in terms of both the stream function ψ, and the velocity potential ϕ,

$$u = \frac{\partial \psi}{\partial y} \qquad v = -\frac{\partial \psi}{\partial x} \qquad (5.4)$$

$$u = -\frac{\partial \phi}{\partial x} \qquad v = -\frac{\partial \phi}{\partial y} \qquad (6.29)$$

Substituting for u and v from Eq. 5.4 into the irrotationality condition,

$$\frac{\partial v}{\partial x} - \frac{\partial u}{\partial y} = 0 \qquad (6.23)$$

we obtain

$$\frac{\partial^2 \psi}{\partial x^2} + \frac{\partial^2 \psi}{\partial y^2} = \nabla^2 \psi = 0 \qquad (6.31)$$

Substituting for u and v from Eq. 6.29 into the continuity equation,

$$\frac{\partial u}{\partial x} + \frac{\partial v}{\partial y} = 0 \qquad (5.3)$$

we obtain

$$\frac{\partial^2 \phi}{\partial x^2} + \frac{\partial^2 \phi}{\partial y^2} = \nabla^2 \phi = 0 \qquad (6.32)$$

Equations 6.31 and 6.32 are forms of Laplace's equation—an equation that arises in many areas of the physical sciences and engineering. Any function ψ or ϕ that satisfies Laplace's equation represents a possible two-dimensional, incompressible, irrotational flow field.

[8]Examples of rotational and irrotational motion are shown in the NCFMF video *Vorticity*. (See http://web.mit.edu/fluids/www/Shapiro/ncfmf.html for free online viewing of this film.)
[9]Anyone interested in a detailed study of potential flow theory may find [4–6] of interest.

Table 6.1 summarizes the results of our discussion of the stream function and velocity potential for two dimensional flows.

The same rules (of when incompressibility and irrotationality apply, and with the appropriate form of Laplace's equation) are valid for the stream function and velocity potential when expressed in cylindrical coordinates,

$$V_r = \frac{1}{r} \frac{\partial \psi}{\partial \theta} \quad \text{and} \quad V_\theta = -\frac{\partial \psi}{\partial r} \tag{5.8}$$

and

$$V_r = -\frac{\partial \phi}{\partial r} \quad \text{and} \quad V_\theta = -\frac{1}{r} \frac{\partial \phi}{\partial \theta} \tag{6.33}$$

In Section 5-2 we showed that the stream function ψ is constant along any streamline. For ψ = constant, $d\psi = 0$ and

$$d\psi = \frac{\partial \psi}{\partial x} dx + \frac{\partial \psi}{\partial y} dy = 0$$

The slope of a streamline—a line of constant ψ—is given by

$$\left. \frac{dy}{dx} \right)_\psi = -\frac{\partial \psi / dx}{\partial x / \partial y} = -\frac{-v}{u} = \frac{v}{u} \tag{6.34}$$

Along a line of constant ϕ, $d\phi = 0$ and

$$d\phi = \frac{\partial \phi}{\partial x} dx + \frac{\partial \phi}{\partial y} dy = 0$$

Consequently, the slope of a potential line—a line of constant ϕ—is given by

$$\left. \frac{dy}{dx} \right)_\phi = -\frac{\partial \phi / \partial x}{\partial \phi / \partial y} = -\frac{u}{v} \tag{6.35}$$

(The last equality of Eq. 6.35 follows from use of Eq. 6.29.)

Comparing Eqs. 6.34 and 6.35, we see that the slope of a constant ψ line at any point is the negative reciprocal of the slope of the constant ϕ line at that point; this means that *lines of constant ψ and constant ϕ are orthogonal*. This property of potential lines and streamlines is useful in graphical analyses of flow fields.

TABLE 6.1 Definitions of ψ and ϕ, and Conditions Necessary for Satisfying Laplace's Equation

Definition	Always satisfies ...	Satisfies Laplace equation ... $\dfrac{\partial^2(\ )}{\partial x^2} + \dfrac{\partial^2(\ )}{\partial y^2} = \nabla^2(\ ) = 0$
Stream function ψ $u = \dfrac{\partial \psi}{\partial y} \quad v = -\dfrac{\partial \psi}{\partial x}$	... incompressibility: $\dfrac{\partial u}{\partial x} + \dfrac{\partial v}{\partial y} = \dfrac{\partial^2 \psi}{\partial x \partial y} - \dfrac{\partial^2 \psi}{\partial y \partial x} \equiv 0$	... only if irrotational: $\dfrac{\partial v}{\partial x} - \dfrac{\partial u}{\partial y} = -\dfrac{\partial^2 \psi}{\partial x \partial x} - \dfrac{\partial^2 \psi}{\partial y \partial y} = 0$
Velocity potential ϕ $u = -\dfrac{\partial \phi}{\partial x} \quad v = -\dfrac{\partial \phi}{\partial y}$	... irrotationality: $\dfrac{\partial v}{\partial x} - \dfrac{\partial u}{\partial y} = -\dfrac{\partial^2 \phi}{\partial x \partial y} - \dfrac{\partial^2 \phi}{\partial y \partial x} \equiv 0$	... only if incompressible: $\dfrac{\partial u}{\partial x} + \dfrac{\partial v}{\partial y} = -\dfrac{\partial^2 \phi}{\partial x \partial x} - \dfrac{\partial^2 \phi}{\partial y \partial y} = 0$

Example 6.10   Velocity Potential

Consider the flow field given by $\psi = ax^2 - ay^2$, where $a = 3 \text{ s}^{-1}$. Show that the flow is irrotational. Determine the velocity potential for this flow.

GIVEN: Incompressible flow field with $\psi = ax^2 - ay^2$, where $a = 3 \text{ s}^{-1}$.

FIND: (a) Whether or not the flow is irrotational.
   (b) The velocity potential for this flow.

SOLUTION:
If the flow is irrotational, $\nabla^2 \psi = 0$. Checking for the given flow,

$$\nabla^2 \psi = \frac{\partial^2}{\partial x^2}(ax^2 - ay^2) + \frac{\partial^2}{\partial y^2}(ax^2 - ay^2) = 2a - 2a = 0$$

so that the flow *is* irrotational. As an alternative proof, we can compute the fluid particle rotation (in the xy plane, the only component of rotation is ω_z):

$$2\omega_z = \frac{\partial v}{\partial x} - \frac{\partial u}{\partial y} \qquad \text{and} \qquad u = \frac{\partial \psi}{\partial y} \quad v = -\frac{\partial \psi}{\partial x}$$

then

$$u = \frac{\partial}{\partial y}(ax^2 - ay^2) = -2ay \qquad \text{and} \qquad v = -\frac{\partial}{\partial x}(ax^2 - ay^2) = -2ax$$

so

$$2\omega_z = \frac{\partial v}{\partial x} - \frac{\partial u}{\partial y} = \frac{\partial}{\partial x}(-2ax) - \frac{\partial}{\partial y}(-2ay) = -2a + 2a = 0 \qquad\qquad\underleftarrow{\hspace{4cm}} 2\omega_z$$

Once again, we conclude that the flow is irrotational. Because it is irrotational, ϕ must exist, and

$$u = -\frac{\partial \phi}{\partial x} \qquad \text{and} \qquad v = -\frac{\partial \phi}{\partial y}$$

Consequently, $u = -\dfrac{\partial \phi}{\partial x} = -2ay$ and $\dfrac{\partial \phi}{\partial x} = 2ay$. Integrating with respect to x gives $\phi = 2axy + f(y)$, where $f(y)$ is an arbitrary function of y. Then

$$v = -2ax = -\frac{\partial \phi}{\partial y} = -\frac{\partial}{\partial x}[2axy + f(y)]$$

Therefore, $-2ax = -2ax - \dfrac{\partial f(y)}{\partial y} = -2ax - \dfrac{df}{dy}$, so $\dfrac{df}{dy} = 0$ and $f = \text{constant}$. Thus

$$\phi = 2axy + \text{constant} \qquad\underleftarrow{\hspace{4cm}} \phi$$

We also can show that lines of constant ψ and constant ϕ are orthogonal.

$$\psi = ax^2 - ay^2 \qquad \text{and} \qquad \phi = 2axy$$

For $\psi = \text{constant}$, $d\psi = 0 = 2ax\,dx - 2ay\,dy$; hence $\left.\dfrac{dy}{dx}\right)_{\psi = c} = \dfrac{x}{y}$

For $\phi = \text{constant}$, $d\phi = 0 = 2ay\,dx + 2ax\,dy$; hence $\left.\dfrac{dy}{dx}\right)_{\phi = c} = -\dfrac{y}{x}$

The slopes of lines of constant ϕ and constant ψ are negative reciprocals. Therefore lines of constant ϕ are orthogonal to lines of constant ψ.

> This problem illustrates the relations among the stream function, velocity potential, and velocity field.
>
> 🖱 The stream function ψ and velocity potential ϕ are shown in the *Excel* workbook. By entering the equations for ψ and ϕ, other fields can be plotted.

Elementary Plane Flows

The ψ and ϕ functions for five elementary two-dimensional flows—a uniform flow, a source, a sink, a vortex, and a doublet—are summarized in Table 6.2. The ψ and ϕ functions can be obtained from the velocity field for each elementary flow. (We saw in Example 6.10 that we can obtain ϕ from u and v.)

TABLE 6.2 Elementary Plane Flows

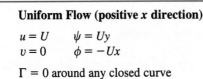

Uniform Flow (positive x direction)

$$u = U \qquad \psi = Uy$$
$$v = 0 \qquad \phi = -Ux$$

$\Gamma = 0$ around any closed curve

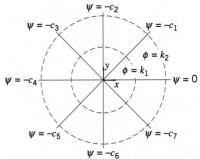

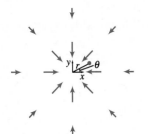

Source Flow (from origin)

$$V_r = \frac{q}{2\pi r} \qquad \psi = \frac{q}{2\pi}\theta$$

$$V_\theta = 0 \qquad \phi = -\frac{q}{2\pi}\ln r$$

Origin is singular point
q is volume flow rate per unit depth
$\Gamma = 0$ around any closed curve

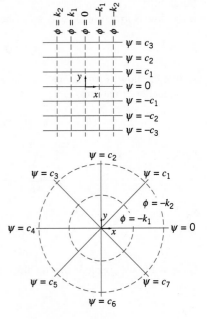

Sink Flow (toward origin)

$$V_r = -\frac{q}{2\pi r} \qquad \psi = -\frac{q}{2\pi}\theta$$

$$V_\theta = 0 \qquad \phi = \frac{q}{2\pi}\ln r$$

Origin is singular point
q is volume flow rate per unit depth
$\Gamma = 0$ around any closed curve

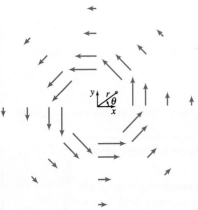

**Irrotational Vortex
(counterclockwise, center at origin)**

$$V_r = 0 \qquad \psi = -\frac{K}{2\pi}\ln r$$

$$V_\theta = \frac{K}{2\pi r} \qquad \phi = -\frac{K}{2\pi}\theta$$

Origin is singular point
K is strength of the vortex
$\Gamma = K$ around any closed
    curve enclosing origin
$\Gamma = 0$ around any closed
    curve not enclosing origin

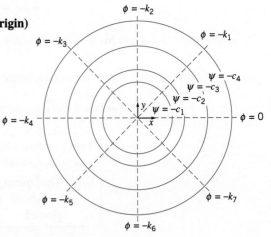

TABLE 6.2 Elementary Plane Flows (*continued*)

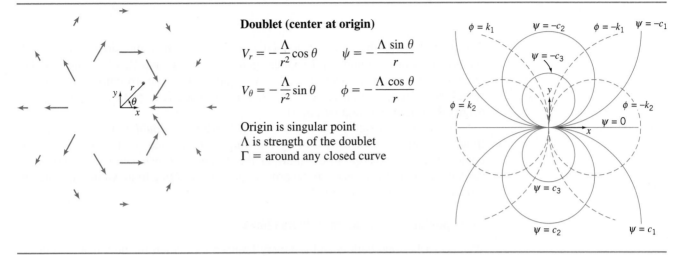

Doublet (center at origin)

$$V_r = -\frac{\Lambda}{r^2}\cos\theta \qquad \psi = -\frac{\Lambda\sin\theta}{r}$$

$$V_\theta = -\frac{\Lambda}{r^2}\sin\theta \qquad \phi = -\frac{\Lambda\cos\theta}{r}$$

Origin is singular point
Λ is strength of the doublet
Γ = around any closed curve

A *uniform flow* of constant velocity parallel to the x axis satisfies the continuity equation and the irrotationality condition identically. In Table 6.2 we have shown the ψ and ϕ functions for a uniform flow in the positive x direction.

For a uniform flow of constant magnitude V, inclined at angle α to the x axis,

$$\psi = (V\cos\alpha)y - (V\sin\alpha)x$$
$$\phi = -(V\sin\alpha)y - (V\cos\alpha)x$$

A simple *source* is a flow pattern in the xy plane in which flow is radially outward from the z axis and symmetrical in all directions. The strength, q, of the source is the volume flow rate per unit depth. At any radius, r, from a source, the tangential velocity, V_θ, is zero; the radial velocity, V_r, is the volume flow rate per unit depth, q, divided by the flow area per unit depth, $2\pi r$. Thus $V_r = q/2\pi r$ for a source. Knowing V_r and V_θ, obtaining ψ and ϕ from Eqs. 5.8 and 6.33, respectively, is straightforward.

In a simple *sink*, flow is radially inward; a sink is a negative source. The ψ and ϕ functions for a sink shown in Table 6.2 are the negatives of the corresponding functions for a source flow.

The origin of either a sink or a source is a singular point, since the radial velocity approaches infinity as the radius approaches zero. Thus, while an actual flow may resemble a source or a sink for some values of r, sources and sinks have no exact physical counterparts. The primary value of the concept of sources and sinks is that, when combined with other elementary flows, they produce flow patterns that adequately represent realistic flows.

A flow pattern in which the streamlines are concentric circles is a vortex; in a *free (irrotational) vortex*, fluid particles do not rotate as they translate in circular paths around the vortex center. There are a number of ways of obtaining the velocity field, for example, by combining the equation of motion (Euler's equation) and the Bernoulli equation to eliminate the pressure. Here, though, for circular streamlines, we have $V_r = 0$ and $V_\theta = f(\theta)$ only. We also have previously introduced the condition of irrotationality in cylindrical coordinates,

$$\frac{1}{r}\frac{\partial rV_\theta}{\partial r} - \frac{1}{r}\frac{\partial V_r}{\partial\theta} = 0 \qquad (6.24)$$

Hence, using the known forms of V_r and V_θ, we obtain

$$\frac{1}{r}\frac{d(rV_\theta)}{dr} = 0$$

Integrating this equation gives

$$V_\theta r = \text{constant}$$

The strength, K, of the vortex is defined as $K = 2\pi r V_\theta$; the dimensions of K are L^2/t (volume flow rate per unit depth). Once again, knowing V_r and V_θ, obtaining ψ and ϕ from Eqs. 5.8 and 6.33, respectively, is straightforward. The irrotational vortex is a reasonable approximation to the flow field in a tornado (except in the region of the origin; the origin is a singular point).

The final "elementary" flow listed in Table 6.2 is the *doublet* of strength Λ. This flow is produced mathematically by allowing a source and a sink of numerically equal strengths to merge. In the limit, as the distance, δs, between them approaches zero, their strengths increase so the product $q\delta s/2\pi$ tends to a finite value, Λ, which is termed the strength of the doublet.

Superposition of Elementary Plane Flows

We saw earlier that both ϕ and ψ satisfy Laplace's equation for flow that is both incompressible and irrotational. Since Laplace's equation is a linear, homogeneous partial differential equation, solutions may be superposed (added together) to develop more complex and interesting patterns of flow. Thus if ψ_1 and ψ_2 satisfy Laplace's equation, then so does $\psi_3 = \psi_1 + \psi_2$. The elementary plane flows are the building blocks in this superposition process. There is one note of caution: While Laplace's equation for the stream function, and the stream function-velocity field equations (Eq. 5.3) are linear, the Bernoulli equation is not; hence, in the superposition process we will have $\psi_3 = \psi_1 + \psi_2$, $u_3 = u_1 + u_2$, and $v_3 = v_1 + v_2$, but $p_3 \neq p_1 + p_2$! We must use the Bernoulli equation, which is nonlinear in V, to find p_3.

We can add together elementary flows to try and generate recognizable flow patterns. The simplest superposition approach is called the *direct* method, in which we try different combinations of elementary flows and see what kinds of flow patterns are produced. This sounds like a random process, but with a little experience it becomes a quite logical process. For example, look at some of the classic examples listed in Table 6.3. The source and uniform flow combination makes sense—we would intuitively expect a source to partially push its way upstream, and to divert the flow around it. The source, sink, and uniform flow (generating what is called a Rankine body) is also not surprising—the entire flow out of the source makes its way into the sink, leading to a closed streamline. *Any streamline can be interpreted as a solid surface because there is no flow across it;* we can therefore pretend that this closed streamline represents a solid. We could easily generalize this source-sink approach to any number of sources and sinks distributed along the x axis, and as long as the sum of the source and sink strengths added up to zero, we would generate a closed streamline body shape. The doublet-uniform flow (with or without a vortex) generates a very interesting result: flow over a cylinder (with or without circulation)! We first saw the flow without circulation in Fig. 2.12*a*. The flow with a clockwise vortex produces a top-to-bottom asymmetry. This is because in the region above the cylinder the velocities due to the uniform flow and vortex are in the same overall direction and lead to a high velocity; below the cylinder they are in opposite directions and therefore lead to a low velocity. As we have learned, whenever velocities are high, streamlines will be close together, and vice versa—explaining the pattern shown. More importantly, from the Bernoulli equation we know that whenever the velocity is high the pressure will be low, and vice versa—hence, we can anticipate that the cylinder with circulation will experience a net upward force (lift) due to pressure. This approach, of looking at streamline patterns to see where we have regions of high or low velocity and hence low or high pressure, is very useful. We will examine these last two flows in Examples 6.11 and 6.12. The last example in Table 6.3, the vortex pair, hints at a way to create flows that simulate the presence of a wall or walls: for

TABLE 6.3 Superposition of Elementary Plane Flows

Source and Uniform Flow (flow past a half-body)

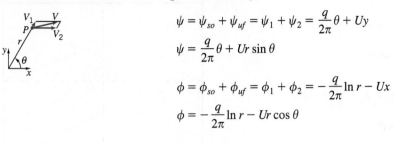

$$\psi = \psi_{so} + \psi_{uf} = \psi_1 + \psi_2 = \frac{q}{2\pi}\theta + Uy$$

$$\psi = \frac{q}{2\pi}\theta + Ur\sin\theta$$

$$\phi = \phi_{so} + \phi_{uf} = \phi_1 + \phi_2 = -\frac{q}{2\pi}\ln r - Ux$$

$$\phi = -\frac{q}{2\pi}\ln r - Ur\cos\theta$$

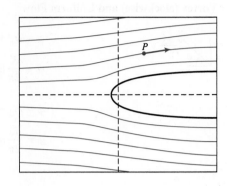

Source and Sink (equal strength, separation distance on x axis = 2a)

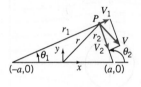

$$\psi = \psi_{so} + \psi_{si} = \psi_1 + \psi_2 = \frac{q}{2\pi}\theta_1 - \frac{q}{2\pi}\theta_2$$

$$\psi = \frac{q}{2\pi}(\theta_1 - \theta_2)$$

$$\phi = \phi_{so} + \phi_{si} = \phi_1 + \phi_2 = -\frac{q}{2\pi}\ln r_1 + \frac{q}{2\pi}\ln r_2$$

$$\phi = \frac{q}{2\pi}\ln\frac{r_2}{r_1}$$

Source, Sink, and Uniform Flow (flow past a Rankine body)

$$\psi = \psi_{so} + \psi_{si} + \psi_{uf} = \psi_1 + \psi_2 + \psi_3$$

$$= \frac{q}{2\pi}\theta_1 - \frac{q}{2\pi}\theta_2 + Uy$$

$$\psi = \frac{q}{2\pi}(\theta_1 - \theta_2) + Ur\sin\theta$$

$$\phi = \phi_{so} + \phi_{si} + \phi_{uf} = \phi_1 + \phi_2 + \phi_3$$

$$= -\frac{q}{2\pi}\ln r_1 + \frac{q}{2\pi}\ln r_2 - Ux$$

$$\phi = \frac{q}{2\pi}\ln\frac{r_2}{r_1} - Ur\cos\theta$$

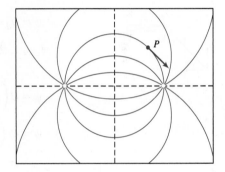

(continued)

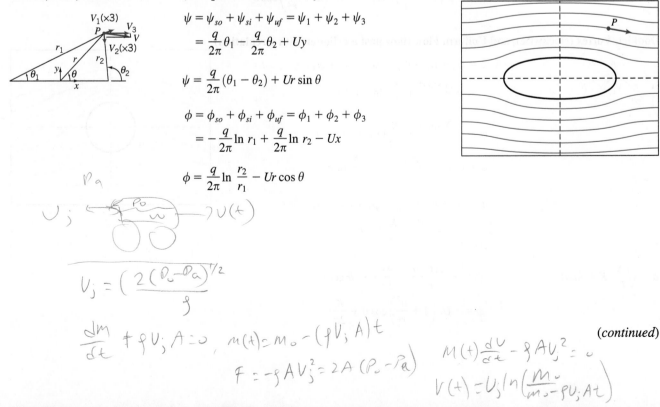

TABLE 6.3 Superposition of Elementary Plane Flows (*continued*)

Vortex (clockwise) and Uniform Flow

$$\psi = \psi_v + \psi_{uf} = \psi_1 + \psi_2 = \frac{K}{2\pi}\ln r + Uy$$

$$\psi = \frac{K}{2\pi}\ln r + Ur\sin\theta$$

$$\phi = \phi_v + \phi_{uf} = \phi_1 + \phi_2 = \frac{K}{2\pi}\theta - Ux$$

$$\phi = \frac{K}{2\pi}\theta - Ur\cos\theta$$

Doublet and Uniform Flow (flow past a cylinder)

$$\psi = \psi_d + \ldots$$

$$= -\frac{\Lambda\sin\ldots}{r}$$

$$\psi = U\left(r - \frac{}{Ur}\right)\ldots$$

$$\psi = Ur\left(1 - \frac{a^2}{r^2}\right)\sin\theta \quad a = \sqrt{\frac{\Lambda}{U}}$$

$$\phi = \phi_d + \phi_{uf} = \phi_1 + \phi_2 = -\frac{\Lambda\cos\theta}{r} - Ux$$

$$= -\frac{\Lambda\cos\theta}{r} - Ur\cos\theta$$

$$\phi = -U\left(r + \frac{\Lambda}{Ur}\right)\cos\theta = -Ur\left(1 + \frac{a^2}{r^2}\right)\cos\theta$$

Doublet, Vortex (clockwise), and Uniform Flow (flow past a cylinder with circulation)

$$a = \sqrt{\frac{\Lambda}{U}}; \ K < 4\pi a U$$

$$\phi = -\frac{\Lambda\cos\theta}{r} + \frac{K}{2\pi}\theta - Ur\cos\theta$$

$$\phi = -Ur\left(1 + \frac{a^2}{r^2}\right)\cos\theta + \frac{K}{2\pi}\theta$$

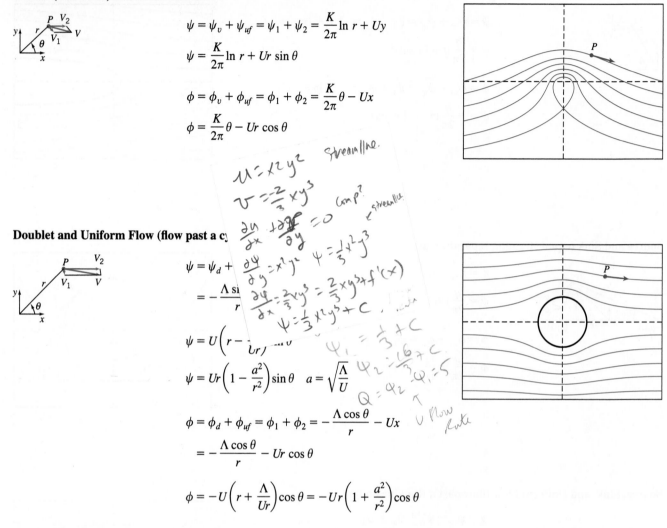

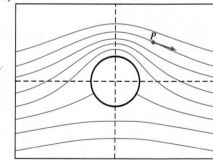

TABLE 6.3 Superposition of Elementary Plane Flows (*continued*)

Source and Vortex (spiral vortex)

$$\psi = \psi_{so} + \psi_v = \psi_1 + \psi_2 = \frac{q}{2\pi}\theta - \frac{K}{2\pi}\ln r$$

$$\phi = \phi_{so} + \phi_v = \phi_1 + \phi_2 = -\frac{q}{2\pi}\ln r - \frac{K}{2\pi}\theta$$

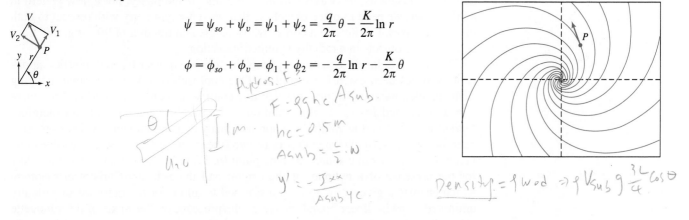

Sink and Vortex

$$\psi = \psi_{si} + \psi_v = \psi_1 + \psi_2 = -\frac{q}{2\pi}\theta - \frac{K}{2\pi}\ln r$$

$$\phi = \phi_{si} + \phi_v = \phi_1 + \phi_2 = \frac{q}{2\pi}\ln r - \frac{K}{2\pi}\theta$$

Vortex Pair (equal ... tion distance on x axis = 2a)

$$\psi - \psi_{v1} + \psi_{v2} = \psi_1 + \psi_2 = -\frac{K}{2\pi}\ln r_1 + \frac{K}{2\pi}\ln r_2$$

$$\psi = \frac{K}{2\pi}\ln\frac{r_2}{r_1}$$

$$\phi = \phi_{v1} + \phi_{v2} = \phi_1 + \phi_2 = -\frac{K}{2\pi}\theta_1 + \frac{K}{2\pi}\theta_2$$

$$\phi = \frac{K}{2\pi}(\theta_2 - \theta_1)$$

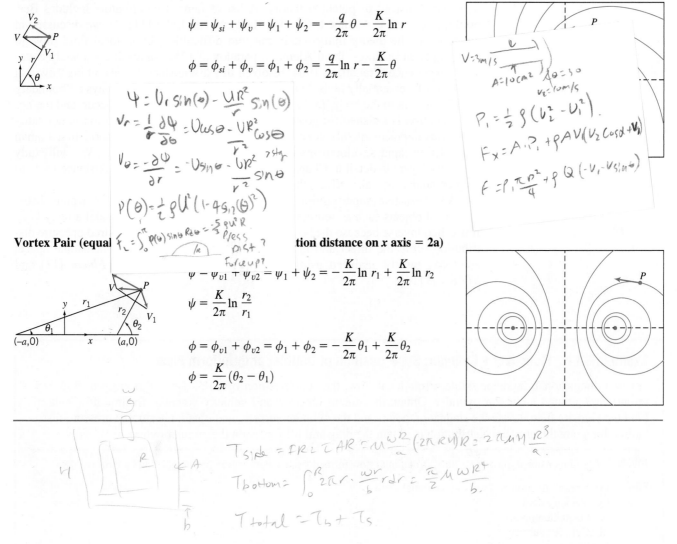

the y-axis to be a streamline (and thus a wall), simply make sure that any objects (e.g., a source, a vortex) in the positive x quadrants have mirror-image objects in the negative x quadrants; the y axis will thus be a line of symmetry. For a flow pattern in a $90°$ corner, we need to place objects so that we have symmetry with respect to both the x and y axes. For flow in a corner whose angle is a fraction of $90°$ (e.g., $30°$), we need to place objects in a radially symmetric fashion.

Because Laplace's equation appears in many engineering and physics applications, it has been extensively studied. One approach is to use conformal mapping with complex notation. It turns out that *any* continuous complex function $f(z)$ (where $z = x + iy$, and $i = \sqrt{-1}$) is a solution of Laplace's equation, and can therefore represent both ϕ and ψ. With this approach many elegant mathematical results have been derived [7–10]. We mention only two: the circle theorem, which enables any given flow [e.g., from a source at some point (a, b)] to be easily transformed to allow for the presence of a cylinder at the origin; and the Schwarz-Christoffel theorem, which enables a given flow to be transformed to allow for the presence of virtually unlimited stepwise linear boundaries (e.g., the presence on the x axis of the silhouette of a building).

Much of this analytical work was done centuries ago, when it was called "hydrodynamics" instead of potential theory. A list of famous contributors includes Bernoulli, Lagrange, d'Alembert, Cauchy, Rankine, and Euler [11]. As we discussed in Section 2-6, the theory immediately ran into difficulties: In an ideal fluid flow no body experiences drag—the d'Alembert paradox of 1752—a result completely counter to experience. Prandtl, in 1904, resolved this discrepancy by describing how real flows may be essentially inviscid almost everywhere, but there is always a "boundary layer" adjacent to the body. In this layer significant viscous effects occur, and the no-slip condition is satisfied (in potential flow theory the no-slip condition is not satisfied). Development of this concept, and the Wright brothers' historic first human flight, led to rapid developments in aeronautics starting in the 1900s. We will study boundary layers in detail in Chapter 9, where we will see that their existence leads to drag on bodies, and also affects the lift of bodies.

An alternative superposition approach is the *inverse* method in which distributions of objects such as sources, sinks, and vortices are used to model a body [12]. It is called inverse because the body shape is deduced based on a desired pressure distribution. Both the direct and inverse methods, including three-dimensional space, are today mostly analyzed using computer applications such as *Fluent* [13] and *STAR-CD* [14].

Example 6.11   Flow over a Cylinder: Superposition of Doublet and Uniform Flow

For two-dimensional, incompressible, irrotational flow, the superposition of a doublet and a uniform flow represents flow around a circular cylinder. Obtain the stream function and velocity potential for this flow pattern. Find the velocity field, locate the stagnation points and the cylinder surface, and obtain the surface pressure distribution. Integrate the pressure distribution to obtain the drag and lift forces on the circular cylinder.

GIVEN: Two-dimensional, incompressible, irrotational flow formed from superposition of a doublet and a uniform flow.

FIND: (a) Stream function and velocity potential.
   (b) Velocity field.
   (c) Stagnation points.
   (d) Cylinder surface.
   (e) Surface pressure distribution.
   (f) Drag force on the circular cylinder.
   (g) Lift force on the circular cylinder.

SOLUTION:

Stream functions may be added because the flow field is incompressible and irrotational. Thus from Table 6.2, the stream function for the combination is

$$\psi = \psi_d + \psi_{uf} = -\frac{\Lambda \sin \theta}{r} + Ur \sin \theta \qquad\qquad \psi$$

The velocity potential is

$$\phi = \phi_d + \phi_{uf} = -\frac{\Lambda \cos \theta}{r} - Ur \cos \theta \qquad\qquad \phi$$

The corresponding velocity components are obtained using Eqs. 6.30 as

$$V_r = -\frac{\partial \phi}{\partial r} = -\frac{\Lambda \cos \theta}{r^2} + U \cos \theta$$

$$V_\theta = -\frac{1}{r}\frac{\partial \phi}{\partial \theta} = -\frac{\Lambda \sin \theta}{r^2} - U \sin \theta$$

The velocity field is

$$\vec{V} = V_r \hat{e}_r + V_\theta \hat{e}_\theta = \left(-\frac{\Lambda \cos \theta}{r^2} + U \cos \theta\right)\hat{e}_r + \left(-\frac{\Lambda \sin \theta}{r^2} - U \sin \theta\right)\hat{e}_\theta \qquad \vec{V}$$

Stagnation points are where $\vec{V} = V_r \hat{e}_r + V_\theta \hat{e}_\theta = 0$

$$V_r = -\frac{\Lambda \cos \theta}{r^2} + U \cos \theta = \cos \theta \left(U - \frac{\Lambda}{r^2}\right)$$

Thus $V_r = 0$ when $r = \sqrt{\dfrac{\Lambda}{U}} = a$. Also,

$$V_\theta = -\frac{\Lambda \sin \theta}{r^2} - U \sin \theta = -\sin \theta \left(U + \frac{\Lambda}{r^2}\right)$$

Thus $V_\theta = 0$ when $\theta = 0, \pi$.
Stagnation points are $(r, \theta) = (a, 0), (a, \pi)$. $\qquad\qquad$ Stagnation points

Note that $V_r = 0$ along $r = a$, so this represents flow around a circular cylinder, as shown in Table 6.3. Flow is irrotational, so the Bernoulli equation may be applied between any two points. Applying the equation between a point far upstream and a point on the surface of the cylinder (neglecting elevation differences), we obtain

$$\frac{p_\infty}{\rho} + \frac{U^2}{2} = \frac{p}{\rho} + \frac{V^2}{2}$$

Thus,

$$p - p_\infty = \frac{1}{2}\rho(U^2 - V^2)$$

Along the surface, $r = a$, and

$$V^2 = V_\theta^2 = \left(-\frac{\Lambda}{a^2} - U\right)^2 \sin^2 \theta = 4U^2 \sin^2 \theta$$

since $\Lambda = Ua^2$. Substituting yields

$$p - p_\infty = \frac{1}{2}\rho(U^2 - 4U^2 \sin^2 \theta) = \frac{1}{2}\rho U^2(1 - 4\sin^2 \theta)$$

or

$$\frac{p - p_\infty}{\frac{1}{2}\rho U^2} = 1 - 4\sin^2 \theta \qquad\qquad \text{Pressure distribution}$$

Drag is the force component parallel to the freestream flow direction. The drag force is given by

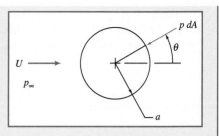

$$F_D = \int_A -p \, dA \cos \theta = \int_0^{2\pi} -pa \, d\theta \, b \cos \theta$$

since $dA = a \, d\theta \, b$, where b is the length of the cylinder normal to the diagram. Substituting $p = p_\infty + \frac{1}{2}\rho U^2 (1 - 4 \sin^2 \theta)$,

$$F_D = \int_0^{2\pi} -p_\infty ab \cos \theta \, d\theta + \int_0^{2\pi} -\frac{1}{2}\rho U^2 (1 - 4 \sin^2 \theta) ab \cos \theta \, d\theta$$

$$= -p_\infty \, ab \sin \theta \big]_0^{2\pi} - \frac{1}{2}\rho U^2 ab \sin \theta \big]_0^{2\pi} + \frac{1}{2}\rho U^2 ab \frac{4}{3} \sin^3 \theta \big]_0^{2\pi}$$

$$F_D = 0 \qquad\longleftarrow \hspace{5cm} F_D$$

Lift is the force component normal to the freestream flow direction. (By convention, positive lift is an upward force.) The lift force is given by

$$F_L = \int_A p \, dA(-\sin \theta) = -\int_0^{2\pi} pa \, d\theta \, b \sin \theta$$

Substituting for p gives

$$F_L = -\int_0^{2\pi} p_\infty ab \sin \theta \, d\theta - \int_0^{2\pi} \frac{1}{2}\rho U^2 (1 - 4 \sin^2 \theta) ab \sin \theta \, d\theta$$

$$= p_\infty a \, b \cos \theta \big]_0^{2\pi} + \frac{1}{2}\rho U^2 ab \cos \theta \big]_0^{2\pi} + \frac{1}{2}\rho U^2 ab \left[\frac{4 \cos^3 \theta}{3} - 4 \cos \theta \right]_0^{2\pi}$$

$$F_L = 0 \qquad\longleftarrow \hspace{5cm} F_L$$

This problem illustrates:

   ✓ How elementary plane flows can be combined to generate interesting and useful flow patterns.

   ✓ d'Alembert's paradox, that potential flows over a body do not generate drag.

   The stream function and pressure distribution are plotted in the *Excel* workbook.

Example 6.12   Flow over a Cylinder with Circulation: Superposition of Doublet, Uniform Flow, and Clockwise Free Vortex

For two-dimensional, incompressible, irrotational flow, the superposition of a doublet, a uniform flow, and a free vortex represents the flow around a circular cylinder with circulation. Obtain the stream function and velocity potential for this flow pattern, using a clockwise free vortex. Find the velocity field, locate the stagnation points and the cylinder surface, and obtain the surface pressure distribution. Integrate the pressure distribution to obtain the drag and lift forces on the circular cylinder. Relate the lift force on the cylinder to the circulation of the free vortex.

GIVEN: Two-dimensional, incompressible, irrotational flow formed from superposition of a doublet, a uniform flow, and a clockwise free vortex.

FIND: (a) Stream function and velocity potential.
(b) Velocity field.
(c) Stagnation points.
(d) Cylinder surface.
(e) Surface pressure distribution.
(f) Drag force on the circular cylinder.
(g) Lift force on the circular cylinder.
(h) Lift force in terms of circulation of the free vortex.

SOLUTION:

Stream functions may be added because the flow field is incompressible and irrotational. From Table 6.2, the stream function and velocity potential for a clockwise free vortex are

$$\psi_{fv} = \frac{K}{2\pi} \ln r \qquad \phi_{fv} = \frac{K}{2\pi} \theta$$

Using the results of Example 6.11, the stream function for the combination is

$$\psi = \psi_d + \psi_{uf} + \psi_{fv}$$

$$\psi = -\frac{\Lambda \sin \theta}{r} + U r \sin \theta + \frac{K}{2\pi} \ln r \qquad\qquad \underleftarrow{\hspace{3cm}} \quad \psi$$

The velocity potential for the combination is

$$\phi = \phi_d + \phi_{uf} + \phi_{fv}$$

$$\phi = -\frac{\Lambda \cos \theta}{r} - U r \cos \theta + \frac{K}{2\pi} \theta \qquad\qquad \underleftarrow{\hspace{3cm}} \quad \phi$$

The corresponding velocity components are obtained using Eqs. 6.30 as

$$V_r = -\frac{\partial \phi}{\partial r} = -\frac{\Lambda \cos \theta}{r^2} + U \cos \theta \tag{1}$$

$$V_\theta = -\frac{1}{r} \frac{\partial \phi}{\partial \theta} = -\frac{\Lambda \sin \theta}{r^2} - U \sin \theta - \frac{K}{2\pi r} \tag{2}$$

The velocity field is

$$\vec{V} = V_r \, \hat{e}_r + V_\theta \, \hat{e}_\theta$$

$$\vec{V} = \left(-\frac{\Lambda \cos \theta}{r^2} + U \cos \theta \right) \hat{e}_r + \left(-\frac{\Lambda \sin \theta}{r} - U \sin \theta - \frac{K}{2\pi r} \right) \hat{e}_\theta \underleftarrow{\hspace{2cm}} \quad \vec{V}$$

Stagnation points are located where $\vec{V} = V_r \, \hat{e}_r + V_\theta \, \hat{e}_\theta = 0$. From Eq. 1,

$$V_r = -\frac{\Lambda \cos \theta}{r^2} + U \cos \theta = \cos \theta \left(U - \frac{\Lambda}{r^2} \right)$$

Thus $V_r = 0$ when $r = \sqrt{\Lambda/U} = a$ $\qquad\qquad \underleftarrow{\hspace{3cm}}$ Cylinder surface

The stagnation points are located on $r = a$. Substituting into Eq. 2 with $r = a$,

$$V_\theta = -\frac{\Lambda \sin \theta}{a^2} - U \sin \theta - \frac{K}{2\pi a}$$

$$= -\frac{\Lambda \sin \theta}{\Lambda/U} - U \sin \theta - \frac{K}{2\pi a}$$

$$V_\theta = -2U \sin \theta - \frac{K}{2\pi a}$$

Thus $V_\theta = 0$ along $r = a$ when

$$\sin \theta = -\frac{K}{4\pi Ua} \quad \text{or} \quad \theta = \sin^{-1}\left[\frac{-K}{4\pi Ua}\right]$$

Stagnation points: $\quad r = a \quad \theta = \sin^{-1}\left[\frac{-K}{4\pi Ua}\right]$ ⟵ Stagnation points

As in Example 6.11, $V_r = 0$ along $r = a$, so this flow field once again represents flow around a circular cylinder, as shown in Table 6.3. For $K = 0$ the solution is identical to that of Example 6.11.

The presence of the free vortex ($K > 0$) moves the stagnation points below the center of the cylinder. Thus the free vortex alters the vertical symmetry of the flow field. The flow field has two stagnation points for a range of vortex strengths between $K = 0$ and $K = 4\pi Ua$.

A single stagnation point is located at $\theta = -\pi/2$ when $K = 4\pi Ua$.

Even with the free vortex present, the flow field is irrotational, so the Bernoulli equation may be applied between any two points. Applying the equation between a point far upstream and a point on the surface of the cylinder we obtain

$$\frac{p_\infty}{\rho} + \frac{U^2}{2} + gz = \frac{p}{\rho} + \frac{V^2}{2} + gz$$

Thus, neglecting elevation differences,

$$p - p_\infty = \frac{1}{2}\rho\,(U^2 - V^2) = \frac{1}{2}\rho U^2\left[1 - \left(\frac{U}{V}\right)^2\right]$$

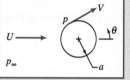

Along the surface $r = a$ and $V_r = 0$, so

$$V^2 = V_\theta^2 = \left(-2U \sin \theta - \frac{K}{2\pi a}\right)^2$$

and

$$\left(\frac{V}{U}\right)^2 = 4 \sin^2 \theta + \frac{2K}{\pi Ua} \sin \theta + \frac{K^2}{4\pi^2 U^2 a^2}$$

Thus

$$p = p_\infty + \frac{1}{2}\rho U^2\left(1 - 4\sin^2\theta - \frac{2K}{\pi Ua}\sin\theta - \frac{K^2}{4\pi^2 U^2 a^2}\right)$$ ⟵ $p(\theta)$

Drag is the force component parallel to the freestream flow direction. As in Example 6.11, the drag force is given by

$$F_D = \int_A -p\,dA\cos\theta = \int_0^{2\pi} -pa\,d\theta b\cos\theta$$

since $dA = a\,d\theta\,b$, where b is the length of the cylinder normal to the diagram.

Comparing pressure distributions, the free vortex contributes only to the terms containing the factor K. The contribution of these terms to the drag force is

$$\frac{F_{D_{fv}}}{\frac{1}{2}\rho U^2} = \int_0^{2\pi}\left(\frac{2K}{\pi Ua}\sin\theta + \frac{K^2}{4\pi^2 U^2 a^2}\right)ab\cos\theta\,d\theta \tag{3}$$

$$\frac{F_{D_{fv}}}{\frac{1}{2}\rho U^2} = \frac{2K}{\pi Ua}ab\left.\frac{\sin^2\theta}{2}\right]_0^{2\pi} + \frac{K^2}{4\pi^2 U^2 a^2}ab\sin\theta\Big]_0^{2\pi} = 0$$ ⟵ F_D

Lift is the force component normal to the freestream flow direction. (Upward force is defined as positive lift.) The lift force is given by

$$F_L = \int_A -p\,dA\sin\theta = \int_0^{2\pi} -pa\,d\theta\,b\sin\theta$$

Comparing pressure distributions, the free vortex contributes only to the terms containing the factor K. The contribution of these terms to the lift force is

$$\frac{F_{L_{fv}}}{\frac{1}{2}\rho U^2} = \int_0^{2\pi} \left(\frac{2K}{\pi Ua} \sin\theta + \frac{K^2}{4\pi^2 U^2 a^2} \right) ab \sin\theta \, d\theta$$

$$= \frac{2K}{\pi Ua} \int_0^{2\pi} ab \sin^2\theta \, d\theta + \frac{K^2}{4\pi^2 U^2 a^2} \int_0^{2\pi} ab \sin\theta \, d\theta$$

$$= \frac{2Kb}{\pi U} \left[\frac{\theta}{2} - \frac{\sin^2\theta}{4} \right]_0^{2\pi} - \frac{K^2 b}{4\pi^2 U^2 a} \cos\theta \Big]_0^{2\pi}$$

$$\frac{F_{L_{fv}}}{\frac{1}{2}\rho U^2} = \frac{2Kb}{\pi U} \left[\frac{2\pi}{2} \right] = \frac{2Kb}{U}$$

Then $F_{L_{fv}} = \rho U K b$ ⟵——————————————————— F_L

The *circulation* is defined by Eq. 5.18 as

$$\Gamma \equiv \oint \vec{V} \cdot d\vec{s}$$

On the cylinder surface, $r = a$, and $\vec{V} = V_\theta \, \hat{e}_\theta$, so

$$\Gamma = \int_0^{2\pi} \left(-2U \sin\theta - \frac{K}{2\pi a} \right) \hat{e}_\theta \cdot a \, d\theta \, \hat{e}_\theta$$

$$= -\int_0^{2\pi} 2Ua \sin\theta \, d\theta - \int_0^{2\pi} \frac{K}{2\pi} \, d\theta$$

$$\Gamma = -K$$ ⟵——————————————————— Circulation

Substituting into the expression for lift,

$$F_L = \rho U K b = \rho U(-\Gamma)b = -\rho U \, \Gamma b$$

or the lift force per unit length of cylinder is

$$\frac{F_L}{b} = -\rho U \Gamma$$ ⟵——————————————————— $\frac{F_L}{b}$

This problem illustrates:
- ✓ Once again d'Alembert's paradox, that potential flows do not generate drag on a body.
- ✓ That the lift per unit length is $-\rho U \Gamma$. It turns out that this expression for lift is the same for *all* bodies in an ideal fluid flow, regardless of shape!
- The stream function and pressure distribution are plotted in the *Excel* workbook.

6-8 SUMMARY AND USEFUL EQUATIONS

In this chapter we have:

✓ Derived Euler's equations in vector form and in rectangular, cylindrical, and streamline coordinates.

✓ Obtained Bernoulli's equation by integrating Euler's equation along a steady-flow streamline, and discussed its restrictions. We have also seen how for a steady, incompressible flow through a stream tube the first law of thermodynamics reduces to the Bernoulli equation if certain restrictions apply.

✓ Defined the static, dynamic, and stagnation (or total) pressures.

✓ Defined the energy and hydraulic grade lines.

✓ *Derived an unsteady flow Bernoulli equation, and discussed its restrictions.

✓ *Observed that for an irrotational flow that is steady and incompressible, the Bernoulli equation applies between *any* two points in the flow.

✓ *Defined the velocity potential ϕ and discussed its restrictions.

*We have also explored in detail two-dimensional, incompressible and irrotational flows, and learned that for these flows: the stream function ψ and the velocity potential ϕ satisfy Laplace's equation; ψ and ϕ can be derived from the velocity components, and vice versa, and the iso-lines of the stream function ψ and the velocity potential ϕ are orthogonal. We explored for such flows how to combine potential flows to generate various flow patterns, and how to determine the pressure distribution and lift and drag on, for example, a cylindrical shape.

Note: Most of the Useful Equations in the table below have a number of constraints or limitations—*be sure to refer to their page numbers for details*!

Useful Equations		
The Euler equation for incompressible, inviscid flow:	$\rho \dfrac{D\vec{V}}{Dt} = \rho\vec{g} - \nabla p$ $\qquad$ (6.1)	Page 216
The Euler equation (rectangular coordinates):	$\rho\left(\dfrac{\partial u}{\partial t} + u\dfrac{\partial u}{\partial x} + v\dfrac{\partial u}{\partial y} + w\dfrac{\partial u}{\partial z}\right) = \rho g_x - \dfrac{\partial p}{\partial x}$ $\qquad$ (6.2a) $\rho\left(\dfrac{\partial v}{\partial t} + u\dfrac{\partial v}{\partial x} + v\dfrac{\partial v}{\partial y} + w\dfrac{\partial v}{\partial z}\right) = \rho g_y - \dfrac{\partial p}{\partial y}$ $\qquad$ (6.2b) $\rho\left(\dfrac{\partial w}{\partial t} + u\dfrac{\partial w}{\partial x} + v\dfrac{\partial w}{\partial y} + w\dfrac{\partial w}{\partial z}\right) = \rho g_z - \dfrac{\partial p}{\partial z}$ $\qquad$ (6.2c)	Page 216
The Euler equation (cylindrical coordinates):	$\rho a_r = \rho\left(\dfrac{\partial V_r}{\partial t} + V_r\dfrac{\partial V_r}{\partial r} + \dfrac{V_\theta}{r}\dfrac{\partial V_r}{\partial \theta} + V_z\dfrac{\partial V_r}{\partial z} - \dfrac{V_\theta^2}{r}\right) = \rho g_r - \dfrac{\partial p}{\partial r}$ $\qquad$ (6.3a) $\rho a_\theta = \rho\left(\dfrac{\partial V_\theta}{\partial t} + V_r\dfrac{\partial V_\theta}{\partial r} + \dfrac{V_\theta}{r}\dfrac{\partial V_\theta}{\partial \theta} + V_z\dfrac{\partial V_\theta}{\partial z} + \dfrac{V_r V_\theta}{r}\right) = \rho g_\theta - \dfrac{1}{r}\dfrac{\partial p}{\partial \theta}$ $\qquad$ (6.3b) $\rho a_z = \rho\left(\dfrac{\partial V_z}{\partial t} + V_r\dfrac{\partial V_z}{\partial r} + \dfrac{V_\theta}{r}\dfrac{\partial V_z}{\partial \theta} + V_z\dfrac{\partial V_z}{\partial z}\right) = \rho g_z - \dfrac{\partial p}{\partial z}$ $\qquad$ (6.3c)	Page 217

*These topics apply to sections that may be omitted without loss of continuity in the text material.

The Bernoulli equation (steady, incompressible, inviscid, along a streamline):	$\dfrac{p}{\rho} + \dfrac{V^2}{2} + gz = \text{constant}$	(6.8)	Page 221
Definition of total head of a flow:	$\dfrac{p}{\rho g} + \dfrac{V^2}{2g} + z = H$	(6.16a)	Page 236
Definition of energy grade line (EGL):	$EGL = \dfrac{p}{\rho g} + \dfrac{V^2}{2g} + z$	(6.16b)	Page 237
Definition of hydraulic grade line (HGL):	$HGL = \dfrac{p}{\rho g} + z$	(6.16c)	Page 237
Relation between EGL, HGL, and dynamic pressure:	$EGL - HGL = \dfrac{V^2}{2g}$	(6.16d)	Page 237
The unsteady Bernoulli equation (incompressible, inviscid, along a streamline):	$\dfrac{p_1}{\rho} + \dfrac{V_1^2}{2} + gz_1 = \dfrac{p_2}{\rho} + \dfrac{V_2^2}{2} + gz_2 + \displaystyle\int_1^2 \dfrac{\partial V}{\partial t}\,ds$	(6.21)	Page W-16
Definition of stream function (2D, incompressible flow):	$u = \dfrac{\partial \psi}{\partial y} \qquad v = -\dfrac{\partial \psi}{\partial x}$	(5.4)	Page 241
Definition of velocity potential (2D irrotational flow):	$u = -\dfrac{\partial \phi}{\partial x} \qquad v = -\dfrac{\partial \phi}{\partial y}$	(6.29)	Page 241
Definition of stream function (2D, incompressible flow, cylindrical coordinates):	$V_r = \dfrac{1}{r}\dfrac{\partial \psi}{\partial \theta} \quad \text{and} \quad V_\theta = -\dfrac{\partial \psi}{\partial r}$	(5.8)	Page 242
Definition of velocity potential (2D irrotational flow, cylindrical coordinates):	$V_r = -\dfrac{\partial \phi}{\partial r} \quad \text{and} \quad V_\theta = -\dfrac{1}{r}\dfrac{\partial \phi}{\partial \theta}$	(6.33)	Page 242

REFERENCES

1. Shaw, R., "The Influence of Hole Dimensions on Static Pressure Measurements," *J. Fluid Mech., 7*, Part 4, April 1960, pp. 550–564.

2. Chue, S. H., "Pressure Probes for Fluid Measurement," *Progress in Aerospace Science, 16*, 2, 1975, pp. 147–223.

3. United Sensor Corporation, 3 Northern Blvd., Amherst, NH 03031.

4. Robertson, J. M., *Hydrodynamics in Theory and Application.* Englewood Cliffs, NJ: Prentice-Hall, 1965.

5. Streeter, V. L., *Fluid Dynamics.* New York: McGraw-Hill, 1948.

6. Vallentine, H. R., *Applied Hydrodynamics.* London: Butterworths, 1959.

7. Lamb, H., *Hydrodynamics.* New York: Dover, 1945.

8. Milne-Thomson, L. M., *Theoretical Hydrodynamics*, 4th ed. New York: Macmillan, 1960.

9. Karamcheti, K., *Principles of Ideal-Fluid Aerodynamics.* New York: Wiley, 1966.

10. Kirchhoff, R. H., *Potential Flows: Computer Graphic Solutions.* New York: Marcel Dekker, 1985.

11. Rouse, H., and S. Ince, *History of Hydraulics.* New York: Dover, 1957.

12. Kuethe, A. M., and C.-Y. Chow, *Foundations of Aerodynamics: Bases of Aerodynamic Design*, 4th ed. New York: Wiley, 1986.

13. *Fluent.* Fluent Incorporated, Centerra Resources Park, 10 Cavendish Court, Lebanon, NH 03766 (www.fluent.com).

14. *STAR-CD.* Adapco, 60 Broadhollow Road, Melville, NY 11747 (www.cd-adapco.com).

PROBLEMS

6.1 Consider the flow field with velocity given by $\vec{V} = [A(y^2 - x^2) - Bx]\hat{i} + [2Axy + By]\hat{j}$; $A = 1$ ft$^{-1}\cdot$s^{-1}, $B = 1$ ft$^{-1}\cdot$s^{-1}; the coordinates are measured in feet. The density is 2 slug/ft^3, and gravity acts in the negative y direction. Calculate the acceleration of a fluid particle and the pressure gradient at point $(x, y) = (1, 1)$.

6.2 An incompressible frictionless flow field is given by $\vec{V} = (Ax - By)\hat{i} - Ay\hat{j}$, where $A = 1$ s^{-1}, $B = 3$ s^{-1}, and the coordinates are measured in meters. Find the magnitude and direction of the acceleration of a fluid particle at point $(x, y) = (0.7, 2)$. Find the pressure gradient at the same point, if $\vec{g} = -g\hat{j}$ and the fluid is water.

6.3 A horizontal flow of water is described by the velocity field $\vec{V} = (Ax + Bt)\hat{i} + (-Ay + Bt)\hat{j}$, where $A = 5$ s^{-1}, $B = 10$ ft$\cdot$s^{-2}, x and y are in feet, and t is in seconds. Find expressions for the local acceleration, the convective acceleration, and the total acceleration. Evaluate these at point $(2, 2)$ at $t = 5$ seconds. Evaluate ∇p at the same point and time.

6.4 A velocity field in a fluid with density of 1500 kg/m^3 is given by $\vec{V} = (Ax - By)t\,\hat{i} - (Ay + Bx)t\,\hat{j}$, where $A = 1$ s^{-2}, $B = 2$ s^{-2}, x and y are in meters, and t is in seconds. Body forces are negligible. Evaluate ∇p at point $(x, y) = (1, 2)$ at $t = 1$ s.

6.5 Consider the flow field with velocity given by $\vec{V} = [A(x^2 - y^2) - 3Bx]\hat{i} - [2Axy - 3By]\hat{j}$, where $A = 1$ ft$^{-1}\cdot$s^{-1}, $B = 1$ s^{-1}, and the coordinates are measured in feet. The density is 2 slug/ft^3 and gravity acts in the negative y direction. Determine the acceleration of a fluid particle and the pressure gradient at point $(x, y) = (1, 1)$.

6.6 Consider the flow field with velocity given by $\vec{V} = Ax\sin(2\pi\omega t)\hat{i} - Ay\sin(2\pi\omega t)\hat{j}$, where $A = 2$ s^{-1} and $\omega = 1$ s^{-1}. The fluid density is 2 kg/m^3. Find expressions for the local acceleration, the convective acceleration, and the total acceleration.

Evaluate these at point $(1, 1)$ at $t = 0$, 0.5 and 1 seconds. Evaluate ∇p at the same point and times.

6.7 The x component of velocity in an incompressible flow field is given by $u = Ax$, where $A = 2$ s^{-1} and the coordinates are measured in meters. The pressure at point $(x, y) = (0, 0)$ is $p_0 = 190$ kPa (gage). The density is $\rho = 1.50$ kg/m^3 and the z axis is vertical. Evaluate the simplest possible y component of velocity. Calculate the fluid acceleration and determine the pressure gradient at point $(x, y) = (2, 1)$. Find the pressure distribution along the positive x axis.

6.8 The velocity field for a plane source located distance $h = 1$ m above an infinite wall aligned along the x axis is given by

$$\vec{V} = \frac{q}{2\pi[x^2 + (y - h)^2]}\left[x\hat{i} + (y - h)\hat{j}\right]$$
$$+ \frac{q}{2\pi[x^2 + (y + h)^2]}\left[x\hat{i} + (y + h)\hat{j}\right]$$

where $q = 2$ m^3/s/m. The fluid density is 1000 kg/m^3 and body forces are negligible. Derive expressions for the velocity and acceleration of a fluid particle that moves along the wall, and plot from $x = 0$ to $x = +10h$. Verify that the velocity and acceleration normal to the wall are zero. Plot the pressure gradient $\partial p/\partial x$ along the wall. Is the pressure gradient along the wall adverse (does it oppose fluid motion) or not?

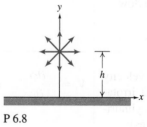

P 6.8

6.9 The velocity distribution in a two-dimensional steady flow field in the xy plane is $\vec{V} = (Ax - B)\hat{i} + (C - Ay)\hat{j}$, where $A = 2$ s^{-1}, $B = 5$ m·s^{-1}, and $C = 3$ m·s^{-1}; the coordinates are measured in meters, and the body force distribution is $\vec{g} = -g\hat{k}$. Does the velocity field represent the flow of an incompressible fluid? Find the stagnation point of the flow field. Obtain an expression for the pressure gradient in the flow field. Evaluate the difference in pressure between point $(x, y) = (1, 3)$ and the origin, if the density is 1.2 kg/m^3.

6.10 In a frictionless, incompressible flow, the velocity field in m/s and the body force are given by $\vec{V} = Ax\hat{i} - Ay\hat{j}$ and $\vec{g} = -g\hat{k}$; the coordinates are measured in meters. The pressure is p_0 at point $(x, y, z) = (0, 0, 0)$. Obtain an expression for the pressure field, $p(x, y, z)$.

6.11 An incompressible liquid with density of 900 kg/m^3 and negligible viscosity flows steadily through a horizontal pipe of constant diameter. In a porous section of length $L = 0.3$ m, liquid is removed at a constant rate per unit length so that the uniform axial velocity in the pipe is $u(x) = U(1 - x/2L)$, where $U = 5$ m/s. Develop expressions for the acceleration of a fluid particle along the centerline of the porous section and for the pressure gradient along the centerline. Evaluate the outlet pressure if the pressure at the inlet to the porous section is 35 kPa (gage).

6.12 For the flow of Problem 4.118 show that the uniform radial velocity is $V_r = Q/2\pi rh$. Obtain expressions for the r component of acceleration of a fluid particle in the gap and for the pressure variation as a function of radial distance from the central holes.

6.13 The velocity field for a plane vortex sink is given by $\vec{V} = (-q/2\pi r)\hat{e}_r + (K/2\pi r)\hat{e}_\theta$, where $q = 2$ m^3/s/m and $K = 1$ m^3/s/m. The fluid density is 1000 kg/m^3. Find the acceleration at $(1, 0)$, $(1, \pi/2)$, and $(2, 0)$. Evaluate ∇p under the same conditions.

6.14 An incompressible, inviscid fluid flows into a horizontal round tube through its porous wall. The tube is closed at the left end and the flow discharges from the tube to the atmosphere at the right end. For simplicity, consider the x component of velocity in the tube uniform across any cross-section. The density of the fluid is ρ, the tube diameter and length are D and L respectively, and the uniform inflow velocity is v_0. The flow is steady. Obtain an algebraic expression for the x component of acceleration of a fluid particle located at position x, in terms of v_0, x, and D. Find an expression for the pressure gradient, $\partial p/\partial x$, at position x. Integrate to obtain an expression for the gage pressure at $x = 0$.

6.15 An incompressible liquid with negligible viscosity and density $\rho = 850$ kg/m^3 flows steadily through a horizontal pipe. The pipe cross-section area linearly varies from 100 cm^2 to 25 cm^2 over a length of 2 m. Develop an expression for and plot the pressure gradient and pressure versus position along the pipe, if the inlet centerline velocity is 1 m/s and inlet pressure is 250 kPa.

6.16 An incompressible liquid with negligible viscosity and density $\rho = 750$ kg/m^3 flows steadily through a 10-m-long convergent-divergent section of pipe for which the area varies as

$$A(x) = A_0(1 + e^{-x/a} - e^{-x/2a})$$

where $A_0 = 0.1$ m^2 and $a = 1$ m. Develop an expression for and plot the pressure gradient and pressure versus position along the pipe, if the inlet centerline velocity is 1 m/s and inlet pressure is 200 kPa.

6.17 A nozzle for an incompressible, inviscid fluid of density $\rho = 1000$ kg/m^3 consists of a converging section of pipe. At the inlet the diameter is $D_i = 100$ mm, and at the outlet the diameter is $D_o = 20$ mm. The nozzle length is $L = 500$ mm, and the diameter decreases linearly with distance x along the nozzle. Derive and plot the acceleration of a fluid particle, assuming uniform flow at each section, if the speed at the inlet is $V_i = 1$ m/s. Plot the pressure gradient through the nozzle, and find its maximum absolute value. If the pressure gradient must be no greater than 5 MPa/m in absolute value, how long would the nozzle have to be?

6.18 A diffuser for an incompressible, inviscid fluid of density $\rho = 1000$ kg/m^3 consists of a diverging section of pipe. At the inlet the diameter is $D_i = 0.25$ m, and at the outlet the diameter is $D_o = 0.75$ m. The diffuser length is $L = 1$ m, and the diameter increases linearly with distance x along the diffuser. Derive and plot the acceleration of a fluid particle, assuming uniform flow at each section, if the speed at the inlet is $V_i = 5$ m/s. Plot the pressure gradient through the diffuser, and find its maximum value. If the pressure gradient must be no greater than 25 kPa/m, how long would the diffuser have to be?

6.19 Consider the flow of Problem 5.46. Evaluate the magnitude and direction of the net pressure force that acts on the upper plate between r_i and R, if $r_i = R/2$.

6.20 Consider again the flow field of Problem 5.59. Assume the flow is incompressible with $\rho = 1.23$ kg/m^3 and friction is negligible. Further assume the vertical air flow velocity is $v_0 = 15$ mm/s, the half-width of the cavity is $L = 22$ mm, and its height is $h = 1.2$ mm. Calculate the pressure gradient at $(x, y) = (L, h)$. Obtain an equation for the flow streamlines in the cavity.

6.21 A liquid layer separates two plane surfaces as shown. The lower surface is stationary; the upper surface moves downward at constant speed V. The moving surface has width w, perpendicular to the plane of the diagram, and $w \gg L$. The incompressible liquid layer, of density ρ, is squeezed from between the surfaces. Assume the flow is uniform at any cross-section and neglect viscosity as a first approximation. Use a suitably chosen control volume to show that $u = Vx/b$ within the gap, where $b = b_0 - Vt$. Obtain an algebraic expression for the acceleration of a fluid particle located at x. Determine the pressure gradient, $\partial p/\partial x$, in the liquid layer. Find the pressure distribution, $p(x)$. Obtain an expression for the net pressure force that acts on the upper (moving) flat surface.

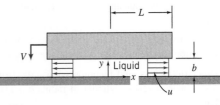

P6.21

6.22 A rectangular microcircuit "chip" floats on a thin layer of air, $h = 0.5$ mm thick, above a porous surface. The chip width is $b = 20$ mm, as shown. Its length, L, is very long in the direction perpendicular to the diagram. There is no flow in the z direction. Assume flow in the x direction in the gap under the chip is uniform. Flow is incompressible and frictional effects may be neglected. Use a suitably chosen control volume to show that $U(x) = qx/h$ in the gap. Find a general expression for the acceleration of a fluid particle in the gap. Evaluate the maximum acceleration. Obtain an expression for the pressure gradient $\partial p/\partial x$ and sketch the pressure distribution under the chip. Show p_{atm} on your sketch. Is the net pressure force on the chip directed upward or downward? Explain. For the conditions shown, with $q = 0.06$ m³/s/m, estimate the mass per unit length of the chip.

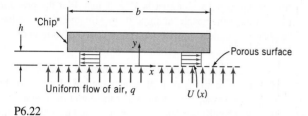

P6.22

6.23 Heavy weights can be moved with relative ease on air cushions by using a load pallet as shown. Air is supplied from the plenum through porous surface AB. It enters the gap vertically at uniform speed, q. Once in the gap, all air flows in the positive x direction (there is no flow across the plane at $x = 0$). Assume air flow in the gap is incompressible and uniform at each cross section, with speed $u(x)$, as shown in the enlarged view. Although the gap is narrow ($h \ll L$), neglect frictional effects as a first approximation. Use a suitably chosen control volume to show that $u(x) = qx/h$ in the gap. Calculate the acceleration of a fluid particle in the gap. Evaluate the pressure gradient, $\partial p/\partial x$, and sketch the pressure distribution within the gap. Be sure to indicate the pressure at $x = L$.

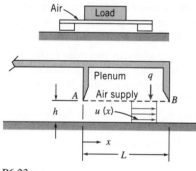

P6.23

6.24 Air at 20 psia and 100°F flows around a smooth corner at the inlet to a diffuser. The air speed is 150 ft/s, and the radius of curvature of the streamlines is 3 in. Determine the magnitude of the centripetal acceleration experienced by a fluid particle rounding the corner. Express your answer in gs. Evaluate the pressure gradient, $\partial p/\partial r$.

6.25 The velocity field for a plane doublet is given in Table 6.2. Find an expression for the pressure gradient at any point (r, θ).

6.26 Steady, frictionless, and incompressible flow from right to left over a stationary circular cylinder of radius a is given by the velocity field

$$\vec{V} = U\left[\left(\frac{a}{r}\right)^2 - 1\right]\cos\theta\,\hat{e}_r + U\left[\left(\frac{a}{r}\right)^2 + 1\right]\sin\theta\,\hat{e}_\theta$$

Consider flow along the streamline forming the cylinder surface, $r = a$. Express the components of the pressure gradient in terms of angle θ. Plot speed V as a function of r along the radial line $\theta = \pi/2$ for $r > a$.

6.27 To model the velocity distribution in the curved inlet section of a wind tunnel, the radius of curvature of the streamlines is expressed as $R = LR_0/2y$. As a first approximation, assume the air speed along each streamline is $V = 20$ m/s. Evaluate the pressure change from $y = 0$ to the tunnel wall at $y = L/2$, if $L = 150$ mm and $R_0 = 0.6$ m.

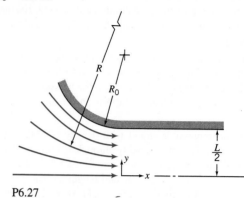

P6.27

6.28 Repeat Example 6.1, but with the somewhat more realistic assumption that the flow is similar to a free vortex (irrotational) profile, $V_\theta = c/r$ (where c is a constant), as shown in Fig. P6.28. In doing so, prove that the flow rate is given by $Q = k\sqrt{\Delta p}$, where k is

$$k = w\ln\left(\frac{r_2}{r_1}\right)\sqrt{\frac{2r_2^2 r_1^2}{\rho(r_2^2 - r_1^2)}}$$

and w is the depth of the bend.

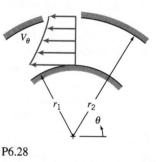

P6.28

6.29 Using the analyses of Example 6.1 and Problem 6.28, plot the discrepancy (percent) between the flow rates obtained from assuming uniform flow and the free vortex (irrotational) profile as a function of inner radius r_1.

6.30 The velocity field in a two-dimensional, steady, inviscid flow field in the horizontal xy plane is given by $\vec{V} = (Ax + B)\hat{i} - Ay\hat{j}$, where $A = 1$ s⁻¹ and $B = 2$ m/s; x and y are measured in meters. Show that streamlines for this flow are given by $(x + B/A)y = $ constant. Plot streamlines passing through points $(x, y) = (1, 1)$, $(1, 2)$, and $(2, 2)$. At point $(x, y) = (1, 2)$, evaluate and plot the acceleration vector and the velocity vector. Find the component of acceleration along the streamline at the same point; express it as a vector. Evaluate the pressure gradient along the streamline at the same point if the fluid is air. What statement, if any, can you make about the relative value of the pressure at points $(1, 1)$ and $(2, 2)$?

6.31 A velocity field is given by $\vec{V} = [Ax^3 + Bxy^2]\hat{i} + [Ay^3 + Bx^2y]\hat{j}$; $A = 0.2$ m⁻²·s⁻¹, B is a constant, and the coordinates are measured in meters. Determine the value and units for B if this velocity field is to represent an incompressible flow.

Calculate the acceleration of a fluid particle at point $(x, y) = (2, 1)$. Evaluate the component of particle acceleration normal to the velocity vector at this point.

6.32 The x component of velocity in a two-dimensional, incompressible flow field is given by $u = Ax^2$; the coordinates are measured in feet and $A = 1$ ft$^{-1} \cdot$s^{-1}. There is no velocity component or variation in the z direction. Calculate the acceleration of a fluid particle at point $(x, y) = (1, 2)$. Estimate the radius of curvature of the streamline passing through this point. Plot the streamline and show both the velocity vector and the acceleration vector on the plot. (Assume the simplest form of the y component of velocity.)

6.33 The x component of velocity in a two-dimensional, incompressible flow field is given by $u = Axy$; the coordinates are measured in meters and $A = 2$ m$^{-1} \cdot$s^{-1}. There is no velocity component or variation in the z direction. Calculate the acceleration of a fluid particle at point $(x, y) = (2, 1)$. Estimate the radius of curvature of the streamline passing through this point. Plot the streamline and show both the velocity vector and the acceleration vector on the plot. (Assume the simplest form of the y component of velocity.)

6.34 The x component of velocity in a two-dimensional incompressible flow field is given by $u = -\Lambda(x^2 - y^2)/(x^2 + y^2)^2$, where u is in m/s, the coordinates are measured in meters, and $\Lambda = 2$ m$^3 \cdot$s^{-1}. Show that the simplest form of the y component of velocity is given by $v = -2\Lambda xy/(x^2 + y^2)^2$. There is no velocity component or variation in the z direction. Calculate the acceleration of fluid particles at points $(x, y) = (0, 1)$, $(0, 2)$, and $(0, 3)$. Estimate the radius of curvature of the streamlines passing through these points. What does the relation among the three points and their radii of curvature suggest to you about the flow field? Verify this by plotting these streamlines. [Hint: You will need to use an integrating factor.]

6.35 The y component of velocity in a two-dimensional incompressible flow field is given by $v = -Axy$, where v is in m/s, the coordinates are measured in meters, and $A = 1$ m$^{-1} \cdot$s^{-1}. There is no velocity component or variation in the z direction. Calculate the acceleration of a fluid particle at point $(x, y) = (1, 2)$. Estimate the radius of curvature of the streamline passing through this point. Plot the streamline and show both the velocity vector and the acceleration vector on the plot. (Assume the simplest form of the x component of velocity.)

6.36 Consider the velocity field $\vec{V} = A[x^4 - 6x^2y^2 + y^4]\hat{i} + B[x^3y - xy^3]\hat{j}$; $A = 2$ m$^{-3} \cdot$s^{-1}, B is a constant, and the coordinates are measured in meters. Find B for this to be an incompressible flow. Obtain the equation of the streamline through point $(x, y) = (1, 2)$. Derive an algebraic expression for the acceleration of a fluid particle. Estimate the radius of curvature of the streamline at $(x, y) = (1, 2)$.

6.37 Water flows at a speed of 10 ft/s. Calculate the dynamic pressure of this flow. Express your answer in in. of mercury.

6.38 Calculate the dynamic pressure that corresponds to a speed of 100 km/hr in standard air. Express your answer in millimeters of water.

6.39 You present your open hand out of the window of an automobile perpendicular to the airflow. Assuming for simplicity that the air pressure on the entire front surface is stagnation pressure

(with respect to automobile coordinates), with atmospheric pressure on the rear surface, estimate the net force on your hand when driving at (a) 30 mph and (b) 60 mph. Do these results roughly correspond with your experience? Do the simplifications tend to make the calculated force an over- or underestimate?

6.40 A jet of air from a nozzle is blown at right angles against a wall in which two pressure taps are located. A manometer connected to the tap directly in front of the jet shows a head of 0.15 in. of mercury above atmospheric. Determine the approximate speed of the air leaving the nozzle if it is at 50°F and 14.7 psia. At the second tap a manometer indicates a head of 0.10 in. of mercury above atmospheric; what is the approximate speed of the air there?

6.41 A pitot-static tube is used to measure the speed of air at standard conditions at a point in a flow. To ensure that the flow may be assumed incompressible for calculations of engineering accuracy, the speed is to be maintained at 100 m/s or less. Determine the manometer deflection, in millimeters of water, that corresponds to the maximum desirable speed.

6.42 The inlet contraction and test section of a laboratory wind tunnel are shown. The air speed in the test section is $U = 22.5$ m/s. A total-head tube pointed upstream indicates that the stagnation pressure on the test section centerline is 6.0 mm of water below atmospheric. The corrected barometric pressure and temperature in the laboratory are 99.1 kPa (abs) and 23°C. Evaluate the dynamic pressure on the centerline of the wind tunnel test section. Compute the static pressure at the same point. Qualitatively compare the static pressure at the tunnel wall with that at the centerline. Explain why the two may not be identical.

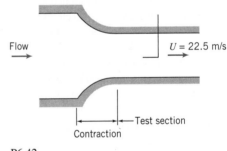

P6.42

6.43 Maintenance work on high-pressure hydraulic systems requires special precautions. A small leak can result in a high-speed jet of hydraulic fluid that can penetrate the skin and cause serious injury (therefore troubleshooters are cautioned to use a piece of paper or cardboard, *not a finger*, to search for leaks). Calculate and plot the jet speed of a leak versus system pressure, for pressures up to 40 MPa (gage). Explain how a high-speed jet of hydraulic fluid can cause injury.

6.44 An open-circuit wind tunnel draws in air from the atmosphere through a well-contoured nozzle. In the test section, where the flow is straight and nearly uniform, a static pressure tap is drilled into the tunnel wall. A manometer connected to the tap shows that static pressure within the tunnel is 45 mm of water below atmospheric. Assume that the air is incompressible, and at 25°C, 100 kPa (abs). Calculate the air speed in the wind-tunnel test section.

6.45 The wheeled cart shown in Problem 4.123 rolls with negligible resistance. The cart is to accelerate to the right. The jet speed is $V = 40$ m/s. The jet area remains constant at $A = 25$ mm^2. Neglect viscous forces between the water and vane. When the cart attains speed $U = 15$ m/s, calculate the stagnation pressure of the water leaving the nozzle with respect to a fixed observer, the stagnation pressure of the water jet leaving the nozzle with respect to an observer on the vane, the absolute velocity of the jet leaving the vane with respect to a fixed observer, and the stagnation pressure of the jet leaving the vane with respect to a fixed observer. How would viscous forces affect the latter stagnation pressure, i.e., would viscous forces increase, decrease, or leave unchanged this stagnation pressure? Justify your answer.

6.46 Water flows steadily up the vertical 0.1-m-diameter pipe and out the nozzle, which is 0.05 m in diameter, discharging to atmospheric pressure. The stream velocity at the nozzle exit must be 20 m/s. Calculate the minimum gage pressure required at section ①. If the device were inverted, what would be the required minimum pressure at section ① to maintain the nozzle exit velocity at 20 m/s?

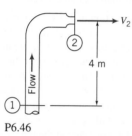

P6.46

6.47 Water flows in a circular duct. At one section the diameter is 0.3 m, the static pressure is 260 kPa (gage), the velocity is 3 m/s, and the elevation is 10 m above ground level. At a section downstream at ground level, the duct diameter is 0.15 m. Find the gage pressure at the downstream section if frictional effects may be neglected.

6.48 You are on a date. Your date runs out of gas unexpectedly. You come to your own rescue by siphoning gas from another car. The height difference for the siphon is about 6 in. The hose diameter is 1 in. What is your gasoline flow rate?

6.49 A pipe ruptures and benzene shoots 25 ft into the air. What is the pressure inside the pipe?

6.50 A can of Coke has a small pinhole leak in it. The Coke is being sprayed vertically in the air to a height of 20 in. What is the pressure inside the can of Coke?

6.51 The water flow rate through the siphon is 0.7 ft^3/s, its temperature is 70°F, and the pipe diameter is 2 in. Compute the maximum allowable height, h, so that the pressure at point A is above the vapor pressure of the water. (Assume the flow is frictionless.)

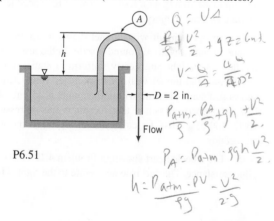

P6.51

6.52 Water flows from a very large tank through a 5-cm-diameter tube. The dark liquid in the manometer is mercury. Estimate the velocity in the pipe and the rate of discharge from the tank. (Assume the flow is frictionless.)

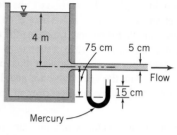

P6.52

6.53 A stream of liquid moving at low speed leaves a nozzle pointed directly downward. The velocity may be considered uniform across the nozzle exit and the effects of friction may be ignored. At the nozzle exit, located at elevation z_0, the jet velocity and area are V_0 and A_0, respectively. Determine the variation of jet area with elevation.

6.54 In a laboratory experiment, water flows radially outward at moderate speed through the space between circular plane parallel disks. The perimeter of the disks is open to the atmosphere. The disks have diameter $D = 150$ mm and the spacing between the disks is $h = 0.8$ mm. The measured mass flow rate of water is $\dot{m} = 305$ g/s. Assuming frictionless flow in the space between the disks, estimate the theoretical static pressure between the disks at radius $r = 50$ mm. In the laboratory situation, where *some* friction is present, would the pressure measured at the same location be above or below the theoretical value? Why?

6.55 Consider steady, frictionless, incompressible flow of air over the wing of an airplane. The air approaching the wing is at 75 kPa (gage), 4°C, and has a speed of 60 m/s relative to the wing. At a certain point in the flow, the pressure is 3 kPa (gage). Calculate the speed of the air relative to the wing at this point.

6.56 A mercury barometer is carried in a car on a day when there is no wind. The temperature is 20°C and the corrected barometer height is 761 mm of mercury. One window is open slightly as the car travels at 105 km/hr. The barometer reading in the moving car is 5 mm lower than when the car is stationary. Explain what is happening. Calculate the local speed of the air flowing past the window, *relative to* the automobile.

6.57 A fire nozzle is coupled to the end of a hose with inside diameter $D = 3$ in. The nozzle is contoured smoothly and has outlet diameter $d = 1$ in. The design inlet pressure for the nozzle is $p_1 = 100$ psi (gage). Evaluate the maximum flow rate the nozzle could deliver.

6.58 An Indianapolis racing car travels at 98.3 m/s along a straightaway. The team engineer wishes to locate an air inlet on the body of the car to obtain cooling air for the driver's suit. The plan is to place the inlet at a location where the air speed is 25.5 m/s along the surface of the car. Calculate the static pressure at the proposed inlet location. Express the pressure rise above ambient as a fraction of the freestream dynamic pressure.

6.59 Steady, frictionless, and incompressible flow from left to right over a stationary circular cylinder, of radius a, is represented by the velocity field

$$\vec{V} = U\left[1 - \left(\frac{a}{r}\right)^2\right]\cos\theta\,\hat{e}_r - U\left[1 + \left(\frac{a}{r}\right)^2\right]\sin\theta\,\hat{e}_\theta$$

Obtain an expression for the pressure distribution along the streamline forming the cylinder surface, $r = a$. Determine the locations where the static pressure on the cylinder is equal to the freestream static pressure.

6.60 The velocity field for a plane doublet is given in Table 6.2. If $\Lambda = 3$ m³·s⁻¹, the fluid density is $\rho = 1.5$ kg/m³, and the pressure at infinity is 100 kPa, plot the pressure along the x axis from $x = -2.0$ m to -0.5 m and $x = 0.5$ m to 2.0 m.

6.61 The velocity field for a plane source at a distance h above an infinite wall aligned along the x axis was given in Problem 6.8. Using the data from that problem, plot the pressure distribution along the wall from $x = -10h$ to $x = +10h$ (assume the pressure at infinity is atmospheric). Find the net force on the wall if the pressure on the lower surface is atmospheric. Does the force tend to pull the wall towards the source, or push it away?

6.62 A fire nozzle is coupled to the end of a hose with inside diameter $D = 75$ mm. The nozzle is smoothly contoured and its outlet diameter is $d = 25$ mm. The nozzle is designed to operate at an inlet water pressure of 700 kPa (gage). Determine the design flow rate of the nozzle. (Express your answer in L/s.) Evaluate the axial force required to hold the nozzle in place. Indicate whether the hose coupling is in tension or compression.

6.63 A smoothly contoured nozzle, with outlet diameter $d = 20$ mm, is coupled to a straight pipe by means of flanges. Water flows in the pipe, of diameter $D = 50$ mm, and the nozzle discharges to the atmosphere. For steady flow and neglecting the effects of viscosity, find the volume flow rate in the pipe corresponding to a calculated axial force of 45.5 N needed to keep the nozzle attached to the pipe.

6.64 Water flows steadily through a 3.25-in-diameter pipe and discharges through a 1.25-in-diameter nozzle to atmospheric pressure. The flow rate is 24.5 gpm. Calculate the minimum static pressure required in the pipe to produce this flow rate. Evaluate the axial force of the nozzle assembly on the pipe flange.

6.65 Water flows steadily through the reducing elbow shown. The elbow is smooth and short, and the flow accelerates, so the effect of friction is small. The volume flow rate is $Q = 20$ gpm. The elbow is in a horizontal plane. Estimate the gage pressure at section ①. Calculate the x component of the force exerted *by* the reducing elbow *on* the supply pipe.

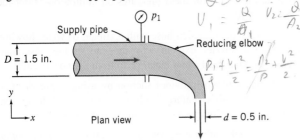

P6.65

6.66 A flow nozzle is a device for measuring the flow rate in a pipe. This particular nozzle is to be used to measure low-speed air

flow for which compressibility may be neglected. During operation, the pressures p_1 and p_2 are recorded, as well as upstream temperature, T_1. Find the mass flow rate in terms of $\Delta p = p_2 - p_1$ and T_1, the gas constant for air, and device diameters D_1 and D_2. Assume the flow is frictionless. Will the actual flow be more or less than this predicted flow? Why?

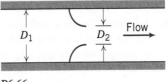

P6.66

6.67 The branching of a blood vessel is shown. Blood at a pressure of 100 mm Hg flows in the main vessel at 4 L/min. Estimate the blood pressure in each branch, assuming that blood vessels behave as rigid tubes, that we have frictionless flow, and that the vessel lies in the horizontal plane. What is the force generated at the branch by the blood? You may approximate blood to have the same density as water.

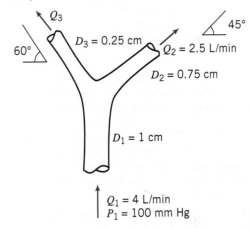

P6.67

6.68 A water jet is directed upward from a well-designed nozzle of area $A_1 = 600$ mm²; the exit jet speed is $V_1 = 6.3$ m/s. The flow is steady and the liquid stream does not break up. Point ② is located $H = 1.55$ m above the nozzle exit plane. Determine the velocity in the undisturbed jet at point ②. Calculate the pressure that would be sensed by a stagnation tube located there. Evaluate the force that would be exerted on a flat plate placed normal to the stream at point ②. Sketch the pressure distribution on the plate.

6.69 An object, with a flat horizontal lower surface, moves downward into the jet of the spray system of Problem 4.77 with speed $U = 5$ ft/s. Determine the minimum supply pressure needed to produce the jet leaving the spray system at $V = 15$ ft/s. Calculate the maximum pressure exerted by the liquid jet on the flat object at the instant when the object is $h = 1.5$ ft above the jet exit. Estimate the force of the water jet on the flat object.

6.70 Water flows out of a kitchen faucet of 1.25 cm diameter at the rate of 0.1 L/s. The bottom of the sink is 45 cm below the faucet outlet. Will the cross-sectional area of the fluid stream increase, decrease, or remain constant between the faucet outlet and the bottom of the sink? Explain briefly. Obtain an expression for the stream cross section as a function of distance y above the sink bottom. If a plate is held directly under the faucet, how will the force required to hold the plate in a horizontal position vary with height above the sink? Explain briefly.

6.71 An old magic trick uses an empty thread spool and a playing card. The playing card is placed against the bottom of the spool. Contrary to intuition, when one blows downward through the central hole in the spool, the card is not blown away. Instead it is "sucked" up against the spool. Explain.

6.72 The tank, of diameter D, has a well-rounded nozzle with diameter d. At $t = 0$, the water level is at height h_0. Develop an expression for dimensionless water height, h/h_0, at any later time. For $D/d = 10$, plot h/h_0 as a function of time with h_0 as a parameter for $0.1 \le h_0 \le 1$ m. For $h_0 = 1$ m, plot h/h_0 as a function of time with D/d as a parameter for $2 \le D/d \le 10$.

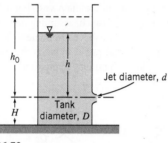

P6.72

6.73 A horizontal axisymmetric jet of air with 0.4 in. diameter strikes a stationary vertical disk of 7.5 in. diameter. The jet speed is 225 ft/s at the nozzle exit. A manometer is connected to the center of the disk. Calculate (a) the deflection, if the manometer liquid has SG = 1.75, (b) the force exerted by the jet on the disk, and (c) the force exerted on the disk if it is assumed that the stagnation pressure acts on the entire forward surface of the disk. Sketch the streamline pattern and plot the distribution of pressure on the face of the disk.

6.74 The water level in a large tank is maintained at height H above the surrounding level terrain. A rounded nozzle placed in the side of the tank discharges a horizontal jet. Neglecting friction, determine the height h at which the orifice should be placed so the water strikes the ground at the maximum horizontal distance X from the tank. Plot jet speed V and distance X as functions of h $(0 < h < H)$.

6.75 The flow over a Quonset hut may be approximated by the velocity distribution of Problem 6.59 with $0 \le \theta \le \pi$. During a storm the wind speed reaches 100 km/hr; the outside temperature is 5°C. A barometer inside the hut reads 720 mm of mercury; pressure p_∞ is also 720 mm Hg. The hut has a diameter of 6 m and a length of 18 m. Determine the net force tending to lift the hut off its foundation.

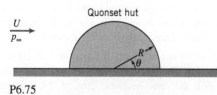

P6.75

6.76 Many recreation facilities use inflatable "bubble" structures. A tennis bubble to enclose four courts is shaped roughly as a circular semicylinder with a diameter of 30 m and a length of 70 m. The blowers used to inflate the structure can maintain the

air pressure inside the bubble at 10 mm of water above ambient pressure. The bubble is subjected to a wind that blows at 60 km/hr in a direction perpendicular to the axis of the semicylindrical shape. Using polar coordinates, with angle θ measured from the ground on the upwind side of the structure, the resulting pressure distribution may be expressed as

$$\frac{p - p_\infty}{\frac{1}{2}\rho V_w^2} = 1 - 4\sin^2\theta$$

where p is the pressure at the surface, p_∞ the atmospheric pressure, and V_w the wind speed. Determine the net vertical force exerted on the structure.

6.77 Water flows at low speed through a circular tube with inside diameter of 2 in. A smoothly contoured body of 1.5 in. diameter is held in the end of the tube where the water discharges to atmosphere. Neglect frictional effects and assume uniform velocity profiles at each section. Determine the pressure measured by the gage and the force required to hold the body.

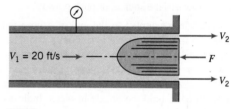

P6.77

6.78 High-pressure air forces a stream of water from a tiny, rounded or... ...e is high enough that gravity ... owly, so that the expansion ... ial volume of air in the tank ... f air is $\Psi(t)$; the total volun ... c expression for the mass f ... ind an algebraic expression ... water inside the tank. Deve ... nd solve for the water mas ... m³, $\Psi_t = 10$ m³, $A = 25$ mr ... s in the tank versus time fc ...

$$\frac{p_1}{\rho} + \frac{V_1^2}{2} = \frac{p_2}{\rho} + \frac{V_2^2}{2}$$

$$p_1 = \frac{\rho}{2}(V_2^2 - V_1^2)$$

$$V_2 = V_1\left(\frac{D^2}{D^2 - d^2}\right)$$

$$F = p_1 A_1 + \rho(V_1^2 A_1 - V_2^2 A_2)$$

6.79 Rep ... pands so rapidly that the expansion may be treated as adiabatic.

6.80 Describe the pressure distribution on the exterior of a multistory building in a steady wind. Identify the locations of the maximum and minimum pressures on the outside of the building. Discuss the effect of these pressures on infiltration of outside air into the building.

6.81 Imagine a garden hose with a stream of water flowing out through a nozzle. Explain why the end of the hose may be unstable when held a half meter or so from the nozzle end.

6.82 An aspirator provides suction by using a stream of water flowing through a venturi. Analyze the shape and dimensions of such a device. Comment on any limitations on its use.

6.83 A tank with a *reentrant* orifice called a *Borda mouthpiece* is shown. The fluid is inviscid and incompressible. The reentrant orifice essentially eliminates flow along the tank walls, so the pressure there is nearly hydrostatic. Calculate the *contraction coefficient, $C_c = A_j/A_0$. Hint:* Equate the unbalanced hydrostatic pressure force and momentum flux from the jet.

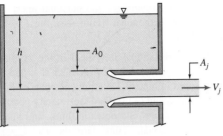

P6.83

6.84 Carefully sketch the energy grade lines (EGL) and hydraulic grade lines (HGL) for the system shown in Fig. 6.6 if the pipe is horizontal (i.e., the outlet is at the base of the reservoir), and a water turbine (extracting energy) is located at point ②, or at point ③. In Chapter 8 we will investigate the effects of friction on internal flows. Can you anticipate and sketch the effect of friction on the EGL and HGL for the two cases?

6.85 Carefully sketch the energy grade lines (EGL) and hydraulic grade lines (HGL) for the system shown in Fig. 6.6 if a pump (adding energy to the fluid) is located at point ②, or at point ③, such that flow is *into* the reservoir. In Chapter 8 we will investigate the effects of friction on internal flows. Can you anticipate and sketch the effect of friction on the EGL and HGL for the two cases?

*6.86 Compressed air is used to accelerate water from a tube. Neglect the velocity in the reservoir and assume the flow in the tube is uniform at any section. At a particular instant, it is known that $V = 6$ ft/s and $dV/dt = 7.5$ ft/s². The cross-sectional area of the tube is $A = 32$ in². Determine the pressure in the tank at this instant.

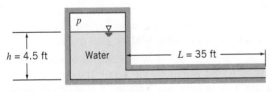

P6.86, 6.87, 6.90

*6.87 If the water in the pipe in Problem 6.86 is initially at rest and the air pressure is 3 psig, what will be the initial acceleration of the water in the pipe?

*6.88 Apply the unsteady Bernoulli equation to the U-tube manometer of constant diameter shown. Assume that the manometer is initially deflected and then released. Obtain a differential equation for *l* as a function of time.

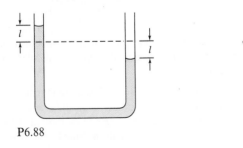

P6.88

*6.89 Consider the reservoir and disk flow system with the reservoir level maintained constant. Flow between the disks is started from rest at $t = 0$. Evaluate the rate of change of volume flow rate at $t = 0$, if $r_1 = 50$ mm.

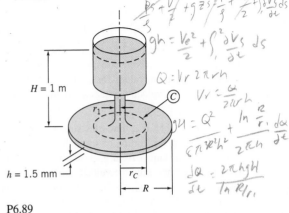

P6.89

*6.90 If the water in the pipe of Problem 6.86 is initially at rest, and the air pressure is maintained at 1.5 psig, derive a differential equation for the velocity V in the pipe as a function of time, integrate, and plot V versus t for $t = 0$ to 5 s.

*6.91 Consider the tank of Problem 4.44. Using the Bernoulli equation for unsteady flow along a streamline, evaluate the minimum diameter ratio, D/d, required to justify the assumption that flow from the tank is quasi-steady.

*6.92 Two circular disks, of radius R, are separated by distance b. The upper disk moves toward the lower one at constant speed V. The space between the disks is filled with a frictionless, incompressible fluid, which is squeezed out as the disks come together. Assume that, at any radial section, the velocity is uniform across the gap width b. However, note that b is a function of time. The pressure surrounding the disks is atmospheric. Determine the gage pressure at $r = 0$.

*6.93 Determine whether the Bernoulli equation can be applied between different radii for the vortex flow fields (a) $\vec{V} = \omega r \, \hat{e}_\theta$ and (b) $\vec{V} = \hat{e}_\theta \, K/2\pi r$.

*6.94 Consider the flow represented by the stream function $\psi = A x^2 y$, where A is a dimensional constant equal to 2.5 $m^{-1} \cdot s^{-1}$. The density is 1200 kg/m³. Is the flow rotational? Can the pressure difference between points $(x, y) = (1, 4)$ and $(2, 1)$ be evaluated? If so, calculate it, and if not, explain why.

*6.95 The velocity field for a two-dimensional flow is $\vec{V} = (Ax - By)t\hat{i} - (Bx + Ay)t\hat{j}$, where $A = 1 \ s^{-2}$ $B = 2 \ s^{-2}$, t is in seconds, and the coordinates are measured in meters. Is this a possible incompressible flow? Is the flow steady or unsteady? Show that the flow is irrotational and derive an expression for the velocity potential.

*6.96 Using Table 6.2, find the stream function and velocity potential for a plane source, of strength q, near a 90° corner. The source is equidistant h from each of the two infinite planes that make up the corner. Find the velocity distribution along one of the planes, assuming $p = p_0$ at infinity. By choosing suitable values for q and h, plot the streamlines and lines of constant velocity potential. (Hint: Use the *Excel* workbook of Example 6.10.)

---

*These problems require material from sections that may be omitted without loss of continuity in the text material.

*6.97 The flow field for a plane source at a distance h above an infinite wall aligned along the x axis is given by

$$\vec{V} = \frac{q}{2\pi[x^2 + (y-h)^2]}[x\hat{i} + (y-h)\hat{j}]$$
$$+ \frac{q}{2\pi[x^2 + (y+h)^2]}[x\hat{i} + (y+h)\hat{j}]$$

where q is the strength of the source. The flow is irrotational and incompressible. Derive the stream function and velocity potential. By choosing suitable values for q and h, plot the streamlines and lines of constant velocity potential. (Hint: Use the *Excel* workbook of Example 6.10.)

*6.98 Using Table 6.2, find the stream function and velocity potential for a plane vortex, of strength K, near a 90° corner. The vortex is equidistant h from each of the two infinite planes that make up the corner. Find the velocity distribution along one of the planes, assuming $p = p_0$ at infinity. By choosing suitable values for K and h, plot the streamlines and lines of constant velocity potential. (Hint: Use the *Excel* workbook of Example Problem 6.10.)

*6.99 The stream function of a flow field is $\psi = x^3 - 10x^3y^2 + 5xy^4$, where $A = 1$ m$^{-1} \cdot$s^{-1}, $B = \frac{1}{3}$ m$^{-1} \cdot$s^{-1}, and the coordinates are measured in meters. Find an expression for the velocity potential.

*6.100 A flow field is represented by the stream function $\psi = x^5 - 10x^3y^2 + 5xy^4$. Find the corresponding velocity field. Show that this flow field is irrotational and obtain the potential function.

*6.101 Consider the flow field represented by the potential function $\phi = Ax^2 + Bxy - Ay^2$. Verify that this is an incompressible flow and determine the corresponding stream function.

*6.102 Consider the flow field presented by the potential function $\phi = x^6 - 15x^4y^2 + 15x^2y^4 - y^6$. Verify that this is an incompressible flow and obtain the corresponding stream function.

*6.103 Show that $f(z) = z^6$ (where z is the complex number $z = x + iy$) leads to a valid velocity potential (the real part of f) and a corresponding stream function (the imaginary part of f) of an irrotational and incompressible flow. Then show that the real and imaginary parts of df/dz yield u and $-v$, respectively.

*6.104 Show that *any* differentiable function $f(z)$ of the complex number $z = x + iy$ leads to a valid potential (the real part of f) and a corresponding stream function (the imaginary part of f) of an incompressible, irrotational flow. To do so, prove using the chain rule that $f(z)$ automatically satisfies the Laplace equation. Then show that $df/dz = u - iv$.

*6.105 Consider the flow field represented by the velocity potential $\phi = Ax + Bx^2 - By^2$, where $A = 1$ m$\cdot$s^{-1}, $B = 1$ m$^{-1}\cdot$s^{-1}, and the coordinates are measured in meters. Obtain expressions for the velocity field and the stream function. Calculate the pressure difference between the origin and point $(x, y) = (1, 2)$.

*6.106 An incompressible flow field is characterized by the stream function $\psi = 3Ax^2y - Ay^3$, where $A = 1$ m$^{-1}\cdot$s^{-1}. Show that this flow field is irrotational. Derive the velocity potential for the flow. Plot the streamlines and potential lines, and visually verify that they are orthogonal. (Hint: Use the *Excel* workbook of Example 6.10.)

*6.107 A flow field is represented by the potential function $\phi = Ay^3 - Bx^2y$, where $A = 1/3$ m$^{-1}\cdot$s^{-1}, $B = 1$ m$^{-1}\cdot$s^{-1}, and

the coordinates are measured in meters. Obtain an expression for the magnitude of the velocity vector. Find the stream function for the flow. Plot the streamlines and potential lines, and visually verify that they are orthogonal. (Hint: Use the *Excel* workbook of Example 6.10.)

*6.108 A certain irrotational flow field in the xy plane has the stream function $\psi = Bxy$, where $B = 0.25$ s^{-1}, and the coordinates are measured in meters. Determine the rate of flow between points $(x, y) = (2, 2)$ and $(3, 3)$. Find the velocity potential for this flow. Plot the streamlines and potential lines, and visually verify that they are orthogonal. (Hint: Use the *Excel* workbook of Example 6.10.)

*6.109 The velocity distribution in a two-dimensional, steady, inviscid flow field in the xy plane is $\vec{V} = (Ax + B)\hat{i} + (C - Ay)\hat{j}$, where $A = 3$ s^{-1}, $B = 6$ m/s, $C = 4$ m/s, and the coordinates are measured in meters. The body force distribution is $\vec{B} = -g\hat{k}$ and the density is 825 kg/m^3. Does this represent a possible incompressible flow field? Plot a few streamlines in the upper half plane. Find the stagnation point(s) of the flow field. Is the flow irrotational? If so, obtain the potential function. Evaluate the pressure difference between the origin and point $(x, y, z) = (2, 2, 2)$.

*6.110 Consider the flow past a circular cylinder, of radius a, used in Example 6.11. Show that $V_r = 0$ along the lines $(r, \theta) = (r, \pm\pi/2)$. Plot V_θ/U versus radius for $r \geq a$, along the line $(r, \theta) = (r, \pi/2)$. Find the distance beyond which the influence of the cylinder is less than 1 percent of U.

*6.111 Consider flow around a circular cylinder with freestream velocity from right to left and a counterclockwise free vortex. Show that the lift force on the cylinder can be expressed as $F_L = -\rho U\Gamma$, as illustrated in Example 6.12.

*6.112 A crude model of a tornado is formed by combining a sink, of strength $q = 2800$ m^2/s, and a free vortex, of strength $K = 5600$ m^2/s. Obtain the stream function and velocity potential for this flow field. Estimate the radius beyond which the flow may be treated as incompressible. Find the gage pressure at that radius.

*6.113 A source and a sink with strengths of equal magnitude, $q = 3\pi$ m^2/s, are placed on the x axis at $x = -a$ and $x = a$, respectively. A uniform flow, with speed $U = 20$ m/s, in the positive x direction, is added to obtain the flow past a Rankine body. Obtain the stream function, velocity potential, and velocity field for the combined flow. Find the value of ψ = constant on the stagnation streamline. Locate the stagnation points if $a = 0.3$ m.

*6.114 Consider again the flow past a Rankine body of Problem 6.113. The half-width, h, of the body in the y direction is given by the transcendental equation

$$\frac{h}{a} = \cot\left(\frac{\pi Uh}{q}\right)$$

Evaluate the half-width, h. Find the local velocity and the pressure at points $(x, y) = (0, \pm h)$. Assume the fluid density is that of standard air.

*6.115 A flow field is formed by combining a uniform flow in the positive x direction, with $U = 10$ m/s, and a counterclockwise vortex, with strength $K = 16\pi$ m^2/s, located at the origin. Obtain the stream function, velocity potential, and velocity field for the

*These problems require material from sections that may be omitted without loss of continuity in the text material.

combined flow. Locate the stagnation point(s) for the flow. Plot the streamlines and potential lines. (Hint: Use the *Excel* workbook of Example 6.10.)

*6.116 Consider the flow field formed by combining a uniform flow in the positive x direction with a sink located at the origin. Let $U = 50$ m/s and $q = 90$ m²/s. Use a suitably chosen control volume to evaluate the net force per unit depth needed to hold in place (in standard air) the surface shape formed by the stagnation streamline.

*6.117 Consider the flow field formed by combining a uniform flow in the positive x direction and a source located at the origin. Let $U = 30$ m/s and $q = 150$ m²/s. Plot the ratio of the local

velocity to the freestream velocity as a function of θ along the stagnation streamline. Locate the points on the stagnation streamline where the velocity reaches its maximum value. Find the gage pressure there if the fluid density is 1.2 kg/m³.

*6.118 Consider the flow field formed by combining a uniform flow in the positive x direction and a source located at the origin. Obtain expressions for the stream function, velocity potential, and velocity field for the combined flow. If $U = 25$ m/s, determine the source strength if the stagnation point is located at $x = -1$ m. Plot the streamlines and potential lines. (Hint: Use the *Excel* workbook of Example 6.10.)

83) $\int_{A_0} \rho \, dA_1 = \dot{m} V_j = \rho V_j A_j V_j = \rho U_j V_j^2$

$P_1 A_0 = \rho g h = \rho A_j V_j^2$

$\dfrac{P_0}{A_j} = \dfrac{V_j^2}{g h}$

$\dfrac{P_1}{\rho} = \dfrac{V_j^2}{2}$

$P_1 = \rho g h$

$\dfrac{V^2}{2} = g h$

$\dfrac{A_0}{A_j} = \dfrac{V_j^2}{g h} = 2$

Chapter 7

Dimensional Analysis and Similitude

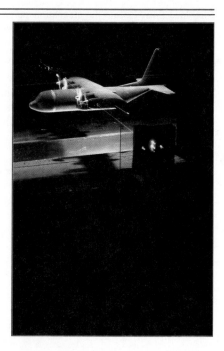

CASE STUDY

T. Rex

Tyrannosaurus rex. (California Academy of Sciences)

Dimensional analysis, the main topic of this chapter, is used in many scientific pursuits. It has even been used to try to determine the speed at which dinosaurs such as Tyrannosaurus rex may have been able to run [1]. The only data available on these creatures are in the fossil record—the most pertinent data being the dinosaurs' average leg length l and stride s. Could these data be used to extract the dinosaurs' speed? Comparing data on l and s and the speed V of quadrupeds (e.g., horses, dogs) and bipeds (e.g., humans) does not indicate a pattern, unless dimensional analysis is used to learn that all of the data should be plotted in the following way: Plot the dimensionless quantity V^2/gl (where V is the measured speed of the animal and g is the acceleration of gravity) against the dimensionless ratio s/l. When this is done, "magically" the data for most animals fall approximately on one curve! Hence, the running behavior of most animals can be obtained from the graph: In this case, the dinosaurs' value of s/l allows a corresponding value of V^2/gl to be interpolated from the curve, leading to an estimate for V of dinosaurs (because l and g are known). Based on this, in contrast to the *Jurassic Park* movies, it seems likely that humans could easily outrun T. rex!

In previous chapters we have mentioned several instances in which we claim a simplified flow exists. For example, we have stated that a flow with typical speed V will be essentially incompressible if the Mach number, $M \equiv V/c$ (where c is the speed of sound), is less than about 0.3 and that we can neglect viscous effects in most of a flow if the Reynolds number, $Re = \rho V L / \mu$ (L is a typical or "characteristic" size scale of the flow), is "large." We will also make extensive use of the Reynolds number based on pipe diameter, D ($Re = \rho VD/\mu$), to predict with a high degree of accuracy whether the pipe flow is laminar or turbulent. It turns out that there are many such interesting dimensionless groupings in engineering science—for example, in heat transfer, the value of the Biot number, $Bi = hL/k$, of a hot body, size L and conductivity k, indicates whether that body will tend to cool on the outside surface first or will basically cool uniformly when it's plunged into a cool fluid with convection coefficient h. (Can you figure out what a high Bi number predicts?) How do we obtain these groupings, and why do their values have such powerful predictive power?

The answers to these questions will be provided in this chapter when we introduce the method of dimensional analysis. This is a technique for gaining insight into fluid flows (in fact, into many engineering and scientific phenomena) before we do either extensive theoretical analysis or experimentation; it also enables us to extract trends from data that would otherwise remain disorganized and incoherent.

We will also discuss modeling. For example, how do we correctly perform tests on the drag on a 3/8-scale model of an automobile in a wind tunnel to predict what the drag would be on the full-size automobile at the same speed? *Must* we use the same speed for model and full-size automobile? How do we scale up the measured model drag to find the automobile drag?

7-1 NONDIMENSIONALIZING THE BASIC DIFFERENTIAL EQUATIONS

Before describing dimensional analysis let us see what we can learn from our previous analytical descriptions of fluid flow. Consider, for example, a steady incompressible two-dimensional flow of a Newtonian fluid with constant viscosity (already quite a list of assumptions!). The mass conservation equation (Eq. 5.1c) becomes

$$\frac{\partial u}{\partial x} + \frac{\partial v}{\partial y} = 0 \tag{7.1}$$

and the Navier–Stokes equations (Eqs. 5.27) reduce to

$$\rho\left(u\frac{\partial u}{\partial x} + v\frac{\partial u}{\partial y}\right) = -\frac{\partial p}{\partial x} + \mu\left(\frac{\partial^2 u}{\partial x^2} + \frac{\partial^2 u}{\partial y^2}\right) \tag{7.2}$$

and

$$\rho\left(u\frac{\partial v}{\partial x} + v\frac{\partial v}{\partial y}\right) = -\rho g - \frac{\partial p}{\partial y} + \mu\left(\frac{\partial^2 v}{\partial x^2} + \frac{\partial^2 v}{\partial y^2}\right) \tag{7.3}$$

As we discussed in Section 5-4, these equations form a set of coupled nonlinear partial differential equations for u, v, and p, and are difficult to solve for most flows. Equation 7.1 has dimensions of 1/time, and Eqs. 7.2 and 7.3 have dimensions of force/volume. Let us see what happens when we convert them into dimensionless equations. (Even if you did not study Section 5-4 you will be able to understand the following material.)

To nondimensionalize these equations, divide all lengths by a reference length, L, and all velocities by a reference speed, V_∞, which usually is taken as the freestream velocity. Make the pressure nondimensional by dividing by ρV_∞^2 (twice the freestream dynamic pressure). Denoting nondimensional quantities with asterisks, we obtain

$$x^* = \frac{x}{L}, \ y^* = \frac{y}{L}, \ u^* = \frac{u}{V_\infty}, v^* = \frac{v}{V_\infty} \ \text{ and } \ p^* = \frac{p}{\rho V_\infty^2} \tag{7.4}$$

so that $x = x^*L$, $y = y^*L$, $u = u^*V_\infty$, and so on. We can then substitute into Eqs. 7.1 through 7.3; below we show two representative substitutions:

$$u\frac{\partial u}{\partial x} = u^*V_\infty \frac{\partial(u^*V_\infty)}{\partial(x^*L)} = \frac{V_\infty^2}{L}u^*\frac{\partial u^*}{\partial x^*}$$

and

$$\frac{\partial^2 u}{\partial x^2} = \frac{\partial(u^*V_\infty)}{\partial(x^*L)^2} = \frac{V_\infty}{L^2}\frac{\partial^2 u^*}{\partial x^{*2}}$$

Using this procedure, the equations become

$$\frac{V_\infty}{L}\frac{\partial u^*}{\partial x^*} + \frac{V_\infty}{L}\frac{\partial v^*}{\partial y^*} = 0 \tag{7.5}$$

$$\frac{\rho V_\infty^2}{L}\left(u^*\frac{\partial u^*}{\partial x^*} + v^*\frac{\partial u^*}{\partial y^*}\right) = -\frac{\rho V_\infty^2}{L}\frac{\partial p^*}{\partial x^*} + \frac{\mu V_\infty}{L^2}\left(\frac{\partial^2 u^*}{\partial x^{*2}} + \frac{\partial^2 u^*}{\partial y^{*2}}\right) \tag{7.6}$$

$$\frac{\rho V_\infty^2}{L}\left(u^*\frac{\partial v^*}{\partial x^*} + v^*\frac{\partial v^*}{\partial y^*}\right) = -\rho g - \frac{\rho V_\infty^2}{L}\frac{\partial p^*}{\partial y^*} + \frac{\mu V_\infty}{L^2}\left(\frac{\partial^2 v^*}{\partial x^{*2}} + \frac{\partial^2 v^*}{\partial y^{*2}}\right) \tag{7.7}$$

Dividing Eq. 7.5 by V_∞/L and Eqs. 7.6 and 7.7 by $\rho V_\infty^2/L$ gives

$$\frac{\partial u^*}{\partial x^*} + \frac{\partial v^*}{\partial y^*} = 0 \tag{7.8}$$

$$u^*\frac{\partial u^*}{\partial x^*} + v^*\frac{\partial u^*}{\partial y^*} = -\frac{\partial p^*}{\partial x^*} + \frac{\mu}{\rho V_\infty L}\left(\frac{\partial^2 u^*}{\partial x^{*2}} + \frac{\partial^2 u^*}{\partial y^{*2}}\right) \tag{7.9}$$

$$u^*\frac{\partial v^*}{\partial x^*} + v^*\frac{\partial v^*}{\partial y^*} = -\frac{gL}{V_\infty^2} - \frac{\partial p^*}{\partial y^*} + \frac{\mu}{\rho V_\infty L}\left(\frac{\partial^2 v^*}{\partial x^{*2}} + \frac{\partial^2 v^*}{\partial y^{*2}}\right) \tag{7.10}$$

Equations 7.8, 7.9, and 7.10 are the nondimensional forms of our original equations (Eqs. 7.1, 7.2, 7.3). As such, we can think about their solution (with appropriate boundary conditions) as an exercise in applied mathematics. Equation 7.9 contains a dimensionless coefficient $\mu/\rho V_\infty L$ (which we recognize as the inverse of the Reynolds number) in front of the second-order (viscous) terms; Eq. 7.10 contains this and another dimensionless coefficient, gL/V_∞^2 (which we will discuss shortly) for the gravity force term. We recall from the theory of differential equations that the mathematical form of the solution of such equations is very sensitive to the values of the coefficients in the equations (e.g., certain second-order partial differential equations can be elliptic, parabolic, or hyperbolic depending on coefficient values).

These equations tell us that the solution, and hence the actual flow pattern they describe, depends on the values of the two coefficients. For example, if $\mu/\rho V_\infty L$ is very small (i.e., we have a high Reynolds number), the second-order differentials, representing viscous forces, can be neglected, at least in most of the flow, and we end up with a form of Euler's equations (Eqs. 6.2). We say "in most of the flow" because we have already learned that in reality for this case we will have a boundary layer in which there *is* significant effect of viscosity; in addition, from a mathematical point of view, it is always dangerous to neglect higher-order derivatives, even if their coefficients are small, because reduction to a lower-order equation means we lose a boundary condition (specifically the no-slip condition). We can predict that if $\mu/\rho V_\infty L$ is large or small, then viscous forces will be significant or not, respectively; if gLV_∞^2 is large or small, we can predict that gravity forces will be significant or not, respectively. We can thus gain insight even before attempting a solution to the differential equations. Note that for completeness, we would have to apply the same nondimensionalizing approach to the boundary conditions of the problem, which often introduce further dimensionless coefficients.

Writing nondimensional forms of the governing equations, then, can yield insight into the underlying physical phenomena, and indicate which forces are dominant. If we had two geometrically similar but different scale flows satisfying Eqs. 7.8, 7.9, and 7.10 (for example, a model and a prototype), the equations would only yield the same mathematical results if the two flows had the same values for the two coefficients (i.e., had the same relative importance of gravity, viscous, and inertia forces). This nondimensional form of the equations is also the starting point in numerical methods, which is very often the only way of obtaining their solution. Additional derivations and examples of establishing similitude from the governing equations of a problem are presented in [2] and [3].

We will now see how the method of dimensional analysis can be used instead of the above procedure to find appropriate dimensionless groupings of physical parameters. As we have mentioned, using dimensionless groupings is very useful for experimental measurements, and we will see in the next two sections that we can obtain them even when we do not have the governing equations such as Eqs. 7.1, 7.2, and 7.3 to work from.

7-2   NATURE OF DIMENSIONAL ANALYSIS

Most phenomena in fluid mechanics depend in a complex way on geometric and flow parameters. For example, consider the drag force on a stationary smooth sphere immersed in a uniform stream. What experiments must be conducted to determine the drag force on the sphere? To answer this question, we must specify what we believe are the parameters that are important in determining the drag force. Clearly, we would expect the drag force to depend on the size of the sphere (characterized by the diameter, D), the fluid speed, V, and the fluid viscosity, μ. In addition, the density of the fluid, ρ, also might be important. Representing the drag force by F, we can write the symbolic equation

$$F = f(D, V, \rho, \mu)$$

Although we may have neglected parameters on which the drag force depends, such as surface roughness (or may have included parameters on which it does not depend), we have set up the problem of determining the drag force for a stationary sphere in terms of quantities that are both controllable and measurable in the laboratory.

We could set up an experimental procedure for finding the dependence of F on V, D, ρ, and μ. To see how the drag, F, is affected by fluid speed, V, we could place a sphere in a wind tunnel and measure F for a range of V values. We could then run more tests in which we explore the effect on F of sphere diameter, D, by using different diameter spheres. We are already generating a lot of data: If we ran the wind tunnel at, say, 10 different speeds, for 10 different sphere sizes, we'd have 100 data points. We could present these results on one graph (e.g., we could plot 10 curves of F vs. V, one for each sphere size), but acquiring the data would already be time consuming: If we assume each run takes $\frac{1}{2}$ hour, we have already accumulated 50 hours of work! We still wouldn't be finished—we would have to book time using, say, a water tank, where we could repeat all these runs for a different value of ρ and of μ. In principle, we would next have to search out a way to use other fluids to be able to do experiments for a range of ρ and μ values (say, 10 of each). At the end of the day (actually, at the end of about $2\frac{1}{2}$ years of 40-hour weeks!) we would have performed about 10^4 tests. Then we would have to try and make sense of the data: How do we plot, say, curves of F vs. V, with D, ρ, and μ all being parameters? This is a daunting task, even for such a seemingly simple phenomenon as the drag on a sphere!

Fortunately we do not have to do all this work. As we will see in Example 7.1, using dimensional analysis, all the data for drag on a smooth sphere can be plotted as a single relationship between two nondimensional parameters in the form

$$\frac{F}{\rho V^2 D^2} = f\left(\frac{\rho VD}{\mu}\right)$$

The form of the function f still must be determined experimentally, but the point is that all spheres, in all fluids, for most velocities will fall on the same curve. Rather than needing to conduct 10^4 experiments, we could establish the nature of the function as accurately with only about 10 tests. The time saved in performing only 10 rather than 10^4 tests is obvious. Even more important is the greater experimental convenience. No longer must we find fluids with 10 different values of density and viscosity. Nor must we make 10 spheres of different diameters. Instead, only the parameter $\rho VD/\mu$ must be varied. This can be accomplished simply by using *one* sphere (e.g., 1 in. diameter), in *one* fluid (e.g., air), and only changing the speed, for example.

Figure 7.1 shows some classic data for flow over a sphere (the factors $\frac{1}{2}$ and $\pi/4$ have been added to the denominator of the parameter on the left to make it take the form of a commonly used nondimensional group, the drag coefficient, C_D, that we will discuss in detail in Chapter 9). If we performed the experiments as outlined above, our results would fall on the same curve, within experimental error. The data points represent results obtained by various workers for several different fluids and spheres. Note that we end up with a curve that can be used to obtain the drag force on a very wide range of sphere/fluid combinations. For example, it could be used to obtain the drag on a hot-air balloon due to a crosswind, or on a red-blood cell (assuming it could be modeled as a sphere) as it moves through the aorta—in either case, given the fluid (ρ and μ), the flow speed V, and the sphere diameter D, we could compute a value for $\rho VD/\mu$, then read the corresponding value for C_D, and finally compute the drag force F.

In Section 7-3 we introduce the *Buckingham Pi* theorem, a formalized procedure for deducing the dimensionless groups appropriate for a given fluid mechanics or other engineering problem. This section, and Section 7-4, may seem a bit difficult to follow; we suggest you read them once, then study Examples 7.1, 7.2, and 7.3 to see how practical and useful the method in fact is, before returning to the two sections for a reread.

The Buckingham Pi theorem is a statement of the relation between a function expressed in terms of dimensional parameters and a related function expressed in terms of nondimensional parameters. The Buckingham Pi theorem allows us to develop the important nondimensional parameters quickly and easily.

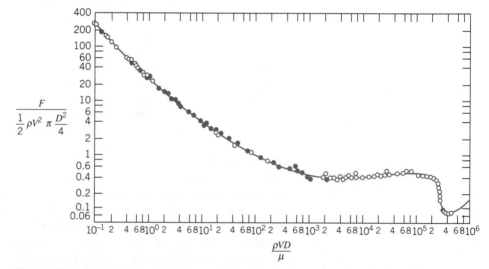

Fig. 7.1 Experimentally derived relation between the nondimensional parameters [4].

7-3 **BUCKINGHAM PI THEOREM**

In the previous section we discussed how the drag F on a sphere depends on the sphere diameter D, fluid density ρ and viscosity μ, and fluid speed V, or

$$F = F(D, \rho, \mu, V)$$

with theory or experiment being needed to determine the nature of function f. More formally, we write

$$g(F, D, \rho, \mu, V) = 0$$

where g is an unspecified function, different from f. The Buckingham Pi theorem [5] states that we can transform a relationship between n parameters of the form

$$g(q_1, q_2, \ldots, q_n) = 0$$

into a corresponding relationship between $n - m$ independent dimensionless Π parameters in the form

$$G(\Pi_1, \Pi_2, \ldots, \Pi_{n-m}) = 0$$

or

$$\Pi_1 = G_1(\Pi_2, \ldots, \Pi_{n-m})$$

where m is *usually* the minimum number, r, of independent dimensions (e.g., mass, length, time) required to define the dimensions of all the parameters $q_1, q_2, \ldots, q_n$. (Sometimes $m \neq r$; we will see this in Example 7.3.) For example, for the sphere problem, we will see (in Example 7.1) that

$$g(F, D, \rho, \mu, V) = 0 \qquad \text{or} \qquad F = F(D, \rho, \mu, V)$$

leads to

$$G\left(\frac{F}{\rho V^2 D^2}, \frac{\mu}{\rho V D}\right) = 0 \qquad \text{or} \qquad \frac{F}{\rho V^2 D^2} = G_1\left(\frac{\mu}{\rho V D}\right)$$

The theorem does not predict the functional form of G or G_1. The functional relation among the independent dimensionless Π parameters must be determined experimentally.

The $n - m$ dimensionless Π parameters obtained from the procedure are independent. A Π parameter is not independent if it can be formed from any combination of one or more of the other Π parameters. For example, if

$$\Pi_5 = \frac{2\Pi_1}{\Pi_2 \Pi_3} \qquad \text{or} \qquad \Pi_6 = \frac{\Pi_1^{3/4}}{\Pi_3^2}$$

then neither Π_5 nor Π_6 is independent of the other dimensionless parameters.

Several methods for determining the dimensionless parameters are available. A detailed procedure is presented in the next section.

7-4 **DETERMINING THE Π GROUPS**

Regardless of the method to be used to determine the dimensionless parameters, one begins by listing all dimensional parameters that are known (or believed) to affect the given flow phenomenon. Some experience admittedly is helpful in compiling the list. Students, who do not have this experience, often are troubled by the need to apply engineering judgment in an apparent massive dose. However, it is difficult to go wrong if a generous selection of parameters is made.

If you suspect that a phenomenon depends on a given parameter, include it. If your suspicion is correct, experiments will show that the parameter must be included to get consistent results. If the parameter is extraneous, an extra Π parameter may result, but experiments will later show that it may be eliminated. Therefore, do not be afraid to include *all* the parameters that you feel are important.

The six steps listed below (which may seem a bit abstract but are actually easy to do) outline a recommended procedure for determining the Π parameters:

Step 1. *List all the dimensional parameters involved.* (Let *n* be the number of parameters.) If all of the pertinent parameters are not included, a relation may be obtained, but it will not give the complete story. If parameters that actually have no effect on the physical phenomenon are included, either the process of dimensional analysis will show that these do not enter the relation sought, or one or more dimensionless groups will be obtained that experiments will show to be extraneous.

Step 2. *Select a set of fundamental (primary) dimensions, e.g., MLt or FLt.* (Note that for heat transfer problems you may also need *T* for temperature, and in electrical systems, *q* for charge.)

Step 3. *List the dimensions of all parameters in terms of primary dimensions.* (Let *r* be the number of primary dimensions.) Either force or mass may be selected as a primary dimension.

Step 4. *Select a set of r dimensional parameters that includes all the primary dimensions.* These parameters will all be combined with each of the remaining parameters, one of those at a time, and so will be called repeating parameters. No repeating parameter should have dimensions that are a power of the dimensions of another repeating parameter; for example, do not include both an area (L^2) and a second moment of area (L^4) as repeating parameters. The repeating parameters chosen may appear in all the dimensionless groups obtained; consequently, do *not* include the dependent parameter among those selected in this step.

Step 5. *Set up dimensional equations, combining the parameters selected in Step 4 with each of the other parameters in turn, to form dimensionless groups.* (There will be $n - m$ equations.) Solve the dimensional equations to obtain the $n - m$ dimensionless groups.

Step 6. *Check to see that each group obtained is dimensionless.* If mass was initially selected as a primary dimension, it is wise to check the groups using force as a primary dimension, or vice versa.

The functional relationship among the Π parameters must be determined experimentally. The detailed procedure for determining the dimensionless Π parameters is illustrated in Examples 7.1 and 7.2.

Example 7.1   Drag Force on a Smooth Sphere

As noted in Section 7-2, the drag force, F, on a smooth sphere depends on the relative speed, V, the sphere diameter, D, the fluid density, ρ, and the fluid viscosity, μ. Obtain a set of dimensionless groups that can be used to correlate experimental data.

GIVEN: $F = f(\rho, V, D, \mu)$ for a smooth sphere.

FIND: An appropriate set of dimensionless groups.

SOLUTION:
(Circled numbers refer to steps in the procedure for determining dimensionless Π parameters.)

① $F \qquad V \qquad D \qquad \rho \qquad \mu$ $\qquad\qquad\qquad$ $n = 5$ dimensional parameters

② Select primary dimensions M, L, and t.

③ $\quad F \qquad\; V \qquad D \qquad\; \rho \qquad\;\; \mu$

$\qquad \dfrac{ML}{t^2} \quad \dfrac{L}{t} \qquad L \qquad \dfrac{M}{L^3} \quad \dfrac{M}{Lt}$ $\qquad\qquad$ $r = 3$ primary dimensions

④ Select repeating parameters ρ, V, D. $m = r = 3$ repeating parameters

⑤ Then $n - m = 2$ dimensionless groups will result. Setting up dimensional equations, we obtain

$$\Pi_1 = \rho^a V^b D^c F \quad \text{and} \quad \left(\frac{M}{L^3}\right)^a \left(\frac{L}{t}\right)^b (L)^c \left(\frac{ML}{t^2}\right) = M^0 L^0 t^0$$

Equating the exponents of M, L, and t results in

$$\begin{array}{llll}
M: & a + 1 = 0 & a = -1 \\
L: & -3a + b + c + 1 = 0 & c = -2 \\
t: & -b - 2 = 0 & b = -2
\end{array}\left.\vphantom{\begin{array}{l}1\\2\\3\end{array}}\right\} \quad \text{Therefore,} \quad \Pi_1 = \frac{F}{\rho V^2 D^2}$$

Similarly,

$$\Pi_2 = \rho^d V^e D^f \mu \quad \text{and} \quad \left(\frac{M}{L^3}\right)^d \left(\frac{L}{t}\right)^e (L)^f \left(\frac{M}{Lt}\right) = M^0 L^0 t^0$$

$$\begin{array}{llll}
M: & d + 1 = 0 & d = -1 \\
L: & -3d + e + f - 1 = 0 & f = -1 \\
t: & -e - 1 = 0 & e = -1
\end{array}\left.\vphantom{\begin{array}{l}1\\2\\3\end{array}}\right\} \quad \text{Therefore,} \quad \Pi_2 = \frac{\mu}{\rho VD}$$

⑥ Check using F, L, t dimensions

$$[\Pi_1] = \left[\frac{F}{\rho V^2 D^2}\right] \quad \text{and} \quad F \frac{L^4}{Ft^2} \left(\frac{t}{L}\right)^2 \frac{1}{L^2} = 1$$

where [ ] means "has dimensions of," and

$$[\Pi_2] = \left[\frac{\mu}{\rho VD}\right] \quad \text{and} \quad \frac{Ft}{L^2} \frac{L^4}{Ft^2} \frac{t}{L} \frac{1}{L} = 1$$

The functional relationship is $\Pi_1 = f(\Pi_2)$, or

$$\frac{F}{\rho V^2 D^2} = f\left(\frac{\mu}{\rho VD}\right)$$

as noted before. The form of the function, f, must be determined experimentally (see Fig. 7.1).

> The *Excel* workbook for this Example is convenient for computing the values of a, b, and c for this and other problems.

Example 7.2   Pressure Drop in Pipe Flow

The pressure drop, Δp, for steady, incompressible viscous flow through a straight horizontal pipe depends on the pipe length, l, the average velocity, $\overline{V}$, the fluid viscosity, μ, the pipe diameter, D, the fluid density, ρ, and the average "roughness" height, e. Determine a set of dimensionless groups that can be used to correlate data.

GIVEN: $\Delta p = f(\rho, \overline{V}, D, l, \mu, e)$ for flow in a circular pipe.

FIND: A suitable set of dimensionless groups.

SOLUTION:
(Circled numbers refer to steps in the procedure for determining dimensionless Π parameters.)

① Δp ρ μ $\overline{V}$ l D e $n = 7$ dimensional parameters

② Choose primary dimensions M, L, and t.

③ Δp ρ μ $\overline{V}$ l D e

   $\dfrac{M}{Lt^2}$ $\dfrac{M}{L^3}$ $\dfrac{M}{Lt}$ $\dfrac{L}{t}$ L L L $r = 3$ primary dimensions

④ Select repeating parameters $\rho, \overline{V}, D$. $m = r = 3$ repeating parameters

⑤ Then $n - m = 4$ dimensionless groups will result. Setting up dimensional equations we have:

$$\Pi_1 = \rho^a \overline{V}^b D^c \Delta p \quad \text{and}$$

$$\left(\frac{M}{L^3}\right)^a \left(\frac{L}{t}\right)^b (L)^c \left(\frac{M}{Lt^2}\right) = M^0 L^0 t^0$$

$$\begin{aligned} M: &\quad 0 = a + 1 \\ L: &\quad 0 = -3a + b + c - 1 \\ t: &\quad 0 = -b - 2 \end{aligned} \Bigg\} \quad \begin{aligned} a &= -1 \\ b &= -2 \\ c &= 0 \end{aligned}$$

Therefore, $\Pi_1 = \rho^{-1} \overline{V}^{-2} D^0 \Delta p = \dfrac{\Delta p}{\rho \overline{V}^2}$

$$\Pi_2 = \rho^d \overline{V}^e D^f \mu \quad \text{and}$$

$$\left(\frac{M}{L^3}\right)^d \left(\frac{L}{t}\right)^e (L)^f \frac{M}{Lt} = M^0 L^0 t^0$$

$$\begin{aligned} M: &\quad 0 = d + 1 \\ L: &\quad 0 = -3d + e + f - 1 \\ t: &\quad 0 = -e - 1 \end{aligned} \Bigg\} \quad \begin{aligned} d &= -1 \\ e &= -1 \\ f &= -1 \end{aligned}$$

Therefore, $\Pi_2 = \dfrac{\mu}{\rho \overline{V} D}$

$$\Pi_3 = \rho^g \overline{V}^h D^i l \quad \text{and}$$

$$\left(\frac{M}{L^3}\right)^g \left(\frac{L}{t}\right)^h (L)^i L = M^0 L^0 t^0$$

$$\begin{aligned} M: &\quad 0 = g \\ L: &\quad 0 = -3g + h + i + 1 \\ t: &\quad 0 = -h \end{aligned} \Bigg\} \quad \begin{aligned} g &= 0 \\ h &= 0 \\ i &= -1 \end{aligned}$$

Therefore, $\Pi_3 = \dfrac{l}{D}$

$$\Pi_4 = \rho^j \overline{V}^k D^l e \quad \text{and}$$

$$\left(\frac{M}{L^3}\right)^j \left(\frac{L}{t}\right)^k (L)^l L = M^0 L^0 t^0$$

$$\begin{aligned} M: &\quad 0 = j \\ L: &\quad 0 = -3j + k + l + 1 \\ t: &\quad 0 = -k \end{aligned} \Bigg\} \quad \begin{aligned} j &= 0 \\ k &= 0 \\ l &= -1 \end{aligned}$$

Therefore, $\Pi_4 = \dfrac{e}{D}$

⑥ Check, using F, L, t dimensions

$$[\Pi_1] = \left[\frac{\Delta p}{\rho \overline{V}^2}\right] \quad \text{and} \quad \frac{F}{L^2} \frac{L^4}{Ft^2} \frac{t^2}{L^2} = 1$$

$$[\Pi_2] = \left[\frac{\mu}{\rho \overline{V} D}\right] \quad \text{and} \quad \frac{Ft}{L^2} \frac{L^4}{Ft^2} \frac{t}{L} \frac{1}{L} = 1$$

$$[\Pi_3] = \left[\frac{l}{D}\right] \quad \text{and} \quad \frac{L}{L} = 1$$

$$[\Pi_4] = \left[\frac{e}{D}\right] \quad \text{and} \quad \frac{L}{L} = 1$$

Finally, the functional relationship is

$$\Pi_1 = f(\Pi_2, \ \Pi_3, \ \Pi_4)$$

or

$$\frac{\Delta p}{\rho \overline{V}^2} = f\left(\frac{\mu}{\rho \overline{V} D}, \frac{l}{D}, \frac{e}{D}\right)$$

> **Notes:**
> - ✓ As we shall see when we study pipe flow in detail in Chapter 8, this relationship correlates the data well.
> - ✓ Each Π group is unique (e.g., there is only *one* possible dimensionless grouping of $\mu, \rho, \overline{V}$, and D).
> - ✓ We can often deduce Π groups by inspection, e.g., l/D is the obvious unique grouping of l with $\rho, \overline{V}$, and D.
> - 🐭 The *Excel* workbook for Example 7.1 is convenient for computing the values of a, b, and c for this problem.

The procedure outlined above, where m is taken equal to r (the fewest independent dimensions required to specify the dimensions of all parameters involved), almost always produces the correct number of dimensionless Π parameters. In a few cases, trouble arises because the number of primary dimensions differs when variables are expressed in terms of different systems of dimensions (e.g., MLt or FLt). The value of m can be established with certainty by determining the rank of the dimensional matrix; that rank is m. Although not needed in most applications, for completeness, this procedure is illustrated in Example 7.3.

The $n - m$ dimensionless groups obtained from the procedure are independent but not unique. If a different set of repeating parameters is chosen, different groups result. The repeating parameters are so named because they may appear in all the dimensionless groups obtained. Based on experience, viscosity should appear in only one dimensionless parameter. Therefore μ should *not* be chosen as a repeating parameter.

When we have a choice, it usually works out best to choose density ρ (dimensions M/L^3 in the MLt system), speed V (dimensions L/t), and characteristic length L (dimension L) as repeating parameters because experience shows this generally leads to a set of dimensionless parameters that are suitable for correlating a wide range of experimental data; in addition, ρ, V, and L are usually fairly easy to measure or otherwise obtain. The values of the dimensionless parameters obtained using these repeating parameters almost always have a very tangible meaning, telling you the relative strength of various fluid forces (e.g., viscous) to inertia forces—we will discuss several "classic" ones shortly.

It's also worth stressing that, given the parameters you're combining, *we can often determine the unique dimensional parameters by inspection*. For example, if we had repeating parameters ρ, V, and L and were combining them with a parameter A_f, representing the frontal area of an object, it's fairly obvious that only the combination A_f/L^2 is dimensionless; experienced fluid mechanicians also know that ρV^2 produces dimensions of stress, so any time a stress or force parameter arises, dividing by ρV^2 or $\rho V^2 L^2$ will produce a dimensionless quantity.

We will find useful a measure of the magnitude of fluid inertia forces, obtained from Newton's second law, $F = ma$; the dimensions of inertia force are thus MLt^{-2}. Using ρ, V, and L to build the dimensions of ma leads to the unique combination $\rho V^2 L^2$ (only ρ has dimension M, and only V^2 will produce dimension t^{-2}; L^2 is then required to leave us with MLt^{-2}).

If $n - m = 1$, then a single dimensionless Π parameter is obtained. In this case, the Buckingham Pi theorem indicates that the single Π parameter must be a constant.

Example 7.3   Capillary Effect: Use of Dimensional Matrix

When a small tube is dipped into a pool of liquid, surface tension causes a meniscus to form at the free surface, which is elevated or depressed depending on the contact angle at the liquid-solid-gas interface. Experiments indicate that the magnitude of this capillary effect, Δh, is a function of the tube diameter, D, liquid specific weight, γ, and surface tension, σ. Determine the number of independent Π parameters that can be formed and obtain a set.

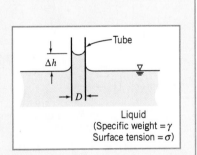

GIVEN: $\Delta h = f(D, \gamma, \sigma)$

FIND: (a) Number of independent Π parameters.
        (b) One set of Π parameters.

SOLUTION:

(Circled numbers refer to steps in the procedure for determining dimensionless π parameters.)

① Δh D γ σ $n = 4$ dimensional parameters

② Choose primary dimensions (use both M, L, t and F, L, t dimensions to illustrate the problem in determining m).

③ (a) M, L, t

$$\Delta h \quad D \quad \gamma \quad \sigma$$

$$L \quad L \quad \frac{M}{L^2 t^2} \quad \frac{M}{t^2}$$

$r = 3$ primary dimensions

    (b) F, L, t

$$\Delta h \quad D \quad \gamma \quad \sigma$$

$$L \quad L \quad \frac{F}{L^3} \quad \frac{F}{L}$$

$r = 2$ primary dimensions

Thus for each set of primary dimensions we ask, "Is m equal to r?" Let us check each dimensional matrix to find out. The dimensional matrices are

	Δh	D	γ	σ
M	0	0	1	1
L	1	1	-2	0
t	0	0	-2	-2

	Δh	D	γ	σ
F	0	0	1	1
L	1	1	-3	-1

The rank of a matrix is equal to the order of its largest nonzero determinant.

$$\begin{vmatrix} 0 & 1 & 1 \\ 1 & -2 & 0 \\ 0 & -2 & -2 \end{vmatrix} = 0 - (1)(-2) + (1)(-2) = 0$$

$$\begin{vmatrix} -2 & 0 \\ -2 & -2 \end{vmatrix} = 4 \neq 0 \quad \therefore \; m = 2$$
$$m \neq r$$

$$\begin{vmatrix} 1 & 1 \\ -3 & -1 \end{vmatrix} = -1 + 3 = 2 \neq 0$$

$$\therefore \; m = 2$$
$$m = r$$

④ $m = 2$. Choose D, γ as repeating parameters.

⑤ $n - m = 2$ dimensionless groups will result.

$$\Pi_1 = D^a \gamma^b \Delta h \quad \text{and}$$
$$(L)^a \left(\frac{M}{L^2 t^2}\right)^b (L) = M^0 L^0 t^0$$

$\left.\begin{array}{ll} M: & b + 0 = 0 \\ L: & a - 2b + 1 = 0 \\ t: & -2b + 0 = 0 \end{array}\right\} \begin{array}{l} b = 0 \\ a = -1 \end{array}$

Therefore, $\Pi_1 = \dfrac{\Delta h}{D}$

$$\Pi_2 = D^c \gamma^d \sigma \quad \text{and}$$
$$(L)^c \left(\frac{M}{L^2 t^2}\right)^d \frac{M}{t^2} = M^0 L^0 t^0$$

$\left.\begin{array}{ll} M: & d + 1 = 0 \\ L: & c - 2d = 0 \\ t: & -2d - 2 = 0 \end{array}\right\} \begin{array}{l} d = -1 \\ c = -2 \end{array}$

Therefore, $\Pi_2 = \dfrac{\sigma}{D^2 \gamma}$

⑥ Check, using F, L, t dimensions

$$[\Pi_1] = \left[\frac{\Delta h}{D}\right] \quad \text{and} \quad \frac{L}{L} = 1$$

$$[\Pi_2] = \left[\frac{\sigma}{D^2 \gamma}\right] \quad \text{and} \quad \frac{F}{L} \frac{1}{L^2} \frac{L^3}{F} = 1$$

$m = 2$. Choose D, γ as repeating parameters.

$n - m = 2$ dimensionless groups will result.

$$\Pi_1 = D^e \gamma^f \Delta h \quad \text{and}$$
$$(L)^e \left(\frac{F}{L^3}\right)^f L = F^0 L^0 t^0$$

$\left.\begin{array}{ll} F: & f = 0 \\ L: & e - 3f + 1 = 0 \end{array}\right\} \; e = -1$

Therefore, $\Pi_1 = \dfrac{\Delta h}{D}$

$$\Pi_2 = D^g \gamma^h \sigma \quad \text{and}$$
$$(L)^g \left(\frac{F}{L^3}\right)^h \frac{F}{L} = F^0 L^0 t^0$$

$\left.\begin{array}{ll} F: & h + 1 = 0 \\ L: & g - 3h - 1 = 0 \end{array}\right\} \begin{array}{l} h = -1 \\ g = -2 \end{array}$

Therefore, $\Pi_2 = \dfrac{\sigma}{D^2 \gamma}$

Check, using M, L, t dimensions

$$[\Pi_1] = \left[\frac{\Delta h}{D}\right] \quad \text{and} \quad \frac{L}{L} = 1$$

$$[\Pi_2] = \left[\frac{\sigma}{D^2 \gamma}\right] \quad \text{and} \quad \frac{M}{t^2} \frac{1}{L^2} \frac{L^2 t^2}{M} = 1$$

Therefore, both systems of dimensions yield the same dimensionless Π parameters. The predicted functional relationship is

$$\Pi_1 = f(\Pi_2) \qquad \text{or} \qquad \frac{\Delta h}{D} = f\left(\frac{\sigma}{D^2\gamma}\right)$$

Notes:

✓ This result is reasonable on physical grounds. The fluid is static; we would not expect time to be an important dimension.

✓ We analyzed this problem in Example 2.3, where we found that $\Delta h = 4\sigma\cos(\theta)/\rho g D$ (θ is the contact angle). Hence $\Delta h/D$ is *directly proportional* to $\sigma/D^2\gamma$.

✓ The purpose of this problem is to illustrate use of the dimensional matrix to determine the required number of repeating parameters.

7-5 SIGNIFICANT DIMENSIONLESS GROUPS IN FLUID MECHANICS

Over the years, several hundred different dimensionless groups that are important in engineering have been identified. Following tradition, each such group has been given the name of a prominent scientist or engineer, usually the one who pioneered its use. Several are so fundamental and occur so frequently in fluid mechanics that we should take time to learn their definitions. Understanding their physical significance also gives insight into the phenomena we study.

Forces encountered in flowing fluids include those due to inertia, viscosity, pressure, gravity, surface tension, and compressibility. The ratio of any two forces will be dimensionless. We have previously shown that the inertia force is proportional to $\rho V^2 L^2$.

We can now compare the relative magnitudes of various fluid forces to the inertia force, using the following scheme:

Viscous force $\sim$ $\quad \tau A = \mu \dfrac{du}{dy} A \propto \mu \dfrac{V}{L} L^2 = \mu VL \quad$ so $\quad \dfrac{\text{viscous}}{\text{inertia}} \sim \quad \dfrac{\mu VL}{\rho V^2 L^2} = \dfrac{\mu}{\rho VL}$

Pressure force $\sim$ $\quad \Delta p A \propto \Delta p L^2 \quad$ so $\quad \dfrac{\text{pressure}}{\text{inertia}} \sim \quad \dfrac{\Delta p L^2}{\rho V^2 L^2} = \dfrac{\Delta p}{\rho V^2}$

Gravity force $\sim$ $\quad mg \propto g\rho L^3 \quad$ so $\quad \dfrac{\text{gravity}}{\text{inertia}} \sim \quad \dfrac{g\rho L^3}{\rho V^2 L^2} = \dfrac{gL}{V^2}$

Surface tension $\sim$ $\quad \sigma L \quad$ so $\quad \dfrac{\text{surface tension}}{\text{inertia}} \sim \quad \dfrac{\sigma L}{\rho V^2 L^2} = \dfrac{\sigma}{\rho V^2 L}$

Compressibility force $\sim$ $\quad E_v A \propto E_v L^2 \quad$ so $\quad \dfrac{\text{compressibility force}}{\text{inertia}} \sim \dfrac{E_v L^2}{\rho V^2 L^2} = \dfrac{E_v}{\rho V^2}$

All of the dimensionless parameters listed above occur so frequently, and are so powerful in predicting the relative strengths of various fluid forces, that they (slightly modified—usually by taking the inverse) have been given identifying names.

The first parameter, $\mu/\rho VL$, is by tradition inverted to the form $\rho VL/\mu$, and was actually explored independently of dimensional analysis in the 1880s by Osborne Reynolds, the British engineer, who studied the transition between laminar and turbulent flow regimes in a tube. He discovered that the parameter (later named after him)

$$Re = \frac{\rho \overline{V} D}{\mu} = \frac{\overline{V} D}{\nu}$$

is a criterion by which the flow regime may be determined. Later experiments have shown that the *Reynolds number* is a key parameter for other flow cases as well. Thus, in general,

$$Re = \frac{\rho VL}{\mu} = \frac{VL}{\nu} \qquad (7.11)$$

where L is a characteristic length descriptive of the flow field geometry. The Reynolds number is the ratio of inertia forces to viscous forces. Flows with "large" Reynolds number generally are turbulent. Flows in which the inertia forces are "small" compared with the viscous forces are characteristically laminar flows.

In aerodynamic and other model testing, it is convenient to modify the second parameter, $\Delta p/\rho V^2$, by inserting a factor $\frac{1}{2}$ to make the denominator represent the dynamic pressure (the factor, of course, does not affect the dimensions). The ratio

$$Eu = \frac{\Delta p}{\frac{1}{2}\rho V^2} \qquad (7.12)$$

is formed, where Δp is the local pressure minus the freestream pressure, and ρ and V are properties of the freestream flow. This ratio has been named after Leonhard Euler, the Swiss mathematician who did much early analytical work in fluid mechanics. Euler is credited with being the first to recognize the role of pressure in fluid motion; the Euler equations of Chapter 6 demonstrate this role. The *Euler number* is the ratio of pressure forces to inertia forces. The Euler number is often called the *pressure coefficient*, C_p.

In the study of cavitation phenomena, the pressure difference, Δp, is taken as $\Delta p = p - p_v$, where p is the pressure in the liquid stream, and p_v is the liquid vapor pressure at the test temperature. Combining these with ρ and V in the stream yields the dimensionless parameter called the *cavitation number*,

$$Ca = \frac{p - p_v}{\frac{1}{2}\rho V^2} \qquad (7.13)$$

The smaller the cavitation number, the more likely cavitation is to occur. This is usually an unwanted phenomenon.

William Froude was a British naval architect. Together with his son, Robert Edmund Froude, he discovered that the parameter

$$Fr = \frac{V}{\sqrt{gL}} \qquad (7.14)$$

was significant for flows with free surface effects. Squaring the *Froude number* gives

$$Fr^2 = \frac{V^2}{gL}$$

which may be interpreted as the ratio of inertia forces to gravity forces (it is the inverse of the third force ratio, V^2/gL, that we discussed above). The length, L, is a characteristic length descriptive of the flow field. In the case of open-channel flow, the characteristic length is the water depth; Froude numbers less than unity indicate subcritical flow and values greater than unity indicate supercritical flow. We will have much more to say on this in Chapter 11.

By convention, the inverse of the fourth force ratio, $\sigma/\rho V^2 L$, discussed above, is called the *Weber* number; it indicates the ratio of inertia to surface tension forces

$$We = \frac{\rho V^2 L}{\sigma} \qquad (7.15)$$

The value of the Weber number is indicative of the existence of, and frequency of, capillary waves at a free surface.

In the 1870s, the Austrian physicist Ernst Mach introduced the parameter

$$M = \frac{V}{c} \qquad (7.16)$$

where V is the flow speed and c is the local sonic speed. Analysis and experiments have shown that the *Mach number* is a key parameter that characterizes compressibility effects in a flow. The Mach number may be written

$$M = \frac{V}{c} = \frac{V}{\sqrt{\dfrac{dp}{d\rho}}} = \frac{V}{\sqrt{\dfrac{E_v}{\rho}}} \qquad \text{or} \qquad M^2 = \frac{\rho V^2 L^2}{E_v L^2} = \frac{\rho V^2}{E_v}$$

which is the inverse of the final force ratio, $E_v/\rho V^2$, discussed above, and can be interpreted as a ratio of inertia forces to forces due to compressibility. For truly incompressible flow (and note that under some conditions even liquids are quite compressible), $c = \infty$ so that $M = 0$.

Equations 7.11 through 7.16 are some of the most commonly used dimensionless groupings in fluid mechanics because for any flow pattern they immediately (even before performing any experiments or analysis) indicate the relative importance of inertia, viscosity, pressure, gravity, surface tension, and compressibility.

7-6 FLOW SIMILARITY AND MODEL STUDIES

To be useful, a model test must yield data that can be scaled to obtain the forces, moments, and dynamic loads that would exist on the full-scale prototype. What conditions must be met to ensure the similarity of model and prototype flows?

Perhaps the most obvious requirement is that the model and prototype must be geometrically similar. *Geometric similarity* requires that the model and prototype be the same shape, and that all linear dimensions of the model be related to corresponding dimensions of the prototype by a constant scale factor.

A second requirement is that the model and prototype flows must be *kinematically similar*. Two flows are kinematically similar when the velocities at corresponding points are in the same direction and differ only by a constant scale factor. Thus two flows that are kinematically similar also have streamline patterns related by a constant scale factor. Since the boundaries form the bounding streamlines, flows that are kinematically similar must be geometrically similar.

In principle, in order to model the performance in an infinite flow field correctly, kinematic similarity would require that a wind tunnel of infinite cross-section be used to obtain data for drag on an object. In practice, this restriction may be relaxed considerably, permitting use of equipment of reasonable size.

Kinematic similarity requires that the regimes of flow be the same for model and prototype. If compressibility or cavitation effects, which may change even the qualitative patterns of flow, are not present in the prototype flow, they must be avoided in the model flow.

When two flows have force distributions such that identical types of forces are parallel and are related in magnitude by a constant scale factor at all corresponding points, the flows are *dynamically similar*.

The requirements for dynamic similarity are the most restrictive. Kinematic similarity requires geometric similarity; kinematic similarity is a necessary, but not sufficient, requirement for dynamic similarity.

To establish the conditions required for complete dynamic similarity, all forces that are important in the flow situation must be considered. Thus the effects of viscous forces, of pressure forces, of surface tension forces, and so on, must be considered. Test conditions must be established such that all important forces are related by the same scale factor between model and prototype flows. When dynamic similarity exists, data measured in a model flow may be related quantitatively to conditions in the prototype flow. What, then, are the conditions that ensure dynamic similarity between model and prototype flows?

The Buckingham Pi theorem may be used to obtain the governing dimensionless groups for a flow phenomenon; to achieve dynamic similarity between geometrically similar flows, we must make sure that each independent dimensionless group has the same value in the model and in the prototype. Then not only will the forces have the same relative importance, but also the dependent dimensionless group will have the same value in the model and prototype.

For example, in considering the drag force on a sphere in Example 7.1, we began with

$$F = f(D, V, \rho, \mu)$$

The Buckingham Pi theorem predicted the functional relation

$$\frac{F}{\rho V^2 D^2} = f_1 \left(\frac{\rho V D}{\mu} \right)$$

In Section 7-5 we showed that the dimensionless parameters can be viewed as ratios of forces. Thus, in considering a model flow and a prototype flow about a sphere (the flows are geometrically similar), the flows also will be dynamically similar if the value of the independent parameter, $\rho V D/\mu$, is duplicated between model and prototype, i.e., if

$$\left(\frac{\rho V D}{\mu} \right)_{\text{model}} = \left(\frac{\rho V D}{\mu} \right)_{\text{prototype}}$$

Furthermore, if

$$Re_{\text{model}} = Re_{\text{prototype}}$$

then the value of the dependent parameter, $F/\rho V^2 D^2$, in the functional relationship, will be duplicated between model and prototype, i.e.,

$$\left(\frac{F}{\rho V^2 D^2} \right)_{\text{model}} = \left(\frac{F}{\rho V^2 D^2} \right)_{\text{prototype}}$$

and the results determined from the model study can be used to predict the drag on the full-scale prototype.

The actual force on the object caused by the fluid is not the same for the model and prototype, but the value of its dimensionless group is. The two tests can be run using different fluids, if desired, as long as the Reynolds numbers are matched. For experimental convenience, test data can be measured in a wind tunnel in air and the results used to predict drag in water, as illustrated in Example 7.4.

Example 7.4   Similarity: Drag of a Sonar Transducer

The drag of a sonar transducer is to be predicted, based on wind tunnel test data. The prototype, a 1-ft diameter sphere, is to be towed at 5 knots (nautical miles per hour) in seawater at 40°F. The model is 6 in. in diameter. Determine the required test speed in air. If the drag of the model at these test conditions is 0.60 lbf, estimate the drag of the prototype.

Given:
Sonar transducer to be tested in a wind tunnel.

FIND: (a) V_m.
(b) F_p.

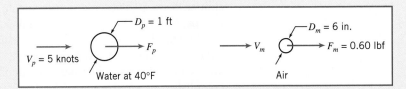

SOLUTION:
Since the prototype operates in water and the model test is to be performed in air, useful results can be expected only if cavitation effects are absent in the prototype flow and compressibility effects are absent from the model test. Under these conditions,

$$\frac{F}{\rho V^2 D^2} = f\left(\frac{\rho V D}{\mu}\right)$$

and the test should be run at

$$Re_{model} = Re_{prototype}$$

to ensure dynamic similarity. For seawater at 40°F, $\rho = 1.99$ slug/ft^3 and $v \approx 1.69 \times 10^{-5}$ ft^2/s. At prototype conditions,

$$V_p = \frac{5 \, \text{nmi}}{\text{hr}} \times \frac{6080 \, \text{ft}}{\text{nmi}} \times \frac{\text{hr}}{3600 \, \text{s}} = 8.44 \text{ ft/s}$$

$$Re_p = \frac{V_p D_p}{v_p} = \frac{8.44 \, \text{ft}}{\text{s}} \times 1 \, \text{ft} \times \frac{\text{s}}{1.69 \times 10^{-5} \, \text{ft}^2} = 4.99 \times 10^5$$

The model test conditions must duplicate this Reynolds number. Thus

$$Re_m = \frac{V_m D_m}{v_m} = 4.99 \times 10^5$$

For air at STP, $\rho = 0.00238$ slug/ft^3 and $v = 1.57 \times 10^{-4}$ ft^2/s. The wind tunnel must be operated at

$$V_m = Re_m \frac{v_m}{D_m} = 4.99 \times 10^5 \times \frac{1.57 \times 10^{-4} \, \text{ft}^2}{\text{s}} \times \frac{1}{0.5 \, \text{ft}}$$

$$V_m = 157 \text{ ft/s} \longleftarrow \underline{\hspace{3cm}} \qquad \qquad \underline{V_m}$$

This speed is low enough to neglect compressibility effects.
At these test conditions, the model and prototype flows are dynamically similar. Hence

$$\left.\frac{F}{\rho V^2 D^2}\right)_m = \left.\frac{F}{\rho V^2 D^2}\right)_p$$

and

$$F_p = F_m \frac{\rho_p}{\rho_m} \frac{V_p^2}{V_m^2} \frac{D_p^2}{D_m^2} = 0.60 \text{ lbf} \times \frac{1.99}{0.00238} \times \frac{(8.44)^2}{(157)^2} \times \frac{1}{(0.5)^2}$$

$$F_p = 5.8 \text{ lbf} \longleftarrow \underline{\hspace{3cm}} \qquad \qquad \underline{F_p}$$

If cavitation were expected—if the sonar probe were operated at high speed near the free surface of the seawater—then useful results could not be obtained from a model test in air.

> This problem:
> ✓ Demonstrates the calculation of prototype values from model test data.
> ✓ "Reinvented the wheel": the results for drag on a smooth sphere are very well known, so we did not need to do a model experiment but instead could have simply read from the graph of Fig. 7.1 the value of $C_D = F_p/(\frac{1}{2}\rho V_p^2 \frac{\pi}{4} D_p^2) \approx 0.1$ corresponding to a Reynolds number of 4.99×10^5. Then $F_p \approx 5.6$ lbf can easily be computed. We will have more to say on drag coefficients in Chapter 9.

Incomplete Similarity

We have shown that to achieve complete dynamic similarity between geometrically similar flows, it is necessary to duplicate the values of the independent dimensionless groups; by so doing the value of the dependent parameter is then duplicated.

In the simplified situation of Example 7.4, duplicating the Reynolds number value between model and prototype ensured dynamically similar flows. Testing in air allowed the Reynolds number to be duplicated exactly (this also could have been accomplished in a water tunnel for this situation). The drag force on a sphere actually depends on the nature of the boundary-layer flow. Therefore, geometric similarity requires that the relative surface roughness of the model and prototype be the same. This means that relative roughness also is a parameter that must be duplicated between model and prototype situations. If we assume that the model was constructed carefully, measured values of drag from model tests could be scaled to predict drag for the operating conditions of the prototype.

In many model studies, to achieve dynamic similarity requires duplication of several dimensionless groups. In some cases, complete dynamic similarity between model and prototype may not be attainable. Determining the drag force (resistance) of a surface ship is an example of such a situation. Resistance on a surface ship arises from skin friction on the hull (viscous forces) and surface wave resistance (gravity forces). Complete dynamic similarity requires that both Reynolds and Froude numbers be duplicated between model and prototype.

In general it is not possible to predict wave resistance analytically, so it must be modeled. This requires that

$$Fr_m = \frac{V_m}{(gL_m)^{1/2}} = Fr_p = \frac{V_p}{(gL_p)^{1/2}}$$

To match Froude numbers between model and prototype therefore requires a velocity ratio of

$$\frac{V_m}{V_p} = \left(\frac{L_m}{L_p}\right)^{1/2}$$

to ensure dynamically similar surface wave patterns.

Hence for any model length scale, matching the Froude numbers determines the velocity ratio. Only the kinematic viscosity can then be varied to match Reynolds numbers. Thus

$$Re_m = \frac{V_m L_m}{\nu_m} = Re_p = \frac{V_p L_p}{\nu_p}$$

leads to the condition that

$$\frac{\nu_m}{\nu_p} = \frac{V_m}{V_p}\frac{L_m}{L_P}$$

If we use the velocity ratio obtained from matching the Froude numbers, equality of Reynolds numbers leads to a kinematic viscosity ratio requirement of

$$\frac{\nu_m}{\nu_p} = \left(\frac{L_m}{L_p}\right)^{1/2}\frac{L_m}{L_p} = \left(\frac{L_m}{L_p}\right)^{3/2}$$

If $L_m/L_p = \frac{1}{100}$ (a typical length scale for ship model tests), then ν_m/ν_p must be $\frac{1}{1000}$. Figure A.3 shows that mercury is the only liquid with kinematic viscosity less than that of water. However, it is only about an order of magnitude less, so the kinematic viscosity ratio required to duplicate Reynolds numbers cannot be attained.

We conclude that we have a problem: it is impossible in practice for this model/ prototype scale of $\frac{1}{100}$ to satisfy both the Reynolds number and Froude number criteria; at best we will be able to satisfy only one of them. In addition, water is the only practical fluid for most model tests of free-surface flows. To obtain complete dynamic similarity then would require a full-scale test. However, all is not lost: Model studies do provide useful information even though complete similarity cannot be obtained. As an example, Fig. 7.2 shows data from a test of a 1:80 scale model of a ship conducted at the U.S. Naval Academy Hydromechanics Laboratory. The plot displays "resistance coefficient" data versus Froude number. The square points are calculated from values of total resistance measured in the test. We would like to obtain the corresponding total resistance curve for the full-scale ship.

If you think about it, we can *only* measure the total drag (the square data points). The total drag is due to both wave resistance (dependent on the Froude number) and friction resistance (dependent on the Reynolds number), and it's not possible to determine experimentally how much each contributes. We *cannot* use the total drag curve of Fig. 7.2 for the full-scale ship because, as we have discussed above, we can never set up the model conditions so that its Reynolds number *and* Froude number match those of the full-scale ship. Nevertheless, we would like to extract from Fig. 7.2 the corresponding total drag curve for the full-scale ship. In many experimental situations we need to use a creative "trick" to come up with a solution. In this case, the experimenters used boundary-layer theory (which we discuss in Chapter 9) to *predict* the viscous resistance component of the model (shown as diamonds in Fig. 7.2); then they estimated the wave resistance (not obtainable from theory) by simply subtracting this theoretical viscous resistance from the experimental total resistance, point by point (shown as circles in Fig. 7.2).

Using this clever idea (typical of the kind of experimental and analytical approaches experimentalists need to employ), Fig. 7.2 therefore gives the wave resistance of the model as a function of Froude number. It is *also* valid for the full-scale ship, because wave resistance depends only on the Froude number! We can now build a graph similar to Fig. 7.2 valid for the full-scale ship: Simply compute from boundary-layer theory the viscous resistance of the full-scale ship and add this to the wave resistance values, point by point. The result is shown in Fig. 7.3. The wave

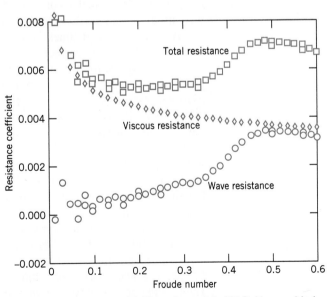

Fig. 7.2 Data from test of 1:80 scale model of U.S. Navy guided missile frigate *Oliver Hazard Perry* (FFG-7). (Data from U.S. Naval Academy Hydromechanics Laboratory, courtesy of Professor Bruce Johnson.)

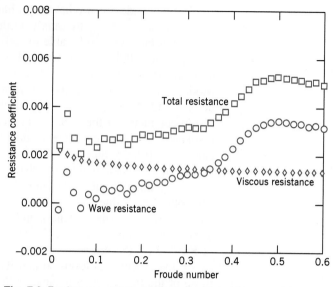

Fig. 7.3 Resistance of full-scale ship predicted from model test results. (Data from U.S. Naval Academy Hydromechanics Laboratory, courtesy of Professor Bruce Johnson.)

resistance points are identical to those in Fig. 7.2; the viscous resistance points are computed from theory (and are different from those of Fig. 7.2); and the predicted total resistance curve for the full-scale ship is finally obtained.

In this example, incomplete modeling was overcome by using analytical computations; the model experiments modeled the Froude number, but not the Reynolds number.

Because the Reynolds number cannot be matched for model tests of surface ships, the boundary-layer behavior is not the same for model and prototype. The model Reynolds number is only $(L_m/L_p)^{3/2}$ as large as the prototype value, so the extent of laminar flow in the boundary layer on the model is too large by a corresponding factor. The method just described assumes that boundary-layer behavior can be scaled. To make this possible, the model boundary layer is "tripped" or "stimulated" to become turbulent at a location that corresponds to the behavior on the full-scale vessel. "Studs" were used to stimulate the boundary layer for the model test results shown in Fig. 7.2.

A correction sometimes is added to the full-scale coefficients calculated from model test data. This correction accounts for roughness, waviness, and unevenness that inevitably are more pronounced on the full-scale ship than on the model. Comparisons between predictions from model tests and measurements made in full-scale trials suggest an overall accuracy within ±5 percent [6].

As we will see in Chapter 11, the Froude number is an important parameter in the modeling of rivers and harbors. In these situations it is not practical to obtain complete similarity. Use of a reasonable model scale would lead to extremely small water depths, so that viscous forces and surface tension forces would have much larger relative effects in the model flow than in the prototype. Consequently, different length scales are used for the vertical and horizontal directions. Viscous forces in the deeper model flow are increased using artificial roughness elements.

Emphasis on fuel economy has made reduction of aerodynamic drag important for automobiles, trucks, and buses. Most work on development of low-drag configurations is done using model tests. Traditionally, automobile models have been built to $\frac{3}{8}$ scale, at which a model of a full-size automobile has a frontal area of about 0.3 m². Thus testing can be done in a wind tunnel with test section area of 6 m² or larger. At $\frac{3}{8}$ scale, a wind speed of about 150 mph is needed to model a prototype automobile traveling at the legal speed limit. Thus there is no problem with compressibility effects, but the scale models are expensive and time-consuming to build.

Fig. 7.4 Full-scale automobile under test in Volvo wind tunnel, using smoke streaklines for flow visualization. (Photograph courtesy of Volvo Cars of North America, Inc.)

A large wind tunnel (test section dimensions are 5.4 m high, 10.4 m wide, and 21.3 m long; maximum air speed is 250 km/hr with the tunnel empty) is used by General Motors to test full-scale automobiles at highway speeds. The large test section allows use of production autos or of full-scale clay mockups of proposed auto body styles. Many other vehicle manufacturers are using comparable facilities; Fig. 7.4 shows a full-size sedan under test in the Volvo wind tunnel. The relatively low speed permits flow visualization using tufts or "smoke" streams.[1] Using full-size "models," stylists and engineers can work together to achieve optimum results.

It is harder to achieve dynamic similarity in tests of trucks and buses; models must be made to smaller scale than those for automobiles.[2] A large scale for truck and bus testing is 1:8. To achieve complete dynamic similarity by matching Reynolds numbers at this scale would require a test speed of 440 mph. This would introduce unwanted compressibility effects, and model and prototype flows would not be kinematically similar. Fortunately, trucks and buses are "bluff" objects. Experiments show that above a certain Reynolds number, their nondimensional drag becomes independent of Reynolds number [9]. (Figure 7.1 actually shows an example of this—for a sphere, the dimensionless drag is approximately constant for $2000 < Re < 2 \times 10^5$.) Although similarity is not complete, measured test data can be scaled to predict prototype drag forces. The procedure is illustrated in Example 7.5.

For additional details on techniques and applications of dimensional analysis consult [10–13].

---

[1] A mixture of liquid nitrogen and steam may be used to produce "smoke" streaklines that evaporate and do not clog the fine mesh screens used to reduce the turbulence level in a wind tunnel. Streaklines may be made to appear "colored" in photos by placing a filter over the camera lens. This and other techniques for flow visualization are detailed in [7] and [8].

[2] The vehicle length is particularly important in tests at large yaw angles to simulate crosswind behavior. Tunnel blockage considerations limit the acceptable model size. See [9] for recommended practices.

Example 7.5 Incomplete Similarity: Aerodynamic Drag on a Bus

The following wind tunnel test data from a 1:16 scale model of a bus are available:

Air Speed (m/s)	18.0	21.8	26.0	30.1	35.0	38.5	40.9	44.1	46.7
Drag Force (N)	3.10	4.41	6.09	7.97	10.7	12.9	14.7	16.9	18.9

Using the properties of standard air, calculate and plot the dimensionless aerodynamic drag coefficient,

$$C_D = \frac{F_D}{\frac{1}{2}\rho V^2 A}$$

versus Reynolds number $Re = \rho V w/\mu$, where w is model width. Find the minimum test speed above which C_D remains constant. Estimate the aerodynamic drag force and power requirement for the prototype vehicle at 100 km/hr. (The width and frontal area of the prototype are 8 ft and 84 ft^2, respectively.)

GIVEN: Data from a wind tunnel test of a model bus. Prototype dimensions are width of 8 ft and frontal area of 84 ft^2. Model scale is 1:16. Standard air is the test fluid.

FIND: (a) Aerodynamic drag coefficient, $C_D = F_D/\frac{1}{2}\rho V^2 A$, versus Reynolds number, $Re = \rho V w/\mu$; plot.
(b) Speed above which C_D is constant.
(c) Estimated aerodynamic drag force and power required for the full-scale vehicle at 100 km/hr.

SOLUTION:
The model width is

$$w_m = \frac{1}{16} w_p = \frac{1}{16} \times 8\text{ ft} \times 0.3048 \frac{\text{m}}{\text{ft}} = 0.152\text{ m}$$

The model area is

$$A_m = \left(\frac{1}{16}\right)^2 A_p = \left(\frac{1}{16}\right)^2 \times 84\text{ ft}^2 \times (0.305)^2 \frac{\text{m}^2}{\text{ft}^2} = 0.0305\text{ m}^2$$

The aerodynamic drag coefficient may be calculated as

$$C_D = \frac{F_D}{\frac{1}{2}\rho V^2 A}$$

$$= \frac{2}{} \times F_D(\text{N}) \times \frac{\text{m}^3}{1.23\text{ kg}} \times \frac{\text{s}^2}{(V)^2\text{ m}^2} \times \frac{1}{0.0305\text{ m}^2} \times \frac{\text{kg} \cdot \text{m}}{\text{N} \cdot \text{s}^2}$$

$$C_D = \frac{53.3\ F_D(\text{N})}{[V(\text{m/s})]^2}$$

The Reynolds number may be calculated as

$$Re = \frac{\rho V w}{\mu} = \frac{V w}{\nu} = \frac{V\text{ m}}{\text{s}} \times 0.152\text{ m} \times \frac{\text{s}}{1.46 \times 10^{-5}\text{ m}^2}$$

$$Re = 1.04 \times 10^4\ V(\text{m/s})$$

The calculated values are plotted in the following figure:

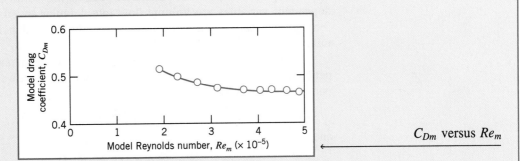

C_{Dm} versus Re_m

The plot shows that the model drag coefficient becomes constant at $C_{Dm} \approx 0.46$ above $Re_m = 4 \times 10^5$, which corresponds to an air speed of approximately 40 m/s. Since the drag coefficient is independent of Reynolds number above $Re \approx 4 \times 10^5$, then for the prototype vehicle ($Re \approx 4.5 \times 10^6$), $C_D \approx 0.46$. The drag force on the full-scale vehicle is

$$F_{Dp} = C_D \frac{1}{2} \rho V_p^2 A_p$$

$$= \frac{0.46}{2} \times 1.23 \frac{kg}{m^3} \left(100 \frac{km}{hr} \times 1000 \frac{m}{km} \times \frac{hr}{3600 \ s} \right)^2 \times 84 \ ft^2 \times (0.305)^2 \frac{m^2}{ft^2} \times \frac{N \cdot s^2}{kg \cdot m}$$

$$F_{Dp} = 1.71 \ kN \longleftarrow \qquad\qquad\qquad F_{Dp}$$

The corresponding power required to overcome aerodynamic drag is

$$\mathscr{P}_p = F_{Dp} V_p$$

$$= 1.71 \times 10^3 \ N \times 100 \frac{km}{hr} \times 1000 \frac{m}{km} \times \frac{hr}{3600 \ s} \times \frac{W \cdot s}{N \cdot m}$$

$$\mathscr{P}_p = 47.5 \ kW \longleftarrow \qquad\qquad\qquad \mathscr{P}_p$$

> This problem illustrates a common phenomenon in aerodynamics: Above a certain minimum Reynolds number the drag coefficient of an object usually approaches a constant—that is, becomes independent of the Reynolds number. Hence, in these situations we do not have to match the Reynolds numbers of the model and prototype in order for them to have the same drag coefficient—a considerable advantage. However, the SAE *Recommended Practices* [9] suggests $Re \geq 2 \times 10^6$ for truck and bus testing.

Scaling with Multiple Dependent Parameters

In some situations of practical importance there may be more than one dependent parameter. In such cases, dimensionless groups must be formed separately for each dependent parameter.

As an example, consider a typical centrifugal pump. The detailed flow pattern within a pump changes with volume flow rate and speed; these changes affect the pump's performance. Performance parameters of interest include the pressure rise (or head) developed, the power input required, and the machine efficiency measured under specific operating conditions.[3] Performance curves are generated by varying an independent parameter such as the volume flow rate. Thus the independent variables are volume flow rate, angular speed, impeller diameter, and fluid properties. Dependent variables are the several performance quantities of interest.

Finding dimensionless parameters begins from the symbolic equations for the dependence of head, h (energy per unit mass, L^2/t^2), and power, $\mathcal{P}$, on the independent parameters, given by

$$h = g_1(Q, \rho, \omega, D, \mu)$$

and

$$\mathcal{P} = g_2(Q, \rho, \omega, D, \mu)$$

Straightforward use of the Pi theorem gives the dimensionless *head coefficient* and *power coefficient* as

$$\frac{h}{\omega^2 D^2} = f_1\left(\frac{Q}{\omega D^3}, \frac{\rho \omega D^2}{\mu}\right) \tag{7.17}$$

and

$$\frac{\mathcal{P}}{\rho \omega^3 D^5} = f_2\left(\frac{Q}{\omega D^3}, \frac{\rho \omega D^2}{\mu}\right) \tag{7.18}$$

The dimensionless parameter $Q/\omega D^3$ in these equations is called the *flow coefficient*. The dimensionless parameter $\rho \omega D^2/\mu$ ($\propto \rho V D/\mu$) is a form of Reynolds number.

Head and power in a pump are developed by inertia forces. Both the flow pattern within a pump and the pump performance change with volume flow rate and speed of rotation. Performance is difficult to predict analytically except at the design point of the pump, so it is measured experimentally. Typical characteristic curves plotted from experimental data for a centrifugal pump tested at constant speed are shown in Fig. 7.5 as functions of volume flow rate. The head, power, and efficiency curves in

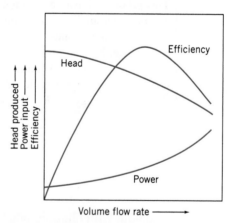

Fig. 7.5 Typical characteristic curves for centrifugal pump tested at constant speed.

---

[3] Efficiency is defined as the ratio of power delivered to the fluid divided by input power, $\eta = \mathcal{P}/\mathcal{P}_{\text{in}}$. For incompressible flow, we will see in Chapter 8 that the energy equation reduces to $\mathcal{P} = \rho Q h$ (when "head" h is expressed as energy per unit mass) or to $\mathcal{P} = \rho g Q H$ (when head H is expressed as energy per unit weight).

Fig. 7.5 are smoothed through points calculated from measured data. Maximum efficiency usually occurs at the design point.

Complete similarity in pump performance tests would require identical flow coefficients and Reynolds numbers. In practice, it has been found that viscous effects are relatively unimportant when two geometrically similar machines operate under "similar" flow conditions. Thus, from Eqs. 7.17 and 7.18, when

$$\frac{Q_1}{\omega_1 D_1^3} = \frac{Q_2}{\omega_2 D_2^3} \tag{7.19}$$

it follows that

$$\frac{h_1}{\omega_1^2 D_1^2} = \frac{h_2}{\omega_2^2 D_2^2} \tag{7.20}$$

and

$$\frac{\mathscr{P}_1}{\rho_1 \omega_1^3 D_1^5} = \frac{\mathscr{P}_2}{\rho_2 \omega_2^3 D_2^5} \tag{7.21}$$

The empirical observation that viscous effects are unimportant under similar flow conditions allows use of Eqs. 7.19 through 7.21 to scale the performance characteristics of machines to different operating conditions, as either the speed or diameter is changed. These useful scaling relationships are known as pump or fan "laws." If operating conditions for one machine are known, operating conditions for any geometrically similar machine can be found by changing D and ω according to Eqs. 7.19 through 7.21. (More details on dimensional analysis, design, and performance curves for fluid machinery are presented in Chapter 10.)

Another useful pump parameter can be obtained by eliminating the machine diameter from Eqs. 7.19 and 7.20. If we designate $\Pi_1 = Q/\omega D^3$ and $\Pi_2 = h/\omega^2 D^2$, then the ratio $\Pi_1^{1/2}/\Pi_2^{3/4}$ is another dimensionless parameter; this parameter is the *specific speed, N_s,*

$$N_s = \frac{\omega Q^{1/2}}{h^{3/4}} \tag{7.22a}$$

The specific speed, as defined in Eq. 7.22a, is a dimensionless parameter (provided that the head, h, is expressed as energy per unit mass). You may think of specific speed as the speed required for a machine to produce unit head at unit volume flow rate. A constant specific speed describes all operating conditions of geometrically similar machines with similar flow conditions.

Although specific speed is a dimensionless parameter, it is common practice to use a convenient but inconsistent set of units in specifying the variables ω and Q, and to use the energy per unit weight H in place of energy per unit mass h in Eq. 7.22a. When this is done the specific speed,

$$N_{s_{cu}} = \frac{\omega Q^{1/2}}{H^{3/4}} \tag{7.22b}$$

is not a unitless parameter and its magnitude depends on the units used to calculate it. Customary units used in U.S. engineering practice for pumps are rpm for ω, gpm for Q, and feet (energy per unit weight) for H. In these customary U.S. units, "low" specific speed means $500 < N_{s_{cu}} < 4000$ and "high" means $10{,}000 < N_{s_{cu}} < 15{,}000$. Example 7.6 illustrates use of the pump scaling laws and specific speed parameter. More details of specific speed calculations and additional examples of applications to fluid machinery are presented in Chapter 10.

Example 7.6   Pump "Laws"

A centrifugal pump has an efficiency of 80 percent at its design-point specific speed of 2000 (units of rpm, gpm, and feet). The impeller diameter is 8 in. At design-point flow conditions, the volume flow rate is 300 gpm of water at 1170 rpm. To obtain a higher flow rate, the pump is to be fitted with a 1750 rpm motor. Use the pump "laws" to find the design-point performance characteristics of the pump at the higher speed. Show that the specific speed remains constant for the higher operating speed. Determine the motor size required.

GIVEN: Centrifugal pump with design specific speed of 2000 (in rpm, gpm, and feet units). Impeller diameter is $D = 8$ in. At the pump's design-point flow conditions, $\omega = 1170$ rpm and $Q = 300$ gpm, with water.

FIND: (a) Performance characteristics,
(b) specific speed, and
(c) motor size required, for similar flow conditions at 1750 rpm.

SOLUTION:

From pump "laws," $Q/\omega D^3 =$ constant, so

$$Q_2 = Q_1 \frac{\omega_2}{\omega_1} \left(\frac{D_2}{D_1}\right)^3 = 300 \text{ gpm} \left(\frac{1750}{1170}\right) (1)^3 = 449 \text{ gpm} \quad\longleftarrow\quad \underline{\underline{Q_2}}$$

The pump head is not specified at $\omega_1 = 1170$ rpm, but it can be calculated from the specific speed, $N_{s_{cu}} = 2000$. Using the given units and the definition of $N_{s_{cu}}$,

$$N_{s_{cu}} = \frac{\omega Q^{1/2}}{H^{3/4}} \qquad \text{so} \qquad H_1 = \left(\frac{\omega_1 Q_1^{1/2}}{N_{s_{cu}}}\right)^{4/3} = 21.9 \text{ ft}$$

Then $H/\omega^2 D^2 =$ constant, so

$$H_2 = H_1 \left(\frac{\omega_2}{\omega_1}\right)^2 \left(\frac{D_2}{D_1}\right)^2 = 21.9 \text{ ft} \left(\frac{1750}{1170}\right)^2 (1)^2 = 49.0 \text{ ft} \quad\longleftarrow\quad \underline{\underline{H_2}}$$

The pump output power is $\mathscr{P}_1 = \rho g Q_1 H_1$, so at $\omega_1 = 1170$ rpm,

$$\mathscr{P}_1 = \frac{1.94 \text{ slug}}{\text{ft}^3} \times \frac{32.2 \text{ ft}}{\text{s}^2} \times \frac{300 \text{ gal}}{\text{min}} \times 21.9 \text{ ft} \times \frac{\text{ft}^3}{7.48 \text{ gal}} \times \frac{\text{min}}{60 \text{ s}} \times \frac{\text{lbf} \cdot \text{s}^2}{\text{slug} \cdot \text{ft}} \times \frac{\text{hp} \cdot \text{s}}{550 \text{ ft} \cdot \text{lbf}}$$

$$\mathscr{P}_1 = 1.66 \text{ hp}$$

But $\mathscr{P}/\rho \omega^3 D^5 =$ constant, so

$$\mathscr{P}_2 = \mathscr{P}_1 \left(\frac{\rho_2}{\rho_1}\right) \left(\frac{\omega_2}{\omega_1}\right)^3 \left(\frac{D_2}{D_1}\right)^5 = 1.66 \text{ hp}(1) \left(\frac{1750}{1170}\right)^3 (1)^5 = 5.55 \text{ hp} \quad\longleftarrow\quad \underline{\underline{\mathscr{P}_2}}$$

The required input power may be calculated as

$$\mathscr{P}_{\text{in}} = \frac{\mathscr{P}_2}{\eta} = \frac{5.55 \text{ hp}}{0.80} = 6.94 \text{ hp} \quad\longleftarrow\quad \underline{\underline{\mathscr{P}_{\text{in}}}}$$

Thus a 7.5-hp motor (the next larger standard size) probably would be specified.
The specific speed at $\omega_2 = 1750$ rpm is

$$N_{s_{cu}} = \frac{\omega Q^{1/2}}{H^{3/4}} = \frac{1750(449)^{1/2}}{(49.0)^{3/4}} = 2000 \quad\longleftarrow\quad \underline{\underline{N_{s_{cu}}}}$$

> This problem illustrates application of the pump "laws" and specific speed to scaling of performance data. Pump and fan "laws" are used widely in industry to scale performance curves for families of machines from a single performance curve, and to specify drive speed and power in machine applications.

Comments on Model Testing

While outlining the procedures involved in model testing, we have tried not to imply that testing is a simple task that automatically gives results that are easily interpreted, accurate, and complete. As in all experimental work, careful planning and execution are needed to obtain valid results. Models must be constructed carefully and accurately, and they must include sufficient detail in areas critical to the phenomenon being measured. Aerodynamic balances or other force measuring systems must be aligned carefully and calibrated correctly. Mounting methods must be devised that offer adequate rigidity and model motion, yet do not interfere with the phenomenon being measured. References [14–16] are considered the standard sources for details of wind tunnel test techniques. More specialized techniques for water impact testing are described in [17].

Experimental facilities must be designed and constructed carefully. The quality of flow in a wind tunnel must be documented. Flow in the test section should be as nearly uniform as possible (unless the desire is to simulate a special profile such as an atmospheric boundary layer), free from angularity, and with little swirl. If they interfere with measurements, boundary layers on tunnel walls must be removed by suction or energized by blowing. Pressure gradients in a wind tunnel test section may cause erroneous drag-force readings due to pressure variations in the flow direction.

Special facilities are needed for unusual conditions or for special test requirements, especially to achieve large Reynolds numbers. Many facilities are so large or specialized that they cannot be supported by university laboratories or private industry. A few examples include [18–20]:

- National Full-Scale Aerodynamics Complex, NASA, Ames Research Center, Moffett Field, California.
  Two wind tunnel test sections, powered by a 125,000 hp electric drive system:
  - 40 ft high and 80 ft wide (12 × 24 m) test section, maximum wind speed of 300 knots.
  - 80 ft high and 120 ft wide (24 × 36 m) test section, maximum wind speed of 137 knots.
- U.S. Navy, David Taylor Research Center, Carderock, Maryland.
  - High-Speed Towing Basin 2968 ft long, 21 ft wide, and 16 ft deep. Towing carriage can travel at up to 100 knots while measuring drag loads to 8000 lbf and side loads to 2000 lbf.
  - 36 in. variable-pressure water tunnel with 50 knot maximum test speed at pressures between 2 and 60 psia.
  - Anechoic Flow Facility with quiet, low-turbulence air flow in 8 ft square by 21 ft-long open-jet test section. Flow noise at maximum speed of 200 ft/s is less than that of conversational speech.
- U.S. Army Corps of Engineers, Sausalito, California.
  - San Francisco Bay and Delta Model with slightly more than 1 acre in area, 1:1000 horizontal scale and 1:100 vertical scale, 13,500 gpm of pumping capacity, use of fresh and salt water, and tide simulation.
- NASA, Langley Research Center, Hampton, Virginia.
  - National Transonic Facility (NTF) with cryogenic technology (temperatures as low as $-300°F$) to reduce gas viscosity, raising Reynolds number by a factor of 6, while halving drive power.

7-7 SUMMARY AND USEFUL EQUATIONS

In this chapter we have:

✓ Obtained dimensionless coefficients by nondimensionalizing the governing differential equations of a problem.

✓ Stated the Buckingham Pi theorem and used it to determine the independent and dependent dimensionless parameters from the physical parameters of a problem.

✓ Defined a number of important dimensionless groups: the Reynolds number, Euler number, cavitation number, Froude number, Weber number, and Mach number, and discussed their physical significance.

We have also explored some ideas behind modeling: geometric, kinematic, and dynamic similarity, incomplete modeling, and predicting prototype results from model tests.

Note: Most of the Useful Equations in the table below have a number of constraints or limitations—*be sure to refer to their page numbers for details!*

Useful Equations		
Reynolds number (inertia to viscous):	$Re = \dfrac{\rho VL}{\mu} = \dfrac{VL}{\nu}$ (7.11)	Page 280
Euler number (pressure to inertia):	$Eu = \dfrac{\Delta p}{\frac{1}{2}\rho V^2}$ (7.12)	Page 280
Cavitation number:	$Ca = \dfrac{p - p_v}{\frac{1}{2}\rho V^2}$ (7.13)	Page 280
Froude number (inertia to gravity):	$Fr = \dfrac{V}{\sqrt{gL}}$ (7.14)	Page 280
Weber number (inertia to surface tension):	$We = \dfrac{\rho V^2 L}{\sigma}$ (7.15)	Page 281
Mach number (inertia to compressibility):	$M = \dfrac{V}{c}$ (7.16)	Page 281
Centrifugal pump specific speed (in terms of head h):	$N_s = \dfrac{\omega Q^{1/2}}{h^{3/4}}$ (7.22a)	Page 291
Centrifugal pump specific speed (in terms of head H):	$N_{s_{cu}} = \dfrac{\omega Q^{1/2}}{H^{3/4}}$ (7.22b)	Page 291

REFERENCES

1. McNiell, Alexander, R., "How Dinosaurs Ran," *Scientific American*, 264, 4, April 1991, pp. 130–136.

2. Kline, S. J., *Similitude and Approximation Theory*. New York: McGraw-Hill, 1965.

3. Hansen, A. G., *Similarity Analysis of Boundary-Value Problems in Engineering*. Englewood Cliffs, NJ: Prentice-Hall, 1964.

4. Schlichting, H., *Boundary Layer Theory*, 7th ed. New York: McGraw-Hill, 1979.

5. Buckingham, E., "On Physically Similar Systems: Illustrations of the Use of Dimensional Equations," *Physical Review, 4*, 4, 1914, pp. 345–376.

6. Todd, L. H., "Resistance and Propulsion," in *Principles of Naval Architecture*, J. P. Comstock, ed. New York: Society of Naval Architects and Marine Engineers, 1967.

7. "Aerodynamic Flow Visualization Techniques and Procedures." Warrendale, PA: Society of Automotive Engineers, SAE Information Report HS J1566, January 1986.

8. Merzkirch, W., *Flow Visualization*, 2nd ed. New York: Academic Press, 1987.

9. "SAE Wind Tunnel Test Procedure for Trucks and Buses," *Recommended Practice* SAE J1252, Warrendale, PA: Society of Automotive Engineers, 1981.

10. Sedov, L. I., *Similarity and Dimensional Methods in Mechanics*. New York: Academic Press, 1959.

11. Birkhoff, G., *Hydrodynamics—A Study in Logic, Fact, and Similitude*, 2nd ed. Princeton, NJ: Princeton University Press, 1960.

12. Ipsen, D. C., *Units, Dimensions, and Dimensionless Numbers*. New York: McGraw-Hill, 1960.

13. Yalin, M. S., *Theory of Hydraulic Models*. New York: Macmillan, 1971.

14. Pankhurst, R. C., and D. W. Holder, *Wind-Tunnel Technique*. London: Pitman, 1965.

15. Rae, W. H., and A. Pope, *Low-Speed Wind Tunnel Testing*, 2nd ed. New York: Wiley-Interscience, 1984.

16. Pope, A., and K. L. Goin, *High-Speed Wind Tunnel Testing*. New York: Krieger, 1978.

17. Waugh, J. G., and G. W. Stubstad, *Hydroballistics Modeling*. San Diego, CA: U.S. Naval Undersea Center, *ca.* 1965.

18. Baals, D. W., and W. R. Corliss, *Wind Tunnels of NASA*. Washington, D.C.: National Aeronautics and Space Administration, SP-440, 1981.

19. Vincent, M., "The Naval Ship Research and Development Center." Carderock, MD: Naval Ship Research and Development Center, Report 3039 (Revised), November 1971.

20. Smith, B. E., P. T. Zell, and P. M. Shinoda, "Comparison of Model- and Full-Scale Wind-Tunnel Performance," *Journal of Aircraft*, 27, 3, March 1990, pp. 232–238.

[handwritten: dynamic sim $\Rightarrow \dfrac{V_m \cdot D_m}{V_m} = \dfrac{U_p D_p}{V_m}$]

PROBLEMS

Many of the Problems in this chapter involve obtaining the Π groups that characterize a problem. The *Excel* workbook used in Example 7.1 is useful for performing the computations involved. To avoid needless duplication, the mouse symbol will only be used next to Problems when it has an *additional* benefit (e.g., for graphing).

7.1 The slope of the free surface of a steady wave in one-dimensional flow in a shallow liquid layer is described by the equation

$$\frac{\partial h}{\partial x} = -\frac{u}{g}\frac{\partial u}{\partial x}$$

Use a length scale, L, and a velocity scale, V_0, to nondimensionalize this equation. Obtain the dimensionless groups that characterize this flow.

7.2 The propagation speed of small-amplitude surface waves in a region of uniform depth is given by

$$c^2 = \left(\frac{\sigma}{\rho}\frac{2\pi}{\lambda} + \frac{g\lambda}{2\pi}\right)\tanh\frac{2\pi h}{\lambda}$$

where h is depth of the undisturbed liquid and λ is wavelength. Using L as a characteristic length and V_0 as a characteristic velocity, obtain the dimensionless groups that characterize the equation.

7.3 The equation describing small amplitude vibration of a beam is

$$\rho A\frac{\partial^2 y}{\partial t^2} + EI\frac{\partial^4 y}{\partial x^4} = 0$$

where y is the beam deflection at location x and time t, ρ and E are the density and modulus of elasticity of the beam material, respectively, and A and I are the beam cross-section area and second moment of area, respectively. Use the beam length L, and frequency of vibration ω, to nondimensionalize this equation. Obtain the dimensionless groups that characterize the equation.

7.4 One-dimensional unsteady flow in a thin liquid layer is described by the equation

$$\frac{\partial u}{\partial t} + u\frac{\partial u}{\partial x} = -g\frac{\partial h}{\partial x}$$

Use a length scale, L, and a velocity scale, V_0, to nondimensionalize this equation. Obtain the dimensionless groups that characterize this flow.

7.5 By using order of magnitude analysis, the continuity and Navier–Stokes equations can be simplified to the Prandtl boundary-layer equations. For steady, incompressible, and two-dimensional flow, neglecting gravity, the result is

$$\frac{\partial u}{\partial x} + \frac{\partial v}{\partial y} = 0$$

$$u\frac{\partial u}{\partial x} + v\frac{\partial u}{\partial y} = -\frac{1}{\rho}\frac{\partial p}{\partial x} + v\frac{\partial^2 u}{\partial y^2}$$

Use L and V_0 as characteristic length and velocity, respectively. Nondimensionalize these equations and identify the similarity parameters that result.

7.6 In atmospheric studies the motion of the earth's atmosphere can sometimes be modeled with the equation

$$\frac{D\vec{V}}{Dt} + 2\vec{\Omega} \times \vec{V} = -\frac{1}{\rho}\nabla p$$

where $\vec{V}$ is the large-scale velocity of the atmosphere across the earth's surface, ∇p is the climatic pressure gradient, and $\vec{\Omega}$ is the earth's angular velocity. What is the meaning of the term $\vec{\Omega} \times \vec{V}$? Use the pressure difference, Δp, and typical length scale, L (which could, for example, be the magnitude of, and distance between, an atmospheric high and low, respectively), to nondimensionalize this equation. Obtain the dimensionless groups that characterize this flow.

7.7 The equation describing motion of fluid in a pipe due to an applied pressure gradient, when the flow starts from rest, is

$$\frac{\partial u}{\partial t} = -\frac{1}{\rho}\frac{\partial p}{\partial x} + \nu\left(\frac{\partial^2 u}{\partial r^2} + \frac{1}{r}\frac{\partial u}{\partial r}\right)$$

Use the average velocity $\overline{V}$, pressure drop Δp, pipe length L, and diameter D to nondimensionalize this equation. Obtain the dimensionless groups that characterize this flow.

7.8 An unsteady, two dimensional, compressible, inviscid flow can be described by the equation

$$\frac{\partial^2 \psi}{\partial t^2} + \frac{\partial}{\partial t}(u^2 + v^2) + (u^2 - c^2)\frac{\partial^2 \psi}{\partial x^2} + (v^2 - c^2)\frac{\partial^2 \psi}{\partial y^2} + 2uv\frac{\partial^2 \psi}{\partial x \partial y} = 0$$

where ψ is the stream function, u and v are the x and y components of velocity, respectively, c is the local speed of sound, and t is the time. Using L as a characteristic length and c_0 (the speed of sound at the stagnation point) to nondimensionalize this equation, obtain the dimensionless groups that characterize the equation.

7.9 At very low speeds, the drag on an object is independent of fluid density. Thus the drag force, F, on a small sphere is a function only of speed, V, fluid viscosity, μ, and sphere diameter, D. Use dimensional analysis to determine how the drag force F depends on the speed V.

7.10 At relatively high speeds the drag on an object is independent of fluid viscosity. Thus the aerodynamic drag force, F, on an automobile, is a function only of speed, V, air density ρ, and vehicle size, characterized by its frontal area A. Use dimensional analysis to determine how the drag force F depends on the speed V.

7.11 Experiments show that the pressure drop for flow through an orifice plate of diameter d mounted in a length of pipe of diameter D may be expressed as $\Delta p = p_1 - p_2 = f(\rho, \mu, \overline{V}, d, D)$. You are asked to organize some experimental data. Obtain the resulting dimensionless parameters.

7.12 The speed, V, of a free-surface wave in shallow liquid is a function of depth, D, density, ρ, gravity, g, and surface tension, σ. Use dimensional analysis to find the functional dependence of V on the other variables. Express V in the simplest form possible.

7.13 The wall shear stress, τ_w, in a boundary layer depends on distance from the leading edge of the body, x, the density, ρ, and viscosity, μ, of the fluid, and the freestream speed of the flow, U. Obtain the dimensionless groups and express the functional relationship among them.

7.14 The boundary-layer thickness, δ, on a smooth flat plate in an incompressible flow without pressure gradients depends on the freestream speed, U, the fluid density, ρ, the fluid viscosity, μ, and the distance from the leading edge of the plate, x. Express these variables in dimensionless form.

7.15 If an object is light enough it can be supported on the surface of a fluid by surface tension. Tests are to be done to investigate this phenomenon. The weight, W, supportable in this way depends on the object's perimeter, p, and the fluid's density, ρ, surface tension σ, and gravity, g. Determine the dimensionless parameters that characterize this problem.

7.16 The mean velocity, $\overline{u}$, for turbulent flow in a pipe or a boundary layer may be correlated using the wall shear stress, τ_w, distance from the wall, y, and the fluid properties, ρ and μ. Use

dimensional analysis to find one dimensionless parameter containing $\overline{u}$ and one containing y that are suitable for organizing experimental data. Show that the result may be written

$$\frac{\overline{u}}{u_*} = f\left(\frac{yu_*}{\nu}\right)$$

where $u_* = (\tau_w/\rho)^{1/2}$ is the *friction velocity*.

7.17 The speed, V, of a free-surface gravity wave in deep water is a function of wavelength, λ, depth, D, density, ρ, and acceleration of gravity, g. Use dimensional analysis to find the functional dependence of V on the other variables. Express V in the simplest form possible.

7.18 The torque, T, of a handheld automobile buffer is a function of rotational speed, ω, applied normal force, F, automobile surface roughness, e, buffing paste viscosity, μ, and surface tension, σ. Determine the dimensionless parameters that characterize this problem.

7.19 Measurements of the liquid height upstream from an obstruction placed in an open-channel flow can be used to determine volume flow rate. (Such obstructions, designed and calibrated to measure rate of open-channel flow, are called *weirs*.) Assume the volume flow rate, Q, over a weir is a function of upstream height, h, gravity, g, and channel width, b. Use dimensional analysis to find the functional dependence of Q on the other variables.

7.20 Capillary waves are formed on a liquid free surface as a result of surface tension. They have short wavelengths. The speed of a capillary wave depends on surface tension, σ, wavelength, λ, and liquid density, ρ. Use dimensional analysis to express wave speed as a function of these variables.

7.21 The load-carrying capacity, W, of a journal bearing is known to depend on its diameter, D, length, l, and clearance, c, in addition to its angular speed, ω, and lubricant viscosity, μ. Determine the dimensionless parameters that characterize this problem.

7.22 The time, t, for oil to drain out of a viscosity calibration container depends on the fluid viscosity, μ, and density, ρ, the orifice diameter, d, and gravity, g. Use dimensional analysis to find the functional dependence of t on the other variables. Express t in the simplest possible form.

7.23 The power, $\mathcal{P}$, used by a vacuum cleaner is to be correlated with the amount of suction provided (indicated by the pressure drop, Δp, below the ambient room pressure). It also depends on impeller diameter, D, and width, d, motor speed, ω, air density, ρ, and cleaner inlet and exit widths, d_i and d_o, respectively. Determine the dimensionless parameters that characterize this problem.

7.24 The power per unit cross-sectional area, E, transmitted by a sound wave is a function of wave speed, V, medium density, ρ, wave amplitude, r, and wave frequency, n. Determine, by dimensional analysis, the general form of the expression for E in terms of the other variables.

7.25 You are asked to find a set of dimensionless parameters to organize data from a laboratory experiment, in which a tank is drained through an orifice from initial liquid level h_0. The time, τ, to drain the tank depends on tank diameter, D, orifice diameter, d, acceleration of gravity, g, liquid density, ρ, and liquid viscosity, μ. How many dimensionless parameters will result? How many repeating variables must be selected to determine the dimensionless parameters? Obtain the Π parameter that contains the viscosity.

7.26 The power, $\mathcal{P}$, required to drive a fan is believed to depend on fluid density, ρ, volume flow rate, Q, impeller diameter, D, and angular velocity, ω. Use dimensional analysis to determine the dependence of $\mathcal{P}$ on the other variables.

7.27 A continuous belt moving vertically through a bath of viscous liquid drags a layer of liquid, of thickness h, along with it. The volume flow rate of liquid, Q, is assumed to depend on μ, ρ, g, h, and V, where V is the belt speed. Apply dimensional analysis to predict the form of dependence of Q on the other variables.

7.28 In a fluid mechanics laboratory experiment a tank of water, with diameter D, is drained from initial level h_0. The smoothly rounded drain hole has diameter d. Assume the mass flow rate from the tank is a function of h, D, d, g, ρ, and μ, where g is the acceleration of gravity and ρ and μ are fluid properties. Measured data are to be correlated in dimensionless form. Determine the number of dimensionless parameters that will result. Specify the number of repeating parameters that must be selected to determine the dimensionless parameters. Obtain the Π parameter that contains the viscosity.

7.29 Small droplets of liquid are formed when a liquid jet breaks up in spray and fuel injection processes. The resulting droplet diameter, d, is thought to depend on liquid density, viscosity, and surface tension, as well as jet speed, V, and diameter, D. How many dimensionless ratios are required to characterize this process? Determine these ratios.

7.30 The diameter, d, of the dots made by an ink jet printer depends on the ink viscosity, μ, density, ρ, and surface tension, σ, the nozzle diameter, D, the distance, L, of the nozzle from the paper surface, and the ink jet velocity, V. Use dimensional analysis to find the Π parameters that characterize the ink jet's behavior.

7.31 The sketch shows an air jet discharging vertically. Experiments show that a ball placed in the jet is suspended in a stable position. The equilibrium height of the ball in the jet is found to depend on D, d, V, ρ, μ, and W, where W is the weight of the ball. Dimensional analysis is suggested to correlate experimental data. Find the Π parameters that characterize this phenomenon.

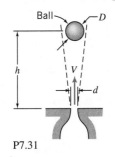

P7.31

7.32 The terminal speed V of shipping boxes sliding down an incline on a layer of air (injected through numerous pinholes in the incline surface) depends on the box mass, m, and base area, A, gravity, g, the incline angle, θ, the air viscosity, μ, and the air layer thickness, δ. Use dimensional analysis to find the Π parameters that characterize this phenomenon.

7.33 The diameter, d, of bubbles produced by a bubble-making toy depends on the soapy water viscosity, μ, density, ρ, and surface tension, σ, the ring diameter, D, and the pressure differential, Δp, generating the bubbles. Use dimensional analysis to find the Π parameters that characterize this phenomenon.

7.34 A washing machine agitator is to be designed. The power, $\mathcal{P}$, required for the agitator is to be correlated with the amount of water used (indicated by the depth, H, of the water). It also depends on the agitator diameter, D, height, h, maximum angular velocity, ω_{max}, and frequency of oscillations, f, and water density, ρ, and viscosity, μ. Determine the dimensionless parameters that characterize this problem.

7.35 The time, t, for a flywheel, with moment of inertia, I, to reach angular velocity, ω, from rest, depends on the applied torque, T, and the following flywheel bearing properties: the oil viscosity, μ, gap, δ, diameter, D, and length, L. Use dimensional analysis to find the Π parameters that characterize this phenomenon.

7.36 A large tank of liquid under pressure is drained through a smoothly contoured nozzle of area A. The mass flow rate is thought to depend on nozzle area, A, liquid density, ρ, difference in height between the liquid surface and nozzle, h, tank gage pressure, Δp, and gravitational acceleration, g. Determine how many independent Π parameters can be formed for this problem. Find the dimensionless parameters. State the functional relationship for the mass flow rate in terms of the dimensionless parameters.

7.37 The ventilation in the clubhouse on a cruise ship is insufficient to clear cigarette smoke (the ship is not yet completely smoke-free). Tests are to be done to see if a larger extractor fan will work. The concentration of smoke, c (particles per cubic meter) depends on the number of smokers, N, the pressure drop produced by the fan, Δp, the fan diameter, D, motor speed, ω, the particle and air densities, ρ_p, and ρ, respectively, gravity, g, and air viscosity, μ. Determine the dimensionless parameters that characterize this problem.

7.38 Spin plays an important role in the flight trajectory of golf, Ping-Pong, and tennis balls. Therefore, it is important to know the rate at which spin decreases for a ball in flight. The aerodynamic torque, T, acting on a ball in flight, is thought to depend on flight speed, V, air density, ρ, air viscosity, μ, ball diameter, D, spin rate (angular speed), ω, and diameter of the dimples on the ball, d. Determine the dimensionless parameters that result.

7.39 The power loss, $\mathcal{P}$, in a journal bearing depends on length, l, diameter, D, and clearance, c, of the bearing, in addition to its angular speed, ω. The lubricant viscosity and mean pressure are also important. Obtain the dimensionless parameters that characterize this problem. Determine the functional form of the dependence of $\mathcal{P}$ on these parameters.

7.40 The thrust of a marine propeller is to be measured during "open-water" tests at a variety of angular speeds and forward speeds ("speeds of advance"). The thrust, F_T, is thought to depend on water density, ρ, propeller diameter, D, speed of advance, V, acceleration of gravity, g, angular speed, ω, pressure in the liquid, p, and liquid viscosity, μ. Develop a set of dimensionless parameters to characterize the performance of the propeller. (One of the resulting parameters, gD/V^2, is known as the *Froude speed of advance*.)

7.41 In a fan-assisted convection oven, the heat transfer rate to a roast, $\dot{Q}$ (energy per unit time), is thought to depend on the specific heat of air, c_p, temperature difference, Θ, a length scale, L, air density, ρ, air viscosity, μ, and air speed, V. How many basic dimensions are included in these variables? Determine the number of Π parameters needed to characterize the oven. Evaluate the Π parameters.

7.42 The power, $\mathcal{P}$, required to drive a propeller is known to depend on the following variables: freestream speed, V, propeller diameter, D, angular speed, ω, fluid viscosity, μ, fluid density, ρ, and speed of sound in the fluid, c. How many dimensionless groups are required to characterize this situation? Obtain these dimensionless groups.

7.43 The rate dT/dt at which the temperature T at the center of a rice kernel falls during a food technology process is critical—too high a value leads to cracking of the kernel, and too low a value makes the process slow and costly. The rate depends on the rice specific heat, c, thermal conductivity, k, and size, L, as well as the cooling air specific heat, c_p, density, ρ, viscosity, μ, and speed, V. How many basic dimensions are included in these variables? Determine the Π parameters for this problem.

7.44 When a valve is closed suddenly in a pipe with flowing water, a water hammer pressure wave is set up. The very high pressures generated by such waves can damage the pipe. The maximum pressure, p_{max}, generated by water hammer is a function of liquid density, ρ, initial flow speed, U_0, and liquid bulk modulus, E_v. How many dimensionless groups are needed to characterize water hammer? Determine the functional relationship among the variables in terms of the necessary Π groups.

7.45 The fluid velocity u at any point in a boundary layer depends on the distance y of the point above the surface, the free-stream velocity U and free-stream velocity gradient dU/dx, the fluid kinematic viscosity v, and the boundary layer thickness δ. How many dimensionless groups are required to describe this problem? Find: (a) two Π groups by inspection, (b) one Π that is a standard fluid mechanics group, and (c) any remaining Π groups using the Buckingham Pi theorem.

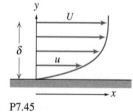

P7.45

7.46 An airship is to operate at 20 m/s in air at standard conditions. A model is constructed to $\frac{1}{20}$-scale and tested in a wind tunnel at the same air temperature to determine drag. What criterion should be considered to obtain dynamic similarity? If the model is tested at 75 m/s, what pressure should be used in the wind tunnel? If the model drag force is 250 N, what will be the drag of the prototype?

7.47 The designers of a large tethered pollution-sampling balloon wish to know what the drag will be on the balloon for the maximum anticipated wind speed of 5 m/s (the air is assumed to be at 20°C). A $\frac{1}{20}$-scale model is built for testing in water at 20°C. What water speed is required to model the prototype? At this speed the model drag is measured to be 2 kN. What will be the corresponding drag on the prototype?

7.48 An ocean-going vessel is to be powered by a rotating circular cylinder. Model tests are planned to estimate the power required to rotate the prototype cylinder. A dimensional analysis is needed to scale the power requirements from model test results

to the prototype. List the parameters that should be included in the dimensional analysis. Perform a dimensional analysis to identify the important dimensionless groups.

7.49 To match the Reynolds number in an air flow and a water flow using the same size model, which flow will require the higher flow speed? How much higher must it be?

7.50 Measurements of drag force are made on a model automobile in a towing tank filled with fresh water. The model length scale is $\frac{1}{5}$ that of the prototype. State the conditions required to ensure dynamic similarity between the model and prototype. Determine the fraction of the prototype speed in air at which the model test should be made in water to ensure dynamically similar conditions. Measurements made at various speeds show that the dimensionless force ratio becomes constant at model test speeds above $V_m = 4$ m/s. The drag force measured during a test at this speed is $F_{Dm} = 182$ N. Calculate the drag force expected on the prototype vehicle operating at 90 km/hr in air.

7.51 On a cruise ship, passengers complain about the noise emanating from the ship's propellers (probably due to turbulent flow effects between propeller and ship). You have been hired to find out the source of this noise. You will study the flow pattern around the propellers and have decided to use a 1:10 scale water tank. If the ship's propellers rotate at 125 rpm, estimate the model propeller rotation speed if a) the Froude number or b) the Reynolds number is the governing dimensionless group. Which is most likely to lead to the best modeling?

7.52 A $\frac{1}{5}$-scale model of a torpedo is tested in a wind tunnel to determine the drag force. The prototype operates in water, has 533 mm diameter, and is 6.7 m long. The desired operating speed of the prototype is 28 m/s. To avoid compressibility effects in the wind tunnel, the maximum speed is limited to 110 m/s. However, the pressure in the wind tunnel can be varied while holding the temperature constant at 20°C. At what minimum pressure should the wind tunnel be operated to achieve a dynamically similar test? At dynamically similar test conditions, the drag force on the model is measured as 618 N. Evaluate the drag force expected on the full-scale torpedo.

7.53 The drag of an airfoil at zero angle of attack is a function of density, viscosity, and velocity, in addition to a length parameter. A $\frac{1}{10}$-scale model of an airfoil was tested in a wind tunnel at a Reynolds number of 5.5×10^6, based on chord length. Test conditions in the wind tunnel air stream were 15°C and 10 atmospheres absolute pressure. The prototype airfoil has a chord length of 2 m, and it is to be flown in air at standard conditions. Determine the speed at which the wind tunnel model was tested, and the corresponding prototype speed.

7.54 Consider a smooth sphere, of diameter D, immersed in a fluid moving with speed V. The drag force on a 10-ft diameter weather balloon in air moving at 5 ft/s is to be calculated from test data. The test is to be performed in water using a 2-in. diameter model. Under dynamically similar conditions, the model drag force is measured as 0.85 lbf. Evaluate the model test speed and the drag force expected on the full-scale balloon.

7.55 An airplane wing, with chord length of 1.5 m and span of 9 m, is designed to move through standard air at a speed of 7.5 m/s. A $\frac{1}{10}$-scale model of this wing is to be tested in a water tunnel. What speed is necessary in the water tunnel to achieve dynamic similarity? What will be the ratio of forces measured in the model flow to those on the prototype wing?

7.56 The fluid dynamic characteristics of a golf ball are to be tested using a model in a wind tunnel. Dependent parameters are the drag force, F_D, and lift force, F_L, on the ball. The independent parameters should include angular speed, ω, and dimple depth, d. Determine suitable dimensionless parameters and express the functional dependence among them. A golf pro can hit a ball at $V = 240$ ft/s and $\omega = 9000$ rpm. To model these conditions in a wind tunnel with maximum speed of 80 ft/s, what diameter model should be used? How fast must the model rotate? (The diameter of a U.S. golf ball is 1.68 in.)

7.57 A water pump with impeller diameter 60 cm is to be designed to move 0.4 m^3/s when running at 800 rpm. Testing is performed on a $\frac{1}{2}$ scale model running at 2000 rpm using air (20°C) as the fluid. For similar conditions (neglecting Reynolds number effects), what will be the model flow rate? If the model draws 75 W, what will be the power requirement of the prototype?

7.58 A model test is performed to determine the flight characteristics of a Frisbee. Dependent parameters are drag force, F_D, and lift force, F_L. The independent parameters should include angular speed, ω, and roughness height, h. Determine suitable dimensionless parameters and express the functional dependence among them. The test (using air) on a $\frac{1}{4}$-scale model Frisbee is to be geometrically, kinematically, and dynamically similar to the prototype. The prototype values are $V_p = 5$ m/s and $\omega_p = 100$ rpm. What values of V_m and ω_m should be used?

7.59 A model hydrofoil is to be tested at 1:20 scale. The test speed is chosen to duplicate the Froude number corresponding to the 60 knot prototype speed. To model cavitation correctly, the cavitation number also must be duplicated. At what ambient pressure must the test be run? Water in the model test basin can be heated to 130°F, compared to 45°F for the prototype.

7.60 SAE 10W oil at 25°C flowing in a 25-mm diameter horizontal pipe, at an average speed of 1 m/s, produces a pressure drop of 450 kPa (gage) over a 150-m length. Water at 15°C flows through the same pipe under dynamically similar conditions. Using the results of Example 7.2, calculate the average speed of the water flow and the corresponding pressure drop.

7.61 In some speed ranges, vortices are shed from the rear of bluff cylinders placed across a flow. The vortices alternately leave the top and bottom of the cylinder, as shown, causing an alternating force normal to the freestream velocity. The vortex shedding frequency, f, is thought to depend on ρ, d, V, and μ. Use dimensional analysis to develop a functional relationship for f. Vortex shedding occurs in standard air on two cylinders with a diameter ratio of 2. Determine the velocity ratio for dynamic similarity, and the ratio of vortex shedding frequencies.

P7.61

7.62 A $\frac{1}{8}$-scale model of a tractor-trailer rig is tested in a pressurized wind tunnel. The rig width, height, and length are $W = 0.305$ m, $H = 0.476$ m, and $L = 2.48$ m, respectively. At wind speed $V = 75.0$ m/s, the model drag force is $F_D = 128$ N. (Air density in the tunnel is $\rho = 3.23$ kg/m^3.) Calculate the aerodynamic drag coefficient for the model. Compare the Reynolds numbers for the model test and for the prototype vehicle at 55 mph. Calculate the aerodynamic drag force on the prototype vehicle at a road speed of 55 mph into a headwind of 10 mph.

7.63 On a cruise ship, passengers complain about the amount of smoke that becomes entrained behind the cylindrical smoke stack. You have been hired to study the flow pattern around the stack, and have decided to use a 1:12.5 scale model of the 4.75 m smoke stack. What range of wind tunnel speeds could you use if the ship speed for which the problem occurs is 15 knots to 25 knots?

7.64 The aerodynamic behavior of a flying insect is to be investigated in a wind tunnel using a ten-times scale model. If the insect flaps its wings 50 times a second when flying at 4 ft/s, determine the wind tunnel air speed and wing oscillation frequency required for dynamic similarity. Do you expect that this would be a successful or practical model for generating an easily measurable wing lift? If not, can you suggest a different fluid (e.g., water, or air at a different pressure and/or temperature) that would produce a better modeling?

7.65 A model test of a tractor-trailer rig is performed in a wind tunnel. The drag force, F_D, is found to depend on frontal area, A, wind speed, V, air density, ρ, and air viscosity, μ. The model scale is 1:4; frontal area of the model is $A = 0.625$ m^2. Obtain a set of dimensionless parameters suitable to characterize the model test results. State the conditions required to obtain dynamic similarity between model and prototype flows. When tested at wind speed $V = 89.6$ m/s, in standard air, the measured drag force on the model was $F_D = 2.46$ kN. Assuming dynamic similarity, estimate the aerodynamic drag force on the full-scale vehicle at $V = 22.4$ m/s. Calculate the power needed to overcome this drag force if there is no wind.

7.66 Tests are performed on a 1:5 scale boat model. What must be the kinematic viscosity of the model fluid if friction and wave drag phenomena are to be correctly modeled? The full size boat will be used in a freshwater lake where the average water temperature is 10°C.

7.67 Your favorite professor likes mountain climbing, so there is always a possibility that the professor may fall into a crevasse in some glacier. If that happened today, and the professor was trapped in a slowly moving glacier, you are curious to know whether the professor would reappear at the downstream drop-off of the glacier during this academic year. Assuming ice is a Newtonian fluid with the density of glycerine but a million times as viscous, you decide to build a glycerin model and use dimensional analysis and similarity to estimate when the professor would reappear. Assume the real glacier is 15 m deep and is on a slope that falls 1.5 m in a horizontal distance of 1850 m. Develop the dimensionless parameters and conditions expected to govern dynamic similarity in this problem. If the model professor reappears in the laboratory after 9.6 hours, when should you return to the end of the real glacier to provide help to your favorite professor?

7.68 An automobile is to travel through standard air at 60 mph. To determine the pressure distribution, a $\frac{1}{5}$-scale model is to be tested in water. What factors must be considered to ensure kinematic similarity in the tests? Determine the water speed that should be used. What is the corresponding ratio of drag force between prototype and model flows? The lowest pressure coefficient is $C_p = -1.4$ at the location of the minimum static pressure on the surface. Estimate the minimum tunnel pressure required to avoid cavitation, if the onset of cavitation occurs at a cavitation number of 0.5.

7.69 A 1:30 scale model of a submarine is to be tested in a towing tank under two conditions: motion at the free surface and motion far below the free surface. The tests are performed in fresh water. On the surface, the submarine cruises at 20 knots. At what speed should the model be towed to ensure dynamic similarity? Far below the surface, the sub cruises at 0.5 knots. At what speed should the model be towed to ensure dynamic similarity? What must the drag of the model be multiplied by under each condition to give the drag of the full-scale submarine?

7.70 Consider water flow around a circular cylinder, of diameter D and length l. In addition to geometry, the drag force is known to depend on liquid speed, V, density, ρ, and viscosity, μ. Express drag force, F_D, in dimensionless form as a function of all relevant variables. The static pressure distribution on a circular cylinder, measured in the laboratory, can be expressed in terms of the dimensionless pressure coefficient; the lowest pressure coefficient is $C_p = -2.4$ at the location of the minimum static pressure on the cylinder surface. Estimate the maximum speed at which a cylinder could be towed in water at atmospheric pressure, without causing cavitation, if the onset of cavitation occurs at a cavitation number of 0.5.

7.71 A $\frac{1}{10}$-scale model of a tractor-trailer rig is tested in a wind tunnel. The model frontal area is $A_m = 0.1 \text{ m}^2$. When tested at $V_m = 75$ m/s in standard air, the measured drag force is $F_D = 350$ N. Evaluate the drag coefficient for the model conditions given. Assuming that the drag coefficient is the same for model and prototype, calculate the drag force on a prototype rig at a highway speed of 90 km/hr. Determine the air speed at which a model should be tested to ensure dynamically similar results if the prototype speed is 90 km/hr. Is this air speed practical? Why or why not?

7.72 A circular container, partially filled with water, is rotated about its axis at constant angular speed, ω. At any time, τ, from the start of rotation, the speed, V_θ, at distance r from the axis of rotation, was found to be a function of τ, ω, and the properties of the liquid. Write the dimensionless parameters that characterize this problem. If, in another experiment, honey is rotated in the same cylinder at the same angular speed, determine from your dimensionless parameters whether honey will attain steady motion as quickly as water. Explain why the Reynolds number would not be an important dimensionless parameter in scaling the steady-state motion of liquid in the container.

7.73 It is recommended in [9] that the frontal area of a model be less than 5 percent of the wind tunnel test section area and $Re = Vw/\nu > 2 \times 10^6$, where w is the model width. Further, the model height must be less than 30 percent of the test section height, and the maximum projected width of the model at maximum yaw (20°) must be less than 30 percent of the test section width. The maximum air speed should be less than 300 ft/s to avoid compressibility effects. A model of a tractor-trailer rig is to be tested in a wind tunnel that has a test section 1.5 ft high and 2 ft wide. The height, width, and length of the full-scale rig are 13 ft 6 in., 8 ft, and 65 ft, respectively. Evaluate the scale ratio of the largest model that meets the recommended criteria. Assess whether an adequate Reynolds number can be achieved in this test facility.

7.74 The power, $\mathscr{P}$, required to drive a fan is assumed to depend on fluid density, ρ, volume flow rate, Q, impeller diameter, D, and angular speed, ω. If a fan with $D_1 = 200$ mm delivers $Q_1 = 0.4 \text{ m}^3$/s of air at $\omega_1 = 2400$ rpm, what volume flow rate could be expected for a geometrically similar fan with $D_2 = 400$ mm at $\omega_2 = 1850$ rpm?

7.75 Over a certain range of air speeds, V, the lift, F_L, produced by a model of a complete aircraft in a wind tunnel depends on the air speed, air density, ρ, and a characteristic length (the wing base chord length, $c = 150$ mm). The following experimental data is obtained for air at standard atmospheric conditions:

V (m/s)	10	15	20	25	30	35	40	45	50
F_L (N)	2.2	4.8	8.7	13.3	19.6	26.5	34.5	43.8	54

Plot the lift versus speed curve. By using *Excel* to perform a trendline analysis on this curve, generate and plot data for the lift produced by the prototype, which has a wing base chord length of 5 m, over a speed range of 75 m/s to 250 m/s.

7.76 The pressure rise, Δp, of a liquid flowing steadily through a centrifugal pump depends on pump diameter, D, angular speed of the rotor, ω, volume flow rate, Q, and density, ρ. The table gives data for the prototype and for a geometrically similar model pump. For conditions corresponding to dynamic similarity between the model and prototype pumps, calculate the missing values in the table.

Variable	Prototype	Model
Δp		29.3 kPa
Q	1.25 m³/min	
ρ	800 kg/m³	999 kg/m³
ω	183 rad/s	367 rad/s
D	150 mm	50 mm

7.77 Tests are performed on a 1-m long ship model in a water tank. Results obtained (after doing some data analysis) are as follows:

V (m/s)	3	6	9	12	15	18	20
D_{Wave} (N)	0	0.125	0.5	1.5	3	4	5.5
$D_{Friction}$ (N)	0.1	0.35	0.75	1.25	2	2.75	3.25

The assumption is that wave drag modeling is done using the Froude number, and friction drag by the Reynolds number. The full size ship will be 50 m long when built. Estimate the total drag when it is cruising at 15 knots, and at 20 knots, in a freshwater lake.

7.78 A centrifugal water pump running at speed $\omega = 750$ rpm has the following data for flow rate Q and pressure head Δp:

Q (m³/hr)	0	100	150	200	250	300	325	350
Δp (kPa)	361	349	328	293	230	145	114	59

The pressure head Δp is a function of flow rate, Q, and speed, ω, and also impeller diameter, D, and water density, ρ. Plot the pressure head versus flow rate curve. Find the two Π parameters for this problem, and from the above data plot one against the other. By using *Excel* to perform a trendline analysis on this latter curve, generate and plot data for pressure head versus flow rate for impeller speeds of 500 rpm and 1000 rpm.

7.79 An axial-flow pump is required to deliver 0.75 m³/s of water at a head of 15 J/kg. The diameter of the rotor is 0.25 m, and it is to be driven at 500 rpm. The prototype is to be modeled on a small test apparatus having a 2.25 kW, 1000 rpm power supply. For similar performance between the prototype and the model, calculate the head, volume flow rate, and diameter of the model.

7.80 A model propeller 2 ft in diameter is tested in a wind tunnel. Air approaches the propeller at 150 ft/s when it rotates at 2000 rpm. The thrust and torque measured under these conditions are 25 lbf and 7.5 lbf·ft, respectively. A prototype 10 times as large as the model is to be built. At a dynamically similar operating point, the approach air speed is to be 400 ft/s. Calculate the speed, thrust, and torque of the prototype propeller under these conditions, neglecting the effect of viscosity but including density.

7.81 Consider again Problem 7.40. Experience shows that for ship-size propellers, viscous effects on scaling are small. Also, when cavitation is not present, the nondimensional parameter containing pressure can be ignored. Assume that torque, T, and power, $\mathscr{P}$, depend on the same parameters as thrust. For conditions under which effects of μ and p can be neglected, derive scaling "laws" for propellers, similar to the pump "laws" of Section 7-6, that relate thrust, torque, and power to the angular speed and diameter of the propeller.

7.82 Water drops are produced by a mechanism that it is believed follows the pattern $d_p = D(We)^{-3/5}$. In this formula, d_p is the drop size, D is proportional to a length scale, and We is the Weber number. In scaling up, if the large-scale characteristic length scale was increased by 10 and the large-scale velocity decreased by a factor of 4, how would the small- and large-scale drops differ from each other for the same material, for example, water?

7.83 Closed-circuit wind tunnels can produce higher speeds than open-circuit tunnels with the same power input because energy is

recovered in the diffuser downstream from the test section. The *kinetic energy ratio* is a figure of merit defined as the ratio of the kinetic energy flux in the test section to the drive power. Estimate the kinetic energy ratio for the 40 ft × 80 ft wind tunnel at NASA-Ames described on page 293.

7.84 A 1:16 model of a 20-m long truck is tested in a wind tunnel at a speed of 80 m/s, where the axial static pressure gradient is −1.2 mm of water per meter. The frontal area of the prototype is 10 m². Estimate the horizontal buoyancy correction for this situation. Express the correction as a fraction of the measured C_D, if $C_D = 0.85$.

7.85 A 1:16 model of a bus is tested in a wind tunnel in standard air. The model is 152 mm wide, 200 mm high, and 762 mm long. The measured drag force at 26.5 m/s wind speed is 6.09 N. The longitudinal pressure gradient in the wind tunnel test section is −11.8 N/m²/m. Estimate the correction that should be made to the measured drag force to correct for horizontal buoyancy caused by the pressure gradient in the test section. Calculate the drag coefficient for the model. Evaluate the aerodynamic drag force on the prototype at 100 km/hr on a calm day.

7.86 Frequently one observes a flag on a pole flapping in the wind. Explain why this occurs.

7.87 Explore the variation in wave propagation speed given by the equation of Problem 7.2 for a free-surface flow of water. Find the operating depth to minimize the speed of capillary waves (waves with small wavelength, also called ripples). First assume wavelength is much smaller than water depth. Then explore the effect of depth. What depth do you recommend for a water table used to visualize compressible-flow wave phenomena? What is the effect of reducing surface tension by adding a surfactant?

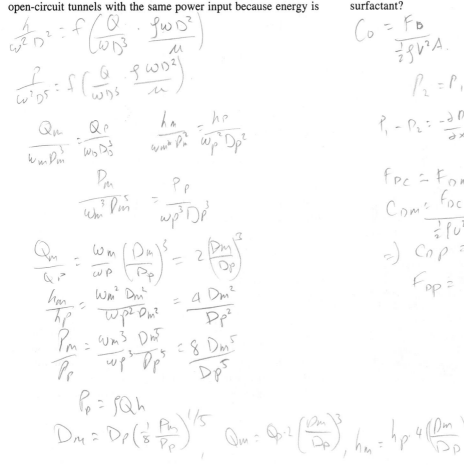

Internal Incompressible Viscous Flow

CASE STUDY

The Fountains at the Bellagio in Las Vegas

The fountains at the Bellagio in Las Vegas.

Any visitor to Las Vegas will be familiar with the water fountains at the Bellagio hotel. These are a set of high-powered water jets designed and built by the WET Design Company that are choreographed to vary in their strength and direction to selected pieces of music.

WET developed many innovations to make the fountains. Traditional fountains use pumps and pipes, which must be matched for optimum flow (one of the topics discussed in this chapter). Many of WET's designs use compressed air instead of water pumps, which allows energy to be continuously generated and accumulated, ready for instant output. This innovative use of compressed air allowed the fountains to become a reality—with the traditional systems of pipes or pumps, a fountain such as the Bellagio's would be impractical and expensive. For example, it would be difficult to obtain the 240-foot heights the fountains achieve without expensive, large, and noisy water pumps. The "Shooter" that WET developed works on the principle of introducing a large bubble of compressed air into the piping, which forces trapped water through a nozzle at high pressure. The ones installed at the Bellagio are able to shoot about 75 gallons per second of water over 240 feet

in the air. In addition to providing a spectacular effect, they require only about 1/10th the energy of traditional water pumps to produce the same effect. Other air-powered devices produce pulsing water jets, achieving a maximum height of 125 feet. In addition to their power, these innovations lead to a saving of 80 percent or more in energy costs and have project construction costs that are about 50 percent less than traditional pipe-pump fountains.

Flows completely bounded by solid surfaces are called internal flows. Thus internal flows include many important and practical flows such as those through pipes, ducts, nozzles, diffusers, sudden contractions and expansions, valves, and fittings.

Internal flows may be laminar or turbulent. Some laminar flow cases may be solved analytically. In the case of turbulent flow, analytical solutions are not possible, and we must rely heavily on semi-empirical theories and on experimental data. The nature of laminar and turbulent flows was discussed in Section 2-6. For internal flows, the flow regime (laminar or turbulent) is primarily a function of the Reynolds number.

In this chapter we will only consider incompressible flows; hence we will study the flow of liquids as well as gases that have negligible heat transfer and for which the Mach number $M < 0.3$; a value of $M = 0.3$ in air corresponds to a speed of approximately 100 m/s. Following a brief introduction, this chapter is divided into the following parts:

PART A: Part A discusses fully developed laminar flow of a Newtonian fluid between parallel plates and in a pipe. These two cases can be studied analytically.

PART B: Part B is about laminar and turbulent flows in pipes and ducts. The laminar flow analysis follows from Part A; the turbulent flow (which is the most common) is too complex to be analyzed, so experimental data will be used to develop solution techniques.

PART C: Part C is a discussion of methods of flow measurement.

8-1   INTRODUCTION

Laminar versus Turbulent Flow

As discussed previously in Section 2-6, the pipe flow regime (laminar or turbulent) is determined by the Reynolds number, $Re = \rho \overline{V} D/\mu$. One can demonstrate, by the classic Reynolds experiment,[1] the qualitative difference between laminar and turbulent flows. In this experiment water flows from a large reservoir through a clear tube. A thin filament of dye injected at the entrance to the tube allows visual observation of the flow. At low flow rates (low Reynolds numbers) the dye injected into the flow remains in a single filament along the tube; there is little dispersion of dye because the flow is laminar. A laminar flow is one in which the fluid flows in laminae, or layers; there is no macroscopic mixing of adjacent fluid layers.

As the flow rate through the tube is increased, the dye filament eventually becomes unstable and breaks up into a random motion throughout the tube; the line of dye is stretched and twisted into myriad entangled threads, and it quickly disperses throughout the entire flow field. This behavior of turbulent flow is caused by small,

[1]This experiment is demonstrated in the NCFMF video *Turbulence*. (See http://web.mit.edu/fluids/www/Shapiro/ncfmf.html for free online viewing of this film; it is old but good!)

high-frequency velocity fluctuations superimposed on the mean motion of a turbulent flow, as illustrated earlier in Fig. 2.15; the mixing of fluid particles from adjacent layers of fluid results in rapid dispersion of the dye. We mentioned in Chapter 2 an everyday example of the difference between laminar and turbulent flow—when you gently turn on the kitchen faucet (not aerated). For very low flow rates, the water exits smoothly (indicating laminar flow in the pipe); for higher flow rates, the flow is churned up (turbulent flow).

Under normal conditions, transition to turbulence occurs at $Re \approx 2300$ for flow in pipes: For water flow in a 1-in. diameter pipe, this corresponds to an average speed of 0.3 ft/s. With great care to maintain the flow free from disturbances, and with smooth surfaces, experiments have been able to maintain laminar flow in a pipe to a Reynolds number of about 100,000! However, most engineering flow situations are not so carefully controlled, so we will take $Re \approx 2300$ as our benchmark for transition to turbulence. Transition Reynolds numbers for some other flow situations are given in the Examples. Turbulence occurs when the viscous forces in the fluid are unable to damp out random fluctuations in the fluid motion (generated, for example, by roughness of a pipe wall), and the flow becomes chaotic. For example, a high viscosity fluid such as motor oil is able to damp out fluctuations more effectively than a low viscosity fluid such as water and therefore remains laminar even at relatively high flow rates. On the other hand, a high density fluid will generate significant inertia forces due to the random fluctuations in the motion, and this fluid will transition to turbulence at a relatively low flow rate.

The Entrance Region

Figure 8.1 illustrates laminar flow in the entrance region of a circular pipe. The flow has uniform velocity U_0 at the pipe entrance. Because of the no-slip condition at the wall, we know that the velocity at the wall must be zero along the entire length of the pipe. A boundary layer (Section 2-6) develops along the walls of the channel. The solid surface exerts a retarding shear force on the flow; thus the speed of the fluid in the neighborhood of the surface is reduced. At successive sections along the pipe in this entry region, the effect of the solid surface is felt farther out into the flow.

For incompressible flow, mass conservation requires that, as the speed close to the wall is reduced, the speed in the central frictionless region of the pipe must increase slightly to compensate; for this inviscid central region, then, the pressure (as indicated by the Bernoulli equation) must also drop somewhat.

Sufficiently far from the pipe entrance, the boundary layer developing on the pipe wall reaches the pipe centerline and the flow becomes entirely viscous. The velocity profile shape then changes slightly after the inviscid core disappears. When the profile shape no longer changes with increasing distance x, the flow is called *fully developed*. The distance downstream from the entrance to the location at which fully developed flow begins is called the *entrance length*. The actual shape of the fully developed velocity profile depends on whether the flow is laminar or turbulent. In Fig. 8.1 the profile is shown qualitatively for a laminar flow. Although the velocity profiles for some fully developed laminar flows can be obtained by simplifying the complete equations of motion from Chapter 5, turbulent flows cannot be so treated.

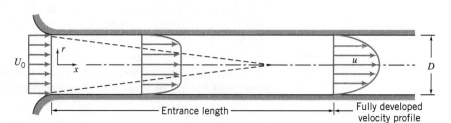

Fig. 8.1 Flow in the entrance region of a pipe.

For laminar flow, it turns out that entrance length, L, is a function of Reynolds number,

$$\frac{L}{D} \simeq 0.06 \frac{\rho \overline{V} D}{\mu} \tag{8.1}$$

where $\overline{V} \equiv Q/A$ is the average velocity (because flow rate $Q = A\overline{V} = AU_0$, we have $\overline{V} = U_0$). Laminar flow in a pipe may be expected only for Reynolds numbers less than 2300. Thus the entrance length for laminar pipe flow may be as long as

$$L \simeq 0.06 \, Re \, D \le (0.06)(2300) \, D = 138D$$

or nearly 140 pipe diameters. If the flow is turbulent, enhanced mixing among fluid layers[2] causes more rapid growth of the boundary layer. Experiments show that the mean velocity profile becomes fully developed within 25 to 40 pipe diameters from the entrance. However, the details of the turbulent motion may not be fully developed for 80 or more pipe diameters. We are now ready to study laminar internal flows (Part A), as well as laminar and turbulent flows in pipes and ducts (Part B). For these we will be focusing on what happens after the entrance region, i.e., fully developed flows.

PART A   FULLY DEVELOPED LAMINAR FLOW

In this section we consider a few classic examples of fully developed laminar flows. Our intent is to obtain detailed information about the velocity field because knowledge of the velocity field permits calculation of shear stress, pressure drop, and flow rate.

8-2

FULLY DEVELOPED LAMINAR FLOW BETWEEN INFINITE PARALLEL PLATES

The flow between parallel plates is appealing because the geometry is the simplest possible, but why *would* there be a flow at all? The answer is that flow could be generated by applying a pressure gradient parallel to the plates, or by moving one plate parallel with respect to the other, or by having a body force (e.g., gravity) parallel to the plates, or by a combination of these driving mechanisms. We will consider all of these possibilities.

Both Plates Stationary

Fluid in high-pressure hydraulic systems (such as the brake system of an automobile) often leaks through the annular gap between a piston and cylinder. For very small gaps (typically 0.005 mm or less), this flow field may be modeled as flow between infinite parallel plates, as indicated in the sketch of Fig. 8.2. To calculate the leakage flow rate, we must first determine the velocity field.

Let us consider the fully developed laminar flow between horizontal infinite parallel plates. The plates are separated by distance a, as shown in Fig. 8.3. The plates are considered infinite in the z direction, with no variation of any fluid property in this direction. The flow is also assumed to be steady and incompressible. Before starting our analysis, what do we know about the flow field? For one thing we know that the x component of velocity must be zero at both the upper and lower plates as a result of the no-slip condition at the wall. The boundary conditions are then

$$\text{at} \quad y = 0 \qquad u = 0$$

$$\text{at} \quad y = a \qquad u = 0$$

Since the flow is fully developed, the velocity cannot vary with x and, hence, depends on y only, so that $u = u(y)$. Furthermore, there is no component of velocity in either the y

---

[2]This mixing is illustrated extremely well in the introductory portion of the NCFMF video *Turbulence*. (See http://web.mit.edu/fluids/www/Shapiro/ncfmf.html for free online viewing of this film.)

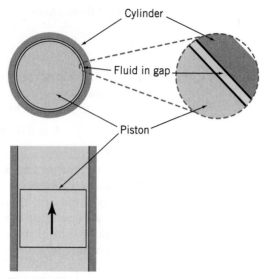

Fig. 8.2 Piston-cylinder approximated as parallel plates.

or z direction $(v = w = 0)$. In fact, for fully developed flow only the pressure can and will change (in a manner to be determined from the analysis) in the x direction.

This is an obvious case for using the Navier-Stokes equations in rectangular coordinates (Eqs. 5.27). Using the above assumptions, these equations can be greatly simplified and then solved using the boundary conditions (see Problem 8.16). In this section we will instead take a longer route—using a differential control volume—to bring out some important features of the fluid mechanics.

For our analysis we select a differential control volume of size $d\forall = dx\,dy\,dz$, and apply the x component of the momentum equation.

Basic equation:

$$
\overset{= 0(3)}{F_{S_x}} + \overset{= 0(1)}{\cancel{F_{B_x}}} = \cancel{\frac{\partial}{\partial t}} \int_{CV} u\,\rho\,d\forall + \int_{CS} u\,\rho\vec{V}\cdot d\vec{A} \tag{4.18a}
$$

Assumptions: (1) Steady flow (given)
(2) Fully developed flow (given)
(3) $F_{B_x} = 0$ (given)

The very nature of fully developed flow is that the velocity profile is the same at all locations along the flow; hence there is no change in momentum. Equation 4.18a then reduces to the simple result that the sum of the surface forces on the control volume is zero,

$$
F_{S_x} = 0 \tag{8.2}
$$

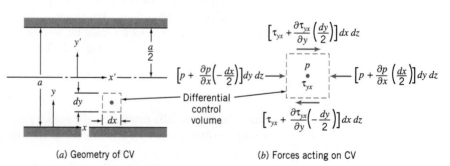

(a) Geometry of CV   (b) Forces acting on CV

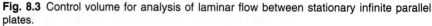

Fig. 8.3 Control volume for analysis of laminar flow between stationary infinite parallel plates.

The next step is to sum the forces acting on the control volume in the x direction. We recognize that normal forces (pressure forces) act on the left and right faces and tangential forces (shear forces) act on the top and bottom faces.

If the pressure at the center of the element is p, then the pressure force on the left face is

$$dF_L = \left(p - \frac{\partial p}{\partial x}\frac{dx}{2}\right)dy\,dz$$

and the pressure force on the right face is

$$dF_R = -\left(p + \frac{\partial p}{\partial x}\frac{dx}{2}\right)dy\,dz$$

If the shear stress at the center of the element is τ_{yx}, then the shear force on the bottom face is

$$dF_B = -\left(\tau_{yx} - \frac{d\tau_{yx}}{dy}\frac{dy}{2}\right)dx\,dz$$

and the shear force on the top face is

$$dF_T = \left(\tau_{yx} + \frac{d\tau_{yx}}{dy}\frac{dy}{2}\right)dx\,dz$$

Note that in expanding the shear stress, τ_{yx}, in a Taylor series about the center of the element, we have used the total derivative rather than a partial derivative. We did this because we recognized that τ_{yx} is only a function of y, since $u = u(y)$.

Using the four surface forces dF_L, dF_R, dF_B, and dF_T in Eq. 8.2, this equation simplifies to

$$\frac{\partial p}{\partial x} = \frac{d\tau_{yx}}{dy} \tag{8.3}$$

This equation states that because there is no change in momentum, the net pressure force (which is actually $-\partial p/\partial x$) balances the net friction force (which is actually $-d\tau_{yx}/dy$). Equation 8.3 has an interesting feature: The left side is at most a function of x only (this follows immediately from writing the y component of the momentum equation); the right side is at most a function of y only (the flow is fully developed, so it does not change with x). Hence, the only way the equation can be valid for all x and y is for each side to in fact be constant:

$$\frac{d\tau_{yx}}{dy} = \frac{\partial p}{\partial x} = \text{constant}$$

Integrating this equation, we obtain

$$\tau_{yx} = \left(\frac{\partial p}{\partial x}\right)y + c_1$$

which indicates that the shear stress varies linearly with y. We wish to find the velocity distribution. To do so, we need to relate the shear stress to the velocity field. For a Newtonian fluid we can use Eq. 2.15 because we have a one-dimensional flow [or we could have started with the full stress equation (Eq. 5.25a) and simplified],

$$\tau_{yx} = \mu\frac{du}{dy} \tag{2.15}$$

so we get

$$\mu\frac{du}{dy} = \left(\frac{\partial p}{\partial x}\right)y + c_1$$

Integrating again

$$u = \frac{1}{2\mu}\left(\frac{\partial p}{\partial x}\right)y^2 + \frac{c_1}{\mu}\,y + c_2 \tag{8.4}$$

It is interesting to note that if we had started with the Navier-Stokes equations (Eqs. 5.27) instead of using a differential control volume, after only a few steps (i.e., simplifying and integrating twice) we would have obtained Eq. 8.4 (see Problem 8.16). To evaluate the constants, c_1 and c_2, we must apply the boundary conditions. At $y = 0$, $u = 0$. Consequently, $c_2 = 0$. At $y = a$, $u = 0$. Hence

$$0 = \frac{1}{2\mu}\left(\frac{\partial p}{\partial x}\right)a^2 + \frac{c_1}{\mu}\,a$$

This gives

$$c_1 = -\frac{1}{2}\left(\frac{\partial p}{\partial x}\right)a$$

and hence,

$$u = \frac{1}{2\mu}\left(\frac{\partial p}{\partial x}\right)y^2 - \frac{1}{2\mu}\left(\frac{\partial p}{\partial x}\right)ay = \frac{a^2}{2\mu}\left(\frac{\partial p}{\partial x}\right)\left[\left(\frac{y}{a}\right)^2 - \left(\frac{y}{a}\right)\right] \tag{8.5}$$

At this point we have the velocity profile. This is key to finding other flow properties, as we next discuss.

Shear Stress Distribution

The shear stress distribution is given by

$$\tau_{yx} = \left(\frac{\partial p}{\partial x}\right)y + c_1 = \left(\frac{\partial p}{\partial x}\right)y - \frac{1}{2}\left(\frac{\partial p}{\partial x}\right)a = a\left(\frac{\partial p}{\partial x}\right)\left[\frac{y}{a} - \frac{1}{2}\right] \tag{8.6a}$$

Volume Flow Rate

The volume flow rate is given by

$$Q = \int_A \vec{V} \cdot d\vec{A}$$

For a depth l in the z direction,

$$Q = \int_0^a ul\,dy \qquad \text{or} \qquad \frac{Q}{l} = \int_0^a \frac{1}{2\mu}\left(\frac{\partial p}{\partial x}\right)(y^2 - ay)\,dy$$

Thus the volume flow rate per unit depth is given by

$$\frac{Q}{l} = -\frac{1}{12\mu}\left(\frac{\partial p}{\partial x}\right)a^3 \tag{8.6b}$$

Flow Rate as a Function of Pressure Drop

Since $\partial p/\partial x$ is constant, the pressure varies linearly with x and

$$\frac{\partial p}{\partial x} = \frac{p_2 - p_1}{L} = \frac{-\Delta p}{L}$$

Substituting into the expression for volume flow rate gives

$$\frac{Q}{l} = -\frac{1}{12\mu}\left[\frac{-\Delta p}{L}\right]a^3 = \frac{a^3 \Delta p}{12\mu L} \tag{8.6c}$$

Average Velocity

The average velocity magnitude, $\overline{V}$, is given by

$$\overline{V} = \frac{Q}{A} = -\frac{1}{12\mu}\left(\frac{\partial p}{\partial x}\right)\frac{a^3 l}{la} = -\frac{1}{12\mu}\left(\frac{\partial p}{\partial x}\right)a^2 \tag{8.6d}$$

Point of Maximum Velocity

To find the point of maximum velocity, we set du/dy equal to zero and solve for the corresponding y. From Eq. 8.5

$$\frac{du}{dy} = \frac{a^2}{2\mu}\left(\frac{\partial p}{\partial x}\right)\left[\frac{2y}{a^2} - \frac{1}{a}\right]$$

Thus,

$$\frac{du}{dy} = 0 \quad \text{at} \quad y = \frac{a}{2}$$

At

$$y = \frac{a}{2}, \quad u = u_{\max} = -\frac{1}{8\mu}\left(\frac{\partial p}{\partial x}\right)a^2 = \frac{3}{2}\overline{V} \tag{8.6e}$$

Transformation of Coordinates

In deriving the above relations, the origin of coordinates, $y = 0$, was taken at the bottom plate. We could just as easily have taken the origin at the centerline of the channel. If we denote the coordinates with origin at the channel centerline as x, y', the boundary conditions are $u = 0$ at $y' = \pm a/2$.

To obtain the velocity profile in terms of x, y', we substitute $y = y' + a/2$ into Eq. 8.5. The result is

$$u = \frac{a^2}{2\mu}\left(\frac{\partial p}{\partial x}\right)\left[\left(\frac{y'}{a}\right)^2 - \frac{1}{4}\right] \tag{8.7}$$

Equation 8.7 shows that the velocity profile for laminar flow between stationary parallel plates is parabolic, as shown in Fig. 8.4.

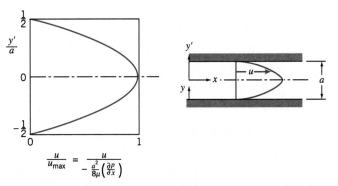

Fig. 8.4 Dimensionless velocity profile for fully developed laminar flow between infinite parallel plates.

Since all stresses were related to velocity gradients through Newton's law of viscosity, and the additional stresses that arise as a result of turbulent fluctuations have not been accounted for, *all of the results in this section are valid for laminar flow only*. Experiments show that laminar flow between stationary parallel plates becomes turbulent for Reynolds numbers (defined as $Re = \rho \overline{V} a / \mu$) greater than approximately 1400. Consequently, the Reynolds number should be checked after using Eqs. 8.6 to ensure a valid solution.

EXAMPLE 8.1   Leakage Flow Past a Piston

A hydraulic system operates at a gage pressure of 20 MPa and 55°C. The hydraulic fluid is SAE 10W oil. A control valve consists of a piston 25 mm in diameter, fitted to a cylinder with a mean radial clearance of 0.005 mm. Determine the leakage flow rate if the gage pressure on the low-pressure side of the piston is 1.0 MPa. (The piston is 15 mm long.)

GIVEN: Flow of hydraulic oil between piston and cylinder, as shown. Fluid is SAE 10W oil at 55°C.

FIND: Leakage flow rate, Q.

SOLUTION:

The gap width is very small, so the flow may be modeled as flow between parallel plates. Equation 8.6c may be applied.

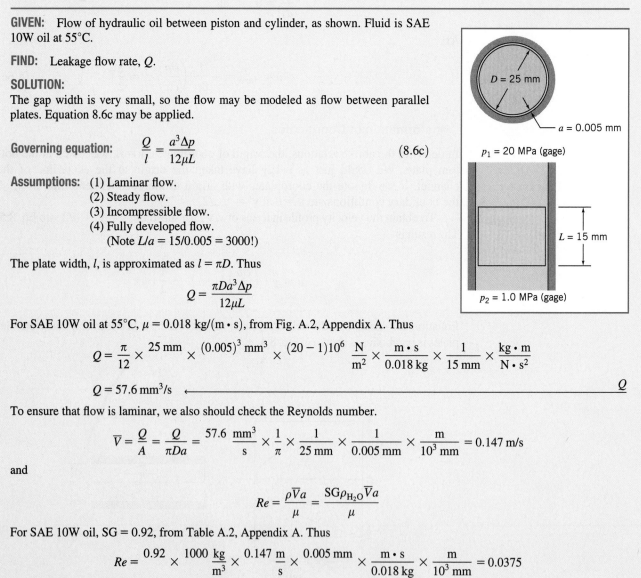

Governing equation: $\dfrac{Q}{l} = \dfrac{a^3 \Delta p}{12 \mu L}$ (8.6c)

Assumptions: (1) Laminar flow.
(2) Steady flow.
(3) Incompressible flow.
(4) Fully developed flow.
(Note $L/a = 15/0.005 = 3000!$)

The plate width, l, is approximated as $l = \pi D$. Thus

$$Q = \frac{\pi D a^3 \Delta p}{12 \mu L}$$

For SAE 10W oil at 55°C, $\mu = 0.018$ kg/(m · s), from Fig. A.2, Appendix A. Thus

$$Q = \frac{\pi}{12} \times 25 \text{ mm} \times (0.005)^3 \text{ mm}^3 \times (20-1)10^6 \frac{\text{N}}{\text{m}^2} \times \frac{\text{m} \cdot \text{s}}{0.018 \text{ kg}} \times \frac{1}{15 \text{ mm}} \times \frac{\text{kg} \cdot \text{m}}{\text{N} \cdot \text{s}^2}$$

$$Q = 57.6 \text{ mm}^3/\text{s} \longleftarrow \hspace{6cm} Q$$

To ensure that flow is laminar, we also should check the Reynolds number.

$$\overline{V} = \frac{Q}{A} = \frac{Q}{\pi D a} = 57.6 \frac{\text{mm}^3}{\text{s}} \times \frac{1}{\pi} \times \frac{1}{25 \text{ mm}} \times \frac{1}{0.005 \text{ mm}} \times \frac{\text{m}}{10^3 \text{ mm}} = 0.147 \text{ m/s}$$

and

$$Re = \frac{\rho \overline{V} a}{\mu} = \frac{\text{SG} \rho_{\text{H}_2\text{O}} \overline{V} a}{\mu}$$

For SAE 10W oil, SG = 0.92, from Table A.2, Appendix A. Thus

$$Re = 0.92 \times 1000 \frac{\text{kg}}{\text{m}^3} \times 0.147 \frac{\text{m}}{\text{s}} \times 0.005 \text{ mm} \times \frac{\text{m} \cdot \text{s}}{0.018 \text{ kg}} \times \frac{\text{m}}{10^3 \text{ mm}} = 0.0375$$

Thus flow is surely laminar, since $Re \ll 1400$.

Upper Plate Moving with Constant Speed, *U*

The second basic way to generate flow between infinite parallel plates is to have one plate move parallel to the other, either with or without an applied pressure gradient. We will next analyze this problem for the case of laminar flow.

Such a flow commonly occurs, for example, in a journal bearing (a commonly used type of bearing, e.g., the main crankshaft bearings in the engine of an automobile). In such a bearing, an inner cylinder, the journal, rotates inside a stationary member. At light loads, the centers of the two members essentially coincide, and the small clearance gap is symmetric. Since the gap is small, it is reasonable to "unfold" the bearing and to model the flow field as flow between infinite parallel plates, as indicated in the sketch of Fig. 8.5.

Let us now consider a case where the upper plate is moving to the right with constant speed, *U*. All we have done in going from a stationary upper plate to a moving upper plate is to change one of the boundary conditions. The boundary conditions for the moving plate case are

$$u = 0 \qquad \text{at} \qquad y = 0$$
$$u = U \qquad \text{at} \qquad y = a$$

Since only the boundary conditions have changed, there is no need to repeat the entire analysis of the previous section. The analysis leading to Eq. 8.4 is equally valid for the moving plate case. Thus the velocity distribution is given by

$$u = \frac{1}{2\mu}\left(\frac{\partial p}{\partial x}\right)y^2 + \frac{c_1}{\mu}\,y + c_2 \qquad (8.4)$$

and our only task is to evaluate constants c_1 and c_2 by using the appropriate boundary conditions. [Note once again that using the full Navier-Stokes equations (Eqs. 5.27) would have led very quickly to Eq. 8.4.]

At $y = 0$, $u = 0$. Consequently, $c_2 = 0$.

At $y = a$, $u = U$. Consequently,

$$U = \frac{1}{2\mu}\left(\frac{\partial p}{\partial x}\right)a^2 + \frac{c_1}{\mu}\,a \qquad \text{and thus} \qquad c_1 = \frac{U\mu}{a} - \frac{1}{2}\left(\frac{\partial p}{\partial x}\right)a$$

Hence,

$$u = \frac{1}{2\mu}\left(\frac{\partial p}{\partial x}\right)y^2 + \frac{Uy}{a} - \frac{1}{2\mu}\left(\frac{\partial p}{\partial x}\right)ay = \frac{Uy}{a} + \frac{1}{2\mu}\left(\frac{\partial p}{\partial x}\right)(y^2 - ay)$$

$$u = \frac{Uy}{a} + \frac{a^2}{2\mu}\left(\frac{\partial p}{\partial x}\right)\left[\left(\frac{y}{a}\right)^2 - \left(\frac{y}{a}\right)\right] \qquad (8.8)$$

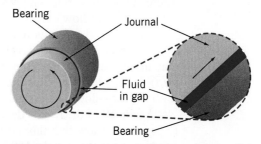

Fig. 8.5 Journal bearing approximated as parallel plates.

It is reassuring to note that Eq. 8.8 reduces to Eq. 8.5 for a stationary upper plate (set $U = 0$). From Eq. 8.8, for zero pressure gradient (for $\partial p/\partial x = 0$) the velocity varies linearly with y. This was the case treated earlier in Chapter 2; this linear profile is called a *Couette* flow, after a 19th-century physicist.

We can obtain additional information about the flow from the velocity distribution of Eq. 8.8.

Shear Stress Distribution

The shear stress distribution is given by $\tau_{yx} = \mu(du/dy)$,

$$\tau_{yx} = \mu \frac{U}{a} + \frac{a^2}{2}\left(\frac{\partial p}{\partial x}\right)\left[\frac{2y}{a^2} - \frac{1}{a}\right] = \mu \frac{U}{a} + a\left(\frac{\partial p}{\partial x}\right)\left[\frac{y}{a} - \frac{1}{2}\right] \qquad (8.9a)$$

Volume Flow Rate

The volume flow rate is given by $Q = \int_A \vec{V} \cdot d\vec{A}$. For depth l in the z direction

$$Q = \int_0^a ul\,dy \qquad \text{or} \qquad \frac{Q}{l} = \int_0^a \left[\frac{Uy}{a} + \frac{1}{2\mu}\left(\frac{\partial p}{\partial x}\right)(y^2 - ay)\right]dy$$

Thus the volume flow rate per unit depth is given by

$$\frac{Q}{l} = \frac{Ua}{2} - \frac{1}{12\mu}\left(\frac{\partial p}{\partial x}\right)a^3 \qquad (8.9b)$$

Average Velocity

The average velocity magnitude, $\overline{V}$, is given by

$$\overline{V} = \frac{Q}{A} = l\left[\frac{Ua}{2} - \frac{1}{12\mu}\left(\frac{\partial p}{\partial x}\right)a^3\right]\bigg/la = \frac{U}{2} - \frac{1}{12\mu}\left(\frac{\partial p}{\partial x}\right)a^2 \qquad (8.9c)$$

Point of Maximum Velocity

To find the point of maximum velocity, we set du/dy equal to zero and solve for the corresponding y. From Eq. 8.8

$$\frac{du}{dy} = \frac{U}{a} + \frac{a^2}{2\mu}\left(\frac{\partial p}{\partial x}\right)\left[\frac{2y}{a^2} - \frac{1}{a}\right] = \frac{U}{a} + \frac{a}{2\mu}\left(\frac{\partial p}{\partial x}\right)\left[2\left(\frac{y}{a}\right) - 1\right]$$

Thus,

$$\frac{du}{dy} = 0 \qquad \text{at} \qquad y = \frac{a}{2} - \frac{U/a}{(1/\mu)(\partial p/\partial x)}$$

There is no simple relation between the maximum velocity, u_{max}, and the mean velocity, $\overline{V}$, for this flow case.

Equation 8.8 suggests that the velocity profile may be treated as a combination of a linear and a parabolic velocity profile; the last term in Eq. 8.8 is identical to that in Eq. 8.5. The result is a family of velocity profiles, depending on U and $(1/\mu)(\partial p/\partial x)$; three profiles are sketched in Fig. 8.6. (As shown in Fig. 8.6, some reverse flow—flow in the negative x direction—can occur when $\partial p/\partial x > 0$.)

Again, all of the results developed in this section are valid for laminar flow only. Experiments show that this flow becomes turbulent (for $\partial p/\partial x = 0$) at a Reynolds number of approximately 1500, where $Re = \rho Ua/\mu$ for this flow case. Not much information is available for the case where the pressure gradient is not zero.

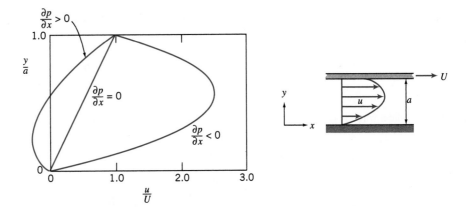

Fig. 8.6 Dimensionless velocity profile for fully developed laminar flow between infinite parallel plates: upper plate moving with constant speed, *U*.

EXAMPLE 8.2 Torque and Power in a Journal Bearing

A crankshaft journal bearing in an automobile engine is lubricated by SAE 30 oil at 210°F. The bearing diameter is 3 in., the diametral clearance is 0.0025 in., and the shaft rotates at 3600 rpm; it is 1.25 in. long. The bearing is under no load, so the clearance is symmetric. Determine the torque required to turn the journal and the power dissipated.

GIVEN: Journal bearing, as shown. Note that the gap width, *a*, is *half* the diametral clearance. Lubricant is SAE 30 oil at 210°F. Speed is 3600 rpm.

FIND: (a) Torque, *T*.
(b) Power dissipated.

$L = 1.25$ in. $D = 3$ in. $a = \dfrac{0.0025}{2}$ in. ω

SOLUTION:

Torque on the journal is caused by viscous shear in the oil film. The gap width is small, so the flow may be modeled as flow between infinite parallel plates:

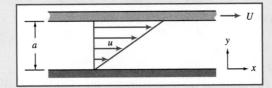

Governing equation:
$$\tau_{yx} = \mu \frac{U}{a} + a \overbrace{\left(\frac{\partial p}{\partial x}\right)}^{=\,0(6)}\left[\frac{y}{a} - \frac{1}{2}\right] \qquad (8.9a)$$

Assumptions:
(1) Laminar flow.
(2) Steady flow.
(3) Incompressible flow.
(4) Fully developed flow.
(5) Infinite width ($L/a = 1.25/0.00125 = 1000$, so this is a reasonable assumption).
(6) $\partial p/\partial x = 0$ (flow is symmetric in the actual bearing at no load).

Then

$$\tau_{yx} = \mu \frac{U}{a} = \mu \frac{\omega R}{a} = \mu \frac{\omega D}{2a}$$

For SAE 30 oil at 210°F (99°C), $\mu = 9.6 \times 10^{-3}$ N · s/m^2 (2.01×10^{-4} lbf · s/ft^2), from Fig. A.2, Appendix A. Thus,

$$\tau_{yx} = \frac{2.01 \times 10^{-4}}{\text{ft}^2} \frac{\text{lbf} \cdot \text{s}}{} \times \frac{3600}{\text{min}} \frac{\text{rev}}{} \times \frac{2\pi}{\text{rev}} \frac{\text{rad}}{} \times \frac{\text{min}}{60 \text{ s}} \times 3 \text{ in.} \times \frac{1}{2} \times \frac{1}{0.00125 \text{ in.}}$$

$$\tau_{yx} = 90.9 \text{ lbf/ft}^2$$

The total shear force is given by the shear stress times the area. It is applied to the journal surface. Therefore, for the torque

$$T = FR = \tau_{yx}\pi DLR = \frac{\pi}{2}\tau_{yx}D^2L$$

$$= \frac{\pi}{2} \times 90.9 \frac{\text{lbf}}{\text{ft}^2} \times (3)^2 \text{ in.}^2 \times \frac{\text{ft}^2}{144 \text{ in.}^2} \times 1.25 \text{ in.}$$

$$T = 11.2 \text{ in.} \cdot \text{lbf} \quad\longleftarrow\rule{6cm}{0.4pt} \hfill T$$

The power dissipated in the bearing is

$$\dot{W} = FU = FR\omega = T\omega$$

$$= 11.2 \text{ in.} \cdot \text{lbf} \times \frac{3600}{\text{min}} \frac{\text{rev}}{} \times \frac{\text{min}}{60 \text{ s}} \times \frac{2\pi}{\text{rev}} \frac{\text{rad}}{} \times \frac{\text{ft}}{12 \text{ in.}} \times \frac{\text{hp} \cdot \text{s}}{550 \text{ ft} \cdot \text{lbf}}$$

$$\dot{W} = 0.640 \text{ hp} \quad\longleftarrow\rule{6cm}{0.4pt} \hfill \dot{W}$$

To ensure laminar flow, check the Reynolds number.

$$Re = \frac{\rho U a}{\mu} = \frac{\text{SG}\rho_{\text{H}_2\text{O}} U a}{\mu} = \frac{\text{SG}\rho_{\text{H}_2\text{O}}\omega R a}{\mu}$$

Assume, as an approximation, the specific gravity of SAE 30 oil is the same as that of SAE 10W oil. From Table A.2, Appendix A, SG = 0.92. Thus

$$Re = 0.92 \times 1.94 \frac{\text{slug}}{\text{ft}^3} \times \frac{(3600)2\pi}{60} \frac{\text{rad}}{\text{s}} \times 1.5 \text{ in.} \times 0.00125 \text{ in.}$$

$$\times \frac{\text{ft}^2}{2.01 \times 10^{-4} \text{ lbf} \cdot \text{s}} \times \frac{\text{ft}^2}{144 \text{ in.}^2} \times \frac{\text{lbf} \cdot \text{s}^2}{\text{slug} \cdot \text{ft}}$$

$$Re = 43.6$$

Therefore, the flow is laminar, since $Re \ll 1500$.

> In this problem we approximated the circular-streamline flow in a small annular gap as a linear flow between infinite parallel plates. As we saw in Example 5.10, for the small value of the gap width a to radius R ratio a/R (in this problem <1%), the error in shear stress is about $\frac{1}{2}$ of this ratio. Hence, the error introduced is insignificant—much less than the uncertainty associated with obtaining a viscosity for the oil.

We have seen how steady, one-dimensional laminar flows between two plates can be generated by applying a pressure gradient, by moving one plate with respect to the other, or by having both driving mechanisms present. To finish our discussion of this type of flow, Example 8.3 examines a *gravity-driven* steady, one-dimensional laminar flow down a vertical wall. Once again, the direct approach would be to start with the two-dimensional rectangular coordinate form of the Navier-Stokes equations (Eqs. 5.27; see Problem 8.36); instead we will use a differential control volume.

EXAMPLE 8.3   Laminar Film on a Vertical Wall

A viscous, incompressible, Newtonian liquid flows in steady, laminar flow down a vertical wall. The thickness, δ, of the liquid film is constant. Since the liquid free surface is exposed to atmospheric pressure, there is no pressure gradient. For this gravity-driven flow, apply the momentum equation to differential control volume $dx\,dy\,dz$ to derive the velocity distribution in the liquid film.

GIVEN: Fully developed laminar flow of incompressible, Newtonian liquid down a vertical wall; thickness, δ, of the liquid film is constant and $\partial p / \partial x = 0$.

FIND: Expression for the velocity distribution in the film.

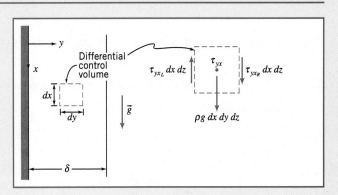

SOLUTION:

The x component of the momentum equation for a control volume is

$$F_{S_x} + F_{B_x} = \frac{\partial}{\partial t} \int_{CV} u\,\rho\,d\mathcal{V} + \int_{CS} u\,\rho\vec{V} \cdot d\vec{A} \qquad (4.18a)$$

Under the conditions given we are dealing with a steady, incompressible, fully developed laminar flow.

For steady flow, $\dfrac{\partial}{\partial t} \displaystyle\int_{CV} u\,\rho\,d\mathcal{V} = 0$

For fully developed flow, $\displaystyle\int_{CS} u\,\rho\vec{V} \cdot d\vec{A} = 0$

Thus the momentum equation for the present case reduces to

$$F_{S_x} + F_{B_x} = 0$$

The body force, F_{B_x}, is given by $F_{B_x} = \rho g\,d\mathcal{V} = \rho g\,dx\,dy\,dz$. The only surface forces acting on the differential control volume are shear forces on the vertical surfaces. (Since we have a free-surface flow, with straight streamlines, the pressure is atmospheric throughout; no net pressure forces act on the control volume.)

   If the shear stress at the center of the differential control volume is τ_{yx}, then,

$$\text{shear stress on left face is } \tau_{yx_L} = \left(\tau_{yx} - \frac{d\tau_{yx}}{dy}\,\frac{dy}{2} \right),$$

and

$$\text{shear stress on right face is } \tau_{yx_R} = \left(\tau_{yx} + \frac{d\tau_{yx}}{dy}\,\frac{dy}{2} \right)$$

The direction of the shear stress vectors is taken consistent with the sign convention of Section 2-3. Thus on the left face, a minus y surface, τ_{yx_L} acts upward, and on the right face, a plus y surface, τ_{yx_R} acts downward.

   The surface forces are obtained by multiplying each shear stress by the area over which it acts. Substituting into $F_{S_x} + F_{B_x} = 0$, we obtain

$$-\tau_{yx_L}\,dx\,dz + \tau_{yx_R}\,dx\,dz + \rho g\,dx\,dy\,dz = 0$$

or

$$-\left(\tau_{yx} - \frac{d\tau_{yx}}{dy}\,\frac{dy}{2} \right) dx\,dz + \left(\tau_{yx} + \frac{d\tau_{yx}}{dy}\,\frac{dy}{2} \right) dx\,dz + \rho g\,dx\,dy\,dz = 0$$

Simplifying gives

$$\frac{d\tau_{yx}}{dy} + \rho g = 0 \quad \text{or} \quad \frac{d\tau_{yx}}{dy} = -\rho g$$

Since

$$\tau_{yx} = \mu \frac{du}{dy} \quad \text{then} \quad \mu \frac{d^2 u}{dy^2} = -\rho g \quad \text{and} \quad \frac{d^2 u}{dy^2} = -\frac{\rho g}{\mu}$$

Integrating with respect to y gives

$$\frac{du}{dy} = -\frac{\rho g}{\mu}y + c_1$$

Integrating again, we obtain

$$u = -\frac{\rho g}{\mu}\frac{y^2}{2} + c_1 y + c_2$$

To evaluate constants c_1 and c_2, we apply appropriate boundary conditions:

(i) $y = 0$, $u = 0$ (no-slip)

(ii) $y = \delta$, $\dfrac{du}{dy} = 0$ (neglect air resistance, i.e., assume zero shear stress at free surface)

From boundary condition (i), $c_2 = 0$

From boundary condition (ii), $0 = -\dfrac{\rho g}{\mu}\delta + c_1$ or $c_1 = \dfrac{\rho g}{\mu}\delta$

Hence,

$$u = -\frac{\rho g}{\mu}\frac{y^2}{2} + \frac{\rho g}{\mu}\delta y \quad \text{or} \quad u = \frac{\rho g}{\mu}\delta^2\left[\left(\frac{y}{\delta}\right) - \frac{1}{2}\left(\frac{y}{\delta}\right)^2\right] \qquad\qquad u(y)$$

Using the velocity profile it can be shown that:

$$\text{the volume flow rate is } Q/l = \frac{\rho g}{3\mu}\delta^3$$

$$\text{the maximum velocity is } U_{\max} = \frac{\rho g}{2\mu}\delta^2$$

$$\text{the average velocity is } \overline{V} = \frac{\rho g}{3\mu}\delta^2$$

Flow in the liquid film is laminar for $Re = \overline{V}\delta/\nu \leq 1000$ [1].

> Notes:
> ✓ This problem is a special case ($\theta = 90°$) of the inclined plate flow analyzed in Example 5.9 that we solved using the Navier-Stokes equations.
> ✓ This problem and Example 5.9 demonstrate that use of the differential control volume approach or the Navier-Stokes equations, leads to the same result.

8-3 FULLY DEVELOPED LAMINAR FLOW IN A PIPE

As a final example of fully developed laminar flow, let us consider fully developed laminar flow in a pipe. Here the flow is axisymmetric. Consequently it is most convenient to work in cylindrical coordinates. This is yet another case where we could use the Navier-Stokes equations, this time in cylindrical coordinates (Eqs. B.3). Instead we will again take the longer route—using a differential control volume—to bring out some important features of the fluid mechanics. The development will be very similar to that for parallel plates in the previous section; cylindrical coordinates just make the analysis a little trickier mathematically. Since the flow is axisymmetric, the control volume will be a differential annulus, as shown in Fig. 8.7. The control volume length is dx and its thickness is dr.

For a fully developed steady flow, the x component of the momentum equation (Eq. 4.18a), when applied to the differential control volume, once again reduces to

$$F_{S_x} = 0$$

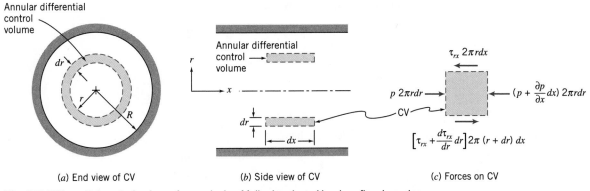

Fig. 8.7 Differential control volume for analysis of fully developed laminar flow in a pipe.

The next step is to sum the forces acting on the control volume in the x direction. We know that normal forces (pressure forces) act on the left and right ends of the control volume, and that tangential forces (shear forces) act on the inner and outer cylindrical surfaces.

If the pressure at the left face of the control volume is p, then the pressure force on the left end is

$$dF_L = p2\pi r\, dr$$

The pressure force on the right end is

$$dF_R = -\left(p + \frac{\partial p}{\partial x}\, dx\right) 2\pi r\, dr$$

If the shear stress at the inner surface of the annular control volume is τ_{rx}, then the shear force on the inner cylindrical surface is

$$dF_I = -\tau_{rx}2\pi r\, dx$$

The shear force on the outer cylindrical surface is

$$dF_O = \left(\tau_{rx} + \frac{d\tau_{rx}}{dr}\, dr\right) 2\pi\, (r + dr)\, dx$$

The sum of the x components of force, dF_L, dF_R, dF_I, and dF_O, acting on the control volume must be zero. This leads to the condition that

$$-\frac{\partial p}{\partial x}\, 2\pi r\, dr\, dx + \tau_{rx}2\pi\, dr\, dx + \frac{d\tau_{rx}}{dr}\, 2\pi r\, dr\, dx = 0$$

Dividing this equation by $2\pi r\, dr\, dx$ and solving for $\partial p/\partial x$ gives

$$\frac{\partial p}{\partial x} = \frac{\tau_{rx}}{r} + \frac{d\tau_{rx}}{dr} = \frac{1}{r}\frac{d(r\tau_{rx})}{dr}$$

Comparing this to the corresponding equation for parallel plates (Eq. 8.3) shows the mathematical complexity introduced because we have cylindrical coordinates. The left side of the equation is at most a function of x only (the pressure is uniform at each section); the right side is at most a function of r only (because the flow is fully developed). Hence, the only way the equation can be valid for all x and r is for both sides to in fact be constant:

$$\frac{1}{r}\frac{d(r\tau_{rx})}{dr} = \frac{\partial p}{\partial x} = \text{constant} \quad \text{or} \quad \frac{d(r\tau_{rx})}{dr} = r\frac{\partial p}{\partial x}$$

We are not quite finished, but already we have an important result: *In a constant diameter pipe, the pressure drops uniformly along the pipe length* (except for the entrance region).

Integrating this equation, we obtain

$$r\tau_{rx} = \frac{r^2}{2}\left(\frac{\partial p}{\partial x}\right) + c_1$$

or

$$\tau_{rx} = \frac{r}{2}\left(\frac{\partial p}{\partial x}\right) + \frac{c_1}{r} \tag{8.10}$$

Since $\tau_{rx} = \mu\, du/dr$, we have

$$\mu\frac{du}{dr} = \frac{r}{2}\left(\frac{\partial p}{\partial x}\right) + \frac{c_1}{r}$$

and

$$u = \frac{r^2}{4\mu}\left(\frac{\partial p}{\partial x}\right) + \frac{c_1}{\mu}\ln r + c_2 \tag{8.11}$$

We need to evaluate constants c_1 and c_2. However, we have only the one boundary condition that $u = 0$ at $r = R$. What do we do? Before throwing in the towel, let us look at the solution for the velocity profile given by Eq. 8.11. Although we do not know the velocity at the pipe centerline, we do know from physical considerations that the velocity must be finite at $r = 0$. The only way that this can be true is for c_1 to be zero. (We could have also concluded that $c_1 = 0$ from Eq. 8.10—which would otherwise yield an infinite stress at $r = 0$.) Thus, from physical considerations, we conclude that $c_1 = 0$, and hence

$$u = \frac{r^2}{4\mu}\left(\frac{\partial p}{\partial x}\right) + c_2$$

The constant, c_2, is evaluated by using the available boundary condition at the pipe wall: at $r = R$, $u = 0$. Consequently,

$$0 = \frac{R^2}{4\mu}\left(\frac{\partial p}{\partial x}\right) + c_2$$

This gives

$$c_2 = -\frac{R^2}{4\mu}\left(\frac{\partial p}{\partial x}\right)$$

and hence

$$u = \frac{r^2}{4\mu}\left(\frac{\partial p}{\partial x}\right) - \frac{R^2}{4\mu}\left(\frac{\partial p}{\partial x}\right) = \frac{1}{4\mu}\left(\frac{\partial p}{\partial x}\right)(r^2 - R^2)$$

or

$$u = -\frac{R^2}{4\mu}\left(\frac{\partial p}{\partial x}\right)\left[1 - \left(\frac{r}{R}\right)^2\right] \tag{8.12}$$

Since we have the velocity profile, we can obtain a number of additional features of the flow.

Shear Stress Distribution

The shear stress is

$$\tau_{rx} = \mu\frac{du}{dr} = \frac{r}{2}\left(\frac{\partial p}{\partial x}\right) \tag{8.13a}$$

Volume Flow Rate

The volume flow rate is

$$Q = \int_A \vec{V} \cdot d\vec{A} = \int_0^R u 2\pi r \, dr = \int_0^R \frac{1}{4\mu} \left(\frac{\partial p}{\partial x} \right) (r^2 - R^2) 2\pi r \, dr$$

$$Q = -\frac{\pi R^4}{8\mu} \left(\frac{\partial p}{\partial x} \right) \tag{8.13b}$$

Flow Rate as a Function of Pressure Drop

We proved that in fully developed flow the pressure gradient, $\partial p/\partial x$, is constant. Therefore, $\partial p/\partial x = (p_2 - p_1)/L = -\Delta p/L$. Substituting into Eq. 8.13b for the volume flow rate gives

$$Q = -\frac{\pi R^4}{8\mu} \left[\frac{-\Delta p}{L} \right] = \frac{\pi \Delta p R^4}{8\mu L} = \frac{\pi \Delta p D^4}{128\mu L} \tag{8.13c}$$

for laminar flow in a horizontal pipe. Note that Q is a sensitive function of D; $Q \sim D^4$, so, for example, doubling the diameter D increases the flow rate Q by a factor of 16.

Average Velocity

The average velocity magnitude, $\overline{V}$, is given by

$$\overline{V} = \frac{Q}{A} = \frac{Q}{\pi R^2} = -\frac{R^2}{8\mu} \left(\frac{\partial p}{\partial x} \right) \tag{8.13d}$$

Point of Maximum Velocity

To find the point of maximum velocity, we set du/dr equal to zero and solve for the corresponding r. From Eq. 8.12

$$\frac{du}{dr} = \frac{1}{2\mu} \left(\frac{\partial p}{\partial x} \right) r$$

Thus,

$$\frac{du}{dr} = 0 \quad \text{at} \quad r = 0$$

At $r = 0$,

$$u = u_{max} = U = -\frac{R^2}{4\mu} \left(\frac{\partial p}{\partial x} \right) = 2\overline{V} \tag{8.13e}$$

The velocity profile (Eq. 8.12) may be written in terms of the maximum (centerline) velocity as

$$\frac{u}{U} = 1 - \left(\frac{r}{R} \right)^2 \tag{8.14}$$

The parabolic velocity profile, given by Eq. 8.14 for fully developed laminar pipe flow, was sketched in Fig. 8.1.

EXAMPLE 8.4   Capillary Viscometer

A simple and accurate viscometer can be made from a length of capillary tubing. If the flow rate and pressure drop are measured, and the tube geometry is known, the viscosity of a Newtonian liquid can be computed from Eq. 8.13c. A test of a certain liquid in a capillary viscometer gave the following data:

Flow rate:	880 mm³/s	Tube length:	1 m
Tube diameter:	0.50 mm	Pressure drop:	1.0 MPa

Determine the viscosity of the liquid.

GIVEN: Flow in a capillary viscometer.
The flow rate is $Q = 880$ mm³/s.

FIND: The fluid viscosity.

SOLUTION:
Equation 8.13c may be applied.

Governing equation:
$$Q = \frac{\pi \Delta p D^4}{128 \mu L} \tag{8.13c}$$

Assumptions: (1) Laminar flow.
(2) Steady flow.
(3) Incompressible flow.
(4) Fully developed flow.
(5) Horizontal tube.

Then

$$\mu = \frac{\pi \Delta p D^4}{128 \, LQ} = \frac{\pi}{128} \times 1.0 \times 10^6 \, \frac{N}{m^2} \times (0.50)^4 \, mm^4 \times \frac{s}{880 \, mm^3} \times \frac{1}{1 \, m} \times \frac{m}{10^3 \, mm}$$

$$\mu = 1.74 \times 10^{-3} \, N \cdot s/m^2 \qquad\qquad \mu$$

Check the Reynolds number. Assume the fluid density is similar to that of water, 999 kg/m³. Then

$$\overline{V} = \frac{Q}{A} = \frac{4Q}{\pi D^2} = \frac{4}{\pi} \times 880 \, \frac{mm^3}{s} \times \frac{1}{(0.50)^2 \, mm^2} \times \frac{m}{10^3 \, mm} = 4.48 \, m/s$$

and

$$Re = \frac{\rho \overline{V} D}{\mu} = 999 \, \frac{kg}{m^3} \times 4.48 \, \frac{m}{s} \times 0.50 \, mm \times \frac{m^2}{1.74 \times 10^{-3} \, N \cdot s} \times \frac{m}{10^3 \, mm} \times \frac{N \cdot s^2}{kg \cdot m}$$

$$Re = 1290$$

Consequently, since $Re < 2300$, the flow is laminar.

> This problem is a little oversimplified. To design a capillary viscometer the entrance length, liquid temperature, and kinetic energy of the flowing liquid would all need to be considered.

PART B   FLOW IN PIPES AND DUCTS

In this section we will be interested in determining the factors that affect the pressure in an incompressible fluid as it flows in a pipe or duct (we will refer to "pipe" but imply "duct," too). If we ignore friction for a moment (and assume steady flow and consider a streamline in the flow), the Bernoulli equation from Chapter 6 applies,

$$\frac{p}{\rho} + \frac{V^2}{2} + gz = \text{constant} \tag{6.8}$$

From this equation we can see what *tends* to lead to a *pressure decrease* along the streamline in this frictionless flow: a *reduction of area* at some point in the pipe (causing an increase in the velocity V), or the pipe having a *positive incline* (so z increases). Conversely, the pressure will tend to increase if the flow area is increased or the pipe slopes downward. We say "tends to" because one factor may counteract another; for example, we may have a downward sloping pipe (tending to increase pressure) with a reduction in diameter (tending to decrease pressure).

In reality, flows in pipes and ducts experience significant friction and are often turbulent, so the Bernoulli equation does not apply (it doesn't even make sense to use V; instead we will use $\overline{V}$, to represent the average velocity at a point along the pipe). We will learn that, in effect, friction effects lead to a continual reduction in the value of the Bernoulli constant of Eq. 6.8 (this represents a "loss" of mechanical energy). We have already seen that, in contrast to the Bernoulli equation, for laminar flow there is a pressure drop even for a horizontal, constant diameter pipe; in this section we will see that turbulent flows experience an even larger pressure drop. We will need to replace the Bernoulli equation with an energy equation that incorporates the effects of friction.

In summary, we can state that *three* factors tend to reduce the pressure in a pipe flow: a decrease in pipe area, an upward slope, and friction. For now we will focus on pressure loss due to friction and so will analyze pipes that are of constant area and that are horizontal.

We have already seen in the previous section that for laminar flow we can theoretically deduce the pressure drop. Rearranging Eq. 8.13c to solve for the pressure drop Δp,

$$\Delta p = \frac{128 \mu L Q}{\pi D^4}$$

We would like to develop a similar expression that applies for turbulent flows, but we will see that this is not possible analytically; instead, we will develop expressions based on a combination of theoretical and experimental approaches. Before proceeding, we note that it is conventional to break losses due to friction into two categories: *major losses*, which are losses due to friction in the constant-area sections of the pipe; and *minor losses* (sometimes larger than "major" losses), which are losses due to valves, elbows, and so on (and we will treat the pressure drop at the entrance region as a minor loss term).

Since circular pipes are most common in engineering applications, the basic analysis will be performed for circular geometries. The results can be extended to other geometries by introducing the hydraulic diameter, which is treated in Section 8-7. (Open channel flows will be treated in Chapter 11, and compressible flow in ducts will be treated in Chapter 13.)

8-4   ## SHEAR STRESS DISTRIBUTION IN FULLY DEVELOPED PIPE FLOW

We consider again fully developed flow in a horizontal circular pipe, except now we may have laminar or turbulent flow. In Section 8-3 we showed that a force balance between friction and pressure forces leads to Eq. 8.10:

$$\tau_{rx} = \frac{r}{2} \left(\frac{\partial p}{\partial x} \right) + \frac{c_1}{r} \tag{8.10}$$

Because we cannot have infinite stress at the centerline, the constant of integration c_1 must be zero, so

$$\tau_{rx} = \frac{r}{2} \frac{\partial p}{\partial x} \tag{8.15}$$

Equation 8.15 indicates that *for both laminar and turbulent fully developed flows the shear stress varies linearly across the pipe,* from zero at the centerline to a maximum at the pipe wall. The stress on the wall, τ_w (equal and opposite to the stress in the fluid at the wall), is given by

$$\tau_w = -[\tau_{rx}]_{r=R} = -\frac{R}{2}\frac{\partial p}{\partial x} \tag{8.16}$$

For *laminar* flow we used our familiar stress equation $\tau_{rx} = \mu \, du/dr$ in Eq. 8.15 to eventually obtain the laminar velocity distribution. This led to a set of usable equations, Eqs. 8.13, for obtaining various flow characteristics; e.g., Eq. 8.13c gave a relationship for the flow rate Q, a result first obtained experimentally by Jean Louis Poiseuille, a French physician, and independently by Gotthilf H. L. Hagen, a German engineer, in the 1850s [2].

Unfortunately there is no equivalent stress equation for *turbulent* flow, so we cannot replicate the laminar flow analysis to derive turbulent equivalents of Eqs. 8.13. All we can do in this section is indicate some classic semi-empirical results.

As we discussed in Section 2-6, and illustrated in Fig. 2.17, turbulent flow is represented at each point by the time-mean velocity $\bar{u}$ plus (for a two-dimensional flow) randomly fluctuating velocity components u' and v' in the x and y directions (in this context y is the distance inwards from the pipe wall). These components continuously transfer momentum between adjacent fluid layers, tending to reduce any velocity gradient present. This effect shows up as an apparent stress, first introduced by Osborne Reynolds, and called the *Reynolds stress*.[3] This stress is given by $-\rho\overline{u'v'}$, where the overbar indicates a time average. Hence, we find

$$\tau = \tau_{\text{lam}} + \tau_{\text{turb}} = \mu\frac{d\bar{u}}{dy} - \rho\overline{u'v'} \tag{8.17}$$

Do not misunderstand the minus sign in Eq. 8.17—it turns out that u' and v' are negatively correlated, so that $\tau_{\text{turb}} = -\rho\overline{u'v'}$ is positive. In Fig. 8.8, experimental measurements of the Reynolds stress for fully developed turbulent pipe flow at two Reynolds numbers are presented; $Re_U = UD/\nu$, where U is the centerline velocity. The turbulent shear stress has been nondimensionalized with the wall shear stress. Recall that Eq. 8.15 showed that the shear stress in the fluid varies linearly from τ_w at the pipe wall ($y/R \to 0$) to zero at the centerline ($y/R = 1$); from Fig. 8.8 we see that the Reynolds stress has almost the same trend, so that the friction is almost all due to Reynolds stress. What Fig. 8.8 *doesn't* show is that close to the wall ($y/R \to 0$) the

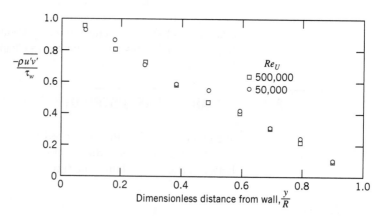

Fig. 8.8 Turbulent shear stress (Reynolds stress) for fully developed turbulent flow in a pipe. (Data from [5].)

---

[3] The Reynolds stress terms arise from consideration of the complete equations of motion for turbulent flow [4].

Reynolds stress drops to zero. This is because the no-slip condition holds, so not only does the mean velocity $\bar{u} \to 0$, but also the fluctuating velocity components u' and $v' \to 0$ (the wall tends to suppress the fluctuations). Hence, the turbulent stress, $\tau_{\text{turb}} = -\rho\overline{u'v'} \to 0$, as we approach the wall, and is zero at the wall. Since the Reynolds stress is zero at the wall, Eq. 8.17 shows that the wall shear is given by $\tau_w = \mu(d\bar{u}/dy)_{y=0}$. In the region very close to the wall, called the *wall layer*, viscous shear is dominant. In the region between the wall layer and the central portion of the pipe both viscous and turbulent shear are important.

8-5 TURBULENT VELOCITY PROFILES IN FULLY DEVELOPED PIPE FLOW

Except for flows of very viscous fluids in small diameter ducts, internal flows generally are turbulent. As noted in the discussion of shear stress distribution in fully developed pipe flow (Section 8-4), in turbulent flow there is no universal relationship between the stress field and the mean velocity field. Thus, for turbulent flows we are forced to rely on experimental data.

Dividing Eq. 8.17 by ρ gives

$$\frac{\tau}{\rho} = v\,\frac{d\bar{u}}{dy} - \overline{u'v'} \tag{8.18}$$

The term τ/ρ arises frequently in the consideration of turbulent flows; it has dimensions of velocity squared. In particular, the quantity $(\tau_w/\rho)^{1/2}$ is called the *friction velocity* and is denoted by the symbol u_*. It is a constant for a given flow.

The velocity profile for fully developed turbulent flow through a smooth pipe is shown in Fig. 8.9. The plot is semilogarithmic; $\bar{u}/u_*$ is plotted against $\log(yu_*/v)$. The nondimensional parameters $\bar{u}/u_*$ and yu_*/v arise from dimensional analysis if one reasons that the velocity in the neighborhood of the wall is determined by the conditions at the wall, the fluid properties, and the distance from the wall. It is simply fortuitous that the dimensionless plot of Fig. 8.9 gives a fairly accurate representation of the velocity profile in a pipe away from the wall; note the small deviations in the region of the pipe centerline.

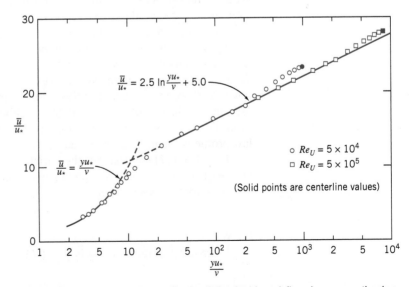

Fig. 8.9 Turbulent velocity profile for fully developed flow in a smooth pipe. (Data from [5].)

In the region very close to the wall where viscous shear is dominant, the mean velocity profile follows the linear viscous relation

$$u^+ = \frac{\bar{u}}{u_*} = \frac{yu_*}{\nu} = y^+ \tag{8.19}$$

where y is distance measured from the wall ($y = R - r$; R is the pipe radius), and $\bar{u}$ is mean velocity. Equation 8.19 is valid for $0 \le y^+ \le 5$–7; this region is called the *viscous sublayer*.

For values of $yu_*/\nu > 30$, the data are quite well represented by the semilogarithmic curve-fit equation

$$\frac{\bar{u}}{u_*} = 2.5 \ln \frac{yu_*}{\nu} + 5.0 \tag{8.20}$$

In this region both viscous and turbulent shear are important (although turbulent shear is expected to be significantly larger). There is considerable scatter in the numerical constants of Eq. 8.20; the values given represent averages over many experiments [6]. The region between $y^+ = 5 - 7$ and $y^+ = 30$ is referred to as the *transition region*, or *buffer layer*.

If Eq. 8.20 is evaluated at the centerline ($y = R$ and $u = U$) and the general expression of Eq. 8.20 is subtracted from the equation evaluated at the centerline, we obtain

$$\frac{U - \bar{u}}{u_*} = 2.5 \ln \frac{R}{y} \tag{8.21}$$

where U is the centerline velocity. Equation 8.21, referred to as the *defect law*, shows that the velocity defect (and hence the general shape of the velocity profile in the neighborhood of the centerline) is a function of the distance ratio only and does not depend on the viscosity of the fluid.

The velocity profile for turbulent flow through a smooth pipe may also be approximated by the empirical *power-law* equation

$$\frac{\bar{u}}{U} = \left(\frac{y}{R}\right)^{1/n} = \left(1 - \frac{r}{R}\right)^{1/n} \tag{8.22}$$

where the exponent, n, varies with the Reynolds number. In Fig. 8.10 the data of Laufer [5] are shown on a plot of $\ln y/R$ versus $\ln \bar{u}/U$. If the power-law profile were an accurate representation of the data, all data points would fall on a straight line of slope n. Clearly the data for $Re_U = 5 \times 10^4$ deviate from the best-fit straight line in the neighborhood of the wall.

Hence the power-law profile is not applicable close to the wall ($y/R < 0.04$). Since the velocity is low in this region, the error in calculating integral quantities such as mass, momentum, and energy fluxes at a section is relatively small. The power-law profile gives an infinite velocity gradient at the wall and hence cannot be used in calculations of wall shear stress. Although the profile fits the data close to the centerline, it fails to give zero slope there. Despite these shortcomings, the power-law profile is found to give adequate results in many calculations.

Data from [7] suggest that the variation of power-law exponent n with Reynolds number (based on pipe diameter, D, and centerline velocity, U) for fully developed flow in smooth pipes is given by

$$n = -1.7 + 1.8 \log Re_U \tag{8.23}$$

for $Re_U > 2 \times 10^4$.

Since the average velocity is $\bar{V} = Q/A$, and

$$Q = \int_A \vec{V} \cdot d\vec{A}$$

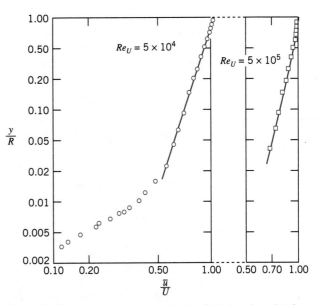

Fig. 8.10 Power-law velocity profiles for fully developed turbulent flow in a smooth pipe. (Data from [5].)

the ratio of the average velocity to the centerline velocity may be calculated for the power-law profiles of Eq. 8.22 assuming the profiles to be valid from wall to centerline. The result is

$$\frac{\overline{V}}{U} = \frac{2n^2}{(n+1)(2n+1)} \tag{8.24}$$

From Eq. 8.24, we see that as n increases (with increasing Reynolds number) the ratio of the average velocity to the centerline velocity increases; with increasing Reynolds number the velocity profile becomes more blunt or "fuller" (for $n = 6$, $\overline{V}/U = 0.79$ and for $n = 10$, $\overline{V}/U = 0.87$). As a representative value, 7 often is used for the exponent; this gives rise to the term "a one-seventh power profile" for fully developed turbulent flow:

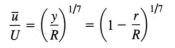

$$\frac{\overline{u}}{U} = \left(\frac{y}{R}\right)^{1/7} = \left(1 - \frac{r}{R}\right)^{1/7}$$

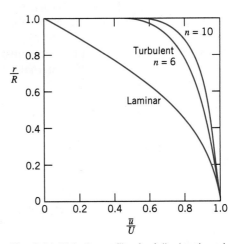

Fig. 8.11 Velocity profiles for fully developed pipe flow.

Velocity profiles for $n = 6$ and $n = 10$ are shown in Fig. 8.11. The parabolic profile for fully developed laminar flow is included for comparison. It is clear that the turbulent profile has a much steeper slope near the wall. This is consistent with our discussion leading to Eq. 8.17—the fluctuating velocity components u' and v' continuously transfer momentum between adjacent fluid layers, tending to reduce the velocity gradient.

8-6 ENERGY CONSIDERATIONS IN PIPE FLOW

We have so far used the momentum and conservation of mass equations, in control volume form, to discuss viscous flow. It is obvious that viscous effects will have an important effect on energy considerations. In Section 6-5 we discussed the Energy Grade Line (EGL),

$$EGL = \frac{p}{\rho g} + \frac{V^2}{2g} + z \qquad (6.16b)$$

and saw that this is a measure of the total mechanical energy ("pressure," kinetic and potential, per unit mass) in a flow. We can expect that instead of being constant (which it was for inviscid flow), the EGL will continuously decrease in the direction of flow as friction "eats" the mechanical energy (Examples 8.9 and 8.10 have sketches of such EGL—and HGL—curves; you may wish to preview them). We can now consider the energy equation (the first law of thermodynamics) to obtain information on the effects of friction.

Consider, for example, steady flow through the piping system, including a reducing elbow, shown in Fig. 8.12. The control volume boundaries are shown as dashed lines. They are normal to the flow at sections ① and ② and coincide with the inside surface of the pipe wall elsewhere.

Basic equation:

$$= 0(1) = 0(2) = 0(1) = 0(3)$$

$$\dot{Q} - \cancel{\dot{W_s}} - \cancel{\dot{W}_{shear}} - \cancel{\dot{W}_{other}} = \frac{\partial}{\partial t} \iiint_{CV} e\, \rho\, dV + \int_{CS} (e + pv)\, \rho \vec{V} \cdot d\vec{A} \qquad (4.56)$$

$$e = u + \frac{V^2}{2} + gz$$

Assumptions: (1) $\dot{W}_s = 0$, $\dot{W}_{other} = 0$.
(2) $\dot{W}_{shear} = 0$ (although shear stresses are present at the walls of the elbow, the velocities are zero there, so there is no possibility of work).
(3) Steady flow.
(4) Incompressible flow.
(5) Internal energy and pressure uniform across sections ① and ②.

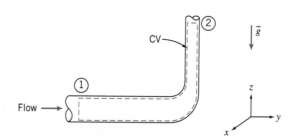

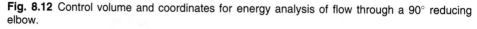

Fig. 8.12 Control volume and coordinates for energy analysis of flow through a 90° reducing elbow.

Under these assumptions the energy equation reduces to

$$\dot{Q} = \dot{m}(u_2 - u_1) + \dot{m}\left(\frac{p_2}{\rho} - \frac{p_1}{\rho}\right) + \dot{m}g(z_2 - z_1)$$

$$+ \int_{A_2} \frac{V_2^2}{2}\,\rho V_2\,dA_2 - \int_{A_1} \frac{V_1^2}{2}\,\rho V_1\,dA_1 \qquad (8.25)$$

Note that we have *not* assumed the velocity to be uniform at sections ① and ②, since we know that for viscous flows the velocity at a cross-section cannot be uniform. However, it is convenient to introduce the average velocity into Eq. 8.25 so that we can eliminate the integrals. To do this, we define a kinetic energy coefficient.

Kinetic Energy Coefficient

The *kinetic energy coefficient*, α, is defined such that

$$\int_A \frac{V^2}{2}\,\rho V\,dA = \alpha \int_A \frac{\overline{V}^2}{2}\,\rho V\,dA = \alpha \dot{m}\frac{\overline{V}^2}{2} \qquad (8.26a)$$

or

$$\alpha = \frac{\displaystyle\int_A \rho V^3\,dA}{\dot{m}\,\overline{V}^2} \qquad (8.26b)$$

We can think of α as a correction factor that allows us to use the average velocity $\overline{V}$ in the energy equation to compute the kinetic energy at a cross section.

For laminar flow in a pipe (velocity profile given by Eq. 8.12), $\alpha = 2.0$.

In turbulent pipe flow, the velocity profile is quite flat, as shown in Fig. 8.11. We can use Eq. 8.26b together with Eqs. 8.22 and 8.24 to determine α. Substituting the power-law velocity profile of Eq. 8.22 into Eq. 8.26b, we obtain

$$\alpha = \left(\frac{U}{\overline{V}}\right)^3 \frac{2n^2}{(3+n)(3+2n)} \qquad (8.27)$$

Equation 8.24 gives $\overline{V}/U$ as a function of the power-law exponent n; combining this with Eq. 8.27 leads to a fairly complicated expression in n. The overall result is that in the realistic range of n, from $n = 6$ to $n = 10$ for high Reynolds numbers, α varies from 1.08 to 1.03; for the one-seventh power profile ($n = 7$), $\alpha = 1.06$. Because α is reasonably close to unity for high Reynolds numbers, and because the change in kinetic energy is usually small compared with the dominant terms in the energy equation, *we shall almost always use the approximation $\alpha = 1$ in our pipe flow calculations.*

Head Loss

Using the definition of α, the energy equation (Eq. 8.25) can be written

$$\dot{Q} = \dot{m}(u_2 - u_1) + \dot{m}\left(\frac{p_2}{\rho} - \frac{p_1}{\rho}\right) + \dot{m}g(z_2 - z_1) + \dot{m}\left(\frac{\alpha_2 \overline{V}_2^2}{2} - \frac{\alpha_1 V_1^2}{2}\right)$$

Dividing by the mass flow rate gives

$$\frac{\delta Q}{dm} = u_2 - u_1 + \frac{p_2}{\rho} - \frac{p_1}{\rho} + gz_2 - gz_1 + \frac{\alpha_2 \overline{V}_2^2}{2} - \frac{\alpha_1 \overline{V}_1^2}{2}$$

Rearranging this equation, we write

$$\left(\frac{p_1}{\rho} + \alpha_1 \frac{\overline{V}_1^2}{2} + gz_1\right) - \left(\frac{p_2}{\rho} + \alpha_2 \frac{\overline{V}_2^2}{2} + gz_2\right) = (u_2 - u_1) - \frac{\delta Q}{dm} \qquad (8.28)$$

In Eq. 8.28, the term

$$\left(\frac{p}{\rho} + \alpha \frac{\overline{V}^2}{2} + gz \right)$$

represents the mechanical energy per unit mass at a cross section. (Compare it to the EGL expression, Eq. 6.16b, for computing "mechanical" energy, which we discussed at the beginning of this section. The differences are that in the EGL we divide by g to obtain the EGL in units of feet or meters, and here $\alpha \overline{V}^2$ allows for the fact that in a pipe flow we have a velocity profile, not a uniform flow.) The term $u_2 - u_1 - \delta Q/dm$ is equal to the difference in mechanical energy per unit mass between sections ① and ②. It represents the (irreversible) conversion of mechanical energy at section ① to unwanted thermal energy ($u_2 - u_1$) and loss of energy via heat transfer ($-\delta Q/dm$). We identify this group of terms as the total energy loss per unit mass and designate it by the symbol h_{l_T}. Then

$$\left(\frac{p_1}{\rho} + \alpha_1 \frac{\overline{V}_1^2}{2} + gz_1 \right) - \left(\frac{p_2}{\rho} + \alpha_2 \frac{\overline{V}_2^2}{2} + gz_2 \right) = h_{l_T} \qquad (8.29)$$

The dimensions of energy per unit mass FL/M are equivalent to dimensions of L^2/t^2. Equation 8.29 is one of the most important and useful equations in fluid mechanics. It enables us to compute the loss of mechanical energy caused by friction between two sections of a pipe. We recall our discussion at the beginning of Part B, where we discussed what would cause the pressure to change. We hypothesized a frictionless flow (i.e., described by the Bernoulli equation, or Eq. 8.29 with $\alpha = 1$ and $h_{l_T} = 0$) so that the pressure could only change if the velocity changed (if the pipe had a change in diameter), or if the potential changed (if the pipe was not horizontal). Now, with friction, Eq. 8.29 indicates that the pressure will change even for a constant area horizontal pipe—mechanical energy will be continuously changed into thermal energy.

As the empirical science of hydraulics developed during the nineteenth century, it was common practice to express the energy balance in terms of energy per unit *weight* of flowing liquid (e.g., water) rather than energy per unit *mass*, as in Eq. 8.29. When Eq. 8.29 is divided by the acceleration of gravity, g, we obtain

$$\left(\frac{p_1}{\rho g} + \alpha_1 \frac{\overline{V}_1^2}{2g} + z_1 \right) - \left(\frac{p_2}{\rho g} + \alpha_2 \frac{\overline{V}_2^2}{2g} + z_2 \right) = \frac{h_{l_T}}{g} = H_{l_T} \qquad (8.30)$$

Each term in Eq. 8.30 has dimensions of energy per unit weight of flowing fluid. Then the net dimensions of $H_{l_T} = h_{l_T}/g$ are $(L^2/t^2)(t^2/L) = L$, or feet of flowing liquid. Since the term head loss is in common use, we shall use it when referring to either H_{l_T} (with dimensions of energy per unit weight or length) or $h_{l_T} = gH_{l_T}$ (with dimensions of energy per unit mass).

Equation 8.29 (or Eq. 8.30) can be used to calculate the pressure difference between any two points in a piping system, provided the head loss, h_{l_T} (or H_{l_T}), can be determined. We shall consider calculation of head loss in the next section.

8-7   CALCULATION OF HEAD LOSS

Total head loss, h_{l_T}, is regarded as the sum of major losses, h_l, due to frictional effects in fully developed flow in constant-area tubes, and minor losses, h_{l_m}, resulting from entrances, fittings, area changes, and so on. Consequently, we consider the major and minor losses separately.

Major Losses: Friction Factor

The energy balance, expressed by Eq. 8.29, can be used to evaluate the major head loss. For fully developed flow through a constant-area pipe, $h_{l_m} = 0$, and $\alpha_1 \ (\overline{V}_1^2/2) = \alpha_2 \ (\overline{V}_2^2/2)$; Eq. 8.29 reduces to

$$\frac{p_1 - p_2}{\rho} = g(z_2 - z_1) + h_l \tag{8.31}$$

If the pipe is horizontal, then $z_2 = z_1$ and

$$\frac{p_1 - p_2}{\rho} = \frac{\Delta p}{\rho} = h_l \tag{8.32}$$

Thus the major head loss can be expressed as the pressure loss for fully developed flow through a horizontal pipe of constant area.

Since head loss represents the energy converted by frictional effects from mechanical to thermal energy, head loss for fully developed flow in a constant-area duct depends only on the details of the flow through the duct. Head loss is independent of pipe orientation.

a. Laminar Flow

In laminar flow, we saw in Section 8-3 that the pressure drop may be computed analytically for fully developed flow in a horizontal pipe. Thus, from Eq. 8.13c,

$$\Delta p = \frac{128 \mu L Q}{\pi D^4} = \frac{128 \mu L \overline{V} (\pi D^2/4)}{\pi D^4} = 32 \frac{L}{D} \frac{\mu \overline{V}}{D}$$

Substituting in Eq. 8.32 gives

$$h_l = 32 \frac{L}{D} \frac{\mu \overline{V}}{\rho D} = \frac{L}{D} \frac{\overline{V}^2}{2} \left(64 \frac{\mu}{\rho \overline{V} D} \right) = \left(\frac{64}{Re} \right) \frac{L}{D} \frac{\overline{V}^2}{2} \tag{8.33}$$

(We shall see the reason for writing h_l in this form shortly.)

b. Turbulent Flow

In turbulent flow we cannot evaluate the pressure drop analytically; we must resort to experimental results and use dimensional analysis to correlate the experimental data. In fully developed turbulent flow, the pressure drop, Δp, caused by friction in a horizontal constant-area pipe is known to depend on pipe diameter, D, pipe length, L, pipe roughness, e, average flow velocity, $\overline{V}$, fluid density, ρ, and fluid viscosity, μ. In functional form

$$\Delta p = \Delta p(D, L, e, \overline{V}, \rho, \mu)$$

We applied dimensional analysis to this problem in Example 7.2. The results were a correlation of the form

$$\frac{\Delta p}{\rho \overline{V}^2} = f \left(\frac{\mu}{\rho \overline{V} D}, \frac{L}{D}, \frac{e}{D} \right)$$

We recognize that $\mu/\rho \overline{V} D = 1/Re$, so we could just as well write

$$\frac{\Delta p}{\rho \overline{V}^2} = \phi \left(Re, \frac{L}{D}, \frac{e}{D} \right)$$

Substituting from Eq. 8.32, we see that

$$\frac{h_l}{\overline{V}^2} = \phi \left(Re, \frac{L}{D}, \frac{e}{D} \right)$$

TABLE 8.1 Roughness for Pipes of Common Engineering Materials (Data from [8])

Pipe	Roughness, e	
	Feet	**Millimeters**
Riveted steel	10.003–0.03	0.9–9
Concrete	0.001–0.01	0.3–3
Wood stave	0.0006–0.003	0.2–0.9
Cast iron	0.00085	0.26
Galvanized iron	0.0005	0.15
Asphalted cast iron	0.0004	0.12
Commercial steel or wrought iron	0.00015	0.046
Drawn tubing	0.000005	0.0015

Although dimensional analysis predicts the functional relationship, we must obtain actual values experimentally.

Experiments show that the nondimensional head loss is directly proportional to L/D. Hence we can write

$$\frac{h_l}{\overline{V}^2} = \frac{L}{D}\,\phi_1\left(Re,\ \frac{e}{D}\right)$$

Since the function, ϕ_1, is still undetermined, it is permissible to introduce a constant into the left side of the above equation. By convention the number $\frac{1}{2}$ is introduced into the denominator so that the left side of the equation is the ratio of the head loss to the kinetic energy per unit mass of flow. Then

$$\frac{h_l}{\frac{1}{2}\overline{V}^2} = \frac{L}{D}\,\phi_2\left(Re,\ \frac{e}{D}\right)$$

The unknown function, $\phi_2\ (Re,\ e/D)$, is defined as the *friction factor*, f,

$$f \equiv \phi_2\left(Re,\ \frac{e}{D}\right)$$

and

$$h_l = f\,\frac{L}{D}\,\frac{\overline{V}^2}{2} \tag{8.34}$$

or

$$H_l = f\,\frac{L}{D}\,\frac{\overline{V}^2}{2g} \tag{8.35}$$

The friction factor[4] is determined experimentally. The results, published by L. F. Moody [8], are shown in Fig. 8.13.

To determine head loss for fully developed flow with known conditions, the Reynolds number is evaluated first. Roughness, e, is obtained from Table 8.1. Then the friction factor, f, can be read from the appropriate curve in Fig. 8.13, at the known values of Re and e/D. Finally, head loss can be found using Eq. 8.34 or Eq. 8.35.

---

[4] The friction factor defined by Eq. 8.34 is the *Darcy friction factor*. The *Fanning friction factor*, less frequently used, is defined in Problem 8.83.

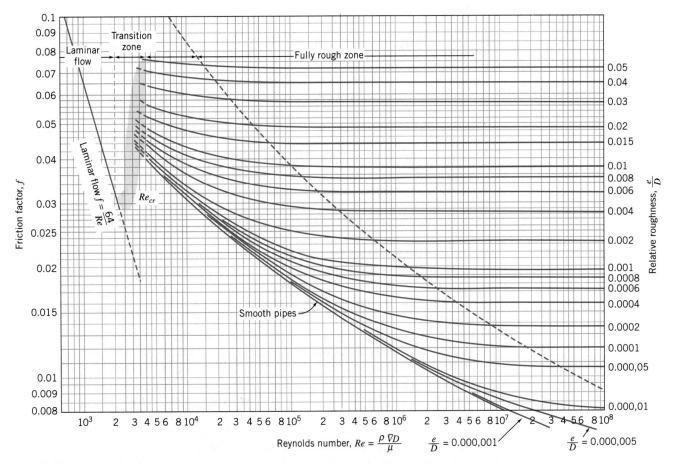

Fig. 8.13 Friction factor for fully developed flow in circular pipes. (Data from [8], used by permission.)

Several features of Fig. 8.13 require some discussion. The friction factor for laminar flow may be obtained by comparing Eqs. 8.33 and 8.34:

$$h_l = \left(\frac{64}{Re}\right)\frac{L}{D}\frac{\bar{V}^2}{2} = f\,\frac{L}{D}\,\frac{\bar{V}^2}{2}$$

Consequently, for laminar flow

$$f_{\text{laminar}} = \frac{64}{Re} \qquad (8.36)$$

Thus, in laminar flow, the friction factor is a function of Reynolds number only; it is independent of roughness. Although we took no notice of roughness in deriving Eq. 8.33, experimental results verify that the friction factor is a function only of Reynolds number in laminar flow.

The Reynolds number in a pipe may be changed most easily by varying the average flow velocity. If the flow in a pipe is originally laminar, increasing the velocity until the critical Reynolds number is reached causes transition to occur; the laminar flow gives way to turbulent flow. The effect of transition on the velocity profile was discussed in Section 8-5. Figure 8.11 shows that the velocity gradient at the tube wall is much larger for turbulent flow than for laminar flow. This change in velocity profile causes the wall shear stress to increase sharply, with the same effect on the friction factor.

As the Reynolds number is increased above the transition value, the velocity profile continues to become fuller, as noted in Section 8-5. For values of relative roughness $e/D \leq 0.001$, the friction factor at first tends to follow the smooth pipe curve, along which friction factor is a function of Reynolds number only. However, as the Reynolds number increases, the velocity profile becomes still fuller. The size of the thin viscous sublayer near the tube wall decreases. As roughness elements begin to poke through this layer, the effect of roughness becomes important, and the friction factor becomes a function of both the Reynolds number *and* the relative roughness.

At very large Reynolds number, most of the roughness elements on the tube wall protrude through the viscous sublayer; the drag and, hence, the pressure loss, depend only on the size of the roughness elements. This is termed the "fully rough" flow regime; the friction factor depends only on e/D in this regime.

For values of relative roughness $e/D \gtrsim 0.001$, as the Reynolds number is increased above the transition value, the friction factor is greater than the smooth pipe value. As was the case for lower values of e/D, the value of Reynolds number at which the flow regime becomes fully rough decreases with increasing relative roughness.

To summarize the preceding discussion, we see that as Reynolds number is increased, the friction factor decreases as long as the flow remains laminar. At transition, f increases sharply. In the turbulent flow regime, the friction factor decreases gradually and finally levels out at a constant value for large Reynolds number.

Bear in mind that the actual loss of energy is h_l (Eq. 8.34), which is proportional to f and $\overline{V}^2$. Hence, for laminar flow $h_l \propto \overline{V}$ (because $f = 64/Re$, and $Re \propto \overline{V}$); for the transition region there is a sudden increase in h_l; for the fully rough zone $h_l \propto \overline{V}^2$ (because $f \approx$ const.), and for the rest of the turbulent region h_l increases at a rate somewhere between $\overline{V}$ and $\overline{V}^2$. We conclude that the head loss *always* increases with flow rate, and more rapidly when the flow is turbulent.

To avoid having to use a graphical method for obtaining f for turbulent flows, various mathematical expressions have been fitted to the data. The most widely used formula for friction factor is from Colebrook [9],

$$\frac{1}{\sqrt{f}} = -2.0 \log\left(\frac{e/D}{3.7} + \frac{2.51}{Re\sqrt{f}}\right) \qquad (8.37)$$

Equation 8.37 is implicit in f, but these days most scientific calculators have an equation-solving feature that can be easily used to find f for a given roughness ratio e/D and Reynolds number Re (and some calculators have the Colebrook equation itself built in!). Certainly a spreadsheet such as *Excel*, or other mathematical computer applications, can also be used (there is an *Excel* add-in for computing f for laminar and turbulent flows available on the Web site). Even without using these automated approaches, Eq. 8.37 is not difficult to solve for f—all we need to do is iterate. Equation 8.37 is quite stable—almost any initial guess value for f in the right side will, after very few iterations, lead to a converged value for f to three significant figures. From Fig. 8.13, we can see that for turbulent flows $f < 0.1$; hence $f = 0.1$ would make a good initial value. Another strategy is to use Fig. 8.13 to obtain a good first estimate; then usually one iteration using Eq. 8.37 yields a good value for f. As an alternative, Haaland [10] developed the following equation,

$$\frac{1}{\sqrt{f}} = -1.8 \log\left[\left(\frac{e/D}{3.7}\right)^{1.11} + \frac{6.9}{Re}\right]$$

as an approximation to the Colebrook equation; for $Re > 3000$, it gives results within about 2 percent of the Colebrook equation, without the need to iterate.

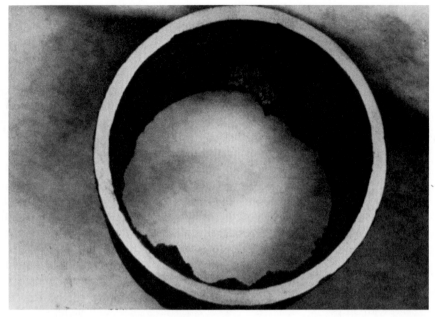

Fig. 8.14 Pipe section removed after 40 years of service as a water line, showing formation of scale. (Photo courtesy of Alan T. McDonald.)

For turbulent flow in smooth pipes, the Blasius correlation, valid for $Re \leq 10^5$, is

$$f = \frac{0.316}{Re^{0.25}} \tag{8.38}$$

When this relation is combined with the expression for wall shear stress (Eq. 8.16), the expression for head loss (Eq. 8.32), and the definition of friction factor (Eq. 8.34), a useful expression for the wall shear stress is obtained as

$$\tau_w = 0.0332 \rho \overline{V}^2 \left(\frac{v}{R\overline{V}} \right)^{0.25} \tag{8.39}$$

This equation will be used later in our study of turbulent boundary-layer flow over a flat plate (Chapter 9).

All of the e values given in Table 8.1 are for new pipes, in relatively good condition. Over long periods of service, corrosion takes place and, particularly in hard water areas, lime deposits and rust scale form on pipe walls. Corrosion can weaken pipes, eventually leading to failure. Deposit formation increases wall roughness appreciably, and also decreases the effective diameter. These factors combine to cause e/D to increase by factors of 5 to 10 for old pipes (see Problem 10.65). An example is shown in Fig. 8.14.

Curves presented in Fig. 8.13 represent average values for data obtained from numerous experiments. The curves should be considered accurate within approximately ± 10 percent, which is sufficient for many engineering analyses. If more accuracy is needed, actual test data should be used.

Minor Losses

The flow in a piping system may be required to pass through a variety of fittings, bends, or abrupt changes in area. Additional head losses are encountered, primarily as a result of flow separation. (Energy eventually is dissipated by violent mixing in the separated zones.) These losses will be minor (hence the term *minor losses*) if the piping system includes long lengths of constant-area pipe. Depending on the device, minor losses traditionally are computed in one of two ways, either

$$h_{l_m} = K \frac{\overline{V}^2}{2} \tag{8.40a}$$

where the *loss coefficient*, K, must be determined experimentally for each situation, or

$$h_{l_m} = f \frac{L_e}{D} \frac{\overline{V}^2}{2} \tag{8.40b}$$

where L_e is an *equivalent length* of straight pipe.

For flow through pipe bends and fittings, the loss coefficient, K, is found to vary with pipe size (diameter) in much the same manner as the friction factor, f, for flow through a straight pipe. Consequently, the equivalent length, L_e/D, tends toward a constant for different sizes of a given type of fitting.

Experimental data for minor losses are plentiful, but they are scattered among a variety of sources. Different sources may give different values for the same flow configuration. The data presented here should be considered as representative for some commonly encountered situations; in each case the source of the data is identified.

a. Inlets and Exits

A poorly designed inlet to a pipe can cause appreciable head loss. If the inlet has sharp corners, flow separation occurs at the corners, and a *vena contracta* is formed. The fluid must accelerate locally to pass through the reduced flow area at the vena contracta. Losses in mechanical energy result from the unconfined mixing as the flow stream decelerates again to fill the pipe. Three basic inlet geometries are shown in Table 8.2. From the table it is clear that the loss coefficient is reduced significantly when the inlet is rounded even slightly. For a well-rounded inlet ($r/D \geq 0.15$) the entrance loss coefficient is almost negligible. Example 8.9 illustrates a procedure for experimentally determining the loss coefficient for a pipe inlet.

The kinetic energy per unit mass, $\alpha \overline{V}^2/2$, is completely dissipated by mixing when flow discharges from a duct into a large reservoir or plenum chamber. The situation corresponds to flow through an abrupt expansion with $AR = 0$ (Fig. 8.15). The minor loss coefficient thus equals α, which as we saw in the previous section we usually set to 1 for turbulent flow. No improvement in minor loss coefficient for an exit is possible; however, addition of a diffuser can reduce $\overline{V}^2/2$ and therefore h_{l_m} considerably (see Example 8.10).

TABLE 8.2 Minor Loss Coefficients for Pipe Entrances (Data from [11].)

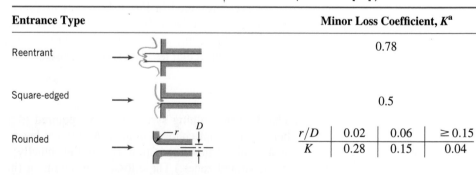

Entrance Type		Minor Loss Coefficient, K[a]		
Reentrant		0.78		
Square-edged		0.5		
Rounded	r/D	0.02	0.06	≥ 0.15
	K	0.28	0.15	0.04

[a]Based on $h_{l_m} = K(\overline{V}^2/2)$, where $\overline{V}$ is the mean velocity in the pipe.

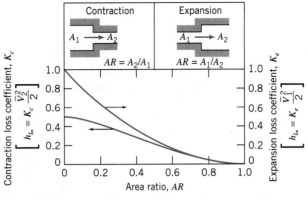

Fig. 8.15 Loss coefficients for flow through sudden area changes. (Data from [1].)

b. Enlargements and Contractions

Minor loss coefficients for sudden expansions and contractions in circular ducts are given in Fig. 8.15. Note that both loss coefficients are based on the *larger* $\overline{V}^2/2$. Thus losses for a sudden expansion are based on $\overline{V}_1^2/2$, and those for a contraction are based on $\overline{V}_2^2/2$.

Losses caused by area change can be reduced somewhat by installing a nozzle or diffuser between the two sections of straight pipe. Data for nozzles are given in Table 8.3. Note that the final column (data for the included angle $\theta = 180°$) agrees with the data of Fig. 8.15.

Losses in diffusers depend on a number of geometric and flow variables. Diffuser data most commonly are presented in terms of a pressure recovery coefficient, C_p, defined as the ratio of static pressure rise to inlet dynamic pressure,

$$C_p \equiv \frac{p_2 - p_1}{\frac{1}{2}\rho\overline{V}_1^2} \tag{8.41}$$

This shows what fraction of the inlet kinetic energy shows up as a pressure rise. It is not difficult to show (using the Bernoulli and continuity equations; see Problem 8.181) that the ideal (frictionless) pressure recovery coefficient is given by

$$C_{p_i} = 1 - \frac{1}{AR^2} \tag{8.42}$$

where AR is the area ratio. Hence, the ideal pressure recovery coefficient is a function only of the area ratio. In reality a diffuser typically has turbulent flow, and the static pressure rise in the direction of flow may cause flow separation from the walls if the diffuser is poorly designed; flow pulsations can even occur. For these reasons the

TABLE 8.3 Loss Coefficients (K) for Gradual Contractions: Round and Rectangular Ducts (Data from [12].)

	Included Angle, θ, Degrees						
A_2/A_1	10	15–40	50–60	90	120	150	180
0.50	0.05	0.05	0.06	0.12	0.18	0.24	0.26
0.25	0.05	0.04	0.07	0.17	0.27	0.35	0.41
0.10	0.05	0.05	0.08	0.19	0.29	0.37	0.43

Note: Coefficients are based on $h_{l_m} = K(\overline{V}_2^2/2)$.

actual C_p will be somewhat less than indicated by Eq. 8.42. For example, data for conical diffusers with fully developed turbulent pipe flow at the inlet are presented in Fig. 8.16 as a function of geometry. Note that more tapered diffusers (small divergence angle ϕ or large dimensionless length N/R_1) are more likely to approach the ideal constant value for C_p. As we make the cone shorter, for a given fixed area ratio we start to see a drop in C_p—we can consider the cone length at which this starts to happen the optimum length (it is the shortest length for which we obtain the maximum coefficient for a given area ratio—closest to that predicted by Eq. 8.42). We can relate C_p to the head loss. If gravity is neglected, and $\alpha_1 = \alpha_2 = 1.0$, the head loss equation, Eq. 8.29, reduces to

$$\left[\frac{p_1}{\rho} + \frac{\overline{V}_1^2}{2}\right] - \left[\frac{p_2}{\rho} + \frac{\overline{V}_2^2}{2}\right] = h_{l_T} = h_{l_m}$$

Thus,

$$h_{l_m} = \frac{\overline{V}_1^2}{2} - \frac{\overline{V}_2^2}{2} - \frac{p_2 - p_1}{\rho}$$

$$h_{l_m} = \frac{\overline{V}_1^2}{2}\left[\left(1 - \frac{\overline{V}_2^2}{\overline{V}_1^2}\right) - \frac{p_2 - p_1}{\frac{1}{2}\rho\overline{V}_1^2}\right] = \frac{\overline{V}_1^2}{2}\left[\left(1 - \frac{\overline{V}_2^2}{\overline{V}_1^2}\right) - C_p\right]$$

From continuity, $A_1\overline{V}_1 = A_2\overline{V}_2$, so

$$h_{l_m} = \frac{\overline{V}_1^2}{2}\left[1 - \left(\frac{A_1}{A_2}\right)^2 - C_p\right]$$

or

$$h_{l_m} = \frac{\overline{V}_1^2}{2}\left[\left(1 - \frac{1}{(AR)^2}\right) - C_p\right] \tag{8.43}$$

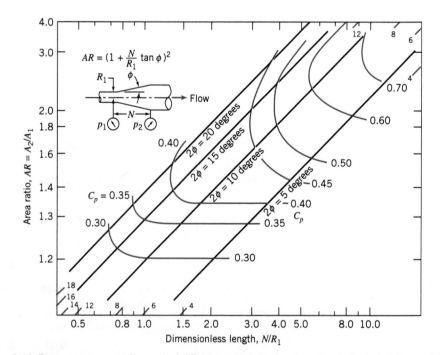

Fig. 8.16 Pressure recovery for conical diffusers with fully developed turbulent pipe flow at inlet. (Data from [13].)

The frictionless result (Eq. 8.42) is obtained from Eq. 8.43 if $h_{l_m} = 0$. We can combine Eqs. 8.42 and 8.43 to obtain an expression for the head loss in terms of the actual and ideal C_p values:

$$h_{l_m} = (C_{p_i} - C_p) \frac{\bar{V}_1^2}{2} \qquad (8.44)$$

Performance maps for plane wall and annular diffusers [14] and for radial diffusers [15] are available in the literature.

Diffuser pressure recovery is essentially independent of Reynolds number for inlet Reynolds numbers greater than 7.5×10^4 [16]. Diffuser pressure recovery with uniform inlet flow is somewhat better than that for fully developed inlet flow. Performance maps for plane wall, conical, and annular diffusers for a variety of inlet flow conditions are presented in [17].

Since static pressure rises in the direction of flow in a diffuser, flow may separate from the walls. For some geometries, the outlet flow is distorted. The flow regime behavior of plane wall diffusers is illustrated well in the NCFMF video *Flow Visualization* (see http://web.mit.edu/fluids/www/Shapiro/ncfmf.html for free online viewing of this film). For wide angle diffusers, vanes or splitters can be used to suppress stall and improve pressure recovery [18].

c. Pipe Bends

The head loss of a bend is larger than for fully developed flow through a straight section of equal length. The additional loss is primarily the result of secondary flow,[5] and is represented most conveniently by an equivalent length of straight pipe. The equivalent length depends on the relative radius of curvature of the bend, as shown in Fig. 8.17a for 90° bends. An approximate procedure for computing the resistance of bends with other turning angles is given in [11].

Because they are simple and inexpensive to construct in the field, miter bends often are used in large pipe systems. Design data for miter bends are given in Fig. 8.17b. Note that you get what you pay for: From Fig. 8.17a the equivalent length for pipe bends varies from about 10 to about 40 diameters; for the cheaper 90° meterbend of Fig. 8.17b we get a much larger equivalent length of 60 diameters.

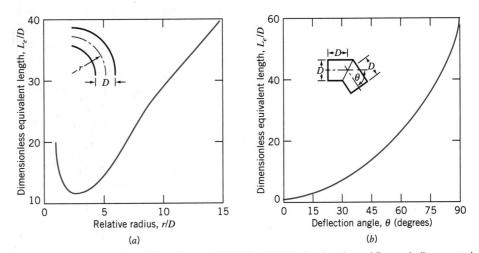

Fig. 8.17 Representative total resistance (L_e/D) for (a) 90° pipe bends and flanged elbows, and (b) miter bends. (Data from [11].)

---

[5] Secondary flows are shown in the NCFMF video *Secondary Flow*. (See http://web.mit.edu/fluids/www/Shapiro/ncfmf.html for free online viewing of this film.)

TABLE 8.4 Representative Dimensionless Equivalent Lengths (L_e/D) for Valves and Fittings (Data from [11].)

Fitting Type	Equivalent Length,[a] L_e/D
Valves (fully open)	
Gate valve	8
Globe valve	340
Angle valve	150
Ball valve	3
Lift check valve: globe lift	600
angle lift	55
Foot valve with strainer: poppet disk	420
hinged disk	75
Standard elbow: 90°	30
45°	16
Return bend, close pattern	50
Standard tee: flow through run	20
flow through branch	60

[a]Based on $h_{l_m} = f(L_e/D)(\overline{V}^2/2)$.

d. Valves and Fittings

Losses for flow through valves and fittings also may be expressed in terms of an equivalent length of straight pipe. Some representative data are given in Table 8.4.

All resistances are given for fully open valves; losses increase markedly when valves are partially open. Valve design varies significantly among manufacturers. Whenever possible, resistances furnished by the valve supplier should be used if accurate results are needed.

Fittings in a piping system may have threaded, flanged, or welded connections. For small diameters, threaded joints are most common; large pipe systems frequently have flanged or welded joints.

In practice, insertion losses for fittings and valves vary considerably, depending on the care used in fabricating the pipe system. If burrs from cutting pipe sections are allowed to remain, they cause local flow obstructions, which increase losses appreciably.

Although the losses discussed in this section were termed "minor losses," they can be a large fraction of the overall system loss. Thus a system for which calculations are to be made must be checked carefully to make sure all losses have been identified and their magnitudes estimated. If calculations are made carefully, the results will be of satisfactory engineering accuracy. You may expect to predict actual losses within ±10 percent.

We include here one more device that changes the energy of the fluid—except this time the energy of the fluid will be increased, so it creates a "negative energy loss."

Pumps, Fans, and Blowers in Fluid Systems

In many practical flow situations (e.g., the cooling system of an automobile engine, the HVAC system of a building), the driving force for maintaining the flow against friction is a pump (for liquids) or a fan or blower (for gases). Here we will consider pumps, although all the results apply equally to fans and blowers. We generally neglect heat transfer and internal energy changes of the fluid (we will incorporate them later into the definition of the pump efficiency), so the first law of thermodynamics applied across the pump is

$$\dot{W}_{\text{pump}} = \dot{m}\left[\left(\frac{p}{\rho} + \frac{\overline{V}^2}{2} + gz\right)_{\text{discharge}} - \left(\frac{p}{\rho} + \frac{\overline{V}^2}{2} + gz\right)_{\text{suction}}\right]$$

We can also compute the head Δh_{pump} (energy/mass) produced by the pump,

$$\Delta h_{\text{pump}} = \frac{\dot{W}_{\text{pump}}}{\dot{m}} = \left(\frac{p}{\rho} + \frac{\overline{V}^2}{2} + gz\right)_{\text{discharge}} - \left(\frac{p}{\rho} + \frac{\overline{V}^2}{2} + gz\right)_{\text{suction}} \quad (8.45)$$

In many cases the inlet and outlet diameters (and therefore velocities) and elevations are the same or negligibly different, so Eq. 8.45 simplifies to

$$\Delta h_{\text{pump}} = \frac{\Delta p_{\text{pump}}}{\rho} \tag{8.46}$$

It is interesting to note that a pump adds energy to the fluid in the form of a gain in pressure—the everyday, invalid perception is that pumps add kinetic energy to the fluid. (It *is* true that when a pump-pipe system is first started up, the pump does work to accelerate the fluid to its steady speed; this is when a pump driven by an electric motor is most in danger of burning out the motor.)

The idea is that in a pump-pipe system the head produced by the pump (Eq. 8.45 or 8.46) is needed to overcome the head loss for the pipe system. Hence, the flow rate in such a system depends on the pump characteristics and the major and minor losses of the pipe system. We will learn in Chapter 10 that the head produced by a given pump is not constant, but varies with flow rate through the pump, leading to the notion of "matching" a pump to a given system to achieve the desired flow rate.

A useful relation is obtained from Eq. 8.46 if we multiply by $\dot{m} = \rho Q$ (Q is the flow rate) and recall that $\dot{m}\,\Delta h_{\text{pump}}$ is the power supplied to the fluid,

$$\dot{W}_{\text{pump}} = Q\Delta p_{\text{pump}} \tag{8.47}$$

We can also define the pump efficiency:

$$\eta = \frac{\dot{W}_{\text{pump}}}{\dot{W}_{\text{in}}} \tag{8.48}$$

where $\dot{W}_{\text{pump}}$ is the power reaching the fluid, and $\dot{W}_{\text{in}}$ is the power input (usually electrical) to the pump.

We note that, when applying the energy equation (Eq. 8.29) to a pipe system, we may sometimes choose points 1 and 2 so that a pump is included in the system. For these cases we can simply include the head of the pump as a "negative loss":

$$\left(\frac{p_1}{\rho} + \alpha_1 \frac{\overline{V}_1^2}{2} + gz_1\right) - \left(\frac{p_2}{\rho} + \alpha_2 \frac{\overline{V}_2^2}{2} + gz_2\right) = h_{l_T} - \Delta h_{\text{pump}} \tag{8.49}$$

Noncircular Ducts

The empirical correlations for pipe flow also may be used for computations involving noncircular ducts, provided their cross sections are not too exaggerated. Thus ducts of square or rectangular cross section may be treated if the ratio of height to width is less than about 3 or 4.

The correlations for turbulent pipe flow are extended for use with noncircular geometries by introducing the *hydraulic diameter*, defined as

$$D_h \equiv \frac{4A}{P} \tag{8.50}$$

in place of the diameter, D. In Eq. 8.50, A is cross-sectional area, and P is *wetted perimeter*, the length of wall in contact with the flowing fluid at any cross-section. The factor 4 is introduced so that the hydraulic diameter will equal the duct diameter for a circular cross-section. For a circular duct, $A = \pi D^2/4$ and $P = \pi D$, so that

$$D_h = \frac{4A}{P} = \frac{4\left(\dfrac{\pi}{4}\right)D^2}{\pi D} = D$$

For a rectangular duct of width b and height h, $A = bh$ and $P = 2(b + h)$, so

$$D_h = \frac{4bh}{2(b + h)}$$

If the *aspect ratio*, *ar*, is defined as $ar = h/b$, then

$$D_h = \frac{2h}{1 + ar}$$

for rectangular ducts. For a square duct, $ar = 1$ and $D_h = h$.

As noted, the hydraulic diameter concept can be applied in the approximate range $\frac{1}{4} < ar < 4$. Under these conditions, the correlations for pipe flow give acceptably accurate results for rectangular ducts. Since such ducts are easy and cheap to fabricate from sheet metal, they are commonly used in air conditioning, heating, and ventilating applications. Extensive data on losses for air flow are available (e.g., see [12, 19]).

Losses caused by secondary flows increase rapidly for more extreme geometries, so the correlations are not applicable to wide, flat ducts, or to ducts of triangular or other irregular shapes. Experimental data must be used when precise design information is required for specific situations.

8-8 ## SOLUTION OF PIPE FLOW PROBLEMS

Section 8-7 provides us with a complete scheme for solving many different pipe flow problems. For convenience we collect together the relevant computing equations.

The *energy equation*, relating the conditions at any two points 1 and 2 for a single-path pipe system, is

$$\left(\frac{p_1}{\rho} + \alpha_1 \frac{\overline{V}_1^2}{2} + gz_1\right) - \left(\frac{p_2}{\rho} + \alpha_2 \frac{\overline{V}_2^2}{2} + gz_2\right) = h_{l_T} = \sum h_l + \sum h_{l_m} \quad (8.29)$$

This equation expresses the fact that there will be a loss of mechanical energy ("pressure," kinetic and/or potential) in the pipe. Recall that for turbulent flows $\alpha \approx 1$. Note that by judicious choice of points 1 and 2 we can analyze not only the entire pipe system, but also just a certain section of it that we may be interested in. The *total head loss* is given by the sum of the major and minor losses. (Remember that we can also include "negative losses" for any pumps present between points 1 and 2. The relevant form of the energy equation is then Eq. 8.49.)

Each *major loss* is given by

$$h_l = f \frac{L}{D} \frac{\overline{V}^2}{2} \quad (8.34)$$

where the *friction factor* is obtained from

$$f = \frac{64}{Re} \quad \text{for laminar flow } (Re < 2300) \quad (8.36)$$

or

$$\frac{1}{\sqrt{f}} = -2.0 \log\left(\frac{e/D}{3.7} + \frac{2.51}{Re\sqrt{f}}\right) \quad \text{for turbulent flow } (Re \geq 2300) \quad (8.37)$$

and Eqs. 8.36 and 8.37 are presented graphically in the Moody chart (Fig. 8.13).

Each *minor loss* is given either by

$$h_{l_m} = K \frac{\overline{V}^2}{2} \quad (8.40a)$$

α = 1 for Turbulent Flow

where K is the device *loss coefficient*, or

$$h_{l_m} = f \frac{L_e}{D} \frac{\overline{V}^2}{2} \tag{8.40b}$$

where L_e is the additional *equivalent length* of pipe.

We also note that the flow rate Q is related to the average velocity $\overline{V}$ at each pipe cross-section by

$$Q = \pi \frac{D^2}{4} \overline{V}$$

We will apply these equations first to single-path systems.

Single-Path Systems

In single-path pipe problems we generally know the system configuration (type of pipe material and hence pipe roughness, the number and type of elbows, valves, and other fittings, etc., and changes of elevation), as well as the fluid (ρ and μ) we will be working with. Although not the only possibilities, usually the goal is to determine one of the following:

(a) The pressure drop Δp, for a given pipe (L and D), and flow rate Q.
(b) The pipe length L, for a given pressure drop Δp, pipe diameter D, and flow rate Q.
(c) The flow rate Q, for a given pipe (L and D), and pressure drop Δp.
(d) The pipe diameter D, for a given pipe length L, pressure drop Δp, and flow rate Q.

Each of these cases often arises in real-world situations. For example, case (a) is a necessary step in selecting the correct size pump to maintain the desired flow rate in a system—the pump must be able to produce the system Δp at the specified flow rate Q. (We will discuss this in more detail in Chapter 10.) Cases (a) and (b) are computationally straightforward; we will see that cases (c) and (d) can be a little tricky to evaluate. We will discuss each case, and present an Example for each. The Examples present solutions as you might do them using a calculator, but there is also an *Excel* workbook for each. (Remember that the Web site has an *Excel* add-in that once installed will automatically compute f from Re and e/D!) The advantage of using a computer application such as a spreadsheet is that we do not have to use either the Moody chart (Fig. 8.13) or solve the implicit Colebrook equation (Eq. 8.37) to obtain turbulent friction factors—the application can find them for us! In addition, as we'll see, cases (c) and (d) involve significant iterative calculations that can be avoided by use of a computer application. Finally, once we have a solution using a computer application, engineering "what-ifs" become easy, e.g., if we double the head produced by a pump, how much will the flow rate in a given system increase?

a. Find Δp for a Given L, D, and Q

These types of problems are quite straightforward—the energy equation (Eq. 8.29) can be solved directly for $\Delta p = (p_1 - p_2)$ in terms of known or computable quantities. The flow rate leads to the Reynolds number (or numbers if there is a diameter change) and hence the friction factor (or factors) for the flow; tabulated data can be used for minor loss coefficients and equivalent lengths. The energy equation can then be used to directly obtain the pressure drop. Example 8.5 illustrates this type of problem.

b. Find L for a Given Δp, D, and Q

These types of problems are also straightforward—the energy equation (Eq. 8.29) can be solved directly for L in terms of known or computable quantities. The flow rate again leads to the Reynolds number and hence the friction factor for the flow.

Tabulated data can be used for minor loss coefficients and equivalent lengths. The energy equation can then be rearranged and solved directly for the pipe length. Example 8.6 illustrates this type of problem.

c. Find Q for a Given Δp, L, and D

These types of problems require either manual iteration or use of a computer application such as *Excel*. The unknown flow rate or velocity is needed before the Reynolds number and hence the friction factor can be found. To manually iterate we first solve the energy equation directly for $\overline{V}$ in terms of known quantities and the unknown friction factor f. To start the iterative process we make a guess for f (a good choice is to take a value from the fully turbulent region of the Moody chart because many practical flows are in this region) and obtain a value for $\overline{V}$. Then we can compute a Reynolds number and hence obtain a new value for f. We repeat the iteration process $f \rightarrow \overline{V} \rightarrow Re \rightarrow f$ until convergence (usually only two or three iterations are necessary). A much quicker procedure is to use a computer application. For example, spreadsheets (such as *Excel*) have built-in solving features for solving one or more algebraic equations for one or more unknowns. Example 8.7 illustrates this type of problem.

d. Find D for a Given Δp, L, and Q

These types of problems arise, for example, when we have designed a pump-pipe system and wish to choose the best pipe diameter—the best being the minimum diameter (for minimum pipe cost) that will deliver the design flow rate. We need to manually iterate, or use a computer application such as *Excel*. The unknown diameter is needed before the Reynolds number and relative roughness, and hence the friction factor, can be found. To manually iterate we could first solve the energy equation directly for D in terms of known quantities and the unknown friction factor f, and then iterate from a starting guess for f in a similar way to case (c) above: $f \rightarrow D \rightarrow Re$ and $e/D \rightarrow f$. In practice this is a little unwieldy, so instead to manually find a solution we make successive guesses for D until the corresponding pressure drop Δp (for the given flow rate Q) computed from the energy equation matches the design Δp. As in case (c) a much quicker procedure is to use a computer application. For example, spreadsheets (such as *Excel*) have built-in solving features for solving one or more algebraic equations for one or more unknowns. Example 8.8 illustrates this type of problem.

In choosing a pipe size, it is logical to work with diameters that are available commercially. Pipe is manufactured in a limited number of standard sizes. Some data for standard pipe sizes are given in Table 8.5. For data on extra strong or double extra strong pipes, consult a handbook, e.g., [11]. Pipe larger than 12 in. nominal diameter is produced in multiples of 2 in. up to a nominal diameter of 36 in. and in multiples of 6 in. for still larger sizes.

TABLE 8.5 Standard Sizes for Carbon Steel, Alloy Steel, and Stainless Steel Pipe (Data from [11].)

Nominal Pipe Size (in.)	Inside Diameter (in.)	Nominal Pipe Size (in.)	Inside Diameter (in.)
$\frac{1}{8}$	0.269	$2\frac{1}{2}$	2.469
$\frac{1}{4}$	0.364	3	3.068
$\frac{3}{8}$	0.493	4	4.026
$\frac{1}{2}$	0.622	5	5.047
$\frac{3}{4}$	0.824	6	6.065
1	1.049	8	7.981
$1\frac{1}{2}$	1.610	10	10.020
2	2.067	12	12.000

EXAMPLE 8.5 Pipe Flow into a Reservoir: Pressure Drop Unknown

A 100-m length of smooth horizontal pipe is attached to a large reservoir. A pump is attached to the end of the pipe to pump water into the reservoir at a volume flow rate of $0.01 \, \text{m}^3/\text{s}$. What pressure (gage) must the pump produce at the pipe to generate this flow rate? The inside diameter of the smooth pipe is 75 mm.

GIVEN: Water is pumped at $0.01 \, \text{m}^3/\text{s}$ through a 75-mm diameter smooth pipe, with $L = 100$ m, into a constant-level reservoir of depth $d = 10$ m.

FIND: Pump pressure, p_1, required to maintain the flow.

SOLUTION:

Governing equations:

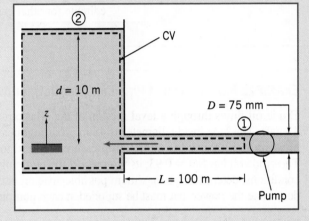

$$\left(\frac{p_1}{\rho} + \alpha_1 \frac{\overline{V}_1^2}{2} + gz_1 \right) - \left(\frac{p_2}{\rho} + \alpha_2 \frac{\overline{V}_2^2}{2} + gz_2 \right) = h_{l_T} = h_l + h_{l_m}$$

$$(8.29)$$

where

$$h_l = f \frac{L}{D} \frac{\overline{V}^2}{2} \quad (8.34) \qquad \text{and} \qquad h_{l_m} = K \frac{\overline{V}^2}{2} \quad (8.40a)$$

For the given problem, $p_1 = p_{\text{pump}}$ and $p_2 = 0$ (gage), so $\Delta p = p_1 - p_2 = p_{\text{pump}}$, $\overline{V}_1 = \overline{V}$, $\overline{V}_2 \approx 0$, K (exit loss) $= 1.0$, and $\alpha_1 \approx 1.0$. If we set $z_1 = 0$, then $z_2 = d$. Simplifying Eq. 8.29 gives

$$\frac{\Delta p}{\rho} + \frac{\overline{V}^2}{2} - gd = f \frac{L}{D} \frac{\overline{V}^2}{2} + \frac{\overline{V}^2}{2} \tag{1}$$

The left side of the equation is the loss of mechanical energy between points ① and ②; the right side is the major and minor losses that contributed to the loss. Solving for the pressure drop, $\Delta p = p_{\text{pump}}$,

$$p_{\text{pump}} = \Delta p = \rho \left(gd + f \frac{L}{D} \frac{\overline{V}^2}{2} \right)$$

Everything on the right side of the equation is known or can be readily computed. The flow rate Q leads to $\overline{V}$,

$$\overline{V} = \frac{Q}{A} = \frac{4Q}{\pi D^2} = \frac{4}{\pi} \times \frac{0.01 \, \text{m}^3}{\text{s}} \times \frac{1}{(0.075)^2 \, \text{m}^2} = 2.26 \, \text{m/s}$$

This in turn [assuming water at 20°C, $\rho = 999 \, \text{kg/m}^3$, and $\mu = 1.0 \times 10^{-3} \, \text{kg/(m·s)}$] leads to the Reynolds number

$$Re = \frac{\rho \overline{V} D}{\mu} = \frac{999 \, \text{kg}}{\text{m}^3} \times \frac{2.26 \, \text{m}}{\text{s}} \times 0.075 \, \text{m} \times \frac{\text{m·s}}{1.0 \times 10^{-3} \text{kg}} = 1.70 \times 10^5$$

For turbulent flow in a smooth pipe ($e = 0$), from Eq. 8.37, $f = 0.0162$. Then

$$p_{\text{pump}} = \Delta p = \rho \left(gd + f \frac{L}{D} \frac{\overline{V}^2}{2} \right)$$

$$= \frac{999 \, \text{kg}}{\text{m}^3} \left(\frac{9.81 \, \text{m}}{\text{s}^2} \times 10 \, \text{m} + (0.0162) \times \frac{100 \, \text{m}}{0.075 \, \text{m}} \times \frac{(2.26)^2 \text{m}^2}{2 \, \text{s}^2} \right) \times \frac{\text{N·s}^2}{\text{kg·m}}$$

$$p_{\text{pump}} = 1.53 \times 10^5 \, \text{N/m}^2 \, \text{(gage)}$$

Hence,

$$p_{\text{pump}} = 153 \, \text{kPa (gage)} \quad \longleftarrow$$ p_{pump}

This problem illustrates the method for manually calculating pressure drop. The *Excel* workbook for this problem automatically computes Re and f from the given data. It then solves Eq. 1 directly for pressure p_{pump} without having to explicitly solve for it first. The workbook can be easily used to see, for example, how the pump pressure p_{pump} required to maintain flow Q is affected by changing the diameter D; it is easily editable for other case (a) type problems.

EXAMPLE 8.6   Flow in a Pipeline: Length Unknown

Crude oil flows through a level section of the Alaskan pipeline at a rate of 1.6 million barrels per day (1 barrel = 42 gal). The pipe inside diameter is 48 in.; its roughness is equivalent to galvanized iron. The maximum allowable pressure is 1200 psi; the minimum pressure required to keep dissolved gases in solution in the crude oil is 50 psi. The crude oil has SG = 0.93; its viscosity at the pumping temperature of 140°F is $\mu = 3.5 \times 10^{-4}$ lbf · s/ft². For these conditions, determine the maximum possible spacing between pumping stations. If the pump efficiency is 85 percent, determine the power that must be supplied at each pumping station.

GIVEN: Flow of crude oil through horizontal section of Alaskan pipeline.

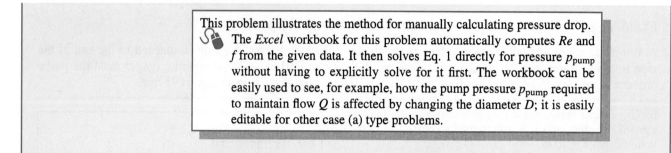

$D = 48$ in. (roughness of galvanized iron), SG = 0.93, $\mu = 3.5 \times 10^{-4}$ lbf · s/ft²

FIND: (a) Maximum spacing, L.
(b) Power needed at each pump station.

SOLUTION:

As shown in the figure, we assume that the Alaskan pipeline is made up of repeating pump-pipe sections. We can draw two control volumes: CV_1, for the pipe flow (state ② to state ①); CV_2, for the pump (state ① to state ②).

First we apply the energy equation for steady, incompressible pipe flow to CV_1.

Governing equations:

$$\left(\frac{p_2}{\rho} + \alpha_2 \frac{\overline{V}_2^2}{2} + \cancel{g z_2}\right) - \left(\frac{p_1}{\rho} + \alpha_1 \frac{\overline{V}_1^2}{2} + \cancel{g z_1}\right) = h_{l_T} = h_l + h_{l_m} \tag{8.29}$$

where

$$h_l = f \frac{L}{D} \frac{\overline{V}^2}{2} \quad (8.34) \qquad \text{and} \qquad h_{l_m} = K \frac{\overline{V}^2}{2} \quad (8.40a)$$

Assumptions: (1) $\alpha_1 \overline{V}_1^2 = \alpha_2 \overline{V}_2^2$.
(2) Horizontal pipe, $z_1 = z_2$.
(3) Neglect minor losses.
(4) Constant viscosity.

Then, using CV_1

$$\Delta p = p_2 - p_1 = f \frac{L}{D} \rho \frac{\overline{V}^2}{2} \tag{1}$$

or

$$L = \frac{2D}{f}\frac{\Delta p}{\rho \overline{V}^2} \quad \text{where } f = f(Re, e/D)$$

$$Q = 1.6 \times 10^6 \frac{\text{bbl}}{\text{day}} \times 42 \frac{\text{gal}}{\text{bbl}} \times \frac{\text{ft}^3}{7.48 \text{ gal}} \times \frac{\text{day}}{24 \text{ hr}} \times \frac{\text{hr}}{3600 \text{ s}} = 104 \text{ ft}^3/\text{s}$$

so

$$\overline{V} = \frac{Q}{A} = \frac{104 \text{ ft}^3}{\text{s}} \times \frac{4}{\pi(4)^2 \text{ ft}^2} = 8.27 \text{ ft/s}$$

$$Re = \frac{\rho \overline{V} D}{\mu} = \frac{(0.93)1.94 \text{ slug}}{\text{ft}^3} \times \frac{8.27 \text{ ft}}{\text{s}} \times 4 \text{ ft} \times \frac{\text{ft}^2}{3.5 \times 10^{-4} \text{ lbf} \cdot \text{s}} \times \frac{\text{lbf} \cdot \text{s}^2}{\text{slug} \cdot \text{ft}}$$

$$Re = 1.71 \times 10^5$$

From Table 8.1, $e = 0.0005$ ft and hence $e/D = 0.00012$. Then from Eq. 8.37, $f = 0.017$ and thus

$$L = \frac{2}{0.017} \times 4 \text{ ft} \times \frac{(1200 - 50) \text{ lbf}}{\text{in.}^2} \times \frac{\text{ft}^3}{(0.93)1.94 \text{ slug}} \times \frac{\text{s}^2}{(8.27)^2 \text{ ft}^2}$$

$$\times \frac{144 \text{ in.}^2}{\text{ft}^2} \times \frac{\text{slug} \cdot \text{ft}}{\text{lbf} \cdot \text{s}^2} = 6.32 \times 10^5 \text{ ft}$$

$$L = 632,000 \text{ ft } (120 \text{ mi}) \longleftarrow \hspace{5cm} L$$

To find the pumping power we can apply the first law of thermodynamics to CV_2. This control volume consists only of the pump, and we saw in Section 8-7 that this law simplifies to

$$\dot{W}_{\text{pump}} = Q\Delta p_{\text{pump}} \tag{8.47}$$

and the pump efficiency is

$$\eta = \frac{\dot{W}_{\text{pump}}}{\dot{W}_{\text{in}}} \tag{8.48}$$

We recall that $\dot{W}_{\text{pump}}$ is the power reaching the fluid, and $\dot{W}_{\text{in}}$ is the power input. Because we have a repeating system the pressure rise through the pump (i.e., from state ① to state ②) equals the pressure drop in the pipe (i.e., from state ② to state ①),

$$\Delta p_{\text{pump}} = \Delta p$$

so that

$$\dot{W}_{\text{pump}} = Q\Delta p_{\text{pump}} = \frac{104 \text{ ft}^3}{\text{s}} \times \frac{(1200 - 50) \text{ lbf}}{\text{in.}^2} \times \frac{144 \text{ in.}^2}{\text{ft}^2} \times \frac{\text{hp} \cdot \text{s}}{550 \text{ ft} \cdot \text{lbf}} \approx 31,300 \text{ hp}$$

and the required power input is

$$\dot{W}_{\text{in.}} = \frac{\dot{W}_{\text{pump}}}{\eta} = \frac{31300 \text{ hp}}{0.85} = 36,800 \text{ hp} \longleftarrow \hspace{3cm} \dot{W}_{\text{needed}}$$

This problem illustrates the method for manually calculating pipe length L. The *Excel* workbook for this problem automatically computes Re and f from the given data. It then solves Eq. 1 directly for L without having to explicitly solve for it first. The workbook can be easily used to see, for example, how the flow rate Q depends on L; it may be edited for other case (b) type problems.

EXAMPLE 8.7   Flow from a Water Tower: Flow Rate Unknown

A fire protection system is supplied from a water tower and standpipe 80 ft tall. The longest pipe in the system is 600 ft and is made of cast iron about 20 years old. The pipe contains one gate valve; other minor losses may be neglected. The pipe diameter is 4 in. Determine the maximum rate of flow (gpm) through this pipe.

GIVEN: Fire protection system, as shown.

FIND: Q, gpm.

SOLUTION:

Governing equations:

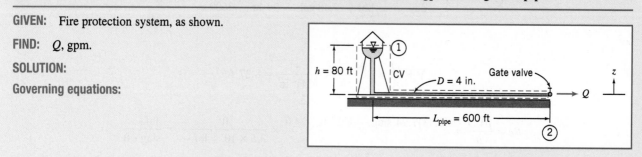

$$\left(\frac{\cancel{p_1}}{\rho} + \alpha_1 \cancel{\frac{\overline{V_1^2}}{2}} + gz_1\right) - \left(\frac{\cancel{p_2}}{\rho} + \alpha_2 \frac{\overline{V_2^2}}{2} + gz_2\right) = h_{l_T} = h_l + h_{l_m} \qquad \overset{\approx 0(2)}{} \tag{8.29}$$

where

$$h_l = f\frac{L}{D}\frac{\overline{V}^2}{2} \quad (8.34) \qquad \text{and} \qquad h_{l_m} = f\frac{L_e}{D}\frac{\overline{V}^2}{2} \quad (8.40\,b)$$

Assumptions: (1) $p_1 = p_2 = p_{atm}$
(2) $\overline{V}_1 = 0$, and $\alpha_2 \simeq 1.0$.

Then Eq. 8.29 can be written as

$$g(z_1 - z_2) - \frac{\overline{V_2^2}}{2} = h_{l_T} = f\left(\frac{L}{D} + \frac{L_e}{D}\right)\frac{\overline{V_2^2}}{2} \tag{1}$$

For a fully open gate valve, from Table 8.4, $L_e/D = 8$. Thus

$$g(z_1 - z_2) = \frac{\overline{V_2^2}}{2}\left[f\left(\frac{L}{D} + 8\right) + 1\right]$$

To manually iterate, we solve for $\overline{V}_2$ and obtain

$$\overline{V}_2 = \left[\frac{2g(z_1 - z_2)}{f(L/D + 8) + 1}\right]^{1/2} \tag{2}$$

To be conservative, assume the standpipe is the same diameter as the horizontal pipe. Then

$$\frac{L}{D} = \frac{600 \text{ ft} + 80 \text{ ft}}{4 \text{ in.}} \times \frac{12 \text{ in.}}{\text{ft}} = 2040$$

Also

$$z_1 - z_2 = h = 80 \text{ ft}$$

To solve Eq. 2 manually we need to iterate. To start, we make an estimate for f by assuming the flow is fully turbulent (where f is constant). This value can be obtained from solving Eq. 8.37 using a calculator or from Fig. 8.13. For a large value of Re (e.g., 10^8), and a roughness ratio $e/D \approx 0.005$ ($e = 0.00085$ ft for cast iron is obtained from Table 8.1, and doubled to allow for the fact that the pipe is old), we find that $f \approx 0.03$. Thus a first iteration for $\overline{V}_2$ from Eq. 2 is

$$\overline{V}_2 = \left[2 \times 32.2 \frac{\text{ft}}{\text{s}^2} \times 80 \text{ ft} \times \frac{1}{0.03(2040 + 8) + 1}\right]^{1/2} = 9.08 \text{ ft/s}$$

Now obtain a new value for f:

$$Re = \frac{\rho\overline{V}D}{\mu} = \frac{\overline{V}D}{\nu} = 9.08 \frac{\text{ft}}{\text{s}} \times \frac{\text{ft}}{3} \times \frac{\text{s}}{1.21 \times 10^{-5} \text{ ft}^2} = 2.50 \times 10^5$$

For $e/D = 0.005$, $f = 0.0308$ from Eq. 8.37. Thus we obtain

$$\overline{V}_2 = \left[2 \times 32.2 \, \frac{\text{ft}}{\text{s}^2} \times 80 \, \text{ft} \times \frac{1}{0.0308 \, (2040 + 8) + 1}\right]^{1/2} = 8.97 \, \text{ft/s}$$

The values we have obtained for $\overline{V}_2$ (9.08 ft/s and 8.97 ft/s) differ by less than 2%—an acceptable level of accuracy. If this accuracy had not been achieved we would continue iterating until this, or any other accuracy we desired, was achieved (usually only one or two more iterations at most are necessary for reasonable accuracy). Note that instead of starting with a fully rough value for f, we could have started with a guess value for $\overline{V}_2$ of, say, 1 ft/s or 10 ft/s. The volume flow rate is

$$Q = \overline{V}_2 A = \overline{V}_2 \frac{\pi D^2}{4} = \frac{8.97 \, \text{ft}}{\text{s}} \times \frac{\pi}{4} \left(\frac{1}{3}\right)^2 \text{ft}^2 \times 7.48 \, \frac{\text{gal}}{\text{ft}^3} \times 60 \, \frac{\text{s}}{\text{min}}$$

$$Q = 351 \, \text{gpm} \xleftarrow{\hspace{7cm}} Q$$

> This problem illustrates the method for manually iterating to calculate flow rate. The *Excel* workbook for this problem automatically iterates to solve for the flow rate Q. It solves Eq. 1 without having to obtain the explicit equation (Eq. 2) for $\overline{V}_2$ (or Q) first. The workbook can be easily used to perform numerous "what-ifs" that would be extremely time-consuming to do manually, e.g., to see how Q is affected by changing the roughness e/D. For example, it shows that replacing the old cast-iron pipe with a new pipe ($e/D \approx 0.0025$) would increase the flow rate from 351 gpm to about 386 gpm, a 10% increase! The workbook can be modified to solve other case (c) type problems.

EXAMPLE 8.8 Flow in an Irrigation System: Diameter Unknown

Spray heads in an agricultural spraying system are to be supplied with water through 500 ft of drawn aluminum tubing from an engine-driven pump. In its most efficient operating range, the pump output is 1500 gpm at a discharge pressure not exceeding 65 psig. For satisfactory operation, the sprinklers must operate at 30 psig or higher pressure. Minor losses and elevation changes may be neglected. Determine the smallest standard pipe size that can be used.

GIVEN: Water supply system, as shown.

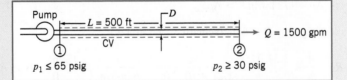

FIND: Smallest standard D.

SOLUTION:

Δp, L, and Q are known. D is unknown, so iteration is needed to determine the minimum standard diameter that satisfies the pressure drop constraint at the given flow rate. The maximum allowable pressure drop over the length, L, is

$$\Delta p_{\text{max}} = p_{1\text{max}} - p_{2\text{min}} = (65 - 30) \, \text{psi} = 35 \, \text{psi}$$

Governing equations:
$$\left(\frac{p_1}{\rho} + \alpha_1 \frac{\overline{V}_1^2}{2} + \cancel{g z_1}\right) - \left(\frac{p_2}{\rho} + \alpha_2 \frac{\overline{V}_2^2}{2} + \cancel{g z_2}\right) = h_{l_T} \qquad (8.29)$$
$$= 0(3)$$
$$h_{l_T} = h_l + \cancel{h_{l_m}} = f \frac{L}{D} \frac{\overline{V}_2^2}{2}$$

Assumptions: (1) Steady flow.
(2) Incompressible flow.
(3) $h_{l_T} = h_l$, i.e., $h_{l_m} = 0$.
(4) $z_1 = z_2$.
(5) $\overline{V}_1 = \overline{V}_2 = \overline{V}; \alpha_1 \simeq \alpha_2$.

Then

$$\Delta p = p_1 - p_2 = f \frac{L}{D} \frac{\rho \overline{V}^2}{2} \qquad (1)$$

Equation 1 is difficult to solve for D because both $\overline{V}$ and f depend on D! The best approach is to use a computer application such as *Excel* to automatically solve for D. For completeness here we show the manual iteration procedure. The first step is to express Eq. 1 and the Reynolds number in terms of Q instead of $\overline{V}$ (Q is constant but $\overline{V}$ varies with D). We have $\overline{V} = Q/A = 4Q/\pi D^2$ so that

$$\Delta p = f \frac{L}{D} \frac{\rho}{2} \left(\frac{4Q}{\pi D^2} \right)^2 = \frac{8 f L \rho Q^2}{\pi^2 D^5} \qquad (2)$$

The Reynolds number in terms of Q is

$$Re = \frac{\rho \overline{V} D}{\mu} = \frac{\overline{V} D}{v} = \frac{4Q}{\pi D^2} \frac{D}{v} = \frac{4Q}{\pi v D}$$

Finally, Q must be converted to cubic feet per second.

$$Q = 1500 \frac{\text{gal}}{\text{min}} \times \frac{\text{min}}{60 \text{ s}} \times \frac{\text{ft}^3}{7.48 \text{ gal}} = 3.34 \text{ ft}^3/\text{s}$$

For an initial guess, take nominal 4 in. (4.026 in. i.d.) pipe:

$$Re = \frac{4Q}{\pi v D} = \frac{4}{\pi} \times 3.34 \frac{\text{ft}^3}{\text{s}} \times \frac{\text{s}}{1.21 \times 10^{-5} \text{ ft}^2} \times \frac{1}{4.026 \text{ in.}} \times \frac{12 \text{ in.}}{\text{ft}} = 1.06 \times 10^6$$

For drawn tubing, $e = 5 \times 10^{-6}$ ft (Table 8.1) and hence $e/D = 1.5 \times 10^{-5}$, so $f \simeq 0.012$ (Eq. 8.37), and

$$\Delta p = \frac{8 f L \rho Q^2}{\pi^2 D^5} = \frac{8}{\pi^2} \times 0.012 \times 500 \text{ ft} \times 1.94 \frac{\text{slug}}{\text{ft}^3} \times (3.34)^2 \frac{\text{ft}^6}{\text{s}^2}$$

$$\times \frac{1}{(4.026)^5 \text{in.}^5} \times \frac{1728 \text{ in.}^3}{\text{ft}^3} \times \frac{\text{lbf} \cdot \text{s}^2}{\text{slug} \cdot \text{ft}}$$

$$\Delta p = 172 \text{ lbf/in.}^2 > \Delta p_{max}$$

Since this pressure drop is too large, try $D = 6$ in. (actually 6.065 in. i.d.):

$$Re = \frac{4}{\pi} \times 3.34 \frac{\text{ft}^3}{\text{s}} \times \frac{\text{s}}{1.21 \times 10^{-5} \text{ ft}^2} \times \frac{1}{6.065 \text{ in.}} \times \frac{12 \text{ in.}}{\text{ft}} = 6.95 \times 10^5$$

For drawn tubing with $D = 6$ in., $e/D = 1.0 \times 10^{-5}$, so $f \simeq 0.013$ (Eq. 8.37), and

$$\Delta p = \frac{8}{\pi^2} \times 0.013 \times 500 \text{ ft} \times 1.94 \frac{\text{slug}}{\text{ft}^3} \times (3.34)^2 \frac{\text{ft}^6}{\text{s}^2}$$

$$\times \frac{1}{(6.065)^5 \text{ in.}^5} \times (12)^3 \frac{\text{in.}^3}{\text{ft}^3} \times \frac{\text{lbf} \cdot \text{s}^2}{\text{slug} \cdot \text{ft}}$$

$$\Delta p = 24.0 \text{ lbf/in.}^2 < \Delta p_{max}$$

Since this is less than the allowable pressure drop, we should check a 5 in. (nominal) pipe. With an actual i.d. of 5.047 in.,

$$Re = \frac{4}{\pi} \times 3.34 \frac{\text{ft}^3}{\text{s}} \times \frac{\text{s}}{1.21 \times 10^{-5} \text{ ft}^2} \times \frac{1}{5.047 \text{ in.}} \times \frac{12 \text{ in.}}{\text{ft}} = 8.36 \times 10^5$$

For drawn tubing with $D = 5$ in., $e/D = 1.2 \times 10^{-5}$, so $f \simeq 0.0122$ (Eq. 8.37), and

$$\Delta p = \frac{8}{\pi^2} \times 0.0122 \times 500 \text{ ft} \times 1.94 \frac{\text{slug}}{\text{ft}^3} \times (3.34)^2 \frac{\text{ft}^6}{\text{s}^2}$$

$$\times \frac{1}{(5.047)^5 \text{ in.}^5} \times (12)^3 \frac{\text{in.}^3}{\text{ft}^3} \times \frac{\text{lbf} \cdot \text{s}^2}{\text{slug} \cdot \text{ft}}$$

$$\Delta p = 56.4 \text{ lbf/in.}^2 > \Delta p_{max}$$

Thus the criterion for pressure drop is satisfied for a minimum nominal diameter of 6 in. pipe. ⟵————————————— D

This problem illustrates the method for manually iterating to calculate pipe diameter.

The *Excel* workbook for this problem automatically iterates to solve for the exact pipe diameter D that satisfies Eq. 1, without having to obtain the explicit equation (Eq. 2) for D first. Then all that needs to be done is to select the smallest standard pipe size that is equal to or greater than this value. For the given data, $D = 5.58$ in., so the appropriate pipe size is 6 in. The workbook can be used to perform numerous "what-ifs" that would be extremely time-consuming to do manually, e.g., to see how the required D is affected by changing the pipe length L. For example, it shows that reducing L to 250 ft would allow 5 in. (nominal) pipe to be used. The workbook can be modified for solving other case (d) type problems.

We have solved Examples 8.7 and 8.8 by iteration (manual, or using *Excel*). Several specialized forms of friction factor versus Reynolds number diagrams have been introduced to solve problems of this type without the need for iteration. For examples of these specialized diagrams, see [20] and [21].

Examples 8.9 and 8.10 illustrate the evaluation of minor loss coefficients and the application of a diffuser to reduce exit kinetic energy from a flow system.

EXAMPLE 8.9 Calculation of Entrance Loss Coefficient

Reference [22] reports results of measurements made to determine entrance losses for flow from a reservoir to a pipe with various degrees of entrance rounding. A copper pipe 10 ft long, with 1.5 in. i.d., was used for the tests. The pipe discharged to atmosphere. For a square-edged entrance, a discharge of 0.566 ft³/s was measured when the reservoir level was 85.1 ft above the pipe centerline. From these data, evaluate the loss coefficient for a square-edged entrance.

GIVEN: Pipe with square-edged entrance discharging from reservoir as shown.

FIND: $K_{entrance}$.

SOLUTION:
Apply the energy equation for steady, incompressible pipe flow.

Governing equations:

$$\underbrace{\frac{p_1}{\rho}}_{\approx 0(2)} + \alpha_1 \frac{V_1^2}{2} + gz_1 = \underbrace{\frac{p_2}{\rho}}_{= 0} + \alpha_2 \frac{V_2^2}{2} + gz_2 + h_{l_T}$$

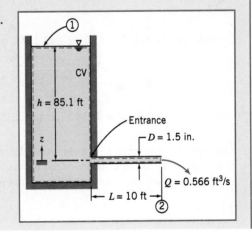

$$h_{l_T} = f \frac{L}{D} \frac{\overline{V}_2^2}{2} + K_{entrance} \frac{\overline{V}_2^2}{2}$$

Assumptions: (1) $p_1 = p_2 = p_{atm}$.

(2) $\overline{V}_1 \approx 0$.

Substituting for h_{l_T} and dividing by g gives $z_1 = h = \alpha_2 \dfrac{\overline{V}_2^2}{2g} + f \dfrac{L}{D} \dfrac{\overline{V}_2^2}{2g} + K_{entrance} \dfrac{\overline{V}_2^2}{2g}$

or

$$K_{entrance} = \frac{2gh}{\overline{V}_2^2} - f\frac{L}{D} - \alpha_2 \tag{1}$$

The average velocity is

$$\overline{V}_2 = \frac{Q}{A} = \frac{4Q}{\pi D^2}$$

$$\overline{V}_2 = \frac{4}{\pi} \times \frac{0.566 \ \text{ft}^3}{\text{s}} \times \frac{1}{(1.5)^2 \ \text{in.}^2} \times \frac{1.44 \ \text{in.}^2}{\text{ft}^2} = 46.1 \ \text{ft/s}$$

Assume $T = 70°F$, so $\nu = 1.05 \times 10^{-5} \ \text{ft}^2/\text{s}$ (Table A.7). Then

$$Re = \frac{\overline{V}D}{\nu} = \frac{46.1 \ \text{ft}}{\text{s}} \times \frac{1.5 \ \text{in.}}{1} \times \frac{\text{s}}{1.05 \times 10^{-5} \ \text{ft}^2} \times \frac{\text{ft}}{12 \ \text{in.}} = 5.49 \times 10^5$$

For drawn tubing, $e = 5 \times 10^{-6}$ ft (Table 8.1), so $e/D = 0.000,04$ and $f = 0.0135$ (Eq. 8.37).

In this problem we need to be careful in evaluating the kinetic energy correction factor α_2, as it is a significant factor in computing $K_{entrance}$ from Eq. 1. We recall from Section 8-6 and previous Examples that we have usually assumed $\alpha \approx 1$, but here we will compute a value from Eq. 8.27:

$$\alpha = \left(\frac{U}{\overline{V}}\right)^3 \frac{2n^2}{(3+n)(3+2n)} \tag{8.27}$$

To use this equation we need values for the turbulent power-law coefficient n and the ratio of centerline to mean velocity $U/\overline{V}$. For n, from Section 8-5

$$n = -1.7 + 1.8 \ \log(Re_U) \approx 8.63 \tag{8.23}$$

where we have used the approximation $Re_U \approx Re_{\overline{V}}$. For $\overline{V}/U$, we have

$$\frac{\overline{V}}{U} = \frac{2n^2}{(n+1)(2n+1)} = 0.847 \tag{8.24}$$

Using these results in Eq. 8.27 we find $\alpha = 1.04$. Substituting into Eq. 1, we obtain

$$K_{entrance} = 2 \times \frac{32.2 \ \text{ft}}{\text{s}^2} \times 85.1 \ \text{ft} \times \frac{\text{s}^2}{(46.1)^2 \ \text{ft}^2} - (0.0135) \frac{10 \ \text{ft}}{1.5 \ \text{in.}} \times \frac{12 \ \text{in.}}{\text{ft}} - 1.04$$

$$K_{entrance} = 0.459 \longleftarrow \underline{\hspace{4cm}} K_{entrance}$$

This coefficient compares favorably with that shown in Table 8.2. The hydraulic and energy grade lines are shown below. The large head loss in a square-edged entrance is due primarily to separation at the sharp inlet corner and formation of a vena contracta immediately downstream from the corner. The effective flow area reaches a minimum at the vena contracta, so the flow velocity is a maximum there. The flow expands again following the vena contracta to fill the pipe. The uncontrolled expansion following the vena contracta is responsible for most of the head loss. (See Example 8.12.)

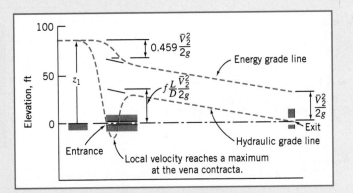

Rounding the inlet corner reduces the extent of separation significantly. This reduces the velocity increase through the vena contracta and consequently reduces the head loss caused by the entrance. A "well-rounded" inlet almost eliminates flow separation; the flow pattern approaches that shown in Fig. 8.1. The added head loss in a well-rounded inlet compared with fully developed flow is the result of higher wall shear stresses in the entrance length.

> This problem:
>
> ✓ Illustrates a method for obtaining the value of a minor loss coefficient from experimental data.
> ✓ Shows how the EGL and HGL lines first introduced in Section 6-5 for inviscid flow are modified by the presence of major and minor losses. The EGL line continuously drops as mechanical energy is consumed—quite sharply when, for example, we have a square-edged entrance loss; the HGL at each location is lower than the EGL by an amount equal to the local dynamic head $\overline{V}^2/2g$—at the vena contracta, for example, the HGL experiences a large drop, then recovers.

EXAMPLE 8.10 Use of Diffuser to Increase Flow Rate

Water rights granted to each citizen by the Emperor of Rome gave permission to attach to the public water main a calibrated, circular, tubular bronze nozzle [23]. Some citizens were clever enough to take unfair advantage of a law that regulated flow rate by such an indirect method. They installed diffusers on the outlets of the nozzles to increase their discharge. Assume the static head available from the main is $z_0 = 1.5$ m and the nozzle exit diameter is $D = 25$ mm. (The discharge is to atmospheric pressure.) Determine the increase in flow rate when a diffuser with $N/R_1 = 3.0$ and $AR = 2.0$ is attached to the end of the nozzle.

GIVEN: Nozzle attached to water main as shown.

FIND: Increase in discharge when diffuser with $N/R_1 = 3.0$ and $AR = 2.0$ is installed.

SOLUTION:
Apply the energy equation for steady, incompressible pipe flow.

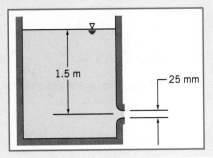

Governing equation: $\dfrac{p_0}{\rho} + \alpha_0 \dfrac{\overline{V}_0^2}{2} + gz_0 = \dfrac{p_1}{\rho} + \alpha_1 \dfrac{\overline{V}_1^2}{2} + gz_1 + h_{l_T}$ (8.29)

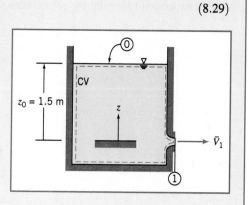

Assumptions: (1) $\overline{V}_0 \approx 0$.
　　　　　　　　(2) $\alpha_1 \approx 1$.

For the nozzle alone,

$$\underset{\approx 0(1)}{\cancel{\dfrac{p_0}{\rho}}} + \underset{\approx 1(2)}{\alpha_0 \cancel{\dfrac{\overline{V}_0^2}{2}}} + gz_0 = \cancel{\dfrac{p_1}{\rho}} + \cancel{\alpha_1} \dfrac{\overline{V}_1^2}{2} + \underset{= 0}{\cancel{gz_1}} + h_{l_T}$$

$$h_{l_T} = K_{\text{entrance}} \dfrac{\overline{V}_1^2}{2}$$

Thus

$$gz_0 = \dfrac{\overline{V}_1^2}{2} + K_{\text{entrance}} \dfrac{\overline{V}_1^2}{2} = (1 + K_{\text{entrance}}) \dfrac{\overline{V}_1^2}{2} \qquad (1)$$

Solving for the velocity and substituting the value of $K_{\text{entrance}} \approx 0.04$ (from Table 8.2),

$$\overline{V}_1 = \sqrt{\dfrac{2gz_0}{1.04}} = \sqrt{\dfrac{2}{1.04} \times 9.81 \,\dfrac{\text{m}}{\text{s}^2} \times 1.5 \,\text{m}} = 5.32 \;\text{m/s}$$

$$Q = \overline{V}_1 A_1 = \overline{V}_1 \dfrac{\pi D_1^2}{4} = 5.32 \,\dfrac{\text{m}}{\text{s}} \times \dfrac{\pi}{4} \times (0.025)^2 \;\text{m}^2 = 0.00261 \;\text{m}^3/\text{s} \longleftarrow \qquad Q$$

For the nozzle with diffuser attached,

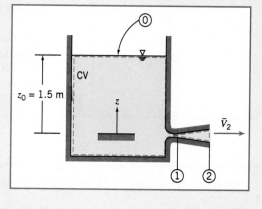

$$\underset{\approx 0(2)}{\cancel{\dfrac{p_0}{\rho}}} + \alpha_0 \cancel{\dfrac{\overline{V}_0^2}{2}} + gz_0 = \cancel{\dfrac{p_1}{\rho}} + \underset{\approx 1(2)}{\cancel{\alpha_2}} \dfrac{\overline{V}_2^2}{2} + \underset{= 0}{\cancel{gz_2}} = h_{l_T}$$

$$h_{l_T} = K_{\text{entrance}} \dfrac{\overline{V}_1^2}{2} + K_{\text{diffuser}} \dfrac{\overline{V}_1^2}{2}$$

or

$$gz_0 = \dfrac{\overline{V}_2^2}{2} + (K_{\text{entrance}} + K_{\text{diffuser}}) \dfrac{\overline{V}_1^2}{2} \qquad (2)$$

From continuity $\overline{V}_1 A_1 = \overline{V}_2 A_2$, so

$$\overline{V}_2 = \overline{V}_1 \dfrac{A_1}{A_2} = \overline{V}_1 \dfrac{1}{AR}$$

and Eq. 2 becomes

$$gz_0 = \left[\dfrac{1}{(AR)^2} + K_{\text{entrance}} + K_{\text{diffuser}} \right] \dfrac{\overline{V}_1^2}{2} \qquad (3)$$

Figure 8.16 gives data for $C_p = \dfrac{p_2 - p_1}{\frac{1}{2}\rho \overline{V}_1^2}$ for diffusers.

To obtain K_{diffuser}, apply the energy equation from ① to ②.

$$\dfrac{p_1}{\rho} + \alpha_1 \dfrac{\overline{V}_1^2}{2} + \cancel{gz_1} = \dfrac{p_2}{\rho} + \alpha_2 \dfrac{\overline{V}_2^2}{2} + \cancel{gz_2} + K_{\text{diffuser}} \dfrac{\overline{V}_1^2}{2}$$

Solving, with $\alpha_2 \approx 1$, we obtain

$$K_{\text{diffuser}} = 1 - - \frac{\overline{V}_2^2}{\overline{V}_1^2} - \frac{p_2 - p_1}{\frac{1}{2}\rho\overline{V}_1^2} = 1 - \left(\frac{A_1}{A_2}\right)^2 - C_p = 1 - \frac{1}{(AR)^2} - C_p$$

From Fig. 8.16, $C_p = 0.45$, so

$$K_{\text{diffuser}} = 1 - \frac{1}{(2.0)^2} - 0.45 = 0.75 - 0.45 = 0.3$$

Solving Eq. 3 for the velocity and substituting the values of K_{entrance} and K_{diffuser}, we obtain

$$\overline{V}_1^2 = \frac{2gz_0}{0.25 + 0.04 + 0.3}$$

so

$$\overline{V}_1 = \sqrt{\frac{2gz_0}{0.59}} = \sqrt{\frac{2}{0.59} \times 9.81\,\frac{\text{m}}{\text{s}^2} \times 1.5\,\text{m}} = 7.06\ \text{m/s}$$

and

$$Q_d = \overline{V}_1 A_1 = \overline{V}_1 \frac{\pi D_1^2}{4} = 7.06\,\frac{\text{m}}{\text{s}} \times \frac{\pi}{4} \times (0.025)^2\ \text{m}^2 = 0.00347\ \text{m}^3/\text{s} \qquad \underline{\qquad Q_d}$$

The flow rate increase that results from adding the diffuser is

$$\frac{\Delta Q}{Q} = \frac{Q_d - Q}{Q} = \frac{Q_d}{Q} - 1 = \frac{0.00347}{0.00261} - 1 = 0.330 \quad \text{or} \quad 33 \text{ percent} \qquad \underline{\qquad \frac{\Delta Q}{Q}}$$

Addition of the diffuser significantly increases the flow rate! There are two ways to explain this.

First, we can sketch the EGL and HGL curves—approximately to scale—as shown below. We can see that, as required, the HGL at the exit is zero for both flows (recall that the HGL is the sum of static pressure and potential heads). However, the pressure rises through the diffuser, so the pressure at the diffuser inlet will be, as shown, quite low (below atmospheric). Hence, with the diffuser, the Δp driving force for the nozzle is much larger than that for the bare nozzle, leading to a much greater velocity, and flow rate, at the nozzle exit plane—it is as if the diffuser acted as a suction device on the nozzle.

Second, we can examine the energy equations for the two flows (for the bare nozzle Eq. 1, and for the nozzle with diffuser Eq. 3). These equations can be rearranged to yield equations for the velocity at the nozzle exit,

$$\overline{V}_1 = \sqrt{\frac{2gz_0}{1 + K_{\text{entrance}}}} \quad \text{(bare nozzle)} \qquad \overline{V}_1 = \sqrt{\frac{2gz_0}{\sqrt{\frac{1}{(AR)^2} + K_{\text{diffuser}} + K_{\text{entrance}}}}} \quad \text{(nozzle + diffuser)}$$

Comparing these two expressions, we see that the diffuser introduces an extra term (its loss coefficient $K_{\text{diffuser}} = 0.3$) to the denominator, tending to reduce the nozzle velocity, but on the other hand we replace the term 1 (representing loss of the bare nozzle exit plane kinetic energy) with $1/(AR)^2 = 0.25$ (representing a smaller loss, of the diffuser exit plane kinetic energy). The net effect is that we replace 1 in the denominator with $0.25 + 0.3 = 0.55$, leading to a net increase in the nozzle velocity. The resistance to flow introduced by adding the diffuser is more than made up by the fact that we "throw away" much less kinetic energy at the exit of the device (the exit velocity for the bare nozzle is 5.32 m/s, whereas for the diffuser it is 1.77 m/s).

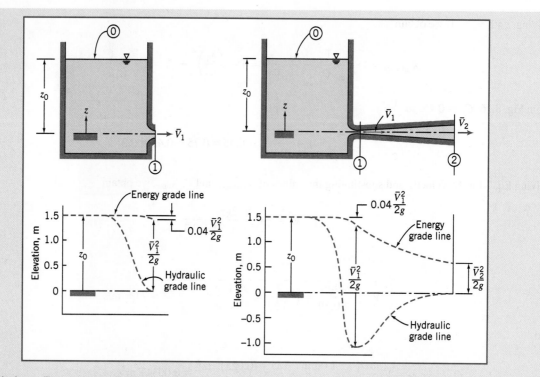

Water Commissioner Frontinus standardized conditions for all Romans in 97 A.D. He required that the tube attached to the nozzle of each customer's pipe be the same diameter for at least 50 lineal feet from the public water main (see Problem 8.137).

*Multiple-Path Systems

Many real-world pipe systems (e.g., the pipe network that supplies water to the apartments in a large building) consist of a network of pipes of various diameters assembled in a complicated configuration that may contain parallel and series connections. As an example, consider part of a system as shown in Fig. 8.18. Water is supplied at some pressure from a manifold at point 1, and flows through the components shown to the drain at point 5. Some water flows through pipes A, B, C, and D, constituting a *series* of pipes (and pipe B has a lower flow rate than the others); some flows through A, E, F or G, H, C, and D (F and G are *parallel*), and these two main branches are in *parallel*. We analyze this type of problem in a similar way to how we analyze DC resistor circuits in electrical theory: by applying a few basic rules to the system. The electrical potential at each point in the circuit is analogous to the HGL (or static pressure head if we neglect gravity) at corresponding points in the system. The current in each resistor is analogous to the flow rate in each pipe section. We have the additional difficulty in pipe systems that the resistance to flow in each pipe is a function of the flow rate (electrical resistors are usually considered constant).

The simple rules for analyzing networks can be expressed in various ways. We will express them as follows:

1. The net flow out of any node (junction) is zero.
2. Each node has a unique pressure head (HGL).

For example, in Fig. 8.18 rule 1 means that the flow into node 2 from pipe A must equal the sum of outflows to pipes B and E. Rule 2 means that the pressure head at

---

*This section may be omitted without loss of continuity in the text material.

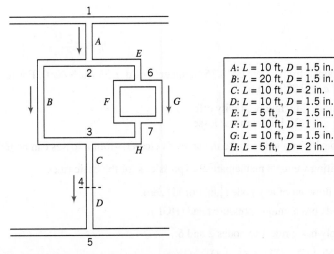

Fig. 8.18 Schematic of part of a pipe network.

node 7 must be equal to the head at node 6 less the losses through pipe F or pipe G, as well as equal to the head at node 3 plus the loss in pipe H.

These rules apply in addition to all the pipe-flow constraints we have discussed (e.g., for $Re \geq 2300$ the flow will be turbulent, and the fact that we may have significant minor losses from features such as sudden expansions). We can anticipate that the flow in pipe F (diameter 1 in.) will be a good deal less than the flow in pipe G (diameter 1.5 in), and the flow through branch E will be larger than that through branch B (why?).

The problems that arise with pipe networks can be as varied as those we discussed when studying single-path systems, but the most common involve finding the flow delivered to each pipe, given an applied pressure difference. We examine this case in Example 8.11. Obviously, pipe networks are much more difficult and time-consuming to analyze than single-path problems, almost always requiring iterative solution methods, and in practice are usually only solved using the computer. A number of computer schemes for analyzing networks have been developed [24], and many engineering consulting companies use proprietary software applications for such analysis. A spreadsheet such as *Excel* is also very useful for setting up and solving such problems.

EXAMPLE 8.11 Flow Rates in a Pipe Network

In the section of a cast-iron water pipe network shown in Fig. 8.18, the static pressure head (gage) available at point 1 is 100 ft of water, and point 5 is a drain (atmospheric pressure). Find the flow rates (gpm) in each pipe.

GIVEN: Pressure head h_{1-5} of 100 ft across pipe network.

FIND: The flow rate in each pipe.

SOLUTION:

Governing equations:

For each pipe section,

$$\left(\frac{p_1}{\rho} + \alpha_1 \frac{\overline{V}_1^2}{2} + \cancel{gz_1}\right)^{=0(1)} - \left(\frac{p_2}{\rho} + \alpha_2 \frac{\overline{V}_2^2}{2} + \cancel{gz_2}\right)^{=0(1)} = h_{l_T} = h_l + \cancel{\sum h_{l_m}}^{=0(2)}$$

$$(8.29)$$

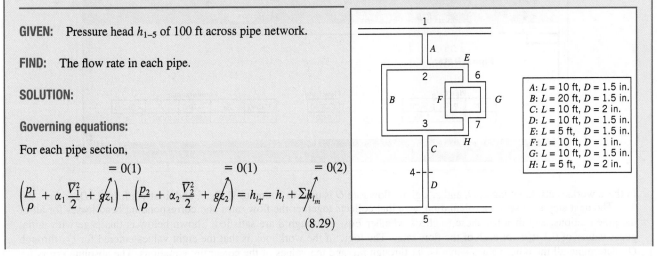

where

$$h_l = f \frac{L}{D} \frac{\overline{V}^2}{2} \qquad (8.34)$$

and f is obtained from either Eq. 8.36 (laminar) or Eq. 8.37 (turbulent). For the cast-iron pipe, Table 8.1 gives a roughness for cast iron of $e = 0.00085$ ft.

Assumptions: (1) Ignore gravity effects.
                   (2) Ignore minor losses.

(Assumption 2 is applied to make the analysis clearer—minor losses can be incorporated easily later.)

In addition we have mathematical expressions for the basic rules

1. The net flow out of any node (junction) is zero.
2. Each node has a unique pressure head (HGL).

We can apply basic rule 1 to nodes 2 and 6:

Node 2: $Q_A = Q_B + Q_E$ (1)   Node 6: $Q_E = Q_F + Q_G$ (2)

and we also have the obvious constraints

$Q_A = Q_C$ (3) $Q_A = Q_D$ (4) $Q_E = Q_H$ (5)

We can apply basic rule 2 to obtain the following pressure drop constraints:

h_{1-5}: $h = h_A + h_B + h_C + h_D$ (6) h_{2-3}: $h_B = h_E + h_F + h_H$ (7) h_{6-7}: $h_F = h_G$ (8)

This set of eight equations (as well as Eqs. 8.29 and 8.34 for each pipe section!) must be solved iteratively. If we were to manually iterate, we would use Eqs. 3, 4, and 5 to immediately reduce the number of unknowns and equations to five (Q_A, Q_B, Q_E, Q_F, Q_G). There are several approaches to the iteration, one of which is:

1. Make a guess for Q_A, Q_B, and Q_F.
2. Eqs. 1 and 2 then lead to values for Q_E and Q_G.
3. Eqs. 6, 7, and 8 are finally used as a check to see if rule 2 (for unique pressure heads at the nodes) is satisfied.
4. If any of Eqs. 6, 7, or 8 are not satisfied, use knowledge of pipe flow to adjust the values of Q_A, Q_B, or Q_F.
5. Repeat steps 2 through 5 until convergence occurs.

An example of applying step 4 would be if Eq. 8 were not satisfied. Suppose $h_F > h_G$; then we would have selected too large a value for Q_F, and would reduce this slightly, and recompute all flow rates and heads.

This iterative process is obviously quite unrealistic for manual calculation (remember that obtaining each head loss h from each Q involves a good amount of calculation). Fortunately, we can use a spreadsheet such as *Excel* to automate all these calculations—it will simultaneously solve for all eight unknowns automatically! The first step is to set up one worksheet for each pipe section for computing the pipe head h given the flow rate Q. A typical such worksheet is shown below:

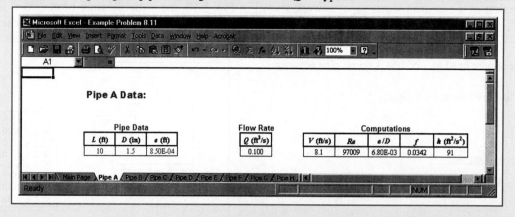

In these worksheets, knowing L, D, and e, a given flow rate Q is used to compute $\overline{V}$, Re, f, and finally h from L, D, and e.

The next step is to set up a calculation page that collects together the flow rates and corresponding head losses for all of the pipe sections, and then use these to check whether Eqs. 1 through 8 are satisfied. Shown below is this page with initial guess values of 0.1 ft³/s for each of the flow rates. The logic of the workbook is that the eight values entered for Q_A through Q_H determine all the other values—that is, h_A through h_H, and the values of the constraint equations. The absolute errors for each of the constraint equations are shown, as well as their sum. We can then use *Excel*'s *Solver* feature (repeatedly as necessary) to minimize the total error (currently 735%) by varying Q_A through Q_H.

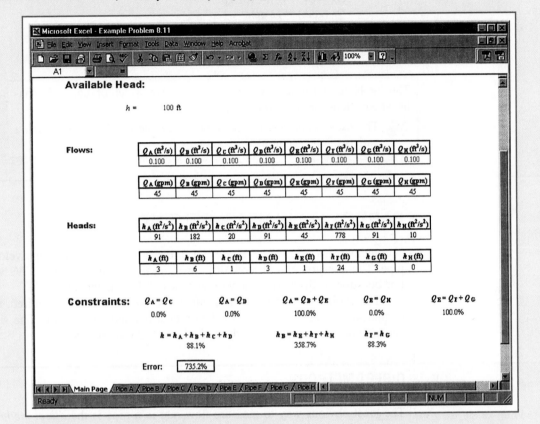

The final results obtained by *Excel* are:

The flow rates are:

$$Q_A = Q_C = Q_D = 167 \text{ gpm}$$
$$Q_B \text{ (gpm)} = 72 \text{ gpm}$$
$$Q_E \text{ (gpm)} = Q_H \text{(gpm)} = 95 \text{ gpm}$$
$$Q_F \text{ (gpm)} = 24 \text{ gpm}$$
$$Q_G \text{ (gpm)} = 71 \text{ gpm}$$

> This problem illustrates use of *Excel* to solve a set of coupled, non-linear equations for unknown flow rates.
>
> The *Excel* workbook for this problem can be modified for solving a variety of other multiple-path systems.

PART C   FLOW MEASUREMENT

Throughout this text we have referred to the flow rate Q or average velocity $\overline{V}$ in a pipe. The question arises: How does one measure these quantities? We will address this question by discussing the various types of flow meters available.

The choice of a flow meter is influenced by the accuracy required, range, cost, complication, ease of reading or data reduction, and service life. The simplest and cheapest device that gives the desired accuracy should be chosen.

8-9   DIRECT METHODS

The most obvious way to measure flow rate in a pipe is the *direct method*—simply measure the amount of fluid that accumulates in a container over a fixed time period! Tanks can be used to determine flow rate for steady liquid flows by measuring the volume or mass of liquid collected during a known time interval. If the time interval is long enough to be measured accurately, flow rates may be determined precisely in this way.

Compressibility must be considered in volume measurements for gas flows. The densities of gases generally are too small to permit accurate direct measurement of mass flow rate. However, a volume sample often can be collected by displacing a "bell," or inverted jar over water (if the pressure is held constant by counterweights). If volume or mass measurements are set up carefully, no calibration is required; this is a great advantage of direct methods.

In specialized applications, particularly for remote or recording uses, *positive displacement* flow meters may be specified, in which the fluid moves a component such as a reciprocating piston or oscillating disk as it passes through the device. Common examples include household water and natural gas meters, which are calibrated to read directly in units of product, or gasoline metering pumps, which measure total flow and automatically compute the cost. Many positive-displacement meters are available commercially. Consult manufacturers' literature or References (e.g., [25]) for design and installation details.

8-10   RESTRICTION FLOW METERS FOR INTERNAL FLOWS

Most restriction flow meters for internal flow (except the laminar flow element, discussed shortly) are based on acceleration of a fluid stream through some form of nozzle, as shown schematically in Fig. 8.19. The idea is that the change in velocity leads

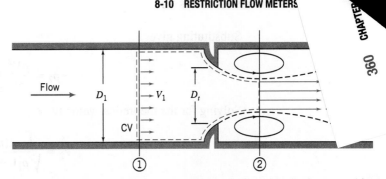

Fig. 8.19 Internal flow through a generalized nozzle, showing control volume used for analysis.

to a change in pressure. This Δp can be measured using a pressure gage (electronic or mechanical) or a manometer, and the flow rate inferred using either a theoretical analysis or an experimental correlation for the device. Flow separation at the sharp edge of the nozzle throat causes a recirculation zone to form, as shown by the dashed lines downstream from the nozzle. The mainstream flow continues to accelerate from the nozzle throat to form a *vena contracta* at section ② and then decelerates again to fill the duct. At the vena contracta, the flow area is a minimum, the flow streamlines are essentially straight, and the pressure is uniform across the channel section.

The theoretical flow rate may be related to the pressure differential between sections ① and ② by applying the continuity and Bernoulli equations. Then empirical correction factors may be applied to obtain the actual flow rate.

Basic equations:

We will need mass-conservation,

$$\sum_{CS} \vec{V} \cdot \vec{A} = 0 \tag{4.13b}$$

[we can use this instead of Eq. 4.12, because of assumption (5) below] and the Bernoulli equation,

$$\frac{p_1}{\rho} + \frac{V_1^2}{2} + \cancel{g}z_1 = \frac{p_2}{\rho} + \frac{V_2^2}{2} + \cancel{g}z_2 \tag{6.8}$$

which we can use if assumption (4) is valid. For the short section of pipe considered, this is reasonable.

Assumptions: (1) Steady flow.
(2) Incompressible flow.
(3) Flow along a streamline.
(4) No friction.
(5) Uniform velocity at sections ① and ②.
(6) No streamline curvature at sections ① or ②, so pressure is uniform across those sections.
(7) $z_1 = z_2$.

Then, from the Bernoulli equation,

$$p_1 - p_2 = \frac{\rho}{2} \left(V_2^2 - V_1^2\right) = \frac{\rho V_2^2}{2} \left[1 - \left(\frac{V_1}{V_2}\right)^2 \right]$$

and from continuity

$$(-\rho V_1 A_1) + (\rho V_2 A_2) = 0$$

or

$$V_1 A_1 = V_2 A_2 \qquad \text{so} \qquad \left(\frac{V_1}{V_2}\right)^2 = \left(\frac{A_2}{A_1}\right)^2$$

Substituting gives

$$p_1 - p_2 = \frac{\rho V_2^2}{2}\left[1 - \left(\frac{A_2}{A_1}\right)^2\right]$$

Solving for the theoretical velocity, V_2,

$$V_2 = \sqrt{\frac{2(p_1 - p_2)}{\rho[1 - (A_2/A_1)^2]}} \tag{8.51}$$

The theoretical mass flow rate is then given by

$$\dot{m}_{\text{theoretical}} = \rho V_2 A_2$$

$$= \rho\sqrt{\frac{2(p_1 - p_2)}{\rho[1 - (A_2/A_1)^2]}}\,A_2$$

or

$$\dot{m}_{\text{theoretical}} = \frac{A_2}{\sqrt{1 - (A_2/A_1)^2}}\sqrt{2\rho(p_1 - p_2)} \tag{8.52}$$

Equation 8.52 shows that, under our set of assumptions, for a given fluid (ρ) and flow meter geometry (A_1 and A_2), the flow rate is directly proportional to the square root of the pressure drop across the meter taps,

$$\dot{m}_{\text{theoretical}} \propto \sqrt{\Delta p}$$

which is the basic idea of these devices. This relationship limits the flow rates that can be measured accurately to approximately a 4:1 range.

Several factors limit the utility of Eq. 8.52 for calculating the actual mass flow rate through a meter. The actual flow area at section ② is unknown when the vena contracta is pronounced (e.g., for orifice plates when D_t is a small fraction of D_1). The velocity profiles approach uniform flow only at large Reynolds numbers. Frictional effects can become important (especially downstream from the meter) when the meter contours are abrupt. Finally, the location of pressure taps influences the differential pressure reading.

The theoretical equation is adjusted for Reynolds number and diameter ratio D_t/D_1 by defining an empirical *discharge coefficient C* such that, replacing Eq. 8.52, we have

$$\dot{m}_{\text{actual}} = \frac{CA_t}{\sqrt{1 - (A_t/A_1)^2}}\sqrt{2\rho(p_1 - p_2)} \tag{8.53}$$

Letting $\beta = D_t/D_1$, then $(A_t/A_1)^2 = (D_t/D_1)^4 = \beta^4$, so

$$\dot{m}_{\text{actual}} = \frac{CA_t}{\sqrt{1 - \beta^4}}\sqrt{2\rho(p_1 - p_2)} \tag{8.54}$$

In Eq. 8.54, $1/\sqrt{1 - \beta^4}$ is the *velocity-of-approach factor*. The discharge coefficient and velocity-of-approach factor frequently are combined into a single *flow coefficient*,

$$K \equiv \frac{C}{\sqrt{1 - \beta^4}} \tag{8.55}$$

In terms of this flow coefficient, the actual mass flow rate is expressed as

$$\dot{m}_{\text{actual}} = KA_t\sqrt{2\rho(p_1 - p_2)} \tag{8.56}$$

For standardized metering elements, test data [25, 26] hav
empirical equations that predict discharge and flow coefficie
pipe diameter, and Reynolds number. The accuracy of the equati
ranges) usually is adequate so that the meter can be used witho
Reynolds number, pipe size, or bore diameter fall outside the sp
equation, the coefficients must be measured experimentally.

For the turbulent flow regime (pipe Reynolds number greater tl ⌐, ine discharge coefficient may be expressed by an equation of the form [25]

$$C = C_\infty + \frac{b}{Re_{D_1}^n} \tag{8.57}$$

The corresponding form for the flow-coefficient equation is

$$K = K_\infty + \frac{1}{\sqrt{1 - \beta^4}} \frac{b}{Re_{D_1}^n} \tag{8.58}$$

In Eqs. 8.57 and 8.58, subscript ∞ denotes the coefficient at infinite Reynolds number; constants b and n allow for scaling to finite Reynolds numbers. Correlating equations and curves of coefficients versus Reynolds number are given in the next three subsections, following a general comparison of the characteristics of specific metering elements.

As we have noted, selection of a flow meter depends on factors such as cost, accuracy, need for calibration, and ease of installation and maintenance. Some of these factors are compared for *orifice plate*, *flow nozzle*, and *venturi* meters in Table 8.6. Note that a high head loss means that the running cost of the device is high—it will consume a lot of the fluid energy. A high initial cost must be amortized over the life of the device. This is an example of a common cost calculation for a company (and an individual!)—between a high initial but low running cost, or low initial but high running cost.

Flow meter coefficients reported in the literature have been measured with fully developed turbulent velocity distributions at the meter inlet (Section ①). If a flow meter is to be installed downstream from a valve, elbow, or other disturbance, a straight section of pipe must be placed in front of the meter. Approximately 10 diameters of straight pipe are required for venturi meters, and up to 40 diameters for orifice plate or flow nozzle meters. When a meter has been properly installed, the flow rate may be computed from Eq. 8.54 or 8.56, after choosing an appropriate value for the empirical discharge coefficient, C, or flow coefficient, K, defined in Eqs. 8.53 and 8.55, respectively. Some design data for incompressible flow are given in the next few sections. The same basic methods can be extended to compressible flows, but these will not be treated here. For complete details, see [25] or [26].

TABLE 8.6 Characteristics of Orifice, Flow Nozzle, and Venturi Flow Meters

Flow Meter Type	Diagram	Head Loss	Initial Cost
Orifice		High	Low
Flow Nozzle		Intermediate	Intermediate
Venturi		Low	High

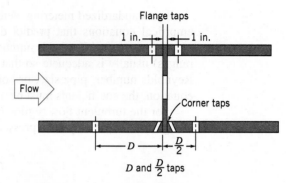

Fig. 8.20 Orifice geometry and pressure tap locations [25].

The Orifice Plate

The orifice plate (Fig. 8.20) is a thin plate that may be clamped between pipe flanges. Since its geometry is simple, it is low in cost and easy to install or replace. The sharp edge of the orifice will not foul with scale or suspended matter. However, suspended matter can build up at the inlet side of a concentric orifice in a horizontal pipe; an eccentric orifice may be placed flush with the bottom of the pipe to avoid this difficulty. The primary disadvantages of the orifice are its limited capacity and the high permanent head loss caused by the uncontrolled expansion downstream from the metering element.

Pressure taps for orifices may be placed in several locations, as shown in Fig. 8.20 (see [25] or [26] for additional details). Since the location of the pressure taps influences the empirically determined flow coefficient, one must select handbook values of C or K consistent with the location of pressure taps.

The correlating equation recommended for a concentric orifice with corner taps [25] is

$$C = 0.5959 + 0.0312\beta^{2.1} - 0.184\beta^8 + \frac{91.71\beta^{2.5}}{Re_{D_1}^{0.75}} \qquad (8.59)$$

Equation 8.59 is the form of Eq. 8.57 for the discharge coefficient C for the orifice plate; it predicts orifice discharge coefficients within ± 0.6 percent for $0.2 < \beta < 0.75$ and for $10^4 < Re_{D_1} < 10^7$. Some flow coefficients calculated from Eq. 8.59 and 8.55 are presented in Fig. 8.21.

A similar correlating equation is available for orifice plates with D and $D/2$ taps. Flange taps require a different correlation for every line size. Pipe taps, located at $2\frac{1}{2}$ and $8\,D$, no longer are recommended for accurate work.

Example 8.12, which appears later in this section, illustrates the application of flow coefficient data to orifice sizing.

The Flow Nozzle

Flow nozzles may be used as metering elements in either plenums or ducts, as shown in Fig. 8.22; the nozzle section is approximately a quarter ellipse. Design details and recommended locations for pressure taps are given in [26].

The correlating equation recommended for an ASME long-radius flow nozzle [25] is

$$C = 0.9975 - \frac{6.53\beta^{0.5}}{Re_{D_1}^{0.5}} \qquad (8.60)$$

Equation 8.60 is the form of Eq. 8.57 for the discharge coefficient C for the flow nozzle; it predicts discharge coefficients for flow nozzles within ± 2.0 percent for

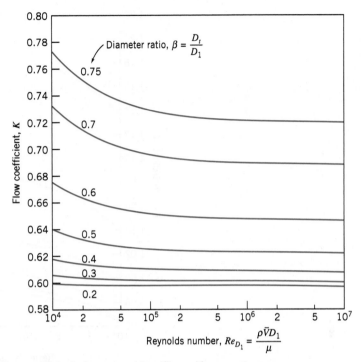

Fig. 8.21 Flow coefficients for concentric orifices with corner taps.

$0.25 < \beta < 0.75$ for $10^4 < Re_{D_1} < 10^7$. Some flow coefficients calculated from Eq. 8.60 and Eq. 8.55 are presented in Fig. 8.23. (K can be greater than one when the velocity-of-approach factor exceeds one.)

a. Pipe Installation

For pipe installation, K is a function of β and Re_{D_1}. Figure 8.23 shows that K is essentially independent of Reynolds number for $Re_{D_1} > 10^6$. Thus at high flow rates, the flow rate may be computed directly using Eq. 8.56. At lower flow rates, where K is a weak function of Reynolds number, iteration may be required.

b. Plenum Installation

For plenum installation, nozzles may be fabricated from spun aluminum, molded fiberglass, or other inexpensive materials. Thus they are simple and cheap to make and

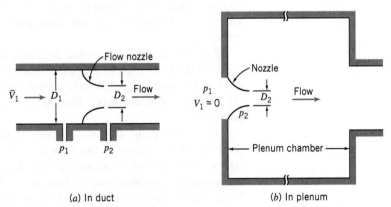

(a) In duct   (b) In plenum

Fig. 8.22 Typical installations of nozzle flow meters.

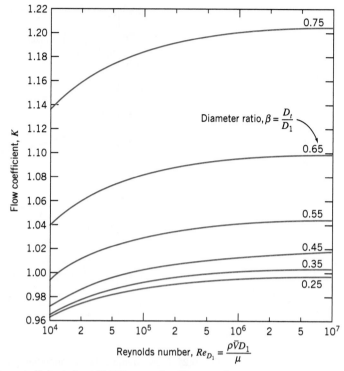

Fig. 8.23 Flow coefficients for ASME long-radius flow nozzles.

install. Since the plenum pressure is equal to p_2, the location of the downstream pressure tap is not critical. Meters suitable for a wide range of flow rates may be made by installing several nozzles in a plenum. At low flow rates, most of them may be plugged. For higher flow rates, more nozzles may be used.

For plenum nozzles $\beta = 0$, which is outside the range of applicability of Eq. 8.58. Typical flow coefficients are in the range, $0.95 < K < 0.99$; the larger values apply at high Reynolds numbers. Thus the mass rate of flow can be computed within approximately ± 2 percent using Eq. 8.56 with $K = 0.97$.

The Venturi

Venturi meters, as sketched in Table 8.6, are generally made from castings and machined to close tolerances to duplicate the performance of the standard design. As a result, venturi meters are heavy, bulky, and expensive. The conical diffuser section downstream from the throat gives excellent pressure recovery; therefore, overall head loss is low. Venturi meters are also self-cleaning because of their smooth internal contours.

Experimental data show that discharge coefficients for venturi meters range from 0.980 to 0.995 at high Reynolds numbers ($Re_{D_1} > 2 \times 10^5$). Thus $C = 0.99$ can be used to measure mass flow rate within about ± 1 percent at high Reynolds number [25]. Consult manufacturers' literature for specific information at Reynolds numbers below 10^5.

The orifice plate, flow nozzle, and venturi all produce pressure differentials proportional to the square of the flow rate, according to Eq. 8.56. In practice, a meter size must be chosen to accommodate the highest flow rate expected. Because the relationship of pressure drop to flow rate is nonlinear, the range of flow rate that can be measured accurately is limited. Flow meters with single throats usually are considered only for flow rates over a 4:1 range [25].

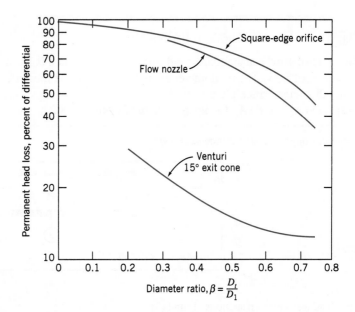

Fig. 8.24 Permanent head loss produced by various flow metering elements [25].

The unrecoverable loss in head across a metering element may be expressed as a fraction of the differential pressure, Δp, across the element. Pressure losses are displayed as functions of diameter ratio in Fig. 8.24 [25]. Note that the venturi meter has a much lower permanent head loss than the orifice (which has the highest loss) or nozzle, confirming the trends we summarized in Table 8.6.

The Laminar Flow Element

The *laminar flow element*[6] is designed to produce a pressure differential directly proportional to flow rate. The idea is that the laminar flow element (LFE) contains a metering section in which the flow passes through a large number of tubes or passages (these often look like a bunch of straws) that are each narrow enough that the flow through them is laminar, regardless of the flow conditions in the main pipe (recall that $Re_{tube} = \rho V_{tube} D_{tube}/\mu$, so if D_{tube} is made small enough we can ensure that $Re_{tube} < Re_{crit} \approx 2300$). For each laminar flow tube we can apply the results of Section 8-3, specifically

$$Q_{tube} = \frac{\pi D_{tube}^4}{128\mu L_{tube}}\Delta p \; \propto \; \Delta p \qquad (8.13c)$$

so the flow rate in each tube is a linear function of the pressure drop across the device. The flow rate in the whole pipe will be the sum of each of these tube flows, and so will also be a linear function of pressure drop. Usually this linear relation is provided in a calibration from the manufacturer, and the LFE can be used over a 10:1 range of flow rates. The relationship between pressure drop and flow rate for laminar flow also depends on viscosity, which is a strong function of temperature. Therefore, the fluid temperature must be known to obtain accurate metering with an LFE.

A laminar flow element costs approximately as much as a venturi, but it is much lighter and smaller. Thus the LFE is becoming widely used in applications where compactness and extended range are important.

---

[6] Patented and manufactured by Meriam Instrument Co., 10920 Madison Ave., Cleveland, Ohio 44102.

EXAMPLE 8.12 Flow through an Orifice Meter

An air flow rate of 1 m³/s at standard conditions is expected in a 0.25-m diameter duct. An orifice meter is used to measure the rate of flow. The manometer available to make the measurement has a maximum range of 300 mm of water. What diameter orifice plate should be used with corner taps? Analyze the head loss if the flow area at the vena contracta is $A_2 = 0.65 \, A_t$. Compare with data from Fig. 8.24.

GIVEN: Flow through duct and orifice as shown.

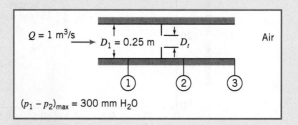

FIND: (a) D_t.
(b) Head loss between sections ① and ③.
(c) Degree of agreement with data from Fig. 8.24.

SOLUTION:
The orifice plate may be designed using Eq. 8.56 and data from Fig. 8.21.

Governing equation:
$$\dot{m}_{actual} = KA_t \sqrt{2\rho(p_1 - p_2)} \tag{8.56}$$

Assumptions: (1) Steady flow.
(2) Incompressible flow.

Since $A/A_1 = (D_t/D_1)^2 = \beta^2$,

$$\dot{m}_{actual} = K\beta^2 A_1 \sqrt{2\rho(p_1 - p_2)}$$

or

$$K\beta^2 = \frac{\dot{m}_{actual}}{A_1\sqrt{2\rho(p_1-p_2)}} = \frac{\rho Q}{A_1\sqrt{2\rho(p_1-p_2)}} = \frac{Q}{A_1}\sqrt{\frac{\rho}{2(p_1-p_2)}}$$

$$= \frac{Q}{A_1}\sqrt{\frac{\rho}{2g\rho_{H_2O}\Delta h}}$$

$$= \frac{1}{s}\frac{m^3}{\pi} \times \frac{4}{\pi} \frac{1}{(0.25)^2\,m^2}\left[\frac{1}{2} \times 1.23\,\frac{kg}{m^3} \times \frac{s^2}{9.81\,m} \times \frac{m^3}{999\,kg} \times \frac{1}{0.30\,m}\right]^{1/2}$$

$$K\beta^2 = 0.295 \quad \text{or} \quad K = \frac{0.295}{\beta^2} \tag{1}$$

Since K is a function of both β (Eq. 1) and Re_{D_1} (Fig. 8.21), we must iterate to find β. The duct Reynolds number is

$$Re_{D_1} = \frac{\rho\overline{V}_1 D_1}{\mu} = \frac{\rho\,(Q/A_1)\,D_1}{\mu} = \frac{4Q}{\pi\nu D_1}$$

$$Re_{D_1} = \frac{4}{\pi} \times \frac{1\,m^3}{s} \times \frac{s}{1.46\times10^{-5}\,m^2} \times \frac{1}{0.25\,m} = 3.49\times10^5$$

Guess $\beta = 0.75$. From Fig. 8.21, K should be 0.72. From Eq. 1,

$$K = \frac{0.295}{(0.75)^2} = 0.524$$

Thus our guess for β is too large. Guess $\beta = 0.70$. From Fig. 8.21, K should be 0.69. From Eq. 1,

$$K = \frac{0.295}{(0.70)^2} = 0.602$$

Thus our guess for β is still too large. Guess $\beta = 0.65$. From Fig. 8.21, K should be 0.67. From Eq. 1,

$$K = \frac{0.295}{(0.65)^2} = 0.698$$

There is satisfactory agreement with $\beta \simeq 0.66$ and

$$D_t = \beta D_1 = 0.66(0.25\ \text{m}) = 0.165\ \text{m} \longleftarrow \qquad D_t$$

To find the permanent head loss for this device, we could simply use the diameter ratio $\beta \approx 0.66$ in Fig. 8.24; but instead we will find it from the given data. To evaluate the permanent head loss, apply Eq. 8.29 between sections ① and ③.

Governing equation:
$$\left(\frac{p_1}{\rho} + \alpha_1 \frac{\overline{V}_1^2}{2} + \cancel{g z_1}\right) - \left(\frac{p_3}{\rho} + \alpha_3 \frac{\overline{V}_3^2}{2} + \cancel{g z_3}\right) = h_{l_T} \tag{8.29}$$

Assumptions: (3) $\alpha_1 \overline{V}_1^2 = \alpha_3 \overline{V}_3^2$.
(4) Neglect Δz.

Then

$$h_{l_T} = \frac{p_1 - p_3}{\rho} = \frac{p_1 - p_2 - (p_3 - p_2)}{\rho} \tag{2}$$

Equation 2 indicates our approach: We will find $p_1 - p_3$ by using $p_1 - p_2 = 300\ \text{mm}\ H_2O$, and obtain a value for $p_3 - p_2$ by applying the x component of the momentum equation to a control volume between sections ② and ③.

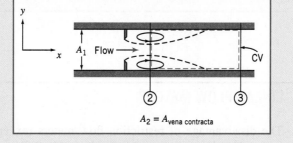

Governing equation:
$$= 0(5) \quad = 0(1)$$
$$F_{S_x} + \cancel{F_{B_x}} = \cancel{\frac{\partial}{\partial t} \int_{CV}} u\,\rho d\Psi + \int_{CS} u\,\rho \overline{V} \cdot d\vec{A} \tag{4.18a}$$

Assumptions: (5) $F_{B_x} = 0$
(6) Uniform flow at sections ② and ③.
(7) Pressure uniform across duct at sections ② and ③.
(8) Neglect friction force on CV.

Then, simplifying and rearranging,

$$(p_2 - p_3)A_1 = u_2(-\rho \overline{V}_2 A_2) + u_3(\rho \overline{V}_3 A_3) = (u_3 - u_2)\rho Q = (\overline{V}_3 - \overline{V}_2)\rho Q$$

or

$$p_3 - p_2 = (\overline{V}_2 - \overline{V}_3)\frac{\rho Q}{A_1}$$

Now $\overline{V}_3 = Q/A_1$, and

$$\overline{V}_2 = \frac{Q}{A_2} = \frac{Q}{0.65\,A_t} = \frac{Q}{0.65\beta^2\,A_1}$$

Thus,

$$p_3 - p_2 = \frac{\rho Q^2}{A_1^2}\left[\frac{1}{0.65\,\beta^2} - 1\right]$$

$$p_3 - p_2 = 1.23\,\frac{\text{kg}}{\text{m}^3} \times (1)^2\,\frac{\text{m}^6}{\text{s}^2} \times \frac{4^2}{\pi^2}\frac{1}{(0.25)^4\,\text{m}^4}\left[\frac{1}{0.65(0.66)^2} - 1\right]\frac{\text{N}\cdot\text{s}^2}{\text{kg}\cdot\text{m}}$$

$$p_3 - p_2 = 1290\,\text{N/m}^2$$

The diameter ratio, β, was selected to give maximum manometer deflection at maximum flow rate. Thus

$$p_1 - p_2 = \rho_{\text{H}_2\text{O}}g\Delta h = 999\,\frac{\text{kg}}{\text{m}^3} \times 9.81\,\frac{\text{m}}{\text{s}^2} \times 0.30\,\text{m} \times \frac{\text{N}\cdot\text{s}^2}{\text{kg}\cdot\text{m}} = 2940\,\text{N/m}^2$$

Substituting into Eq. 2 gives

$$h_{l_T} = \frac{p_1 - p_3}{\rho} = \frac{p_1 - p_2 - (p_3 - p_2)}{\rho}$$

$$h_{l_T} = \frac{(2940 - 1290)}{\text{m}^2}\,\frac{\text{N}}{} \times \frac{\text{m}^3}{1.23\,\text{kg}} = 1340\,\text{N}\cdot\text{m/kg} \longleftarrow \hspace{3cm} h_{l_T}$$

To compare with Fig. 8.24, express the permanent pressure loss as a fraction of the meter differential

$$\frac{p_1 - p_3}{p_1 - p_2} = \frac{(2940 - 1290)\,\text{N/m}^2}{2940\,\text{N/m}^2} = 0.561$$

The fraction from Fig. 8.24 is about 0.57. This is satisfactory agreement!

This problem illustrates flow meter calculations and shows use of the momentum equation to compute the pressure rise in a sudden expansion.

8-11   LINEAR FLOW METERS

The disadvantage of restriction flow meters (except the LFE) is that the measured output (Δp) is not linear with the flow rate Q. Several flow meter types produce outputs that are directly proportional to flow rate. These meters produce signals without the need to measure differential pressure. The most common linear flow meters are discussed briefly in the following paragraphs.

Float meters may be used to indicate flow rate directly for liquids or gases. An example is shown in Fig. 8.25 In operation, the ball or float is carried upward in the tapered clear tube by the flowing fluid until the drag force and float weight are in equilibrium. Such meters (often called *rotameters*) are available with factory calibration for a number of common fluids and flow rate ranges.

A free-running vaned impeller may be mounted in a cylindrical section of tube (Fig. 8.26) to make a *turbine flow meter*. With proper design, the rate of rotation of the impeller may be made closely proportional to volume flow rate over a wide range.

Rotational speed of the turbine element can be sensed using a magnetic or modulated carrier pickup external to the meter. This sensing method therefore requires no penetrations or seals in the duct. Thus turbine flow meters can be used safely to measure flow rates in corrosive or toxic fluids. The electrical signal can be displayed, recorded, or integrated to provide total flow information.

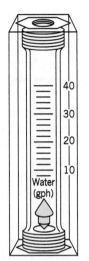

Fig. 8.25 Float-type variable-area flow meter. (Courtesy of Dwyer Instrument Co., Michigan City, Indiana.)

An interesting device is the *vortex flow meter*. This device takes advantage of the fact that a uniform flow will generate a vortex street when it encounters a bluff body such as a cylinder perpendicular to the flow. A vortex street is a series of alternating vortices shed from the rear of the body; the alternation generates an oscillating sideways force on, and therefore oscillation of, the cylinder (the classic example of this being the "singing" of telephone wires in a high wind). It turns out that the dimensionless group characterizing this phenomenon is the Strouhal number, $St = fL/V$ (f is the vortex shedding frequency, L is the cylinder diameter, and V is the freestream velocity), and it is approximately constant ($St \approx 0.21$). Hence we have a device for which $V \propto f$. Measurement of f thus directly indicates the velocity $\overline{V}$ (however, the velocity profile does affect the shedding frequency so calibration is required). The cylinder used in a flow meter is usually quite short in length—10 mm or less—and placed perpendicular to the flow (and for some devices is not a cylinder at all but some other small bluff object). The oscillation can be measured using a strain gage or other sensor. Vortex flow meters can be used over a 20:1 range of flow rates [25].

The *electromagnetic flow meter* uses the principle of magnetic induction. A magnetic field is created across a pipe. When a conductive fluid passes through the field, a voltage is generated at right angles to the field and velocity vectors. Electrodes placed on a pipe diameter are used to detect the resulting signal voltage. The signal voltage is proportional to the average axial velocity when the profile is axisymmetric.

Magnetic flow meters may be used with liquids that have electrical conductivities above 100 microsiemens per meter (1 siemen = 1 ampere per volt). The minimum flow speed should be above about 0.3 m/s, but there are no restrictions on Reynolds number. The flow rate range normally quoted is 10:1 [25].

Ultrasonic flow meters also respond to average velocity at a pipe cross section. Two principal types of ultrasonic meters are common: Propagation time is measured for clean liquids, and reflection frequency shift (Doppler effect) is measured for flows carrying particulates. The speed of an acoustic wave increases in the flow direction and decreases when transmitted against the flow. For clean liquids, an acoustic path inclined to the pipe axis is used to infer flow velocity. Multiple paths are used to estimate the volume flow rate accurately.

Doppler effect ultrasonic flow meters depend on reflection of sonic waves (in the MHz range) from scattering particles in the fluid. When the particles move at flow speed, the frequency shift is proportional to flow speed; for a suitably chosen path, output is proportional to volume flow rate. One or two transducers may be used; the meter may be clamped to the outside of the pipe. Ultrasonic meters may require calibration in place. Flow rate range is 10:1 [25].

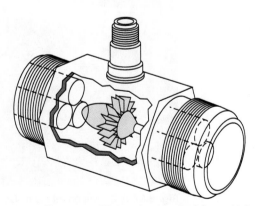

Fig. 8.26 Turbine flow meter. (Courtesy of Potter Aeronautical Corp., Union, New Jersey.)

8-12   **TRAVERSING METHODS**

In situations such as in air handling or refrigeration equipment, it may be impractical or impossible to install fixed flow meters. In such cases it may be possible to obtain flow rate data using traversing techniques.

To make a flow rate measurement by traverse, the duct cross-section is conceptually subdivided into segments of equal area. The velocity is measured at the center of each area segment using a pitot tube, a total head tube, or a suitable anemometer. The volume flow rate for each segment is approximated by the product of the measured velocity and the segment area. The flow rate through the entire duct is the sum of these segmental flow rates. Details of recommended procedures for flow rate measurements by the traverse method are given in [27].

Use of *pitot* or *pitot-static tubes* for traverse measurements requires direct access to the flow field. Pitot tubes give uncertain results when pressure gradients or streamline curvature are present, and their response times are slow. Two types of anemometers—*thermal anemometers* and *laser Doppler anemometers* (LDAs)—overcome these difficulties partially, although they introduce new complications.

Thermal anemometers use tiny elements (either hot-wire or hot-film elements) that are heated electrically. Sophisticated electronic feedback circuits are used to maintain the temperature of the element constant and to sense the input heating rate needed to do this. The heating rate is related to the local flow velocity by calibration (a higher velocity leads to more heat transfer). The primary advantage of thermal anemometers is the small size of the sensing element. Sensors as small as 0.002 mm in diameter and 0.1 mm long are available commercially. Because the thermal mass of such tiny elements is extremely small, their response to fluctuations in flow velocity is rapid. Frequency responses to the 50 kHz range have been

Fig. 8.27 A 2-component Laser Doppler Anemometer Probe Volume. (Courtesy Dr. Frank W. Chambers, Oklahoma State University)

quoted [28]. Thus thermal anemometers are ideal for measuring turbulence quantities. Insulating coatings may be applied to permit their use in conductive or corrosive gases or liquids.

Because of their fast response and small size, thermal anemometers are used extensively for research. Numerous schemes have been published for treating the resulting data [29]. Digital processing techniques, including fast Fourier transforms, can be applied to the signals to obtain mean values and moments, and to analyze frequency content and correlations.

Laser Doppler anemometers are becoming widely used for specialized applications where direct physical access to the flow field is difficult or impossible. One or more laser beams are focused to a small volume in the flow at the location of interest (as shown in Fig 8.27). Laser light is scattered from particles that are present in the flow (dust or particulates) or introduced for this purpose. A frequency shift is caused by the local flow speed (Doppler effect). Scattered light and a reference beam are collected by receiving optics. The frequency shift is proportional to the flow speed; this relationship may be calculated, so there is no need for calibration. Since velocity is measured directly, the signal is unaffected by changes in temperature, density, or composition in the flow field. The primary disadvantages of LDAs are that the optical equipment is expensive and fragile, and that extremely careful alignment is needed (as the authors can attest).

8-13 SUMMARY AND USEFUL EQUATIONS

In this chapter we have:

✓ Defined many terms used in the study of internal incompressible viscous flow, such as: the entrance length, fully developed flow, the friction velocity, Reynolds stress, the kinetic energy coefficient, the friction factor, major and minor head losses, and hydraulic diameter.

✓ Analyzed laminar flow between parallel plates and in pipes and observed that we can obtain the velocity distribution analytically, and from this derive: the average velocity, the maximum velocity and its location, the flow rate, the wall shear stress, and the shear stress distribution.

✓ Studied turbulent flow in pipes and ducts and learned that semi-empirical approaches are needed, e.g., the power-law velocity profile.

✓ Written the energy equation in a form useful for analyzing pipe flows.

✓ Discussed how to incorporate pumps, fans, and blowers into a pipe flow analysis.

✓ Described various flow measurement devices: direct measurement, restriction devices (orifice plate, nozzle, and venturi), linear flow meters (rotameters, various electromagnetic or acoustic devices, and the vortex flow meter), and traversing devices (pitot tubes and laser-Doppler anemometers).

We have learned that pipe and duct flow problems often need iterative solution—the flow rate Q is not a linear function of the driving force (usually Δp), except for laminar flows (which are not common in practice). *We have also seen that pipe networks can be analyzed using the same techniques as a single-pipe system, with the addition of a few basic rules, and that in practice a computer application such as *Excel* is needed to solve all but the simplest networks.

*This topic applies to a section that may be omitted without loss of continuity in the text material.

Note: Most of the Useful Equations in the table below have a number of constraints or limitations—*be sure to refer to their page numbers for details!*

Useful Equations		
Velocity profile for pressure-driven laminar flow between stationary parallel plates:	$$u = \frac{a^2}{2\mu} \left(\frac{\partial p}{\partial x}\right) \left[\left(\frac{y}{a}\right)^2 - \left(\frac{y}{a}\right) \right] \qquad (8.5)$$	Page 308
Flow rate for pressure-driven laminar flow between stationary parallel plates:	$$\frac{Q}{l} = -\frac{1}{12\mu} \left[\frac{-\Delta p}{L}\right] a^3 = \frac{a^3 \Delta p}{12\mu L} \qquad (8.6c)$$	Page 308
Velocity profile for pressure-driven laminar flow between stationary parallel plates (centered coordinates):	$$u = \frac{a^2}{2\mu} \left(\frac{\partial p}{\partial x}\right) \left[\left(\frac{y'}{a}\right)^2 - \frac{1}{4} \right] \qquad (8.7)$$	Page 309
Velocity profile for pressure-driven laminar flow between parallel plates (upper plate moving):	$$u = \frac{Uy}{a} + \frac{a^2}{2\mu} \left(\frac{\partial p}{\partial x}\right) \left[\left(\frac{y}{a}\right)^2 - \left(\frac{y}{a}\right) \right] \qquad (8.8)$$	Page 311
Flow rate for pressure-driven laminar flow between parallel plates (upper plate moving):	$$\frac{Q}{l} = \frac{Ua}{2} - \frac{1}{12\mu}\left(\frac{\partial p}{\partial x}\right) a^3 \qquad (8.9b)$$	Page 312
Velocity profile for laminar flow in a pipe:	$$u = -\frac{R^2}{4\mu} \left(\frac{\partial p}{\partial x}\right) \left[1 - \left(\frac{r}{R}\right)^2 \right] \qquad (8.12)$$	Page 318
Flow rate for laminar flow in a pipe:	$$Q = -\frac{\pi R^4}{8\mu} \left[\frac{-\Delta p}{L}\right] = \frac{\pi \Delta p R^4}{8\mu L} = \frac{\pi \Delta p D^4}{128\mu L} \qquad (8.13c)$$	Page 319
Velocity profile for laminar flow in a pipe (normalized form):	$$\frac{u}{U} = 1 - \left(\frac{r}{R}\right)^2 \qquad (8.14)$$	Page 319
Velocity profile for turbulent flow in a smooth pipe (power-law equation):	$$\frac{\bar{u}}{U} = \left(\frac{y}{R}\right)^{1/n} = \left(1 - \frac{y}{R}\right)^{1/n} \qquad (8.22)$$	Page 324
Head loss equation:	$$\left(\frac{p_1}{\rho} + \alpha_1 \frac{\bar{V}_1^2}{2} + gz_1\right) - \left(\frac{p_2}{\rho} + \alpha_2 \frac{\bar{V}_2^2}{2} + gz_2\right) = h_{l_T} \qquad (8.29)$$	Page 328
Major head loss equation:	$$h_l = f \frac{L}{D} \frac{\bar{V}^2}{2} \qquad (8.34)$$	Page 330
Friction factor (laminar flow):	$$f_{\text{laminar}} = \frac{64}{Re} \qquad (8.36)$$	Page 331

Friction factor (turbulent flow—Colebrook equation):	$$\frac{1}{\sqrt{f}} = -2.0 \log\left(\frac{e/D}{3.7} + \frac{2.51}{Re\sqrt{f}}\right) \qquad (8.37)$$	Page 332
Minor loss using loss coefficient K:	$$h_{l_m} = K\frac{\overline{V}^2}{2} \qquad (8.40a)$$	Page 334
Minor loss using equivalent length L_e:	$$h_{l_m} = f\frac{L_e}{D}\frac{\overline{V}^2}{2} \qquad (8.40b)$$	Page 334
Diffuser pressure recovery coefficient:	$$C_p \equiv \frac{p_2 - p_1}{\frac{1}{2}\rho\overline{V}_1^2} \qquad (8.41)$$	Page 335
Ideal diffuser pressure recovery coefficient:	$$C_{p_i} = 1 - \frac{1}{AR^2} \qquad (8.42)$$	Page 335
Head loss in diffuser in terms of pressure recovery coefficients:	$$h_{l_m} = (C_{p_i} - C_p)\frac{\overline{V}_1^2}{2} \qquad (8.44)$$	Page 337
Pump work:	$$\dot{W}_{\text{pump}} = Q\Delta p_{\text{pump}} \qquad (8.47)$$	Page 339
Pump efficiency:	$$\eta = \frac{\dot{W}_{\text{pump}}}{\dot{W}_{\text{in}}} \qquad (8.48)$$	Page 339
Hydraulic diameter:	$$D_h \equiv \frac{4A}{P} \qquad (8.50)$$	Page 339
Mass flow rate equation for a flow meter (in terms of discharge coefficient C):	$$\dot{m}_{\text{actual}} = \frac{CA_t}{\sqrt{1-\beta^4}}\sqrt{2\rho(p_1 - p_2)} \qquad (8.54)$$	Page 360
Mass flow rate equation for a flow meter (in terms of flow coefficient K):	$$\dot{m}_{\text{actual}} = KA_t\sqrt{2\rho(p_1 - p_2)} \qquad (8.56)$$	Page 360
Discharge coefficient (as a function of Re):	$$C = C_\infty + \frac{b}{Re_{D_1}^n} \qquad (8.57)$$	Page 361
Flow coefficient (as a function of Re):	$$K = K_\infty + \frac{1}{\sqrt{1-\beta^4}}\frac{b}{Re_{D_1}^n} \qquad (8.58)$$	Page 361

REFERENCES

1. Streeter, V. L., ed., *Handbook of Fluid Dynamics*. New York: McGraw-Hill, 1961.

2. Rouse, H., and S. Ince, *History of Hydraulics*. New York: Dover, 1957.

3. Moin, P., and J. Kim, "Tackling Turbulence with Super-computers," *Scientific American*, 276, 1, January 1997, pp. 62–68.

4. Panton, R. L., *Incompressible Flow*, 2nd ed. New York: Wiley, 1996.

5. Laufer, J., "The Structure of Turbulence in Fully Developed Pipe Flow," U.S. National Advisory Committee for Aeronautics (NACA), Technical Report 1174, 1954.

6. Tennekes, H., and J. L. Lumley, *A First Course in Turbulence*. Cambridge, MA: The MIT Press, 1972.

7. Hinze, J. O., *Turbulence*, 2nd ed. New York: McGraw-Hill, 1975.

8. Moody, L. F., "Friction Factors for Pipe Flow," *Transactions of the ASME*, 66, 8, November 1944. pp. 671–684.

9. Colebrook, C. F., "Turbulent Flow in Pipes, with Particular Reference to the Transition Region between the Smooth and Rough Pipe Laws," *Journal of the Institution of Civil Engineers, London*, 11, 1938–39, pp. 133–156.

10. Haaland, S. E., "Simple and Explicit Formulas for the Friction Factor in Turbulent Flow," *Transactions of ASME, Journal of Fluids Engineering*, 103, 1983, pp. 89–90.

11. "Flow of Fluids through Valves, Fittings, and Pipe," New York: Crane Company, Technical Paper No. 410, 1982.

12. *ASHRAE Handbook—Fundamentals*. Atlanta, GA: American Society of Heating, Refrigerating, and Air Conditioning Engineers, Inc., 1981.

13. Cockrell, D. J., and C. I. Bradley, "The Response of Diffusers to Flow Conditions at Their Inlet," Paper No. 5, *Symposium on Internal Flows*, University of Salford, Salford, England, April 1971. pp. A32–A41.

14. Sovran, G., and E. D. Klomp, "Experimentally Determined Optimum Geometries for Rectilinear Diffusers with Rectangular, Conical, or Annular Cross-Sections," in *Fluid Mechanics of Internal Flows*, G. Sovran, ed. Amsterdam: Elsevier, 1967.

15. Feiereisen, W. J., R. W. Fox, and A. T. McDonald, "An Experimental Investigation of Incompressible Flow without Swirl in R-Radial Diffusers," *Proceedings, Second International Japan Society of Mechanical Engineers Symposium on Fluid Machinery and Fluidics*, Tokyo, Japan, September 4–9, 1972. pp. 81–90.

16. McDonald, A. T., and R. W. Fox, "An Experimental Investigation of Incompressible Flow in Conical Diffusers,"

International Journal of Mechanical Sciences, 8, 2, February 1966. pp. 125–139.

17. Runstadler, P. W., Jr., "Diffuser Data Book," Hanover, NH: Creare, Inc., Technical Note 186, 1975.

18. Reneau, L. R., J. P. Johnston, and S. J. Kline, "Performance and Design of Straight, Two-Dimensional Diffusers," *Transactions of the ASME, Journal of Basic Engineering*, 89D, 1, March 1967. pp. 141–150.

19. *Aerospace Applied Thermodynamics Manual*. New York: Society of Automotive Engineers, 1969.

20. Daily, J. W., and D. R. F. Harleman, *Fluid Dynamics*. Reading, MA: Addison-Wesley, 1966.

21. White, F. M., *Fluid Mechanics*, 6th ed. New York: McGraw-Hill, 2007.

22. Hamilton, J. B., "The Suppression of Intake Losses by Various Degrees of Rounding," University of Washington, Seattle, WA, Experiment Station Bulletin 51, 1929.

23. Herschel, C., *The Two Books on the Water Supply of the City of Rome, from Sextus Julius Frontinus (ca. 40–103 A.D.)*. Boston, 1899.

24. Lam, C. F., and M. L. Wolla, "Computer Analysis of Water Distribution Systems: Part 1, Formulation of Equations," *Proceedings of the ASCE, Journal of the Hydraulics Division*, 98, HY2, February 1972. pp. 335–344.

25. Miller, R. W., *Flow Measurement Engineering Handbook*. 3rd ed. New York: McGraw Hill, 1996.

26. Bean, H. S., ed., *Fluid Meters, Their Theory and Application*. New York: American Society of Mechanical Engineers, 1971.

27. ISO 7145, *Determination of Flowrate of Fluids in Closed Conduits or Circular Cross Sections—Method of Velocity Determination at One Point in the Cross Section*, ISO UDC 532.57.082.25:532.542, 1st ed. Geneva: International Standards Organization, 1982.

28. Goldstein, R. J., ed., *Fluid Mechanics Measurements*, 2nd ed. Washington, D.C.: Taylor & Francis, 1996.

29. Bruun, H. H., *Hot-Wire Anemometry—Principles and Signal Analysis*. New York: Oxford University Press, 1995.

30. Swamee, P. K., and A. K. Jain, "Explicit Equations for Pipe-Flow Problems," *Proceedings of the ASCE, Journal of the Hydraulics Division, 102*, HY5, May 1976. pp. 657–664.

31. Potter, M. C., and J. F. Foss, *Fluid Mechanics*. New York: Ronald, 1975.

PROBLEMS

8.1 Standard air enters a 6-in. diameter duct. Find the volume flow rate at which the flow becomes turbulent. At this flow rate, estimate the entrance length required to establish fully developed flow.

8.2 Consider incompressible flow in a circular channel. Derive general expressions for Reynolds number in terms of (a) volume flow rate and tube diameter and (b) mass flow rate and tube

diameter. The Reynolds number is 1800 in a section where the tube diameter is 10 mm. Find the Reynolds number for the same flow rate in a section where the tube diameter is 6 mm.

8.3 Standard air flows in a pipe system in which diameter is decreased in two stages from 1 in., to $\frac{1}{2}$ in., to $\frac{1}{4}$ in. Each section is 5 ft long. As the flow rate is increased, which section will become turbulent first? Determine the flow rates at which one, two, then all three sections first become turbulent. At each of these flow rates, determine which sections, if any, attain fully developed flow.

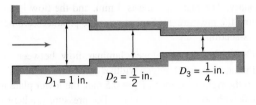

P8.3

8.4 For flow in circular tubes, transition to turbulence usually occurs around $Re \approx 2300$. Investigate the circumstances under which the flows of (a) standard air and (b) water at 15°C become turbulent. On log-log graphs, plot: the average velocity, the volume flow rate, and the mass flow rate, at which turbulence first occurs, as functions of tube diameter.

8.5 For the laminar flow in the section of pipe shown in Fig. 8.1, sketch the expected wall shear stress, pressure, and centerline velocity as functions of distance along the pipe. Explain significant features of the plots, comparing them with fully developed flow. Can the Bernoulli equation be applied anywhere in the flow field? If so, where? Explain briefly.

8.6 An incompressible fluid flows between two infinite stationary parallel plates. The velocity profile is given by $u = u_{max}(Ay^2 + By + C)$, where A, B, and C are constants and y is measured upward from the lower plate. The total gap width is h units. Use appropriate boundary conditions to express the magnitude and units of the constants in terms of h. Develop an expression for volume flow rate per unit depth and evaluate the ratio $\overline{V}/u_{max}$.

8.7 The velocity profile for fully developed flow between stationary parallel plates is given by $u = a(h^2/4 - y^2)$, where a is a constant, h is the total gap width between plates, and y is the distance measured from the center of the gap. Determine the ratio $\overline{V}/u_{max}$.

8.8 A fluid flows steadily between two parallel plates. The flow is fully developed and laminar. The distance between the plates is h.
(a) Derive an equation for the shear stress as a function of y. Sketch this function.
(b) For $\mu = 2.4 \times 10^{-5}$ lbf · s/ft², $\partial p/\partial x = -4.0$ lbf/ft²/ft, and $h = 0.05$ in., calculate the maximum shear stress, in lbf/ft².

8.9 Viscous oil flows steadily between parallel plates. The flow is fully developed and laminar. The pressure gradient is 1.25 kPa/m and the channel [...] he magnitude and direction [...] ate surface. Find the vol [...] nel ($\mu = 0.50$ N · s/m²).

8.10 A viscous oil fl[...] lel plates. The flow is lam [...] gap width between the plat[...] 0.5 N · s/m² and the pressu[...] the magnitude and direction [...] nd the volume flow rate thr[...]

8.11 Oil is confined in [...] av-ing a radial clearance o [...] dy

force of 4500 lbf is applied to the piston. Assume the properties of SAE 30 oil at 120°F. Estimate the rate at which oil leaks past the piston.

8.12 A hydraulic jack supports a load of 9,000 kg. The following data are given:

Diameter of piston	100 mm
Radial clearance between piston and cylinder	0.05 mm
Length of piston	120 mm

Estimate the rate of leakage of hydraulic fluid past the piston, assuming the fluid is SAE 30 oil at 30°C.

8.13 A high pressure in a system is created by a small piston-cylinder assembly. The piston diameter is 6 mm and it extends 50 mm into the cylinder. The radial clearance between the piston and cylinder is 0.002 mm. Neglect elastic deformations of the piston and cylinder caused by pressure. Assume the fluid properties are those of SAE 10W oil at 35°C. When the pressure in the cylinder is 600 MPa, estimate the leakage rate.

8.14 A hydrostatic bearing is to support a load of 50,000 N per meter of length perpendicular to the diagram. The bearing is supplied with SAE 30 oil at 35°C and 700 kPa (gage) through the central slit. Since the oil is viscous and the gap is small, the flow may be considered fully developed. Calculate (a) the required width of the bearing pad, (b) the resulting pressure gradient, dp/dx, and (c) the gap height, if $Q = 1$ mL/min per meter of length.

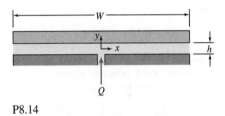

P8.14

8.15 The basic component of a pressure gage tester consists of a piston-cylinder apparatus as shown. The piston, 6 mm in diameter, is loaded to develop a pressure of known magnitude. (The piston length is 25 mm.) Calculate the mass, M, required to produce 1.5 MPa (gage) in the cylinder. Determine the leakage flow rate as a function of radial clearance, a, for this load if the liquid is SAE 30 oil at 20°C. Specify the maximum allowable radial clearance so the vertical movement of the piston due to leakage will be less than 1 mm/min.

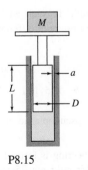

P8.15

8.16 In Section 8-2 we derived the velocity profile between parallel plates (Eq. 8.5) by using a differential control volume. Instead, following the procedure we used in Example 5.9, derive Eq.

[handwritten overlay:]
$\Sigma F_y = \frac{\pi D^2}{4}(p - p_{atm}) - Mg = 0$

$M = \frac{\pi D^2}{4g} p_{gage}$

$\frac{Q}{L} = \frac{a^3 \Delta p}{12\mu L} \Rightarrow Q = \frac{\pi a^3 \Delta p D}{\mu L} \sim a^3$

$Q = \frac{\pi D^2}{4} v$

$a = \left[\frac{12\mu QL}{\pi D \Delta p}\right]^{1/3}$

8.5 by starting with the Navier-Stokes equations (Eqs. 5.27). Be sure to state all assumptions.

8.17 Viscous liquid, at volume flow rate Q, is pumped through the central opening into the narrow gap between the parallel disks shown. The flow rate is low, so the flow is laminar, and the pressure gradient due to convective acceleration in the gap is negligible compared with the gradient caused by viscous forces (this is termed *creeping flow*). Obtain a general expression for the variation of average velocity in the gap between the disks. For creeping flow, the velocity profile at any cross section in the gap is the same as for fully developed flow between stationary parallel plates. Evaluate the pressure gradient, dp/dr, as a function of radius. Obtain an expression for $p(r)$. Show that the net force required to hold the upper plate in the position shown is

$$F = \frac{3\mu Q R^2}{h^3}\left[1 - \left(\frac{R_0}{R}\right)^2\right]$$

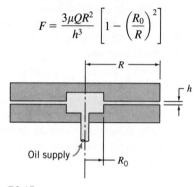

Oil supply

R_0

P8.17

8.18 Consider the simple power-law model for a non-Newtonian fluid given by Eq. 2.16. Extend the analysis of Section 8-2 to show that the velocity profile for fully developed laminar flow of a power-law fluid between stationary parallel plates separated by distance $2h$ may be written

$$u = \left(\frac{h}{k}\frac{\Delta p}{L}\right)^{1/n}\frac{nh}{n+1}\left[1 - \left(\frac{y}{h}\right)^{(n+1)/n}\right]$$

where y is the coordinate measured from the channel centerline. Plot the profiles u/U_{max} versus y/h for $n = 0.7$, 1.0, and 1.3.

8.19 Using the profile of Problem 8.18, show that the flow rate for fully developed laminar flow of a power-law fluid between stationary parallel plates may be written as

$$Q = \left(\frac{h}{k}\frac{\Delta p}{L}\right)^{1/n}\frac{2nwh^2}{2n+1}$$

Here w is the plate width. In such an experimental setup the following data on applied pressure difference Δp and flow rate Q were obtained:

Δp (kPa)	10	20	30	40	50	60	70	80	90	100
Q (L/min)	0.451	0.759	1.01	1.15	1.41	1.57	1.66	1.85	2.05	2.25

Determine if the fluid is pseudoplastic or dilatant, and obtain an experimental value for n.

8.20 A sealed journal bearing is formed from concentric cylinders. The inner and outer radii are 25 and 26 mm, the journal length is 100 mm, and it turns at 2800 rpm. The gap is filled with oil in laminar motion. The velocity profile is linear across the gap. The torque needed to turn the journal is 0.2 N·m. Calculate the viscosity of the oil. Will the torque increase or decrease with time? Why?

8.21 Water at 60°C flows between two large flat plates. The lower plate moves to the left at a speed of 0.3 m/s; the upper plate is stationary. The plate spacing is 3 mm, and the flow is laminar. Determine the pressure gradient required to produce zero net flow at a cross-section.

8.22 Consider fully developed laminar flow between infinite parallel plates separated by gap width $d = 10$ mm. The upper plate moves to the right with speed $U_2 = 0.5$ m/s; the lower plate moves to the left with speed $U_1 = 0.25$ m/s. The pressure gradient in the direction of flow is zero. Develop an expression for the velocity distribution in the gap. Find the volume flow rate per unit depth passing a given cross-section.

8.23 Two immiscible fluids are contained between infinite parallel plates. The plates are separated by distance $2h$, and the two fluid layers are of equal thickness h; the dynamic viscosity of the upper fluid is three times that of the lower fluid. If the lower plate is stationary and the upper plate moves at constant speed $U = 20$ ft/s, what is the velocity at the interface? Assume laminar flows, and that the pressure gradient in the direction of flow is zero.

8.24 Two immiscible fluids are contained between infinite parallel plates. The plates are separated by distance $2h$, and the two fluid layers are of equal thickness $h = 2.5$ mm. The dynamic viscosity of the upper fluid is twice that of the lower fluid, which is $\mu_{lower} = 0.5$ N·s/m^2. If the plates are stationary and the applied pressure gradient is -1000 N/m^2/m, find the velocity at the interface. What is the maximum velocity of the flow? Plot the velocity distribution.

8.25 The dimensionless velocity profile for fully developed laminar flow between infinite parallel plates with the upper plate moving at constant speed U is shown in Fig. 8.6. Find the pressure gradient $\partial p/\partial x$ at which (a) the upper plate and (b) the lower plate experience zero shear stress, in terms of U, a, and μ. Plot the dimensionless velocity profiles for these cases.

8.26 The record-read head for a computer disk-drive memory storage system rides above the spinning disk on a very thin film of air (the film thickness is 0.25 μm). The head location is 25 mm from the disk centerline; the disk spins at 8500 rpm. The record-read head is 5 mm square. For standard air in the gap between the head and disk, determine (a) the Reynolds number of the flow, (b) the viscous shear stress, and (c) the power required to overcome viscous shear.

8.27 Consider steady, incompressible, and fully developed laminar flow of a viscous liquid down an incline with no pressure gradient. The velocity profile was derived in Example 5.9. Plot the velocity profile. Calculate the kinematic viscosity of the liquid if the film thickness on a 30° slope is 0.8 mm and the maximum

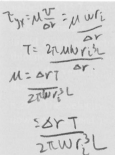

ped laminar flow of a viscous he liquid layer is of constant differential control volume to an expression for the volume

flow of a thin viscous film s developed in Example 5.9.

Consider a film 7 mm thick, of liquid with SG = 1.2 and dynamic viscosity of $1.60 \, N \cdot s/m^2$. Derive an expression for the shear stress distribution within the film. Calculate the maximum shear stress within the film and indicate its direction. Evaluate the volume flow rate in the film, in mm^3/s per millimeter of surface width. Calculate the film Reynolds number based on average velocity.

8.30   Two immiscible fluids of equal density are flowing down a surface inclined at a 30° angle. The two fluid layers are of equal thickness $h = 2.5$ mm; the kinematic viscosity of the upper fluid is twice that of the lower fluid, which is $v_{lower} = 2 \times 10^{-4} \, m^2/s$. Find the velocity at the interface and the velocity at the free surface. Plot the velocity distribution.

8.31   Consider fully developed flow between parallel plates with the upper plate moving at $U = 5$ ft/s; the spacing between the plates is $a = 0.1$ in. Determine the flow rate per unit depth for the case of zero pressure gradient. If the fluid is air, evaluate the shear stress on the lower plate and plot the shear stress distribution across the channel for the zero pressure gradient case. Will the flow rate increase or decrease if the pressure gradient is adverse? Determine the pressure gradient that will give zero shear stress at $y = 0.25a$. Plot the shear stress distribution across the channel for the latter case.

8.32   Water at 15°C flows between parallel plates with gap width $b = 2.5$ mm. The upper plate moves with speed $U = 0.25$ m/s in the positive x direction. The pressure gradient is $\partial p/\partial x = -175$ Pa/m. Locate the point of maximum velocity and determine its magnitude (let $y = 0$ at the bottom plate). Determine the volume of flow that passes a given cross-section ($x = $ constant) in 10 s. Plot the velocity and shear stress distributions.

8.33   The velocity profile for fully developed flow of air between parallel plates with the upper plate moving is given by Eq. 8.8. Assume $U = 2$ m/s and $a = 2.5$ mm. Find the pressure gradient for which there is no net flow in the x direction. Plot the expected velocity distribution and the expected shear stress distribution across the channel for this flow. For the case where $u = 2U$ at $y/a = 0.5$, plot the expected velocity distribution and shear stress distribution across the channel. Comment on features of the plots.

8.34   The velocity profile for fully developed flow of water between parallel plates with the upper plate moving is given by Eq. 8.8. Assume $U = 2$ m/s and $a = 2.5$ mm. Determine the volume flow rate per unit depth for zero pressure gradient. Evaluate the shear stress on the lower plate and sketch the shear stress distribution across the channel. Would the volume flow rate increase or decrease with a mild adverse pressure gradient? Calculate the pressure gradient that will give zero shear stress at $y/a = 0.25$. Sketch the shear stress distribution for this case.

8.35   A continuous belt, passing upward through a chemical bath at speed U_0, picks up a liquid film of thickness h, density ρ, and viscosity μ. Gravity tends to make the liquid drain down, but the movement of the belt keeps the liquid from running off completely. Assume that the flow is fully developed and laminar with zero pressure gradient, and that the atmosphere produces no shear stress at the outer surface of the film. State clearly the boundary conditions to be satisfied by the velocity at $y = 0$ and $y = h$.

Obtain an expression for the velocity profile.

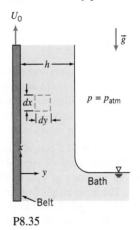

P8.35

8.36   In Example 8.3 we derived the velocity profile for laminar flow on a vertical wall by using a differential control volume. Instead, following the procedure we used in Example 5.9, derive the velocity profile by starting with the Navier-Stokes equations (Eqs. 5.27). Be sure to state all assumptions.

8.37   Microchips are supported on a thin air film on a smooth horizontal surface during one stage of the manufacturing process. The chips are 11.7 mm long and 9.35 mm wide and have a mass of 0.325 g. The air film is 0.125 mm thick. The initial speed of a chip is $V_0 = 1.75$ mm/s; the chip slows as the result of viscous shear in the air film. Analyze the chip motion during deceleration to develop a differential equation for chip speed V versus time t. Calculate the time required for a chip to lose 5 percent of its initial speed. Plot the variation of chip speed versus time during deceleration. Explain why it looks as you have plotted it.

8.38   Free-surface waves begin to form on a laminar liquid film flowing down an inclined surface whenever the Reynolds number, based on mass flow per unit width of film, is larger than about 33. Estimate the maximum thickness of a laminar film of water that remains free from waves while flowing down a vertical surface.

8.39   A viscous-shear pump is made from a stationary housing with a close-fitting rotating drum inside. The clearance is small compared with the diameter of the drum, so flow in the annular space may be treated as flow between parallel plates. Fluid is dragged around the annulus by viscous forces. Evaluate the performance characteristics of the shear pump (pressure differential, input power, and efficiency) as functions of volume flow rate. Assume that the depth normal to the diagram is b.

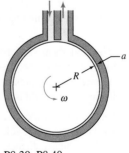

P8.39, P8.40

8.40 The efficiency of the viscous-shear pump of Fig. P8.39 is given by

$$\eta = 6q\,\frac{(1-2q)}{(4-6q)}$$

where $q = Q/abR\omega$ is a dimensionless flow rate (Q is the flow rate at pressure differential Δp, and b is the depth normal to the diagram). Plot the efficiency versus dimensionless flow rate, and find the flow rate for maximum efficiency. Explain why the efficiency peaks, and why it is zero at certain values of q.

8.41 The clamping force to hold a part in a metal-turning operation is provided by high-pressure oil supplied by a pump. Oil leaks axially through an annular gap with diameter D, length L, and radial clearance a. The inner member of the annulus rotates at angular speed ω. Power is required both to pump the oil and to overcome viscous dissipation in the annular gap. Develop expressions in terms of the specified geometry for the pump power, $\mathscr{P}_p$, and the viscous dissipation power, $\mathscr{P}_v$. Show that the total power requirement is minimized when the radial clearance, a, is chosen such that $\mathscr{P}_v = 3\mathscr{P}_p$.

8.42 An inventor proposes to make a "viscous timer" by placing a weighted cylinder inside a slightly larger cylinder containing viscous liquid, creating a narrow annular gap close to the wall. Analyze the flow field created when the apparatus is inverted and the mass begins to fall under gravity. Would this system make a satisfactory timer? If so, for what range of time intervals? What would be the effect of a temperature change on measured time?

8.43 Automotive design is tending toward all-wheel drive to improve vehicle performance and safety when traction is poor. An all-wheel drive vehicle must have an interaxle differential to allow operation on dry roads. Numerous vehicles are being built using multiplate viscous drives for interaxle differentials. Perform the analysis and design needed to define the torque transmitted by the differential for a given speed difference, in terms of the design parameters. Identify suitable dimensions for a viscous differential to transmit a torque of 150 N·m at a speed loss of 125 rpm, using lubricant with the properties of SAE 30 oil. Discuss how to find the ... differential, if the plate co...

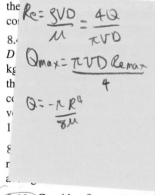

8.4... a shaft of diameter D ... ent of inertia $I = 0.055$ kg ... stationary housing such th ... fluid in the gap has vis- c... given an initial angular v... ne for the shaft to slow to 1...

8... in a pipe, determine the r... ich the velocity equals the a...

8.46 Consider first water and then SAE 10W lubricating oil flowing at 40°C in a 6-mm diameter tube. Determine the maximum flow rate (and the corresponding pressure gradient, $\partial p/\partial x$) for each fluid at which laminar flow would be expected.

8.47 A hypodermic needle, with inside diameter $d = 0.005$ in. and length $L = 1$ in., is used to inject saline solution with viscosity five times that of water. The plunger diameter is $D = 0.375$ in.; the maximum force that can be exerted by a thumb on the plunger

is $F = 7.5$ lbf. Estimate the volume flow rate of saline that can be produced.

8.48 In engineering science there are often analogies to be made between disparate phenomena. For example, the applied pressure difference Δp and corresponding volume flow rate Q in a tube can be compared to the applied DC voltage V across and current I through an electrical resistor, respectively. By analogy, find a formula for the "resistance" of laminar flow of fluid of viscosity μ in a tube length of L and diameter D, corresponding to electrical resistance R. For a tube 100 mm long with inside diameter 0.3 mm, find the maximum flow rate and pressure difference for which this analogy will hold for (a) kerosine and (b) castor oil (both at 40°C). When the flow exceeds this maximum, why does the analogy fail?

8.49 Consider fully developed laminar flow in the annulus between two concentric pipes. The outer pipe is stationary, and the inner pipe moves in the x direction with speed V. Assume the axial pressure gradient is zero ($\partial p/\partial x = 0$). Obtain a general expression for the shear stress, τ, as a function of the radius, r, in terms of a constant, C_1. Obtain a general expression for the velocity profile, $u(r)$, in terms of two constants, C_1 and C_2. Obtain expressions for C_1 and C_2.

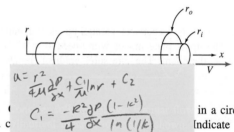

8.50 ... in a circular pipe. Use a c... Indicate the forces acting ... mentum equation, develop ... on.

8.51 Consider fully developed laminar flow in the annular space formed by the two concentric cylinders shown in the diagram for Problem 8.49, but with pressure gradient, $\partial p/\partial x$, and the inner cylinder stationary. Let $r_0 = R$ and $r_i = kR$. Show that the velocity profile is given by

$$u = -\frac{R^2}{4\mu}\frac{\partial p}{\partial x}\left[1 - \left(\frac{r}{R}\right)^2 + \left(\frac{1-k^2}{\ln(1/k)}\right)\ln\frac{r}{R}\right]$$

Obtain an expression for the location of the maximum velocity as a function of k. Plot the location of maximum velocity ($\alpha = r/R$) as a function of radius ratio k. Compare the limiting case, $k \to 0$, with the corresponding expression for flow in a circular pipe.

8.52 For the flow of Problem 8.51 show that the volume flow rate is given by

$$Q = -\frac{\pi R^4}{8\mu}\frac{\partial p}{\partial x}\left[(1-k^4) - \frac{(1-k^2)^2}{\ln(1/k)}\right]$$

Find an expression for the average velocity. Compare the limiting case, $k \to 0$, with the corresponding expression for flow in a circular pipe.

8.53 It has been suggested in the design of an agricultural sprinkler that a structural member be held in place by a wire placed along the centerline of a pipe; it is surmised that a relatively small wire would have little effect on the pressure drop for a given flow rate. Using the result of Problem 8.52, derive an expression giving the percentage change in pressure drop as a function of the ratio of wire diameter to pipe diameter for laminar flow. Plot the percentage change in pressure drop as a function of radius ratio k for $0.001 \leq k \leq 0.10$.

8.54 In a food industry plant two immiscible fluids are pumped through a tube such that fluid 1 ($\mu_1 = 0.02$ lbf · s/ft^2) forms an inner core and fluid 2 ($\mu_2 = 0.03$ lbf · s/ft^2) forms an outer annulus. The tube has $D = 0.2$ in. diameter and length $L = 50$ ft. Derive and plot the velocity distribution if the applied pressure difference, Δp, is 1 psi.

8.55 A horizontal pipe carries fluid in fully developed turbulent flow. The static pressure difference measured between two sections is 35 kPa. The distance between the sections is 10 m and the pipe diameter is 150 mm. Calculate the shear stress, τ_w, that acts on the walls.

8.56 One end of a horizontal pipe is attached using glue to a pressurized tank containing liquid, and the other has a cap attached. The inside diameter of the pipe is 2.5 cm, and the tank pressure is 250 kPa (gage). Find the force the glue must withstand, and the force it must withstand when the cap is off and the liquid is discharging to atmosphere.

8.57 The pressure drop between two taps separated in the streamwise direction by 30 ft in a horizontal, fully developed channel flow of water is 1 psi. The cross-section of the channel is a 1 in. $\times 9\frac{1}{2}$ in. rectangle. Calculate the average wall shear stress.

8.58 Kerosine is pumped through a smooth tube with inside diameter $D = 30$ mm at close to the critical Reynolds number. The flow is unstable and fluctuates between laminar and turbulent states, causing the pressure gradient to intermittently change from approximately -4.5 kPa/m to -11 kPa/m. Which pressure gradient corresponds to laminar, and which to turbulent, flow? For each flow, compute the shear stress at the tube wall, and sketch the shear stress distributions.

8.59 A liquid drug, with the viscosity and density of water, is to be administered through a hypodermic needle. The inside diameter of the needle is 0.25 mm and its length is 50 mm. Determine (a) the maximum volume flow rate for which the flow will be laminar, (b) the pressure drop required to deliver the maximum flow rate, and (c) the corresponding wall shear stress.

8.60 Consider the empirical "power-law" profile for turbulent pipe flow, Eq. 8.22. For $n = 7$ determine the value of r/R at which u is equal to the average velocity, $\overline{V}$. Plot the results over the range $6 \leq n \leq 10$ and compare with the case of fully developed laminar pipe flow, Eq. 8.14.

8.61 Laufer [5] measured the following data for mean velocity in fully developed turbulent pipe flow at $Re_U = 50,000$:

$\bar{u}/U$	0.996	0.981	0.963	0.937	0.907	0.866	0.831
y/r	0.898	0.794	0.691	0.588	0.486	0.383	0.280
$\bar{u}/U$	0.792	0.742	0.700	0.650	0.619	0.551	
y/R	0.216	0.154	0.093	0.062	0.041	0.024	

In addition, Laufer measured the following data for mean velocity in fully developed turbulent pipe flow at $Re_U = 500,000$:

$\bar{u}/U$	0.997	0.988	0.975	0.959	0.934	0.908
y/R	0.898	0.794	0.691	0.588	0.486	0.383
$\bar{u}/U$	0.874	0.847	0.818	0.771	0.736	0.690
y/R	0.280	0.216	0.154	0.093	0.062	0.037

Using *Excel*'s trendline analysis, fit each set of data to the "power-law" profile for turbulent flow, Eq. 8.22, and obtain a value of n for each set. Do the data tend to confirm the validity of Eq. 8.22? Plot the data and their corresponding trendlines on the same graph.

8.62 Equation 8.23 gives the power-law velocity profile exponent, n, as a function of centerline Reynolds number, Re_U, for fully developed turbulent flow in smooth pipes. Equation 8.24 relates mean velocity, $\overline{V}$, to centerline velocity, U, for various values of n. Prepare a plot of $\overline{V}/U$ as a function of Reynolds number, $Re_{\overline{V}}$.

8.63 A momentum coefficient, β, is defined by

$$\int_A u \, \rho u \, dA = \beta \int_A \overline{V} \rho u \, dA = \beta \dot{m} \overline{V}$$

Evaluate β for a laminar velocity profile, Eq. 8.14, and for a "power-law" turbulent velocity profile, Eq. 8.22. Plot β as a function of n for turbulent power-law profiles over the range $6 \leq n \leq 10$ and compare with the case of fully developed laminar pipe flow.

8.64 Consider fully developed laminar flow of water between stationary parallel plates. The maximum flow speed, plate spacing, and width are 20 ft/s, 0.075 in. and 1.25 in. respectively. Find the kinetic energy coefficient, α.

8.65 Consider fully developed laminar flow in a circular tube. Evaluate the kinetic energy coefficient for this flow.

8.66 Show that the kinetic energy coefficient, α, for the "power law" turbulent velocity profile of Eq. 8.22 is given by Eq. 8.27. Plot α as a function of $Re_{\overline{V}}$, for $Re_{\overline{V}} = 1 \times 10^4$ to 1×10^7. When analyzing pipe flow problems it is common practice to assume $\alpha \approx 1$. Plot the error associated with this assumption as a function of $Re_{\overline{V}}$, for $Re_{\overline{V}} = 1 \times 10^4$ to 1×10^7.

8.67 Measurements are made for the flow configuration shown in Fig. 8.12. At the inlet, section ①, the pressure is 70 kPa (gage), the average velocity is 1.75 m/s, and the elevation is 2.25 m. At the outlet, section ②, the pressure, average velocity, and elevation are 45 kPa (gage), 3.5 m/s, and 3 m, respectively. Calculate the head loss in meters. Convert to units of energy per unit mass.

8.68 Water flows in a horizontal constant-area pipe; the pipe diameter is 50 mm and the average flow speed is 1.5 m/s. At the pipe inlet the gage pressure is 588 kPa, and the outlet is at atmospheric pressure. Determine the head loss in the pipe. If the pipe is now aligned so that the outlet is 25 m above the inlet, what will the inlet pressure need to be to maintain the same flow rate? If the pipe is now aligned so that the outlet is 25 m below the inlet, what will the inlet pressure need to be to maintain the same flow rate? Finally, how much lower than the inlet must the outlet be so that the same flow rate is maintained if both ends of the pipe are at atmospheric pressure (i.e., gravity feed)?

8.69 For the flow configuration of Fig. 8.12, it is known that the head loss is 1 m. The pressure drop from inlet to outlet is 50 kPa, the velocity doubles from inlet to outlet, and the elevation increase is 2 m. Compute the inlet water velocity.

8.70 Consider the pipe flow from the water tower of Example 8.7. After another 10 years the pipe roughness has increased such that the flow is fully turbulent and $f = 0.04$. Find by how much the flow rate is decreased.

8.71 Consider the pipe flow from the water tower of Problem 8.70. To increase delivery, the pipe length is reduced from 600 ft to 300 ft (the flow is still fully turbulent and $f \approx 0.04$). What is the flow rate?

8.72 The average flow speed in a constant-diameter section of the Alaskan pipeline is 2.5 m/s. At the inlet, the pressure is 8.25 MPa (gage) and the elevation is 45 m; at the outlet, the pressure is 350 kPa (gage) and the elevation is 115 m. Calculate the head loss in this section of pipeline.

8.73 Water flows fr[...] . The tube is located 2.5 m[...] tank. The head loss is 2 J/[...] in the tube.

8.74 At the inlet to[...] askan pipeline, the pressure[...] at the outlet the elevation is[...] pipe-line is 6.9 kJ/kg. Calc[...]

8.75 Water flows a[...] meter garden hose. The pres[...] s 12.3 psi. Calculate the hea[...]

8.76 Water is pump[...] oir 20 m above a pump to a free discharge 35 m above the pump. The pressure on the intake side of the pump is 150 kPa and the pressure on the discharge side is 450 kPa. All pipes are commercial steel of 15 cm diameter. Determine (a) the head supplied by the pump and (b) the total head loss between the pump and point of free discharge.

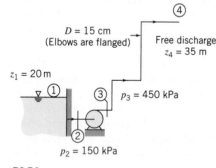

$D = 15$ cm (Elbows are flanged) — (4) Free discharge $z_4 = 35$ m

$z_1 = 20$ m — (1) — (3) $p_3 = 450$ kPa

(2)

$p_2 = 150$ kPa

P8.76

8.77 Laufer [5] measured the following data for mean velocity near the wall in fully developed turbulent pipe flow at $Re_U = 50,000$ ($U = 9.8$ ft/s and $R = 4.86$ in.) in air:

$\frac{\bar{u}}{U}$	0.343	0.318	0.300	0.264	0.228	0.221	0.179	0.152	0.140
$\frac{y}{R}$	0.0082	0.0075	0.0071	0.0061	0.0055	0.0051	0.0041	0.0034	0.0030

Plot the data and obtain the best-fit slope, $d\bar{u}/dy$. Use this to estimate the wall shear stress from $\tau_w = \mu \, d\bar{u}/dy$. Compare this value to that obtained using the friction factor f computed using (a) the

Colebrook formula (Eq. 8.37), and (b) the Blasius correlation (Eq. 8.38).

8.78 A small-diameter capillary tube made from drawn aluminum is used in place of an expansion valve in a home refrigerator. The inside diameter is 0.5 mm. Calculate the corresponding relative roughness. Comment on whether this tube may be considered "smooth" with regard to fluid flow.

8.79 A smooth, 75-mm diameter pipe carries water (65°C) horizontally. When the mass flow rate is 0.075 kg/s, the pressure drop is measured to be 7.5 Pa per 100 m of pipe. Based on these measurements, what is the friction factor? What is the Reynolds number? Does this Reynolds number generally indicate laminar or turbulent flow? Is the flow actually laminar or turbulent?

8.80 Usi[...] the Moody chart of Fig. 8.13.

8.81 The[...] mputing the turbulent fric[...] t expression [30] that gives[...]

Compare[...] with Eq. 8.37 by computing[...] nction of Re and e/D, for[...] 0.001, 0.01, and 0.05. Wh[...] hese Re and e/D values? Plot[...] as a p[...]

8.82 We saw in Section 8-7 that instead of the implicit Colebrook equation (Eq. 8.37) for computing the turbulent friction factor f, an explicit expression that gives reasonable accuracy is

$$\frac{1}{\sqrt{f}} = -1.8 \log \left[\left(\frac{e/D}{3.7} \right)^{1.11} + \frac{6.9}{Re} \right]$$

Compare the accuracy of this expression for f with Eq. 8.37 by computing the percentage discrepancy as a function of Re and e/D, for $Re = 10^4$ to 10^8, and $e/D = 0, 0.0001, 0.001, 0.01,$ and 0.05. What is the maximum discrepancy for these Re and e/D values? Plot f against Re with e/D as a parameter.

8.83 The Moody diagram gives the Darcy friction factor, f, in terms of Reynolds number and relative roughness. The *Fanning friction factor* for pipe flow is defined as

$$f_F = \frac{\tau_w}{\frac{1}{2} \rho \bar{V}^2}$$

where τ_w is the wall shear stress in the pipe. Show that the relation between the Darcy and Fanning friction factors for fully developed pipe flow is given by $f = 4 f_F$.

8.84 Water flows through a 25-mm diameter tube that suddenly enlarges to a diameter of 50 mm. The flow rate through the enlargement is 1.25 Liter/s. Calculate the pressure rise across the enlargement. Compare with the value for frictionless flow.

8.85 Water flows at 0.003 mm³/s through a gradual contraction, in which the pipe diameter is reduced from 5 cm to 2.5 cm, with a 120° included angle. If the pressure before the contraction is 200 kPa, estimate the pressure after the contraction. Recompute the answer if the included angle is changed to 180° (a sudden contraction).

8.86 Air at standard conditions flows through a sudden expansion in a circular duct. The upstream and downstream duct diameters are 75 mm and 225 mm, respectively. The pressure downstream is 5 mm of water higher than that upstream. Determine the average speed of the air approaching the expansion and the volume flow rate.

8.87 Water flows through a 2-in. diameter tube that suddenly contracts to 1 in. diameter. The pressure drop across the contraction is 0.5 psi. Determine the volume flow rate.

8.88 In an undergraduate laboratory you have been assigned the task of developing a crude flow meter for measuring the flow in a 400-mm diameter water pipe system. You are to install a 200-mm diameter section of pipe, and a water manometer to measure the pressure drop at the sudden contraction. Derive an expression for the theoretical calibration constant k in $Q = k\sqrt{\Delta h}$, where Q is the volume flow rate in L/min, and Δh is the manometer deflection in mm. Plot the theoretical calibration curve for a flow rate range of 0 to 200 L/min. Would you expect this to be a practical device for measuring flow rate?

8.89 Flow through a sudden contraction is shown. The minimum flow area at the vena contracta is given in terms of the area ratio by the contraction coefficient [31],

$$C_c = \frac{A_c}{A_2} = 0.62 + 0.38\left(\frac{A_2}{A_1}\right)^3$$

The loss in a sudden contraction is mostly a result of the vena contracta: The fluid accelerates into the contraction, there is flow separation (as shown by the dashed lines), and the vena contracta acts as a miniature sudden expansion with significant secondary flow losses. Use these assumptions to obtain and plot estimates of the minor loss coefficient for a sudden contraction, and compare with the data presented in Fig. 8.15.

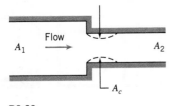

P8.89

8.90 Water flows from the tank shown through a very short pipe. Assume the flow is quasi-steady. Estimate the flow rate at the instant shown. How could you improve the flow system if a larger flow rate were desired?

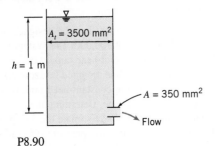

P8.90

8.91 Consider again flow through the elbow analyzed in Example 4.6. Using the given conditions, calculate the minor head loss coefficient for the elbow.

8.92 Air flows out of a clean room test chamber through a 150-mm diameter duct of length L. The original duct had a square-edged entrance, but this has been replaced with a well-rounded one. The pressure in the chamber is 2.5 mm of water above ambient. Losses from friction are negligible compared with the entrance and exit losses. Estimate the increase in volume flow rate that results from the change in entrance contour.

8.93 A water tank (open to the atmosphere) contains water to a depth of 10 ft. A $\frac{1}{2}$-in. diameter hole is punched in the bottom. Modeling the hole as square-edged, estimate the flow rate (gpm) exiting the tank. If you were to stick a short section of pipe into the hole, by how much would the flow rate change? If instead you were to machine the inside of the hole to give it a rounded edge ($r = 0.01$ in.), by how much would the flow rate change?

8.94 A conical diffuser is used to expand a pipe flow from a diameter of 100 mm to a diameter of 150 mm. Find the minimum length of the diffuser if we want a loss coefficient (a) $K_{\text{diffuser}} \leq 0.2$, (b) $K_{\text{diffuser}} \leq 0.35$.

8.95 A conical diffuser of length 6 in. is used to expand a pipe flow from a diameter of 2 in. to a diameter of 3.5 in. For a water flow rate of 750 gal/min, estimate the static pressure rise. What is the approximate value of the loss coefficient?

8.96 Space has been found for a conical diffuser 0.45 m long in the clean room ventilation system described in Problem 8.92. The best diffuser of this size is to be used. Assume that data from Fig. 8.16 may be used. Determine the appropriate diffuser angle and area ratio for this installation and estimate the volume flow rate that will be delivered after it is installed.

8.97 By applying the basic equations to a control volume starting at the expansion and ending downstream, analyze flow through a sudden expansion (assume the inlet pressure p_1 acts on the area A_2 at the expansion). Develop an expression for and plot the minor head loss across the expansion as a function of area ratio, and compare with the data of Fig. 8.15.

8.98 Water at 45°C enters a shower head through a circular tube with 15.8 mm inside diameter. The water leaves in 24 streams, each of 1.05 mm diameter. The volume flow rate is 5.67 L/min. Estimate the minimum water pressure needed at the inlet to the shower head. Evaluate the force needed to hold the shower head onto the end of the circular tube. Indicate clearly whether this is a compression or a tension force.

8.99 Analyze flow through a sudden expansion to obtain an ex- $\frac{P_1}{\rho} + \partial\frac{V_1^2}{2} + gz_1 - \left(\frac{P_2}{\rho} + \partial_2\frac{V_2^2}{2} + gz_2\right)$ velocity $\overline{V}_1$ in terms of the pr $= \text{hf hem}$ AR, fluid density ρ, and lo tionless, would the flow ra $V_1 = \frac{Q}{A}$ change be higher or lower th if the flow were friction- le $V_2 = \frac{V_1 A_1}{A_2}$ rger or smaller pressure ch

$P_1 = \frac{\rho}{2}(V_2^2 + k V_2^2 - V_1^2) = \frac{\rho}{2}\left(\frac{(1+k)V_2^2}{+V_1^2}\right)$ e from a large reservoir

$R_x = P_1 g A_1 + g Q(V_1 - V_2)$ l nozzle of 1 in. diameter. e exit plane. Calculate the n of 2-in. diameter pipe is a sudden expansion. Determine the location and estimate the magnitude of the minimum pressure with the sudden expansion in place. If the flow were frictionless (with the sudden expansion in place), would the minimum pressure be higher, lower, or the same? Would the flow rate be higher, lower, or the same?

8.101 Water flows steadily from a large tank through a length of smooth plastic tubing, then discharges to atmosphere. The tubing inside diameter is 3.18 mm, and its length is 15.3 m. Calculate the maximum volume flow rate for which flow in the tubing will remain laminar. Estimate the water level in the tank below which flow will be laminar (for laminar flow, $\alpha = 2$ and $K_{ent} = 1.4$).

8.102 You are asked to compare the behavior of fully developed laminar flow and fully developed turbulent flow in a horizontal pipe under different conditions. For the same flow rate, which will have the larger centerline velocity? Why? If the pipe discharges to atmosphere, what would you expect the trajectory of the discharge stream to look like (for the same flow rate)? Sketch your expectations for each case. For the same flow rate, which flow would give the larger wall shear stress? Why? Sketch the shear stress distribution τ/τ_w as a function of radius for each flow. For the same Reynolds number, which flow would have the larger pressure drop per unit length? Why? For a given imposed pressure differential, which flow would have the larger flow rate? Why?

Most of the remaining problems in this chapter involve determination of the turbulent friction factor f from the Reynolds number Re and dimensionless roughness e/D. For approximate calculations, f can be read from Fig. 8.13; a more accurate approach is to use this value (or some other value, even $f = 1$) as the first value for iterating in Eq. 8.37. The most convenient approach is to use solution of Eq. 8.37 programmed into (or built-into) your calculator, or programmed into an *Excel* workbook. Hence, most of the remaining problems benefit from use of *Excel*. To avoid needless duplication, the mouse symbol will only be used next to remaining problems in this chapter when it has an *additional* benefit (e.g., for iterating to a solution, or for graphing).

8.103 Estimate the minimum level in the water tank of Problem 8.101 such that the flow will be turbulent.

8.104 A laboratory experiment is set up to measure pressure drop for flow of water through a smooth tube. The tube diameter is 15.9 mm, and its length is 3.56 m. Flow enters the tube from a reservoir through a square-edged entrance. Calculate the volume flow rate needed to obtain turbulent flow in the tube. Evaluate the reservoir height differential required to obtain turbulent flow in the tube.

8.105 As discussed in Problem 8.48, the applied pressure difference, Δp, and corresponding volume flow rate, Q, for laminar flow in a tube can be compared to the applied DC voltage V across, and current I through, an electrical resistor, respectively. Investigate whether or not this analogy is valid for turbulent flow by plotting the "resistance" $\Delta p/Q$ as a function of Q for turbulent flow of kerosine (at 40°C) in a tube 100 mm long with inside diameter 0.3 mm.

8.106 Plot the required reservoir depth of water to create flow in a smooth tube of diameter 10 mm and length 100 m, for a flow rate range of 1 L/min through 10 L/min.

8.107 Oil with kinematic viscosity $v = 0.00005 \text{ m}^2/\text{s}$ flows at 0.003 m³/s in a 25-m long horizontal steel pipe of 4 cm diameter. By what percentage ratio will the energy loss increase if the same flow rate is maintained while the pipe diameter is reduced to 1 cm?

8.108 A water system is used in a laboratory to study flow in a smooth pipe. To obtain a reasonable range, the maximum Reynolds number in the pipe must be 100,000. The system is supplied from an overhead constant-head tank. The pipe system consists of a square-edged entrance, two 45° standard elbows, two 90° standard elbows, and a fully open gate valve. The pipe diameter is 15.9 mm, and the total length of pipe is 9.8 m. Calculate the minimum height of the supply tank above the pipe system discharge to reach the desired Reynolds number.

8.109 Water is to flow by gravity from one reservoir to a lower one through a straight, inclined galvanized iron pipe. The pipe diameter is 50 mm, and the total length is 250 m. Each reservoir is open to the atmosphere. Plot the required elevation difference Δz as a function of flow rate Q, for Q ranging from 0 to 0.01 m³/s. Estimate the fraction of Δz due to minor losses.

8.110 Water from a pump flows through a 9-in. diameter commercial steel pipe for a distance of 4 miles from the pump discharge to a reservoir open to the atmosphere. The level of the water in the reservoir is 50 ft above the pump discharge, and the average speed of the water in the pipe is 10 ft/s. Calculate the pressure at the pump discharge.

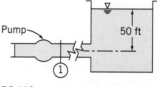

P8.110

8.111 A 5-cm diameter potable water line is to be run through a maintenance room in a commercial building. Three possible layouts for the water line are proposed, as shown. Which is the best option, based on minimizing losses? Assume galvanized iron, and a flow rate of 350 L/min.

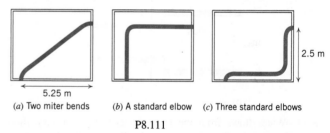

(a) Two miter bends   (b) A standard elbow   (c) Three standard elbows

P8.111

8.112 In a certain air-conditioning installation, a flow rate of 35 m³/min of air at standard conditions is required. A smooth sheet metal duct 0.3 m square is to be used. Determine the pressure drop for a 30 m horizontal duct run.

8.113 A pipe friction experiment is to be designed, using water, to reach a Reynolds number of 100,000. The system will use 5 cm smooth PVC pipe from a constant-head tank to the flow bench and 20 m of smooth 2.5 cm PVC line mounted horizontally for the test section. The water level in the constant-head tank is 0.5 m above the entrance to the 5 cm PVC line. Determine the required average speed of water in the 2.5 cm pipe. Estimate the feasibility of using a constant-head tank. Calculate the pressure difference expected between taps 5 m apart in the horizontal test section.

8.114 A system for testing variable-output pumps consists of the pump, four standard elbows, and an open gate valve forming a closed circuit as shown. The circuit is to absorb the energy added by the pump. The tubing is 75-mm diameter cast iron, and the total length of the circuit is 20 m. Plot the pressure difference required from the pump for water flow rates Q ranging from 0.01 m^3/s to 0.06 m^3/s.

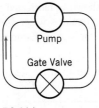

P8.114

8.115 Consider flow of standard air at 1250 ft^3/min. Compare the pressure drop per unit length of a round duct with that for rectangular ducts of aspect ratio 1, 2, and 3. Assume that all ducts are smooth, with cross-sectional areas of 1 ft^2.

8.116 Two reservoirs are connected by three clean cast-iron pipes in series, $L_1 = 600$ m, $D_1 = 0.3$ m, $L_2 = 900$ m, $D_2 = 0.4$ m, $L_3 = 1500$ m, and $D_3 = 0.45$ m. When the discharge is 0.11 m^3/s of water at 15°C, determine the difference in elevation between the reservoirs.

8.117 Water, at volume flow rate $Q = 0.75$ ft^3/s, is delivered by a fire hose and nozzle assembly. The hose ($L = 250$ ft, $D = 3$ in and $e/D = 0.004$) is made up of four 60 ft sections joined by couplings. The entrance is square-edged; the minor loss coefficient for each coupling is $K_c = 0.5$, based on mean velocity through the hose. The nozzle loss coefficient is $K_n = 0.02$, based on velocity in the exit jet, of $D_2 = 1$ in. diameter. Estimate the supply pressure required at this flow rate.

8.118 Data were obtained from measurements on a vertical section of old, corroded, galvanized iron pipe of 25 mm inside diameter. At one section the pressure was $p_1 = 700$ kPa (gage); at a second section, 6 m lower, the pressure was $p_2 = 525$ kPa (gage). The volume flow rate of water was 0.2 m^3/min. Estimate the relative roughness of the pipe. What percent savings in pumping power would result if the pipe were restored to its new, clean relative roughness?

8.119 Flow in a tube may alternate between laminar and turbulent states for Reynolds numbers in the transition zone. Design a bench-top experiment consisting of a constant-head cylindrical transparent plastic tank with depth graduations, and a length of plastic tubing (assumed smooth) attached at the base of the tank through which the water flows to a measuring container. Select tank and tubing dimensions so that the system is compact, but will operate in the transition zone range. Design the experiment so that you can easily increase the tank head from a low range (laminar flow) through transition to turbulent flow, and vice versa. (Write instructions for students on recognizing when the flow is laminar or turbulent.) Generate plots (on the same graph) of tank depth against Reynolds number, assuming laminar or turbulent flow.

8.120 A small swimming pool is drained using a garden hose. The hose has 20 mm inside diameter, a roughness height of 0.2 mm, and is 30 m long. The free end of the hose is located 3 m below the elevation of the bottom of the pool. The average velocity at the hose discharge is 1.2 m/s. Estimate the depth of the water in the swimming pool. If the flow were inviscid, what would be the velocity?

8.121 A compressed air drill requires 0.25 kg/s of air at 650 kPa (gage) at the drill. The hose from the air compressor to the drill is 40 mm inside diameter. The maximum compressor discharge gage pressure is 670 kPa; air leaves the compressor at 40°C. Neglect changes in density and any effects of hose curvature. Calculate the longest hose that may be used.

8.122 What flow rate (gpm) will be produced in a 4-in. diameter water pipe for which there is a pressure drop of 40 psi over a 300 ft length? The pipe roughness is 0.01 ft. The water is at 68°F.

8.123 When you drink you beverage with a straw, you need to overcome both gravity and friction in the straw. Estimate the fraction of the total effort you put into quenching your thirst of each factor, making suitable assumptions about the liquid and straw properties, and your drinking rate (for example, how long it would take you to drink a 12 oz drink if you drank it all in one go (quite a feat with a straw). Is the flow laminar or turbulent? (Ignore minor losses.)

8.124 Gasoline flows in a long, underground pipeline at a constant temperature of 15°C. Two pumping stations at the same elevation are located 13 km apart. The pressure drop between the stations is 1.4 MPa. The pipeline is made from 0.6-m diameter pipe. Although the pipe is made from commercial steel, age and corrosion have raised the pipe roughness to approximately that for galvanized iron. Compute the volume flow rate.

8.125 Water flows steadily in a horizontal 125-mm diameter cast-iron pipe. The pipe is 150 m long and the pressure drop between sections ① and ② is 150 kPa. Find the volume flow rate through the pipe.

8.126 Water flows steadily in a 125-mm diameter cast-iron pipe 150 m long. The pressure drop between sections ① and ② is 150 kPa, and section ② is located 15 m above section ①. Find the volume flow rate.

8.127 Two open standpipes of equal diameter are connected by a straight tube as shown. Water flows by gravity from one standpipe to the other. For the instant shown, estimate the rate of change of water level in the left standpipe.

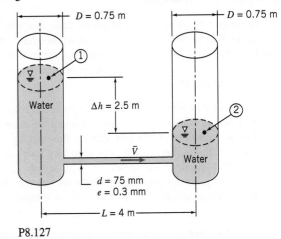

P8.127

8.128 Two galvanized iron pipes of diameter D are connected to a large water reservoir as shown. Pipe A has length L and pipe B has length $2L$. Both pipes discharge to atmosphere. Which pipe will pass the larger flow rate? Justify (without calculating the flow rate in each pipe). Compute the flow rates if $H = 35$ ft, $D = 2$ in., and $L = 200$ ft.

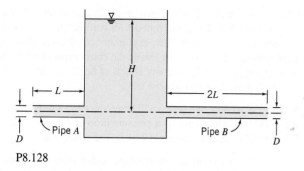

P8.128

8.129 Galvanized iron drainpipes of diameter 7.5 cm are located at the four corners of a building, but three of them become clogged with debris. Find the rate of downpour (cm/min) at which the single functioning drainpipe can no longer drain the roof. The building roof area is 500 m², and the height is 5 m. Assume the drainpipes are the same height as the building, and that both ends are open to atmosphere. Ignore minor losses.

8.130 A mining engineer plans to do hydraulic mining with a high-speed jet of water. A lake is located $H = 300$ m above the mine site. Water will be delivered through $L = 900$ m of fire hose; the hose has inside diameter $D = 75$ mm and relative roughness $e/D = 0.01$. Couplings, with equivalent length $L_e = 20\ D$, are located every 10 m along the hose. The nozzle outlet diameter is $d = 25$ mm. Its minor loss coefficient is $K = 0.02$ based on outlet velocity. Estimate the maximum outlet velocity that this system could deliver. Determine the maximum force exerted on a rock face by this water jet.

8.131 Investigate the effect of tube roughness on flow rate by computing the flow generated by a pressure difference $\Delta p = 100$ kPa applied to a length $L = 100$ m of tubing, with diameter $D = 25$ mm. Plot the flow rate against tube relative roughness e/D for e/D ranging from 0 to 0.05 (this could be replicated experimentally by progressively roughening the tube surface). Is it possible that this tubing could be roughened so much that the flow could be slowed to a laminar flow rate?

8.132 Investigate the effect of tube length on water flow rate by computing the flow generated by a pressure difference $\Delta p = 100$ kPa applied to a length L of smooth tubing, of diameter $D = 25$ mm. Plot the flow rate against tube length for flow ranging from low speed laminar to fully turbulent.

8.133 For the pipe flow into a reservoir of Example 8.5 consider the effect of pipe roughness on flow rate, assuming the pressure of the pump is maintained at 153 kPa. Plot the flow rate against pipe roughness ranging from smooth ($e = 0$) to very rough ($e = 3.75$ mm). Also consider the effect of pipe length (again assuming the pump always produces 153 kPa) for smooth pipe. Plot the flow rate against pipe length for $L = 100$ m through $L = 1000$ m.

8.134 Water for a fire protection system is supplied from a water tower through a 150 mm cast-iron pipe. A pressure gage at a fire hydrant indicates 600 kPa when no water is flowing. The total pipe length between the elevated tank and the hydrant is 200 m. Determine the height of the water tower above the hydrant. Calculate the maximum volume flow rate that can be achieved when the system is flushed by opening the hydrant wide (assume minor losses are 10 percent of major losses at this condition). When a fire hose is attached to the hydrant, the volume flow rate is 0.75 m³/min. Determine the reading of the pressure gage at this flow condition.

8.135 The siphon shown is fabricated from 50 mm i.d. drawn aluminum tubing. The liquid is water at 15°C. Compute the volume flow rate through the siphon. Estimate the minimum pressure inside the tube.

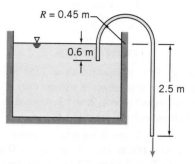

P8.135

8.136 A large c[...] diameter cast iron drainpip[...] the depth of water is 3.5 m, [...] ntrance is a) reentrant, b) squa[...]

8.137 Consider [...] ussed in Example 8.10. Ass[...] constant-diameter pipe req[...] relative roughness of the pi[...] er delivered by the pipe u[...] le. What would be the effect[...] of the 50 ft pipe?

8.138 A 7500 gallon tank of kerosine is to be emptied by a gravity feed using a drain hose of diameter 1 in., roughness 0.01 in., and length 50 ft. The top of the tank is open to the atmosphere and the hose exits to an open chamber. If the kerosense level is initially 10 ft above the drain exit, estimate (by assuming steady flow) the initial drainage rate. Estimate the flow rate when the kerosene level is down to 5 ft, and down to 1 ft. Based on these three estimates, make a rough estimate of the time it took to drain to the 1 ft level.

8.139 In Example 8.10 we found that the flow rate from a water main could be increased (by as much as 33 percent) by attaching a diffuser to the outlet of the nozzle installed into the water main. We read that the Roman water commissioner required that the tube attached to the nozzle of each customer's pipe be the same diameter for at least 50 feet from the public water main. Was the commissioner overly conservative? Using the data of the problem, estimate the length of pipe (with $e/D = 0.01$) at which the system of pipe and diffuser would give a flow rate equal to that with the nozzle alone. Plot the volume flow ratio Q/Q_i as a function of L/D, where L is the length of pipe between the nozzle and the diffuser, Q_i is the volume flow rate for the nozzle alone, and Q is the actual volume flow rate with the pipe inserted between nozzle and diffuser.

8.140 You are watering your lawn with an *old* hose. Because lime deposits have built up over the years, the 0.75 in. i.d. hose now has an average roughness height of 0.022 in. One 50 ft length of the hose, attached to your spigot, delivers 15 gpm of water (60°F). Compute the pressure at the spigot, in psi. Estimate the delivery if two 50 ft lengths of the hose are connected. Assume that the pressure at the spigot varies with flow rate and the water main pressure remains constant at 50 psig.

8.141 Your boss, from the "old school," claims that for pipe flow the flow rate, $Q \propto \sqrt{\Delta p}$, where Δp is the pressure difference driving the flow. You dispute this, so perform some calculations. You take a 1-in. diameter commercial steel pipe and assume an initial flow rate of 1.25 gal/min of water. You then increase the applied pressure in equal increments and compute the new flow rates so you can plot Q versus Δp, as computed by you and your boss. Plot the two curves on the same graph. Was your boss right?

8.142 A hydraulic press is powered by a remote high-pressure pump. The gage pressure at the pump outlet is 3000 psi, whereas the pressure required for the press is 2750 psi (gage), at a flow rate of 0.02 ft³/s. The press and pump are connected by 165 ft of smooth, drawn steel tubing. The fluid is SAE 10W oil at 100°F. Determine the minimum tubing diameter that may be used.

8.143 A pump is located 4.5 m to one side of, and 3.5 m above a reservoir. The pump is designed for a flow rate of 6 L/s. For satisfactory operation, the static pressure at the pump inlet must not be lower than −6 m of water gage. Determine the smallest standard commercial steel pipe that will give the required performance.

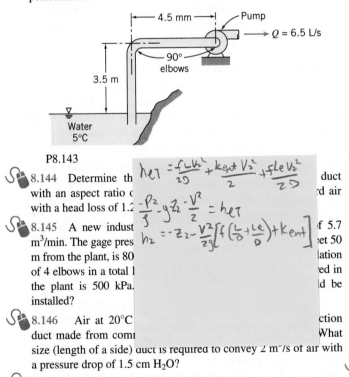

P8.143

8.144 Determine th[...] duct with an aspect ratio [...] d air with a head loss of 1.2[...]

8.145 A new indust[...] f 5.7 m³/min. The gage pres[...] et 50 m from the plant, is 80[...] lation of 4 elbows in a total l[...] ed in the plant is 500 kPa. [...] d be installed?

8.146 Air at 20°C [...] ction duct made from com[...] What size (length of a side) duct is required to convey 2 m³/s of air with a pressure drop of 1.5 cm H₂O?

8.147 Investigate the effect of tube diameter on water flow rate by computing the flow generated by a pressure difference, $\Delta p = 100 \, kPa$, applied to a length $L = 100$ m of smooth tubing. Plot the flow rate against tube diameter for a range that includes laminar and turbulent flow.

8.148 What diameter water pipe is required to handle 1200 gpm and a 50 psi pressure drop? The pipe length is 500 ft, and roughness is 0.01 ft. The water is at 68°F.

8.149 A large reservoir supplies water for a community. A portion of the water supply system is shown. Water is pumped from the reservoir to a large storage tank before being sent on to the water treatment facility. The system is designed to provide 1310 L/s of water at 20°C. From B to C the system consists of a square-edged entrance, 760 m of pipe, three gate valves, four 45° elbows, and two 90° elbows. Gage pressure at C is 197 kPa. The system between F and G contains 760 m of pipe, two gate valves, and four 90° elbows. All pipe is 508 mm diameter, cast iron. Calculate the average velocity of water in the pipe, the gage pressure at section F, the power input to the pump (its efficiency is 80 percent), and the wall shear stress in section FG.

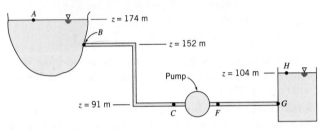

P8.149

8.150 An air-pipe friction experiment consists of a smooth brass tube with 63.5 mm inside diameter; the distance between pressure taps is 1.52 m. The pressure drop is indicated by a manometer filled with Meriam red oil. The centerline velocity U is measured with a pitot cylinder. At one flow condition, $U = 23.1$ m/s and the pressure drop is 12.3 mm of oil. For this condition, evaluate the Reynolds number based on average flow velocity. Calculate the friction factor and compare with the value obtained from Eq. 8.37 (use $n = 7$ in the power-law velocity profile).

*8.151 Oil has been flowing from a large tank on a hill to a tanker at the wharf. The compartment in the tanker is nearly full and an operator is in the process of stopping the flow. A valve on the wharf is closed at a rate such that 1 MPa is maintained in the line immediately upstream of the valve. Assume:

Length of line from tank to valve	3 km
Inside diameter of line	200 mm
Elevation of oil surface in tank	60 m
Elevation of valve on wharf	6 m
Instantaneous flow rate	2.5 m³/min
Head loss in line (exclusive of valve being closed) at this rate of flow	23 m of oil
Specific gravity of oil	0.88

Calculate the initial instantaneous rate of change of volume flow rate.

*8.152 Problem 8.151 describes a situation in which flow in a long pipeline from a hilltop tank is slowed gradually to avoid a large pressure rise. Expand this analysis to predict and plot the closing schedule (valve loss coefficient versus time) needed to maintain the maximum pressure at the valve at or below a given value throughout the process of stopping the flow from the tank.

---

*These problems require material from sections that may be omitted without loss of continuity in the text material.

8.153   A pump draws water at a steady flow rate of 25 lbm/s through a piping system. The pressure on the suction side of the pump is −2.5 psig. The pump outlet pressure is 50 psig. The inlet pipe diameter is 3 in.; the outlet pipe diameter is 2 in. The pump efficiency is 70 percent. Calculate the power required to drive the pump.

8.154   The pressure rise across a water pump is 75 kPa when the volume flow rate is 25 L/s. If the pump efficiency is 80 percent, determine the power input to the pump.

8.155   A 2.5 (nominal) in. pipeline conveying water contains 290 ft of straight galvanized pipe, 2 fully open gate valves, 1 fully open angle valve, 7 standard 90° elbows, 1 square-edged entrance from a reservoir, and 1 free discharge. The entrance and exit conditions are:

Location	Elevation	Pressure
Entrance	50.0 ft	20 psig
Discharge	94.0 ft	0 psig

A centrifugal pump is installed in the line to move the water. What pressure rise must the pump deliver so the volume flow rate will be $Q = 0.439 \ \text{ft}^3/\text{s}$?

8.156   Cooling water is pumped from a reservoir to rock drills on a construction job using the pipe system shown. The flow rate must be 600 gpm and water must leave the spray nozzle at 120 ft/s. Calculate the minimum pressure needed at the pump outlet. Estimate the required power input if the pump efficiency is 70 percent.

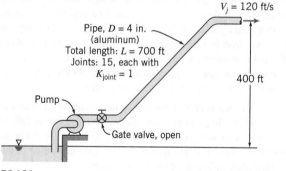

$V_j = 120 \ \text{ft/s}$

Pipe, $D = 4$ in. (aluminum)
Total length: $L = 700$ ft
Joints: 15, each with $K_{\text{joint}} = 1$

400 ft

Pump

Gate valve, open

P8.156

8.157   You are asked to size a pump for installation in the water supply system of the Sears Tower in Chicago. The system requires 100 gpm of water pumped to a reservoir at the top of the tower 340 m above the street. City water pressure at the street-level pump inlet is 400 kPa (gage). Piping is to be commercial steel. Determine the minimum diameter required to keep the average water velocity below 3.5 m/s in the pipe. Calculate the pressure rise required across the pump. Estimate the minimum power needed to drive the pump.

8.158   Air conditioning for the Purdue University campus is provided by chilled water pumped through a main supply pipe. The pipe makes a loop 3 miles in length. The pipe diameter is 2 ft and the material is steel. The maximum design volume flow rate is 11,200 gpm. The circulating pump is driven by an electric motor. The efficiencies of pump and motor are $\eta_p = 0.80$ and $\eta_m = 0.90$, respectively. Electricity cost is 12¢/(kW · hr). Determine (a) the pressure drop, (b) the rate of energy addition to the water, and (c) the daily cost of electrical energy for pumping.

8.159   A fire nozzle is supplied through 100 m of 3.5-cm diameter, smooth, rubber-lined hose. Water from a hydrant is supplied to a booster pump on board the pumper truck at 350 kPa (gage). At design conditions, the pressure at the nozzle inlet is 700 kPa (gage), and the pressure drop along the hose is 750 kPa per 100 m of length. Determine (a) the design flow rate, (b) the nozzle exit velocity, assuming no losses in the nozzle, and (c) the power required to drive the booster pump, if its efficiency is 70 percent.

8.160   Heavy crude oil (SG = 0.925 and $v = 1.0 \times 10^{-4} \ \text{m}^2/\text{s}$) is pumped through a pipeline laid on flat ground. The line is made from steel pipe with 600 mm i.d. and has a wall thickness of 12 mm. The allowable tensile stress in the pipe wall is limited to 275 MPa by corrosion considerations. It is important to keep the oil under pressure to ensure that gases remain in solution. The minimum recommended pressure is 500 kPa. The pipeline carries a flow of 400,000 barrels (in the petroleum industry, a "barrel" is 42 gal) per day. Determine the maximum spacing between pumping stations. Compute the power added to the oil at each pumping station.

8.161   According to the Purdue student newspaper, the volume flow rate through the fountain in the Engineering Mall is 550 gpm. Each water stream can rise to a height of 10 m. Estimate the daily cost to operate the fountain. Assume that the pump motor efficiency is 90 percent, the pump efficiency is 80 percent, and the cost of electricity is 12¢/(kW · hr).

8.162   Petroleum products are transported over long distances by pipeline, e.g., the Alaskan pipeline (see Example 8.6). Estimate the energy needed to pump a typical petroleum product, expressed as a fraction of the throughput energy carried by the pipeline. State and critique your assumptions clearly.

8.163   The pump testing system of Problem 8.114 is run with a pump that generates a pressure difference given by $\Delta p = 750 - 15 \times 10^4 Q^2$ where Δp is in kPa, and the generated flow rate is $Q \ \text{m}^3/\text{s}$. Find the water flow rate, pressure difference, and power supplied to the pump if it is 70 percent efficient.

8.164   A water pump can generate a pressure difference Δp (psi) given by $\Delta p = 145 - 0.1 \ Q^2$, where the flow rate is $Q \ \text{ft}^3/\text{s}$. It supplies a pipe of diameter 20 in., roughness 0.5 in., and length 2500 ft. Find the flow rate, pressure difference, and the power supplied to the pump if it is 70 percent efficient. If the pipe were replaced with one of roughness 0.25 in., how much would the flow increase, and what would the required power be?

8.165   A square cross-section duct (0.5 m × 0.5 m × 30 m) is used to convey air ($\rho = 1.1 \ \text{kg/m}^3$) into a clean room in an electronics manufacturing facility. The air is supplied by a fan and passes through a filter installed in the duct. The duct friction factor is $f = 0.03$, the filter has a loss coefficient of $K = 12$, and the clean room is kept at a positive gage pressure of 50 Pa. The fan performance is given by $\Delta p = 1020 - 25Q - 30 \ Q^2$, where Δp (Pa) is the pressure generated by the fan at flow rate $Q \ (\text{m}^3/\text{s})$. Determine the flow rate delivered to the room.

8.166   The head versus capacity curve for a certain fan may be approximated by the equation $H = 30 - 10^{-7} \ Q^2$, where H is the output static head in inches of water and Q is the air flow rate in ft^3/min. The fan outlet dimensions are 8 × 16 in. Determine the air flow rate delivered by the fan into a 200 ft straight length of 8 × 16 in. rectangular duct.

*8.167 The water pipe system shown is constructed from 75 mm galvanized iron pipe. Minor losses may be neglected. The inlet is at 250 kPa (gage), and all exits are at atmospheric pressure. Find the flow rates Q_0, Q_1, Q_2, and Q_3. If the flow in the 400 m branch is closed off ($Q_1 = 0$), find the increase in flows Q_2, and Q_3.

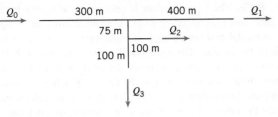

P8.167

*8.168 A cast-iron pipe system consists of a 150 ft section of water pipe, after which the flow branches into two 150 ft sections, which then meet in a final 150 ft section. Minor losses may be neglected. All sections are 1.5 in. diameter, except one of the two branches, which is 1 in. diameter. If the applied pressure across the system is 50 psi, find the overall flow rate and the flow rates in each of the two branches.

*8.169 A swimming pool has a partial-flow filtration system. Water at 75°F is pumped from the pool through the system shown. The pump delivers 30 gpm. The pipe is nominal 3/4 in. PVC (i.d. = 0.824 in.). The pressure loss through the filter is approximately $\Delta p = 0.6 Q^2$, where Δp is in psi and Q is in gpm. Determine the pump pressure and the flow rate through each branch of the system.

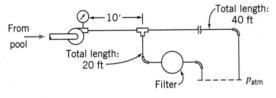

P8.169

8.170 Why does the shower temperature change when a toilet is flushed? Sketch pressure curves for the hot and cold water supply systems to explain what happens.

8.171 Water at 65°C flows through a 75-mm diameter orifice installed in a 150-mm i.d. pipe. The flow rate is 20 L/s. Determine the pressure difference between the corner taps.

8.172 A square-edged orifice with corner taps and a water manometer are used to meter compressed air. The following data are given:

Inside diameter of air line	150 mm
Orifice plate diameter	100 mm
Upstream pressure	600 kPa
Temperature of air	25°C
Manometer deflection	750 mm H$_2$O

Calculate the volume flow rate in the line, expressed in cubic meters per hour.

8.173 A venturi meter with a 30-in. diameter throat is placed in a 6-in.-diameter line carrying water at 75°F. The pressure drop

between the upstream tap and the venturi throat is 12 in. of mercury. Compute the rate of flow.

8.174 A smooth 200 m pipe, 100 mm diameter connects two reservoirs (the entrance and exit of the pipe are sharp-edged). At the midpoint of the pipe is an orifice plate with diameter 40 mm. If the water levels in the reservoirs differ by 30 m, estimate the pressure differential indicated by the orifice plate and the flow rate.

8.175 Gasoline flows through a 2 × 1 in. venturi meter. The differential pressure is 380 mm of mercury. Find the volume flow rate.

8.176 Consider a horizontal 50 × 25 mm venturi with water flow. For a differential pressure of 150 kPa, calculate the volume flow rate.

8.177 Air flow rate in a test of an internal combustion engine is to be measured using a flow nozzle installed in a plenum. The engine displacement is 1.6 liters, and its maximum operating speed is 6000 rpm. To avoid loading the engine, the maximum pressure drop across the nozzle should not exceed 0.25 m of water. The manometer can be read to ±0.5 mm of water. Determine the flow nozzle diameter that should be specified. Find the minimum rate of air flow that can be metered to ±2 percent using this setup.

8.178 Air flows through the venturi meter described in Problem 8.173. Assume that the upstream pressure is 60 psi, and that the temperature is everywhere constant at 68°F. Determine the maximum possible mass flow rate of air for which the assumption of incompressible flow is a valid engineering approximation. Compute the corresponding differential pressure reading on a mercury manometer.

8.179 Water at 70°F flows steadily through a venturi. The pressure upstream from the throat is 5 psig. The throat area is 0.025 ft^2; the upstream area is 0.1 ft^2. Estimate the maximum flow rate this device can handle without cavitation.

8.180 Consider a flow nozzle installation in a pipe. Apply the basic equations to the control volume indicated, to show that the permanent head loss across the meter can be expressed, in dimensionless form, as the head loss coefficient,

$$C_1 = \frac{p_1 - p_3}{p_1 - p_2} = \frac{1 - A_2/A_1}{1 + A_2/A_1}$$

Plot C_l as a function of diameter ratio, D_2/D_1.

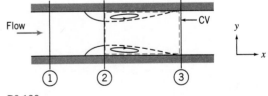

P8.180

8.181 Derive Eq. 8.42, the pressure loss coefficient for a diffuser assuming ideal (frictionless) flow.

8.182 In some western states, water for mining and irrigation was sold by the "miner's inch," the rate at which water flows through an opening in a vertical plank of 1 in.^{2} area, up to 4 in. tall, under a head of 6 to 9 in. Develop an equation to predict the flow rate through such an orifice. Specify clearly the aspect ratio

---

*These problems require material from sections that may be omitted without loss of continuity in the text material.

of the opening, thickness of the plank, and datum level for measurement of head (top, bottom, or middle of the opening). Show that the unit of measure varies from 38.4 (in Colorado) to 50 (in Arizona, Idaho, Nevada, and Utah) miner's inches equal to 1 ft^3/s.

8.183 Drinking straws are to be used to improve the air flow in a pipe-flow experiment. Packing a section of the air pipe with drinking straws to form a "laminar flow element" might allow the air flow rate to be measured directly, and simultaneously would act as a flow straightener. To evaluate this idea, determine (a) the Reynolds number for flow in each drinking straw, (b) the friction factor for flow in each straw, and (c) the gage pressure at the exit from the drinking straws. (For laminar flow in a tube, the entrance loss coefficient is $K_{ent} = 1.4$ and $\alpha = 2.0$.) Comment on the utility of this idea.

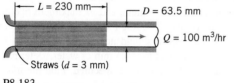

P8.183

8.184 The volume flow rate in a circular duct may be measured by "pitot traverse," i.e., by measuring the velocity in each of several area segments across the duct, then summing. Comment on

the way such a traverse should be set up. Quantify and plot the expected error in measurement of flow rate as a function of the number of radial locations used in the traverse.

8.185 The chilled-water pipeline system that provides air conditioning for the Purdue University campus is described in Problem 8.158. The pipe diameter is selected to minimize total cost (capital cost plus operating cost). Annualized costs are compared, since capital cost occurs once and operating cost continues for the life of the system. The optimum diameter depends on both cost factors and operating conditions; the analysis must be repeated when these variables change. Perform a pipeline optimization analysis. Solve Problem 8.158, arranging your calculations to study the effect of pipe diameter on annual pumping cost. (Assume friction factor remains constant.) Obtain an expression for total annual cost per unit delivery (e.g., dollars per cubic meter), assuming construction cost varies as the square of pipe diameter. Obtain an analytical relation for the pipe diameter that yields minimum total cost per unit delivery. Assume the present chilled-water pipeline was optimized for a 20 year life with 5 percent annual interest. Repeat the optimization for a design to operate at 30 percent larger flow rate. Plot the annual cost of electrical energy for pumping and the capital cost, using the flow conditions of Problem 8.158, with pipe diameter varied from 300 to 900 mm. Show how the diameter may be chosen to minimize total cost. How sensitive are the results to interest rate?

Chapter 9

External Incompressible Viscous Flow

CASE STUDY

The Blended Wing-Body Aircraft

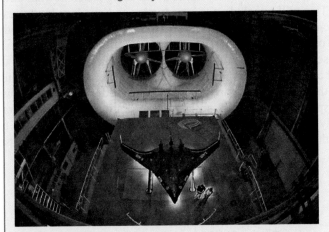

The X-48B prototype in the full-scale NASA tunnel. (Courtesy of Boeing/Bob Ferguson)

Researchers are testing a 6.3-m wingspan ($8\frac{1}{2}$ percent scale) prototype of the X-48B, a blended wing-body (BWB) aircraft that may have military and commercial applications. Boeing Phantom Works partnered with NASA and the U.S. Air Force Research Laboratory

(AFRL) to study the advanced concept, fuel-efficient blended wing-body. It is called a blended wing-body because it looks more like a modified triangular-shaped wing than traditional aircraft, which essentially consist of a tube and wing with a tail.

The big difference between this aircraft and the traditional tube and wing aircraft, apart from the fact that the tube is absorbed into the wing shape, is that it does not have a tail. Traditional aircraft need a tail for stability and control; the X-48B uses a number of different multiple-control surfaces to control the vehicle.

There will be a number of advantages to the BWB if it proves feasible. Apart from possible fuel savings of up to 30 percent due to improved streamlining, the interior of a commercial BWB airplane would be radically different from that of current airplanes. Passengers would enter a room like a movie theater rather than a cramped half-cylinder, there would be no windows (video screens would be connected to external cameras instead), and passengers would be seated in the large movie theater–like room (because seating is not only in the central core but also well out into the blended wings).

External flows are flows over bodies immersed in an unbounded fluid. The flow over a sphere (Fig. 2.14*b*) and the flow over a streamlined body (Fig. 2.16) are examples of external flows, which were discussed qualitatively in Chapter 2. More interesting examples are the flow fields around such objects as airfoils (Fig. 9.1), automobiles, and airplanes. Our objective in this chapter is to quantify the behavior of viscous, incompressible fluids in external flow.

A number of phenomena that occur in external flow over a body are illustrated in the sketch of viscous flow at high Reynolds number over an airfoil (Fig. 9.1). The free-stream flow divides at the stagnation point and flows around the body. Fluid at the surface takes on the velocity of the body as a result of the no-slip condition. Boundary layers form on both the upper and lower surfaces of the body. (The boundary-layer thickness on both surfaces in Fig. 9.1 is exaggerated greatly for clarity.) The flow in the boundary layers initially is laminar. Transition to turbulent flow occurs at some distance from the stagnation point, depending on free-stream conditions, surface roughness, and pressure gradient. The transition points are indicated by "T" in the figure. The turbulent boundary layer following transition grows more rapidly than the laminar layer. A slight displacement of the streamlines of the external flow is caused by the thickening boundary layers on the surface. In a region of increasing pressure (an *adverse pressure gradient*—so-called because it opposes the fluid motion, tending to decelerate the fluid particles) flow separation may occur. Separation points are indicated by "S" in the figure. Fluid that was in the boundary layers on the body surface forms the viscous wake behind the separation points.

This chapter has two parts. Part A is a review of boundary-layer flows. Here we discuss in a little more detail the ideas introduced in Chapter 2, and then apply the fluid mechanics concepts we have learned to analyze the boundary layer for flow along a flat plate—the simplest possible boundary layer, because the pressure field is constant. We will be interested in seeing how the boundary-layer thickness grows, what the surface friction will be, and so on. We will explore a classic analytical solution for a laminar boundary layer, and see that we need to resort to approximate methods when the boundary layer is turbulent (and we will also be able to use these approximate methods for laminar boundary layers, to avoid using the somewhat difficult analytical method). This will conclude our introduction to boundary layers, except we will briefly discuss the effect of pressure gradients (present for *all* body shapes except flat plates) on boundary-layer behavior.

In Part B we will discuss the force on a submerged body, such as the airfoil of Fig. 9.1. We will see that this force results from both shear and pressure forces acting on the body surface, and that both of these are profoundly affected by the fact that we have a boundary layer, especially when this causes flow separation and a wake. Traditionally the force a body experiences is decomposed into the component parallel to the flow, the *drag*, and the component perpendicular to the flow, the *lift*. Because

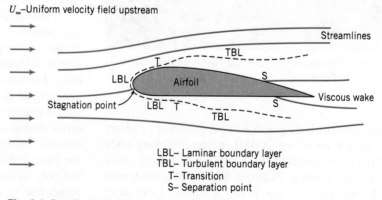

Fig. 9.1 Details of viscous flow around an airfoil.

most bodies do have a point of separation and a wake, it is difficult to use analysis to determine the force components, so we will present approximate analyses and experimental data for various interesting body shapes.

PART A   BOUNDARY LAYERS

9-1   THE BOUNDARY-LAYER CONCEPT

The concept of a boundary layer was first introduced by Ludwig Prandtl [1], a German aerodynamicist, in 1904.

Prior to Prandtl's historic breakthrough, the science of fluid mechanics had been developing in two rather different directions. *Theoretical hydrodynamics* evolved from Euler's equation of motion for a nonviscous fluid (Eq. 6.1, published by Leonhard Euler in 1755). Since the results of hydrodynamics contradicted many experimental observations (especially, as we saw in Chapter 6, that under the assumption of inviscid flow no bodies experience drag!), practicing engineers developed their own empirical art of *hydraulics*. This was based on experimental data and differed significantly from the purely mathematical approach of theoretical hydrodynamics.

Although the complete equations describing the motion of a viscous fluid (the Navier-Stokes equations, Eqs. 5.26, developed by Navier, 1827, and independently by Stokes, 1845) were known prior to Prandtl, the mathematical difficulties in solving these equations (except for a few simple cases) prohibited a theoretical treatment of viscous flows. Prandtl showed [1] that many viscous flows can be analyzed by dividing the flow into two regions, one close to solid boundaries, the other covering the rest of the flow. Only in the thin region adjacent to a solid boundary (the boundary layer) is the effect of viscosity important. In the region outside of the boundary layer, the effect of viscosity is negligible and the fluid may be treated as inviscid.

The boundary-layer concept provided the link that had been missing between theory and practice (for one thing, it introduced the theoretical possibility of drag!). Furthermore, the boundary-layer concept permitted the solution of viscous flow problems that would have been impossible through application of the Navier-Stokes equations to the complete flow field.[1] Thus the introduction of the boundary-layer concept marked the beginning of the modern era of fluid mechanics.

The development of a boundary layer on a solid surface was discussed in Section 2-6. In the boundary layer both viscous and inertia forces are important. Consequently, it is not surprising that the Reynolds number (which represents the ratio of inertia to viscous forces) is significant in characterizing boundary-layer flows. The characteristic length used in the Reynolds number is either the length in the flow direction over which the boundary layer has developed or some measure of the boundary-layer thickness.

As is true for flow in a duct, flow in a boundary layer may be laminar or turbulent. There is no unique value of Reynolds number at which transition from laminar to turbulent flow occurs in a boundary layer. Among the factors that affect boundary-layer transition are pressure gradient, surface roughness, heat transfer, body forces, and freestream disturbances. Detailed consideration of these effects is beyond the scope of this book.

In many real flow situations, a boundary layer develops over a long, essentially flat surface. Examples include flow over ship and submarine hulls, aircraft wings, and atmospheric motions over flat terrain. Since the basic features of all these flows are illustrated in the simpler case of flow over a flat plate, we consider this first. The simplicity of the flow over an infinite flat plate is that the velocity U outside the boundary layer is constant, and therefore, because this region is steady, inviscid, and

---

[1] Today, computer solutions of the Navier-Stokes equations are common.

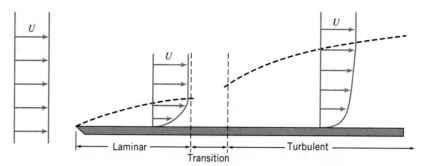

Fig. 9.2 Boundary layer on a flat plate (vertical thickness exaggerated greatly).

incompressible, the pressure will also be constant. This constant pressure is the pressure felt by the boundary layer—obviously the simplest pressure field possible. This is a *zero pressure gradient flow*.

A qualitative picture of the boundary-layer growth over a flat plate is shown in Fig. 9.2. The boundary layer is laminar for a short distance downstream from the leading edge; transition occurs over a region of the plate rather than at a single line across the plate. The transition region extends downstream to the location where the boundary-layer flow becomes completely turbulent.

For incompressible flow over a smooth flat plate (zero pressure gradient), in the absence of heat transfer, transition from laminar to turbulent flow in the boundary layer can be delayed to a Reynolds number, $Re_x = \rho U x / \mu$, greater than one million if external disturbances are minimized. (The length x is measured from the leading edge.) For calculation purposes, under typical flow conditions, transition usually is considered to occur at a length Reynolds number of 500,000. For air at standard conditions, with freestream velocity $U = 30$ m/s, this corresponds to $x \approx 0.24$ m. In the qualitative picture of Fig. 9.2, we have shown the turbulent boundary layer growing faster than the laminar layer. In later sections of this chapter we shall show that this is indeed true.

In the next section we discuss various ways to quantify the thickness of a boundary layer.

9-2 BOUNDARY-LAYER THICKNESSES

The boundary layer is the region adjacent to a solid surface in which viscous stresses are present, as opposed to the free stream where viscous stresses are negligible. These stresses are present because we have shearing of the fluid layers, i.e., a velocity gradient, in the boundary layer. As indicated in Fig. 9.2, both laminar and turbulent layers have such gradients, but the difficulty is that the gradients only asymptotically approach zero as we reach the edge of the boundary layer. Hence, the location of the edge, i.e., of the boundary-layer thickness, is not very obvious—we cannot simply define it as where the boundary-layer velocity u equals the freestream velocity U. Because of this, several boundary-layer definitions have been developed: the disturbance thickness δ, the displacement thickness δ^*, and the momentum thickness θ. (Each of these increases as we move down the plate, in a manner we have yet to determine.)

The most straightforward definition is the disturbance thickness, δ. This is usually defined as the distance from the surface at which the velocity is within 1% of the free stream, $u \approx 0.99U$ (as shown in Fig. 9.3b). The other two definitions are based on the notion that the boundary layer retards the fluid, so that the mass flux and momentum flux are both less than they would be in the absence of the boundary layer. We imagine that the flow remains at uniform velocity U, but the surface of the plate is moved upwards to reduce either the mass or momentum flux by the same amount that the boundary layer actually does. The *displacement thickness*, δ^*, is the distance the plate would be moved so that the loss of mass flux (due to reduction in uniform flow area) is

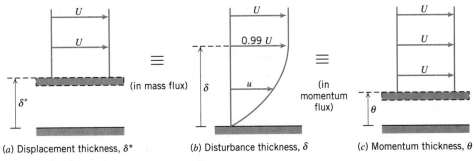

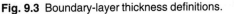

(a) Displacement thickness, δ^* (b) Disturbance thickness, δ (c) Momentum thickness, θ

Fig. 9.3 Boundary-layer thickness definitions.

equivalent to the loss the boundary layer causes. The mass flux if we had no boundary layer would be $\int_0^\infty \rho U\, dy\, w$, where w is the width of the plate perpendicular to the flow. The actual flow mass flux is $\int_0^\infty \rho u\, dy\, w$. Hence, the loss due to the boundary layer is $\int_0^\infty \rho(U-u)\, dy\, w$. If we imagine keeping the velocity at a constant U, and instead move the plate up a distance δ^* (as shown in Fig. 9.3a), the loss of mass flux would be $\rho U \delta^*\, w$. Setting these losses equal to one another gives

$$\rho U \delta^*\, w = \int_0^\infty \rho(U-u)\, dy\, w$$

For incompressible flow, $\rho = $ constant, and

$$\delta^* = \int_0^\infty \left(1 - \frac{u}{U}\right) dy \approx \int_0^\delta \left(1 - \frac{u}{U}\right) dy \qquad (9.1)$$

Since $u \approx U$ at $y = \delta$, the integrand is essentially zero for $y \geq \delta$. Application of the displacement-thickness concept is illustrated in Example 9.1.

The *momentum thickness*, θ, is the distance the plate would be moved so that the loss of momentum flux is equivalent to the loss the boundary layer actually causes. The momentum flux if we had no boundary layer would be $\int_0^\infty \rho u U\, dy\, w$ (the actual mass flux is $\int_0^\infty \rho u\, dy\, w$, and the momentum per unit mass flux of the uniform flow is U itself). The actual momentum flux of the boundary layer is $\int_0^\infty \rho u^2\, dy\, w$. Hence, the loss of momentum in the boundary layer is $\int_0^\infty \rho u(U-u)\, dy\, w$. If we imagine keeping the velocity at a constant U, and instead move the plate up a distance θ (as shown in Fig. 9.3c), the loss of momentum flux would be $\int_0^\theta \rho U U\, dy\, w = \rho U^2\, \theta w$. Setting these losses equal to one another gives

$$\rho U^2 \theta = \int_0^\infty \rho u(U-u)\, dy$$

and

$$\theta = \int_0^\infty \frac{u}{U}\left(1 - \frac{u}{U}\right) dy \approx \int_0^\delta \frac{u}{U}\left(1 - \frac{u}{U}\right) dy \qquad (9.2)$$

Again, the integrand is essentially zero for $y \geq \delta$.

The displacement and momentum thicknesses, δ^* and θ, are *integral thicknesses*, because their definitions, Eqs. 9.1 and 9.2, are in terms of integrals across the boundary layer. Because they are defined in terms of integrals for which the integrand vanishes in the free-stream, they are appreciably easier to evaluate accurately from experimental data than the boundary-layer disturbance thickness, δ. This fact, coupled with their physical significance, accounts for their common use in specifying boundary-layer thickness.

We have seen that the velocity profile in the boundary layer merges into the local freestream velocity asymptotically. Little error is introduced if the slight difference between velocities at the edge of the boundary layer is ignored for an approximate analysis. Simplifying assumptions usually made for engineering analyses of boundary-layer development are:

1. $u \rightarrow U$ at $y = \delta$
2. $\partial u / \partial y \rightarrow 0$ at $y = \delta$
3. $v \ll U$ within the boundary layer

Results of the analyses developed in the next two sections show that the boundary layer is very thin compared with its development length along the surface. Therefore it is also reasonable to assume:

4. Pressure variation across the thin boundary layer is negligible. The freestream pressure distribution is *impressed* on the boundary layer.

EXAMPLE 9.1   Boundary Layer in Channel Flow

A laboratory wind tunnel has a test section that is 305 mm square. Boundary-layer velocity profiles are measured at two cross-sections and displacement thicknesses are evaluated from the measured profiles. At section ①, where the freestream speed is $U_1 = 26$ m/s, the displacement thickness is $\delta_1^* = 1.5$ mm. At section ②, located downstream from section ①, $\delta_2^* = 2.1$ mm. Calculate the change in static pressure between sections ① and ②. Express the result as a fraction of the freestream dynamic pressure at section ①. Assume standard atmosphere conditions.

GIVEN: Flow of standard air in laboratory wind tunnel. Test section is $L = 305$ mm square. Displacement thicknesses are $\delta_1^* = 1.5$ mm and $\delta_2^* = 2.1$ mm. Freestream speed is $U_1 = 26$ m/s.

FIND: Change in static pressure between sections ① and ②. (Express as a fraction of freestream dynamic pressure at section ①.)

SOLUTION:

The idea here is that at each location the boundary-layer displacement thickness effectively reduces the area of uniform flow, as indicated in the following figures: Location ② has a smaller effective flow area than location ① (because $\delta_2^* > \delta_1^*$). Hence, from mass conservation the uniform velocity at location ② will be higher. Finally, from the Bernoulli equation the pressure at location ② will be lower than that at location ①.

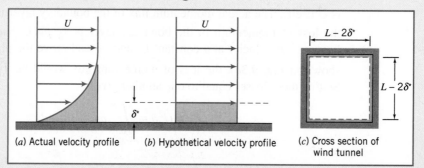

(a) Actual velocity profile   (b) Hypothetical velocity profile   (c) Cross section of wind tunnel

Apply the continuity and Bernoulli equations to freestream flow outside the boundary-layer displacement thickness, where viscous effects are negligible.

Governing equations:

$$\frac{\partial}{\partial t} \underset{\text{CV}}{\iiint} \rho \, d\forall + \int_{\text{CS}} \rho \vec{V} \cdot d\vec{A} = 0 \qquad (4.12)$$

$$\frac{p_1}{\rho} + \frac{V_1^2}{2} + g z_1 = \frac{p_2}{\rho} + \frac{V_2^2}{2} + g z_2 \qquad (4.24)$$

Assumptions: (1) Steady flow.
                   (2) Incompressible flow.

(3) Flow uniform at each section outside $\delta*$.
(4) Flow along a streamline between sections ① and ②.
(5) No frictional effects in freestream.
(6) Negligible elevation changes.

From the Bernoulli equation we obtain

$$p_1 - p_2 = \frac{1}{2}\rho\left(V_2^2 - V_1^2\right) = \frac{1}{2}\,\rho\left(U_2^2 - U_1^2\right) = \frac{1}{2}\rho U_1^2\left[\left(\frac{U_2}{U_1}\right)^2 - 1\right]$$

or

$$\frac{p_1 - p_2}{\frac{1}{2}\rho U_1^2} = \left(\frac{U_2}{U_1}\right)^2 - 1$$

From continuity, $V_1 A_1 = U_1 A_1 = V_2 A_2 = U_2 A_2$, so $U_2/U_1 = A_1/A_2$, where $A = (L - 2\delta*)^2$ is the effective flow area. Substituting gives

$$\frac{p_1 - p_2}{\frac{1}{2}\,\rho U_1^2} = \left(\frac{A_1}{A_2}\right)^2 - 1 = \left[\frac{(L - 2\delta_1^*)^2}{(L - 2\delta_2^*)^2}\right]^2 - 1$$

$$\frac{p_1 - p_2}{\frac{1}{2}\,\rho U_1^2} = \left[\frac{305 - 2(1.5)}{305 - 2(2.1)}\right]^4 - 1 = 0.0161 \qquad \text{or} \qquad 1.61 \text{ percent} \quad\longleftarrow\quad \dfrac{p_1 - p_2}{\frac{1}{2}\,\rho U_1^2}$$

> Notes:
> ✓ This problem illustrates a basic application of the displacement-thickness concept. It is somewhat unusual in that, because the flow is confined, the reduction in flow area caused by the boundary layer leads to the result that the pressure in the inviscid flow region drops (if only slightly). In most applications the pressure distribution is determined from the inviscid flow and *then* applied to the boundary layer.
> ✓ We saw a similar phenomenon in Section 8-1, where we discovered that the centerline velocity at the entrance of a pipe increases due to the boundary layer "squeezing" the effective flow area.

9-3   LAMINAR FLAT-PLATE BOUNDARY LAYER: EXACT SOLUTION (ON THE WEB)

9-4   MOMENTUM INTEGRAL EQUATION

Blasius' exact solution, discussed in Section 9-3 (on the Web), analyzed a laminar boundary layer on a flat plate. Even this simplest case (i.e., constant free-stream velocity U and pressure p, laminar flow) involved a rather subtle mathematical transformation of two differential equations. The solution was based on the insight that the laminar boundary-layer velocity profile is self-similar—only its scale changes as we move along the plate. Numerical integration was necessary to obtain results for the boundary-layer thickness $\delta(x)$, velocity profile u/U versus y/δ, and wall shear stress $\tau_w(x)$.

We would like to obtain a method for analyzing the general case—that is, for laminar *and* turbulent boundary layers, for which the free-stream velocity $U(x)$ and pressure $p(x)$ are known functions of position along the surface x (such as on the curved surface of an airfoil or on the flat but divergent surfaces of a flow diffuser). The approach is one in which we will again apply the basic equations to a control volume. The derivation, from the mass conservation (or continuity) equation and the momentum equation, will take several pages.

Consider incompressible, steady, two-dimensional flow over a solid surface. The boundary-layer thickness, δ, grows in some manner with increasing distance, x. For

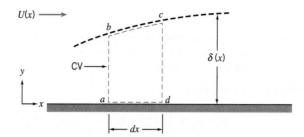

Fig. 9.4 Differential control volume in a boundary layer.

our analysis we choose a differential control volume, of length dx, width w, and height $\delta(x)$, as shown in Fig. 9.4. The freestream velocity is $U(x)$.

We wish to determine the boundary-layer thickness, δ, as a function of x. There will be mass flow across surfaces ab and cd of differential control volume $abcd$. What about surface bc? Surface bc is *not* a streamline (we showed this in Example 9.2, on the Web); it is the imaginary boundary that separates the viscous boundary layer and the inviscid free-stream flow. Thus there will be mass flow across surface bc. Since control surface ad is adjacent to a solid boundary, there will not be flow across ad. Before considering the forces acting on the control volume and the momentum fluxes through the control surface, let us apply the continuity equation to determine the mass flux through each portion of the control surface.

a. Continuity Equation

Basic equation:

$$\overset{=\;0(1)}{\cancel{\frac{\partial}{\partial t}} \int_{CV} \rho \, d\forall} + \int_{CS} \rho \vec{V} \cdot d\vec{A} = 0 \tag{4.12}$$

Assumptions: (1) Steady flow.
(2) Two-dimensional flow.

Then

$$\int_{CS} \rho \vec{V} \cdot d\vec{A} = 0$$

Hence

$$\dot{m}_{ab} + \dot{m}_{bc} + \dot{m}_{cd} = 0$$

or

$$\dot{m}_{bc} = -\dot{m}_{ab} - \dot{m}_{cd}$$

Now let us evaluate these terms for the differential control volume of width w:

Surface	Mass Flux
ab	Surface ab is located at x. Since the flow is two-dimensional (no variation with z), the mass flux through ab is $$\dot{m}_{ab} = -\left\{ \int_0^{\delta} \rho u \, dy \right\} w$$
cd	Surface cd is located at $x + dx$. Expanding $\dot{m}$ in a Taylor series about location x, we obtain $$\dot{m}_{x+dx} = \dot{m}_x + \frac{\partial \dot{m}}{\partial x}\bigg]_x dx$$

and hence

$$\dot{m}_{cd} = \left\{ \int_0^\delta \rho u \, dy + \frac{\partial}{\partial x} \left[\int_0^\delta \rho u \, dy \right] dx \right\} w$$

bc   Thus for surface *bc* we obtain, from the continuity equation and the above results,

$$\dot{m}_{bc} = -\left\{ \frac{\partial}{\partial x} \left[\int_0^\delta \rho u \, dy \right] dx \right\} w$$

(Note that the velocity u and boundary-layer thickness δ, the upper limit on the integral, both depend on x.)

Now let us consider the momentum fluxes and forces associated with control volume *abcd*. These are related by the momentum equation.

b. Momentum Equation

Apply the x component of the momentum equation to control volume *abcd*:

Basic equation:

$$F_{S_x} + \cancelto{=\,0(3)}{F_{B_x}} = \cancelto{=\,0(1)}{\frac{\partial}{\partial t} \int_{CV} u \, \rho \, d\mathcal{V}} + \int_{CS} u \, \rho \vec{V} \cdot d\vec{A} \qquad (4.18a)$$

Assumption: (3) $F_{B_x} = 0$.

Then

$$F_{S_x} = \mathrm{mf}_{ab} + \mathrm{mf}_{bc} + \mathrm{mf}_{cd}$$

where mf represents the x component of momentum flux.

To apply this equation to differential control volume *abcd*, we must obtain expressions for the x momentum flux through the control surface and also the surface forces acting on the control volume in the x direction. Let us consider the momentum flux first and again consider each segment of the control surface.

Surface	Momentum Flux (mf)

ab   Surface *ab* is located at x. Since the flow is two-dimensional, the x momentum flux through *ab* is

$$\mathrm{mf}_{ab} = -\left\{ \int_0^\delta u \, \rho u \, dy \right\} w$$

cd   Surface *cd* is located at $x + dx$. Expanding the x momentum flux (mf) in a Taylor series about location x, we obtain

$$\mathrm{mf}_{x+dx} = \mathrm{mf}_x + \frac{\partial \mathrm{mf}}{\partial x} \bigg]_x dx$$

or

$$\mathrm{mf}_{cd} = \left\{ \int_0^\delta u \, \rho u \, dy + \frac{\partial}{\partial x} \left[\int_0^\delta u \, \rho u \, dy \right] dx \right\} w$$

bc   Since the mass crossing surface *bc* has velocity component U in the x direction, the x momentum flux across *bc* is given by

$$\mathrm{mf}_{bc} = U \dot{m}_{bc}$$

$$\mathrm{mf}_{bc} = -U \left\{ \frac{\partial}{\partial x} \left[\int_0^\delta \rho u \, dy \right] dx \right\} w$$

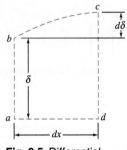

Fig. 9.5 Differential control volume.

From the above we can evaluate the net x momentum flux through the control surface as

$$\int_{CS} u\,\rho\vec{V}\cdot d\vec{A} = -\left\{\int_0^\delta u\,\rho u\,dy\right\}w + \left\{\int_0^\delta u\,\rho u\,dy\right\}w$$

$$+\left\{\frac{\partial}{\partial x}\left[\int_0^\delta u\,\rho u\,dy\right]dx\right\}w - U\left\{\frac{\partial}{\partial x}\left[\int_0^\delta \rho u\,dy\right]dx\right\}w$$

Collecting terms, we find that

$$\int_{CS} u\,\rho\vec{V}\cdot d\vec{A} = \left\{\frac{\partial}{\partial x}\left[\int_0^\delta u\,\rho u\,dy\right]dx - U\frac{\partial}{\partial x}\left[\int_0^\delta \rho u\,dy\right]dx\right\}w$$

Now that we have a suitable expression for the x momentum flux through the control surface, let us consider the surface forces acting on the control volume in the x direction. (For convenience the differential control volume has been redrawn in Fig. 9.5.) Note that surfaces ab, bc, and cd all experience normal forces (i.e., pressure) that generate force in the x direction. In addition, a shear force acts on surface ad. Since, by definition of the boundary layer, the velocity gradient goes to zero at the edge of the boundary layer, the shear force acting along surface bc is negligible.

Surface	Force
ab	If the pressure at x is p, then the force acting on surface ab is given by $$F_{ab} = pw\delta$$ (The boundary layer is very thin; its thickness has been greatly exaggerated in all the sketches we have made. Because it is thin, pressure variations in the y direction may be neglected, and we assume that within the boundary layer, $p = p(x)$ only.)
cd	Expanding in a Taylor series, the pressure at $x + dx$ is given by $$p_{x+dx} = p + \frac{dp}{dx}\bigg]_x dx$$ The force on surface cd is then given by $$F_{cd} = -\left(p + \frac{dp}{dx}\bigg]_x dx\right)w(\delta + d\delta)$$
bc	The average pressure acting over surface bc is $$p + \frac{1}{2}\frac{dp}{dx}\bigg]_x dx$$ Then the x component of the normal force acting over bc is given by $$F_{bc} = \left(p + \frac{1}{2}\frac{dp}{dx}\bigg]_x dx\right)w\,d\delta$$
ad	The average shear force acting on ad is given by $$F_{ad} = -\left(\tau_w + \frac{1}{2}\,d\tau_w\right)w\,dx$$

Summing these x components, we obtain the total force acting in the x direction on the control volume,

$$F_{S_x} = \left\{ -\frac{dp}{dx}\,\delta\,dx - \frac{1}{2}\frac{dp}{dx}\,dx\overset{\approx 0}{\cancel{d\delta}} - \tau_w\,dx - \frac{1}{2}\overset{\approx 0}{\cancel{d\tau_w}}\,dx \right\} w$$

where we note that $dx\,d\delta \ll \delta\,dx$ and $d\tau_w \ll \tau_w$, and so neglect the second and fourth terms.

Substituting the expressions, for $\int_{CS} u\,\rho\vec{V}\cdot d\vec{A}$ and F_{S_x} into the x momentum equation (Eq. 4.18a), we obtain

$$\left\{ -\frac{dp}{dx}\,\delta\,dx - \tau_w\,dx \right\} w = \left\{ \frac{\partial}{\partial x}\left[\int_0^\delta u\,\rho u\,dy \right] dx - U\frac{\partial}{\partial x}\left[\int_0^\delta \rho u\,dy \right] dx \right\} w$$

Dividing this equation by $w\,dx$ gives

$$-\delta\frac{dp}{dx} - \tau_w = \frac{\partial}{\partial x}\int_0^\delta u\,\rho u\,dy - U\frac{\partial}{\partial x}\int_0^\delta \rho u\,dy \tag{9.16}$$

Equation 9.16 is a "momentum integral" equation that gives a relation between the x components of the forces acting in a boundary layer and the x momentum flux.

The pressure gradient, dp/dx, can be determined by applying the Bernoulli equation to the inviscid flow outside the boundary layer: $dp/dx = -\rho U\,dU/dx$. If we recognize that $\delta = \int_0^\delta dy$, then Eq. 9.16 can be written as

$$\tau_w = -\frac{\partial}{\partial x}\int_0^\delta u\,\rho u\,dy + U\frac{\partial}{\partial x}\int_0^\delta \rho u\,dy + \frac{dU}{dx}\int_0^\delta \rho U\,dy$$

Since

$$U\frac{\partial}{\partial x}\int_0^\delta \rho u\,dy = \frac{\partial}{\partial x}\int_0^\delta \rho u U\,dy - \frac{dU}{dx}\int_0^\delta \rho u\,dy$$

we have

$$\tau_w = \frac{\partial}{\partial x}\int_0^\delta \rho u(U - u)\,dy + \frac{dU}{dx}\int_0^\delta \rho(U - u)\,dy$$

and

$$\tau_w = \frac{\partial}{\partial x}U^2\int_0^\delta \rho\,\frac{u}{U}\left(1 - \frac{u}{U}\right)dy + U\frac{dU}{dx}\int_0^\delta \rho\left(1 - \frac{u}{U}\right)dy$$

Using the definitions of displacement thickness, δ^* (Eq. 9.1), and momentum thickness, θ (Eq. 9.2), we obtain

$$\frac{\tau_w}{\rho} = \frac{d}{dx}(U^2\theta) + \delta^* U\frac{dU}{dx} \tag{9.17}$$

Equation 9.17 is the *momentum integral equation*. This equation will yield an ordinary differential equation for boundary-layer thickness δ as a function of x. Where does δ appear in Eq. 9.17? It appears in the upper limits of the integrals that define δ^* and θ! All we need to do is provide a suitable expression for the velocity profile u/U and somehow relate the wall stress τ_w to other variables—not necessarily easy tasks! Once the boundary-layer thickness is determined, expressions for the momentum thickness, displacement thickness, and wall shear stress can then be obtained.

Equation 9.17 was obtained by applying the basic equations (continuity and x momentum) to a differential control volume. Reviewing the assumptions we made in the derivation, we see that the equation is restricted to steady, incompressible, two-dimensional flow with no body forces parallel to the surface.

We have not made any specific assumption relating the wall shear stress, τ_w, to the velocity field. Thus Eq. 9.17 is valid for either a laminar or turbulent boundary-layer flow. In order to use this equation to estimate the boundary-layer thickness as a function of x, we must first:

1. Obtain a first approximation to the free-stream velocity distribution, $U(x)$. This is determined from inviscid flow theory (the velocity that would exist in the absence of a boundary layer) and depends on body shape.

2. Assume a reasonable velocity-profile shape inside the boundary layer.

3. Derive an expression for τ_w using the results obtained from item **2**.

To illustrate the application of Eq. 9.17 to boundary-layer flows, we consider first the case of flow with zero pressure gradient over a flat plate (Section 9-5)—the results we obtain for a laminar boundary layer can then be compared to the exact Blasius results. The effects of pressure gradients in boundary-layer flow are then discussed in Section 9-6.

9-5   USE OF THE MOMENTUM INTEGRAL EQUATION FOR FLOW WITH ZERO PRESSURE GRADIENT

For the special case of a flat plate (zero pressure gradient) the free-stream pressure p and velocity U are both constant, so for item **1** we have $U(x) = U = $ constant.

The momentum integral equation then reduces to

$$\tau_w = \rho U^2 \frac{d\theta}{dx} = \rho U^2 \frac{d}{dx} \int_0^\delta \frac{u}{U} \left(1 - \frac{u}{U}\right) dy \tag{9.18}$$

The velocity distribution, u/U, in the boundary layer is assumed to be similar for all values of x and normally is specified as a function of y/δ. (Note that u/U is dimensionless and δ is a function of x only.) Consequently, it is convenient to change the variable of integration from y to y/δ. Defining

$$\eta = \frac{y}{\delta}$$

we get

$$dy = \delta \, d\eta$$

and the momentum integral equation for zero pressure gradient is written

$$\tau_w = \rho U^2 \frac{d\theta}{dx} = \rho U^2 \frac{d\delta}{dx} \int_0^1 \frac{u}{U} \left(1 - \frac{u}{U}\right) d\eta \tag{9.19}$$

We wish to solve this equation for the boundary-layer thickness as a function of x. To do this, we must satisfy the remaining items:

2. Assume a velocity distribution in the boundary layer—a functional relationship of the form

$$\frac{u}{U} = f\left(\frac{y}{\delta}\right)$$

    a. The assumed velocity distribution should satisfy the following approximate physical boundary conditions:

$$\text{at } y = 0, \quad u = 0$$

$$\text{at } y = \delta, \quad u = U$$

$$\text{at } y = \delta, \quad \frac{\partial u}{\partial y} = 0$$

b. Note that once we have assumed a velocity distribution, from the definition of the momentum thickness (Eq. 9.2), the numerical value of the integral in Eq. 9.19 is simply

$$\int_0^1 \frac{u}{U}\left(1 - \frac{u}{U}\right) d\eta = \frac{\theta}{\delta} = \text{constant} = \beta$$

and the momentum integral equation becomes

$$\tau_w = \rho U^2 \frac{d\delta}{dx} \beta$$

3. Obtain an expression for τ_w in terms of δ. This will then permit us to solve for $\delta(x)$, as illustrated below.

Laminar Flow

For laminar flow over a flat plate, a reasonable assumption for the velocity profile is a polynomial in y:

$$u = a + by + cy^2$$

The physical boundary conditions are:

$$\text{at } y = 0, \qquad u = 0$$
$$\text{at } y = \delta, \qquad u = U$$
$$\text{at } y = \delta, \qquad \frac{\partial u}{\partial y} = 0$$

Evaluating constants a, b, and c gives

$$\frac{u}{U} = 2\left(\frac{y}{\delta}\right) - \left(\frac{y}{\delta}\right)^2 = 2\eta - \eta^2 \qquad (9.20)$$

Equation 9.20 satisfies item **2**. For item **3**, we recall that the wall shear stress is given by

$$\tau_w = \mu \frac{\partial u}{\partial y}\bigg)_{y=0}$$

Substituting the assumed velocity profile, Eq. 9.20, into this expression for τ_w gives

$$\tau_w = \mu \frac{\partial u}{\partial y}\bigg]_{y=0} = \mu \frac{U \,\partial(u/U)}{\delta \,\partial(y/\delta)}\bigg]_{y/\delta=0} = \frac{\mu U}{\delta} \frac{d(u/U)}{d\eta}\bigg]_{\eta=0}$$

or

$$\tau_w = \frac{\mu U}{\delta} \frac{d}{d\eta}(2\eta - \eta^2)\bigg]_{\eta=0} = \frac{\mu U}{\delta}(2 - 2\eta)\bigg]_{\eta=0} = \frac{2\mu U}{\delta}$$

Note that this shows that the wall stress τ_w is a function of x, since the boundary-layer thickness $\delta = \delta(x)$. Now that we have completed items **1**, **2**, and **3**, we can return to the momentum integral equation

$$\tau_w = \rho U^2 \frac{d\delta}{dx} \int_0^1 \frac{u}{U}\left(1 - \frac{u}{U}\right) d\eta \qquad (9.19)$$

Substituting for τ_w and u/U, we obtain

$$\frac{2\mu U}{\delta} = \rho U^2 \frac{d\delta}{dx} \int_0^1 (2\eta - \eta^2)(1 - 2\eta + \eta^2) \, d\eta$$

or

$$\frac{2\mu U}{\delta \rho U^2} = \frac{d\delta}{dx} \int_0^1 (2\eta - 5\eta^2 + 4\eta^3 - \eta^4)\, d\eta$$

Integrating and substituting limits yields

$$\frac{2\mu}{\delta \rho U} = \frac{2}{15}\frac{d\delta}{dx} \quad \text{or} \quad \delta\, d\delta = \frac{15\mu}{\rho U}\, dx$$

which is a differential equation for δ. Integrating again gives

$$\frac{\delta^2}{2} = \frac{15\mu}{\rho U}\, x + c$$

If we assume that $\delta = 0$ at $x = 0$, then $c = 0$, and thus

$$\delta = \sqrt{\frac{30\mu x}{\rho U}}$$

Note that this shows that the laminar boundary-layer thickness δ grows as $\sqrt{x}$; it has a parabolic shape. Traditionally this is expressed in dimensionless form:

$$\frac{\delta}{x} = \sqrt{\frac{30\mu}{\rho U x}} = \frac{5.48}{\sqrt{Re_x}} \tag{9.21}$$

Equation 9.21 shows that the ratio of laminar boundary-layer thickness to distance along a flat plate varies inversely with the square root of length Reynolds number. It has the same form as the exact solution derived from the complete differential equations of motion by H. Blasius in 1908. Remarkably, Eq. 9.21 is only in error (the constant is too large) by about 10 percent compared with the exact solution (Section 9-3 on the Web). Table 9.2 summarizes corresponding results calculated using other approximate velocity profiles and lists results obtained from the exact solution. (The only thing that changes in the analysis when we choose a different velocity profile is the value of β in $\tau_w = \rho U^2 d\delta/dx\, \beta$ in item **2b** on page 401.) The shapes of the approximate profiles may be compared readily by plotting u/U versus y/δ.

TABLE 9.2 Results of the Calculation of Laminar Boundary-Layer Flow over a Flat Plate at Zero Incidence Based on Approximate Velocity Profiles

Velocity Distribution $\frac{u}{U} = f\left(\frac{y}{\delta}\right) = f(\eta)$	$\beta \equiv \dfrac{\theta}{\delta}$	$\dfrac{\delta^*}{\delta}$	$H \equiv \dfrac{\delta^*}{\theta}$	Constant a in $\dfrac{\delta}{x} = \dfrac{a}{\sqrt{Re_x}}$	Constant b in $C_f = \dfrac{b}{\sqrt{Re_x}}$
$f(\eta) = \eta$	$\dfrac{1}{6}$	$\dfrac{1}{2}$	3.00	3.46	0.577
$f(\eta) = 2\eta - \eta^2$	$\dfrac{2}{15}$	$\dfrac{1}{3}$	2.50	5.48	0.730
$f(\eta) = \dfrac{3}{2}\eta - \dfrac{1}{2}\eta^3$	$\dfrac{39}{280}$	$\dfrac{3}{8}$	2.69	4.64	0.647
$f(\eta) = 2\eta - 2\eta^3 + \eta^4$	$\dfrac{37}{315}$	$\dfrac{3}{10}$	2.55	5.84	0.685
$f(\eta) = \sin\left(\dfrac{\pi}{2}\eta\right)$	$\dfrac{4 - \pi}{2\pi}$	$\dfrac{\pi - 2}{\pi}$	2.66	4.80	0.654
Exact	0.133	0.344	2.59	5.00	0.664

Once we know the boundary-layer thickness, all details of the flow may be determined. The wall shear stress, or "skin friction," coefficient is defined as

$$C_f \equiv \frac{\tau_w}{\frac{1}{2}\rho U^2} \tag{9.22}$$

Substituting from the velocity profile and Eq. 9.21 gives

$$C_f = \frac{\tau_w}{\frac{1}{2}\rho U^2} = \frac{2\mu(U/\delta)}{\frac{1}{2}\rho U^2} = \frac{4\mu}{\rho U \delta} = 4\frac{\mu}{\rho U x}\frac{x}{\delta} = 4\frac{1}{Re_x}\frac{\sqrt{Re_x}}{5.48}$$

Finally,

$$C_f = \frac{0.730}{\sqrt{Re_x}} \tag{9.23}$$

Once the variation of τ_w is known, the viscous drag on the surface can be evaluated by integrating over the area of the flat plate, as illustrated in Example 9.3.

Equation 9.21 can be used to calculate the thickness of the laminar boundary layer at transition. At $Re_x = 5 \times 10^5$, with $U = 30$ m/s, for example, $x = 0.24$ m for air at standard conditions. Thus

$$\frac{\delta}{x} = \frac{5.48}{\sqrt{Re_x}} = \frac{5.48}{\sqrt{5 \times 10^5}} = 0.00775$$

and the boundary-layer thickness is

$$\delta = 0.00775x = 0.00775(0.24 \text{ m}) = 1.86 \text{ mm}$$

The boundary-layer thickness at transition is less than 1 percent of the development length, x. These calculations confirm that viscous effects are confined to a very thin layer near the surface of a body.

The results in Table 9.2 indicate that reasonable results may be obtained with a variety of approximate velocity profiles.

EXAMPLE 9.3   Laminar Boundary Layer on a Flat Plate: Approximate Solution Using Sinusoidal Velocity Profile

Consider two-dimensional laminar boundary-layer flow along a flat plate. Assume the velocity profile in the boundary layer is sinusoidal,

$$\frac{u}{U} = \sin\left(\frac{\pi}{2}\frac{y}{\delta}\right)$$

Find expressions for:

(a) The rate of growth of δ as a function of x.
(b) The displacement thickness, δ^*, as a function of x.
(c) The total friction force on a plate of length L and width b.

GIVEN: Two-dimensional, laminar boundary-layer flow along a flat plate. The boundary-layer velocity profile is

$$\frac{u}{U} = \sin\left(\frac{\pi}{2}\frac{y}{\delta}\right) \qquad \text{for } 0 \leq y \leq \delta$$

and

$$\frac{u}{U} = 1 \qquad \text{for } y > \delta$$

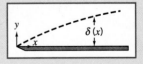

FIND: (a) $\delta(x)$. (b) $\delta^*(x)$.
(c) Total friction force on a plate of length L and width b.

SOLUTION:

For flat plate flow, $U =$ constant, $dp/dx = 0$, and

$$\tau_w = \rho U^2 \frac{d\theta}{dx} = \rho U^2 \frac{d\delta}{dx} \int_0^1 \frac{u}{U}\left(1 - \frac{u}{U}\right) d\eta \tag{9.19}$$

Assumptions: (1) Steady flow.
(2) Incompressible flow.

Substituting $\dfrac{u}{U} = \sin\dfrac{\pi}{2}\eta$ into Eq. 9.19, we obtain

$$\tau_w = \rho U^2 \frac{d\delta}{dx} \int_0^1 \sin\frac{\pi}{2}\eta\left(1 - \sin\frac{\pi}{2}\eta\right) d\eta = \rho U^2 \frac{d\delta}{dx} \int_0^1 \left(\sin\frac{\pi}{2}\eta - \sin^2\frac{\pi}{2}\eta\right) d\eta$$

$$= \rho U^2 \frac{d\delta}{dx} \frac{2}{\pi}\left[-\cos\frac{\pi}{2}\eta - \frac{1}{2}\frac{\pi}{2}\eta + \frac{1}{4}\sin\pi\eta\right]_0^1 = \rho U^2 \frac{d\delta}{dx} \frac{2}{\pi}\left[0 + 1 - \frac{\pi}{4} + 0 + 0 - 0\right]$$

$$\tau_w = 0.137\rho U^2 \frac{d\delta}{dx} = \beta\rho U^2 \frac{d\delta}{dx}; \quad \beta = 0.137$$

Now

$$\tau_w = \mu \frac{\partial u}{\partial y}\bigg]_{y=0} = \mu \frac{U}{\delta} \frac{\partial(u/U)}{\partial(y/\delta)}\bigg]_{y=0} = \mu \frac{U}{\delta} \frac{\pi}{2}\cos\frac{\pi}{2}\eta\bigg]_{\eta=0} = \frac{\pi\mu U}{2\delta}$$

Therefore,

$$\tau_w = \frac{\pi\mu U}{2\delta} = 0.137\rho U^2 \frac{d\delta}{dx}$$

Separating variables gives

$$\delta\, d\delta = 11.5 \frac{\mu}{\rho U}\, dx$$

Integrating, we obtain

$$\frac{\delta^2}{2} = 11.5 \frac{\mu}{\rho U}\, x + c$$

But $c = 0$, since $\delta = 0$ at $x = 0$, so

$$\delta = \sqrt{23.0 \frac{x\mu}{\rho U}}$$

or

$$\frac{\delta}{x} = 4.80\sqrt{\frac{\mu}{\rho Ux}} = \frac{4.80}{\sqrt{Re_x}} \qquad\qquad\qquad \delta(x)$$

The displacement thickness, δ^*, is given by

$$\delta^* = \delta \int_0^1 \left(1 - \frac{u}{U}\right) d\eta$$

$$= \delta \int_0^1 \left(1 - \sin\frac{\pi}{2}\eta\right) d\eta = \delta\left[\eta + \frac{2}{\pi}\cos\frac{\pi}{2}\eta\right]_0^1$$

$$\delta^* = \delta\left[1 - 0 + 0 - \frac{2}{\pi}\right] = \delta\left[1 - \frac{2}{\pi}\right]$$

Since, from part (a),

$$\frac{\delta}{x} = \frac{4.80}{\sqrt{Re_x}}$$

then

$$\frac{\delta^*}{x} = \left(1 - \frac{2}{\pi}\right) \frac{4.80}{\sqrt{Re_x}} = \frac{1.74}{\sqrt{Re_x}} \longleftarrow \qquad \delta^*(x)$$

The total friction force on one side of the plate is given by

$$F = \int_{A_p} \tau_w \, dA$$

Since $dA = b\,dx$ and $0 \le x \le L$, then

$$F = \int_0^L \tau_w b \, dx = \int_0^L \rho U^2 \frac{d\theta}{dx} b \, dx = \rho U^2 b \int_0^{\theta_L} d\theta = \rho U^2 b \theta_L$$

$$\theta_L = \int_0^{\delta_L} \frac{u}{U}\left(1 - \frac{u}{U}\right) dy = \delta_L \int_0^1 \frac{u}{U}\left(1 - \frac{u}{U}\right) d\eta = \beta \delta_L$$

From part (a), $\beta = 0.137$ and $\delta_L = \dfrac{4.80L}{\sqrt{Re_L}}$, so

$$F = \frac{0.658 \rho U^2 bL}{\sqrt{Re_L}} \longleftarrow \qquad F$$

> This problem illustrates application of the momentum integral equation to the laminar boundary layer on a flat plate.
>
> The *Excel* workbook for this Example plots the growth of δ and δ^* in the boundary layer, and the exact solution (Eq. 9.13 on the Web). It also shows wall shear stress distributions for the sinusoidal velocity profile and the exact solution.

Turbulent Flow

For the flat plate, we still have for item **1** that $U = $ constant. As for the laminar boundary layer, we need to satisfy item **2** (an approximation for the turbulent velocity profile) and item **3** (an expression for τ_w) in order to solve Eq. 9.19 for $\delta(x)$:

$$\tau_w = \rho U^2 \frac{d\delta}{dx} \int_0^1 \frac{u}{U}\left(1 - \frac{u}{U}\right) d\eta \tag{9.19}$$

Details of the turbulent velocity profile for boundary layers at zero pressure gradient are very similar to those for turbulent flow in pipes and channels. Data for turbulent boundary layers plot on the universal velocity profile using coordinates of $\bar{u}/u_*$ versus yu_*/v, as shown in Fig. 8.9. However, this profile is rather complex mathematically for easy use with the momentum integral equation. The momentum integral equation is approximate; hence, an acceptable velocity profile for turbulent boundary layers on smooth flat plates is the empirical power-law profile. An exponent of $\frac{1}{7}$ is typically used to model the turbulent velocity profile. Thus

$$\frac{u}{U} = \left(\frac{y}{\delta}\right)^{1/7} = \eta^{1/7} \tag{9.24}$$

However, this profile does not hold in the immediate vicinity of the wall, since at the wall it predicts $du/dy = \infty$. Consequently, we cannot use this profile in the definition of τ_w to obtain an expression for τ_w in terms of δ as we did for laminar boundary-layer flow. For turbulent boundary-layer flow we adapt the expression developed for pipe flow,

$$\tau_w = 0.0332 \rho \overline{V}^2 \left[\frac{\nu}{R\overline{V}} \right]^{0.25} \tag{8.39}$$

For a $\frac{1}{7}$-power profile in a pipe, Eq. 8.24 gives $\overline{V}/U = 0.817$. Substituting $\overline{V} = 0.817U$ and $R = \delta$ into Eq. 8.39, we obtain

$$\tau_w = 0.0233 \rho U^2 \left(\frac{\nu}{U\delta} \right)^{1/4} \tag{9.25}$$

Substituting for τ_w and u/U into Eq. 9.19 and integrating, we obtain

$$0.0233 \left(\frac{\nu}{U\delta} \right)^{1/4} = \frac{d\delta}{dx} \int_0^1 \eta^{1/7} \left(1 - \eta^{1/7} \right) d\eta = \frac{7}{72} \frac{d\delta}{dx}$$

Thus we obtain a differential equation for δ:

$$\delta^{1/4} \, d\delta = 0.240 \left(\frac{\nu}{U} \right)^{1/4} dx$$

Integrating gives

$$\frac{4}{5} \delta^{5/4} = 0.240 \left(\frac{\nu}{U} \right)^{1/4} x + c$$

If we assume that $\delta \simeq 0$ at $x = 0$ (this is equivalent to assuming turbulent flow from the leading edge), then $c = 0$ and

$$\delta = 0.382 \left(\frac{\nu}{U} \right)^{1/5} x^{4/5}$$

Note that this shows that the turbulent boundary-layer thickness δ grows as $x^{4/5}$; it grows almost linearly (recall that δ grows more slowly, as $\sqrt{x}$, for the laminar boundary layer). Traditionally this is expressed in dimensionless form:

$$\frac{\delta}{x} = 0.382 \left(\frac{\nu}{Ux} \right)^{1/5} = \frac{0.382}{Re_x^{1/5}} \tag{9.26}$$

Using Eq. 9.25, we obtain the skin friction coefficient in terms of δ:

$$C_f = \frac{\tau_w}{\frac{1}{2}\rho U^2} = 0.0466 \left(\frac{\nu}{U\delta} \right)^{1/4}$$

Substituting for δ, we obtain

$$C_f = \frac{\tau_w}{\frac{1}{2}\rho U^2} = \frac{0.0594}{Re_x^{1/5}} \tag{9.27}$$

Experiments show that Eq. 9.27 predicts turbulent skin friction on a flat plate very well for $5 \times 10^5 < Re_x < 10^7$. This agreement is remarkable in view of the approximate nature of our analysis.

Application of the momentum integral equation for turbulent boundary-layer flow is illustrated in Example 9.4.

EXAMPLE 9.4   Turbulent Boundary Layer on a Flat Plate: Approximate Solution Using $\frac{1}{7}$-power Velocity Profile

Water flows at $U = 1$ m/s past a flat plate with $L = 1$ m in the flow direction. The boundary layer is tripped so it becomes turbulent at the leading edge. Evaluate the disturbance thickness, δ, displacement thickness, δ^*, and wall shear stress, τ_w, at $x = L$. Compare with laminar flow maintained to the same position. Assume a $\frac{1}{7}$-power turbulent velocity profile.

GIVEN: Flat-plate boundary-layer flow; turbulent flow from the leading edge. Assume $\frac{1}{7}$-power velocity profile.

FIND: (a) Disturbance thickness, δ_L.
(b) Displacement thickness, δ^*_L.
(c) Wall shear stress, $\tau_w(L)$.
(d) Comparison with results for laminar flow from the leading edge.

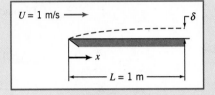

SOLUTION:

Apply results from the momentum integral equation.

Governing equation:

$$\frac{\delta}{x} = \frac{0.382}{Re_x^{1/5}} \tag{9.26}$$

$$\delta^* = \int_0^\infty \left(1 - \frac{u}{U}\right) dy \tag{9.1}$$

$$C_f = \frac{\tau_w}{\frac{1}{2}\rho U^2} = \frac{0.0594}{Re_x^{1/5}} \tag{9.27}$$

At $x = L$, with $\nu = 1.00 \times 10^{-6}$ m²/s for water ($T = 20°C$),

$$Re_L = \frac{UL}{\nu} = \frac{1 \text{ m}}{\text{s}} \times 1 \text{ m} \times \frac{\text{s}}{10^{-6} \text{ m}^2} = 10^6$$

From Eq. 9.26,

$$\delta_L = \frac{0.382}{Re_L^{1/5}} L = \frac{0.382}{(10^6)^{1/5}} \times 1 \text{ m} = 0.0241 \text{ m} \quad \text{or} \quad \delta_L = 24.1 \text{ mm} \longleftarrow \underline{\quad \delta_L \quad}$$

Using Eq. 9.1, with $u/U = (y/\delta)^{1/7} = \eta^{1/7}$, we obtain

$$\delta_L^* = \int_0^\infty \left(1 - \frac{u}{U}\right) dy = \delta_L \int_0^1 \left(\frac{u}{U}\right) d\left(\frac{y}{\delta}\right) = \delta_L \int_0^1 (1 - \eta^{1/7}) d\eta = \delta_L \left[\eta - \frac{7}{8}\eta^{8/7}\right]_0^1$$

$$\delta_L^* = \frac{\delta_L}{8} = \frac{24.1 \text{ mm}}{8} = 3.01 \text{ mm} \longleftarrow \underline{\quad \delta_L^* \quad}$$

From Eq. 9.27,

$$C_f = \frac{0.0594}{(10^6)^{1/5}} = 0.00375$$

$$\tau_w = C_f \frac{1}{2}\rho U^2 = 0.00375 \times \frac{1}{2} \times 999 \frac{\text{kg}}{\text{m}^3} \times \frac{(1)^2 \text{ m}^2}{\text{s}^2} \times \frac{\text{N} \cdot \text{s}^2}{\text{kg} \cdot \text{m}}$$

$$\tau_w = 1.87 \text{ N/m}^2 \longleftarrow \underline{\quad \tau_w(L) \quad}$$

For laminar flow, use Blasius solution values. From Eq. 9.13 (on the Web),

$$\delta_L = \frac{5.0}{\sqrt{Re_L}} L = \frac{5.0}{(10^6)^{1/2}} \times 1 \text{ m} = 0.005 \text{ m} \quad \text{or} \quad 5.00 \text{ mm}$$

From Example 9.2, $\delta^*/\delta = 0.344$, so

$$\delta^* = 0.344 \, \delta = 0.344 \times 5.0 \text{ mm} = 1.72 \text{ mm}$$

From Eq. 9.15, $C_f = \dfrac{0.664}{\sqrt{Re_x}}$, so

$$\tau_w = C_f \frac{1}{2} \rho U^2 = \frac{0.664}{\sqrt{10^6}} \times \frac{1}{2} \times 999 \frac{\text{kg}}{\text{m}^3} \times (1)^2 \frac{\text{m}^2}{\text{s}^2} \times \frac{\text{N} \cdot \text{s}^2}{\text{kg} \cdot \text{m}} = 0.332 \text{ N/m}^2$$

Comparing values at $x = L$, we obtain

$$\text{Disturbance thickness,} \quad \frac{\delta_{\text{turbulent}}}{\delta_{\text{laminar}}} = \frac{24.1 \text{ mm}}{5.00 \text{ mm}} = 4.82$$

$$\text{Displacement thickness,} \quad \frac{\delta^*_{\text{turbulent}}}{\delta^*_{\text{laminar}}} = \frac{3.01 \text{ mm}}{1.72 \text{ mm}} = 1.75$$

$$\text{Wall shear stress,} \quad \frac{\tau_{w,\,\text{turbulent}}}{\tau_{w,\,\text{laminar}}} = \frac{1.87 \text{ N/m}^2}{0.332 \text{ N/m}^2} = 5.63$$

> This problem illustrates application of the momentum integral equation to the turbulent boundary layer on a flat plate. Compared to a laminar boundary layer, it is clear that the turbulent boundary layer grows much more rapidly—because the turbulent wall stress is significantly greater than the laminar wall stress.
>
> The *Excel* workbook for this Example plots the $\frac{1}{7}$-power-law turbulent boundary layer (Eq. 9.26) and the laminar boundary layer (Eq. 9.13 on the Web). It also shows the wall stress distributions for both cases.

Summary of Results for Boundary-Layer Flow with Zero Pressure Gradient

Use of the momentum integral equation is an approximate technique to predict boundary-layer development; the equation predicts trends correctly. Parameters of the laminar boundary layer vary as $Re_x^{-1/2}$; those for the turbulent boundary layer vary as $Re_x^{-1/5}$. Thus the turbulent boundary layer develops more rapidly than the laminar boundary layer.

Laminar and turbulent boundary layers were compared in Example 9.4. Wall shear stress is much higher in the turbulent boundary layer than in the laminar layer. This is the primary reason for the more rapid development of turbulent boundary layers.

The agreement we have obtained with experimental results shows that use of the momentum integral equation is an effective approximate method that gives us considerable insight into the general behavior of boundary layers.

9-6   PRESSURE GRADIENTS IN BOUNDARY-LAYER FLOW

The boundary layer (laminar or turbulent) with a uniform flow along an infinite flat plate is the easiest one to study because the pressure gradient is zero—the fluid particles in the boundary layer are slowed only by shear stresses, leading to boundary-layer growth. We now consider the effects caused by a pressure gradient, which will be present for all bodies except, as we have seen, a flat plate.

A *favorable pressure gradient* is one in which the pressure decreases in the flow direction (i.e., $\partial p/\partial x < 0$); it is called favorable because it tends to overcome the slowing of fluid particles caused by friction in the boundary layer. This pressure gradient arises when the free-stream velocity U is increasing with x, for example in the converging flow field in a nozzle. On the other hand, an *adverse pressure gradient* is one in which pressure increases in the flow direction (i.e., $\partial p/\partial x > 0$); it is called adverse because it will cause fluid particles in the boundary-layer to slow down at a greater rate than that due to boundary-layer friction alone. If the adverse pressure gradient is severe enough, the fluid particles in the boundary layer will actually be brought to rest. When this occurs, the particles will be forced away from the body surface (a phenomenon called *flow separation*) as they make room for following particles, ultimately leading to a *wake* in which flow is turbulent. Examples of this are when the walls of a diffuser diverge too rapidly and when an airfoil has too large an angle of attack; both of these are generally very undesirable!

This description, of the adverse pressure gradient and friction in the boundary layer together forcing flow separation, certainly makes intuitive sense; the question arises whether we can more formally see when this occurs. For example, can we have flow separation and a wake for uniform flow over a flat plate, for which $\partial p/\partial x = 0$? We can gain insight into this question by considering when the velocity in the boundary layer will become zero. Consider the velocity u in the boundary layer at an infinitesimal distance Δy above the plate. This will be

$$u_{y=\Delta y} = u_0 + \left.\frac{\partial u}{\partial y}\right)_{y=0} \Delta y = \left.\frac{\partial u}{\partial y}\right)_{y=0} \Delta y$$

where $u_0 = 0$ is the velocity at the surface of the plate. It is clear that $u_{y=\Delta y}$ will be zero (i.e., separation will occur) only when $\partial u/\partial y)_{y=0} = 0$. Hence, we can use this as our litmus test for flow separation. We recall that the velocity gradient near the surface in a laminar boundary layer, and in the viscous sublayer of a turbulent boundary layer, was related to the wall shear stress by

$$\tau_w = \mu \left.\frac{\partial u}{\partial y}\right)_{y=0}$$

Further, we learned in the previous section that the wall shear stress for the flat plate is given by

$$\frac{\tau_w(x)}{\rho U^2} = \frac{\text{constant}}{\sqrt{Re_x}}$$

for a laminar boundary layer and

$$\frac{\tau_w(x)}{\rho U^2} = \frac{\text{constant}}{Re_x^{1/5}}$$

for a turbulent boundary layer. We see that for the flow over a flat plate, the wall stress is always $\tau_w > 0$. Hence, $\partial u/\partial y)_{y=0} > 0$ always; and therefore, finally, $u_{y=\Delta y} > 0$ always. We conclude that for uniform flow over a flat plate the flow *never* separates, and we never develop a wake region, whether the boundary layer is laminar or turbulent, regardless of plate length.

We conclude that flow will not separate for flow over a flat plate, when $\partial p/\partial x = 0$. Clearly, for flows in which $\partial p/\partial x < 0$ (whenever the free-stream velocity is increasing), we can be sure that there will be no flow separation; for flows in which $\partial p/\partial x > 0$ (i.e., adverse pressure gradients) we *could* have flow separation. We should not conclude that an adverse pressure gradient *always* leads to flow separation and a wake; we have only concluded that it is a necessary condition for flow separation to occur.

To illustrate these results consider the variable cross-sectional flow shown in Fig. 9.6. Outside the boundary layer the velocity field is one in which the flow accelerates (Region 1), has a constant velocity region (Region 2), and then a deceleration region (Region 3). Corresponding to these, the pressure gradient is favorable, zero, and adverse, respectively, as shown. (Note that the straight wall is not a simple flat plate—it has these various pressure gradients because the flow above the wall is not a uniform flow.) From our discussions above, we conclude that separation cannot occur

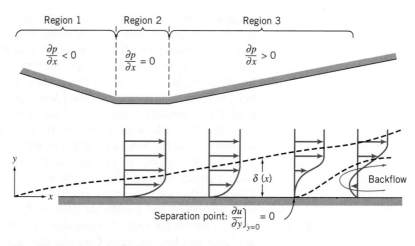

Fig. 9.6 Boundary-layer flow with pressure gradient (boundary-layer thickness exaggerated for clarity).

in Region 1 or 2, but can (as shown) occur in Region 3. Could we avoid flow separation in a device like this? Intuitively, we can see that if we make the divergent section less severe, we may be able to eliminate flow separation. In other words, we may eliminate flow separation if we make the adverse pressure gradient $\partial p/\partial x$ small enough. The final question remaining is how small the adverse pressure gradient needs to be to accomplish this. This, and a more rigorous proof that we must have $\partial p/\partial x > 0$ for a chance of flow separation, is beyond the scope of this text [3]. We conclude that flow separation is possible, but not guaranteed, when we have an adverse pressure gradient.

The nondimensional velocity profiles for laminar and turbulent boundary-layer flow over a flat plate are shown in Fig. 9.7a. The turbulent profile is much fuller (more blunt) than the laminar profile. At the same free-stream speed, the momentum flux within the turbulent boundary layer is greater than within the laminar layer (Fig. 9.7b). Separation occurs when the momentum of fluid layers near the surface is reduced to zero by the combined action of pressure and viscous forces. As shown in Fig. 9.7b, the momentum of the fluid near the surface is significantly greater for the turbulent profile. Consequently, the turbulent layer is better able to resist separation in an adverse pressure gradient. We shall discuss some consequences of this behavior in Section 9-7.

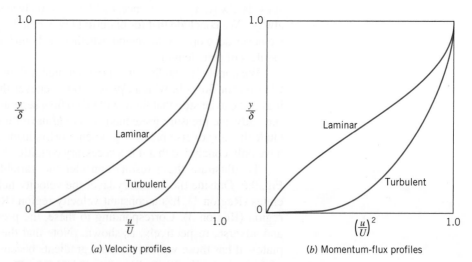

Fig. 9.7 Nondimensional profiles for flat plate boundary-layer flow.

Adverse pressure gradients cause significant changes in velocity profiles for both laminar and turbulent boundary-layer flows. Approximate solutions for nonzero pressure gradient flow may be obtained from the momentum integral equation

$$\frac{\tau_w}{\rho} = \frac{d}{dx}(U^2\theta) + \delta^* \ U\frac{dU}{dx} \tag{9.17}$$

Expanding the first term, we can write

$$\frac{\tau_w}{\rho} = U^2 \ \frac{d\theta}{dx} + (\delta^* + 2\theta) \ U\frac{dU}{dx}$$

or

$$\frac{\tau_w}{\rho U^2} = \frac{C_f}{2} = \frac{d\theta}{dx} + (H+2) \ \frac{\theta}{U}\frac{dU}{dx} \tag{9.28}$$

where $H = \delta^*/\theta$ is a velocity-profile "shape factor." The shape factor increases in an adverse pressure gradient. For turbulent boundary-layer flow, H increases from 1.3 for a zero pressure gradient to approximately 2.5 at separation. For laminar flow with zero pressure gradient, $H = 2.6$; at separation $H = 3.5$.

The free-stream velocity distribution, $U(x)$, must be known before Eq. 9.28 can be applied. Since $dp/dx = -\rho U \ dU/dx$, specifying $U(x)$ is equivalent to specifying the pressure gradient. We can obtain a first approximation for $U(x)$ from ideal flow theory for an inviscid flow under the same conditions. As pointed out in Chapter 6, for frictionless irrotational flow (potential flow), the stream function, ψ, and the velocity potential, ϕ, satisfy Laplace's equation. These can be used to determine $U(x)$ over the body surface.

Much effort has been devoted to calculation of velocity distributions over bodies of known shape (the "direct" problem) and to the determination of body shapes to produce a desired pressure distribution (the "inverse" problem). Smith and coworkers [6] have developed calculation methods that use singularities distributed over the body surface to solve the direct problem for two-dimensional or axisymmetric body shapes. A type of finite-element method that uses singularities defined on discrete surface panels (the "panel" method [7]) recently has gained increased popularity for application to three-dimensional flows. Recall also that in Section 5-5 we briefly reviewed some basic ideas of CFD (Computational Fluid Dynamics).

Once the velocity distribution, $U(x)$, is known, Eq. 9.28 can be integrated to determine $\theta(x)$, if H and C_f can be correlated with θ. A detailed discussion of various calculation methods for flows with nonzero pressure gradient is beyond the scope of this book. Numerous solutions for laminar flows are given in [8]. Calculation methods for turbulent boundary-layer flow based on the momentum integral equation are reviewed in [9].

Because of the importance of turbulent boundary layers in engineering flow situations, the state of the art of calculation schemes is advancing rapidly. Numerous calculation schemes have been proposed [10, 11]; most such schemes for turbulent flow use models to predict turbulent shear stress and then solve the boundary-layer equations numerically [12, 13]. Continuing improvement in size and speed of computers is beginning to make possible the solution of the full Navier-Stokes equations using numerical methods [14, 15].

PART B FLUID FLOW ABOUT IMMERSED BODIES

Whenever there is relative motion between a solid body and the viscous fluid surrounding it, the body will experience a net force $\vec{F}$. The magnitude of this force depends on many factors—certainly the relative velocity $\vec{V}$, but also the body shape and size, and the fluid properties (ρ, μ, etc.). As the fluid flows around the body, it will generate surface stresses on each element of the surface, and it is these that lead to the net force. The surface stresses are composed of tangential stresses due to viscous action and normal stresses due to the local pressure. We might be tempted to think that we can analytically derive the net force by integrating these over the body surface. The first step might be: Given the shape of the body (and assuming that the Reynolds number is high enough that we can use inviscid flow theory), compute the pressure distribution. Then integrate the pressure over the body surface to obtain the contribution of pressure forces to the net force $\vec{F}$. (As we discussed in Chapter 6, this step was developed very early in the history of fluid mechanics; it led to the result that no bodies experience drag!) The second step might be: Use this pressure distribution to find the surface viscous stress τ_w (at least in principle, using, for example, Eq. 9.17). Then integrate the viscous stress over the body surface to obtain its contribution to the net force $\vec{F}$. This procedure sounds conceptually straightforward, but in practice is quite difficult except for the simplest body shapes. In addition, even if possible, it leads to erroneous results in most cases because it takes no account of a very important consequence of the existence of boundary layers—flow separation. This causes a wake, which not only creates a low-pressure region usually leading to large drag on the body, but also radically changes the overall flow field and hence the inviscid flow region and pressure distribution on the body.

For these reasons we must usually resort to experimental methods to determine the net force for most body shapes (although CFD approaches are improving rapidly). Traditionally the net force $\vec{F}$ is resolved into the drag force, F_D, defined as the component of the force parallel to the direction of motion, and the lift force, F_L (if it exists for a body), defined as the component of the force perpendicular to the direction of motion. In Sections 9-7 and 9-8 we will examine these forces for a number of different body shapes.

9-7   DRAG

Drag is the component of force on a body acting parallel to the direction of relative motion. In discussing the need for experimental results in fluid mechanics (Chapter 7), we considered the problem of determining the drag force, F_D, on a smooth sphere of diameter d, moving through a viscous, incompressible fluid with speed V; the fluid density and viscosity were ρ and μ, respectively. The drag force, F_D, was written in the functional form

$$F_D = f_1(d, V, \mu, \rho)$$

Application of the Buckingham Pi theorem resulted in two dimensionless Π parameters that were written in functional form as

$$\frac{F_D}{\rho V^2 d^2} = f_2\left(\frac{\rho V d}{\mu}\right)$$

Note that d^2 is proportional to the cross-sectional area ($A = \pi d^2/4$) and therefore we could write

$$\frac{F_D}{\rho V^2 A} = f_3\left(\frac{\rho V d}{\mu}\right) = f_3(Re) \tag{9.29}$$

Although Eq. 9.29 was obtained for a sphere, the form of the equation is valid for incompressible flow over *any* body; the characteristic length used in the Reynolds number depends on the body shape.

The *drag coefficient*, C_D, is defined as

$$C_D \equiv \frac{F_D}{\frac{1}{2}\rho V^2 A} \tag{9.30}$$

The number $\frac{1}{2}$ has been inserted (as was done in the defining equation for the friction factor) to form the familiar dynamic pressure. Then Eq. 9.29 can be written as

$$C_D = f(Re) \tag{9.31}$$

We have not considered compressibility or free-surface effects in this discussion of the drag force. Had these been included, we would have obtained the functional form

$$C_D = f(Re, Fr, M)$$

At this point we shall consider the drag force on several bodies for which Eq. 9.31 is valid. The total drag force is the sum of friction drag and pressure drag. However, the drag coefficient is a function only of the Reynolds number.

We now consider the drag force and drag coefficient for a number of bodies, starting with the simplest: a flat plate parallel to the flow (which has only friction drag); a flat plate normal to the flow (which has only pressure drag); and cylinders and spheres (the simplest 2D and 3D bodies, which have both friction and pressure drag). We will also briefly discuss streamlining.

Pure Friction Drag: Flow over a Flat Plate Parallel to the Flow

This flow situation was considered in detail in Section 9-5. Since the pressure gradient is zero (and in any event the pressure forces are perpendicular to the plate and therefore do not contribute to drag), the total drag is equal to the friction drag. Thus

$$F_D = \int_{\text{plate surface}} \tau_w \, dA$$

and

$$C_D = \frac{F_D}{\frac{1}{2}\rho V^2 \, A} = \frac{\int_{\text{PS}} \tau_w \, dA}{\frac{1}{2}\rho V^2 \, A} \tag{9.32}$$

where A is the total surface area in contact with the fluid (i.e., the *wetted area*). The drag coefficient for a flat plate parallel to the flow depends on the shear stress distribution along the plate.

For laminar flow over a flat plate, the shear stress coefficient was given by

$$C_f = \frac{\tau_w}{\frac{1}{2}\rho U^2} = \frac{0.664}{\sqrt{Re_x}} \tag{9.15}$$

The drag coefficient for flow with free-stream velocity V, over a flat plate of length L and width b, is obtained by substituting for τ_w from Eq. 9.15 into Eq. 9.32. Thus

$$C_D = \frac{1}{A}\int_A 0.664 \, Re_x^{-0.5} \, dA = \frac{1}{bL}\int_0^L 0.664 \left(\frac{V}{\nu}\right)^{-0.5} x^{-0.5} b \, dx$$

$$= \frac{0.664}{L}\left(\frac{\nu}{V}\right)^{0.5}\left[\frac{x^{0.5}}{0.5}\right]_0^L = 1.33 \left(\frac{\nu}{VL}\right)^{0.5}$$

$$C_D = \frac{1.33}{\sqrt{Re_L}} \tag{9.33}$$

Assuming the boundary layer is turbulent from the leading edge, the shear stress coefficient, based on the approximate analysis of Section 9-5, is given by

$$C_f = \frac{\tau_w}{\frac{1}{2}\rho U^2} = \frac{0.0594}{Re_x^{1/5}} \tag{9.27}$$

Substituting for τ_w from Eq. 9.27 into Eq. 9.32, we obtain

$$C_D = \frac{1}{A} \int_A 0.0594 \, Re_x^{-0.2} \, dA = \frac{1}{bL} \int_0^L 0.0594 \left(\frac{V}{\nu}\right)^{-0.2} x^{-0.2} b \, dx$$

$$= \frac{0.0594}{L} \left(\frac{\nu}{V}\right)^{0.2} \left[\frac{x^{0.8}}{0.8}\right]_0^L = 0.0742 \left(\frac{\nu}{VL}\right)^{0.2}$$

$$C_D = \frac{0.0742}{Re_L^{1/5}} \tag{9.34}$$

Equation 9.34 is valid for $5 \times 10^5 < Re_L < 10^7$.

For $Re_L < 10^9$ the empirical equation given by Schlichting [3]

$$C_D = \frac{0.455}{(\log Re_L)^{2.58}} \tag{9.35}$$

fits experimental data very well.

For a boundary layer that is initially laminar and undergoes transition at some location on the plate, the turbulent drag coefficient must be adjusted to account for the laminar flow over the initial length. The adjustment is made by subtracting the quantity B/Re_L from the C_D determined for completely turbulent flow. The value of B depends on the Reynolds number at transition; B is given by

$$B = Re_{\mathrm{tr}}(C_{D_{\mathrm{turbulent}}} - C_{D_{\mathrm{laminar}}}) \tag{9.36}$$

For a transition Reynolds number of 5×10^5, the drag coefficient may be calculated by making the adjustment to Eq. 9.34, in which case

$$C_D = \frac{0.0742}{Re_L^{1/5}} - \frac{1740}{Re_L} \qquad (5 \times 10^5 < Re_L < 10^7) \tag{9.37a}$$

or to Eq. 9.35, in which case

$$C_D = \frac{0.455}{(\log Re_L)^{2.58}} - \frac{1610}{Re_L} \qquad (5 \times 10^5 < Re_L < 10^9) \tag{9.37b}$$

The variation in drag coefficient for a flat plate parallel to the flow is shown in Fig. 9.8.

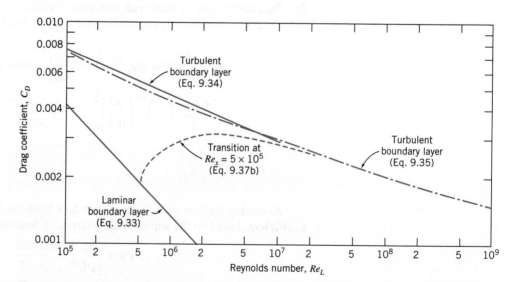

Fig. 9.8 Variation of drag coefficient with Reynolds number for a smooth flat plate parallel to the flow.

In the plot of Fig. 9.8, transition was assumed to occur at $Re_x = 5 \times 10^5$ for flows in which the boundary layer was initially laminar. The actual Reynolds number at which transition occurs depends on a combination of factors, such as surface roughness and free-stream disturbances. Transition tends to occur earlier (at lower Reynolds number) as surface roughness or free-stream turbulence is increased. For transition at other than $Re_x = 5 \times 10^5$, the constant in the second term of Eqs. 9.37 is modified using Eq. 9.36. Figure 9.8 shows that the drag coefficient is less, for a given length of plate, when laminar flow is maintained over the longest possible distance. However, at large $Re_L (> 10^7)$ the contribution of the laminar drag is negligible.

EXAMPLE 9.5   Skin Friction Drag on a Supertanker

A supertanker is 360 m long and has a beam width of 70 m and a draft of 25 m. Estimate the force and power required to overcome skin friction drag at a cruising speed of 13 kt in seawater at 10°C.

GIVEN: Supertanker cruising at $U = 13$ kt.

FIND: (a) Force.
(b) Power required to overcome skin friction drag.

SOLUTION:
Model the tanker hull as a flat plate, of length L and width $b = B + 2D$, in contact with water. Estimate skin friction drag from the drag coefficient.

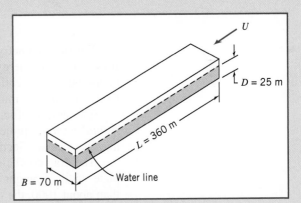

Governing equations:
$$C_D = \frac{F_D}{\frac{1}{2}\rho U^2 A} \qquad (9.32)$$

$$C_D = \frac{0.455}{(\log Re_L)^{2.58}} - \frac{1610}{Re_L} \qquad (9.37b)$$

The ship speed is 13 kt (nautical miles per hour), so

$$U = \frac{13 \text{ nm}}{\text{hr}} \times \frac{6076 \text{ ft}}{\text{nm}} \times \frac{0.305 \text{ m}}{\text{ft}} \times \frac{\text{hr}}{3600 \text{ s}} = 6.69 \text{ m/s}$$

From Appendix A, at 10°C, $v = 1.37 \times 10^{-6}$ m²/s for seawater. Then

$$Re_L = \frac{UL}{v} = \frac{6.69 \text{ m}}{\text{s}} \times 360 \text{ m} \times \frac{\text{s}}{1.37 \times 10^{-6} \text{ m}^2} = 1.76 \times 10^9$$

Assuming Eq. 9.37b is valid,

$$C_D = \frac{0.455}{(\log 1.76 \times 10^9)^{2.58}} - \frac{1610}{1.76 \times 10^9} = 0.00147$$

and from Eq. 9.32,

$$F_D = C_D A \frac{1}{2}\rho U^2$$

$$= 0.00147 \times (360 \text{ m})(70 + 50) \text{ m} \times \frac{1}{2} \times 1020 \frac{\text{kg}}{\text{m}^3} \times (6.69)^2 \frac{\text{m}^2}{\text{s}^2} \times \frac{\text{N} \cdot \text{s}^2}{\text{kg} \cdot \text{m}}$$

$$F_D = 1.45 \text{ MN} \longleftarrow \underline{\hspace{7cm}} \quad F_D$$

The corresponding power is

$$\mathcal{P} = F_D U = 1.45 \times 10^6 \text{ N} \times \frac{6.69 \text{ m}}{\text{s}} \times \frac{\text{W} \cdot \text{s}}{\text{N} \cdot \text{m}}$$

$$\mathcal{P} = 9.70 \text{ MW} \longleftarrow \underline{\hspace{7cm}} \quad \mathcal{P}$$

This problem illustrates application of drag coefficient equations for a flat plate parallel to the flow.

✓ The power required (about 13,000 hp) is very large because although the friction stress is small, it acts over a substantial area.

✓ The boundary layer is turbulent for almost the entire length of the ship (transition occurs at $x \approx 0.1$ m).

Pure Pressure Drag: Flow over a Flat Plate Normal to the Flow

In flow over a flat plate normal to the flow (Fig. 9.9), the wall shear stress is perpendicular to the flow direction and therefore does not contribute to the drag force. The drag is given by

$$F_D = \int_{\text{surface}} p \, dA$$

For this geometry the flow separates from the edges of the plate; there is back-flow in the low energy wake of the plate. Although the pressure over the rear surface of the plate is essentially constant, its magnitude cannot be determined analytically. Consequently, we must resort to experiments to determine the drag force.

The drag coefficient for flow over an immersed object usually is based on the *frontal area* (or projected area) of the object. (For airfoils and wings, the *planform area* is used; see Section 9-8.)

The drag coefficient for a finite plate normal to the flow depends on the ratio of plate width to height and on the Reynolds number. For *Re* (based on height) greater than about 1000, the drag coefficient is essentially independent of Reynolds number. The variation of C_D with the ratio of plate width to height (*b/h*) is shown in Fig. 9.10. (The ratio *b/h* is defined as the *aspect ratio* of the plate.) For *b/h* = 1.0, the drag coefficient is a minimum at $C_D = 1.18$; this is just slightly higher than for a circular disk ($C_D = 1.17$) at large Reynolds number.

The drag coefficient for all objects with sharp edges is essentially independent of Reynolds number (for *Re* ≳ 1000) because the separation points and therefore the size of the wake are fixed by the geometry of the object. Drag coefficients for selected objects are given in Table 9.3.

Friction and Pressure Drag: Flow over a Sphere and Cylinder

We have looked at two special flow cases in which either friction or pressure drag was the sole form of drag present. In the former case, the drag coefficient was a strong function of Reynolds number, while in the latter case, C_D was essentially independent of Reynolds number for *Re* ≳ 1000.

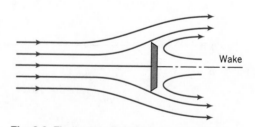

Fig. 9.9 Flow over a flat plate normal to the flow.

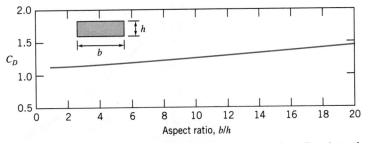

Fig. 9.10 Variation of drag coefficient with aspect ratio for a flat plate of finite width normal to the flow with $Re_h > 1000$ [16].

In the case of flow over a sphere, both friction drag and pressure drag contribute to total drag. The drag coefficient for flow over a smooth sphere is shown in Fig. 9.11 as a function of Reynolds number.[2]

At very low Reynolds number,[3] $Re \le 1$, there is no flow separation from a sphere; the wake is laminar and the drag is predominantly friction drag. Stokes has shown analytically, for very low Reynolds number flows where inertia forces may be

TABLE 9.3 Drag Coefficient Data for Selected Objects ($Re \gtrsim 10^3$)[a]

Object	Diagram		$C_D(Re \gtrsim 10^3)$
Square prism		$b/h = \infty$	2.05
		$b/h = 1$	1.05
Disk			1.17
Ring			1.20[b]
Hemisphere (open end facing flow)			1.42
Hemisphere (open end facing downstream)			0.38
C-section (open side facing flow)			2.30
C-section (open side facing downstream)			1.20

[a] Data from [16].
[b] Based on ring area.

[2] An approximate curve fit to the data of Fig. 9.11 is presented in Problem 9.130.

[3] See the NCFMF video *The Fluid Dynamics of Drag* or [17] for a good discussion of drag on spheres and other shapes. Another excellent NCFMF video is *Low Reynolds Number Flows*. See also [18]. (See http://web.mit.edu/fluids/www/Shapiro/ncfmf.html for free online viewing of these films; they are old but good!)

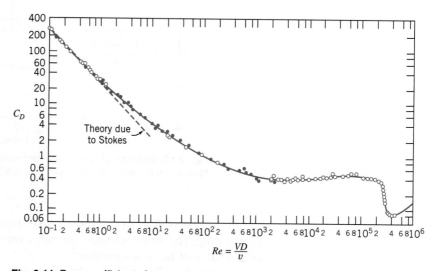

Fig. 9.11 Drag coefficient of a smooth sphere as a function of Reynolds number [3].

neglected, that the drag force on a sphere of diameter d, moving at speed V, through a fluid of viscosity μ, is given by

$$F_D = 3\pi\mu V d$$

The drag coefficient, C_D, defined by Eq. 9.30, is then

$$C_D = \frac{24}{Re}$$

As shown in Fig. 9.11, this expression agrees with experimental values at low Reynolds number but begins to deviate significantly from the experimental data for $Re > 1.0$.

As the Reynolds number is further increased, the drag coefficient drops continuously up to a Reynolds number of about 1000, but not as rapidly as predicted by Stokes' theory. A turbulent wake (not incorporated in Stokes' theory) develops and grows at the rear of the sphere as the separation point moves from the rear of the sphere toward the front; this wake is at a relatively low pressure, leading to a large pressure drag. By the time $Re \approx$ 1000, about 95% of total drag is due to pressure. For $10^3 < Re < 3 \times 10^5$ the drag coefficient is approximately constant. In this range the entire rear of the sphere has a low-pressure turbulent wake, as indicated in Fig. 9.12, and most of the drag is caused by the front-rear pressure asymmetry. Note that $C_D \propto 1/Re$ corresponds to $F_D \propto V$, and that $C_D \sim$ const. corresponds to $F_D \propto V^2$, indicating a quite rapid increase in drag.

For Reynolds numbers larger than about 3×10^5, transition occurs and the boundary layer on the forward portion of the sphere becomes turbulent. The point of separation then moves downstream from the sphere midsection, and the size of the wake decreases. The net pressure force on the sphere is reduced (Fig. 9.12), and the drag coefficient decreases abruptly.

A turbulent boundary layer, since it has more momentum flux than a laminar boundary layer, can better resist an adverse pressure gradient, as discussed in Section 9-6. Consequently, turbulent boundary-layer flow is desirable on a blunt body because it delays separation and thus reduces the pressure drag.

Transition in the boundary layer is affected by roughness of the sphere surface and turbulence in the flow stream. Therefore, the reduction in drag associated with a turbulent boundary layer does not occur at a unique value of Reynolds number. Experiments with smooth spheres in a flow with low turbulence level show that transition may be delayed to a critical Reynolds number, Re_D, of about 4×10^5. For rough surfaces and/or highly turbulent free-stream flow, transition can occur at a critical Reynolds number as low as 50,000.

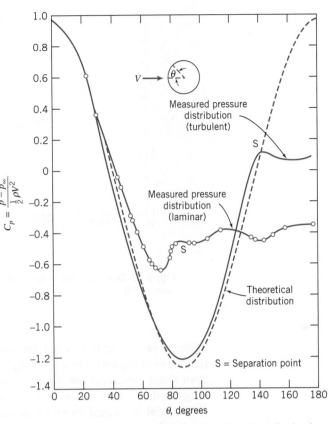

Fig. 9.12 Pressure distribution around a smooth sphere for laminar and turbulent boundary-layer flow, compared with inviscid flow [18].

The drag coefficient of a sphere with turbulent boundary-layer flow is about one-fifth that for laminar flow near the critical Reynolds number. The corresponding reduction in drag force can affect the range of a sphere (e.g., a golf ball) appreciably. The "dimples" on a golf ball are designed to "trip" the boundary layer and, thus, to guarantee turbulent boundary-layer flow and minimum drag. To illustrate this effect graphically, we obtained samples of golf balls without dimples some years ago. One of our students volunteered to hit drives with the smooth balls. In 50 tries with each type of ball, the average distance with the standard balls was 215 yards; the average with the smooth balls was only 125 yards!

Adding roughness elements to a sphere also can suppress local oscillations in location of the transition between laminar and turbulent flow in the boundary layer. These oscillations can lead to variations in drag and to random fluctuations in lift (see Section 9-8). In baseball, the "knuckle ball" pitch is intended to behave erratically to confuse the batter. By throwing the ball with almost no spin, the pitcher relies on the seams to cause transition in an unpredictable fashion as the ball moves on its way to the batter. This causes the desired variation in the flight path of the ball.

Figure 9.13 shows the drag coefficient for flow over a smooth cylinder. The variation of C_D with Reynolds number shows the same characteristics as observed in the flow over a smooth sphere, but the values of C_D are about twice as high.

Flow about a smooth circular cylinder may develop a regular pattern of alternating vortices downstream. The *vortex trail*[4] causes an oscillatory lift force on the

---

[4] The regular pattern of vortices in the wake of a cylinder sometimes is called a *Karman vortex street* in honor of the prominent fluid mechanician, Theodore von Kármán, who was first to predict the stable spacing of the vortex trail on theoretical grounds in 1911; see [19].

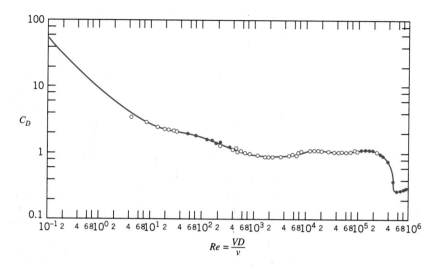

Fig. 9.13 Drag coefficient for a smooth circular cylinder as a function of Reynolds number [3].

cylinder perpendicular to the stream motion. Vortex shedding excites oscillations that cause telegraph wires to "sing" and ropes on flag poles to "slap" annoyingly. Sometimes structural oscillations can reach dangerous magnitudes and cause high stresses; they can be reduced or eliminated by applying roughness elements or fins—either axial or helical (sometimes seen on chimneys or automobile antennas)—that destroy the symmetry of the cylinder and stabilize the flow.

Experimental data show that regular vortex shedding occurs most strongly in the range of Reynolds number from about 60 to 5000. For $Re > 1000$ the dimensionless frequency of vortex shedding, expressed as a Strouhal number, $St = fD/V$, is approximately equal to 0.21 [3].

Roughness affects drag of cylinders and spheres similarly: the critical Reynolds number is reduced by the rough surface, and transition from laminar to turbulent flow in the boundary layers occurs earlier. The drag coefficient is reduced by a factor of about 4 when the boundary layer on the cylinder becomes turbulent.

EXAMPLE 9.6   Aerodynamic Drag and Moment on a Chimney

A cylindrical chimney 1 m in diameter and 25 m tall is exposed to a uniform 50 km/hr wind at standard atmospheric conditions. End effects and gusts may be neglected. Estimate the bending moment at the base of the chimney due to wind forces.

GIVEN: Cylindrical chimney, $D = 1$ m, $L = 25$ m, in uniform flow with

$$V = 50 \text{ km/hr} \qquad p = 101 \text{ kPa (abs)} \qquad T = 15°C$$

Neglect end effects.

FIND: Bending moment at bottom of chimney.

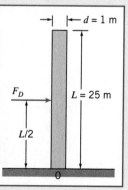

SOLUTION:

The drag coefficient is given by $C_D = F_D / \frac{1}{2}\rho V^2 A$, and thus $F_D = C_D A \frac{1}{2}\rho V^2$. Since the force per unit length is uniform over the entire length, the resultant force, F_D, will act at the midpoint of the chimney. Hence the moment about the chimney base is

$$M_0 = F_D\,\frac{L}{2} = C_D A\,\frac{1}{2}\rho V^2\,\frac{L}{2} = C_D A\,\frac{L}{4}\,\rho V^2$$

$$V = \frac{50\ \text{km}}{\text{hr}} \times \frac{10^3\ \text{m}}{\text{km}} \times \frac{\text{hr}}{3600\ \text{s}} = 13.9\ \text{m/s}$$

For air at standard conditions, $\rho = 1.23\ \text{kg/m}^3$, and $\mu = 1.79 \times 10^{-5}\ \text{kg/(m} \cdot \text{s})$. Thus

$$Re = \frac{\rho V D}{\mu} = \frac{1.23\ \text{kg}}{\text{m}^3} \times \frac{13.9\ \text{m}}{\text{s}} \times \frac{1\ \text{m}}{} \times \frac{\text{m} \cdot \text{s}}{1.79 \times 10^{-5}\ \text{kg}} = 9.55 \times 10^5$$

From Fig. 9.13, $C_D \approx 0.35$. For a cylinder, $A = DL$, so

$$M_0 = C_D A\,\frac{L}{4}\rho V^2 = C_D DL\,\frac{L}{4}\rho V^2 = C_D D\,\frac{L^2}{4}\,\rho V^2$$

$$= \frac{1}{4} \times 0.35 \times 1\ \text{m} \times (25)^2\ \text{m}^2 \times 1.23\,\frac{\text{kg}}{\text{m}^3} \times (13.9)^2\,\frac{\text{m}^2}{\text{s}^2} \times \frac{\text{N} \cdot \text{s}^2}{\text{kg} \cdot \text{m}}$$

$$M_0 = 13.0\ \text{kN} \cdot \text{m} \longleftarrow \hspace{4cm} M_0$$

> This problem illustrates application of drag-coefficient data to calculate the force and moment on a structure. We modeled the wind as a uniform flow; more realistically, the lower atmosphere is often modeled as a huge turbulent boundary layer, with a power-law velocity profile, $u \sim y^{1/n}$ (y is the elevation). See Problem 9.135, where this is analyzed for the case $n = 7$.

EXAMPLE 9.7   Deceleration of an Automobile by a Drag Parachute

A dragster weighing 1600 lbf attains a speed of 270 mph in the quarter mile. Immediately after passing through the timing lights, the driver opens the drag chute, of area $A = 25\ \text{ft}^2$. Air and rolling resistance of the car may be neglected. Find the time required for the machine to decelerate to 100 mph in standard air.

GIVEN: Dragster weighing 1600 lbf, moving with initial speed $V_0 = 270$ mph, is slowed by the drag force on a chute of area $A = 25\ \text{ft}^2$. Neglect air and rolling resistance of the car. Assume standard air.

FIND: Time required for the machine to decelerate to 100 mph.

SOLUTION:
Taking the car as a system and writing Newton's second law in the direction of motion gives

$$-F_D = ma = m\,\frac{dV}{dt}$$

$V_0 = 270\ \text{mph}$
$V_f = 100\ \text{mph}$
$\rho = 0.00238\ \text{slug/ft}^3$

Since $C_D = \dfrac{F_D}{\frac{1}{2}\rho V^2 A}$, then $F_D = \frac{1}{2}C_D\,\rho V^2 A$.

Substituting into Newton's second law gives

$$-\frac{1}{2}C_D\,\rho V^2 A = m\,\frac{dV}{dt}$$

Separating variables and integrating, we obtain

$$-\frac{1}{2}\,C_D\,\rho\,\frac{A}{m}\int_0^t dt = \int_{V_0}^{V_f}\frac{dV}{V^2}$$

$$-\frac{1}{2}\,C_D\,\rho\,\frac{A}{m}\,t = -\frac{1}{V}\Bigg]_{V_0}^{V_f} = -\frac{1}{V_f}+\frac{1}{V_0} = -\frac{(V_0-V_f)}{V_f V_0}$$

Finally,

$$t = \frac{(V_0-V_f)}{V_f V_0}\,\frac{2m}{C_D\,\rho A} = \frac{(V_0-V_f)}{V_f V_0}\,\frac{2W}{C_D\,\rho A g}$$

Model the drag chute as a hemisphere (with open end facing flow). From Table 9.3, $C_D = 1.42$ (assuming $Re > 10^3$). Then, substituting numerical values,

$$t = \frac{(270-100)\,\text{mph}}{}\times 2 \times 1600\,\text{lbf} \times \frac{1}{100\,\text{mph}}\times\frac{\text{hr}}{270\,\text{mi}}\times\frac{1}{1.2}\times\frac{\text{ft}^3}{0.00238\,\text{slug}}$$

$$\times\frac{1}{25\,\text{ft}^2}\times\frac{\text{s}^2}{32.2\,\text{ft}}\times\frac{\text{slug}\cdot\text{ft}}{\text{lbf}\cdot\text{s}^2}\times\frac{\text{mi}}{5280\,\text{ft}}\times\frac{3600}{\text{hr}}\,\frac{\text{s}}{}$$

$$t = 5.05\,\text{s} \longleftarrow \qquad\qquad\qquad\qquad\qquad\qquad\qquad t$$

Check the assumption on Re:

$$Re = \frac{DV}{\nu} = \left[\frac{4A}{\pi}\right]^{1/2}\frac{V}{\nu}$$

$$= \left[\frac{4}{\pi}\times 25\,\text{ft}^2\right]^{1/2}\times 100\,\frac{\text{mi}}{\text{hr}}\times\frac{\text{hr}}{3600\,\text{s}}\times 5280\,\frac{\text{ft}}{\text{mi}}\times\frac{\text{s}}{1.57\times 10^{-4}\,\text{ft}^2}$$

$$Re = 5.27\times 10^6$$

Hence the assumption is valid.

> This problem illustrates application of drag-coefficient data to calculate the drag on a vehicle parachute.
>
> The *Excel* workbook for this Example plots the dragster velocity (and distance traveled) as a function of time; it also allows "what-ifs," e.g., we can find the parachute area A required to slow the dragster to 60 mph in 5 sec.

All experimental data presented in this section are for single objects immersed in an unbounded fluid stream. The objective of wind tunnel tests is to simulate the conditions of an unbounded flow. Limitations on equipment size make this goal unreachable in practice. Frequently it is necessary to apply corrections to measured data to obtain results applicable to unbounded flow conditions.

In numerous realistic flow situations, interactions occur with nearby objects or surfaces. Drag can be reduced significantly when two or more objects, moving in tandem, interact. This phenomenon is well known to bicycle riders and those interested in automobile racing, where "drafting" is a common practice. Drag reductions of 80 percent may be achieved with optimum spacing [20]. Drag also can be increased significantly when spacing is not optimum.

Drag can be affected by neighbors alongside as well. Small particles falling under gravity travel more slowly when they have neighbors than when they are isolated. This phenomenon, which is illustrated in the NCFMF video *Low Reynolds Number Flows* (see http://web.mit.edu/fluids/www/Shapiro/ncfmf.html for free on-line viewing of this film; it is old but good!), has important applications to mixing and sedimentation processes.

Experimental data for drag coefficients on objects must be selected and applied carefully. Due regard must be given to the differences between the actual conditions and the more controlled conditions under which measurements were made.

Streamlining

The extent of the separated flow region behind many of the objects discussed in the previous section can be reduced or eliminated by streamlining, or fairing, the body shape. We have seen that due to the convergent body shape at the rear of any object (after all, every object is of finite length!), the streamlines will diverge, so that the velocity will decrease, and therefore, more importantly (as shown by the Bernoulli equation, applicable in the freestream region) the pressure will increase. Hence, we initially have an adverse pressure gradient at the rear of the body, leading to boundary-layer separation and ultimately to a low-pressure wake leading to large pressure drag. Streamlining is the attempt to reduce the drag on a body. We can reduce the drag on a body by making the rear of the body more tapered (e.g., we can reduce the drag on a sphere by making it "teardrop" shaped), which will reduce the adverse pressure gradient and hence make the turbulent wake smaller. However, as we do so, we are in danger of increasing the skin friction drag simply because we have increased the surface area. In practice, there is an optimum amount of fairing or tapering at which the total drag (the sum of pressure and skin friction drag) is minimized. These effects are discussed at length in the NCFMF video series *The Fluid Dynamics of Drag*. (See http://web.mit.edu/fluids/www/Shapiro/ncfmf.html for free online viewing of this film.)

The pressure gradient around a "teardrop" shape (a "streamlined" cylinder) is less severe than that around a cylinder of circular section. The trade-off between pressure and friction drag for this case is illustrated by the results presented in Fig. 9.14, for tests at $Re_c = 4 \times 10^5$. (This Reynolds number is typical of that for a strut on an early aircraft.) From the figure, the minimum drag coefficient is $C_D \approx 0.06$, which occurs when the ratio of thickness to chord is $t/c \approx 0.25$. This value is

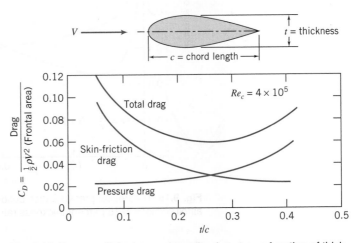

Fig. 9.14 Drag coefficient on a streamlined strut as a function of thickness ratio, showing contributions of skin friction and pressure to total drag [19].

approximately 20 percent of the minimum drag coefficient for a circular cylinder of the same thickness! Hence, even a small aircraft will typically have fairings on many structural members, e.g., the struts that make up the landing wheel assembly, leading to significant fuel savings.

The maximum thickness for the shapes shown in Fig. 9.14 is located approximately 25 percent of the chord distance from the leading edge. Most of the drag on the thinner sections is due to skin friction in the turbulent boundary layers on the tapered rear sections. Interest in low-drag airfoils increased during the 1930s. The National Advisory Committee for Aeronautics (NACA) developed several series of "laminar-flow" airfoils for which transition was postponed to 60 or 65 percent chord length aft from the airfoil nose.

Pressure distribution and drag coefficients[5] for two symmetric airfoils of infinite span and 15 percent thickness at zero angle of attack are presented in Fig. 9.15. Transition on the conventional (NACA 0015) airfoil takes place where the pressure gradient becomes adverse, at $x/c = 0.13$, near the point of maximum thickness. Thus most of the airfoil surface is covered with a turbulent boundary layer; the drag coefficient is $C_D \approx 0.0061$. The point of maximum thickness has been moved aft on the airfoil (NACA 66_2–015) designed for laminar flow. The boundary layer is maintained in the laminar regime by the favorable pressure gradient to $x/c = 0.63$. Thus the bulk of the flow is laminar; $C_D \approx 0.0035$ for this section, based on planform area. The

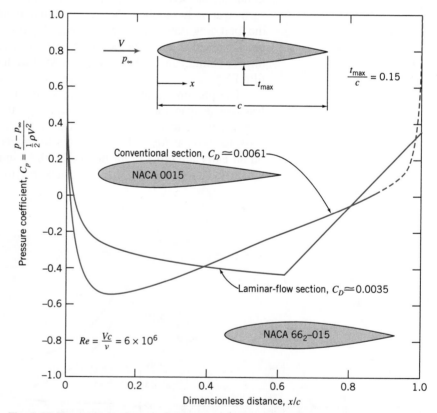

Fig. 9.15 Theoretical pressure distributions at zero angle of attack for two symmetric airfoil sections of 15 percent thickness ratio. (Data from [21].)

[5] Note that drag coefficients for airfoils are based on the *planform* area. i.e., $C_D = F_D/\frac{1}{2}\rho V^2 A_p$, where A_p is the maximum projected wing area.

Fig. 9.16 Nearly optimum shape for low-drag strut [24].

drag coefficient based on frontal area is $C_{D_f} = C_D/0.15 = 0.0233$, or about 40 percent of the optimum for the shapes shown in Fig. 9.14.

Tests in special wind tunnels have shown that laminar flow can be maintained up to length Reynolds numbers as high as 30 million by appropriate profile shaping. Because they have favorable drag characteristics, laminar-flow airfoils are used in the design of most modern subsonic aircraft.

Recent advances have made possible development of low-drag shapes even better than the NACA 60-series shapes. Experiments [21] led to the development of a pressure distribution that prevented separation while maintaining the turbulent boundary layer in a condition that produces negligible skin friction. Improved methods for calculating body shapes that produced a desired pressure distribution [23, 24] led to development of nearly optimum shapes for thick struts with low drag. Figure 9.16 shows an example of the results.

Reduction of aerodynamic drag also is important for road vehicle applications. Interest in fuel economy has provided significant incentive to balance efficient aerodynamic performance with attractive design for automobiles. Drag reduction also has become important for buses and trucks.

Practical considerations limit the overall length of road vehicles. Fully streamlined tails are impractical for all but land-speed-record cars. Consequently, it is not possible to achieve results comparable to those for optimum airfoil shapes. However, it is possible to optimize both front and rear contours within given constraints on overall length [25–27].

Much attention has been focused on front contours. Studies on buses have shown that drag reductions up to 25 percent are possible with careful attention to front contour [27]. Thus it is possible to reduce the drag coefficient of a bus from about 0.65 to less than 0.5 with practical designs. Highway tractor-trailer rigs have higher drag coefficients—C_D values from 0.90 to 1.1 have been reported. Commercially available add-on devices offer improvements in drag of up to 15 percent, particularly for windy conditions where yaw angles are nonzero. The typical fuel saving is half the percentage by which aerodynamic drag is reduced.

Front contours and details are important for automobiles. A low nose and smoothly rounded contours are the primary features that promote low drag. Radii of "A-pillar" and windshield header, and blending of accessories to reduce parasite and interference drag have received increased attention. As a result, drag coefficients have been reduced from about 0.55 to 0.30 or less for recent production vehicles. Recent advances in computational methods have led to development of computer-generated optimum shapes. A number of designs have been proposed, with claims of C_D values below 0.2 for vehicles complete with running gear.

9-8   LIFT

For most objects in relative motion in a fluid, the most significant fluid force is the drag. However, there are some objects, such as airfoils, for which the lift is significant.[6] Lift is defined as the component of fluid force perpendicular to the fluid motion. For an airfoil, the *lift coefficient*, C_L, is defined as

$$C_L \equiv \frac{F_L}{\frac{1}{2}\,\rho V^2\, A_p} \qquad\qquad (9.38)$$

It is worth noting that the lift coefficient defined above and the drag coefficient (Eq. 9.30) are each defined as the ratio of an actual force (lift or drag) divided by the product of dynamic pressure and area. This denominator can be viewed as the force that would be generated if we imagined bringing to rest the fluid directly approaching the area (recall that the dynamic pressure is the difference between total and static pressures). This gives us a "feel" for the meaning of the coefficients: They indicate the ratio of the actual force to this (unrealistic but nevertheless intuitively meaningful) force. We note also that the coefficient definitions include V^2 in the denominator, so that F_L (or F_D) being proportional to V^2 corresponds to a constant C_L (or C_D), and that F_L (or F_D) increasing with V at a lower rate than quadratic corresponds to a decrease in C_L (or C_D) with V.

The lift and drag coefficients for an airfoil are functions of both Reynolds number and angle of attack; the angle of attack, α, is the angle between the airfoil chord and the free-stream velocity vector. The *chord* of an airfoil is the straight line joining the leading edge and the trailing edge. The wing section shape is obtained by combining a *mean line* and a thickness distribution (see [21] for details). When the airfoil has a symmetric section, the mean line and the chord line both are straight lines, and they coincide. An airfoil with a curved mean line is said to be *cambered*.

The area at right angles to the flow changes with angle of attack. Consequently, the planform area, A_p (the maximum projected area of the wing), is used to define lift and drag coefficients for an airfoil.

The phenomenon of aerodynamic lift is commonly explained by the velocity increase causing pressure to decrease (the Bernoulli effect) over the top surface of the airfoil and the velocity decrease (causing pressure to increase) along the bottom surface of the airfoil. The resulting pressure distributions are shown clearly in the video *Boundary Layer Control*. Because of the pressure differences relative to atmosphere, the upper surface of the airfoil may be called the *suction surface* and the lower surface the *pressure surface*.

As shown in Example 6.12, lift on a body can also be related to the circulation around the profile: In order for lift to be generated, there must be a net circulation around the profile. One may imagine the circulation to be caused by a vortex "bound" within the profile.

Advances continue in computational methods and computer hardware. However, most airfoil data available in the literature were obtained from wind tunnel tests. Reference 21 contains results from a large number of tests conducted by NACA (the National Advisory Committee for Aeronautics—the predecessor to NASA). Data for some representative NACA profile shapes are described in the next few paragraphs.

Lift and drag coefficient data for typical conventional and laminar-flow profiles are plotted in Fig. 9.17 for a Reynolds number of 9×10^6 based on chord length. The section shapes in Fig. 9.17 are designated as follows:

---

[6]Flow over an airfoil is shown in the NCFMF video *Boundary Layer Control*. (see http://web.mit.edu/fluids/www/Shapiro/ncfmf.html for free online viewing of this film.)

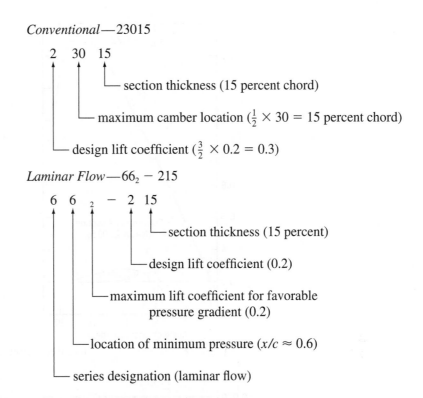

Conventional—23015

Laminar Flow—66_2 − 215

Both sections are cambered to give lift at zero angle of attack. As the angle of attack is increased, the Δp between the upper and lower surfaces increases, causing the lift coefficient to increase smoothly until a maximum is reached. Further increases in angle of attack produce a sudden decrease in C_L. The airfoil is said to have *stalled* when C_L drops in this fashion.

Airfoil stall results when flow separation occurs over a major portion of the upper surface of the airfoil. As the angle of attack is increased, the stagnation point moves back along the lower surface of the airfoil, as shown schematically for the symmetric laminar-flow section in Fig. 9.18a. Flow on the upper surface then must accelerate sharply to round the nose of the airfoil.[7] The effect of angle of attack on the theoretical upper-surface pressure distribution is shown in Fig. 9.18b. The minimum pressure becomes lower, and its location moves forward on the upper surface. A severe adverse pressure gradient appears following the point of minimum pressure; finally, the adverse pressure gradient causes the flow to separate completely from the upper surface and the airfoil stalls (the uniform pressure in the turbulent wake will be approximately equal to the pressure just before separation, i.e., low).

Movement of the minimum pressure point and accentuation of the adverse pressure gradient are responsible for the sudden increase in C_D for the laminar-flow section, which is apparent in Fig. 9.17. The sudden rise in C_D is caused by early transition from laminar to turbulent boundary-layer flow on the upper surface. Aircraft with laminar-flow sections are designed to cruise in the low-drag region.

Because laminar-flow sections have very sharp leading edges, all of the effects we have described are exaggerated, and they stall at lower angles of attack than conventional sections, as shown in Fig. 9.17. The maximum possible lift coefficient, $C_{L_{max}}$, also is less for laminar-flow sections.

Plots of C_L versus C_D (called lift-drag polars) often are used to present airfoil data in compact form. A polar plot is given in Fig. 9.19 for the two sections we have

---

[7] Flow patterns and pressure distributions for airfoil sections are shown in the NCFMF video *Boundary Layer Control*. (See http://web.mit.edu/fluids/www/Shapiro/ncfmf.html for free online viewing of this film.)

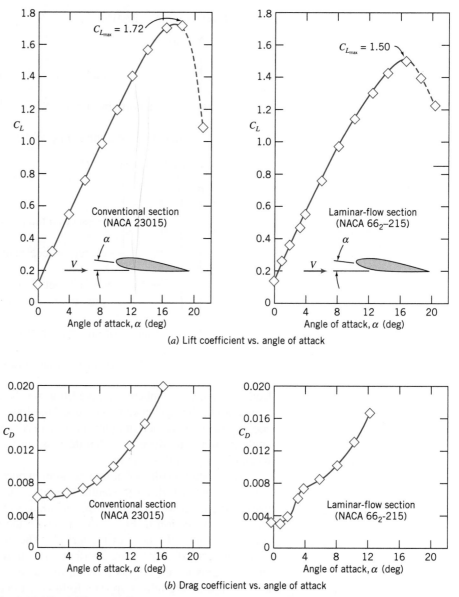

Fig. 9.17 Lift and drag coefficients versus angle of attack for two airfoil sections of 15 percent thickness ratio at $Re_c = 9 \times 10^6$. (Data from [21].)

discussed. The lift/drag ratio, C_L/C_D, is shown at the design lift coefficient for both sections. This ratio is very important in the design of aircraft: The lift coefficient determines the lift of the wing and hence the load that can be carried, and the drag coefficient indicates a large part (in addition to that caused by the fuselage, etc.) of the drag the airplane engines have to work against in order to generate the needed lift; hence, in general, a high C_L/C_D is the goal, at which the laminar airfoil clearly excels.

Recent improvements in modeling and computational capabilities have made it possible to design airfoil sections that develop high lift while maintaining very low drag [23, 24]. Boundary-layer calculation codes are used with inverse methods for calculating potential flow to develop pressure distributions and the resulting body shapes that postpone transition to the most rearward location possible. The turbulent boundary layer following transition is maintained in a state of incipient separation with nearly zero skin friction by appropriate shaping of the pressure distribution.

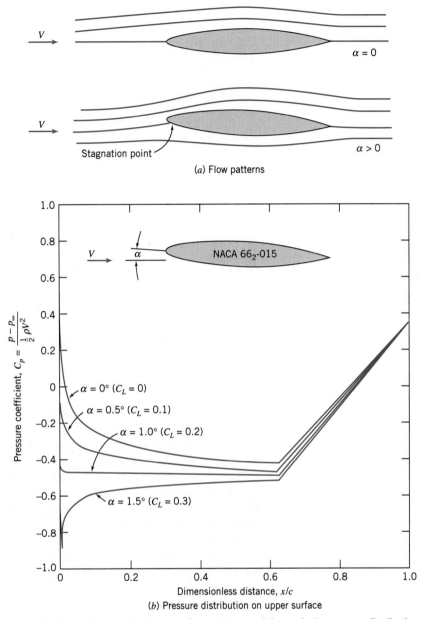

Fig. 9.18 Effect of angle of attack on flow pattern and theoretical pressure distribution for a symmetric laminar-flow airfoil of 15 percent thickness ratio. (Data from [21].)

Such computer-designed airfoils have been used on racing cars to develop very high negative lift (downforce) to improve high-speed stability and cornering performance [23]. Airfoil sections especially designed for operation at low Reynolds number were used for the wings and propeller on the Kremer prize-winning man-powered "Gossamer Condor" [28], which now hangs in the National Air and Space Museum in Washington, D.C.

All real airfoils—*wings*—are of finite span and have less lift and more drag than their airfoil section data would indicate. There are several ways to explain this. If we consider the pressure distribution near the end of the wing, the low pressure on the upper and high pressure on the lower surface cause flow to occur around the wing tip, leading to *trailing vortices* (as shown in Fig. 9.20), and the pressure difference is reduced, leading to less lift. These trailing vortices can also be explained more abstractly, in terms of circulation: We learned in Section 6-6 that circulation around a

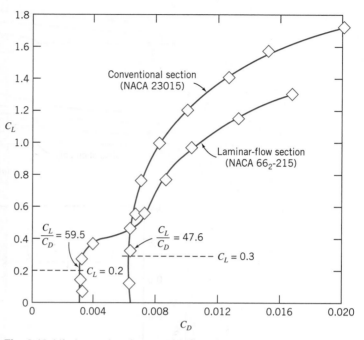

Fig. 9.19 Lift-drag polars for two airfoil sections of 15 percent thickness ratio. (Data from [21].)

wing section is present whenever we have lift, and that the circulation is solenoidal—that is, it cannot end in the fluid; hence, the circulation extends beyond the wing in the form of trailing vortices. Trailing vortices can be very strong and persistent, possibly being a hazard to other aircraft for 5 to 10 miles behind a large airplane—air speeds of greater than 200 mph have been measured.[8]

Trailing vortices reduce lift because of the loss of pressure difference, as we just mentioned. This reduction and an increase in drag (called *induced drag*) can also be explained in the following way: The "downwash" velocities induced by the vortices mean that the effective angle of attack is reduced—the wing "sees" a flow at approximately the mean of the upstream and downstream directions—explaining why the wing has less lift than its section data would suggest. This also causes the lift

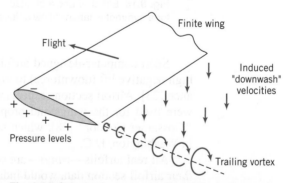

Fig. 9.20 Schematic representation of the trailing vortex system of a finite wing.

[8] Sforza, P. M., "Aircraft Vortices: Benign or Baleful?" *Space/Aeronautics, 53,* 4, April 1970, pp. 42–49. See also the University of Iowa video *Form Drag, Lift, and Propulsion.*

force (which is perpendicular to the effective angle of attack) to "lean backwards" a little, resulting in some of the lift appearing as drag.

Loss of lift and increase in drag caused by finite-span effects are concentrated near the tip of the wing; hence, it is clear that a short, stubby wing will experience these effects more severely than a very long wing. We should therefore expect the effects to correlate with the wing *aspect ratio*, defined as

$$AR \equiv \frac{b^2}{A_p} \tag{9.39}$$

where A_p is planform area and b is wingspan. For a rectangular planform of wingspan b and chord length c,

$$AR = \frac{b^2}{A_p} = \frac{b^2}{bc} = \frac{b}{c}$$

The maximum lift/drag ratio ($L/D = C_L/C_D$) for a modern low-drag section may be as high as 400 for infinite aspect ratio. A high-performance sailplane (glider) with $AR = 40$ might have $L/D = 40$, and a typical light plane ($AR \approx 12$) might have $L/D \approx 20$ or so. Two examples of rather poor shapes are lifting bodies used for reentry from the upper atmosphere, and water skis, which are *hydrofoils* of low aspect ratio. For both of these shapes, L/D typically is less than unity.

Variations in aspect ratio are seen in nature. Soaring birds, such as the albatross or California condor, have thin wings of long span. Birds that must maneuver quickly to catch their prey, such as owls, have wings of relatively short span, but large area, which gives low *wing loading* (ratio of weight to planform area) and thus high maneuverability.

It makes sense that as we try to generate more lift from a finite wing (by, for example, increasing the angle of attack), the trailing vortices and therefore the downwash increase; we also learned that the downwash causes the effective angle of attack to be less than that of the corresponding airfoil section (i.e., when $AR = \infty$), ultimately leading to loss of lift and to induced drag. Hence, we conclude that the effects of the finite aspect ratio can be characterized as a reduction $\Delta\alpha$ in the effective angle of attack, and that this (which is usually undesirable) becomes worse as we generate more lift (i.e., as the lift coefficient C_L increases) and as the aspect ratio AR is made smaller. Theory and experiment indicate that

$$\Delta\alpha \approx \frac{C_L}{\pi AR} \tag{9.40}$$

Compared with an airfoil section ($AR = \infty$), the geometric angle of attack of a wing (finite AR) must be increased by this amount to get the same lift, as shown in Fig. 9.21. It also means that instead of being perpendicular to the motion, the lift force leans angle $\Delta\alpha$ backwards from the perpendicular—we have an induced drag component of the drag coefficient. From simple geometry

$$\Delta C_D \approx C_L\Delta\alpha \approx \frac{C_L^2}{\pi AR} \tag{9.41}$$

This also is shown in Fig. 9.21.

When written in terms of aspect ratio, the drag of a wing of finite span becomes [21]

$$C_D = C_{D,\infty} + C_{D,i} = C_{D,\infty} + \frac{C_L^2}{\pi AR} \tag{9.42}$$

where $C_{D,\infty}$ is the section drag coefficient at C_L, $C_{D,i}$ is the induced drag coefficient at C_L, and AR is the aspect ratio of the finite-span wing.

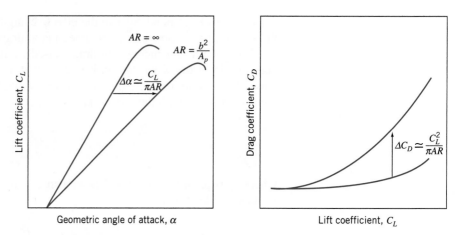

Fig. 9.21 Effect of finite aspect ratio on lift and drag coefficients for a wing.

Drag on airfoils arises from viscous and pressure forces. Viscous drag changes with Reynolds number but only slightly with angle of attack. These relationships and some commonly used terminology are illustrated in Fig. 9.22.

A useful approximation to the drag polar for a complete aircraft may be obtained by adding the induced drag to the drag at zero lift. The drag at any lift coefficient is obtained from

$$C_D = C_{D,0} + C_{D,i} = C_{D,0} + \frac{C_L^2}{\pi AR} \qquad (9.43)$$

where $C_{D,0}$ is the drag coefficient at zero lift and AR is the aspect ratio.

It is possible to increase the *effective* aspect ratio for a wing of given geometric ratio by adding an *endplate* or *winglet* to the wing tip. An endplate may be a simple plate attached at the tip, perpendicular to the wing span, as on the rear-mounted wing of a racing car (see Fig. 9.26). An endplate functions by blocking the flow that tends to migrate from the high-pressure region below the wing tip to the low-pressure region above the tip when the wing is producing lift. When the endplate is added, the strength of the trailing vortex and the induced drag are reduced.

Winglets are short, aerodynamically contoured wings set perpendicular to the wing at the tip. Like the endplate, the winglet reduces the strength of the trailing vortex system and the induced drag. The winglet also produces a small component of force in the flight direction, which has the effect of further reducing the overall drag of the aircraft. The contour and angle of attack of the winglet are adjusted based on wind tunnel tests to provide optimum results.

As we have seen, aircraft can be fitted with low-drag airfoils to give excellent performance at cruise conditions. However, since the maximum lift coefficient is low

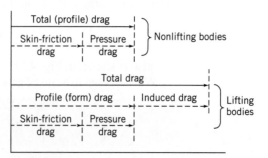

Fig. 9.22 Drag breakdown on nonlifting and lifting bodies.

for thin airfoils, additional effort must be expended to obtain acceptably low landing speeds. In steady-state flight conditions, lift must equal aircraft weight. Thus,

$$W = F_L = C_L \tfrac{1}{2} \rho V^2 A$$

Minimum flight speed is therefore obtained when $C_L = C_{L_{max}}$. Solving for V_{min},

$$V_{min} = \sqrt{\frac{2W}{\rho C_{L_{max}} A}} \tag{9.44}$$

According to Eq. 9.44, the minimum landing speed can be reduced by increasing either $C_{L_{max}}$ or wing area. Two basic techniques are available to control these variables: variable-geometry wing sections (e.g., obtained through the use of flaps) or boundary-layer control techniques.

Flaps are movable portions of a wing trailing edge that may be extended during landing and takeoff to increase effective wing area. The effects on lift and drag of two typical flap configurations are shown in Fig. 9.23, as applied to the NACA 23012 airfoil section. The maximum lift coefficient for this section is increased from 1.52 in the "clean" condition to 3.48 with double-slotted flaps. From Eq. 9.44, the corresponding reduction in landing speed would be 34 percent.

Figure 9.23 shows that section drag is increased substantially by high-lift devices. From Fig. 9.23b, section drag at $C_{L_{max}}$ ($C_D \approx 0.28$) with double-slotted flaps is about 5 times as high as section drag at $C_{L_{max}}$ ($C_D \approx 0.055$) for the clean airfoil. Induced drag due to lift must be added to section drag to obtain total drag. Because induced drag is proportional to C_L^2 (Eq. 9.41), total drag rises sharply at low aircraft speeds. At speeds near stall, drag may increase enough to exceed the thrust available from the engines. To avoid this dangerous region of unstable operation, the Federal Aviation Administration (FAA) limits operation of commercial aircraft to speeds above 1.2 times stall speed.

Although details are beyond the scope of this book, the basic purpose of all boundary-layer control techniques is to delay separation or reduce drag, by adding momentum to the boundary layer through blowing, or by removing low-momentum boundary-layer fluid by suction.[9] Many examples of practical boundary-layer control systems may be seen on commercial transport aircraft at your local airport. Two typical systems are shown in Fig. 9.24.

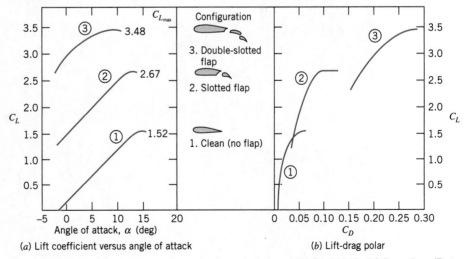

(a) Lift coefficient versus angle of attack   (b) Lift-drag polar

Fig. 9.23 Effect of flaps on aerodynamic characteristics of NACA 23012 airfoil section. (Data from [21].)

[9] See the excellent NCFMF video *Boundary Layer Control* for a review of these techniques. (See http://web.mit.edu/fluids/www/Shapiro/ncfmf.html for free online viewing of this film.)

Fig. 9.24 (a) Application of high-lift boundary-layer control devices to reduce landing speed of a jet transport aircraft. The wing of the Boeing 777 is highly mechanized. In the landing configuration, large slotted trailing-edge flaps roll out from under the wing and deflect downward to increase wing area and camber, thus increasing the lift coefficient. Slats at the leading edge of the wing move forward and down, to increase the effective radius of the leading edge and prevent flow separation, and to open a slot that helps keep air flow attached to the wing's upper surface. After touchdown, spoilers (not shown in use) are raised in front of each flap to decrease lift and ensure that the plane remains on the ground, despite use of the lift-augmenting devices. (This photograph was taken during a flight test. Flow cones are attached to the flaps and ailerons to identify regions of separated flow on these surfaces.) (Photograph courtesy of Boeing Airplane Company.)

Fig. 9.24 (b) Application of high-lift boundary-layer control devices to reduce takeoff speed of a jet transport aircraft. This is another view of the Boeing 777 wing. In the takeoff configuration, large slotted trailing-edge flaps deflect to increase the lift coefficient. The low-speed aileron near the wing-tip also deflects to improve span loading during takeoff. This view also shows the single-slotted outboard flap, the high-speed aileron, and nearest the fuselage, the double-slotted inboard flap. (Photograph courtesy of Boeing Airplane Company.)

EXAMPLE 9.8 Optimum Cruise Performance of a Jet Transport

Jet engines burn fuel at a rate proportional to thrust delivered. The optimum cruise condition for a jet aircraft is at maximum speed for a given thrust. In steady level flight, thrust and drag are equal. Hence, optimum cruise occurs at the speed when the ratio of drag force to air speed is minimized.

A Boeing 727-200 jet transport has wing planform area $A_p = 1600$ ft^2, and aspect ratio $AR = 6.5$. Stall speed at sea level for this aircraft with flaps up and a gross weight of 150,000 lbf is 175 mph. Below $M = 0.6$, drag due to compressibility effects is negligible, so Eq. 9.43 may be used to estimate total drag on the aircraft. $C_{D,0}$ for the aircraft is constant at 0.0182. Assume sonic speed at sea level is $c = 759$ mph.

Evaluate the performance envelope for this aircraft at sea level by plotting drag force versus speed, between stall and $M = 0.6$. Use this graph to estimate optimum cruise speed for the aircraft at sea-level conditions. Comment on stall speed and optimum cruise speed for the aircraft at 30,000 ft altitude on a standard day.

GIVEN: Boeing 727-200 jet transport at sea-level conditions.

$$W = 150,000 \text{ lbf}, \quad A = 1600 \text{ ft}^2, \quad AR = 6.5, \text{ and } C_{D,0} = 0.182$$

Stall speed is $V_{stall} = 175$ mph, and compressibility effects on drag are negligible for $M \leq 0.6$ (sonic speed at sea level is $c = 759$ mph).

FIND: (a) Drag force as a function of speed from V_{stall} to $M = 0.6$; plot results.
(b) Estimate of optimum cruise speed at sea level.
(c) Stall speed and optimum cruise speed at 30,000 ft altitude.

SOLUTION:
For steady, level flight, weight equals lift and thrust equals drag.

Governing equations:
$$F_L = C_L A \tfrac{1}{2} \rho V^2 = W \qquad C_D = C_{D,0} + \frac{C_L^2}{\pi AR}$$

$$F_D = C_D A \tfrac{1}{2} \rho V^2 = T \qquad M = \frac{V}{c}$$

At sea level, $\rho = 0.00238$ slug/ft^3, and $c = 759$ mph.

Since $F_L = W$ for level flight at any speed, then

$$C_L = \frac{W}{\frac{1}{2}\rho V^2 A} = \frac{2W}{\rho V^2 A}$$

At stall speed, $V = 175$ mph, so

$$C_L = 2 \times \frac{150,000 \text{ lbf}}{} \times \frac{\text{ft}^3}{0.00238 \text{ slug}} \left[\frac{\text{hr}}{V \text{ mi}} \times \frac{\text{mi}}{5280 \text{ ft}} \times 3600 \frac{\text{s}}{\text{hr}} \right]^2 \frac{1}{1600 \text{ ft}^2} \times \frac{\text{slug} \cdot \text{ft}}{\text{lbf} \cdot \text{s}^2}$$

$$C_L = \frac{3.65 \times 10^4}{[V(\text{mph})]^2} = \frac{3.65 \times 10^4}{(175)^2} = 1.196, \text{ and}$$

$$C_D = C_{D,0} + \frac{C_L^2}{\pi AR} = 0.0182 + \frac{(1.196)^2}{\pi(6.5)} = 0.0882$$

Then

$$F_D = W \frac{C_D}{C_L} = 150,000 \text{ lbf} \left(\frac{0.0882}{1.19} \right) = 11,100 \text{ lbf}$$

At $M = 0.6$, $V = Mc = (0.6)759$ mph $= 455$ mph, so $C_L = 0.177$ and

$$C_D = 0.0182 + \frac{(0.177)^2}{\pi(6.5)} = 0.0197$$

so

$$F_D = 150,000 \text{ lbf} \left(\frac{0.0197}{0.177} \right) = 16,700 \text{ lbf}$$

Similar calculations lead to the following table (computed using *Excel*):

V (mph)	175	200	300	400	455
C_L	1.196	0.916	0.407	0.229	0.177
C_D	0.0882	0.0593	0.0263	0.0208	0.0197
F_D (lbf)	11,100	9,710	9,700	13,600	16,700

These data may be plotted as:

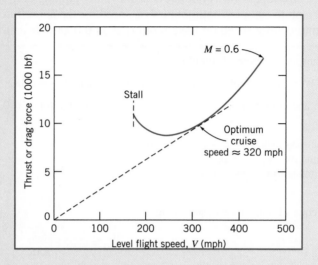

From the plot, the optimum cruise speed at sea level is estimated as 320 mph (and using *Excel* we obtain 323 mph).

At 30,000 ft (9,140 m) altitude, the density is only about 0.375 times sea level density, from Table A.3. The speeds for corresponding forces are calculated from

$$F_L = C_L A \tfrac{1}{2}\rho V^2 \quad \text{or} \quad V = \sqrt{\frac{2F_L}{C_L \rho A}} \quad \text{or} \quad \frac{V_{30}}{V_{SL}} = \sqrt{\frac{\rho_{SL}}{\rho_{30}}} = \sqrt{\frac{1}{0.375}} = 1.63$$

Thus, speeds increase 63 percent at 30,000 ft altitude:
$$V_{\text{stall}} \approx 285 \text{ mph}$$
$$V_{\text{cruise}} \approx 522 \text{ mph}$$

This problem illustrates that high-altitude flight increases the optimum cruising speed—in general this speed depends on aircraft configuration, gross weight, segment length, and winds aloft.

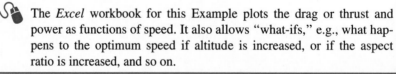 The *Excel* workbook for this Example plots the drag or thrust and power as functions of speed. It also allows "what-ifs," e.g., what happens to the optimum speed if altitude is increased, or if the aspect ratio is increased, and so on.

Aerodynamic lift is an important consideration in the design of high-speed land vehicles such as racing cars and land-speed-record machines. A road vehicle generates lift by virtue of its shape [29]. A representative centerline pressure distribution measured in the wind tunnel for an automobile is shown in Fig. 9.25 [30].

The pressure is low around the nose because of streamline curvature as the flow rounds the nose. The pressure reaches a maximum at the base of the windshield, again as a result of streamline curvature. Low-pressure regions also occur at the

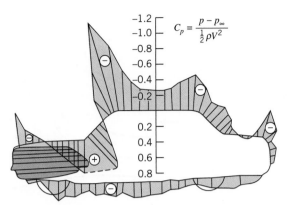

$$C_p = \frac{p - p_\infty}{\frac{1}{2}\rho V^2}$$

Fig. 9.25 Pressure distribution along the centerline of an automobile [30].

windshield header and over the top of the automobile. The air speed across the top is approximately 30 percent higher than the free-stream air speed. The same effect occurs around the "A-pillars" at the windshield edges. The drag increase caused by an added object, such as an antenna, spotlight, or mirror at that location, thus would be $(1.3)^2 \approx 1.7$ times the drag the object would experience in an undisturbed flow field. Thus the *parasite drag* of an added component can be much higher than would be predicted from its drag calculated for free flow.

At high speeds, aerodynamic lift forces can unload tires, causing serious reductions in steering control and reducing stability to a dangerous extent. Lift forces on early racing cars were counteracted somewhat by "spoilers," at considerable penalty in drag. In 1965 Jim Hall introduced the use of movable inverted airfoils on his Chaparral sports cars to develop aerodynamic downforce and provide aerodynamic braking [31]. Since then the developments in application of aerodynamic devices have been rapid. Aerodynamic design is used to reduce lift on all modern racing cars, as exemplified in Fig. 9.26. Liebeck airfoils [23] are used frequently for high-speed automobiles. Their high lift coefficients and relatively low drag allow downforce equal to or greater than the car weight to be developed at racing speeds. "Ground effect" cars use venturi-shaped ducts under the car and side skirts to seal leakage flows. The net result of these aerodynamic effects is that the downward force (which

Fig. 9.26 Contemporary racing car (Schumacher's Formula 1 Ferrari) showing aerodynamic features. The car's front and rear wings are designed to provide significant downforce at speed to improve traction. Also visible are fairings to direct hot air from the radiators around the rear tires, and at the front of the car, cool air toward the brakes. Not shown are other aerodynamic features such as the fuselage bottom, which is designed to route the airflow carefully, using diffusers, to develop the most negative pressure, and to cause this negative pressure to act over the largest possible area under the car, to develop additional downforce. (Photograph © Wayne P. Johnson)

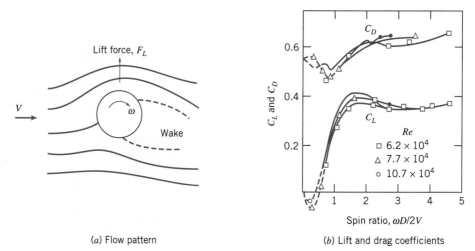

(a) Flow pattern   (b) Lift and drag coefficients

Fig. 9.27 Flow pattern, lift, and drag coefficients for a smooth spinning sphere in uniform flow. (Data from [19].)

increases with speed) generates excellent traction without adding significant weight to the vehicle, allowing faster speeds through curves and leading to lower lap times.

Another method of boundary-layer control is use of moving surfaces to reduce skin friction effects on the boundary layer [32]. This method is hard to apply to practical devices, because of geometric and weight complications, but it is very important in recreation. Most golfers, tennis players, soccer players, and baseball pitchers can attest to this! Tennis and soccer players use spin to control the trajectory and bounce of a shot. In golf, a drive can leave the tee at 275 ft/s or more, with backspin of 9000 rpm! Spin provides significant aerodynamic lift that substantially increases the carry of a drive. Spin is also largely responsible for hooking and slicing when shots are not hit squarely. The baseball pitcher uses spin to throw a curve ball.

Flow about a spinning sphere is shown in Fig. 9.27a. Spin alters the pressure distribution and also affects the location of boundary-layer separation. Separation is delayed on the upper surface of the sphere in Fig. 9.27a, and it occurs earlier on the lower surface. Thus pressure (because of the Bernoulli effect) is reduced on the upper surface and increased on the lower surface; the wake is deflected downward as shown. Pressure forces cause a lift in the direction shown; spin in the opposite direction would produce negative lift—a downward force. The force is directed perpendicular to both V and the spin axis.

Lift and drag data for spinning smooth spheres are presented in Fig. 9.27b. The most important parameter is the *spin ratio*, $\omega D/2V$, the ratio of surface speed to free-stream flow speed; Reynolds number plays a secondary role. At low spin ratio, lift is negative in terms of the directions shown in Fig. 9.27a. Only above $\omega D/2V \approx 0.5$ does lift become positive and continue to increase as spin ratio increases. Lift coefficient levels out at about 0.35. Spin has little effect on sphere drag coefficient, which varies from about 0.5 to about 0.65 over the range of spin ratio shown.

Earlier we mentioned the effect of dimples on the drag of a golf ball. Experimental data for lift and drag coefficients for spinning golf balls are presented in Fig. 9.28 for subcritical Reynolds numbers between 126,000 and 238,000. Again the independent variable is spin ratio; a much smaller range of spin ratio, typical of golf balls, is presented in Fig. 9.28.

A clear trend is evident: The lift coefficient increases consistently with spin ratio for both hexagonal and "conventional" (round) dimples. The lift coefficient on a golf ball with hexagonal dimples is significantly—as much as 15 percent—higher than on a ball with round dimples. The advantage for hexagonal dimples continues to the

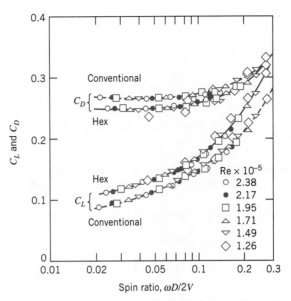

Fig. 9.28 Comparison of conventional and hex-dimpled golf balls [33].

largest spin ratios that were measured. The drag coefficient for a ball with hexagonal dimples is consistently 5 to 7 percent lower than the drag coefficient for a ball with round dimples at low spin ratios, but the difference becomes less pronounced as spin ratio increases.

The combination of higher lift and lower drag increases the carry of a golf shot. A recent design—the Callaway HX—has improved performance further by using a "tubular lattice network" using ridges of hexagons and pentagons (at a precise height of 0.0083 in.) instead of dimples, so that there are no flat spots at all on the surface [34]. Callaway claims the HX flies farther than any ball they ever tested.

EXAMPLE 9.9   Lift of a Spinning Ball

A smooth tennis ball, with 57 g mass and 64 mm diameter, is hit at 25 m/s with topspin of 7500 rpm. Calculate the aerodynamic lift acting on the ball. Evaluate the radius of curvature of its path at maximum elevation in a vertical plane. Compare with the radius for no spin.

GIVEN: Tennis ball in flight, with $m = 57$ g and $D = 64$ mm, hit with $V = 25$ m/s and topspin of 7500 rpm.

FIND: (a) Aerodynamic lift acting on ball.
(b) Radius of curvature of path in vertical plane.
(c) Comparison with radius for no spin.

SOLUTION:
Assume ball is smooth.
Use data from Fig. 9.27 to find lift: $C_L = f\left(\dfrac{\omega D}{2V}, Re_D\right)$.

From given data (for standard air, $\nu = 1.46 \times 10^{-5} \, \text{m}^2/\text{s}$),

$$\frac{\omega D}{2V} = \frac{1}{2} \times 7500 \, \frac{\text{rev}}{\text{min}} \times 0.064 \, \text{m} \times \frac{\text{s}}{25 \, \text{m}} \times \frac{2\pi \, \text{rad}}{\text{rev}} \times \frac{\text{min}}{60 \, \text{s}} = 1.01$$

$$Re_D = \frac{VD}{\nu} = 25 \, \frac{\text{m}}{\text{s}} \times 0.064 \, \text{m} \times \frac{\text{s}}{1.46 \times 10^{-5} \, \text{m}^2} = 1.10 \times 10^5$$

From Fig. 9.27, $C_L \approx 0.3$, so

$$F_L = C_L A \frac{1}{2} \rho V^2$$

$$= C_L \frac{\pi D^2}{4} \frac{1}{2} \rho V^2 = \frac{\pi}{8} C_L D^2 \rho V^2$$

$$F_L = \frac{\pi}{8} \times 0.3 \times (0.064)^2 \, \text{m}^2 \times 1.23 \, \frac{\text{kg}}{\text{m}^3} \times (25)^2 \, \frac{\text{m}^2}{\text{s}^2} \times \frac{\text{N} \cdot \text{s}^2}{\text{kg} \cdot \text{m}} = 0.371 \, \text{N} \qquad \longleftarrow \qquad F_L$$

Because the ball is hit with topspin, this force acts downward.

Use Newton's second law to evaluate the curvature of the path. In the vertical plane,

$$\sum F_z = -F_L - mg = ma_z = -m \frac{V^2}{R} \qquad \text{or} \qquad R = \frac{V^2}{g + F_L/m}$$

$$R = (25)^2 \, \frac{\text{m}^2}{\text{s}^2} \left[\cfrac{1}{9.81 \, \dfrac{\text{m}}{\text{s}^2} + 0.371 \, \text{N} \times \dfrac{1}{0.057 \, \text{kg}} \times \dfrac{\text{kg} \cdot \text{m}}{\text{N} \cdot \text{s}^2}} \right]$$

$$R = 38.3 \, \text{m (with spin)} \qquad \longleftarrow \qquad R$$

$$R = (25)^2 \, \frac{\text{m}^2}{\text{s}^2} \times \frac{\text{s}^2}{9.81 \, \text{m}} = 63.7 \, \text{m (without spin)} \qquad \longleftarrow \qquad R$$

Thus topspin has a significant effect on trajectory of the shot!

It has long been known that a spinning projectile in flight is affected by a force perpendicular to the direction of motion and to the spin axis. This effect, known as the *Magnus effect*, is responsible for the systematic drift of artillery shells.

Cross flow about a rotating circular cylinder is qualitatively similar to flow about the spinning sphere shown schematically in Fig. 9.27*a*. If the velocity of the upper surface of a cylinder is in the same direction as the free-stream velocity, separation is

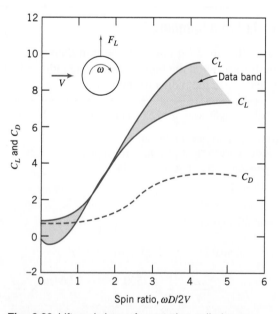

Fig. 9.29 Lift and drag of a rotating cylinder as a function of relative rotational speed; Magnus force. (Data from [35].)

delayed on the upper surface; it occurs earlier on the lower surface. Thus the wake is deflected and the pressure distribution on the cylinder surface is altered when rotation is present. Pressure is reduced on the upper surface and increased on the lower surface, causing a net lift force acting upward. Spin in the opposite direction reverses these effects and causes a downward lift force.

Lift and drag coefficients for the rotating cylinder are based on projected area, *LD*. Experimentally measured lift and drag coefficients for subcritical Reynolds numbers between 40,000 and 660,000 are shown as functions of spin ratio in Fig. 9.29. When surface speed exceeds flow speed, the lift coefficient increases to surprisingly high values, while in two-dimensional flow, drag is affected only moderately. Induced drag, which must be considered for finite cylinders, can be reduced by using end disks larger in diameter than the body of the cylinder.

The power required to rotate a cylinder may be estimated from the skin friction drag of the cylinder surface. Hoerner [35] suggests basing the skin friction drag estimate on the tangential surface speed and surface area. Goldstein [19] suggests that the power required to spin the cylinder, when expressed as an equivalent drag coefficient, may represent 20 percent or more of the aerodynamic C_D of a stationary cylinder.

9-9   SUMMARY AND USEFUL EQUATIONS

In this chapter we have:

✓ Defined and discussed various terms commonly used in aerodynamics, such as: boundary-layer disturbance, displacement and momentum thicknesses; flow separation; streamlining; skin friction and pressure drag and drag coefficient; lift and lift coefficient; wing chord, span and aspect ratio; and induced drag.

  ✓ Derived expressions for the boundary-layer thickness on a flat plate (zero pressure gradient) using exact* and approximate methods (using the momentum integral equation).

  ✓ Learned how to estimate the lift and drag from published data for a variety of objects.

While investigating the above phenomena, we developed insight into some of the basic concepts of aerodynamic design, such as how to minimize drag, how to determine the optimum cruising speed of an airplane, and so on.

Note: Most of the Useful Equations in the table below have a number of constraints or limitations—*be sure to refer to their page numbers for details!*

Useful Equations		
Definition of displacement thickness:	$\delta^* = \int_0^\infty \left(1 - \frac{u}{U}\right) dy \approx \int_0^\delta \left(1 - \frac{u}{U}\right) dy$ (9.1)	Page 393
Definition of momentum thickness:	$\theta = \int_0^\infty \frac{u}{U}\left(1 - \frac{u}{U}\right) dy \approx \int_0^\delta \frac{u}{U}\left(1 - \frac{u}{U}\right) dy$ (9.2)	Page 393
Boundary-layer thickness (laminar, exact—Blasius):	$\delta \approx \dfrac{5.0}{\sqrt{U/\nu x}} = \dfrac{5.0x}{\sqrt{Re_x}}$ (9.13)	Page W-20
Wall stress (laminar, exact—Blasius):	$\tau_w = 0.332U\sqrt{\rho\mu U/x} = \dfrac{0.332\rho U^2}{\sqrt{Re_x}}$ (9.14)	Page W-21

---

* This topic applies to a section that may be omitted without loss of continuity in the text material.

Skin friction coefficient (laminar, exact—Blasius):	$$C_f = \frac{\tau_w}{\frac{1}{2}\rho U^2} = \frac{0.664}{\sqrt{Re_x}} \qquad (9.15)$$	Page W-21
Momentum integral equation:	$$\frac{\tau_w}{\rho} = \frac{d}{dx}(U^2\theta) + \delta^* U \frac{dU}{dx} \qquad (9.17)$$	Page 399
Boundary-layer thickness for flat plate (laminar, approximate—polynomial velocity profile):	$$\frac{\delta}{x} = \sqrt{\frac{30\mu}{\rho U x}} = \frac{5.48}{\sqrt{Re_x}} \qquad (9.21)$$	Page 402
Definition of skin friction coefficient:	$$C_f \equiv \frac{\tau_w}{\frac{1}{2}\rho U^2} \qquad (9.22)$$	Page 403
Skin friction coefficient for flat plate (laminar, approximate—polynomial velocity profile):	$$C_f = \frac{0.730}{\sqrt{Re_x}} \qquad (9.23)$$	Page 403
Boundary-layer thickness for flat plate (turbulent, approximate—$\frac{1}{7}$th power-law velocity profile):	$$\frac{\delta}{x} = 0.382 \left(\frac{v}{Ux}\right)^{1/5} = \frac{0.382}{Re_x^{1/5}} \qquad (9.26)$$	Page 406
Skin friction coefficient for flat plate (turbulent, approximate—$\frac{1}{7}$th power-law velocity profile):	$$C_f = \frac{\tau_w}{\frac{1}{2}\rho U^2} = \frac{0.0594}{Re_x^{1/5}} \qquad (9.27)$$	Page 406
Definition of drag coefficient:	$$C_D \equiv \frac{F_D}{\frac{1}{2}\rho V^2 A} \qquad (9.30)$$	Page 412
Drag coefficient for flat plate (entirely laminar, based on Blasius solution):	$$C_D = \frac{1.33}{\sqrt{Re_L}} \qquad (9.33)$$	Page 413
Drag coefficient for flat plate (entirely turbulent, based on $\frac{1}{7}$th power-law velocity profile):	$$C_D = \frac{0.0742}{Re_L^{1/5}} \qquad (9.34)$$	Page 414
Drag coefficient for flat plate (empirical, $Re_L < 10^9$):	$$C_D = \frac{0.455}{(\log Re_L)^{2.58}} \qquad (9.35)$$	Page 414

Drag coefficient for flat plate (based on $\frac{1}{7}$th power-law velocity profile, $5 \times 10^5 \leq Re_L \leq 10^7$):	$$C_D = \frac{0.0742}{Re_L^{1/5}} - \frac{1740}{Re_L}$$ (9.37a)	Page 414
Drag coefficient for flat plate (empirical, $5 \times 10^5 < Re_L < 10^9$):	$$C_D = \frac{0.455}{(\log Re_L)^{2.58}} - \frac{1610}{Re_L}$$ (9.37b)	Page 414
Definition of lift coefficient:	$$C_L \equiv \frac{F_L}{\frac{1}{2}\,\rho V^2\, A_p}$$ (9.38)	Page 426
Definition of aspect ratio:	$$AR \equiv \frac{b^2}{A_p}$$ (9.39)	Page 431
Drag coefficient of a wing (finite span airfoil, using $C_{D,\infty}$):	$$C_D = C_{D,\infty} + C_{D,i} = C_{D,\infty} + \frac{C_L^2}{\pi\,AR}$$ (9.42)	Page 431
Drag coefficient of a wing (finite span airfoil, using $C_{D,0}$):	$$C_D = C_{D,0} + C_{D,i} = C_{D,0} + \frac{C_L^2}{\pi AR}$$ (9.43)	Page 432

REFERENCES

1. Prandtl, L., "Fluid Motion with Very Small Friction (in German)," *Proceedings of the Third International Congress on Mathematics*, Heidelberg, 1904; English translation available as NACA TM 452, March 1928.

2. Blasius, H., "The Boundary Layers in Fluids with Little Friction (in German)," *Zeitschrift für Mathematik und Physik, 56*, 1, 1908, pp. 1–37; English translation available as NACA TM 1256, February 1950.

3. Schlichting, H., *Boundary-Layer Theory*, 7th ed. New York: McGraw-Hill, 1979.

4. Stokes, G. G., "On the Effect of the Internal Friction of Fluids on the Motion of Pendulums," *Cambridge Philosophical Transactions, IX*, 8, 1851.

5. Howarth, L., "On the Solution of the Laminar Boundary-Layer Equations," *Proceedings of the Royal Society of London, A164*, 1938, pp. 547–579.

6. Hess, J. L., and A. M. O. Smith, "Calculation of Potential Flow about Arbitrary Bodies," in *Progress in Aeronautical Sciences*, Vol. 8, D. Kuchemann et al., eds. Elmsford, NY: Pergamon Press, 1966.

7. Kraus, W., "Panel Methods in Aerodynamics," in *Numerical Methods in Fluid Dynamics*, H. J. Wirz and J. J. Smolderen, eds. Washington, D.C.: Hemisphere, 1978.

8. Rosenhead, L., ed., *Laminar Boundary Layers*. London: Oxford University Press, 1963.

9. Rotta, J. C., "Turbulent Boundary Layers in Incompressible Flow," in *Progress in Aeronautical Sciences*, A. Ferri, et al., eds. New York: Pergamon Press, 1960, pp. 1–220.

10. Kline, S. J., et al., eds., *Proceedings, Computation of Turbulent Boundary Layers—1968 AFOSR-IFP-Stanford Conference*, Vol. I: Methods, Predictions, Evaluation, and Flow Structure, and Vol. II: Compiled Data. Stanford, CA: Thermosciences Division, Department of Mechanical Engineering, Stanford University, 1969.

11. Kline, S. J., et al., eds., *Proceedings, 1980–81 AFOSR-HTTM-Stanford Conference on Complex Turbulent Flows: Comparison of Computation and Experiment*, three volumes. Stanford, CA: Thermosciences Division, Department of Mechanical Engineering, Stanford University, 1982.

12. Cebeci, T., and P. Bradshaw, *Momentum Transfer in Boundary Layers*. Washington, D.C.: Hemisphere, 1977.

13. Bradshaw, P., T. Cebeci, and J. H. Whitelaw, *Engineering Calculation Methods for Turbulent Flow*. New York: Academic Press, 1981.

14. *Fluent*. Fluent Incorporated, Centerra Resources Park, 10 Cavendish Court, Lebanon, NH 03766 (www.fluent.com).

15. *STAR-CD*. Adapco, 60 Broadhollow Road, Melville, NY 11747 (www.cd-adapco.com).

16. Hoerner, S. F., *Fluid-Dynamic Drag*, 2nd ed. Midland Park, NJ: Published by the author, 1965.

17. Shapiro, A. H., *Shape and Flow, the Fluid Dynamics of Drag*. New York: Anchor, 1961 (paperback).

18. Fage, A., "Experiments on a Sphere at Critical Reynolds Numbers," Great Britain, *Aeronautical Research Council, Reports and Memoranda*, No. 1766, 1937.

19. Goldstein, S., ed., *Modern Deyelopments in Fluid Dynamics*, Vols. I and II. Oxford: Clarendon Press, 1938. (Reprinted in paperback by Dover, New York, 1967.)

20. Morel, T., and M. Bohn, "Flow over Two Circular Disks in Tandem," *Transactions of the ASME, Journal of Fluids Engineering, 102*, 1, March 1980, pp. 104–111.

21. Abbott, I. H., and A. E. von Doenhoff, *Theory of Wing Sections, Including a Summary of Airfoil Data*. New York: Dover, 1959 (paperback).

22. Stratford, B. S., "An Experimental Flow with Zero Skin Friction," *Journal of Fluid Mechanics, 5*, Pt. 1, January 1959, pp. 17–35.

23. Liebeck, R. H., "Design of Subsonic Airfoils for High Lift," *AIAA Journal of Aircraft, 15*, 9, September 1978, pp. 547–561.

24. Smith, A. M. O., "Aerodynamics of High-Lift Airfoil Systems," in *Fluid Dynamics of Aircraft Stalling*, AGARD CP-102, 1973, pp. 10–1 through 10–26.

25. Morel, T., "Effect of Base Slant on Flow in the Near Wake of an Axisymmetric Cylinder," *Aeronautical Quarterly, XXXI*, Pt. 2, May 1980, pp. 132–147.

26. Hucho, W. H., "The Aerodynamic Drag of Cars—Current Understanding, Unresolved Problems, and Future Prospects," in *Aerodynamic Drag Mechanisms of Bluff Bodies and Road Vehicles*, G. Sovran, T. Morel, and W. T. Mason, eds. New York: Plenum, 1978.

27. McDonald, A. T., and G. M. Palmer, "Aerodynamic Drag Reduction of Intercity Buses," *Transactions, Society of Automotive Engineers, 89*, Section 4, 1980, pp. 4469–4484 (SAE Paper No. 801404).

28. Grosser, M., *Gossamer Odyssey*. Boston: Houghton Mifflin, 1981.

29. Carr, G. W., "The Aerodynamics of Basic Shapes for Road Vehicles. Part 3: Streamlined Bodies," The Motor Industry Research Association, Warwickshire, England, Report No. 107/4, 1969.

30. Goetz, H., "The Influence of Wind Tunnel Tests on Body Design, Ventilation, and Surface Deposits of Sedans and Sports Cars," SAE Paper No. 710212, 1971.

31. Hall, J., "What's Jim Hall Really Like?" *Automobile Quarterly, VIII*, 3, Spring 1970, pp. 282–293.

32. Moktarian, F., and V. J. Modi, "Fluid Dynamics of Airfoils with Moving Surface Boundary-Layer Control," *AIAA Journal of Aircraft, 25*, 2, February 1988, pp. 163–169.

33. Mehta, R. D., "Aerodynamics of Sports Balls," in *Annual Review of Fluid Mechanics*, ed. by M. van Dyke, et al. Palo Alto, CA: Annual Reviews, 1985, *17*, pp. 151–189.

34. "The Year in Ideas," *New York Times Magazine*, December 9, 2001, pp. 58–60.

35. Hoerner, S. F., and H. V. Borst, *Fluid-Dynamic Lift*. Bricktown, NJ: Hoerner Fluid Dynamics, 1975.

36. Chow, C.-Y., *An Introduction to Computational Fluid Mechanics*. New York: Wiley, 1980.

37. Carr, G. W., "The Aerodynamics of Basic Shapes for Road Vehicles, Part 1: Simple Rectangular Bodies," The Motor Industry Research Association, Warwickshire, England, Report No. 1968/2, 1967.

PROBLEMS

9.1   A model of a river towboat is to be tested at 1:18 scale. The boat is designed to travel at 3.5 m/s in fresh water at 10°C. Estimate the distance from the bow where transition occurs. Where should transition be stimulated on the model towboat?

9.2   The roof of a minivan is approximated as a horizontal flat plate. Plot the length of the laminar boundary layer as a function of minivan speed, V, as the minivan accelerates from 10 mph to 90 mph.

9.3   The takeoff speed of a Boeing 757 is 260 km/hr. At approximately what distance will the boundary layer on the wings become turbulent? If it cruises at 850 km/hr at 10,000 m, at approximately what distance will the boundary layer on the wings now become turbulent?

9.4   For flow around a sphere the boundary layer becomes turbulent around $Re_D \approx 2.5 \times 10^5$. Find the speeds at which (a) an American golf ball ($D = 1.68$ in.), (b) a British golf ball ($D = 41.1$ mm), and (c) a soccer ball ($D = 8.75$ in.) develop turbulent boundary layers. Assume standard atmospheric conditions.

9.5   A student is to design an experiment involving dragging a sphere through a tank of fluid to illustrate (a) "creeping flow" ($Re_D < 1$) and (b) flow for which the boundary layer becomes turbulent ($Re_D \approx 2.5 \times 10^5$). She proposes to use a smooth sphere of diameter 1 cm in SAE 10 oil at room temperature. Is this realistic for both cases? If either case is unrealistic, select an alternative reasonable sphere diameter and common fluid for that case.

9.6 A 4 ft × 8 ft sheet of plywood is attached to the roof of your vehicle after being purchased at the hardware store. At what speed (mph) will the boundary layer first start becoming turbulent? At what speed is about 90% of the boundary layer turbulent?

9.7 The extent of the laminar boundary layer on the surface of an aircraft or missile varies with altitude. For a given speed, will the laminar boundary-layer length increase or decrease with altitude? Why? Plot the ratio of laminar boundary-layer length at altitude z, to boundary-layer length at sea level, as a function of z, up to altitude $z = 30$ km, for a standard atmosphere.

9.8 Plot on one graph the length of the laminar boundary layer on a flat plate, as a function of freestream velocity, for (a) water and standard air at (b) sea level and (c) 10 km altitude. Use log-log axes, and compute data for the boundary-layer length ranging from 0.01 m to 10 m.

9.9 The most general sinusoidal velocity profile for laminar boundary-layer flow on a flat plate is $u = A \sin(By) + C$. State three boundary conditions applicable to the laminar boundary-layer velocity profile. Evaluate constants A, B, and C.

9.10 Velocity profiles in laminar boundary layers often are approximated by the equations

Linear: $\dfrac{u}{U} = \dfrac{y}{\delta}$

Sinusoidal: $\dfrac{u}{U} = \sin\left(\dfrac{\pi}{2}\dfrac{y}{\delta}\right)$

Parabolic: $\dfrac{u}{U} = 2\left(\dfrac{y}{\delta}\right) - \left(\dfrac{y}{\delta}\right)^2$

Compare the shapes of these velocity profiles by plotting y/δ (on the ordinate) versus u/U (on the abscissa).

9.11 An approximation for the velocity profile in a laminar boundary layer is

$$\frac{u}{U} = \frac{3}{2}\frac{y}{\delta} - \frac{1}{2}\left(\frac{y}{\delta}\right)^3$$

Does this expression satisfy boundary conditions applicable to the laminar boundary-layer velocity profile? Evaluate δ^*/δ and θ/δ.

9.12 An approximation for the velocity profile in a laminar boundary layer is

$$\frac{u}{U} = 2\frac{y}{\delta} - 2\left(\frac{y}{\delta}\right)^3 + \left(\frac{y}{\delta}\right)^4$$

Does this expression satisfy boundary conditions applicable to the laminar boundary-layer velocity profile? Evaluate δ^*/δ and θ/δ.

9.13 A simplistic laminar boundary-layer model is

$$\frac{u}{U} = \sqrt{2}\frac{y}{\delta} \qquad 0 < y \le \frac{\delta}{2}$$

$$\frac{u}{U} = (2 - \sqrt{2})\frac{y}{\delta} + (\sqrt{2} - 1) \qquad \frac{\delta}{2} < y \le \delta$$

Does this expression satisfy boundary conditions applicable to the laminar boundary-layer velocity profile? Evaluate δ^*/δ and θ/δ.

9.14 The velocity profile in a turbulent boundary layer often is approximated by the $\frac{1}{7}$-power-law equation

$$\frac{u}{U} = \left(\frac{y}{\delta}\right)^{1/7}$$

Compare the shape of this profile with the parabolic laminar boundary-layer velocity profile (Problem 9.10) by plotting y/δ (on the ordinate) versus u/U (on the abscissa) for both profiles.

9.15 Evaluate θ/δ for each of the laminar boundary-layer velocity profiles given in Problem 9.10.

9.16 Evaluate δ^*/δ for each of the laminar boundary-layer velocity profiles given in Problem 9.10.

9.17 Evaluate δ^*/δ and θ/δ for the turbulent $\frac{1}{7}$-power-law velocity profile given in Problem 9.14. Compare with ratios for the parabolic laminar boundary-layer velocity profile given in Problem 9.10.

9.18 A fluid, with density $\rho = 800$ kg/m³, flows at $U = 3$ m/s over a flat plate 3 m long and 1 m wide. At the trailing edge the boundary-layer thickness is $\delta = 25$ mm. Assume the velocity profile is linear, as shown, and that the flow is two-dimensional (flow conditions are independent of z). Using control volume *abcd*, shown by dashed lines, compute the mass flow rate across surface *ab*. Determine the drag force on the upper surface of the plate. Explain how this (viscous) drag can be computed from the given data even though we do not know the fluid viscosity (see Problem 9.41).

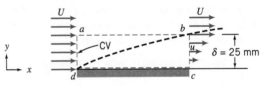

P9.18

9.19 The flat plate of Problem 9.18 is turned so that the 1 m side is parallel to the flow (the width becomes 3 m). Should we expect that the drag increases or decreases? Why? The trailing edge boundary-layer thickness is now $\delta = 14$ mm. Assume again that the velocity profile is [...] nsional (flow conditions ar[...] of Problem 9.18.

9.20 S[...] city profile at section *bc* g[...] Problem 9.10.

9.21 T[...] nnel is 1.5 meters long, pre[...] at the outlet. The tunnel cr[...] wind tunnel is to operate w[...] y of 50 m/s in the test secti[...] a wind tunnel is boundary[...] splacement thickness redu[...] (the test area, in which we[...] the uniform flow will be accelerated. If these effects are pronounced, we end up with a smaller useful test cross section with a velocity somewhat higher than anticipated. If the boundary-layer thickness is 10 mm at the entrance and 25 mm at the exit, and the boundary-layer velocity profile is given by $u/U = (y/\delta)^{1/7}$, estimate the displacement thickness at the end of the test section and the percent change in the uniform velocity between the inlet and outlet.

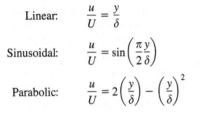

9.22 Laboratory wind tunnels have test sections 25 cm square and 50 cm long. With nominal air speed $U_1 = 25$ m/s at the test section inlet, turbulent boundary layers form on the top, bottom, and side walls of the tunnel. The boundary-layer thickness is $\delta_1 = 20$ mm at the inlet and $\delta_2 = 30$ mm at the outlet from the test section. The boundary-layer velocity profiles are of power-law form, with $u/U = (y/\delta)^{1/7}$. Evaluate the freestream velocity, U_2, at the exit from the wind-tunnel test section. Determine the change in static pressure along the test section.

9.23   Air flows in a horizontal cylindrical duct of diameter $D = 100$ mm. At a section a few meters from the entrance, the turbulent boundary layer is of thickness $\delta_1 = 5.25$ mm, and the velocity in the inviscid central core is $U_1 = 12.5$ m/s. Farther downstream the boundary layer is of thickness $\delta_2 = 24$ mm. The velocity profile in the boundary layer is approximated well by the $\frac{1}{7}$-power expression. Find the velocity, U_2, in the inviscid central core at the second section, and the pressure drop between the two sections.

9.24   The square test section of a small laboratory wind tunnel has sides of width $W = 12$ in. At one measurement location, the turbulent boundary layers on the tunnel walls are $\delta_1 = 0.4$ in. thick. The velocity profile is approximated well by the $\frac{1}{7}$-power expression. At this location the freestream air speed is $U_1 = 60$ ft/s, and the static pressure is $p_1 = -1$ in. H_2O (gage). At a second measurement location downstream, the boundary-layer thickness is $\delta_2 = 0.5$ in. Evaluate the air speed in the freestream at the second section. Calculate the difference in static pressure from section ① to section ②.

9.25   Air flows in the entrance region of a square duct, as shown. The velocity is uniform, $U_0 = 100$ ft/s, and the duct is 3 in. square. At a section 1 ft downstream from the entrance, the displacement thickness, δ^*, on each wall measures 0.035 in. Determine the pressure change between sections ① and ②.

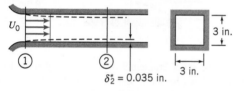

$\delta_2^* = 0.035$ in.

P9.25

9.26   Flow of air develops in a flat horizontal duct following a well-rounded entrance section. The duct height is $H = 300$ mm. Turbulent boundary layers grow on the duct walls, but the flow is not yet fully developed. Assume that the velocity profile in each boundary layer is $u/U = (y/\delta)^{1/7}$. The inlet flow is uniform at $\overline{V} = 10$ m/s at section ①. At section ②, the boundary-layer thickness on each wall of the channel is $\delta_2 = 100$ mm. Show that for this flow, $\delta^* = \delta/8$. Evaluate the static gage pressure at section ①. Find the average wall shear stress between the entrance and section ②, located at $L = 5$ m.

9.27   A laboratory wind tunnel has a square test section, with sides of width $W = 305$ mm and length $L = 610$ mm. When the freestream air speed at the test section entrance is $U_1 = 24.4$ m/s, the head loss from the atmosphere is 6.5 mm H_2O. Turbulent boundary layers form on the top, bottom, and side walls of the test section. Measurements show the boundary-layer thicknesses are $\delta_1 = 20.3$ mm at the entrance and $\delta_2 = 25.4$ mm at the outlet from the test section. The velocity profiles are of $\frac{1}{7}$-power form. Evaluate the freestream air speed at the outlet from the test section. Determine the static pressures at the test section inlet and outlet.

9.28   Flow of air develops in a horizontal cylindrical duct, of diameter $D = 400$ mm, following a well-rounded entrance. A turbulent boundary grows on the duct wall, but the flow is not yet fully developed. Assume that the velocity profile in the boundary layer is $u/U = (y/\delta)^{1/7}$. The inlet flow is at $\overline{V} = 15$ m/s at section ①. At section ②, the boundary-layer thickness is $\delta_2 = 100$ mm. Evaluate the static gage pressure at section ②, located at $L = 6$ m. Find the average wall shear stress.

9.29   Air flows into the inlet contraction section of a wind tunnel in an undergraduate laboratory. From the inlet the air enters the test section, which is square in cross-section with side dimensions of 305 mm. The test section is 609 mm long. At one operating condition air leaves the contraction at 50.2 m/s with negligible boundary-layer thickness. Measurements show that boundary layers at the downstream end of the test section are 20.3 mm thick. Evaluate the displacement thickness of the boundary layers at the downstream end of the wind tunnel test section. Calculate the change in static pressure along the wind tunnel test section. Estimate the approximate total drag force caused by skin friction on each wall of the wind tunnel.

*9.30   Using numerical results for the Blasius exact solution for laminar boundary-layer flow on a flat plate, plot the dimensionless velocity profile, u/U (on the abscissa), versus dimensionless distance from the surface, y/δ (on the ordinate). Compare with the approximate parabolic velocity profile of Problem 9.10.

*9.31   Using numerical results obtained by Blasius (Table 9.1), evaluate the distribution of shear stress in a laminar boundary layer on a flat plate. Plot τ/τ_w versus y/δ. Compare with results derived from the approximate sinusoidal velocity profile given in Problem 9.10.

*9.32   Using numerical results obtained by Blasius (Table 9.1), evaluate the distribution of shear stress in a laminar boundary layer on a flat plate. Plot τ/τ_w versus y/δ. Compare with results derived from the approximate parabolic velocity profile given in Problem 9.10.

*9.33   Using numerical results obtained by Blasius (Table 9.1), evaluate the vertical component of velocity in a laminar boundary layer on a flat plate. Plot v/U versus y/δ for $Re_x = 10^5$.

*9.34   Verify that the y component of velocity for the Blasius solution to the Prandtl boundary-layer equations is given by Eq. 9.10. Obtain an algebraic expression for the x component of the acceleration of a fluid particle in the laminar boundary layer. Plot a_x versus η to determine the maximum x component of acceleration at a given x.

9.35   Numerical results of the Blasius solution to the Prandtl boundary-layer equations are presented in Table 9.1. Consider steady, incompressible flow of standard air over a flat plate at freestream speed $U = 15$ ft/s. At $x = 7.5$ in., estimate the distance from the surface at which $u = 0.95\,U$. Evaluate the slope of the streamline through this point. Obtain an algebraic expression for the local skin friction, $\tau_w(x)$. Obtain an algebraic expression for the total skin friction drag force on the plate. Evaluate the momentum thickness at $L = 3$ ft.

*9.36   The Blasius exact solution involves solving a nonlinear equation, Eq. 9.11, with initial and boundary conditions given by Eq. 9.12. Set up an *Excel* workbook to obtain a numerical solution of this system. The workbook should consist of columns for η, f,

---

[5] Note that drag coefficients for airfoils are based on the *planform* area. i.e., $C_D = F_D/\frac{1}{2}\rho V^2 A_p$, where A_p is the maximum projected wing area.

f', and f''. The rows should consist of values of these, with a suitable step size for η (e.g., for 1000 rows the step size for η would be 0.01 to generate data through $\eta = 10$, to go a little beyond the data in Table 9.1). The values of f and f' for the first row are zero (from the initial conditions, Eq. 9.12); a guess value is needed for f'' (try 0.5). Subsequent row values for f, f', and f'' can be obtained from previous row values using Euler's finite difference method for approximating first derivatives (and Eq. 9.11). Finally, a solution can be found by using *Excel*'s *Goal Seek* or *Solver* functions to vary the initial value of f'' until f' = 1 for large η (e.g., $\eta = 10$, boundary condition of Eq. 9.12). Plot the results. Note: Because Euler's method is relatively crude, the results will agree with Blasius' only to within about 1%.

9.37 Consider flow of air over a flat plate. On one graph, plot the laminar boundary-layer thickness as a function of distance along the plate (up to transition) for freestream speeds $U = 1$ m/s, 2 m/s, 3 m/s, 4 m/s, 5 m/s, and 10 m/s.

*9.38 A thin flat plate, $L = 0.25$ m long and $b = 1$ m wide, is installed in a water tunnel as a splitter. The freestream speed is $U = 1.75$ m/s and the velocity profile in the boundary layer is approximated as parabolic. Plot δ, δ^*, and τ_w versus x/L for the plate.

9.39 Consider flow over the splitter plate of Problem 9.38. Show algebraically that the total drag force on one side of the splitter plate may be written $F_D = \rho U^2 \theta_L b$. Evaluate θ_L and the total drag for the given conditions.

9.40 A thin flat plate is installed in a water tunnel as a splitter. The plate is 0.3 m long and 1 m wide. The freestream speed is 1.6 m/s. Laminar boundary layers form on both sides of the plate. The boundary-layer velocity profile is approximated as parabolic. Determine the total viscous drag force on the plate assuming that pressure drag is negligible.

9.41 In Problems 9.18 and 9.19 the drag on the upper surface of a flat plate with flow (fluid density $\rho = 800$ kg/m^3) at freestream speed $U = 3$ m/s, was determined from momentum flux calculations. The drag was determined for the plate with its long edge (3 m) and its short edge (1 m) parallel to the flow. If the fluid viscosity $\mu = 0.02$ N · s/m^2, compute the drag using boundary-layer equations.

9.42 Assume laminar boundary-layer flow to estimate the drag on the plate shown when it is placed parallel to a 5-m/s air flow. The air is at 20°C and 1 atm.

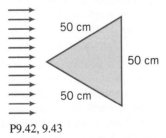

P9.42, 9.43

9.43 Assume laminar boundary-layer flow to estimate the drag on the plate shown when it is placed parallel to a 5-m/s air flow, except that the base rather than the tip faces the flow. Would you expect this to be larger than, the same as, or lower than the drag for Problem 9.42?

9.44 Assume laminar boundary-layer flow to estimate the drag on the plate shown when it is placed parallel to a 7.5-m/s air flow.

The air is at 20°C and 1 atm. (Note that the shape is given by $x = y^2/25$, where x and y are in cm.)

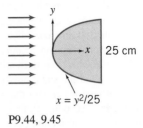

P9.44, 9.45

9.45 Assume laminar boundary-layer flow to estimate the drag on the plate shown when it is placed parallel to a 7.5-m/s air flow, except that the base rather than the tip faces the flow. Would you expect this to be larger than, the same as, or lower than the drag for Problem 9.44?

9.46 Assume laminar boundary-layer flow to estimate the drag on four square plates (each 7.5 cm × 7.5 cm) placed parallel to a 1-m/s water flow, for the two configurations shown. Before calculating, which configuration do you expect to experience the lowest drag? Assume the plates attached with string are far enough apart for wake effects to be negligible, and that the water is at 20°C.

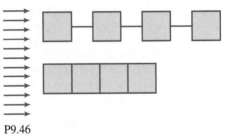

P9.46

9.47 A horizontal surface, with length $L = 1.8$ m and width $b = 0.9$ m, is immersed in a stream of standard air flowing at $U = 3.2$ m/s. Assume a laminar boundary layer forms and approximate the velocity profile as sinusoidal. Plot δ, δ^*, and τ_w versus x/L for the plate.

9.48 The velocity profile in a laminar boundary-layer flow at zero pressure gradient is approximated by the linear expression given in Problem 9.10. Use the momentum integral equation with this profile to obtain expressions for δ/x and C_f.

9.49 A horizontal surface, with length $L = 0.8$ m and width $b = 1.9$ m, is immersed in a stream of standard air flowing at $U = 5.3$ m/s. Assume a laminar boundary layer forms and approximate the velocity profile as linear. Plot δ, δ^*, and τ_w versus x/L for the plate.

9.50 For the flow conditions of Problem 9.49, develop an algebraic expression for the variation of wall shear stress with distance along the surface. Integrate to obtain an algebraic expression for the total skin-friction drag on the surface. Evaluate the drag for the given conditions.

9.51 Water at 10°C flows over a flat plate at a speed of 0.8 m/s. The plate is 0.35 m long and 1 m wide. The boundary layer on each surface of the plate is laminar. Assume that the velocity profile may be approximated as linear. Determine the drag force on the plate.

9.52 Standard air flows from the atmosphere into the wide, flat channel shown. Laminar boundary layers form on the top and bottom walls of the channel (ignore boundary-layer effects on the side walls). Assume the boundary layers behave as on a flat plate, with linear velocity profiles. At any axial distance from the inlet, the static pressure is uniform across the channel. Assume uniform flow at section ①. Indicate where the Bernoulli equation can be applied in this flow field. Find the static pressure (gage) and the displacement thickness at section ②. Plot the stagnation pressure (gage) across the channel at section ②, and explain the result. Find the static pressure (gage) at section ① and compare to the static pressure (gage) at section ②.

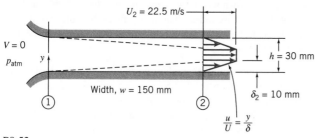

P9.52

9.53 Consider flow of air over a flat plate of length 5 m. On one graph, plot the boundary-layer thickness as a function of distance along the plate for free-stream speed $U = 10$ m/s assuming (a) a completely laminar boundary layer, (b) a completely turbulent boundary layer, and (c) a laminar boundary layer that becomes turbulent at $Re_x = 5 \times 10^5$. Use *Excel's Goal Seek* or *Solver* to find the speeds U for which transition occurs at the trailing edge, and at $x = 4$ m, 3 m, 2 m, and 1 m.

*9.54 A developing boundary layer of standard air on a flat plate is shown in Fig. P9.18. The free-stream flow outside the boundary layer is undisturbed with $U = 165$ ft/s. The plate is 10 ft wide perpendicular to the diagram. Assume flow in the boundary layer is turbulent, with a $\frac{1}{7}$-power velocity profile, and that $\delta = 0.75$ in. at surface *bc*. Calculate the mass flow rate across surface *ad* and the mass flux across surface *ab*. Evaluate the *x* momentum flux across surface *bc*. Determine the drag force exerted on the flat plate between *d* and *c*. Estimate the distance from the leading edge at which transition from laminar to turbulent flow may be expected.

9.55 For the flow conditions of Example 9.4, develop an algebraic expression for the variation of wall shear stress with distance along the surface. Integrate to obtain an algebraic expression for the total skin friction drag on the surface. Evaluate the drag for the given conditions.

9.56 Assume the flow conditions given in Example 9.4. Plot δ, δ^*, and τ_w versus x/L for the plate.

9.57 Repeat Problem 9.42, except that the air flow is now at 25 m/s (assume turbulent boundary-layer flow).

9.58 Repeat Problem 9.44, except that the air flow is now at 25 m/s (assume turbulent boundary-layer flow).

9.59 Repeat Problem 9.46, except that the water flow is now at 10 m/s (assume turbulent boundary-layer flow).

9.60 The velocity profile in a turbulent boundary-layer flow at zero pressure gradient is approximated by the $\frac{1}{6}$-power profile

expression,

$$\frac{u}{U} = \eta^{1/6}, \quad \text{where} \quad \eta = \frac{y}{\delta}$$

Use the momentum integral equation with this profile to obtain expressions for δ/x and C_f. Compare with results obtained in Section 9-5 for the $\frac{1}{7}$-power profile.

9.61 For the flow conditions of Example 9.4, but using the $\frac{1}{6}$-power velocity profile of Problem 9.60, develop an algebraic expression for the variation of wall shear stress with distance along the surface. Integrate to obtain an algebraic expression for the total skin friction drag on the surface. Evaluate the drag for the given conditions.

9.62 Repeat Problem 9.60, using the $\frac{1}{8}$-power profile expression.

9.63 Standard air flows over a horizontal smooth flat plate at free-stream speed $U = 20$ m/s. The plate length is $L = 1.5$ m and its width is $b = 0.8$ m. The pressure gradient is zero. The boundary layer is tripped so that it is turbulent from the leading edge; the velocity profile is well represented by the $\frac{1}{7}$-power expression. Evaluate the boundary-layer thickness, δ, at the trailing edge of the plate. Calculate the wall shear stress at the trailing edge of the plate. Estimate the skin friction drag on the portion of the plate between $x = 0.5$ m and the trailing edge.

9.64 Air at standard conditions flows over a flat plate. The free-stream speed is 10 m/s. Find δ and τ_w at $x = 1$ m from the leading edge assuming (a) completely laminar flow (assume a parabolic velocity profile) and (b) completely turbulent flow (assume a $\frac{1}{7}$-power velocity profile).

9.65 A uniform flow of standard air at 60 m/s enters a plane-wall diffuser with negligible boundary-layer thickness. The inlet width is 75 mm. The diffuser walls diverge slightly to accommodate the boundary-layer growth so that the pressure gradient is negligible. Assume flat-plate boundary-layer behavior. Explain why the Bernoulli equation is applicable to this flow. Estimate the diffuser width 1.2 m downstream from the entrance.

9.66 A laboratory wind tunnel has a flexible upper wall that can be adjusted to compensate for boundary-layer growth, giving zero pressure gradient along the test section. The wall boundary layers are well represented by the $\frac{1}{7}$-power velocity profile. At the inlet the tunnel cross section is square, with height H_1 and width W_1, each equal to 305 mm. With free-stream speed $U_1 = 26.5$ m/s, measurements show that $\delta_1 = 12.2$ mm and downstream, $\delta_6 = 16.6$ mm. Calculate the height of the tunnel walls at section ⑥. Determine the equivalent length of flat plate that would produce the inlet boundary layer thickness. Estimate the streamwise distance between sections ① and ⑥ in the tunnel.

9.67 Small wind tunnels in an undergraduate laboratory have 305-mm square test sections. Measurements show the boundary layers on the tunnel walls are fully turbulent and well represented by $\frac{1}{7}$-power profiles. At cross section ① with free-stream speed $U_1 = 26.1$ m/s, data show that $\delta_1 = 12.2$ mm; at section ②, located downstream, $\delta_2 = 16.6$ mm. Evaluate the change in static pressure between sections ① and ②. Estimate the distance between the two sections.

9.68 Air flows in a cylindrical duct of diameter $D = 150$ mm. At section ①, the turbulent boundary layer is of thickness $\delta_1 = 10$ mm, and the velocity in the inviscid central core is $U_1 = 25$ m/s. Further downstream, at section ②, the boundary layer is of thickness $\delta_2 = 30$ mm. The velocity profile in the boundary layer is approximated well by the $\frac{1}{7}$-power expression. Find the velocity,

U_2, in the inviscid central core at the second section, and the pressure drop between the two sections. Does the magnitude of the pressure drop indicate that we are justified in approximating the flow between sections ① and ② as one with zero pressure gradient? Estimate the length of duct between sections ① and ②. Estimate the distance downstream from section ① at which the boundary-layer thickness is $\delta = 20$ mm.

9.69 Perform a cost-effectiveness analysis on a typical large tanker used for transporting petroleum. Determine, as a percentage of the petroleum cargo, the amount of petroleum that is consumed in traveling a distance of 2000 miles. Use data from Example 9.5, and the following: Assume the petroleum cargo constitutes 75% of the total weight, the propeller efficiency is 70%, the wave drag and power to run auxiliary equipment constitute losses equivalent to an additional 20%, the engines have a thermal efficiency of 40%, and the petroleum energy is 20,000 Btu/lbm. Also compare the performance of this tanker to that of the Alaskan Pipeline, which requires about 120 Btu of energy for each ton-mile of petroleum delivery.

9.70 Consider the linear, sinusoidal, and parabolic laminar boundary-layer approximations of Problem 9.10. Compare the momentum fluxes of these profiles. Which is most likely to separate first when encountering an adverse pressure gradient?

*9.71 Table 9.1 shows the numerical results obtained from Blasius exact solution of the laminar boundary-layer equations. Plot the velocity distribution (note that from Eq. 9.13 we see that $\eta \approx 5.0\frac{y}{\delta}$). On the same graph, plot the turbulent velocity distribution given by the $\frac{1}{7}$-power expression of Eq. 9.24. Which is most likely to separate first when encountering an adverse pressure gradient? To justify your answer, compare the momentum fluxes of these profiles (the laminar data can be integrated using a numerical method such as Simpson's rule).

9.72 Consider the plane-wall diffuser shown in Fig. P9.72. First, assume the fluid is inviscid. Describe the flow pattern, including the pressure distribution, as the diffuser angle ϕ is increased from zero degrees (parallel walls). Second, modify your description to allow for boundary layer effects. Which fluid (inviscid or viscous) will generally have the highest exit pressure?

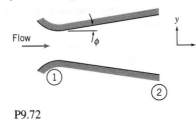

P9.72

9.73 Boundary-layer separation occurs when the shear stress at the surface becomes zero. Assume a polynomial representation for the laminar boundary layer of the form, $u/U = a + b\lambda + c\lambda^2 + d\lambda^3$, where $\lambda = y/\delta$. Specify boundary conditions on the velocity profile at separation. Find appropriate constants, a, b, c, and d, for the separation profile. Calculate the shape factor H at separation. Plot the profile and compare with the parabolic approximate profile.

9.74 For flow over a flat plate with zero pressure gradient, will the shear stress increase, decrease, or remain constant along the plate? Justify your answer. Does the momentum flux increase,

decrease, or remain constant as the flow proceeds along the plate? Justify your answer. Compare the behavior of laminar flow and turbulent flow (both from the leading edge) over a flat plate. At a given distance from the leading edge, which flow will have the larger boundary-layer thickness? Does your answer depend on the distance along the plate? How would you justify your answer?

9.75 Cooling air is supplied through the wide, flat channel shown. For minimum noise and disturbance of the outlet flow, laminar boundary layers must be maintained on the channel walls. Estimate the maximum inlet flow speed at which the outlet flow will be laminar. Assuming parabolic velocity profiles in the laminar boundary layers, evaluate the pressure drop, $p_1 - p_2$. Express your answer in inches of water.

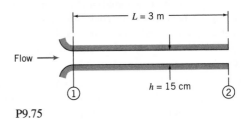

P9.75

9.76 A laboratory wind tunnel has a test section that is square in cross section, with inlet width, W_1, and height, H_1, each equal to 305 mm. At freestream speed $U_1 = 24.5$ m/s, measurements show the boundary-layer thickness is $\delta_1 = 9.75$ mm with a $\frac{1}{7}$-power turbulent velocity profile. The pressure gradient in this region is given approximately by $dp/dx = -0.035$ mm H_2O/mm. Evaluate the reduction in effective flow area caused by the boundary layers on the tunnel bottom, top, and walls at section ①. Calculate the rate of change of boundary-layer momentum thickness, $d\theta/dx$, at section ①. Estimate the momentum thickness at the end of the test section, located $L = 254$ mm downstream.

9.77 The variable-wall concept is proposed to maintain constant boundary-layer thickness in the wind tunnel of Problem 9.76. Beginning with the initial conditions of Problem 9.76, evaluate the freestream velocity distribution needed to maintain constant boundary-layer thickness. Assume constant width, W_1. Estimate the top-height settings along the test section from $x = 0$ at section ① to $x = 254$ mm at section ② downstream.

9.78 A vertical stabilizing fin on a land-speed-record car is $L = 1.65$ m long and $H = 0.785$ m tall. The automobile is to be driven at the Bonneville Salt Flats in Utah, where the elevation is 1340 m and the summer temperature reaches 50°C. The car speed is 560 km/hr. Evaluate the length Reynolds number of the fin. Estimate the location of transition from laminar to turbulent flow in the boundary layers. Calculate the power required to overcome skin friction drag on the fin.

9.79 Repeat Problem 9.46, except that the water flow is now at 10 m/s (use formulas for C_D from Section 9-7).

9.80 A towboat for river barges is tested in a towing tank. The towboat model is built at a scale ratio of 1:13.5. Dimensions of the model are overall length 11.1 ft, beam 3.11 ft, and draft 0.62 ft. (The model displacement in fresh water is 1200 lb.) Estimate the average length of wetted surface on the hull. Calculate the skin friction drag force on the prototype at a speed of 8 mph relative to the water.

---

* This problem requires material from sections that may be omitted without loss of continuity in the text material.

9.81 A jet transport aircraft cruises at 40,000 ft altitude in steady level flight at 500 mph. Model the aircraft fuselage as a circular cylinder with diameter $D = 12$ ft and length $L = 125$ ft. Neglecting compressibility effects, estimate the skin friction drag force on the fuselage. Evaluate the power needed to overcome this force.

9.82 Resistance of a barge is to be determined from model test data. The model is constructed to a scale ratio of 1:13.5, and has length, beam, and draft of 22.0, 4.00, and 0.667 ft, respectively. The test is to simulate performance of the prototype at 8 mph. What must be the model speed in order for the model and prototype to exhibit similar wave drag behavior? Is the boundary layer on the prototype predominantly laminar or turbulent? Does the model boundary layer become turbulent at the comparable point? If not, the model boundary layer could be artificially triggered to turbulent by placing a tripwire across the hull. Where would this be placed? Estimate the skin-friction drag on model and prototype.

9.83 A flat-bottomed barge, 80 ft long and 35 ft wide, submerged to a depth of 5 ft, is to be pushed up a river (the river water is at 60°F). Estimate and plot the power required to overcome skin friction for speeds ranging up to 15 mph.

9.84 You are asked by the Purdue crew to estimate the skin friction drag on their eight-seat racing shell. The hull of the shell may be approximated as half a circular cylinder with 457 mm diameter and 7.32 m length. The speed of the shell through the water is 6.71 m/s. Estimate the location of transition from laminar to turbulent flow in the boundary layer on the hull of the shell. Calculate the thickness of the turbulent boundary layer at the rear of the hull. Determine the total skin friction drag on the hull under the given conditions.

9.85 A nuclear submarine cruises fully submerged at 27 knots. The hull is approximately a circular cylinder with diameter $D = 11.0$ m and length $L = 107$ m. Estimate the percentage of the hull length for which the boundary layer is laminar. Calculate the skin friction drag on the hull and the power consumed.

9.86 A sheet of plastic material 10 mm thick, with specific gravity SG = 1.5, is dropped into a large tank containing water. The sheet is 0.5 m by 1 m. Estimate the terminal speed of the sheet as it falls with (a) the short side vertical and (b) the long side vertical. Assume that the drag is due only to skin friction, and that the boundary layers are turbulent from the leading edge.

9.87 The 600-seat jet transport aircraft proposed by Airbus Industrie has a fuselage that is 70 m long and 7.5 m in diameter. The aircraft is to operate 14 hr per day, 6 days per week; it will cruise at 257 m/s ($M = 0.87$) at 12 km altitude. The engines consume fuel at the rate of 0.06 kg per hour for each N of thrust produced. Estimate the skin friction drag force on the aircraft fuselage at cruise. Calculate the annual fuel savings for the aircraft if friction drag on the fuselage could be reduced 1 percent by modifying the surface coating.

9.88 A supertanker displacement is approximately 600,000 metric tons. This ship has length $L = 300$ m, beam (width) $b = 80$ m, and draft (depth) $D = 25$ m. The ship steams at 14 knots through seawater at 4°C. For these conditions, estimate (a) the thickness of the boundary layer at the stern of the ship, (b) the total skin friction drag acting on the ship, and (c) the power required to overcome the drag force.

9.89 In Section 7-6 the wave resistance and viscous resistance on a model and prototype ship were discussed. For the prototype, $L = 409$ ft and $A = 19,500$ ft². From the data of Figs. 7.2 and 7.3, plot on one graph the wave, viscous, and total resistance (lbf) experienced by the prototype, as a function of speed. Plot a similar graph for the model. Discuss your results. Finally, plot the power (hp) required for the prototype ship to overcome the total resistance.

9.90 As a part of the 1976 bicentennial celebration, an enterprising group hung a giant American flag (59 m high and 112 m wide) from the suspension cables of the Verrazano Narrows Bridge. They apparently were reluctant to make holes in the flag to alleviate the wind force, and hence they effectively had a flat plate normal to the flow. The flag tore loose from its mountings when the wind speed reached 16 km/hr. Estimate the wind force acting on the flag at this wind speed. Should they have been surprised that the flag blew down?

*9.91 Fishing net is made of 1/32-in. diameter nylon thread assembled in a rectangular pattern. The horizontal and vertical distances between adjacent thread centerlines are 3/8 in. Estimate the drag on a 5 ft × 40 ft section of this net when it is dragged (perpendicular to the flow) through 60°F water at 7 knots. What is the power required to maintain this motion?

9.92 A rotary mixer is constructed from two circular disks as shown. The mixer is rotated at 60 rpm in a large vessel containing a brine solution (SG = 1.1). Neglect the drag on the rods and the motion induced in the liquid. Estimate the minimum torque and power required to drive the mixer.

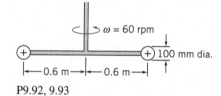

P9.92, 9.93

9.93 As a young design engineer you decide to make the rotary mixer look more "cool" by replacing the disks with rings. The rings may have the added benefit of making the mixer mix more effectively. If the mixer absorbs 350 W at 60 rpm, redesign the device. There is a design constraint that the outer diameter of the rings not exceed 125 mm.

9.94 The vertical component of the landing speed of a parachute is to be less than 6 m/s. The total mass of chute and jumper is 120 kg. Determine the minimum diameter of the open parachute.

9.95 An emergency braking parachute system on a military aircraft consists of [a parachute] of diameter 6 m. If the airplane mass is 85[00 kg] ... he time and distance at w[hich] ... /hr by the parachute alon[e] ... ance and versus time. Wha[t] ... ed? An engineer proposes t[o] ... placing the large parachute ... each of diameter 3.75 m. W[hat] ... e and distance to slow to 10[0 km/hr] ...

9.96 As ... [as]ked to design an emergenc[y] ... th a military aircraft of m[ass] ... /hr, and the parachute system alone must slow ... .00 km/hr in less than 1200 m. Find the minimum diameter required for a single parachute, and for three non-interfering parachutes. Plot the airplane speed versus distance and versus time. What is the maximum "g-force" experienced?

9.97 It has been proposed to use surplus 55 gal oil drums to make simple windmills for underdeveloped countries. Two possible configurations are shown. Estimate which would be better, why, and by how much. The diameter and length of a 55 gal drum are $D = 24$ in. and $H = 29$ in.

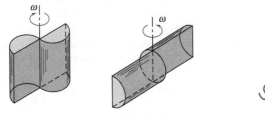

P.9.97

9.98 The resistance to motion of a good bicycle on smooth pavement is nearly all due to aerodynamic drag. Assume that the total mass of rider and bike is $M = 100$ kg. The frontal area measured from a photograph is $A = 0.46$ m². Experiments on a hill, where the road grade is 8 percent, show that terminal speed is $V_t = 15$ m/s. From these data, the drag coefficient is estimated as $C_D = 1.2$. Verify this calculation of drag coefficient. Estimate the distance needed for the bike and rider to decelerate from 15 to 10 m/s while coasting after reaching level road.

9.99 Ballistic data obtained on a firing range show that aerodynamic drag reduces the speed of a .44 magnum revolver bullet from 250 m/s to 210 m/s as it travels over a horizontal distance of 150 m. The diameter and mass of the bullet are 11.2 mm and 15.6 g, respectively. Evaluate the average drag coefficient for the bullet.

9.100 A cyclist is able to attain a maximum speed of 30 km/hr on a calm day. The total mass of rider and bike is 65 kg. The rolling resistance of the tires is $F_R = 7.5$ N, and the drag coefficient and frontal area are $C_D = 1.2$ and $A = 0.25$ m². The cyclist bets that today, even though there is a headwind of 10 km/hr, she can maintain a speed of 24 km/hr. She also bets that, cycling with wind support, she can attain a top speed of 40 km/hr. Which, if any, bets does she win?

9.101 Consider the cyclist in Problem 9.100. Determine the maximum speeds she is actually able to attain today (with the 10 km/hr wind) cycling into the wind, and cycling with the wind. If she were to replace the tires with high-tech ones that had a rolling resistance of only 3.5 N, determine her maximum speed on a calm day, cycling into the wind, and cycling with the wind. If she in addition attaches an aerodynamic fairing that reduces the drag coefficient to $C_D = 0.9$, what will be her new maximum speeds?

9.102 Consider the cyclist in Problem 9.100. She is having a bad day, because she has to climb a hill with a 5° slope. What is the speed she is able to ~~ there is~~ also a headwind of ~~hill, and~~ turns around and he ~~hard as~~ possible, what will b ~~hen the~~ wind is present)? Wl ~~cides to~~ coast down the hill (v

***9.103** At a surprise ~~of 9-in.~~ diameter helium ba ~~a short~~ string. The first one ~~e other~~

[handwritten notes overlaid]
$F_D = \frac{1}{2}\rho A V^2 C_D$, $A = \frac{\pi D^2}{4}$
$k = \frac{V}{\omega}\left(\frac{\omega}{\omega} - k\right)^2 C_{Dopen}$
$= \left(\frac{V}{\omega} + R\right)^2 C_{Dnotopen}$
$k = J$
$T_+ = \left(\frac{1}{2}\rho A V_{min}^2 C_{Dopen}\right)$
$- \left(\frac{1}{2}\rho A V_{min}^2 C_{Dnotopen}\right)R$

eight are tied at 3 ft. spacings, so the last is tied at a height of 63 ft. Being quite a nerdy engineer, you notice that in the steady wind, each balloon is blown by the wind so it looks like the angles the strings make with the vertical are about 5°, 10°, 20°, 30°, 35°, 45°, 50°, 60° and 65°. Estimate and plot the wind velocity profile for the 63 ft. range. Assume the helium is at 70°F and 1.5 psig, and that each balloon is made of 1/10 oz. of latex.

9.104 A 1-ft diameter hollow plastic sphere containing pollution test equipment is being dragged through the Hudson River in New York by a diver riding an underwater jet device. The sphere (with an effective specific gravity of $SG = 0.25$) is fully submerged, and is tethered to the diver by a thin 4-ft long wire. What is the relative velocity of the diver and sphere if the angle the wire makes with the horizontal is 45°? The water is at 50°F.

***9.105** A circular disk is hung in an air stream from a pivoted strut as shown. In a wind-tunnel experiment, performed in air at 15 m/s with a 25-mm diameter disk, α was measured at 10°. For these conditions determine the mass of the disk. Assume the drag coefficient for the disk applies when the component of wind speed normal to the disk is used. Assume drag on the strut and friction in the pivot are negligible. Plot a theoretical curve of α as a function of air speed.

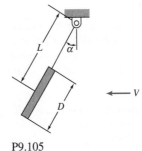

P9.105

9.106 An anemometer to measure wind speed is made from four hemispherical cups of 50 mm diameter, as shown. The center of each cup is placed at $R = 80$ mm from the pivot. Find the theoretical calibration constant k in the calibration equation $V = k\omega$, where V (km/hr) is the wind speed and ω (rpm) is the rotation speed. In your analysis base the torque calculations on the drag generated at the instant when two of the cups are orthogonal, and the other two cups are parallel, and ignore friction in the bearings. Explain why, in the absence of friction, at any given wind speed, the anemometer runs at constant speed rather than accelerating without limit. If the actual anemometer bearing has (constant) friction such that the anemometer needs a minimum wind speed of 1 km/hr to begin rotating, compare the rotation speeds with and without friction for $V = 10$ km/hr.

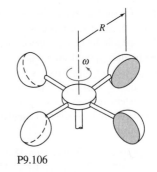

P9.106

9.107 A simple but effective anemometer to measure wind speed can be made from a thin plate hinged to deflect in the wind. Consider a thin plate made from brass that is 20 mm high and 10 mm wide. Derive a relationship for wind speed as a function of deflection angle, θ. What thickness of brass should be used to give $\theta = 30°$ at 10 m/s?

9.108 Experimental data [16] suggest that the maximum and minimum drag area ($C_D A$) for a skydiver varies from about 0.85 m² for a prone, spread-eagle position to about 0.11 m² for vertical fall. Estimate the terminal speeds for a 75 kg skydiver in each position. Calculate the time and distance needed for the skydiver to reach 95 percent of terminal speed at an altitude of 3000 m on a standard day.

9.109 An F-4 aircraft is slowed after landing by dual parachutes deployed from the rear. Each parachute is 12 ft in diameter. The F-4 weighs 32,000 lbf and lands at 160 knots. Estimate the time and distance required to decelerate the aircraft to 100 knots, assuming that the brakes are not used and the drag of the aircraft is negligible.

9.110 A vehicle is built to try for the land-speed record at the Bonneville salt flats, elevation 4400 ft. The engine delivers 500 hp to the rear wheels, and careful streamlining has resulted in a drag coefficient of 0.15, based on a 15 ft² frontal area. Compute the theoretical maximum ground speed of the car (a) in still air and (b) with a 20 mph headwind.

9.111 Compare and plot the power (hp) required by a typical large American sedan of the 1970s and a current midsize sedan to overcome aerodynamic drag versus road speed in standard air, for a speed range of 20 mph to 100 mph. Use the following as representative values:

	Weight (lbf)	Drag Coefficient	Frontal Area (ft²)
1970's Sedan	4500	0.5	24
Current Sedan	3500	0.3	20

If rolling resistance is 1.5 percent of curb weight, determine for each vehicle the speed at which the aerodynamic force exceeds frictional resistance.

9.112 A bus travels at 50 mph in standard air. The frontal area of the vehicle is 80 ft², and the drag coefficient is 0.95. How much power is required to overcome aerodynamic drag? Estimate the maximum speed of the bus if the engine is rated at 450 hp. A young engineer proposes adding fairings on the front and rear of the bus to reduce the drag coefficient. Tests indicate that this would reduce the drag coefficient to 0.85 without changing the frontal area. What would be the required power at 50 mph, and the new top speed? If the fuel cost for the bus is currently $200/day, how long would the modification take to pay for itself if it costs $4,500 to install?

9.113 A tractor-trailer rig has frontal area $A = 102$ ft² and drag coefficient $C_D = 0.9$. Rolling resistance is 6 lbf per 1000 lbf of vehicle weight. The specific fuel consumption of the diesel engine is 0.34 lbm of fuel per horsepower hour, and drivetrain efficiency is 92 percent. The density of diesel fuel is 6.9 lbm/gal. Estimate the fuel economy of the rig at 55 mph if its gross weight is 72,000 lbf. An air fairing system reduces aerodynamic drag 15 percent. The truck travels 120,000 miles per year. Calculate the fuel saved per year by the roof fairing.

9.114 A 165 hp sports car of frontal area 18.5 ft², with a drag coefficient of 0.32, requires 12 hp to cruise at 55 mph. At what speed does aerodynamic drag first exceed rolling resistance? (The rolling resistance is 1% of the car weight, and the car mass is 2750 lb.) Find the drivetrain efficiency. What is the maximum acceleration at 55 mph? What is the maximum speed? Which redesign will lead to a higher maximum speed: improving the drive train efficiency by 5% from its current value, reducing the drag coefficient to 0.29, or reducing the rolling resistance to 0.93% of the car weight?

9.115 A round thin disk of radius R is oriented perpendicular to a fluid stream. The pressure distributions on the front and back surfaces are measured and presented in the form of pressure coefficients. The data are modeled with the following expressions for the front and back surfaces, respectively:

$$\text{Front Surface} \quad C_p = 1 - \left(\frac{r}{R}\right)^6$$

$$\text{Rear Surface} \quad C_p = -0.42$$

Calculate the drag coefficient for the disk.

9.116 Repeat the analysis for the frictionless anemometer of Problem 9.106, except this time base the torque calculations on the more realistic model that the average torque is obtained by integrating, over one revolution, the instantaneous torque generated by each cup (i.e., as the cup's orientation to the wind varies).

9.117 An object of mass m, with cross-sectional area equal to half the size of the chute, falls down a mail chute. The motion is steady. The wake area is $\frac{3}{4}$ the size of the chute at its maximum area. Use the assumption of constant pressure in the wake. Apply the continuity, Bernoulli, and momentum equations to develop an expression for terminal speed of the object in terms of its mass and other quantities.

9.118 An object falls in air down a long vertical chute. The speed of the object is constant at 3 m/s. The flow pattern around the object is shown. The static pressure is uniform across sections ① and ②; pressure is atmospheric at section ①. The effective flow area at section ② is 20 percent of the chute area. Frictional effects between sections ① and ② are negligible. Evaluate the flow speed relative to the object at section ②. Calculate the static pressure at section ②. Determine the mass of the object.

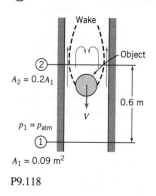

P9.118

9.119 A large paddle wheel is immersed in the current of a river to generate power. Each paddle has area A and drag coefficient C_D; the center of each paddle is located at radius R from the centerline of the paddle wheel. Assume the equivalent of one paddle is submerged continuously in the flowing stream. Obtain an expression for the drag force on a single paddle in terms of geometric variables, current speed, V, and linear speed of the paddle center, $U = R\omega$. Develop expressions for the torque and power produced by the paddle wheel. Find the speed at which the paddle wheel should rotate to obtain maximum power output from the wheel in a given current.

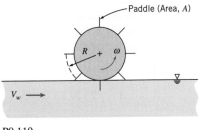

P9.119

9.120 A light plane tows an advertising banner over a football stadium on a Saturday afternoon. The banner is 4 ft tall and 45 ft long. According to Hoerner [16], the drag coefficient based on area (Lh) for such a banner is approximated by $C_D = 0.05 \, L/h$, where L is the banner length and h is the banner height. Estimate the power required to tow the banner at $V = 55$ mph. Compare with the drag of a rigid flat plate. Why is the drag larger for the banner?

9.121 The antenna on a car is 10 mm in diameter and 1.8 m long. Estimate the bending moment that tends to snap it off if the car is driven at 120 km/hr on a standard day.

9.122 A large three-blade horizontal axis wind turbine (HAWT) can be damaged if the wind speed is too high. To avoid this, the blades of the turbine can be oriented so that they are parallel to the flow. Find the bending moment at the base of each blade when the wind speed is 45 m/s. Model each blade as a flat plate 35 m wide and 0.45 m long.

9.123 The HAWT of Problem 9.122 is not self-starting. The generator is used as an electric motor to get the turbine up to the operating speed of 20 rpm. To make this easier, the blades are aligned so they lie in the plane of rotation. Assuming an overall efficiency of motor and drive train of 65%, find the power required to maintain the turbine at the operating speed. As an approximation, model each blade as a series of flat plates (the outer region of each blade moves at a significantly higher speed than the inner region).

9.124 Consider small oil droplets (SG = 0.85) rising in water. Develop a relation for calculating terminal speed of a droplet (in m/s) as a function of droplet diameter (in mm) assuming Stokes flow. For what range of droplet diameter is Stokes flow a reasonable assumption?

9.125 Standard air is drawn into a low-speed wind tunnel. A 30-mm diameter sphere is mounted on a force balance to measure lift and drag. An oil-filled manometer is used to measure static pressure inside the tunnel; the reading is −40 mm of oil (SG = 0.85). Calculate the freestream air speed in the tunnel, the Reynolds number of flow over the sphere, and the drag force on the sphere. Are the boundary layers on the sphere laminar or turbulent? Explain.

9.126 A spherical hydrogen-filled balloon, 0.6 m in diameter, exerts an upward force of 1.3 N on a restraining string when held stationary in standard air with no wind. With a wind speed of 3 m/s, the string holding the balloon makes an angle of 60° with the horizontal. Calculate the drag coefficient of the balloon under these conditions, neglecting the weight of the string.

*9.127 A field hockey ball has diameter $D = 73$ mm and mass $m = 160$ g. When struck well, it leaves the stick with initial speed $U_0 = 50$ m/s. The ball is essentially smooth. Estimate the distance traveled in horizontal flight before the speed of the ball is reduced 10 percent by aerodynamic drag.

9.128 Compute the terminal speed of a 3-mm diameter raindrop (assume spherical) in standard air.

9.129 A small sphere ($D = 6$ mm) is observed to fall through castor oil at a terminal speed of 60 mm/s. The temperature is 20°C. Compute the drag coefficient for the sphere. Determine the density of the sphere. If dropped in water, would the sphere fall slower or faster? Why?

9.130 The following curve-fit for the drag coefficient of a smooth sphere as a function of Reynolds number has been proposed by Chow [36]:

$C_D = 24/Re$	$Re \le 1$
$C_D = 24/Re^{0.646}$	$1 < Re \le 400$
$C_D = 0.5$	$400 < Re \le 3 \times 10^5$
$C_D = 0.000366 \, Re^{0.4275}$	$3 \times 10^5 < Re \le 2 \times 10^6$
$C_D = 0.18$	$Re > 2 \times 10^6$

Use data from Fig. 9.11 to estimate the magnitude and location of the maximum error between the curve fit and data.

9.131 Problem 9.105 showed a circular disk hung in an air stream from a cylindrical strut. Assume the strut is $L = 40$ mm long and $d = 3$ mm in diameter. Solve Problem 9.105 including the effect of drag on the support.

9.132 A tennis ball with a mass of 57 g and diameter of 64 mm is dropped in standard sea level air. Calculate the terminal velocity of the ball. Assuming as an approximation that the drag coefficient remains constant at its terminal-velocity value, estimate the time and distance required for the ball to reach 95% of its terminal speed.

9.133 A model airfoil of chord 15 cm and span 60 cm is placed in a wind tunnel with an air flow of 30 m/s (the air is at 20°C). It is mounted on a cylindrical support rod 2 cm in diameter and 25 cm tall. Instruments at the base of the rod indicate a vertical force of 50 N and a horizontal force of 6 N. Calculate the lift and drag coefficients of the airfoil.

9.134 A water tower consists of a 12-m diameter sphere on top of a vertical tower 30 m tall and 2 m in diameter. Estimate the bending moment exerted on the base of the tower due to the aerodynamic force imposed by a 100 km/hr wind on a standard day. Neglect interference at the joint between the sphere and tower.

9.135 Consider a cylindrical flag pole of height H. For constant drag coefficient, evaluate the drag force and bending moment on the pole if wind speed varies as $u/U = (y/H)^{1/7}$, where y is distance measured from the ground. Compare with drag and moment for a uniform wind profile with constant speed U.

9.136 A cast-iron "12-pounder" cannonball rolls off the deck of a ship and falls into the ocean at a location where the depth is 1000 m. Estimate the time that elapses before the cannonball hits the sea bottom.

9.137 The Stokes drag law for smooth spheres is to be verified experimentally by dropping steel ball bearings in glycerin.

Evaluate the largest diameter steel ball for which $Re < 1$ at terminal speed. Calculate the height of glycerin column needed for a bearing to reach 95 percent of terminal speed.

9.138 The plot shows pressure difference versus angle, measured for air flow around a circular cylinder at $Re = 80,000$. Use these data to estimate C_D for this flow. Compare with data from Fig. 9.13. How can you explain the difference?

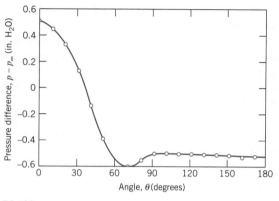

P9.138

9.139 Consider the tennis ball of Problem 9.132. Use the equations for drag coefficient given in Problem 9.130, and a numerical integration scheme (e.g., Simpson's rule) to compute the time and distance required for the ball to reach 95% of its terminal speed.

9.140 The air bubble of Problem 3.11 expands as it rises in water. Find the time it takes for the bubble to reach the surface. Repeat for bubbles of diameter 5 mm and 15 mm. Compute and plot the depth of the bubbles as a function of time.

9.141 Consider the tennis ball of Problem 9.132. Suppose it is hit so that it has an initial upward speed of 50 m/s. Estimate the maximum height of the ball, assuming (a) a constant drag coefficient and (b) using the equations for drag coefficient given in Problem 9.130, and a numerical integration scheme (e.g., a Simpson's rule).

9.142 Approximate dimensions of a rented rooftop carrier are shown. Estimate the drag force on the carrier ($r = 10$ cm) at 100 km/hr. If the drivetrain efficiency of the vehicle is 0.85 and the brake specific fuel consumption of its engine is 0.3 kg/(kW · hr), estimate the additional rate of fuel consumption due to the carrier. Compute the effect on fuel economy if the auto achieves 12.75 km/L without the carrier. The rental company offers you a cheaper, square-edged carrier at a price $5 less than the current carrier. Estimate the extra cost of using this carrier instead of the round-edged one for a 750 km trip, assuming fuel is $3.50 per gallon. Is the cheaper carrier really cheaper?

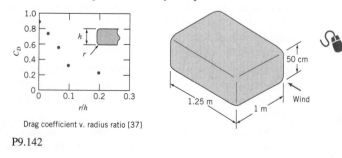

Drag coefficient v. radius ratio [37]

P9.142

9.143 Coastdown tests, performed on a level road on a calm day, can be used to measure aerodynamic drag and rolling resistance coefficients for a full-scale vehicle. Rolling resistance is estimated from dV/dt measured at low speed, where aerodynamic drag is small. Rolling resistance then is deducted from dV/dt measured at high speed to determine the aerodynamic drag. The following data were obtained during a test with a vehicle, of weight $W = 25,000$ lbf and frontal area $A = 79$ ft^2:

V(mph)	5	55
$\dfrac{dV}{dt}\left(\dfrac{\text{mph}}{\text{s}}\right)$	−0.150	−0.475

Estimate the aerodynamic drag coefficient for this vehicle. At what speed does the aerodynamic drag first exceed rolling resistance?

9.144 A spherical sonar transducer with 0.375 m diameter is to be towed in seawater. The transducer must be fully submerged at 31.1 knots. To avoid cavitation, the minimum pressure on the surface of the transducer must be greater than 30 kPa (abs). Calculate the hydrodynamic drag force acting on the transducer at the required towing speed. Estimate the minimum depth to which the transducer must be submerged to avoid cavitation.

9.145 While walking across campus one windy day, Floyd Fluids speculates about using an umbrella as a "sail" to propel a bicycle along the sidewalk. Develop an algebraic expression for the speed a bike could reach on level ground with the umbrella "propulsion system." The frontal area of bike and rider is estimated as 0.3 m^2, and the drag coefficient is about 1.2. Assume rolling resistance is 0.75% of the bike and rider weight; the combined mass is 75 kg. Evaluate the bike speed that could be achieved with an umbrella 1.22 m in diameter in a wind that blows at 24 km/hr. Discuss the practicality of this propulsion system.

9.146 Motion of a small rocket was analyzed in Example 4.12 assuming negligible aerodynamic drag. This was not realistic at the final calculated speed of 369 m/s. Use Euler's finite difference method for approximating the first derivatives, in an *Excel* workbook, to solve the equation of motion for the rocket. Plot the rocket speed as a function of time, assuming $C_D = 0.3$ and a rocket diameter of 700 mm. Compare with the results for $C_D = 0$.

9.147 Towers for television transmitters may be up to 500 m in height. In the winter, ice forms on structural members. When the ice thaws, chunks break off and fall to the ground. How far from the base of a tower would you recommend placing a fence to limit danger to pedestrians from falling ice chunks?

9.148 Wiffle™ balls made from light plastic with numerous holes are used to practice baseball and golf. Explain the purpose of the holes and why they work. Explain how you could test your hypothesis experimentally.

9.149 Design a wind anemometer that uses aerodynamic drag to move or deflect a member or linkage, producing an output that can be related to wind speed, for the range from 1 to 10 m/s in standard air. Consider three alternative design concepts. Select the best concept and prepare a detailed design. Specify the shape, size, and material for each component. Quantify the relation between wind speed and anemometer output. Present results as a theoretical "calibration curve" of anemometer output versus wind speed. Discuss reasons why you rejected the alternative designs and chose your final design concept.

9.150 The "shot tower," used to produce spherical lead shot, has been recognized as a mechanical engineering landmark. In a shot tower, molten lead is dropped from a high tower; as the lead solidifies, surface tension pulls each shot into a spherical shape. Discuss the possibility of increasing the "hang time," or of using a shorter tower, by dropping molten lead into an air stream that is moving upward. Support your discussion with appropriate calculations.

9.151 An antique airplane carries 50 m of external guy wires stretched normal to the direction of motion. The wire diameter is 5 mm. Estimate the maximum power saving that results from an optimum streamlining of the wires at a plane speed of 175 km/hr in standard air at sea level.

9.152 Why do modern guns have rifled barrels?

9.153 Why is it possible to kick a football farther in a spiral motion than in an end-over-end tumbling motion?

9.154 An airplane with an effective lift area of 25 m² is fitted with airfoils of NACA 23012 section (Fig. 9.23). The maximum flap setting that can be used at takeoff corresponds to configuration ② in Fig. 9.23. Determine the maximum gross mass possible for the airplane if its takeoff speed is 150 km/hr at sea level (neglect added lift due to ground effect). Find the minimum takeoff speed required for this gross mass if the airplane is instead taking off from Denver (elevation approximately 1.6 km).

9.155 How do cab-mounted wind deflectors for tractor-trailer trucks work? Explain using diagrams of the flow pattern around the truck and pressure distribution on the surface of the truck.

9.156 An aircraft is in level flight at 225 km/hr through air at standard conditions. The lift coefficient at this speed is 0.45 and the drag coefficient is 0.065. The mass of the aircraft is 900 kg. Calculate the effective lift area for the craft, and the required engine thrust and power.

9.157 The foils of a surface-piercing hydrofoil watercraft have a total effective area of 0.7 m². Their coefficients of lift and drag are 1.6 and 0.5, respectively. The total mass of the craft in running trim is 1800 kg. Determine the minimum speed at which the craft is supported by the hydrofoils. At this speed, find the power required to overcome water resistance. If the craft is fitted with a 110 kW engine, estimate its top speed.

9.158 A high school project involves building a model ultralight airplane. Some of the students propose making an airfoil from a sheet of plastic 1.5 m long by 2 m wide at an angle of attack of 12°. At this airfoil's aspect ratio and angle of attack the lift and drag coefficients are $C_L = 0.72$ and $C_D = 0.17$. If the airplane is designed to fly at 12 m/s, what is the maximum total payload? What will be the required power to maintain flight? Does this proposal seem feas

$F_L = C_L A \frac{1}{2} \rho V^2$

9.159 The U.S ___ ng planform area $A = 27.9$ m ___ ent of $C_L =$ 1.6. When fully ___ 500 kg. The airframe is capa ___ al accelerations. However, ___ vers during training. Consi ___ the aircraft banked. Find th ___ ich the pilot

$F_D = F_L \frac{C_D}{C_L}$

$GF_B = \mu_k F_L + F_D$

can produce a $5g$ total acceleration. Calculate the corresponding flight radius. Discuss the effect of altitude on these results.

9.160 A light airplane, with mass $M = 1000$ kg, has a conventional-section (NACA 23015) wing of planform area $A = 10$ m². Find the angle of attack of the wing for a cruising speed of $V = 63$ m/s. What is the required power? Find the maximum instantaneous vertical "g force" experienced at cruising speed if the angle of attack is suddenly increased.

9.161 The teacher of the students designing the airplane of Problem 9.158 is not happy with the idea of using a sheet of plastic for the airfoil. He asks the students to evaluate the expected maximum total payload, and required power to maintain flight, if the sheet of plastic is replaced with a conventional section (NACA 23015) airfoil with the same aspect ratio and angle of attack. What are the results of the analysis?

9.162 A light airplane has 10 m effective wingspan and 1.8 m chord. It was originally designed to use a conventional (NACA 23015) airfoil section. With this airfoil, its cruising speed on a standard day near sea level is 225 km/hr. A conversion to a laminar-flow (NACA 66₂-215) section airfoil is proposed. Determine the cruising speed that could be achieved with the new airfoil section for the same power.

9.163 Assume the Boeing 727 aircraft has wings with NACA 23012 section, planform area of 1600 ft², double-slotted flaps, and effective aspect ratio of 6.5. If the aircraft flies at 150 knots in standard air at 175,000 lb gross weight, estimate the thrust required to maintain level flight.

9.164 Instead of a new laminar-flow airfoil, a redesign of the light airplane of Problem 9.162 is proposed in which the current conventional airfoil section is replaced with another conventional airfoil section of the same area, but with aspect ratio $AR = 8$. Determine the cruising speed that could be achieved with this new airfoil for the same power.

9.165 An airplane with mass of 10,000 lb is flown at constant elevation and speed on a circular path at 150 mph. The flight circle has a radius of 3,250 ft. The plane has lifting area of 225 ft² and is fitted with NACA 23015 section airfoils with effective aspect ratio of 7. Estimate the drag on the aircraft and the power required.

9.166 Find the minimum and maximum speeds at which the airplane of Problem 9.165 can fly on a 3,250 ft radius circular flight path, and estimate the drag on the aircraft and power required at these extremes.

9.167 The glide angle for unpowered flight is such that lift, drag, and weight are in equilibrium. Show that the glide slope angle, θ, is such that $\tan \theta = C_D/C_L$. The minimum glide slope occurs at the speed where C_L/C_D is a maximum. For the conditions of Example 9.8, evaluate the minimum glide slope angle for a Boeing 727-200. How far could this aircraft glide from an initial altitude of 10 km on a standard day?

9.168 Jim Hall's Chaparral 2F sports-racing cars in the 1960s pioneered use of airfoils mounted above the rear suspension to enhance stability and improve braking performance. The airfoil was effectively 6 ft wide (span) and had a 1 ft chord. Its angle of attack was variable between 0 and minus 12 degrees. Assume lift and drag coefficient data are given by curves (for conventional section) in Fig. 9.17. Consider a car speed of 120 mph on a calm day.

For an airfoil deflection of 12° down, calculate (a) the maximum downward force and (b) the maximum increase in deceleration force produced by the airfoil.

9.169 Some cars come with a "spoiler," a wing section mounted on the rear of the vehicle that salespeople sometimes claim significantly increases traction of the tires at highway speeds. Investigate the validity of this claim. Are these devices really just cosmetic?

9.170 The wing loading of the Gossamer Condor is 0.4 lbf/ft^2 of wing area. Crude measurements showed drag was approximately 6 lbf at 12 mph. The total weight of the Condor was 200 lbf. The effective aspect ratio of the Condor is 17. Estimate the minimum power required to fly the aircraft. Compare to the 0.39 hp that pilot Brian Allen could sustain for 2 hr.

9.171 How does a Frisbee™ fly? What causes it to curve left or right? What is the effect of spin on its flight?

9.172 Roadside signs tend to oscillate in a twisting motion when a strong wind blows. Discuss the phenomena that must occur to cause this behavior.

9.173 An automobile travels down the road with a bicycle attached to a carrier across the rear of the trunk. The bicycle wheels rotate slowly. Explain why and in what direction the rotation occurs.

9.174 Air moving over an automobile is accelerated to speeds higher than the travel speed, as shown in Fig. 9.25. This causes changes in interior pressure when windows are opened or closed. Use the data of Fig. 9.25 to estimate the pressure reduction when a window is opened slightly at a speed of 100 km/hr. What is the air speed in the freestream near the window opening?

9.175 A class demonstration showed that lift is present when a cylinder rotates in an air stream. A string wrapped around a paper cylinder and pulled causes the cylinder to spin and move forward simultaneously. Assume a cylinder of 2 in. diameter and 10 in.

length is given a rotational speed of 300 rpm and a forward speed of 4 ft/s. Estimate the approximate lift force that acts on the cylinder.

9.176 A golf ball (diameter $D = 43$ mm) with circular dimples is hit from a sand trap at 20 m/s with backspin of 2000 rpm. The mass of the ball is 48 g. Evaluate the lift and drag forces acting on the ball. Express your results as fractions of the weight of the ball.

9.177 Rotating cylinders were proposed as a means of ship propulsion in 1924 by the German engineer, Flettner. The original Flettner rotor ship had two rotors, each about 3 m in diameter and 15 m high, rotating at up to 750 rpm. Calculate the maximum lift and drag forces that act on each rotor in a 50 km/hr wind. Compare the total force to that produced at the optimum L/D at the same wind speed. Estimate the power needed to spin the rotor at 750 rpm.

9.178 American and British golf balls have slightly different diameters but the same mass (see Problems 1.39 and 1.42). Assume a professional golfer hits each type of ball from a tee at 85 m/s with backspin of 9000 rpm. Evaluate the lift and drag forces on each ball. Express your answers as fractions of the weight of each ball. Estimate the radius of curvature of the trajectory of each ball. Which ball should have the longer range for these conditions?

9.179 A baseball pitcher throws a ball at 80 mph. Home plate is 60 ft away from the pitcher's mound. What spin should be placed on the ball for maximum horizontal deviation from a straight path? (A baseball has a mass of 5 oz and a circumference of 9 in.) How far will the ball deviate from a straight line?

9.180 A soccer player takes a free kick. Over a distance of 10 m, the ball veers to the right by about 1 m. Estimate the spin the player's kick put on the ball if its speed is 30 m/s. The ball has a mass of 420 gm and has a circumference of 70 cm.

Chapter 10

Fluid Machinery

CASE STUDY

The Little Engine That Could!

Silicon gas-turbine engines suitable for powering laptops or cell phones; a 6-mm-diameter turbine assembly.
(Courtesy of Dr. Alan Epstein, M.I.T.)

Alan Epstein, a professor of aeronautics and astronautics at the Massachusetts Institute of Technology, and his team have done a lot of research on tiny gas-turbine engines made of silicon. They are about the size of a quarter (as shown in the figure) and can be easily mass produced. Unlike conventional large turbines that are assembled from many components, these turbines are built basically from a solid piece of silicon. Professor Epstein discovered that the basic concepts of turbine theory (discussed in this chapter) apply even to his microturbines; the fluid mechanics turns out to be the same as that for larger engines, as long as the passages made for gas flow are larger than about 1 μm in diameter (smaller than this and noncontinuum molecular kinetics is needed).

The rotor and its airfoils are carved out of a single wafer, as shown in the figure. Additional "plumbing" and bearings are etched onto the wafers that are to sandwich the rotor. Combustion occurs just outside the rotor, at the same wafer level, spinning it by pushing on its airfoils from the outside. At more than a *million* rpm, these turbines make no audible noise (it's there, but not even your dog can hear it)! Electricity will then be generated using, for example, a tiny generator. The fuel source could be packaged with the engine or come as a replaceable cartridge like a cigarette lighter. In terms of power density, the little engine will easily beat batteries, with an output of somewhere between 50 and 100 watts!

Humans have sought to control nature since antiquity. Early humans carried water by the bucket; as larger groups formed, this process was mechanized. The first fluid machines developed as bucket wheels and screw pumps to lift water. The Romans introduced paddle wheels around 70 B.C. to obtain energy from streams [1]. Later, windmills were developed to harness wind power, but the low power density of the wind limited output to a few hundred horsepower. Development of water wheels made it possible to extract thousands of horsepower at a single site.

Today we take many fluid machines for granted. On a typical day we draw pressurized water from the tap, use a blower to dry our hair, drive a car in which fluid machines operate the lubrication, cooling, and power steering systems, and work in a comfortable environment provided by air circulation. The list could be extended indefinitely.

A fluid machine is a device that either performs work on, or extracts work (or power) from, a fluid. As you can imagine, this is a very large field of study, so we will limit ourselves mostly to incompressible flows. Within incompressible flows, we will focus on such common machines as pumps and fans that perform work on a fluid, and machines such as water turbines used for extracting work or power from a fluid.

First the terminology of the field is introduced and machines are classified by operating principle and physical characteristics. Rather than attempt a treatment of the entire field, we focus on machines in which energy transfer to or from the fluid is through a rotating element. Basic equations are reviewed and then simplified to forms useful for analysis of fluid machines. Performance characteristics of typical machines are considered. Examples are given of pump and turbine applications in typical systems. Problems ranging from simple applications to system design conclude the chapter.

10-1   INTRODUCTION AND CLASSIFICATION OF FLUID MACHINES

Fluid machines may be broadly classified as either *positive displacement* or *dynamic*. In positive-displacement machines, energy transfer is accomplished by volume changes that occur due to movement of the boundary in which the fluid is confined. This includes piston-cylinder arrangements, gear pumps (for example, the oil pump for a car engine), and lobe pumps (for example, those used in medicine for circulating blood through a machine). We will not analyze these devices in this chapter; we will review them briefly in Section 10-5. Dynamic fluid-handling devices that direct the flow with blades or vanes attached to a rotating member are termed *turbomachines*. In contrast to positive-displacement machinery, there is no closed volume in a turbomachine. All work interactions in a turbomachine result from dynamic effects of the rotor on the fluid stream. These devices are very widely used in industry for power generation (for example, water and steam turbines) and in numerous other applications (for example, the turbocharger of a high-performance car). The emphasis in this chapter is on dynamic machines.

A further distinction among types of turbomachines is based on the geometry of the flow path. In *radial-flow* machines, the flow path is essentially radial, with significant changes in radius from inlet to outlet. (Such machines sometimes are called *centrifugal* machines.) In *axial-flow* machines, the flow path is nearly parallel to the machine centerline, and the radius of the flow path does not vary significantly. In *mixed-flow* machines the flow-path radius changes only moderately. Schematic diagrams of typical turbomachines are shown in Figs. 10.1 through 10.3.

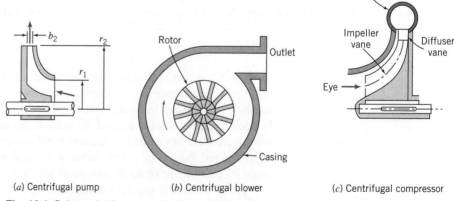

(a) Centrifugal pump   (b) Centrifugal blower   (c) Centrifugal compressor

Fig. 10.1 Schematic diagrams of typical centrifugal-flow turbomachines, adapted from [2].

Machines for Doing Work on a Fluid

Machines that add energy to a fluid by performing work on it are called *pumps* when the flow is liquid or slurry, and *fans, blowers*, or *compressors* for gas- or vapor-handling units, depending on pressure rise. Fans usually have small pressure rise (less than 1 inch of water) and blowers have moderate pressure rise (perhaps 1 inch of mercury); pumps and compressors may have very high pressure rises. Current industrial systems operate at pressures up to 150,000 psi (10^4 atmospheres).

The rotating element of a pump is frequently called the *impeller*; the impeller is contained within the pump *housing* or *casing*. The shaft that transfers mechanical energy to the impeller usually must penetrate the casing; a system of bearings and seals is required to complete the mechanical design of the unit.

Three typical centrifugal machines are shown schematically in Fig. 10.1. Flow enters each machine nearly axially at small radius through the *eye* of the rotor, diagram (*a*), at radius r_1. Flow is turned and leaves through the impeller discharge at radius r_2, where the width is b_2. Flow leaving the impeller is collected in the *scroll* or *volute*, which gradually increases in area as it nears the outlet of the machine, diagram (*b*). The impeller usually has vanes; it may be *shrouded* (enclosed) as shown in diagram (*a*), or *open* as shown in diagram (*c*). The impeller vanes may be relatively straight, or they may curve to become non-radial at the outlet. Diagram (*c*) shows that there may be a diffuser between the impeller discharge and the volute. This *radial* diffuser may be *vaneless* or it may have vanes.

Typical axial-flow and mixed-flow turbomachines are shown schematically in Fig. 10.2. Diagram (*a*) shows a typical axial-flow compressor *stage*.[1] Flow enters nearly parallel to the rotor axis and maintains nearly the same radius through the stage. The mixed-flow pump in diagram (*b*) shows the flow being turned outward and moving to larger radius as it passes through the stage.

The pressure rise that can be achieved efficiently in a single stage is limited, depending on the type of machine. However, stages may be combined to produce multi-stage machines, virtually without limit on pressure rise. Axial-flow compressors, as typically found in turbojet engines, are examples of multi-stage compressors. Centrifugal pumps frequently are built with multiple stages in a single housing.

Fans, blowers, compressors, and pumps are found in many sizes and types, ranging from simple household units to complex industrial units of large capacity. Torque and power requirements for idealized pumps and turboblowers can be analyzed by applying the angular-momentum principle using a suitable control volume.

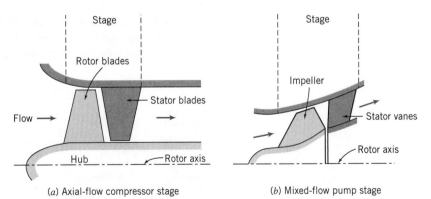

(a) Axial-flow compressor stage   (b) Mixed-flow pump stage

Fig. 10.2 Schematic diagrams of typical axial-flow and mixed-flow turbomachines, adapted from [2].

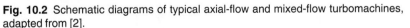

[1] The combination of a stationary blade row and a moving blade row is called a *stage*. (The stationary blades may be guide vanes placed before the rotor; more commonly they are *antiswirl vanes* placed after the rotor.)

Propellers are essentially axial-flow devices that operate without an outer housing. Propellers may be designed to operate in gases or liquids. As you might expect, propellers designed for these very different applications are quite distinct. Marine propellers tend to have wide blades compared with their radii, giving high *solidity*. Aircraft propellers tend to have long, thin blades with relatively low solidity.

Machines for Extracting Work (Power) from a Fluid

Machines that extract energy from a fluid in the form of work (or power) are called *turbines*. The assembly of *vanes, blades,* or *buckets* attached to the turbine shaft is called the *rotor, wheel,* or *runner.* In *hydraulic turbines* the working fluid is water, so the flow is incompressible. In *gas turbines* and *steam turbines* the density of the working fluid may change significantly.

The two most general classifications of turbines are *impulse* and *reaction* turbines. Impulse turbines are driven by one or more high-speed free jets. Each jet is accelerated in a nozzle external to the turbine wheel. If friction and gravity are neglected, neither the fluid pressure nor speed relative to the runner changes as the fluid passes over the turbine buckets. Thus for an impulse turbine, the fluid acceleration and accompanying pressure drop take place in nozzles external to the blades and the runner does not flow full of fluid; work is extracted as a result of the large momentum change of the fluid.

Several typical hydraulic turbines are shown schematically in Fig. 10.3. Diagram (*a*) shows an impulse turbine driven by a single jet, which lies in the plane of the turbine runner. Water from the jet strikes each bucket in succession, is turned, and leaves the bucket with relative velocity nearly opposite to that with which it entered the bucket. Spent water falls into the *tailrace* (not shown).

In reaction turbines, part of the pressure change takes place externally and part takes place within the moving blades. External acceleration occurs and the flow is turned to enter the runner in the proper direction as it passes through nozzles or stationary blades called *guide vanes* or *wicket gates*. Additional fluid acceleration relative to the rotor occurs within the moving blades, so both the relative velocity and the pressure of the stream change across the runner. Because reaction turbines flow full of fluid, they generally can produce more power for a given overall size than impulse turbines.

A reaction turbine of the Francis type is shown in Fig. 10.3*b*. Incoming water flows circumferentially through the turbine casing. It enters the periphery of the stationary guide vanes and flows toward the runner. Water enters the runner nearly radially and is turned downward to leave nearly axially; the flow pattern may be thought of as a centrifugal pump in reverse. Water leaving the runner flows through a diffuser known as a *draft tube* before entering the tailrace.

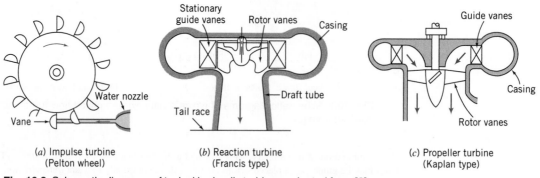

(*a*) Impulse turbine
(Pelton wheel)

(*b*) Reaction turbine
(Francis type)

(*c*) Propeller turbine
(Kaplan type)

Fig. 10.3 Schematic diagrams of typical hydraulic turbines, adapted from [2].

Diagram (*c*) shows a propeller turbine of the Kaplan type. The water entry is similar to that in the Francis turbine just described. However, it is turned to flow nearly axially before encountering the turbine runner. Flow leaving the runner may pass through a draft tube.

Thus turbines range from simple windmills to complex gas and steam turbines with many stages of carefully designed blading. These devices also can be analyzed in idealized form by applying the angular-momentum principle.

Dimensionless parameters such as *specific speed, flow coefficient, torque coefficient, power coefficient*, and *pressure ratio* frequently are used to characterize the performance of turbomachines. These parameters were introduced in Chapter 7; their development and use will be considered in more detail later in this chapter.

10-2   SCOPE OF COVERAGE

According to Japikse [3], "Turbomachinery represents a \$400 billion market (possibly much more) with enormous worldwide growth at this time. It is estimated that industrial centrifugal pumps alone consume 5% of all the energy produced in the USA." Therefore, proper design, construction, selection, and application of pumps and compressors are economically significant.

Design of actual machines involves diverse technical knowledge, including fluid mechanics, materials, bearings, seals, and vibrations. These topics are covered in numerous specialized texts. Our objective here is to present only enough detail to illustrate the analytical basis of fluid flow design and to discuss briefly the limitations on results obtained from simple analytical models. For more detailed design information consult the references.

Applications or "system" engineering requires a wealth of experience. Much of this experience must be gained by working with other engineers in the field. Our coverage is not intended to be comprehensive; instead we discuss only the most important considerations for successful system application of pumps, compressors, and turbines.

In this chapter our treatment deals almost exclusively with *incompressible flows*. The material in this chapter is of a different nature than that in the previous chapters. Chapters 1 through 9 covered much of the fundamental material of fluid mechanics, with detailed analytical results in most cases. This chapter will also involve significant amounts of analysis, but the inherent complexity of the topic means there will be many occasions when we need to resort to empirical results and correlations. To the student, this may appear as so much "hand-waving," but combining theory and experiment to deduce results is a very common approach in engineering science.

10-3   TURBOMACHINERY ANALYSIS

The analysis method used for turbomachinery is chosen according to the information sought. If overall information on flow rate, pressure change, torque, and power is desired, then a finite-control-volume analysis may be used. If detailed information is desired about blade angles or velocity profiles, then individual blade elements must be analyzed using an infinitesimal control volume or other detailed procedure. We consider only idealized flow processes in this book, so we concentrate on the approach using the finite control volume, applying the angular-momentum principle. The analysis that follows applies to machines both for doing work on, and extracting work from, a fluid flow.

The Angular-Momentum Principle

The angular-momentum principle was applied to finite control volumes in Chapter 4. The result was Eq. 4.46,

$$\vec{r} \times \vec{F}_S + \int_{CV} \vec{r} \times \vec{g} \, \rho \, dV + \vec{T}_{\text{shaft}} = \frac{\partial}{\partial t} \int_{CV} \vec{r} \times \vec{V} \rho \, dV + \int_{CS} \vec{r} \times \vec{V} \rho \vec{V} \cdot d\vec{A} \quad (4.46)$$

Equation 4.46 states that the moment of surface forces and body forces, plus the applied torque, lead to a change in the angular momentum of the flow. [The surface forces are due to friction and pressure, the body force is due to gravity, the applied torque could be positive or negative (depending on whether we are doing work on or extracting work from the fluid, respectively), and the angular-momentum change can arise as a change in angular momentum within the control volume, or flux of angular momentum across the control surface.]

In the next section Eq. 4.46 is simplified for analysis of turbomachinery.

Euler Turbomachine Equation

For turbomachinery analysis, it is convenient to choose a fixed control volume enclosing the rotor to evaluate shaft torque. Because we are looking at control volumes for which we expect large shaft torques, as a first approximation torques due to surface forces may be ignored. This means we are neglecting friction and torque generated by pressure changes. The body force may be neglected by symmetry. Then, for steady flow, Eq. 4.46 becomes

$$\vec{T}_{\text{shaft}} = \int_{CS} \vec{r} \times \vec{V} \, \rho \vec{V} \cdot d\vec{A} \quad (10.1a)$$

Equation 10.1a states: For a turbomachine with work *input*, the torque *required* causes a change in the fluid angular momentum; for a turbomachine with work *output*, the torque *produced* is due to the change in fluid angular momentum. Let us write this equation in scalar form and illustrate its application to axial- and radial-flow machines.

As shown in Fig. 10.4, we select a *fixed* control volume enclosing a generalized turbomachine rotor. The fixed coordinate system is chosen with the z axis aligned with the axis of rotation of the machine. The idealized velocity components are shown in the figure. The fluid enters the rotor at radial location r_1, with uniform absolute velocity $\vec{V}_1$; the fluid leaves the rotor at radial location r_2, with uniform absolute velocity $\vec{V}_2$.

The integrand on the right side of Eq. 10.1a is the product of $\vec{r} \times \vec{V}$ with the mass flow rate at each section. For *uniform flow* into the rotor at section ①, and out

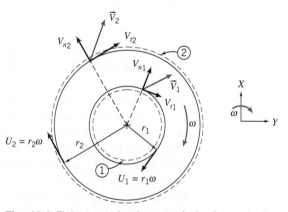

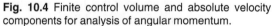

Fig. 10.4 Finite control volume and absolute velocity components for analysis of angular momentum.

of the rotor at section ②, Eq. 10.1a becomes

$$T_{\text{shaft}}\hat{k} = (r_2 V_{t_2} - r_1 V_{t_1})\dot{m}\,\hat{k} \tag{10.1b}$$

(Note that in $\vec{r} \times \vec{V}$ the position vector $\vec{r}$ is purely radial, so only the tangential velocity component V_t counts.) In scalar form,

$$T_{\text{shaft}} = (r_2 V_{t_2} - r_1 V_{t_1})\dot{m} \tag{10.1c}$$

The assumptions we made in deriving this equation are: *steady, frictionless flow; uniform flow* at inlet and exit; and *negligible pressure effects.* Equation 10.1c is the basic relationship between torque and angular momentum for all turbomachines. It often is called the *Euler turbomachine equation.*

Each velocity that appears in Eq. 10.1c is the tangential component of the absolute velocity of the fluid crossing the control surface. The tangential velocities are chosen positive when in the same direction as the *blade speed, U.* This sign convention gives $T_{\text{shaft}} > 0$ for pumps, fans, blowers, and compressors and $T_{\text{shaft}} < 0$ for turbines.

The rate of work done on a turbomachine rotor (the *mechanical power, $\dot{W}_m$*) is given by the dot product of rotor angular velocity, $\vec{\omega}$, and applied torque, $\vec{T}_{\text{shaft}}$. Using Eq. 10.1b, we obtain

$$\dot{W}_m = \vec{\omega} \cdot \vec{T}_{\text{shaft}} = \omega\hat{k} \cdot T_{\text{shaft}}\hat{k} = \omega\hat{k} \cdot (r_2 V_{t_2} - r_1 V_{t_1})\dot{m}\hat{k}$$

or

$$\dot{W}_m = \omega T_{\text{shaft}} = \omega(r_2 V_{t_2} - r_1 V_{t_1})\dot{m} \tag{10.2a}$$

According to Eq. 10.2a, the angular momentum of the fluid is increased by the addition of shaft work. For a pump, $\dot{W}_m > 0$ and the angular momentum of the fluid must increase. For a turbine, $\dot{W}_m < 0$ and the angular momentum of the fluid must decrease.

Equation 10.2a may be written in two other useful forms. Introducing $U = r\omega$, where U is the tangential speed of the rotor at radius r, we have

$$\dot{W}_m = (U_2 V_{t_2} - U_1 V_{t_1})\dot{m} \tag{10.2b}$$

Dividing Eq. 10.2b by $\dot{m}g$, we obtain a quantity with the dimensions of length, which may be viewed as the theoretical *head* added to the flow.[2]

$$H = \frac{\dot{W}_m}{\dot{m}g} = \frac{1}{g}(U_2 V_{t_2} - U_1 V_{t_1}) \tag{10.2c}$$

Equations 10.1 and 10.2 are simplified forms of the angular-momentum equation for a control volume. They all are written for a fixed control volume under the assumptions of steady, uniform flow at each section. The equations show that only the difference in the product rV_t or UV_t, between the outlet and inlet sections, is important in determining the torque applied to the rotor or the mechanical power. Although $r_2 > r_1$ in Fig. 10.4, no restriction has been made on geometry; the fluid may enter and leave at the same or different radii.

Velocity Diagrams

The equations that we have derived also suggest the importance of clearly defining the velocity components of the fluid and rotor at the inlet and outlet sections. For this purpose, it is useful to develop *velocity diagrams* (frequently called *velocity polygons*) for the inlet and outlet flows. Figure 10.5 shows the velocity diagrams and introduces the notation for blade and flow angles.

---

[2] Since $\dot{W}_m$ has dimensions of energy per unit time and $\dot{m}g$ is weight flow per unit time, *head, H,* is actually energy per unit weight of flowing fluid.

Machines are designed such that at *design condition* the fluid moves smoothly (without disturbances) through the blades. In the idealized situation at the *design speed*, flow relative to the rotor is assumed to enter and leave tangent to the blade profile at each section. (This idealized inlet condition is sometimes called *shockless* entry flow.) At speeds other than design speed (and sometimes in reality, even at design speed!), the fluid may impact the blades at inlet, exit at an angle relative to the blade, or may have significant flow separation, leading to machine inefficiency. Figure 10.5 is representative of a typical radial flow machine. We assume the fluid is moving without major flow disturbances through the machine, as shown in Fig. 10.5a, with blade inlet and exit angles β_1 and β_2, respectively, relative to the circumferential direction. Note that although angles β_1 and β_2 are both less than 90° in Fig. 10.5, in general they can be less than, equal to, or greater than 90°, and the analysis that follows applies to all of these possibilities.

The runner speed at inlet is $U_1 = \omega r_1$, and therefore it is specified by the impeller geometry and the machine operating speed. The absolute fluid velocity is the vector sum of the impeller velocity and the flow velocity relative to the blade. The absolute inlet velocity $\vec{V}_1$ may be determined graphically, as shown in Fig. 10.5b. The angle of the absolute fluid velocity, α_1, is measured from the direction normal to the flow area, as shown.[3] Note that for a given machine, angles α_1 and α_2 will vary with flow rate Q (through $\vec{V}_1$ and $\vec{V}_2$) and rotor speed ω (through U_1 and U_2). The tangential component of the absolute velocity, V_{t_1}, and the component normal to the flow area, V_{n_1}, are also shown in Fig. 10.5b. Note from the geometry of the figure that at each section the normal component of the *absolute* velocity, V_n, and the normal component of the velocity *relative to the blade*, V_{rb_n}, are equal (because the blade has no normal velocity).

When the inlet flow is swirl-free, the absolute inlet velocity will be purely radial. The inlet blade angle may be specified for the design flow rate and pump speed to provide shockless entry flow. Swirl, which may be present in the inlet flow, or introduced by *inlet guide vanes*, causes the absolute inlet flow direction to differ from radial.

The velocity diagram is constructed similarly at the outlet section. The runner speed at the outlet is $U_2 = \omega r_2$, which again is known from the geometry and operating speed of the turbomachine. The relative flow is assumed to leave the impeller tangent to the blades, as shown in Fig. 10.5c. This idealizing assumption of perfect guidance fixes the direction of the relative outlet flow at design conditions.

For a centrifugal pump or reaction turbine, the velocity relative to the blade generally changes in magnitude from inlet to outlet. The continuity equation must be

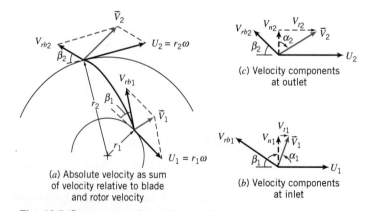

(c) Velocity components at outlet

(a) Absolute velocity as sum of velocity relative to blade and rotor velocity

(b) Velocity components at inlet

Fig. 10.5 Geometry and notation used to develop velocity diagrams for typical radial-flow machines.

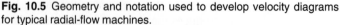

[3] The notation varies from book to book, so be careful when comparing references.

applied, using the impeller geometry, to determine the normal component of velocity at each section. The normal component, together with the outlet blade angle, is sufficient to establish the velocity relative to the blade at the impeller outlet for a radial-flow machine. The velocity diagram is completed by the vector addition of the velocity relative to the blade and the wheel velocity, as shown in Fig. 10.5c.

The inlet and outlet velocity diagrams provide all the information needed to calculate the ideal torque or power, absorbed or delivered by the impeller, using Eqs. 10.1 or 10.2. The results represent the performance of a turbomachine under idealized conditions at the design operating point, since we have assumed:

✓ Negligible torque due to surface forces (viscous and pressure).
✓ Inlet and exit flow tangent to blades.
✓ Uniform flow at inlet and exit.

An actual turbomachine is not likely to conform to all of these assumptions, so the results of our analysis represent the upper limit of the performance of actual machines.

Performance of an actual machine may be estimated using the same basic approach, but accounting for variations in flow properties across the blade span at the inlet and outlet sections, and for deviations between the blade angles and the flow directions. Such detailed calculations are beyond the scope of this book.

The alternative is to measure the overall performance of a machine on a suitable test stand. Manufacturers' data are examples of measured performance information.

In Example 10.1 the angular-momentum principle is applied to an idealized centrifugal pump. In Example 10.2 velocity diagrams are utilized in the analysis of flow through an axial-flow fan.

EXAMPLE 10.1   Idealized Centrifugal Pump

A centrifugal pump is used to pump 150 gpm of water. The water enters the impeller axially through a 1.25-in. diameter inlet. The inlet velocity is axial and uniform. The impeller outlet diameter is 4 in. Flow leaves the impeller at 10 ft/s relative to the blades, which are radial at the exit. The impeller speed is 3450 rpm. Determine the impeller exit width, b_2, the torque input, and the power predicted by the Euler turbine equation.

GIVEN: Flow as shown in the figure: $V_{rb_2} = 10$ ft/s, $Q = 150$ gpm.

FIND: (a) b_2.
(b) T_{shaft}.
(c) $\dot{W}_m$.

SOLUTION:
Apply the angular-momentum equation to a fixed control volume.

Governing equations:

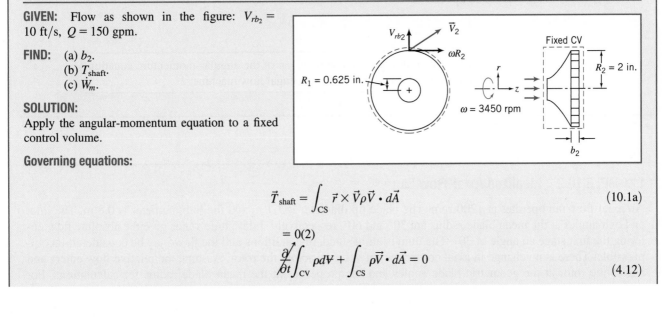

$$\vec{T}_{\text{shaft}} = \int_{CS} \vec{r} \times \vec{V} \rho \vec{V} \cdot d\vec{A} \qquad (10.1a)$$

$$\frac{\overset{= 0(2)}{\cancel{\partial}}}{\cancel{\partial t}} \int_{CV} \rho \, d\mkern-10mu\forall + \int_{CS} \rho \vec{V} \cdot d\vec{A} = 0 \qquad (4.12)$$

Assumptions: (1) Neglect torques due to body and surface forces.
(2) Steady flow.
(3) Uniform flow at inlet and outlet sections.
(4) Incompressible flow.

Then, from continuity,

$$(-\rho V_1 \pi R_1^2) + (\rho V_{rb_2} 2\pi R_2 b_2) = 0$$

or

$$\dot{m} = \rho Q = \rho V_{rb_2} 2\pi R_2 b_2$$

so that

$$b_2 = \frac{Q}{2\pi R_2 V_{rb_2}} = \frac{1}{2\pi} \times 150 \,\frac{\text{gal}}{\text{min}} \times \frac{1}{2 \,\text{in.}} \times \frac{\text{s}}{10 \,\text{ft}} \times \frac{\text{ft}^3}{7.48 \,\text{gal}} \times \frac{\text{min}}{60 \,\text{s}} \times \frac{12 \,\text{in.}}{\text{ft}}$$

$$b_2 = 0.0319 \text{ ft or } 0.383 \text{ in.} \longleftarrow \hspace{4cm} b_2$$

The angular-momentum equation, Eq. 10.1a, simplifies to Eq. 10.1b for uniform flow, or in scalar form to Eq. 10.1c,

$$T_{\text{shaft}} = (r_2 V_{t_2} - r_1 V_{t_1})\dot{m} \hspace{4cm} (10.1c)$$

For an axial inlet the tangential velocity $V_{t_1} = 0$, and for radial exit blades $V_{t_2} = R_2\omega$, so Eq. 10.1c reduces to

$$T_{\text{shaft}} = R_2^2 \omega \dot{m} = \omega R_2^2 \rho Q$$

where we have used continuity ($\dot{m} = \rho Q$).
Thus,

$$T_{\text{shaft}} = \omega R_2^2 \rho Q = 3450 \,\frac{\text{rev}}{\text{min}} \times (2)^2 \text{in.}^2 \times 1.94 \,\frac{\text{slug}}{\text{ft}^3} \times 150 \,\frac{\text{gal}}{\text{min}}$$

$$\times \, 2\pi \,\frac{\text{rad}}{\text{rev}} \times \frac{\text{min}^2}{3600 \,\text{s}^2} \times \frac{\text{ft}^3}{7.48 \,\text{gal}} \times \frac{\text{ft}^2}{144 \,\text{in.}^2} \times \frac{\text{lbf} \cdot \text{s}^2}{\text{slug} \cdot \text{ft}}$$

$$T_{\text{shaft}} = 6.51 \text{ ft} \cdot \text{lbf} \longleftarrow \hspace{4cm} T_{\text{shaft}}$$

and

$$\dot{W}_m = \omega T_{\text{shaft}} = 3450 \,\frac{\text{rev}}{\text{min}} \times 6.51 \text{ ft} \cdot \text{lbf} \times 2\pi \,\frac{\text{rad}}{\text{rev}} \times \frac{\text{min}}{60 \,\text{s}} \times \frac{\text{hp} \cdot \text{s}}{550 \,\text{ft} \cdot \text{lbf}}$$

$$\dot{W}_m = 4.28 \text{ hp} \longleftarrow \hspace{4cm} \dot{W}_m$$

This problem illustrates the application of the angular-momentum equation for a fixed control volume to a centrifugal flow machine.

EXAMPLE 10.2 Idealized Axial-Flow Fan

An axial-flow fan operates at 1200 rpm. The blade tip diameter is 1.1 m and the hub diameter is 0.8 m. The inlet and exit angles at the mean blade radius are 30° and 60°, respectively. Inlet guide vanes give the absolute flow entering the first stage an angle of 30°. The fluid is air at standard conditions and the flow may be considered incompressible. There is no change in axial component of velocity across the rotor. Assume the relative flow enters and leaves the rotor at the geometric blade angles and use properties at the mean blade radius for calculations. For these idealized conditions, draw the inlet velocity diagram, determine the volume flow rate of the fan, and sketch the rotor blade shapes. Using the data so obtained, draw the outlet velocity diagram and calculate the minimum torque and power needed to drive the fan.

GIVEN: Flow through rotor of axial-flow fan.

Tip diameter: 1.1 m
Hub diameter: 0.8 m
Operating speed: 1200 rpm
Absolute inlet angle: 30°
Blade inlet angle: 30°
Blade outlet angle: 60°

Fluid is air at standard conditions. Use properties at mean diameter of blades.

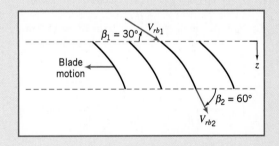

FIND:
(a) Inlet velocity diagram.
(b) Volume flow rate.
(c) Rotor blade shape.

(d) Outlet velocity diagram.
(e) Rotor torque.
(f) Power required.

SOLUTION:
Apply the angular-momentum equation to a fixed control volume.

Governing equations:

$$\vec{T}_{shaft} = \int_{CS} \vec{r} \times \vec{V} \, \rho \vec{V} \cdot d\vec{A} \tag{10.1a}$$

$$\frac{\overset{= \; 0(2)}{\cancel{\frac{\partial}{\partial t}} \int_{CV} \rho \, d\forall}}{} + \int_{CS} \rho \vec{V} \cdot d\vec{A} = 0 \tag{4.12}$$

Assumptions:
(1) Neglect torques due to body or surface forces.
(2) Steady flow.
(3) Uniform flow at inlet and outlet sections.
(4) Incompressible flow.
(5) No change in axial flow area.
(6) Use mean radius of rotor blades, R_m.

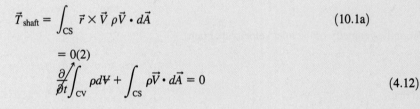

The blade shapes are
(Note that for an axial-flow machine the normal velocity components are parallel to the axis, not normal to the circumferential surface!)

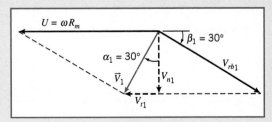

The inlet velocity diagram is
From continuity

$$(-\rho V_{n_1} A_1) + (\rho V_{n_2} A_2) = 0$$

or

$$Q = V_{n_1} A_1 = V_{n_2} A_2$$

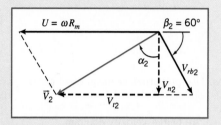

Since $A_1 = A_2$, then $V_{n_1} = V_{n_2}$, and the outlet velocity diagram is as shown in the following figure:
At the mean blade radius,

$$U = R_m \omega = \frac{D_m}{2}\omega$$

$$U = \frac{\frac{1}{2}(1.1 + 0.8)\text{ m}}{2} \times 1200\ \frac{\text{rev}}{\text{min}} \times 2\pi\ \frac{\text{rad}}{\text{rev}} \times \frac{\text{min}}{60\text{ s}} = 59.7\text{ m/s}$$

From the geometry of the inlet velocity diagram,

$$U = V_{n_1}(\tan\ \alpha_1 + \cot\ \beta_1)$$

so that

$$V_{n_1} = \frac{U}{\tan\ \alpha_1 + \cot\ \beta_1} = 59.7\ \frac{\text{m}}{\text{s}} \times \frac{1}{\tan 30° + \cot 30°} = 25.9\text{ m/s}$$

Consequently,

$$V_1 = \frac{V_{n_1}}{\cos\ \alpha_1} = 25.9\ \frac{\text{m}}{\text{s}} \times \frac{1}{\cos 30°} = 29.9\text{ m/s}$$

$$V_{t_1} = V_1 \sin\ \alpha_1 = 29.9\ \frac{\text{m}}{\text{s}} \times \sin 30° = 15.0\text{ m/s}$$

and

$$V_{rb_1} = \frac{V_{n_1}}{\sin\ \beta_1} = 25.9\ \frac{\text{m}}{\text{s}} \times \frac{1}{\sin 30°} = 51.8\text{ m/s}$$

The volume flow rate is

$$Q = V_{n_1} A_1 = \frac{\pi}{4} V_{n_1}(D_t^2 - D_h^2) = \frac{\pi}{4} \times 25.9\ \frac{\text{m}}{\text{s}}[(1.1)^2 - (0.8)^2]\text{ m}^2$$

$$Q = 11.6\text{ m}^3/\text{s} \underleftarrow{\hspace{6cm}} Q$$

From the geometry of the outlet velocity diagram,

$$\tan\alpha_2 = \frac{V_{t_2}}{V_{n_2}} = \frac{U - V_{n_2}\cot\beta_2}{V_{n_2}} = \frac{U - V_{n_1}\cot\beta_2}{V_{n_1}}$$

or

$$\alpha_2 = \tan^{-1}\left[\frac{59.7\,\dfrac{m}{s} - 25.9\,\dfrac{m}{s} \times \cot 60°}{25.9\,\dfrac{m}{s}}\right] = 59.9°$$

and

$$V_2 = \frac{V_{n_2}}{\cos\alpha_2} = \frac{V_{n_1}}{\cos\alpha_2} = 25.9\,\frac{m}{s} \times \frac{1}{\cos 59.9°} = 51.6\,m/s$$

Finally,

$$V_{t_2} = V_2 \sin\alpha_2 = 51.6\,\frac{m}{s} \times \sin 59.9° = 44.6\,m/s$$

The angular-momentum equation, Eq. 10.1a, simplifies to Eq. 10.1b for uniform flow, or in scalar form to Eq. 10.1c,

$$T_{shaft} = (r_2 V_{t_2} - r_1 V_{t_1})\dot{m} \tag{10.1c}$$

For this machine we have $r_1 = R_1 \approx R_m$ and $r_2 = R_2 \approx R_m$, so Eq. 10.1c reduces to

$$T_{shaft} = R_m(V_{t_2} - V_{t_1})\dot{m} = R_m(V_{t_2} - V_{t_1})\rho Q$$

where we have used continuity ($\dot{m} = \rho Q$).

Hence

$$T_{shaft} = \rho Q R_m(V_{t_2} - V_{t_1})$$

$$= 1.23\,\frac{kg}{m^3} \times 11.6\,\frac{m^3}{s} \times \frac{0.95\,m}{2} \times (44.6 - 15.0)\,\frac{m}{s} \times \frac{N \cdot s^2}{kg \cdot m}$$

$$T_{shaft} = 201\,N \cdot m \qquad\qquad\qquad\qquad\qquad\qquad\qquad\qquad T_{shaft}$$

Thus the torque *on* the CV is in the same sense as $\vec{\omega}$. The power required is

$$\dot{W}_m = \vec{\omega} \cdot \vec{T} = \omega T_{shaft} = 1200\,\frac{rev}{min} \times 2\pi\,\frac{rad}{rev} \times \frac{min}{60\,s} \times 201\,N \cdot m \times \frac{W \cdot s}{N \cdot m}$$

$$\dot{W}_m = 25.3\,kW \qquad\qquad\qquad\qquad\qquad\qquad\qquad\qquad\qquad \dot{W}_m$$

> This problem illustrates construction of velocity diagrams and application of the angular-momentum equation for a fixed control volume to an axial-flow machine under idealized conditions.

Figure 10.5 represents the flow through a simple centrifugal pump impeller. If the fluid enters the impeller with a purely radial absolute velocity, then the fluid entering the impeller has no angular momentum and V_{t_1} is identically zero.

With $V_{t_1} = 0$, the increase in head (from Eq. 10.2c) is given by

$$H = \frac{U_2 V_{t_2}}{g} \tag{10.3}$$

From the exit velocity diagram of Fig. 10.5c,

$$V_{t_2} = U_2 - V_{rb_2}\cos\beta_2 = U_2 - \frac{V_{n_2}}{\sin\beta_2}\cos\beta_2 = U_2 - V_{n_2}\cot\beta_2 \tag{10.4}$$

Then

$$H = \frac{U_2^2 - U_2 V_{n_2} \cot \beta_2}{g} \qquad (10.5)$$

For an impeller of width w, the volume flow rate is

$$Q = \pi D_2 w V_{n_2} \qquad (10.6)$$

To express the increase in head in terms of volume flow rate, we substitute for V_{n_2} in terms of Q from Eq. 10.6. Thus

$$H = \frac{U_2^2}{g} - \frac{U_2 \cot \beta_2}{\pi D_2 w g} Q \qquad (10.7a)$$

Equation 10.7a is of the form

$$H = C_1 - C_2 Q \qquad (10.7b)$$

where constants C_1 and C_2 are functions of *machine geometry* and *speed*,

$$C_1 = \frac{U_2^2}{g} \quad \text{and} \quad C_2 = \frac{U_2 \cot \beta}{\pi D_2 w g}$$

Thus Eq. 10.7a predicts a linear variation of head, H, with volume flow rate, Q. Note that this linear relation is an idealized model; actual devices may have only an approximate linear variation and may be better modeled with a curve-fitting method based on measured data. (We will see an example of this in Example 10.4.)

Constant $C_1 = U_2^2/g$ represents the ideal head developed by the pump for zero flow rate; this is called the *shutoff head*. The slope of the curve of head versus flow rate (the $H - Q$ curve) depends on the sign and magnitude of C_2.

For radial outlet vanes, $\beta_2 = 90°$ and $C_2 = 0$. The tangential component of the absolute velocity at the outlet is equal to the wheel speed and is independent of flow rate. From Eq. 10.7a, the ideal head is independent of flow rate. This characteristic $H - Q$ curve is plotted in Fig. 10.6.

If the vanes are *backward curved* (as shown in Fig. 10.5a), $\beta_2 < 90°$ and $C_2 > 0$. Then the tangential component of the absolute outlet velocity is less than the wheel speed and it decreases in proportion to the flow rate. From Eq. 10.7a, the ideal head decreases linearly with increasing flow rate. The corresponding $H - Q$ curve is plotted in Fig. 10.6.

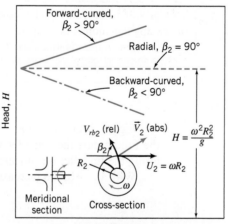

Fig. 10.6 Idealized relationship between head and volume flow rate for centrifugal pump with forward-curved, radial, and backward-curved impeller blades.

If the vanes are *forward curved*, then $\beta_2 > 90°$ and $C_2 < 0$. The tangential component of the absolute fluid velocity at the outlet is greater than the wheel speed and it increases as the flow rate increases. From Eq. 10.7a, the ideal head increases linearly with increasing flow rate. The corresponding $H - Q$ curve is plotted in Fig. 10.6.

The characteristics of a radial-flow machine can be altered by changing the outlet vane angle; the idealized model developed above predicts the trends as the outlet vane angle is changed.

The predictions of the idealized angular-momentum theory for a centrifugal pump are summarized in Fig. 10.6. Forward-curved vanes are almost never used in practice because they tend to have an unstable operating point.

Hydraulic Power

The torque and power predicted by applying the angular-momentum equation to a turbomachine rotor (Eqs. 10.1c and 10.2a) are idealized values. In practice, rotor power and the rate of change of fluid energy are not equal. Energy *transfer* between rotor and fluid causes losses because of viscous effects, departures from uniform flow, and departures of flow direction from the blade angles. Kinetic energy *transformation* to pressure rise (which is ultimately the goal of these turbomachines) by diffusion in the fixed casing introduces more losses. Energy *dissipation* occurs in seals and bearings and in fluid friction between the rotor and housing of the machine ("windage" losses). Applying the first law of thermodynamics to a control volume surrounding the rotor shows that these "losses" in mechanical energy are irreversible conversions from mechanical energy to thermal energy. As was the case for the pipe flows discussed in Chapter 8, the thermal energy appears either as internal energy in the fluid stream or as heat transfer to the surroundings.

Because of these losses, in a pump the actual power delivered to the fluid is less than predicted by the angular-momentum equation. In the case of a turbine, the actual power delivered to the shaft is less than the power given up by the fluid stream.

We can define the power, head, and efficiency of a turbomachine based on whether the machine does work on the fluid or extracts work (or power) from the fluid.

Machines for Doing Work on a Fluid

For a pump, the *hydraulic power* is given by the rate of mechanical energy input to the fluid,

$$\dot{W}_h = \rho Q g H_p \tag{10.8a}$$

where

$$H_p = \left(\frac{p}{\rho g} + \frac{\overline{V}^2}{2g} + z\right)_{\text{discharge}} - \left(\frac{p}{\rho g} + \frac{\overline{V}^2}{2g} + z\right)_{\text{suction}} \tag{10.8b}$$

For a pump the *head* rise measured on a test stand is less than that produced by the impeller. The rate of mechanical energy input is greater than the rate of head rise produced by the impeller. The mechanical input power needed to drive the pump is related to the hydraulic power by defining *pump efficiency* as

$$\eta_p = \frac{\dot{W}_h}{\dot{W}_m} = \frac{\rho Q g H_p}{\omega T} \tag{10.8c}$$

To evaluate the actual change in head across a machine from Eq. 10.8b, we must know the pressure, fluid velocity, and elevation at two measurement sections. Fluid velocity can be calculated from the measured volume flow rate and passage diameters. (Suction and discharge lines for pumps usually have different inside diameters.)

Static pressure usually is measured in straight sections of pipe upstream from the pump inlet and downstream from the pump outlet, after diffusion has occurred within the pump casing. The elevation of each pressure gage may be recorded, or the static pressure readings may be corrected to the same elevation. (The pump centerline provides a convenient reference level.)

Machines for Extracting Work (Power) from a Fluid

For a hydraulic turbine the *hydraulic power* is defined as the rate of mechanical energy removal from the flowing fluid stream,

$$\dot{W}_h = \rho Q g H_t \tag{10.9a}$$

where

$$H_t = \left(\frac{p}{\rho g} + \frac{\overline{V}^2}{2g} + z\right)_{\text{inlet}} - \left(\frac{p}{\rho g} + \frac{\overline{V}^2}{2g} + z\right)_{\text{outlet}} \tag{10.9b}$$

For a hydraulic turbine the power output obtained from the rotor (the mechanical power) is less than the rate of energy transfer from the fluid to the rotor, because the rotor must overcome friction and windage losses.

The mechanical power output obtained from the turbine is related to the hydraulic power by defining *turbine efficiency* as

$$\eta_t = \frac{\dot{W}_m}{\dot{W}_h} = \frac{\omega T}{\rho Q g H_t} \tag{10.9c}$$

Equations 10.9a and 10.9b show that *to obtain maximum power output from a hydraulic turbine, it is important to minimize the mechanical energy in the flow leaving the turbine.* This is accomplished by making the outlet pressure, flow speed, and elevation as small as practical. The turbine must be set as close to the tailwater level as possible, allowing for the level increase when the river floods. Tests to measure turbine efficiency may be performed at various output power levels and at different constant head conditions (see the discussion of Figs. 10.12 and 10.13).

The trends predicted by the idealized angular-momentum theory, especially Eq. 10.7b and Fig. 10.6, are compared with experimental results in the next section.

10-4   **PERFORMANCE CHARACTERISTICS**

To specify fluid machines for flow systems, the designer must know the pressure rise (or head), torque, power requirement, and efficiency of a machine. For a given machine each of these characteristics is a function of flow rate; the characteristics for similar machines depend upon size and operating speed. In this section we define *performance characteristics* for pumps and turbines and review experimentally measured trends for typical machines. We discuss *dimensionless parameters* to illustrate the similarities among families of machines and the trends in design features as functions of flow rate and head rise. We review *scaling laws* and present examples to illustrate their use. The section concludes with a discussion of *cavitation* and the net head that must be available at the inlet of a pump to assure satisfactory cavitation-free operation.

Performance Parameters

The idealized analyses presented in Section 10-3 are useful to predict trends and to approximate the design-point performance of an energy-absorbing or energy-producing machine. However, the complete performance of a real machine, including operation at off-design conditions, must be determined experimentally. We consider the performance parameters of a turbomachine based on whether the machine does work on the fluid or extracts work (or power) from the fluid.

Machines for Doing Work on a Fluid

To determine performance, a pump, fan, blower, or compressor must be set up on an instrumented test stand with the capability of measuring flow rate, speed, input torque, and pressure rise. The test must be performed according to a standardized procedure corresponding to the machine being tested [4, 5]. Measurements are made as flow rate is varied from shutoff (zero flow) to maximum delivery by varying the load from maximum to minimum (by starting with a valve that is closed and opening it to fully open in stages). Power input to the machine is determined from a calibrated motor or calculated from measured speed and torque, and then efficiency is computed as illustrated in Example 10.3. Finally, the calculated characteristics are plotted in the desired engineering units or nondimensionally. If appropriate, smooth curves may be faired through the plotted points or curve-fits may be made to the results, as illustrated in Example 10.4.

EXAMPLE 10.3   Calculation of Pump Characteristics from Test Data

The flow system used to test a centrifugal pump at a nominal speed of 1750 rpm is shown. The liquid is water at 80°F, and the suction and discharge pipe diameters are 6 in. Data measured during the test are given in the table. The electric motor is supplied at 460 V, 3-phase, and has a power factor of 0.875 and a constant efficiency of 90 percent.

Rate of Flow (gpm)	Suction Pressure (psig)	Discharge Pressure (psig)	Motor Current (amp)
0	0.65	53.3	18.0
500	0.25	48.3	26.2
800	−0.35	42.3	31.0
1000	−0.92	36.9	33.9
1100	−1.24	33.0	35.2
1200	−1.62	27.8	36.3
1400	−2.42	15.3	38.0
1500	−2.89	7.3	39.0

Calculate the net head delivered and the pump efficiency at a volume flow rate of 1000 gpm. Plot the pump head, power input, and efficiency as functions of volume flow rate.

GIVEN: Pump test flow system and data shown.

FIND: (a) Pump head and efficiency at $Q = 1000$ gpm.
    (b) Pump head, power input, and efficiency as a function of volume flow rate. Plot the results.

SOLUTION:

Governing equations:

$$\dot{W}_h = \rho Q g H_p \qquad \eta_p = \frac{\dot{W}_h}{\dot{W}_m} = \frac{\rho Q g H_p}{\omega T}$$

$$H_p = \left(\frac{p}{\rho g} + \frac{\overline{V}^2}{2g} + z \right)_d - \left(\frac{p}{\rho g} + \frac{\overline{V}^2}{2g} + z \right)_s$$

Assumptions: (1) Steady flow.
(2) Uniform flow at each section.
(3) $\overline{V}_2 = \overline{V}_1$.
(4) Correct all heads to the same elevation.

Since $\overline{V}_1 = \overline{V}_2$, the pump head is

$$H_p = \frac{1}{g}\left[\left(\frac{p}{\rho} + gz\right)_d - \left(\frac{p}{\rho} + gz\right)_s\right] = \frac{p_2 - p_1}{\rho g}$$

where the discharge and suction pressures, *corrected to the same elevation*, are designated p_2 and p_1, respectively.

Correct measured static pressures to the pump centerline:

$$p_1 = p_s + \rho g z_s$$

$$p_1 = \frac{-0.92\ \text{lbf}}{\text{in.}^2} + 1.94\ \frac{\text{slug}}{\text{ft}^3} \times 32.2\ \frac{\text{ft}}{\text{s}^2} \times 1.0\ \text{ft} \times \frac{\text{lbf} \cdot \text{s}^2}{\text{slug} \cdot \text{ft}} \times \frac{\text{ft}^2}{144\ \text{in.}^2} = -0.49\ \text{psig}$$

and

$$p_2 = p_d + \rho g z_d$$

$$p_2 = \frac{36.9\ \text{lbf}}{\text{in.}^2} + 1.94\ \frac{\text{slug}}{\text{ft}^3} \times 32.2\ \frac{\text{ft}}{\text{s}^2} \times 3.0\ \text{ft} \times \frac{\text{lbf} \cdot \text{s}^2}{\text{slug} \cdot \text{ft}} \times \frac{\text{ft}^2}{144\ \text{in.}^2} = 38.2\ \text{psi}$$

Calculate the pump head:

$$H_p = (p_2 - p_1)/\rho g$$

$$H_p = \frac{[38.2 - (-0.49)]\ \text{lbf}}{\text{in.}^2} \times \frac{\text{ft}^3}{1.94\ \text{slug}} \times \frac{\text{s}^2}{32.2\ \text{ft}} \times \frac{144\ \text{in.}^2}{\text{ft}^2} \times \frac{\text{slug} \cdot \text{ft}}{\text{lbf} \cdot \text{s}^2} = 89.2\ \text{ft} \qquad\qquad\qquad H_p$$

Compute the hydraulic power delivered to the fluid:

$$\dot{W}_h = \rho Q g H_p = Q(p_2 - p_1)$$

$$= \frac{1000\ \text{gal}}{\text{min}} \times \frac{[38.2 - (-0.49)]\ \text{lbf}}{\text{in.}^2} \times \frac{\text{ft}^3}{7.48\ \text{gal}} \times \frac{\text{min}}{60\ \text{s}} \times \frac{144\ \text{in.}^2}{\text{ft}^2} \times \frac{\text{hp} \cdot \text{s}}{550\ \text{ft} \cdot \text{lbf}}$$

$$\dot{W}_h = 22.6\ \text{hp}$$

Calculate the motor power output (the mechanical power input to the pump) from electrical information:

$$\mathscr{P}_{\text{in}} = \eta\sqrt{3}(PF)EI$$

$$\mathscr{P}_{\text{in}} = 0.90 \times \sqrt{3} \times 0.875 \times 460\ \text{V} \times 33.9\ \text{A} \times \frac{\text{W}}{\text{VA}} \times \frac{\text{hp}}{746\ \text{W}} = 28.5\ \text{hp}$$

The corresponding pump efficiency is

$$\eta_p = \frac{\dot{W}_h}{\dot{W}_m} = \frac{22.6\ \text{hp}}{28.5\ \text{hp}} = 0.792 \quad \text{or} \quad 79.2\ \text{percent} \qquad\qquad\qquad \eta_p$$

Results from similar calculations at the other volume flow rates are plotted below:

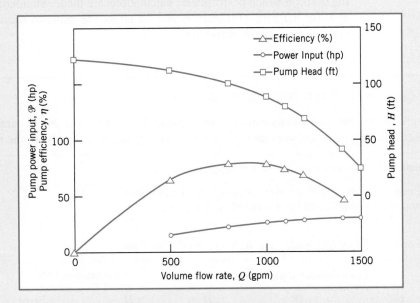

This problem illustrates the data reduction procedure used to obtain the performance curves for a pump from experimental data. The results calculated and plotted in this example are typical for a centrifugal pump driven at constant speed:
- ✓ The pressure rise is highest at shutoff (zero flow rate).
- ✓ Pressure rise decreases steadily as flow rate is increased; compare this typical experimental curve to the linear behavior predicted by Eq. 10.7b, and shown in Fig. 10.6, for idealized backward-curved impeller blades (used in most centrifugal pumps).
- ✓ Required power input increases with flow rate; the increase is generally nonlinear.
- ✓ Efficiency is zero at shutoff, rises to a peak as flow rate is increased, then drops off at larger flow rates; it stays near its maximum over a range of flow rates (in this example, from about 800 to 1100 gpm).

This example is a little oversimplified because it is assumed that the electric motor efficiency is constant. In practice, motor efficiency varies with load, so must be either computed at each load from motor speed and torque measurements, or obtained from a calibration curve.

🖱 The *Excel* workbook for this Example was used for the calculations for each flow rate, and for generating the graph. It can be modified for use with other pump data.

The basic procedure used to calculate machine performance was illustrated for a centrifugal pump in Example 10.3. The difference in static pressures between the pump suction and discharge was used to calculate the head rise produced by the pump. For pumps, dynamic pressure rise (or fluid kinetic energy change) typically is a small fraction of the head rise developed by the pump, so it may be neglected compared with the head rise.

The test and data reduction procedures for fans, blowers, and compressors are basically the same as for centrifugal pumps. However, blowers, and especially fans, add relatively small amounts of static head to gas or vapor flows. For these machines, the dynamic head may increase from inlet to discharge, and it may be appreciable compared with the static head rise. For these reasons, it is important to state clearly the basis on which performance calculations are made. Standard definitions are available for machine efficiency based on either the static-to-static pressure rise or the static-to-total pressure rise [6].

EXAMPLE 10.4   Curve-Fit to Pump Performance Data

Pump test data were given and performance was calculated in Example 10.3. Fit a parabolic curve, $H = H_0 - AQ^2$, to these calculated pump performance results and compare the fitted curve with the measured data.

GIVEN: Pump test data and performance calculated in Example 10.3.

FIND: (a) Parabolic curve, $H = H_0 - AQ^2$, fitted to the pump performance data.
   (b) Comparison of the curve-fit with the calculated performance.

SOLUTION:

The curve-fit may be obtained by fitting a linear curve to H versus Q^2. Tabulating,

From calculated performance:			From the curve fit:	
Q (gpm)	Q^2 (gpm^2)	H (ft)	H (ft)	Error (%)
0	0	123	127	2.8
500	25×10^4	113	116	3.1
800	64×10^4	100	99.8	−0.5
1000	100×10^4	89.2	84.6	−5.2
1100	121×10^4	80.9	75.7	−6.5
1200	144×10^4	69.8	65.9	−5.6
1400	196×10^4	42.8	43.9	2.5
1500	225×10^4	25.5	31.7	24.2
			Intercept =	127
			Slope =	-4.23×10^{-5}
			r^2 =	0.984

Using the method of least squares, the equation for the fitted curve is obtained as

$$H \text{ (ft)} = 127 - 4.23 \times 10^{-5} \, [Q(\text{gpm})]^2$$

with coefficient of determination $r^2 = 0.984$. (The closer r^2 is to unity, its maximum possible value, the better the fit.)

Always compare the results of a curve-fit with the data used to develop the fit. The figure shows the curve-fit (the solid line) and the experimental values (the points).

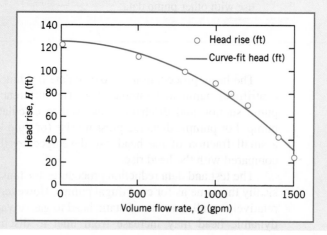

This problem illustrates that the pump test data for Example 10.3 can be fitted quite well to a parabolic curve. As with fitting a curve to any experimental data, our justifications for choosing a parabolic function in this case are:

✓ Experimental observation—the experimental data *looks* parabolic.

✓ Theory or concept—we will see later in this section that similarity rules suggest such a relation between head and flow rate.

The *Excel* workbook for this Example was used for the least-squares calculations, and for generating the graph. It can be modified for use with other pump data.

Typical characteristic curves for a centrifugal pump tested at constant speed were shown qualitatively in Fig. 7.5;[4] the head versus capacity curve is reproduced in Fig. 10.7 to compare with characteristics predicted by the idealized analysis. Figure 10.7 shows that the head at any flow rate in the real machine may be significantly lower than is predicted by the idealized analysis. Some of the causes are:

1. At very low flow rate some fluid recirculates in the impeller.
2. Friction loss and leakage loss both increase with flow rate.
3. "Shock loss" results from mismatch between the direction of the relative velocity and the tangent to the impeller blade at the inlet.[5]

Curves such as those in Figs. 7.5 and 10.7 are measured at constant (design) speed with a single impeller diameter. It is common practice to vary pump capacity by changing the impeller size in a given casing. To present information compactly, data from tests of several impeller diameters may be plotted on a single graph, as shown in Fig. 10.8. As before, for each diameter, head is plotted versus flow rate; each curve is labeled with the corresponding diameter. Efficiency contours are

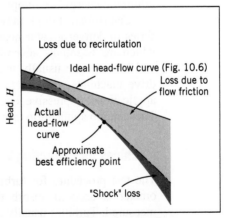

Fig. 10.7 Comparison of ideal and actual head-flow curves for a centrifugal pump with backward-curved impeller blades [8].

[4] The only important pump characteristic not shown in Fig. 7.5 is the net positive suction head (*NPSH*) required to prevent cavitation. Cavitation and *NPSH* will be treated later in this section.

[5] This loss is largest at high and low flow rates; it decreases essentially to zero as optimum operating conditions are approached [7].

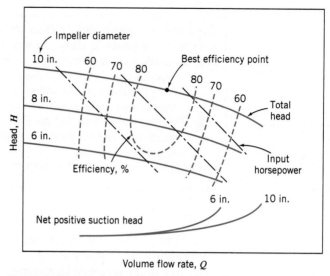

Fig. 10.8 Typical pump performance curves from tests with three impeller diameters at constant speed [8].

plotted by joining points having the same constant efficiency. Power-requirement contours are also plotted. Finally, the *NPSH* requirements (which we have not yet defined—we will discuss its meaning later in this section) are shown for the extreme diameters; in Fig. 10.8, the curve for the 8 in. impeller would lie between the curves for the 6 in. and 10 in. impellers.

For this typical machine, head is a maximum at shutoff and decreases continuously as flow rate increases. Input power is minimum at shutoff and increases as delivery is increased. Consequently, to minimize the starting load, it may be advisable to start the pump with the outlet valve closed. (However, the valve should not be left closed for long, lest the pump overheat as energy dissipated by friction is transferred to the water in the housing.) Pump efficiency increases with capacity until the *best efficiency point* (BEP) is reached, then decreases as flow rate is increased further. For minimum energy consumption, it is desirable to operate as close to BEP as possible.

Centrifugal pumps may be combined in parallel to deliver greater flow or in series to deliver greater head. A number of manufacturers build multi-stage pumps, which are essentially several pumps arranged in series within a single casing. Pumps and blowers are usually tested at several constant speeds. Common practice is to drive machines with electric motors at nearly constant speed, but in some system applications impressive energy savings can result from variable-speed operation. These pump application topics are discussed in Section 10-5.

Machines for Extracting Work (Power) from a Fluid

The test procedure for turbines is similar to that for pumps, except that a dynamometer is used to absorb the turbine power output while speed and torque are measured. Turbines usually are intended to operate at a constant speed that is a fraction or multiple of the electric power frequency to be produced. Therefore turbine tests are run at constant speed under varying load, while water usage is measured and efficiency is calculated.

The impulse turbine is a relatively simple turbomachine, so we use it to illustrate typical test results. Impulse turbines are chosen when the head available exceeds about 300 m. Most impulse turbines used today are improved versions of the *Pelton wheel* developed in the 1880s by American mining engineer Lester Pelton [9]. An impulse turbine is supplied with water under high head through a long conduit called

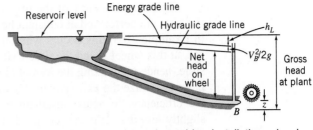

Fig. 10.9 Schematic of impulse-turbine installation, showing definitions of gross and net heads [7].

a *penstock*. The water is accelerated through a nozzle and discharges as a high-speed free jet at atmospheric pressure. The jet strikes deflecting buckets attached to the rim of a rotating wheel (Fig. 10.3a). Its kinetic energy is given up as it is turned by the buckets. Turbine output is controlled at essentially constant jet speed by changing the flow rate of water striking the buckets. A variable-area nozzle may be used to make small and gradual changes in turbine output. Larger or more rapid changes must be accomplished by means of jet deflectors, or auxiliary nozzles, to avoid sudden changes in flow speed and the resulting high pressures in the long water column in the penstock. Water discharged from the wheel at relatively low speed falls into the tailrace. The tailrace level is set to avoid submerging the wheel during flooded conditions. When large amounts of water are available, additional power can be obtained by connecting two wheels to a single shaft or by arranging two or more jets to strike a single wheel.

Figure 10.9 illustrates an impulse-turbine installation and the definitions of gross and net head [7]. The *gross head* available is the difference between the levels in the supply reservoir and the tailrace. The effective or *net head, H*, used to calculate efficiency, is the total head at the *entrance* to the nozzle, measured at the nozzle centerline [7]. Hence not all of the net head is converted into work at the turbine: Some is lost to turbine inefficiency, some is lost in the nozzle itself, and some is lost as residual kinetic energy in the exit flow. In practice, the penstock usually is sized so that at rated power the net head is 85–95 percent of the gross head.

In addition to nozzle loss, windage, bearing friction, and surface friction between the jet and bucket reduce performance compared with the ideal, frictionless case. Figure 10.10 shows typical results from tests performed at constant head.

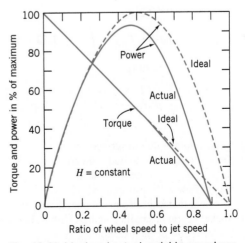

Fig. 10.10 Ideal and actual variable-speed performance for an impulse turbine [10].

The peak efficiency of the impulse turbine corresponds to the peak power, since the tests are performed at constant head and flow rate. For the ideal turbine, as shown in Example 10.5, this occurs when the wheel speed is half the jet speed. As we will see, at this wheel speed the fluid exits the turbine at the lowest absolute velocity possible, hence minimizing the loss of kinetic energy at the exit. As indicated in Eq. 10.2a, if we minimize the exit velocity $\vec{V}_2$ we will maximize the turbine work $\dot{W}_m$, and hence the efficiency. In actual installations, peak efficiency occurs at a wheel speed only slightly less than half the jet speed. This condition fixes the wheel speed once the jet speed is determined for a given installation. For large units, overall efficiency may be as high as 88 percent [11].

EXAMPLE 10.5   Optimum Speed for Impulse Turbine

A Pelton wheel is a form of impulse turbine well adapted to situations of high head and low flow rate. Consider the Pelton wheel and single-jet arrangement shown, in which the jet stream strikes the bucket tangentially and is turned through angle θ. Obtain an expression for the torque exerted by the water stream on the wheel and the corresponding power output. Show that the power is a maximum when the bucket speed, $U = R\omega$, is half the jet speed, V.

GIVEN: Pelton wheel and single jet shown.

FIND: (a) Expression for torque exerted on the wheel.
(b) Expression for power output.
(c) Ratio of wheel speed U to jet speed V for maximum power.

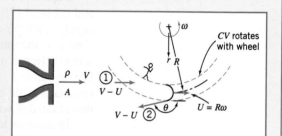

SOLUTION:

As an illustration of its use, we start with the angular-momentum equation, Eq. 4.52 (on the Web site), for a rotating CV as shown, rather than the inertial CV form, Eq. 4.46, that we used in deriving the Euler turbomachine equation in Section 10.3.

Governing equation:

$$\overbrace{\vec{r} \times \vec{F}_s}^{=\,0(1)} + \overbrace{\int_{CV} \vec{r} \times \vec{g}\, \rho\, d\mathcal{V}}^{=\,0(2)} + \vec{T}_{shaft} - \int_{CV} \vec{r} \times [2\vec{\omega} \times \vec{V}_{xyz} + \vec{\omega} \times (\vec{\omega} \times \vec{r}) + \overbrace{\dot{\vec{\omega}} \times \vec{r}}^{\approx\,0(3)}]\, \rho\, d\mathcal{V}$$

$$= \overbrace{\frac{\partial}{\partial t}\int_{CV} \vec{r} \times \vec{V}_{xyz}\, \rho\, d\mathcal{V}}^{=\,0(4)} + \int_{CS} \vec{r} \times \vec{V}_{xyz}\, \rho\vec{V}_{xyz} \cdot d\vec{A}$$

$$\tag{4.52}$$

Assumptions: (1) Neglect torque due to surface forces.
(2) Neglect torque due to body forces.
(3) Neglect mass of water on wheel.
(4) Steady flow with respect to wheel.
(5) All water that issues from the nozzle acts upon the buckets.
(6) Bucket height is small compared with R, hence $r_1 \approx r_2 \approx R$.
(7) Uniform flow at each section.
(8) No change in jet speed relative to bucket.

Then, since all water from the jet crosses the buckets,

$$\vec{T}_{shaft} = \vec{r}_1 \times \vec{V}_1(-\rho VA) + \vec{r}_2 \times \vec{V}_2(+\rho VA)$$

$$\vec{r}_1 = R\hat{e}_r \qquad\qquad \vec{r}_2 = R\hat{e}_r$$

$$\vec{V}_1 = (V - U)\hat{e}_\theta \qquad \vec{V}_2 = (V - U)\cos\theta\,\hat{e}_\theta + (V - U)\sin\theta\,\hat{e}_r$$

$$T_{shaft}\hat{k} = R(V - U)\hat{k}(-\rho VA) + R(V - U)\cos\theta\,\hat{k}(\rho VA)$$

so that finally

$$T_{shaft}\hat{k} = -R(1 - \cos\theta)\rho VA(V - U)\hat{k}$$

This is the external torque of the shaft on the control volume, i.e., on the wheel. The torque exerted by the water on the wheel is equal and opposite,

$$\vec{T}_{out} = -\vec{T}_{shaft} = R(1 - \cos\theta)\rho VA(V - U)\hat{k} = \rho QR(V - U)(1 - \cos\theta)\hat{k} \qquad \longleftarrow \quad \vec{T}_{out}$$

The corresponding power output is

$$\dot{W}_{out} = \vec{\omega} \cdot \vec{T}_{out} = R\omega(1 - \cos\theta)\rho VA(V - U) = \rho QU(V - U)(1 - \cos\theta) \qquad \longleftarrow \quad \dot{W}_{out}$$

To find the condition for maximum power, differentiate the expression for power with respect to wheel speed U and set the result equal to zero. Thus

$$\frac{d\dot{W}}{dU} = \rho Q(V - U)(1 - \cos\theta) + \rho QU(-1)(1 - \cos\theta) = 0$$

$$\therefore (V - U) - U = V - 2U = 0$$

Thus for maximum power, $\quad U/V = \frac{1}{2}$ or $U = V/2$. $\qquad \longleftarrow \qquad\qquad U/V$

Note: Turning the flow through $\theta = 180°$ would give maximum power with $U = V/2$. Under these conditions, theoretically the *absolute* velocity of the fluid at the exit (computed in the direction of U) would be $U - (V - U) = V/2 - (V - V/2) = 0$, so that the fluid would exit with zero kinetic energy, maximizing the power output. In practice, it is possible to deflect the jet stream through angles up to 165°. With $\theta = 165°$, $1 - \cos\theta \approx 1.97$, or about 1.5 percent below the value for maximum power.

This problem illustrates the use of the angular-momentum equation for a rotating control volume, Eq. 4.52 (on the Web), to analyze flow through an ideal impulse turbine.

✓ The peak power occurs when the wheel speed is half the jet speed, which is a useful design criterion when selecting a turbine for a given available head.

✓ This problem also could be analyzed starting with an inertial control volume, i.e., using the Euler turbomachine equation (Problem 10.16).

In practice, hydraulic turbines usually are run at a constant speed, and output is varied by changing the opening area of the needle valve jet nozzle. Nozzle loss increases slightly and mechanical losses become a larger fraction of output as the valve is closed, so efficiency drops sharply at low load, as shown in Fig. 10.11. For this Pelton wheel, efficiency remains above 85 percent from 40 to 113 percent of full load.

At lower heads, reaction turbines provide better efficiency than impulse turbines. In contrast to flow in a centrifugal pump, used for doing work on a fluid, flow in a work-producing reaction turbine enters the rotor at the largest (outer) radial section and discharges at the smallest (inner) radial section after transferring most of its energy to the rotor. Reaction turbines tend to be high flow, low head machines. A typical reaction turbine installation is shown schematically in Fig. 10.12, where the terminology used to define the heads is indicated.

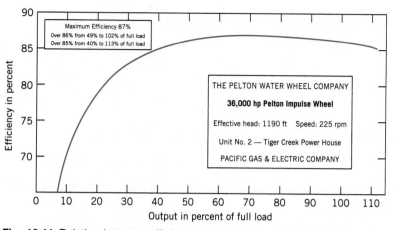

Fig. 10.11 Relation between efficiency and output for a typical Pelton water turbine (adapted from [11]).

Reaction turbines flow full of water. Consequently, it is possible to use a diffuser or draft tube to regain a fraction of the kinetic energy that remains in water leaving the rotor. The draft tube forms an integral part of the installation design. As shown in Fig. 10.12, the *gross head* available is the difference between the supply reservoir head and the tailrace head. The *effective head* or *net head, H*, used to calculate efficiency, is the difference between the elevation of the energy grade line just upstream of the turbine and that of the draft tube discharge (section *C*). The benefit of the draft tube is clear: the net head available for the turbine is equal to the gross head minus losses in the supply pipework and the kinetic energy loss at the turbine exit; without the draft tube the exit velocity and kinetic energy would be relatively large, but with the draft tube they are small, leading to increased turbine efficiency. Put another way, the draft tube diffuser, through a Bernoulli effect, reduces the turbine exit pressure, leading to a larger pressure drop across the turbine, and increased power output. (We saw a similar Bernoulli effect used by ancient Romans in Example 8.10.)

An efficient mixed-flow turbine runner was developed by James B. Francis using a careful series of experiments at Lowell, Massachusetts, during the 1840s [9]. An efficient axial-flow propeller turbine, with adjustable blades, was developed by German professor Victor Kaplan between 1910 and 1924. The *Francis Turbine* (Fig. 10.3*b*) is usually chosen when $15 \leq H \leq 300$ m, and the *Kaplan Turbine* (Fig. 10.3*c*) is usually chosen for heads of 15 m or less. Performance of reaction turbines may be measured in the same manner as performance of the impulse turbine. However, because the gross heads are less, any change in water level during operation is more significant. Consequently, measurements are made at a series of heads to completely define the performance of a reaction turbine.

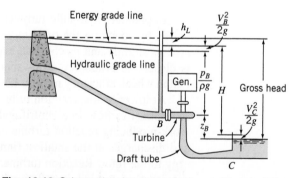

Fig. 10.12 Schematic of typical reaction turbine installation, showing definitions of head terminology [7].

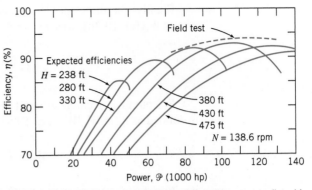

Fig. 10.13 Performance of typical reaction turbine as predicted by model tests (expected efficiencies) and confirmed by field test [10].

An example of the data presentation for a reaction turbine is given in Fig. 10.13, where efficiency is shown at various output powers for a series of constant heads [10]. The reaction turbine has higher maximum efficiency than the impulse turbine, but efficiency varies more sharply with load.

As a sharp-eyed reader, you will have noticed that Fig. 10.13 contained both model-test (expected efficiencies) and full-scale results. You should be asking, "How are model tests designed and conducted, and how are model test results scaled to predict prototype performance?" To answer these questions, read on.

Dimensional Analysis and Specific Speed

Dimensional analysis for turbomachines was introduced in Chapter 7, where dimensionless flow, head, and power coefficients were derived in generalized form. The independent parameters were the flow coefficient and a form of Reynolds number. The dependent parameters were the head and power coefficients.

Our objective here is to develop the forms of dimensionless coefficients in common use, and to give examples illustrating their use in selecting a machine type, designing model tests, and scaling results. Since we developed an idealized theory for turbomachines in Section 10-3, we can gain additional physical insight by developing dimensionless coefficients directly from the resulting computing equations.

The dimensionless *flow coefficient*, Φ, is defined by normalizing the volume flow rate using the exit area and the wheel speed at the outlet. Thus

$$\Phi = \frac{Q}{A_2 U_2} = \frac{V_{n_2}}{U_2} \tag{10.10}$$

where V_{n_2} is the velocity component perpendicular to the exit area. This component is also referred to as the *meridional velocity* at the wheel exit plane. It appears in true projection in the *meridional plane*, which is any radial cross-section through the centerline of a machine.

A dimensionless *head coefficient*, Ψ, may be obtained by normalizing the head, H (Eq. 10.2c), with U_2^2/g. Thus

$$\Psi = \frac{gH}{U_2^2} \tag{10.11}$$

A dimensionless *torque coefficient*, τ, may be obtained by normalizing the torque, T (Eq. 10.1c), with $\rho A_2 U_2^2 R_2$. Thus

$$\tau = \frac{T}{\rho A_2 U_2^2 R_2} \tag{10.12}$$

Finally, the dimensionless *power coefficient*, Π, is obtained by normalizing the power $\dot{W}$ (Eq. 10.2b), with $\dot{m}\ U_2^2 = \rho Q U_2^2$. Thus

$$\Pi = \frac{\dot{W}}{\rho Q U_2^2} = \frac{\dot{W}}{\rho \omega^2 Q R_2^2} \qquad (10.13)$$

For pumps, mechanical input power exceeds hydraulic power, and the efficiency is defined as $\eta_p = \dot{W}_h / \dot{W}_m$ (Eq. 10.8c). Hence

$$\dot{W}_m = T\omega = \frac{1}{\eta_p}\ \dot{W}_h = \frac{\rho Q g H_p}{\eta_p} \qquad (10.14)$$

Introducing dimensionless coefficients Φ (Eq. 10.10), Ψ (Eq. 10.11), and τ (Eq. 10.12) into Eq. 10.14, we obtain an analogous relation among the dimensionless coefficients as

$$\tau = \frac{\Psi\Phi}{\eta_p} \qquad (10.15)$$

For turbines, mechanical output power is less than hydraulic power, and the efficiency is defined as $\eta_t = \dot{W}_m / \dot{W}_h$ (Eq. 10.9c). Hence,

$$\dot{W}_m = T\omega = \eta_t \dot{W}_h = \eta_t \rho Q g H_t \qquad (10.16)$$

Introducing dimensionless coefficients Φ, Ψ, and τ into Eq. 10.16, we obtain an analogous relation among the dimensionless coefficients as

$$\tau = \eta_t\, \Psi\Phi \qquad (10.17)$$

The dimensionless coefficients form the basis for designing model tests and scaling the results. As shown in Chapter 7, the flow coefficient Φ is treated as the independent parameter. Then, if viscous effects are neglected, the head, torque, and power coefficients are treated as multiple dependent parameters. Under these assumptions, dynamic similarity is achieved when the flow coefficient is matched between model and prototype machines.

As discussed in Chapter 7, a useful parameter called *specific speed* can be obtained by combining the flow and head coefficients and eliminating the machine size. The result was

$$N_S = \frac{\omega Q^{1/2}}{h^{3/4}} \qquad (7.22a)$$

When head is expressed as energy per unit mass (i.e., with dimensions equivalent to L^2/t^2, or g times head in height of liquid), and ω is expressed in radians per second, the specific speed defined by Eq. 7.22a is dimensionless.

Although specific speed is a dimensionless parameter, it is common practice to use an "engineering" equation form of Eq. 7.22a in which ω and Q are specified in units that are convenient but inconsistent, and energy per unit mass, h, is replaced with energy per unit weight of fluid, H. When this is done, the specific speed is not a unitless parameter and the magnitude of the specific speed depends on the units used to calculate it. Customary units used in U.S. engineering practice for pumps are rpm for ω, gpm for Q, and feet (energy per unit weight) for H. In practice, the symbol N is used to represent rate of rotation (ω) in rpm. Thus, the dimensional specific speed for pumps, expressed in U.S. customary units, as an "engineering" equation, becomes

$$N_{S_{cu}} = \frac{N(\text{rpm})[Q(\text{gpm})]^{1/2}}{[H(\text{ft})]^{3/4}} \qquad (7.22b)$$

Values of the dimensionless specific speed, N_S (Eq. 7.22a), must be multiplied by 2733 to obtain the values of specific speed corresponding to this commonly used but inconsistent set of units (see Example 10.6).

For hydraulic turbines, we use the fact that power output is proportional to flow rate and head, $\mathcal{P} \propto \rho Q h$ in consistent units. Substituting $\mathcal{P}/\rho h$ for Q in Eq. 7.22a gives

$$N_S = \omega(\mathcal{P}/\rho h)^{1/2}/h^{3/4} = \omega\mathcal{P}^{1/2}/(\rho^{1/2}h^{5/4}) \qquad (10.18a)$$

as the nondimensional form of the specific speed.

In U.S. engineering practice it is customary to drop the factor $\rho^{1/2}$ (water is invariably the working fluid in the turbines to which the specific speed is applied) and to use head H in place of energy per unit mass h. Customary units used in U.S. engineering practice for hydraulic turbines are rpm for ω, horsepower for $\mathcal{P}$, and feet for H. In practice, the symbol N is used to represent rate of rotation (ω) in rpm. Thus the dimensional specific speed for a hydraulic turbine, expressed in U.S. customary units, as an "engineering" equation, becomes

$$N_{S_{cu}} = \frac{N(\text{rpm})[\mathcal{P}(\text{hp})]^{1/2}}{[H(\text{ft})]^{5/4}} \qquad (10.18b)$$

Values of the dimensionless specific speed for a hydraulic turbine, N_S (Eq. 10.18a), must be multiplied by 43.46 to obtain the values of specific speed corresponding to this commonly used but inconsistent set of units.

Specific speed may be thought of as *the operating speed at which a pump produces unit head at unit volume flow rate* (or, for a hydraulic turbine, unit power at unit head). To see this, solve for N in Eqs. 7.22b and 10.18b, respectively. For pumps

$$N(\text{rpm}) = N_{S_{cu}} \frac{[H(\text{ft})]^{3/4}}{[Q(\text{gpm})]^{1/2}}$$

and for hydraulic turbines

$$N(\text{rpm}) = N_{S_{cu}} \frac{[H(\text{ft})]^{5/4}}{[\mathcal{P}(\text{hp})]^{1/2}}$$

Holding specific speed constant describes all operating conditions of geometrically similar machines with similar flow conditions.

It is customary to characterize a machine by its specific speed at the design point. This specific speed has been found to characterize the hydraulic design features of a machine. Low specific speeds correspond to efficient operation of radial-flow machines. High specific speeds correspond to efficient operation of axial-flow machines. For a specified head and flow rate, one can choose either a low specific speed machine (which operates at low speed) or a high specific speed machine (which operates at higher speed).

Typical proportions for commercial pump designs and their variation with dimensionless specific speed are shown in Fig. 10.14. In this figure, the size of each machine has been adjusted to give the same head and flow rate for rotation at a speed corresponding to the specific speed. Thus it can be seen that if the machine's size and weight are critical, one should choose a higher specific speed. Figure 10.14 shows the

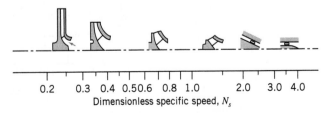

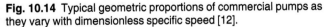

Fig. 10.14 Typical geometric proportions of commercial pumps as they vary with dimensionless specific speed [12].

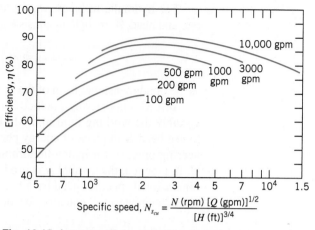

Fig. 10.15 Average efficiencies of commercial pumps as they vary with specific speed and pump size [10].

trend from radial (purely centrifugal pumps), through mixed-flow, to axial-flow geometries as specific speed increases.

The corresponding efficiency trends for typical pumps are shown in Fig. 10.15, which shows that pump capacity generally increases as specific speed increases. The figure also shows that at any given specific speed, efficiency is higher for large pumps than for small ones. Physically this *scale effect* means that viscous losses become less important as the pump size is increased.

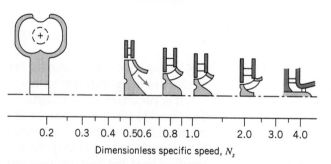

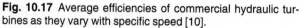

Fig. 10.16 Typical geometric proportions of commercial hydraulic turbines as they vary with dimensionless specific speed [12].

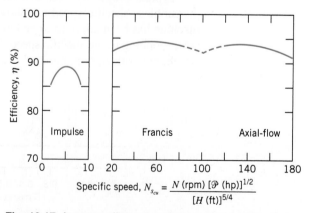

Fig. 10.17 Average efficiencies of commercial hydraulic turbines as they vary with specific speed [10].

Characteristic proportions of hydraulic turbines also are correlated by specific speed, as shown in Fig. 10.16. As in Fig. 10.14, the machine size has been scaled in this illustration to deliver approximately the same power at unit head when rotating at a speed equal to the specific speed. The corresponding efficiency trends for typical turbine types are shown in Fig. 10.17.

Several variations of specific speed, calculated directly from engineering units, are widely used in practice. The most commonly used forms of specific speed for pumps are defined and compared in Example 10.6.

EXAMPLE 10.6   Comparison of Specific Speed Definitions

At the best efficiency point, a centrifugal pump, with impeller diameter $D = 8$ in., produces $H = 21.9$ ft at $Q = 300$ gpm with $N = 1170$ rpm. Compute the corresponding specific speeds using: (a) U.S. customary units, (b) SI units (rad/s, m^3/s, m^2/s^2), and (c) European units (rev/s, m^3/s, m^2/s^2). Develop conversion factors to relate the specific speeds.

GIVEN: Centrifugal pump at best efficiency point (BEP). Assume the pump characteristics are $H = 21.9$ ft, $Q = 300$ gpm, and $N = 1170$ rpm.

FIND: (a) The specific speed in U.S. customary units.
(b) The specific speed in SI units.
(c) The specific speed in European units.
(d) Appropriate conversion factors to relate the specific speeds.

SOLUTION:

Governing equations: $N_s = \dfrac{\omega Q^{1/2}}{h^{3/4}}$ and $N_{S_{cu}} = \dfrac{N Q^{1/2}}{H^{3/4}}$

From the given information, the specific speed in U.S. customary units is

$$N_{S_{cu}} = 1170 \text{ rpm} \times (300)^{1/2} \text{ gpm}^{1/2} \times \frac{1}{(21.9)^{3/4} \text{ ft}^{3/4}} = 2000 \quad \longleftarrow \underline{\hspace{4cm} N_{S_{cu}}}$$

Convert information to SI units:

$$\omega = 1170 \frac{\text{rev}}{\text{min}} \times \frac{2\pi \text{ rad}}{\text{rev}} \times \frac{\text{min}}{60 \text{ s}} = 123 \text{ rad/s}$$

$$Q = \frac{300 \text{ gal}}{\text{min}} \times \frac{\text{ft}^3}{7.48 \text{ gal}} \times \frac{\text{min}}{60 \text{ s}} \times (0.305)^3 \frac{\text{m}^3}{\text{ft}^3} = 0.0190 \text{ m}^3/\text{s}$$

$$H = 21.9 \text{ ft} \times 0.305 \frac{\text{m}}{\text{ft}} = 6.68 \text{ m}$$

The energy per unit mass is

$$h = gH = 9.81 \frac{\text{m}}{\text{s}^2} \times 6.68 \text{ m} = 65.5 \text{ m}^2/\text{s}^2$$

The dimensionless specific speed is

$$N_s = 123 \frac{\text{rad}}{\text{s}} \times (0.0190)^{1/2} \frac{\text{m}^{3/2}}{\text{s}^{1/2}} \times \frac{(\text{s}^2)^{3/4}}{(65.5)^{3/4} (\text{m}^2)^{3/4}} = 0.736 \quad \longleftarrow \underline{\hspace{3cm} N_s \text{ (SI)}}$$

Convert the operating speed to hertz:

$$\omega = 1170 \frac{\text{rev}}{\text{min}} \times \frac{\text{min}}{60 \text{ s}} \times \frac{\text{Hz} \cdot \text{s}}{\text{rev}} = 19.5 \text{ Hz}$$

Finally, the specific speed in European units is

$$N_s(\text{Eur}) = \frac{19.5 \text{ Hz}}{} \times (0.0190)^{1/2} \frac{\text{m}^{3/2}}{\text{s}^{1/2}} \times \frac{(\text{s}^2)^{3/4}}{(65.5)^{3/4}(\text{m}^2)^{3/4}} = 0.117 \qquad \longleftarrow \qquad N_s(\text{Eur})$$

To relate the specific speeds, form ratios:

$$\frac{N_{s_{cu}}}{N_s(\text{Eur})} = \frac{2000}{0.117} = 17{,}100$$

$$\frac{N_{s_{cu}}}{N_s(\text{SI})} = \frac{2000}{0.736} = 2720$$

This problem demonstrates the use of "engineering" equations to calculate specific speed for pumps from each of three commonly used sets of units and to compare the results. (Three significant figures have been used for all calculations in this example. Slightly different results would be obtained if more significant figures were carried in intermediate calculations.)

Similarity Rules

Pump manufacturers offer a limited number of casing sizes and designs. Frequently, casings of different sizes are developed from a common design by increasing or decreasing all dimensions by the same scale ratio. Additional variation in characteristic curves may be obtained by varying the operating speed or by changing the impeller size within a given pump housing. The dimensionless parameters developed in Chapter 7 form the basis for predicting changes in performance that result from changes in pump size, operating speed, or impeller diameter.

To achieve dynamic similarity requires geometric and kinematic similarity. Assuming similar pumps and flow fields, and neglecting viscous effects, as shown in Chapter 7, we obtain dynamic similarity when the dimensionless flow coefficient is held constant. Dynamically similar operation is assured when two flow conditions satisfy the relation

$$\frac{Q_1}{\omega_1 D_1^3} = \frac{Q_2}{\omega_2 D_2^3} \tag{10.19a}$$

The dimensionless head and power coefficients depend only on the flow coefficient, i.e.,

$$\frac{h}{\omega^2 D^2} = f_1\left(\frac{Q}{\omega D^3}\right) \quad \text{and} \quad \frac{\mathcal{P}}{\rho \omega^3 D^5} = f_2\left(\frac{Q}{\omega D^3}\right)$$

Hence, when we have dynamic similarity, as shown in Example 7.6, pump characteristics at a new condition (subscript 2) may be related to those at an old condition (subscript 1) by

$$\frac{h_1}{\omega_1^2 D_1^2} = \frac{h_2}{\omega_2^2 D_2^2} \tag{10.19b}$$

and

$$\frac{\mathcal{P}_1}{\rho_1 \omega_1^3 D_1^5} = \frac{\mathcal{P}_2}{\rho_2 \omega_2^3 D_2^5} \tag{10.19c}$$

These scaling relationships may be used to predict the effects of changes in pump operating speed, pump size, or impeller diameter within a given housing.

The simplest situation is when we keep the *same* pump and only the *pump speed* is changed. Then geometric similarity is assured. Kinematic similarity holds if there is no cavitation; flows are then dynamically similar when the flow coefficients are matched. For this case of speed change with fixed diameter, Eqs. 10.19 become

$$\frac{Q_2}{Q_1} = \frac{\omega_2}{\omega_1} \tag{10.20a}$$

$$\frac{h_2}{h_1} = \frac{H_2}{H_1} = \left(\frac{\omega_2}{\omega_1}\right)^2 \tag{10.20b}$$

$$\frac{\mathscr{P}_2}{\mathscr{P}_1} = \left(\frac{\omega_2}{\omega_1}\right)^3 \tag{10.20c}$$

In Example 10.4, it was shown that a pump performance curve could be modeled within engineering accuracy by the parabolic relationship, $H = H_0 - AQ^2$. Since this representation contains two parameters, the pump curve for the new operating condition could be derived by scaling any two points from the performance curve measured at the original operating condition. Usually, the *shutoff condition* and the *best efficiency point* are chosen for scaling. These points are represented by points B and C in Fig. 10.18.

As shown by Eq. 10.20a, the flow rate increases by the ratio of operating speeds, so

$$Q_{B'} = \frac{\omega_2}{\omega_1} Q_B = 0 \quad \text{and} \quad Q_{C'} = \frac{\omega_2}{\omega_1} Q_C$$

Thus, point B' is located directly above point B and point C' moves to the right of point C (in this example $\omega_2 > \omega_1$).

The head increases by the square of the speed ratio, so

$$H_{B'} = H_B \left(\frac{\omega_2}{\omega_1}\right)^2 \quad \text{and} \quad H_{C'} = H_C \left(\frac{\omega_2}{\omega_1}\right)^2$$

Points C and C', where dynamically similar flow conditions are present, are termed *homologous* points for the pump.

We can relate the old operating condition (e.g., running at speed $N_1 = 1170$ rpm, as shown in Fig. 10.18) to the new, primed one (e.g., running at speed $N_2 = 1750$ rpm in Fig. 10.18) using the parabolic relation and Eqs. 10.20a and 10.20b,

$$H = H' \left(\frac{\omega_1}{\omega_2}\right)^2 = H_0 - AQ^2 = H_0' \left(\frac{\omega_1}{\omega_2}\right)^2 - AQ'^2 \left(\frac{\omega_1}{\omega_2}\right)^2$$

or

$$H' = H_0' - AQ'^2 \tag{10.21}$$

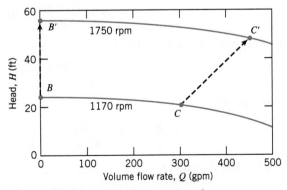

Fig. 10.18 Schematic of a pump performance curve, illustrating the effect of a change in pump operating speed.

so that for a given pump the factor A remains unchanged as we change pump speed (as we will verify in Example 10.7).

Efficiency remains relatively constant between dynamically similar operating points when only the pump operating speed is changed. Application of these ideas is illustrated in Example 10.7.

EXAMPLE 10.7   Scaling Pump Performance Curves

When operated at $N = 1170$ rpm, a centrifugal pump, with impeller diameter $D = 8$ in., has shutoff head $H_0 = 25.0$ ft of water. At the same operating speed, best efficiency occurs at $Q = 300$ gpm, where the head is $H = 21.9$ ft of water. Fit these data at 1170 rpm with a parabola. Scale the results to a new operating speed of 1750 rpm. Plot and compare the results.

GIVEN: Centrifugal pump (with $D = 8$ in. impeller) operated at $N = 1170$ rpm.

Q (gpm)	0	300
H (ft of water)	25.0	21.9

FIND: (a) The equation of a parabola through the pump characteristics at 1170 rpm.
   (b) The corresponding equation for a new operating speed of 1750 rpm.
   (c) Comparison (plot) of the results.

SOLUTION:

Assume a parabolic variation in pump head of the form, $H = H_0 - AQ^2$. Solving for A gives

$$A_1 = \frac{H_0 - H}{Q^2} = \frac{(25.0 - 21.9)\text{ ft}}{} \times \frac{1}{(300)^2(\text{gpm})^2} = 3.44 \times 10^{-5}\text{ ft/(gpm)}^2$$

The desired equation is

$$H\text{ (ft)} = 25.0 - 3.44 \times 10^{-5}\,[Q\text{ (gpm)}]^2$$

The pump remains the same, so the two flow conditions are geometrically similar. Assuming no cavitation occurs, the two flows also will be kinematically similar. Then dynamic similarity will be obtained when the two flow coefficients are matched. Denoting the 1170 rpm condition by subscript 1 and the 1750 rpm condition by subscript 2, we have

$$\frac{Q_2}{\omega_2 D_2^3} = \frac{Q_1}{\omega_1 D_1^3} \quad \text{or} \quad \frac{Q_2}{Q_1} = \frac{\omega_2}{\omega_1} = \frac{N_2}{N_1}$$

since $D_2 = D_1$. For the shutoff condition,

$$Q_2 = \frac{N_2}{N_1}\,Q_1 = \frac{1750\text{ rpm}}{1170\text{ rpm}} \times 0\text{ gpm} = 0\text{ gpm}$$

From the best efficiency point, the new flow rate is

$$Q_2 = \frac{N_2}{N_1}\,Q_1 = \frac{1750\text{ rpm}}{1170\text{ rpm}} \times 300\text{ gpm} = 449\text{ gpm}$$

The pump heads are related by

$$\frac{h_2}{h_1} = \frac{H_2}{H_1} = \frac{N_2^2 D_2^2}{N_1^2 D_1^2} \quad \text{or} \quad \frac{H_2}{H_1} = \frac{N_2^2}{N_1^2} = \left(\frac{N_2}{N_1}\right)^2$$

since $D_2 = D_1$. For the shutoff condition,

$$H_2 = \left(\frac{N_2}{N_1}\right)^2 H_1 = \left(\frac{1750\text{ rpm}}{1170\text{ rpm}}\right)^2 25.0\text{ ft} = 55.9\text{ ft}$$

At the best efficiency point,

$$H_2 = \left(\frac{N_2}{N_1}\right)^2 H_1 = \left(\frac{1750 \text{ rpm}}{1170 \text{ rpm}}\right)^2 21.9 \text{ ft} = 49.0 \text{ ft}$$

The curve parameter at 1750 rpm may now be found. Solving for A, we find

$$A_2 = \frac{H_{02} - H_2}{Q_2^2} = \frac{(55.9 - 49.0) \text{ ft}}{} \times \frac{1}{(449)^2 (\text{gpm})^2} = 3.44 \times 10^{-5} \text{ ft/(gpm)}^2$$

Note that A_2 at 1750 rpm is the same as A_1 at 1170 rpm. Thus we have demonstrated that the coefficient A in the parabolic equation does not change when the pump speed is changed. The "engineering" equations for the two curves are

$$H_1 = 25.0 - 3.44 \times 10^{-5} [Q \text{ (gpm)}]^2 \quad \text{(at 1170 rpm)}$$

and

$$H_2 = 55.9 - 3.44 \times 10^{-5} [Q \text{ (gpm)}]^2 \quad \text{(at 1750 rpm)}$$

The pump curves are compared in the following plot:

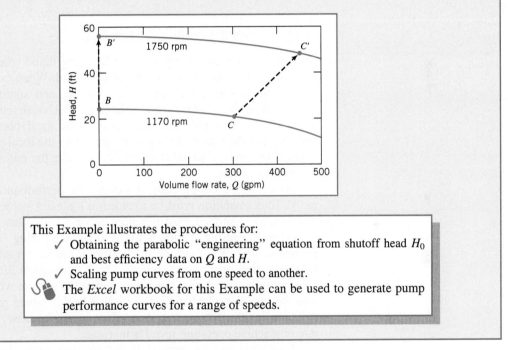

This Example illustrates the procedures for:
  ✓ Obtaining the parabolic "engineering" equation from shutoff head H_0 and best efficiency data on Q and H.
  ✓ Scaling pump curves from one speed to another.
  🖱 The *Excel* workbook for this Example can be used to generate pump performance curves for a range of speeds.

In principle, geometric similarity would be maintained when pumps of the *same geometry*, differing in size only by a scale ratio, were tested at the *same operating speed*. The flow, head, and power would be predicted to vary with *pump size* as

$$Q_2 = Q_1 \left(\frac{D_2}{D_1}\right)^3, \quad H_2 = H_1 \left(\frac{D_2}{D_1}\right)^2, \quad \text{and} \quad \mathscr{P}_2 = \mathscr{P}_1 \left(\frac{D_2}{D_1}\right)^5 \qquad (10.22)$$

It is impractical to manufacture and test a series of pump models that differ in size by only a scale ratio. Instead it is common practice to test a given pump casing at a fixed speed with several impellers of different diameter [13]. Because pump casing width is the same for each test, impeller width also must be the same; only impeller diameter D is changed. As a result, volume flow rate scales in proportion to D^2, not to D^3. Pump input power at fixed speed scales as the product of flow rate and head, so it becomes proportional to D^4. Using this modified scaling method frequently gives results of acceptable accuracy, as demonstrated in several end-of-chapter problems where the method is checked against measured performance data from Appendix D.

It is not possible to compare the efficiencies at the two operating conditions directly. However, viscous effects should become relatively less important as the pump size increases. Thus efficiency should improve slightly as diameter is increased.

Moody [14] suggested an empirical equation that may be used to estimate the maximum efficiency of a prototype pump based on test data from a geometrically similar model of the prototype pump. His equation is written

$$\frac{1 - \eta_p}{1 - \eta_m} = \left(\frac{D_m}{D_p}\right)^{1/5} \tag{10.23}$$

To develop Eq. 10.23, Moody assumed that only the surface resistance changes with model scale so that losses in passages of the same roughness vary as $1/D^5$. Unfortunately, it is difficult to maintain the same relative roughness between model and prototype pumps. Further, the Moody model does not account for any difference in mechanical losses between model and prototype, nor does it allow determination of off-peak efficiencies. Nevertheless, scaling of the maximum-efficiency point is useful to obtain a general estimate of the efficiency curve for the prototype pump.

Cavitation and Net Positive Suction Head

Cavitation can occur in any machine handling liquid whenever the local static pressure falls below the vapor pressure of the liquid. When this occurs, the liquid can locally flash to vapor, forming a vapor cavity and significantly changing the flow pattern from the noncavitating condition. The vapor cavity changes the effective shape of the flow passage, thus altering the local pressure field. Since the size and shape of the vapor cavity are influenced by the local pressure field, the flow may become unsteady. The unsteadiness may cause the entire flow to oscillate and the machine to vibrate.

As cavitation commences, it reduces the performance of a pump or turbine rapidly. Thus cavitation must be avoided to maintain stable and efficient operation. In addition, local surface pressures may become high when the vapor cavity implodes or collapses, causing erosion damage or surface pitting. The damage may be severe enough to destroy a machine made from a brittle low-strength material. Obviously cavitation also must be avoided to assure long machine life.

In a pump, cavitation tends to begin at the section where the flow is accelerated into the impeller. Cavitation in a turbine begins where pressure is lowest. The tendency to cavitate increases as local flow speeds increase; this occurs whenever flow rate or machine operating speed is increased.

Cavitation can be avoided if the pressure everywhere in the machine is kept above the vapor pressure of the operating liquid. At constant speed, this requires that a pressure somewhat greater than the vapor pressure of the liquid be maintained at a pump inlet (the *suction*). Because of pressure losses in the inlet piping, the suction pressure may be sub-atmospheric. Therefore it is important to carefully limit the pressure drop in the inlet piping system.

Net positive suction head (NPSH) is defined as the difference between the absolute stagnation pressure in the flow at the pump suction and the liquid vapor pressure, expressed as head of flowing liquid [15].[6] Hence the *NPSH* is a measure of the difference between the maximum possible pressure in the given flow and the pressure at which the liquid will start flashing over to a vapor; the larger the *NPSH*, the less likely cavitation is to occur. The *net positive suction head required (NPSHR)* by a specific pump to suppress cavitation varies with the liquid pumped, and with the

---

[6] *NPSH* may be expressed in any convenient units of measure, such as height of the flowing liquid, e.g., ft of water (hence the term *suction head*), psia, or kPa (abs). When expressed as *head, NPSH* is measured relative to the pump impeller centerline.

liquid temperature and pump condition (e.g., as critical geometric features of the pump are affected by wear). *NPSHR* may be measured in a pump test facility by controlling the input pressure. The results are plotted on the pump performance curve. Typical pump characteristic curves for three impellers tested in the same housing were shown in Fig. 10.8. Experimentally determined *NPSHR* curves for the largest and smallest impeller diameters are plotted near the bottom of the figure.

The *net positive suction head available (NPSHA)* at the pump inlet must be greater than the *NPSHR* to suppress cavitation. Pressure drop in the inlet piping and pump entrance increases as volume flow rate increases. Thus for any system, the *NPSHA* decreases as flow rate is raised. The *NPSHR* of the pump increases as the flow rate is raised. Therefore, as the system flow rate is increased, the curves for *NPSHA* and *NPSHR* versus flow rate ultimately cross. Hence, for any inlet system, there is a flow rate that cannot be exceeded if flow through the pump is to remain free from cavitation. Inlet pressure losses may be reduced by increasing the diameter of the inlet piping; for this reason many centrifugal pumps have larger flanges or couplings at the inlet than at the outlet.

EXAMPLE 10.8   Calculation of Net Positive Suction Head (*NPSH*)

A Peerless Type 4AE11 centrifugal pump (Fig. D.3, Appendix D) is tested at 1750 rpm using a flow system with the layout of Example 10.3. The water level in the inlet reservoir is 3.5 ft above the pump centerline; the inlet line consists of 6 ft of 5 in. diameter straight cast-iron pipe, a standard elbow, and a fully open gate valve. Calculate the net positive suction head available (*NPSHA*) at the pump inlet at a volume flow rate of 1000 gpm of water at 80°F. Compare with the net positive suction head required (*NPSHR*) by the pump at this flow rate. Plot *NPSHA* and *NPSHR* for water at 80°F and 180°F versus volume flow rate.

GIVEN: A Peerless Type 4AE11 centrifugal pump (Fig. D.3, Appendix D) is tested at 1750 rpm using a flow system with the layout of Example 10.3. The water level in the inlet reservoir is 3.5 ft. above the pump centerline; the inlet line has 6 ft of 5 in. diameter straight cast-iron pipe, a standard elbow, and a fully open gate valve.

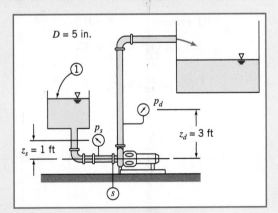

FIND: (a) *NPSHA* at Q = 1000 gpm of water at 80°F.
(b) Comparison with *NPSHR* for this pump at Q = 1000 gpm.
(c) Plot of *NPSHA* and *NPSHR* for water at 80°F and 180°F versus volume flow rate.

SOLUTION:
Net positive suction head (*NPSH*) is defined as the difference between the absolute stagnation pressure in the flow at the pump suction and the liquid vapor pressure, expressed as head of flowing liquid. Therefore it is necessary to calculate the head at the pump suction.

Apply the energy equation for steady, incompressible pipe flow to compute the pressure at the pump inlet and thus the *NPSHA*. Denote the reservoir level as ① and the pump suction as ⓢ, as shown above.

Governing equation:

$$p_1 + \frac{1}{2}\rho\overline{V}_1^2 + \rho g z_1 = p_s + \frac{1}{2}\rho\overline{V}_s^2 + \rho g_s + \rho h_{\ell_T}$$

with $\overline{V}_1^2 \approx 0$

Assumption: $\overline{V}_1$ is negligible. Thus

$$p_s = p_1 + \rho g(z_1 - z_s) - \frac{1}{2}\rho\overline{V}_s^2 - \rho h_{\ell_T} \tag{1}$$

The total head loss is

$$h_{\ell_T} = \left(\sum K + \sum f\frac{L_e}{D} + f\frac{L}{D}\right)\frac{1}{2}\rho\overline{V}_s^2 \tag{2}$$

Substituting Eq. 2 into Eq. 1 and dividing by ρg,

$$H_s = H_1 + z_1 - z_s - \left(\sum K + \sum f\frac{L_e}{D} + f\frac{L}{D} + 1\right)\frac{\overline{V}_s^2}{2g} \tag{3}$$

Evaluating the friction factor and head loss,

$$f = f(Re, e/D); \quad Re = \frac{\rho\overline{V}D}{\mu} = \frac{\overline{V}D}{\nu}; \quad \overline{V} = \frac{Q}{A}; \quad A = \frac{\pi D^2}{4}$$

For 5 in. (nominal) pipe, $D = 5.047$ in.

$$D = 5.047 \text{ in.} \times \frac{\text{ft}}{12 \text{ in.}} = 0.421 \text{ ft}, \quad A = \frac{\pi D^2}{4} = 0.139 \text{ ft}^2$$

$$\overline{V} = \frac{1000 \text{ gal}}{\text{min}} \times \frac{\text{ft}^3}{7.48 \text{ gal}} \times \frac{1}{0.139 \text{ ft}^2} \times \frac{\text{min}}{60 \text{ s}} = 16.0 \text{ ft/s}$$

From Table A.7, for water at $T = 80°F$, $\nu = 0.927 \times 10^{-5}$ ft^2/s.
   The Reynolds number is

$$Re = \frac{\overline{V}D}{\nu} = \frac{16.0 \text{ ft}}{\text{s}} \times \frac{0.421 \text{ ft}}{} \times \frac{\text{s}}{0.927 \times 10^{-5} \text{ ft}^2} = 7.27 \times 10^5$$

From Table 8.1, $e = 0.00085$ ft, so $e/D = 0.00202$. From Eq. 8.37, $f = 0.0237$. The minor loss coefficients are

$$\text{Entrance} \qquad K = 0.5$$

$$\text{Standard elbow} \quad \frac{L_e}{D} = 30$$

$$\text{Open gate value} \quad \frac{L_e}{D} = 8$$

Substituting,

$$\left(\sum K + \sum f\frac{L_e}{D} + f\frac{L}{D} + 1\right) = 0.5 + 0.0237(30 + 8) + 0.0237\left(\frac{6}{0.421}\right) + 1 = 2.74$$

The heads are

$$H_1 = \frac{p_{\text{atm}}}{\rho g} = \frac{14.7 \text{ lbf}}{\text{in.}^2} \times \frac{144 \text{ in.}^2}{\text{ft}^2} \times \frac{\text{ft}^3}{1.93 \text{ slug}} \times \frac{\text{s}^2}{32.2 \text{ ft}} \times \frac{\text{slug} \cdot \text{ft}}{\text{lbf} \cdot \text{s}^2} = 34.1 \text{ ft (abs)}$$

$$\frac{\overline{V}_s^2}{2g} = \frac{1}{2} \times (16.0)^2 \frac{\text{ft}^2}{\text{s}^2} \times \frac{\text{s}^2}{32.2 \text{ ft}} = 3.98 \text{ ft}$$

Thus,

$$H_s = 34.1 \text{ ft} + 3.5 \text{ ft} - (2.74)3.98 \text{ ft} = 26.7 \text{ ft (abs)}$$

To obtain *NPHSA*, add velocity head and subtract vapor head. Thus

$$NPHSA = H_s + \frac{\overline{V}_s^2}{2g} - H_v$$

The vapor pressure for water at 80°F is $p_v = 0.507$ psia. The corresponding head is $H_v = 1.17$ ft of water. Thus,

$$NPSHA = 26.7 + 3.98 - 1.17 = 29.5 \text{ ft} \longleftarrow \underline{\qquad\qquad\qquad\qquad} \quad NPSHA$$

The pump curve (Fig. D.3, Appendix D) shows that at 1000 gpm the pump requires

$$NPSHR = 10.0 \text{ ft} \longleftarrow \underline{\qquad\qquad\qquad\qquad} \quad NPSHR$$

Results of similar computations for water at 80°F are plotted in the figure on the left below. (*NPSHR* values are obtained from the pump curves in Fig. D.3, Appendix D.)

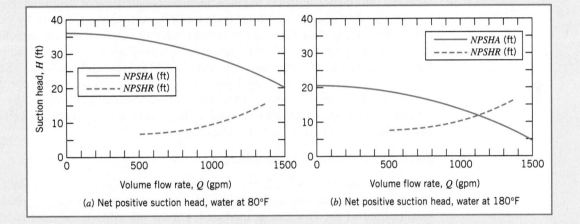

(a) Net positive suction head, water at 80°F   (b) Net positive suction head, water at 180°F

Results of computation for water at 180°F are plotted in the figure on the right above. The vapor pressure for water at 180°F is $p_v = 7.51$ psia. The corresponding head is $H_v = 17.3$ ft of water. This high vapor pressure reduces the *NPSHA*, as shown in the plot.

This problem illustrates the procedures used for checking whether a given pump is in danger of experiencing cavitation:

✓ Equation 3 and the plots show that the *NPSHA* decreases as flow rate Q (or $\overline{V}_s$) increases; on the other hand, the *NPSHR* increases with Q, so if the flow rate is high enough, a pump will likely experience cavitation (when *NPSHA* < *NPSHR*).

✓ The *NPSHR* for any pump increases with flow rate Q because local fluid velocities within the pump increase, causing locally reduced pressures and tending to promote cavitation.

✓ For this pump, at 80°F, the pump appears to have *NPSHA* > *NPSHR* at all flow rates, so it would never experience cavitation; at 180°F, cavitation would occur around 1100 gpm, but from Fig. D.3, the pump best efficiency is around 900 gpm, so it would probably not be run at 1100 gpm—the pump would probably not cavitate even with the hotter water.

The *Excel* workbook for this Example can be used to generate the *NPSHA* and *NPSHR* curves for a variety of pumps and water temperatures.

| 10-5 | APPLICATIONS TO FLUID SYSTEMS |

We define a *fluid system* as the combination of a fluid machine and a network of pipes or channels that convey fluid. The engineering application of fluid machines in an actual system requires matching the machine and system characteristics, while satisfying constraints of energy efficiency, capital economy, and durability. We have alluded to the vast assortment of hardware offered by competing suppliers; this variety verifies the commercial importance of fluid machinery in modern engineering systems.

Usually it is more economical to specify a production machine rather than a custom unit, because products of established vendors have known, published performance characteristics, and they must be durable to survive in the marketplace. Application engineering consists of making the best selection from catalogs of available products. In addition to machine characteristic curves, all manufacturers provide a wealth of dimensional data, alternative configuration and mounting schemes, and technical information bulletins to guide intelligent application of their products.

This section consists of a brief review of relevant theory, followed by example applications using data taken from manufacturer literature. Two subsections treat machines for doing work on a fluid (pumps, fans, blowers, compressors, and propellers) and machines for extracting work from a fluid (turbines and windmills). Selected performance curves for centrifugal pumps and fans are presented in Appendix D. These may be studied as typical examples of performance data supplied by manufacturers. The curves may also be used to help solve the equipment selection and system design problems at the end of the chapter.

Machines for Doing Work on a Fluid

We will consider various machines for doing work on a fluid, but we first make a few general points. As we saw in Example 10.3, a typical pump, for example, produces a smaller head as the flow rate is increased. On the other hand, the head (which includes major and minor losses) required to maintain flow in a pipe system increases with the flow rate. Hence, as shown graphically[7] in Fig. 10.19, a pump-system will run at the *operating point*, the flow rate at which the pump head rise and required system head match. (Figure 10.19 also shows a pump efficiency curve, indicating that, for optimum pump selection, a pump should be chosen that has maximum efficiency at the operating point flow rate.) The pump-system shown in Fig. 10.19 is stable. If for some reason the flow rate falls below the operating flow rate, the pump pressure head rises above the required system head, and so the flow rate increases back to the operating point. Conversely, if the flow rate momentarily increases, the required head exceeds the head provided by the pump, and the flow rate decreases back to the operating point. This notion of an operating point applies to each machine we will consider (although, as we will see, the operating points are not always stable).

The system pressure requirement at a given flow rate is composed of frictional pressure drop (major loss due to friction in straight sections of constant area and minor loss due to entrances, fittings, valves, and exits) and pressure changes due to gravity (static lift may be positive or negative). It is useful to discuss the two limiting cases of pure friction and pure lift before considering their combination.

The *all-friction* system head versus flow curve, with no static lift, starts at zero flow and head, as shown in Fig. 10.20*a*. For this system the total head required is the sum of major and minor losses,

$$h_{l_T} = \sum h_l + \sum h_{l_m} = \sum f \frac{L}{D} \frac{\overline{V}^2}{2} + \sum \left(f \frac{L_e}{D} \frac{\overline{V}^2}{2} + K \frac{\overline{V}^2}{2} \right)$$

---

[7] While a graphical representation is useful for visualizing the pump-system matching, we typically use analytical or numerical methods to determine the operating point (*Excel* is very useful for this).

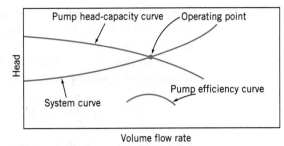

Fig. 10.19 Superimposed system head-flow and pump head-capacity curves.

For turbulent flow (the usual flow regime in engineering systems), as we learned in Chapter 8 (see Fig. 8.13), the friction factors approach constant and the minor loss coefficients K and equivalent lengths L_e are also constant. Hence $h_{l_T} \sim \overline{V}^2 \sim Q^2$ so that the system curve is approximately parabolic. (In reality, because the friction factors f only approach constants as the regime becomes fully turbulent, it turns out that $Q^{1.75} < h_{l_T} < Q^2$.) This means the system curve with pure friction becomes steeper as flow rate increases. To develop the friction curve, losses are computed at various flow rates and then plotted.

Pressure change due to elevation difference is independent of flow rate. Thus the *pure lift* system head-flow curve is a horizontal straight line. The gravity head is evaluated from the change in elevation in the system.

All actual flow systems have some frictional pressure drop and some elevation change. Thus all system head-flow curves may be treated as the sum of a frictional component and a static-lift component. The head for the complete system at any flow rate is the sum of the frictional and lift heads. The system head-flow curve is plotted in Fig. 10.20b.

Whether the resulting system curve is *steep* or *flat* depends on the relative importance of friction and gravity. Friction drop may be relatively unimportant in the

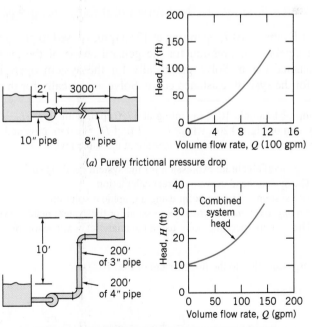

(a) Purely frictional pressure drop

(b) Combination of frictional and gravity pressure changes

Fig. 10.20 Schematic diagrams illustrating basic types of system head-flow curves (adapted from [8]).

water supply to a high-rise building (e.g., the Sears Tower in Chicago, which is nearly 400 m tall), and gravity lift may be negligible in an air-handling system for a one-story building.

In Section 8-7 we obtained a form of the energy equation for a control volume consisting of a pump-pipe system,

$$\left(\frac{p_1}{\rho} + \alpha_1 \frac{\overline{V}_1^2}{2} + gz_1\right) - \left(\frac{p_2}{\rho} + \alpha_2 \frac{\overline{V}_2^2}{2} + gz_2\right) = h_{l_T} - \Delta h_{\text{pump}} \tag{8.49}$$

Replacing Δh_{pump} with h_a, representing the head added by any machine (not only a pump) that does work on the fluid, and rearranging Eq. 8.49, we obtain a more general expression

$$\frac{p_1}{\rho} + \alpha_1 \frac{\overline{V}_1^2}{2} + gz_1 + h_a = \frac{p_2}{\rho} + \alpha_2 \frac{\overline{V}_2^2}{2} + gz_2 + h_{l_T} \tag{10.24a}$$

Dividing by g gives

$$\frac{p_1}{\rho g} + \alpha_1 \frac{\overline{V}_1^2}{2g} + z_1 + H_a = \frac{p_2}{\rho g} + \alpha_2 \frac{\overline{V}_2^2}{2g} + z_2 + \frac{h_{l_T}}{g} \tag{10.24b}$$

where H_a is the energy per unit weight (i.e, the head, with dimensions of L) added by the machine.

a. Pumps

The pump operating point is defined by superimposing the system curve and the pump performance curve, as shown in Fig. 10.19. The point of intersection is the only condition where the pump and system flow rates are equal and the pump and system heads are equal simultaneously. The procedure used to determine the match point for a pumping system is illustrated in Example 10.9.

EXAMPLE 10.9   Finding the Operating Point for a Pumping System

The pump of Example 10.7, operating at 1750 rpm, is used to pump water through the pipe system of Fig. 10.20a. Develop an algebraic expression for the general shape of the system resistance curve. Calculate and plot the system resistance curve. Solve graphically for the system operating point. Obtain an approximate analytical expression for the system resistance curve. Solve analytically for the system operating point.

GIVEN: Pump of Example 10.7, operating at 1750 rpm, with $H = H_0 - AQ^2$, where $H_0 = 55.9$ ft and $A = 3.44 \times 10^{-5}$ ft/(gpm)^2. System of Fig. 10.20a, where $L_1 = 2$ ft of $D_1 = 10$ in. pipe and $L_2 = 3000$ ft of $D_2 = 8$ in. pipe, conveying water between two large reservoirs whose surfaces are at the same level.

FIND: (a) A general algebraic expression for the system head curve.
(b) The system head curve by direct calculation.
(c) The system operating point using a graphical solution.
(d) An *approximate* analytical expression for the system head curve.
(e) The system operating point using the analytical expression of part (d).

SOLUTION:
Apply the energy equation to the flow system of Fig. 10.20a.

Governing equation:

$$\frac{p_0}{\rho g} + \alpha_0 \frac{\overline{V}_0^2}{2g} + z_0 + H_a = \frac{p_3}{\rho g} + \alpha_3 \frac{\overline{V}_3^2}{2g} + z_3 + \frac{h_{l_T}}{g} \tag{10.24b}$$

where z_0 and z_3 are the surface elevations of the supply and discharge reservoirs, respectively.

Assumptions: (1) $p_0 = p_3 = p_{atm}$.
(2) $\overline{V}_0 = \overline{V}_3 = 0$.
(3) $z_0 = z_3$ (given).

Simplifying, we obtain

$$H_a = \frac{h_{l_T}}{g} = \frac{h_{lT_{01}}}{g} + \frac{h_{lT_{23}}}{g} = H_{l_T} \tag{1}$$

where sections ① and ② are located just upstream and downstream from the pump, respectively.
The total head losses are the sum of the major and minor losses, so

$$h_{lT_{01}} = K_{ent} \frac{\overline{V}_1^2}{2} + f_1 \frac{L_1}{D_1} \frac{\overline{V}_1^2}{2} = \left(K_{ent} + f_1 \frac{L_1}{D_1} \right) \frac{\overline{V}_1^2}{2}$$

$$h_{lT_{23}} = f_2 \frac{L_2}{D_2} \frac{\overline{V}_2^2}{2} + K_{exit} \frac{\overline{V}_2^2}{2} = \left(f_2 \frac{L_2}{D_2} + K_{exit} \right) \frac{\overline{V}_2^2}{2}$$

From continuity, $\overline{V}_1 A_1 = \overline{V}_2 A_2$, so $\overline{V}_1 = \overline{V}_2 \dfrac{A_2}{A_1} = \overline{V}_2 \left(\dfrac{D_2}{D_1} \right)^2$.

Hence

$$H_{l_T} = \frac{h_{l_T}}{g} = \left(K_{ent} + f_1 \frac{L_1}{D_1} \right) \frac{\overline{V}_2^2}{2g} \left(\frac{D_2}{D_1} \right)^4 + \left(f_2 \frac{L_2}{D_2} + K_{exit} \right) \frac{\overline{V}_2^2}{2g}$$

or, upon simplifying,

$$H_{l_T} = \left[\left(K_{ent} + f_1 \frac{L_1}{D_1} \right) \left(\frac{D_2}{D_1} \right)^4 + f_2 \frac{L_2}{D_2} + K_{exit} \right] \frac{\overline{V}_2^2}{2g} \qquad\qquad H_{l_T}$$

This is the head loss equation for the system. At the operating point, as indicated in Eq. 1, the head loss is equal to the head produced by the pump, given by

$$H_a = H_0 - AQ^2 \tag{2}$$

where $H_0 = 55.9$ ft and $A = 3.44 \times 10^{-5}$ ft/(gpm)^2.
The head loss in the system and head produced by the pump can be computed for a range of flow rates:

Q (gpm)	$\overline{V}_1$ (ft/s)	Re_1 (1000)	f_1 (–)	$\overline{V}_2$ (ft/s)	Re_2 (1000)	f_2 (–)	H_{l_T} (ft)	H_a (ft)
0	0.00	0	–	0.00	0	–	0.0	55.9
100	0.41	32	0.026	0.64	40	0.025	0.7	55.6
200	0.82	63	0.023	1.28	79	0.023	2.7	54.5
300	1.23	95	0.022	1.91	119	0.023	5.9	52.8
400	1.63	127	0.022	2.55	158	0.022	10.3	50.4
500	2.04	158	0.021	3.19	198	0.022	15.8	47.3
600	2.45	190	0.021	3.83	237	0.022	22.6	43.5
700	2.86	222	0.021	4.47	277	0.022	30.6	39.0
800	3.27	253	0.021	5.11	317	0.022	39.7	33.9
900	3.68	285	0.021	5.74	356	0.021	50.1	28.0
1000	4.09	317	0.021	6.38	396	0.021	61.7	21.5
1100	4.49	348	0.020	7.02	435	0.021	74.4	
1200	4.90	380	0.020	7.66	475	0.021	88.4	
1300	5.31	412	0.020	8.30	515	0.021	103	
1400	5.72	443	0.020	8.94	554	0.021	120	
1500	6.13	475	0.020	9.57	594	0.021	137	

The pump curve and the system resistance curve are plotted below:

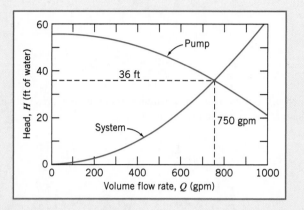

The graphical solution is shown on the plot. At the operating point, $H \approx 36$ ft and $Q \approx 750$ gpm.

We can obtain more accuracy from the graphical solution using the following approach: Because the Reynolds number corresponds to the fully turbulent regime, $f \approx$ const., we can simplify the equation for the head loss and write it in the form

$$H_{l_T} \approx CQ^2 \tag{3}$$

where $C = 8/\pi^2 D_2^4 g$ times the term in square brackets in the expression for H_{l_T}. We can obtain a value for C directly from Eq. 3 by using values for H_{l_T} and Q from the table at a point close to the anticipated operating point. For example, from the $Q = 700$ gpm data point,

$$C = \frac{H_{l_T}}{Q^2} = \frac{30.6 \text{ ft}}{700^2 \text{ (gpm)}^2} = 6.24 \times 10^{-5} \text{ ft/(gpm)}^2$$

Hence, the approximate analytical expression for the system head curve is

$$H_{l_T} = 6.24 \times 10^{-5} \text{ ft/(gpm)}^2 \, [Q \text{ (gpm)}]^2 \qquad \longleftarrow \qquad H_{l_T}$$

Using Eqs. 2 and 3 in Eq. 1, we obtain

$$H_0 - AQ^2 = CQ^2$$

Solving for Q, the volume flow rate at the operating point, gives

$$Q = \left[\frac{H_0}{A + C}\right]^{1/2}$$

For this case,

$$Q = \left[55.9 \text{ ft} \times \frac{\text{(gpm)}^2}{(3.44 \times 10^{-5} + 6.24 \times 10^{-5}) \text{ ft}}\right]^{1/2} = 760 \text{ gpm} \qquad \longleftarrow \qquad Q$$

The volume flow rate may be substituted into either expression for head to calculate the head at the operating point as

$$H = CQ^2 = 6.24 \times 10^{-5} \, \frac{\text{ft}}{\text{(gpm)}^2} \times (760)^2 \text{(gpm)}^2 = 36.0 \text{ ft} \qquad \longleftarrow \qquad H$$

We can see that in this problem our reading of the operating point from the graph was pretty good: The reading of head was in agreement with the calculated head; the reading of flow rate was less than 2% different from the calculated result.

Note that both sets of results are approximate. We can get a more accurate, and easier, result by using *Excel*'s *Solver* or *Goal Seek* to find the operating point, allowing for the fact that the friction factors vary, however slightly, with Reynolds number. Doing so yields an operating point flow rate of 761 gpm and head of 36.0 ft.

This problem illustrates the procedures used to find the operating point of a pump and flow system.

- ✓ The approximate methods—graphical, and assuming friction losses are proportional to Q^2—yielded results close to the detailed computation using *Excel*. We conclude that since most pipe flow friction coefficients are accurate to only about $\pm 10\%$ anyway, the approximate methods are accurate enough. On the other hand, use of *Excel*, when available, is easier as well as being more accurate.
- ✓ Equation 3, for the head loss in the system, must be replaced with an equation of the form $H = Z_0 + CQ^2$ when the head H required by the system has a component Z_0 due to gravity as well as a component due to head losses.

The *Excel* workbook for this Example was used to generate the tabulated results as well as the most accurate solution. It can be adapted for use with other pump-pipe systems.

The shapes of both the pump curve and the system curve can be important to system stability in certain applications. The pump curve shown in Fig. 10.19 is typical of the curve for a new centrifugal pump of intermediate specific speed, for which the head decreases smoothly and monotonically as the flow rate increases from shutoff. Two effects take place gradually as the system ages: the pump wears and its performance decreases (it produces less pressure head so the pump curve gradually moves downward toward lower head at each flow rate) and the system head increases (the system curve gradually moves toward higher head at each flow rate because of pipe aging[8]). The effect of these changes is to move the operating point toward lower flow rates over time. The magnitude of the change in flow rate depends on the shapes of the pump and system curves.

The capacity losses, as pump wear occurs, are compared for steep (friction dominated) and flat (gravity dominated) system curves in Fig. 10.21. The loss in capacity is greater for the flat system curve than for the steep system curve.

The pump efficiency curve is also plotted in Fig. 10.19. The original system operating point usually is chosen to coincide with the maximum efficiency by careful choice of pump size and operating speed. Pump wear increases internal leakage, thus reducing delivery and lowering peak efficiency. In addition, as shown in Fig. 10.21, the operating point moves toward lower flow rate, away from the best efficiency point. Thus the reduced system performance may not be accompanied by reduced energy usage.

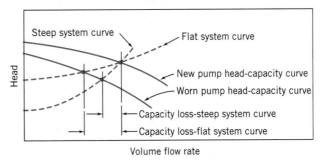

Fig. 10.21 Effect of pump wear on flow delivery to system.

[8] As the pipe ages, mineral deposits form on the wall (see Fig. 8.14), raising the relative roughness and reducing the pipe diameter compared with the as-new condition. See Problem 10.65 for typical friction-factor data.

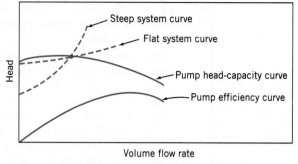

Fig. 10.22 Operation of low specific speed pump near shutoff.

Sometimes it is necessary to satisfy a high-head, low-flow requirement; this forces selection of a pump with low specific speed. Such a pump may have a performance curve with a slightly rising head near shutoff, as shown in Fig. 10.22. When the system curve is steep, the operating point is well defined and no problems with system operation should result. However, use of the pump with a flat system curve could easily cause problems, especially if the actual system curve were slightly above the computed curve or the pump delivery were below the charted head-capacity performance.

If there are two points of intersection of the pump and system curves, the system may operate at either point, depending on conditions at startup; a disturbance could cause the system operating point to shift to the second point of intersection. Under certain conditions, the system operating point can alternate between the two points of intersection, causing unsteady flow and unsatisfactory performance.

Instead of a single pump of low specific speed, a multi-stage pump may be used in this situation. Since the flow rate through all stages is the same, but the head per stage is less than in the single-stage unit, the specific speed of the multi-stage pump is higher (see Eq. 7.22a).

The head-flow characteristic curve of some high specific speed pumps shows a dip at capacities below the peak efficiency point, as shown in Fig. 10.23. Caution is needed in applying such pumps if it is ever necessary to operate the pump at or near the dip in the head-flow curve. No trouble should occur if the system characteristic is steep, for there will be only one point of intersection with the pump curve. Unless this intersection is near point *B*, the system should return to stable, steady-state operation following any transient disturbance.

Operation with a flat system curve is more problematic. It is possible to have one, two, or three points of intersection of the pump and system curves, as suggested in the figure. Points *A* and *C* are stable operating points, but point *B* is unstable: If the

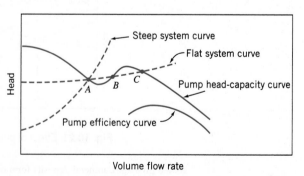

Fig. 10.23 Operation of high specific speed pump near the dip.

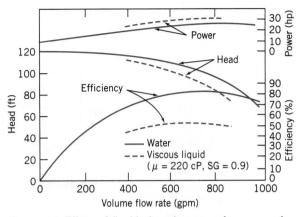

Fig. 10.24 Effect of liquid viscosity on performance of a centrifugal pump [5].

flow rate momentarily falls below Q_B, for whatever reason, the flow rate will continue to fall (to Q_A) because the head provided by the pump is now less than that required by the system; conversely, if the flow surges above Q_B, the flow rate will continue to increase (to Q_C) because the pump head exceeds the required head. With the flat system curve, the pump may "hunt" or oscillate periodically or aperiodically.

Several other factors can adversely influence pump performance: pumping hot liquid, pumping liquid with entrained vapor, and pumping liquid with high viscosity. According to [5], the presence of small amounts of entrained gas can drastically reduce performance. As little as 4 percent vapor can reduce pump capacity by more than 40 percent. Air can enter the suction side of the pumping circuit where pressure is below atmospheric if any leaks are present.

Adequate submergence of the suction pipe is necessary to prevent air entrainment. Insufficient submergence can cause a vortex to form at the pipe inlet. If the vortex is strong, air can enter the suction pipe. References 16 and 17 give guidelines for adequate suction-basin design to eliminate the likelihood of vortex formation.

Increased fluid viscosity may dramatically reduce the performance of a centrifugal pump [17]. Typical experimental test results are plotted in Fig. 10.24. In the figure, pump performance with water ($\mu = 1$ cP) is compared with performance in pumping a more viscous liquid ($\mu = 220$ cP). The increased viscosity reduces the head produced by the pump. At the same time the input power requirement is increased. The result is a dramatic drop in pump efficiency at all flow rates.

Heating a liquid raises its vapor pressure. Thus to pump a hot liquid requires additional pressure at the pump inlet to prevent cavitation. (See Example 10.8.)

In some systems, such as city water supply or chilled-water circulation, there may be a wide range in demand with a relatively constant system resistance. In these cases, it may be possible to operate constant-speed pumps in series or parallel to supply the system requirements without excessive energy dissipation due to outlet throttling. Two or more pumps may be operated in parallel or series to supply flow at high demand conditions, and fewer units can be used when demand is low.

For pumps in *series*, the combined performance curve is derived by adding the head rises at each flow rate (Fig. 10.25). The increase in flow rate gained by operating pumps in series depends upon the resistance of the system being supplied. For two pumps in series, delivery will increase at any system head. The characteristic curves for one pump and for two identical pumps in series are

$$H_1 = H_0 - AQ^2$$

and

$$H_{2s} = 2(H_0 - AQ^2) = 2H_0 - 2AQ^2$$

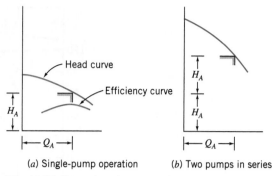

(a) Single-pump operation   (b) Two pumps in series

Fig. 10.25 Operation of two centrifugal pumps in series.

Figure 10.25 is a schematic illustrating the application of two identical pumps in series. A reasonable match to the system requirement is possible—while keeping efficiency high—if the system curve is relatively steep.

In an actual system, it is not appropriate simply to connect two pumps in series. If only one pump were powered, flow through the second, unpowered pump would cause additional losses, raising the system resistance. It also is desirable to arrange the pumps and piping so that each pump can be taken out of the pumping circuit for maintenance, repair, or replacement when needed. Thus a system of bypasses, valves, and check valves may be necessary in an actual installation [13, 17].

Pumps also may be combined in *parallel*. The resulting performance curve, shown in Fig. 10.26, is obtained by adding the pump capacities at each head. The characteristic curves for one pump and for two identical pumps in parallel are

$$H_1 = H_0 - AQ^2$$

and

$$H_{2p} = H_0 - A\left(\frac{Q}{2}\right)^2 = H_0 - \frac{1}{4}AQ^2$$

The schematic in Fig. 10.26 shows that the parallel combination may be used most effectively to increase system capacity when the system curve is relatively flat.

An actual system installation with parallel pumps also requires more thought to allow satisfactory operation with only one pump powered. It is necessary to prevent backflow through the pump that is not powered. To prevent backflow, and to permit pump removal, a more complex and expensive piping setup is needed.

Many other piping arrangements and pump combinations are possible. Pumps of different sizes, heads, and capacities may be combined in series, parallel, or series-parallel arrangements. Obviously the complexity of the piping and control system increases rapidly. In many applications the complexity is due to a requirement that the system

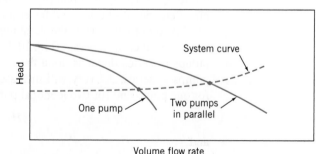

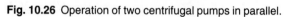

Fig. 10.26 Operation of two centrifugal pumps in parallel.

TABLE 10.1 Power Requirements for Constant- and Variable-Speed Drive Pumps

Throttle Valve Control with Constant-Speed (1750 rpm) Motor

Flow Rate (gpm)	System Head (ft)	Valve[a] Efficiency (%)	Pump Head (ft)	Pump Efficiency (%)	Pump Power (bhp)	Motor Efficiency (%)	Motor Input (hp)	Power Input[b] (hp)
1700	180	100.0	180	80.0	96.7	90.8	106.5	106.7
1500	150	78.1	192	78.4	92.9	90.7	102.4	102.6
1360	131	66.2	198	76.8	88.6	90.7	97.7	97.9
1100	102	49.5	206	72.4	79.1	90.6	87.3	87.5
900	83	39.5	210	67.0	71.3	90.3	79.0	79.1
600	62	29.0	214	54.0	60.1	90.0	66.8	66.9

Variable-Speed Drive with Energy-Efficient Motor

Flow Rate (gpm)	Pump/System Head (ft)	Pump Efficiency (%)	Pump Power (bhp)	Motor speed (rpm)	Motor Efficiency (%)	Motor Input (hp)	Control Efficiency (%)	Power Input (hp)
1700	180	80.0	96.7	1750	93.7	103.2	97.0	106.4
1500	150	79.6	71.5	1580	94.0	76.0	96.1	79.1
1360	131	78.8	57.2	1470	93.9	60.9	95.0	64.1
1100	102	78.4	36.2	1275	93.8	38.6	94.8	40.7
900	83	77.1	24.5	1140	92.3	26.5	92.8	28.6
600	62	72.0	13.1	960	90.0	14.5	89.1	16.3

[a]Valve efficiency is the ratio of system pressure to pump pressure.
[b]Power input is motor input divided by 0.998 starter efficiency.

handle a variety of flow rates—a range of flow rates can be generated by using pumps in parallel and in series, and by using throttling valves. Throttling valves are usually necessary because constant-speed motors drive most pumps, so simply using a network of pumps (with some on and others off) without throttling valves only allows the flow rate to be varied in discrete steps. The disadvantage of throttling valves is that they can be a major loss of energy, so that a given flow rate will require a larger power supply than would otherwise be the case. Some typical data for a throttling valve, given in Table 10.1 [18], show a decreasing valve efficiency (the percentage of pump pressure available that is not consumed by the valve) as the valve is used to reduce the flow rate.

Use of *variable-speed operation* allows infinitely variable control of system flow rate with high energy efficiency and without extra plumbing complexity. A further advantage is that a variable-speed drive system offers much simplified control of system flow rate. The cost of efficient variable-speed drive systems continues to decrease because of advances in power electronic components and circuits. The system flow rate can be controlled by varying pump operating speed with impressive savings in pumping power and energy usage. The input power reduction afforded by use of a variable-speed drive is illustrated in Table 10.1 [18]. At 1100 gpm the power input is cut almost 54 percent for the variable-speed system; the reduction at 600 gpm is more than 75 percent.

The reduction in input power requirement at reduced flow with the variable-speed drive is impressive. The energy savings, and therefore the cost savings, depend on the specific duty cycle on which the machine operates. Reference 18 presents information on mean duty cycles for centrifugal pumps used in the chemical process industry; Fig. 10.27 is a plot showing the histogram of these data. The plot shows that although the system must be designed and installed to deliver full rated capacity, this condition seldom occurs. Instead, more than half the time, the system operates at 70 percent capacity or below. The energy savings that result from use of a variable-speed drive for this duty cycle are estimated in Example 10.10.

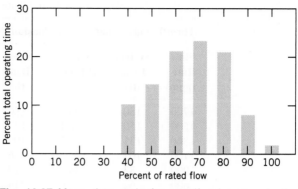

Fig. 10.27 Mean duty cycle for centrifugal pumps in the chemical and petroleum industries [18].

EXAMPLE 10.10   Energy Savings with Variable-Speed Centrifugal Pump Drive

Combine the information on mean duty cycle for centrifugal pumps given in Fig. 10.27 with the drive data in Table 10.1. Estimate the annual savings in pumping energy and cost that could be achieved by implementing a variable-speed drive system.

GIVEN: Consider the variable-flow, variable-pressure pumping system of Table 10.1. Assume the system operates on the typical duty cycle shown in Fig. 10.27, 24 hours per day, year round.

FIND: (a) An estimate of the reduction in annual energy usage obtained with the variable-speed drive.
(b) The energy costs and the cost saving due to variable-speed operation.

SOLUTION:
Full-time operation involves 365 days × 24 hours per day, or 8760 hours per year. Thus the percentages in Fig. 10.27 may be multiplied by 8760 to give annual hours of operation.

First plot the pump input power versus flow rate using data from Table 10.1 to allow interpolation, as shown below.

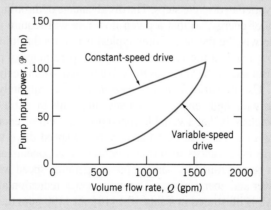

Illustrate the procedure using operation at 70 percent flow rate as a sample calculation. At 70 percent flow rate, the pump delivery is 0.7 × 1700 gpm = 1190 gpm. From the plot, the pump input power requirement at this flow rate is 90 hp for the constant-speed drive. At this flow rate, the pump operates 23 percent of the time, or 0.23 × 8760 = 2015 hours per year. The total energy consumed at this duty point is 90 hp × 2015 hr = 1.81×10^5 hp · hr. The electrical energy consumed is

$$E = \frac{1.81 \times 10^5 \text{ hp} \cdot \text{hr}}{} \times 0.746 \frac{\text{kW} \cdot \text{hr}}{\text{hp} \cdot \text{hr}} = 1.35 \times 10^5 \text{ kW} \cdot \text{hr}$$

The corresponding cost of electricity [at $0.12/(kW · hr)] is

$$C = \frac{1.35 \times 10^5 \text{ kW} \cdot \text{hr}}{} \times \frac{\$0.12}{\text{kW} \cdot \text{hr}} = \$16,250$$

The following tables were prepared using similar calculations:

Constant-Speed Drive, 8760 hr/yr					
Flow (%)	Flow (gpm)	Time (%)	Time (hr)	Power (hp)	Energy (hp · hr)
100	1700	2	175	109	1.91×10^4
90	1530	8	701	103	7.20×10^4
80	1360	21	1840	96	17.7×10^4
70	1190	23	2015	90	18.1×10^4
60	1020	21	1840	84	15.4×10^4
50	850	15	1314	77	10.2×10^4
40	680	10	876	71	6.21×10^4
				Total:	76.7×10^4

Summing the last column of the table shows that for the constant-speed drive system the annual energy consumption is 7.67×10^5 hp · hr. The electrical energy consumption is

$$E = \frac{7.67 \times 10^5 \text{ hp} \cdot \text{hr}}{} \times \frac{0.746 \text{ kW} \cdot \text{hr}}{\text{hp} \cdot \text{hr}} = 572,000 \text{ kW} \cdot \text{hr} \qquad\qquad\qquad E_{\text{CSD}}$$

At $0.12 per kilowatt hour, the energy cost for the constant-speed drive system is

$$C = \frac{572,000 \text{ kW} \cdot \text{hr}}{} \times \frac{\$0.12}{\text{kW} \cdot \text{hr}} = \$68,700 \qquad\qquad\qquad C_{\text{CSD}}$$

Variable-Speed Drive, 8760 hr/yr					
Flow (%)	Flow (gpm)	Time (%)	Time (hr)	Power (hp)	Energy (hp · hr)
100	1700	2	175	109	1.90×10^4
90	1530	8	701	81	5.71×10^4
80	1360	21	1840	61	11.2×10^4
70	1190	23	2015	46	9.20×10^4
60	1020	21	1840	34	6.29×10^4
50	850	15	1314	26	3.37×10^4
40	680	10	876	19	1.68×10^4
				Total:	39.4×10^4

Summing the last column of the table shows that for the variable-speed drive system, the annual energy consumption is 3.94×10^5 hp · hr. The electrical energy consumption is

$$E = \frac{3.94 \times 10^5 \text{ hp} \cdot \text{hr}}{} \times \frac{0.746 \text{ kW} \cdot \text{hr}}{\text{hp} \cdot \text{hr}} = 294,000 \text{ kW} \cdot \text{hr} \qquad\qquad\qquad E_{\text{VSD}}$$

At $0.12 per kilowatt hour, the energy cost for the variable-speed drive system is only

$$C = \frac{294,000 \text{ kW} \cdot \text{hr}}{} \times \frac{\$0.12}{\text{kW} \cdot \text{hr}} = \$35,250 \qquad\qquad\qquad C_{\text{VSD}}$$

Thus, in this application, the variable-speed drive reduces energy consumption by 278,000 kW · hr (47 percent). The cost saving is an impressive $33,450 annually. One could afford to install a variable-speed drive even at considerable cost penalty. The savings in energy cost are appreciable each year and continue throughout the life of the system.

> This problem illustrates the energy and cost savings that can be gained by the use of variable-speed pump drives. We see that the specific benefits depend on the system and its operating duty cycle.
>
> The *Excel* workbook for this Example was used for plotting the graph, for obtaining the interpolated data, and for performing all calculations. It can be easily modified for other such analyses. Note that results were rounded down to three significant figures *after* calculation.

b. Fans, Blowers, and Compressors

Fans are designed to handle air or vapor. Fan sizes range from that of the cooling fan in a notebook computer, which moves a cubic meter of air per hour and requires a few watts of power, to that of the ventilation fans for the Channel Tunnel, which move thousands of cubic meters of air per minute and require many hundreds of kilowatts of power. Fans are produced in varieties similar to those of pumps: They range from radial-flow (centrifugal) to axial-flow devices. As with pumps, the characteristic curve shapes for fans depend on the fan type. Some typical performance curves for centrifugal fans are presented in Appendix D. The curves may be used to choose fans to solve some of the equipment-selection and system-design problems at the end of the chapter.

An exploded view of a medium-size centrifugal fan is shown in Fig. 10.28. Some commonly used terminology is shown on the figure.

The pressure rise produced by fans is several orders of magnitude less than that for pumps. Another difference between fans and pumps is that measurement of flow rate is more difficult in gases and vapors than in liquids. There is no convenient analog to the "catch the flow in a bucket" method of measuring liquid flow rates! Consequently, fan testing requires special facilities and procedures [6, 20]. Because the pressure rise produced by a fan is small, usually it is impractical to measure flow rate with a restriction flow meter such as an orifice, flow nozzle, or venturi. It may be necessary to use an auxiliary fan to develop enough pressure rise to permit measurement of flow rate with acceptable accuracy using a restriction flow meter. An alternative is to use an instrumented duct in which the flow rate is calculated from a pitot traverse. Appropriate standards may be consulted to obtain complete information on specific fan-test methods and data-reduction procedures for each application [6, 20].

Because the pressure change across a fan is small, the dynamic pressure at the fan exit may be an appreciable fraction of the pressure rise. Consequently, it is necessary to carefully specify the basis on which pressure measurements are made. Data for both static and total pressure rise and for efficiency, based on both pressure rises, are frequently plotted on the same characteristic graph (Fig. 10.29).

The coordinates may be plotted in physical units (e.g., inches of water, cubic feet per minute, and horsepower) or as dimensionless flow and pressure coefficients. The difference between the total and static pressures is the dynamic pressure, so the vertical distance between these two curves is proportional to Q^2.

Centrifugal fans are used frequently; we will use them as examples. The centrifugal fan developed from simple paddle-wheel designs, in which the wheel was a disk carrying radial flat plates. (This primitive form still is used in non-clogging fans such as in commercial clothes dryers.) Refinements have led to the three general types shown in Figs. 10.30a through c, with backward-curved, radial-tipped, and forward-curved blades. All the fans illustrated have blades that are curved at their inlet edges

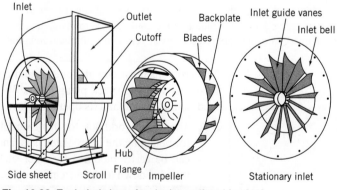

Fig. 10.28 Exploded view of typical centrifugal fan [19].

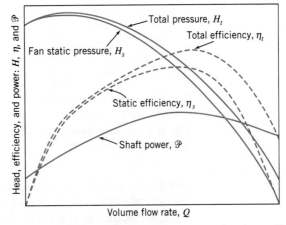

Fig. 10.29 Typical characteristic curves for fan with backward-curved blades [21].

to approximate shockless flow between the blade and the inlet flow direction. These three designs are typical of fans with sheet-metal blades, which are relatively simple to manufacture and thus relatively inexpensive. The forward-curved design illustrated in the figure has very closely spaced blades; it is frequently called a *squirrel-cage* fan because of its resemblance to the exercise wheels found in animal cages.

As fans become larger in size and power demand, efficiency becomes more important. The streamlined *airfoil blades* shown in Fig. 10.30*d* are much less sensitive to inlet flow direction and improve efficiency markedly compared with the thin blades shown in diagrams *a* through *c*. The added expense of airfoil blades for large metal fans may be life-cycle cost effective. Airfoil blades are being used more frequently on small fans as impellers molded from plastic become common.

As is true for pumps, the total pressure rise across a fan is approximately proportional to the absolute velocity of the fluid at the exit from the wheel. Therefore the characteristic curves produced by the basic blade shapes tend to differ from each other. The typical curve shapes are shown in Fig. 10.31, where both pressure rise and power requirements are sketched. Fans with backward-curved blade tips typically have a power curve that reaches a maximum and then decreases as flow rate increases. If the fan drive is sized properly to handle the peak power, it is impossible to overload the drive with this type of fan.

The power curves for fans with radial and forward-curved blades rise as flow rate increases. If the fan operating point is higher than the design flow rate, the motor

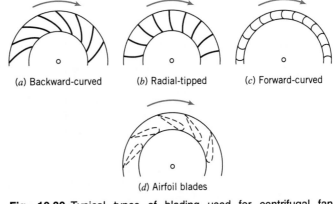

Fig. 10.30 Typical types of blading used for centrifugal fan wheels [21].

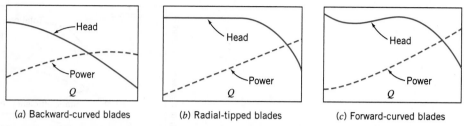

| (a) Backward-curved blades | (b) Radial-tipped blades | (c) Forward-curved blades |

Fig. 10.31 General features of performance curves for centrifugal fans with backward-, radial-, and forward-curved blades [21].

may be overloaded. Such fans cannot be run for long periods at low back pressures. An example of this would be when a fan is run without a load to resist the flow—in other words, the fan is almost "free-wheeling." Because the power drawn by the fan monotonically increases with flow rate, the fan motor could eventually burn out under this free-wheeling condition.

Fans with backward-curved blades are best for installations with large power demand and continuous operation. The forward-curved blade fan is preferred where low first cost and small size are important and where service is intermittent. Forward-curved blades require lower tip speed to produce a specified head; lower blade tip speed means reduced noise. Thus forward-curved blades may be specified for heating and air conditioning applications to minimize noise.

Characteristic curves for axial-flow (*propeller*) fans differ markedly from those for centrifugal fans. The power curve, Fig. 10.32, is especially different, as it tends to decrease continuously as flow rate increases. Thus it is impossible to overload a properly sized drive for an axial-flow fan.

The simple propeller fan is often used for ventilation; it may be free-standing or mounted in an opening, as a window fan, with no inlet or outlet duct work. Ducted axial-flow fans have been studied extensively and developed to high efficiency [22]. Modern designs, with airfoil blades, mounted in ducts and often fitted with guide vanes, can deliver large volumes against high resistances with high efficiency. The primary deficiency of the axial-flow fan is the non-monotonic slope of the pressure characteristic: in certain ranges of flow rate the fan may pulsate. Because axial-flow fans tend to have high rotational speeds, they can be noisy.

Selection and installation of a fan always requires compromise. To minimize energy consumption, it is desirable to operate a fan at its highest efficiency point. To reduce the fan size for a given capacity, it is tempting to operate at higher flow rate than that at maximum efficiency. In an actual installation, this tradeoff must be made considering such factors as available space, initial cost, and annual hours of operation. It is not wise to operate a fan at a flow rate below maximum efficiency. Such a fan

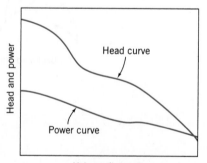

Fig. 10.32 Characteristic curves for a typical axial-flow fan [21].

would be larger than necessary and some designs, particularly those with forward-curved blades, can be unstable and noisy when operated in this region.

It is necessary to consider the duct system at both the inlet and the outlet of the fan to develop a satisfactory installation. Anything that disrupts the uniform flow at the fan inlet is likely to impair performance. Nonuniform flow at the inlet causes the wheel to operate unsymmetrically and may decrease capacity dramatically. Swirling flow also adversely affects fan performance. Swirl in the direction of rotation reduces the pressure developed; swirl in the opposite direction can increase the power required to drive the fan.

The fan specialist may not be allowed total freedom in designing the best flow system for the fan. Sometimes a poor flow system can be improved without too much effort by adding splitters or straightening vanes to the inlet. Some fan manufacturers offer guide vanes that can be installed for this purpose.

Flow conditions at the fan discharge also affect installed performance. Every fan produces nonuniform outlet flow. When the fan is connected to a length of straight duct, the flow becomes more uniform and some excess kinetic energy is transformed to static pressure. If the fan discharges directly into a large space with no duct, the excess kinetic energy of the nonuniform flow is dissipated. A fan in a flow system with no discharge ducting may fall considerably short of the performance measured in a laboratory test setup.

The flow pattern at the fan outlet may be affected by the amount of resistance present downstream. The effect of the system on fan performance may be different at different points along the fan pressure-flow curve. Thus, it may not be possible to accurately predict the performance of a fan, *as installed*, on the basis of curves measured in the laboratory.

Fans may be scaled up or down in size or speed using the basic laws developed for fluid machines in Chapter 7. It is possible for two fans to operate with fluids of significantly different density,[9] so pressure is used instead of head (which uses density) as a dependent parameter and density must be retained in the dimensionless groups. The dimensionless groups appropriate for fan scaling are

$$\Pi_1 = \frac{Q}{\omega D^3}, \quad \Pi_2 = \frac{p}{\rho \omega^2 D^2}, \quad \text{and} \quad \Pi_3 = \frac{\mathscr{P}}{\rho \omega^3 D^5} \qquad (10.25)$$

Once again dynamic similarity is assured when the flow coefficients are matched. Thus when

$$Q' = Q\left(\frac{\omega'}{\omega}\right)\left(\frac{D'}{D}\right)^3 \qquad (10.26a)$$

then

$$p' = p\left(\frac{\rho'}{\rho}\right)\left(\frac{\omega'}{\omega}\right)^2\left(\frac{D'}{D}\right)^2 \qquad (10.26b)$$

and

$$\mathscr{P}' = \mathscr{P}\left(\frac{\rho'}{\rho}\right)\left(\frac{\omega'}{\omega}\right)^3\left(\frac{D'}{D}\right)^5 \qquad (10.26c)$$

As a first approximation, the efficiency of the scaled fan is assumed to remain constant, so

$$\eta' = \eta \qquad (10.26d)$$

---

[9] Density of the flue gas handled by an induced-draft fan on a steam powerplant may be 40 percent less than the density of the air handled by the forced-draft fan in the same plant.

When head is replaced by pressure, and density is included, the expression defining the specific speed of a fan becomes

$$N_s = \frac{\omega Q^{1/2} \rho^{3/4}}{p^{3/4}}$$

(10.27)

A fan scale-up with density variation is the subject of Example 10.11.

EXAMPLE 10.11   Scaling of Fan Performance

Performance curves [21] are given below for a centrifugal fan with $D = 36$ in. and $N = 600$ rpm, as measured on a test stand using cool air ($\rho = 0.075$ lbm/ft^3). Scale the data to predict the performance of a similar fan with $D' = 42$ in., $N' = 1150$ rbm, and $\rho' = 0.045$ lbm/ft^3. Estimate the delivery and power of the larger fan when it operates at a system pressure equivalent to 7.4 in. of H$_2$O. Check the specific speed of the fan at the new operating point.

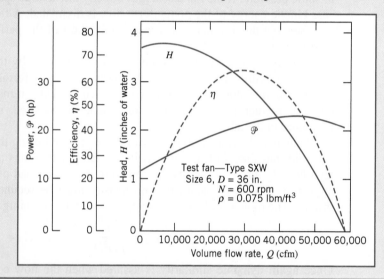

GIVEN: Performance data as shown for centrifugal fan with $D = 36$ in., $N = 600$ rpm, and $\rho = 0.075$ lbm/ft^3.

FIND: (a) The predicted performance of a geometrically similar fan with $D' = 42$ in., at $N' = 1150$ rpm, with $\rho' = 0.045$ lbm/ft^3.
(b) An estimate of the delivery and input power requirement if the larger fan operates against a system resistance of 7.4 in. H$_2$O.
(c) The specific speed of the larger fan at this operating point.

SOLUTION:
Develop the performance curves at the new operating condition by scaling the test data point-by-point. Using Eqs. 10.26 and the data from the curves at $Q = 30,000$ cfm, the new volume flow rate is

$$Q' = Q\left(\frac{N'}{N}\right)\left(\frac{D'}{D}\right)^3 = 30,000 \text{ cfm}\left(\frac{1150}{600}\right)\left(\frac{42}{36}\right)^3 = 91,300 \text{ cfm}$$

The fan pressure rise is

$$p' = p\frac{\rho'}{\rho}\left(\frac{N'}{N}\right)^2\left(\frac{D'}{D}\right)^2 = 2.96 \text{ in. H}_2\text{O}\left(\frac{0.045}{0.075}\right)\left(\frac{1150}{600}\right)^2\left(\frac{42}{36}\right)^2 = 8.88 \text{ in. H}_2\text{O}$$

and the new power input is

$$\mathscr{P}' = \mathscr{P}\left(\frac{\rho'}{\rho}\right)\left(\frac{N'}{N}\right)^3\left(\frac{D'}{D}\right)^5 = 21.4 \text{ hp}\left(\frac{0.045}{0.075}\right)\left(\frac{1150}{600}\right)^3\left(\frac{42}{36}\right)^5 = 195 \text{ hp}$$

We assume the efficiency remains constant between the two scaled points, so

$$\eta' = \eta = 0.64$$

Similar calculations at other operating points give the results tabulated below:

Q (cfm)	p (in. H₂O)	𝒫 (hp)	η (%)	Q' (cfm)	p' (in. H₂O)	𝒫' (hp)
0	3.68	11.1	0	0	11.0	101
10,000	3.75	15.1	37	30,400	11.3	138
20,000	3.50	18.6	59	60,900	10.5	170
30,000	2.96	21.4	65	91,300	8.88	195
40,000	2.12	23.1	57	122,000	6.36	211
50,000	1.02	23.1	34	152,000	3.06	211
60,000	0	21.0	0	183,000	0	192

To allow interpolation among the calculated points, it is convenient to plot the results:

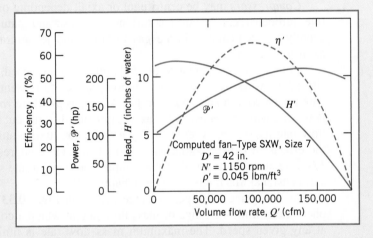

From the head-capacity curve, the larger fan should deliver 110,000 cfm at 7.5 in. H₂O system head, with an efficiency of about 58 percent.

This operating point is only slightly to the right of peak efficiency for this fan, so it is a reasonable point at which to operate the fan. The specific speed of the fan at this operating point (in U.S. customary units) is given by direct substitution into Eq. 10.27:

$$N_{s_{cu}} = \frac{\omega Q^{1/2} \, \rho^{3/4}}{p^{3/4}} = \frac{(1150 \text{ rpm})(110,000 \text{ cfm})^{1/2}(0.045 \text{ lbm/ft}^3)^{3/4}}{(7.5 \text{ in. H}_2\text{O})^{3/4}} = 8223 \qquad \longleftarrow \qquad N_{s_{cu}}$$

In nondimensional (SI) units,

$$N_s = \frac{(120 \text{ rad/s})(3110 \text{ m}^3/\text{s})^{1/2}(0.721 \text{ kg/m}^3)^{3/4}}{(1.86 \times 10^3 \text{ N/m}^2)^{3/4}} = 18.5 \qquad \longleftarrow \qquad N_s(\text{SI})$$

This problem illustrates the procedure for scaling performance of fans operating on gases with two different densities.

The *Excel* workbook for this Example was used for plotting the graphs, for obtaining the interpolated data, and for performing all calculations. It can be easily modified for other such analyses.

Three methods are available to control fan delivery: motor speed control, inlet dampers, and outlet throttling. Speed control was treated thoroughly in the section on pumps. The same benefits of reduced energy usage and noise are obtained with fans, and the cost of variable-speed drive systems continues to drop.

Inlet dampers may be used effectively on some large centrifugal fans. However, they decrease efficiency and cannot be used to reduce the fan flow rate below about 40 percent of rated capacity. Outlet throttling is cheap but wasteful of energy. For further details, consult either Reference 19 or 21; both are particularly comprehensive. Osborne [23] also treats noise, vibration, and the mechanical design of fans.

Fans also may be combined in series, parallel, or more complex arrangements to match varying system resistance and flow needs. These combinations may be analyzed using the methods described for pumps. References 24 and 25 are excellent sources for loss data on air flow systems.

Blowers have performance characteristics similar to fans, but they operate (typically) at higher speeds and increase the fluid pressure more than do fans. Jorgensen [19] divides the territory between fans and compressors at an arbitrary pressure level that changes the air density by 5 percent; he does not demarcate between fans and blowers.

Compressors may be centrifugal or axial, depending on specific speed. Automotive turbochargers, small gas-turbine engines, and natural-gas pipeline boosters usually are centrifugal. Large gas turbines and jet aircraft engines frequently are axial-flow machines.

Compressor performance depends on operating speed, mass flow rate, and density of the working fluid. It is common practice to present compressor performance data on the coordinates shown in Fig. 10.33, as *pressure ratio* versus *corrected mass flow rate*, with *corrected speed* as a parameter. It turns out that normalizing the mass flow rate by $\sqrt{T}/p$, where T and p are absolute temperature and pressure, removes the effects of density variations. Normalizing the compressor operating speed with $1/\sqrt{T}$ relates the tip speed of the compressor wheel to the speed of sound (this forms a dimensional Mach number—see Chapter 12).

At first glance, the performance curves in Fig. 10.33 appear incomplete. Two phenomena limit the range of mass flow rate at which a compressor can be operated at any given speed. The maximum mass flow rate is limited by choking—the approach to $M = 1$ at some point in the machine—see Chapter 13. Performance deteriorates rapidly as the choking limit is approached.

The mass flow rate is limited at the low end by either *rotating stall* or *surge* in the compressor. Rotating stall occurs when cells of separated flow form and block a segment of the compressor rotor. The effect is to reduce performance and unbalance the rotor; this causes severe vibration and can quickly lead to damage. Thus it is impossible to operate a compressor with rotating stall and it must be avoided.

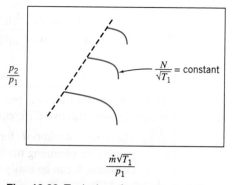

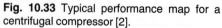

Fig. 10.33 Typical performance map for a centrifugal compressor [2].

Centrifugal and axial compressors may also be limited by surge, a cyclic pulsation phenomenon that causes the mass flow rate through the machine to vary, and can even reverse it! Surge is accompanied by loud noises and can damage the compressor or related components; it too must be avoided.

In general, as shown in Fig. 10.33, the higher the performance, the more narrow the range in which the compressor may be operated successfully. Thus a compressor must be carefully matched to its flow system to assure satisfactory operation. Compressor matching in natural gas pipeline applications is discussed by Vincent–Genod [26]. Perhaps the most common application of high-speed fluid machinery today is in automotive turbochargers (worldwide many millions of cars are sold each year with turbochargers). Automotive turbocharger matching is described in manufacturers' literature [27].

c. Positive-Displacement Pumps

Pressure is developed in positive-displacement pumps through volume reductions caused by movement of the boundary in which the fluid is confined. In contrast to turbomachines, positive displacement pumps can develop high pressures at relatively low speeds because the pumping effect depends on volume change instead of dynamic action.

Positive-displacement pumps frequently are used in hydraulic systems at pressures ranging up to 40 MPa (6000 psi). A principal advantage of hydraulic power is the high *power density* (power per unit weight or unit size) that can be achieved: for a given power output, a hydraulic system can be lighter and smaller than a typical electric-drive system.

Numerous types of positive-displacement pumps have been developed. A few examples include piston pumps, vane pumps, and gear pumps. Within each type, pumps may be fixed- or variable-displacement. A comprehensive classification of pump types is given in [16].

The performance characteristics of most positive-displacement pumps are similar; in this section we shall focus on gear pumps. This pump type typically is used, for example, to supply pressurized lubricating oil in internal combustion engines. Figure 10.34 is a schematic diagram of a typical gear pump. Oil enters the space between the gears at the bottom of the pump cavity. Oil is carried outward and upward by the teeth of the rotating gears and exits through the outlet port at the top of the cavity. Pressure is generated as the oil is forced toward the pump outlet; leakage and backflow are prevented by the closely fitting gear teeth at the center of the pump, and by the small clearances maintained between the side faces of the gears and the pump

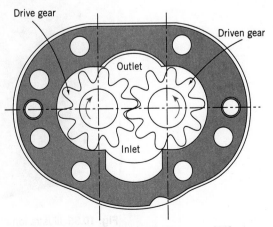

Fig. 10.34 Schematic of typical gear pump [28].

housing. The close clearances require the hydraulic fluid to be kept extremely clean by full-flow filtration.

Figure 10.35 is a photo showing the parts of an actual gear pump; it gives a good idea of the robust housing and bearings needed to withstand the large pressure forces developed within the pump. It also shows pressure-loaded side plates designed to "float"—to allow thermal expansion—while maintaining the smallest possible side clearance between gears and housing. Many ingenious designs have been developed for pumps; details are beyond the scope of our treatment here, which will focus on performance characteristics. For more details consult Reference 28 or 29.

Typical performance curves of pressure versus delivery for a medium-duty gear pump are shown in Fig. 10.36. The pump size is specified by its displacement per revolution and the working fluid is characterized by its viscosity and temperature. Curves for tests at three constant speeds are presented in the diagram. At each speed, delivery decreases slightly as pressure is raised. The pump displaces the same volume, but as pressure is raised, both leakage and backflow increase, so delivery decreases slightly. Leakage fluid ends up in the pump housing, so a case drain must be provided to return this fluid to the system reservoir.

Volumetric efficiency—shown by the dashed curves—is defined as actual volumetric delivery divided by pump displacement. Volumetric efficiency decreases as pressure is raised or pump speed is reduced. *Overall efficiency*—shown by the solid curves—is defined as power delivered to the fluid divided by power input to the pump. Overall efficiency tends to rise (and reaches a maximum at intermediate pressure) as pump speed increases.

Thus far we have shown pumps of fixed displacement only. The extra cost and complication of variable-displacement pumps is motivated by the energy saving they permit during partial-flow operation. In a variable-displacement pump, delivery can be varied to accommodate the load. Load sensing can be used to reduce the delivery pressure and thus the energy expenditure still further during part-load operation. Some pump designs allow pressure relief to further reduce power loss during standby operation.

Figure 10.37 illustrates system losses with a fixed-displacement pump compared with losses for variable-displacement and variable-pressure pumps. Assume the pressure and flow required by the load at partial-flow operation correspond to point L on the diagram. A fixed-displacement pump will operate along curve CD; its delivery

Fig. 10.35 Illustration of gear pump with pressure-loaded side plates [28]. (Photo courtesy Sauer Sundstrand Company.)

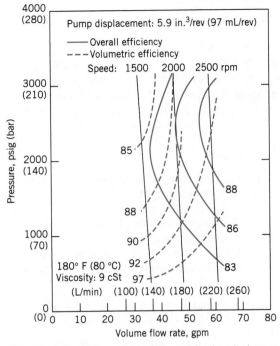

Fig. 10.36 Performance characteristics of typical gear pump [28].

will be at point A. Since the load requires only the flow at L, the remaining flow (between L and A) must be bypassed back to the reservoir. Its pressure is dissipated by throttling. Consequently the system power loss will be the area beneath line LA.

A variable-displacement pump operating at constant pressure will deliver just enough flow to supply the load, but at a pressure represented by point B. The system power loss will be proportional to the area to the left of line BL. Control of delivery pressure using load sensing can be used to reduce power loss. With a load sensing pump of variable displacement, the pressure supplied is only slightly higher than is needed to move the load. A pump with load sensing would operate at the flow and pressure of point B'. The system loss would be reduced significantly to the area to the left of line $B'L$.

The best system choice depends on the operating duty cycle. Complete details of these and other hydraulic power systems are presented in [28].

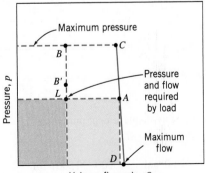

Fig. 10.37 Pressure-flow diagram illustrating system losses at part load [28].

EXAMPLE 10.12 Performance of a Positive-Displacement Pump

A hydraulic pump, with the performance characteristics of Fig. 10.36, operates at 2000 rpm in a system that requires $Q = 20$ gpm at $p = 1500$ psig to the load at one operating condition. Check the volume of oil per revolution delivered by this pump. Compute the required pump power input, the power delivered to the load, and the power dissipated by throttling at this condition. Compare with the power dissipated by using (i) a variable-displacement pump at 3000 psig and (ii) a pump with load sensing that operates at 100 psi above the load requirement.

GIVEN: Hydraulic pump, with performance characteristics of Fig. 10.36, operating at 2000 rpm. System requires $Q = 20$ gpm at $p = 1500$ psig.

FIND: (a) The volume of oil per revolution delivered by this pump.
(b) The required pump power input.
(c) The power delivered to the load.
(d) The power dissipated by throttling at this condition.
(e) The power dissipated using:
   (i) a variable-displacement pump at 3000 psig, and
   (ii) a pump with load sensing that operates at 100 psi above the load pressure requirement.

SOLUTION:

To estimate the maximum delivery, extrapolate the curve of pressure versus flow rate to zero pressure. Under these conditions, $Q = 48.5$ gpm at $N = 2000$ rpm with negligible Δp. Thus

$$\Psi = \frac{Q}{N} = \frac{48.5}{min} \frac{gal}{min} \times \frac{min}{2000 \ rev} \times \frac{231 \ in.^3}{gal} = 5.60 \ in.^3/rev \quad\longleftarrow \quad \Psi$$

The volumetric efficiency of the pump at maximum flow is

$$\eta_V = \frac{\Psi_{calc}}{\Psi_{pump}} = \frac{5.60}{5.9} = 0.949$$

The operating point of the pump may be found from Fig. 10.36. At 1500 psig, it operates at $Q \approx 46.5$ gpm. The power delivered to the fluid is

$$\mathcal{P}_{fluid} = \rho Q g H_p = Q \Delta p_p$$

$$= \frac{46.5}{min} \frac{gal}{min} \times \frac{1500}{in.^2} \frac{lbf}{in.^2} \times \frac{ft^3}{7.48 \ gal} \times \frac{min}{60 \ s} \times \frac{144 \ in.^2}{ft^2} \times \frac{hp \cdot s}{550 \ ft \cdot lbf}$$

$$\mathcal{P}_{fluid} = 40.7 \ hp$$

From the graph, at this operating point, the pump efficiency is approximately $\eta = 0.84$. Therefore the required input power is

$$\mathcal{P}_{input} = \frac{\mathcal{P}_{fluid}}{\eta} = \frac{40.7 \ hp}{0.84} = 48 \ hp \quad\longleftarrow\quad \mathcal{P}_{input}$$

The power delivered to the load is

$$\mathcal{P}_{load} = Q_{load} \Delta p_{load}$$

$$= \frac{20.0}{min} \frac{gal}{min} \times \frac{1500}{in.^2} \frac{lbf}{in.^2} \times \frac{ft^3}{7.48 \ gal} \times \frac{min}{60 \ s} \times \frac{144 \ in.^2}{ft^2} \times \frac{hp \cdot s}{550 \ ft \cdot lbf}$$

$$\mathcal{P}_{load} = 17.5 \ hp \quad\longleftarrow\quad \mathcal{P}_{load}$$

The power dissipated by throttling is

$$\mathcal{P}_{dissipated} = \mathcal{P}_{fluid} - \mathcal{P}_{load} = 40.7 - 17.5 = 23.2 \ hp \quad\longleftarrow\quad \mathcal{P}_{dissipated}$$

The dissipation with the variable-displacement pump is

$$\mathcal{P}_{var-disp} = Q_{load}(p_{oper} - p_{load})$$

$$= \frac{20.0}{min} \frac{gal}{min} \times \frac{(3000 - 1500)}{in.^2} \frac{lbf}{in.^2} \times \frac{ft^3}{7.48 \ gal} \times \frac{min}{60 \ s} \times \frac{144 \ in.^2}{ft^2} \times \frac{hp \cdot s}{550 \ ft \cdot lbf}$$

$$\mathcal{P}_{var-disp} = 17.5 \ hp \quad\longleftarrow\quad \mathcal{P}_{var-disp}$$

The dissipation with the variable-displacement pump is therefore less than the 23.2 hp dissipated with the constant-displacement pump and throttle. The saving is approximately 6 hp.

The final computation is for the load-sensing pump. If the pump pressure is 100 psi above that required by the load, the excess energy dissipation is

$$\mathscr{P}_{\text{load-sense}} = Q_{\text{load}}(p_{\text{oper}} - p_{\text{load}})$$
$$= 20.0 \, \frac{\text{gal}}{\text{min}} \times 100 \, \frac{\text{lbf}}{\text{in.}^2} \times \frac{\text{ft}^3}{7.48 \, \text{gal}} \times \frac{\text{min}}{60 \, \text{s}} \times 144 \, \frac{\text{in.}^2}{\text{ft}^2} \times \frac{\text{hp} \cdot \text{s}}{550 \, \text{ft} \cdot \text{lbf}}$$

$$\mathscr{P}_{\text{load-sense}} = 1.17 \, \text{hp} \quad \longleftarrow \qquad \qquad \qquad \mathscr{P}_{\text{load-sense}}$$

> This problem contrasts the performance of a system with a pump of constant displacement to that of a system with variable-displacement and load-sensing pumps. The specific savings depend on the system operating point and on the duty cycle of the system.

d. Propellers

It has been suggested that a propeller may be considered an axial-flow machine without a housing [10]. In common with other propulsion devices, a propeller produces thrust by imparting linear momentum to a fluid. Thrust production always leaves the stream with some kinetic energy and angular momentum that are not recoverable, so the process is never 100 percent efficient.

The one-dimensional flow model shown schematically in Fig. 10.38 is drawn in absolute coordinates on the left and as seen by an observer moving with the propeller, at speed V, on the right. The wake is modeled as a uniform flow as shown, and in the new coordinates the flow is steady. The actual propeller is replaced conceptually by a thin *actuator disk*, across which flow speed is continuous but pressure rises abruptly. Relative to the propeller, the upstream flow is at speed V and ambient pressure. The axial speed at the actuator disk is $V + \Delta V/2$, with a corresponding reduction in pressure. Downstream, the speed is $V + \Delta V$ and the pressure returns to ambient. (Example 10.13 shows that half the speed increase occurs before and half after the actuator disk.) The contraction of the slipstream area to satisfy continuity and the pressure rise across the propeller disk are shown in the figure.

Not shown in the figure are the swirl velocities that result from the torque required to turn the propeller. The kinetic energy of the swirl in the slipstream also is lost unless it is removed by a counter-rotating propeller or partially recovered in stationary guide vanes.

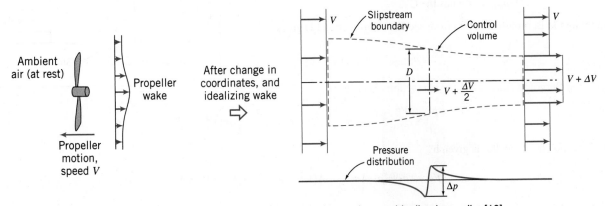

Fig. 10.38 One-dimensional flow model and control volume used to analyze an idealized propeller [10].

As for all turbomachinery, propellers may be analyzed in two ways. Application of linear momentum in the axial direction, using a finite control volume, provides overall relations among slipstream speed, thrust, useful power output, and minimum residual kinetic energy in the slipstream. A more detailed *blade element* theory is needed to calculate the interaction between a propeller blade and the stream. A general relation for ideal propulsive efficiency can be derived using the control volume approach, as shown following Example 10.13.

EXAMPLE 10.13   Control Volume Analysis of Idealized Flow through a Propeller

Consider the one-dimensional model for the idealized flow through a propeller shown in Fig. 10.38. The propeller advances into still air at steady speed V_1. Obtain expressions for the pressure immediately upstream and the pressure immediately downstream from the actuator disk. Write the thrust on the propeller as the product of this pressure difference times the disk area. Equate this expression for thrust to one obtained by applying the linear momentum equation to the control volume. Show that half the velocity increase occurs ahead of and half behind the propeller disk.

GIVEN: Propeller advancing into still air at speed V_1, as shown in Fig. 10.38.

FIND: (a) Expressions for the pressures immediately upstream and immediately downstream from the actuator disk.
   (b) Expression for the air speed at the actuator disk. Then show that half the velocity increase occurs ahead of the actuator disk and half occurs behind the actuator disk.

SOLUTION:
Apply the Bernoulli equation and the x component of linear momentum using the CV shown.

Governing equations:

$$\frac{p}{\rho} + \frac{V^2}{2} + \overset{\approx\,0(5)}{\cancel{gz}} = \text{constant}$$

$$F_{S_x} + \overset{=\,0(5)}{\cancel{F_{B_x}}} = \overset{=\,0(1)}{\cancel{\frac{\partial}{\partial t}\int_{CV} u_{xyz}\,\rho\,dV}} + \int_{CS} u_{xyz}\,\rho\vec{V}\cdot d\vec{A}$$

Assumptions: (1) Steady flow relative to the CV.
   (2) Incompressible flow.
   (3) Flow along a streamline.
   (4) Frictionless flow.
   (5) Horizontal flow: neglect changes in z; $F_{B_x} = 0$.
   (6) Uniform flow at each section.
   (7) p_{atm} surrounds the CV.

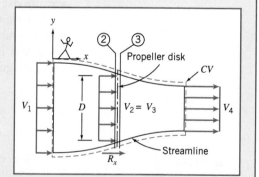

Applying the Bernoulli equation from section ① to section ② gives

$$\frac{p_{atm}}{\rho} + \frac{V_1^2}{2} = \frac{p_2}{\rho} + \frac{V_2^2}{2}; \qquad p_{2(gage)} = \frac{1}{2}\rho\,(V_1^2 - V_2^2)$$

Applying Bernoulli from section ③ to section ④ gives

$$\frac{p_3}{\rho} + \frac{V_3^2}{2} = \frac{p_{atm}}{\rho} + \frac{V_4^2}{2}; \qquad p_{3(gage)} = \frac{1}{2}\rho\,(V_4^2 - V_3^2)$$

The thrust on the propeller is given by

$$F_T = (p_3 - p_2)A = \frac{1}{2}\rho A(V_4^2 - V_1^2) \qquad (V_3 = V_2 = V)$$

From the momentum equation, using *relative* velocities,

$$R_x = F_T = u_1(-\dot{m}) + u_4(+\dot{m}) = \rho V A(V_4 - V_1) \qquad \{u_1 = V_1, \ u_4 = V_4\}$$

$$F_T = \rho V A(V_4 - V_1)$$

Equating these two expressions for F_T,

$$F_T = \frac{1}{2}\rho A(V_4^2 - V_1^2) = \rho V A(V_4 - V_1) \quad \text{or} \quad \frac{1}{2}(V_4 + V_1)(V_4 - V_1) = V(V_4 - V_1)$$

Thus, $V = \frac{1}{2}(V_1 + V_4)$, so

$$\Delta V_{12} = V - V_1 = \frac{1}{2}(V_1 + V_4) - V_1 = \frac{1}{2}(V_4 - V_1) = \frac{\Delta V}{2}$$

$$\Delta V_{34} = V_4 - V = V_4 - \frac{1}{2}(V_1 + V_4) = \frac{1}{2}(V_4 - V_1) = \frac{\Delta V}{2} \qquad \longleftarrow \underline{\text{Velocity Increase}}$$

> The purpose of this problem is to apply the continuity, momentum, and Bernoulli equations to an idealized flow model of a propeller, and to verify the Rankine theory of 1885 that half the velocity change occurs on either side of the propeller disk.

The continuity and momentum equations in control volume form were applied in Example 10.13 to the propeller flow shown in Fig. 10.38. The results obtained are discussed further below. The thrust produced is

$$F_T = \dot{m}\Delta V \tag{10.28}$$

For incompressible flow, in the absence of friction and heat transfer, the energy equation indicates that the minimum required input to the propeller is the power required to increase the kinetic energy of the flow, which may be expressed as

$$\mathcal{P}_{\text{input}} = \dot{m}\left[\frac{(V + \Delta V)^2}{2} - \frac{V^2}{2}\right] = \dot{m}\left[\frac{2V\Delta V + (\Delta V)^2}{2}\right] = \dot{m}V\Delta V\left[1 + \frac{\Delta V}{2V}\right] \tag{10.29}$$

The useful power produced is the product of thrust and speed of advance, V, of the propeller. Using Eq. 10.28, this may be written as

$$\mathcal{P}_{\text{useful}} = F_T V = \dot{m}V\Delta V \tag{10.30}$$

Combining Eqs. 10.29 and 10.30, and simplifying, gives the propulsive efficiency as

$$\eta = \frac{\mathcal{P}_{\text{useful}}}{\mathcal{P}_{\text{input}}} = \frac{1}{1 + \dfrac{\Delta V}{2V}} \tag{10.31}$$

Equations 10.28 through 10.31 are applicable to any device that creates thrust by increasing the speed of a fluid stream. Thus they apply equally well to propeller-driven or jet-propelled aircraft, boats, or ships.

Equation 10.31 for propulsive efficiency is of fundamental importance. It indicates that propulsive efficiency can be increased by reducing ΔV or by increasing V. At constant thrust, as shown by Eq. 10.28, ΔV can be reduced if $\dot{m}$ is increased, i.e., if more fluid is accelerated over a smaller speed increase. More mass flow can be handled if propeller diameter is increased, but overall size and tip speed ultimately limit this approach. The same principle is used to increase the propulsive efficiency of a *turbofan* engine by using a large fan to move additional air flow outside the engine core.

Propulsive efficiency also can be increased by increasing the speed of motion relative to the fluid. Speed of advance may be limited by cavitation in marine applications. Flight speed is limited for propeller-driven aircraft by compressibility effects at the propeller tips, but progress is being made in the design of propellers to maintain high efficiency with low noise levels while operating with transonic flow at the blade tips. Jet-propelled aircraft can fly much faster than propeller-driven craft, giving them superior propulsive efficiency.

A more detailed *blade element* theory may be used to calculate the interaction between a propeller blade and the stream. If the blade spacing is large and the *disk loading*[10] is light, blades can be considered independent and relations can be derived for the torque required and the thrust produced by a propeller. These approximate relations are most accurate for low-solidity propellers.[11] Aircraft propellers typically are of fairly low solidity, having long, thin blades.

A schematic diagram of an element of a rotating propeller blade is shown in Fig. 10.39. The blade is set at angle θ to the plane of the propeller disk. Flow is shown as it would be seen by an observer *on* the propeller blade.

The relative speed of flow, V_r, passing over the blade element depends on both the blade peripheral speed, ωr, and the *speed of advance, V*. Consequently, for a given blade setting, the angle of attack, α, depends on *both V and ωr*. Thus, the performance of a propeller is influenced by both ω and V.

Even if the geometry of the propeller is adjusted to give constant geometric pitch,[12] the flow field in which it operates may not be uniform. Thus, the angle of attack across the blade elements may vary from the ideal, and can be calculated only with the aid of a comprehensive computer code that can predict local flow directions and speeds.

Propeller performance characteristics usually are measured experimentally. Figure 10.40 shows typical measured characteristics for a marine propeller [10], and for an aircraft propeller [30]. The variables used to plot the characteristics are almost dimensionless: by convention, rotational speed, n, is expressed in revolutions per second (rather than as ω, in radians per second). The independent variable is the *speed of advance coefficient, J*,

$$J \equiv \frac{V}{nD} \tag{10.32}$$

Dependent variables are the *thrust coefficient, C_F*, the *torque coefficient, C_T*, the *power coefficient, C_P*, and the *propeller efficiency, η*, defined as

$$C_F = \frac{F_T}{\rho n^2 D^4}, \quad C_T = \frac{T}{\rho n^2 D^5}, \quad C_P = \frac{\mathcal{P}}{\rho n^3 D^5}, \quad \text{and} \quad \eta = \frac{F_T V}{\mathcal{P}_{\text{input}}} \tag{10.33}$$

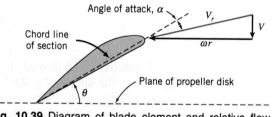

Fig. 10.39 Diagram of blade element and relative flow velocity vector.

---

[10] *Disk loading* is the propeller thrust divided by the swept area of the actuator disk.

[11] *Solidity* is defined as the ratio of projected blade area to the swept area of the actuator disk.

[12] *Pitch* is defined as the distance a propeller would travel in still fluid per revolution if it advanced along the blade setting angle θ. The pitch, H, of this blade element is equal to $2\pi r \tan \theta$. To obtain constant pitch along the blade, θ must follow the relation, $\tan \theta = H/2\pi r$, from hub to tip. Thus the geometric blade angle is smallest at the tip and increases steadily toward the root.

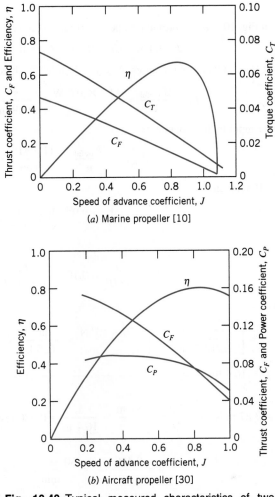

Fig. 10.40 Typical measured characteristics of two propellers.

The performance curves for both propellers show similar trends. Both thrust and torque coefficients are highest, and efficiency is zero, at zero speed of advance. This corresponds to the largest angle of attack for each blade element ($\alpha = \alpha_{max} = \theta$). Efficiency is zero because no useful work is being done by the stationary propeller. As advance speed increases, thrust and torque decrease smoothly. Efficiency increases to a maximum at an optimum advance speed and then decreases to zero as thrust tends to zero. (For example, if the blade element section is symmetric, this would theoretically occur when $\alpha = 0$, or when $\tan \theta = V/\omega r$.)

EXAMPLE 10.14   Sizing a Marine Propeller

Consider the supertanker of Example 9.5. Assume the total power required to overcome viscous resistance and wave drag is 11.4 MW. Use the performance characteristics of the marine propeller shown in Fig. 10.40a to estimate the diameter and operating speed required to propel the supertanker using a single propeller.

GIVEN: Supertanker of Example 9.5, with total propulsion power requirement of 11.4 MW to overcome viscous and wave drag, and performance data for the marine propeller shown in Fig. 10.40a.

FIND: (a) An estimate of the diameter of a single propeller required to power the ship.
(b) The operating speed of this propeller.

SOLUTION:
From the curves in Fig. 10.40*a*, at optimum propeller efficiency, the coefficients are

$$J = 0.85, \quad C_F = 0.10, \quad C_T = 0.020, \quad \text{and} \quad \eta = 0.66$$

The ship steams at $V = 6.69$ m/s and requires $\mathcal{P}_{useful} = 11.4$ MW. Therefore, the propeller thrust must be

$$F_T = \frac{\mathcal{P}_{useful}}{V} = \frac{11.4 \times 10^6 \text{ W}}{} \times \frac{\text{s}}{6.69 \text{ m}} \times \frac{\text{N} \cdot \text{m}}{\text{W} \cdot \text{s}} = 1.70 \text{ MN}$$

The required power input to the propeller is

$$\mathcal{P}_{input} = \frac{\mathcal{P}_{useful}}{\eta} = \frac{11.4 \text{ MW}}{0.66} = 17.3 \text{ MW}$$

From $J = \dfrac{V}{nD} = 0.85$, then

$$nD = \frac{V}{J} = 6.69 \frac{\text{m}}{\text{s}} \times \frac{1}{0.85} = 7.87 \text{ m/s}$$

Since

$$C_F = \frac{F_T}{\rho n^2 D^4} = 0.10 = \frac{F_T}{\rho (n^2 D^2) D^2} = \frac{F_T}{\rho (nD)^2 D^2}$$

solving for D gives

$$D = \left[\frac{F_T}{\rho (nD)^2 C_F} \right]^{1/2} = \left[1.70 \times 10^6 \text{ N} \times \frac{\text{m}^3}{1025 \text{ kg}} \times \frac{\text{s}^2}{(7.87)^2 \text{ m}^2} \times \frac{1}{0.10} \times \frac{\text{kg} \cdot \text{m}}{\text{N} \cdot \text{s}^2} \right]^{1/2}$$

$$D = 16.4 \text{ m} \qquad \longleftarrow \hspace{10cm} D$$

From $nD = \dfrac{V}{J} = 7.87$ m/s, $n = \dfrac{nD}{D} = \dfrac{7.87 \frac{\text{m}}{\text{s}}}{} \times \dfrac{1}{16.4 \text{ m}} = 0.480$ rev/s
so that

$$n = \frac{0.480 \text{ rev}}{\text{s}} \times \frac{60 \text{ s}}{\text{min}} = 28.8 \text{ rev/min} \qquad \longleftarrow \hspace{7cm} n$$

The required propeller is quite large, but still smaller than the 25 m draft of the supertanker. The ship would need to take on seawater for ballast to keep the propeller submerged when not carrying a full cargo of petroleum.

> This problem illustrates the use of normalized coefficient data for the preliminary sizing of a marine propeller. This preliminary design process would be repeated, using data for other propeller types, to find the optimum combination of propeller size, speed, and efficiency.

Marine propellers tend to have high solidity. This packs a lot of lifting surface within the swept area of the disk to keep the pressure difference small across the propeller and to avoid cavitation. Cavitation tends to unload the blades of a marine propeller, reducing both the torque required and the thrust produced [10]. Cavitation becomes more prevalent along the blades as the cavitation number,

$$Ca = \frac{p - p_v}{\frac{1}{2} \rho V^2} \tag{10.34}$$

is reduced. Inspection of Eq. 10.34 shows that Ca decreases when p is reduced by operating near the free surface or by increasing V. Those who have operated motor boats also are aware that local cavitation can be caused by distorted flow approaching the propeller, e.g., from turning sharply.

Compressibility affects aircraft propellers when tip speeds approach the *critical Mach number* at which the local Mach number approaches $M = 1$ at some point on the blade. Under these conditions, torque increases because of increased drag, thrust drops because of reduced section lift, and efficiency drops drastically.

If a propeller operates within the boundary layer of a propelled body, where the relative flow is slowed, its apparent thrust and torque may increase compared with those in a uniform freestream at the same rate of advance. The residual kinetic energy in the slipstream also may be reduced. The combination of these effects may increase the overall propulsive efficiency of the combined body and propeller. Advanced computer codes are used in the design of modern ships (and submarines, where noise may be an overriding consideration) to optimize performance of each propeller/hull combination.

For certain special applications, a propeller may be placed within a *shroud* or *duct*. Such configurations may be integrated into a hull (e.g., as a bow thruster to increase maneuverability), built into the wing of an aircraft, or placed on the deck of a hovercraft. Thrust may be improved by the favorable pressure forces on the duct lip, but efficiency may be reduced by the added skin-friction losses encountered in the duct.

Machines for Extracting Work (Power) from a Fluid

a. Hydraulic Turbines

Falling water has long been considered a source of "free," renewable energy. In reality, power produced by hydraulic turbines is not free; operating costs are low, but considerable capital investment is required to prepare the site and install the equipment. At a minimum, the water inlet works, supply penstock, turbine(s), powerhouse, and controls must be provided. An economic analysis is necessary to determine the feasibility of developing any candidate site. In addition to economic factors, hydroelectric power plants must also be evaluated for their environmental impact—in recent years it has been found that such plants are not entirely benign, and can be damaging, for example, to salmon runs.

Early in the industrial revolution water wheels were used to power grain mills and textile machinery. These plants had to be located at the site of the falling water, which limited use of water power to relatively small and local enterprises. The introduction of alternating current in the 1880s made it possible to transmit electrical energy efficiently over long distances. Since then nearly 40 percent of the available hydroelectric power resources in the United States have been developed and connected to the utility grid [31]. Hydroelectric power accounts for about 16 percent of the electrical energy produced in this country.

The United States has abundant and relatively cheap supplies of fossil fuels, mostly coal. Therefore at present the remaining hydropower resources in the United States are not considered economical compared to fossil-fired plants.

Worldwide, only about 20 percent of available hydropower resources have been developed commercially [31]. Considerably more hydropower will likely be developed in coming decades as countries become more industrialized. Many developing countries do not have their own supplies of fossil fuel. Hydropower may offer many such countries their only practical path to increased utility development. Consequently the design and installation of hydroelectric plants are likely to be important future engineering activities in developing countries.

To evaluate a candidate site for hydropower potential, one must know the average stream flow rate and the gross head available to make preliminary estimates of turbine type, number of turbines, and potential power production. Economic analyses are beyond the scope of this book, but we consider the fluids engineering fundamentals of impulse turbine performance to optimize the efficiency.

Hydraulic turbines convert the potential energy of stored water to mechanical work. To maximize turbine efficiency, it is always a design goal to discharge water

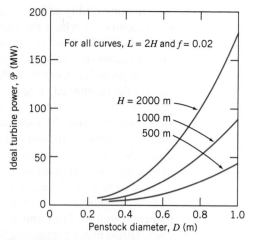

Fig. 10.41 Maximum hydraulic impulse turbine power output versus penstock diameter.

from a turbine at ambient pressure, as close to the tailwater elevation as possible, and with the minimum possible residual kinetic energy.

Conveying water flow into the turbine with minimum energy loss also is important. Numerous design details must be considered, such as inlet geometry, trash racks, etc. [31]. References 1, 8, 10, and 31–37 contain a wealth of information about turbine siting, selection, hydraulic design, and optimization of hydropower plants. The number of large manufacturers has dwindled to just a few, but small-scale units are becoming plentiful [34]. The enormous cost of a commercial-scale hydro plant justifies the use of comprehensive scale-model testing to finalize design details. See [31] for detailed coverage of hydraulic power generation.

Hydraulic losses in long supply pipes (known as *penstocks*) must be considered when designing the installation for high-head machines such as impulse turbines; an optimum diameter for the inlet pipe that maximizes turbine output power can be determined for these units, as shown in Example 10.15.

Turbine power output is proportional to volume flow rate times the pressure difference across the nozzle. At zero flow, the full hydrostatic head is available but power is zero. As flow rate increases, the net head at the nozzle inlet decreases. Power first increases, reaches a maximum, then decreases again as flow rate increases. As we will see in Example 10.15, for a given penstock diameter, the theoretical maximum power is obtained when the system is designed so that one-third of the gross head is dissipated by friction losses in the penstock. In practice, penstock diameter is chosen larger than the theoretical minimum, and only 10–15 percent of the gross head is dissipated by friction [7].

A certain minimum penstock diameter is required to produce a given power output. The minimum diameter depends on the desired power output, the available head, and the penstock material and length. Some representative values are shown in Fig. 10.41.

EXAMPLE 10.15   Performance and Optimization of an Impulse Turbine

Consider the hypothetical impulse turbine installation shown. Analyze flow in the penstock to develop an expression for the optimum turbine output power as a function of jet diameter, D_j. Obtain an expression for the ratio of jet diameter, D_j, to penstock diameter, D, at which output power is maximized. Under conditions of maximum power output, show that the head loss in the penstock is one-third of the available head. Develop a parametric equation for the minimum penstock diameter needed to produce a specified power output, using gross head and penstock length as parameters.

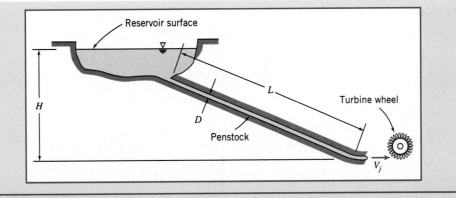

GIVEN: Impulse turbine installation shown.

FIND: (a) Expression for optimum turbine output power as a function of jet diameter.
(b) Expression for the ratio of jet diameter, D_j, to penstock diameter, D, at which output power is maximized.
(c) Ratio of head loss in penstock to available head for condition of maximum power.
(d) Parametric equation for the minimum penstock diameter needed to produce a specified output power, using gross head and penstock length as parameters.

SOLUTION:
According to the results of Example 10.5, the output power of an idealized impulse turbine is given by $\mathcal{P}_{\text{out}} = \rho Q U (V - U)$ $(1 - \cos \theta)$. For optimum power output, $U = V/2 = V_j/2$, and

$$\mathcal{P}_{\text{out}} = \rho Q \frac{V}{2} \left(V - \frac{V}{2} \right) (1 - \cos \theta) = \rho A_j V_j \frac{V_j}{2} \frac{V_j}{2} (1 - \cos \theta)$$

$$\mathcal{P}_{\text{out}} = \rho A_j \frac{V_j^3}{4} (1 - \cos \theta)$$

Thus output power is proportional to $A_j V_j^3$.

Apply the energy equation for steady incompressible pipe flow through the penstock to analyze V_j^2 at the nozzle outlet. Designate the free surface of the reservoir as section ①; there $\overline{V}_1 \approx 0$.

Governing equation:

$$\overset{\approx\ 0}{\frac{p_1}{\rho} + \alpha_1 \frac{\overline{V}_1^2}{2}} + gz_1 - \left(\frac{p_j}{\rho} + \alpha_j \frac{\overline{V}_j^2}{2} + gz_j \right) = h_{l_T} = \left(K_{\text{ent}} + f\frac{L}{D} \right) \frac{\overline{V}_p^2}{2} + K_{\text{nozzle}} \frac{\overline{V}_j^2}{2}$$

Assumptions: (1) Steady flow.
(2) Incompressible flow.
(3) Fully developed flow.
(4) Atmospheric pressure at jet exit.
(5) $\alpha_j = 1$, so $\overline{V}_j = V_j$.
(6) Uniform flow in penstock, so $\overline{V}_p = V$.
(7) $K_{\text{ent}} \ll f\dfrac{L}{D}$.
(8) $K_{\text{nozzle}} = 1$.

Then

$$g(z_1 - z_j) = gH = f\frac{L}{D} \frac{V^2}{2} + \frac{V_j^2}{2} \quad \text{or} \quad V_j^2 = 2gH - f\frac{L}{D} V^2 \qquad (1)$$

Hence the available head is partly consumed in friction in the supply penstock, and the rest is available as kinetic energy at the jet exit—in other words, the jet kinetic energy is reduced by the loss in the penstock. However, this loss itself is a function of jet speed, as we see from continuity:

$$VA = V_j A_j, \quad \text{so} \quad V = V_j \frac{A_j}{A} = V_j \left(\frac{D_j}{D} \right)^2 \quad \text{and} \quad V_j^2 = 2gH - f\frac{L}{D} V_j^2 \left(\frac{D_j}{D} \right)^4$$

Solving for V_j, we obtain

$$V_j = \left[\frac{2gH}{\left\{ 1 + f\frac{L}{D}\left(\frac{D_j}{D}\right)^4 \right\}} \right]^{1/2} \tag{2}$$

The turbine power can be written as

$$\mathcal{P} = \rho A_j \frac{V_j^3}{4}(1-\cos\theta) = \rho\frac{\pi}{16}D_j^2 \left[\frac{2gH}{\left\{ 1 + f\frac{L}{D}\left(\frac{D_j}{D}\right)^4 \right\}} \right]^{3/2}(1-\cos\theta)$$

$$\mathcal{P} = C_1 D_j^2 \left[1 + f\frac{L}{D}\left(\frac{D_j}{D}\right)^4 \right]^{-3/2} \qquad\qquad \overset{\longleftarrow}{}\ \mathcal{P}$$

where $C_1 = \rho\pi(2gH)^{3/2}(1-\cos\theta)/16 = $ constant.

   To find the condition for maximum power output, at fixed penstock diameter, D, differentiate with respect to D_j and set equal to zero,

$$\frac{d\mathcal{P}}{dD_j} = 2C_1 D_j \left[1 + f\frac{L}{D}\left(\frac{D_j}{D}\right)^4 \right]^{-3/2} - \frac{3}{2}C_1 D_j^2 \left[1 + f\frac{L}{D}\left(\frac{D_j}{D}\right)^4 \right]^{-5/2} 4f\frac{L}{D}\frac{D_j^3}{D^4} = 0$$

Thus,

$$1 + f\frac{L}{D}\left(\frac{D_j}{D}\right)^4 = 3f\frac{L}{D}\left(\frac{D_j}{D}\right)^4$$

Solving for D_j/D, we obtain

$$\frac{D_j}{D} = \left[\frac{1}{2f\frac{L}{D}} \right]^{1/4} \qquad\qquad \overset{\longleftarrow}{}\ \frac{D_j}{D}$$

At this optimum value of D_j/D, the jet speed is given by Eq. 2 as

$$V_j = \left[\frac{2gH}{\left\{ 1 + f\frac{L}{D}\left(\frac{D_j}{D}\right)^4 \right\}} \right]^{1/2} = \sqrt{\frac{4}{3}gH}$$

The head loss at maximum power is then obtained from Eq. 1 after rearranging

$$h_l = f\frac{L}{D}\frac{V^2}{2} = gH - \frac{V_j^2}{2} = gH - \frac{2}{3}gH = \frac{1}{3}gH$$

and

$$\frac{h_l}{gH} = \frac{1}{3} \qquad\qquad \overset{\longleftarrow}{}\ \frac{h_l}{gH}$$

Under the conditions of maximum power

$$\mathcal{P}_{max} = \rho V_j^3 \frac{A_j}{4}(1-\cos\theta) = \rho\left(\frac{4}{3}gH\right)^{3/2}\frac{\pi}{16}\left[\frac{D^5}{2fL}\right]^{1/2}(1-\cos\theta)$$

Finally, to solve for minimum penstock diameter for fixed output power, the equation may be written in the form

$$D \propto \left(\frac{L}{H}\right)^{1/5}\left(\frac{\mathcal{P}}{H}\right)^{2/5} \qquad\qquad \overset{\longleftarrow}{}\ D$$

This problem illustrates the optimization of an idealized impulse turbine. The analysis determines the minimum penstock diameter needed to obtain a specified power output. In practice, larger diameters than this are used, reducing the frictional head loss below that computed here.

b. Wind-Power Machines

Windmills (or more properly, wind turbines) have been used for centuries to harness the power of natural winds. Two well-known examples are shown in Fig. 10.42.

Dutch windmills (Fig. 10.42a) turned slowly so the power could be used to turn stone wheels for milling grain, hence the name "windmill." They evolved into large structures; the practical maximum size was limited by the materials of the day. Calvert [39] reports that, based on his laboratory-scale tests, a traditional Dutch windmill of 26 m diameter produced 41 kW in a wind of 36 km/hr at an angular speed of 20 rpm.

American multi-blade windmills (Fig. 10.42b) were found on many American farms between about 1850 and 1950. They performed valuable service in powering water pumps before rural electrification.

The recent emphasis on renewable resources has revived interest in windmill design and optimization. Horizontal-axis wind turbine (HAWT) and vertical-axis wind turbine (VAWT) configurations have been studied extensively. Most HAWT designs feature 2- or 3-bladed propellers turning at high speed. The large modern HAWT, shown in Fig. 10.43a, is capable of producing power in any wind above a light breeze.

The final example (Fig. 10.43b) is a *Darrieus* VAWT. This device uses a modern symmetric airfoil section for the rotor, which is formed into a *troposkien* shape.[13] In contrast to the other designs, the Darrieus VAWT is not capable of starting from rest;

(a) Traditional Dutch mill   (b) American farm windmill

Fig. 10.42 Examples of well-known windmills [38]. (Photo courtesy of (a) Netherlands Board of Tourism, (b) U.S. Department of Agriculture.)

[13] This shape (which would be assumed by a flexible cord whirled about a vertical axis) minimizes bending stresses in the Darrieus turbine rotor.

(a) Horizontal-axis wind turbine   (b) Vertical-axis wind turbine

Fig. 10.43 Examples of modern wind turbine designs [40]. (Photos courtesy U.S. Department of Energy.)

it can only produce usable power above a certain minimum angular speed. It may be combined with a self-starting turbine, such as a *Savonius rotor*, to provide starting torque (see illustration for Problem 9.97 or [41]).

A horizontal-axis wind turbine may be analyzed as a propeller operated in reverse. The Rankine model of one-dimensional flow incorporating an idealized actuator disk is shown in Fig. 10.44. The simplified notation of the figure is frequently used for analysis of wind turbines.

The wind speed far upstream is V. The stream is decelerated to $V(1 - a)$ at the turbine disk and to $V(1 - 2a)$ in the wake of the turbine (a is called the *interference factor*). Thus the stream tube of air captured by the wind turbine is small upstream and its diameter increases as it moves downstream.

Straightforward application of linear momentum to a CV (see Example 10.16) predicts the axial thrust on a turbine of radius R to be

$$F_T = 2\pi R^2 \, \rho V^2 \, a(1 - a) \qquad (10.35)$$

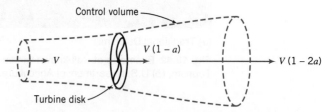

Fig. 10.44 Control volume and simplified notation used to analyze wind turbine performance.

Application of the energy equation, assuming no losses (no change in internal energy or heat transfer), gives the power taken from the fluid stream as

$$\mathscr{P} = 2\pi R^2 \rho V^3 a(1-a)^2 \tag{10.36}$$

The efficiency of a wind turbine is most conveniently defined with reference to the kinetic energy flux contained within a stream tube the size of the actuator disk. This kinetic energy flux is

$$KEF = \frac{1}{2}\rho V^3 \pi R^2 \tag{10.37}$$

Combining Eqs. 10.36 and 10.37 gives the efficiency (or alternatively, the *power coefficient* [40]) as

$$\eta = \frac{\mathscr{P}}{KEF} = 4a(1-a)^2 \tag{10.38}$$

Betz [see 40] was the first to derive this result and to show that the theoretical efficiency is maximized when $a = 1/3$. The maximum theoretical efficiency is $\eta = 0.593$.

If the wind turbine is lightly loaded (a is small), it will affect a large mass of air per unit time, but the energy extracted per unit mass will be small and the efficiency low. Most of the kinetic energy in the initial air stream will be left in the wake and wasted. If the wind turbine is heavily loaded ($a \approx 1/2$), it will affect a much smaller mass of air per unit time. The energy removed per unit mass will be large, but the power produced will be small compared with the kinetic energy flux through the undisturbed area of the actuator disk. Thus a peak efficiency occurs at intermediate disk loadings.

The Rankine model includes some important assumptions that limit its applicability [40]. First, the wind turbine is assumed to affect only the air contained within the stream tube defined in Fig. 10.44. Second, the kinetic energy produced as swirl behind the turbine is not accounted for. Third, any radial pressure gradient is ignored. Glauert [see 30] partially accounted for the wake swirl to predict the dependence of ideal efficiency on *tip-speed ratio*, $X = \omega R/V$, as shown in Fig. 10.45 (ω is the angular velocity of the turbine).

As the tip-speed ratio increases, ideal efficiency increases, approaching the peak value ($\eta = 0.593$) asymptotically. (Physically, the swirl left in the wake is reduced as the tip-speed ratio increases.) Reference 40 presents a summary of the detailed blade-element theory used to develop the limiting efficiency curve shown in Fig. 10.45.

Each type of wind turbine has its most favorable range of application. The traditional American multi-bladed windmill has a large number of blades and operates

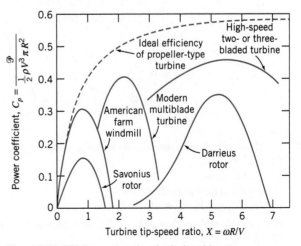

Fig. 10.45 Efficiency trends of wind turbine types versus tip-speed ratio [40].

at relatively slow speed. Its solidity, σ (the ratio of blade area to the swept area of the turbine disk, πR^2) is high. Because of its relatively slow operating speed, its tip-speed ratio and theoretical performance limit are low. Its relatively poor performance, compared with its theoretical limit, is largely caused by use of crude blades, which are simple bent sheet metal surfaces rather than airfoil shapes.

It is necessary to increase the tip-speed ratio considerably to reach a more favorable operating range. Modern high-speed wind-turbine designs use carefully shaped airfoils and operate at tip-speed ratios up to 7 [42].

EXAMPLE 10.16   Performance of an Idealized Windmill

Develop general expressions for thrust, power output, and efficiency of an idealized windmill, as shown in Fig. 10.44. Calculate the thrust, ideal efficiency, and actual efficiency for the Dutch windmill tested by Calvert ($D = 26$ m, $N = 20$ rpm, $V = 36$ km/hr, and $\mathscr{P}_{output} = 41$ kW).

GIVEN: Idealized windmill, as shown in Fig. 10.44, and Dutch windmill tested by Calvert:

$$D = 26 \text{ m} \quad N = 20 \text{ rpm} \quad V = 36 \text{ km/hr} \quad \mathscr{P}_{output} = 41 \text{ kW}$$

FIND: (a) General expressions for the ideal thrust, power output, and efficiency.
   (b) The thrust, power output, and ideal and actual efficiencies for the Dutch windmill tested by Calvert.

SOLUTION:
Apply the continuity, momentum (x component), and energy equations, using the CV and coordinates shown.

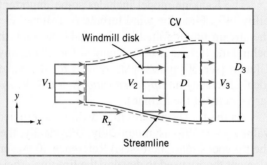

Governing equations:

$$\frac{\partial}{\partial t}\int_{CV} \rho \, d\forall + \int_{CS} \rho \vec{V} \cdot d\vec{A} = 0 \quad {}^{=0(3)}$$

$$F_{S_x} + F_{B_x} = \frac{\partial}{\partial t}\int_{CS} u \, \rho \, d\forall + \int_{CS} u \, \rho \vec{V} \cdot d\vec{A} \quad {}^{=0(2)}{}^{=0(3)}$$

$$\dot{Q} - \dot{W}_s = \frac{\partial}{\partial t}\int_{CV} e \, \rho \, d\forall + \int_{CS} \left(e + \frac{p}{\rho}\right) \rho \vec{V} \cdot d\vec{A} \quad {}^{=0(7)}{}^{=0(3)}$$

Assumptions: (1) Atmospheric pressure acts on CV; $F_{S_x} = R_x$.
   (2) $F_{B_x} = 0$.
   (3) Steady flow.
   (4) Uniform flow at each section.
   (5) Incompressible flow of standard air.
   (6) $V_1 - V_2 = V_2 - V_3 = \frac{1}{2}(V_1 - V_3)$, as shown by Rankine.
   (7) $Q = 0$.
   (8) No change in internal energy for frictionless incompressible flow.

In terms of the interference factor, a, $V_1 = V$, $V_2 = (1 - a) V$, and $V_3 = (1 - 2a) V$.

From continuity, for uniform flow at each cross section, $V_1 A_1 = V_2 A_2 = V_3 A_3$.

From momentum,

$$R_x = u_1(-\rho V_1 A_1) + u_3(+\rho V_3 A_3) = (V_3 - V_1)\rho V_2 A_2 \qquad \{u_1 = V_1, \; u_3 = V_3\}$$

R_x is the external force acting *on* the control volume. The thrust force exerted *by* the CV *on* the surroundings is

$$K_x = -R_x = (V_1 - V_3)\rho V_2 A_2$$

In terms of the interference factor, the equation for thrust may be written in the general form,

$$K_x = \rho V^2 \, \pi R^2 2a(1 - a) \qquad\qquad\qquad\qquad K_x$$

(Set dK_x/da equal to zero to show that maximum thrust occurs when $a = \frac{1}{2}$.)

The energy equation becomes

$$-\dot{W}_s = \frac{V_1^2}{2} \, (-\rho V_1 A_1) + \frac{V_3^2}{2} \, (+\rho V_3 A_3) = \rho V_2 \pi R^2 \, \frac{1}{2} \, (V_3^2 - V_1^2)$$

The ideal output power, $\mathcal{P}$, is equal to $\dot{W}_s$. In terms of the interference factor,

$$\mathcal{P} = \dot{W}_s = \rho V(1 - a)\pi R^2 \left[\frac{V^2}{2} - \frac{V^2}{2} \, (1 - 2a)^2 \right] = \rho V^3(1 - a) \, \frac{\pi R^2}{2} \, [1 - (1 - 2a)^2]$$

After simplifying algebraically,

$$\mathcal{P}_{\text{ideal}} = 2\rho V^3 \pi R^2 a(1 - a)^2 \qquad\qquad\qquad\qquad \mathcal{P}_{\text{ideal}}$$

The kinetic energy flux through a stream tube of undistorted flow, equal in area to the actuator disk, is

$$KEF = \rho V \pi R^2 \, \frac{V^2}{2} = \frac{1}{2}\rho V^3 \pi R^2$$

Thus the ideal efficiency may be written

$$\eta = \frac{\mathcal{P}_{\text{ideal}}}{KEF} = \frac{2\rho V^3 \pi R^2 a(1 - a)^2}{\frac{1}{2}\rho V^3 \pi R^2} = 4a(1 - a)^2 \qquad\qquad \eta$$

To find the condition for maximum possible efficiency, set $d\eta/da$ equal to zero. The maximum efficiency is $\eta = 0.593$, which occurs when $a = 1/3$.

The Dutch windmill tested by Calvert had a tip-speed ratio of

$$X = \frac{NR}{V} = 20 \, \frac{\text{rev}}{\text{min}} \times 2\pi \, \frac{\text{rad}}{\text{rev}} \times \frac{\text{min}}{60 \, \text{s}} \times 13 \, \text{m} \times \frac{\text{s}}{10 \, \text{m}} = 2.72 \qquad\qquad X$$

The maximum theoretically attainable efficiency at this tip-speed ratio, accounting for swirl (Fig. 10.45), would be about 0.53.

The actual efficiency of the Dutch windmill is

$$\eta_{\text{actual}} = \frac{\mathcal{P}_{\text{actual}}}{KEF}$$

Based on Calvert's test data, the kinetic energy flux is

$$KEF = \frac{1}{2}\rho V^3 \pi R^2$$

$$= \frac{1}{2} \times 1.23 \, \frac{\text{kg}}{\text{m}^3} \times (10)^3 \, \frac{\text{m}^3}{\text{s}^3} \times \pi(13)^2 \, \text{m}^2 \times \frac{\text{N} \cdot \text{s}^2}{\text{kg} \cdot \text{m}} \times \frac{\text{W} \cdot \text{s}}{\text{N} \cdot \text{m}}$$

$$KEF = 3.27 \times 10^5 \, \text{W} \quad \text{or} \quad 327 \, \text{kW}$$

Substituting into the definition of actual efficiency,

$$\eta_{\text{actual}} = \frac{41 \, \text{kW}}{327 \, \text{kW}} = 0.125 \qquad\qquad\qquad\qquad \eta_{\text{actual}}$$

Thus the actual efficiency of the Dutch windmill is about 24 percent of the maximum efficiency theoretically attainable at this tip-speed ratio.

The actual thrust on the Dutch windmill can only be estimated, because the interference factor, a, is not known. The maximum possible thrust would occur at $a = 1/2$, in which case,

$$K_x = \rho V^2 \pi R^2 \, 2a(1 - a)$$

$$= 1.23 \, \frac{\text{kg}}{\text{m}^3} \times (10)^2 \, \frac{\text{m}^2}{\text{s}^2} \times \pi (13)^2 \, \text{m}^2 \times 2 \left(\frac{1}{2}\right) \left(1 - \frac{1}{2}\right) \times \frac{\text{N} \cdot \text{s}^2}{\text{kg} \cdot \text{m}}$$

$$K_x = 3.27 \times 10^4 \, \text{N} \quad \text{or} \quad 32.7 \, \text{kN} \longleftarrow \underline{\hspace{4cm}} K_x$$

This does not sound like a large thrust force, considering the size ($D = 26$ m) of the windmill. However, $V = 36$ km/hr is only a moderate wind. The actual machine would have to withstand much more severe wind conditions during storms.

> This problem illustrates application of the concepts of ideal thrust, power, and efficiency for a windmill, and calculation of these quantities for an actual machine.

10-6 SUMMARY AND USEFUL EQUATIONS

In this chapter, we:

- ✓ Defined the two major types of fluid machines: positive displacement machines, and turbomachines.
- ✓ Defined, within the turbomachine category: radial, axial, and mixed flow types, pumps, fans, blowers, compressors, and impulse and reaction turbines.
- ✓ Discussed various features of turbomachines, such as impellers, rotors, runners, scrolls (volutes), compressor stages, and draft tubes.
- ✓ Discussed various defining parameters, such as pump efficiency, solidity, hydraulic power, mechanical power, turbine efficiency, shutoff head, shock loss, specific speed, cavitation, *NPSHR*, and *NPSHA*.
- ✓ Used the angular-momentum equation for a control volume to derive the Euler turbomachine equation.
- ✓ Drew velocity diagrams and applied the Euler turbomachine equation to the analysis of various idealized machines to derive ideal torque, head, and power.
- ✓ Evaluated the performance—head, power, and efficiency—of various actual machines from measured data.
- ✓ Defined and used dimensionless parameters to scale the performance of a fluid machine from one size, operating speed, and set of operating conditions to another.
- ✓ Examined pumps for their compliance with the constraint that the net positive suction head available exceeds that required to avoid cavitation.
- ✓ Matched fluid machines for doing work on a fluid to pipe systems to obtain the operating point (flow rate and head).
- ✓ Predicted the effects of installing fluid machines in series and parallel on the operating point of a system.

With these concepts and techniques, we learned how to use manufacturers' literature and other data to perform preliminary analyses and make appropriate selections of pumps, fans, hydraulic and wind turbines, and other fluid machines.

Note: Most of the Useful Equations in the table below have a number of constraints or limitations—*be sure to refer to their page numbers for details!*

Useful Equations		
Euler turbomachine equation:	$$T_{\text{shaft}} = (r_2 V_{t_2} - r_1 V_{t_1})\dot{m} \qquad (10.1c)$$	Page 463
Turbomachine theoretical power:	$$\dot{W}_m = (U_2 V_{t_2} - U_1 V_{t_1})\dot{m} \qquad (10.2b)$$	Page 463
Turbomachine theoretical head:	$$H = \frac{\dot{W}_m}{\dot{m}g} = \frac{1}{g}(U_2 V_{t_2} - U_1 V_{t_1}) \qquad (10.2c)$$	Page 463
Pump power, head, and efficiency:	$$\dot{W}_h = \rho Q g H_p \qquad (10.8a)$$ $$H_p = \left(\frac{p}{\rho g} + \frac{\overline{V}^2}{2g} + z\right)_{\text{discharge}} - \left(\frac{p}{\rho g} + \frac{\overline{V}^2}{2g} + z\right)_{\text{suction}} \qquad (10.8b)$$ $$\eta_p = \frac{\dot{W}_h}{\dot{W}_m} = \frac{\rho Q g H_p}{\omega T} \qquad (10.8c)$$	Page 471
Turbine power, head, and efficiency:	$$\dot{W}_h = \rho Q g H_t \qquad (10.9a)$$ $$H_t = \left(\frac{p}{\rho g} + \frac{\overline{V}^2}{2g} + z\right)_{\text{inlet}} - \left(\frac{p}{\rho g} + \frac{\overline{V}^2}{2g} + z\right)_{\text{outlet}} \qquad (10.9b)$$ $$\eta_t = \frac{\dot{W}_m}{\dot{W}_h} = \frac{\omega T}{\rho Q g H_t} \qquad (10.9c)$$	Page 472
Dimensionless flow coefficient:	$$\Phi = \frac{Q}{A_2 U_2} = \frac{V_{n_2}}{U_2} \qquad (10.10)$$	Page 483
Dimensionless head coefficient:	$$\Psi = \frac{gH}{U_2^2} \qquad (10.11)$$	Page 483
Dimensionless torque coefficient:	$$\tau = \frac{T}{\rho A_2 U_2^2 R_2} \qquad (10.12)$$	Page 483
Dimensionless power coefficient:	$$\Pi = \frac{\dot{W}}{\rho Q \, U_2^2} = \frac{\dot{W}}{\rho \omega^2 \, Q R_2^2} \qquad (10.13)$$	Page 484

Centrifugal pump specific speed (in terms of head h):	$$N_S = \frac{\omega Q^{1/2}}{h^{3/4}}$$ (7.22a)	Page 484
Centrifugal pump specific speed (in terms of head H):	$$N_{S_{cu}} = \frac{N(\text{rpm})[Q(\text{gpm})]^{1/2}}{[H(\text{ft})]^{3/4}}$$ (7.22b)	Page 484
Centrifugal turbine specific speed (in terms of head h):	$$N_S = \omega(\mathscr{P}/\rho h)^{1/2}/h^{3/4} = \omega\mathscr{P}^{1/2}/(\rho^{1/2}h^{5/4})$$ (10.18a)	Page 485
Centrifugal turbine specific speed (in terms of head H):	$$N_{S_{cu}} = \frac{N(\text{rpm})[\mathscr{P}(\text{hp})]^{1/2}}{[H(\text{ft})]^{5/4}}$$ (10.18b)	Page 485
Propeller speed of advance coefficient:	$$J \equiv \frac{V}{nD}$$ (10.32)	Page 522
Propeller thrust, torque, power, and efficiency coefficients:	$$C_F = \frac{F_T}{\rho n^2 D^4}, \quad C_T = \frac{T}{\rho n^2 D^5}, \quad C_P = \frac{\mathscr{P}}{\rho n^3 D^5}, \quad \text{and} \quad \eta = \frac{F_T V}{\mathscr{P}_{\text{input}}}$$ (10.33)	Page 522
Cavitation number:	$$Ca = \frac{p - p_v}{\frac{1}{2}\rho V^2}$$ (10.34)	Page 524

REFERENCES

1. Wilson, D. G., "Turbomachinery—From Paddle Wheels to Turbojets," *Mechanical Engineering, 104*, 10, October 1982, pp. 28–40.

2. Logan, E. S., Jr., *Turbomachinery: Basic Theory and Applications*. New York: Dekker, 1981.

3. Japikse, D. "Teaching Design in an Engineering Education Curriculum: A Design Track Syllabus," TM-519, Concepts ETI Inc., White River Jct., VT 05001.

4. American Society of Mechanical Engineers, *Performance Test Codes: Centrifugal Pumps*, ASME PTC 8.2-1990. New York: ASME, 1990.

5. American Institute of Chemical Engineers, *Equipment Testing Procedure: Centrifugal Pumps (Newtonian Liquids)*. New York: AIChE, 1984.

6. Air Movement and Control Association, *Laboratory Methods of Testing Fans for Rating*. AMCA Standard 210-74, ASHRAE Standard 51-75. Atlanta, GA: ASHRAE, 1975.

7. Daugherty, R. L., J. B. Franzini, and E. J. Finnemore, *Fluid Mechanics with Engineering Applications*, 8th ed. New York: McGraw-Hill, 1985.

8. Peerless Pump,* Brochure B-4003, "System Analysis for Pumping Equipment Selection," 1979.

9. Rouse, H., and S. Ince, *History of Hydraulics*. Iowa City, IA: Iowa University Press, 1957.

10. Daily, J. W., "Hydraulic Machinery," in Rouse, H., ed., *Engineering Hydraulics*. New York: Wiley, 1950.

11. Russell, G. E., *Hydraulics*, 5th ed. New York: Henry Holt, 1942.

* Peerless Pump Company, a member of the Sterling Group, P.O. Box 7026, Indianapolis, IN 46206–7026, U.S.A.

12. Sabersky, R. H., A. J. Acosta, E. G. Hauptmann, and E. M. Gates, *Fluid Flow: A First Course in Fluid Mechanics*, 4th ed. Englewood Cliffs, NJ: Prentice-Hall, 1999.

13. Hodge, B. K., *Analysis and Design of Energy Systems*, 2nd ed. Englewood Cliffs, NJ: Prentice-Hall, 1990.

14. Moody, L. F., "Hydraulic Machinery," in *Handbook of Applied Hydraulics*, ed. by C. V. Davis. New York: McGraw-Hill, 1942.

15. Hydraulic Institute, *Hydraulic Institute Standards*. New York: Hydraulic Institute, 1969.

16. Dickinson, C., *Pumping Manual*, 8th ed. Surrey, England: Trade & Technical Press, Ltd., 1988.

17. Hicks, T. G., and T. W. Edwards, *Pump Application Engineering*. New York: McGraw-Hill, 1971.

18. Armintor, J. K., and D. P. Conners, "Pumping Applications in the Petroleum and Chemical Industries," *IEEE Transactions on Industry Applications, IA-23*, 1, January 1987.

19. Jorgensen, R., ed., *Fan Engineering*, 8th ed. Buffalo, NY: Buffalo Forge, 1983.

20. American Society of Mechanical Engineers, *Power Test Code for Fans*. New York: ASME, Power Test Codes, PTC 11-1946.

21. Berry, C. H., *Flow and Fan: Principles of Moving Air through Ducts*, 2nd ed. New York: Industrial Press, 1963.

22. Wallis, R. A., *Axial Flow Fans and Ducts*. New York: Wiley, 1983.

23. Osborne, W. C., *Fans*, 2nd ed. London: Pergamon Press, 1977.

24. American Society of Heating, Refrigeration, and Air Conditioning Engineers, *Handbook of Fundamentals*. Atlanta, GA: ASHRAE, 1980.

25. Idelchik, I. E., *Handbook of Hydraulic Resistance*, 2nd ed. New York: Hemisphere, 1986.

26. Vincent-Genod, J., *Fundamentals of Pipeline Engineering*. Houston: Gulf Publishing Co., 1984.

27. Warner-Ishi Turbocharger brochure.**

28. Lambeck, R. R., *Hydraulic Pumps and Motors: Selection and Application for Hydraulic Power Control Systems*. New York: Dekker, 1983.

29. Warring, R. H., ed., *Hydraulic Handbook*, 8th ed. Houston: Gulf Publishing Co., 1983.

30. Durand, W. F., ed., *Aerodynamic Theory*, 6 Volumes. New York: Dover, 1963.

31. Gulliver, J. S., and R. E. A. Arndt, *Hydropower Engineering Handbook*. New York: McGraw-Hill, 1990.

32. Fritz, J. J., *Small and Mini Hydropower Systems: Resource Assessment and Project Feasibility*. New York: McGraw-Hill, 1984.

33. Gladwell, J. S., *Small Hydro: Some Practical Planning and Design Considerations*. Idaho Water Resources Institute. Moscow, ID: University of Idaho, April 1980.

34. McGuigan, D., *Small Scale Water Power*. Dorchester: Prism Press, 1978.

35. Olson, R. M., and S. J. Wright, *Essentials of Engineering Fluid Mechanics*, 5th ed. New York: Harper & Row, 1990.

36. Quick, R. S., "Problems Encountered in the Design and Operation of Impulse Turbines," *Transactions of the ASME*, 62, 1940, pp. 15–27.

37. Warnick, C. C., *Hydropower Engineering*. Englewood Cliffs, NJ: Prentice-Hall, 1984.

38. Putnam, P. C., *Power from the Wind*. New York: Van Nostrand, 1948.

39. Calvert, N.G., *Windpower Principles: Their Application on the Small Scale*. London: Griffin, 1978.

40. Avallone, E. A., T. Baumeister, III, and Sadegh, A. eds., *Marks' Standard Handbook for Mechanical Engineers*, 11th ed. New York: McGraw-Hill, 2007.

41. Eldridge, F. R., *Wind Machines*, 2nd ed. New York: Van Nostrand Reinhold, 1980.

42. Migliore, P. G., "Comparison of NACA 6-Series and 4-Digit Airfoils for Darrieus Wind Turbines," *Journal of Energy*, 7, 4, Jul-Aug 1983, pp. 291–292.

43. White, F. M., *Fluid Mechanics*, 6th ed. New York: McGraw-Hill, 2007.

44. Sovern, D. T., and G. J. Poole, "Column Separation in Pumped Pipelines," in Kienow, K. K., ed., *Pipeline Design and Installation*, Proceedings of the International Conference on Pipeline Design and Installation, Las Vegas, Nevada, March 25–27, 1990. New York: American Society of Civil Engineers, 1990, pp. 230–243.

45. Drella, M., "Aerodynamics of Human-Powered Flight," in *Annual Review of Fluid Mechanics*, 22, pp. 93–110. Palo Alto, CA: Annual Reviews, 1990.

46. U.S. Department of the Interior, "Selecting Hydraulic Reaction Turbines," A Water Resources Technical Publication, *Engineering Monograph No. 20*. Denver, CO: U.S. Department of the Interior, Bureau of Reclamation, 1976.

47. Abbott, I. H., and A. E. von Doenhoff, *Theory of Wing Sections, Including a Summary of Airfoil Data*. New York: Dover, 1959.

PROBLEMS

10.1 Consider the centrifugal pump impeller dimensions given in Example 10.1. Estimate the ideal head rise and mechanical power input if the outlet blade angle is changed to $60°$, $70°$, $80°$, or $85°$.

10.2 The geometry of a centrifugal water pump is $r_1 = 4$ in., $r_2 = 7.5$ in., $b_1 = b_2 = 1.5$ in., $\beta_1 = 30°$, $\beta_2 = 20°$, and it runs at speed 1500 rpm. Estimate the discharge required for axial entry, the horsepower generated in the water, and the head produced.

10.3 A centrifugal pump running at 3500 rpm pumps water at a rate of 150 gpm. The water enters axially, and leaves the impeller at 17.5 ft/s relative to the blades, which are radial at the exit. If the pump requires 6.75 hp, and is 67 percent efficient, estimate the basic dimensions (impeller exit diameter and width), using the Euler turbomachine equation.

10.4 Dimensions of a centrifugal pump impeller are

** Warner-Ishi, P.O. Box 580, Shelbyville, IL 62565-0580, U.S.A.

Parameter	Inlet, Section ①	Outlet, Section ②
Radius, r (mm)	175	500
Blade width, b (mm)	50	30
Blade angle, β (deg)	65	70

The pump handles water and is driven at 750 rpm. Calculate the theoretical head and mechanical power input if the flow rate is 0.75 m³/s.

10.5 Dimensions of a centrifugal pump impeller are

Parameter	Inlet, Section ①	Outlet, Section ②
Radius, r (in.)	3	9.75
Blade width, b (in.)	1.5	1.125
Blade angle, β (deg)	60	70

The pump is driven at 1250 rpm while pumping water. Calculate the theoretical head and mechanical power input if the flow rate is 1500 gpm.

10.6 Dimensions of a centrifugal pump impeller are

Parameter	Inlet, Section ①	Outlet, Section ②
Radius, r (in.)	15	45
Blade width, b (in.)	4.75	3.25
Blade angle, β (deg)	40	60

The pump is driven at 575 rpm and the fluid is water. Calculate the theoretical head and mechanical power if the flow rate is 80,000 gpm.

10.7 A centrifugal water pump, with 15 cm diameter impeller and axial inlet flow, is driven at 1750 rpm. The impeller vanes are backward-curved ($\beta_2 = 65°$) and have axial width $b_2 = 2$ cm. For a volume flow rate of 225 m³/hr determine the theoretical head rise and power input to the pump.

10.8 For the impeller of Problem 10.5, determine the rotational speed for which the tangential component of the inlet velocity is zero if the volume flow rate is 4000 gpm. Calculate the theoretical head and mechanical power input.

10.9 Consider the geometry of the idealized centrifugal pump described in Problem 10.11. Draw inlet and outlet velocity diagrams assuming b = constant. Calculate the inlet blade angles required for "shockless" entry flow at the design flow rate. Evaluate the theoretical power input to the pump at the design flow rate.

10.10 For the impeller of Problem 10.4, operating at 750 rpm, determine the volume flow rate for which the tangential component of the inlet velocity is zero. Calculate the theoretical head and mechanical power input.

10.11 Consider a centrifugal pump whose geometry and flow conditions are

Impeller inlet radius, R_1	1 in.
Impeller outlet radius, R_2	7.5 in.
Impeller outlet width, b_2	0.375 in.
Design speed, N	2000 rpm
Design flow rate, Q	8000 gpm
Backward-curved vanes (outlet blade angle), β_2	75°
Required flow rate range	50–150% of design

Assume ideal pump behavior with 100 percent efficiency. Find the shutoff head. Calculate the absolute and relative discharge velocities, the total head, and the theoretical power required at the design flow rate.

10.12 For the impeller of Problem 10.6, determine the inlet blade angle for which the tangential component of the inlet velocity is zero if the volume flow rate is 125,000 gpm. Calculate the theoretical head and mechanical power input.

10.13 Consider the centrifugal pump impeller dimensions given in Example 10.1. Construct the velocity diagram for shockless flow at the impeller inlet, if b = constant. Calculate the effective flow angle with respect to the radial impeller blades for the case of no inlet swirl. Investigate the effects on flow angle of (a) variations in impeller width and (b) inlet swirl velocities.

10.14 A centrifugal pump runs at 1750 rpm while pumping water at a rate of 50 L/s. The water enters axially, and leaves tangential to the impeller blades. The impeller exit diameter and width are 300 mm and 10 mm, respectively. If the pump requires 45 kW, and is 75 percent efficient, estimate the exit angle of the impeller blades.

10.15 A centrifugal water pump designed to operate at 1300 rpm has dimensions

Parameter	Inlet	Outlet
Radius, r (mm)	100	175
Blade width, b (mm)	10	7.5
Blade angle, β (deg)		40

Draw the inlet velocity diagram for a volume flow rate of 35 L/s. Determine the inlet blade angle for which the entering velocity has no tangential component. Draw the outlet velocity diagram. Determine the outlet absolute flow angle (measured relative to the normal direction). Evaluate the hydraulic power delivered by the pump, if its efficiency is 75 percent. Determine the head developed by the pump.

10.16 Repeat the analysis for determining the optimum speed for an impulse turbine of Example 10.5, using the Euler turbomachine equation.

10.17 A centrifugal water pump designed to operate at 1200 rpm has dimensions

Parameter	Inlet	Outlet
Radius, r (mm)	90	150
Blade width, b (mm)	10	7.5
Blade angle, β (deg)	25	45

Determine the flow rate at which the entering velocity has no tangential component. Draw the outlet velocity diagram, and determine the outlet absolute flow angle (measured relative to the normal direction) at this flow rate. Evaluate the hydraulic power delivered by the pump if its efficiency is 70 percent. Determine the head developed by the pump.

10.18 Gasoline is pumped by a centrifugal pump. When the flow rate is 0.025 m³/s, the pump requires 15 kW input, and its efficiency is 85 percent. Calculate the pressure rise produced by the pump. Express this result as (a) ft of water and (b) ft of gasoline.

10.19 A centrifugal pump designed to deliver water at 30 L/s has dimensions

Parameter	Inlet	Outlet
Radius, r (mm)	75	150
Blade width, b (mm)	7.5	6.25
Blade angle, β (deg)	25	40

Draw the inlet velocity diagram. Determine the design speed if the entering velocity has no tangential component. Draw the outlet velocity diagram. Determine the outlet absolute flow angle (measured relative to the normal direction). Evaluate the theoretical head developed by the pump. Estimate the minimum mechanical power delivered to the pump.

10.20 The theoretical head delivered by a centrifugal pump at shutoff depends on the discharge radius and angular speed of the impeller. For preliminary design, it is useful to have a plot showing the theoretical shutoff characteristics and approximating the actual performance. Prepare a log-log plot of impeller radius versus theoretical head rise at shutoff with standard motor speeds as parameters. Assume the fluid is water and the actual head at the design flow rate is 70 percent of the theoretical shutoff head. (Show these as dashed lines on the plot.) Explain how this plot might be used for preliminary design.

10.21 In the water pump of Problem 10.7, the pump casing acts as a diffuser, which converts 60 percent of the absolute velocity head at the impeller outlet to static pressure rise. The head loss through the pump suction and discharge channels is 0.75 times the radial component of velocity head leaving the impeller. Estimate the volume flow rate, head rise, power input, and pump efficiency at the maximum efficiency point. Assume the torque to overcome bearing, seal, and spin losses is 10 percent of the ideal torque at $Q = 0.065$ m³/s.

10.22 Use data from Appendix D to choose points from the performance curves for a Peerless horizontal split case Type 4AE12 pump at 1750 and 3550 nominal rpm. Obtain and plot curve-fits for total head versus delivery at each speed for this pump, with a 12.12-in. diameter impeller.

10.23 Use data from Appendix D to choose points from the performance curves for a Peerless horizontal split case Type 16A18B pump at 705 and 880 nominal rpm. Obtain and plot curve-fits of total head versus delivery for this pump, with an 18.0-in. diameter impeller.

10.24 Data from tests of a suction pump operated at 1750 rpm with a 35-cm diameter impeller are

Flow rate, Q (m³/s × 10³)	17	26	38	45	63
Total head, H (m)	60	59	54	50	37
Power input, $\mathcal{P}$ (kW)	19	22	26	30	34

Plot the performance curves for this pump; include a curve of efficiency versus volume flow rate. Locate the best efficiency point and specify the pump rating at this point.

10.25 Data from tests of a suction pump operated at 1750 rpm with a 35-cm diameter impeller are

Flow rate, Q (m³/s × 10³)	18	28	35	50	58	81
Total head, H (m)	62	62	61	57	53	41
Power input, $\mathcal{P}$ (kW)	22	26	30	34	37	45

Plot the performance curves for this pump; include a curve of efficiency versus volume flow rate. Locate the best efficiency point and specify the pump rating at this point.

10.26 Data measured during tests of a centrifugal pump at 2750 rpm are

Parameter	Inlet, Section ①	Outlet, Section ②
Gage pressure, p (psi)	17.5	75
Elevation above datum, z (ft)	8.25	30
Average speed of flow, $\overline{V}$ (ft/s)	9	12

The flow rate is 65 gpm and the torque applied to the pump shaft is 6.25 lbf · ft. Evaluate the total dynamic heads at the pump inlet and outlet, the hydraulic power input to the fluid, and the pump efficiency. Specify the electric motor size needed to drive the pump. If the electric motor efficiency is 85 percent, calculate the electric power requirement.

10.27 Data measured during tests of a centrifugal pump driven at 3000 rpm are

Parameter	Inlet, Section ①	Outlet, Section ②
Gage pressure, p (psi)	12.5	
Elevation above datum, z (ft)	6.5	32.5
Average speed of flow, $\overline{V}$ (ft/s)	6.5	15

The flow rate is 65 gpm and the torque applied to the pump shaft is 4.75 lbf · ft. The pump efficiency is 75 percent, and the electric motor efficiency is 85 percent. Find the electric power required, and the gage pressure at section ②.

10.28 Write the turbine specific speed in terms of the flow coefficient and the head coefficient.

10.29 Write the pump specific speed in terms of the flow coefficient and the head coefficient.

10.30 The *kilogram force* (kgf), defined as the force exerted by a kilogram mass in standard gravity, is commonly used in European practice. The *metric horsepower* (hpm) is defined as 1 hpm ≡ 75 m · kgf/s. Develop a conversion relating metric horsepower to U.S. horsepower. Relate the specific speed for a hydraulic turbine—calculated in units of rpm, metric horsepower, and meters—to the specific speed calculated in U.S. customary units.

10.31 Typical performance curves for a centrifugal pump, tested with three different impeller diameters in a single casing, are shown. Specify the flow rate and head produced by the pump at its best efficiency point with a 12-in. diameter impeller. Scale these data to predict the performance of this pump when tested with 11 in. and 13 in. impellers. Comment on the accuracy of the scaling procedure.

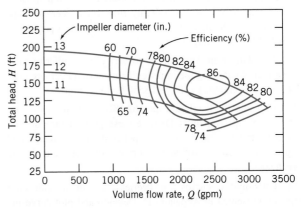

P10.31

10.32 A small centrifugal pump, when tested at $N = 2875$ rpm with water, delivered $Q = 0.016$ m³/s and $H = 40$ m at its best efficiency point ($\eta = 0.70$). Determine the specific speed of the pump at this test condition. Sketch the impeller shape you expect. Compute the required power input to the pump.

10.33 A pump with $D = 500$ mm delivers $Q = 0.725$ m³/s of water at $H = 10$ m at its best efficiency point. If the specific speed of the pump is 1.74, and the required input power is 90 kW, determine the shutoff head, H_0, and best efficiency, η. What type of pump is this? If the pump is now run at 900 rpm, by scaling the performance curve, estimate the new flow rate, head, shutoff head, and required power.

10.34 At its best efficiency point ($\eta = 0.85$), a mixed-flow pump, with $D = 400$ mm, delivers $Q = 1.20$ m^3/s of water at $H = 50$ m when operating at $N = 1500$ rpm. Calculate the specific speed of this pump. Estimate the required power input. Determine the curve-fit parameters of the pump performance curve based on the shutoff point and the best efficiency point. Scale the performance curve to estimate the flow, head, efficiency, and power input required to run the same pump at 750 rpm.

10.35 A centrifugal water pump operates at 1750 rpm; the impeller has backward-curved vanes with $\beta_2 = 60°$ and $b_2 = 1.25$ cm. At a flow rate of 0.025 m^3/s, the radial outlet velocity is $V_{n_2} = 3.5$ m/s. Estimate the head this pump could deliver at 1150 rpm.

10.36 A pumping system must be specified for a lift station at a wastewater treatment facility. The average flow rate is 110 million liters per day and the required lift is 10 m. Non-clogging impellers must be used; about 65 percent efficiency is expected. For convenient installation, electric motors of 37.5 kW or less are desired. Determine the number of motor/pump units needed and recommend an appropriate operating speed.

10.37 A set of seven 35 hp motor-pump units is used to deliver water through an elevation of 50 ft. The efficiency of the pumps is specified to be 60 percent. Estimate the delivery (gallons per day) and select an appropriate operating speed.

10.38 Appendix D contains area bound curves for pump model selection and performance curves for individual pump models. Use these data and the similarity rules to predict and plot the curves of head H (ft) versus Q (gpm) of a Peerless Type 10AE12 pump, with impeller diameter $D = 12$ in., for nominal speeds of 1000, 1200, 1400, and 1600 rpm.

10.39 Appendix D contains area bound curves for pump model selection and performance curves for individual pump models. Use these data to verify the similarity rules for a Peerless Type 4AE12 pump, with impeller diameter $D = 11.0$ in., operated at 1750 and 3550 nominal rpm.

10.40 Use data from Appendix D to verify the similarity rules for the effect of changing the impeller diameter of a Peerless Type 4AE12 pump operated at 1750 and 3550 nominal rpm.

10.41 Consider the Peerless Type 16A18B horizontal split case centrifugal pump (Appendix D). Use these performance data to verify the similarity rules for (a) impeller diameter change and (b) operating speeds of 705 and 880 rpm (note the scale change between speeds).

10.42 Performance curves for Peerless horizontal split case pumps are presented in Appendix D. Develop and plot curve-fits for a Type 16A18B pump, with impeller diameter $D = 18.0$ in., driven at 705 and 880 nominal rpm. Verify the effects of pump speed on scaling pump curves using the procedure described in Example 10.7.

10.43 Performance curves for Peerless horizontal split case pumps are presented in Appendix D. Develop and plot a curve-fit for a Type 10AE12 pump driven at 1150 nominal rpm using the procedure described in Example 10.7.

10.44 Problem 10.20 suggests that pump head at best efficiency is typically about 70 percent of shutoff head. Use pump data from Appendix D to evaluate this suggestion. A further suggestion in Section 10-4 is that the appropriate scaling for tests of a pump casing with different impeller diameters is $Q \propto D^2$. Use pump data to evaluate this suggestion.

10.45 Catalog data for a centrifugal water pump at design conditions are $Q = 250$ gpm and $\Delta p = 18.6$ psi at 1750 rpm. A laboratory flume requires 200 gpm at 32 ft of head. The only motor available develops 3 hp at 1750 rpm. Is this motor suitable for the laboratory flume? How might the pump/motor match be improved?

10.46 A reaction turbine is designed to produce 17.5 MW at 120 rpm under 45 m of head. Laboratory facilities are available to provide 10 m of head and to absorb 35 kW from the model turbine. Assume comparable efficiencies for the model and prototype turbines. Determine the appropriate model test speed, scale ratio, and volume flow rate.

10.47 A 1/3 scale model of a centrifugal water pump, when running at $N_m = 100$ rpm, produces a flow rate of $Q_m = 1$ m^3/s with a head of $H_m = 4.5$ m. Assuming the model and prototype efficiencies are comparable, estimate the flow rate, head, and power requirement if the design speed is 125 rpm.

10.48 A centrifugal pump is to operate at $Q = 250$ cfs, $H = 400$ ft, and $N = 870$ rpm. A model test is planned in a facility where the maximum water flow rate is 5 cfs and a 300 hp dynamometer is available. Assume the model and prototype efficiencies are comparable. Determine the appropriate model test speed and scale ratio.

10.49 White [43] suggests modeling the efficiency for a centrifugal pump using the curve-fit, $\eta = aQ - bQ^3$, where a and b are constants. Describe a procedure to evaluate a and b from experimental data. Evaluate a and b using data for the Peerless Type 10AE12 pump, with impeller diameter $D = 12.0$ in., at 1760 rpm (Appendix D). Plot and illustrate the accuracy of the curve-fit by comparing measured and predicted efficiencies for this pump.

10.50 Sometimes the variation of water viscosity with temperature can be used to achieve dynamic similarity. A model pump delivers 20 gpm of water at 59°F against a head of 60 ft, when operating at 3500 rpm. Determine the water temperature that must be used to obtain dynamically similar operation at 1750 rpm. Estimate the volume flow rate and head produced by the pump at the lower-speed test condition. Comment on the *NPSH* requirements for the two tests.

10.51 A four-stage boiler feed pump has suction and discharge lines of 10 cm and 7.5 cm inside diameter. At 3500 rpm, the pump is rated at 0.025 m^3/s against a head of 125 m while handling water at 115°C. The inlet pressure gage, located 50 cm below the impeller centerline, reads 150 kPa. The pump is to be factory certified by tests at the same flow rate, head rise, and speed, but using water at 27°C. Calculate the *NPSHA* at the pump inlet in the field installation. Evaluate the suction head that must be used in the factory test to duplicate field suction conditions.

10.52 Data from tests of a pump operated at 1500 rpm, with a 30-cm diameter impeller, are

Flow rate, Q (m^3/s $\times 10^3$)	10	20	30	40	50	60	70
Net positive suction head required, *NPSR* (m)	2.2	2.4	2.6	3.1	3.6	4.1	5.1

Develop and plot a curve-fit equation for *NPSHR* versus volume flow rate in the form $NPSHR = a + bQ^2$, where a and b are constants. If the $NPSHA = 6$ m, estimate the maximum allowable flow rate of this pump.

10.53 A large deep fryer at a snack-food plant contains hot oil that is circulated through a heat exchanger by pumps. Solid particles and water droplets coming from the food product are observed in the flowing oil. What special factors must be considered in specifying the operating conditions for the pumps?

10.54 The net positive suction head required (*NPSHR*) by a pump may be expressed approximately as a parabolic function of volume flow rate. The *NPSHR* for a particular pump operating at 1750 rpm is given as $H_r = H_0 + AQ^2$, where $H_0 = 3$ m of water and $A = 3000$ m/(m^3/s)^2. Assume the pipe system supplying the pump suction consists of a reservoir, whose surface is 6 m above the pump centerline, a square entrance, 6 m of 15 cm cast-iron pipe, and a 90° elbow. Calculate the maximum volume flow rate at 20°C for which the suction head is sufficient to operate this pump without cavitation.

10.55 For the pump and flow system of Problem 10.54, calculate the maximum flow rate for hot water at various temperatures and plot versus water temperature. (Be sure to consider the density variation as water temperature is varied.)

10.56 A centrifugal pump, operating at $N = 2265$ rpm, lifts water between two reservoirs connected by 300 ft of 6 in. and 100 ft of 3 in. cast-iron pipe in series. The gravity lift is 25 ft. Estimate the head requirement, power needed, and hourly cost of electrical energy to pump water at 200 gpm to the higher reservoir. Assume that electricity costs 12¢/kW·hr, and that the electric motor efficiency is 85 percent.

10.57 Part of the water supply for the South Rim of Grand Canyon National Park is taken from the Colorado River [44]. A flow rate of 600 gpm, taken from the river at elevation 3734 ft, is pumped to a storage tank atop the South Rim at 7022 ft elevation. Part of the pipeline is above ground and part is in a hole directionally drilled at angles up to 70° from the vertical; the total pipe length is approximately 13,200 ft. Under steady flow operating conditions, the frictional head loss is 290 ft of water in addition to the static lift. Estimate the diameter of the commercial steel pipe in the system. Compute the pumping power requirement if the pump efficiency is 61 percent.

10.58 A centrifugal pump is installed in a piping system with $L = 300$ m of $D = 40$ cm cast-iron pipe. The downstream reservoir surface is 15 m lower than the upstream reservoir. Determine and plot the system head curve. Find the volume flow rate (magnitude and direction) through the system when the pump is not operating. Estimate the friction loss, power requirement, and hourly energy cost to pump water at 1 m^3/s through this system.

10.59 A Peerless horizontal split-case type 4AE12 pump with 11.0-in. diameter impeller, operating at 1750 rpm, lifts water between two reservoirs connected by 200 ft of 4 in. and 200 ft of 3 in. cast-iron pipe in series. The gravity lift is 10 ft. Plot the system head curve and determine the pump operating point.

*10.60 A pump transfers water from one reservoir to another through two cast-iron pipes in series. The first is 3000 ft of 9 in. pipe and the second is 1000 ft of 6 in. pipe. A constant flow rate of 75 gpm is tapped off at the junction between the two pipes.

Obtain and plot the system head versus flow rate curve. Find the delivery if the system is supplied by the pump of Example 10.7, operating at 1750 rpm.

10.61 Performance data for a pump are

H (m)	27.5	27	25	22	18	13	6.5
Q (m³/s)	0	0.025	0.050	0.075	0.100	0.125	0.150

The pump is to be used to move water between two open reservoirs with an elevation increase of 7.5 m. The connecting pipe system consists of 500 m of commercial steel pipe containing two 90° elbows and an open gate valve. Find the flow rate if we use a) 20 cm, b) 30 cm, and c) 40 cm pipe.

10.62 Performance data for a pump are

H (ft)	179	176	165	145	119	84	43
Q (gpm)	0	500	1000	1500	2000	2500	3000

Estimate the delivery when the pump is used to move water between two open reservoirs, through 1200 ft of 12 in. commercial steel pipe containing two 90° elbows and an open gate valve, if the elevation increase is 50 ft. Determine the gate valve loss coefficient needed to reduce the volume flow rate by half.

10.63 Consider again the pump and piping system of Problem 10.62. Determine the volume flow rate and gate valve loss coefficient for the case of two identical pumps installed in *series*.

10.64 Consider again the pump and piping system of Problem 10.62. Determine the volume flow rate and gate valve loss coefficient for the case of two identical pumps installed in *parallel*.

10.65 The resistance of a given pipe increases with age as deposits form, increasing the roughness and reducing the pipe diameter (see Fig. 8.14). Typical multipliers to be applied to the friction factor are given in [16]:

Pipe Age (years)	Small Pipes, 4–10 in.	Large Pipes, 12–60 in.
New	1.00	1.00
10	2.20	1.60
20	5.00	2.00
30	7.25	2.20
40	8.75	2.40
50	9.60	2.86
60	10.0	3.70
70	10.1	4.70

Consider again the pump and piping system of Problem 10.62. Estimate the percentage reductions in volume flow rate that occur after (a) 20 years and (b) 40 years of use, if the pump characteristics remain constant. Repeat the calculation if the pump head is reduced 10 percent after 20 years of use and 25 percent after 40 years.

10.66 Consider again the pump and piping system of Problem 10.63. Estimate the percentage reductions in volume flow rate that occur after (a) 20 years and (b) 40 years of use, if the pump characteristics remain constant. Repeat the calculation if the pump head is reduced 10 percent after 20 years of use and 25 percent after 40 years. (Use the data of Problem 10.65 for increase in pipe friction factor with age.)

10.67 Consider again the pump and piping system of Problem 10.64. Estimate the percentage reductions in volume flow rate that occur after (a) 20 years and (b) 40 years of use, if the pump characteristics remain constant. Repeat the calculation if the pump head is reduced 10 percent after 20 years of use and 25 percent after 40 years. (Use the data of Problem 10.65 for increase in pipe friction factor with age.)

10.68 The city of Englewood, Colorado, diverts water for municipal use from the South Platte River at elevation 5280 ft [44]. The water is pumped to storage reservoirs at 5310 ft elevation. The inside diameter of the steel water line is 27 in.; its length is 5800 ft. The facility is designed for an initial capacity (flow rate) of 31 cfs, with an ultimate capacity of 38 cfs. Calculate and plot the system resistance curve. Specify an appropriate pumping system. Estimate the pumping power required for steady-state operation, at both the initial and ultimate flow rates.

10.69 A pump in the system shown draws water from a sump and delivers it to an open tank through 1250 ft of new, 4 in. nominal diameter, schedule 40 steel pipe. The vertical suction pipe is 5 ft long and includes a foot valve with hinged disk and a 90° standard elbow. The discharge line includes two 90° standard elbows, an angle lift check valve, and a fully open gate valve. The design flow rate is 200 gpm. Find the head losses in the suction and discharge lines. Calculate the *NPSHA*. Select a pump suitable for this application.

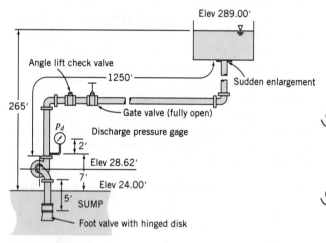

P10.69, 10.70

10.70 Consider the flow system and data of Problem 10.69 and the data for pipe aging given in Problem 10.65. Select pump(s) that will maintain the system flow at the desired rate for (a) 10 years and (b) 20 years. Compare the delivery produced by these pumps with the delivery by the pump sized for new pipes only.

10.71 Consider the flow system described in Problem 8.155. Select a pump appropriate for this application. Check the *NPSHR* versus the *NPSHA* for this system.

10.72 Consider the flow system shown in Problem 8.110. Assume the minimum *NPSHR* at the pump inlet is 15 ft of water. Select a pump appropriate for this application. Use the data for increase in friction factor with pipe age given in Problem 10.65 to determine and compare the system flow rate after 10 years of operation.

10.73 Consider the flow system shown in Problem 8.156. Select an appropriate pump for this application. Check the pump efficiency and power requirement compared with those in the problem statement.

10.74 A fire nozzle is supplied through 300 ft of 3-in. diameter canvas hose (with *e* = 0.001 ft). Water from a hydrant is supplied at 50 psig to a booster pump on board the pumper truck. At design operating conditions, the pressure at the nozzle inlet is 100 psig, and the pressure drop along the hose is 33 psi per 100 ft of length. Calculate the design flow rate and the maximum nozzle exit speed. Select a pump appropriate for this application, determine its efficiency at this operating condition, and calculate the power required to drive the pump.

10.75 Consider the pipe network of Problem 8.168. Select a pump suitable to deliver a total flow rate of 300 gpm through the pipe network.

10.76 A pumping system with two different static lifts is shown. Each reservoir is supplied by a line consisting of 300 m of 20 cm cast-iron pipe. Evaluate and plot the system head versus flow curve. Explain what happens when the pump head is less than the height of the upper reservoir. Calculate the flow rate delivered at a pump head of 26 m.

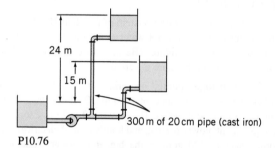

P10.76

10.77 Consider the chilled water circulation system of Problem 8.158. Select pumps that may be combined in parallel to supply the total flow requirement. Calculate the power required for 3 pumps in parallel. Also calculate the volume flow rates and power required when only 1 or 2 of these pumps operates.

10.78 Consider the flow system shown in Problem 8.76. Evaluate the *NPSHA* at the pump inlet. Select a pump appropriate for this application. Use the data on pipe aging from Problem 10.65 to estimate the reduction in flow rate after 10 years of operation.

10.79 Consider the gasoline pipeline flow of Problem 8.124. Select pumps that, combined in parallel, supply the total flow requirement. Calculate the power required for 4 pumps in parallel. Also calculate the volume flow rates and power required when only 1, 2, or 3 of these pumps operates.

10.80 Water for the sprinkler system at a lakeside summer home is to be drawn from the adjacent lake. The home is located on a bluff 80 ft above the lake surface. The pump is located on level ground 10 ft above the lake surface. The sprinkler system requires 10 gpm at 50 psig. The piping system is to be 1-in. diameter galvanized iron. The inlet section (between the lake and pump inlet) includes a reentrant inlet, one standard 45° elbow, one standard 90° elbow, and 50 ft of pipe. The discharge section (between the pump outlet and the sprinkler connection) includes two standard 45° elbows and 120 ft of pipe. Evaluate the head loss on the suction side of the pump. Calculate the gage pressure at the pump inlet. Determine the hydraulic power requirement of the pump. If the pipe diameter were increased to 1.5 in., would the power requirement of the pump increase, decrease, or stay the same? What difference would it make if the pump were located halfway up the hill?

10.81 Water is pumped from a lake (at $z = 0$) to a large storage tank located on a bluff above the lake. The pipe is 3-in. diameter galvanized iron. The inlet section (between the lake and the pump) includes one rounded inlet, one standard 90° elbow, and 50 ft of pipe. The discharge section (between the pump outlet and the discharge to the open tank) includes two standard 90° elbows, one gate valve, and 150 ft of pipe. The pipe discharge (into the side of the tank) is at $z = 70$ ft. Calculate the system flow curve. Estimate the system operating point. Determine the power input to the pump if its efficiency at the operating point is 80 percent. Sketch the system curve when the water level in the upper tank reaches $z = 90$ ft. If the water level in the upper tank is at $z = 75$ ft and the valve is partially closed to reduce the flow rate to 0.1 ft³/s, sketch the system curve for this operating condition. Would you expect the pump efficiency to be higher for the first or second operating condition? Why?

10.82 Manufacturer's data for the "Little Giant Water Wizard" submersible utility pump are

Discharge height (ft)	1	2	5	10	15	20	26.3
Water flow rate (gpm)	20.4	20	19	16	13	8	0

The Owner's Manual also states, "Note: These ratings are based on discharge into 1 in. pipe with friction loss neglected. Using $\frac{3}{4}$ in. garden hose adaptor, performance will be reduced approximately 15%." Plot a performance curve for the pump. Develop a curve-fit equation for the performance curve; show the curve-fit on the plot. Calculate and plot the pump delivery versus discharge height through a 50 ft length of smooth $\frac{3}{4}$ in. garden hose. Compare with the curve for delivery into 1 in. pipe.

10.83 Consider the swimming pool filtration system of Problem 8.169. Assume the pipe used is $\frac{3}{4}$ in. nominal PVC (smooth plastic). Specify the speed and impeller diameter and estimate the efficiency of a suitable pump.

10.84 Consider the fire hose and nozzle of Problem 8.159. Specify an appropriate pump and impeller diameter to supply four such hoses simultaneously. Calculate the power input to the pump.

10.85 Performance data for a centrifugal fan of 1 m diameter, tested at 650 rpm, are

Volume flow rate Q (m³/s)	3	4	5	6	7	8
Static pressure rise, Δp (mm H₂O)	53	51	45	35	23	11
Power output $\mathcal{P}$ (kW)	2.05	2.37	2.60	2.62	2.61	2.4

Plot the performance data versus volume flow rate. Calculate static efficiency and show the curve on the plot. Find the best efficiency point and specify the fan rating at this point.

10.86 Using the fan of Problem 10.85 determine the minimum-size square sheet-metal duct that will carry a flow of 5.75 m³/s over a distance of 15 m. Estimate the increase in delivery if the fan speed is increased to 800 rpm.

10.87 Consider the fan and performance data of Problem 10.85. At $Q = 5.75$ m³/s, the dynamic pressure is equivalent to 4 mm of water. Evaluate the fan outlet area. Plot total pressure rise and input horsepower for this fan versus volume flow rate. Calculate the fan total efficiency and show the curve on the plot. Find the best efficiency point and specify the fan rating at this point.

10.88 The performance data of Problem 10.85 are for a 1-m diameter fan wheel. This fan also is manufactured with 1.025, 1.125-, 1.250-, and 1.375-m diameter wheels. Pick a standard fan to deliver 14 m³/s against a 25-mm H₂O static pressure rise. Assume standard air at the fan inlet. Determine the required fan speed and the input power needed.

10.89 Performance characteristics of a Buffalo Forge axial flow fan are presented on the next page. The fan is used to power a wind tunnel with 1-ft square test section. The tunnel consists of a smooth inlet contraction, two screens (each with loss coefficient $K = 0.12$), the test section, and a diffuser where the cross section is expanded to 24 in. diameter at the fan inlet. Flow from the fan is discharged back to the room. Calculate and plot the system characteristic curve of pressure loss versus volume flow rate. Estimate the maximum air flow speed available in this wind tunnel test section.

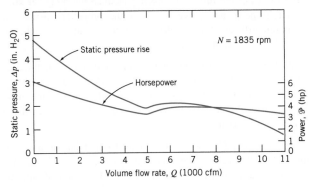

P10.89, 10.90

10.90 Consider again the axial-flow fan and wind tunnel of Problem 10.89. Scale the performance of the fan as it varies with operating speed. Develop and plot a "calibration curve" showing test section flow speed (in m/s) versus fan speed (in rpm).

10.91 Experimental test data for an aircraft engine fuel pump are presented below. This gear pump is required to supply jet fuel at 450 pounds per hour and 150 psig to the engine fuel controller. Tests were conducted at 10, 96, and 100 percent of the rated pump speed of 4536 rpm. At each constant speed, the back pressure on the pump was set, and the flow rate measured. On one graph, plot curves of pressure versus delivery at the three constant speeds. Estimate the pump displacement volume per revolution. Calculate the volumetric efficiency at each test point and sketch contours of constant η_v. Evaluate the energy loss caused by valve throttling at 100 percent speed and full delivery to the engine.

Pump Speed (rpm)	Back Pressure (psig)	Fuel Flow (pph*)	Pump Speed (rpm)	Back Pressure (psig)	Fuel Flow (pph)	Pump Speed (rpm)	Back Pressure (psig)	Fuel Flow (pph)
	200	1810		200	1730		200	89
4536	300	1810	4355	300	1750	453	250	73
(100%)	400	1810	(96%)	400	1735	(10%)	300	58.5
	500	1790		500	1720		350	45
	900	1720		900	1635		400	30

* Fuel flow rate measured in pounds per hour (pph).

10.92 The propeller on an airboat used in the Florida Everglades moves air at the rate of 90 lbm/s. When at rest, the speed of the slipstream behind the propeller is 90 mph at a location where the pressure is atmospheric. Calculate (a) the propeller diameter, (b) the thrust produced at rest, and (c) the thrust produced when the airboat is moving ahead at 30 mph if the mass flow rate through the propeller remains constant.

10.93 An air boat in the Florida Everglades is powered by a propeller, with $D = 1.5$ m, driven at maximum speed, $N = 1800$ rpm, by a 125 kW engine. Estimate the maximum thrust produced by the propeller at (a) standstill and (b) $V = 12.5$ m/s.

10.94 A jet-propelled aircraft traveling at 450 mph takes in 90 lbm/s of air and discharges it at 1200 mph relative to the aircraft. Determine the propulsive efficiency (defined as the ratio of the useful work output to the mechanical energy input to the fluid) of the aircraft.

10.95 Drag data for model and prototype guided missile frigates are presented in Figs. 7.2 and 7.3. Dimensions of the prototype vessel are given in Problem 9.89. Use these data, with the propeller performance characteristics of Fig. 10.40, to size a single propeller to power the full-scale vessel. Calculate the propeller size, operating speed, and power input, if the propeller operates at maximum efficiency when the vessel travels at its maximum speed, $V = 37.6$ knots.

10.96 The propulsive efficiency, η, of a propeller is defined as the ratio of the useful work produced to the mechanical energy input to the fluid. Determine the propulsive efficiency of the moving airboat of Problem 10.92. What would be the efficiency if the boat were not moving?

10.97 The propeller for the Gossamer Condor human-powered aircraft has $D = 12$ ft and rotates at $N = 107$ rpm. Additional details on the aircraft are given in Problem 9.170. Estimate the dimensionless performance characteristics and efficiency of this propeller at cruise conditions. Assume the pilot expends 70 percent of maximum power at cruise. (See Reference 45 for more information on human-powered flight.)

10.98 Equations for the thrust, power, and efficiency of propulsion devices were derived in Section 10-5. Show that these equations may be combined for the condition of constant thrust to obtain

$$\eta = \frac{2}{1 + \left(1 + \dfrac{F_T}{\dfrac{\rho V^2}{2} \dfrac{\pi D^2}{4}}\right)^{1/2}}$$

Interpret this result physically.

10.99 Preliminary calculations for a hydroelectric power generation site show a net head of 2350 ft is available at a water flow rate of 75 ft³/s. Compare the geometry and efficiency of Pelton wheels designed to run at (a) 450 rpm and (b) 600 rpm.

10.100 Conditions at the inlet to the nozzle of a Pelton wheel are $p = 700$ psig and $V = 15$ mph. The jet diameter is $d = 7.5$ in. and the nozzle loss coefficient is $K_{nozzle} = 0.04$. The wheel diameter is $D = 8$ ft. At this operating condition, $\eta = 0.86$. Calculate (a) the power output, (b) the normal operating speed, (c) the approximate runaway speed, (d) the torque at normal operating speed, and (e) the approximate torque at zero speed.

10.101 The reaction turbines at Niagara Falls are of the Francis type. The impeller outside diameter is 176 in. Each turbine produces 72,500 hp at 107 rpm, with 93.8 percent efficiency under 214 ft of net head. Calculate the specific speed of these units. Evaluate the volume flow rate to each turbine. Estimate the penstock size if it is 1300 ft long and the net head is 85 percent of the gross head.

10.102 Francis turbine Units 19, 20, and 21, installed at the Grand Coulee Dam on the Columbia River, are *very* large [46]. Each runner is 32.6 ft in diameter and contains 550 tons of cast steel. At rated conditions, each turbine develops 820,000 hp at 72 rpm under 285 ft of head. Efficiency is nearly 95 percent at rated conditions. The turbines operate at heads from 220 to 355 ft. Calculate the specific speed at rated operating conditions. Estimate the maximum water flow rate through each turbine.

10.103 Measured data for performance of the reaction turbines at Shasta Dam near Redding, California are shown in Fig. 10.13. Each turbine is rated at 103,000 hp when operating at 138.6 rpm under a net head of 380 ft. Evaluate the specific speed and compute the shaft torque developed by each turbine at rated operating conditions. Calculate and plot the water flow rate per turbine required to produce rated output power as a function of head.

10.104 Figure 10.11 contains data for the efficiency of a large Pelton water wheel installed in the Tiger Creek Power House of Pacific Gas & Electric Company near Jackson, California. This unit is rated at 36,000 hp when operated at 225 rpm under a net head of 1190 ft of water. Assume reasonable flow angles and nozzle loss coefficient. Determine the rotor diameter and estimate the jet diameter and the volume flow rate.

10.105 An impulse turbine is to develop 15 MW from a single wheel at a location where the net head is 350 m. Determine the appropriate speed, wheel diameter, and jet diameter for single- and multiple-jet operation. Compare with a double-overhung wheel installation. Estimate the required water consumption.

10.106 Tests of a model impulse turbine under a net head of 20 m produced the following results:

Wheel Speed (rpm)	No-Load Discharge (m³/hr)	Net Brake Scale Reading (N) ($R = 2$ m)					
300	10	33	72	107	140	194	233
325	11.4	29	63	96	124	175	213
Discharge (m³/hr)		44	86	124	157	211	257

Calculate and plot the machine power output and efficiency versus water flow rate.

10.107 In U.S. customary units, the common definition of specific speed for a hydraulic turbine is given by Eq. 10.18b. Develop a conversion between this definition and a truly dimensionless one in SI units. Evaluate the specific speed of an impulse turbine, operating at 400 rpm under a net head of 1190 ft with 86 percent efficiency, when supplied by a single 6-in. diameter jet. Use both U.S. customary and SI units. Estimate the wheel diameter.

10.108 According to a spokesperson for Pacific Gas & Electric Company, the Tiger Creek plant, located east of Jackson. California, is one of 71 PG&E hydroelectric powerplants. The plant has 1219 ft of gross head, consumes 750 cfs of water, is rated at 60 MW, and operates at 58 MW. The plant is claimed to produce 968 kW · hr/(acre · ft) of water and 336.4×10^6 kW · hr/yr of operation. Estimate the net head at the site, the turbine specific speed, and its efficiency. Comment on the internal consistency of these data.

10.109 Design the piping system to supply a water turbine from a mountain reservoir. The reservoir surface is 1000 ft above the turbine site. The turbine efficiency is 80 percent, and it must produce 35 hp of mechanical power. Define the minimum standard-size pipe required to supply water to the turbine and the required volume flow rate of water. Discuss the effects of turbine efficiency, pipe roughness, and installing a diffuser at the turbine exit on the performance of the installation.

10.110 The National Aeronautics & Space Administration (NASA) and the U.S. Department of Energy (DOE) co-sponsor a large demonstration wind turbine generator at Plum Brook, near Sandusky, Ohio [41]. The turbine has two blades, with $D = 38$ m, and delivers maximum power when the wind speed is above $V = 29$ km/hr. It is designed to produce 100 kW with powertrain efficiency of 0.75. The rotor is designed to operate at a constant speed of 40 rpm in winds over 6 mph by controlling system load and adjusting blade angles. For the maximum power condition, estimate the rotor tip speed and power coefficient.

10.111 A small hydraulic impulse turbine is supplied with water through a penstock with diameter D and length L; the jet diameter is d. The elevation difference between the reservoir surface and nozzle centerline is Z. The nozzle head loss coefficient is K_{nozzle} and the loss coefficient from the reservoir to the penstock entrance is $K_{entrance}$. Determine the water jet speed, the volume flow rate, and the hydraulic power of the jet, for the case where $Z = 300$ ft, $L = 1000$ ft, $D = 6$ in., $K_{entrance} = 0.5$, $K_{nozzle} = 0.04$, and $d = 2$ in., if the pipe is made from commercial steel. Plot the jet power as a function of jet diameter to determine the optimum jet diameter and the resulting hydraulic power of the jet. Comment on the effects of varying the loss coefficients and pipe roughness.

10.112 A model of an American multiblade farm windmill is to be built for display. The model, with $D = 1$ m, is to develop full power at $V = 10$ m/s wind speed. Calculate the angular speed of the model for optimum power generation. Estimate the power output.

10.113 A typical American multiblade farm windmill has $D = 7$ ft and is designed to produce maximum power in winds with $V = 15$ mph. Estimate the rate of water delivery, as a function of the height to which the water is pumped, for this windmill.

10.114 The largest known Darrieus vertical axis wind turbine was built by the U.S. Department of Energy near Sandia, New Mexico [42]. This machine is 60 ft tall and 30 ft in diameter; the area swept by the rotor is almost 1200 ft². Estimate the maximum power this wind turbine can produce in a 20 mph wind.

10.115 Aluminum extrusions, patterned after NACA symmetric airfoil sections, frequently are used to form Darrieus wind turbine "blades." Below are section lift and drag coefficient data [47] for a NACA 0012 section, tested at Re $= 6 \times 10^6$ with standard roughness (the section stalled for $\alpha > 12°$):

Angle of attack, α (deg)	0	2	4	6	8	10	12
Lift coefficient, C_L (—)	0	0.23	0.45	0.68	0.82	0.94	1.02
Drag coefficient. C_D (—)	0.0098	0.0100	0.0119	0.0147	0.0194	—	—

Analyze the air flow relative to a blade element of a Darrieus wind turbine rotating about its troposkien axis. Develop a numerical model for the blade element. Calculate the power coefficient developed by the blade element as a function of tip-speed ratio. Compare your result with the general trend of power output for Darrieus rotors shown in Fig. 10.45.

10.116 Lift and drag data for the NACA 23015 airfoil section are presented in Fig. 9.17. Consider a two-blade horizontal-axis propeller wind turbine with NACA 23015 blade section. Analyze the air flow relative to a blade element of the rotating wind turbine. Develop a numerical model for the blade element. Calculate the power coefficient developed by the blade element as a function of tip-speed ratio. Compare your result with the general trend of power output for high-speed two-bladed turbine rotors shown in Fig. 10.45.

Chapter 11

Open-Channel Flow

11-1 STEADY UNIFORM FLOW

11-2 SPECIFIC ENERGY, MOMENTUM EQUATION, AND SPECIFIC FORCE

11-3 STEADY, GRADUALLY VARIED FLOW

11-4 RAPIDLY VARIED FLOW

11-5 DISCHARGE MEASUREMENT

11-6 SUMMARY AND USEFUL EQUATIONS

Open channels are conduits for flows that have a free surface or boundary exposed to the atmosphere. *Open-channel flow* refers to a liquid flow whose surface is exposed to the atmosphere. Flow in a pipe conduit that is not flowing full, thus having a free surface, is also an open-channel flow. The motion of flowing liquid in an open channel is usually caused by gravitational effects, with a pressure distribution that is generally hydrostatic in the vertical direction. Open-channel flows are almost always

turbulent and unaffected by surface tension; however, flows can be density stratified. Some examples of open-channel flows are:

✓ Rivulets flowing across a field
✓ Flows in gutters along rooftops or streets
✓ Flows in water supply, irrigation, and flood control channels
✓ Flows in streams and rivers.

Throughout the history of humankind, open channels have been very important for the purposes of water supply and flood control.

The topic of open-channel flow is covered in detail in a number of texts [1–7]; in this chapter we will do a brief survey of the topic and discuss flows that do not vary, that gradually vary, and that rapidly vary as they progress along a channel. (The material for this chapter is a condensed version of Chapter 5 of *Water Resources Engineering* by Mays [8].)

11-1 STEADY UNIFORM FLOW

This section describes the continuity, energy, and momentum equations for steady uniform flow in open channels. The physical picture of uniform flow (Fig. 11.1a), in which the channel cross-section slope and boundary roughness are constant along the length of the channel is a special case of the more general case shown in Fig. 11.1b.

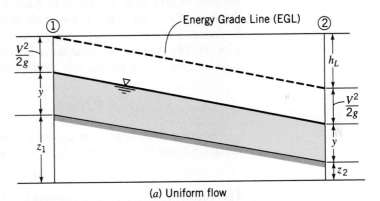

(a) Uniform flow

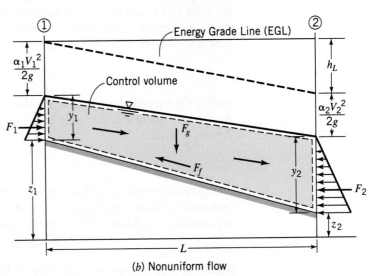

(b) Nonuniform flow

Fig. 11.1 Open-channel flow: uniform and nonuniform flow.

In uniform flow the water depth is constant. The expression *uniform flow* in this chapter has a different meaning than in earlier chapters. In earlier chapters it meant that the *velocity* was uniform *at a section* of the flow; in this chapter we use it to mean that the *flow* is the same *at all sections*. This means that the velocity may or may not be uniform at the sections—we may have a velocity gradient at all of the sections. However, the flow is one-dimensional; it is essentially fully developed. Hence for the flow shown in Fig. 11.1a, we have $A_1 = A_2$ (cross-section areas), $Q_1 = Q_2$ (flow rates), $\overline{V}_1 = \overline{V}_2$ (average velocity, $\overline{V} = Q/A$), and $y_1 = y_2$ (flow depth). The depth of flow in uniform open-channel flow is also referred to as the *normal depth*. Figure 11.1b shows steady, gradually varied (nonuniform) flow, by which we mean that flow conditions change in the direction of flow; we will use this control volume to derive the energy equation for open-channel flow and will discuss nonuniform flow in Section 11-3. Figure 11.2 shows an open-channel flow, in an aqueduct of the Central Arizona Project.

Energy

The energy equation for open-channel flow can be derived (using the control volume of Fig. 11.1b) in a similar manner as the energy equation for pipe flow.

The energy equation for one-dimensional flow in an open channel is the same as that for pipe flow discussed in Chapter 8. We use the following form:

$$\left(\frac{p_1}{\rho g} + \alpha_1 \frac{\overline{V}_1^2}{2g} + z_1\right) - \left(\frac{p_2}{\rho g} + \alpha_2 \frac{\overline{V}_2^2}{2g} + z_2\right) = H_l \qquad (8.30)$$

(Note that for convenience we have dropped the T subscript in H_{l_T} in Eq. 8.30.) As in the case of pipe flow, the effect of friction is to decrease the mechanical energy of the flow. We recall that p is the static pressure, $\overline{V}$ is the average velocity, z is the elevation, and α is the kinetic energy coefficient (usually we have turbulent flow, so $\alpha \approx 1$). The pressure distribution is assumed to be hydrostatic, so that $p = \rho g y$ at each location, where y is the flow depth. Hence the energy equation becomes

$$y_1 + z_1 + \alpha_1 \frac{\overline{V}_1^2}{2g} = y_2 + z_2 + \alpha_2 \frac{\overline{V}_2^2}{2g} + H_l \qquad (11.1)$$

Equation 11.1 applies to constant depth or varying depth flows. For constant depth (uniform) flows, we have $\overline{V}_1 = \overline{V}_2 = V$, and $y_1 = y_2$, so

$$H_l = z_1 - z_2$$

This equation states that for a constant depth (uniform) flow the flow rate is such that the head loss is equal to the decrease in height of the channel. By dividing both sides by L, the length of the control volume (channel), the following headloss per unit length of channel, S_f, is obtained as

$$S_f = \frac{H_l}{L} = \frac{z_1 - z_2}{L}$$

so that the *friction slope equals the channel bottom slope*. The channel bottom slope $S_0 = \tan \theta$, where θ is the angle of inclination. If θ is small ($<10°$), then $\tan \theta \approx \sin \theta = (z_1 - z_2)/L$.

Momentum

The forces acting upon the fluid control volume in Figure 11.1b are friction, gravity, and hydrostatic pressure. The friction force, F_f, is the product of the wall shear stress τ_0 and the area over which it acts, PL, where P is the wetted perimeter of the cross-section, thus

$$F_f = -\tau_0 PL$$

where the negative sign indicates that the friction force acts opposite to the direction of flow. The gravity force F_g relates to the weight of the fluid γAL, where γ is the specific weight of the fluid (weight per unit volume). The gravity force on the fluid is the

Fig. 11.2 Hayden-Rhodes Aqueduct, Central Arizona Project. (Courtesy of the U.S. Bureau of Reclamation (1985), photograph by Joe Madrigal Jr.)

component of the weight acting in the direction of flow, that is,

$$F_g = \gamma AL \sin \theta$$

The hydrostatic forces are denoted as F_1 and F_2, and are identical for uniform flow so that $F_1 - F_2 = 0$.

The general form of the integral momentum equation in the x direction is

$$F_x = F_{S_x} + F_{B_x} = \frac{\partial}{\partial t} \int_{\text{CV}} u \rho \, d\Psi + \int_{\text{CS}} u \rho \vec{V} \cdot d\vec{A} \qquad (4.18a)$$

The right side of Eq. 4.18a is zero because the flow is steady and conditions are the same at inlet and exit; there is no change of momentum for the control volume. For the left side, the surface forces consist of F_1, F_2, and F_f and the body force is F_g. Hence we obtain

$$F_1 + F_g + F_f - F_2 = 0$$

or, since $F_1 = F_2$, then $F_g + F_f = 0$ and so

$$\gamma AL \sin\theta - \tau_0 PL = 0$$

For small θ, $S_0 \approx \sin\theta$ so

$$\gamma ALS_0 = \tau_0 PL \qquad (11.2)$$

which states that for steady uniform flow the friction and gravity forces are in balance and $S_0 = S_f$. Solving Eq. 11.2 for the wall shear stress (for steady uniform flow) yields

$$\tau_0 = \frac{\gamma ALS_0}{PL}$$

or

$$\tau_0 = \gamma RS_0 = \gamma RS_f \qquad (11.3)$$

where $R = A/P$ is the hydraulic radius. (Note that the hydraulic diameter D_h defined in Eq. 8.50 is *four* times the hydraulic radius, $D_h = 4R$!) Equation 11.3 expresses the effects of friction through the wall shear stress τ_0 as represented from a momentum viewpoint and through the rate of energy dissipation S_f represented from an energy viewpoint. Consequently Eq. 11.3 expresses a linkage between the momentum and energy principles.

The shear stress τ_0 for fully turbulent flow can be expressed as a function of density, velocity, and resistance coefficient C_f as

$$\tau_0 = C_f \rho \frac{V^2}{2} \qquad (11.4)$$

Equating Eqs. 11.3 and 11.4 yields

$$C_f \rho \frac{V^2}{2} = \gamma RS_0$$

and solving for the velocity gives

$$V = \sqrt{\frac{2g}{C_f}} \sqrt{RS_0} \qquad (11.5)$$

Defining $C = \sqrt{2g/C_f}$, Eq. 11.5 can be simplified to the well known *Chezy equation*

$$V = C\sqrt{RS_0} \qquad (11.6)$$

where C is referred to as the *Chezy coefficient*.

Robert Manning [11] derived the following empirical relation for C based upon experiments:

$$C = \frac{1}{n} R^{1/6} \qquad (11.7)$$

where n is the Manning's roughness coefficient. Values of n are listed in Table 11.1. Values of n for natural channels have been also published by the U.S. Geological Survey [12]. Substituting C from Eq. 11.7 into Eq. 11.6 results in the *Manning equation*

$$V = \frac{1}{n} R^{2/3} S_0^{1/2} \tag{11.8}$$

which is valid for SI units and $S_0 = S_f$.

Manning's equation in SI units can also be expressed as

$$Q = \frac{1}{n} A R^{2/3} S_0^{1/2} \tag{11.9}$$

For V in ft/sec and R in feet (U.S. Customary units), Eq. 11.8 can be rewritten as

$$V = \frac{1.49}{n} R^{2/3} S_0^{1/2} \tag{11.10}$$

and Eq. 11.9 can be written as

$$Q = \frac{1.49}{n} A R^{2/3} S_0^{1/2} \tag{11.11}$$

where A is in ft^2 and $S_0 = S_f$. Note that many of the above equations, and many that follow, are "engineering" equations; that is, *the user needs to be aware of the required units of each term in the equation*. Table 11.2 lists the geometric function for channel elements (including other data we will use later).

To determine the normal depth (for uniform flow), Eq. 11.9 or Eq. 11.11 can be solved for a specified discharge. Because the original shear stress τ_0 in Eq. 11.4 is for fully turbulent flow, Manning's equation is valid only for fully turbulent flow. Henderson [2] presented the following criterion for fully turbulent flow in an open channel:

$$n^6 \sqrt{RS_f} \geq 1.9 \times 10^{-3} \quad (R \text{ in feet}) \tag{11.12a}$$

$$n^6 \sqrt{RS_f} \geq 1.1 \times 10^{-3} \quad (R \text{ in meters}) \tag{11.12b}$$

TABLE 11.1 A Selection of Manning's Roughness Coefficients

		Manning's n		
		Depth Ranges		
Lining Category	Lining Type	0–0.5 ft (0–15 cm)	0.5–2.0 ft (15–60 cm)	>2.0 ft (>60 cm)
Rigid	Concrete	0.015	0.013	0.013
	Grouted riprap	0.040	0.030	0.028
	Stone masonry	0.042	0.032	0.030
	Soil cement	0.025	0.022	0.020
	Asphalt	0.018	0.016	0.016
Unlined	Bare soil	0.023	0.020	0.020
	Rock cut	0.045	0.035	0.025
Temporary	Woven paper net	0.016	0.015	0.015
	Jute net	0.028	0.022	0.019
	Fiberglass roving	0.028	0.021	0.019
	Straw with net	0.065	0.033	0.025
	Curled wood mat	0.066	0.035	0.028
	Synthetic mat	0.036	0.025	0.021
Gravel riprap	1 in (2.5 cm) D_{50}	0.044	0.033	0.030
	2 in (5 cm) D_{50}	0.066	0.041	0.034
Rock riprap	6 in (15 cm) D_{50}	0.104	0.069	0.035
	12 in (30 cm) D_{50}	—	0.078	0.040

Source: [9], [10]

TABLE 11.2 Geometric Functions for Channel Elements

Section:	Rectangle	Trapezoid	Triangle	Circle

Area A	$B_w y$	$(B_w + zy)y$	zy^2	$\dfrac{1}{8}(\theta - \sin\theta)d_o^2$
Wetted perimeter P	$B_w + 2y$	$B_w + 2y\sqrt{1+z^2}$	$2y\sqrt{1+z^2}$	$\dfrac{1}{2}\theta d_o$
Hydraulic radius R	$\dfrac{B_w y}{B_w + 2y}$	$\dfrac{(B_w + zy)y}{B_w + 2y\sqrt{1+z^2}}$	$\dfrac{zy}{2y\sqrt{1+z^2}}$	$\dfrac{1}{4}\left(1 - \dfrac{\sin\theta}{\theta}\right)d_o$
Top width B	B_w	$B_w + 2zy$	$2zy$	$\left[\sin\left(\dfrac{\theta}{2}\right)\right]d_o$ or $2\sqrt{y(d_o - y)}$
$\dfrac{2dR}{3Rdy} + \dfrac{1}{A}\dfrac{dA}{dy}$	$\dfrac{5B_w + 6y}{3y(B_w + 2y)}$	$\dfrac{(B_w + 2zy)(5B_w + 6y\sqrt{1+z^2}) + 4zy^2\sqrt{1+z^2}}{3y(B_w + zy)(B_w + 2y\sqrt{1+z^2})}$	$\dfrac{8}{3y}$	$\dfrac{4(2\sin\theta + 3\theta - 5\theta\cos\theta)}{3d_o\theta(\theta - \sin\theta)\sin(\theta/2)}$
				where $\theta = 2\cos^{-1}\left(1 - \dfrac{2y}{d_o}\right)$

Source: Chow [1] (with additions).

EXAMPLE 11.1   Flow Rate in a Rectangular Channel

An 8-ft wide rectangular channel with a bed slope of 0.0004 ft/ft has a depth of flow of 2 ft. Assuming steady uniform flow, determine the discharge in the channel. The Manning roughness coefficient is $n = 0.015$.

GIVEN: Geometry of rectangular channel and flow depth.

FIND: Flow rate Q.

SOLUTION:
Use the appropriate form of Manning's equation. For a problem in U.S. customary units, this is Eq. 11.11.

Governing equations: $Q = \dfrac{1.49}{n}AR^{2/3}S_0^{1/2}$ $R = \dfrac{B_w y}{B_w + 2y}$ (Table 11.2)

Using this equation with the given data

$$Q = \frac{1.49}{n}AR^{2/3}S_0^{1/2}$$

$$= \frac{1.49}{0.015} \times \left(8\text{ ft} \times 2\text{ ft}\right) \times \left(\frac{8\text{ ft} \times 2\text{ ft}}{8\text{ ft} + 2\times 2\text{ ft}}\right)^{2/3} \times \left(0.0004\,\frac{\text{ft}}{\text{ft}}\right)^{1/2}$$

$$Q = 38.5 \text{ ft}^3/\text{s} \qquad\qquad\qquad\qquad\qquad\qquad\qquad Q$$

This Example demonstrates use of Manning's equation to solve for flow rate Q. Note that as this is an "engineering" equation, the units do not cancel.

EXAMPLE 11.2   Normal Depth in a Rectangular Channel

Determine the normal depth (for uniform flow) if the channel described in Example 11.1 has a flow rate of 100 cfs.

GIVEN: Geometric data on rectangular channel of Example 11.1.

FIND: Normal depth for a flow rate $Q = 100 \text{ ft}^3/\text{s}$.

SOLUTION:

Use the appropriate form of Manning's equation. For a problem in U.S. customary units, this is Eq. 11.11.

Governing equations:

$$Q = \frac{1.49}{n} AR^{2/3} S_0^{1/2} \qquad R = \frac{B_w y}{B_w + 2y} \qquad \text{(Table 11.2)}$$

Combining these equations

$$Q = \frac{1.49}{n} AR^{2/3} S_0^{1/2} = \frac{1.49}{n} (B_w y) \left(\frac{B_w y}{B_w + 2y} \right)^{2/3} S_0^{1/2}$$

Hence, after rearranging

$$\left(\frac{Q \cdot n}{1.49 \, B_w^{5/3} S_0^{1/2}} \right)^3 (B_w + 2y)^2 = y^5$$

Substituting $Q = 100 \text{ ft}^3/\text{s}$, $n = 0.015$, $B_w = 8$ ft, and $S_0 = 0.0004$ and simplifying (remembering this is an "engineering" equation, in which we insert values without units)

$$3.89(8 + 2y)^2 = y^5$$

This nonlinear equation can be solved for y using a numerical method such as the Newton-Raphson method (or better yet using your calculator's solving feature or *Excel*'s *Goal Seek* or *Solver*!), we find

$y = 3.94 \text{ ft} \longleftarrow$ ⟍ $\overline{\qquad\qquad\qquad\qquad\qquad\qquad\qquad\qquad\qquad}^{\; y}$

> **Notes:**
> ✓ This Example demonstrates use of Manning's equation for finding the normal depth.
> ✓ This relatively simple physical problem still involved solving a non-linear algebraic equation.
> 🖱 The *Excel* workbook for this problem can be used for solving similar problems.

11-2   SPECIFIC ENERGY, MOMENTUM EQUATION, AND SPECIFIC FORCE

We are now ready to see what happens when the flow does *not* remain constant depth. To help with this, we define some useful terms—specific energy and specific force—and derive the appropriate form of the momentum equation.

Specific Energy

The *total head* or *energy head*, H, at any location in an open-channel flow can be defined from Eq. 11.1 as

$$H = y + z + \frac{V^2}{2g} \qquad (11.13)$$

which assumes that the velocity distribution at all sections is uniform (i.e., the kinetic energy coefficient $\alpha = 1$) and the pressure distribution is hydrostatic (i.e., $p = \gamma y$).

Using the channel bottom as the datum (i.e., $z = 0$), then define the total head above the channel bottom as the *specific energy*,

$$E = y + \frac{V^2}{2g} \qquad (11.14)$$

Using continuity ($V = Q/A$), the specific energy can be expressed in terms of the discharge as

$$E = y + \frac{Q^2}{2gA^2} \qquad (11.15)$$

The specific energy is the energy of the flow due to its depth and speed. *Specific energy curves*, such as are shown in Figs. 11.3 and 11.4, can be derived using Eq. 11.15. We make two comments here. First, in Eq. 11.15, we need to be aware that the flow area A itself is a monotonic function of depth y; for any channel shape, A increases with y. Hence, Eq. 11.15 indicates that the specific energy is a combination of a linear increase with depth and a hyperbolic-type decrease with depth. This explains the nature of the curves shown in the figures. Second, it is interesting to note that for a given flow with specific energy E and flow rate Q, *there are two possible depths y for uniform flow*. Figure 11.3 shows an example of this; given energy $E = E_1 = E_2$ and flow rate Q, we can have flow at depth y_1 or depth y_2; the first flow has large depth and is moving slowly, and the second flow is shallow but fast moving. We will see later that we can switch from one flow to another.

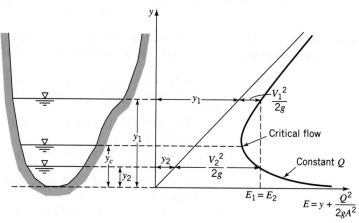

Fig. 11.3 Specific energy.

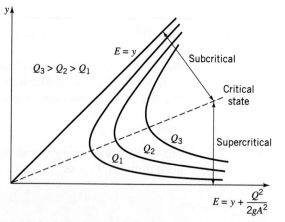

Fig. 11.4 Specific energy showing subcritical and supercritical flow ranges.

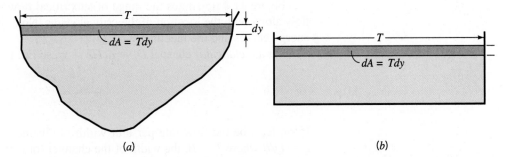

Fig. 11.5 Definition of top width ($T = dA/dy$). (a) Natural channel; (b) Rectangular channel.

Critical flow occurs when the specific energy is minimum for a given discharge (i.e., $dE/dy = 0$), so that

$$\frac{dE}{dy} = 1 - \frac{Q^2}{gA^3}\frac{dA}{dy} = 0 \tag{11.16}$$

We introduce the notion of the *top width T*. By definition, the incremental increase in cross-sectional area of flow dA, due to an incremental increase in the depth dy, is $dA = Tdy$ (see Fig. 11.5), so that $T = dA/dy$. Hence Eq. 11.16 can be expressed as

$$1 - \frac{TQ^2}{gA^3} = 0$$

or

$$\frac{TQ^2}{gA^3} = 1$$

To denote critical conditions use T_c, A_c, V_c, and y_c, so

$$\frac{T_c Q^2}{gA_c^3} = 1 \tag{11.17}$$

or

$$\frac{V_c^2}{g} = \frac{A_c}{T_c} \tag{11.18}$$

Equation 11.17 or 11.18 can be used to determine the critical depth and/or the critical velocity.

Rearranging Eq. 11.18 yields

$$\frac{V_c^2}{g(A_c/T_c)} = 1$$

The *hydraulic depth* is defined as $D = A/T$ so Eq. 11.18 becomes

$$\frac{V_c^2}{gD_c} = 1$$

or

$$\frac{V_c}{\sqrt{gD_c}} = 1 \tag{11.19}$$

This is basically the *Froude number*, *Fr*, which is 1 at critical flow:

$$Fr = \frac{V}{\sqrt{gD}} \begin{cases} < 1 \text{ subcritical flow} \\ = 1 \text{ critical flow} \\ > 1 \text{ supercritical flow} \end{cases} \tag{11.20}$$

Figure 11.4 illustrates the range of subcritical flow and the range of supercritical flow along with the location of the critical states. Note the relationship of the specific energy curves and the fact that $Q_3 > Q_2 > Q_1$.

For a *rectangular* channel $D_c = A_c/T_c = y_c$, so Eq. 11.19 for critical flow becomes

$$\frac{V_c}{\sqrt{gy_c}} = 1 \qquad (11.21)$$

If we let q be the flow rate per unit width of channel for a rectangular channel, i.e. $q = Q/B$ where $T = B$, the width of the channel (or $q = Q/T$), then Eq. 11.17 can be rearranged, $T_cQ^2/(gT_c^3 y_c^3) = q^2/(gy_c^3) = 1$, and solved for y_c to yield

$$y_c = \left(\frac{q^2}{g}\right)^{1/3} \qquad (11.22)$$

EXAMPLE 11.3   Critical Depth for a Rectangular Channel

Compute the critical depth for the channel and flow rate in Example 11.1.

GIVEN: Geometry of rectangular channel and flow rate of Example 11.1.

FIND: Critical depth.

SOLUTION:
Use the critical flow value of the Froude number (Eq. 11.20), expressed for a rectangular channel (Eq. 11.21); alternatively, use Eq. 11.22.

Governing equations: $\dfrac{V_c}{\sqrt{gy_c}} = 1$ (11.21)

or, alternatively,

$$y_c = \left(\frac{q^2}{g}\right)^{1/3} \qquad (11.22)$$

Using Eq. 11.21, $V = \dfrac{Q}{A} = \dfrac{Q}{By_c} = \sqrt{gy_c}$

where $B = 8$ ft is the channel width and $Q = 100$ ft^3/s is the flow rate. Solving for y_c

$$y_c = \left(\frac{Q}{B\sqrt{g}}\right)^{2/3}$$

$$= \left(100 \; \frac{\text{ft}^3}{\text{s}} \times \frac{1}{8 \; \text{ft}} \times \frac{\text{s}}{\sqrt{32.2 \; \text{ft}^{1/2}}}\right)^{2/3}$$

$$y_c = 1.69 \; \text{ft}$$

Alternatively, from Eq. 11.22, $y_c = \left(\dfrac{q^2}{g}\right)^{1/3}$

where q is the flow per unit width of the rectangular channel

$$q = \frac{Q}{B} = \frac{100 \; \text{ft}^3}{\text{s}} \times \frac{1}{8 \; \text{ft}} = 12.5 (\text{ft}^3/\text{s})/\text{ft}$$

Hence

$$y_c = \left(\frac{q^2}{g}\right)^{1/3} = \left(12.5^2 \left(\frac{\text{ft}^3}{\text{s} \cdot \text{ft}}\right)^2 \times \frac{\text{s}^2}{32.2 \; \text{ft}}\right)^{1/3}$$

$$y_c = 1.69 \; \text{ft} \quad \longleftarrow \hspace{5cm} y_c$$

> This Example demonstrates computation of the critical depth for flow in a rectangular channel.

EXAMPLE 11.4   Specific Energy Curves for a Rectangular Channel

For a rectangular channel of 20 ft width, construct a family of specific energy curves for $Q = 0$, 50, 100, and 300 cfs. Draw the locus of the critical depth points on these curves. For each flow rate, what is the minimum specific energy found from these curves?

GIVEN: Rectangular channel and range of flow rates.

FIND: Curves of specific energy, including locus of critical depth points. For each flow rate, find the minimum specific energy.

SOLUTION:

Use the flow rate form of the specific energy equation (Eq. 11.15) for generating the curves. The minimum specific energy occurs at critical depth (obtained from Eq. 11.22).

Governing equations:

$$E = y + \frac{Q^2}{2gA^2} \tag{11.15}$$

$$y_c = \left(\frac{q^2}{g}\right)^{1/3} \tag{11.22}$$

For the specific energy curves, express E as a function of depth y

$$E = y + \frac{Q^2}{2gA^2} = y + \frac{Q^2}{2g(By)^2} = y + \left(\frac{Q^2}{2gB^2}\right)\frac{1}{y^2}$$

The table and corresponding graph were generated from this equation using *Excel*.

Computed Specific Energy Values

Depth, y (ft)	Specific Energy, E (ft-lb/lb)			
	Q = 0	Q = 50	Q = 100	Q = 300
0.5	0.50	0.89	2.05	14.86
0.6	0.60	0.87	1.68	10.57
0.8	0.80	0.95	1.41	6.41
1.0	1.00	1.10	1.39	4.59
1.2	1.20	1.27	1.47	3.69
1.4	1.40	1.45	1.60	3.23
1.6	1.60	1.64	1.75	3.00
1.8	1.80	1.83	1.92	2.91
2.0	2.00	2.02	2.10	2.90
2.2	2.20	2.22	2.28	2.94
2.4	2.40	2.42	2.47	3.02
2.6	2.60	2.61	2.66	3.13
2.8	2.80	2.81	2.85	3.26
3.0	3.00	3.01	3.04	3.40
3.5	3.50	3.51	3.53	3.79
4.0	4.00	4.01	4.02	4.22
4.5	4.50	4.50	4.52	4.68
5.0	5.00	5.00	5.02	5.14

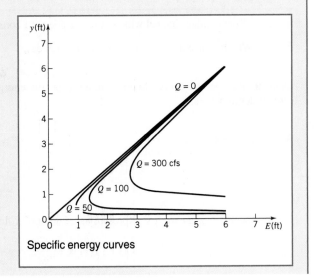

Specific energy curves

For the minimum specific energy we first need the critical depth.

For $Q = 50$ ft^3/s:

$$y_c = \left(\frac{q^2}{g}\right)^{1/3} = \left(\frac{(Q/B)^2}{g}\right)^{1/3} = \left(\frac{Q^2}{gB^2}\right)^{1/3}$$

$$= \left[50^2\left(\frac{ft^3}{s}\right)^2 \times \frac{s^2}{32.2\,ft} \times \frac{1}{20^2\,ft^2}\right]^{1/3}$$

$$y_c = 0.579\ \text{ft}$$

Then the minimum specific energy is

$$E_{min} = y_c + \left(\frac{Q^2}{2gB^2}\right)\frac{1}{y_c^2}$$

$$= 0.579\ \text{ft} + \left[50^2\left(\frac{ft^3}{s}\right)^2 \times \frac{1}{2} \times \frac{s^2}{32.2\,ft} \times \frac{1}{20^2\,ft^2}\right] \times \frac{1}{0.579^2\,ft^2}$$

$$E_{min} = 0.869\ \text{ft}$$

Repeating these calculations for $Q = 100$ ft^3/s and $Q = 300$ ft^3/s, and summarizing

For $Q = 50$ ft^3/s $y_c = 0.579$ ft $E_{min} = 0.869$ ft

For $Q = 100$ ft^3/s $y_c = 0.919$ ft $E_{min} = 1.379$ ft

For $Q = 300$ ft^3/s $y_c = 1.91$ ft $E_{min} = 2.868$ ft   ← E_{min}

> This Example demonstrates computation of the specific energy curves, and finding the minimum specific energy.
>
> 🖱 The *Excel* workbook for this problem can be used for solving similar problems.

EXAMPLE 11.5   Critical Depth for Flow in a Rectangular Channel

A rectangular channel 2 m wide has a flow of 2.4 m^3/s at a depth of 1.0 m. Determine if critical depth occurs at (a) a section where a hump of height $\Delta z = 20$ cm is installed across the channel bed, (b) a side wall constriction (with no humps) reducing the channel width to 1.7 m, and (c) both the hump and side wall constrictions combined. Neglect head losses of the hump and constriction caused by friction, expansion, and contraction.

GIVEN: Rectangular channel with a hump, a side wall constriction, or both.

FIND: Whether or not critical flow occurs in each case.

SOLUTION:

Compare the specific energy to the minimum specific energy for the given flow rate in each case to establish whether or not critical depth occurs.

Governing equations:

$$E = y + \frac{Q^2}{2gA^2} \tag{11.15}$$

$$y_c = \left(\frac{q^2}{g}\right)^{1/3} \tag{11.22}$$

For the specific energy we first express E as a function of flow per unit width q

$$E = y + \frac{Q^2}{2gA^2} = y + \frac{Q^2}{2g(By)^2} = y + \left(\frac{q^2}{2g}\right)\frac{1}{y^2}$$

The minimum specific energy, E_{min}, occurs when $y = y_c$. Hence, combining the above equation and Eq. 11.22

$$E_{min} = y_c + \left(\frac{q^2}{2g}\right)\frac{1}{y_c^2} = \left(\frac{q^2}{g}\right)^{1/3} + \left(\frac{q^2}{2g}\right)\left(\frac{g}{q^2}\right)^{2/3}$$

$$E_{min} = \frac{3}{2}\left(\frac{q^2}{g}\right)^{1/3} \quad \text{or} \quad E_{min} = \frac{3}{2}y_c$$

This important result is illustrated in the figure, which shows the normal depth y plotted against specific energy E for a given flow rate per unit width q.

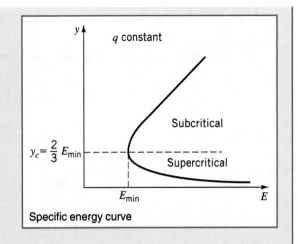

Specific energy curve

(a) For a hump of $\Delta z = 20$ cm:
We can define a quantity Δz_{crit} as the change in elevation that will cause the flow to be at critical depth by comparing the actual flow specific energy to the critical specific energy

$$E = E_{min} + \Delta z_{crit}$$

or

$$\Delta z_{crit} = E - E_{min}$$

For the given flow

$$E = y + \left(\frac{Q^2}{2gB^2}\right)\frac{1}{y^2}$$

$$= 1.0 \text{ m} + \left[2.4^2\left(\frac{m^3}{s}\right)^2 \times \frac{1}{2} \times \frac{s^2}{9.81 \text{ m}} \times \frac{1}{2^2 \text{ m}^2}\right] \times \frac{1}{1.0^2 \text{ m}^2}$$

$$E = 1.073 \text{ m}$$

On the other hand

$$E_{min} = \frac{3}{2}\left(\frac{q^2}{g}\right)^{1/3} = \frac{3}{2}\left(\frac{(Q/B)^2}{g}\right)^{1/3} = \frac{3}{2}\left(\frac{Q^2}{gB^2}\right)^{1/3}$$

$$= \frac{3}{2}\left[2.4^2\left(\frac{m^3}{s}\right)^2 \times \frac{s^2}{9.81 \text{ m}} \times \frac{1}{2^2 \text{ m}^2}\right]^{1/3}$$

$$E_{min} = 0.791 \text{ m}$$

Hence
$$\Delta z_{crit} = E - E_{min} = 1.073 - 0.791 \text{ m} = 0.282 \text{ m}$$

This shows that an elevation change of $\Delta z_{crit} = 0.282$ m is required to attain critical conditions. The hump height is $\Delta z = 20$ cm $= 0.2$ m < 0.282 m $= \Delta z_{crit}$.
Hence the hump is insufficient to make the flow reach critical state. ←——————————————————————

(b) A side wall constriction (with no humps) reducing the channel width to 1.7 m:
For flow at the constriction ($B = 1.7$ m)

$$E_{min} = \frac{3}{2}\left(\frac{q^2}{g}\right)^{1/3} = \frac{3}{2}\left(\frac{Q^2}{gB^2}\right)^{1/3}$$

$$= \frac{3}{2}\left[2.4^2\left(\frac{m^3}{s}\right)^2 \times \frac{s^2}{9.81 \text{ m}} \times \frac{1}{1.7^2 \text{ m}^2}\right]^{1/3}$$

$$E_{min} = 0.882 \text{ m}$$

On the other hand, for the given flow we still have $E = 1.073$ m. Note that because energy losses are negligible (by assumption), the specific energy in the constriction and upstream of the constriction must be equal.

Hence at the constriction $\qquad E = 1.073 \text{ m} > 0.882 \text{ m} = E_{\min}$ ←───────────────

so critical flow does not occur.

We might inquire as to what constriction *would* cause critical flow. To find this, solve

$$E_{\min} = \frac{3}{2} \left(\frac{q^2}{g} \right)^{1/3} = \frac{3}{2} \left(\frac{Q^2}{gB^2} \right)^{1/3}$$

for B with $\qquad\qquad\qquad E_{\min} = E = 1.073 \text{ m}.$

Hence

$$\frac{Q^2}{gB_c^2} = \left(\frac{2}{3} E_{\min} \right)^3$$

$$B_c = \frac{Q}{\sqrt{\dfrac{8}{27} gE_{\min}^3}}$$

$$= \left(\frac{27}{8} \right)^{1/2} \times \frac{2.4}{} \left(\frac{\text{m}^3}{\text{s}} \right) \times \frac{\text{s}}{9.81^{1/2} \text{ m}^{1/2}} \times \frac{1}{1.073^{3/2} \text{ m}^{3/2}}$$

$$B_c = 1.27 \text{ m}$$

where B_c is the width required to attain critical conditions.

(c) For a hump of $\Delta z = 20$ cm and the constriction to $B = 1.7$ m:

We have already seen in case (a) that the hump is insufficient by itself to create critical conditions. From case (b) we saw that at the constriction the minimum specific energy is $E_{\min} = 0.882$ m rather than $E_{\min} = 0.791$ m in the main flow. Hence we can compute a new value for Δz_{crit} (the change in elevation that will cause the flow to be at critical depth)

$$\Delta z_{\text{crit}} = E - E_{\min}$$

For the constriction

$$\Delta z_{\text{crit}} = E - E_{\min} = 1.073 - 0.882 \text{ m} = 0.191 \text{ m}$$

This shows that an elevation change of $\Delta z_{\text{crit}} = 0.191$ m is required to attain critical conditions at the constriction. The hump height is $\Delta z = 20$ cm $= 0.2$ m > 0.191 m $= \Delta z_{\text{crit}}$.

Hence the hump and constriction together are sufficient to make the flow reach critical state. ←───────────────

This Example illustrates how to determine whether or not a channel hump or constriction, or both, lead to critical flow conditions.

Momentum Equation for Varying Flow

For a short horizontal reach of channel (Fig. 11.6), we can apply the x component of the momentum equation for a control volume, Eq. 4.18a,

$$F_x = F_{S_x} + F_{B_x} = \frac{\partial}{\partial t} \int_{\text{CV}} u \, \rho \, d\forall + \int_{\text{CS}} u \, \rho \vec{V} \cdot d\vec{A} \qquad (4.18a)$$

The unsteady term on the right of Eq. 4.18a is zero for steady flow. For the momentum flux term, the momentum entering from upstream is $\rho \beta_1 \overline{V}_1 Q$ and the momentum leaving the control volume is $\rho \beta_2 \overline{V}_2 Q$, where β is called the *momentum correction factor* that accounts for the nonuniformity of velocity,

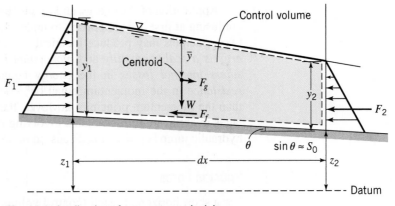

Fig. 11.6 Application of momentum principle.

$$\int_{CS} u\rho \vec{V} \cdot d\vec{A} = \rho\beta\overline{V}Q$$

(see Problem 8.63 for an example of computing β). Hence the momentum flux term in Eq. 4.18a becomes

$$\int_{CS} u\rho \vec{V} \cdot d\vec{A} = -\rho\beta_1\overline{V}_1Q + \rho\beta_2\overline{V}_2Q \qquad (11.23)$$

The forces acting in the x direction on the control volume are

$$F_{S_x} + F_{B_x} = F_1 - F_2 - F_f + F_g \qquad (11.24)$$

The hydrostatic forces are

$$F_1 = \gamma A_1\overline{y}_1 \qquad (11.25)$$

and

$$F_2 = \gamma A_2\overline{y}_2 \qquad (11.26)$$

where $\overline{y}_1$ and $\overline{y}_2$ are the distances to the centroids. The gravity force F_g due to the weight W of the water is $W \sin\theta = \rho gA dx \sin\theta$, where $W = \rho gA dx$. Because the channel slope is small, $S_0 \approx \sin\theta$, and the force due to gravity can be written as

$$F_g = \rho g\overline{A}dxS_0 \qquad (11.27)$$

where $\overline{A} = (A_1 + A_2)/2$ is the average cross-sectional area of flow. The external force due to friction created by shear between the channel bottom and sides of the control volume is $-\tau_0 P dx$ where τ_0 is the bed shear stress and P is the wetted perimeter. From Eq. 11.3, $\tau_0 = \gamma RS_f = \rho g(A/P)S_f$, so the friction force is then

$$F_f = -\rho gAS_f dx \qquad (11.28)$$

For convenience we will continue to use the symbols F_g and F_f.

Substituting equations 11.23 through 11.26 into Eq. 4.18a, with steady flow, gives

$$\gamma A_1\overline{y}_1 - \gamma A_2\overline{y}_2 + F_g - F_f = -\rho\beta_1\overline{V}_1Q + \rho\beta_2\overline{V}_2Q \qquad (11.29)$$

which is the *momentum equation for steady state open-channel flow.*

Ignoring the small difference between the energy coefficient α and the momentum coefficient β in gradually varied flow, the internal energy losses are practically identical with the losses due to external forces [1]. Recall that for uniform flow, $F_g = F_f$.

Application of the energy and momentum principles in open-channel flow can be confusing at first. It is important to understand the basic differences, even though the two principles may produce identical or very similar results. Keep in mind that *energy is a scalar quantity* and *momentum is a vector quantity* and that *energy considers internal losses* in the energy equation and *momentum considers external resistance* in the momentum equation. The energy principle is simpler and clearer than the momentum principle; however, the momentum principle has certain advantages in application to problems involving high internal-energy changes, such as the hydraulic jump [1], which is discussed in Section 11-4 on rapidly varied flow.

Specific Force

For a short horizontal reach (control volume) with $\theta = 0$ and the gravity force $F_g = W \sin \theta = 0$, the external force of friction F_f can be neglected so $F_f = 0$ and $F_g = 0$. Also assuming $\beta_1 = \beta_2 = 1$ and denoting $\overline{V} = V$, the momentum equation (Eq. 11.29) reduces to

$$\gamma A_1 \bar{y}_1 - \gamma A_2 \bar{y}_2 = -\rho V_1 Q + \rho V_2 Q \tag{11.30}$$

Substituting $V_1 = Q/A_1$ and $V_2 = Q/A_2$, dividing through by γ and substituting $1/g = \rho/\gamma$, and then rearranging yields

$$\frac{Q^2}{gA_1} + A_1 \bar{y}_1 = \frac{Q^2}{gA_2} + A_2 \bar{y}_2 \tag{11.31}$$

The *specific force F* (Fig. 11.7) is defined as

$$F = \frac{Q^2}{gA} + A\bar{y} \tag{11.32}$$

which has units of ft^3 or m^3. The minimum value of the specific force with respect to the depth is determined using

$$\frac{dF}{dy} = \frac{d\left(\dfrac{Q^2}{gA}\right)}{dy} + \frac{d(A\bar{y})}{dy} = 0$$

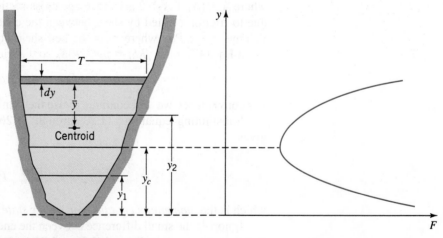

Fig. 11.7 Specific force curves.

which results in

$$\frac{dF}{dy} = -\frac{TQ^2}{gA^2} + A = 0 \qquad (11.33)$$

Refer to [1] or [5] for the proof and further explanation of the steps involved in obtaining Eq. 11.33 from Eq. 11.32. Equation 11.33 reduces to $-V^2/g + A/T = 0$ where the hydraulic depth $D = A/T$, so

$$\frac{V^2}{g} = D \quad \text{or} \quad \frac{V^2}{gD} = 1$$

which we have already shown is the criterion for critical flow (Eq. 11.20). Therefore, at critical flow the specific force is a minimum for a given discharge.

Summarizing, critical flow is characterized by the following conditions:

✓ Specific energy is minimum for a given discharge.
✓ Specific force is minimum for a given discharge.
✓ Velocity head is equal to half the hydraulic depth.
✓ Froude number is equal to unity.

Two additional conditions that are not proven here are [1]:

✓ The discharge is maximum for a given specific energy.
✓ The velocity of flow in a channel of small slope with uniform velocity distribution is equal to the celerity of small gravity waves in shallow water caused by local disturbances.

When flow is at or near the critical state, minor changes in specific energy near critical flow cause major changes in depth (see Figures 11.3 and 11.4), causing the flow to be unstable. Figure 11.8 illustrates examples of locations of critical flow.

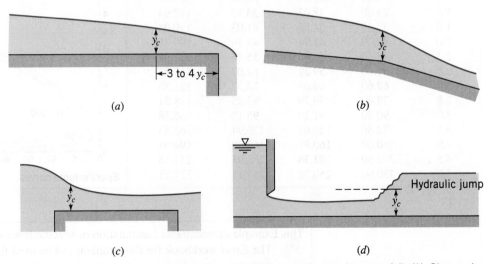

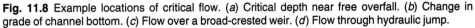

Fig. 11.8 Example locations of critical flow. (*a*) Critical depth near free overfall. (*b*) Change in grade of channel bottom. (*c*) Flow over a broad-crested weir. (*d*) Flow through hydraulic jump.

EXAMPLE 11.6 Computation of Specific Force Curves

Compute the specific force curves for the channel and flow rates used in Example 11.4.

GIVEN: Rectangular channel (20 ft wide), and flow rates $Q = 0, 50, 100$, and 300 cfs.

FIND: Specific force curves.

SOLUTION:
Use the given data and Eq. 11.32.

Governing equation:

$$F = \frac{Q^2}{gA} + A\bar{y}$$

(11.32)

The area A and centroid $\bar{y}$ can be written in terms of normal depth y, so

$$F = \frac{Q^2}{gBy} + (By)\frac{y}{2}$$

$$F = \frac{Q^2}{gBy} + \frac{By^2}{2}$$

The table and corresponding graph shown below can now be easily obtained using *Excel*.

Computed Specific Force Curve Values

Depth, y (ft)	Specific Force, F (ft³)			
	Q = 0	Q = 50	Q = 100	Q = 300
0.1	0.10	38.92	155.38	1397.62
0.2	0.40	19.81	78.04	699.16
0.4	1.60	11.30	40.42	350.98
0.6	3.60	10.07	29.48	236.52
0.8	6.40	11.25	25.81	181.09
1.0	10.00	13.88	25.53	149.75
1.2	14.40	17.63	27.34	130.86
1.4	19.60	22.37	30.69	119.42
1.6	25.60	28.03	35.30	112.94
1.8	32.40	34.56	41.03	110.04
2.0	40.00	41.94	47.76	109.88
2.2	48.40	50.16	55.46	111.92
2.4	57.60	59.22	64.07	115.83
2.6	67.60	69.09	73.57	121.35
2.8	78.40	79.79	83.95	128.31
3.0	90.00	91.29	95.18	136.58
3.5	122.50	123.61	126.94	162.43
4.0	160.00	160.97	163.88	194.94
4.5	202.50	203.36	205.95	233.56
5.0	250.00	250.78	253.11	277.95

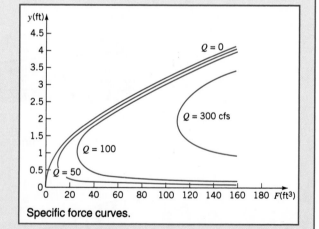

Specific force curves.

This Example demonstrates computation of specific force curves.
The *Excel* workbook for this problem can be used for plotting similar curves.

11-3 STEADY, GRADUALLY VARIED FLOW

Several types of open-channel flow problems can be solved in hydraulic engineering practice using the concepts of nonuniform flow. The first to be discussed are *gradually varied flow problems* in which the change in the water surface profile is small enough that it is possible to integrate the relevant differential equation from one section to an adjacent section for the change in depth or change in water surface elevation. Consider the energy equation (Eq. 11.1) previously derived for nonuniform flow using the control volume approach (with $\alpha_1 = \alpha_2 = 1$):

$$y_1 + z_1 + \frac{\overline{V}_1^2}{2g} = y_2 + z_2 + \frac{\overline{V}_2^2}{2g} + H_l \tag{11.1}$$

Because $H_l = S_f L = S_f \Delta x$ letting $\Delta y = y_2 - y_1$ and $\Delta z = z_1 - z_2 = S_0 \Delta x$, then Eq. 11.1 can be expressed as

$$S_0 \Delta x + \frac{\overline{V}_1^2}{2g} = \Delta y + \frac{\overline{V}_2^2}{2g} + S_f \Delta x \tag{11.34}$$

Rearranging yields

$$\Delta y = S_0 \Delta x - S_f \Delta x - \left(\frac{\overline{V}_2^2}{2g} - \frac{\overline{V}_1^2}{2g} \right)$$

and then dividing through by Δx results in

$$\frac{\Delta y}{\Delta x} = S_0 - S_f - \left(\frac{\overline{V}_2^2}{2g} - \frac{\overline{V}_1^2}{2g} \right) \frac{1}{\Delta x} \tag{11.35}$$

Taking the limit as $\Delta x \to 0$, we get

$$\lim_{\Delta x \to 0} \left(\frac{\Delta y}{\Delta x} \right) = \frac{dy}{dx}$$

and

$$\lim_{\Delta x \to 0} \left(\frac{\overline{V}_2^2}{2g} - \frac{\overline{V}_1^2}{2g} \right) \left(\frac{1}{\Delta x} \right) = \frac{d}{dx} \left(\frac{\overline{V}^2}{2g} \right)$$

Substituting these into Eq. 11.35 and rearranging yields

$$\frac{dy}{dx} + \frac{d}{dx} \left(\frac{\overline{V}^2}{2g} \right) = S_0 - S_f \tag{11.36}$$

The second term $d/dx(\overline{V}^2/2g)$ can be expressed as $\left[d\left(\overline{V}^2/2g \right)/dy \right] dy/dx$, so that Eq. 11.36 can be simplified to

$$\frac{dy}{dx} \left[1 + \frac{d\left(\frac{\overline{V}^2}{2g} \right)}{dy} \right] = S_0 - S_f \tag{11.37}$$

or

$$\frac{dy}{dx} = \frac{S_0 - S_f}{\left[1 + \frac{d\left(\frac{\overline{V}^2}{2g} \right)}{dy} \right]} \tag{11.38}$$

Equations 11.37 and 11.38 are two expressions of *the differential equation for gradually varied flow*. Equation 11.38 can also be expressed in terms of the Froude number. First observe that

$$\frac{d}{dy}\left(\frac{\overline{V}^2}{2g}\right) = \frac{d}{dy}\left(\frac{Q^2}{2gA^2}\right) = -\left(\frac{Q^2}{gA^3}\right)\frac{dA}{dy} \tag{11.39}$$

We already introduced the notion of the width of flow, T, to be given by $T = dA/dy$ (see Fig. 11.5). Also $A/T = D$, which is the hydraulic depth. Equation 11.39 can now be expressed as

$$\frac{d}{dy}\left(\frac{\overline{V}^2}{2g}\right) = -\left(\frac{Q^2}{gA^3}\right)\frac{Tdy}{dy} = -\frac{Q^2}{gA^2}\left(\frac{T}{A}\right) = -\frac{Q^2}{gA^2D} = -Fr^2 \tag{11.40}$$

where $Fr = \overline{V}/\sqrt{gD} = Q/A\sqrt{gD}$. Substituting Eq. 11.40 into Eq. 11.38 and simplifying, we find that the gradually varied flow equation in terms of the Froude number is

$$\frac{dy}{dx} = \frac{S_0 - S_f}{1 - Fr^2}$$

EXAMPLE 11.7   Vena Contracta at the Exit of a Sluice Gate

Consider a vertical sluice gate in a wide rectangular channel ($R = A/P = By/(B + 2y) = y$ because $B \gg 2y$). The flow downstream of a sluice gate is basically a jet that possesses a vena contracta (see figure). The distance from the sluice gate to the vena contracta as a rule is approximated as the same as the sluice gate opening [1]. The coefficients of contraction for vertical sluice gates are approximately 0.6, ranging from 0.598 to 0.611 [2].

Find the distance from the vena contracta to a point b downstream where the depth of flow is known to be 0.5 m deep. The depth of flow at the vena contracta is 0.457 m for a flow rate of 4.646 m³/s per meter of width. The channel bed slope is 0.0003 and Manning's roughness factor is $n = 0.020$.

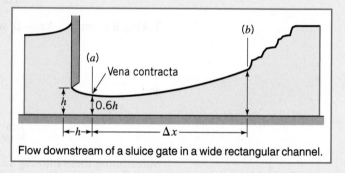

Flow downstream of a sluice gate in a wide rectangular channel.

GIVEN: Rectangular channel and data on sluice gate (coefficient of contraction and vena contracta geometry).

FIND: Distance downstream of sluice gate at which flow depth is 0.5 m.

SOLUTION:
Use the appropriate form of the energy equation (Eq. 11.34) and Manning's equation (Eq. 11.8) to relate conditions at points a and b.

Governing equations:

$$S_0\Delta x + \frac{\overline{V}_1^2}{2g} = \Delta y + \frac{\overline{V}_2^2}{2g} + S_f\Delta x \tag{11.34}$$

$$\overline{V} = \frac{1}{n}R^{2/3}S_0^{1/2} \tag{11.8}$$

The distance Δx from y_a to y_b can be obtained from Eq. 11.34,

$$S_0 \Delta x + \frac{\overline{V}_a^2}{2g} = \Delta y + \frac{\overline{V}_b^2}{2g} + S_f \Delta x$$

where $\Delta y = y_b - y_a$. Solving for Δx

$$\Delta x = \frac{\Delta y + \left(\dfrac{\overline{V}_b^2}{2g} - \dfrac{\overline{V}_a^2}{2g} \right)}{S_0 - S_f} \tag{1}$$

This equation can be used to compute Δx once all terms on the right are known. The depths y_a and y_b are given and hence Δy can be obtained. The channel bed slope S_0 is also given. Hence we need estimates of $\overline{V}_a$ and $\overline{V}_b$, as well as the friction slope S_f. The velocities can be obtained from the given flow rate per unit width, q,

$$\overline{V} = \frac{q}{y}$$

The table below shows a summary of the calculations for $\overline{V}$ and $\overline{V}^2/(2g)$ at locations a and b. (The table also shows computation of the hydraulic radius R, which will be used in obtaining S_f.)

Location	y (m)	$R = y$ (m)	$\overline{V}$(m/s)	$\overline{V}^2/(2g)$(m)
a	0.457	0.457	10.2	5.27
b	0.500	0.500	9.29	4.40

For the friction slope S_f we use Manning's equation with S_f replacing S_0 (recall from the discussion of Manning's equation in Section 11-1 that the equation was derived for friction and gravity effects in balance)

$$\overline{V} = \frac{1}{n} R^{2/3} S_f^{1/2}$$

or

$$S_f = \left(\frac{n\overline{V}}{R^{2/3}} \right)^2$$

The problem with this equation is that $\overline{V}$ and R (and hence S_f!) vary along the vena contracta. As an approximation we use an averaged version of the equation,

$$S_{f_{ave}} \approx \left(\frac{n\overline{V}_{ave}}{R_{ave}^{2/3}} \right)^2$$

with (from the table)

$$\overline{V}_{ave} = \frac{\overline{V}_a + \overline{V}_b}{2} = \frac{10.2 + 9.29}{2} \text{ m/s} = 9.73 \text{ m/s}$$

and

$$R_{ave} = \frac{R_a + R_b}{2} = \frac{0.457 + 0.500}{2} \text{ m} = 0.479 \text{ m}$$

Hence (remembering that Manning's equation is an "engineering" equation)

$$S_f \approx S_{f_{ave}} = \left(0.020 \times \frac{9.73 \text{ m}}{\text{s}} \times \frac{1}{0.479^{2/3}} \frac{1}{\text{m}^{2/3}} \right)^2$$

$$S_f = 0.101 \text{ m/m}$$

Using the above results in Eq. 1,

$$\Delta x = \frac{\Delta y + \left(\dfrac{\overline{V}_b^2}{2g} - \dfrac{\overline{V}_a^2}{2g}\right)}{S_0 - S_f} = \frac{(0.500 - 0.457)\text{m} + (4.40 - 5.27)\text{m}}{+ (0.0003 - 0.101)\text{m/m}}$$

$$\Delta x = 8.21 \text{ m}$$

Finally we can compute the distance x_b from the sluice gate to point b

$$x_b = h + \Delta x = \frac{y_a}{0.6} + \Delta x = \frac{0.457}{0.6} + 8.21 \text{ m}$$

$$x_b = 8.97 \text{ m} \qquad \longleftarrow \qquad\qquad\qquad\qquad\qquad\qquad\qquad\qquad x_b$$

> This Example illustrates use of a version of the energy equation and Manning's equation to relate conditions at two points in a gradually varying flow.

11-4   RAPIDLY VARIED FLOW

Rapidly varied flow occurs when a water flow depth changes abruptly over a very short distance. The following are characteristic features of rapidly varied flow [1]:

✓ Curvature of the flow is pronounced, so that the pressure distribution cannot be assumed to be hydrostatic.

✓ The rapid variation occurs over a relatively short distance so that boundary friction is comparatively small and usually insignificant.

✓ Rapid changes of water area occur in rapidly varied flow, causing the velocity distribution coefficients α and β to be much greater than 1.0.

Examples of rapidly varied flow are hydraulic jumps, transitions in channels, flow over spillways, flow in channels of nonlinear alignment, and flow through nonprismatic channel sections such as flow in channel junctions, flow through trash racks, and flow between bridge piers.

The discussion presented in this chapter is limited to the hydraulic jump. The *hydraulic jump* occurs when a rapid change in flow depth occurs from a small depth to a large depth such that there is an abrupt rise in water surface. A hydraulic jump occurs wherever supercritical flow changes to subcritical flow. Hydraulic jumps can occur in canals downstream of regulating sluices, at the foot of spillways, or where a steep channel slope suddenly becomes flat.

Figure 11.9 illustrates a hydraulic jump along with the specific energy and specific force curves. The depths of flow upstream and downstream of the jump are called *sequent depths* or *conjugate depths*. Because hydraulic jumps are typically short in length, the losses due to shear along the wetted perimeter are small compared to the pressure forces. Neglecting these forces and assuming a horizontal channel ($F_g = 0$), the momentum principle can be applied as in Section 11-2 to derive Eq. 11.31:

$$\frac{Q^2}{gA_1} + A_1\overline{y}_1 = \frac{Q^2}{gA_2} + A_2\overline{y}_2 \tag{11.31}$$

Consider a rectangular channel of width $B > 0$, so $Q = A_1\overline{V}_1 = A_2\overline{V}_2$, $A_1 = By_1$, $A_2 = By_2$, $\overline{y}_1 = y_1/2$ and $\overline{y}_2 = y_2/2$.

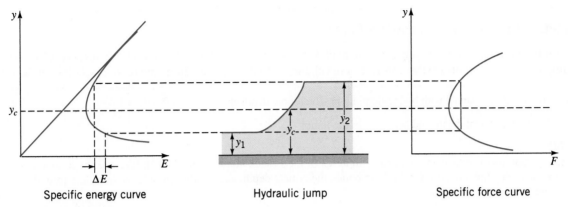

Fig. 11.9 Hydraulic jump.

$$\frac{Q^2}{gBy_1} + By_1\left(\frac{y_1}{2}\right) = \frac{Q^2}{gBy_2} + By_2\left(\frac{y_2}{2}\right)$$

Simplifying yields

$$\frac{Q^2}{g}\left(\frac{1}{y_1} - \frac{1}{y_2}\right) = \frac{1}{2}B^2(y_2^2 - y_1^2)$$

$$\frac{Q^2}{g}(y_2 - y_1) = \frac{1}{2}B^2 y_1 y_2(y_2^2 - y_1^2)$$

$$\frac{B^2 y_1^2 \overline{V}_1^2}{g}(y_2 - y_1) = \frac{1}{2}B^2 y_1 y_2(y_2 + y_1)(y_2 - y_1)$$

$$\frac{y_1 \overline{V}_1^2}{g} = \frac{1}{2}y_2(y_2 + y_1)$$

Dividing by y_1^2, we get

$$\frac{2\overline{V}_1^2}{gy_1} = \frac{y_2}{y_1}\left(\frac{y_2}{y_1} + 1\right) \tag{11.41}$$

The Froude number for a rectangular channel is $Fr_1 = \overline{V}_1/\sqrt{gD_1} = \overline{V}_1/\sqrt{gy_1}$; therefore Eq. 11.41 reduces to

$$\left(\frac{y_2}{y_1}\right)^2 + \frac{y_2}{y_1} - 2Fr_1^2 = 0$$

or

$$\frac{y_2}{y_1} = \frac{1}{2}\left(-1 + \sqrt{1 + 8Fr_1^2}\right) \tag{11.42}$$

Alternatively, $Q = B^2 y_2^2 \overline{V}_2^2$ and $Fr_2 = V_2/\sqrt{gy_2}$ could have been used to derive

$$\frac{y_1}{y_2} = \frac{1}{2}\left(-1 + \sqrt{1 + 8Fr_2^2}\right) \tag{11.43}$$

Equations 11.42 and 11.43 can be used to find the sequent depths of a hydraulic jump. It's interesting to note that the hydraulic jump has a close analog in supersonic flow: the *normal shock*. As we will learn in Chapter 13, instead of a sudden increase in depth, a supersonic flow can experience a sudden large increase in pressure; in both the hydraulic jump and the normal shock, there is a sudden reduction in speed.

EXAMPLE 11.8 Hydraulic Jump in a Rectangular Channel Flow

A hydraulic jump occurs in a rectangular channel 3.0 m wide. The water depth before the jump is 0.6 m, and after the jump is 1.6 m. Compute (a) the flow rate in the channel, (b) the critical depth, and (c) the head loss in the jump.

GIVEN: Rectangular channel with hydraulic jump in which flow depth changes from 0.6 m to 1.6 m.

FIND: Flow rate, critical depth, and head loss in the jump.

SOLUTION:
Use the equation that relates depths y_1 and y_2 in terms of the Froude number (Eq. 11.42); then use the Froude number (Eq. 11.20) to obtain the flow rate; use Eq. 11.22 to obtain the critical depth; and finally compute the head loss from the change in specific energy through the jump.

Governing equations:

$$\frac{y_2}{y_1} = \frac{1}{2}\left(-1 + \sqrt{1 + 8Fr_1^2}\right) \tag{11.42}$$

$$Fr = \frac{\overline{V}}{\sqrt{gD}} \tag{11.20}$$

$$y_c = \left(\frac{q^2}{g}\right)^{1/3} \tag{11.22}$$

$$E = y + \frac{\overline{V}^2}{2g} \tag{11.14}$$

(a) From Eq. 11.42

$$Fr_1 = \sqrt{\frac{\left(1 + 2\dfrac{y_2}{y_1}\right)^2 - 1}{8}}$$

$$= \sqrt{\frac{\left(1 + 2 \times \dfrac{1.6\,\text{m}}{0.6\,\text{m}}\right)^2 - 1}{8}}$$

$$Fr_1 = 2.21$$

As expected, $Fr_1 > 1$ (supercritical flow). We can now use the definition of Froude number for open-channel flow to find $\overline{V}_1$

$$Fr_1 = \frac{\overline{V}_1}{\sqrt{gD_1}} = \frac{\overline{V}_1}{\sqrt{gy_1}}$$

where $D_1 = y_1$ is the hydraulic depth. Hence

$$\overline{V}_1 = Fr_1\sqrt{gy_1} = 2.21 \times \sqrt{\frac{9.81\,\text{m}}{\text{s}^2} \times 0.6\,\text{m}} = 5.36\,\text{m/s}$$

From this we can obtain the flow rate Q

$$Q = By_1\overline{V}_1 = 3.0\,\text{m} \times 0.6\,\text{m} \times \frac{5.36\,\text{m}}{\text{s}}$$

$$Q = 9.65\,\text{m}^3/\text{s} \qquad\qquad\qquad Q$$

(b) The critical depth can be obtained from Eq. 11.22

$$y_c = \left(\frac{q^2}{g}\right)^{1/3} = \left(\frac{Q^2}{gB^2}\right)^{1/3}$$

$$= \left(9.65^2 \frac{m^6}{s^2} \times \frac{9.81 \ s^2}{m} \times 3.0^2 \frac{1}{m^2}\right)^{1/3}$$

$$y_c = 1.02 \ m \quad \longleftarrow \qquad\qquad\qquad\qquad\qquad\qquad\qquad y_c$$

Note that as illustrated in Fig. 11.9, $y_1 < y_c < y_2$.

(c) The head loss can be found from the change in specific energy

$$H_l = E_1 - E_2 = \left(y_1 + \frac{\overline{V}_1^2}{2g}\right) - \left(y_2 + \frac{\overline{V}_2^2}{2g}\right)$$

with $\overline{V}_2 = Q/(By_1) = 2.01 \ m/s$,

$$H_l = \left(0.6 \ m + 5.36^2 \frac{m^2}{s^2} \times \frac{1}{2} \times \frac{s^2}{9.81 \ m}\right) - \left(1.6 \ m + 2.01^2 \frac{m^2}{s^2} \times \frac{1}{2} \times \frac{s^2}{9.81 \ m}\right)$$

$$H_l = 0.258 \ m \quad \longleftarrow \qquad\qquad\qquad\qquad\qquad\qquad\qquad H_l$$

> This Example illustrates computation of flow rate, critical depth, and head loss for a hydraulic jump.

EXAMPLE 11.9 Hydraulic Jump Head Loss as a Function of y_1 and y_2

Derive an equation to approximate the head loss (energy loss) of a hydraulic jump in a horizontal rectangular channel in terms of the depths before and after the jump, y_1 and y_2, only.

GIVEN: Horizontal rectangular channel with a hydraulic jump.

FIND: An expression for the head loss through the hydraulic jump in terms of the depths before and after the jump, y_1 and y_2.

SOLUTION:
Use energy and momentum equations to relate conditions before and afer the jump.

Governing equations:

Energy loss:
$$H_l = E_1 - E_2 = \left(y_1 + \frac{\overline{V}_1^2}{2g}\right) - \left(y_2 + \frac{\overline{V}_2^2}{2g}\right)$$

Momentum:
$$\gamma A_1 \bar{y}_1 - \gamma A_2 \bar{y}_2 + F_g - F_f = -\rho\beta_1\overline{V}_1 Q + \rho\beta_2\overline{V}_2 Q \qquad (11.29)$$

In the energy loss expression, we can use $\overline{V} = q/y$ in two places, so

$$H_l = \left(y_1 + \frac{q^2}{2gy_1^2}\right) - \left(y_2 + \frac{q^2}{2gy_2^2}\right) = \frac{q^2}{2g}\left(\frac{1}{y_1^2} - \frac{1}{y_2^2}\right) + (y_1 - y_2)$$

$$H_l = \frac{q^2}{2g}\left(\frac{y_2^2 - y_1^2}{y_1^2 y_2^2}\right) + (y_1 - y_2) \qquad\qquad (1)$$

We now need to replace q with an expression involving y_1 and y_2 only.

The momentum equation (Eq. 11.29) expresses the fact that, on a control volume surrounding the hydraulic jump, the surface and body forces lead to a change in momentum between locations 1 and 2. The term $\gamma A_1 \bar{y}_1 - \gamma A_2 \bar{y}_2$ is the net hydrostatic force, the term F_g is the body force, and the term F_f is the friction force. The term $-\rho\beta_1\bar{V}_1 Q + \rho\beta_2\bar{V}_2 Q$ computes the difference between the momentum flux at locations 1 and 2. In this problem the slope is zero so $F_g = 0$, the friction force F_f is negligible if we choose points immediately before and immediately after the jump, and for turbulent flow we usually set the momentum correction factor $\beta \approx 1$. Hence, Eq. 11.29 simplifies to

$$\gamma A_1 \bar{y}_1 - \gamma A_2 \bar{y}_2 = -\rho \bar{V}_1 Q + \rho \bar{V}_2 Q$$

which is Eq. 11.30 that we derived in Section 11-2 for the same set of constraints. Note that $\gamma = g\rho$ and for a rectangular channel $\bar{y} = y/2$, and $A = By$. Using these in the above equation we find

$$gBy_1 \frac{y_1}{2} - gBy_2 \frac{y_2}{2} = Q(\bar{V}_2 - \bar{V}_1)$$

or, dividing by B and rearranging

$$\frac{q}{g} = \frac{y_1^2 - y_2^2}{2(\bar{V}_2 - \bar{V}_1)} = \frac{y_1^2 - y_2^2}{2\left(\dfrac{q}{y_2} - \dfrac{q}{y_1}\right)}$$

Once again rearranging and simplifying

$$\frac{q^2}{g} = \frac{y_1^2 - y_2^2}{2\left(\dfrac{1}{y_2} - \dfrac{1}{y_1}\right)} = \frac{(y_1^2 - y_2^2)y_1 y_2}{2(y_1 - y_2)}$$

$$\frac{q^2}{g} = \frac{(y_1 + y_2)y_1 y_2}{2} \qquad\qquad (2)$$

Combining Eq. 1 (energy) with Eq. 2 (momentum), we obtain

$$H_l = \frac{q^2}{2g}\left(\frac{y_2^2 - y_1^2}{y_1^2 y_2^2}\right) + (y_1 - y_2)$$

$$= \frac{(y_1 + y_2)y_1 y_2}{4}\left(\frac{y_2^2 - y_1^2}{y_1^2 y_2^2}\right) + (y_1 - y_2)$$

$$= \frac{(y_1 + y_2)(y_2^2 - y_1^2) + 4y_1 y_2(y_1 - y_2)}{4y_1 y_2} = \frac{y_2^3 - 3y_2^2 y_1 + 3y_2 y_1^2 + y_2^3}{4y_1 y_2}$$

$$H_l = \frac{(y_2 - y_1)^3}{4y_1 y_2} \longleftarrow \qquad\qquad H_l$$

11-5   DISCHARGE MEASUREMENT USING WEIRS

A *weir* is a device (or overflow structure) that is placed normal to the direction of flow. The weir essentially backs up water so that in flowing over the weir the water goes through critical depth. Weirs have been used for the measurement of water flow in open channels for many years. Weirs can generally be classified as *sharp-crested weirs* and *broad-crested weirs*. Weirs are discussed in detail in Bos [13], Brater [14], and Replogle [15].

A *sharp-crested weir* is basically a thin plate mounted perpendicular to the flow with the top of the plate having a beveled, sharp edge, which makes the nappe spring clear from the plate (see Fig. 11.10). The rate of flow is determined by measuring the

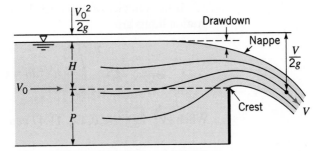

Fig. 11.10 Flow over sharp-crested weir.

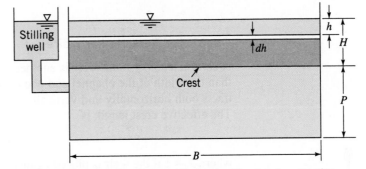

Fig. 11.11 Rectangular sharp-crested weir without end contraction.

head, typically in a stilling well (see Fig. 11.11) at a distance upstream from the crest. The head H is measured using a gauge.

Suppressed Rectangular Weir

These sharp-crested weirs are as wide as the channel and the width of the nappe is the same length as the crest. Referring to Fig. 11.10, consider an elemental area $dA = Bdh$ and assume the velocity is $\sqrt{2gh}$; then the elemental flow is

$$dQ = Bdh\sqrt{2gh} = B\sqrt{2g}h^{1/2}\,dh \qquad (11.44)$$

The discharge is expressed by integrating Eq. 11.44 over the area above the top of the weir crest:

$$Q = \int\limits_0^H dQ = \sqrt{2g}B\int\limits_0^H h^{1/2}dh = \frac{2}{3}\sqrt{2g}BH^{3/2} \qquad (11.45)$$

Friction effects have been neglected in the derivation of Eq. 11.45. The drawdown effect shown in Fig. 11.10 and the crest contraction indicate that the streamlines are not parallel or normal to the area in the plane. To account for these effects a coefficient of discharge C_d is used, so that

$$Q = C_d\frac{2}{3}\sqrt{2g}BH^{3/2}$$

where C_d is approximately 0.62. This is the basic equation for a suppressed rectangular weir, which can be expressed more generally as

$$Q = C_wBH^{3/2} \qquad (11.46)$$

where the C_w is the weir coefficient, $C_w = \frac{2}{3}C_d\sqrt{2g}$. For U.S. customary units, $C_w \approx 3.33$, and for SI units $C_w \approx 1.84$.

If the velocity of approach V_a where H is measured is appreciable, then the integration limits are

$$Q = \sqrt{2g}B \int_{V_a^2/2g}^{H+V_a^2/2g} h^{1/2}dh = C_wB\left[\left(H + \frac{V_a^2}{2g}\right)^{3/2} - \left(\frac{V_a^2}{2g}\right)^{3/2}\right] \qquad (11.47)$$

When $(V_a^2/2g)^{3/2} \approx 0$, Eq. 11.47 can be simplified to

$$Q = C_wB\left(H + \frac{V_a^2}{2g}\right)^{3/2}$$

Contracted Rectangular Weirs

A *contracted horizontal weir* is another sharp crested weir with a crest that is shorter than the width of the channel and one or two beveled end sections so that water contracts both horizontally and vertically. This forces the nappe width to be less than B. The effective crest length is

$$B' = B - 0.1\,nH$$

where $n = 1$ if the weir is placed against one side wall of the channel so that the contraction on one side is suppressed and $n = 2$ if the weir is positioned so that it is not placed against a side wall.

Triangular Weir

Triangular or *V-notch weirs* are sharp-crested weirs that are used for relatively small flows, but have the advantage that they can also function for reasonably large flows as well. Referring to Fig. 11.12, the rate of discharge through an elemental area, dA, is

$$dQ = C_d\sqrt{2gh}dA$$

where $dA = 2xdh$, and $x = (H - h)\tan(\theta/2)$ so $dA = 2(H - h)\tan(\theta/2)dh$. Then

$$dQ = C_d\sqrt{2gh}\left[2(H - h)\tan\left(\frac{\theta}{2}\right)dh\right]$$

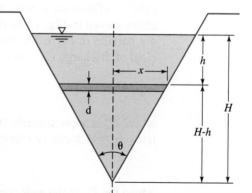

Fig. 11.12 Triangular sharp-crested weir.

$$\text{and} \qquad Q = C_d 2\sqrt{2g}\tan\left(\frac{\theta}{2}\right)\int_0^H (H-h)h^{1/2}dh$$

$$= C_d\left(\frac{8}{15}\right)\sqrt{2g}\tan\left(\frac{\theta}{2}\right)H^{5/2}$$

$$Q = C_w H^{5/2}$$

The value of C_w for a value of $\theta = 90°$ (the most common) is $C_w = 2.50$ for U.S. customary units and $C_w = 1.38$ for SI units.

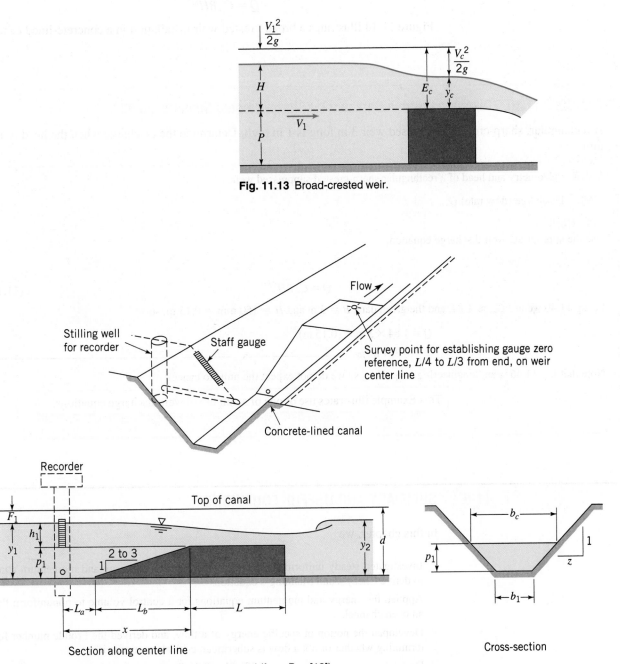

Fig. 11.13 Broad-crested weir.

Fig. 11.14 Broad-crested weir in concrete-lined canal (from Bos [13]).

Broad-Crested Weir

Broad-crested weirs (refer to Fig. 11.13) are essentially critical-depth weirs in that if the weirs are high enough, critical depth occurs on the crest of the weir. For critical flow conditions $y_c = (q^2/g)^{1/3}$ and $E = \frac{3}{2}y_c$ for rectangular channels:

$$Q = B \cdot q = B\sqrt{gy_c^3} = B\sqrt{g\left(\frac{2}{3}E\right)^3} = B\left(\frac{2}{3}\right)^{3/2}\sqrt{g}E^{3/2}$$

or, assuming the approach velocity is negligible:

$$Q = B\left(\frac{2}{3}\right)^{3/2}\sqrt{g}H^{3/2}$$

$$Q = C_wBH^{3/2}$$

Figure 11.14 illustrates a broad-crested weir installation in a concrete-lined canal.

EXAMPLE 11.10 Discharge from a Rectangular Sharp-Crested Suppressed Weir

A rectangular, sharp-crested suppressed weir 3 m long is 1 m high. Determine the discharge when the head is 150 mm.

GIVEN: Geometry and head of a rectangular sharp-crested suppressed weir.

FIND: Discharge (flow rate) Q.

SOLUTION:
Use the appropriate weir discharge equation.

Governing equations:

$$Q = C_wBH^{3/2} \tag{11.46}$$

In Eq. 11.46 we use $C_w \approx 1.84$, and the given data, $B = 3$ m and $H = 150$ mm $= 0.15$ m, so

$$Q = 1.84 \times 3\,\text{m} \times (0.15\,\text{m})^{3/2}$$

$$Q = 0.321\,\text{m}^3/\text{s} \longleftarrow \hspace{4cm} Q$$

Note that Eq. 11.46 is an "engineering" equation, so we do not expect the units to cancel.

> This Example illustrates use of one of a number of weir discharge equations.

11-6 SUMMARY AND USEFUL EQUATIONS

In this chapter, we:

✓ Investigated steady uniform flow in a channel, and used energy and momentum concepts to derive Chezy's and Manning's equations.

✓ Applied the energy and momentum equations for a control volume to nonuniform flow in an open channel.

✓ Developed the notion of specific energy of a flow, and derived the Froude number for determining whether or not a flow is subcritical, critical, or supercritical.

✓ Derived an expression for the specific force of a flow.

✓ Investigated some basic concepts of gradually varied flows.

✓ Investigated rapidly varied flows, especially the hydraulic jump.

We also learned how to use many of the important concepts mentioned above in analyzing a range of real-world open-channel flow problems.

Note: Most of the Useful Equations in the table below have a number of constraints—*be sure to refer to their page numbers for details!*

Useful Equations		
The Chezy equation:	$V = C\sqrt{RS_0}$ (11.6)	Page 550
The Chezy coefficient:	$C = \dfrac{1}{n}R^{1/6}$ (11.7)	Page 550
The Manning equation for velocity (SI units):	$V = \dfrac{1}{n}R^{2/3}S_0^{1/2}$ (11.8)	Page 551
The Manning equation for flow rate (SI units):	$Q = \dfrac{1}{n}AR^{2/3}S_0^{1/2}$ (11.9)	Page 551
The Manning equation for velocity (British units):	$V = \dfrac{1.49}{n}R^{2/3}S_0^{1/2}$ (11.10)	Page 551
The Manning equation for flow rate (British units):	$Q = \dfrac{1.49}{n}AR^{2/3}S_0^{1/2}$ (11.11)	Page 551
Criterion for turbulent flow:	$n^6\sqrt{RS_f} \geq 1.9 \times 10^{-3}\,(R\text{ in feet})$ (11.12a) $n^6\sqrt{RS_f} \geq 1.1 \times 10^{-3}\,(R\text{ in meters})$ (11.12b)	Page 551
Total head (or energy head):	$H = y + z + \dfrac{V^2}{2g}$ (11.13)	Page 554
Specific energy (in terms of velocity):	$E = y + \dfrac{V^2}{2g}$ (11.14)	Page 554
Criteria for critical flow:	$Fr = \dfrac{V}{\sqrt{gD}} \begin{cases} <1 \text{ subcritical flow} \\ =1 \text{ critical flow} \\ >1 \text{ supercritical flow} \end{cases}$ (11.20)	Page 556
Criterion for critical flow (rectangular channel):	$\dfrac{V_c}{\sqrt{gy_c}} = 1$ (11.21)	Page 556

Momentum equation for steady-state open-channel flow:	$\gamma A_1 \bar{y}_1 - \gamma A_2 \bar{y}_2 + F_g - F_f = -\rho \beta_1 \bar{V}_1 Q + \rho \beta_2 \bar{V}_2 Q$ (11.29)	Page 562
Specific force:	$$F = \frac{Q^2}{gA} + A\bar{y} \qquad (11.32)$$	Page 563
Hydraulic jump depth change (in terms of Fr_1):	$$\frac{y_2}{y_1} = \frac{1}{2}\left(-1 + \sqrt{1 + 8Fr_1^2}\right) \qquad (11.42)$$	Page 570
Hydraulic jump depth change (in terms of Fr_2):	$$\frac{y_1}{y_2} = \frac{1}{2}\left(-1 + \sqrt{1 + 8Fr_2^2}\right) \qquad (11.43)$$	Page 570

REFERENCES

1. Chow. V. T., *Open-Channel Hydraulics*. New York: McGraw-Hill, 1959.

2. Henderson, F. M., *Open-Channel Flow*. New York: Macmillan, 1966.

3. French, R. H., *Open-Channel Hydraulics*. New York: McGraw-Hill, 1985.

4. Townson, J. M., *Free-Surface Hydraulics*. London: Unwin Hyman, 1991.

5. Chaudhry, M. H., *Open-Channel Flow*. Englewood Cliffs, NJ: Prentice Hall, 1993.

6. Jain, S. C., *Open Channel Flow*. New York: Wiley, 2001.

7. Sturm, T. W., *Open Channel Hydraulics*. New York: McGraw-Hill, 2001.

8. Mays, L. W., *Water Resources Engineering*. 2005 ed. New York: Wiley, 2005.

9. Linsley, R. K., J. B. Franzini, D. L. Freyberg, and G. Tchobanoglous, *Water Resources Engineering*. New York: McGraw-Hill, 1991.

10. Chen, Y. H., and G. K. Cotton, *Design of Roadside Channels with Flexible Linings*, Hydraulic Engineering Circular 15,

FHWA-IP-87-7, Federal Highway Administration, McClean, VA, 1988.

11. Manning, R., "On the Flow of Water in Open Channels and Pipes." *Transactions Institute of Civil Engineers of Ireland*, vol. 20, pp. 161–209, Dublin, 1891; Supplement, vol. 24, pp. 179–207, 1895.

12. Barnes, H. H., Jr., *Roughness Characteristics of Natural Channels*. U.S. Geological Survey, Water Supply Paper 1849, Washington, DC: U.S. Government Printing Office, 1962.

13. Bos, M. G., J. A. Replogle, and A. J. Clemmens, *Flow Measuring Flumes for Open Channel System*. New York: John Wiley and Sons, 1984.

14. Brater, E. F., H. W. King, J. E. Lindell, and C. Y. Wei, *Handbook of Hydraulics*, 7th edition, New York: McGraw-Hill, 1996.

15. Replogle, J. A., A. J. Clemmens, and C. A. Pugh, "Hydraulic Design of Flow Measuring Structures." *Hydraulic Design Handbook*, edited by L. W. Mays, New York: McGraw-Hill, 1999.

PROBLEMS

11.1 A 2-m-wide rectangular channel with a bed slope of 0.0005 has a depth of flow of 1.5 m. Manning's roughness coefficient is 0.015. Determine the steady uniform discharge in the channel.

11.2 Determine the uniform flow depth in a rectangular channel 2.5 m wide with a discharge of 3 m³/s. The slope is 0.0004 and Manning's roughness factor is 0.015.

11.3 Determine the uniform flow depth in a trapezoidal channel with a bottom width of 8 ft and side slopes of 1 vertical to 2 horizontal. The discharge is 100 ft³/s. Manning's roughness factor is 0.015 and the channel bottom slope is 0.0004.

11.4 Determine the uniform flow depth in a trapezoidal channel with a bottom width of 2.5 m and side slopes of 1 vertical to 2 horizontal with a discharge of 3 m³/s. The slope is 0.0004 and Manning's roughness factor is 0.015.

11.5 A partially open sluice gate in a 3-m-wide rectangular channel carries water at 8.5 m³/sec. The upstream depth is 2 m. Find the downstream depth and Froude number.

11.6 A rectangular flume built of concrete, with 1 ft per 1000 ft slope, is 6 ft wide. Water flows at a normal depth of 3 ft. Compute the discharge.

11.7 A rectangular flume built of timber is 3 ft wide. The flume is to handle a flow of 90 ft³/sec at a normal depth of 6 ft. Determine the slope required.

11.8 A channel with square cross section is to carry 20 m³/sec of water at normal depth on a slope of 0.003. Compare the dimensions of the channel required for (a) concrete and (b) soil cement.

11.9 Water flows in a trapezoidal channel at a normal depth of 1.2 m. The bottom width is 2.4 m and the sides slope at 1:1 (45°). The flow rate is 7.1 m³/sec. The channel is excavated from bare soil. Find the bed slope.

11.10 A triangular channel with side angles of 45° is to carry 10 m³/sec at a slope of 0.001. The channel is concrete. Find the required dimensions.

11.11 A semicircular trough of corrugated steel, with diameter $D = 1$ m, carries water at depth $y_n = 0.25$ m. The slope is 0.01. Find the discharge.

11.12 Find the discharge at which the channel of Problem 11.11 flows full.

11.13 The flume of Problem 11.6 is fitted with a new plastic film liner ($n = 0.010$). Find the new depth of flow if the discharge remains constant at 85.5 ft³/sec.

11.14 Discharge through the channel of Problem 11.9 is increased to 15 m³/sec. Find the corresponding normal depth, if the bed slope is 0.00193.

11.15 The channel of Problem 11.9 has 0.00193 bed slope. Find the normal depth for the given discharge after a new plastic liner ($n = 0.010$) is installed.

11.16 Consider again the semicircular channel of Problem 11.11. Find the normal depth that corresponds to a discharge of 0.3 m³/sec.

11.17 Consider a symmetric open channel of triangular cross section. Show that for a given flow area, the wetted perimeter is minimized when the sides meet at a right angle.

11.18 A trapezoidal channel with a bottom width of 20 ft, side slopes of 1 to 2, channel bottom slope of 0.0016, and a Manning's n of 0.025 carries a discharge of 400 cfs. Compute the critical depth and velocity of this channel.

11.19 Compute the normal depth and velocity of the channel of Problem 11.18.

11.20 Derive an expression for the hydraulic radius of a trapezoidal channel with bottom width B_w liquid depth y, and side slope angle θ. Verify the equation given in Table 11.2. Plot the ratio R/y for $B_w = 2$ m with side slope angles of 30° and 60° for $0.5 < y < 3$ m.

11.21 Verify the equation given in Table 11.2 for the hydraulic radius of a circular channel. Evaluate and plot the ratio R/d_o, for liquid depths between 0 and d_o.

11.22 Determine the cross-section of the greatest hydraulic efficiency for a trapezoidal channel with side slope of 1 vertical to 2 horizontal if the design discharge is 10 m³/s. The channel slope is 0.001 and Manning's roughness factor is 0.020.

11.23 For a trapezoidal shaped channel ($n = 0.014$ and slope $S_o = 0.0002$ with a 20-ft bottom width and side slopes of 1 vertical to 1.5 horizontal), determine the normal depth for a discharge of 1000 cfs.

11.24 Show that the best hydraulic trapezoidal section is one-half of a hexagon.

11.25 Solve Example 11.4 for discharges of 0, 25, 75, 125, and 200 ft³/s.

11.26 Rework Example 11.5 for a 30-cm-high hump and a side wall constriction that reduces the channel width to 1.6 m.

11.27 Compute the critical depth for the channel in Problem 11.1.

11.28 Compute the critical depth for the channel in Problem 11.2.

11.29 Rework Example 11.6 with discharges of 0, 25, 75, 125, and 200 cfs.

11.30 Resolve Example 11.7 for a channel bed slope of 0.003.

11.31 Once again consider the trapezoidal channel in Problem 11.8 with a dam placed in the channel so that water backs up to a depth of 5 ft immediately behind the dam. How far upstream would you expect the depth to be 4.80 ft? Consider an energy correction coefficient of 1.1.

11.32 A rectangular channel carries a discharge of 10 ft³/sec per foot of width. Determine the minimum specific energy possible for this flow. Compute the corresponding flow depth and speed.

11.33 Flow in the channel of Problem 11.32 ($E_{min} = 2.19$ ft) is to be at twice the minimum specific energy. Compute the alternate depths for this E.

11.34 Water flows at 300 ft³/sec in a trapezoidal channel with bottom width of 8 ft. The sides are sloped at 2:1. Find the critical depth for this channel.

11.35 For a channel of nonrectangular cross section, critical depth occurs at minimum specific energy. Obtain a general equation for critical depth in a triangular channel in terms of Q, g, and z.

11.36 For a channel of nonrectangular cross section, critical depth occurs at minimum specific energy. Obtain a general equation for critical depth in a channel of trapezoidal section in terms of Q, g, B_w, and z.

11.37 Consider the Venturi flume shown. The bed is horizontal and flow may be considered frictionless. The upstream depth is 1 ft and the downstream depth is 0.75 ft. The upstream breadth is 2 ft and the breadth of the throat is 1 ft. Estimate the flow rate through the flume.

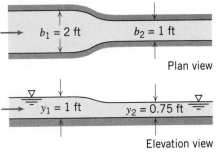

P11.37

11.38 A rectangular channel 10 ft wide carries 100 cfs on a horizontal bed at 1.0 ft depth. A smooth bump across the channel rises 4 in. above the channel bottom. Find the elevation of the liquid free surface above the bump.

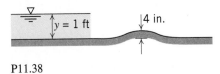

P11.38

11.39   A rectangular channel 10 ft wide carries a discharge of 20 ft^3/sec at 0.9 ft depth. A smooth bump 0.2 ft high is placed on the floor of the channel. Estimate the local change in flow depth caused by the bump.

11.40   At a section of a 10-ft-wide rectangular channel, the depth is 0.3 ft for a discharge of 20 ft^3/sec. A smooth bump 0.1 ft high is placed on the floor of the channel. Determine the local change in flow depth caused by the bump.

11.41   Water, at 3 ft/sec and 2 ft depth, approaches a smooth rise in a wide channel. Estimate the stream depth after the 0.5 ft rise.

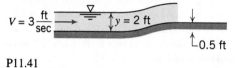

$$V = 3\,\frac{\text{ft}}{\text{sec}} \qquad y = 2 \text{ ft} \qquad 0.5 \text{ ft}$$

P11.41

11.42   Water issues from a sluice gate at 0.6 m depth. The discharge per unit width is 6.0 m^3/sec/m. Estimate the water level far upstream where the flow speed is negligible. Calculate the maximum rate of flow per unit width that could be delivered through the sluice gate.

11.43   A horizontal rectangular channel 3 ft wide contains a sluice gate. Upstream of the gate the depth is 6 ft; the depth downstream is 0.9 ft. Estimate the volume flow rate in the channel.

11.44   Consider a 2.45-m-wide rectangular channel with a bed slope of 0.0004 and a Manning's roughness factor of 0.015. A weir is placed in the channel and the depth upstream of the weir is 1.52 m for a discharge of 5.66 m^3/s. Determine if a hydraulic jump forms upstream of the weir.

11.45   A hydraulic jump occurs in a rectangular channel 4.0 m wide. The water depth before the jump is 0.4 m and after the jump is 1.7 m. Compute the flow rate in the channel, the critical depth, and the headloss in the jump.

11.46   A wide channel carries 20 ft^3/sec per foot of width at a depth of 1 ft at the toe of a hydraulic jump. Determine the depth of the jump and the head loss across it.

11.47   A hydraulic jump occurs in a wide horizontal channel. The discharge is 30 ft^3/sec per foot of width. The upstream depth is 1.3 ft. Determine the depth of the jump.

11.48   A hydraulic jump occurs in a rectangular channel. The flow rate is 200 ft^3/sec, and the depth before the jump is 1.2 ft. Determine the depth behind the jump and the head loss, if the channel is 10 ft wide.

11.49   The hydraulic jump may be used as a crude flow meter. Suppose that in a horizontal rectangular channel 5 ft wide the observed depths before and after a hydraulic jump are 0.66 and 3.0 ft. Find the rate of flow and the head loss.

11.50   A hydraulic jump occurs on a horizontal apron downstream from a wide spillway, at a location where depth is 0.9 m and speed is 25 m/sec. Estimate the depth and speed downstream from the jump. Compare the specific energy downstream of the jump to that upstream.

11.51   A hydraulic jump occurs in a rectangular channel. The flow rate is 6.5 m^3/sec and the depth before the jump is 0.4 m. Determine the depth after the jump and the head loss, if the channel is 1 m wide.

11.52   A rectangular, sharp-crested weir with end contraction is 1.6 m long. How high should it be placed in a channel to maintain an upstream depth of 2.5 m for 0.5 m^3/s flow rate?

11.53   For a sharp-crested suppressed weir ($C_w = 3.33$) of length $B = 8.0$ ft, $P = 2.0$ ft, and $H = 1.0$ ft, determine the discharge over the weir. Neglect the velocity of approach head.

11.54   A rectangular sharp-crested weir with end contractions is 1.5 m long. How high should the weir crest be placed in a channel to maintain an upstream depth of 2.5 m for 0.5 m^3/s flow rate?

11.55   Determine the head on a 60° V-notch weir for a discharge of 150 l/s. Take $C_d = 0.58$.

11.56   The head on a 90° V-notch weir is 1.5 ft. Determine the discharge.

11.57   Determine the weir coefficient of a 90° V-notch weir for a head of 180 mm for a flow rate of 20 l/s.

Chapter 12

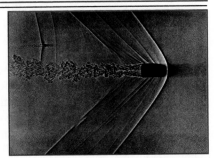

Introduction to Compressible Flow

CASE STUDY

Reducing the Sonic Boom

The SSBD aircraft trailing NASA's F-15B. (Courtesy of NASA.)

Most of us are familiar with the fact that supersonic aircraft generally have very sharp noses and wing leading edges, compared to subsonic aircraft (we will learn some reasons why supersonic aircraft are so shaped in this and the next chapter); compare, for example, the supersonic Concorde to the subsonic Boeing 747. We are also familiar with the notion of a sonic boom, a large window-rattling boom created when the remains of a supersonic jet's oblique shock wave wash over the ground. The sonic boom is an important reason that the Concorde was not allowed to fly supersonically over land, limiting its use and being one factor in the aircraft's limited commercial success.

The Defense Advanced Research Projects Agency (DARPA) and NASA have now shown that modifying an aircraft's shape can also change the shape of its sonic boom, thereby reducing the loudness developed. Their Shaped Sonic Boom Demonstration (SSBD) program found that by designing the aircraft to a specific shape, the pressure waves created by the aircraft can be kept from merging into a shock wave (see the discussion of the Mach cone in Section 12-2); when these weaker waves reach the ground, the loudness of the sonic boom is greatly reduced. For the demonstration, Northrop Grumman modified an F-5E fighter aircraft by installing a specially shaped "nose glove"; compare the nose of the SSBD (the lower aircraft in the figure) to the traditional supersonic nose of a supersonic F-15B.

It is possible that this new nose shape could eventually allow reintroduction of supersonic transports, even for the key routes across the continental United States.

In Chapter 2 we briefly discussed the two most important questions we must ask before analyzing a fluid flow: whether or not the flow is viscous, and whether or not the flow is compressible. We subsequently considered *incompressible, inviscid* flows (Chapter 6) and *incompressible, viscous* flows (Chapters 8 and 9). We are now ready to study flows that experience compressibility effects. Because this is an introductory text, our focus will be mainly on *one-dimensional compressible, inviscid* flows, although we will also review some important *compressible, viscous* flow phenomena. After our consideration of one-dimensional flows, we will introduce some basic concepts of *two-dimensional steady compressible flows*.

We first need to establish what we mean by a "compressible" flow. This is a flow in which there are significant or noticeable changes in fluid density. Just as inviscid fluids do not actually exist, so incompressible fluids do not actually exist. For example, in this text we have treated water as an incompressible fluid, although in fact the density of seawater increases by 1% for each mile or so of depth. Hence, whether or not a given flow can be treated as incompressible is a judgment call: Liquid flows will almost always be considered incompressible (exceptions include phenomena such as the "water hammer" effect in pipes), but gas flows could easily be either incompressible or compressible. We will learn in this chapter (in Example 12.5) that for Mach numbers *M* less than about 0.3, the change in gas density due to the flow will be less than 3 percent; this change is small enough in most engineering applications for the following rule: *A gas flow can be considered incompressible when M < 0.3*.

The consequences of compressibility are not limited simply to density changes. Density changes mean that we can have significant compression or expansion work on a gas, so the thermodynamic state of the fluid will change, meaning that in general *all* properties—temperature, internal energy, entropy, and so on—can change. In particular, density changes create a mechanism (just as viscosity did) for exchange of energy between "mechanical" energies (kinetic, potential, and "pressure") and the thermal internal energy. For this reason, we begin with a review of the thermodynamics needed to study compressible flow.

12-1   REVIEW OF THERMODYNAMICS

The pressure, density, and temperature of a substance may be related by an equation of state. Although many substances are complex in behavior, experience shows that most gases of engineering interest, at moderate pressure and temperature, are well represented by the ideal gas equation of state,

$$p = \rho R T \tag{12.1}$$

where R is a unique constant for each gas;[1] R is given by

$$R = \frac{R_u}{M_m}$$

where R_u is the universal gas constant, $R_u = 8314 \text{ N} \cdot \text{m}/(\text{kgmole} \cdot \text{K}) = 1544 \text{ ft} \cdot \text{lbf}/(\text{lbmole} \cdot {}^\circ\text{R})$ and M_m is the molecular mass of the gas. Although the ideal gas equation is derived using a model that has the unrealistic assumptions that the gas molecules (a) take up zero volume (i.e., they are point masses) and (b) do not interact with one another, many real gases conform to Eq. 12.1, especially if the pressure is "low" enough and/or temperature "high" enough (see, e.g., [1–3]). For example, at room temperature, as long as the pressure is less than about 30 atm, Eq. 12.1 models the air density to better than 1 percent accuracy; similarly, Eq. 12.1 is accurate for air at 1 atm for temperatures that are greater than about −130°C (140 K).

The ideal gas has other features that are useful. In general, the *internal energy* of a simple substance may be expressed as a function of any two independent properties, e.g., $u = u(v, T)$, where $v \equiv 1/\rho$ is the *specific volume*. Then

$$du = \left(\frac{\partial u}{\partial T}\right)_v dT + \left(\frac{\partial u}{\partial v}\right)_T dv$$

---

[1] For air, $R = 287 \text{ N} \cdot \text{m}/(\text{kg} \cdot \text{K}) = 53.3 \text{ ft} \cdot \text{lbf}/(\text{lbm} \cdot {}^\circ\text{R})$.

The *specific heat at constant volume* is defined as $c_v \equiv (\partial u/\partial T)_v$, so that

$$du = c_v \, dT + \left(\frac{\partial u}{\partial v}\right)_T dv$$

In particular, for an ideal gas it can be shown (see, e.g., Chapter 11 of [1]) that the internal energy, u, is a function of temperature only, so $(\partial u/\partial v)_T = 0$, and

$$du = c_v \, dT \qquad (12.2)$$

for an ideal gas. This means that internal energy and temperature changes may be related if c_v is known. Furthermore, since $u = u(T)$, then from Eq. 12.2, $c_v = c_v(T)$.

The *enthalpy* of any substance is defined as $h \equiv u + p/\rho$. For an ideal gas, $p = \rho RT$, and so $h = u + RT$. Since $u = u(T)$ for an ideal gas, h also must be a function of temperature alone.

We can obtain a relation between h and T by recalling once again that for a simple substance any property can be expressed as a function of any two other independent properties [1], e.g., $h = h(v, T)$ as we did for u, or $h = h(p, T)$. We choose the latter in order to develop a useful relation,

$$dh = \left(\frac{\partial h}{\partial T}\right)_p dT + \left(\frac{\partial h}{\partial p}\right)_T dp$$

Since the *specific heat at constant pressure* is defined as $c_p \equiv (\partial h/\partial T)_p$,

$$dh = c_p \, dT + \left(\frac{\partial h}{\partial p}\right)_T dp$$

We have shown that for an ideal gas h is a function of T only. Consequently, $(\partial h/\partial p)_T = 0$ and

$$dh = c_p \, dT \qquad (12.3)$$

Since h is a function of T alone, Eq. 12.3 requires that c_p be a function of T only for an ideal gas.

Although specific heats for an ideal gas are functions of temperature, their difference is a constant for each gas. To see this, from

$$h = u + RT$$

we can write

$$dh = du + R dT$$

Combining this with Eq. 12.2 and Eq. 12.3, we can write

$$dh = c_p \, dT = du + RdT = c_v \, dT + R \, dT$$

Then

$$c_p - c_v = R \qquad (12.4)$$

It may seem a bit odd that we have functions of temperature on the left of Eq. 12.4 but a constant on the right; it turns out that the specific heats of an ideal gas change with temperature at the same rate, so their *difference* is constant.

The *ratio of specific heats* is defined as

$$k \equiv \frac{c_p}{c_v} \qquad (12.5)$$

Using the definition of k, we can solve Eq. 12.4 for either c_p or c_v in terms of k and R. Thus,

$$c_p = \frac{kR}{k-1} \qquad (12.6a)$$

and

$$c_v = \frac{R}{k-1} \tag{12.6b}$$

Although the specific heats of an ideal gas may vary with temperature, for moderate temperature ranges they vary only slightly, and can be treated as constant, so

$$u_2 - u_1 = \int_{u_1}^{u_2} du = \int_{T_1}^{T_2} c_v \, dT = c_v(T_2 - T_1) \tag{12.7a}$$

$$h_2 - h_1 = \int_{h_1}^{h_2} dh = \int_{T_1}^{T_2} c_p \, dT = c_p(T_2 - T_1) \tag{12.7b}$$

Data for M_m, c_p, c_v, R, and k for common gases are given in Table A.6 of Appendix A.

We will find the property *entropy* to be extremely useful in analyzing compressible flows. State diagrams, particularly the temperature-entropy (*Ts*) diagram, are valuable aids in the physical interpretation of analytical results. Since we shall make extensive use of *Ts* diagrams in solving compressible flow problems, let us review briefly some useful relationships involving the property entropy [1–3].

Entropy is defined by the equation

$$\Delta S \equiv \int_{\text{rev}} \frac{\delta Q}{T} \quad \text{or} \quad dS = \left(\frac{\delta Q}{T}\right)_{\text{rev}} \tag{12.8}$$

where the subscript signifies *reversible*.

The inequality of Clausius, deduced from the second law, states that

$$\oint \frac{\delta Q}{T} \leq 0$$

As a consequence of the second law, we can write

$$dS \geq \frac{\delta Q}{T} \quad \text{or} \quad T \, dS \geq \delta Q \tag{12.9a}$$

For *reversible* processes, the equality holds, and

$$T \, ds = \frac{\delta Q}{m} \qquad \text{(reversible process)} \tag{12.9b}$$

The inequality holds for *irreversible* processes, and

$$T \, ds > \frac{\delta Q}{m} \qquad \text{(irreversible process)} \tag{12.9c}$$

For an *adiabatic* process, $\delta Q/m = 0$. Thus

$$ds = 0 \qquad \text{(reversible adiabatic process)} \tag{12.9d}$$

and

$$ds > 0 \qquad \text{(irreversible adiabatic process)} \tag{12.9e}$$

Thus a process that is *reversible and adiabatic* is also *isentropic*; the entropy remains constant during the process. Inequality 12.9e shows that entropy must *increase* for an adiabatic process that is irreversible.

Equations 12.9 show that any two of the restrictions—reversible, adiabatic, or isentropic—imply the third. For example, a process that is isentropic and reversible must also be adiabatic.

A useful relationship among properties (p, v, T, s, u) can be obtained by considering the first and second laws together. The result is the Gibbs, or $T \, ds$, equation

$$T \, ds = du + p \, dv \tag{12.10a}$$

This is a differential relationship among properties, valid for any process between any two equilibrium states. Although it is derived from the first and second laws, it is, in itself, a statement of neither.

An alternative form of Eq. 12.10a can be obtained by substituting

$$du = d(h - pv) = dh - p \, dv - v \, dp$$

to obtain

$$T \, ds = dh - v \, dp \tag{12.10b}$$

For an ideal gas, entropy change can be evaluated from the $T \, ds$ equations as

$$ds = \frac{du}{T} + \frac{p}{T} \, dv = c_v \frac{dT}{T} + R \frac{dv}{v}$$

$$ds = \frac{dh}{T} - \frac{v}{T} \, dp = c_p \frac{dT}{T} - R \frac{dp}{p}$$

For constant specific heats, these equations can be integrated to yield

$$s_2 - s_1 = c_v \ln \frac{T_2}{T_1} + R \ln \frac{v_2}{v_1} \tag{12.11a}$$

$$s_2 - s_1 = c_p \ln \frac{T_2}{T_1} - R \ln \frac{p_2}{p_1} \tag{12.11b}$$

and also

$$s_2 - s_1 = c_v \ln \frac{p_2}{p_1} + c_p \ln \frac{v_2}{v_1} \tag{12.11c}$$

(Equation 12.11c can be obtained from either Eq. 12.11a or 12.11b using Eq. 12.4 and the ideal gas equation, Eq. 12.1, written in the form $pv = RT$, to eliminate T.)

Example 12.1 shows use of the above governing equations (the $T \, ds$ equations) to evaluate property changes during a process.

For an ideal gas with constant specific heats, we can use Eqs. 12.11 to obtain relations valid for an isentropic process. From Eq. 12.11a

$$s_2 - s_1 = 0 = c_v \ln \frac{T_2}{T_1} + R \ln \frac{v_2}{v_1}$$

Then, using Eqs. 12.4 and 12.5,

$$\left(\frac{T_2}{T_1}\right)\left(\frac{v_2}{v_1}\right)^{R/c_v} = 0 \quad \text{or} \quad T_2 v_2^{k-1} = T_1 v_1^{k-1} = Tv^{k-1} = \text{constant}$$

where states 1 and 2 are arbitrary states of the isentropic process. Using $v = 1/\rho$,

$$Tv^{k-1} = \frac{T}{\rho^{k-1}} = \text{constant} \tag{12.12a}$$

We can apply a similar process to Eqs. 12.11b and 12.11c, respectively, and obtain the following useful relations:

$$Tp^{1-k/k} = \text{constant} \tag{12.12b}$$

$$pv^k = \frac{p}{\rho^k} = \text{constant} \tag{12.12c}$$

Equations 12.12 are for an ideal gas undergoing an isentropic process.

Qualitative information that is useful in drawing state diagrams also can be obtained from the $T \, ds$ equations. To complete our review of the thermodynamic fundamentals, we evaluate the slopes of lines of constant pressure and of constant volume on the Ts diagram in Example 12.2.

EXAMPLE 12.1 Property Changes in Compressible Duct Flow

Air flows through a long duct of constant area at 0.15 kg/s. A short section of the duct is cooled by liquid nitrogen that surrounds the duct. The rate of heat loss in this section is 15.0 kJ/s from the air. The absolute pressure, temperature, and velocity entering the cooled section are 188 kPa, 440 K, and 210 m/s, respectively. At the outlet, the absolute pressure and temperature are 213 kPa and 351 K. Compute the duct cross-sectional area and the changes in enthalpy, internal energy, and entropy for this flow.

GIVEN: Air flows steadily through a short section of constant-area duct that is cooled by liquid nitrogen.

$T_1 = 440$ K
$p_1 = 188$ kPa (abs)
$V_1 = 210$ m/s

Flow →   CV

$T_2 = 351$ K
$p_2 = 213$ kPa (abs)

① $\dot{Q} < 0$ ②

FIND: (a) Duct area. (b) Δh. (c) Δu. (d) Δs.

SOLUTION:
The duct area may be found from the continuity equation.

$$= 0(1)$$

Governing equation:

$$\cancel{\frac{\partial}{\partial T} \int_{CV} \rho \, d\mathbf{\forall}} + \int_{CS} \rho \vec{V} \cdot d\vec{A} = 0 \tag{4.12}$$

Assumptions:
(1) Steady flow.
(2) Uniform flow at each section.
(3) Ideal gas with constant specific heats.

Then

$$(-\rho_1 V_1 A_1) + (\rho_2 V_2 A_2) = 0$$

or

$$\dot{m} = \rho_1 V_1 A = \rho_2 V_2 A$$

since $A = A_1 = A_2 = $ constant. Using the ideal gas relation, $p = \rho RT$, we find

$$\rho_1 = \frac{p_1}{RT_1} = 1.88 \times 10^5 \frac{\text{N}}{\text{m}^2} \times \frac{\text{kg} \cdot \text{K}}{287 \, \text{N} \cdot \text{m}} \times \frac{1}{440 \, \text{K}} = 1.49 \, \text{kg/m}^3$$

From continuity,

$$A = \frac{\dot{m}}{\rho_1 V_1} = \frac{0.15 \, \text{kg}}{\text{s}} \times \frac{\text{m}^3}{1.49 \, \text{kg}} \times \frac{\text{s}}{210 \, \text{m}} = 4.79 \times 10^{-4} \text{m}^2 \quad\longleftarrow \qquad\qquad A$$

For an ideal gas, the change in enthalpy is

$$\Delta h = h_2 - h_1 = \int_{T_1}^{T_2} c_p \, dT = c_p (T_2 - T_1) \tag{12.7b}$$

$$\Delta h = 1.00 \, \frac{\text{kJ}}{\text{kg} \cdot \text{K}} \times (351 - 440) \, \text{K} = -89.0 \, \text{kJ/kg} \quad\longleftarrow \qquad\qquad \Delta h$$

Also, the change in internal energy is

$$\Delta u = u_2 - u_1 = \int_{T_1}^{T_2} c_v \, dT = c_v (T_2 - T_1) \tag{12.7a}$$

$$\Delta u = 0.717 \, \frac{\text{kJ}}{\text{kg} \cdot \text{K}} \times (351 - 440) \, \text{K} = -63.8 \, \text{kJ/kg} \quad\longleftarrow \qquad\qquad \Delta u$$

The entropy change may be obtained from Eq. 12.11b,

$$\Delta s = s_2 - s_1 = c_p \ln \frac{T_2}{T_1} - R \ln \frac{p_2}{p_1}$$

$$= 1.00 \ \frac{kJ}{kg \cdot K} \times \ln\left(\frac{351}{440}\right) - 0.287 \ \frac{kJ}{kg \cdot K} \times \ln\left(\frac{2.13 \times 10^5}{1.88 \times 10^5}\right)$$

$$\Delta s = -0.262 \ kJ/(kg \cdot K) \longleftarrow \qquad \Delta s$$

We see that entropy may decrease for a nonadiabatic process in which the gas is cooled.

> This Example illustrates the use of the governing equations for computing property changes of an ideal gas during a process.

EXAMPLE 12.2 Constant-Property Lines on a *Ts* Diagram

For an ideal gas, find the equations for lines of (a) constant volume and (b) constant pressure in the *Ts* plane.

FIND: Equations for lines of (a) constant volume and
(b) constant pressure in the *Ts* plane for an ideal gas.

SOLUTION:
(a) We are interested in the relation between T and s with the volume v held constant. This suggests use of Eq. 12.11a,

$$s_2 - s_1 = c_v \ln \frac{T_2}{T_1} + R \ln \overset{= 0}{\cancel{\frac{v_2}{v_1}}}$$

We relabel this equation so that state 1 is now reference state 0, and state 2 is an arbitrary state,

$$s - s_0 = c_v \ln \frac{T}{T_0} \quad \text{or} \quad T = T_0 e^{(s-s_0)/c_v} \qquad (1)$$

Hence, we conclude that constant volume lines in the *Ts* plane are exponential.

(b) We are interested in the relation between T and s with the pressure p held constant. This suggests use of Eq. 12.11b, and using a similar approach to case (a), we find

$$T = T_0 e^{(s-s_0)/c_p}$$

Hence, we conclude that constant pressure lines in the *Ts* plane are also exponential.

What about the slope of these curves? Because $c_p > c_v$ for all gases, we can see that the exponential, and therefore the slope, of the constant pressure curve, Eq. 2, is smaller than that for the constant volume curve, Eq. 1. This is shown in the sketch below:

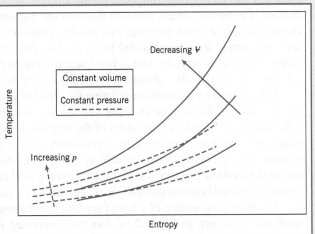

> This Example illustrates use of governing equations to explore relations among properties.

12-2   PROPAGATION OF SOUND WAVES

Speed of Sound

A beginner to compressible flow studies might wonder what on earth sound has to do with the speeds present in a flow. We will see in this chapter and the next that the speed of sound, c, is an important marker in fluid mechanics: Flows with speeds less than the speed of sound are called *subsonic*; flows with speeds greater than the speed of sound are called *supersonic*; and we will learn that the behaviors of subsonic and supersonic flows are completely different. We have previously (in Chapter 2, and in Chapter 7 with Eq. 7.16) defined the Mach number M of a flow, and it is so important for our studies that we redefine it here,

$$M \equiv \frac{V}{c} \tag{12.13}$$

where V is the speed (of the fluid, or in some cases of the aircraft), so that $M < 1$ and $M > 1$ correspond to subsonic and supersonic flow, respectively. In addition, we mentioned in Section 12-1 that we'll demonstrate in Example 12.5 that for $M < 0.3$, we can generally assume incompressible flow. Hence, knowledge of the Mach number value is important in fluid mechanics.

An answer to the question posed at the beginning of this section is that the speed of sound is important in fluid mechanics because this is the speed at which "signals" can travel through the medium. Consider, for example, an object such as an aircraft in motion—the air ultimately has to move out of its way. In Newton's day, it was thought that this happened when the (invisible) air particles literally bounced off the front of the object, like so many balls bouncing off a wall; now we know that in most instances the air starts moving out of the way well before encountering the object (this will *not* be true when we have supersonic flow!). How does the air "know" to move out of the way? It knows because as the object moves, it generates disturbances (infinitesimal pressure waves—sound waves) that emanate from the object in all directions. It is these waves that cumulatively "signal" the air and redirect it around the body as it approaches. These waves travel out at the speed of sound.

[Sound is a pressure wave of very low pressure magnitude, for human hearing typically in the range of about 10^{-9} atm (the threshold of hearing) to about 10^{-3} atm (you will feel pain!). Superimposed on the ambient atmospheric pressure, sound waves consist of extremely small pressure fluctuations. Because the range of human hearing covers about five or six orders of magnitude in pressure, typically we use a dimensionless logarithmic scale, the decibel level, to indicate sound intensity; 0 dB corresponds to the threshold of hearing, and if you listen to your MP3 player at full blast the sound will be at about 100 dB—about 10^{10} the intensity of the threshold of hearing!]

Let us derive a method for computing the speed of sound in any medium (solid, liquid, or gas). As we do so, bear in mind that we are obtaining the speed of a "signal"— a pressure wave—and that the speed of the medium in which the wave travels is a completely different thing. For example, if you watch a soccer player kick the ball (at the speed of light—the watching, that is), a fraction of a second later you will hear the thud of contact as the sound (a pressure wave) travels from the field up to you in the stands, but no air particles traveled between you and the player (all the air particles simply vibrated a bit).

Consider propagation of a sound wave of infinitesimal strength into an undisturbed medium, as shown in Fig. 12.1a. We are interested in relating the speed of wave

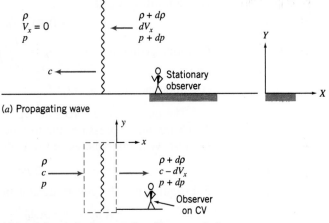

(a) Propagating wave

(b) Inertial control volume moving with wave, velocity c

Fig. 12.1 Propagating sound wave showing control volume chosen for analysis.

propagation, c, to fluid property changes across the wave. If pressure and density in the undisturbed medium ahead of the wave are denoted by p and ρ, passage of the wave will cause them to undergo infinitesimal changes to become $p + dp$ and $\rho + d\rho$. Since the wave propagates into a stationary fluid, the velocity ahead of the wave, V_x, is zero. The magnitude of the velocity behind the wave, $V_x + dV_x$, then will be simply dV_x; in Fig. 12.1a, the direction of the motion behind the wave has been assumed to the left.[2]

The flow of Fig. 12.1a appears unsteady to a stationary observer, viewing the wave motion from a fixed point on the ground. However, the flow appears steady to an observer located *on* an inertial control volume moving with a segment of the wave, as shown in Fig. 12.1b. The velocity approaching the control volume is then c, and the velocity leaving is $c - dV_x$.

The basic equations may be applied to the differential control volume shown in Fig. 12.1b (we use V_x for the x component of velocity to avoid confusion with internal energy, u).

a. Continuity Equation

Governing equation:

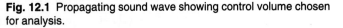

$$\frac{\partial}{\partial T} \int_{CV} \rho \, d\forall + \int_{CS} \rho \vec{V} \cdot d\vec{A} = 0 \qquad (4.12)$$

Assumptions: (1) Steady flow.
(2) Uniform flow at each section.

Then

$$(-\rho c A) + \{(\rho + d\rho)(c - dV_x)A\} = 0 \qquad (12.14a)$$

or

$$-\rho c A + \rho c A - \rho \, dV_x A + d\rho c A - \overset{\approx 0}{\cancel{d\rho \, dV_x A}} = 0$$

or

$$dV_x = \frac{c}{\rho} d\rho \qquad (12.14b)$$

---

[2] The same final result is obtained regardless of the direction initially assumed for motion behind the wave (see Problem 12.28).

b. Momentum Equation

$$= 0(3) = 0(1)$$

Governing equation: $F_{S_x} + \cancel{F_{B_x}} = \cancel{\frac{\partial}{\partial t} \int_{CV} V_x\, \rho dV} + \int_{CS} V_x\, \rho \vec{V} \cdot d\vec{A}$ (4.18a)

Assumption: (3) $F_{B_x} = 0$

The only surface forces acting in the x direction on the control volume of Fig. 12.1*b* are due to pressure (the infinitesimal upper and lower areas have zero friction because we assume the wave is one dimensional).

$$F_{S_x} = pA - (p + dp)A = -A\, dp$$

Substituting into the governing equation gives

$$-A\, dp = c(-\rho cA) + (c - dV_x)\{(\rho + d\rho)(c - dV_x)A\}$$

Using the continuity equation, (Eq. 12.14a), this reduces to

$$-A\, dp = c(-\rho cA) + (c - dV_x)(\rho cA) = (-c + c - dV_x)(\rho cA)$$
$$-A\, dp = -\rho cA\, dV_x$$

or

$$dV_x = \frac{1}{\rho c}\, dp \qquad\qquad (12.14c)$$

Combining Eqs. 12.14b and 12.14c, we obtain

$$dV_x = \frac{c}{\rho}\, d\rho = \frac{1}{\rho c}\, dp$$

from which

$$dp = c^2\, d\rho$$

or

$$c^2 = \frac{dp}{d\rho} \qquad\qquad (12.15)$$

We have derived an expression for the speed of sound in any medium in terms of thermodynamic quantities! Equation 12.15 indicates that the speed of sound depends on how the pressure and density of the medium are related. To obtain the speed of sound in a medium we could measure the time a sound wave takes to travel a prescribed distance, or instead we could apply a small pressure change dp to a sample, measure the corresponding density change $d\rho$, and evaluate c from Eq. 12.15. For example, an *incompressible* medium would have $d\rho = 0$ for any dp, so $c \to \infty$. We can anticipate that solids and liquids (whose densities are difficult to change) will have relatively high c values, and gases (whose densities are easy to change) will have relatively low c values. There is only one problem with Eq. 12.15: For a simple substance, each property depends on any *two* independent properties [1]. For a sound wave, by definition we have an infinitesimal pressure change (i.e., it is *reversible*), and it occurs very quickly, so there is no time for any heat transfer to occur (i.e., it is *adiabatic*). Thus the sound wave propagates *isentropically*. Hence, if we express p as a function of density and entropy, $p = p(\rho, s)$, then

$$dp = \left(\frac{\partial p}{\partial \rho}\right)_s d\rho + \left(\frac{\partial p}{\partial s}\right)_\rho ds = \left(\frac{\partial p}{\partial \rho}\right)_s d\rho$$

so Eq. 12.15 becomes

$$c^2 = \frac{dp}{d\rho} = \frac{\partial p}{\partial \rho}\bigg)_s$$

and

$$c = \sqrt{\frac{\partial p}{\partial \rho}\bigg)_s} \tag{12.16}$$

We can now apply Eq. 12.16 to solids, liquids, and gases. For *solids* and *liquids* data are usually available on the bulk modulus E_v, which is a measure of how a pressure change affects a relative density change,

$$E_v = \frac{dp}{d\rho/\rho} = \rho\frac{dp}{d\rho}$$

For these media

$$c = \sqrt{E_v/\rho} \tag{12.17}$$

For an *ideal gas*, the pressure and density in isentropic flow are related by

$$\frac{p}{\rho^k} = \text{constant} \tag{12.12c}$$

Taking logarithms and differentiating, we obtain

$$\frac{dp}{p} - k\frac{d\rho}{\rho} = 0$$

Therefore,

$$\frac{\partial p}{\partial \rho}\bigg)_s = k\frac{p}{\rho}$$

But $p/\rho = RT$, so finally

$$c = \sqrt{kRT} \tag{12.18}$$

for an ideal gas. The speed of sound in air has been measured precisely by numerous investigators [4]. The results agree closely with the theoretical prediction of Eq. 12.18.

The important feature of sound propagation in an ideal gas, as shown by Eq. 12.18, is that the *speed of sound is a function of temperature only*. The variation in atmospheric temperature with altitude on a standard day was discussed in Chapter 3; the properties are summarized in Table A.3. The corresponding variation in c is computed as an exercise in Problem 12.29 and plotted as a function of altitude.

EXAMPLE 12.3   Speed of Sound in Steel, Water, Seawater, and Air

Find the speed of sound in (a) steel ($E_v \approx 200\,\text{GN/m}^2$), (b) water (at 20°C), (c) seawater (at 20°C), and (d) air at sea level on a standard day.

FIND: Speed of sound in (a) steel ($E_v = 200\,\text{GN/m}^2$), (b) water (at 20°C), (c) seawater (at 20°C), and (d) air at sea level on a standard day.

SOLUTION:
(a) For steel, a solid, we use Eq. 12.17, with ρ obtained from Table A.1(b),

$$c = \sqrt{E_v/\rho} = \sqrt{E_v/SG\rho_{H_2O}}$$

$$c = \sqrt{200 \times 10^9\,\frac{N}{m^2} \times \frac{1}{7.83} \times \frac{m^3}{1000\,kg} \times \frac{kg \cdot m}{N \cdot s^2}} = 5050\,\text{m/s} \longleftarrow \qquad c_{\text{steel}}$$

(b) For water we also use Eq. 12.17, with data obtained from Table A.2,

$$c = \sqrt{E_v/\rho} = \sqrt{E_v/SG\rho_{H_2O}}$$

$$c = \sqrt{2.24 \times 10^9 \frac{N}{m^2} \times \frac{1}{0.998} \times \frac{m^3}{1000 \text{ kg}} \times \frac{kg \cdot m}{N \cdot s^2}} = 1500 \text{ m/s} \quad\longleftarrow\qquad c_{\text{water}}$$

(c) For seawater we again use Eq. 12.17, with data obtained from Table A.2,

$$c = \sqrt{E_v/\rho} = \sqrt{E_v/SG\rho_{H_2O}}$$

$$c = \sqrt{2.42 \times 10^9 \frac{N}{m^2} \times \frac{1}{1.025} \times \frac{m^3}{1000 \text{ kg}} \times \frac{kg \cdot m}{N \cdot s^2}} = 1540 \text{ m/s} \quad\longleftarrow\qquad c_{\text{seawater}}$$

(d) For air we use Eq. 12.18, with the sea level temperature obtained from Table A.3,

$$c = \sqrt{kRT}$$

$$c = \sqrt{1.4 \times 287 \frac{N \cdot m}{kg \cdot K} \times 288 \text{ K} \times \frac{kg \cdot m}{N \cdot s^2}} = 340 \text{ m/s} \quad\longleftarrow\qquad c_{\text{air (288 K)}}$$

> This Example illustrates the relative magnitudes of the speed of sound in typical solids, liquids, and gases ($c_{\text{solids}} > c_{\text{liquids}} > c_{\text{gases}}$). Do not confuse the speed of sound with the *attenuation* of sound—the rate at which internal friction of the medium reduces the sound level—generally, solids and liquids attenuate sound much more rapidly than do gases.

Types of Flow—The Mach Cone

Flows for which $M < 1$ are *subsonic*, while those with $M > 1$ are *supersonic*. Flow fields that have both subsonic and supersonic regions are termed *transonic*. (The transonic regime occurs for Mach numbers between about 0.9 and 1.2.) Although most flows within our experience are subsonic, there are important practical cases where $M \geq 1$ occurs in a flow field. Perhaps the most obvious are supersonic aircraft and transonic flows in aircraft compressors and fans. Yet another flow regime, *hypersonic* flow ($M \gtrsim 5$), is of interest in missile and reentry-vehicle design. (The proposed National Aerospace Plane would have cruised at Mach numbers approaching 20.) Some important qualitative differences between subsonic and supersonic flows can be deduced from the properties of a simple moving sound source.

Consider a point source of sound that emits a pulse every Δt seconds. Each pulse expands outwards from its origination point at the speed of sound c, so at any instant t the pulse will be a sphere of radius ct centered at the pulse's origination point. We want to investigate what happens if the point source itself is moving. There are four possibilities, as shown in Fig. 12.2:

(a) $V = 0$. The point source is *stationary*. Figure 12.2a shows conditions after $3\Delta t$ seconds. The first pulse has expanded to a sphere of radius $c(3\Delta t)$, the second to a sphere of radius $c(2\Delta t)$, and the third to a sphere of radius $c(\Delta t)$; a new pulse is about to be emitted. The pulses constitute a set of ever-expanding concentric spheres.

(b) $0 < V < c$. The point source moves to the left at *subsonic* speed. Figure 12.2b shows conditions after $3\Delta t$ seconds. The source is shown at times $t = 0$, Δt, $2\Delta t$, and $3\Delta t$. The first pulse has expanded to a sphere of radius $c(3\Delta t)$ *centered where the source was*

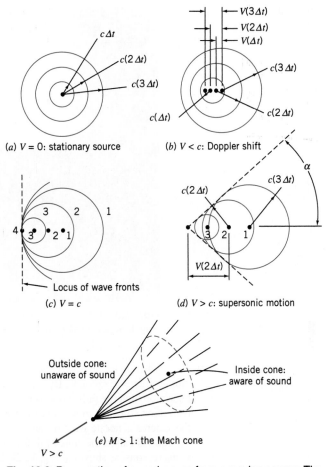

Fig. 12.2 Propagation of sound waves from a moving source: The Mach cone.

originally, the second to a sphere of radius $c(2\Delta t)$ *centered where the source was at time* Δt, and the third to a sphere of radius $c(\Delta t)$ *centered where the source was at time* $2\Delta t$; a new pulse is about to be emitted. The pulses again constitute a set of ever-expanding spheres, except now they are not concentric. The pulses are all expanding at constant speed c. We make two important notes: First, we can see that an observer who is ahead of the source (or whom the source is approaching) will hear the pulses at a higher frequency rate than will an observer who is behind the source (this is the Doppler effect that occurs when a vehicle approaches and passes); second, an observer ahead of the source hears the source *before* the source itself reaches the observer.

(c) $V = c$. The point source moves to the left at *sonic* speed. Figure 12.2c shows conditions after $3\Delta t$ seconds. The source is shown at times $t = 0$ (point 1), Δt (point 2), $2\Delta t$ (point 3), and $3\Delta t$ (point 4). The first pulse has expanded to sphere 1 of radius $c(3\Delta t)$ *centered at point 1*, the second to sphere 2 of radius $c(2\Delta t)$ *centered at point 2*, and the third to sphere 3 of radius $c(\Delta t)$ *centered around the source at point 3*. We can see once more that the pulses constitute a set of ever-expanding spheres, except now they are tangent to one another on the left! The pulses are all expanding at constant speed c, but the source is also moving at speed c, with the result that the source and all its pulses are traveling together to the left. We again make two important notes: First, we can see that an observer who is ahead of the source will *not* hear the pulses before the source reaches her; second, in theory, over time an unlimited number of pulses will accumulate at the front of the source, leading to a sound wave of unlimited amplitude (a source of concern to engineers trying to break the "sound barrier," which many people thought could not be broken—Chuck Yeager in a Bell X-1 was the first to do so in 1947).

Fig. 12.3 An F/A-18 Hornet as it breaks the sound barrier. (Ensign John Gay, USS *Constellation*, U.S. Navy.)

(d) $V > c$. The point source moves to the left at *supersonic* speed. Figure 12.2*d* shows conditions after $3\Delta t$ seconds. By now it is clear how the spherical waves develop. We can see once more that the pulses constitute a set of ever-expanding spheres, except now the source is moving so fast it moves ahead of each sphere that it generates! For supersonic motion, the spheres generate what is called a *Mach cone* tangent to each sphere. The region inside the cone is called the *zone of action* and that outside the cone the *zone of silence*, for obvious reasons, as shown in Fig. 12.2*e*. From geometry, we see from Fig. 12.2*d* that

$$\sin\alpha = \frac{c}{V} = \frac{1}{M}$$

or

$$\alpha = \sin^{-1}\left(\frac{1}{M}\right) \qquad (12.19)$$

Figure 12.3 shows an image of an F/A-18 Hornet just as it accelerates to supersonic speed. The visible vapor pattern is due to the sudden increase in pressure as a shock wave washes over the aircraft (we will see in the next chapter that a shock wave leads to a sudden and large pressure increase). The (invisible) Mach cone emanates from the nose of the aircraft and passes through the periphery of the vapor disk.

EXAMPLE 12.4   Mach Cone of a Bullet

In tests of a protective material, we wish to photograph a bullet as it impacts a jacket made of the material. A camera is set up a perpendicular distance $h = 5$ m from the bullet trajectory. We wish to determine the perpendicular distance d from the target plane at which the camera must be placed such that the sound of the bullet will trigger the camera at the impact time. Note: The bullet speed is measured to be 550 m/s; the delay time of the camera is 0.005 s.

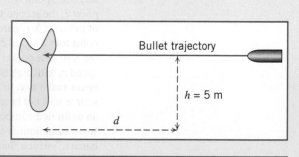

FIND: Location of camera for capturing impact image.

SOLUTION:

The correct value of d is that for which the bullet hits the target 0.005s before the Mach wave reaches the camera. We must first find the Mach number of the bullet; then we can find the Mach angle; finally, we can use basic trigonometry to find d.

Assuming sea level conditions, from Table A.3 we have $T = 288$ K. Hence Eq. 12.18 yields

$$c = \sqrt{kRT}$$

$$c = \sqrt{1.4 \times 287 \frac{N \cdot m}{kg \cdot K} \times 288 \text{ K} \times \frac{kg \cdot m}{N \cdot s^2}} = 340 \text{ m/s}$$

Then we can find the Mach number,

$$M = \frac{V}{c} = \frac{550 \text{ m/s}}{340 \text{ m/s}} = 1.62$$

From Eq. 12.19 we can next find the Mach angle,

$$\alpha = \sin^{-1}\left(\frac{1}{M}\right) = \sin^{-1}\left(\frac{1}{1.62}\right) = 38.2°$$

The distance x traveled by the bullet while the Mach wave reaches the camera is then

$$x = \frac{h}{\tan(\alpha)} = \frac{5 \text{ m}}{\tan(38.2°)} = 6.35 \text{ m}$$

Finally, we must add to this the time traveled by the bullet while the camera is operating, which is 0.005 s $\times$ 550 m/s,

$$d = 0.005 \text{ s} \times \frac{550 \text{ m}}{s} + 6.35 \text{ m} = 2.75 \text{ m} + 6.35 \text{ m}$$

$$d = 9.10 \text{ m} \qquad\qquad\qquad\qquad\qquad\qquad\qquad\qquad d$$

12-3   REFERENCE STATE: LOCAL ISENTROPIC STAGNATION PROPERTIES

In our study of compressible flow, we will discover that, in general, *all* properties (p, T, ρ, u, h, s, V) may be changing as the flow proceeds. We need to obtain reference conditions that we can use to relate conditions in a flow from point to point. For any flow, a reference condition is obtained when the fluid is (in reality or conceptually) brought to rest ($V = 0$). We will call this the *stagnation condition*, and the property values (p_0, T_0, ρ_0, u_0, h_0, s_0) at this state the *stagnation properties*. This process—of bringing the fluid to rest—is not as straightforward as it seems. For example, do we do so while there is friction, or while the fluid is being heated or cooled, or "violently," or in some other way? The simplest process to use is an isentropic process, in which there is no friction, no heat transfer, and no "violent" events. Hence, the properties we obtain will be the *local isentropic stagnation properties*. Why "local"? Because the actual flow can be any kind of flow, e.g., with friction, so it may or may not itself be isentropic. Hence, each point in the flow will have its own, or local, isentropic stagnation properties. This is illustrated in Fig. 12.4, showing a flow from some state ① to some new state ②. The local isentropic stagnation properties for each state, obtained by isentropically bringing the fluid to rest, are also shown. Hence, $s_{0_1} = s_1$ and $s_{0_2} = s_2$. The actual flow may or may not be isentropic. If it *is* isentropic, $s_1 = s_2 = s_{0_1} = s_{0_2}$, so the stagnation states are identical; if it is *not* isentropic, then $s_{0_1} \neq s_{0_2}$. We will see that changes in local isentropic stagnation properties will provide useful information about the flow.

We can obtain information on the reference isentropic stagnation state for *incompressible* flows by recalling the Bernoulli equation from Chapter 6

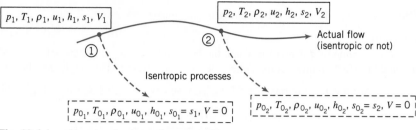

Fig. 12.4 Local isentropic stagnation properties.

$$\frac{p}{\rho} + \frac{V^2}{2} + gz = \text{constant} \tag{6.8}$$

valid for a steady, incompressible, frictionless flow along a streamline. Equation 6.8 is valid for an incompressible isentropic process because it is reversible (frictionless and steady) and adiabatic (we did not include heat transfer considerations in its derivation). As we saw in Section 6-3, the Bernoulli equation leads to

$$p_0 = p + \frac{1}{2}\rho V^2 \tag{6.11}$$

(The gravity term drops out because we assume the reference state is at the same elevation as the actual state, and in any event in external flows it is usually much smaller than the other terms.) In Example 12.6 we compare isentropic stagnation conditions obtained assuming incompressibility (Eq. 6.11), and allowing for compressibility.

For *compressible* flows, we will focus on ideal gas behavior.

Local Isentropic Stagnation Properties for the Flow of an Ideal Gas

For a compressible flow we can derive the isentropic stagnation relations by applying the mass conservation (or continuity) and momentum equations to a differential control volume, and then integrating. For the process shown schematically in Fig. 12.4, we can depict the process from state ① to the corresponding stagnation state by imagining the control volume shown in Fig. 12.5. Consider first the continuity equation.

a. Continuity Equation

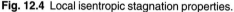

Governing equation: $\quad \cancelto{0(1)}{\dfrac{\partial}{\partial t}} \displaystyle\int_{\text{CV}} \rho \, d\forall + \int_{\text{CS}} \rho \vec{V} \cdot d\vec{A} = 0 \tag{4.12}$

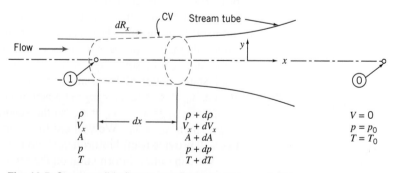

Fig. 12.5 Compressible flow in an infinitesimal stream tube.

Assumptions: (1) Steady flow.
(2) Uniform flow at each section.

Then

$$(-\rho V_x A) + \{(\rho + d\rho)(V_x + dV_x)(A + dA)\} = 0$$

or

$$\rho V_x A = (\rho + d\rho)(V_x + dV_x)(A + dA) \tag{12.20a}$$

b. Momentum Equation

Governing equation: $F_{S_x} + \overset{= 0(3)}{\cancel{F_{B_x}}} = \overset{= 0(1)}{\cancel{\frac{\partial}{\partial t}}} \int_{CV} V_x \rho \, d\cancel{V} + \int_{CS} V_x \rho \vec{V} \cdot d\vec{A} \tag{4.18a}$

Assumptions: (3) $F_{B_x} = 0$.
(4) Frictionless flow.

The surface forces acting on the infinitesimal control volume are

$$F_{S_x} = dR_x + pA - (p + dp)(A + dA)$$

The force dR_x is applied along the stream tube boundary, as shown in Fig. 12.5, where the average pressure is $p + dp/2$, and the area component in the x direction is dA. There is no friction. Thus,

$$F_{S_x} = \left(p + \frac{dp}{2}\right) dA + pA - (p + dp)(A + dA)$$

or

$$F_{S_x} = p\,\cancel{dA} + \overset{\approx 0}{\cancel{\frac{dp\,\cancel{dA}}{2}}} + \cancel{pA} - \cancel{pA} - dp\,A - p\,\cancel{dA} - \overset{\approx 0}{\cancel{dp\,\cancel{dA}}}$$

Substituting this result into the momentum equation gives

$$-dp\,A = V_x\{-\rho V_x A\} + (V_x + dV_x)\{(\rho + d\rho)(V_x + dV_x)(A + dA)\}$$

which may be simplified using Eq. 12.20a to obtain

$$-dp\,A = (-V_x + V_x + dV_x)(\rho V_x A)$$

Finally,

$$dp = -\rho V_x dV_x = -\rho\, d\left(\frac{V_x^2}{2}\right)$$

or

$$\frac{dp}{\rho} + d\left(\frac{V_x^2}{2}\right) = 0 \tag{12.20b}$$

Equation 12.20b is a relation among properties during the deceleration process. (Note that for incompressible flow, it immediately leads to Eq. 6.11.) In developing this relation, we have specified a frictionless deceleration process. Before we can integrate between the initial and final (stagnation) states, we must specify the relation that exists between pressure, p, and density, ρ, along the process path.

Since the deceleration process is isentropic, then p and ρ for an ideal gas are related by the expression

$$\frac{p}{\rho^k} = \text{constant} \tag{12.12c}$$

Our task now is to integrate Eq. 12.20b subject to this relation. Along the stagnation streamline there is only a single component of velocity; V_x is the magnitude of the velocity. Hence we can drop the subscript in Eq. 12.20b.

From $p/\rho^k = $ constant $= C$, we can write

$$p = C\rho^k \quad \text{and} \quad \rho = p^{1/k} C^{-1/k}$$

Then, from Eq. 12.20b,

$$-d\left(\frac{V^2}{2}\right) = \frac{dp}{\rho} = p^{-1/k} C^{1/k} dp$$

We can integrate this equation between the initial state and the corresponding stagnation state

$$-\int_V^0 d\left(\frac{V^2}{2}\right) = C^{1/k} \int_p^{p_0} p^{-1/k} dp$$

to obtain

$$\frac{V^2}{2} = C^{1/k} \frac{k}{k-1} \left[p^{(k-1)/k}\right]_p^{p_0} = C^{1/k} \frac{k}{k-1} \left[p_0^{(k-1)/k} - p^{(k-1)/k}\right]$$

$$\frac{V^2}{2} = C^{1/k} \frac{k}{k-1} p^{(k-1)/k} \left[\left(\frac{p_0}{p}\right)^{(k-1)/k} - 1\right]$$

Since $C^{1/k} = p^{1/k}/\rho$,

$$\frac{V^2}{2} = \frac{k}{k-1} \frac{p^{1/k}}{\rho} p^{(k-1)/k} \left[\left(\frac{p_0}{p}\right)^{(k-1)/k} - 1\right]$$

$$\frac{V^2}{2} = \frac{k}{k-1} \frac{p}{\rho} \left[\left(\frac{p_0}{p}\right)^{(k-1)/k} - 1\right]$$

Since we seek an expression for stagnation pressure, we can rewrite this equation as

$$\left(\frac{p_0}{p}\right)^{(k-1)/k} = 1 + \frac{k-1}{k} \frac{\rho}{p} \frac{V^2}{2}$$

and

$$\frac{p_0}{p} = \left[1 + \frac{k-1}{k} \frac{\rho V^2}{2p}\right]^{k/(k-1)}$$

For an ideal gas, $p = \rho RT$, and hence

$$\frac{p_0}{p} = \left[1 + \frac{k-1}{2} \frac{V^2}{kRT}\right]^{k/(k-1)}$$

Also, for an ideal gas the sonic speed is $c = \sqrt{kRT}$, and thus

$$\frac{p_0}{p} = \left[1 + \frac{k-1}{2} \frac{V^2}{c^2}\right]^{k/(k-1)}$$

$$\frac{p_0}{p} = \left[1 + \frac{k-1}{2} M^2\right]^{k/(k-1)} \tag{12.21a}$$

Equation 12.21a enables us to calculate the local isentropic stagnation pressure at any point in a flow field of an ideal gas, provided that we know the static pressure and Mach number at that point.

We can readily obtain expressions for other isentropic stagnation properties by applying the relation

$$\frac{p}{\rho^k} = \text{constant}$$

between end states of the process. Thus

$$\frac{p_0}{p} = \left(\frac{\rho_0}{\rho}\right)^k \quad \text{and} \quad \frac{\rho_0}{\rho} = \left(\frac{p_0}{p}\right)^{1/k}$$

For an ideal gas, then,

$$\frac{T_0}{T} = \frac{p_0}{p}\frac{\rho}{\rho_0} = \frac{p_0}{p}\left(\frac{p_0}{p}\right)^{-1/k} = \left(\frac{p_0}{p}\right)^{(k-1)/k}$$

Using Eq. 12.21a, we can summarize the equations for determining local isentropic stagnation properties of an ideal gas as

$$\frac{p_0}{p} = \left[1 + \frac{k-1}{2}M^2\right]^{k/(k-1)} \tag{12.21a}$$

$$\frac{T_0}{T} = 1 + \frac{k-1}{2}M^2 \tag{12.21b}$$

$$\frac{\rho_0}{\rho} = \left[1 + \frac{k-1}{2}M^2\right]^{1/(k-1)} \tag{12.21c}$$

From Eqs. 12.21, the ratio of each local isentropic stagnation property to the corresponding static property at any point in a flow field for an ideal gas can be found if the local Mach number is known. We will usually use Eqs. 12.21 in lieu of the continuity and momentum equations for relating the properties at a state to that state's stagnation properties, but it is important to remember that we derived Eqs. 12.21 using these equations *and* the isentropic relation for an ideal gas. Appendix E-1 lists flow functions for property ratios T_0/T, p_0/p, and ρ_0/ρ, in terms of M for isentropic flow of an ideal gas. A table of values, as well as a plot of these property ratios is presented for air ($k = 1.4$) for a limited range of Mach numbers. The associated *Excel* workbook, *Isentropic Relations*, available on the Web site, can be used to print a larger table of values for air and other ideal gases. The calculation procedure is illustrated in Example 12.5.

The Mach number range for validity of the assumption of incompressible flow is investigated in Example 12.6.

EXAMPLE 12.5   Local Isentropic Stagnation Conditions in Channel Flow

Air flows steadily through the duct shown from 350 kPa(abs), 60°C, and 183 m/s at the inlet state to $M = 1.3$ at the outlet, where local isentropic stagnation conditions are known to be 385 kPa(abs) and 350 K. Compute the local isentropic stagnation pressure and temperature at the inlet and the static pressure and temperature at the duct outlet. Locate the inlet and outlet static state points on a Ts diagram, and indicate the stagnation processes.

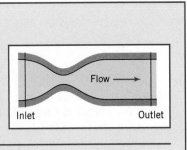

GIVEN: Steady flow of air through a duct as shown in the sketch.

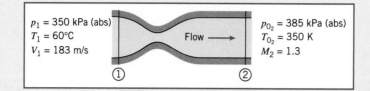

FIND: (a) p_{0_1}.
(b) T_{0_1}.
(c) p_2.
(d) T_2.
(e) State points ① and ② on a Ts diagram; indicate the stagnation processes.

SOLUTION:

To evaluate local isentropic stagnation conditions at section ①, we must calculate the Mach number, $M_1 = V_1/c_1$. For an ideal gas, $c = \sqrt{kRT}$. Then

$$c_1 = \sqrt{kRT_1} = \left[1.4 \times 287 \frac{\text{N} \cdot \text{m}}{\text{kg} \cdot \text{K}} \times (273 + 60) \text{ K} \times \frac{\text{kg} \cdot \text{m}}{\text{N} \cdot \text{s}^2} \right]^{1/2} = 366 \text{ m/s}$$

and

$$M_1 = \frac{V_1}{c_1} = \frac{183}{366} = 0.5$$

Local isentropic stagnation properties can be evaluated from Eqs. 12.21. Thus

$$p_{0_1} = p_1 \left[1 + \frac{k-1}{2} M_1^2 \right]^{k(k-1)} = 350 \text{ kPa } [1 + 0.2(0.5)^2]^{3.5} = 415 \text{ kPa(abs)} \qquad\longleftarrow\qquad p_{0_1}$$

$$T_{0_1} = T_1 \left[1 + \frac{k-1}{2} M_1^2 \right] = 333 \text{ K}[1 + 0.2(0.5)^2] = 350 \text{ K} \qquad\longleftarrow\qquad T_{0_1}$$

At section ②, Eqs. 12.21 can be applied again. Thus from Eq. 12.21a,

$$p_2 = \frac{p_{0_2}}{\left[1 + \frac{k-1}{2} M_2^2 \right]^{k/(k-1)}} = \frac{385 \text{ kPa}}{[1 + 0.2(1.3)^2]^{3.5}} = 139 \text{ kPa(abs)} \qquad\longleftarrow\qquad p_2$$

From Eq. 12.21b,

$$T_2 = \frac{T_{0_2}}{1 + \frac{k-1}{2} M_2^2} = \frac{350 \text{ K}}{1 + 0.2(1.3)^2} = 262 \text{ K} \qquad\longleftarrow\qquad T_2$$

To locate states ① and ② in relation to one another, and sketch the stagnation processes on the Ts diagram, we need to find the change in entropy $s_2 - s_1$. At each state we have p and T, so it is convenient to use Eq. 12.11b,

$$s_2 - s_1 = c_p \ln \frac{T_2}{T_1} - R \ln \frac{p_2}{p_1}$$

$$= 1.00 \frac{\text{kJ}}{\text{kg} \cdot \text{K}} \times \ln\left(\frac{262}{333}\right) - 0.287 \frac{\text{kJ}}{\text{kg} \cdot \text{K}} \times \ln\left(\frac{139}{350}\right)$$

$$s_2 - s_1 = 0.0252 \text{ kJ/(kg} \cdot \text{K)}$$

Hence in this flow we have an increase in entropy. Perhaps there is irreversibility (e.g., friction), or heat is being added, or both. (We will see in Chapter 13 that the fact that $T_{0_1} = T_{0_2}$ for this particular flow means that actually we have an adiabatic flow.) We also found that $T_2 < T_1$ and that $p_2 < p_1$. We can now sketch the Ts diagram (and recall we saw in Example 12.2 that isobars (lines of constant pressure) in Ts space are exponential),

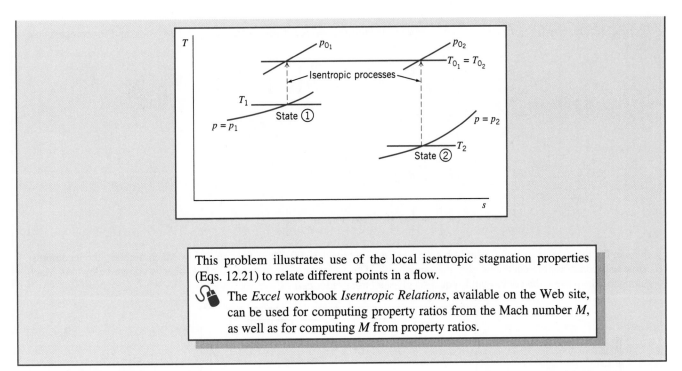

This problem illustrates use of the local isentropic stagnation properties (Eqs. 12.21) to relate different points in a flow.

The *Excel* workbook *Isentropic Relations*, available on the Web site, can be used for computing property ratios from the Mach number M, as well as for computing M from property ratios.

EXAMPLE 12.6 Mach-Number Limit for Incompressible Flow

We have derived equations for p_0/p for both compressible and "incompressible" flows. By writing both equations in terms of Mach number, compare their behavior. Find the Mach number below which the two equations agree within engineering accuracy.

GIVEN: The incompressible and compressible forms of the equations for stagnation pressure, p_0.

Incompressible $$p_0 = p + \frac{1}{2}\rho V^2 \qquad (6.11)$$

Compressible $$\frac{p_0}{p} = \left[1 + \frac{k-1}{2}M^2\right]^{k/(k-1)} \qquad (12.21a)$$

FIND: (a) Behavior of both equations as a function of Mach number.
(b) Mach number below which calculated values of p_0/p agree within engineering accuracy.

SOLUTION:
First, let us write Eq. 6.11 in terms of Mach number. Using the ideal gas equation of state and $c^2 = kRT$,

$$\frac{p_0}{p} = 1 + \frac{\rho V^2}{2p} = 1 + \frac{V^2}{2RT} = 1 + \frac{kV^2}{2kRT} = 1 + \frac{kV^2}{2c^2}$$

Thus,

$$\frac{p_0}{p} = 1 + \frac{k}{2}M^2 \qquad (1)$$

for "incompressible" flow.
Equation 12.21a may be expanded using the binomial theorem,

$$(1 + x)^n = 1 + nx + \frac{n(n-1)}{2!}x^2 + \cdots, |x| < 1$$

For Eq. 12.21a, $x = [(k-1)/2]M^2$, and $n = k/(k-1)$. Thus the series converges for $[(k-1)/2]M^2 < 1$, and for compressible flow,

$$\frac{p_0}{p} = 1 + \left(\frac{k}{k-1}\right)\left[\frac{k-1}{2}M^2\right] + \left(\frac{k}{k-1}\right)\left(\frac{k}{k-1}-1\right)\frac{1}{2!}\left[\frac{k-1}{2}M^2\right]^2$$

$$+ \left(\frac{k}{k-1}\right)\left(\frac{k}{k-1}-1\right)\left(\frac{k}{k-1}-2\right)\frac{1}{3!}\left[\frac{k-1}{2}M^2\right]^3 + \cdots$$

$$= 1 + \frac{k}{2}M^2 + \frac{k}{8}M^4 + \frac{k(2-k)}{48}M^6 + \cdots$$

$$\frac{p_0}{p} = 1 + \frac{k}{2}M^2\left[1 + \frac{1}{4}M^2 + \frac{(2-k)}{24}M^4 + \cdots\right] \tag{2}$$

In the limit, as $M \to 0$, the term in brackets in Eq. 2 approaches 1.0. Thus, for flow at low Mach number, the incompressible and compressible equations give the same result. The variation of p_0/p with Mach number is shown below. As Mach number is increased, the compressible equation gives a larger ratio, p_0/p.

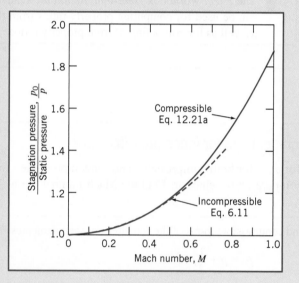

Equations 1 and 2 may be compared quantitatively most simply by writing

$$\frac{p_0}{p} - 1 = \frac{k}{2}M^2 \quad \text{("incompressible")}$$

$$\frac{p_0}{p} - 1 = \frac{k}{2}M^2\left[1 + \frac{1}{4}M^2 + \frac{(2-k)}{24}M^4 + \cdots\right]\text{(compressible)}$$

The term in brackets is approximately equal to 1.02 at $M = 0.3$, and to 1.04 at $M = 0.4$. Thus, for calculations of engineering accuracy, *flow may be considered incompressible if $M < 0.3$.* The two agree within 5 percent for $M \lesssim 0.45$.

12-4   CRITICAL CONDITIONS

Stagnation conditions are extremely useful as reference conditions for thermodynamic properties; this is not true for velocity, since by definition $V = 0$ at stagnation. A useful reference value for velocity is the *critical speed*—the speed V we attain when a flow is either accelerated or decelerated (actually or conceptually) isentropically until we reach $M = 1$. Even if there is no point in a given flow field where the Mach number is equal to unity, such a hypothetical condition still is useful as a reference condition.

Using asterisks to denote conditions at $M = 1$, then by definition

$$V^* \equiv c^*$$

At critical conditions, Eqs. 12.21 for isentropic stagnation properties become

$$\frac{p_0}{p^*} = \left[\frac{k+1}{2}\right]^{k/(k-1)} \tag{12.22a}$$

$$\frac{T_0}{T^*} = \frac{k+1}{2} \tag{12.22b}$$

$$\frac{\rho_0}{\rho^*} = \left[\frac{k+1}{2}\right]^{1/(k-1)} \tag{12.22c}$$

The critical speed may be written in terms of either critical temperature, T^*, or isentropic stagnation temperature, T_0.

For an ideal gas, $c^* = \sqrt{kRT^*}$, and thus $V^* = \sqrt{kRT^*}$. Since, from Eq. 12.22b,

$$T^* = \frac{2}{k+1}T_0$$

we have

$$V^* = c^* = \sqrt{\frac{2k}{k+1}RT_0} \tag{12.23}$$

We shall use both stagnation conditions and critical conditions as reference conditions in the next chapter when we consider a variety of compressible flow.

12-5   SUMMARY AND USEFUL EQUATIONS

In this chapter, we:

- ✓ Reviewed the basic equations used in thermodynamics, including isentropic relations.
- ✓ Introduced some compressible flow terminology, such as definitions of the Mach number and subsonic, supersonic, transonic, and hypersonic flows.
- ✓ Learned about several phenomena having to do with sound, including that the speed of sound in an ideal gas is a function of temperature only ($c = \sqrt{kRT}$), and that the Mach cone and Mach angle determine when a supersonic vehicle is heard on the ground.
- ✓ Learned that there are two useful reference states for a compressible flow: the isentropic stagnation condition, and the isentropic critical condition.

Note: Most of the Useful Equations in the table below have a number of constraints or limitations—*be sure to refer to their page numbers for details!*

Useful Equations		
Definition of Mach number M:	$M \equiv \dfrac{V}{c}$ (12.13)	Page 588
Speed of sound c:	$c = \sqrt{\left.\dfrac{\partial p}{\partial \rho}\right)_s}$ (12.16)	Page 591

Speed of sound c (solids and liquids):	$c = \sqrt{E_v/\rho}$ (12.17)	Page 591
Speed of sound c (ideal gas):	$c = \sqrt{kRT}$ (12.18)	Page 591
Mach cone angle α:	$\alpha = \sin^{-1}\left(\dfrac{1}{M}\right)$ (12.19)	Page 594
Isentropic pressure ratio (ideal gas, constant specific heats):	$\dfrac{p_0}{p} = \left[1 + \dfrac{k-1}{2}M^2\right]^{k/(k-1)}$ (12.21a)	Page 599
Isentropic temperature ratio (ideal gas, constant specific heats):	$\dfrac{T_0}{T} = 1 + \dfrac{k-1}{2}M^2$ (12.21b)	Page 599
Isentropic density ratio (ideal gas, constant specific heats):	$\dfrac{\rho_0}{\rho} = \left[1 + \dfrac{k-1}{2}M^2\right]^{1/(k-1)}$ (12.21c)	Page 599
Critical pressure ratio (ideal gas, constant specific heats):	$\dfrac{p_0}{p^*} = \left[\dfrac{k+1}{2}\right]^{k/(k-1)}$ (12.22a)	Page 603
Critical temperature ratio (ideal gas, constant specific heats):	$\dfrac{T_0}{T^*} = \dfrac{k+1}{2}$ (12.22a)	Page 603
Critical density ratio (ideal gas, constant specific heats):	$\dfrac{\rho_0}{\rho^*} = \left[\dfrac{k+1}{2}\right]^{1/(k-1)}$ (12.22c)	Page 603
Critical velocity V^* (ideal gas, constant specific heats):	$V^* = c^* = \sqrt{\dfrac{2k}{k+1}RT_0}$ (12.23)	Page 603

REFERENCES

1. Cengel, Y. A., and M. A. Boles, *Thermodynamics: An Engineering Approach*, 4th ed. New York: McGraw-Hill, 2002.

2. Borgnake, C., and R. E. Sonntag, *Fundamentals of Thermodynamics*, 7th ed. New York: Wiley, 2008.

3. Moran, M. J., and H. N. Shapiro, *Fundamentals of Engineering Thermodynamics*, 6th ed. New York: Wiley, 2007.

4. Wong, G. S. K., "Speed of Sound in Standard Air," *J. Acoustical Society of America, 79*, 5, May 1986, pp. 1359–1366.

PROBLEMS

12.1 An air flow in a duct passes through a thick filter. What happens to the pressure, temperature, and density of the air as it does so? *Hint*: This is a throttling process.

12.2 Air is expanded in a steady flow process through a turbine. Initial conditions are 1300°C and 2.0 MPa (abs). Final conditions are 500°C and atmospheric pressure. Show this process on a *Ts* diagram. Evaluate the changes in internal energy, enthalpy, and specific entropy for this process.

12.3 A vendor claims that an adiabatic air compressor takes in air at standard atmosphere conditions and delivers the air at 650 kPa (gage) and 285°C. Is this possible? Justify your answer by calculation. Sketch the process on a *Ts* diagram.

12.4 What is the lowest possible delivery temperature generated by an adiabatic air compressor, starting with standard atmosphere conditions and delivering the air at 100 psig? Sketch the process on a *Ts* diagram.

12.5 A test chamber is separated into two equal chambers by a rubber diaphragm. One contains air at 20°C and 200 kPa (absolute), and the other has a vacuum. If the diaphragm is punctured, find the pressure and temperature of the air after it expands to fill the chamber. *Hint*: This is a rapid, violent event, so is irreversible but adiabatic.

12.6 An automobile supercharger is a device that pressurizes the air that is used by the engine for combustion to increase the engine power (how does it differ from a turbocharger?). A supercharger takes in air at 70°F and atmospheric pressure and boosts it to 200 psig, at an intake rate of 0.5 ft³/s. What are the pressure, temperature, and volume flow rate at the exit? (The relatively high exit temperature is the reason an intercooler is also used.) Assuming a 70% efficiency, what is the power drawn by the supercharger? *Hint*: the efficiency is defined as the ratio of the isentropic power to actual power.

12.7 Five kilograms of air is cooled in a closed tank from 250 to 50°C. The initial pressure is 3 MPa. Compute the changes in entropy, internal energy, and enthalpy. Show the process state points on a *Ts* diagram.

12.8 Air is contained in a piston-cylinder device. The temperature of the air is 100°C. Using the fact that for a reversible process the heat transfer $q = \int Tds$, compare the amount of heat (J/kg) required to raise the temperature of the air to 1200°C at (a) constant pressure and (b) constant volume. Verify your results using the first law of thermodynamics. Plot the processes on a *Ts* diagram.

12.9 The four-stroke Otto cycle of a typical automobile engine is sometimes modeled as an ideal air-standard closed system. In this simplified system the combustion process is modeled as a heating process, and the exhaust-intake process as a cooling process of the working fluid (air). The cycle consists of: isentropic compression from state ① ($p_1 = 100$ kPa (abs), $T_1 = 20$°C, $\Psi_1 = 500$ cc) to state ② ($\Psi_2 = \Psi_1/8.5$); isometric (constant volume) heat addition to state ③ ($T_3 = 2750$°C); isentropic expansion to state ④ ($\Psi_4 = \Psi_1$); and isometric cooling back to state ①. Plot the $p\Psi$ and *Ts* diagrams for this cycle, and find the efficiency, defined as the net work (the cycle area in $p\Psi$ space) divided by the heat added.

12.10 The four-stroke cycle of a typical diesel engine is sometimes modeled as an ideal air-standard closed system. In this simplified system the combustion process is modeled as a heating process, and the exhaust-intake process as a cooling process of the working fluid (air). The cycle consists of: isentropic compression from state ① ($p_1 = 100$ kPa (abs), $T_1 = 20$°C, $\Psi_1 = 500$ cc) to state ② ($\Psi_2 = \Psi_1/12.5$); isometric (constant volume) heat addition to state ③ ($T_3 = 3000$°C); isobaric heat addition to state ④ ($\Psi_4 = 1.75\Psi_3$); isentropic expansion to state ⑤; and isometric cooling back to state ①. Plot the $p\Psi$ and *Ts* diagrams for this cycle, and find the efficiency, defined as the net work (the cycle area in $p\Psi$ space) divided by the heat added.

12.11 A tank of volume $\Psi = 10$ m³ contains compressed air at 15°C. The gage pressure in the tank is 4.50 MPa. Evaluate the work required to fill the tank by compressing air from standard atmosphere conditions for (a) isothermal compression and (b) isentropic compression followed by cooling at constant pressure. What is the peak temperature of the isentropic compression process? Calculate the energy removed during cooling for process (b). Assume ideal gas behavior and reversible processes. Label state points on a *Ts* diagram and a $p\Psi$ diagram for each process.

12.12 Air enters a turbine in steady flow at 0.5 kg/s with negligible velocity. Inlet conditions are 1300°C and 2.0 MPa (abs). The air is expanded through the turbine to atmospheric pressure. If the actual temperature and velocity at the turbine exit are 500°C and 200 m/s, determine the power produced by the turbine. Label state points on a *Ts* diagram for this process.

12.13 Natural gas, with the thermodynamic properties of methane, flows in an underground pipeline of 0.6 m diameter. The gage pressure at the inlet to a compressor station is 0.5 MPa; outlet pressure is 8.0 MPa (gage). The gas temperature and speed at inlet are 13°C and 32 m/s, respectively. The compressor efficiency is $\eta = 0.85$. Calculate the mass flow rate of natural gas through the pipeline. Label state points on a *Ts* diagram for compressor inlet and outlet. Evaluate the gas temperature and speed at the compressor outlet and the power required to drive the compressor.

12.14 Over time the efficiency of the compressor of Problem 12.13 drops. At what efficiency will the power required to attain 8.0 MPa (gage) exceed 30 MW? Plot the required power and the gas exit temperature as functions of efficiency.

12.15 In an isothermal process, 0.1 cubic feet of standard air per minute (SCFM) is pumped into a balloon. Tension in the rubber skin of the balloon is given by $\sigma = kA$, where $k = 200$ lbf/ft³, and A is the surface area of the balloon in ft². Compute the time required to increase the balloon radius from 5 to 7 inches.

12.16 For the balloon process of Problem 12.15 we could define a "volumetric ratio" as the ratio of the volume of standard air supplied to the volume increase of the balloon, per unit time. Plot this ratio over time as the balloon radius is increased from 5 to 7 inches.

12.17 A sound pulse level above about 20 Pa can cause permanent hearing damage. Assuming such a sound wave travels through air at 20°C and 100 kPa, estimate the density, temperature, and velocity change immediately after the sound wave passes.

12.18 The bulk modulus E_v of a material indicates how hard it is to compress the material; a large E_v indicates the material requires a large pressure to compress. Is air "stiffer" when suddenly or slowly compressed? To answer this, find expressions in terms of instantaneous pressure p for the bulk modulus of air (kPa) when it is a) rapidly compressed and b) slowly compressed. *Hint*: Rapid compression is approximately isentropic (it is adiabatic because it is too quick for heat transfer to occur), and slow compression is isothermal (there is plenty of time for the air to equilibrate to ambient temperature).

12.19 You have designed a device for determining the bulk modulus, E_v, of a material. It works by measuring the time delay between sending a sound wave into a sample of the material and receiving the wave after it travels through the sample and bounces back. As a test, you use a 1 m rod of steel ($E_v \approx 200$ GN/m^2). What time delay should your device indicate? You now test a 1 m rod (1 cm diameter) of an unknown material and find a time delay of 0.5 ms. The mass of the rod is measured to be 0.25 kg. What is this material's bulk modulus?

12.20 Dolphins often hunt by listening for sounds made by their prey. They "hear" with the lower jaw, which conducts the sound vibrations to the middle ear via a fat-filled cavity in the lower jaw bone. If the prey is 1000 m away, how long after a sound is made does a dolphin hear it? Assume the seawater is at 20°C.

12.21 A submarine sends a sonar signal to detect the enemy. The reflected wave returns after 25 s. Estimate the separation between the submarines. (As an approximation assume the seawater is at 20°C.)

12.22 An airplane flies at 400 mph at 1600 ft altitude on a standard day. The plane climbs to 50,000 ft and flies at 725 mph. Calculate the Mach number of flight in both cases.

12.23 Actual performance characteristics of the Lockheed SR-71 "Blackbird" reconnaissance aircraft never were released. However, it was thought to cruise at $M = 3.3$ at 85,000 ft altitude. Evaluate the speed of sound and flight speed for these conditions. Compare to the muzzle speed of a 30–06 rifle bullet (700 m/s).

12.24 The Boeing 727 aircraft of Example 9.8 cruises at 520 mph at 33,000 ft altitude on a standard day. Calculate the cruise Mach number of the aircraft. If the maximum allowable operating Mach number for the aircraft is 0.9, what is the corresponding flight speed?

12.25 Investigate the effect of altitude on Mach number by plotting the Mach number of a 500 mph airplane as it flies at altitudes ranging from sea level to 10 km.

12.26 You are watching a July 4th fireworks display from a distance of one mile. How long after you see an explosion do you hear it? You also watch New Year's fireworks (same place and distance). How long after you see an explosion do you hear it? Assume it's 75°F in July and 5°F in January.

12.27 Use data for specific volume to calculate and plot the speed of sound in saturated liquid water over the temperature range from 0 to 200°C.

12.28 Re-derive the equation for sonic speed (Eq. 12.18) assuming that the direction of fluid motion behind the sound wave is dV_x to the *right*. Show that the result is identical to that given by Eq. 12.18.

12.29 Compute the speed of sound at sea level in standard air. By scanning data from Table A.3 into your PC (or using Fig. 3.3), evaluate the speed of sound and plot for altitudes to 90 km.

12.30 The temperature varies linearly from sea level to approximately 11 km altitude in the standard atmosphere. Evaluate the *lapse rate*—the rate of decrease of temperature with altitude—in the standard atmosphere. Derive an expression for the rate of change of sonic speed with altitude in an ideal gas under standard atmospheric conditions. Evaluate and plot from sea level to 10 km altitude.

12.31 Air at 77°F flows at $M = 1.9$. Determine the air speed and the Mach angle.

12.32 A projectile is fired into a gas in which the pressure is 50 psia and the density is 0.27 lbm/ft^3. It is observed experimentally that a Mach cone emanates from the projectile with 20° total angle. What is the speed of the projectile with respect to the gas?

12.33 A photograph of a bullet shows a Mach angle of 32°. Determine the speed of the bullet for standard air.

12.34 The National Transonic Facility (NTF) is a high-speed wind tunnel designed to operate with air at cryogenic temperatures to reduce viscosity, thus raising the unit Reynolds number (Re/x) and reducing pumping power requirements. Operation is envisioned at temperatures of −270°F and below. A schlieren photograph taken in the NTF shows a Mach angle of 57° where $T = -270$°F and $p = 1.3$ psia. Evaluate the local Mach number and flow speed. Calculate the unit Reynolds number for the flow.

12.35 An F-4 aircraft makes a high-speed pass over an airfield on a day when $T = 35$°C. The aircraft flies at $M = 1.4$ and 200 m altitude. Calculate the speed of the aircraft. How long after it passes directly over point A on the ground does its Mach cone pass over point A?

12.36 While jogging on the beach (it's a warm summer day, about 30°C) a high-speed jet flies overhead. You guesstimate it's at an altitude of about 3500 m, and count off about 5 s before you hear it. Estimate the speed and Mach number of the jet.

12.37 An aircraft passes overhead at 3 km altitude. The aircraft flies at $M = 1.5$; assume air temperature is constant at 20°C. Find the air speed of the aircraft. A headwind blows at 30 m/s. How long after the aircraft passes directly overhead does its sound reach a point on the ground?

12.38 A supersonic aircraft flies at 3 km altitude at a speed of 1000 m/s on a standard day. How long after passing directly above a ground observer is the sound of the aircraft heard by the ground observer?

12.39 For the conditions of Problem 12.38, find the location at which the sound wave that first reaches the ground observer was emitted.

12.40 The Concorde supersonic transport cruised at $M = 2.2$ at 17 km altitude on a standard day. How long after the aircraft passed directly above a ground observer was the sound of the aircraft heard?

12.41 The airflow around an automobile is assumed to be incompressible. Investigate the validity of this assumption for an automobile traveling at 60 mph. (Relative to the automobile the minimum air velocity is zero, and the maximum is approximately 120 mph.)

12.42 Opponents of supersonic transport aircraft claim that sound waves can be refracted in the upper atmosphere and that, as a result, sonic booms can be heard several hundred miles away from the ground track of the aircraft. Explain the phenomenon of sound wave refraction.

12.43 Plot the percentage discrepancy between the density at the stagnation point and the density at a location where the Mach number is M, of a compressible flow, for Mach numbers ranging from 0.05 to 0.95. Find the Mach numbers at which the discrepancy is 1 percent, 5 percent, and 10 percent.

12.44 An aircraft flies at 250 m/s in air at 28 kPa and $-50°C$. Find the stagnation pressure at the nose of the aircraft.

12.45 Compute the air density in the undisturbed air, and at the stagnation point, of Problem 12.44. What is the percentage increase in density? Can we approximate this as an incompressible flow?

12.46 Find the ratio of static to total pressure for a car moving at 55 mph at sea level and an airplane moving at 550 mph at 30,000 ft.

12.47 For an aircraft traveling at $M = 2$ at an elevation of 12 km, find the dynamic and stagnation pressures.

12.48 A body moves through standard air at 200 m/s. What is the stagnation pressure on the body? Assume (a) compressible flow and (b) incompressible flow.

12.49 Consider flow of standard air at 600 m/s. What is the local isentropic stagnation pressure? The stagnation enthalpy? The stagnation temperature?

12.50 A DC-10 aircraft cruises at 12 km altitude on a standard day. A pitot-static tube on the nose of the aircraft measures stagnation and static pressures of 29.6 kPa and 19.4 kPa. Calculate (a) the flight Mach number of the aircraft, (b) the speed of the aircraft, and (c) the stagnation temperature that would be sensed by a probe on the aircraft.

12.51 An aircraft cruises at $M = 0.65$ at 10 km altitude on a standard day. The aircraft speed is deduced from measurement of the difference between the stagnation and static pressures. What is the value of this difference? Compute the air speed from this actual difference assuming (a) compressibility and (b) incompressibility. Is the discrepancy in air-speed computations significant in this case?

12.52 The Anglo-French Concorde supersonic transport cruised at $M = 2.2$ at 20 km altitude. Evaluate the speed of sound, aircraft flight speed, and Mach angle. What was the maximum air temperature at stagnation points on the aircraft structure?

12.53 Modern high-speed aircraft use "air data computers" to compute air speed from measurement of the difference between the stagnation and static pressures. Plot, as a function of actual Mach number M, for $M = 0.1$ to $M = 0.9$, the percentage error in computing the Mach number assuming incompressibility (i.e., using the Bernoulli equation), from this pressure difference. Plot the percentage error in speed, as a function of speed, of an aircraft cruising at 12 km altitude, for a range of speeds corresponding to the actual Mach number ranging from $M = 0.1$ to $M = 0.9$.

12.54 A supersonic wind tunnel test section is designed to have $M = 2.5$ at 15°C and 35 kPa (abs). The fluid is air. Determine the required inlet stagnation conditions, T_0 and p_0. Calculate the required mass flow rate for a test section area of 0.175 m^2.

12.55 Air flows steadily through a length (①) denotes inlet and (②) denotes exit) of insulated constant-area duct. Properties change along the duct as a result of friction.
(a) Beginning with the control volume form of the first law of thermodynamics, show that the equation can be reduced to

$$h_1 + \frac{V_1^2}{2} = h_2 + \frac{V_2^2}{2} = \text{constant}$$

(b) Denoting the constant by h_0 (the stagnation enthalpy), show that for adiabatic flow of an ideal gas with friction

$$\frac{T_0}{T} = 1 + \frac{k-1}{2}M^2$$

(c) For this flow does $T_{0_1} = T_{0_2}$? $p_{0_1} = p_{0_2}$? Explain these results.

12.56 A new design for a supersonic transport is tested in a wind tunnel at $M = 1.8$. Air is the working fluid. The stagnation temperature and pressure for the wind tunnel are 200 psia and 500°F, respectively. The model wing area is 100 in^2. The measured lift and drag are 12,000 lbf and 1600 lbf, respectively. Find the lift and drag coefficients.

12.57 For aircraft flying at supersonic speeds, lift and drag coefficients are functions of Mach number only. A supersonic transport with wingspan of 75 m is to fly at 780 m/s at 20 km altitude on a standard day. Performance of the aircraft is to be measured from tests of a model with 0.9 m wingspan in a supersonic wind tunnel. The wind tunnel is to be supplied from a large reservoir of compressed air, which can be heated if desired. The static temperature of air in the test section is to be 10°C to avoid freezing of moisture. At what air speed should the wind tunnel tests be run to duplicate the Mach number of the prototype? What must be the stagnation temperature in the reservoir? What pressure is required in the reservoir if the test section pressure is to be 10 kPa (abs)?

12.58 Actual performance characteristics of the Lockheed SR-71 "Blackbird" reconnaissance aircraft were classified. However, it was thought to cruise at $M = 3.3$ at 26 km altitude. Calculate the aircraft flight speed for these conditions. Determine the local isentropic stagnation pressure. Because the aircraft speed is supersonic, a normal shock occurs in front of a total-head tube. The stagnation pressure decreases by 74.7 percent across the shock. Evaluate the stagnation pressure sensed by a probe on the aircraft. What is the maximum air temperature at stagnation points on the aircraft structure?

12.59 Air flows in an insulated duct. At point (①) the conditions are $M_1 = 0.1$, $T_1 = 20°C$, and $p_1 = 1.0$ MPa (abs). Downstream, at point (②), because of friction the conditions are $M_2 = 0.7$, $T_2 = -5.62°C$, and $p_2 = 136.5$ kPa (abs). (Four significant figures are given to minimize roundoff errors.) Compare the stagnation temperatures at points (①) and (②), and explain the result. Compute the stagnation pressures at points (①) and (②). Can you explain how it can be that the velocity *increases* for this frictional flow? Should this process be isentropic or not? Justify your answer by computing the change in entropy between points (①) and (②). Plot static and stagnation state points on a Ts diagram.

12.60 Air is cooled as it flows without friction at a rate of 0.05 kg/s in a duct. At point (①) the conditions are $M_1 = 0.5$, $T_1 = 500°C$, and $p_1 = 500$ kPa (abs). Downstream, at point (②), the conditions are $M_2 = 0.2$, $T_2 = -18.57°C$, and $p_2 = 639.2$ kPa (abs). (Four significant figures are given to minimize roundoff errors.) Compare the stagnation temperatures at points ① and ②, and explain the result. Compute the rate of cooling. Compute the stagnation pressures at points ① and ②. Should this process be isentropic or not? Justify your answer by computing the change in entropy between points ① and ②. Plot static and stagnation state points on a Ts diagram.

12.61 Consider steady, adiabatic flow of air through a long straight pipe with $A = 0.05\ m^2$. At the inlet (section ①) the air is at 200 kPa (abs), 60°C, and 146 m/s. Downstream at section ②, the air is at 95.6 kPa (abs) and 280 m/s. Determine p_{0_1}, p_{0_2}, T_{0_1}, T_{0_2}, and the entropy change for the flow. Show static and stagnation state points on a Ts diagram.

12.62 Air flows steadily through a constant-area duct. At section ①, the air is at 400 kPa (abs), 325 K, and 150 m/s. As a result of heat transfer and friction, the air at section ② downstream is at 275 kPa (abs), 450 K. Calculate the heat transfer per kilogram of air between sections ① and ②, and the stagnation pressure at section ②.

12.63 Air passes through a normal shock in a supersonic wind tunnel. Upstream conditions are $M_1 = 1.8$, $T_1 = 270$ K, and $p_1 = 10.0$ kPa (abs). Downstream conditions are $M_2 = 0.6165$, $T_2 = 413.6$ K, and $p_2 = 36.13$ kPa (abs). (Four significant figures are given to minimize roundoff errors.) Evaluate local isentropic stagnation conditions (a) upstream from, and (b) downstream from, the normal shock. Calculate the change in specific entropy across the shock. Plot static and stagnation state points on a Ts diagram.

12.64 Air enters a turbine at $M_1 = 0.4$, $T_1 = 1250°C$, and $p_1 = 625$ kPa (abs). Conditions leaving the turbine are $M_2 = 0.8$, $T_2 = 650°C$, and $p_2 = 20$ kPa (abs). Evaluate local isentropic stagnation conditions (a) at the turbine inlet and (b) at the turbine outlet.

Calculate the change in specific entropy across the turbine. Plot static and stagnation state points on a Ts diagram.

12.65 A Boeing 747 cruises at $M = 0.87$ at an altitude of 13 km on a standard day. A window in the cockpit is located where the external flow Mach number is 0.2 relative to the plane surface. The cabin is pressurized to an equivalent altitude of 2500 m in a standard atmosphere. Estimate the pressure difference across the window. Be sure to specify the direction of the net pressure force.

12.66 If a window of the cockpit in Problem 12.65 develops a tiny leak the air will start to rush out at critical speed. Find the mass flow rate if the leak area is 1 mm².

12.67 A CO_2 cartridge is used to propel a toy rocket. Gas in the cartridge is pressurized to 45 MPa (gage) and is at 25°C. Calculate the critical conditions (temperature, pressure, and flow speed) that correspond to these stagnation conditions.

12.68 The gas storage reservoir for a high-speed wind tunnel contains helium at 3600 R and 725 psig. Calculate the critical conditions (temperature, pressure, and flow speed) that correspond to these stagnation conditions.

12.69 Stagnation conditions in a solid propellant rocket motor are $T_0 = 3000$ K and $p_0 = 45$ MPa (gage). Critical conditions occur in the throat of the rocket nozzle where the Mach number is equal to one. Evaluate the temperature, pressure, and flow speed at the throat. Assume ideal gas behavior with $R = 323$ J/(kg · K) and $k = 1.2$.

12.70 The hot gas stream at the turbine inlet of a JT9-D jet engine is at 1500°C, 140 kPa (abs), and $M = 0.32$. Calculate the critical conditions (temperature, pressure, and flow speed) that correspond to these conditions. Assume the fluid properties of pure air.

Chapter 13

Compressible Flow

▌CASE STUDY▐

The X-43A/Hyper-X Airplane

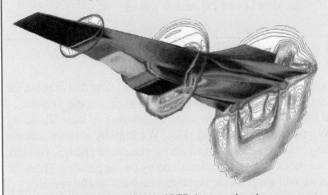

The X-43A/Hyper-X at $M = 7$ (CFD image showing pressure contours). (Courtesy of NASA.)

Superman is faster than a speeding bullet. So how fast is that? It turns out that the highest speed of a bullet is about 1500 m/s, or about Mach number 4.5 at sea level. Can humans keep up with superman? If we're in orbit we can (What is the Mach number of the Space Shuttle in orbit?—it's a trick question!), because there's no drag—once we get up to speed, we can stay there—but flying at hypersonic speeds (i.e., above about $M = 5$) in the atmosphere requires tremendous engine thrust and an engine that can function at all at such speeds. In 2004, an air-breathing X-43A managed to fly at almost Mach 10, or about 7000 mph. The hypersonic scramjet engine in this airplane is actually integrated into the airframe, and the entire lower surface of the vehicle is shaped to make the engine work. The bulge on the underside in the figure is the engine. Unlike the turbojet engines used in many jet aircraft, which have fans and compressors as major components, the scramjet, amazingly, has no moving parts, so if you were to look inside it there wouldn't be much to see! Instead it uses geometry to develop a shock train that reduces the speed of the airflow from hypersonic to supersonic velocities. The scramjet, which is essentially a ramjet with supersonic combustion, doesn't need to slow the flow down to subsonic speeds. The compression ram on the undersurface of the aircraft slows the flow down from hypersonic to supersonic speed before it reaches the engine. It does this by causing a sequence of oblique shocks (discussed in this chapter) that successively slow the flow down and also increase the air density. As the supersonic, relatively high-density air passes through the engine, hydrogen fuel is injected and combusts, creating tremendous thrust at the exhaust. Once at hypersonic speed, the combustion process is self-sustaining.

One of the problems the engineers faced was how to start the engine. First, the airplane has to be accelerated above Mach 4 by conventional means (by a jet engine or rocket, or by piggy-backing another aircraft), and then the scramjet fuel can be started and ignited. This sounds simple enough, but the ignition process has been compared to "lighting a match in a hurricane"! The solution was to ignite using a mixture of pyrophoric silane (which auto-ignites when exposed to air) and hydrogen, then switch to pure hydrogen.

The X-43A/Hyper-X is experimental, but in future we may expect to see scramjets in military applications (aircraft and missiles), then possibly in commercial aircraft. Conceivably, you could live in New York, go to a meeting in Los Angeles, and be back in New York for dinner!

In Chapter 12 we reviewed some basic concepts of compressible flow. The main focus of this chapter is to discuss one-dimensional compressible flow in more detail. The first question we can ask is "What would cause the fluid properties to vary in a one-dimensional compressible flow?" The answer is that various phenomena can cause changes:

✓ Flow with varying area (causing the velocity to change, and hence other property changes).

✓ Flow in a channel with friction (causing the entropy to increase, and hence other property changes).

✓ Flow in a channel with heating or cooling (causing a change in fluid energy, and hence other property changes).

✓ Normal shock (a "violent" adiabatic process that causes the entropy to increase, and hence other property changes).

For simplicity, we will study each of these phenomena separately (bearing in mind that a real flow is likely to experience several of them simultaneously). After completing our treatment of one-dimensional flow, we will introduce some basic concepts of two-dimensional flows: oblique shocks and expansion waves.

13-1   BASIC EQUATIONS FOR ONE-DIMENSIONAL COMPRESSIBLE FLOW

Our first task is to develop general equations for a one-dimensional flow that express the basic laws from Chapter 4: *mass conservation* (continuity), *momentum*, the *first law of thermodynamics*, the *second law of thermodynamics*, and an *equation of state*. To do so, we will use the fixed control volume shown in Fig. 13.1. We initially assume that the flow is affected by *all* of the phenomena mentioned above (i.e., area change, friction, and heat transfer—even the normal shock will be described by this approach). Then, for each individual phenomenon we will simplify the equations to obtain useful results.

As shown in Fig. 13.1, the properties at sections ① and ② are labeled with corresponding subscripts. R_x is the x component of surface force from friction and

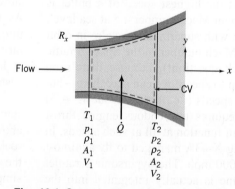

Fig. 13.1 Control volume for analysis of a general one-dimensional flow.

pressure on the sides of the channel. There will also be surface forces from pressures at surfaces ① and ②. Note that the x component of body force is zero, so it is not shown. $\dot{Q}$ is the heat transfer.

a. Continuity Equation

Basic equation:

$$\overbrace{\frac{\partial}{\partial t} \int_{CV} \rho \, d\forall}^{= 0(1)} + \int_{CS} \rho \vec{V} \cdot d\vec{A} = 0 \tag{4.12}$$

Assumptions: (1) Steady flow.
(2) One-dimensional flow.

Then

$$(-\rho_1 V_1 A_1) + (\rho_2 V_2 A_2) = 0$$

or

$$\rho_1 V_1 A_1 = \rho_2 V_2 A_2 = \rho V A = \dot{m} = \text{constant} \tag{13.1a}$$

b. Momentum Equation

Basic equation:

$$F_{S_x} + \overbrace{F_{B_x}}^{= 0(3)} = \overbrace{\frac{\partial}{\partial t} \int_{CV} V_x \rho \, d\forall}^{= 0(1)} + \int_{CS} V_x \rho \vec{V} \cdot d\vec{A} \tag{4.18a}$$

Assumption: (3) $F_{B_x} = 0$

The surface force is caused by pressure forces at surfaces ① and ②, and by the friction and distributed pressure force, R_x, along the channel walls. Substituting gives

$$R_x + p_1 A_1 - p_2 A_2 = V_1(-\rho_1 V_1 A_1) + V_2(\rho_2 V_2 A_2)$$

Using continuity, we obtain

$$R_x + p_1 A_1 - p_2 A_2 = \dot{m} V_2 - \dot{m} V_1 \tag{13.1b}$$

c. First Law of Thermodynamics

Basic equation:

$$\dot{Q} - \overbrace{\dot{W}_s}^{} - \overbrace{\dot{W}_{shear}}^{} - \overbrace{\dot{W}_{other}}^{} = \frac{\partial}{\partial t} \int_{CV} e \rho \, d\forall + \int_{CS} (e + pv) \rho \vec{V} \cdot d\vec{A} \tag{4.56}$$

where

$$e = u + \frac{V^2}{2} + \overbrace{gz}^{\simeq 0(6)}$$

Assumptions: (4) $\dot{W}_s = 0$.
(5) $\dot{W}_{shear} = \dot{W}_{other} = 0$.
(6) Effects of gravity are negligible.

(Note that even if we have friction, there is no friction *work* at the walls because with friction the velocity at the walls must be zero from the no-slip condition.) Under these assumptions, the first law reduces to

$$\dot{Q} = \left(u_1 + p_1 v_1 + \frac{V_1^2}{2} \right)(-\rho_1 V_1 A_1) + \left(u_2 + p_2 v_2 + \frac{V_2^2}{2} \right)(\rho_2 V_2 A_2)$$

(Remember that v here represents the specific volume.) This can be simplified by using $h \equiv u + pv$, and continuity (Eq. 13.1a),

$$\dot{Q} = \dot{m} \left\{ \left(h_2 + \frac{V_2^2}{2} \right) - \left(h_1 + \frac{V_1^2}{2} \right) \right\}$$

We can write the heat transfer on a per unit mass rather than per unit time basis:

$$\frac{\delta Q}{dm} = \frac{1}{\dot{m}} \dot{Q}$$

so

$$\frac{\delta Q}{dm} + h_1 + \frac{V_1^2}{2} = h_2 + \frac{V_2^2}{2} \tag{13.1c}$$

Equation 13.1c expresses the fact that heat transfer changes the total energy (the sum of thermal energy h, and kinetic energy $V^2/2$) of the flowing fluid. This combination, $h + V^2/2$, occurs often in compressible flow, and is called the *stagnation enthalpy*, h_0. This is the enthalpy obtained if a flow is brought adiabatically to rest.

Hence, Eq. 13.1c can also be written

$$\frac{\delta Q}{dm} = h_{0_2} - h_{0_1}$$

We see that heat transfer causes the stagnation enthalpy, and hence, stagnation temperature, T_0, to change.

d. Second Law of Thermodynamics

Basic equation:

$$\overset{= 0(1)}{\frac{\partial}{\partial t} \int_{CV} \cancel{s} \rho \, d\Psi} + \int_{CS} s \, \rho \vec{V} \cdot d\vec{A} \geq \int_{CS} \frac{1}{T} \left(\frac{\dot{Q}}{A} \right) dA \tag{4.58}$$

or

$$s_1(-\rho_1 V_1 A_1) + s_2(\rho_2 V_2 A_2) \geq \int_{CS} \frac{1}{T} \left(\frac{\dot{Q}}{A} \right) dA$$

and, again using continuity,

$$\dot{m}(s_2 - s_1) \geq \int_{CS} \frac{1}{T} \left(\frac{\dot{Q}}{A} \right) dA \tag{13.1d}$$

e. Equation of State

Equations of state are relations among intensive thermodynamic properties. These relations may be available as tabulated data or charts, or as algebraic equations. In general, regardless of the format of the data, as we discussed in Chapter 12 (see references [1]–[3] of that chapter), for a simple substance any property can be expressed as a function of any two other independent properties. For example, we could write $h = h(s, p)$, or $\rho = \rho(s, p)$, and so on.

We will primarily be concerned with ideal gases with constant specific heats, and for these we can write Eqs. 12.1 and 12.7b (renumbered for convenient use in this chapter),

$$p = \rho RT \tag{13.1e}$$

and

$$\Delta h = h_2 - h_1 = c_p \Delta T = c_p (T_2 - T_1) \tag{13.1f}$$

For ideal gases with constant specific heats, the change in entropy, $\Delta s = s_2 - s_1$, for any process can be computed from any of Eqs. 12.11. For example, Eq. 12.11b (renumbered for convenient use in this chapter) is

$$\Delta s = s_2 - s_1 = c_p \ln \frac{T_2}{T_1} - R \ln \frac{p_2}{p_1} \tag{13.1g}$$

We now have a basic set of equations for analyzing one-dimensional compressible flows of an ideal gas with constant specific heats:

$$\rho_1 V_1 A_1 = \rho_2 V_2 A_2 = \rho V A = \dot{m} = \text{constant} \tag{13.1a}$$

$$R_x + p_1 A_1 - p_2 A_2 = \dot{m} V_2 - \dot{m} V_1 \tag{13.1b}$$

$$\frac{\delta Q}{dm} + h_1 + \frac{V_1^2}{2} = h_2 + \frac{V_2^2}{2} \tag{13.1c}$$

$$\dot{m}(s_2 - s_1) \geq \int_{CS} \frac{1}{T} \left(\frac{\dot{Q}}{A} \right) dA \tag{13.1d}$$

$$p = \rho R T \tag{13.1e}$$

$$\Delta h = h_2 - h_1 = c_p \Delta T = c_p (T_2 - T_1) \tag{13.1f}$$

$$\Delta s = s_2 - s_1 = c_p \ln \frac{T_2}{T_1} - R \ln \frac{p_2}{p_1} \tag{13.1g}$$

Note that Eq. 13.1e applies only if we have an ideal gas; Equations 13.1f and 13.1g apply only if we have an ideal gas with constant specific heats. Our task is now to simplify this set of equations for each of the phenomena that can affect the flow:

✓ Flow with varying area.

✓ Flow in a channel with friction.

✓ Flow in a channel with heating or cooling.

✓ Normal shock.

13-2 ISENTROPIC FLOW OF AN IDEAL GAS—AREA VARIATION

The first phenomenon is one in which the flow is changed only by area variation—there is no heat transfer ($\delta Q/dm = 0$) or friction (so that R_x, the x component of surface force, results only from pressure on the sides of the channel), and there are no shocks. The absence of heat transfer, friction, and shocks (which are "violent" and therefore inherently irreversible) means the flow will be reversible and adiabatic, so Eq. 13.1d becomes

$$\dot{m}(s_2 - s_1) = \int_{CS} \frac{1}{T} \left(\frac{\dot{Q}}{A} \right) dA = 0$$

or

$$\Delta s = s_2 - s_1 = 0$$

so such a flow is *isentropic*. This means that Eq. 13.1g leads to the result we saw in Chapter 12,

$$T_1 p_1^{(1-k)/k} = T_2 p_2^{(1-k)/k} = T p^{(1-k)/k} = \text{constant} \qquad (12.12b)$$

or its equivalent (which can be obtained by using the ideal gas equation of state in Eq. 12.12b to eliminate temperature),

$$\frac{p_1}{\rho_1^k} = \frac{p_2}{\rho_2^k} = \frac{p}{\rho^k} = \text{constant} \qquad (12.12c)$$

Hence, the basic set of equations (Eqs. 13.1) becomes:

$$\rho_1 V_1 A_1 = \rho_2 V_2 A_2 = \rho V A = \dot{m} = \text{constant} \qquad (13.2a)$$

$$R_x + p_1 A_1 - p_2 A_2 = \dot{m} V_2 - \dot{m} V_1 \qquad (13.2b)$$

$$h_{0_1} = h_1 + \frac{V_1^2}{2} = h_2 + \frac{V_2^2}{2} = h_{0_2} = h_0 \qquad (13.2c)$$

$$s_2 = s_1 = s \qquad (13.2d)$$

$$p = \rho R T \qquad (13.2e)$$

$$\Delta h = h_2 - h_1 = c_p \Delta T = c_p (T_2 - T_1) \qquad (13.2f)$$

$$\frac{p_1}{\rho_1^k} = \frac{p_2}{\rho_2^k} = \frac{p}{\rho^k} = \text{constant} \qquad (13.2g)$$

Note that Eqs. 13.2c, 13.2d, and 13.2f provide insight into how this process appears on an *hs* diagram and on a *Ts* diagram. From Eq. 13.2c, the total energy, or stagnation enthalpy h_0, of the fluid is constant; the enthalpy and kinetic energy may vary along the flow, but their sum is constant. This means that if the fluid accelerates, its temperature must decrease, and vice versa. Equation 13.2d indicates that the entropy remains constant. These results are shown for a typical process in Fig. 13.2.

Equation 13.2f indicates that the temperature and enthalpy are linearly related; hence, processes plotted on a *Ts* diagram will look very similar to that shown in Fig. 13.2 except for the vertical scale.

Equations 13.2 *could* be used to analyze isentropic flow in a channel of varying area. For example, if we know conditions at section ① (i.e., p_1, ρ_1, T_1, s_1, h_1, V_1, and A_1) we could use these equations to find conditions at some new section ② where the area is A_2: We would have seven equations and seven unknowns (p_2, ρ_2, T_2, s_2, h_2, V_2, and, if desired, the net pressure force on the walls R_x). We stress *could*, because in practice this procedure is unwieldy—we have a set of seven *nonlinear coupled algebraic* equations to solve (however, we will see, for example in Example 13.1, that *Excel* can be used to solve this set of equations). Instead we will

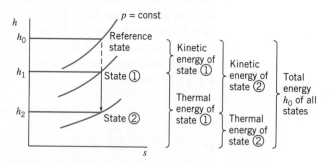

Fig. 13.2 Isentropic flow in the *hs* plane.

usually use some of these equations as convenient but also take advantage of the results we obtained for isentropic flows in Chapter 12, and develop property relations in terms of the local Mach number, the stagnation conditions, and critical conditions.

Before proceeding with this approach, we can gain insight into the isentropic process by reviewing the results we obtained in Chapter 12 when we analyzed a differential control volume (Fig. 12.5). The momentum equation for this was

$$\frac{dp}{\rho} + d\left(\frac{V^2}{2}\right) = 0 \tag{12.20b}$$

(Note that we could also have obtained this equation using our set of equations, Eqs. 13.1. If we applied Eqs. 13.1 to a differential control volume, we could replace ρ_1, V_1, and A_1 with ρ, V, and A, and ρ_2, V_2, and A_2 with $\rho + d\rho$, $V + dV$, and $A + dA$. Then Eq. 13.1a and 13.1b simplify to the above equation.) Then

$$dp = -\rho V\, dV$$

Dividing by ρV^2, we obtain

$$\frac{dp}{\rho V^2} = -\frac{dV}{V} \tag{13.3}$$

A convenient differential form of the continuity equation can be obtained from Eq. 13.2a, in the form

$$\rho A V = \text{constant}$$

Differentiating and dividing by $\rho A V$ yields

$$\frac{d\rho}{\rho} + \frac{dA}{A} + \frac{dV}{V} = 0 \tag{13.4}$$

Solving Eq. 13.4 for dA/A gives

$$\frac{dA}{A} = -\frac{dV}{V} - \frac{d\rho}{\rho}$$

Substituting from Eq. 13.3 gives

$$\frac{dA}{A} = \frac{dp}{\rho V^2} - \frac{d\rho}{\rho}$$

or

$$\frac{dA}{A} = \frac{dp}{\rho V^2}\left[1 - \frac{V^2}{dp/d\rho}\right]$$

Now recall that for an isentropic process, $dp/d\rho = \partial p/\partial\rho)_s = c^2$, so

$$\frac{dA}{A} = \frac{dp}{\rho V^2}\left[1 - \frac{V^2}{c^2}\right] = \frac{dp}{\rho V^2}[1 - M^2]$$

or

$$\frac{dp}{\rho V^2} = \frac{dA}{A}\frac{1}{[1 - M^2]} \tag{13.5}$$

Substituting from Eq. 13.3 into Eq. 13.5, we obtain

$$\frac{dV}{V} = -\frac{dA}{A}\frac{1}{[1 - M^2]} \tag{13.6}$$

Note that for an isentropic flow there can be no friction. Equations 13.5 and 13.6 confirm that for this case, from a momentum point of view we expect an increase in pressure to cause a decrease in speed, and vice versa. Although we cannot use them for computations (we have not so far determined how M varies with A), Eqs. 13.5 and 13.6 give us very interesting insights into how the pressure and velocity change as we change the area of the flow. Three possibilities are discussed below.

Subsonic Flow, $M < 1$

For $M < 1$, the factor $1/[1 - M^2]$ in Eqs. 13.5 and 13.6 is positive, so that a positive dA leads to a positive dp and a negative dV. These mathematical results mean that in a *divergent* section ($dA > 0$) the flow must experience an *increase* in pressure ($dp > 0$) and the velocity must *decrease* ($dV < 0$). Hence *a divergent channel is a subsonic diffuser* (a diffuser is a device that decelerates a flow).

On the other hand, a negative dA leads to a negative dp and a positive dV. These mathematical results mean that in a *convergent* section ($dA < 0$) the flow must experience a *decrease* in pressure ($dp < 0$) and the velocity must *increase* ($dV > 0$). Hence *a convergent channel is a subsonic nozzle* (a nozzle is a device that accelerates a flow).

These results are consistent with our everyday experience and are not surprising—for example, recall the venturi meter in Chapter 8, in which a reduction in area at the throat of the venturi led to a local increase in velocity, and because of the Bernoulli principle, to a pressure drop, and the divergent section led to pressure recovery and flow deceleration. (The Bernoulli principle assumes incompressible flow, which is the limiting case of subsonic flow.)

The subsonic diffuser and nozzle are also shown in Fig. 13.3.

Supersonic Flow, $M > 1$

For $M > 1$, the factor $1/[1 - M^2]$ in Eqs. 13.5 and 13.6 is negative, so that a positive dA leads to a negative dp and a positive dV. These mathematical results mean that in a *divergent* section ($dA > 0$) the flow must experience a *decrease* in pressure ($dp < 0$) and the velocity must *increase* ($dV > 0$). Hence *a divergent channel is a supersonic nozzle*.

On the other hand, a negative dA leads to a positive dp and a negative dV. These mathematical results mean that in a *convergent* section ($dA < 0$) the flow must experience an *increase* in pressure ($dp > 0$) and the velocity must *decrease* ($dV < 0$). Hence *a convergent channel is a supersonic diffuser*.

These results are inconsistent with our everyday experience and are at first a bit surprising—they are the opposite of what we saw in the venturi meter! The results are consistent with the laws of physics; for example, an increase in pressure must lead to a flow deceleration because pressure forces are the only forces acting.

The supersonic nozzle and diffuser are shown in Fig. 13.3.

These somewhat counterintuitive results can be understood when we realize that we are used to assuming that $\rho =$ constant, but we are now in a flow regime where the fluid density is a sensitive function of flow conditions. From Eq. 13.4,

$$\frac{dV}{V} = -\frac{dA}{A} - \frac{d\rho}{\rho}$$

For example, in a supersonic diverging flow (dA positive) the flow actually accelerates (dV also positive) because the density drops sharply ($d\rho$ is negative and large, with the net result that the right side of the equation is positive). We can see examples of supersonic diverging nozzles in the space shuttle main engines, each of which has a nozzle about 10 ft long with an 8 ft exit diameter. The maximum thrust is obtained from the engines when the combustion gases exit at the highest possible speed, which the nozzles achieve.

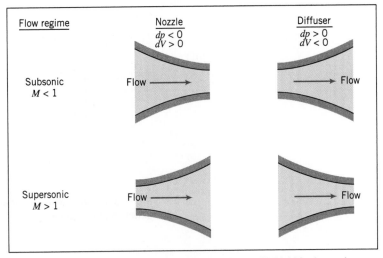

Fig. 13.3 Nozzle and diffuser shapes as a function of initial Mach number.

Sonic Flow, $M = 1$

As we approach $M = 1$, from either a subsonic or supersonic state, the factor $1/[1 - M^2]$ in Eqs. 13.5 and 13.6 approaches infinity, implying that the pressure and velocity changes also approach infinity. This is obviously unrealistic, so we must look for some other way for the equations to make physical sense. The only way we can avoid these singularities in pressure and velocity is if we require that $dA \to 0$ as $M \to 1$. Hence, for an isentropic flow, sonic conditions can only occur where the area is constant! We can be even more specific: We can imagine approaching $M = 1$ from either a subsonic or a supersonic state. A subsonic flow ($M < 1$) would need to be accelerated using a subsonic nozzle, which we have learned is a converging section; a supersonic flow ($M > 1$) would need to be decelerated using a supersonic diffuser, which is also a converging section. Hence, sonic conditions are limited not just to a location of constant area, but one that is a minimum area. The important result is that *for isentropic flow the sonic condition $M = 1$ can only be attained at a throat, or section of minimum area.* (This does *not* mean that a throat *must* have $M = 1$. After all, we may have a low speed flow or even no flow at all in the device!).

We can see that to isentropically accelerate a fluid from rest to supersonic speed we would need to have a subsonic nozzle (converging section) followed by a supersonic nozzle (diverging section), with $M = 1$ at the throat. This device is called a *converging-diverging nozzle* (C-D nozzle). Of course, to create a supersonic flow we need more than just a C-D nozzle: we must also generate and maintain a pressure difference between the inlet and exit. We will discuss shortly C-D nozzles in some detail, and the pressures required to accomplish a change from subsonic to supersonic flow.

We must be careful in our discussion of isentropic flow (especially deceleration), because real fluids can experience nonisentropic phenomena such as boundary-layer separation and shock waves. In practice, supersonic flow cannot be decelerated to exactly $M = 1$ at a throat because sonic flow near a throat is unstable in a rising (adverse) pressure gradient. (It turns out that disturbances that are always present in a real subsonic flow propagate upstream, disturbing the sonic flow at the throat, causing shock waves to form and travel upstream, where they may be disgorged from the inlet of the supersonic diffuser.)

The throat area of a real supersonic diffuser must be slightly larger than that required to reduce the flow to $M = 1$. Under the proper downstream conditions, a weak normal shock forms in the diverging channel just downstream from the throat. Flow leaving the shock is subsonic and decelerates in the diverging channel. Thus

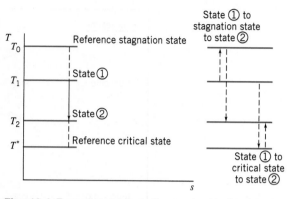

Fig. 13.4 Example of stagnation and critical reference states in the *Ts* plane.

deceleration from supersonic to subsonic flow cannot occur isentropically in practice, since the weak normal shock causes an entropy increase. Normal shocks will be analyzed in Section 13-5.

For accelerating flows (favorable pressure gradients) the idealization of isentropic flow is generally a realistic model of the actual flow behavior. For decelerating flows, the idealization of isentropic flow may not be realistic because of the adverse pressure gradients and the attendant possibility of flow separation, as discussed for incompressible boundary-layer flow in Chapter 9.

Reference Stagnation and Critical Conditions for Isentropic Flow of an Ideal Gas

As we mentioned at the beginning of this section, in principle we could use Eqs. 13.2 to analyze one-dimensional isentropic flow of an ideal gas, but the computations would be somewhat tedious. Instead, because the flow is isentropic, we can use the results of Sections 12-3 (reference stagnation conditions) and 12-4 (reference critical conditions). The idea is illustrated in Fig. 13.4: Instead of using Eqs. 13.2 to compute, for example, properties at state ② from those at state ①, we can use state ① to determine two reference states (the stagnation state and the critical state), and then use these to obtain properties at state ②. We need two reference states because the reference stagnation state does not provide area information (mathematically the stagnation area is infinite).

We will use Eqs. 12.21 (renumbered for convenience),

$$\frac{p_0}{p} = \left[1 + \frac{k-1}{2}M^2\right]^{k/(k-1)} \tag{13.7a}$$

$$\frac{T_0}{T} = 1 + \frac{k-1}{2}M^2 \tag{13.7b}$$

$$\frac{\rho_0}{\rho} = \left[1 + \frac{k-1}{2}M^2\right]^{1/(k-1)} \tag{13.7c}$$

We note that *the stagnation conditions are constant throughout the isentropic flow.* The critical conditions (when $M = 1$) were related to stagnation conditions in Section 12-4,

$$\frac{p_0}{p*} = \left[\frac{k+1}{2}\right]^{k/(k-1)} \tag{12.22a}$$

$$\frac{T_0}{T^*} = \frac{k+1}{2} \tag{12.22b}$$

$$\frac{\rho_0}{\rho^*} = \left[\frac{k+1}{2}\right]^{1/(k-1)} \tag{12.22c}$$

$$V^* = c^* = \sqrt{\frac{2k}{k+1}RT_0} \tag{12.23}$$

Although a particular flow may never attain sonic conditions (as in the example in Fig. 13.4), we will still find the critical conditions useful as reference conditions. Equations 13.7a, 13.7b, and 13.7c relate local properties (p, ρ, T, and V) to stagnation properties (p_0, ρ_0, and T_0) via the Mach number M, and Eqs. 12.22 and 12.23 relate critical properties (p^*, ρ^*, T^*, and V^*) to stagnation properties (p_0, ρ_0, and T_0) respectively, but we have yet to obtain a relation between areas A and A^*. To do this we start with continuity (Eq. 13.2a) in the form

$$\rho A V = \text{constant} = \rho^* A^* V^*$$

Then

$$\frac{A}{A^*} = \frac{\rho^*}{\rho}\frac{V^*}{V} = \frac{\rho^*}{\rho}\frac{c^*}{Mc} = \frac{1}{M}\frac{\rho^*}{\rho}\sqrt{\frac{T^*}{T}}$$

$$\frac{A}{A^*} = \frac{1}{M}\frac{\rho^*}{\rho_0}\frac{\rho_0}{\rho}\sqrt{\frac{T^*/T_0}{T/T_0}}$$

$$\frac{A}{A^*} = \frac{1}{M}\frac{\left[1 + \dfrac{k-1}{2}M^2\right]^{1/(k-1)}}{\left[\dfrac{k+1}{2}\right]^{1/(k-1)}}\left[\frac{1 + \dfrac{k-1}{2}M^2}{\dfrac{k+1}{2}}\right]^{1/2}$$

$$\frac{A}{A^*} = \frac{1}{M}\left[\frac{1 + \dfrac{k-1}{2}M^2}{\dfrac{k+1}{2}}\right]^{(k+1)/2(k-1)} \tag{13.7d}$$

Equations 13.7 form a set that is convenient for analyzing isentropic flow of an ideal gas with constant specific heats, which we usually use instead of the basic equations, Eqs. 13.2. For convenience we list Eqs. 13.7 together:

$$\frac{p_0}{p} = \left[1 + \frac{k-1}{2}M^2\right]^{k/(k-1)} \tag{13.7a}$$

$$\frac{T_0}{T} = 1 + \frac{k-1}{2}M^2 \tag{13.7b}$$

$$\frac{\rho_0}{\rho} = \left[1 + \frac{k-1}{2}M^2\right]^{1/(k-1)} \tag{13.7c}$$

$$\frac{A}{A^*} = \frac{1}{M}\left[\frac{1 + \dfrac{k-1}{2}M^2}{\dfrac{k+1}{2}}\right]^{(k+1)/2(k-1)} \tag{13.7d}$$

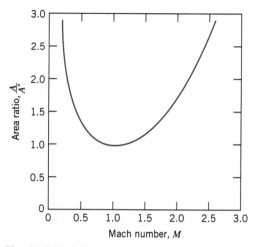

Fig. 13.5 Variation of A/A^* with Mach number for isentropic flow of an ideal gas with $k = 1.4$.

Equations 13.7 provide property relations in terms of the local Mach number, the stagnation conditions, and critical conditions; they are so useful that some calculators have some of them built in (for example, the *HP 48G* series [1]). It is a good idea to program them if your calculator does not already have them. There are even interactive web sites that make them available (see, for example, [2]), and they are fairly easy to define in spreadsheets such as *Excel*. The reader is urged to download the Excel add-ins for these equations from the Web site; with the add-ins, functions are available for computing pressure, temperature, density or area ratios from M, and M from the ratios. While they are somewhat complicated algebraically, they have the advantage over the basic equations, Eq. 13.2, that they are not coupled. Each property can be found directly from its stagnation value and the Mach number. Equation 13.7d shows the relation between Mach number M and area A. The critical area A^* (defined whether or not a given flow ever attains sonic conditions) is used to normalize area A. For each Mach number M we obtain a unique area ratio, but as shown in Fig 13.5 each A/A^* ratio (except 1) has two possible Mach numbers—one subsonic, the other supersonic. The shape shown in Fig. 13.5 *looks* like a converging-diverging section for accelerating from a subsonic to a supersonic flow (with, as necessary, $M = 1$ only at the throat), but in practice this is not the shape to which such a passage would be built. For example, the diverging section usually will have a much less severe angle of divergence to reduce the chance of flow separation (in Fig. 13.5 the Mach number increases linearly, but this is not necessary).

Appendix E-1 lists flow functions for property ratios T_0/T, p_0/p, ρ_0/ρ, and A/A^* in terms of M for isentropic flow of an ideal gas. A table of values, as well as a plot of these property ratios, is presented for air ($k = 1.4$) for a limited range of Mach numbers. The associated *Excel* workbook, *Isentropic Relations*, can be used to print a larger table of values for air and other ideal gases.

Example 13.1 demonstrates use of some of the above equations. As shown in Fig. 13.4, we can use the equations to relate a property at one state to the stagnation value and then from the stagnation value to a second state, but note that we can accomplish this in one step—for example, p_2 can be obtained from p_1 by writing $p_2 = (p_2/p_0)(p_0/p_1)p_1$, where the pressure ratios come from Eq. 13.7a evaluated at the two Mach numbers.

EXAMPLE 13.1   Isentropic Flow in a Converging Channel

Air flows isentropically in a channel. At section ①, the Mach number is 0.3, the area is 0.001 m², and the absolute pressure and the temperature are 650 kPa and 62°C, respectively. At section ②, the Mach number is 0.8. Sketch the channel shape, plot a *Ts* diagram for the process, and evaluate properties at section ②. Verify that the results agree with the basic equations, Eqs. 13.2.

GIVEN: Isentropic flow of air in a channel. At sections ① and ②, the following data are given: $M_1 = 0.3$, $T_1 = 62°C$, $p_1 = 650$ kPa (abs), $A_1 = 0.001$ m², and $M_2 = 0.8$.

FIND: (a)   The channel shape.
(b)   A *Ts* diagram for the process.
(c)   Properties at section ②.
(d)   Show that the results satisfy the basic equations.

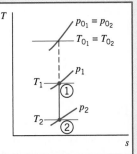

SOLUTION:

To accelerate a subsonic flow requires a converging nozzle. The channel shape must be as shown.

On the *Ts* plane, the process follows an *s* = constant line. Stagnation conditions remain fixed for isentropic flow.

Consequently, the stagnation temperature at section ② can be calculated (for air, $k = 1.4$) from Eq. 13.7b.

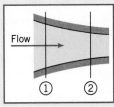

$$T_{0_2} = T_{0_1} = T_1 \left[1 + \frac{k-1}{2} M_1^2\right]$$

$$= (62 + 273) \text{ K}[1 + 0.2(0.3)^2]$$

$$T_{0_2} = T_{0_1} = 341 \text{ K} \longleftarrow \hspace{3cm} T_{0_1}, T_{0_2}$$

For p_{0_2}, from Eq. 13.7a,

$$p_{0_2} = p_{0_1} = p_1 \left[1 + \frac{k-1}{2} M_1^2\right]^{k/(k-1)} = 650 \text{ kPa}[1 + 0.2(0.3)^2]^{3.5}$$

$$p_{0_2} = 692 \text{ kPa (abs)} \longleftarrow \hspace{3cm} p_{0_2}$$

For T_2, from Eq. 13.7b,

$$T_2 = T_{0_2} \Big/ \left[1 + \frac{k-1}{2} M_2^2\right] = 341 \text{ K}/[1 + 0.2(0.8)^2]$$

$$T_2 = 302 \text{ K} \longleftarrow \hspace{3cm} T_2$$

For p_2, from Eq. 13.7a,

$$p_2 = p_{0_2} \Big/ \left[1 + \frac{k-1}{2} M_2^2\right]^{k/k-1} = 692 \text{ kPa}/[1 + 0.2(0.8)^2]^{3.5}$$

$$p_2 = 454 \text{ kPa} \longleftarrow \hspace{3cm} p_2$$

Note that we could have directly computed T_2 from T_1 because T_0 = constant:

$$\frac{T_2}{T_1} = \frac{T_2}{T_0}\Big/\frac{T_0}{T_1} = \left[1 + \frac{k-1}{2} M_1^2\right]\Big/\left[1 + \frac{k-1}{2} M_2^2\right] = [1 + 0.2(0.3)^2]/[1 + 0.2(0.8)^2]$$

$$\frac{T_2}{T_1} = \frac{0.8865}{0.9823} = 0.9025$$

Hence, $\hspace{3cm} T_2 = 0.9025 \, T_1 = 0.9025(273 + 62) \text{ K} = 302 \text{ K}$

Similarly, for p_2,

$$\frac{p_2}{p_1} = \frac{p_2}{p_0}\Big/\frac{p_0}{p_1} = 0.8865^{3.5}/0.9823^{3.5} = 0.6982$$

Hence,

$$p_2 = 0.6982\,p_1 = 0.6982(650\text{ kPa}) = 454\text{ kPa}$$

The density ρ_2 at section ② can be found from Eq. 13.7c using the same procedure we used for T_2 and p_2, or we can use the ideal gas equation of state, Eq. 13.2e,

$$\rho_2 = \frac{p_2}{RT_2} = 4.54 \times 10^5\,\frac{\text{N}}{\text{m}^2} \times \frac{\text{kg}\cdot\text{K}}{287\,\text{N}\cdot\text{m}} \times \frac{1}{302\,\text{K}} = 5.24\text{ kg/m}^3 \longleftarrow \qquad\qquad \rho_2$$

and the velocity at section ② is

$$V_2 = M_2 c_2 = M_2 \sqrt{kRT_2} = 0.8 \times \sqrt{1.4 \times 287\,\frac{\text{N}\cdot\text{m}}{\text{kg}\cdot\text{K}} \times 302\text{ K} \times \frac{\text{kg}\cdot\text{m}}{\text{s}^2\cdot\text{N}}} = 279\text{ m/s} \longleftarrow \qquad V_2$$

The area A_2 can be computed from Eq. 13.7d, noting that A^* is constant for this flow,

$$\frac{A_2}{A_1} = \frac{A_2}{A^*}\frac{A^*}{A_1} = \frac{1}{M_2}\left[\frac{1 + \dfrac{k-1}{2}M_2^2}{\dfrac{k+1}{2}}\right]^{(k+1)/2(k-1)} \Bigg/ \frac{1}{M_1}\left[\frac{1 + \dfrac{k-1}{2}M_1^2}{\dfrac{k+1}{2}}\right]^{(k+1)/2(k-1)}$$

$$= \frac{1}{0.8}\left[\frac{1 + 0.2(0.8)^2}{1.2}\right]^3 \Bigg/ \frac{1}{0.3}\left[\frac{1 + 0.2(0.3)^2}{1.2}\right]^3 = \frac{1.038}{2.035} = 0.5101$$

Hence,

$$A_2 = 0.5101A_1 = 0.5101(0.001\text{ m}^2) = 5.10 \times 10^{-4}\text{ m}^2 \longleftarrow \qquad\qquad A_2$$

Note that $A_2 < A_1$ as expected.

Let us verify that these results satisfy the basic equations.

We first need to obtain ρ_1 and V_1:

$$\rho_1 = \frac{p_1}{RT_1} = 6.5 \times 10^5\,\frac{\text{N}}{\text{m}^2} \times \frac{\text{kg}\cdot\text{K}}{287\,\text{N}\cdot\text{m}} \times \frac{1}{335\,\text{K}} = 6.76\text{ kg/m}^3$$

and

$$V_1 = M_1 c_1 = M_1 \sqrt{kRT_1} = 0.3 \times \sqrt{1.4 \times 287\,\frac{\text{N}\cdot\text{m}}{\text{kg}\cdot\text{K}} \times 335\text{ K} \times \frac{\text{kg}\cdot\text{m}}{\text{s}^2\cdot\text{N}}} = 110\text{ m/s}$$

The mass conservation equation is

$$\rho_1 V_1 A_1 = \rho_2 V_2 A_2 = \rho V A = \dot{m} = \text{constant} \tag{13.2a}$$

$$\dot{m} = \frac{6.76\text{ kg}}{\text{m}^3} \times \frac{110\text{ m}}{\text{s}} \times 0.001\text{ m}^2 = \frac{5.24\text{ kg}}{\text{m}^3} \times \frac{279\text{ m}}{\text{s}} \times 0.00051\text{ m}^2 = 0.744\text{ kg/s} \tag{Check!}$$

We cannot check the momentum equation (Eq. 13.2b) because we do not know the force R_x produced by the walls of the device (we could use Eq. 13.2b to compute this if we wished). The energy equation is

$$h_{0_1} = h_1 + \frac{V_1^2}{2} = h_2 + \frac{V_2^2}{2} = h_{0_2} = h_0 \tag{13.2c}$$

We will check this by replacing enthalpy with temperature using Eq. 13.2f,

$$\Delta h = h_2 - h_1 = c_p \Delta T = c_p(T_2 - T_1) \tag{13.2f}$$

so the energy equation becomes

$$c_p T_1 + \frac{V_1^2}{2} = c_p T_2 + \frac{V_2^2}{2} = c_p T_0$$

Using c_p for air from Table A.6,

$$c_p T_1 + \frac{V_1^2}{2} = 1004 \frac{\text{J}}{\text{kg} \cdot \text{K}} \times 335 \text{ K} + \frac{(110)^2}{2} \left(\frac{\text{m}}{\text{s}}\right)^2 \times \frac{\text{N} \cdot \text{s}^2}{\text{kg} \cdot \text{m}} \times \frac{\text{J}}{\text{N} \cdot \text{m}} = 342 \text{ kJ/kg}$$

$$c_p T_2 + \frac{V_2^2}{2} = 1004 \frac{\text{J}}{\text{kg} \cdot \text{K}} \times 302 \text{ K} + \frac{(278)^2}{2} \left(\frac{\text{m}}{\text{s}}\right)^2 \times \frac{\text{N} \cdot \text{s}^2}{\text{kg} \cdot \text{m}} \times \frac{\text{J}}{\text{N} \cdot \text{m}} = 342 \text{ kJ/kg}$$

$$c_p T_0 = 1004 \frac{\text{J}}{\text{kg} \cdot \text{K}} \times 341 \text{ K} = 342 \text{ kJ/kg} \qquad \text{(Check!)}$$

The final equation we can check is the relation between pressure and density for an isentropic process (Eq. 13.2g),

$$\frac{p_1}{\rho_1^k} = \frac{p_2}{\rho_2^k} = \frac{p}{\rho^k} = \text{constant}$$

$$\frac{p_1}{\rho_1^{1.4}} = \frac{650 \text{ kPa}}{\left(6.76 \frac{\text{kg}}{\text{m}^3}\right)^{1.4}} = \frac{p_2}{\rho_2^{1.4}} = \frac{454 \text{ kPa}}{\left(5.24 \frac{\text{kg}}{\text{m}^3}\right)^{1.4}} = 44.7 \frac{\text{kPa}}{\left(\frac{\text{kg}}{\text{m}^3}\right)^{1.4}} \qquad \text{(Check!)}$$

The basic equations are satisfied by our solution.

> This Example illustrates:
> ✓ Use of the isentropic equations, Eqs. 13.7.
> ✓ That the isentropic equations are consistent with the basic equations, Eqs. 13.2.
> ✓ That the computations can be quite laborious without using preprogrammed isentropic relations (available, for example, in the *Excel* add-ins on the Web site)!
> The *Excel* workbook for this Example is convenient for performing the calculations, using either the isentropic equations or the basic equations.

Isentropic Flow in a Converging Nozzle

Now that we have our computing equations (Eqs. 13.7) for analyzing isentropic flows, we are ready to see how we could obtain flow in a nozzle, starting from rest. We first look at the converging nozzle, and then the C-D nozzle. In either case, to produce a flow we must provide a pressure difference. For example, as illustrated in the converging nozzle shown in Fig. 13.6a, we can do this by providing the gas from a reservoir (or "plenum chamber") at p_0 and T_0, and using a vacuum pump/valve combination to create a low pressure, the "back pressure," p_b. We are interested in what happens to the gas properties as the gas flows through the nozzle, and also in knowing how the mass flow rate increases as we progressively lower the back pressure. (We could also produce a flow by maintaining a constant back pressure, e.g., atmospheric, and increasing the pressure in the plenum chamber.)

Let us call the pressure at the exit plane p_e. We will see that this will often be equal to the applied back pressure, p_b, but not always! The results we obtain as we progressively open the valve from a closed position are shown in Figs. 13.6b and 13.6c. We consider each of the cases shown.

When the valve is closed, there is no flow through the nozzle. The pressure is p_0 throughout, as shown by condition (i) in Fig. 13.6a.

If the back pressure, p_b, is now reduced to slightly less than p_0, there will be flow through the nozzle with a decrease in pressure in the direction of flow, as shown by condition (ii). Flow at the exit plane will be subsonic with the exit-plane pressure equal to the back pressure.

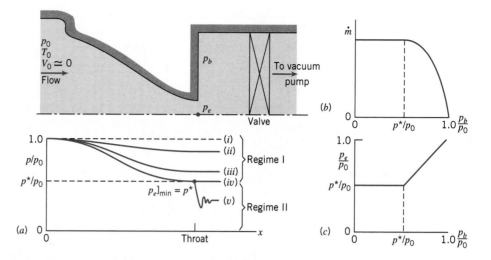

Fig. 13.6 Converging nozzle operating at various back pressures.

What happens as we continue to decrease the back pressure? As expected, the flow rate will continue to increase, and the exit-plane pressure will continue to decrease, as shown by condition (iii) in Fig. 13.6a. [Note that conditions (ii) and (iii) can be described using the Bernoulli equation (Eq. 6.8), as long as the maximum Mach number, at the exit plane, does not exceed $M = 0.3$.]

As we progressively lower the back pressure the flow rate increases, and hence, so do the velocity and Mach number at the exit plane. The question arises: "Is there a limit to the mass flow rate through the nozzle?" or, to put it another way, "Is there an upper limit on the exit Mach number?" The answer to these questions is "Yes!" To see this, recall that for isentropic flow Eq. 13.6 applies:

$$\frac{dV}{V} = -\frac{dA}{A}\frac{1}{[1-M^2]} \tag{13.6}$$

From this we learned that the *only* place we can have sonic conditions ($M = 1$) is where the change in area dA is zero. We *cannot* have sonic conditions anywhere in the converging section. Logically we can see that the *maximum exit Mach number is one*. Because the flow started from rest ($M = 0$), if we had $M > 1$ at the exit, we would have had to pass through $M = 1$ somewhere in the converging section, which would be a violation of Eq. 13.6.

Hence, the maximum flow rate occurs when we have sonic conditions at the exit plane, when $M_e = 1$, and $p_e = p_b = p^*$, the critical pressure. This is shown as condition (iv) in Fig. 13.6a, and is called a "choked flow," beyond which the flow rate cannot be increased. From Eq. 13.7a with $M = 1$ (or from Eq. 12.21a),

$$\frac{p_e}{p_0}\bigg|_{\text{choked}} = \frac{p^*}{p_0} = \left(\frac{2}{k+1}\right)^{k/(k-1)} \tag{13.8}$$

For air, $k = 1.4$, so $p_e/p_0]_{\text{choked}} = 0.528$. For example, if we wish to have sonic flow at the exit of a nozzle from a plenum chamber that is at atmospheric pressure, we would need to maintain a back pressure of about 7.76 psia, or about 6.94 psig vacuum. This does not sound difficult for a vacuum pump to generate, but actually takes a lot of power to maintain, because we will have a large mass flow rate through the pump. For the maximum, or choked, mass flow rate we have

$$\dot{m}_{\text{choked}} = \rho^* V^* A^*$$

Using the ideal gas equation of state, Eq. 13.2e, and the stagnation to critical pressure and temperature ratios, Eqs. 13.7a and 13.7b respectively, with $M = 1$ (or Eqs. 12.21a and 12.21b respectively), with $A^* = A_e$, it can be shown that this becomes

$$\dot{m}_{choked} = A_e p_0 \sqrt{\frac{k}{RT_0}} \left(\frac{2}{k+1}\right)^{(k+1)/2(k-1)} \tag{13.9a}$$

Note that for a given gas (k and R) the maximum flow rate in the converging nozzle depends *only* on the size of the exit area (A_e) and the conditions in the reservoir (p_0, T_0).

For air, for convenience we write an "engineering" form of Eq. 13.9a,

$$\dot{m}_{choked} = 0.04 \frac{A_e p_0}{\sqrt{T_0}} \tag{13.9b}$$

with $\dot{m}_{choked}$ in kg/s, A_e in m^2, p_0 in Pa, and T_0 in K, and

$$\dot{m}_{choked} = 76.6 \frac{A_e p_0}{\sqrt{T_0}} \tag{13.9c}$$

with $\dot{m}_{choked}$ in lbm/s, A_e in ft^2, p_0 in psia, and T_0 in °R.

Suppose we now insist on lowering the back pressure below this "benchmark" level of p^*. Our next question is "What will happen to the flow in the nozzle?" The answer is "Nothing!" The flow remains choked: the mass flow rate does not increase, as shown in Fig. 13.6b, and the pressure distribution in the nozzle remains unchanged, with $p_e = p^* > p_b$, as shown in condition (v) in Figs. 13.6a and 13.6c. After exiting, the flow adjusts down to the applied back pressure, but does so in a nonisentropic, three-dimensional manner in a series of expansion waves and shocks, and for this part of the flow our one-dimensional, isentropic flow concepts no longer apply. We will return to this discussion in Section 13-6.

This idea of choked flow seems a bit strange, but can be explained in at least two ways. First, we have already discussed that to increase the mass flow rate beyond choked would require $M_e > 1$, which is not possible. Second, once the flow reaches sonic conditions, it becomes "deaf" to downstream conditions: Any change (i.e., a reduction) in the applied back pressure propagates in the fluid at the speed of sound in all directions, as we discussed in Chapter 12, so it gets "washed" downstream by the fluid which is moving at the speed of sound at the nozzle exit.

Flow through a converging nozzle may be divided into two regimes:

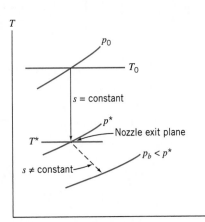

Fig. 13.7 Schematic Ts diagram for choked flow through a converging nozzle.

1. In Regime I, $1 \geq p_b/p_0 \geq p^*/p_0$. Flow to the throat is isentropic and $p_e = p_b$.
2. In Regime II, $p_b/p_0 < p^*/p_0$. Flow to the throat is isentropic, and $M_e = 1$. A nonisentropic expansion occurs in the flow leaving the nozzle and $p_e = p^* > p_b$ (entropy increases because this is adiabatic but irreversible).

The flow processes corresponding to Regime II are shown on a Ts diagram in Fig. 13.7. Two problems involving converging nozzles are solved in Examples 13.2 and 13.3.

Although isentropic flow is an idealization, it often is a very good approximation for the actual behavior of nozzles. Since a nozzle is a device that accelerates a flow, the internal pressure gradient is favorable. This tends to keep the wall boundary layers thin and to minimize the effects of friction.

EXAMPLE 13.2 Isentropic Flow in a Converging Nozzle

A converging nozzle, with a throat area of 0.001 m^2, is operated with air at a back pressure of 591 kPa (abs). The nozzle is fed from a large plenum chamber where the absolute stagnation pressure and temperature are 1.0 MPa and 60°C. The exit Mach number and mass flow rate are to be determined.

GIVEN: Air flow through a converging nozzle at the conditions shown: Flow is isentropic.

FIND: (a) M_e.
(b) $\dot{m}$.

$p_0 = 1.0 \text{ MPa (abs)}$
$T_0 = 333\text{K}$
$p_b = 591 \text{ kPa (abs)}$
p_e

SOLUTION:
The first step is to check for choking. The pressure ratio is

$$\frac{p_b}{p_0} = \frac{5.91 \times 10^5}{1.0 \times 10^6} = 0.591 > 0.528$$

so the flow is *not* choked. Thus $p_b = p_e$, and the flow is isentropic, as sketched on the Ts diagram.

Since $p_0 = $ constant, M_e may be found from the pressure ratio,

$$\frac{p_0}{p_e} = \left[1 + \frac{k-1}{2} M_e^2\right]^{k/(k-1)}$$

T
p_0
T_0
p_e
T_e
T^*
s

Solving for M_e, since $p_e = p_b$, we obtain

$$1 + \frac{k-1}{2} M_e^2 = \left(\frac{p_0}{p_b}\right)^{(k-1)/k}$$

and

$$M_e = \left\{\left[\left(\frac{p_0}{p_b}\right)^{(k-1)/k} - 1\right]\frac{2}{k-1}\right\}^{1/2} = \left\{\left[\left(\frac{1.0 \times 10^6}{5.91 \times 10^5}\right)^{0.286} - 1\right]\frac{2}{1.4-1}\right\}^{1/2} = 0.90 \longleftarrow \qquad M_e$$

The mass flow rate is

$$\dot{m} = \rho_e V_e A_e = \rho_e M_e c_e A_e$$

We need T_e to find ρ_e and c_e. Since $T_0 = $ constant,

$$\frac{T_0}{T_e} = 1 + \frac{k-1}{2} M_e^2$$

or

$$T_e = \frac{T_0}{1 + \frac{k-1}{2} M_e^2} = \frac{(273 + 60) \text{ K}}{1 + 0.2(0.9)^2} = 287 \text{ K}$$

$$c_e = \sqrt{kRT_e} = \left[1.4 \times 287 \frac{\text{N} \cdot \text{m}}{\text{kg} \cdot \text{K}} \times 287 \text{ K} \times \frac{\text{kg} \cdot \text{m}}{\text{N} \cdot \text{s}^2}\right]^{1/2} = 340 \text{ m/s}$$

and

$$\rho_e = \frac{p_e}{RT_e} = 5.91 \times 10^5 \; \frac{N}{m^2} \times \frac{kg \cdot K}{287 \, N \cdot m} \times \frac{1}{287 \, K} = 7.18 \; kg/m^3$$

Finally,

$$\dot{m} = \rho_e M_e c_e A_e = \frac{7.18 \; kg}{m^3} \times 0.9 \times \frac{340 \; m}{s} \times 0.001 \; m^2 = 2.20 \; kg/s \longleftarrow \qquad \dot{m}$$

> This problem illustrates use of the isentropic equations, Eqs. 13.7, for a flow that is not choked.
>
> The *Excel* workbook for this Example is convenient for performing the calculations (using either the isentropic equations or the basic equations). (The *Excel* add-ins for isentropic flow, on the Web site, also make calculations much easier.)

EXAMPLE 13.3   Choked Flow in a Converging Nozzle

Air flows isentropically through a converging nozzle. At a section where the nozzle area is 0.013 ft², the local pressure, temperature, and Mach number are 60 psia, 40°F, and 0.52, respectively. The back pressure is 30 psia. The Mach number at the throat, the mass flow rate, and the throat area are to be determined.

GIVEN: Air flow through a converging nozzle at the conditions shown:

$M_1 = 0.52$
$T_1 = 40°F$
$p_1 = 60 \text{ psia}$
$A_1 = 0.013 \text{ ft}^2$

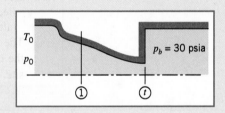

FIND: (a) M_t.   (b) $\dot{m}$.   (c) A_t.

SOLUTION:

First we check for choking, to determine if flow is isentropic down to p_b. To check, we evaluate the stagnation conditions.

$$p_0 = p_1 \left[1 + \frac{k-1}{2} M_1^2 \right]^{k/(k-1)} = 60 \text{ psia } [1 + 0.2(0.52)^2]^{3.5} = 72.0 \text{ psia}$$

The back pressure ratio is

$$\frac{p_b}{p_0} = \frac{30.0}{72.0} = 0.417 < 0.528$$

so the flow is choked! For choked flow,

$$M_t = 1.0 \longleftarrow \qquad M_t$$

The Ts diagram is

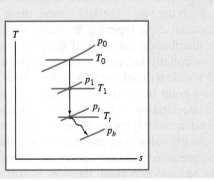

The mass flow rate may be found from conditions at section ①, using $\dot{m} = \rho_1 V_1 A_1$.

$$V_1 = M_1 c_1 = M_1 \sqrt{kRT_1}$$

$$= 0.52 \left[1.4 \times 53.3 \frac{\text{ft} \cdot \text{lbf}}{\text{lbm} \cdot {}^\circ\text{R}} \times (460 + 40){}^\circ\text{R} \times 32.2 \frac{\text{lbm}}{\text{slug}} \times \frac{\text{slug} \cdot \text{ft}}{\text{lbf} \cdot \text{s}^2} \right]^{1/2}$$

$$V_1 = 570 \text{ ft/s}$$

$$\rho_1 = \frac{p_1}{RT_1} = 60 \frac{\text{lbf}}{\text{in.}^2} \times \frac{\text{lbm} \cdot {}^\circ\text{R}}{53.3 \text{ ft} \cdot \text{lbf}} \times \frac{1}{500{}^\circ\text{R}} \times \frac{144 \text{ in.}^2}{\text{ft}^2} = 0.324 \text{ lbm/ft}^3$$

$$\dot{m} = \rho_1 V_1 A_1 = 0.324 \frac{\text{lbm}}{\text{ft}^3} \times \frac{570 \text{ ft}}{\text{s}} \times 0.013 \text{ ft}^2 = 2.40 \text{ lbm/s} \longleftarrow \qquad \dot{m}$$

From Eq. 13.6,

$$\frac{A_1}{A^*} = \frac{1}{M_1} \left[\frac{1 + \dfrac{k-1}{2} M_1^2}{\dfrac{k+1}{2}} \right]^{(k+1)/2(k-1)} = \frac{1}{0.52} \left[\frac{1 + 0.2(0.52)^2}{1.2} \right]^{3.00} = 1.303$$

For choked flow, $A_t = A^*$. Thus,

$$A_t = A^* = \frac{A_1}{1.303} = \frac{0.013 \text{ ft}^2}{1.303} = 9.98 \times 10^{-3} \text{ ft}^2 \longleftarrow \qquad A_t$$

This problem illustrates use of the isentropic equations, Eqs. 13.7, for a flow that is choked.

✓ Because the flow is choked, we could also have used Eq. 13.9a for $\dot{m}$ (after finding T_0).

The *Excel* workbook for this Example is convenient for performing the calculations. (The *Excel* add-ins for isentropic flow, on the Web site, also make calculations much easier.)

Isentropic Flow in a Converging-Diverging Nozzle

Having considered isentropic flow in a converging nozzle, we turn now to isentropic flow in a converging-diverging (C-D) nozzle. As in the previous case, flow through the converging-diverging passage of Fig. 13.8 is induced by a vacuum pump downstream, and is controlled by the valve shown; upstream stagnation conditions are constant. Pressure in the exit plane of the nozzle is p_e; the nozzle discharges to back pressure p_b. As for the converging nozzle, we wish to see, among other things, how the flow rate varies with the driving force, the applied pressure difference ($p_0 - p_b$). Consider the effect of gradually reducing the back pressure. The results are illustrated graphically in Fig. 13.8. Let us consider each of the cases shown.

With the valve initially closed, there is no flow through the nozzle; the pressure is constant at p_0. Opening the valve slightly (p_b slightly less than p_0) produces pressure distribution curve (*i*). If the flow rate is low enough, the flow will be subsonic and essentially incompressible at all points on this curve. Under these conditions, the C-D nozzle will behave as a venturi, with flow accelerating in the converging portion until a point of maximum velocity and minimum pressure is reached at the throat, then decelerating in the diverging portion to the nozzle exit. (This behavior is described accurately by the Bernoulli equation, Eq. 6.8.)

As the valve is opened farther and the flow rate is increased, a more sharply defined pressure minimum occurs, as shown by curve (*ii*). Although compressibility effects become important, the flow is still subsonic everywhere, and flow decelerates

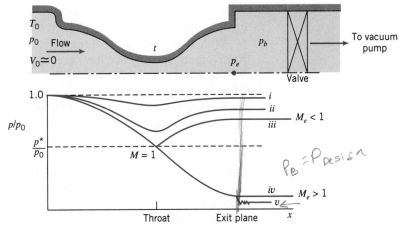

Fig. 13.8 Pressure distributions for isentropic flow in a converging-diverging nozzle.

in the diverging section. (Clearly, this behavior is *not* described accurately by the Bernoulli equation.) Finally, as the valve is opened farther, curve (*iii*) results. At the section of minimum area the flow finally reaches $M = 1$, and the nozzle is choked— the flow rate is the maximum possible for the given nozzle and stagnation conditions.

All flows with pressure distributions (*i*), (*ii*), and (*iii*) are isentropic; as we progress from (*i*) to (*ii*) to (*iii*) we are generating increasing mass flow rates. Finally, when curve (*iii*) is reached, critical conditions are present at the throat. For this flow rate, the flow is choked, and

$$\dot{m} = \rho^* V^* A^*$$

where $A^* = A_t$, just as it was for the converging nozzle, and for this maximum possible flow rate Eq. 13.9a applies (with A_e replaced with the throat area A_t),

$$\dot{m}_{choked} = A_t p_0 \sqrt{\frac{k}{RT_0}} \left(\frac{2}{k+1}\right)^{(k+1)/2(k-1)} \tag{13.10a}$$

Note that for a given gas (k and R) the maximum flow rate in the C-D nozzle depends *only* on the size of the throat area (A_t) and the conditions in the reservoir (p_0, T_0).

For air, for convenience we write an "engineering" form of Eq. 13.10a,

$$\dot{m}_{choked} = 0.04 \frac{A_t p_0}{\sqrt{T_0}} \tag{13.10b}$$

with $\dot{m}_{choked}$ in kg/s, A_t in m², p_0 in Pa, and T_0 in K, and

$$\dot{m}_{choked} = 76.6 \frac{A_t p_0}{\sqrt{T_0}} \tag{13.10c}$$

with $\dot{m}_{choked}$ in lbm/s, A_t in ft², p_0 in psia, and T_0 in °R.

Any attempt to increase the flow rate by further lowering the back pressure will fail, for the two reasons we discussed earlier: once we attain sonic conditions, downstream changes can no longer be transmitted upstream; and we cannot exceed sonic conditions at the throat, because this would require passing through the sonic state somewhere in the converging section, which is not possible in isentropic flow. (Of course, we *could* increase the choked mass flow rate through a given C-D nozzle to any level desired by, for example, increasing the reservoir pressure.)

With sonic conditions at the throat, we consider what *can* happen to the flow in the diverging section. We have previously discussed (see Fig. 13.3) that a diverging section will decelerate a subsonic flow ($M < 1$) but will accelerate a supersonic flow ($M > 1$)—very different behaviors! The question arises: "Does a sonic flow behave as a subsonic or as a supersonic flow as it enters a diverging section?" The answer to this question is that it can behave like either one, depending on the downstream pressure! We have already seen subsonic flow behavior [curve (*iii*)]: the applied back pressure leads to a gradual downstream pressure increase, decelerating the flow. We now consider accelerating the choked flow.

To accelerate flow in the diverging section requires a pressure decrease. This condition is illustrated by curve (*iv*) in Fig. 13.8. The flow will accelerate isentropically in the nozzle provided the exit pressure is set at p_{iv}. Thus, we see that with a throat Mach number of unity, there are two possible isentropic flow conditions in the converging-diverging nozzle. This is consistent with the results of Fig. 13.5, where we found two Mach numbers for each A/A^* in isentropic flow.

Lowering the back pressure below condition (*iv*), say to condition (*v*), has no effect on flow in the nozzle. The flow is isentropic from the plenum chamber to the nozzle exit [as in condition (*iv*)] and then it undergoes a three-dimensional irreversible expansion to the lower back pressure. A nozzle operating under these conditions is said to be *underexpanded*, since additional expansion takes place outside the nozzle.

A converging-diverging nozzle generally is intended to produce supersonic flow at the exit plane. If the back pressure is set at p_{iv}, flow will be isentropic through the nozzle, and supersonic at the nozzle exit. Nozzles operating at $p_b = p_{iv}$ [corresponding to curve (*iv*) in Fig. 13.8] are said to operate at *design conditions*.

Flow leaving a C-D nozzle is supersonic when the back pressure is at or below nozzle design pressure. The exit Mach number is fixed once the area ratio, A_e/A^*, is specified. All other exit plane properties (for isentropic flow) are uniquely related to stagnation properties by the fixed exit plane Mach number.

The assumption of isentropic flow for a real nozzle at design conditions is a reasonable one. However, the one-dimensional flow model is inadequate for the design of relatively short nozzles to produce uniform supersonic exit flow.

Rocket-propelled vehicles use C-D nozzles to accelerate the exhaust gases to the maximum possible speed to produce high thrust. A propulsion nozzle is subject to varying ambient conditions during flight through the atmosphere, so it is impossible to attain the maximum theoretical thrust over the complete operating range. Because only a single supersonic Mach number can be obtained for each area ratio, nozzles for developing supersonic flow in wind tunnels often are built with interchangeable test sections, or with variable geometry.

You probably have noticed that nothing has been said about the operation of converging-diverging nozzles with back pressure in the range $p_{iii} > p_b > p_{iv}$. For such cases the flow cannot expand isentropically to p_b. Under these conditions a shock (which may be treated as an irreversible discontinuity involving entropy increase) occurs somewhere within the flow. Following a discussion of normal shocks in Section 13-5, we shall return to complete the discussion of converging-diverging nozzle flows in Section 13-6.

Nozzles operating with $p_{iii} > p_b > p_{iv}$ are said to be *overexpanded* because the pressure at some point in the nozzle is less than the back pressure. Obviously, an overexpanded nozzle could be made to operate at a new design condition by removing a portion of the diverging section.

In Example 13.4, we consider isentropic flow in a C-D nozzle; in Example 13.5, we consider choked flow in a C-D nozzle.

EXAMPLE 13.4   Isentropic Flow in a Converging-Diverging Nozzle

Air flows isentropically in a converging-diverging nozzle, with exit area of 0.001 m². The nozzle is fed from a large plenum where the stagnation conditions are 350 K and 1.0 MPa (abs). The exit pressure is 954 kPa (abs) and the Mach number at the throat is 0.68. Fluid properties and area at the nozzle throat and the exit Mach number are to be determined.

GIVEN: Isentropic flow of air in C-D nozzle as shown:

$$T_0 = 350\,\text{K}$$
$$p_0 = 1.0\,\text{MPa (abs)}$$
$$p_b = 954\,\text{kPa (abs)}$$
$$M_t = 0.68 \quad A_e = 0.001\,\text{m}^2$$

FIND: (a) Properties and area at nozzle throat.
　　　　　(b) M_e.

SOLUTION:
Stagnation temperature is constant for isentropic flow. Thus, since

$$\frac{T_0}{T} = 1 + \frac{k-1}{2}M^2$$

then

$$T_t = \frac{T_0}{1 + \dfrac{k-1}{2}M_t^2} = \frac{350\,\text{K}}{1 + 0.2(0.68)^2} = 320\,\text{K} \longleftarrow \underline{\qquad T_t}$$

Also, since p_0 is constant for isentropic flow, then

$$p_t = p_0 \left(\frac{T_t}{T_0}\right)^{k/(k-1)} = p_0\left[\frac{1}{1 + \dfrac{k-1}{2}M_t^2}\right]^{k/(k-1)}$$

$$p_t = 1.0 \times 10^6\,\text{Pa}\left[\frac{1}{1 + 0.2(0.68)^2}\right]^{3.5} = 734\,\text{kPa (abs)} \longleftarrow \underline{\qquad p_t}$$

so

$$\rho_t = \frac{p_t}{RT_t} = \frac{7.34 \times 10^5\,\text{N}}{\text{m}^2} \times \frac{\text{kg} \cdot \text{K}}{287\,\text{N} \cdot \text{m}} \times \frac{1}{320\,\text{K}} = 7.99\,\text{kg/m}^3 \longleftarrow \underline{\qquad \rho_t}$$

and

$$V_t = M_t c_t = M_t \sqrt{kRT_t}$$

$$V_t = 0.68\left[14 \times \frac{287\,\text{N} \cdot \text{m}}{\text{kg} \cdot \text{K}} \times 320\,\text{K} \times \frac{\text{kg} \cdot \text{m}}{\text{N} \cdot \text{s}^2}\right]^{1/2} = 244\,\text{m/s} \longleftarrow \underline{\qquad V_t}$$

From Eq. 13.7d we can obtain a value of A_t/A^*

$$\frac{A_t}{A^*} = \frac{1}{M_t}\left[\frac{1 + \dfrac{k-1}{2}M_t^2}{\dfrac{k+1}{2}}\right]^{(k+1)/2(k-1)} = \frac{1}{0.68}\left[\frac{1 + 0.2(0.68)^2}{1.2}\right]^{3.00} = 1.11$$

but at this point A^* is not known.
　　　Since $M_t < 1$, flow at the exit must be subsonic. Therefore, $p_e = p_b$. Stagnation properties are constant, so

$$\frac{p_0}{p_e} = \left[1 + \frac{k-1}{2}M_e^2\right]^{k/(k-1)}$$

Solving for M_e gives

$$M_e = \left\{\left[\left(\frac{p_0}{p_e}\right)^{(k-1)/k} - 1\right]\frac{2}{k-1}\right\}^{1/2} = \left\{\left[\left(\frac{1.0 \times 10^6}{9.54 \times 10^5}\right)^{0.286} - 1\right](5)\right\}^{1/2} = 0.26 \longleftarrow \underline{\qquad M_e}$$

The Ts diagram for this flow is

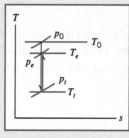

Since A_e and M_e are known, we can compute A^*. From Eq. 13.7d

$$\frac{A_e}{A^*} = \frac{1}{M_e}\left[\frac{1 + \frac{k-1}{2}M_e^2}{\frac{k+1}{2}}\right]^{(k+1)/2(k-1)} = \frac{1}{0.26}\left[\frac{1 + 0.2(0.26)^2}{1.2}\right]^{3.00} = 2.317$$

Thus,

$$A^* = \frac{A_e}{2.317} = \frac{0.001\ \text{m}^2}{2.317} = 4.32 \times 10^{-4}\ \text{m}^2$$

and

$$A_t = 1.110A^* = (1.110)(4.32 \times 10^{-4}\ \text{m}^2) = 4.80 \times 10^{-4}\ \text{m}^2 \longleftarrow \quad A_t$$

> This problem illustrates use of the isentropic equations, Eqs. 13.7, for flow in a C-D nozzle that is not choked.
> ✓ Note that use of Eq. 13.7d allowed us to obtain the throat area without needing to first compute other properties.
> The *Excel* workbook for this Example is convenient for performing the calculations (using either the isentropic equations or the basic equations). (The *Excel* add-ins for isentropic flow, on the Web site, also make calculations much easier.)

EXAMPLE 13.5   Isentropic Flow in a Converging-Diverging Nozzle: Choked Flow

The nozzle of Example 13.4 has a design back pressure of 87.5 kPa (abs) but is operated at a back pressure of 50.0 kPa (abs). Assume flow within the nozzle is isentropic. Determine the exit Mach number and mass flow rate.

GIVEN: Air flow through C-D nozzle as shown:

$T_0 = 350\ \text{K}$

$p_0 = 1.0\ \text{MPa (abs)}$

$p_e(\text{design}) = 87.5\ \text{kPa (abs)}$

$p_b = 50.0\ \text{kPa (abs)}$

$A_e = 0.001\ \text{m}^2$

$A_t = 4.8 \times 10^{-4}\text{m}^2$ (Example 13.4)

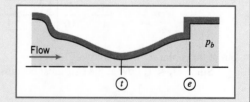

FIND: (a) M_e.
(b) $\dot{m}$.

SOLUTION:

The operating back pressure is *below* the design pressure. Consequently, the nozzle is underexpanded, and the Ts diagram and pressure distribution will be as shown:

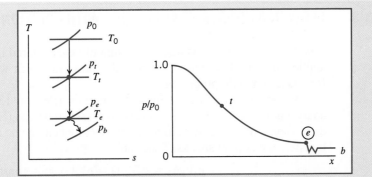

Flow *within* the nozzle will be isentropic, but the irreversible expansion from p_e to p_b will cause an entropy increase; $p_e = p_e(\text{design}) = 87.5\ \text{kPa (abs)}$.

Since stagnation properties are constant for isentropic flow, the exit Mach number can be computed from the pressure ratio. Thus

$$\frac{p_0}{p_e} = \left[1 + \frac{k-1}{2}\,M_e^2\right]^{k/(k-1)}$$

or

$$M_e = \left\{\left[\left(\frac{p_0}{p_e}\right)^{(k-1)/k} - 1\right]\frac{2}{k-1}\right\}^{1/2} = \left\{\left[\left(\frac{1.0\times10^6}{8.75\times10^4}\right)^{0.286} - 1\right]\frac{2}{0.4}\right\}^{1/2} = 2.24 \longleftarrow \qquad M_e$$

Because the flow is choked we can use Eq. 13.10b for the mass flow rate,

$$\dot{m}_{\text{chocked}} = 0.04\,\frac{A_t p_0}{\sqrt{T_0}} \qquad\qquad (13.10b)$$

(with $\dot{m}_{\text{choked}}$ in kg/s, A_t in m^2, p_0 in Pa, and T_0 in K), so

$$\dot{m}_{\text{chocked}} = 0.04 \times 4.8\times10^{-4} \times 1\times10^6/\sqrt{350}$$

$$\dot{m} = \dot{m}_{\text{chocked}} = 1.04\ \text{kg/s} \longleftarrow \qquad\qquad\qquad \dot{m}$$

This problem illustrates use of the isentropic equations, Eqs. 13.7, for flow in a C-D nozzle that is choked.

  ✓ Note that we used Eq. 13.10b, an "engineering equation"—that is, an equation containing a coefficient that has units. While useful here, generally these equations are no longer used in engineering because their correct use depends on using input variable values in specific units.

The *Excel* workbook for this Example is convenient for performing the calculations (using either the isentropic equations or the basic equations). (The *Excel* add-ins for isentropic flow, on the Web site, also make calculations much easier.)

We have now completed our study of idealized one-dimensional isentropic flow in channels of varying area. In real channels, we will have friction and quite possibly heat transfer. Our next tasks are to study effects of these phenomena on a flow. As we mentioned at the beginning of this chapter, in this introductory text we cannot study flows that experience *all* these phenomena: In the next section, we consider the effect of friction alone, in Section 13-4 we study the effect of heat transfer alone, and in Section 13-5 we study the effect of normal shocks (and see in Section 13-6 how these affect the C-D nozzle, in more detail than we did in this section).

13-3 FLOW IN A CONSTANT-AREA DUCT WITH FRICTION

Gas flow in constant-area ducts is commonly encountered in a variety of engineering applications. In this section we consider flows in which wall friction is responsible for changes in fluid properties.

As for isentropic flow with area variation (Section 13-2), our starting point in analyzing flows with friction is the set of basic equations (Eqs. 13.1), describing one-dimensional motion that is affected by several phenomena: area change, friction, heat transfer, and normal shocks. These are

$$\rho_1 V_1 A_1 = \rho_2 V_2 A_2 = \rho V A = \dot{m} = \text{constant} \tag{13.1a}$$

$$R_x + p_1 A_1 - p_2 A_2 = \dot{m} V_2 - \dot{m} V_1 \tag{13.1b}$$

$$\frac{\delta Q}{dm} + h_1 + \frac{V_1^2}{2} = h_2 + \frac{V_2^2}{2} \tag{13.1c}$$

$$\dot{m}(s_2 - s_1) \ge \int_{\text{CS}} \frac{1}{T}\left(\frac{\dot{Q}}{A}\right) dA \tag{13.1d}$$

$$p = \rho R T \tag{13.1e}$$

$$\Delta h = h_2 - h_1 = c_p \Delta T = c_p(T_2 - T_1) \tag{13.1f}$$

$$\Delta s = s_2 - s_1 = c_p \ln \frac{T_2}{T_1} - R \ln \frac{p_2}{p_1} \tag{13.1g}$$

Equation 13.1a is *continuity*, Eq. 13.1b is a *momentum equation*, Eq. 13.1c is an *energy equation*, Eq. 13.1d is the *second law of thermodynamics*, and Eqs. 13.1e, 13.1f, and 13.1g are useful *property relations* for an ideal gas with constant specific heats.

We must simplify these equations for flow in a constant-area duct with friction. We must think about what happens to the heat that friction generates. There are two obvious cases we can consider: In the first we assume that the flow is *adiabatic*, so any heat generated remains in the fluid; in the second we assume that the flow remains *isothermal*, so the fluid either gives off heat or absorbs heat as necessary. While some flows may be neither adiabatic nor isothermal, many real-world flows are. Flow in a relatively short duct will be approximately adiabatic; flow in a very long duct (e.g., an uninsulated natural gas pipeline) will be approximately isothermal (the pipeline will be at the ambient temperature). We consider first adiabatic flow.

Basic Equations for Adiabatic Flow

We can simplify Eqs. 13.1 for frictional adiabatic flow in a constant-area duct of an ideal gas with constant specific heats, as shown in Fig. 13.9.

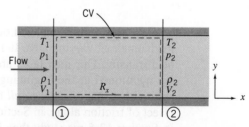
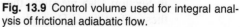

Fig. 13.9 Control volume used for integral analysis of frictional adiabatic flow.

We now have $A_1 = A_2 = A$. In addition, for no heat transfer we have $\delta Q/dm = 0$. Finally, the force R_x is now due only to friction (no x component of surface force is caused by pressure on the parallel sides of the channel). Hence, for this flow our equations simplify to

$$\rho_1 V_1 = \rho_2 V_2 = \rho V \equiv G = \frac{\dot{m}}{A} = \text{constant} \tag{13.11a}$$

$$R_x + p_1 A - p_2 A = \dot{m} V_2 - \dot{m} V_1 \tag{13.11b}$$

$$h_{0_1} = h_1 + \frac{V_1^2}{2} = h_2 + \frac{V_2^2}{2} = h_{0_2} = h_0 \tag{13.11c}$$

$$s_2 > s_1 \tag{13.11d}$$

$$p = \rho R T \tag{13.11e}$$

$$\Delta h = h_2 - h_1 = c_p \Delta T = c_p (T_2 - T_1) \tag{13.11f}$$

$$\Delta s = s_2 - s_1 = c_p \ln \frac{T_2}{T_1} - R \ln \frac{p_2}{p_1} \tag{13.11g}$$

Equations 13.11 can be used to analyze frictional adiabatic flow in a channel of constant area. For example, if we know conditions at section ① (i.e., p_1, ρ_1, T_1, s_1, h_1, and V_1), we can use these equations to find conditions at some new section ② after the fluid has experienced a total friction force R_x. It is the effect of friction that causes fluid properties to change along the duct. For a known friction force we have six equations (not including the constraint of Eq. 13.11d) and six unknowns (p_2, ρ_2, T_2, s_2, h_2, and V_2). In practice this procedure is unwieldy—as for isentropic flow we have a set of *nonlinear coupled algebraic* equations to solve, and as for isentropic flow we will eventually develop alternative approaches. For now, let's see what Eqs. 13.11 indicate will happen to the flow.

Adiabatic Flow: The Fanno Line

If we were to attempt the calculations described above, as the flow progresses down the duct (i.e., for increasing values of R_x), we would develop a relationship between T and s shown qualitatively in Fig. 13.10 for two possibilities: a flow that was initially subsonic (starting at some point ①), and flow that was initially supersonic (starting at some point ①'). The locus of all possible downstream states is referred to as the *Fanno line*. Detailed calculations show some interesting features of Fanno-line flow. At the point of maximum entropy, the Mach number is unity. On the upper branch of the curve, the Mach number is always less than unity, and it increases monotonically as we proceed to the right along the curve. At every point on the lower portion of the curve, the Mach number is greater than unity; the Mach number decreases monotonically as we move to the right along the curve.

For any initial state on a Fanno line, each point on the Fanno line represents a mathematically possible downstream state. In Fig. 13.10 we generated the curves by repeatedly solving Eqs. 13.11 for increasing values of the friction force, R_x; the total friction force increases as we progress down the duct because we are including more and more surface area. Note the arrows in Fig. 13.10, indicating that, as required by Eq. 13.11d, the entropy must increase for this flow. In fact it is because we *do* have friction (an irreversibility) present in an adiabatic flow that this *must* happen. Referring again to Fig. 13.10, we see that for an initially subsonic flow (state ①), the effect of friction is to increase the Mach number toward unity. For a flow that is initially supersonic (state ①'), the effect of friction is to decrease the Mach number toward unity.

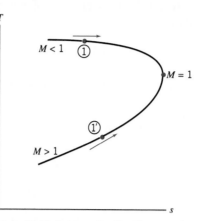

Fig. 13.10 Schematic Ts diagram for frictional adiabatic (Fanno-line) flow in a constant-area duct.

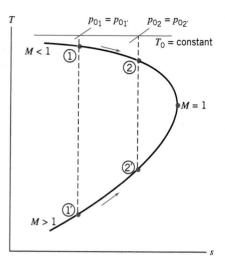

Fig. 13.11 Schematic of Fanno-line flow on Ts plane, showing reduction in local isentropic stagnation pressure caused by friction.

In developing the simplified form of the first law for Fanno-line flow, Eq. 13.11c, we found that stagnation enthalpy remains constant. Consequently, when the fluid is an ideal gas with constant specific heats, stagnation temperature must also remain constant. What happens to stagnation pressure? Friction causes the local isentropic stagnation pressure to decrease for all Fanno-line flows, as shown in Fig. 13.11. Since entropy must increase in the direction of flow, the flow process must proceed to the right on the Ts diagram. In Fig. 13.11, a path from state ① to state ② is shown on the subsonic portion of the curve. The corresponding local isentropic stagnation pressures, p_{0_1} and p_{0_2}, clearly show that $p_{0_2} < p_{0_1}$. An identical result is obtained for flow on the supersonic branch of the curve from state ①′ to state ②′. Again $p_{0_{2'}} < p_{0_{1'}}$. Thus p_0 decreases for any Fanno-line flow.

The effects of friction on flow properties in Fanno-line flow are summarized in Table 13.1.

In deducing the effect of friction on flow properties for Fanno-line flow, we used the shape of the Fanno line on the Ts diagram and the basic governing equations (Eqs. 13.11). You should follow through the logic indicated in the right column of the table. Note that the effect of friction is to accelerate a subsonic flow! This seems a real puzzle—a violation of Newton's second law—until we realize that the pressure

TABLE 13.1 Summary of Effects of Friction on Properties in Fanno-Line Flow

Property	Subsonic $M < 1$	Supersonic $M > 1$	Obtained from:
Stagnation temperature	T_0 = Constant	T_0 = Constant	Energy equation
Entropy	$s \Uparrow$	$s \Uparrow$	$T\,ds$ equation
Stagnation pressure	$p_0 \Downarrow$	$p_0 \Downarrow$	T_0 = constant; $s \Uparrow$
Temperature	$T \Downarrow$	$T \Uparrow$	Shape of Fanno line
Velocity	$V \Uparrow$	$V \Downarrow$	Energy equation, and trend of T
Mach number	$M \Uparrow$	$M \Downarrow$	Trends of V, T, and definition of M
Density	$\rho \Downarrow$	$\rho \Uparrow$	Continuity equation, and effect on V
Pressure	$p \Downarrow$	$p \Uparrow$	Equation of state, and effects on ρ, T

is dropping quite rapidly, so the pressure gradient more than cancels the drag due to friction. We can also note that the density is decreasing in this flow (largely because of the pressure drop) mandating (from continuity) that the velocity must be increasing. All properties simultaneously affect one another (as expressed in the coupled set of equations, Eqs. 13.11), so it is not possible to conclude that the change in any one property is solely responsible for changes in any of the others.

We have noted that entropy must increase in the direction of flow: It is the effect of friction that causes the change in flow properties along the Fanno-line curve. From Fig. 13.11, we see that there is a maximum entropy point corresponding to $M = 1$ for each Fanno line. The maximum entropy point is reached by increasing the amount of friction (through addition of duct length), just enough to produce a Mach number of unity (choked flow) at the exit. If we insist on adding duct beyond this critical duct length, at which the flow is choked, one of two things happens: if the inlet flow is subsonic, the additional length forces the sonic condition to move down to the new exit, and the flow rate in the duct (and Mach number at each location) decreases; if the inlet flow is supersonic, the additional length causes a normal shock to appear somewhere in the duct, and the shock moves upstream as more duct is added (for more details see Section 13-6).

To compute the critical duct length, we must analyze the flow in detail, accounting for friction. This analysis requires that we begin with a differential control volume, develop expressions in terms of Mach number, and integrate along the duct to the section where $M = 1$. This is our next task, and it will involve quite a bit of algebraic manipulation, so first we will demonstrate use of some of Eqs. 13.11 in Example 13.6.

EXAMPLE 13.6 Frictional Adiabatic Flow in a Constant-Area Channel

Air flow is induced in an insulated tube of 7.16 mm diameter by a vacuum pump. The air is drawn from a room, where $p_0 = 101$ kPa (abs) and $T_0 = 23°C$, through a smoothly contoured converging nozzle. At section ①, where the nozzle joins the constant-area tube, the static pressure is 98.5 kPa (abs). At section ②, located some distance downstream in the constant-area tube, the air temperature is 14°C. Determine the mass flow rate, the local isentropic stagnation pressure at section ②, and the friction force on the duct wall between sections ① and ②.

GIVEN: Air flow in insulated tube

FIND: (a) $\dot{m}$.
(b) Stagnation pressure at section ②.
(c) Force on duct wall.

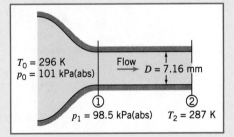

SOLUTION:
The mass flow rate can be obtained from properties at section ①. For isentropic flow through the converging nozzle, local isentropic stagnation properties remain constant. Thus,

$$\frac{p_{0_1}}{p_1} = \left(1 + \frac{k-1}{2} M_1^2\right)^{k/(k-1)}$$

and

$$M_1 = \left\{\frac{2}{k-1}\left[\left(\frac{p_{0_1}}{p_1}\right)^{(k-1)/k} - 1\right]\right\}^{1/2} = \left\{\frac{2}{0.4}\left[\left(\frac{1.01 \times 10^5}{9.85 \times 10^4}\right)^{0.286} - 1\right]\right\}^{1/2} = 0.190$$

$$T_1 = \frac{T_{0_1}}{1 + \frac{k-1}{2} M_1^2} = \frac{(273 + 23)\ \text{K}}{1 + 0.2(0.190)^2} = 294\ \text{K}$$

For an ideal gas,

$$\rho_1 = \frac{p_1}{RT_1} = 9.85 \times 10^4 \frac{N}{m^2} \times \frac{kg \cdot k}{287\,N \cdot m} \times \frac{1}{294\,K} = 1.17\,kg/m^3$$

$$V_1 = M_1 c_1 = M_1 \sqrt{kRT_1} = (0.190)\left[1.4 \times 287 \frac{N \cdot m}{kg \cdot K} \times 294\,K \times \frac{kg \cdot m}{N \cdot s^2}\right]^{1/2}$$

$$V_1 = 65.3\,m/s$$

The area, A_1, is

$$A_1 = A = \frac{\pi D^2}{4} = \frac{\pi}{4}(7.16 \times 10^{-3})^2\,m^2 = 4.03 \times 10^{-5}\,m^2$$

From continuity,

$$\dot{m} = \rho_1 V_1 A_1 = 1.17 \frac{kg}{m^3} \times 65.3 \frac{m}{s} \times 4.03 \times 10^{-5}\,m^2$$

$$\dot{m} = 3.08 \times 10^{-3}\,kg/s \quad\longleftarrow\qquad\qquad \dot{m}$$

Flow is adiabatic, so T_0 is constant, and

$$T_{0_2} = T_{0_1} = 296\,K \qquad\qquad\qquad\qquad T_{0_2}$$

Then

$$\frac{T_{0_2}}{T_2} = 1 + \frac{k-1}{2}M_2^2$$

Solving for M_2 gives

$$M_2 = \left[\frac{2}{k-1}\left(\frac{T_{0_2}}{T_2} - 1\right)\right]^{1/2} = \left[\frac{2}{0.4}\left(\frac{296}{287} - 1\right)\right]^{1/2} = 0.396 \quad\longleftarrow\qquad M_2$$

$$V_2 = M_2 c_2 = M_2 \sqrt{kRT_2} = (0.396)\left[1.4 \times 287 \frac{N \cdot m}{kg \cdot K} \times 287\,K \times \frac{kg \cdot m}{N \cdot s^2}\right]^{1/2}$$

$$V_2 = 134\,m/s \quad\longleftarrow\qquad\qquad\qquad\qquad V_2$$

From continuity, Eq. 13.11a, $\rho_1 V_1 = \rho_2 V_2$, so

$$\rho_2 = \rho_1 \frac{V_1}{V_2} = 1.17 \frac{kg}{m^3} \times \frac{65.3}{134} = 0.570\,kg/m^3 \quad\longleftarrow\qquad \rho_2$$

and

$$p_2 = \rho_2 RT_2 = 0.570 \frac{kg}{m^3} \times 287 \frac{N \cdot m}{kg \cdot K} \times 287\,K = 47.0\,kPa(abs) \quad\longleftarrow\qquad p_2$$

The local isentropic stagnation pressure is

$$p_{0_2} = p_2\left(1 + \frac{k-1}{2}M_2^2\right)^{k/(k-1)} = 4.70 \times 10^4\,Pa[1 + 0.2(0.396)^2]^{3.5}$$

$$p_{0_2} = 52.4\,kPa\,(abs) \quad\longleftarrow\qquad\qquad\qquad p_{0_2}$$

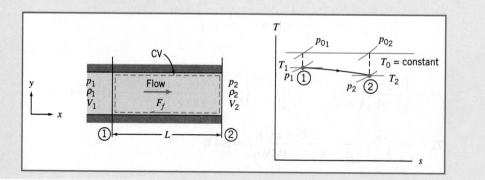

The friction force may be obtained using the momentum equation (Eq.13.11b),

$$R_x + p_1 A - p_2 A = \dot{m} V_2 - \dot{m} V_2 \tag{13.11b}$$

which we apply to the control volume shown above (except we replace R_x from Fig. 13.9 with $-F_f$ because we know the friction force F_f on the fluid acts in the negative x direction).

$$-F_f = (p_2 - p_1)A + \dot{m}(V_2 - V_1)$$

$$-F_f = (4.70 - 9.85)10^4 \, \frac{\text{N}}{\text{m}^2} \times 4.03 \times 10^{-5} \, \text{m}^2 + 3.08 \times 10^{-3} \, \frac{\text{kg}}{\text{s}} \times (134 - 65.3) \, \frac{\text{m}}{\text{s}} \times \frac{\text{N} \cdot \text{s}^2}{\text{kg} \cdot \text{m}}$$

or

$$F_f = 1.86 \, \text{N} \quad \text{(to the left, as shown)}$$

This is the force exerted on the control volume by the duct wall. The force of the *fluid* on the *duct* is

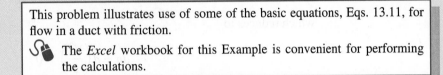

$$K_x = -F_f = 1.86 \, \text{N} \qquad \text{(to the right)} \qquad \qquad K_x$$

> This problem illustrates use of some of the basic equations, Eqs. 13.11, for flow in a duct with friction.
>
> The *Excel* workbook for this Example is convenient for performing the calculations.

Fanno-Line Flow Functions for One-Dimensional Flow of an Ideal Gas

The primary independent variable in Fanno-line flow is the friction force, F_f. Knowledge of the total friction force between any two points in a Fanno-line flow enables us to predict downstream conditions from known upstream conditions. The total friction force is the integral of the wall shear stress over the duct surface area. Since wall shear stress varies along the duct, we must develop a differential equation and then integrate to find property variations. To set up the differential equation, we use the differential control volume shown in Fig. 13.12.

Comparing Fig. 13.12 to Fig. 13.9 we see that we can use the basic equations, Eqs. 13.11, for flow in a duct with friction, if we replace T_1, p_1, ρ_1, V_1, with T, p, ρ, V, and T_2, p_2, ρ_2, V_2, with $T + dT$, $p + dp$, $\rho + d\rho$, $V + dV$, and also R_x with $-dF_f$.

The continuity equation (Eq. 13.11a) becomes

$$\rho V = (\rho + d\rho)(V + dV) = \frac{\dot{m}}{A}$$

so

$$\rho V = \rho V + \rho \, dV + d\rho \, V + d\rho \, dV$$

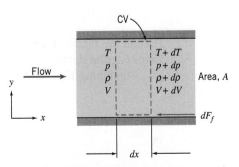

Fig. 13.12 Differential control volume used for analysis of Fanno-line flow.

which reduces to

$$\rho \, dV + V \, d\rho = 0 \qquad (13.12a)$$

since products of differentials are negligible. The momentum equation (Eq. 13.11b) becomes

$$-dF_f + pA - (p + dp)A = \dot{m}(V + dV) - \dot{m}V$$

which reduces to

$$-\frac{dF_f}{A} - dp = \rho V \, dV \qquad (13.12b)$$

after using continuity ($\dot{m} = \rho A V$). The first law of thermodynamics (Eq. 13.11c) becomes

$$h + \frac{V^2}{2} = (h + dh) + \frac{(V + dV)^2}{2}$$

which reduces to

$$dh + d\left(\frac{V^2}{2}\right) = 0 \qquad (13.12c)$$

since products of differentials are negligible.

Equations 13.12 are differential equations that we can integrate to develop useful relations, but before doing so we need to see how we can relate the friction force F_f to other flow properties. First, we note that

$$dF_f = \tau_w \, dA_w = \tau_w P \, dx \qquad (13.13)$$

where P is the wetted perimeter of the duct. To obtain an expression for τ_w in terms of flow variables at each cross section, we assume changes in flow variables with x are gradual and use correlations developed in Chapter 8 for fully developed, incompressible duct flow. For incompressible flow, the local wall shear stress can be written in terms of flow properties and friction factor. From Eqs. 8.16, 8.32, and 8.34 we have, for incompressible flow,

$$\tau_w = -\frac{R}{2}\frac{dp}{dx} = \frac{\rho R}{2}\frac{dh_l}{dx} = \frac{f\rho V^2}{8} \qquad (13.14)$$

where f is the friction factor for pipe flow, given by Eq. 8.36 for laminar flow and Eq. 8.37 for turbulent flow, plotted in Fig. 8.13. (We assume that this correlation of experimental data also applies to compressible flow. This assumption, when checked against experimental data, shows surprisingly good agreement for subsonic flows; data for supersonic flow are sparse.)

Ducts of other than circular shape can be included in our analysis by introducing the hydraulic diameter

$$D_h = \frac{4A}{P} \qquad (8.50)$$

(Recall the factor of 4 was included in Eq. 8.50 so that D_h would reduce to diameter D for circular ducts.)

Combining Eqs. 8.50, 13.13, and 13.14, we obtain

$$dF_f = \tau_w P \, dx = f\frac{\rho V^2}{8}\frac{4A}{D_h} \, dx$$

or

$$dF_f = \frac{fA}{D_h}\frac{\rho V^2}{2} \, dx \qquad (13.15)$$

Substituting this result into the momentum equation (Eq. 13.12b), we obtain

$$-\frac{f}{D_h}\frac{\rho V^2}{2}dx - dp = \rho V\, dV$$

or, after dividing by p,

$$\frac{dp}{p} = -\frac{f}{D_h}\frac{\rho V^2}{2p}dx - \frac{\rho V\, dV}{p}$$

Noting that $p/\rho = RT = c^2/k$, and $V\, dV = d(V^2/2)$, we obtain

$$\frac{dp}{p} = -\frac{f}{D_h}\frac{kM^2}{2}dx - \frac{k}{c^2}d\left(\frac{V^2}{2}\right)$$

and finally,

$$\frac{dp}{p} = -\frac{f}{D_h}\frac{kM^2}{2}dx - \frac{kM^2}{2}\frac{d(V^2)}{V^2} \tag{13.16}$$

To relate M and x, we must eliminate dp/p and $d(V^2)/V^2$ from Eq. 13.16. From the definition of Mach number, $M = V/c$, so $V^2 = M^2c^2 = M^2 kRT$, and after differentiating this equation and dividing by the original equation,

$$\frac{d(V^2)}{V^2} = \frac{dT}{T} + \frac{d(M^2)}{M^2} \tag{13.17a}$$

From the continuity equation, Eq. 13.12a, $d\rho/\rho = -dV/V$ and so

$$\frac{d\rho}{\rho} = -\frac{1}{2}\frac{d(V^2)}{V^2}$$

From the ideal gas equation of state, $p = \rho RT$,

$$\frac{dp}{p} = \frac{d\rho}{\rho} + \frac{dT}{T}$$

Combining these three equations, we obtain

$$\frac{dp}{p} = \frac{1}{2}\frac{dT}{T} - \frac{1}{2}\frac{d(M^2)}{M^2} \tag{13.17b}$$

Substituting Eqs. 13.17 into Eq. 13.16 gives

$$\frac{1}{2}\frac{dT}{T} - \frac{1}{2}\frac{d(M^2)}{M^2} = -\frac{f}{D_h}\frac{kM^2}{2}dx - \frac{kM^2}{2}\frac{dT}{T} - \frac{kM^2}{2}\frac{d(M^2)}{M^2}$$

This equation can be simplified to

$$\left(\frac{1 + kM^2}{2}\right)\frac{dT}{T} = -\frac{f}{D_h}\frac{kM^2}{2}dx + \left(\frac{1 - kM^2}{2}\right)\frac{d(M^2)}{M^2} \tag{13.18}$$

We have been successful in reducing the number of variables somewhat. However, to relate M and x, we must obtain an expression for dT/T in terms of M. Such an expression can be obtained most readily from the stagnation temperature equation

$$\frac{T_0}{T} = 1 + \frac{k-1}{2}M^2 \tag{12.21b}$$

Since stagnation temperature is constant for Fanno-line flow,

$$T\left(1 + \frac{k-1}{2}M^2\right) = \text{constant}$$

and after differentiating this equation and dividing by the original equation,

$$\frac{dT}{T} + \frac{M^2 \frac{(k-1)}{2}}{\left(1 + \frac{k-1}{2}M^2\right)} \frac{d(M^2)}{M^2} = 0$$

Substituting for dT/T into Eq. 13.18 yields

$$\frac{M^2 \frac{(k-1)}{2}\left(\frac{1+kM^2}{2}\right)}{\left(1 + \frac{k-1}{2}M^2\right)} \frac{d(M^2)}{M^2} = \frac{f}{D_h}\frac{kM^2}{2}dx - \left(\frac{1-kM^2}{2}\right)\frac{d(M^2)}{M^2}$$

Combining terms, we obtain

$$\frac{(1-M^2)}{\left(1 + \frac{k-1}{2}M^2\right)} \frac{d(M^2)}{kM^4} = \frac{f}{D_h}dx \qquad (13.19)$$

We have (finally!) obtained a differential equation that relates changes in M with x. Now we must integrate the equation to find M as a function of x.

Integrating Eq. 13.19 between states ① and ② would produce a complicated function of both M_1 and M_2. The function would have to be evaluated numerically for each new combination of M_1 and M_2 encountered in a problem. Calculations can be simplified considerably using critical conditions (where, by definition, $M = 1$). All Fanno-line flows tend toward $M = 1$, so integration is between a section where the Mach number is M and the section where sonic conditions occur (the critical conditions). Mach number will reach unity when the maximum possible length of duct is used, as shown schematically in Fig. 13.13.

The task is to perform the integration

$$\int_M^1 \frac{(1-M^2)}{kM^4\left(1 + \frac{k-1}{2}M^2\right)}d(M^2) = \int_0^{L_{\max}} \frac{f}{D_h}dx \qquad (13.20)$$

The left side may be integrated by parts. On the right side, the friction factor, f, may vary with x, since Reynolds number will vary along the duct. Note, however, that since ρV is constant along the duct (from continuity), the variation in Reynolds number is caused solely by variations in fluid absolute viscosity.

For a mean friction factor, $\bar{f}$, defined over the duct length as

$$\bar{f} = \frac{1}{L_{\max}} \int_0^{L_{\max}} f\,dx$$

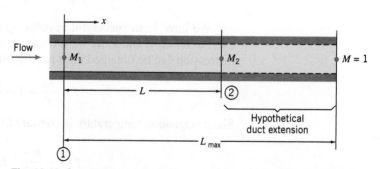

Fig. 13.13 Coordinates and notation used for analysis of Fanno-line flow.

integration of Eq. 13.20 leads to

$$\frac{1 - M^2}{kM^2} + \frac{k+1}{2k} \ln\left[\frac{(k+1)M^2}{2\left(1 + \dfrac{k-1}{2}M^2\right)}\right] = \frac{\bar{f}L_{max}}{D_h} \qquad (13.21a)$$

Equation 13.21a gives the maximum $\bar{f}L/D_h$ corresponding to any initial Mach number.

Since $\bar{f}L_{max}/D_h$ is a function of M, the duct length, L, required for the Mach number to change from M_1 to M_2 (as illustrated in Fig. 13.13) may be found from

$$\frac{\bar{f}L}{D_h} = \left(\frac{\bar{f}L_{max}}{D_h}\right)_{M_1} - \left(\frac{\bar{f}L_{max}}{D_h}\right)_{M_2}$$

Critical conditions are appropriate reference conditions to use in developing property ratio flow functions in terms of local Mach number. Thus, for example, since T_0 is constant, we can write

$$\frac{T}{T^*} = \frac{T/T_0}{T^*/T_0} = \frac{\left(\dfrac{k+1}{2}\right)}{\left(1 + \dfrac{k-1}{2}M^2\right)} \qquad (13.21b)$$

Similarly,

$$\frac{V}{V^*} = \frac{M\sqrt{kRT}}{\sqrt{kRT^*}} = M\sqrt{\frac{T}{T^*}} = \left[\frac{\left(\dfrac{k+1}{2}\right)M^2}{1 + \dfrac{k-1}{2}M^2}\right]^{1/2}$$

From continuity, $V/V^* = \rho^*/\rho$, so

$$\frac{V}{V^*} = \frac{\rho^*}{\rho} = \left[\frac{\left(\dfrac{k+1}{2}\right)M^2}{1 + \dfrac{k-1}{2}M^2}\right]^{1/2} \qquad (13.21c)$$

From the ideal gas equation of state,

$$\frac{p}{p^*} = \frac{\rho}{\rho^*}\frac{T}{T^*} = \frac{1}{M}\left[\frac{\left(\dfrac{k+1}{2}\right)}{1 + \dfrac{k-1}{2}M^2}\right]^{1/2} \qquad (13.21d)$$

The ratio of local stagnation pressure to the reference stagnation pressure is given by

$$\frac{p_0}{p_0^*} = \frac{p_0}{p}\frac{p}{p^*}\frac{p^*}{p_0^*}$$

$$\frac{p_0}{p_0^*} = \left(1 + \frac{k-1}{2}M^2\right)^{k/(k-1)}\frac{1}{M}\left[\frac{\left(\dfrac{k+1}{2}\right)}{1 + \dfrac{k-1}{2}M^2}\right]^{1/2}\frac{1}{\left(\dfrac{k+1}{2}\right)^{k/(k-1)}}$$

or

$$\frac{p_0}{p_0^*} = \frac{1}{M}\left[\left(\frac{2}{k+1}\right)\left(1 + \frac{k-1}{2}M^2\right)\right]^{(k+1)/2(k-1)} \tag{13.21e}$$

Equations 13.21 form a complete set for analyzing flow of an ideal gas in a duct with friction, which we usually use instead of (or in addition to) the basic equations, Eqs. 13.11. For convenience we list them together:

$$\frac{\bar{f}L_{max}}{D_h} = \frac{1-M^2}{kM^2} + \frac{k+1}{2k}\ln\left[\frac{(k+1)M^2}{2\left(1 + \frac{k-1}{2}M^2\right)}\right] \tag{13.21a}$$

$$\frac{T}{T^*} = \frac{\left(\frac{k+1}{2}\right)}{\left(1 + \frac{k-1}{2}M^2\right)} \tag{13.21b}$$

$$\frac{V}{V^*} = \frac{\rho^*}{\rho} = \left[\frac{\left(\frac{k+1}{2}\right)M^2}{1 + \frac{k-1}{2}M^2}\right]^{1/2} \tag{13.21c}$$

$$\frac{p}{p^*} = \frac{1}{M}\left[\frac{\left(\frac{k+1}{2}\right)}{1 + \frac{k-1}{2}M^2}\right]^{1/2} \tag{13.21d}$$

$$\frac{p_0}{p_0^*} = \frac{1}{M}\left[\left(\frac{2}{k+1}\right)\left(1 + \frac{k-1}{2}M^2\right)\right]^{(k+1)/2(k-1)} \tag{13.21e}$$

Equations 13.21, the Fanno-line relations, provide property relations in terms of the local Mach number and critical conditions. They are obviously quite algebraically complicated, but unlike Eqs. 13.11 are not coupled. It is a good idea to program them into your calculator. They are also fairly easy to define in spreadsheets such as *Excel*. The reader is urged to download the *Excel* add-ins for these equations from the Web site; with the add-ins, functions are available for computing the friction factor, temperature, velocity, pressure, and stagnation pressure ratios from M, and M from these ratios. It is important to remember that, as demonstrated in Fig. 12.4, the properties at a state, in any flow process, may be related to that state's isentropic stagnation properties through use of Eqs. 12.21. Appendix E-2 lists flow functions for property ratios p_0/p_0^*, T/T^*, p/p^*, ρ/ρ^*, (V^*/V), and $\bar{f}L_{max}/D_h$ in terms of M for Fanno-line flow of an ideal gas. A table of values, as well as a plot of these property ratios, is presented for air ($k = 1.4$) for a limited range of Mach numbers. The associated *Excel* workbook, *Fanno-Line Relations*, can be used to print a larger table of values for air and other ideal gases.

Example 13.7 Frictional Adiabatic Flow in a Constant-Area Channel: Solution Using Fanno-Line Flow Functions

Air flow is induced in a smooth insulated tube of 7.16 mm diameter by a vacuum pump. Air is drawn from a room, where $p_0 = 760$ mm Hg (abs) and $T_0 = 23°C$, through a smoothly contoured converging nozzle. At section ①, where the nozzle joins the constant-area tube, the static pressure is -18.9 mm Hg (gage). At section ②, located some distance downstream in the constant-area tube, the static pressure is -412 mm Hg (gage). The duct walls are smooth; assume the average friction factor, f, is the value at section ①. Determine the length of duct required for choking from section ①, the Mach number at section ②, and the duct length, L_{12}, between sections ① and ②. Sketch the process on a Ts diagram.

Given:

Air flow (with friction) in an insulated constant-area tube.

Gage pressures: $p_1 = -18.9$ mm Hg, and $p_2 = -412$ mm Hg.
$M_3 = 1.0$

FIND: (a) L_{13}. (b) M_2. (c) L_{12}. (d) Sketch the Ts diagram.

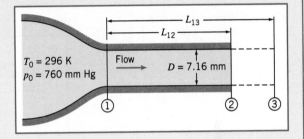

SOLUTION:

Flow in the constant-area tube is frictional and adiabatic, a Fanno-line flow. To find the friction factor, we need to know the flow conditions at section ①. If we assume flow in the nozzle is isentropic, local properties at the nozzle exit may be computed using isentropic relations. Thus

$$\frac{p_{0_1}}{p_1} = \left(1 + \frac{k-1}{2}M_1^2\right)^{k/(k-1)}$$

Solving for M_1, we obtain

$$M_1 = \left\{\frac{2}{k-1}\left[\left(\frac{p_{0_1}}{p_1}\right)^{(k-1)/k} - 1\right]\right\}^{1/2} = \left\{\frac{2}{0.4}\left[\left(\frac{760}{760-18.9}\right)^{0.286} - 1\right]\right\}^{1/2} = 0.190$$

$$T_1 = \frac{T_{0_1}}{1 + \frac{k-1}{2}M_1^2} = \frac{296 \text{ K}}{1 + 0.2(0.190)^2} = 294 \text{ K}$$

$$V_1 = M_1 c_1 = M_1\sqrt{kRT_1} = 0.190\left[1.4 \times 287 \frac{\text{N} \cdot \text{m}}{\text{kg} \cdot \text{K}} \times 294 \times \frac{\text{kg} \cdot \text{m}}{\text{N} \cdot \text{s}^2}\right]^{1/2}$$

$$V_1 = 65.3 \text{ m/s}$$

Using the density of mercury at room temperature (23°C),

$$p_1 = g\rho_{Hg}h_1 = g\,SG\,\rho_{H_2O}h_1$$

$$= 9.81 \frac{\text{m}}{\text{s}^2} \times 13.5 \times 1000 \frac{\text{kg}}{\text{m}^3} \times (760-18.9)10^{-3}\text{ m} \times \frac{\text{N} \cdot \text{s}^2}{\text{kg} \cdot \text{m}}$$

$$p_1 = 98.1 \text{ kPa(abs)}$$

$$\rho_1 = \frac{p_1}{RT_1} = 9.81 \times 10^4 \frac{\text{N}}{\text{m}^2} \times \frac{\text{kg} \cdot \text{K}}{287 \text{ N} \cdot \text{m}} \times \frac{1}{294 \text{ K}} = 1.16 \text{ kg/m}^3$$

At $T = 294$ K (21°C), $\mu = 1.82 \times 10^{-5}$ kg/(m · s) from Table A.10, Appendix A. Thus

$$Re_1 = \frac{\rho_1 V_1 D_1}{\mu_1} = 1.16 \frac{\text{kg}}{\text{m}^3} \times 65.3 \frac{\text{m}}{\text{s}} \times 0.00716 \text{ m} \times \frac{\text{m} \cdot \text{s}}{1.82 \times 10^{-5}\text{ kg}} = 2.98 \times 10^4$$

From Eq. 8.37 (turbulent flow), for smooth pipe, $f = 0.0235$.

From Appendix E-2 at $M_1 = 0.190, p/p^* = 5.745$ (Eq. 13.21d), and $\bar{f}L_{max}/D_h = 16.38$ (Eq. 13.21a). Thus, assuming $\bar{f} = f_1$,

$$L_{13} = (L_{max})_1 = \left(\frac{\bar{f}L_{max}}{D_h}\right)_1 \frac{D_h}{f_1} = 16.38 \times \frac{0.00716\,\text{m}}{0.0235} = 4.99\,\text{m} \quad \longleftarrow \qquad L_{13}$$

Since p^* is constant for all states on the same Fanno line, conditions at section ② can be determined from the pressure ratio, $(p/p^*)_2$. Thus

$$\left(\frac{p}{p^*}\right)_2 = \frac{p_2}{p^*} = \frac{p_2}{p_1}\frac{p_1}{p^*} = \frac{p_2}{p_1}\left(\frac{p}{p^*}\right)_1 = \left(\frac{760 - 412}{760 - 18.9}\right) 5.745 = 2.698$$

where we used Eq. 13.21d to obtain the value of p/p^* at section ①. For $p/p^* = 2.698$ at section ②, Eq. 13.21d yields $M_2 = 0.400$ (after obtaining an initial guess value from the plot in Appendix E-2, and iterating).

$$M_2 = 0.400 \quad \longleftarrow \qquad M_2$$

The Ts diagram for this flow is

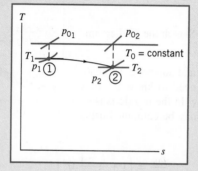

At $M_2 = 0.400$, $\bar{f}L_{max}/D_h = 2.309$ (Eq. 13.21a, Appendix E-2). Thus

$$L_{23} = (L_{max})_2 = \left(\frac{\bar{f}L_{max}}{D_h}\right)_2 \frac{D_h}{f_1} = 2.309 \times \frac{0.00716\,\text{m}}{0.0235} = 0.704\,\text{m}$$

Finally,

$$L_{12} = L_{13} - L_{23} = (4.99 - 0.704)\,\text{m} = 4.29\,\text{m} \quad \longleftarrow \qquad L_{12}$$

> This problem illustrates use of the Fanno-line equations, Eqs. 13.21.
> ✓ These equations give the same results as the basic equations, Eqs. 13.11, as can be seen by comparing, for example, the value of M_2 obtained in this Example and in Example 13.6.
> ✓ The computations can be quite laborious without using preprogrammed Fanno-line relations (available, for example, in the *Excel* add-ins on the Web site)!
> The *Excel* workbook for this Example is convenient for performing the calculations, either using the Fanno-line relations or the basic equations.

Isothermal Flow (on the Web)

13-4 FRICTIONLESS FLOW IN A CONSTANT-AREA DUCT WITH HEAT EXCHANGE

To explore the effects of heat exchange on a compressible flow, we apply the basic equations to steady, one-dimensional, frictionless flow of an ideal gas with constant specific heats through the finite control volume shown in Fig. 13.14.

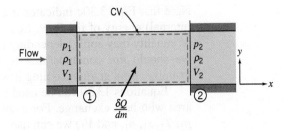

Fig. 13.14 Control volume used for integral analysis of frictionless flow with heat exchange.

As in Section 13-2 (effects of area variation only) and Section 13-3 (effects of friction only), our starting point in analyzing frictionless flows with heat exchange is the set of basic equations (Eqs. 13.1), describing one-dimensional motion that is affected by several phenomena: area change, friction, heat transfer, and normal shocks. These are

$$\rho_1 V_1 A_1 = \rho_2 V_2 A_2 = \rho V A = \dot{m} = \text{constant} \tag{13.1a}$$

$$R_x + p_1 A_1 - p_2 A_2 = \dot{m} V_2 - \dot{m} V_1 \tag{13.1b}$$

$$\frac{\delta Q}{dm} + h_1 + \frac{V_1^2}{2} = h_2 + \frac{V_2^2}{2} \tag{13.1c}$$

$$\dot{m}(s_2 - s_1) \geq \int_{CS} \frac{1}{T}\left(\frac{\dot{Q}}{A}\right) dA \tag{13.1d}$$

$$p = \rho R T \tag{13.1e}$$

$$\Delta h = h_2 - h_1 = c_p \Delta T = c_p (T_2 - T_1) \tag{13.1f}$$

$$\Delta s = s_2 - s_1 = c_p \ln \frac{T_2}{T_1} - R \ln \frac{p_2}{p_1} \tag{13.1g}$$

We recall that Eq. 13.1a is *continuity*, Eq. 13.1b is a *momentum equation*, Eq. 13.1c is an *energy equation*, Eq. 13.1d is the *second law of thermodynamics*, and Eqs. 13.1e, 13.1f, and 13.1g are useful *property relations* for an ideal gas with constant specific heats.

Basic Equations for Flow with Heat Exchange

We simplify Eqs. 13.1 using the facts that $A_1 = A_2 = A$ and that $R_x = 0$. In addition we have the relation $h_0 = h + V^2/2$. Equations 13.1 become for this flow

$$\rho_1 V_1 = \rho_2 V_2 = \rho V A \equiv G = \frac{\dot{m}}{A} = \text{constant} \tag{13.30a}$$

$$p_1 A - p_2 A = \dot{m} V_2 - \dot{m} V_1 \tag{13.30b}$$

$$\frac{\delta Q}{dm} = \left(h_2 + \frac{V_2^2}{2}\right) - \left(h_1 + \frac{V_1^2}{2}\right) = h_{0_2} - h_{0_1} \tag{13.30c}$$

$$\dot{m}(s_2 - s_1) \geq \int_{CS} \frac{1}{T}\left(\frac{\dot{Q}}{A}\right) dA \tag{13.30d}$$

$$p = \rho R T \tag{13.30e}$$

$$\Delta h = h_2 - h_1 = c_p \Delta T = c_p (T_2 - T_1) \tag{13.30f}$$

$$\Delta s = s_2 - s_1 = c_p \ln \frac{T_2}{T_1} - R \ln \frac{p_2}{p_1} \tag{13.30g}$$

Note that Eq. 13.30c indicates that the heat exchange changes the total (kinetic plus internal) energy of the flow. Equation 13.30d is not very useful here. The inequality or equality may apply, depending on the nature of the heat exchange, but in any event we should *not* conclude that in this flow the entropy necessarily increases. For example, for a gradual cooling it will decrease!

Equations 13.30 can be used to analyze frictionless flow in a channel of constant area with heat exchange. For example, if we know conditions at section ① (i.e., p_1, ρ_1, T_1, s_1, h_1, and V_1) we can use these equations to find conditions at some new section ② after the fluid has experienced a total heat exchange $\delta Q/dm$. For a given heat exchange, we have six equations (not including the constraint of Eq. 13.30d) and six unknowns (p_2, ρ_2, T_2, s_2, h_2, and V_2). It is the effect of heat exchange that causes fluid properties to change along the duct. In practice, as we have seen for other flows, this procedure is unwieldy—we again have a set of *nonlinear coupled algebraic* equations to solve. We will use Eqs. 13.30 in Example 13.8. We will also develop some Mach number-based relations to supplement or replace the basic equations, and show how to use these in Example 13.9.

The Rayleigh Line

If we use Eqs. 13.30 to compute property values as a given flow proceeds with a pre-scribed heat exchange rate, we obtain a curve shown qualitatively in the *Ts* plane in Fig. 13.15. The locus of all possible downstream states is called the *Rayleigh line*. The calculations show some interesting features of Rayleigh-line flow. At the point of maximum temperature (point *a* of Fig. 13.15), the Mach number for an ideal gas is $1/\sqrt{k}$. At the point of maximum entropy (point *b* of Fig. 13.15), $M = 1$. On the upper branch of the curve, Mach number is always less than unity, and it increases monotonically as we proceed to the right along the curve. At every point on the lower portion of the curve, Mach number is greater than unity, and it decreases monotonically as we move to the right along the curve. Regardless of the initial Mach number, with heat addition the flow state proceeds to the right, and with heat rejection the flow state proceeds to the left along the Rayleigh line.

For any initial state in a Rayleigh-line flow, any other point on the Rayleigh line represents a mathematically possible downstream state. Although the Rayleigh line represents all mathematically possible states, are they all physically attainable downstream

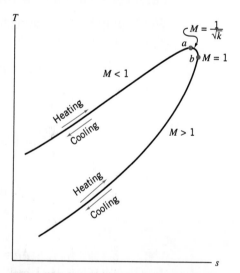

Fig. 13.15 Schematic *Ts* diagram for frictionless flow in a constant-area duct with heat exchange (Rayleigh-line flow).

states? A moment's reflection will indicate that they are. Since we are considering a flow with heat exchange, the second law (Eq. 13.30d) does not impose any restrictions on the sign of the entropy change.

The effects of heat exchange on properties in steady, frictionless, compressible flow of an ideal gas are summarized in Table 13.2; the basis of each indicated trend is discussed in the next few paragraphs.

The direction of entropy change is always determined by the heat exchange; entropy increases with heating and decreases with cooling. Similarly, the first law, Eq. 13.30c, shows that heating increases the stagnation enthalpy and cooling decreases it; since $\Delta h_0 = c_p \Delta T_0$, the effect on stagnation temperature is the same.

The effect of heating and cooling on temperature may be deduced from the shape of the Rayleigh line in Fig. 13.15. We see that except for the region $1/\sqrt{k} < M < 1$ (for air, $1/\sqrt{k} \approx 0.85$), heating causes T to increase, and cooling causes T to decrease. However, we also see the unexpected result that for $1/\sqrt{k} < M < 1$, *heat addition* causes the stream temperature to *decrease*, and *heat rejection* causes the stream temperature to *increase!*

For subsonic flow, the Mach number increases monotonically with heating, until $M = 1$ is reached. For given inlet conditions, all possible downstream states lie on a single Rayleigh line. Therefore, the point $M = 1$ determines the maximum possible heat addition without choking. If the flow is initially supersonic, heating will reduce the Mach number. Again, the maximum possible heat addition without choking is that which reduces the Mach number to $M = 1.0$.

The effect of heat exchange on static pressure is obtained from the shapes of the Rayleigh line and of constant-pressure lines on the Ts plane (see Fig. 13.16). For $M < 1$, pressure falls with heating, and for $M > 1$, pressure increases, as shown by the shapes of the constant-pressure lines. Once the pressure variation has been found, the effect on velocity may be found from the momentum equation,

$$p_1 A - p_2 A = \dot{m} V_2 - \dot{m} V_1 \tag{13.30b}$$

or

$$p + \left(\frac{\dot{m}}{A}\right) V = \text{constant}$$

Thus, since $\dot{m}/A$ is a positive constant, trends in p and V must be opposite. From the continuity equation, Eq. 13.30a, the trend in ρ is opposite to that in V.

TABLE 13.2 Summary of Effects of Heat Exchange on Fluid Properties

Property	Heating		Cooling		Obtained from:
	$M < 1$	$M > 1$	$M < 1$	$M > 1$	
Entropy	$s \Uparrow$	$s \Uparrow$	$s \Downarrow$	$s \Downarrow$	$T ds$ equation
Stagnation temperature	$T_0 \Uparrow$	$T_0 \Uparrow$	$T_0 \Downarrow$	$T_0 \Downarrow$	First law, and $\Delta h_0 = c_p \Delta T_0$
Temperature	$T \Uparrow \left(M < \frac{1}{\sqrt{k}}\right)$ $T \Downarrow \left(\frac{1}{\sqrt{k}} < M < 1\right)$	$T \Uparrow$	$T \Downarrow \left(M < \frac{1}{\sqrt{k}}\right)$ $T \Uparrow \left(\frac{1}{\sqrt{k}} < M < 1\right)$	$T \Downarrow$	Shape of Rayleigh line
Mach number	$M \Uparrow$	$M \Downarrow$	$M \Downarrow$	$M \Uparrow$	Trend on Rayleigh line
Pressure	$p \Downarrow$	$p \Uparrow$	$p \Uparrow$	$p \Downarrow$	Trend on Rayleigh line
Velocity	$V \Uparrow$	$V \Downarrow$	$V \Downarrow$	$V \Uparrow$	Momentum equation, and effect on p
Density	$\rho \Downarrow$	$\rho \Uparrow$	$\rho \Uparrow$	$\rho \Downarrow$	Continuity equation, and effect on V
Stagnation pressure	$p_0 \Downarrow$	$p_0 \Downarrow$	$p_0 \Uparrow$	$p_0 \Uparrow$	Fig. 13.16

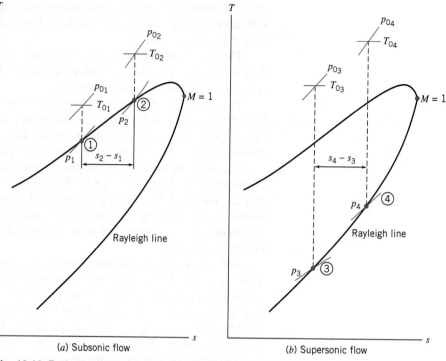

(a) Subsonic flow   (b) Supersonic flow

Fig. 13.16 Reduction in stagnation pressure due to heat addition for two flow cases.

Local isentropic stagnation pressure always decreases with heating. This is illustrated schematically in Fig. 13.16. A reduction in stagnation pressure has obvious practical implications for heating processes, such as combustion chambers. Adding the same amount of energy per unit mass (same change in T_0) causes a larger change in p_0 for supersonic flow; because heating occurs at a lower temperature in supersonic flow, the entropy increase is larger.

EXAMPLE 13.8 Frictionless Flow in a Constant-Area Duct with Heat Addition

Air flows with negligible friction through a duct of area $A = 0.25\ ft^2$. At section ①, flow properties are $T_1 = 600°R$, $p_1 = 20$ psia, and $V_1 = 360$ ft/s. At section ②, $p_2 = 10$ psia. The flow is heated between sections ① and ②. Determine the properties at section ②, the energy added, and the entropy change. Finally, plot the process on a Ts diagram.

GIVEN: Frictionless flow of air in duct shown:

$T_1 = 600°R$
$p_1 = 20$ psia $p_2 = 10$ psia
$V_1 = 360$ ft/s $A_1 = A_2 = A = 0.25\ ft^2$

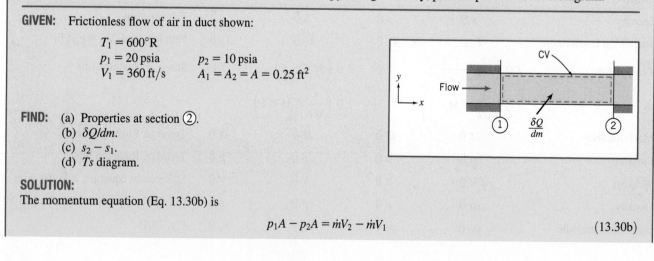

FIND: (a) Properties at section ②.
      (b) $\delta Q/dm$.
      (c) $s_2 - s_1$.
      (d) Ts diagram.

SOLUTION:
The momentum equation (Eq. 13.30b) is

$$p_1 A - p_2 A = \dot{m} V_2 - \dot{m} V_1 \qquad (13.30b)$$

or

$$p_1 - p_2 = \frac{\dot{m}}{A}(V_2 - V_1) = \rho_1 V_1 (V_2 - V_1)$$

Solving for V_2 gives

$$V_2 = \frac{p_1 - p_2}{\rho_1 V_1} + V_1$$

For an ideal gas, Eq. 13.30e,

$$\rho_1 = \frac{p_1}{RT_1} = 20\,\frac{\text{lbf}}{\text{in.}^2} \times 144\,\frac{\text{in.}^2}{\text{ft}^2} \times \frac{\text{lbm} \cdot {}^\circ\text{R}}{53.3\,\text{ft} \cdot \text{lbf}} \times \frac{1}{600{}^\circ\text{R}} = 0.0901\,\text{lbm/ft}^3$$

$$V_2 = (20 - 10)\,\frac{\text{lbf}}{\text{in.}^2} \times 144\,\frac{\text{in.}^2}{\text{ft}^2} \times \frac{\text{ft}^3}{0.0901\,\text{lbm}} \times \frac{\text{s}}{360\,\text{ft}} \times 32.2\,\frac{\text{lbm}}{\text{slug}} \times \frac{\text{slug} \cdot \text{ft}}{\text{lbf} \cdot \text{s}^2} + \frac{360\,\text{ft}}{\text{s}}$$

$$V_2 = 1790\,\text{ft/s} \longleftarrow \underline{\hspace{3cm}} \qquad V_2$$

From continuity, Eq. 13.30a, $G = \rho_1 V_1 = \rho_2 V_2$, so

$$\rho_2 = \rho_1\,\frac{V_1}{V_2} = 0.0901\,\frac{\text{lbm}}{\text{ft}^3}\left(\frac{360}{1790}\right) = 0.0181\,\text{lbm/ft}^3 \longleftarrow \underline{\hspace{2cm}} \qquad \rho_2$$

Solving for T_2, we obtain

$$T_2 = \frac{p_2}{\rho_2 R} = 10\,\frac{\text{lbf}}{\text{in.}^2} \times 144\,\frac{\text{in.}^2}{\text{ft}^2} \times \frac{\text{ft}^3}{0.0181\,\text{lbm}} \times \frac{\text{lbm} \cdot {}^\circ\text{R}}{53.3\,\text{ft} \cdot \text{lbf}} = 1490{}^\circ\text{R} \longleftarrow \underline{\hspace{1cm}} \qquad T_2$$

The local isentropic stagnation temperature is given by Eq. 12.21b,

$$T_{0_2} = T_2\left(1 + \frac{k-1}{2}M_2^2\right)$$

$$c_2 = \sqrt{kRT_2} = 1890\,\text{ft/s}; \qquad M_2 = \frac{V_2}{c_2} = \frac{1790}{1890} = 0.947$$

$$T_{0_2} = 1490{}^\circ\text{R}[1 + 0.2(0.947)^2] = 1760{}^\circ\text{R} \longleftarrow \underline{\hspace{2cm}} \qquad T_{0_2}$$

and

$$p_{0_2} = p_2\left(\frac{T_{0_2}}{T_2}\right)^{k/(k-1)} = 10\,\text{psia}\left(\frac{1760}{1490}\right)^{3.5} = 17.9\,\text{psia} \longleftarrow \underline{\hspace{1cm}} \qquad p_{0_2}$$

The heat addition is obtained from the energy equation (Eq. 13.30c),

$$\frac{\delta Q}{dm} = \left(h_2 + \frac{V_2^2}{2}\right) - \left(h_1 + \frac{V_1^2}{2}\right) = h_{0_2} - h_{0_1} \qquad (13.30c)$$

or

$$\frac{\delta Q}{dm} = h_{0_2} - h_{0_1} = c_p(T_{0_2} - T_{0_1})$$

We already obtained T_{0_2}. For T_{0_1} we have

$$T_{0_1} = T_1\left(1 + \frac{k-1}{2}M_1^2\right)$$

$$c_1 = \sqrt{kRT_1} = 1200\,\text{ft/s}; \qquad M_1 = \frac{V_1}{c_1} = \frac{360}{1200} = 0.3$$

$$T_{0_1} = 600{}^\circ\text{R}[1 + 0.2(0.3)^2] = 611{}^\circ\text{R}$$

so

$$\frac{\delta Q}{dm} = 0.240\,\frac{\text{Btu}}{\text{lbm} \cdot {}^\circ\text{R}}(1760 - 611){}^\circ\text{R} = 276\,\text{Btu/lbm} \longleftarrow \underline{\hspace{2cm}} \qquad \delta Q/dm$$

For the change in entropy (Eq 13.30g),

$$\Delta s = s_2 - s_1 = c_p \ln \frac{T_2}{T_1} - R \ln \frac{p_2}{p_1} = c_p \ln \frac{T_2}{T_1} - (c_p - c_v)\ln \frac{p_2}{p_1} \tag{13.30g}$$

Then

$$s_2 - s_1 = 0.240 \; \frac{\text{Btu}}{\text{lbm} \cdot {}^\circ\text{R}} \times \ln\left(\frac{1490}{600}\right) - (0.240 - 0.71) \; \frac{\text{Btu}}{\text{lbm} \cdot {}^\circ\text{R}} \times \ln\left(\frac{10}{20}\right)$$

$$s_2 - s_1 = 0.266 \; \text{Btu/(lbm} \cdot {}^\circ\text{R}) \longleftarrow \hspace{3cm} s_2 - s_1$$

The process follows a Rayleigh line:

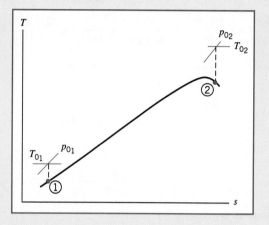

To complete our analysis, let us examine the change in p_0 by comparing p_{0_2} with p_{0_1}.

$$p_{0_1} = p_1 \left(\frac{T_{0_1}}{T_1}\right)^{k/(k-1)} = 20.0 \; \text{pisa} \left(\frac{611}{600}\right)^{3.5} = 21.3 \; \text{psia} \longleftarrow \hspace{2cm} p_{0_1}$$

Comparing, we see that p_{0_2} is less than p_{0_1}.

> This problem illustrates the use of the basic equations, Eqs. 13.30, for analyzing frictionless flow of an ideal gas in a duct with heat exchange.
>
> The *Excel* workbook for this Example is convenient for performing the calculations.

Rayleigh-Line Flow Functions for One-Dimensional Flow of an Ideal Gas

Equations 13.30 are the basic equations for Rayleigh-line flow between two arbitrary states ① and ② in the flow. To reduce labor in solving problems, it is convenient to derive flow functions for property ratios in terms of local Mach number as we did for Fanno-line flow. The reference state is again taken as the critical condition where $M = 1$; properties at the critical condition are denoted by (*).

Dimensionless properties (such as p/p^* and T/T^*) may be obtained by writing the basic equations between a point in the flow where properties are M, T, p, etc., and the critical state ($M = 1$, with properties denoted as T^*, p^*, etc.).

The pressure ratio, p/p^*, may be obtained from the momentum equation, Eq. 13.30b,

$$pA - p^*A = \dot{m}V^* - \dot{m}V$$

or

$$p + \rho V^2 = p^* + p^* V^{*2}$$

Substituting $\rho = p/RT$, and factoring out pressures yields

$$p\left[1 + \frac{V^2}{RT}\right] = p^*\left[1 + \frac{V^{*2}}{RT^*}\right]$$

Noting that $V^2/RT = k(V^2/kRT) = kM^2$, we find

$$p[1 + kM^2] = p^*[1 + k]$$

and finally,

$$\frac{p}{p^*} = \frac{1 + k}{1 + kM^2} \tag{13.31a}$$

From the ideal gas equation of state,

$$\frac{T}{T^*} = \frac{p}{p^*}\frac{\rho^*}{\rho}$$

From the continuity equation, Eq. 13.30a,

$$\frac{\rho^*}{\rho} = \frac{V}{V^*} = M\frac{c}{c^*} = M\sqrt{\frac{T}{T^*}}$$

Then, substituting for ρ^*/ρ, we obtain

$$\frac{T}{T^*} = \frac{p}{p^*}M\sqrt{\frac{T}{T^*}}$$

Squaring and substituting from Eq. 13.31a gives

$$\frac{T}{T^*} = \left[\frac{p}{p^*}M\right]^2 = \left[M\left(\frac{1+k}{1+kM^2}\right)\right]^2 \tag{13.31b}$$

From continuity, using Eq. 13.31b,

$$\frac{\rho^*}{\rho} = \frac{V}{V^*} = \frac{M^2(1+k)}{1+kM^2} \tag{13.31c}$$

The dimensionless stagnation temperature, T_0/T_0^*, can be determined from

$$\frac{T_0}{T_0^*} = \frac{T_0}{T}\frac{T}{T^*}\frac{T^*}{T_0^*}$$

$$= \left(1 + \frac{k-1}{2}M^2\right)\left[M\left(\frac{1+k}{1+kM^2}\right)\right]^2\frac{1}{\left(\dfrac{k+1}{2}\right)}$$

$$\frac{T_0}{T_0^*} = \frac{2(k+1)M^2\left(1 + \dfrac{k-1}{2}M^2\right)}{(1+kM^2)^2} \tag{13.31d}$$

Similarly,

$$\frac{p_0}{p_0^*} = \frac{p_0}{p}\frac{p}{p^*}\frac{p^*}{p_0^*}$$

$$= \left(1 + \frac{k-1}{2}M^2\right)^{k/(k-1)}\left(\frac{1+k}{1+kM^2}\right)\frac{1}{\left(\dfrac{k+1}{2}\right)^{k/(k-1)}}$$

$$\frac{p_0}{p_0^*} = \frac{1+k}{1+kM^2}\left[\left(\frac{2}{k+1}\right)\left(1 + \frac{k-1}{2}M^2\right)\right]^{k/(k-1)} \tag{13.31e}$$

For convenience we collect together the equations:

$$\frac{p}{p^*} = \frac{1+k}{1+kM^2} \tag{13.31a}$$

$$\frac{T}{T^*} = \left[M \left(\frac{1+k}{1+kM^2} \right) \right]^2 \tag{13.31b}$$

$$\frac{\rho^*}{\rho} = \frac{V}{V^*} = \frac{M^2(1+k)}{1+kM^2} \tag{13.31c}$$

$$\frac{T_0}{T_0^*} = \frac{2(k+1)M^2 \left(1 + \frac{k-1}{2}M^2 \right)}{(1+kM^2)^2} \tag{13.31d}$$

$$\frac{p_0}{p_0^*} = \frac{1+k}{1+kM^2} \left[\left(\frac{2}{k+1} \right) \left(1 + \frac{k-1}{2}M^2 \right) \right]^{k/k-1} \tag{13.31e}$$

Equations 13.31, the Rayleigh-line relations, provide property ratios in terms of the local Mach number and critical conditions. They are obviously complicated, but can be programmed into your calculator. They are also fairly easy to define in spreadsheets such as *Excel*. The reader is urged to download the *Excel* add-ins for these equations from the Web site; with the add-ins, functions are available for computing the pressure, temperature, density, and stagnation temperature and pressure ratios from M, and M from these ratios. In Example 13.9 we will explore their use. Appendix E-3 lists flow functions for property ratios T_0/T_0^*, p_0/p_0^*, T/T^*, p/p^*, and ρ^*/ρ (V/V^*), in terms of M for Rayleigh-line flow of an ideal gas. A table of values, as well as a plot of these property ratios, is presented for air ($k = 1.4$) for a limited range of Mach numbers. The associated *Excel* workbook, *Rayleigh-Line Relations*, can be used to print a larger table of values for air and other ideal gases.

EXAMPLE 13.9 **Frictionless Flow in a Constant-Area Duct with Heat Addition: Solution Using Rayleigh-Line Flow Functions**

Air flows with negligible friction in a constant-area duct. At section ①, properties are $T_1 = 60°C$, $p_1 = 135$ kPa (abs), and $V_1 = 732$ m/s. Heat is added between section ① and section ②, where $M_2 = 1.2$. Determine the properties at section ②, the heat exchange per unit mass, and the entropy change, and sketch the process on a Ts diagram.

GIVEN: Frictionless flow of air as shown:

$T_1 = 333$ K $\qquad M_2 = 1.2$
$p_1 = 135$ kPa (abs)
$V_1 = 732$ m/s

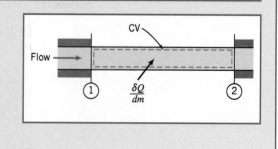

FIND: (a) Properties at section ②.
(b) $\delta Q/dm$.
(c) $s_2 - s_1$.
(d) Ts diagram.

SOLUTION:

To obtain property ratios, we need both Mach numbers.

$$c_1 = \sqrt{kRT_1} = \left[1.4 \times 287 \frac{\text{N} \cdot \text{m}}{\text{kg} \cdot \text{K}} \times 333 \text{ K} \times \frac{\text{kg} \cdot \text{m}}{\text{N} \cdot \text{s}^2} \right]^{1/2} = 366 \text{ m/s}$$

$$M_1 = \frac{V_1}{c_1} = 732 \frac{\text{m}}{\text{s}} \times \frac{\text{s}}{366 \text{ m}} = 2.00$$

From the Rayleigh-line flow functions of Appendix E-3 we find the following:

M	T_0/T_0^*	p_0/p_0^*	T/T^*	p/p^*	V/V^*
2.00	0.7934	1.503	0.5289	0.3636	1.455
1.20	0.9787	1.019	0.9119	0.7958	1.146

Using these data and recognizing that critical properties are constant, we obtain

$$\frac{T_2}{T_1} = \frac{T_2/T^*}{T_1/T^*} = \frac{0.9119}{0.5289} = 1.72; \quad T_2 = 1.72 T_1 = (1.72)333 \text{ K} = 573 \text{ K} \quad \longleftarrow \quad T_2$$

$$\frac{p_2}{p_1} = \frac{p_2/p^*}{p_1/p^*} = \frac{0.7958}{0.3636} = 2.19; \quad p_2 = 2.19 p_1 = (2.19)135 \text{ kPa}$$

$$p_2 = 296 \text{ kPa (abs)} \quad \longleftarrow \quad p_2$$

$$\frac{V_2}{V_1} = \frac{V_2/V^*}{V_1/V^*} = \frac{1.146}{1.455} = 0.788; \quad V_2 = 0.788 V_1 = (0.788)732 \text{ m/s}$$

$$V_2 = 577 \text{ m/s} \quad \longleftarrow \quad V_2$$

$$\rho_2 = \frac{p_2}{RT_2} = 2.96 \times 10^5 \frac{\text{N}}{\text{m}^2} \times \frac{\text{kg} \cdot \text{K}}{287 \text{ N} \cdot \text{m}} \times \frac{1}{573 \text{ K}} = 1.80 \text{ kg/m}^3 \quad \longleftarrow \quad \rho_2$$

The heat addition may be determined from the energy equation, Eq. 13.30c,

$$\frac{\delta Q}{dm} = h_{0_2} - h_{0_1} = c_p(T_{0_2} - T_{0_1})$$

From the isentropic-stagnation functions (Eq. 12.21b) at $M = 2.0$,

$$\frac{T}{T_0} = \frac{T_1}{T_{0_1}} = 0.5556; \quad T_{0_1} = \frac{T_1}{0.5556} = \frac{333 \text{ K}}{0.5556} = 599 \text{ K}$$

and at $M = 1.2$,

$$\frac{T}{T_0} = \frac{T_2}{T_{0_2}} = 0.7664; \quad T_{0_2} = \frac{T_2}{0.7764} = \frac{573 \text{ K}}{0.7764} = 738 \text{ K} \quad \longleftarrow \quad T_{0_2}$$

Substituting gives

$$\frac{\delta Q}{dm} = c_p(T_{0_2} - T_{0_1}) = 1.00 \frac{\text{kJ}}{\text{kg} \cdot \text{K}} \times (738 - 599) \text{ K} = 139 \text{ kJ/kg} \quad \longleftarrow \quad \delta Q/dm$$

For the change in entropy (Eq. 13.30g),

$$s_2 - s_1 = c_p \ln \frac{T_2}{T_1} - R \ln \frac{p_2}{p_1}$$

$$= 1.00 \frac{\text{kJ}}{\text{kg} \cdot \text{K}} \times \ln\left(\frac{573}{333}\right) - 287 \frac{\text{N} \cdot \text{m}}{\text{kg} \cdot \text{K}} \times \ln\left(\frac{2.96 \times 10^5}{1.35 \times 10^5}\right) \times \frac{\text{kJ}}{1000 \text{ N} \cdot \text{m}}$$

$$s_2 - s_1 = 0.137 \text{ kJ/(kg} \cdot \text{K)} \quad \longleftarrow \quad s_2 - s_1$$

Finally, check the effect on p_0. From the isentropic-stagnation function (Eq. 12.21a), at $M = 2.0$,

$$\frac{p}{p_0} = \frac{p_1}{p_{0_1}} = 0.1278; \qquad p_{0_1} = \frac{p_1}{0.1278} = \frac{135 \text{ kPa}}{0.1278} = 1.06 \text{ MPa (abs)}$$

and at $M = 1.2$,

$$\frac{p}{p_0} = \frac{p_2}{p_{0_2}} = 0.4124; \qquad p_{0_2} = \frac{p_2}{0.4124} = \frac{296 \text{ kPa}}{0.4124} = 718 \text{ kPa (abs)} \quad \longleftarrow \qquad p_{0_2}$$

Thus, $p_{0_2} < p_{0_1}$, as expected for a heating process.

The process follows the supersonic branch of a Rayleigh line:

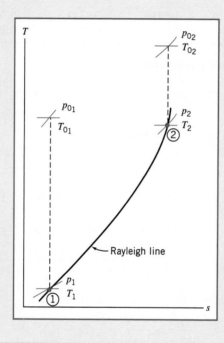

This problem illustrates the use of the Rayleigh-line equations, Eqs. 13.31, for analyzing frictionless flow of an ideal gas in a duct with heat exchange.

🖱 The *Excel* workbook for this Example is convenient for performing the calculations. (Alternatively, the Rayleigh-line *Excel* add-ins, available on the Web site, are useful for these calculations.)

13-5   NORMAL SHOCKS

We have previously mentioned normal shocks in the section on nozzle flow. In practice, these irreversible discontinuities can occur in any supersonic flow field, in either internal flow or external flow.[1] Knowledge of property changes across shocks and of shock behavior is important in understanding the design of supersonic diffusers, e.g., for inlets on high performance aircraft, and supersonic wind tunnels. Accordingly, the purpose of this section is to analyze the normal shock process.

---

[1] The NCFMF video *Channel Flow of a Compressible Fluid* shows several examples of shock formation in internal flow. (See http://web.mit.edu/fluids/www/Shapiro/ncfmf.html for free online viewing of this film; it is old but good!)

Before applying the basic equations to normal shocks, it is important to form a clear physical picture of the shock itself. Although it is physically impossible to have discontinuities in fluid properties, the normal shock is nearly discontinuous. The thickness of a shock is about 0.2 μm (10^{-5} in.), or roughly 4 times the mean free path of the gas molecules [3]. Large changes in pressure, temperature, and other properties occur across this small distance. Fluid particle decelerations through the shock reach tens of millions of *g*s! These considerations justify treating the normal shock as an abrupt discontinuity; we are interested in changes occurring across the shock rather than in the details of its structure.

Consider the short control volume surrounding a normal shock standing in a passage of arbitrary shape shown in Fig. 13.17. You may be exhausted by this procedure by now, but as for isentropic flow with area variation (Section 13-2), frictional flow (Section 13-3), and flow with heat exchange (Section 13-4), our starting point in analyzing this normal shock is the set of basic equations (Eqs. 13.1), describing one-dimensional motion that may be affected by several phenomena: area change, friction, and heat transfer. These are

$$\rho_1 V_1 A_1 = \rho_2 V_2 A_2 = \rho V A = \dot{m} = \text{constant} \tag{13.1a}$$

$$R_x + p_1 A_1 - p_2 A_2 = \dot{m} V_2 - \dot{m} V_1 \tag{13.1b}$$

$$\frac{\delta Q}{dm} + h_1 + \frac{V_1^2}{2} = h_2 + \frac{V_2^2}{2} \tag{13.1c}$$

$$\dot{m}(s_2 - s_1) \geq \int_{\text{CS}} \frac{1}{T}\left(\frac{\dot{Q}}{A}\right) dA \tag{13.1d}$$

$$p = \rho R T \tag{13.1e}$$

$$\Delta h = h_2 - h_1 = c_p \Delta T = c_p(T_2 - T_1) \tag{13.1f}$$

$$\Delta s = s_2 - s_1 = c_p \ln \frac{T_2}{T_1} - R \ln \frac{p_2}{p_1} \tag{13.1g}$$

We recall that Equation 13.1a is *continuity*, Eq. 13.1b is a *momentum equation*, Eq. 13.1c is an *energy equation*, Eq. 13.1d is the *second law of thermodynamics*, and Eqs. 13.1e, 13.1f, and 13.1g are useful *property relations* for an ideal gas with constant specific heats.

We must simplify these equations for flow through a normal shock.

Basic Equations for a Normal Shock

We can now simplify Eqs. 13.1 for flow of an ideal gas with constant specific heats through a normal shock. The most important simplifying feature is that the width of the control volume is infinitesimal (in reality about 0.2 μm as we indicated), so

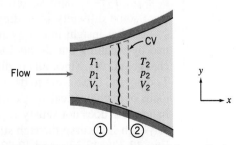

Fig. 13.17 Control volume used for analysis of normal shock.

$A_1 \approx A_2 \approx A$, the force due to the walls $R_x \approx 0$ (because the control volume wall surface area is infinitesimal), and the heat exchange with the walls $\delta Q/dm \approx 0$, for the same reason. Hence, for this flow our equations become

$$\rho_1 V_1 = \rho_2 V_2 = \frac{\dot{m}}{A} = \text{constant} \tag{13.32a}$$

$$p_1 A - p_2 A = \dot{m} V_2 - \dot{m} V_1$$

or, using Eq. 13.32a,

$$p_1 + \rho_1 V_1^2 = p_2 + \rho_2 V_2^2 \tag{13.32b}$$

$$h_{0_1} = h_1 + \frac{V_1^2}{2} = h_2 + \frac{V_2^2}{2} = h_{0_2} \tag{13.32c}$$

$$s_2 > s_1 \tag{13.32d}$$

$$p = \rho R T \tag{13.32e}$$

$$\Delta h = h_2 - h_1 = c_p \Delta T = c_p (T_2 - T_1) \tag{13.32f}$$

$$\Delta s = s_2 - s_1 = c_p \ln \frac{T_2}{T_1} - R \ln \frac{p_2}{p_1} \tag{13.32g}$$

Equations 13.32 can be used to analyze flow through a normal shock. For example, if we know conditions before the shock, at section ① (i.e., p_1, ρ_1, T_1, s_1, h_1, and V_1), we can use these equations to find conditions after the shock, at section ②. We have six equations (not including the constraint of Eq. 13.32d) and six unknowns (p_2, ρ_2, T_2, s_2, h_2, and V_2). Hence, for given upstream conditions there is a single unique downstream state. In practice this procedure is unwieldy—as we have seen in earlier sections, we have a set of *nonlinear coupled algebraic* equations to solve.

We can certainly use these equations for analyzing normal shocks, but we will usually find it more useful to develop normal shock functions based on M_1, the upstream Mach number. Before doing this, let us consider the set of equations. We have repeatedly stated in this chapter that changes in a one-dimensional flow can be caused by area variation, friction, or heat transfer, but in deriving Eqs. 13.32 we have eliminated all three causes! In this case, then, what is causing the flow to change? Perhaps there are no changes through a normal shock! Indeed, if we examine each of these equations we see that each one is satisfied—has a possible "solution"—if all properties at location ② are equal to the corresponding properties at location ① (e.g., $p_2 = p_1$, $T_2 = T_1$) *except* for Eq. 13.32d, which expresses the second law of thermodynamics. Nature is telling us that in the absence of area change, friction, and heat transfer, flow properties will not change *except* in a very abrupt, irreversible manner, for which the entropy increases. In fact, all properties except T_0 *do* change through the shock. We must find a solution in which *all* of Eqs. 13.32 are satisfied. (Incidentally, because all the equations except Eq. 13.32d are satisfied by $p_2 = p_1$, $T_2 = T_1$, and so on, numerical searching methods such as *Excel*'s *Solver* have some difficulty in finding the correct solution!)

Further insight into the equations governing a normal shock, Eqs. 13.32, can be had by recalling our discussion of Fanno-line (friction) and Rayleigh-line (heat exchange) curves. Since all conditions at state ① are known, we can locate state ① on a *Ts* diagram. If we were to draw a Fanno-line curve through state ①, we would have a locus of mathematical states that satisfy Eqs. 13.32a and 13.32c through 13.32g. (The Fanno-line does not satisfy Eq. 13.32b, which assumes no friction force.) Drawing a Rayleigh-line curve through state ① gives a locus of mathematical states that satisfy Eqs. 13.32a, 13.32b, and 13.32d through 13.32g. (The Rayleigh-line does not satisfy Eq. 13.32c, which assumes no heat exchange.) These curves are shown in Fig. 13.18.

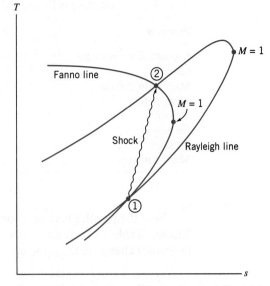

Fig. 13.18 Intersection of Fanno line and Rayleigh line as a solution of the normal-shock equations.

The normal shock must satisfy all seven of Eqs. 13.32a through 13.32g. Consequently, for a given state ①, the end state (state ②) of the normal shock must lie on both the Fanno line and the Rayleigh line passing through state ①. Hence, the intersection of the two lines at state ② represents conditions downstream from the shock, corresponding to upstream conditions at state ①. In Fig. 13.18, flow through the shock has been indicated as occurring from state ① to state ②. This is the only possible direction of the shock process, as dictated by the second law ($s_2 > s_1$).

From Fig. 13.18 we note also that flow through a normal shock involves a change from supersonic to subsonic speeds. Normal shocks can occur only in a flow that is initially supersonic.

As an aid in summarizing the effects of a normal shock on the flow properties, a schematic of the normal-shock process is illustrated on the Ts plane of Fig. 13.19. This figure, together with the governing basic equations, is the basis for Table 13.3. You should follow through the logic indicated in the table.

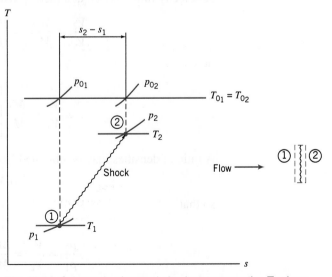

Fig. 13.19 Schematic of normal-shock process on the Ts plane.

TABLE 13.3 Summary of Property Changes across a Normal Shock

Property	Effect	Obtained from:
Stagnation temperature	$T_0 = \text{Constant}$	Energy equation
Entropy	$s \Uparrow$	Second law
Stagnation pressure	$p_0 \Downarrow$	Ts diagram
Temperature	$T \Uparrow$	Ts diagram
Velocity	$V \Downarrow$	Energy equation, and effect on T
Density	$\rho \Uparrow$	Continuity equation, and effect on V
Pressure	$p \Uparrow$	Momentum equation, and effect on V
Mach number	$M \Downarrow$	$M = V/c$, and effects on V and T

Note the parallel between normal shocks (Table 13.3) and supersonic flow with friction (Table 13.1). Both represent irreversible processes in supersonic flow, and all properties change in the same directions.

Normal-Shock Flow Functions for One-Dimensional Flow of an Ideal Gas

We have mentioned that the basic equations, Eqs. 13.32, can be used to analyze flows that experience a normal shock. As in previous flows, it is often more convenient to use Mach number-based equations, in this case based on the incoming Mach number, M_1. This involves three steps: First, we obtain property ratios (e.g., T_2/T_1 and p_2/p_1) in terms of M_1 and M_2, then we develop a relation between M_1 and M_2, and finally, we use this relation to obtain expressions for property ratios in terms of upstream Mach number, M_1.

The temperature ratio can be expressed as

$$\frac{T_2}{T_1} = \frac{T_2}{T_{0_2}} \frac{T_{0_2}}{T_{0_1}} \frac{T_{0_1}}{T_1}$$

Since stagnation temperature is constant across the shock, we have

$$\frac{T_2}{T_1} = \frac{1 + \dfrac{k-1}{2} M_1^2}{1 + \dfrac{k-1}{2} M_2^2} \tag{13.33}$$

A velocity ratio may be obtained by using

$$\frac{V_2}{V_1} = \frac{M_2 c_2}{M_1 c_1} = \frac{M_2}{M_1} \frac{\sqrt{kRT_2}}{\sqrt{kRT_1}} = \frac{M_2}{M_1} \sqrt{\frac{T_2}{T_1}}$$

or

$$\frac{V_2}{V_1} = \frac{M_2}{M_1} \left[\frac{1 + \dfrac{k-1}{2} M_1^2}{1 + \dfrac{k-1}{2} M_2^2} \right]^{1/2}$$

A ratio of densities may be obtained from the continuity equation

$$\rho_1 V_1 = \rho_2 V_2 \tag{13.32a}$$

so that

$$\frac{\rho_2}{\rho_1} = \frac{V_1}{V_2} = \frac{M_1}{M_2} \left[\frac{1 + \dfrac{k-1}{2} M_2^2}{1 + \dfrac{k-1}{2} M_1^2} \right]^{1/2} \tag{13.34}$$

Finally, we have the momentum equation,

$$p_1 + \rho_1 V_1^2 = p_2 + \rho_2 V_2^2 \tag{13.32b}$$

Substituting $\rho = p/RT$, and factoring out pressures, gives

$$p_1 \left[1 + \frac{V_1^2}{RT_1} \right] = p_2 \left[1 + \frac{V_2^2}{RT_2} \right]$$

Since

$$\frac{V^2}{RT} = k \frac{V^2}{kRT} = kM^2$$

then

$$p_1 \left[1 + kM_1^2 \right] = p_2 \left[1 + kM_2^2 \right]$$

Finally,

$$\frac{p_2}{p_1} = \frac{1 + kM_1^2}{1 + kM_2^2} \tag{13.35}$$

To solve for M_2 in terms of M_1, we must obtain another expression for one of the property ratios given by Eqs. 13.33 through 13.35.

From the ideal gas equation of state, the temperature ratio may be written as

$$\frac{T_2}{T_1} = \frac{p_2/\rho_2 R}{p_1/\rho_1 R} = \frac{p_2}{p_1}\frac{\rho_1}{\rho_2}$$

Substituting from Eqs. 13.34 and 13.35 yields

$$\frac{T_2}{T_1} = \left[\frac{1 + kM_1^2}{1 + kM_2^2} \right] \frac{M_2}{M_1} \left[\frac{1 + \dfrac{k-1}{2}M_1^2}{1 + \dfrac{k-1}{2}M_2^2} \right]^{1/2} \tag{13.36}$$

Equations 13.33 and 13.36 are two equations for T_2/T_1. We can combine them and solve for M_2 in terms of M_1. Combining and canceling gives

$$\left[\frac{1 + \dfrac{k-1}{2}M_1^2}{1 + \dfrac{k-1}{2}M_2^2} \right]^{1/2} = \frac{M_2}{M_1} \left[\frac{1 + kM_1^2}{1 + kM_2^2} \right]$$

Squaring, we obtain

$$\frac{1 + \dfrac{k-1}{2}M_1^2}{1 + \dfrac{k-1}{2}M_2^2} = \frac{M_2^2}{M_1^2} \left[\frac{1 + 2kM_1^2 + k^2M_1^4}{1 + 2kM_2^2 + k^2M_2^4} \right]$$

which may be solved explicitly for M_2^2. Two solutions are obtained:

$$M_2^2 = M_1^2 \tag{13.37a}$$

and

$$M_2^2 = \frac{M_1^2 + \dfrac{2}{k-1}}{\dfrac{2k}{k-1}M_1^2 - 1} \tag{13.37b}$$

Obviously, the first of these is trivial. The second expresses the unique dependence of M_2 on M_1.

Now, having a relationship between M_2 and M_1, we can solve for property ratios across a shock. Knowing M_1, we obtain M_2 from Eq. 13.37b; the property ratios can be determined subsequently from Eqs. 13.33 through 13.35.

Since the stagnation temperature remains constant, the stagnation temperature ratio across the shock is unity. The ratio of stagnation pressures is evaluated as

$$\frac{p_{0_2}}{p_{0_1}} = \frac{p_{0_2}}{p_2}\frac{p_2}{p_1}\frac{p_1}{p_{0_1}} = \frac{p_2}{p_1}\left[\frac{1+\dfrac{k-1}{2}M_2^2}{1+\dfrac{k-1}{2}M_1^2}\right]^{k/(k-1)} \tag{13.38}$$

Combining Eqs. 13.35 and 13.37b, we obtain (after considerable algebra)

$$\frac{p_2}{p_1} = \frac{1+kM_1^2}{1+kM_2^2} = \frac{2k}{k+1}M_1^2 - \frac{k-1}{k+1} \tag{13.39}$$

Using Eqs. 13.37b and 13.39, we find that Eq. 13.38 becomes

$$\frac{p_{0_2}}{p_{0_1}} = \frac{\left[\dfrac{\dfrac{k+1}{2}M_1^2}{1+\dfrac{k-1}{2}M_1^2}\right]^{k/(k-1)}}{\left[\dfrac{2k}{k+1}M_1^2 - \dfrac{k-1}{k+1}\right]^{1/(k-1)}} \tag{13.40}$$

After substituting for M_2^2 from Eq. 13.37b into Eqs. 13.33 and 13.34, we summarize the set of Mach number-based equations (renumbered for convenience) for use with an ideal gas passing through a normal shock:

$$M_2^2 = \frac{M_1^2 + \dfrac{2}{k-1}}{\dfrac{2k}{k-1}M_1^2 - 1} \tag{13.41a}$$

$$\frac{p_{0_2}}{p_{0_1}} = \frac{\left[\dfrac{\dfrac{k+1}{2}M_1^2}{1+\dfrac{k-1}{2}M_1^2}\right]^{k/(k-1)}}{\left[\dfrac{2k}{k+1}M_1^2 - \dfrac{k-1}{k+1}\right]^{1/(k-1)}} \tag{13.41b}$$

$$\frac{T_2}{T_1} = \frac{\left(1+\dfrac{k-1}{2}M_1^2\right)\left(kM_1^2 - \dfrac{k-1}{2}\right)}{\left(\dfrac{k+1}{2}\right)^2 M_1^2} \tag{13.41c}$$

$$\frac{p_2}{p_1} = \frac{2k}{k+1}M_1^2 - \frac{k-1}{k+1} \tag{13.41d}$$

$$\frac{\rho_2}{\rho_1} = \frac{V_1}{V_2} = \frac{\dfrac{k+1}{2}M_1^2}{1+\dfrac{k-1}{2}M_1^2} \tag{13.41e}$$

Equations 13.41, while quite complex algebraically, provide explicit property relations in terms of the incoming Mach number, M_1. They are so useful that some calculators have some of them built in (e.g., the *HP 48G* series [1]); it is a good idea to program them if your calculator does not already have them. There are also interactive Web sites that make them available (see, e.g., [2]), and they are fairly easy to define in spreadsheets such as *Excel*. The reader is urged to download the *Excel* add-ins for these equations from the Web site; with the add-ins, functions are available for computing M_2, and the stagnation pressure, temperature, pressure, and density/velocity ratios, from M_1, and M_1 from these ratios. Appendix E-4 lists flow functions for M_2 and property ratios p_{0_2}/p_{0_1}, T_2/T_1, p_2/p_1, and ρ_2/ρ_1 (V_1/V_2) in terms of M_1 for normal-shock flow of an ideal gas. A table of values, as well as a plot of these property ratios, is presented for air ($k = 1.4$) for a limited range of Mach numbers. The associated *Excel* workbook, *Normal-Shock Relations*, can be used to print a larger table of values for air and other ideal gases.

A problem involving a normal shock is solved in Example 13.10.

EXAMPLE 13.10   Normal Shock in a Duct

A normal shock stands in a duct. The fluid is air, which may be considered an ideal gas. Properties upstream from the shock are $T_1 = 5°C$, $p_1 = 65.0$ kPa (abs), and $V_1 = 668$ m/s. Determine properties downstream and $s_2 - s_1$. Sketch the process on a *Ts* diagram.

GIVEN: Normal shock in a duct as shown:

$$T_1 = 5°C$$
$$P_1 = 65.0 \text{ kPa (abs)}$$
$$V_1 = 668 \text{ m/s}$$

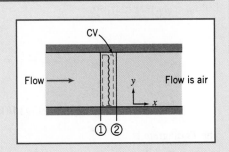

FIND: (a) Properties at section ②.
(b) $s_2 - s_1$.
(c) *Ts* diagram.

SOLUTION:
First compute the remaining properties at section ①. For an ideal gas,

$$\rho_1 = \frac{p_1}{RT_1} = 6.5 \times 10^4 \frac{\text{N}}{\text{m}^2} \times \frac{\text{kg} \cdot \text{K}}{287 \text{ N} \cdot \text{m}} \times \frac{1}{278} = 0.815 \text{ kg/m}^3$$

$$c_1 = \sqrt{kRT_1} = \left[1.4 \times 287 \frac{\text{N} \cdot \text{m}}{\text{kg} \cdot \text{K}} \times 278 \text{ K} \times \frac{\text{kg} \cdot \text{m}}{\text{N} \cdot \text{s}^2} \right]^{1/2} = 334 \text{ m/s}$$

Then

$$M_1 = \frac{V_1}{c_1} = \frac{668}{334} = 2.00, \text{ and (using isentropic stagnation relations, Eqs. 12.21b and 12.21a)}$$

$$T_{0_1} = T_1 \left(1 + \frac{k-1}{2} M_1^2 \right) = 278 \text{ K} \left[1 + 0.2(2.0)^2 \right] = 500 \text{ K}$$

$$p_{0_1} = p_1 \left(1 + \frac{k-1}{2} M_1^2 \right)^{k/(k-1)} = 65.0 \text{ kPa} \left[1 + 0.2(2.0)^2 \right]^{3.5} = 509 \text{ kPa (abs)}$$

From the normal-shock flow functions, Eqs. 13.41, at $M_1 = 2.0$,

M_1	M_2	p_{0_2}/p_{0_1}	T_2/T_1	p_2/p_1	V_2/V_1
2.00	0.5774	0.7209	1.687	4.500	0.3750

From these data

$$T_2 = 1.687T_1 = (1.687)278 \text{ K} = 469 \text{ K} \longleftarrow \qquad\qquad T_2$$

$$p_2 = 4.500p_1 = (4.500)65.0 \text{ kPa} = 293 \text{ kPa (abs)} \longleftarrow \qquad\qquad p_2$$

$$V_2 = 0.3750V_1 = (0.3750)668 \text{ m/s} = 251 \text{ m/s} \longleftarrow \qquad\qquad V_2$$

For an ideal gas,

$$\rho_2 = \frac{p_2}{RT_2} = \frac{2.93 \times 10^5 \text{ N}}{\text{m}^2} \times \frac{\text{kg} \cdot \text{K}}{287 \text{ N} \cdot \text{m}} \times \frac{1}{469 \text{ K}} = 2.18 \text{ kg/m}^3 \longleftarrow \qquad \rho_2$$

Stagnation temperature is constant in adiabatic flow. Thus

$$T_{0_2} = T_{0_1} = 500 \text{ K} \longleftarrow \qquad\qquad T_{0_2}$$

Using the property ratios for a normal shock, we obtain

$$p_{0_2} = p_{0_1}\frac{p_{0_2}}{p_{0_1}} = 509 \text{ kPa } (0.7209) = 367 \text{ kPa (abs)} \longleftarrow \qquad\qquad p_{0_2}$$

For the change in entropy (Eq. 13.32g),

$$s_2 - s_1 = c_p \ln \frac{T_2}{T_1} - R \ln \frac{p_2}{p_1}$$

But $s_{0_2} - s_{0_1} = s_2 - s_1$, so

$$s_{0_2} - s_{0_1} = s_2 - s_1 = c_p \ln \overset{=\,0}{\cancel{\frac{T_{0_2}}{T_{0_1}}}} - R \ln \frac{p_{0_2}}{p_{0_1}} = -0.287 \frac{\text{kJ}}{\text{kg} \cdot \text{K}} \times \ln(0.7209)$$

$$s_2 - s_1 = 0.0939 \text{ kJ/(kg} \cdot \text{K)} \longleftarrow \qquad\qquad s_2 - s_1$$

The Ts diagram is

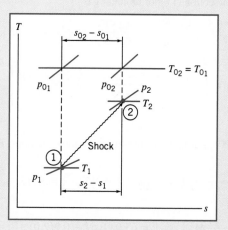

This problem illustrates the use of the normal shock relations, Eqs. 13.41, for analyzing flow of an ideal gas through a normal shock.

The *Excel* workbook for this Example is convenient for performing the calculations. (Alternatively, the normal shock relations *Excel* add-ins, available on the Web site, are useful for these calculations.)

13-6 SUPERSONIC CHANNEL FLOW WITH SHOCKS

Supersonic flow is a necessary condition for a normal shock to occur. The possibility of a normal shock must be considered in any supersonic flow. Sometimes a shock *must* occur to match a downstream pressure condition; it is desirable to determine if a shock will occur and the shock location when it does occur.

In Section 13-5 we showed that stagnation pressure decreases dramatically across a shock: The stronger the shock, the larger the decrease in stagnation pressure. It is necessary to control shock position to obtain acceptable performance from a supersonic diffuser or supersonic wind tunnel.

In this section isentropic flow in a converging-diverging nozzle (Section 13-2) is extended to include shocks. Additional topics (on the Web site) include operation of supersonic diffusers and supersonic wind tunnels, flows with friction, and flows with heat addition.

Flow in a Converging-Diverging Nozzle

Since we have considered normal shocks, we now can complete our discussion of flow in a converging-diverging nozzle operating under varying back pressures, begun in Section 13-2. The pressure distribution through a nozzle for different back pressures is shown in Fig. 13.20.

Four flow regimes are possible. In Regime I the flow is subsonic throughout. The flow rate increases with decreasing back pressure. At condition (*iii*), which forms the dividing line between Regimes I and II, flow at the throat is sonic, and $M_t = 1$.

As the back pressure is lowered below condition (*iii*), a normal shock appears downstream from the throat, as shown by condition (*vi*). There is a pressure rise across the shock. Since the flow is subsonic ($M < 1$) after the shock, the flow decelerates, with an accompanying increase in pressure, through the diverging channel. As the back pressure is lowered further, the shock moves downstream until it appears at the exit plane (condition *vii*). In Regime II, as in Regime I, the exit flow is subsonic, and consequently $p_e = p_b$. Since flow properties at the throat are constant for all conditions in Regime II, the flow rate in Regime II does not vary with back pressure.

In Regime III, as exemplified by condition (*viii*), the back pressure is higher than the exit pressure, but not high enough to sustain a normal shock in the exit plane. The flow adjusts to the back pressure through a series of oblique compression shocks outside the nozzle; these oblique shocks cannot be treated by one-dimensional theory.

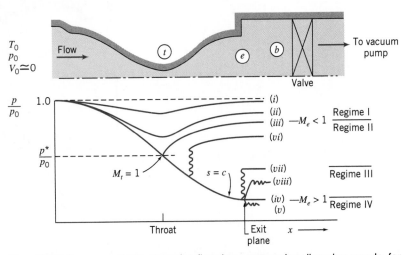

Fig. 13.20 Pressure distributions for flow in a converging-diverging nozzle for different back pressures.

As previously noted in Section 13-2, condition (*iv*) represents the design condition. In Regime IV the flow adjusts to the lower back pressure through a series of oblique expansion waves outside the nozzle; these oblique expansion waves cannot be treated by one-dimensional theory.

The *Ts* diagram for converging-diverging nozzle flow with a normal shock is shown in Fig. 13.21; state ① is located immediately upstream from the shock and state ② is immediately downstream. The entropy increase across the shock moves the subsonic downstream flow to a new isentropic line. The critical temperature is constant, so p_2^* is lower than p_1^*. Since $\rho^* = p^*/RT^*$, the critical density downstream also is reduced. To carry the same mass flow rate, the downstream flow must have a larger critical area. From continuity (and the equation of state), the critical area ratio is the inverse of the critical pressure ratio, i.e., across a shock, $p^*A^* = \text{constant}$.

If the Mach number (or position) of the normal shock in the nozzle is known, the exit-plane pressure can be calculated directly. In the more realistic situation, the exit-plane pressure is specified, and the position and strength of the shock are unknown. The subsonic flow downstream must leave the nozzle at the back pressure, so $p_b = p_e$. Then

$$\frac{p_b}{p_{0_1}} = \frac{p_e}{p_{0_1}} = \frac{p_e}{p_{0_2}}\frac{p_{0_2}}{p_{0_1}} = \frac{p_e}{p_{0_2}}\frac{A_1^*}{A_2^*} = \frac{p_e}{p_{0_2}}\frac{A_t}{A_e}\frac{A_e}{A_2^*} \qquad (13.42)$$

Because we have isentropic flow from state ② (after the shock) to the exit plane, $A_2^* = A_e^*$ and $p_{0_2} = p_{0_e}$. Then from Eq. 13.42 we can write

$$\frac{p_e}{p_{0_1}} = \frac{p_e}{p_{0_2}}\frac{A_t}{A_e}\frac{A_e}{A_2^*} = \frac{p_e}{p_{0_e}}\frac{A_t}{A_e}\frac{A_e}{A_e^*}$$

Rearranging,

$$\frac{p_e}{p_{0_1}}\frac{A_e}{A_t} = \frac{p_e}{p_{0_e}}\frac{A_e}{A_e^*} \qquad (13.43)$$

In Eq. 13.43 the left side contains known quantities, and the right side is a function of the exit Mach number M_e only. The pressure ratio is obtained from the stagnation pressure relation (Eq. 12.21a); the area ratio is obtained from the isentropic area

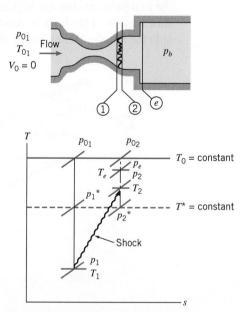

Fig. 13.21 Schematic *Ts* diagram for flow in a converging-diverging nozzle with a normal shock.

relation (Eq. 13.7d). Finding M_e from Eq. 13.43 usually requires iteration. (Problem 13.127 uses *Excel*'s *Solver* feature to perform the iteration.) The magnitude and location of the normal shock can be found once M_e is known by rearranging Eq. 13.43 (remembering that $p_{0_2} = p_{0_e}$),

$$\frac{p_{0_2}}{p_{0_1}} = \frac{A_t}{A_e} \frac{A_e}{A_e^*} \tag{13.44}$$

In Eq. 13.44 the right side is known (the first area ratio is given and the second is a function of M_e only), and the left side is a function of the Mach number before the shock, M_1, only (Eq. 13.41b). Hence, M_1 can be found. The area at which this shock occurs can then be found from the isentropic area relation (Eq. 13.7d, with $A^* = A_t$) for isentropic flow between the throat and state ①.

Supersonic Diffuser (on the Web)

13-7	## OBLIQUE SHOCKS AND EXPANSION WAVES

So far we have considered one-dimensional compressible flows. With the understanding we have developed, we are ready to introduce some basic concepts of two-dimensional flow: *oblique shocks* and *expansion waves*.

Oblique Shocks

In Section 12-2, we discussed the Mach cone, with Mach angle α, that is generated by an airplane flying at $M > 1$, as shown (in airplane coordinates) in Fig. 13.26a. The Mach cone is a weak pressure (sound) wave, so weak that, as shown in Fig. 13.26a, it barely disturbs the streamlines—it is the limiting case of an oblique shock. If we zoom in on the airplane, we see that at the nose of the airplane we have an oblique shock—a shock wave that is aligned, at some angle $\beta < 90°$, to the flow. This oblique shock causes the streamlines to abruptly change direction (usually to follow the surface of the airplane or the airplane's airfoil). Further away from the airplane we still have an oblique shock, but it becomes progressively weaker (β decreases) and the streamlines experience smaller deflections until, far away from the airplane the oblique shock becomes a Mach cone ($\beta \to \alpha$) and the streamlines are essentially unaffected by the airplane.

A supersonic airplane does not necessarily generate an oblique shock that is attached to its nose—we may instead have a detached normal shock ahead of the airplane! In fact, as illustrated in Fig. 13.27, as an airplane accelerates to its supersonic

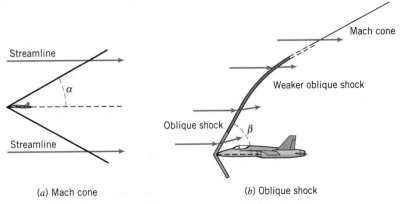

(a) Mach cone   (b) Oblique shock

Fig. 13.26 Mach cone and oblique shock generated by airplane.

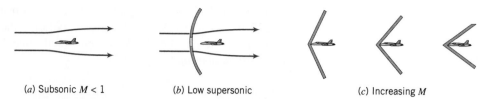

(a) Subsonic M < 1   (b) Low supersonic   (c) Increasing M

Fig. 13.27 Airplane flow patterns as speed increases.

cruising speed the flow will progress from subsonic, through supersonic with a detached normal shock, to attached oblique shocks that become increasingly "pressed" against the airplane's surface.

We can explain these flow phenomena using concepts we developed in our analysis of normal shocks. Consider the oblique shock shown in Fig. 13.28a. It is at some angle β with respect to the incoming supersonic flow, with velocity $\vec{V}_1$, and causes the flow to deflect at some angle θ, with velocity $\vec{V}_2$ after the shock.

It is convenient to orient the xy coordinates orthogonal to the oblique shock, and decompose $\vec{V}_1$ and $\vec{V}_2$ into components normal and tangential to the shock, as shown in Fig. 13.28b, with appropriate subscripts. The control volume is assumed to have arbitrary area A before and after the shock, and infinitesimal thickness across the shock (the upper and lower surfaces in Fig. 13.28b). For this infinitesimal control volume, we can write the basic equations: continuity, momentum, and the first and second laws of thermodynamics.

The continuity equation is

$$\frac{\partial}{\partial t}\overset{=\,0(1)}{\overbrace{\int_{CV}\rho\,dV}} + \int_{CS}\rho\vec{V}\cdot d\vec{A} = 0 \qquad (4.12)$$

Assumption: (1) Steady flow.

Then

$$(-\rho_1 V_{1_n} A) + (\rho_2 V_{2_n} A) = 0$$

(The tangential velocity components V_{1_t} and V_{2_t} flow through an infinitesimal area, so do not contribute to continuity.) Hence,

$$\rho_1 V_{1_n} = \rho_2 V_{2_n} \qquad (13.45a)$$

Next we consider the momentum equation for motion normal and tangential to the shock. We get an interesting result if we look first at the tangential, y component,

$$F_{S_y} + \overset{=\,0(2)}{\overbrace{F_{B_y}}} = \frac{\partial}{\partial t}\int_{CV}\overset{=\,0(1)}{\overbrace{V_y\,\rho\,dV}} + \int_{CS}V_y\,\rho\vec{V}\cdot d\vec{A} \qquad (4.18b)$$

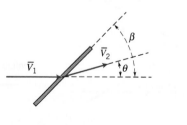

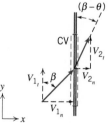

(a) Oblique shock   (b) Oblique shock in shock coordinates

Fig. 13.28 Oblique shock control volume.

Assumption: (2) Negligible body forces.

Then

$$0 = V_{1_t}(-\rho_1 V_{1_n} A) + V_{2_t}(\rho_2 V_{2_n} A)$$

or, using Eq. 13.45a

$$V_{1_t} = V_{2_t} = V_t$$

Hence, we have proved that *the oblique shock has no effect on the velocity component parallel to the shock* (a result that is perhaps not surprising). The momentum equation for the normal, x direction is

$$F_{S_x} + \cancelto{0(2)}{F_{B_x}} = \frac{\partial}{\partial t}\int_{CV} \cancelto{0(1)}{V_x}\,\rho\,d\forall + \int_{CS} V_x\,\rho\vec{V}\cdot d\vec{A} \qquad (4.18a)$$

For our control volume we obtain

$$p_1 A - p_2 A = V_{1_n}(-\rho_1 V_{1_n} A) + V_{2_n}(\rho_2 V_{2_n} A)$$

or, again using Eq. 13.45a,

$$p_1 + \rho_1 V_{1_n}^2 = p_2 + \rho_2 V_{2_n}^2 \qquad (13.45b)$$

The first law of thermodynamics is

$$\cancelto{0(4)}{\dot{Q}} - \cancelto{0(5)}{\dot{W}_s} - \cancelto{0(5)}{\dot{W}_{shear}} - \cancelto{0(5)}{\dot{W}_{other}} = \frac{\partial}{\partial t}\int_{CV} \cancelto{0(1)}{e}\,\rho\,d\forall + \int_{CS} (e + p\upsilon)\,\rho\vec{V}\cdot d\vec{A} \qquad (4.18a)$$

where

$$e = u + \frac{V^2}{2} + \cancelto{0(6)}{gz}$$

Assumptions: (4) Adiabatic flow.
                 (5) No work terms.
                 (6) Negligible gravitational effect.

For our control volume we obtain

$$0 = \left(u_1 + p_1\upsilon_1 + \frac{V_1^2}{2}\right)(-\rho_1 V_{1_n} A) + \left(u_2 + p_2\upsilon_2 + \frac{V_2^2}{2}\right)(\rho_2 V_{2_n} A)$$

(Remember that υ here represents the specific volume.) This can be simplified by using $h \equiv u + p\upsilon$, and continuity (Eq. 13.45a),

$$h_1 + \frac{V_1^2}{2} = h_2 + \frac{V_2^2}{2}$$

But each velocity can be replaced by its Pythagorean sum, so

$$h_1 + \frac{V_{1_n}^2 + V_{1_t}^2}{2} = h_2 + \frac{V_{2_n}^2 + V_{2_t}^2}{2}$$

We have already learned that the tangential velocity is constant, $V_{1_t} = V_{2_t} = V_t$, so the first law simplifies to

$$h_1 + \frac{V_{1_n}^2}{2} = h_2 + \frac{V_{2_n}^2}{2} \qquad (13.45c)$$

Finally, the second law of thermodynamics is

$$\overset{= \, 0(1)}{\frac{\partial}{\partial t} \int_{CV} s\rho \, d\forall} + \int_{CS} s\rho \vec{V} \cdot d\vec{A} \geq \overset{= \, 0(4)}{\int_{CS} \frac{1}{T} \left(\frac{\dot{Q}}{A} \right) dA} \tag{4.58}$$

The shock is irreversible, so Eq. 4.58 for our control volume is

$$s_1(-\rho_1 V_{1_n} A) + s_2(\rho_2 V_{2_n} A) > 0$$

and, again using continuity,

$$s_2 > s_1 \tag{13.45d}$$

The continuity and momentum equations, and the first and second laws of thermodynamics, for an oblique shock, are given by Eqs. 13.45a through 13.45d, respectively. Examination of these equations shows that they are *identical* to the corresponding equations for a normal shock, Eqs. 13.32a through 13.32d, except V_1 and V_2 are replaced with normal velocity components V_{1_n} and V_{2_n}, respectively! Hence, we can use all of the concepts and equations of Section 13-5 for normal shocks, as long as we replace the velocities with their normal components only. The normal velocity components are given by

$$V_{1_n} = V_1 \sin \beta \tag{13.46a}$$

and

$$V_{2_n} = V_2 \sin(\beta - \theta) \tag{13.46b}$$

The corresponding Mach numbers are

$$M_{1_n} = \frac{V_{1_n}}{c_1} = M_1 \sin \beta \tag{13.47a}$$

and

$$M_{2_n} = \frac{V_{2_n}}{c_2} = M_2 \sin(\beta - \theta) \tag{13.47b}$$

The oblique shock equations for an ideal gas with constant specific heats are obtained directly from Eqs. 13.41:

$$M_{2_n}^2 = \frac{M_{1_n}^2 + \dfrac{2}{k-1}}{\dfrac{2k}{k-1} M_{1_n}^2 - 1} \tag{13.48a}$$

$$\frac{p_{0_2}}{p_{0_1}} = \frac{\left[\dfrac{\dfrac{k+1}{2} M_{1_n}^2}{1 + \dfrac{k-1}{2} M_{1_n}^2} \right]^{k/(k-1)}}{\left[\dfrac{2k}{k+1} M_{1_n}^2 - \dfrac{k-1}{k+1} \right]^{1/(k-1)}} \tag{13.48b}$$

$$\frac{T_2}{T_1} = \frac{\left(1 + \dfrac{k-1}{2} M_{1_n}^2 \right) \left(k M_{1_n}^2 - \dfrac{k-1}{2} \right)}{\left(\dfrac{k+1}{2} \right)^2 M_{1_n}^2} \tag{13.48c}$$

$$\frac{p_2}{p_1} = \frac{2k}{k+1} M_{1_n}^2 - \frac{k-1}{k+1} \tag{13.48d}$$

$$\frac{\rho_2}{\rho_1} = \frac{V_{1_n}}{V_{2_n}} = \frac{\dfrac{k+1}{2} M_{1_n}^2}{1 + \dfrac{k-1}{2} M_{1_n}^2} \tag{13.48e}$$

Equations 13.48, along with Eqs. 13.46 and 13.47, can be used to analyze oblique shock problems. Appendix E-5 lists flow functions for M_{2_n} and property ratios p_{0_2}/p_{0_1}, T_2/T_1, p_2/p_1, and ρ_2/ρ_1 (V_1/V_2) in terms of M_{1_n} for oblique-shock flow of an ideal gas. A table of values of these property ratios is presented for air ($k = 1.4$) for a limited range of Mach numbers. The associated *Excel* workbook, *Oblique-Shock Relations*, can be used to print a larger table of values for air and other ideal gases. In essence, as demonstrated in Example 13.11, an oblique shock problem can be analyzed as an equivalent normal shock problem. The reader is urged to download the normal shock *Excel* add-ins from the Web site; they apply to these equations as well as Eqs. 13. 41 for a normal shock.

EXAMPLE 13.11   Comparison of Normal and Oblique Shocks

Air at $-2°C$ and 100 kPa is traveling at a speed of 1650 m/s. Find the pressure, temperature, and speed after the air experiences a normal shock. Compare with the pressure, temperature, and speed (and find the deflection angle θ) if the air instead experiences an oblique shock at angle $\beta = 30°$.

GIVEN: Air flow with:

$$p_1 = 100 \, \text{kPa}$$
$$T_1 = -2°C$$
$$V_1 = 1650 \, \text{m/s}$$

FIND: Downstream pressure, temperature, and speed if it experiences (a) a normal shock and (b) an oblique shock at angle $\beta = 30°$. Also find the deflection angle θ.

SOLUTION:

(a) Normal shock

First compute the speed of sound,

$$c_1 = \sqrt{kRT_1} = \sqrt{1.4 \times 287 \, \frac{\text{N} \cdot \text{m}}{\text{kg} \cdot \text{K}} \times 271 \, \text{K} \times \frac{\text{kg} \cdot \text{m}}{\text{s}^2 \cdot \text{N}}} = 330 \, \text{m/s}$$

Then the upstream Mach number is

$$M_1 = \frac{V_1}{c_1} = \frac{1650 \, \text{m/s}}{330 \, \text{m/s}} = 5.0$$

From the normal-shock flow functions, Eqs. 13.41, at $M_1 = 5.0$

M_1	M_2	p_2/p_1	T_2/T_1	V_2/V_1
5.0	0.4152	29.00	5.800	0.2000

From these data

$$T_2 = 5.800 T_1 = (5.800)271 \, \text{K} = 1572 \, \text{K} = 1299°C \quad \longleftarrow \quad T_2$$
$$p_2 = 29.00 p_1 = (29.00)100 \, \text{kPa} = 2.9 \, \text{MPa} \quad \longleftarrow \quad p_2$$
$$V_2 = 0.200 V_1 = (0.200)1650 \, \text{m/s} = 330 \, \text{m/s} \quad \longleftarrow \quad V_2$$

(b) Oblique shock

First compute the normal and tangential components of velocity,

$$V_{1_n} = V_1 \sin \beta = 1650 \text{ m/s} \times \sin 30° = 825 \text{ m/s}$$
$$V_{1_t} = V_1 \cos \beta = 1650 \text{ m/s} \times \cos 30° = 1429 \text{ m/s}$$

Then the upstream *normal* Mach number is

$$M_{1_n} = \frac{V_{1_n}}{c_1} = \frac{825 \text{ m/s}}{330 \text{ m/s}} = 2.5$$

From the oblique-shock flow functions, Eqs. 13.48, at $M_{1_n} = 2.5$

M_{1_n}	M_{2_n}	p_2/p_1	T_2/T_1	V_{2_n}/V_{1_n}
2.5	0.5130	7.125	2.138	0.300

From these data

$$T_2 = 2.138 T_1 = (2.138)271 \text{ K} = 579 \text{ K} = 306°\text{C} \longleftarrow \qquad T_2$$
$$p_2 = 7.125 p_1 = (7.125)100 \text{ kPa} = 712.5 \text{ kPa} \longleftarrow \qquad p_2$$
$$V_{2_n} = 0.300 V_{1_n} = (0.300)825 \text{ m/s} = 247.5 \text{ m/s}$$
$$V_{2_t} = V_{1_t} = 1429 \text{ m/s} \longleftarrow \qquad V_2$$

The downstream velocity is given by the Pythagorean sum of the velocity components,

$$V_2 = \sqrt{(V_{2_n}^2 + V_{2_t}^2)} = \sqrt{(247.5^2 + 1429^2)} \text{ m/s} = 1450 \text{ m/s}$$

Note that

$$c_2 = \sqrt{kRT_2} = \sqrt{1.4 \times 287 \frac{\text{N} \cdot \text{m}}{\text{kg} \cdot \text{K}} \times 579 \text{ K} \times \frac{\text{kg} \cdot \text{m}}{\text{s}^2 \cdot \text{N}}} = 482 \text{ m/s}$$

so that the downstream Mach number is

$$M_2 = \frac{V_2}{c_2} = \frac{1450 \text{ m/s}}{482 \text{ m/s}} = 3.01$$

Although the downstream normal Mach number must be subsonic, the actual downstream Mach number could be subsonic or supersonic (as in this case).

The deflection angle can be obtained from Eq. 13.46b

$$V_{2_n} = V_2 \sin(\beta - \theta)$$

or

$$\theta = \beta - \sin^{-1}\left(\frac{V_{2_n}}{V_2}\right) = 30° - \sin^{-1}\left(\frac{247.5}{1450}\right) = 30° - 9.8° = 20.2° \longleftarrow \qquad \theta$$

This Example illustrates:
- ✓ That an oblique shock involves deflection of the flow through angle θ.
- ✓ Use of normal shock functions for solution of oblique shock problems.
- ✓ The important result that for a given supersonic flow an oblique shock will always be weaker than a normal shock, because $M_{1_n} < M_1$.
- ✓ That while $M_{2_n} < 1$ always, M_2 can be subsonic or supersonic (as in this case).
- The *Excel* workbook for oblique shocks is convenient for performing these calculations. (Alternatively, the normal shock relations *Excel* add-ins, available on the Web site, are useful for these calculations.)

We can gain further insight into oblique shock behavior by combining some of our earlier equations to relate the deflection angle θ, the Mach number M_1, and the shock angle β. From the oblique shock geometry of Fig. 13.28b,

$$\frac{V_{1_n}}{V_{2_n}} = \frac{V_{1_t} \tan \beta}{V_{2_t} \tan(\beta - \theta)} = \frac{\tan \beta}{\tan(\beta - \theta)}$$

We can also relate the two normal velocities from Eq. 13.48e,

$$\frac{V_{1_n}}{V_{2_n}} = \frac{\dfrac{k+1}{2} M_{1_n}^2}{1 + \dfrac{k-1}{2} M_{1_n}^2} \tag{13.48e}$$

Equating the two expressions for the normal velocity ratio, we have

$$\frac{V_{1_n}}{V_{2_n}} = \frac{\tan \beta}{\tan(\beta - \theta)} = \frac{\dfrac{k+1}{2} M_{1_n}^2}{1 + \dfrac{k-1}{2} M_{1_n}^2}$$

and

$$\tan(\beta - \theta) = \frac{\tan \beta}{\dfrac{(k+1)}{2} M_{1_n}^2} \left(1 + \frac{k-1}{2} M_{1_n}^2\right)$$

Finally, if we use $M_{1_n} = M_1 \sin \beta$ in this expression and further simplify, we obtain (after using a trigonometric identity and more algebra)

$$\tan \theta = \frac{2 \cot \beta (M_1^2 \sin^2 \beta - 1)}{M_1^2(k + \cos 2\beta) + 2} \tag{13.49}$$

Equation 13.49 relates the deflection angle θ to the incoming Mach number M_1 and the oblique shock angle β. For a given Mach number, we can compute θ as a function of β, as shown in Fig. 13.29 for air ($k = 1.4$).

Appendix E-5 presents a table of values of deflection angle θ as a function of Mach number M_1 and oblique shock angle β for air ($k = 1.4$) for a limited range of Mach numbers. The associated *Excel* workbook, *Oblique-Shock Relations*, can be

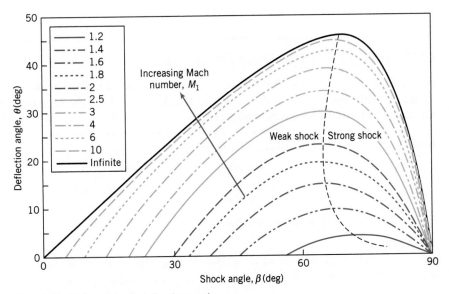

Fig. 13.29 Oblique shock deflection angle.

used to print a larger table of values for air and other ideal gases. The reader is urged to download the oblique shock *Excel* add-in from the Web site; it can be used for solving Eq. 13.49 for the deflection angle θ, oblique shock β, or M_1.

We should note that we used M_1 and shock angle β to compute θ, but in reality the causality is the reverse: it is the deflection θ caused by an object such as the surface of an airplane wing that causes an oblique shock at angle β. We can draw some interesting conclusions from Fig. 13.29:

✓ For a given Mach number and deflection angle, there are generally *two* possible oblique shock angles—we could generate a weak shock (smaller β value, and hence, smaller normal Mach number, M_{1_n}) or a strong shock (larger β value, and hence, larger normal Mach number). In most cases the weak shock appears (exceptions include situations where the downstream pressure is forced to take on a large value as caused by, for example, an obstruction).

✓ For a given Mach number, there is a maximum deflection angle. For example, for air ($k = 1.4$), if $M_1 = 3$, the maximum deflection angle is $\theta_{max} \approx 34°$. Any attempt to deflect the flow at an angle $\theta > \theta_{max}$ would cause a detached normal shock to form instead of an oblique shock.

✓ For zero deflection ($\theta \to 0$), the weak shock becomes a Mach wave and $\beta \to \alpha = \sin^{-1}(1/M_1)$.

Figure 13.29 can be used to explain the phenomena shown in Fig. 13.27. If an airplane (or airplane wing), causing deflection θ, accelerates from subsonic through supersonic speed, we can plot the airplane's progress on Fig. 13.29 as a horizontal line from right to left, through lines of increasing Mach number. For example, for $\theta = 10°$, we obtain the following results: As M_1 increases from subsonic through about 1.4 there is no oblique shock solution—we instead either have no shock (subsonic flow) or a detached normal shock; at some Mach number the normal shock first attaches and becomes an oblique shock (Problem 13.143 shows that for $\theta = 10°$, the normal shock first attaches and becomes oblique at $M_1 \approx 1.42$, with $\beta \approx 67°$); as M_1 increases from 1.6 through 1.8, 2.0, 2.5, etc., toward infinity, from Fig. 13.29, $\beta \approx 51°$, 44°, 39°, 32°, toward 12°, respectively—the oblique shock angle progressively decreases, as we saw in Fig. 13.27.

A problem involving oblique shocks is solved in Example 13.12.

EXAMPLE 13.12   Oblique Shocks on an Airfoil

An airplane travels at a speed of 600 m/s in air at 4°C and 100 kPa. The airplane's airfoil has a sharp leading edge with included angle $\delta = 6°$, and an angle of attack $\alpha = 1°$. Find the pressures on the upper and lower surfaces of the airfoil immediately after the leading edge.

GIVEN: Air flow over sharp leading edge with:

$$p_1 = 100 \text{ kPa} \qquad \delta = 6°$$
$$T_1 = 4°C \qquad \alpha = 1°$$
$$V_1 = 600 \text{ m/s}$$

FIND: Pressure on upper and lower surfaces.

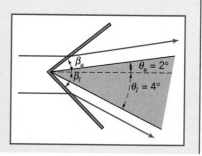

SOLUTION:

For an angle of attack of 1° of an airfoil with leading edge angle 6°, the deflection angles are $\theta_u = 2°$ and $\theta_l = 4°$ as shown.

(a) Upper surface

First compute the speed of sound,

$$c_1 = \sqrt{kRT_1} = \sqrt{1.4 \times 287 \frac{\text{N} \cdot \text{m}}{\text{kg} \cdot \text{K}} \times 277 \text{ K} \times \frac{\text{kg} \cdot \text{m}}{\text{s}^2 \cdot \text{N}}} = 334 \text{ m/s}$$

Then the upstream Mach number is

$$M_1 = \frac{V_1}{c_1} = \frac{600 \text{ m/s}}{334 \text{ m/s}} = 1.80$$

For $M_1 = 1.80$ and $\theta_u = 2°$, we obtain β_u from

$$\tan \theta_u = \frac{2 \cot \beta_u (M_1^2 \sin^2 \beta_u - 1)}{M_1^2 (k + \cos 2\beta_u) + 2} \tag{13.49}$$

This can be solved for β_u using manual iteration or interpolation, or by using, for example, *Excel*'s *Goal Seek* function,

$$\beta_u = 35.5°$$

Then we can find $M_{1_{n(\text{upper})}}$,

$$M_{1_{n(\text{upper})}} = M_1 \sin \beta_u = 1.80 \times \sin 35.5° = 1.045$$

The normal Mach number for the upper oblique shock is close to one—the shock is quite weak.

From the oblique-shock pressure ratio, Eqs. 13.48d, at $M_{1_{n(\text{upper})}} = 1.045$,

$$\frac{p_{2(\text{upper})}}{p_1} = \frac{2k}{k+1} M_{1_{n(\text{upper})}}^2 - \frac{k-1}{k+1} = \frac{2 \times 1.4}{(1.4+1)} (1.045)^2 - \frac{(1.4-1)}{(1.4+1)} = 1.11$$

Hence,

$$p_{2(\text{upper})} = 1.11 \, p_1 = (1.11)100 \text{ kPa} = 111 \text{ kPa} \qquad \longleftarrow \qquad p_{2(\text{upper})}$$

(b) Lower surface

For $M_1 = 1.80$ and $\theta_l = 4°$, we obtain β_l from

$$\tan \theta_l = \frac{2 \cot \beta_l (M_1^2 \sin^2 \beta_l - 1)}{M_1^2 (k + \cos 2\beta_l) + 2} \tag{13.49}$$

and find

$$\beta_l = 37.4°$$

Then we can find $M_{1_{n(\text{lower})}}$,

$$M_{l_{n(\text{lower})}} = M_1 \sin \beta_l = 1.80 \times \sin 37.4° = 1.093$$

The normal Mach number for the lower oblique shock is also close to one.

From the oblique-shock pressure ratio, Eq. 13.48d, at $M_{l_{n(\text{lower})}} = 1.093$,

$$\frac{p_{2(\text{lower})}}{p_1} = \frac{2k}{k+1} M_{1_{n(\text{lower})}}^2 - \frac{k-1}{k+1} = \frac{2 \times 1.4}{(1.4+1)} (1.093)^2 - \frac{(1.4-1)}{(1.4+1)} = 1.23$$

Hence,

$$p_{2(\text{lower})} = 1.23 \, p_1 = (1.23)100 \text{ kPa} = 123 \text{ kPa} \qquad \longleftarrow \qquad p_{2(\text{lower})}$$

This Example illustrates the use of Eq. 13.49 for obtaining oblique shock data from the flow deflection.

The *Excel* workbook for oblique shocks is convenient for performing these calculations. (Alternatively, the normal shock relations and oblique shock relations *Excel* add-ins, available on the Web site, are useful for these calculations.)

Isentropic Expansion Waves

Oblique shock waves occur when a flow is suddenly compressed as it is deflected. We can ask ourselves what happens if we *gradually* redirect a supersonic flow, for example, along a curved surface. The answer is that we may generate *isentropic compression or expansion waves*, as illustrated schematically in Figs. 13.30a and 13.30b, respectively. From Fig. 13.30a we see that a series of compression waves will eventually converge, and their cumulative effect will eventually generate an oblique shock not far from the curved surface. While compression waves do occur, they are not of great interest because the oblique shocks they lead to usually dominate the aerodynamics—at most the waves are a local phenomenon. On the other hand, as shown in Fig. 13.30b, expansion waves in series are divergent and so do not coalesce. Figure 13.30c shows expansion around a sharp-edged corner.

We wish to analyze these isentropic waves to obtain a relation between the deflection angle and the Mach number. First we note that each wave is a Mach wave, so is at angle $\alpha = \sin^{-1}(1/M)$, where M is the Mach number immediately before the wave. Compression waves are convergent because the wave angle α increases as the Mach number decreases. On the other hand, expansion waves are divergent because as the flow expands the Mach number increases, decreasing the Mach angle.

Consider an isentropic wave as shown in Fig. 13.31a. (It happens to be a compression wave, but the analysis that follows applies to both expansion and compression waves.) The speed changes from V to $V + dV$, with deflection $d\theta$. As with the oblique shock analysis for Fig. 13.28a, it is convenient to orient the xy coordinates orthogonal to the wave, as shown in Fig. 13.31b. For this infinitesimal control volume, we can write the basic equations (continuity, momentum, and the first and second laws of thermodynamics). Comparing the isentropic wave control volume of Fig. 13.31b to the control volume for an oblique shock shown in Fig. 13.28, we see that the control volumes have similar features. However, an isentropic wave differs from an oblique shock wave in two important ways:

✓ The wave angle is $\alpha = \sin^{-1}(1/M)$, instead of angle β for the oblique shock.
✓ The changes in velocity and in density, pressure, etc., and the deflection angle, are all infinitesimals.

The second factor is the reason that the flow, which is adiabatic, is isentropic.

With these two differences in mind we repeat the analysis that we performed for the oblique shock. The continuity equation is

$$\frac{\partial}{\partial t} \overset{= 0(1)}{\cancel{\int\!\!\!\int_{CV} \rho \, d\cancel{V}}} + \int_{CS} \rho \vec{V} \cdot d\vec{A} = 0 \qquad (4.12)$$

Assumption: (1) Steady flow.

Then

$$\{-\rho V \sin \alpha \, A\} + \{(\rho + d\rho)(V + dV) \sin(\alpha - d\theta)A\} = 0$$

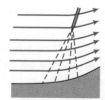  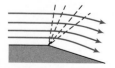

(a) Isentropic compression waves   (b) Isentropic expansion waves   (c) Isentropic expansion at a corner

Fig. 13.30 Isentropic compression and expansion waves.

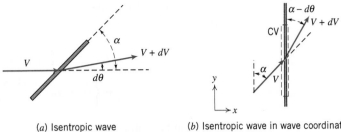

(a) Isentropic wave   (b) Isentropic wave in wave coordinates

Fig. 13.31 Isentropic wave control volume.

or

$$\rho V \sin \alpha = (\rho + d\rho)(V + dV) \sin(\alpha - d\theta) \qquad (13.50)$$

Next we consider the momentum equation for motion normal and tangent to the wave. We look first at the tangential, y component

$$F_{S_y} + \cancel{F_{B_y}}^{= 0(2)} = \cancel{\frac{\partial}{\partial t} \int_{CV} V_y \, \rho \, d\Psi}^{= 0(1)} + \int_{CS} u \, V_y \, \rho \vec{V} \cdot d\vec{A} \qquad (4.18b)$$

Assumption: (2) Negligible body forces.

Then

$$0 = V \cos \alpha \{ -\rho V \sin \alpha A \} + (V + dV) \cos(\alpha - d\theta) \{ (\rho + d\theta)(V + dV) \sin(\alpha - d\theta)A \}$$

or, using continuity (Eq. 13.50),

$$V \cos \alpha = (V + dV) \cos(\alpha - d\theta)$$

Expanding and simplifying [using the facts that, to first order, in the limit as $d\theta \to 0$, $\cos(d\theta) \to 1$, and $\sin(d\theta) \to d\theta$], we obtain

$$d\theta = -\frac{dV}{V \tan \alpha}$$

But $\sin \alpha = 1/M$, so $\tan \alpha = 1/\sqrt{M^2 - 1}$, and

$$d\theta = -\sqrt{M^2 - 1} \, \frac{dV}{V} \qquad (13.51)$$

We skip the analysis of the normal, x component of momentum, and move on to the first law of thermodynamics, which is

$$\cancel{\dot{Q}}^{=0(4)} - \cancel{\dot{W}_s}^{=0(5)} - \cancel{\dot{W}_{shear}}^{=0(5)} - \cancel{\dot{W}_{other}}^{=0(5)} = \cancel{\frac{\partial}{\partial t} \int_{CV} e \, \rho \, d\Psi}^{=0(1)} + \int_{CS} (e + pv)\rho\vec{V} \cdot d\vec{A} \quad (4.18a)$$

where

$$e = u + \frac{V^2}{2} + \cancel{gz}^{=0(6)}$$

Assumptions: (4) Adiabatic flow.
                      (5) No work terms.
                      (6) Negligible gravitational effect.

For our control volume we obtain (using $h \equiv u + pv$, where v represents the specific volume)

$$0 = \left\{ h + \frac{V^2}{2} \right\} \{ -\rho V \sin \alpha A \}$$
$$+ \left\{ (h + dh) + \frac{(V + dV)^2}{2} \right\} \{ (\rho + d\rho)(V + dV) \sin(\alpha - d\theta) A \}$$

This can be simplified, using continuity (Eq. 13.50), to

$$h + \frac{V^2}{2} = (h + dh) + \frac{(V + dV)^2}{2}$$

Expanding and simplifying, in the limit to first order, we obtain

$$dh = -V\, dV$$

If we confine ourselves to ideal gases, $dh = c_p\, dT$, so

$$c_p\, dT = -V\, dV \qquad (13.52)$$

Equation 13.52 relates differential changes in temperature and velocity. We can obtain a relation between M and V using $V = Mc = M\sqrt{kRT}$. Differentiating (and dividing the left side by V and the right by $M\sqrt{kRT}$),

$$\frac{dV}{V} = \frac{dM}{M} + \frac{1}{2}\frac{dT}{T}$$

Eliminating dT using Eq. 13.52,

$$\frac{dV}{V} = \frac{dM}{M} - \frac{1}{2}\frac{V\, dV}{c_p T} = \frac{dM}{M} - \frac{1}{2}\frac{dV}{V}\left(\frac{V^2}{c_p T}\right) = \frac{dM}{M} - \frac{1}{2}\frac{dV}{V}\left(\frac{M^2 c^2}{c_p T}\right)$$

$$\frac{dV}{V} = \frac{dM}{M} - \frac{1}{2}\frac{dV}{V}\left(\frac{M^2 kRT}{c_p T}\right) = \frac{dM}{M} - \frac{1}{2}\frac{dV}{V}M^2 (k - 1)$$

Hence,

$$\frac{dV}{V} = \frac{2}{2 + M^2(k - 1)}\frac{dM}{M} \qquad (13.53)$$

Finally, combining Eqs. 13.51 and 13.53,

$$d\theta = -\frac{2\sqrt{M^2 - 1}}{2 + M^2(k - 1)}\frac{dM}{M} \qquad (13.54)$$

We will generally apply Eq. 13.54 to expansion waves, for which $d\theta$ is negative, so it is convenient to change variables, $d\omega \equiv -d\theta$. Equation 13.54 relates the differential change in Mach number through an isentropic wave to the deflection angle. We can integrate this to obtain the deflection as a function of Mach number, to within a constant of integration. We *could* integrate Eq. 13.54 between the initial and final Mach numbers of a given flow, but it will be more convenient to integrate from a reference state, the critical speed ($M = 1$) to Mach number M, with ω arbitrarily set to zero at $M = 1$,

$$\int_0^\omega d\omega = \int_1^M \frac{2\sqrt{M^2 - 1}}{2 + M^2(k - 1)}\frac{dM}{M}$$

leading to the *Prandtl-Meyer supersonic expansion function*,

$$\omega = \sqrt{\frac{k + 1}{k - 1}} \tan^{-1}\left(\sqrt{\frac{k - 1}{k + 1}(M^2 - 1)} \right) - \tan^{-1}(\sqrt{M^2 - 1}) \qquad (13.55)$$

We use Eq. 13.55 to relate the total deflection caused by isentropic expansion from M_1 to M_2,

$$\text{Deflection} = \omega_2 - \omega_1 = \omega(M_2) - \omega(M_1)$$

Appendix E-6 presents a table of values of the *Prandtl-Meyer supersonic expansion function*, ω, as a function of Mach number M for air ($k = 1.4$) for a limited range of Mach numbers. The associated *Excel* workbook, *Isentropic Expansion Wave Relations*, can be used to print a larger table of values for air and other ideal gases. The reader is urged to download the isentropic expansion wave relations *Excel* add-in from the Web site; it can be used for solving Eq. 13.55 for the Prandtl-Meyer expansion function ω, or M.

We have already indicated that the flow is isentropic. We can verify this by using the second law of thermodynamics,

$$\underbrace{\frac{\partial}{\partial t} \int_{CV} s\,\rho\,d\Psi}_{= 0(1)} + \int_{CS} s\,\rho\,\vec{V} \cdot d\vec{A} \geq \underbrace{\int_{CS} \frac{1}{T}\left(\frac{Q}{A}\right) dA}_{= 0(4)} \qquad (4.58)$$

The wave is reversible, so Eq. 4.58 for our control volume is

$$s\{-\rho V \sin \alpha\, A\} + (s + ds)\{(\rho + d\rho)(V + dV)\sin(\alpha - d\theta)A\} = 0$$

and using continuity (Eq. 13.50), this reduces to

$$ds = 0$$

The flow is demonstrated to be isentropic. Hence, stagnation properties are constant and the local isentropic stagnation property equations (Section 12-3) will be useful here.

$$\frac{p_0}{p} = \left[1 + \frac{k-1}{2} M^2\right]^{k/(k-1)} \qquad (12.21a)$$

$$\frac{T_0}{T} = 1 + \frac{k-1}{2} M^2 \qquad (12.21b)$$

$$\frac{\rho_0}{\rho} = \left[1 + \frac{k-1}{2} M^2\right]^{1/(k-1)} \qquad (12.21c)$$

Equation 13.55, together with Eqs. 12.21a through 12.21c, can be used for analyzing isentropic expansion or compression waves. (We never got around to deriving the normal component of momentum—the above analysis provides a complete set of equations.) A problem involving expansion waves is solved in Example 13.13.

EXAMPLE 13.13   Expansion Wave on an Airfoil

The airplane of Example 13.12 (speed of 600 m/s in air at 4°C and 100 kPa, with a sharp leading edge with included angle $\delta = 6°$) now has an angle of attack $\alpha = 6°$. Find the pressures on the upper and lower surfaces of the airfoil immediately after the leading edge.

GIVEN: Air flow over sharp leading edge with:

$p_1 = 100$ kPa $\delta = 6°$
$T_1 = 4°C$ $\alpha = 6°$
$V_1 = 600$ m/s

FIND: Pressures on upper and lower surfaces.

SOLUTION:

For an angle of attack of $6°$ of an airfoil with leading edge angle $6°$, the deflection angles are $\theta_u = 3°$ and $\theta_l = 9°$ as shown.

(a) Upper surface—isentropic expansion

First compute the speed of sound,

$$c_1 = \sqrt{kRT_1} = \sqrt{1.4 \times 287 \frac{\text{N} \cdot \text{m}}{\text{kg} \cdot \text{K}} \times 277 \text{ K} \times \frac{\text{kg} \cdot \text{m}}{\text{s}^2 \cdot \text{N}}} = 334 \text{ m/s}$$

Then the upstream Mach number is

$$M_1 = \frac{V_1}{c_1} = \frac{600 \text{ m/s}}{334 \text{ m/s}} = 1.80$$

For $M_1 = 1.80$, the Prandtl-Meyer function ω_1 is obtained from

$$\omega_1 = \sqrt{\frac{k+1}{k-1}} \tan^{-1}\left(\sqrt{\frac{k-1}{k+1}(M_1^2 - 1)}\right) - \tan^{-1}\left(\sqrt{M_1^2 - 1}\right) \quad (13.55)$$

so

$$\omega_1 = \sqrt{\frac{1.4+1}{1.4-1}} \tan^{-1}\left(\sqrt{\frac{1.4-1}{1.4+1}(1.80^2 - 1)}\right) - \tan^{-1}\left(\sqrt{1.80^2 - 1}\right) = 20.7°$$

The Prandtl-Meyer function value on the upper surface, ω_u, is then

$$\omega_u = \omega_1 + \theta_u = 20.7° + 3° = 23.7°$$

For this Prandtl-Meyer function value, $M_{2(\text{upper})}$ is obtained from Eq. 13.55:

$$\omega_u = \sqrt{\frac{k+1}{k-1}} \tan^{-1}\left(\sqrt{\frac{k-1}{k+1}(M_{2(\text{upper})}^2 - 1)}\right) - \tan^{-1}\left(\sqrt{(M_{2(\text{upper})}^2 - 1)}\right)$$

This can be solved using manual iteration or interpolation, or by using, for example, *Excel*'s *Goal Seek* function,

$$M_{2(\text{upper})} = 1.90$$

Finally, we can find $p_{2(\text{upper})}$ from repeated use of Eq. 12.21a,

$$p_{2(\text{upper})} = \frac{p_{2(\text{upper})}}{p_0} \frac{p_0}{p_1} p_1 = \left\{\left[1 + \frac{k-1}{2}M_1^2\right]^{k/(k-1)} \middle/ \left[1 + \frac{k-1}{2}M_{2(\text{upper})}^2\right]^{k/(k-1)}\right\} p_1$$

$$= \{[1 + (0.2)1.80^2]^{3.5} / [1 + (0.2)1.90^2]^{3.5}\} \times 100 \text{ kPa}$$

so

$$p_{2(\text{upper})} = 85.8 \text{ kPa} \quad\longleftarrow\quad \underline{\hspace{4cm}} \quad p_{2(\text{upper})}$$

(b) Lower surface—oblique shock

For $M_1 = 1.80$ and $\theta_1 = 9°$, we obtain β_l from

$$\tan \theta_l = \frac{2 \cot \beta_l (M_1^2 \sin^2 \beta_l - 1)}{M_1^2(k + \cos 2\beta_l) + 2} \quad (13.49)$$

and find

$$\beta_l = 42.8°$$

Then we can find $M_{1_{n(\text{lower})}}$,

$$M_{1_{n(\text{lower})}} = M_1 \sin \beta_l = 1.80 \times \sin 42.8° = 1.223$$

From the oblique-shock pressure ratio, Eq. 13.48d, at $M_{1_{n(\text{upper})}} = 1.223$,

$$\frac{p_{2(\text{lower})}}{p_1} = \frac{2k}{k+1}M_{1_{n(\text{lower})}}^2 - \frac{k-1}{k+1} = \frac{2 \times 1.4}{(1.4+1)}(1.223)^2 - \frac{(1.4-1)}{(1.4+1)} = 1.58$$

Hence,

$$p_{2_{(lower)}} = 1.58 p_1 = (1.58)100 \text{ kPa} = 158 \text{ kPa} \quad \longleftarrow \qquad \overline{\quad p_{2_{(lower)}} \quad}$$

> This Example illustrates the use of Eq. 13.55 and the isentropic stagnation relations for analysis of isentropic expansion waves and the use of Eq. 13.49 for an oblique shock.
>
> The *Excel* workbooks for isentropic expansion waves and oblique shocks are convenient for performing these calculations. (Alternatively, the normal and oblique shock relations, and the isentropic expansion wave *Excel* add-ins, available on the Web site, are useful for these calculations.)

Example 13.13 hints at the approach we can use to obtain lift and drag coefficients of a supersonic wing, illustrated in Example 13.14.

EXAMPLE 13.14 Lift and Drag Coefficients of a Supersonic Airfoil

The airplane of Example 13.13 has a symmetric diamond cross section (sharp leading and trailing edges of angle $\delta = 6°$). For a speed of 600 m/s in air at 4°C and 100 kPa, find the pressure distribution on the upper and lower surfaces, and the lift and drag coefficients for an angle of attack of $\alpha = 6°$.

GIVEN: Air flow over symmetric section shown with:

$$p_1 = 100 \text{ kPa} \qquad \delta = 6°$$
$$T_1 = 4°C \qquad \alpha = 6°$$
$$V_1 = 600 \text{ m/s}$$

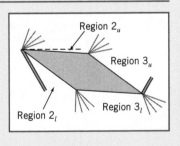

FIND: Pressure distribution, and lift and drag coefficients.

SOLUTION:
We first need to obtain the pressures on the four surfaces of the airfoil. We have already obtained in Example 13.13 the data for Region 2_u and Region 2_l:

$$M_{2_{(upper)}} = 1.90 \qquad p_{2_{(upper)}} = 85.8 \text{ kPa} \quad \longleftarrow \qquad \overline{\quad p_{2_{(upper)}} \quad}$$
$$M_{2_{(lower)}} = 1.489 \qquad p_{2_{(lower)}} = 158 \text{ kPa} \quad \longleftarrow \qquad \overline{\quad p_{2_{(lower)}} \quad}$$

(Note that $M_{2_{(lower)}} = 1.489$ is obtained from $M_{1_n} = 1.223$ in Example 13.13 by direct use of Eqs. 13.48a and 13.47b.) In addition, for Region 2_u, we found the Prandtl-Meyer function to be 23.7°. Hence, for Region 3_u, we can find the value of the Prandtl-Meyer function from the deflection angle. For 6° leading- and trailing-edges, the airfoil angles at the upper and lower surfaces are each 174°. Hence, at the upper and lower surfaces the deflections are each 6°.

For Region 3_u,

$$\omega_{3_{(upper)}} = \omega_{2_{(upper)}} + \theta = 23.7° + 6° = 29.7°$$

For this Prandtl-Meyer function value, $M_{3_{(lower)}}$ is obtained from Eq. 13.55,

$$\omega_{3_{(upper)}} = \sqrt{\frac{k+1}{k-1}} \tan^{-1}\left(\sqrt{\frac{k-1}{k+1}(M_{3_{(upper)}}^2 - 1)}\right) - \tan^{-1}\left(\sqrt{M_{3_{(upper)}}^2 - 1}\right)$$

This can be solved using manual iteration or interpolation, or by using, for example, *Excel*'s *Goal Seek* function,

$$M_{3_{(upper)}} = 2.12$$

Finally, we can find $p_{3_{(upper)}}$ from repeated use of Eq. 12.21a,

$$p_{3_{(upper)}} = \frac{p_{3_{(upper)}}}{p_0} \frac{p_0}{p_1} p_1 = \left\{ \left[1 + \frac{k-1}{2} M_1^2 \right]^{k/(k-1)} \middle/ \left[1 + \frac{k-1}{2} M_{3_{(upper)}}^2 \right]^{k/(k-1)} \right\} p_1$$

$$= \{ [1 + (0.2)1.80^2]^{3.5} / [1 + (0.2)2.12^2]^{3.5} \} \times 100 \text{ kPa}$$

so

$$p_{3_{(upper)}} = 60.9 \text{ kPa} \longleftarrow \qquad\qquad p_{3_{(upper)}}$$

For Region 3_l, we first need to find the Prandtl-Meyer function in the previous region, Region 2_l. For $M_{2_{(lower)}} = 1.223$, we find from Eq. 13.55,

$$\omega_{2_{(lower)}} = \sqrt{\frac{k+1}{k-1}} \tan^{-1}\left(\sqrt{\frac{k-1}{k+1}(M_{2_{(lower)}}^2 - 1)} \right) - \tan^{-1}\left(\sqrt{M_{2_{(lower)}}^2 - 1} \right)$$

$$= \sqrt{\frac{1.4+1}{1.4-1}} \tan^{-1}\left(\sqrt{\frac{1.4-1}{1.4+1}(1.489^2 - 1)} \right) - \tan^{-1}(\sqrt{1.489^2 - 1})$$

so

$$\omega_{2_{(lower)}} = 11.58°$$

Hence, for Region 3_l,

$$\omega_{3_{(lower)}} = \omega_{2_{(lower)}} + \theta = 11.58° + 6° = 17.6°$$

and $M_{3_{(lower)}}$ is obtained from Eq. 13.55,

$$\omega_{3_{(lower)}} = \sqrt{\frac{k+1}{k-1}} \tan^{-1}\left(\sqrt{\frac{k-1}{k+1}\left(M_{3_{(lower)}}^2 - 1\right)} \right) - \tan^{-1}\left(\sqrt{M_{3_{(lower)}}^2 - 1} \right)$$

Once again, this can be solved using manual iteration or interpolation, or by using, for example, *Excel's* *Goal Seek* function,

$$M_{3_{(lower)}} = 1.693$$

Finally, we can find $p_{3_{(lower)}}$ from repeated use of Eq. 12.21a,

$$p_{3_{(lower)}} = \frac{p_{3_{(lower)}}}{p_{0_2}} \frac{p_{0_2}}{p_{2_{(lower)}}} p_{2_{(lower)}} = \left\{ \left[1 + \frac{k-1}{2} M_{2_{(lower)}}^2 \right]^{k/(k-1)} \middle/ \left[1 + \frac{k-1}{2} M_{3_{(lower)}}^2 \right]^{k/(k-1)} \right\} p_{2_{(lower)}}$$

$$= \{ [1 + (0.2)1.489^2]^{3.5} / [1 + (0.2)1.693^2]^{3.5} \} \times 158 \text{ kPa}$$

Hence,

$$p_{3_{(lower)}} = 117 \text{ kPa} \longleftarrow \qquad\qquad p_{3_{(lower)}}$$

(Note that we cannot use p_0, the stagnation pressure of the incoming flow for computing this pressure, because the flow experienced a shock before reaching the lower surface.)

To compute the lift and drag coefficients, we need the lift and drag force.

First we find the vertical and horizontal forces with respect to coordinates orthogonal to the airfoil.

The vertical force (assuming the chord c and span s are in meters) is given by

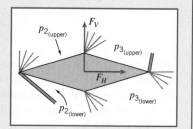

$$F_V = s\frac{c}{2}\{(p_{2_{(lower)}} + p_{3_{(lower)}}) - (p_{2_{(lower)}} + p_{3_{(upper)}})\}$$

$$F_V = s(\text{m})\frac{c(\text{m})}{2}\{(158 + 117) - (85.8 + 60.9)\}(\text{kPa}) = 64.2 \, sc \text{ kN}$$

and the horizontal force by

$$F_H = s\frac{c}{2}\tan 3°\{(p_{2_{(upper)}} + p_{2_{(lower)}}) - (p_{3_{(upper)}} + p_{3_{(lower)}})\}$$

$$F_H = s(\text{m})\frac{c(\text{m})}{2}\tan 3°\{(85.8 + 158) - (60.9 + 117)\}(\text{kPa}) = 1.73 \, sc \text{ kN}$$

The lift and drag forces (per unit plan area) are then

$$F_L = F_V \cos 6° − F_H \sin 6° = 63.6 \, sc \text{ kN}$$

and

$$F_D = F_V \sin 6° + F_H \cos 6° = 8.42 \, sc \text{ kN}$$

The lift and drag coefficients require the air density,

$$\rho = \frac{p}{RT} = 100 \times 10^3 \, \frac{\text{N}}{\text{m}^2} \times \frac{\text{kg} \cdot \text{K}}{287 \, \text{N} \cdot \text{m}} \times \frac{1}{277 \, \text{K}} = 1.258 \text{ kg/m}^3$$

The lift coefficient is then

$$C_L = \frac{F_L}{\frac{1}{2}\rho V^2 sc} = 2 \times \frac{63.6 \times 10^3 \, \text{N}}{1.258 \, \frac{\text{kg}}{\text{m}^3}} \times \frac{\text{m}^3}{(600)^2 \, \frac{\text{s}^2}{\text{m}^2}} \times \frac{\text{kg} \cdot \text{m}}{\text{N} \cdot \text{s}^2} = 0.281 \qquad \longleftarrow \qquad C_L$$

and the drag coefficient is

$$C_D = \frac{F_D}{\frac{1}{2}\rho V^2 sc} = 2 \times \frac{8.42 \times 10^3 \, \text{N}}{1.258 \, \frac{\text{kg}}{\text{m}^3}} \times \frac{\text{m}^3}{(600)^2 \, \frac{\text{s}^2}{\text{m}^2}} \times \frac{\text{kg} \cdot \text{m}}{\text{N} \cdot \text{s}^2} = 0.037 \qquad \longleftarrow \qquad C_D$$

(Note that instead of using $\frac{1}{2}\rho V^2$ in the denominator of the coefficients, we could have used $\frac{1}{2}kp \, M^2$.) The lift-drag ratio is approximately 7.6.

This Example illustrates the use of oblique shock and isentropic expansion wave equations to determine the pressure distribution on an airfoil.

✓ We did not need to analyze the flow after the trailing expansion waves and oblique shock—unlike subsonic flow, the downstream condition has no effect on the airfoil.

✓ Unlike a subsonic flow, a supersonic flow can generate drag even in the absence of boundary layers and flow separation.

✓ Note that, unlike a subsonic flow, a supersonic flow *can* negotiate a sharp corner, even if we include the effect of a viscous boundary layer (as we have not done here). This is because an expanding supersonic flow has a negative pressure gradient, i.e., it is *not* adverse!

✓ An actual airfoil is not likely to have planar surfaces, so more sophisticated techniques than we can cover here are needed. However, this example illustrates the kind of results to be expected when analyzing a supersonic airfoil.

The *Excel* workbooks for oblique shocks and isentropic expansion waves are convenient for performing these calculations. (Alternatively, the normal and oblique shock relations, and the isentropic expansion wave *Excel* add-ins, available on the Web site, are useful for these calculations.)

13-8 SUMMARY AND USEFUL EQUATIONS

In this chapter, we:

✓ Developed a set of governing equations (continuity, the momentum equation, the first and second laws of thermodynamics, and equations of state) for one-dimensional flow of a compressible fluid (in particular an ideal gas) as it may be affected by area change, friction, heat exchange, and normal shocks.

✓ Simplified these equations for isentropic flow affected only by area change, and developed isentropic relations for analyzing such flows.

✓ Simplified the equations for flow affected only by friction, and developed the Fanno-line relations for analyzing such flows.

✓ Simplified the equations for flow affected only by heat exchange, and developed the Rayleigh-line relations for analyzing such flows.

✓ Simplified the equations for flow through a normal shock, and developed normal-shock relations for analyzing such flows.

✓ Introduced some basic concepts of two-dimensional flow: oblique shocks and expansion waves.

While investigating the above flows we developed insight into some interesting compressible flow phenomena, including:

✓ Use of Ts plots in visualizing flow behavior.

✓ Flow through, and necessary shape of, subsonic and supersonic nozzles and diffusers.

✓ The phenomenon of choked flow in converging nozzles and CD nozzles, and the circumstances under which shock waves develop in CD nozzles.

✓ *The phenomena of choked flow in flows with friction and flows with heat exchange.

✓ Computation of pressures and lift and drag coefficients for a supersonic airfoil.

Note: Most of the Useful Equations in the table below have a number of constraints or limitations—*be sure to refer to their page numbers for details*! In particular, most of them assume an ideal gas, with constant specific heats.

	Useful Equations		
One-dimensional flow equations:	$\rho_1 V_1 A_1 = \rho_2 V_2 A_2 = \rho V A = \dot{m} = \text{constant}$	(13.1a)	Page 613
	$R_x + p_1 A_1 - p_2 A_2 = \dot{m}V_2 - \dot{m}V_1$	(13.1b)	
	$\dfrac{\delta Q}{dm} + h_1 + \dfrac{V_1^2}{2} = h_2 + \dfrac{V_2^2}{2}$	(13.1c)	
	$\dot{m}(s_2 - s_1) \geq \displaystyle\int_{CS} \dfrac{1}{T}\left(\dfrac{\dot{Q}}{A}\right)dA$	(13.1d)	
	$p = \rho R T$	(13.1e)	
	$\Delta h = h_2 - h_1 = c_p \Delta T = c_p(T_2 - T_1)$	(13.1f)	
	$\Delta s = s_2 - s_1 = c_p \ln \dfrac{T_2}{T_1} - R \ln \dfrac{p_2}{p_1}$	(13.1g)	
Isentropic relations: [Note: These equations are a little cumbersome for practical use by hand. They are listed (and tabulated and plotted for air) in Appendix E. You are urged to download the *Excel* Add-Ins from the Web site for use in computing with these equations.]	$\dfrac{p_0}{p} = f(M)$	(13.7a)	Page 619
	$\dfrac{T_0}{T} = f(M)$	(13.7b)	
	$\dfrac{\rho_0}{\rho} = f(M)$	(13.7c)	
	$\dfrac{A}{A^*} = f(M)$	(13.7d)	

---

* This topic applies to sections that may be omitted without loss of continuity in the text material.

Pressure ratio for choked converging nozzle, $p_e/p_0\|_{choked}$:	$$\left.\frac{p_e}{p_0}\right\|_{choked} = \frac{p^*}{p_0} = \left(\frac{2}{k+1}\right)^{k/(k-1)} \qquad (13.8)$$	Page 624
Mass flow rate for choked converging nozzle:	$$\dot{m}_{choked} = A_e p_0 \sqrt{\frac{k}{RT_0}} \left(\frac{2}{k+1}\right)^{(k+1)/2(k-1)} \qquad (13.9a)$$	Page 625
Mass flow rate for choked converging nozzle (English Engineering units):	$$\dot{m}_{choked} = 0.04 \frac{A_e p_0}{\sqrt{T_0}} \qquad (13.9b)$$	Page 625
Mass flow rate for choked converging nozzle (SI units):	$$\dot{m}_{choked} = 76.6 \frac{A_e p_0}{\sqrt{T_0}} \qquad (13.9c)$$	Page 625
Mass flow rate for choked converging-diverging nozzle:	$$\dot{m}_{choked} = A_t p_0 \sqrt{\frac{k}{RT_0}} \left(\frac{2}{k+1}\right)^{(k+1)/2(k-1)} \qquad (13.10a)$$	Page 629
Mass flow rate for choked converging-diverging nozzle (English Engineering units):	$$\dot{m}_{choked} = 0.04 \frac{A_t p_0}{\sqrt{T_0}} \qquad (13.10b)$$	Page 629
Mass flow rate for choked converging-diverging nozzle (SI units):	$$\dot{m}_{choked} = 76.6 \frac{A_t p_0}{\sqrt{T_0}} \qquad (13.10c)$$	Page 629
Fanno-line relations (friction): [Note: These equations are too cumbersome for practical use by hand. They are listed (and tabulated and plotted for air) in Appendix E. You are urged to download the *Excel* Add-Ins from the Web site for use in computing with these equations.]	$$\frac{\bar{f}L_{max}}{D_h} = f(M) \qquad (13.21a)$$ $$\frac{T}{T^*} = f(M) \qquad (13.21b)$$ $$\frac{V}{V^*} = \frac{\rho^*}{\rho} = f(M) \qquad (13.21c)$$ $$\frac{p}{p^*} = f(M) \qquad (13.21d)$$ $$\frac{p_0}{p_0^*} = f(M) \qquad (13.21e)$$	Page 644
Isothermal flow relations (friction): [Note: These equations are too cumbersome for practical use by hand. They are listed (and tabulated and plotted for air) in Appendix E. You are urged to download the *Excel* Add-Ins from the Web site for use in computing with these equations.]	$$\frac{p_2}{p_1} = \frac{\rho_2}{\rho_1} = \frac{V_1}{V_2} = \frac{M_1}{M_2} \qquad (13.29a)$$ $$\frac{T_{0_2}}{T_{0_1}} = f\left(\frac{M_1}{M_2}\right) \qquad (13.29b)$$ $$\frac{fL}{D_h} = f\left(\frac{M_1}{M_2}\right) \qquad (13.29c)$$	Page W-26

Rayleigh-line relations (heat transfer): [Note: These equations are too cumbersome for practical use by hand. They are listed (and tabulated and plotted for air) in Appendix E. You are urged to download the *Excel* Add-Ins from the Web site for use in computing with these equations.]	$$\frac{p}{p^*} = f(M) \qquad (13.31a)$$ $$\frac{T}{T^*} = f(M) \qquad (13.31b)$$ $$\frac{\rho^*}{\rho} = \frac{V}{V^*} = f(M) \qquad (13.31c)$$ $$\frac{T_0}{T_0^*} = f(M) \qquad (13.31d)$$ $$\frac{p_0}{p_0^*} = f(M) \qquad (13.31e)$$	Page 654
Normal shock relations: [Note: These equations are too cumbersome for practical use by hand. They are listed (and tabulated and plotted for air) in Appendix E. You are urged to download the *Excel* Add-Ins from the Web site for use in computing with these equations.]	$$M_2 = f(M_1) \qquad (13.41a)$$ $$\frac{p_{0_2}}{p_{0_1}} = f(M_1) \qquad (13.41b)$$ $$\frac{T_2}{T_1} = f(M_1) \qquad (13.41c)$$ $$\frac{p_2}{p_1} = f(M_1) \qquad (13.41d)$$ $$\frac{\rho_2}{\rho_1} = \frac{V_1}{V_2} = f(M_1) \qquad (13.41e)$$	Page 662
Useful relations for determining the normal shock location in converging-diverging nozzle:	$$\frac{p_e}{p_{0_1}} \frac{A_e}{A_t} = \frac{p_e}{p_{0_e}} \frac{A_e}{A_e^*} \qquad (13.43)$$ $$\frac{p_{0_2}}{p_{0_1}} = \frac{A_t}{A_e} \frac{A_e}{A_e^*} \qquad (13.44)$$	Page 666 Page 667
Geometric relations, oblique shock:	$$M_{1_n} = \frac{V_{1_n}}{c_1} = M_1 \sin \beta \qquad (13.47a)$$ $$M_{2_n} = \frac{V_{2_n}}{c_2} = M_2 \sin (\beta - \theta) \qquad (13.47b)$$	Page 670
Oblique shock relations: [Note: These equations are too cumbersome for practical use by hand. They are listed (and tabulated and plotted for air) in Appendix E. You are urged to download the *Excel* Add-Ins from the Web site for use in computing with these equations.]	$$M_{2_n} = f(M_{1_n}) \qquad (13.48a)$$ $$\frac{p_{0_2}}{p_{0_1}} = f(M_{1_n}) \qquad (13.48b)$$ $$\frac{T_2}{T_1} = f(M_{1_n}) \qquad (13.48c)$$ $$\frac{p_2}{p_1} = f(M_{1_n}) \qquad (13.48d)$$ $$\frac{\rho_2}{\rho_1} = \frac{V_{1_n}}{V_{2_n}} = f(M_{1_n}) \qquad (13.48e)$$	Page 670 Page 671

Relation of β, θ, and M_1 for oblique shock:	$\tan\theta = \dfrac{2\cot\beta(M_1^2\sin^2\beta - 1)}{M_1^2(k + \cos 2\beta) + 2}$ (13.49)	Page 673
Prandtl-Meyer expansion function, ω:	$\omega = \sqrt{\dfrac{k+1}{k-1}}\tan^{-1}\left(\sqrt{\dfrac{k-1}{k+1}\,(M^2 - 1)}\right)$ $- \tan^{-1}(\sqrt{M^2 - 1})$ (13.55)	Page 678

REFERENCES

1. *HP 48G Series User's Guide*, Hewlett-Packard Company, Corvallis Division, 1000 N.E. Circle Blvd., Corvallis, OR 97330.

2. *Isentropic Calculator* (http://www.aoe.vt.edu/aoe3114/calc.html), William Devenport, Aerospace and Ocean Engineering, Virginia Polytechnic Institute and State University.

3. Hermann, R., *Supersonic Inlet Diffusers*. Minneapolis, MN: Minneapolis-Honeywell Regulator Co., Aeronautical Division, 1956.

4. Runstadler, P.W., Jr., "Diffuser Data Book," Creare, Inc., Hanover, NH, Technical Note 186, 1975.

5. Seddon, J., and E. L. Goldsmith, *Intake Aerodynamics*. New York: American Institute of Aeronautics and Astronautics, 1985.

6. Shapiro, A. H., *The Dynamics and Thermodynamics of Compressible Fluid Flow*, Vol. 1. New York: Ronald Press, 1953.

7. Zucrow, M. J., and J. D. Hoffman, *Compressible Flow*, Vol. 1. New York: Wiley, 1976.

8. Coles, D., *Channel Flow of a Compressible Fluid*, NCFMF video.

9. Baals, D. W., and W. R. Corliss, *Wind Tunnels of NASA*. Washington, D.C.: National Aeronautics and Space Administration, SP-440, 1981.

10. Pope, A., and K. L. Goin, *High-Speed Wind Tunnel Testing*. New York: Krieger. 1978.

11. Glass, I.I., "Some Aspects of Shock-Wave Research," *AIAA J.*, 25, 2, February 1987, pp. 214–229.

PROBLEMS

Most of the problems in this chapter involve computation of isentropic, Fanno, Rayleigh, normal shock, oblique shock, or isentropic expansion wave effects. The Web site for the text has associated *Excel* workbooks for each of these phenomena, and these are recommended for use while solving the problems (the Web site also has *Excel* add-in functions, which the reader is urged to download and install). To avoid needless duplication, the Mouse symbol will only be used next to problems when *Excel* has an *additional* benefit (e.g., for graphing).

13.1 Air is extracted from a large tank in which the temperature and pressure are 70°C and 101 kPa (abs), respectively, through a nozzle. At one location in the nozzle the static pressure is 25 kPa and the diameter is 15 cm. What is the mass flow rate? Assume isentropic flow.

13.2 Steam flows steadily and isentropically through a nozzle. At an upstream section where the speed is negligible, the temperature and pressure are 900°F and 900 psia. At a section where the nozzle diameter is 0.188 in., the steam pressure is 600 psia. Determine the speed and Mach number at this section and the mass flow rate of steam. Sketch the passage shape.

13.3 Steam flows steadily and isentropically through a nozzle. At an upstream section where the speed is negligible, the temperature and pressure are 450°C and 6 MPa (abs). At a section where the nozzle diameter is 2 cm, the steam pressure is 2 MPa (abs.).

Determine the speed and Mach number at this section and the mass flow rate of steam. Sketch the passage shape.

13.4 At a section in a passage, the pressure is 150 kPa (abs), the temperature is 10°C, and the speed is 120 m/s. For isentropic flow of air, determine the Mach number at the point where the pressure is 50 kPa (abs). Sketch the passage shape.

13.5 At a section in a passage, the pressure is 30 psia, the temperature is 100°F, and the speed is 1750 ft/s. At a section downstream the Mach number is 2.5. Determine the pressure at this downstream location for isentropic flow of air. Sketch the passage shape.

13.6 Air flows isentropically through a converging-diverging nozzle from a large tank containing air at 250°C. At two locations where the area is 1 cm², the static pressures are 200 kPa and 50 kPa. Find the mass flow rate, the throat area, and the Mach numbers at the two locations.

13.7 Air flows steadily and isentropically through a passage. At section ①, where the cross-sectional area is 0.02 m², the air is at 40.0 kPa (abs), 60°C, and $M = 2.0$. At section ② downstream, the speed is 519 m/s. Calculate the Mach number at section ②. Sketch the shape of the passage between sections ① and ②.

13.8 Air flows steadily and isentropically through a passage at 150 lbm/s. At the section where the diameter is $D = 3$ ft, $M = 1.75$,

$T = 32°F$, and $p = 25$ psia. Determine the speed and cross-sectional area downstream where $T = 225°F$. Sketch the flow passage.

13.9 Air, at an absolute pressure of 60.0 kPa and 27°C, enters a passage at 486 m/s, where $A = 0.02$ m². At section ② downstream, $p = 78.8$ kPa (abs). Assuming isentropic flow, calculate the Mach number at section ②. Sketch the flow passage.

13.10 For isentropic flow of air, at a section in a passage, $A = 0.25$ m², $p = 15$ kPa (abs), $T = 10°C$, and $V = 590$ m/s. Find the Mach number and the mass flow rate. At a section downstream the temperature is 137°C and the Mach number is 0.75. Determine the cross-sectional area and pressure at this downstream location. Sketch the passage shape.

13.11 Atmospheric air (101 kPa and 20°C) is drawn into a receiving pipe via a converging nozzle. The throat cross-section diameter is 1 cm. Plot the mass flow rate delivered for the receiving pipe pressure ranging from 100 kPa down to 5 kPa.

13.12 Repeat Problem 13.11 if the converging nozzle is replaced with a converging-diverging nozzle with an exit diameter of 2.5 cm (same throat area).

13.13 A passage is designed to expand air isentropically to atmospheric pressure from a large tank in which properties are held constant at 40°F and 45 psia. The desired flow rate is 2.25 lbm/s. Assuming the passage is 20 ft long, and that the Mach number increases linearly with position in the passage, plot the cross-sectional area and pressure as functions of position.

13.14 Air flows isentropically through a converging nozzle into a receiver in which the absolute pressure is 35 psia. The air enters the nozzle with negligible speed at a pressure of 60 psia and a temperature of 200°F. Determine the mass flow rate through the nozzle for a throat diameter of 4 in.

13.15 Air flows isentropically through a converging nozzle into a receiver where the pressure is 250 kpa (abs). If the pressure is 350 kpa (abs) and the speed is 150 m/s at the nozzle location where the Mach number is 0.5, determine the pressure, speed, and Mach number at the nozzle throat.

13.16 Air is flowing steadily through a series of three tanks. The first very large tank contains air at 650 kPa and 35°C. Air flows from it to a second tank through a converging nozzle with exit area 1 cm². Finally the air flows from the second tank to a third very large tank through an identical nozzle. The flow rate through the two nozzles is the same, and the flow in them is isentropic. The pressure in the third tank is 65 kPa. Find the mass flow rate, and the pressure in the second tank.

13.17 Air flowing isentropically through a converging nozzle discharges to the atmosphere. At the section where the absolute pressure is 250 kPa, the temperature is 20°C and the air speed is 200 m/s. Determine the nozzle throat pressure.

13.18 Air flows from a large tank ($p = 650$ kPa (abs), $T = 550°C$) through a converging nozzle, with a throat area of 600 mm², and discharges to the atmosphere. Determine the mass rate of flow for isentropic flow through the nozzle.

13.19 Air flowing isentropically through a converging nozzle discharges to the atmosphere. At a section the area is $A = 0.05$ m², $T = 3.3°C$, and $V = 200$ m/s. If the flow is just choked, find the pressure and the Mach number at this location. What is the throat area? What is the mass flow rate?

13.20 A converging nozzle is connected to a large tank that contains compressed air at 15°C. The nozzle exit area is 0.001 m². The exhaust is discharged to the atmosphere. To obtain a satisfactory shadow photograph of the flow pattern leaving the nozzle exit, the pressure in the exit plane must be greater than 325 kPa (gage). What pressure is required in the tank? What mass flow rate of air must be supplied if the system is to run continuously? Show static and stagnation state points on a Ts diagram.

13.21 Air, with $p_0 = 650$ kPa (abs) and $T_0 = 350$ K, flows isentropically through a converging nozzle. At the section in the nozzle where the area is 2.6×10^{-3} m², the Mach number is 0.5. The nozzle discharges to a back pressure of 270 kPa (abs). Determine the exit area of the nozzle.

13.22 A large tank supplies air to a converging nozzle that discharges to atmospheric pressure. Assume the flow is reversible and adiabatic. For what range of tank pressures will the flow at the nozzle exit be sonic? If the tank pressure is 600 kPa (abs) and the temperature is 600 K, determine the mass flow rate through the nozzle, if the exit area is 1.29×10^{-3} m².

13.23 Air at 0°C is contained in a large tank on the space shuttle. A converging section with exit area 1×10^{-3} m² is attached to the tank, through which the air exits to space at a rate of 2 kg/s. What are the pressure in the tank, and the pressure, temperature, and speed at the exit?

13.24 A large tank initially is evacuated to −10 kPa (gage). (Ambient conditions are 101 kPa at 20°C.) At $t = 0$, an orifice of 5 mm diameter is opened in the tank wall; the vena contracta area is 65 percent of the geometric area. Calculate the mass flow rate at which air initially enters the tank. Show the process on a Ts diagram. Make a schematic plot of mass flow rate as a function of time. Explain why the plot is nonlinear.

13.25 A-50 cm diameter spherical cavity initially is evacuated. The cavity is to be filled with air for a combustion experiment. The pressure is to be 45 kPa (abs), measured after its temperature reaches T_{atm}. Assume the valve on the cavity is a converging nozzle with throat diameter of 1 mm, and the surrounding air is at standard conditions. For how long should the valve be opened to achieve the desired final pressure in the cavity? Calculate the entropy change for the air in the cavity.

13.26 Air flows isentropically through a converging nozzle attached to a large tank, where the absolute pressure is 171 kPa and the temperature is 27°C. At the inlet section the Mach number is 0.2. The nozzle discharges to the atmosphere; the discharge area is 0.015 m². Determine the magnitude and direction of the force that must be applied to hold the nozzle in place.

13.27 Consider a "rocket cart" propelled by a jet supplied from a tank of compressed air on the cart. Initially, air in the tank is at 1.3 MPa (abs) and 20°C, and the mass of the cart and tank is $M_0 = 25$ kg. The air exhausts through a converging nozzle with exit area $A_e = 30$ mm². Rolling resistance of the cart is $F_R = 6$ N; aerodynamic resistance is negligible. For the instant after air begins to flow through the nozzle: (a) compute the pressure in the nozzle exit plane, (b) evaluate the mass flow rate of air through the nozzle, and (c) calculate the acceleration of the tank and cart assembly.

13.28 A stream of air flowing in a duct ($A = 5 \times 10^{-4}$ m²) is at $p = 300$ kPa (abs), has $M = 0.5$, and flows at $\dot{m} = 0.25$ kg/s.

Determine the local isentropic stagnation temperature. If the cross-sectional area of the passage were reduced downstream, determine the maximum percentage reduction of area allowable without reducing the flow rate (assume isentropic flow). Determine the speed and pressure at the minimum area location.

13.29 An air-jet-driven experimental rocket of 25 kg mass is to be launched from the space shuttle into space. The temperature of the air in the rocket's tank is 125°C. A converging section with exit area 25 mm^2 is attached to the tank, through which the air exits to space at a rate of 0.05 kg/s. What is the pressure in the tank, and the pressure, temperature, and air speed at the exit when the rocket is first released? What is the initial acceleration of the rocket?

13.30 A cylinder of gas used for welding contains helium at 20 MPa (gage) and room temperature. The cylinder is knocked over, its valve is broken off, and gas escapes through a converging passage. The minimum flow diameter is 10 mm at the outlet section where the gas flow is uniform. Find (a) the mass flow rate at which gas leaves the cylinder and (b) the instantaneous acceleration of the cylinder (assume the cylinder axis is horizontal and its mass is 65 kg). Show static and stagnation states and the process path on a Ts diagram.

13.31 A converging nozzle is bolted to the side of a large tank. Air inside the tank is maintained at a constant 50 psia and 100°F. The inlet area of the nozzle is 10 in.^{2} and the exit area is 1 in.^{2} The nozzle discharges to the atmosphere. For isentropic flow in the nozzle, determine the total force on the bolts, and indicate whether the bolts are in tension or compression.

13.32 An insulated spherical air tank with diameter $D = 2$ m is used in a blowdown installation. Initially the tank is charged to 2.75 MPa (abs) at 450 K. The mass flow rate of air from the tank is a function of time; during the first 30 s of blowdown 30 kg of air leaves the tank. Determine the air temperature in the tank after 30 s of blowdown. Estimate the nozzle throat area.

13.33 An ideal gas, with $k = 1.25$, flows isentropically through the converging nozzle shown and discharges into a large duct where the pressure is $p_2 = 25$ psia. The gas is *not* air and the gas constant, R, is unknown. Flow is steady and uniform at all cross-sections. Find the exit area of the nozzle, A_2, and the exit speed, V_2.

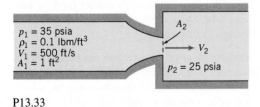

$p_1 = 35$ psia
$\rho_1 = 0.1$ lbm/ft^3
$V_1 = 500$ ft/s
$A_1 = 1$ ft^2

A_2

V_2

$p_2 = 25$ psia

P13.33

13.34 A jet transport aircraft, with pressurized cabin, cruises at 11 km altitude. The cabin temperature and pressure initially are at 25°C and equivalent to 2.5 km altitude. The interior volume of the cabin is 25 m^3. Air escapes through a small hole with effective flow area of 0.002 m^2. Calculate the time required for the cabin pressure to decrease by 40 percent. Plot the cabin pressure as a function of time.

13.35 A large insulated tank, pressurized to 620 kPa (gage), supplies air to a converging nozzle which discharges to atmosphere. The initial temperature in the tank is 127°C. When flow through the nozzle is initiated, what is the Mach number in the exit plane of the nozzle? What is the pressure in the exit plane when the flow is initiated? At what condition will the exit-plane Mach number change? How will the exit-plane pressure vary with time? How will flow rate through the nozzle vary with time? What would you estimate the air temperature in the tank to be when flow through the nozzle approaches zero?

13.36 A converging-diverging nozzle is attached to a very large tank of air in which the pressure is 150 kPa and the temperature is 35°C. The nozzle exhausts to the atmosphere where the pressure is 101 kPa. The exit diameter of the nozzle is 2.75 cm. What is the flow rate through the nozzle? Assume the flow is isentropic.

13.37 At the design condition of the system of Problem 13.36, the exit Mach number is $M_e = 2.0$. Find the pressure in the tank of Problem 13.36 (keeping the temperature constant) for this condition. What is the flow rate? What is the throat area?

13.38 Air escapes from a high-pressure bicycle tire through a hole with diameter $d = 0.254$ mm. The initial pressure in the tire is $p_1 = 620$ kPa (gage). (Assume the temperature remains constant at 27°C.) The internal volume of the tire is approximately 4.26×10^{-4} m^3, and is constant. Estimate the time needed for the pressure in the tire to drop to 310 kPa (gage). Compute the change in specific entropy of the air in the tire during this process. Plot the tire pressure as a function of time.

13.39 A converging-diverging nozzle, designed to expand air to $M = 3.0$, has a 250 mm^2 exit area. The nozzle is bolted to the side of a large tank and discharges to standard atmosphere. Air in the tank is pressurized to 4.5 MPa (gage) at 750 K. Assume flow within the nozzle is isentropic. Evaluate the pressure in the nozzle exit plane. Calculate the mass flow rate of air through the nozzle.

13.40 A converging-diverging nozzle, with a throat area of 2 in.^{2}, is connected to a large tank in which air is kept at a pressure of 80 psia and a temperature of 60°F. If the nozzle is to operate at design conditions (flow is isentropic) and the ambient pressure outside the nozzle is 12.9 psia, calculate the exit area of the nozzle and the mass flow rate.

13.41 Air, at a stagnation pressure of 7.20 MPa (abs) and a stagnation temperature of 1100 K, flows isentropically through a converging-diverging nozzle having a throat area of 0.01 m^2. Determine the speed and the mass flow rate at the downstream section where the Mach number is 4.0.

13.42 Air is to be expanded through a converging-diverging nozzle by a frictionless adiabatic process, from a pressure of 1.10 MPa (abs) and a temperature of 115°C, to a pressure of 141 kPa (abs). Determine the throat and exit areas for a well-designed shockless nozzle, if the mass flow rate is 2 kg/s.

13.43 Air flows isentropically through a converging-diverging nozzle attached to a large tank, in which the pressure is 251 psia and the temperature is 500°R. The nozzle is operating at design conditions for which the nozzle exit pressure, p_e, is equal to the surrounding atmospheric pressure, p_a. The exit area of the nozzle is $A_e = 1.575$ in.^{2}. Calculate the flow rate through the nozzle. Plot the mass flow rate as the temperature of the tank is progressively increased to 2000°R (all pressures remaining the same). Explain this result (e.g., compare the mass flow rates at 500°R and 2000°R).

13.44 A small, solid fuel rocket motor is tested on a thrust stand. The chamber pressure and temperature are 4 MPa and 3250 K. The propulsion nozzle is designed to expand the exhaust gases isentropically to a pressure of 75 kPa. The nozzle exit diameter is 25 cm. Treat the gas as ideal with $k = 1.25$ and $R = 300$ J/(kg $\cdot$ K). Determine the mass flow rate of propellant gas and the thrust force exerted against the test stand.

13.45 Nitrogen, at a pressure and temperature of 371 kPa (abs) and 400 K, enters a nozzle with negligible speed. The exhaust jet is directed against a large flat plate that is perpendicular to the jet axis. The flow leaves the nozzle at atmospheric pressure. The exit area is 0.003 m^2. Find the force required to hold the plate.

13.46 A liquid rocket motor is fueled with hydrogen and oxygen. The chamber temperature and absolute pressure are 3300 K and 6.90 MPa. The nozzle is designed to expand the exhaust gases isentropically to a design back pressure corresponding to an altitude of 10 km on a standard day. The thrust produced by the motor is to be 100 kN at design conditions. Treat the exhaust gases as water vapor and assume ideal gas behavior. Determine the propellant mass flow rate needed to produce the desired thrust, the nozzle exit area, and the area ratio, A_e/A_t.

13.47 A small rocket motor, fueled with hydrogen and oxygen, is tested on a thrust stand at a simulated altitude of 10 km. The motor is operated at chamber stagnation conditions of 1500 K and 8.0 MPa (gage). The combustion product is water vapor, which may be treated as an ideal gas. Expansion occurs through a converging-diverging nozzle with design Mach number of 3.5 and exit area of 700 mm^2. Evaluate the pressure at the nozzle exit plane. Calculate the mass flow rate of exhaust gas. Determine the force exerted by the rocket motor on the thrust stand.

13.48 A CO$_2$ cartridge is used to propel a small rocket cart. Compressed gas, stored at 35 MPa and 20°C, is expanded through a smoothly contoured converging nozzle with 0.5 mm throat diameter. The back pressure is atmospheric. Calculate the pressure at the nozzle throat. Evaluate the mass flow rate of carbon dioxide through the nozzle. Determine the thrust available to propel the cart. How much would the thrust increase if a diverging section were added to the nozzle to expand the gas to atmospheric pressure? What is the exit area? Show stagnation states, static states, and the processes on a Ts diagram.

13.49 Consider the converging-diverging option of Problem 13.48. To what pressure would the compressed gas need to be raised (keeping the temperature at 20°C) to develop a thrust of 15N? (Assume isentropic flow.)

13.50 Room air is drawn into an insulated duct of constant area through a smoothly contoured converging nozzle. Room conditions are $T = 80$°F and $p = 14.7$ psia. The duct diameter is $D = 1$ in. The pressure at the duct inlet (nozzle outlet) is $p_1 = 13$ psia. Find (a) the mass flow rate in the duct and (b) the range of exit pressures for which the duct exit flow is choked.

13.51 Air from a large reservoir at 25 psia and 250°F flows isentropically through a converging nozzle into an insulated pipe at 24 psia. The pipe flow experiences friction effects. Obtain a plot of the Ts diagram for this flow, until $M = 1$. Also plot the pressure and speed distributions from the entrance to the location at which $M = 1$.

13.52 Repeat Problem 13.51 except the nozzle is now a converging-diverging nozzle delivering the air to the pipe at 2.5 psia.

13.53 A Fanno-line flow apparatus in an undergraduate fluid mechanics laboratory consists of a smooth brass tube of 7.16 mm inside diameter, fed by a converging nozzle. The lab temperature and uncorrected barometer reading are 23.5°C and 755.1 mm of mercury. The pressure at the exit from the converging nozzle (entrance to the constant-area duct) is −20.8 mm of mercury (gage). Compute the Mach number at the entrance to the constant-area tube. Calculate the mass flow rate in the tube. Evaluate the pressure at the location in the tube where the Mach number is 0.4.

13.54 Air flows steadily and adiabatically from a large tank through a converging nozzle connected to an insulated constant-area duct. The nozzle may be considered frictionless. Air in the tank is at $p = 145$ psia and $T = 250$°F. The absolute pressure at the nozzle exit (duct inlet) is 125 psia. Determine the pressure at the end of the duct, if the temperature there is 150°F. Find the entropy increase.

13.55 Air flows through a smooth well-insulated 4-in. diameter pipe at 600 lbm/min. At one section the air is at 100 psia and 80°F. Determine the minimum pressure and the maximum speed that can occur in the pipe.

13.56 Measurements are made of compressible flow in a long smooth 7.16 mm i.d. tube. Air is drawn from the surroundings (20°C and 101 kPa) by a vacuum pump downstream. Pressure readings along the tube become steady when the downstream pressure is reduced to 626 mm Hg (vacuum) or below. For these conditions, determine (a) the maximum mass flow rate possible through the tube, (b) the stagnation pressure of the air leaving the tube, and (c) the entropy change of the air in the tube. Show static and stagnation state points and the process path on a Ts diagram.

13.57 A converging-diverging nozzle discharges air into an insulated pipe with area $A = 1$ in^2. At the pipe inlet, $p = 18.5$ psia, $T = 100$°F, and $M = 2.0$. For shockless flow to a Mach number of unity at the pipe exit, calculate the exit temperature, the net force of the fluid on the pipe, and the entropy change.

13.58 Air is drawn from the atmosphere (20°C and 101 kPa) through a converging nozzle into a long insulated 20-mm diameter tube of constant area. Flow in the nozzle is isentropic. The pressure at the inlet to the constant-area tube is $p_1 = 99.4$ kPa. Evaluate the mass flow rate through the tube. Calculate T^* and p^* for the isentropic process. Calculate T^* and p^* for flow leaving the constant-area tube. Show the corresponding static and stagnation state points on a Ts diagram.

13.59 Air flows through a converging nozzle and then a length of insulated duct. The air is supplied from a tank where the temperature is constant at 15°C and the pressure is variable. The outlet end of the duct exhausts to atmosphere. When the exit flow is just choked, pressure measurements show the duct inlet pressure and Mach number are 53.2 psia and 0.30. Determine the pressure in the tank and the temperature, stagnation pressure, and mass flow rate of the outlet flow, if the tube diameter is 0.249 in. Show on a Ts diagram the effect of raising the tank pressure to 100 psia. Sketch the pressure distribution versus distance along the channel for this new flow condition.

13.60 Consider adiabatic flow of air in a constant-area pipe with friction. At one section of the pipe, $p_0 = 100$ psia, $T_0 = 500$°R, and $M = 0.70$. If the cross-sectional area is 1 ft^2 and the Mach number at the exit is $M_2 = 1$, find the friction force exerted on the fluid by the pipe.

13.61 We wish to build a supersonic wind tunnel using an insulated nozzle and constant-area duct assembly. Shock-free operation is desired, with $M_1 = 2.1$ at the test section inlet and $M_2 = 1.1$ at the test section outlet. Stagnation conditions are $T_0 = 295$ K and $p_0 = 101$ kPa (abs). Calculate the outlet pressure and temperature and the entropy change through the test section.

13.62 Consider the laboratory Fanno-line flow channel of Problem 13.53. Assume laboratory conditions are 22.5°C and 760 mm of mercury (uncorrected). The manometer reading at a pressure tap at the end of the converging nozzle is −11.8 mm of mercury (gage). Calculate the Mach number at this location. Determine the duct length required to attain choked flow. Calculate the temperature and stagnation pressure at the choked state in the constant-area duct.

13.63 For the conditions of Problem 13.54, find the length, L, of commercial steel pipe of 2 in. diameter between sections ① and ②.

13.64 Air flows in an insulated duct. At one section, the temperature, absolute pressure, and velocity are 200°C, 2.00 MPa, and 140 m/s. Find the temperature in this duct where the pressure has dropped to 1.26 MPa (abs) as a result of friction. If the duct ($e/D = 0.0003$) has 150 mm diameter, find the distance between the two sections.

13.65 For the conditions of Problem 13.60, determine the duct length. Assume the duct is circular and made from commercial steel. Plot the variations of pressure and Mach number versus distance along the duct.

13.66 Using coordinates T/T_0 and $(s - s*)/c_p$, where $s*$ is the entropy at $M = 1$, plot the Fanno line starting from the inlet conditions specified in Example 13.7. Proceed to $M = 1$.

13.67 Consider the flow described in Example 13.7. Using the flow functions for Fanno-line flow of an ideal gas, plot static pressure, temperature, and Mach number versus L/D measured from the tube inlet; continue until the choked state is reached.

13.68 Using coordinates $T/T*$ and $(s - s*)/c_p$, where $s*$ is the entropy at $M = 1$, plot the Fanno line for air flow for $0.1 < M < 3.0$.

13.69 Air flows through a 40 ft length of insulated constant-area duct with $D = 2.12$ ft. The relative roughness is $e/D = 0.002$. At the duct inlet, $T_1 = 100°$ F and $p_1 = 17.0$ psia. At a location downstream, $p_2 = 14.7$ psia, and the flow is subsonic. Is sufficient information given to solve for M_1 and M_2? Prove your answer graphically. Find the mass flow rate in the duct and T_2.

13.70 Air brought into a tube through a converging-diverging nozzle initially has stagnation temperature and pressure of 550 K and 1.35 MPa (abs.). Flow in the nozzle is isentropic; flow in the tube is adiabatic. At the junction between the nozzle and tube the pressure is 15 kPa. The tube is 1.5 m long and 2.5 cm in diameter. If the outlet Mach number is unity, find the average friction factor over the tube length. Calculate the change in pressure between the tube inlet and discharge.

13.71 For the conditions of Problem 13.57, determine the duct length. Assume the duct is circular and made from commercial steel. Plot the variations of pressure and Mach number versus distance along the duct.

13.72 A smooth constant-area duct assembly ($D = 150$ mm) is to be fed by a converging-diverging nozzle from a tank containing air at 295 K and 1.0 MPa (abs). Shock-free operation is desired. The Mach number at the duct inlet is to be 2.1 and the Mach number at the duct outlet is to be 1.4. The entire assembly will be insulated. Find (a) the pressure required at the duct outlet, (b) the duct length required, and (c) the change in specific entropy. Show the static and stagnation state points and the process path on a Ts diagram.

***13.73** In long, constant-area pipelines, as used for natural gas, temperature is constant. Assume gas leaves a pumping station at 350 kPa and 20°C at $M = 0.10$. At the section along the pipe where the pressure has dropped to 150 kPa, calculate the Mach number of the flow. Is heat added to or removed from the gas over the length between the pressure taps? Justify your answer: Sketch the process on a Ts diagram. Indicate (qualitatively) T_{0_1}, T_{0_2}, and p_{0_2}.

***13.74** Air enters a 15-cm diameter pipe at 15°C, 1.5 MPa, and 60 m/s. The average friction factor is 0.013. Flow is isothermal. Calculate the local Mach number and the distance from the entrance of the channel, at the point where the pressure reaches 500 kPa.

***13.75** Air enters a horizontal channel of constant area at 200°F, 600 psia, and 350 ft/s. Determine the limiting pressure for isothermal flow. Compare with the limiting pressure for frictional adiabatic flow.

***13.76** A clean steel pipe is 950 ft long and 5.25 in. inside diameter. Air at 80°F, 120 psia, and 80 ft/s enters the pipe. Calculate and compare the pressure drops through the pipe for (a) incompressible, (b) isothermal, and (c) adiabatic flows.

***13.77** Natural gas (molecular mass $M_m = 18$ and $k = 1.3$) is to be pumped through a 36 in. i.d. pipe connecting two compressor stations 40 miles apart. At the upstream station the pressure is not to exceed 90 psig, and at the downstream station it is to be at least 10 psig. Calculate the maximum allowable rate of flow (ft³/day at 70°F and 1 atm) assuming sufficient heat exchange through the pipe to maintain the gas at 70°F.

13.78 Air from a large reservoir at 25 psia and 250°F flows isentropically through a converging nozzle into a frictionless pipe at 24 psia. The flow is heated as it flows along the pipe. Obtain a plot of the Ts diagram for this flow, until $M = 1$. Also plot the pressure and speed distributions from the entrance to the location at which $M = 1$.

13.79 Repeat Problem 13.78 except the nozzle is now a converging-diverging nozzle delivering the air to the pipe at 2.5 psia.

13.80 Consider frictionless flow of air in a constant-area duct. At section ①, $M_1 = 0.50$, $p_1 = 1.10$ MPa (abs), and $T_{0_1} = 333$ K. Through the effect of heat exchange, the Mach number at section ② is $M_2 = 0.90$ and the stagnation temperature is $T_{0_2} = 478$ K. Determine the amount of heat exchange per unit mass to or from the fluid between sections ① and ② and the pressure difference, $p_1 - p_2$.

13.81 Air flows without friction through a short duct of constant area. At the duct entrance, $M_1 = 0.30$, $T_1 = 50°C$, and $\rho_1 = 2.16 \text{ kg/m}^3$. As a result of heating, the Mach number and pressure at the tube outlet are $M_2 = 0.60$ and $p_2 = 150$ kPa. Determine the heat addition per unit mass and the entropy change for the process.

13.82 Air flows through a 5-cm-inside diameter pipe with negligible friction. Inlet conditions are $T_1 = 15°C$, $p_1 = 1$ MPa (abs), and $M_1 = 0.35$. Determine the heat exchange per pound of air required to produce $M_2 = 1.0$ at the pipe exit, where $p_2 = 500$ kPa.

13.83 Liquid Freon, used to cool electronic components, flows steadily into a horizontal tube of constant diameter, $D = 0.65$ in. Heat is transferred to the flow, and the liquid boils and leaves the tube as vapor. The effects of friction are negligible compared with the effects of heat addition. Flow conditions are shown. Find (a) the rate of heat transfer and (b) the pressure difference, $p_1 - p_2$.

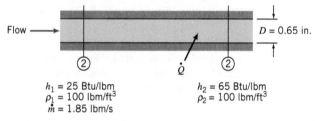

$h_1 = 25 \text{ Btu/lbm}$
$\rho_1 = 100 \text{ lbm/ft}^3$
$\dot{m} = 1.85 \text{ lbm/s}$

$h_2 = 65 \text{ Btu/lbm}$
$\rho_2 = 100 \text{ lbm/ft}^3$

P13.83

13.84 Consider frictionless flow of air in a duct of constant area, $A = 0.087 \text{ ft}^2$. At one section, the static properties are 500°R and 15.0 psia and the Mach number is 0.2. At a section downstream, the static pressure is 10.0 psia. Draw a Ts diagram showing the static and stagnation states. Calculate the flow speed and temperature at the downstream location. Evaluate the rate of heat exchange for the process.

13.85 Air flows at 1.42 kg/s through a 100-mm diameter duct. At the inlet section, the temperature and absolute pressure are 52°C and 60.0 kPa. At the section downstream where the flow is choked, $T_2 = 45°C$. Determine the heat addition per unit mass, the entropy change, and the change in stagnation pressure for the process, assuming frictionless flow.

13.86 A combustor from a JT8D jet engine (as used on the Douglas DC-9 aircraft) has an air flow rate of 15 lbm/s. The area is constant and frictional effects are negligible. Properties at the combustor inlet are 1260°R, 235 psia, and 609 ft/s. At the combustor outlet, $T = 1840°R$ and $M = 0.476$. The heating value of the fuel is 18,000 Btu/lbm; the air-fuel ratio is large enough so properties are those of air. Calculate the pressure at the combustor outlet. Determine the rate of energy addition to the air stream. Find the mass flow rate of fuel required; compare it to the air flow rate. Show the process on a Ts diagram, indicating static and stagnation states and the process path.

13.87 Consider frictionless flow of air in a duct with $D = 10$ cm. At section ①, the temperature and pressure are 0°C and 70 kPa; the mass flow rate is 0.5 kg/s. How much heat may be added without choking the flow? Evaluate the resulting change in stagnation pressure.

13.88 A constant-area duct is fed with air from a converging-diverging nozzle. At the entrance to the duct, the following properties are known: $p_{0_1} = 800$ kPa (abs), $T_{0_1} = 700$ K, and $M_1 = 3.0$. A short distance down the duct (at section ②) $p_2 = 46.4$ kPa. Assuming frictionless flow, determine the speed and Mach number at section ②, and the heat exchange between the inlet and section ②.

13.89 Air flows steadily and without friction at 1.83 kg/s through a duct with cross-sectional area of 0.02 m^2. At the duct inlet, the temperature and absolute pressure are 260°C and 126 kPa. The exit flow discharges subsonically to atmospheric pressure. Determine the Mach number, temperature, and stagnation temperature at the duct outlet and the heat exchange rate.

13.90 In the frictionless flow of air through a 100-mm diameter duct, 1.42 kg/s enters at 52°C and 60.0 kPa (abs). Determine the amount of heat that must be added to choke the flow, and the fluid properties at the choked state.

13.91 Air flows without friction in a short section of constant-area duct. At the duct inlet, $M_1 = 0.30$, $T_1 = 50°C$, and $\rho_1 = 2.16 \text{ kg/m}^3$. At the duct outlet, $M_2 = 0.60$. Determine the heat addition per unit mass, the entropy change, and the change in stagnation pressure for the process.

13.92 Air, from an aircraft inlet system, enters the engine combustion chamber where heat is added during a frictionless process in a tube with constant area of 0.01 m^2. The local isentropic stagnation temperature and Mach number entering the combustor are 427 K and 0.3. The mass flow rate is 0.5 kg/s. When the rate of heat addition is set at 404 kW, flow leaves the combustor at 1026 K and 22.9 kPa (abs). Determine for this process (a) the Mach number at the combustor outlet, (b) the static pressure at the combustor inlet, and (c) the change in local isentropic stagnation pressure during the heat addition process. Show static and stagnation state points and indicate the process path on a Ts diagram.

13.93 Flow in a gas turbine combustor is modeled as steady, one-dimensional, frictionless heating of air in a channel of constant area. For a certain process, the inlet conditions are 500°C, 1.5 MPa (abs), and $M = 0.5$. Calculate the maximum possible heat addition. Find all fluid properties at the outlet section and the reduction in stagnation pressure. Show the process path on a Ts diagram, indicating all static and stagnation state points.

13.94 Consider steady, one-dimensional flow of air in a combustor with constant area of 0.5 ft^2, where hydrocarbon fuel, added to the air stream, burns. The process is equivalent to simple heating because the amount of fuel is small compared to the amount of air; heating occurs over a short distance so that friction is negligible. Properties at the combustor inlet are 818°R, 200 psia, and $M = 0.3$. The speed at the combustor outlet must not exceed 2000 ft/s. Find the properties at the combustor outlet and the heat addition rate. Show the process path on a Ts diagram, indicating static and stagnation state points before and after the heat addition.

13.95 Consider steady flow of air in a combustor where thermal energy is added by burning fuel. Neglect friction. Assume thermodynamic properties are constant and equal to those of pure air. Calculate the stagnation temperature at the burner exit. Compute the Mach number at the burner exit. Evaluate the heat addition per unit mass and the heat exchange rate. Express the rate of heat addition as a fraction of the maximum rate of heat addition possible with this inlet Mach number.

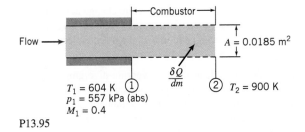

P13.95

13.96 A supersonic wind tunnel is supplied from a high-pressure tank of air at 25°C. The test section temperature is to be maintained above 0°C to prevent formation of ice particles. To accomplish this, air from the tank is heated before it flows into a converging-diverging nozzle which feeds the test section. The heating is done in a short section with constant area. The heater output is $\dot{Q} = 10$ kW. The design Mach number in the wind tunnel test section is to be 3.0. Evaluate the stagnation temperature required at the heater exit. Calculate the maximum mass flow rate at which air can be supplied to the wind tunnel test section. Determine the area ratio, A_e/A_t.

13.97 Frictionless flow of air in a constant-area duct discharges to atmospheric pressure at section ②. Upstream at section ①, $M_1 = 3.0$, $T_1 = 215°R$, and $p_1 = 1.73$ psia. Between sections ① and ②, 48.5 Btu/lbm of air is added to the flow. Determine M_2 and p_2. In addition to a Ts diagram, sketch the pressure distribution versus distance along the channel, labeling sections ① and ②.

13.98 A jet transport aircraft cruises at $M = 0.85$ at an altitude of 40,000 ft. Air for the cabin pressurization system is taken aboard through an inlet duct and slowed isentropically to 100 ft/s relative to the aircraft. Then it enters a compressor where its pressure is raised adiabatically to provide a cabin pressure equivalent to 8000 ft altitude. The air temperature increase across the compressor is 170°F. Finally, the air is cooled to 70°F (in a heat exchanger with negligible friction) before it is added to the cabin air. Sketch a diagram of the system, labeling all components and numbering appropriate cross-sections. Determine the stagnation and static temperature and pressure at each cross-section. Sketch to scale and label a Ts diagram showing the static and stagnation state points and indicating the process paths. Evaluate the work added in the compressor and the energy rejected in the heat exchanger.

13.99 Testing of a demolition explosion is to be evaluated. Sensors indicate that the shock wave generated at the instant of explosion is 30 MPa (abs). If the explosion occurs in air at 20°C and 101 kPa, find the speed of the shock wave, and the temperature and speed of the air just after the shock passes. As an approximation assume $k = 1.4$. (Why is this an approximation?)

13.100 A large tank containing air at 125 psia and 175°F is attached to a converging-diverging nozzle that has a throat area of 1.5 in² through which the air is exiting. A normal shock sits at a point in the nozzle where the area is 2.5 in². The nozzle exit area is 3.5 in². What are the Mach numbers just after the shock and at the exit? What are the stagnation and static pressures before and after the shock?

13.101 A normal shock occurs when a pitot-static tube is inserted into a supersonic wind tunnel. Pressures measured by the tube are $p_{0_2} = 10$ psia and $p_2 = 8$ psia. Before the shock, $T_1 = 285°R$ and $p_1 = 1.5$ psia. Calculate the air speed in the wind tunnel.

13.102 Air flows steadily through a long, insulated constant-area pipe. At section ①, $M_1 = 2.0$, $T_1 = 140°F$, and $p_1 = 35.9$ psia. At section ②, downstream from a normal shock, $V_2 = 1080$ ft/s. Determine the density and Mach number at section ②. Make a qualitative sketch of the pressure distribution along the pipe.

13.103 A total-pressure probe is placed in a supersonic wind tunnel where $T = 530°R$ and $M = 2.0$. A normal shock stands in front of the probe. Behind the shock, $M_2 = 0.577$ and $p_2 = 5.76$ psia. Find (a) the downstream stagnation pressure and stagnation temperature and (b) all fluid properties upstream from the shock. Show static and stagnation state points and the process path on a Ts diagram.

13.104 Air approaches a normal shock at $M_1 = 2.5$, with $T_{0_1} = 1250°R$ and $p_1 = 20$ psia. Determine the speed and temperature of the air leaving the shock and the entropy change across the shock.

13.105 Air undergoes a normal shock. Upstream, $T_1 = 35°C$, $p_1 = 229$ kPa (abs), and $V_1 = 704$ m/s. Determine the temperature and stagnation pressure of the air stream leaving the shock.

13.106 A normal shock stands in a constant-area duct. Air approaches the shock with $T_{0_1} = 550$ K, $p_{0_1} = 650$ kPa (abs), and $M_1 = 2.5$. Determine the static pressure downstream from the shock. Compare the downstream pressure with that reached by decelerating isentropically to the same subsonic Mach number.

13.107 A normal shock occurs in air at a section where $V_1 = 2000$ mph, $T_1 = -15°F$, and $p_1 = 5$ psia. Determine the speed and Mach number downstream from the shock, and the change in stagnation pressure across the shock.

13.108 Air approaches a normal shock with $T_1 = -7.5°F$, $p_1 = 14.7$ psia, and $V_1 = 1750$ mph. Determine the speed immediately downstream from the shock and the pressure change across the shock. Calculate the corresponding pressure change for a frictionless, shockless deceleration between the same speeds.

13.109 A supersonic aircraft cruises at $M = 2.2$ at 12 km altitude. A pitot tube is used to sense pressure for calculating air speed. A normal shock stands in front of the tube. Evaluate the local isentropic stagnation conditions in front of the shock. Estimate the stagnation pressure sensed by the pitot tube. Show static and stagnation state points and the process path on a Ts diagram.

13.110 The Concorde supersonic transport flew at $M = 2.2$ at 20 km altitude. Air is decelerated isentropically by the engine inlet system to a local Mach number of 1.3. The air passed through a normal shock and was decelerated further to $M = 0.4$ at the engine compressor section. Assume, as a first approximation, that this subsonic diffusion process was isentropic and use standard atmosphere data for freestream conditions. Determine the temperature, pressure, and stagnation pressure of the air entering the engine compressor.

13.111 Stagnation pressure and temperature probes are located on the nose of a supersonic aircraft. At 35,000 ft altitude a normal shock stands in front of the probes. The temperature probe indicates $T_0 = 420°F$ behind the shock. Calculate the Mach number and air speed of the plane. Find the static and stagnation pressures behind the shock. Show the process and the static and stagnation state points on a Ts diagram.

13.112 Equations 13.41 are a useful set of equations for analyzing flow through a normal shock. Derive another useful equation,

the Rankine-Hugoniot relation,

$$\frac{p_2}{p_1} = \frac{(k+1)\dfrac{\rho_2}{\rho_1} - (k-1)}{(k+1) - (k-1)\dfrac{\rho_2}{\rho_1}}$$

and use it to find the density ratio for air as $p_2/p_1 \rightarrow \infty$.

13.113 A supersonic wind tunnel is to be operated at $M = 2.2$ in the test section. Upstream from the test section, the nozzle throat area is 0.07 m^2. Air is supplied at stagnation conditions of 500 K and 1.0 MPa (abs). At one flow condition, while the tunnel is being brought up to speed, a normal shock stands at the nozzle exit plane. The flow is steady. For this *starting* condition, immediately downstream from the shock find (a) the Mach number, (b) the static pressure, (c) the stagnation pressure, and (d) the minimum area theoretically possible for the second throat downstream from the test section. On a Ts diagram show static and stagnation state points and the process path.

13.114 Consider a supersonic wind tunnel starting as shown. The nozzle throat area is 1.25 ft^2, and the test section design Mach number is 2.50. As the tunnel starts, a normal shock stands in the divergence of the nozzle where the area is 3.05 ft^2. Upstream stagnation conditions are $T_0 = 1080°$R and $p_0 = 115$ psia. Find the minimum theoretically possible diffuser throat area at this instant. Calculate the entropy increase across the shock.

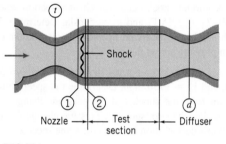

P13.114

13.115 An aircraft is in supersonic flight at 10 km altitude on a standard day. The true air speed of the plane is 659 m/s. Calculate the flight Mach number of the aircraft. A total-head tube attached to the plane is used to sense stagnation pressure which is converted to flight Mach number by an on-board computer. However, the computer programmer has ignored the normal shock that stands in front of the total-head tube and has assumed isentropic flow. Evaluate the pressure sensed by the total-head tube. Determine the erroneous air speed calculated by the computer program.

13.116 A supersonic aircraft cruises at $M = 2.7$ at $60,000$ ft altitude. A normal shock stands in front of a pitot tube on the aircraft; the tube senses a stagnation pressure of 10.4 psia. Calculate the static pressure and temperature behind the shock. Evaluate the loss in stagnation pressure through the shock. Determine the change in specific entropy across the shock. Show static and stagnation states and the process path on a Ts diagram.

13.117 A supersonic aircraft flies at $M_1 = 2.7$ at 20 km altitude on a standard day. Air enters the engine inlet system where it is slowed isentropically to $M_2 = 1.3$. A normal shock occurs at that location. The resulting subsonic flow is decelerated further to $M_4 = 0.40$. The subsonic diffusion is adiabatic but not isentropic; the final pressure is 104 kPa (abs). Evaluate (a) the stagnation

temperature for the flow, (b) the pressure change across the shock, (c) the entropy change, $s_4 - s_1$, and (d) the final stagnation pressure. Sketch the process path on a Ts diagram, indicating all static and stagnation states.

13.118 Air flows through a converging-diverging nozzle with $A_e/A_t = 3.5$. The upstream stagnation conditions are atmospheric; the back pressure is maintained by a vacuum pump. Determine the back pressure required to cause a normal shock to stand in the nozzle exit plane and the flow speed leaving the shock.

13.119 A blast wave propagates outward from an explosion. At large radii, curvature is small and the wave may be treated as a strong normal shock. (The pressure and temperature rise associated with the blast wave decrease as the wave travels outward.) At one instant, a blast wave front travels at $M = 1.60$ with respect to undisturbed air at standard conditions. Find (a) the speed of the air behind the blast wave with respect to the wave and (b) the speed of the air behind the blast wave as seen by an observer on the ground. Draw a Ts diagram for the process as seen by an observer on the wave, indicating static and stagnation state points and property values.

13.120 A converging-diverging nozzle is attached to a large tank of air, in which $T_{0_1} = 300$ K and $p_{0_1} = 250$ kPa (abs). At the nozzle throat the pressure is 132 kPa (abs). In the diverging section, the pressure falls to 68.1 kPa before rising suddenly across a normal shock. At the nozzle exit the pressure is 180 kPa. Find the Mach number immediately behind the shock. Determine the pressure immediately downstream from the shock. Calculate the entropy change across the shock. Sketch the Ts diagram for this flow, indicating static and stagnation state points for conditions at the nozzle throat, both sides of the shock, and the exit plane.

13.121 A converging-diverging nozzle expands air from $250°$F and 50.5 psia to 14.7 psia. The throat and exit plane areas are 0.801 and 0.917 in.^{2}, respectively. Calculate the exit Mach number. Evaluate the mass flow rate through the nozzle.

13.122 A converging-diverging nozzle, with throat area $A_t = 1.0$ in.^{2}, is attached to a large tank in which the pressure and temperature are maintained at 100 psia and $600°$R. The nozzle exit area is 1.58 in.^{2} Determine the exit Mach number at design conditions. Referring to Fig. 13.20, determine the back pressures corresponding to the boundaries of Regimes I, II, III, and IV. Sketch the corresponding plot for this nozzle.

13.123 A converging-diverging nozzle, with $A_e/A_t = 4.0$, is designed to expand air isentropically to atmospheric pressure. Determine the exit Mach number at design conditions and the required inlet stagnation pressure. Referring to Fig. 13.20, determine the back pressures that correspond to the boundaries of Regimes I, II, III, and IV. Sketch the plot of pressure ratio versus axial distance for this nozzle.

13.124 A normal shock occurs in the diverging section of a converging-diverging nozzle where $A = 25$ cm^2 and $M = 2.75$. Upstream, $T_0 = 550$ K and $p_0 = 700$ kPa (abs). The nozzle exit area is 40 cm^2. Assume the flow is isentropic except across the shock. Determine the nozzle exit pressure, throat area, and mass flow rate.

13.125 Air flows adiabatically from a reservoir, where $T = 60°$C and $p = 600$ kPa (abs), through a converging-diverging nozzle with $A_e/A_t = 4.0$. A normal shock occurs where $M = 2.42$. Assuming isentropic flow before and after the shock, determine the back pressure downstream from the nozzle. Sketch the pressure distribution.

13.126 A converging-diverging nozzle is designed to expand air isentropically to atmospheric pressure from a large tank, where $T_0 = 150°C$ and $p_0 = 790$ kPa (abs). A normal shock stands in the diverging section, where $p = 160$ kPa (abs) and $A = 600$ mm^2. Determine the nozzle back pressure, exit area, and throat area.

13.127 A converging-diverging nozzle, with design pressure ratio $p_e/p_0 = 0.128$, is operated with a back pressure condition such that $p_b/p_0 = 0.830$, causing a normal shock to stand in the diverging section. Determine the Mach number at which the shock occurs.

13.128 Air flows through a converging-diverging nozzle, with $A_e/A_t = 3.5$. The upstream stagnation conditions are atmospheric; the back pressure is maintained by a vacuum system. Determine the range of back pressures for which a normal shock will occur within the nozzle and the corresponding mass flow rate, if $A_t = 500$ mm^2.

13.129 A converging-diverging nozzle, with $A_e/A_t = 1.633$, is designed to operate with atmospheric pressure at the exit plane. Determine the range(s) of inlet stagnation pressures for which the nozzle will be free from normal shocks.

13.130 Air flows through a converging-diverging nozzle with $A_e/A_t = 1.87$. Upstream, $T_{0_1} = 240°F$ and $p_{0_1} = 100$ psia. The back pressure is maintained at 40 psia. Determine the Mach number and flow speed in the nozzle exit plane.

13.131 A normal shock occurs in the diverging section of a converging-diverging nozzle where $A = 4.0$ in.^{2} and $M = 2.00$. Upstream, $T_{0_1} = 1000°R$ and $p_{0_1} = 100$ psia. The nozzle exit area is 6.0 in.^{2} Assume that flow is isentropic except across the shock. Find the nozzle exit pressure. Show the processes on a Ts diagram, and indicate the static and stagnation state points.

13.132 Consider flow of air through a converging-diverging nozzle. Sketch the approximate behavior of the mass flow rate versus back pressure ratio, p_b/p_0. Sketch the variation of pressure with distance along the nozzle, and the Ts diagram for the nozzle flow, when the back pressure is p^*.

13.133 Air flows adiabatically from a reservoir, where $T_{0_1} = 60°C$ and $p_{0_1} = 600$ kPa (abs), through a converging-diverging nozzle. The design Mach number of the nozzle is 2.94. A normal shock occurs at the location in the nozzle where $M = 2.42$. Assuming isentropic flow before and after the shock, determine the back pressure downstream from the nozzle. Sketch the pressure distribution.

13.134 A stationary normal shock stands in the diverging section of a converging-diverging nozzle. The Mach number ahead of the shock is 3.0. The nozzle area at the shock is 500 mm^2. The nozzle is fed from a large tank where the pressure is 1000 kPa (gage) and the temperature is 400 K. Find the Mach number, stagnation pressure, and static pressure after the shock. Calculate the nozzle throat area. Evaluate the entropy change across the shock. Finally, if the nozzle exit area is 600 mm^2, estimate the exit Mach number. Would the actual exit Mach number be higher, lower, or the same as your estimate? Why?

*13.135 A supersonic wind tunnel must have two throats, with the second throat larger than the first. Explain why this must be so.

*13.136 A normal shock stands in a section of insulated constant-area duct. The flow is frictional. At section ①, some distance upstream from the shock, $T_1 = 470°R$. At section ④, some distance downstream from the shock, $T_4 = 750°R$ and $M_4 = 1.0$. Denote conditions immediately upstream and downstream from the shock by subscripts ② and ③, respectively. Sketch the pressure distribution along the duct, indicating clearly the locations of sections ① through ④. Sketch a Ts diagram for the flow. Determine the Mach number at section ①.

*13.137 A normal shock stands in a section of insulated constant-area duct. The flow is frictional. At section ①, some distance upstream from the shock, $T_1 = 668°R$, $p_{0_1} = 78.2$ psia, and $M_1 = 2.05$. At section ④, some distance downstream from the shock, $M_4 = 1.00$. Calculate the air speed, V_2, immediately ahead of the shock, where $T_2 = 388°F$. Evaluate the entropy change, $s_4 - s_1$.

13.138 Show that as the upstream Mach number approaches infinity, the Mach number after an oblique shock becomes

$$M_2 \approx \sqrt{\frac{k-1}{2k\sin^2(\beta-\theta)}}$$

13.139 Supersonic air flow at $M_1 = 2.5$ and 80 kPa (abs) is deflected by an oblique shock with angle $\beta = 35°$. Find the Mach number and pressure after the shock, and the deflection angle. Compare these results to those obtained if instead the flow had experienced a normal shock. What is the smallest possible value of angle β for this upstream Mach number?

13.140 Consider supersonic flow of air at $M_1 = 3.0$. What is the range of possible values of the oblique shock angle β? For this range of β, plot the pressure ratio across the shock.

13.141 The air velocities before and after an oblique shock are 1250 m/s and 650 m/s, respectively, and the deflection angle is $\theta = 35°$. Find the oblique shock angle β, and the pressure ratio across the shock.

13.142 The temperature and Mach number before an oblique shock are $T_1 = 10°C$ and $M_1 = 3.25$, respectively, and the pressure ratio across the shock is 5. Find the deflection angle, θ, the shock angle, β, and the Mach number after the shock, M_2.

13.143 An airfoil at zero angle of attack has a sharp leading edge with an included angle of 20°. It is being tested over a range of speeds in a wind tunnel. The air temperature upstream is maintained at 15°C. Determine the Mach number and corresponding air speed at which a detached normal shock first attaches to the leading edge, and the angle of the resulting oblique shock. Plot the oblique shock angle β as a function of upstream Mach number M_1, from the minimum attached-shock value through $M_1 = 7$.

13.144 An airfoil has a sharp leading edge with an included angle of $\delta = 60°$. It is being tested in a wind tunnel running at 1200 m/s (the air pressure and temperature upstream are 75 kPa and 3.5°C). Plot the pressure and temperature in the region adjacent to the upper surface as functions of angle of attack, α, ranging from $\alpha = 0°$ to 30°. What are the maximum pressure and

---

temperature? (Ignore the possibility of a detached shock developing if α is too large; see Problem 13.145.)

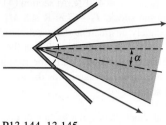

P13.144, 13.145

13.145 The airfoil of Problem 13.144 will develop a detached shock on the lower surface if the angle of attack, α, exceeds a certain value. What is this angle of attack? Plot the pressure and temperature in the region adjacent to the lower surface as functions of angle of attack, α, ranging from $\alpha = 0°$ to the angle at which the shock becomes detached. What are the maximum pressure and temperature?

13.146 The wedge-shaped airfoil shown has chord $c = 1.5$ m and included angle $\delta = 7°$. Find the lift per unit span at a Mach number of 2.75 in air for which the static pressure is 70 kPa.

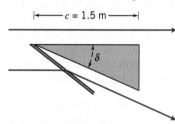

P13.146, 13.155

13.147 The wedge-shaped airfoil shown has chord $c = 2$ m and angles $\delta_{lower} = 15°$ and $\delta_{upper} = 5°$. Find the lift per unit span at a Mach number of 2.75 in air at a static pressure of 75 kPa.

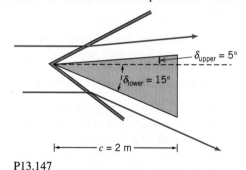

P13.147

13.148 An oblique shock causes a flow that was at $M = 4$ and a static pressure of 75 kPa to slow down to $M = 2.5$. Find the deflection angle and the static pressure after the shock.

13.149 The geometry of the fuselage and engine cowling near the inlet to the engine of a supersonic fighter aircraft is designed so that the incoming air at $M = 3$ is deflected 7.5 degrees, and then experiences a normal shock at the engine entrance. If the incoming air is at 50 kPa, what is the pressure of the air entering the engine? What would be the pressure if the incoming air was slowed down by only a normal shock?

13.150 Air flows isentropically at $M = 2.5$ in a duct. There is a 7.5° contraction that triggers an oblique shock, which in turn reflects off a wall generating a second oblique shock. This second shock is necessary so the flow ends up flowing parallel to the channel walls after the two shocks. Find the Mach number and pressure in the contraction and downstream of the contraction. (Note that the convex corner will have expansion waves to redirect the flow along the upper wall.)

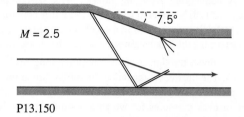

P13.150

13.151 A flow at $M = 2.5$ is deflected by a combination of interacting oblique shocks as shown. The first shock pair is aligned at 50° to the flow. A second oblique shock pair deflects the flow again so it ends up parallel to the original flow. If the pressure before any deflections is 50 kPa, find the pressure after two deflections.

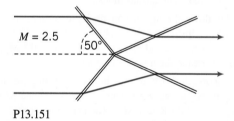

P13.151

13.152 Air flows at Mach number of 1.5, static pressure 95 kPa, and is expanded by angles $\theta_1 = 15°$ and $\theta_2 = 15°$, as shown. Find the pressure changes.

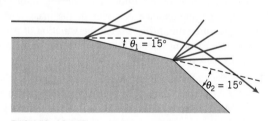

P13.152, 13.153

13.153 Find the incoming and intermediate Mach numbers and static pressures if, after two expansions of $\theta_1 = 15°$ and $\theta_2 = 15°$, the Mach number is 4 and static pressure is 10 kPa.

13.154 Compare the static and stagnation pressures produced by (a) an oblique shock and (b) isentropic *compression* waves as they each deflect a flow at a Mach number of 3.5 through a deflection angle of 35° in air for which the static pressure is 50 kPa.

13.155 Consider the wedge-shaped airfoil of Problem 13.146. Suppose the oblique shock could be replaced by isentropic *compression* waves. Find the lift per unit span at the Mach number of 2.75 in air for which the static pressure is 70 kPa.

13.156 Find the lift and drag per unit span on the airfoil shown for flight at a Mach number of 1.75 in air for which the static pressure is 50 kPa. The chord length is 1 m.

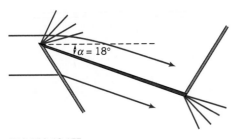

P13.156, 13.157

13.157 Plot the lift and drag per unit span, and the lift/drag ratio, as functions of angle of attack for $\alpha = 0°$ to $18°$, for the airfoil shown, for flight at a Mach number of 1.75 in air for which the static pressure is 50 kPa. The chord length is 1 m.

13.158 Find the drag coefficient of the symmetric, zero angle of attack airfoil shown for a Mach number of 2.0 in air for which the static pressure is 95 kPa and temperature is 0°C. The included angles at the nose and tail are each 10°.

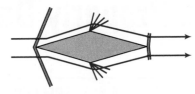

P13.158, 13.159

13.159 Find the lift and drag coefficients of the airfoil of Problem 13.158 if the airfoil now has an angle of attack of 12°.

Appendix A

Fluid Property Data

A-1 SPECIFIC GRAVITY

Specific gravity data for several common liquids and solids are presented in Figs. A.1a and A.1b and in Tables A.1 and A.2. For liquids specific gravity is a function of temperature. (Density data for water and air are given as functions of temperature in Tables A.7 through A.10.) For most liquids specific gravity decreases as temperature increases. Water is unique: It displays a maximum density of 1000 kg/m^3 (1.94 slug/ft^3) at 4°C (39°F). The maximum density of water is used as a reference value to calculate specific gravity. Thus

$$SG \equiv \frac{\rho}{\rho_{H_2O} \text{ (at 4°C)}}$$

Consequently the maximum SG of water is exactly unity.

Specific gravities for solids are relatively insensitive to temperature; values given in Table A.1 were measured at 20°C.

The specific gravity of seawater depends on both its temperature and salinity. A representative value for ocean water is SG = 1.025, as given in Table A.2.

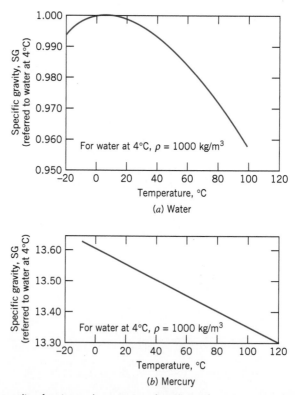

Fig. A.1 Specific gravity of water and mercury as functions of temperature. (Data from [1].) (The specific gravity of mercury varies linearly with temperature. The variation is given by SG = 13.60 − 0.00240 T when T is measured in degrees C.)

TABLE A.1 Specific Gravities of Selected Engineering Materials

(a) Common Manometer Liquids at 20°C (Data from [1, 2, 3].)

Liquid	Specific Gravity
E.V. Hill blue oil	0.797
Meriam red oil	0.827
Benzene	0.879
Dibutyl phthalate	1.04
Monochloronaphthalene	1.20
Carbon tetrachloride	1.595
Bromoethylbenzene (Meriam blue)	1.75
Tetrabromoethane	2.95
Mercury	13.55

(b) Common Materials (Data from [4].)

Material	Specific Gravity (—)
Aluminum	2.64
Balsa wood	0.14
Brass	8.55
Cast Iron	7.08
Concrete (cured)	2.4[a]
Concrete (liquid)	2.5[a]
Copper	8.91
Ice (0°C)	0.917
Lead	11.4
Oak	0.77
Steel	7.83
Styrofoam (1 pcf[b])	0.0160
Styrofoam (3 pcf)	0.0481
Uranium (depleted)	18.7
White pine	0.43

[a]depending on aggregate.
[b]pounds per cubic foot.

TABLE A.2 Physical Properties of Common Liquids at 20°C (Data from [1, 5, 6].)

Liquid	Isentropic Bulk Modulus[a] (GN/m^2)	Specific Gravity (—)
Benzene	1.48	0.879
Carbon tetrachloride	1.36	1.595
Castor oil	2.11	0.969
Crude oil	—	0.82–0.92
Ethanol	—	0.789
Gasoline	—	0.72
Glycerin	4.59	1.26
Heptane	0.886	0.684
Kerosene	1.43	0.82
Lubricating oil	1.44	0.88
Methanol	—	0.796
Mercury	28.5	13.55
Octane	0.963	0.702
Seawater[b]	2.42	1.025
SAE 10W oil	—	0.92
Water	2.24	0.998

[a]Calculated from speed of sound; $1 GN/m^2 = 10^9 N/m^2$ ($1 N/m^2 = 1.45 \times 10^{-4}$ lbf/in.^{2}).
[b]Dynamic viscosity of seawater at 20°C is $\mu = 1.08 \times 10^{-3}$ N · s/m^2. (Thus, the kinematic viscosity of seawater is about 5 percent higher than that of fresh water.)

TABLE A.3 Properties of the U.S. Standard Atmosphere (Data from [7].)

Geometric Altitude (m)	Temperature (K)	p/p_{SL} (—)	ρ/ρ_{SL} (—)
−500	291.4	1.061	1.049
0	288.2	1.000[a]	1.000[b]
500	284.9	0.9421	0.9529
1,000	281.7	0.8870	0.9075
1,500	278.4	0.8345	0.8638
2,000	275.2	0.7846	0.8217
2,500	271.9	0.7372	0.7812
3,000	268.7	0.6920	0.7423
3,500	265.4	0.6492	0.7048
4,000	262.2	0.6085	0.6689
4,500	258.9	0.5700	0.6343
5,000	255.7	0.5334	0.6012
6,000	249.2	0.4660	0.5389
7,000	242.7	0.4057	0.4817
8,000	236.2	0.3519	0.4292
9,000	229.7	0.3040	0.3813
10,000	223.3	0.2615	0.3376
11,000	216.8	0.2240	0.2978
12,000	216.7	0.1915	0.2546
13,000	216.7	0.1636	0.2176
14,000	216.7	0.1399	0.1860
15,000	216.7	0.1195	0.1590
16,000	216.7	0.1022	0.1359
17,000	216.7	0.08734	0.1162
18,000	216.7	0.07466	0.09930
19,000	216.7	0.06383	0.08489
20,000	216.7	0.05457	0.07258
22,000	218.6	0.03995	0.05266
24,000	220.6	0.02933	0.03832
26,000	222.5	0.02160	0.02797
28,000	224.5	0.01595	0.02047
30,000	226.5	0.01181	0.01503
40,000	250.4	0.002834	0.003262
50,000	270.7	0.0007874	0.0008383
60,000	255.8	0.0002217	0.0002497
70,000	219.7	0.00005448	0.00007146
80,000	180.7	0.00001023	0.00001632
90,000	180.7	0.000001622	0.000002588

[a] $p_{SL} = 1.01325 \times 10^5$ N/m² (abs) (=14.696 psia).
[b] $\rho_{SL} = 1.2250$ kg/m³ (= 0.002377 slug/ft³).

| A-2 | **SURFACE TENSION** |

The values of surface tension, σ, for most organic compounds are remarkably similar at room temperature; the typical range is 25 to 40 mN/m. Water is higher, at about 73 mN/m at 20°C. Liquid metals have values in the range between 300 and 600 mN/m; mercury has a value of about 480 mN/m at 20°C. Surface tension decreases with temperature; the decrease is nearly linear with absolute temperature. Surface tension at the critical temperature is zero.

Values of σ are usually reported for surfaces in contact with the pure vapor of the liquid being studied or with air. At low pressures both values are about the same.

TABLE A.4 Surface Tension of Common Liquids at 20°C (Data from [1, 5, 8, 9].)

Liquid	Surface Tension, σ (mN/m)[a]	Contact Angle, θ (degrees)
(a) In contact with air		
Benzene	28.9	
Carbon tetrachloride	27.0	
Ethanol	22.3	
Glycerin	63.0	
Hexane	18.4	
Kerosene	26.8	
Lube oil	25–35	
Mercury	484	140
Methanol	22.6	
Octane	21.8	
Water	72.8	~0
(b) In contact with water		
Benzene	35.0	
Carbon tetrachloride	45.0	
Hexane	51.1	
Mercury	375	140
Methanol	22.7	
Octane	50.8	

[a]1 mN/m = 10^{-3} N/m.

A-3   THE PHYSICAL NATURE OF VISCOSITY

Viscosity is a measure of internal fluid friction, i.e., resistance to deformation. The mechanism of gas viscosity is reasonably well understood, but the theory is poorly developed for liquids. We can gain some insight into the physical nature of viscous flow by discussing these mechanisms briefly.

The viscosity of a Newtonian fluid is fixed by the state of the material. Thus $\mu = \mu(T, p)$. Temperature is the more important variable, so let us consider it first. Excellent empirical equations for viscosity as a function of temperature are available.

Effect of Temperature on Viscosity

a. Gases

All gas molecules are in continuous random motion. When there is bulk motion due to flow, the bulk motion is superimposed on the random motions. It is then distributed throughout the fluid by molecular collisions. Analyses based on kinetic theory predict

$$\mu \propto \sqrt{T}$$

The kinetic theory prediction is in fair agreement with experimental trends, but the constant of proportionality and one or more correction factors must be determined; this limits practical application of this simple equation.

If two or more experimental points are available, the data may be correlated using the empirical Sutherland correlation [7]

$$\mu = \frac{bT^{1/2}}{1 + S/T} \qquad (A.1)$$

Constants b and S may be determined most simply by writing

$$\mu = \frac{bT^{3/2}}{S + T}$$

or

$$\frac{T^{3/2}}{\mu} = \left(\frac{1}{b}\right)T + \frac{S}{b}$$

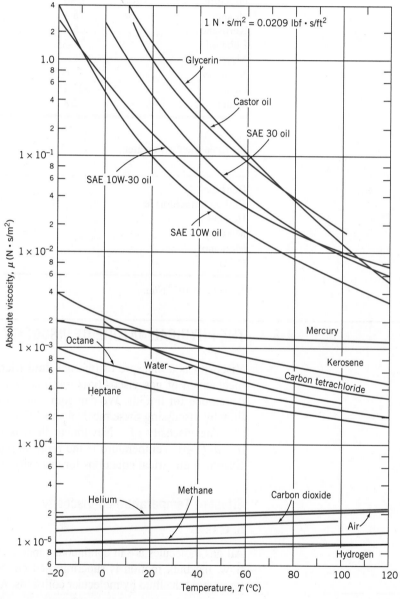

Fig. A.2 Dynamic (absolute) viscosity of common fluids as a function of temperature. (Data from [1, 6, and 10].)

The graphs for air and water were computed from the *Excel* workbook *Absolute Viscosities*, using Eq. A.1 and Eq. A.3, respectively. The workbook can be used to compute viscosities of other fluids if constants b and S (for a gas) or A, B, and C (for a liquid) are known.

(Compare this with $y = mx + c$.) From a plot of $T^{3/2}/\mu$ versus T, one obtains the slope, $1/b$, and the intercept, S/b. For air,

$$b = 1.458 \times 10^{-6} \; \frac{kg}{m \cdot s \cdot K^{1/2}}$$

$$S = 110.4 \; K$$

These constants were used with Eq. A.1 to compute viscosities for the standard atmosphere in [7], the air viscosity values at various temperatures shown in Table A.10, and using appropriate conversion factors, the values shown in Table A.9.

b. Liquids

Viscosities for liquids cannot be estimated well theoretically. The phenomenon of momentum transfer by molecular collisions is overshadowed in liquids by the effects of interacting force fields among the closely packed liquid molecules.

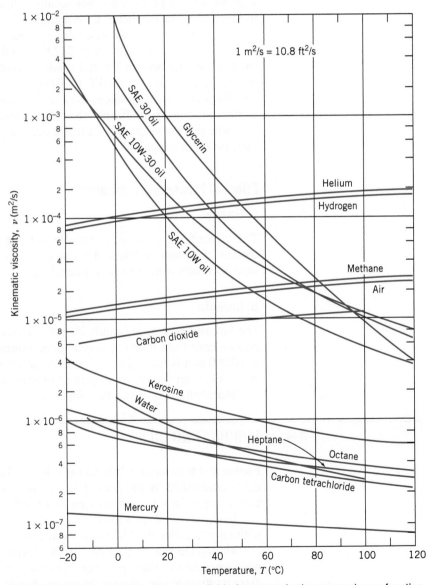

Fig. A.3 Kinematic viscosity of common fluids (at atmospheric pressure) as a function of temperature. (Data from [1, 6, and 10].)

Liquid viscosities are affected drastically by temperature. This dependence on absolute temperature may be represented by the empirical equation

$$\mu = Ae^{B/(T-C)} \tag{A.2}$$

or the equivalent form

$$\mu = A10^{B/(T-C)} \tag{A.3}$$

where T is absolute temperature.

Equation A.3 requires at least three points to fit constants A, B, and C. In theory it is possible to determine the constants from measurements of viscosity at just three temperatures. It is better practice to use more data and to obtain the constants from a statistical fit to the data.

However a curve-fit is developed, always compare the resulting line or curve with the available data. The best way is to critically inspect a plot of the curve-fit compared with the data. In general, curve-fit results will be satisfactory only when the quality of the available data and that of the empirical relation are known to be excellent.

Data for the dynamic viscosity of water are fitted well using constant values $A = 2.414 \times 10^{-5}$ N $\cdot$ s/m^2, $B = 247.8$ K, and $C = 140$ K. Reference 10 states that using these constants in Eq. A.3 predicts water viscosity within $\pm$ 2.5 percent over the temperature range from 0°C to 370°C. Equation A.3 and *Excel* were used to compute the water viscosity values at various temperatures shown in Table A.8, and using appropriate conversion factors, the values shown in Table A.7.

Note that the viscosity of a liquid decreases with temperature, while that of a gas increases with temperature.

Effect of Pressure on Viscosity

a. Gases

The viscosity of gases is essentially independent of pressure between a few hundredths of an atmosphere and a few atmospheres. However, viscosity at high pressures increases with pressure (or density).

b. Liquids

The viscosities of most liquids are not affected by moderate pressures, but large increases have been found at very high pressures. For example, the viscosity of water at 10,000 atm is twice that at 1 atm. More complex compounds show a viscosity increase of several orders of magnitude over the same pressure range.

More information may be found in [11].

A-4 LUBRICATING OILS

Engine and transmission lubricating oils are classified by viscosity according to standards established by the Society of Automotive Engineers [12]. The allowable viscosity ranges for several grades are given in Table A.5.

Viscosity numbers with W (e.g., 20W) are classified by viscosity at 0°F. Those without W are classified by viscosity at 210°F.

Multigrade oils (e.g., 10W-40) are formulated to minimize viscosity variation with temperature. High polymer "viscosity index improvers" are used in blending these multigrade oils. Such additives are highly non-Newtonian; they may suffer permanent viscosity loss caused by shearing.

Special charts are available to estimate the viscosity of petroleum products as a function of temperature. The charts were used to develop the data for typical lubricating oils plotted in Figs. A.2 and A.3. For details, see [15].

TABLE A.5 Allowable Viscosity Ranges for Lubricants (Data from [12–14].)

Engine Oil	SAE Viscosity Grade	Max. Viscosity (cP)[a] at Temp. (°C)	Viscosity (cSt)[b] at 100°C	
			Min	Max
	0W	3250 at −30	3.8	—
	5W	3500 at −25	3.8	—
	10W	3500 at −20	4.1	—
	15W	3500 at −15	5.6	—
	20W	4500 at −10	5.6	—
	25W	6000 at −5	9.3	—
	20	—	5.6	<9.3
	30	—	9.3	<12.5
	40	—	12.5	<16.3
	50	—	16.3	<21.9

Axle and Manual Transmission Lubricant	SAE Viscosity Grade	Max. Temp. (°C) for Viscosity of 150,000 cP	Viscosity (cSt) at 100°C	
			Min	Max
	70W	−55	4.1	—
	75W	−40	4.1	—
	80W	−26	7.0	—
	85W	−12	11.0	—
	90	—	13.5	<24.0
	140	—	24.0	<41.0
	250	—	41.0	—

Automatic Transmission Fluid (Typical)	Maximum Viscosity (cP)	Temperature (°C)	Viscosity (cSt) at 100°C	
			Min	Max
	50000	−40	6.5	8.5
	4000	−23.3	6.5	8.5
	1700	−18	6.5	8.5

[a] centipoise = 1 cP = 1 mPa · s = 10^{-3} Pa · s (= 2.09×10^{-5} lbf · s/ft^2).
[b] centistoke = 10^{-6} m^2/s (= 1.08×10^{-5} ft^2/s).

TABLE A.6 Thermodynamic Properties of Common Gases at STP[a] (Data from [7, 16, 17].)

Gas	Chemical Symbol	Molecular Mass, M_m	R^b $\left(\dfrac{\text{J}}{\text{kg} \cdot \text{K}}\right)$	c_p $\left(\dfrac{\text{J}}{\text{kg} \cdot \text{K}}\right)$	c_v $\left(\dfrac{\text{J}}{\text{kg} \cdot \text{K}}\right)$	$k = \dfrac{c_p}{c_v}$ (—)	R^b $\left(\dfrac{\text{ft} \cdot \text{lbf}}{\text{lbm} \cdot {}^\circ\text{R}}\right)$	c_p $\left(\dfrac{\text{Btu}}{\text{lbm} \cdot {}^\circ\text{R}}\right)$	c_v $\left(\dfrac{\text{Btu}}{\text{lbm} \cdot {}^\circ\text{R}}\right)$
Air	—	28.98	286.9	1004	717.4	1.40	53.33	0.2399	0.1713
Carbon dioxide	CO_2	44.01	188.9	840.4	651.4	1.29	35.11	0.2007	0.1556
Carbon monoxide	CO	28.01	296.8	1039	742.1	1.40	55.17	0.2481	0.1772
Helium	He	4.003	2077	5225	3147	1.66	386.1	1.248	0.7517
Hydrogen	H_2	2.016	4124	14,180	10,060	1.41	766.5	3.388	2.402
Methane	CH_4	16.04	518.3	2190	1672	1.31	96.32	0.5231	0.3993
Nitrogen	N_2	28.01	296.8	1039	742.0	1.40	55.16	0.2481	0.1772
Oxygen	O_2	32.00	259.8	909.4	649.6	1.40	48.29	0.2172	0.1551
Steam[c]	H_2O	18.02	461.4	~2000	~1540	~1.30	85.78	~0.478	~0.368

[a]STP = standard temperature and pressure, $T = 15^\circ\text{C} = 59^\circ\text{F}$ and $p = 101.325$ kPa (abs) = 14.696 psia.

[b]$R \equiv R_u/M_m$; $R_u = 8314.3$ J/(kgmol·K) = 1545.3 ft·lbf/(lbmol·°R); 1 Btu = 778.2 ft·lbf.

[c]Water vapor behaves as an ideal gas when superheated by 55°C (100°F) or more.

TABLE A.7 Properties of Water (U.S. Customary Units)

Temperature, T (°F)	Density, ρ (slug/ft^3)	Dynamic Viscosity, μ (lbf·s/ft^2)	Kinematic Viscosity, ν (ft^2/s)	Surface Tension, σ (lbf/ft)	Vapor Pressure, p_ν (psia)	Bulk Modulus, E_ν (psi)
32	1.94	3.68E-05	1.90E-05	0.00519	0.0886	2.92E + 05
40	1.94	3.20E-05	1.65E-05	0.00514	0.122	
50	1.94	2.73E-05	1.41E-05	0.00509	0.178	
59	1.94	2.38E-05	1.23E-05	0.00504	0.247	
60	1.94	2.35E-05	1.21E-05	0.00503	0.256	
68	1.94	2.10E-05	1.08E-05	0.00499	0.339	
70	1.93	2.05E-05	1.06E-05	0.00498	0.363	3.20E + 05
80	1.93	1.80E-05	9.32E-06	0.00492	0.507	
90	1.93	1.59E-05	8.26E-06	0.00486	0.699	
100	1.93	1.43E-05	7.38E-06	0.00480	0.950	
110	1.92	1.28E-05	6.68E-06	0.00474	1.28	
120	1.92	1.16E-05	6.05E-06	0.00467	1.70	3.32E + 05
130	1.91	1.06E-05	5.54E-06	0.00461	2.23	
140	1.91	9.70E-06	5.08E-06	0.00454	2.89	
150	1.90	8.93E-06	4.70E-06	0.00448	3.72	
160	1.89	8.26E-06	4.37E-06	0.00441	4.75	
170	1.89	7.67E-06	4.06E-06	0.00434	6.00	
180	1.88	7.15E-06	3.80E-06	0.00427	7.52	
190	1.87	6.69E-06	3.58E-06	0.00420	9.34	
200	1.87	6.28E-06	3.36E-06	0.00413	11.5	3.08E + 05
212	1.86	5.84E-06	3.14E-06	0.00404	14.7	

TABLE A.8 Properties of Water (SI Units)

Temperature, T (°C)	Density, ρ (kg/m^3)	Dynamic Viscosity, μ (N·s/m^2)	Kinematic Viscosity, ν (m^2/s)	Surface Tension, σ (N/m)	Vapor Pressure, p_ν (kPa)	Bulk Modulus, E_ν (GPa)
0	1000	1.76E-03	1.76E-06	0.0757	0.661	2.01
5	1000	1.51E-03	1.51E-06	0.0749	0.872	
10	1000	1.30E-03	1.30E-06	0.0742	1.23	
15	999	1.14E-03	1.14E-06	0.0735	1.71	
20	998	1.01E-03	1.01E-06	0.0727	2.34	2.21
25	997	8.93E-04	8.96E-07	0.0720	3.17	
30	996	8.00E-04	8.03E-07	0.0712	4.25	
35	994	7.21E-04	7.25E-07	0.0704	5.63	
40	992	6.53E-04	6.59E-07	0.0696	7.38	
45	990	5.95E-04	6.02E-07	0.0688	9.59	
50	988	5.46E-04	5.52E-07	0.0679	12.4	2.29
55	986	5.02E-04	5.09E-07	0.0671	15.8	
60	983	4.64E-04	4.72E-07	0.0662	19.9	
65	980	4.31E-04	4.40E-07	0.0654	25.0	
70	978	4.01E-04	4.10E-07	0.0645	31.2	
75	975	3.75E-04	3.85E-07	0.0636	38.6	
80	972	3.52E-04	3.62E-07	0.0627	47.4	
85	969	3.31E-04	3.41E-07	0.0618	57.8	
90	965	3.12E-04	3.23E-07	0.0608	70.1	2.12
95	962	2.95E-04	3.06E-07	0.0599	84.6	
100	958	2.79E-04	2.92E-07	0.0589	101	

TABLE A.9 Properties of Air at Atmospheric Pressure (U.S. Customary Units)

Temperature, T (°F)	Density, ρ (slug/ft^3)	Dynamic Viscosity, μ (lbf · s/ft^2)	Kinematic Viscosity, ν (ft^2/s)
40	0.00247	3.63E-07	1.47E-04
50	0.00242	3.69E-07	1.52E-04
59	0.00238	3.74E-07	1.57E-04
60	0.00237	3.74E-07	1.58E-04
68	0.00234	3.79E-07	1.62E-04
70	0.00233	3.80E-07	1.63E-04
80	0.00229	3.85E-07	1.68E-04
90	0.00225	3.91E-07	1.74E-04
100	0.00221	3.96E-07	1.79E-04
110	0.00217	4.02E-07	1.86E-04
120	0.00213	4.07E-07	1.91E-04
130	0.00209	4.12E-07	1.97E-04
140	0.00206	4.18E-07	2.03E-04
150	0.00202	4.23E-07	2.09E-04
160	0.00199	4.28E-07	2.15E-04
170	0.00196	4.33E-07	2.21E-04
180	0.00193	4.38E-07	2.27E-04
190	0.00190	4.43E-07	2.33E-04
200	0.00187	4.48E-07	2.40E-04

TABLE A.10 Properties of Air at Atmospheric Pressure (SI Units)

Temperature, T (°C)	Density, ρ (kg/m^3)	Dynamic Viscosity, μ (N · s/m^2)	Kinematic Viscosity, ν (m^2/s)
0	1.29	1.72E-05	1.33E-05
5	1.27	1.74E-05	1.37E-05
10	1.25	1.76E-05	1.41E-05
15	1.23	1.79E-05	1.45E-05
20	1.21	1.81E-05	1.50E-05
25	1.19	1.84E-05	1.54E-05
30	1.17	1.86E-05	1.59E-05
35	1.15	1.88E-05	1.64E-05
40	1.13	1.91E-05	1.69E-05
45	1.11	1.93E-05	1.74E-05
50	1.09	1.95E-05	1.79E-05
55	1.08	1.98E-05	1.83E-05
60	1.06	2.00E-05	1.89E-05
65	1.04	2.02E-05	1.94E-05
70	1.03	2.04E-05	1.98E-05
75	1.01	2.06E-05	2.04E-05
80	1.00	2.09E-05	2.09E-05
85	0.987	2.11E-05	2.14E-05
90	0.973	2.13E-05	2.19E-05
95	0.960	2.15E-05	2.24E-05
100	0.947	2.17E-05	2.29E-05

REFERENCES

1. *Handbook of Chemistry and Physics*, 62nd ed. Cleveland, OH: Chemical Rubber Publishing Co., 1981–1982.

2. "Meriam Standard Indicating Fluids," Pamphlet No. 920GEN: 430-1, The Meriam Instrument Co., 10920 Madison Avenue, Cleveland, OH 44102.

3. E. Vernon Hill, Inc., P.O. Box 7053, Corte Madera, CA 94925.

4. Avallone, E. A., and T. Baumeister, III, eds., *Marks' Standard Handbook for Mechanical Engineers*, 11th ed. New York: McGraw-Hill, 2007.

5. *Handbook of Tables for Applied Engineering Science*. Cleveland, OH: Chemical Rubber Publishing Co., 1970.

6. Vargaftik, N. B., *Tables on the Thermophysical Properties of Liquids and Gases*, 2nd ed. Washington, D.C.: Hemisphere Publishing Corp., 1975.

7. *The U.S. Standard Atmosphere (1976)*. Washington, D.C.: U.S. Government Printing Office, 1976.

8. Trefethen, L., "Surface Tension in Fluid Mechanics," in *Illustrated Experiments in Fluid Mechanics*. Cambridge, MA: The M.I.T. Press, 1972.

9. Streeter, V. L., ed., *Handbook of Fluid Dynamics*. New York: McGraw-Hill, 1961.

10. Touloukian, Y. S., S. C. Saxena, and P. Hestermans, *Thermophysical Properties of Matter, the TPRC Data Series. Vol. 11—Viscosity*. New York: Plenum Publishing Corp., 1975.

11. Reid, R. C., and T. K. Sherwood, *The Properties of Gases and Liquids*, 2nd ed. New York: McGraw-Hill, 1966.

12. "Engine Oil Viscosity Classification—SAE Standard J300 Jun86," *SAE Handbook*, 1987 ed. Warrendale, PA: Society of Automotive Engineers, 1987.

13. "Axle and Manual Transmission Lubricant Viscosity Classification—SAE Standard J306 Mar85," *SAE Handbook*, 1987 ed. Warrendale, PA: Society of Automotive Engineers, 1987.

14. "Fluid for Passenger Car Type Automatic Transmissions—SAE Information Report J311 Apr86," *SAE Handbook*, 1987 ed. Warrendale, PA: Society of Automotive Engineers, 1987.

15. ASTM Standard D 341–77, "Viscosity-Temperature Charts for Liquid Petroleum Products," American Society for Testing and Materials, 1916 Race Street, Philadelphia, PA 19103.

16. NASA, *Compressed Gas Handbook* (Revised). Washington, D.C.: National Aeronautics and Space Administration, SP-3045, 1970.

17. ASME, *Thermodynamic and Transport Properties of Steam*. New York: American Society of Mechanical Engineers, 1967.

Equations of Motion in Cylindrical Coordinates

The continuity equation in cylindrical coordinates for constant density is

$$\frac{1}{r}\frac{\partial}{\partial r}(rv_r) + \frac{1}{r}\frac{\partial}{\partial \theta}(v_\theta) + \frac{\partial}{\partial z}(v_z) = 0 \tag{B.1}$$

Normal and shear stresses in cylindrical coordinates for constant density and viscosity are

$$\sigma_{rr} = -p + 2\mu\frac{\partial v_r}{\partial r} \qquad\qquad \tau_{r\theta} = \mu\left[r\frac{\partial}{\partial r}\left(\frac{v_\theta}{r}\right) + \frac{1}{r}\frac{\partial v_r}{\partial \theta}\right]$$

$$\sigma_{\theta\theta} = -p + 2\mu\left(\frac{1}{r}\frac{\partial v_\theta}{\partial \theta} + \frac{v_r}{r}\right) \qquad \tau_{\theta z} = \mu\left(\frac{\partial v_\theta}{\partial z} + \frac{1}{r}\frac{\partial v_z}{\partial \theta}\right)$$

$$\sigma_{zz} = -p + 2\mu\frac{\partial v_z}{\partial z} \qquad\qquad \tau_{zr} = \mu\left(\frac{\partial v_r}{\partial z} + \frac{\partial v_z}{\partial r}\right) \tag{B.2}$$

The Navier–Stokes equations in cylindrical coordinates for constant density and viscosity are

r component:

$$\rho\left(\frac{\partial v_r}{\partial t} + v_r\frac{\partial v_r}{\partial r} + \frac{v_\theta}{r}\frac{\partial v_r}{\partial \theta} - \frac{v_\theta^2}{r} + v_z\frac{\partial v_r}{\partial z}\right)$$

$$= \rho g_r - \frac{\partial p}{\partial r} + \mu\left\{\frac{\partial}{\partial r}\left(\frac{1}{r}\frac{\partial}{\partial r}[rv_r]\right) + \frac{1}{r^2}\frac{\partial^2 v_r}{\partial \theta^2} - \frac{2}{r^2}\frac{\partial v_\theta}{\partial \theta} + \frac{\partial^2 v_r}{\partial z^2}\right\} \tag{B.3a}$$

θ component:

$$\rho\left(\frac{\partial v_\theta}{\partial t} + v_r\frac{\partial v_\theta}{\partial r} + \frac{v_\theta}{r}\frac{\partial v_\theta}{\partial \theta} + \frac{v_r v_\theta}{r} + v_z\frac{\partial v_\theta}{\partial z}\right)$$

$$= \rho g_\theta - \frac{1}{r}\frac{\partial p}{\partial \theta} + \mu\left\{\frac{\partial}{\partial r}\left(\frac{1}{r}\frac{\partial}{\partial r}[rv_\theta]\right) + \frac{1}{r^2}\frac{\partial^2 v_\theta}{\partial \theta^2} + \frac{2}{r^2}\frac{\partial v_r}{\partial \theta} + \frac{\partial^2 v_\theta}{\partial z^2}\right\} \tag{B.3b}$$

z component:

$$\rho\left(\frac{\partial v_z}{\partial t} + v_r\frac{\partial v_z}{\partial r} + \frac{v_\theta}{r}\frac{\partial v_z}{\partial \theta} + v_z\frac{\partial v_z}{\partial z}\right)$$

$$= \rho g_z - \frac{\partial p}{\partial z} + \mu\left\{\frac{1}{r}\frac{\partial}{\partial r}\left(r\frac{\partial v_z}{\partial r}\right) + \frac{1}{r^2}\frac{\partial^2 v_z}{\partial \theta^2} + \frac{\partial^2 v_z}{\partial z^2}\right\} \tag{B.3c}$$

Videos for Fluid Mechanics

Listed below by supplier are titles of videos on fluid mechanics. The videos can also be seen online for free at http://web.mit.edu/fluids/www/Shapiro/ncfmf.html.

1. Encyclopaedia Britannica Educational Corporation
    310 South Michigan Avenue
    Chicago, Illinois 60604
        The following twenty-two videos, developed by the National Committee for Fluid Mechanics Films (NCFMF),[1] are available (length as noted):

    Aerodynamic Generation of Sound (44 min, principals: M. J. Lighthill, J. E. Ffowcs-Williams)
    Boundary Layer Control (25 min, principal: D. C. Hazen)
    Cavitation (31 min, principal: P. Eisenberg)
    Channel Flow of a Compressible Fluid (29 min, principal: D. E. Coles)
    Deformation of Continuous Media (38 min, principal: J. L. Lumley)
    Eulerian and Lagrangian Descriptions in Fluid Mechanics (27 min, principal: J. L. Lumley)
    Flow Instabilities (27 min, principal: E. L. Mollo-Christensen)
    Flow Visualization (31 min, principal: S. J. Kline)
    The Fluid Dynamics of Drag[2] (4 parts, 120 min, principal: A. H. Shapiro)
    Fundamentals of Boundary Layers (24 min, principal: F. H. Abernathy)
    Low-Reynolds-Number Flows (33 min, principal: Sir G. I. Taylor)
    Magnetohydrodynamics (27 min, principal: J. A. Shercliff)
    Pressure Fields and Fluid Acceleration (30 min, principal: A. H. Shapiro)
    Rarefied Gas Dynamics (33 min, principals: F. C. Hurlbut, F. S. Sherman)
    Rheological Behavior of Fluids (22 min, principal: H. Markovitz)
    Rotating Flows (29 min, principal: D. Fultz)
    Secondary Flow (30 min, principal: E. S. Taylor)
    Stratified Flow (26 min, principal: R. R. Long)
    Surface Tension in Fluid Mechanics (29 min, principal: L. M. Trefethen)
    Turbulence (29 min, principal: R. W. Stewart)
    Vorticity (2 parts, 44 min, principal: A. H. Shapiro)
    Waves in Fluids (33 min, principal: A. E. Bryson)

2. The University of Iowa
    College of Engineering Fluids Laboratory
    http://css.engineering.uiowa.edu/fluidslab/referenc/instructional.html

        The following six videos were prepared by H. Rouse as a series, in the order listed. They can be downloaded at the above Web site and can be viewed individually without serious loss of continuity.

---

[1] Detailed summaries of the NCFMF videos are contained in *Illustrated Experiments in Fluid Mechanics* (Cambridge, MA: The M.I.T. Press, 1972).

[2] The contents of this video are summarized and illustrated in *Shape and Flow: The Fluid Dynamics of Drag*, by Ascher H. Shapiro (New York: Anchor Books, 1961).

Introduction to the Study of Fluid Motion (24 min). This orientation video shows a variety of familiar flow phenomena. Use of scale models for empirical study of complex phenomena is illustrated and the significance of the Euler, Froude, Mach, and Reynolds numbers as similarity parameters is shown using several sequences of model and prototype flows.

Fundamental Principles of Flow (23 min). The basic concepts and physical relationships needed to analyze fluid motions are developed in this video. The continuity, momentum, and energy equations are derived and used to analyze a jet propulsion device.

Fluid Motion in a Gravitational Field (23 min). Buoyancy effects and free-surface flows are illustrated in this video. The Froude number is shown to be a fundamental parameter for flows with a free surface. Wave motions are shown for open-channel and density-stratified flows.

Characteristics of Laminar and Turbulent Flow (26 min). Dye, smoke, suspended particles, and hydrogen bubbles are used to visualize laminar and turbulent flows. Instabilities that lead to turbulence are shown; production and decay of turbulence and mixing are described.

Form Drag, Lift, and Propulsion (24 min). The effects of boundary-layer separation on flow patterns and pressure distributions are shown for several body shapes. The basic characteristics of lifting shapes, including effects of aspect ratio, are discussed, and the results are applied to analysis of the performance of propellers and torque converters.

Effects of Fluid Compressibility (17 min). The hydraulic analogy between open-channel liquid flow and compressible gas flow is used to show representative wave patterns. Schlieren optical flow visualization is used in a supersonic wind tunnel to show patterns of flow past several bodies at subsonic and supersonic speeds.

Additional videos that can be downloaded for free from
http://www.engineering.uiowa.edu/fluidslab/referenc/processes.html
are as follows:

Fluid Flows in Nature. Examples of fluid flows phenomena in nature.

Fluid Mechanics Terminology. Fundamental fluid dimensions; specific fluid properties (inertia, gravitational attraction, viscosity, elasticity); and specific quantities (velocity, acceleration, mass, force, pressure).

Experimental Fluid Dynamics. The role of experiments; modeling similitude; and characteristics of nondimensional numbers (Eu, Fr, Re, M).

Basic Concepts and Physical Relationships of Fluid Motion. Flow patterns (velocity vectors, streamlines, pathlines; streaklines); local and convective acceleration; relative motion; continuity relationship; vorticity; circulation; and rotational and irrotational flow.

Flow Dynamics. Flow acceleration and pressure-velocity relationship for nonuniform states of motion; dynamic and static pressure principle for simple instruments for the measurement of velocity; pressure and rate of flow; separation; cavitation; integration of the continuity, momentum, and energy equation; and propulsion.

Effect of Viscosity on Flow Pattern. Visualization of viscous effects; Couette, rotational-irrotational, and Poiseuille flow; deformation drag; principle of lubrication; laminar and turbulent flows; establishment of axisymmetric flows; and boundary-layer flow.

Laminar and Turbulent Flows. Flow regimes and transition in pipe flows; velocity distributions; and Moody diagram.

Introduction to Turbulent Flows. Flow regimes and transition in pipe flows and shear layer flows; molecular and eddy viscosity; turbulence intensity; turbulence scales; and production, mixing, and dissipation.

Gravity Action on Liquid Flows. Gravity effects; hydrostatic pressure distribution; fluid-body rotation; confined flow; Bernoulli equation; hydraulic and energy grade lines; liquid jets; free-surface outflows; overflow and underflow; specific energy in open-channel flow; and Froude number.

Gravitational Waves. Wave characteristics; wave propagation (including aspects of generation, celerity, reflection, stability, and reduction to steadiness); type of waves (includes oscillatory, standing, solitary, surge, and the hydraulic jump); and oceanic and atmospheric wave processes driven by saline or thermal effects.

Drag Force. Boundary-layer separation; variation of the pressure distribution and drag force with body form; flow patterns; and drag coefficient.

Flow Circulation. Definition; lift force; cross thrust; forced vibration; and structural failures.

Lift Force and Lifting Vanes. Lift coefficient; lift force; stall; and optimum drag/lift force ratio.

Propulsion. Thrust; propellers; axial-flow machinery; fluid couplings; and torque converters.

Wave Generation in Fluids. Compressibility; analogy between gravitational and elastic waves; effects on fluid patterns; elastic waves; surges; water and blood hammer; and isothermal and adiabatic departure from the constant-density flow.

Shock waves. Analogy with two-dimensional patterns produced by concentric waves; analogy with the surge in open-channel flow; and Schlierern measurements applied to the subsonic and supersonic flows around simple body forms (sphere, plate, cylinder and lifting vanes).

3. American Institute of Aeronautics and Astronautics
370 L'Enfant Promenade, S.W.
Washington, D.C. 20024-2518

America's Wings (29 min). Individuals who made significant contributions to development of aircraft for high-speed flight are interviewed; they discuss and explain their contributions. This is an effective video for a relatively sophisticated audience.

4. Purdue University
Center for Instructional Services
Film Booking
Hicks Undergraduate Library
West Lafayette, Indiana 47907

Tacoma Narrows Bridge Collapse (3 min, silent). This brief video contains spectacular original footage from the spontaneous collapse in a light breeze of the 2800 ft suspension bridge over the Tacoma Narrows, which occurred November 7, 1940. (A video of the collapse can also be seen at http://en.wikipedia.org/wiki/Tacoma_Narrows_Bridge_Collapse#Film_of_collapse.)

Appendix D

Selected Performance Curves for Pumps and Fans

D-1 INTRODUCTION

Many firms, worldwide, manufacture fluid machines in numerous standard types and sizes. Each manufacturer publishes complete performance data to allow application of its machines in systems. This Appendix contains selected performance data for use in solving pump and fan system problems. Two pump types and one fan type are included.

Choice of a manufacturer may be based on established practice, location, or cost. Once a manufacturer is chosen, machine selection is a three-step process:

1. Select a machine type, suited to the application, from a manufacturer's full-line catalog, which gives the ranges of pressure rise (head) and flow rate for each machine type.
2. Choose an appropriate machine model and driver speed from a master selector chart, which superposes the head and flow rate ranges of a series of machines on one graph.
3. Verify that the candidate machine is satisfactory for the intended application, using a detailed performance curve for the specific machine.

It is wise to consult with experienced system engineers, either employed by the machine manufacturer or in your own organization, before making a final purchase decision.

Many manufacturers currently use computerized procedures to select a machine that is most suitable for each given application. Such procedures are simply automated versions of the traditional selection method. Use of the master selector chart and the detailed performance curves is illustrated below for pumps and fans, using data from one manufacturer of each type of machine. Literature of other manufacturers differs in detail but contains the necessary information for machine selection.

D-2 PUMP SELECTION

Representative data are shown in Figs. D.1 through D.10 for Peerless[1] horizontal split case single-stage (series AE) pumps and in Figs. D.11 and D.12 for Peerless multistage (series TU and TUT) pumps.

Figures D.1 and D.2 are master pump selector charts for series AE pumps at 3500 and 1750 nominal rpm. On these charts, the model number (e.g., 6AE14) indicates the discharge line size (6 in. nominal pipe), the pump series (AE), and the maximum impeller diameter (approximately 14 in.).

---

[1] Peerless Pump Company, P.O. Box 7026, Indianapolis, IN 46207-7026.

Figures D.3 through D.10 are detailed performance charts for individual pump models in the AE series.

Figures D.11 and D.12 are master pump selector charts for series TU and TUT pumps at 1750 nominal rpm. Data for two-stage pumps are presented in Fig. D.11, while Fig. D.12 contains data for pumps with three, four, and five stages.

Each pump performance chart contains curves of total head versus volume flow rate; curves for several impeller diameters—tested in the same casing—are presented on a single graph. Each performance chart also contains contours showing pump efficiency and driver power; the net positive suction head (*NPSH*) requirement, as it varies with flow rate, is shown by the curve at the bottom of each chart. The best efficiency point (BEP) for each impeller may be found using the efficiency contours.

Use of the master pump selector chart and detailed performance curves is illustrated in Example D.1.

EXAMPLE D.1   Pump Selection Procedure

Select a pump to deliver 1750 gpm of water at 120 ft total head. Choose the appropriate pump model and driver speed. Specify the pump efficiency, driver power, and *NPSH* requirement.

GIVEN: Select a pump to deliver 1750 gpm of water at 120 ft total head.

FIND: (a) Pump model and driver speed.
(b) Pump efficiency.
(c) Driver power.
(d) *NPSH* requirement.

SOLUTION:

Use the pump selection procedure described in Section D-1. (The numbers below correspond to the numbered steps given in the procedure.)

1. First, select a machine type suited to the application. (This step actually requires a manufacturer's full-line catalog, which is not reproduced here. The Peerless product line catalog specifies a maximum delivery and head of 2500 gpm and 660 ft for series AE pumps. Therefore the required performance can be obtained; assume the selection is to be made from this series.)
2. Second, consult the master pump selector chart. The desired operating point is not within any pump contour on the 3500 rpm selector chart (Fig. D.1). From the 1750 rpm chart (Fig. D.2), select a model 6AE14 pump. From the performance curve for the 6AE14 pump (Fig. D.6), choose a 13 in. impeller.
3. Third, verify the performance of the machine using the detailed performance chart. On the performance chart for the 6AE14 pump, project up from the abscissa at $Q = 1750$ gpm. Project across from $H = 120$ ft on the ordinate. The intersection is the pump performance at the desired operating point:

$$\eta \approx 85.8 \text{ percent} \qquad \mathcal{P} \approx 64 \text{ hp}$$

From the operating point, project down to the *NPSH* requirement curve. At the intersection, read $NPSH \approx 17$ ft.

$\left\{\begin{array}{l}\text{This completes the selection process for this pump. One should consult with experienced system engineers to verify that}\\ \text{the system operating condition has been predicted accurately and the pump has been selected correctly.}\end{array}\right\}$

D-3 FAN SELECTION

Fan selection is similar to pump selection. A representative master fan selection chart is shown in Fig. D.13 for a series of Buffalo Forge[2] axial-flow fans. The chart shows the performance of the entire series of fans as a function of fan size and driver speed.

The master fan selector chart is used to select a fan size and driver speed for detailed consideration. Final evaluation of suitability of the fan model for the application is done using detailed performance charts for the specific model. A sample performance chart for a Buffalo Forge Size 48 Vaneaxial fan is presented in Fig. D.14.

The performance chart is plotted as total pressure rise versus volume flow rate. Figure D.14 contains curves for HB, LB, and MB wheels, operating at various constant speeds; the shaded bands represent measured total efficiency for the fans.

EXAMPLE D.2 Fan Selection Procedure

Select an axial-flow fan to deliver 40,000 cfm of standard air at 1.25 in. H_2O total pressure. Choose the appropriate fan model and driver speed. Specify the fan efficiency and driver power.

GIVEN: Select an axial fan to deliver 40,000 cfm of standard air at 1.25 in. H_2O total head.

FIND: (a) Fan size and driver speed.
(b) Fan efficiency.
(c) Driver power.

SOLUTION:
Use the fan selection procedure described in Section D-1. (The numbers below correspond to the numbered steps given in the procedure.)

1. First, select a machine type suited to the application. (This step actually requires a manufacturer's full-line catalog, which is not reproduced here. Assume the fan selection is to be made from the axial fan data presented in Fig. D.13.)
2. Second, consult the master fan selector chart. The desired operating point is within the contour for the Size 48 fan on the selector chart (Fig. D.13). To achieve the desired performance requires driving the fan at 870 rpm.
3. Third, verify the performance of the machine using the detailed performance chart (Fig. D.14). On the detailed performance chart, project up from the abscissa at $Q = 40,000$ cfm. Project across from $p = 1.25$ in. H_2O on the ordinate. The intersection is the desired operating point.

    These operating conditions cannot be delivered by a Type LB wheel; however, they are close to peak efficiency for either HB or MB wheels. The operating conditions can be delivered at about 72 percent total efficiency using an HB wheel. With an MB wheel, slightly in excess of 75 percent total efficiency may be expected. From the chart, the "efficiency factor" is 4780 at $\eta = 0.75$, and the fan driver power requirement is

$$\mathscr{P} = \frac{\text{Total Pressure} \times \text{Capacity}}{\text{Efficiency Factor}} = \frac{1.25 \text{ in. } H_2O \times 40,000 \text{ cfm}}{4780} = 10.5 \text{ hp}$$

$\left\{ \begin{array}{l} \text{This completes the fan selection process. Again, one should consult with experienced system engineers to verify that the} \\ \text{system operating condition has been predicted accurately and the fan has been selected correctly.} \end{array} \right\}$

---

[2] Buffalo Forge, 465 Broadway, Buffalo, NY 14240.

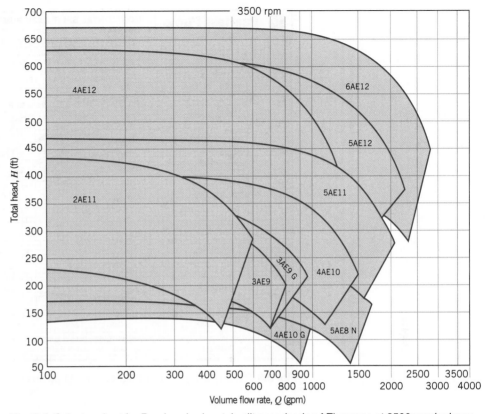

Fig. D.1 Selector chart for Peerless horizontal split case (series AE) pumps at 3500 nominal rpm.

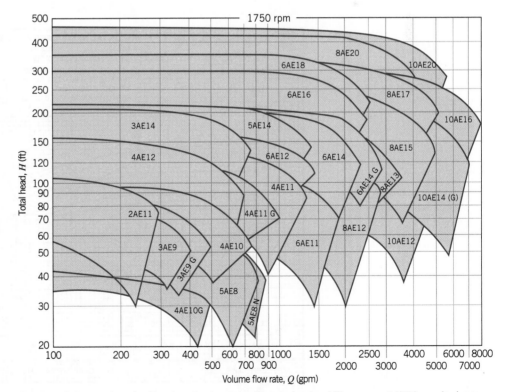

Fig. D.2 Selector chart for Peerless horizontal split case (series AE) pumps at 1750 nominal rpm.

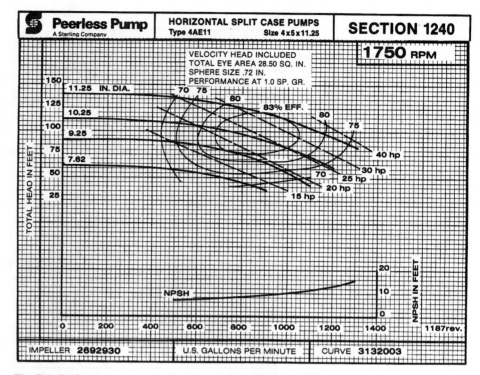

Fig. D.3 Performance curve for Peerless 4AE11 pump at 1750 rpm.

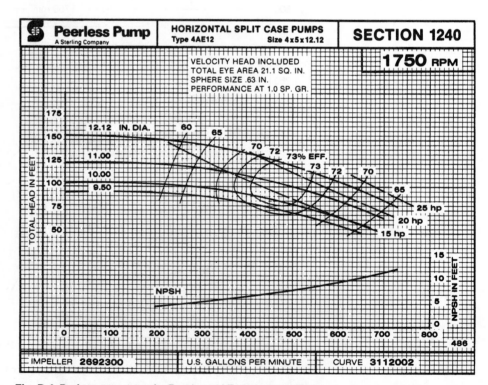

Fig. D.4 Performance curve for Peerless 4AE12 pump at 1750 rpm.

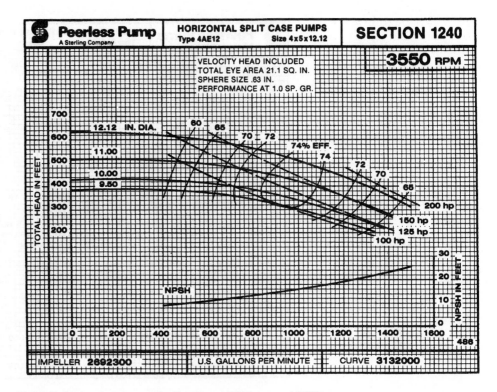

Fig. D.5 Performance curve for Peerless 4AE12 pump at 3550 rpm.

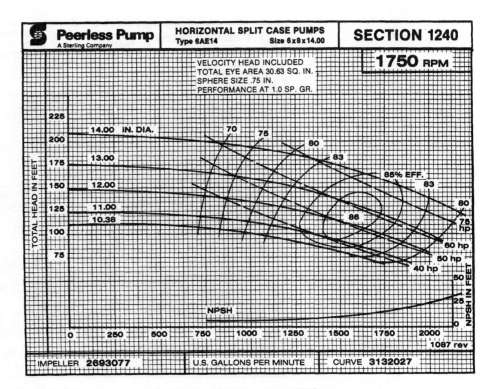

Fig. D.6 Performance curve for Peerless 6AE14 pump at 1750 rpm.

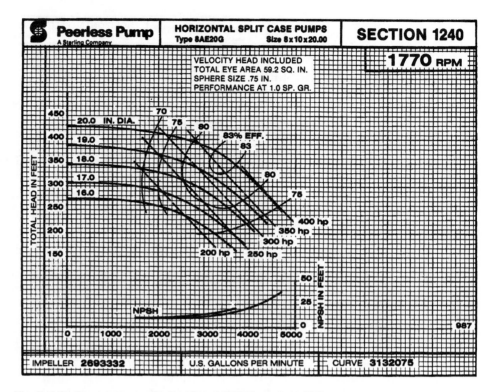

Fig. D.7 Performance curve for Peerless 8AE20G pump at 1770 rpm.

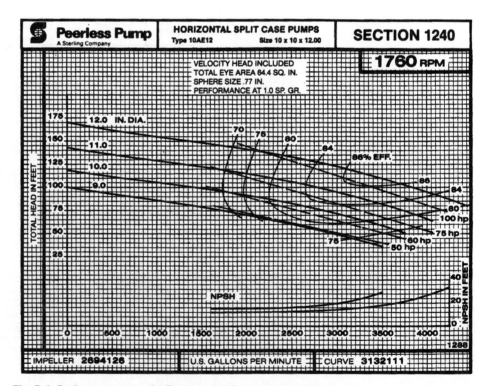

Fig. D.8 Performance curve for Peerless 10AE12 pump at 1760 rpm.

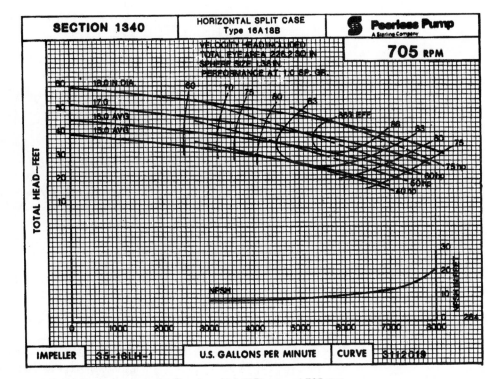

Fig. D.9 Performance curve for Peerless 16A 18B pump at 705 rpm.

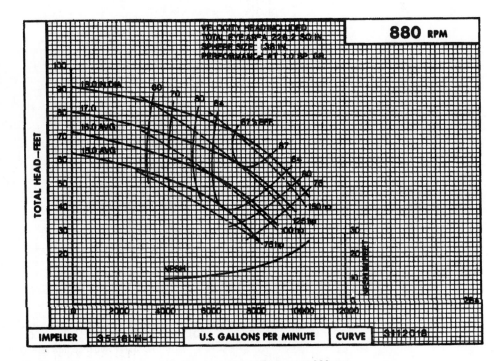

Fig. D.10 Performance curve for Peerless 16A 18B pump at 880 rpm.

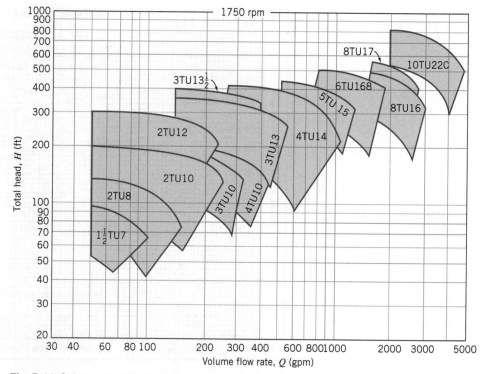
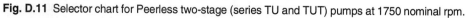

Fig. D.11 Selector chart for Peerless two-stage (series TU and TUT) pumps at 1750 nominal rpm.

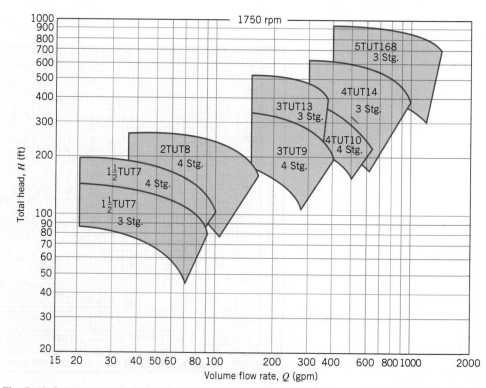

Fig. D.12 Selector chart for Peerless multi-stage (series TU and TUT) pumps at 1750 nominal rpm.

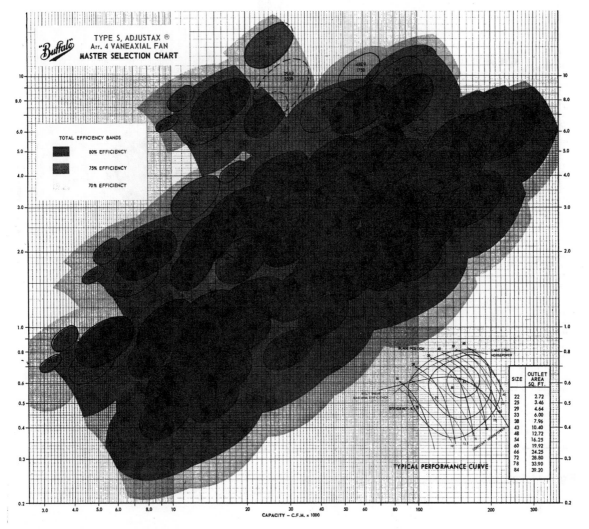

Fig. D.13 Master fan selection chart for Buffalo Forge axial fans.

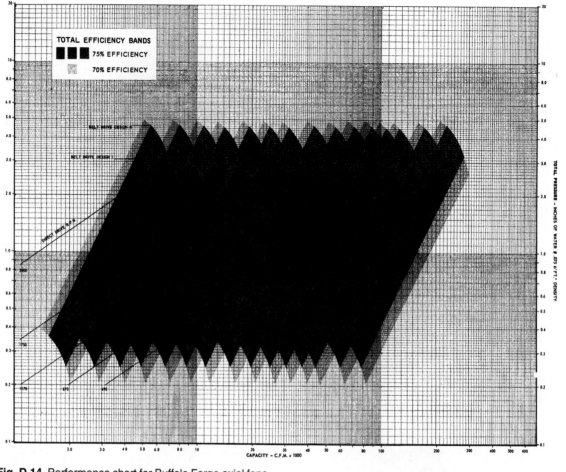

Fig. D.14 Performance chart for Buffalo Forge axial fans.

REFERENCES

1. Peerless Pump literature:
   – Horizontal Split Case Single Stage Double Suction Pumps, Series AE, Brochure B-1200, 1987.
   – Horizontal Split Case Series AE Pumps, 60 Hertz, Performance Curves, Brochure B-1240, n.d.
   – Horizontal Split Case, Multistage Single Suction Pumps, Types TU, TUT, 60 Hertz, Performance Curves, Brochure B-1440, n.d.

2. Buffalo Forge literature:
   – Axial Flow Fans, Bulletin F-305A, 1968.

Appendix E

Flow Functions for Computation of Compressible Flow

E-1   ISENTROPIC FLOW

Isentropic flow functions are computed using the following equations:

$$\frac{T_0}{T} = 1 + \frac{k-1}{2}M^2 \qquad\qquad (12.21b)/(13.7b)$$

$$\frac{p_0}{p} = \left[1 + \frac{k-1}{2}M^2\right]^{k/(k-1)} \qquad\qquad (12.21a)/(13.7a)$$

$$\frac{\rho_0}{\rho} = \left[1 + \frac{k-1}{2}M^2\right]^{1/(k-1)} \qquad\qquad (12.21c)/(13.7c)$$

$$\frac{A}{A^*} = \frac{1}{M}\left[\frac{1 + \dfrac{k-1}{2}M^2}{\dfrac{k+1}{2}}\right]^{(k+1)/2(k-1)} \qquad\qquad (13.7d)$$

Representative values of the isentropic flow functions for $k = 1.4$ are presented in Table E.1 and plotted in Fig. E.1.

TABLE E.1   Isentropic Flow Functions (one-dimensional flow, ideal gas, $k = 1.4$)

M	T/T_0	p/p_0	ρ/ρ_0	A/A^*
0.00	1.0000	1.0000	1.0000	∞
0.50	0.9524	0.8430	0.8852	1.340
1.00	0.8333	0.5283	0.6339	1.000
1.50	0.6897	0.2724	0.3950	1.176
2.00	0.5556	0.1278	0.2301	1.688
2.50	0.4444	0.05853	0.1317	2.637
3.00	0.3571	0.02722	0.07623	4.235
3.50	0.2899	0.01311	0.04523	6.790
4.00	0.2381	0.006586	0.02766	10.72
4.50	0.1980	0.003455	0.01745	16.56
5.00	0.1667	0.001890	0.01134	25.00

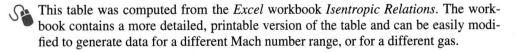 This table was computed from the *Excel* workbook *Isentropic Relations*. The workbook contains a more detailed, printable version of the table and can be easily modified to generate data for a different Mach number range, or for a different gas.

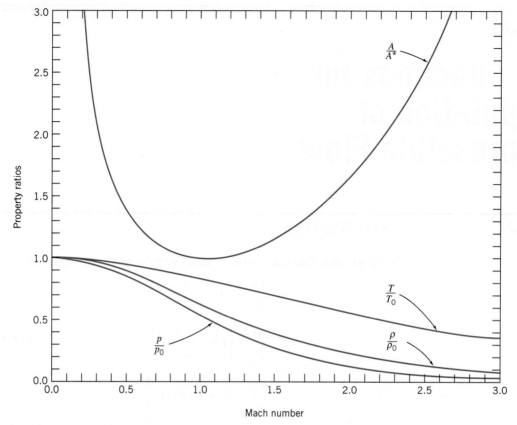

Fig. E.1 Isentropic flow functions.

This graph was generated from the *Excel* workbook. The workbook can be modified easily to generate curves for a different gas.

E-2 FANNO-LINE FLOW

Fanno-line flow functions are computed using the following equations:

$$\frac{p_0}{p_0^*} = \frac{1}{M}\left[\left(\frac{2}{k+1}\right)\left(1 + \frac{k-1}{2}M^2\right)\right]^{(k+1)/2(k-1)} \quad (13.21e)$$

$$\frac{T}{T^*} = \frac{\left(\frac{k+1}{2}\right)}{\left(1 + \frac{k-1}{2}M^2\right)} \quad (13.21b)$$

$$\frac{p}{p^*} = \frac{1}{M}\left[\frac{\left(\frac{k+1}{2}\right)}{1 + \frac{k-1}{2}M^2}\right]^{1/2} \quad (13.21d)$$

$$\frac{V}{V^*} = \frac{\rho^*}{\rho} = \left[\frac{\left(\frac{k+1}{2}\right)M^2}{1 + \frac{k-1}{2}M^2}\right]^{1/2} \quad (13.21c)$$

$$\frac{\bar{f}L_{max}}{D_h} = \frac{1 - M^2}{kM^2} + \frac{k+1}{2k}\ln\left[\frac{(k+1)M^2}{2\left(1 + \frac{k-1}{2}M^2\right)}\right] \quad (13.21a)$$

Representative values of the Fanno-line flow functions for $k = 1.4$ are presented in Table E.2 and plotted in Fig. E.2.

TABLE E.2 Fanno-Line Flow Functions (one-dimensional flow, ideal gas, $k = 1.4$)

M	p_0/p_0^*	T/T^*	p/p^*	V/V^*	$\bar{f}L_{max}/D_h$
0.00	∞	1.200	∞	0.0000	∞
0.50	1.340	1.143	2.138	0.5345	1.069
1.00	1.000	1.000	1.000	1.000	0.0000
1.50	1.176	0.8276	0.6065	1.365	0.1361
2.00	1.688	0.6667	0.4083	1.633	0.3050
2.50	2.637	0.5333	0.2921	1.826	0.4320
3.00	4.235	0.4286	0.2182	1.964	0.5222
3.50	6.790	0.3478	0.1685	2.064	0.5864
4.00	10.72	0.2857	0.1336	2.138	0.6331
4.50	16.56	0.2376	0.1083	2.194	0.6676
5.00	25.00	0.2000	0.08944	2.236	0.6938

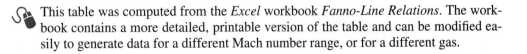

This table was computed from the *Excel* workbook *Fanno-Line Relations*. The workbook contains a more detailed, printable version of the table and can be modified easily to generate data for a different Mach number range, or for a different gas.

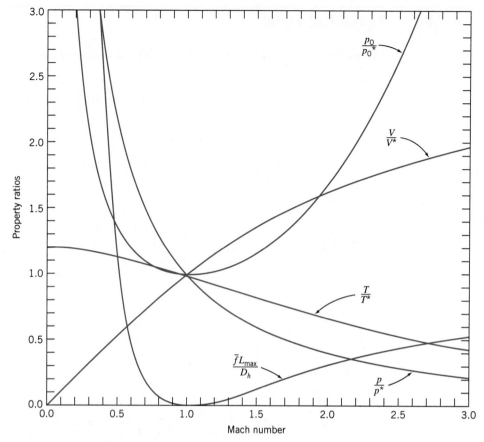

Fig. E.2 Fanno-line flow functions.

This graph was generated from the *Excel* workbook. The workbook can be modified easily to generate curves for a different gas.

| **E-3** | **RAYLEIGH-LINE FLOW** |

Rayleigh-line flow functions are computed using the following equations:

$$\frac{T_0}{T_0^*} = \frac{2(k+1)M^2\left(1 + \frac{k-1}{2}M^2\right)}{(1 + kM^2)^2} \tag{13.31d}$$

$$\frac{p_0}{p_0^*} = \frac{1+k}{1+kM^2}\left[\left(\frac{2}{k+1}\right)\left(1 + \frac{k-1}{2}M^2\right)\right]^{k/(k-1)} \tag{13.31e}$$

$$\frac{T}{T^*} = \left[M\left(\frac{1+k}{1+kM^2}\right)\right]^2 \tag{13.31b}$$

$$\frac{p}{p^*} = \frac{1+k}{1+kM^2} \tag{13.31a}$$

$$\frac{\rho^*}{\rho} = \frac{V}{V^*} = \frac{M^2(1+k)}{1+kM^2} \tag{13.31c}$$

Representative values of the Rayleigh-line flow functions for $k = 1.4$ are presented in Table E.3 and plotted in Fig. E.3.

TABLE E.3 Rayleigh-Line Flow Functions (one-dimensional flow, ideal gas, $k = 1.4$)

M	T_0/T_0^*	p_0/p_0^*	T/T^*	p/p^*	V/V^*
0.00	0.0000	1.268	0.0000	2.400	0.0000
0.50	0.6914	1.114	0.7901	1.778	0.4444
1.00	1.000	1.000	1.000	1.000	1.000
1.50	0.9093	1.122	0.7525	0.5783	1.301
2.00	0.7934	1.503	0.5289	0.3636	1.455
2.50	0.7101	2.222	0.3787	0.2462	1.539
3.00	0.6540	3.424	0.2803	0.1765	1.588
3.50	0.6158	5.328	0.2142	0.1322	1.620
4.00	0.5891	8.227	0.1683	0.1026	1.641
4.50	0.5698	12.50	0.1354	0.08177	1.656
5.00	0.5556	18.63	0.1111	0.06667	1.667

This table was computed from the *Excel* workbook *Rayleigh-Line Relations*. The workbook contains a more detailed, printable version of the table and can be easily modified to generate data for a different Mach number range, or for a different gas.

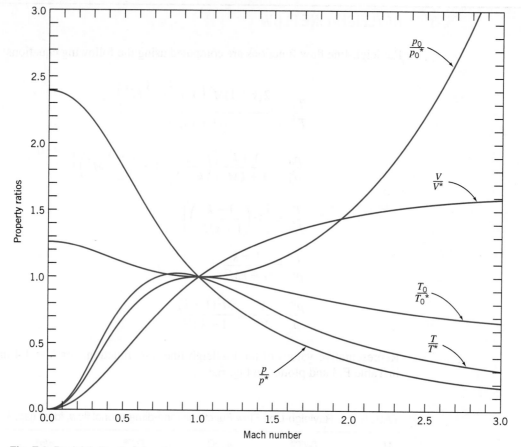

Fig. E.3 Rayleigh-line flow functions.

This graph was generated from the *Excel* workbook. The workbook can be modified easily to generate curves for a different gas.

E-4   NORMAL SHOCK

Normal-shock flow functions are computed using the following equations:

$$M_2^2 = \frac{M_1^2 + \dfrac{2}{k-1}}{\dfrac{2k}{k-1}M_1^2 - 1} \tag{13.41a}$$

$$\frac{p_{0_2}}{p_{0_1}} = \frac{\left[\dfrac{\dfrac{k+1}{2}M_1^2}{1 + \dfrac{k-1}{2}M_1^2}\right]^{k/(k-1)}}{\left[\dfrac{2k}{k+1}M_1^2 - \dfrac{k-1}{k+1}\right]^{1/(k-1)}} \tag{13.41b}$$

$$\frac{T_2}{T_1} = \frac{\left(1 + \dfrac{k-1}{2}M_1^2\right)\left(kM_1^2 - \dfrac{k-1}{2}\right)}{\left(\dfrac{k+1}{2}\right)^2 M_1^2} \tag{13.41c}$$

$$\frac{p_2}{p_1} = \frac{2k}{k+1}M_1^2 - \frac{k-1}{k+1} \tag{13.41d}$$

$$\frac{\rho_2}{\rho_1} = \frac{V_1}{V_2} = \frac{\dfrac{k+1}{2}M_1^2}{1 + \dfrac{k-1}{2}M_1^2} \tag{13.41e}$$

Representative values of the normal-shock flow functions for $k = 1.4$ are presented in Table E.4 and plotted in Fig. E.4.

TABLE E.4 Normal-Shock Flow Functions (one-dimensional flow, ideal gas, $k = 1.4$)

M_1	M_2	p_{0_2}/p_{0_1}	T_2/T_1	p_2/p_1	ρ_2/ρ_1
1.00	1.000	1.000	1.000	1.000	1.000
1.50	0.7011	0.9298	1.320	2.458	1.862
2.00	0.5774	0.7209	1.687	4.500	2.667
2.50	0.5130	0.4990	2.137	7.125	3.333
3.00	0.4752	0.3283	2.679	10.33	3.857
3.50	0.4512	0.2130	3.315	14.13	4.261
4.00	0.4350	0.1388	4.047	18.50	4.571
4.50	0.4236	0.09170	4.875	23.46	4.812
5.00	0.4152	0.06172	5.800	29.00	5.000

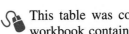 This table was computed from the *Excel* workbook *Normal-Shock Relations*. The workbook contains a more detailed, printable version of the table and can be modified easily to generate data for a different Mach number range, or for a different gas.

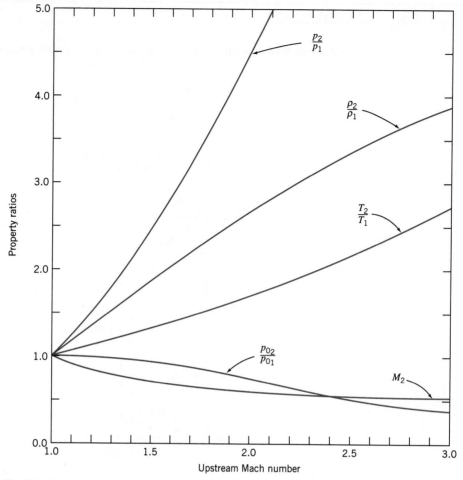

Fig. E.4 Normal-shock flow functions.

This graph was generated from the *Excel* workbook. The workbook can be modified easily to generate curves for a different gas.

E-5 OBLIQUE SHOCK

Oblique-shock flow functions are computed using the following equations:

$$M_{2_n}^2 = \frac{M_{1_n}^2 + \dfrac{2}{k-1}}{\dfrac{2k}{k-1}M_{1_n}^2 - 1} \tag{13.48a}$$

$$\frac{p_{0_2}}{p_{0_1}} = \frac{\left[\dfrac{\dfrac{k+1}{2}M_{1_n}^2}{1 + \dfrac{k-1}{2}M_{1_n}^2}\right]^{k/(k-1)}}{\left[\dfrac{2k}{k+1}M_{1_n}^2 - \dfrac{k-1}{k+1}\right]^{1/(k-1)}} \tag{13.48b}$$

$$\frac{T_2}{T_1} = \frac{\left(1 + \dfrac{k-1}{2}M_{1_n}^2\right)\left(kM_{1_n}^2 - \dfrac{k-1}{2}\right)}{\left(\dfrac{k+1}{2}\right)^2 M_{1_n}^2} \tag{13.48c}$$

$$\frac{p_2}{p_1} = \frac{2k}{k+1}M_{1_n}^2 - \frac{k-1}{k+1} \tag{13.48d}$$

$$\frac{\rho_2}{\rho_1} = \frac{V_{1_n}}{V_{2_n}} = \frac{\dfrac{k+1}{2}M_{1_n}^2}{1 + \dfrac{k-1}{2}M_{1_n}^2} \tag{13.48e}$$

Representative values of the oblique-shock flow functions for $k = 1.4$ are presented in Table E.5 (identical to Table E.4 except for the Mach number notations).

TABLE E.5 Oblique-Shock Flow Functions (ideal gas, $k = 1.4$)

M_{1_n}	M_{2_n}	p_{0_2}/p_{0_1}	T_2/T_1	p_2/p_1	ρ_2/ρ_1
1.00	1.000	1.0000	1.000	1.000	1.000
1.50	0.7011	0.9298	1.320	2.458	1.862
2.00	0.5774	0.7209	1.687	4.500	2.667
2.50	0.5130	0.4990	2.137	7.125	3.333
3.00	0.4752	0.3283	2.679	10.33	3.857
3.50	0.4512	0.2130	3.315	14.13	4.261
4.00	0.4350	0.1388	4.047	18.50	4.571
4.50	0.4236	0.09170	4.875	23.46	4.812
5.00	0.4152	0.06172	5.800	29.00	5.000

The deflection angle θ, oblique-shock angle β, and Mach number M_1 are related using the following equation:

$$\tan \theta = \frac{2 \cot \beta (M_1^2 \sin^2 \beta - 1)}{M_1^2 (k + \cos 2\beta) + 2} \tag{13.49}$$

Representative values of angle θ are presented in Table E.6.

TABLE E.6 Oblique-Shock Deflection Angle θ (deg) (ideal gas, $k = 1.4$)

Shock angle β (deg)	Mach number M_1										
	1.2	1.4	1.6	1.8	2	2.5	3	4	6	10	∞
0	—	—	—	—	—	—	—	—	—	—	—
5	—	—	—	—	—	—	—	—	—	—	4.16
10	—	—	—	—	—	—	—	—	0.64	5.53	8.32
15	—	—	—	—	—	—	—	0.80	7.18	10.5	12.4
20	—	—	—	—	—	—	0.77	7.44	12.4	15.1	16.5
25	—	—	—	—	—	1.93	7.28	12.9	17.1	19.3	20.6
30	—	—	—	—	—	7.99	12.8	17.8	21.5	23.4	24.5
35	—	—	—	1.41	5.75	13.2	17.6	22.2	25.6	27.3	28.3
40	—	—	1.31	6.49	10.6	17.7	21.8	26.2	29.4	31.1	32.0
45	—	—	5.73	10.7	14.7	21.6	25.6	29.8	33.0	34.6	35.5
50	—	3.28	9.31	14.2	18.1	24.9	28.9	33.1	36.2	37.8	38.8
55	—	6.18	12.1	16.9	20.7	27.4	31.5	35.8	39.0	40.7	41.6
60	1.61	8.20	13.9	18.6	22.4	29.2	33.3	37.8	41.1	42.9	43.9
65	3.16	9.27	14.6	19.2	23.0	29.8	34.1	38.7	42.3	44.2	45.3
70	3.88	9.32	14.2	18.5	22.1	28.9	33.3	38.2	42.1	44.2	45.4
75	3.80	8.29	12.5	16.2	19.5	25.9	30.2	35.3	39.5	41.8	43.1
80	3.01	6.25	9.34	12.2	14.8	20.1	23.9	28.7	32.8	35.2	36.6
85	1.66	3.36	5.03	6.61	8.08	11.2	13.6	16.8	19.7	21.6	22.7
90	0	0	0	0	0	0	0	0	0	0	0

Tables E.5 and E.6 were computed from the *Excel* workbook *Oblique-Shock Relations*. The workbook contains a more detailed, printable version of the tables and can be modified easily to generate data for a different Mach number range, or for a different gas.

| E-6 | ISENTROPIC EXPANSION WAVE RELATIONS |

The Prandtl-Meyer supersonic expansion function, ω, is

$$\omega = \sqrt{\frac{k+1}{k-1}}\,\tan^{-1}\left(\sqrt{\frac{k-1}{k+1}\,(M^2-1)}\right) - \tan^{-1}(\sqrt{M^2-1}) \qquad (13.55)$$

Representative values of angle ω are presented in Table E.7.

TABLE E.7 Prandtl-Meyer Supersonic Expansion Function ω (deg) (ideal gas, $k = 1.4$)

M	ω (deg)	M	ω (deg)	M	ω (deg)	M	ω (deg)
1.00	0.00	2.00	26.4	3.00	49.8	4.00	65.8
1.05	0.49	2.05	27.7	3.05	50.7	4.05	66.4
1.10	1.34	2.10	29.1	3.10	51.6	4.10	67.1
1.15	2.38	2.15	30.4	3.15	52.6	4.15	67.7
1.20	3.56	2.20	31.7	3.20	53.5	4.20	68.3
1.25	4.83	2.25	33.0	3.25	54.4	4.25	68.9
1.30	6.17	2.30	34.3	3.30	55.2	4.30	69.5
1.35	7.56	2.35	35.5	3.35	56.1	4.35	70.1
1.40	8.99	2.40	36.7	3.40	56.9	4.40	70.7
1.45	10.4	2.45	37.9	3.45	57.7	4.45	71.3
1.50	11.9	2.50	39.1	3.50	58.5	4.50	71.8
1.55	13.4	2.55	40.3	3.55	59.3	4.55	72.4
1.60	14.9	2.60	41.4	3.60	60.1	4.60	72.9
1.65	16.3	2.65	42.5	3.65	60.9	4.65	73.4
1.70	17.8	2.70	43.6	3.70	61.6	4.70	74.0
1.75	19.3	2.75	44.7	3.75	62.3	4.75	74.5
1.80	20.7	2.80	45.7	3.80	63.0	4.80	75.0
1.85	22.2	2.85	46.8	3.85	63.7	4.85	75.5
1.90	23.6	2.90	47.8	3.90	64.4	4.90	76.0
1.95	25.0	2.95	48.8	3.95	65.1	4.95	76.4
2.00	26.4	3.00	49.8	4.00	65.8	5.00	76.9

This table was computed from the *Excel* workbook *Isentropic Expansion Wave Relations*. The workbook contains a more detailed, printable version of the table and can be easily modified to generate data for a different Mach number range, or for a different gas.

Analysis of Experimental Uncertainty

F-1   INTRODUCTION

Experimental data often are used to supplement engineering analysis as a basis for design. Not all data are equally good; the validity of data should be documented before test results are used for design. Uncertainty analysis is the procedure used to quantify data validity and accuracy.

Analysis of uncertainty also is useful during experiment design. Careful study may indicate potential sources of unacceptable error and suggest improved measurement methods.

F-2   TYPES OF ERROR

Errors always are present when experimental measurements are made. Aside from gross blunders by the experimenter, experimental error may be of two types. Fixed (or systematic) error causes repeated measurements to be in error by the same amount for each trial. Fixed error is the same for each reading and can be removed by proper calibration or correction. Random error (nonrepeatability) is different for every reading and hence cannot be removed. The factors that introduce random error are uncertain by their nature. The objective of uncertainty analysis is to estimate the probable random error in experimental results.

We assume that equipment has been constructed correctly and calibrated properly to eliminate fixed errors. We assume that instrumentation has adequate resolution and that fluctuations in readings are not excessive. We assume also that care is used in making and recording observations so that only random errors remain.

F-3   ESTIMATION OF UNCERTAINTY

Our goal is to estimate the uncertainty of experimental measurements and calculated results due to random errors. The procedure has three steps:

1. Estimate the uncertainty interval for each measured quantity.
2. State the confidence limit on each measurement.
3. Analyze the propagation of uncertainty into results calculated from experimental data.

Below we outline the procedure for each step and illustrate applications with examples.

Step 1 *Estimate the measurement uncertainty interval.* Designate the measured variables in an experiment as $x_1, x_2, \ldots, x_n$. One possible way to find the uncertainty interval for each variable would be to repeat each measurement many times. The result would be a distribution of data for each variable. Random errors in measurement usually produce a *normal (Gaussian)* frequency distribution of measured values. The data scatter for a normal distribution is characterized by the standard deviation, σ. The uncertainty interval for each measured variable, x_i, may be stated as $\pm n\sigma_i$, where $n = 1$, 2, or 3.

For normally distributed data, over 99 percent of measured values of x_i lie within $\pm 3\sigma_i$ of the mean value, 95 percent lie within $\pm 2\sigma_i$, and 68 percent lie within $\pm \sigma_i$ of the mean value of the data set [1]. Thus it would be possible to quantify expected errors within any desired *confidence limit* if a statistically significant set of data were available.

The method of repeated measurements usually is impractical. In most applications it is impossible to obtain enough data for a statistically significant sample owing to the excessive time and cost involved. However, the normal distribution suggests several important concepts:

1. Small errors are more likely than large ones.
2. Plus and minus errors are about equally likely.
3. No finite maximum error can be specified.

A more typical situation in engineering work is a "single-sample" experiment, where only one measurement is made for each point [2]. A reasonable estimate of the measurement uncertainty due to random error in a single-sample experiment usually is plus or minus half the smallest scale division (the *least count*) of the instrument. However, this approach also must be used with caution, as illustrated in the following example.

EXAMPLE F.1 Uncertainty in Barometer Reading

The observed height of the mercury barometer column is $h = 752.6$ mm. The least count on the vernier scale is 0.1 mm, so one might estimate the probable measurement error as ± 0.05 mm.

A measurement probably could not be made this precisely. The barometer sliders and meniscus must be aligned by eye. The slider has a least count of 1 mm. As a conservative estimate, a measurement could be made to the nearest millimeter. The probable value of a single measurement then would be expressed as 752.6 ± 0.5 mm. The relative uncertainty in barometric height would be stated as

$$u_h = \pm \frac{0.5 \text{ mm}}{752.6 \text{ mm}} = \pm 0.000664 \qquad \text{or} \qquad \pm 0.0664 \text{ percent}$$

Comments:

1. An uncertainty interval of ± 0.1 percent corresponds to a result specified to three significant figures; this precision is sufficient for most engineering work.
2. The measurement of barometer height was precise, as shown by the uncertainty estimate. But was it accurate? At typical room temperatures, the observed barometer reading must be reduced by a temperature correction of nearly 3 mm! This is an example of a fixed error that requires a correction factor.

Step 2 *State the confidence limit on each measurement.* The uncertainty interval of a measurement should be stated at specified odds. For example, one may write $h = 752.6 \pm 0.5$ mm (20 to 1). This means that one is willing to bet 20 to 1 that the height of the mercury column actually is within ± 0.5 mm of the stated value. It should be obvious [3] that "... the specification of such odds can only be made by the experimenter based on ... total laboratory experience. There is no substitute for sound engineering judgment in estimating the uncertainty of a measured variable."

The confidence interval statement is based on the concept of standard deviation for a normal distribution. Odds of about 370 to 1 correspond to $\pm 3\sigma$; 99.7 percent of all future readings are expected to fall within the interval. Odds of about 20 to 1 correspond to $\pm 2\sigma$ and odds of 3 to 1 correspond to $\pm \sigma$ confidence limits. Odds of 20 to 1 typically are used for engineering work.

Step 3 *Analyze the propagation of uncertainty in calculations.* Suppose that measurements of independent variables, $x_1, x_2, \ldots, x_n$, are made in the laboratory. The relative uncertainty of each independently measured quantity is estimated as u_i. The measurements are used to calculate some result, R, for the experiment. We wish to analyze how errors in the x_is *propagate* into the calculation of R from measured values.

In general, R may be expressed mathematically as $R = R(x_1, x_2, \ldots, x_n)$. The effect on R of an error in measuring an individual x_i may be estimated by analogy to the derivative of a function [4]. A variation, δx_i, in x_i would cause variation δR_i in R,

$$\delta R_i = \frac{\partial R}{\partial x_i} \delta x_i$$

The relative variation in R is

$$\frac{\delta R_i}{R} = \frac{1}{R} \frac{\partial R}{\partial x_i} \delta x_i = \frac{x_i}{R} \frac{\partial R}{\partial x_i} \frac{\delta x_i}{x_i} \tag{F.1}$$

Equation F.1 may be used to estimate the relative uncertainty in the result due to uncertainty in x_i. Introducing the notation for relative uncertainty, we obtain

$$u_{R_i} = \frac{x_i}{R} \frac{\partial R}{\partial x_i} u_{x_i} \tag{F.2}$$

How do we estimate the relative uncertainty in R caused by the combined effects of the relative uncertainties in all the x_is? The random error in each variable has a range of values within the uncertainty interval. It is unlikely that all errors will have adverse values at the same time. It can be shown [2] that the best representation for the relative uncertainty of the result is

$$u_R = \pm \left[\left(\frac{x_1}{R} \frac{\partial R}{\partial x_1} u_1 \right)^2 + \left(\frac{x_2}{R} \frac{\partial R}{\partial x_2} u_2 \right)^2 + \cdots + \left(\frac{x_n}{R} \frac{\partial R}{\partial x_n} u_n \right)^2 \right]^{1/2} \tag{F.3}$$

EXAMPLE F.2   Uncertainty in Volume of Cylinder

Obtain an expression for the uncertainty in determining the volume of a cylinder from measurements of its radius and height. The volume of a cylinder in terms of radius and height is

$$\forall = \forall(r, h) = \pi r^2 h$$

Differentiating, we obtain

$$d\forall = \frac{\partial \forall}{\partial r} dr + \frac{\partial \forall}{\partial h} dh = 2\pi r h \, dr + \pi r^2 \, dh$$

since

$$\frac{\partial \forall}{\partial r} = 2\pi r h \quad \text{and} \quad \frac{\partial \forall}{\partial h} = \pi r^2$$

From Eq. F.2, the relative uncertainty due to radius is

$$u_{\forall, r} = \frac{\delta \forall_r}{\forall} = \frac{r}{\forall} \frac{\partial \forall}{\partial r} u_r = \frac{r}{\pi r^2 h} (2\pi r h) u_r = 2 u_r$$

and the relative uncertainty due to height is

$$u_{\forall, h} = \frac{\delta \forall_h}{\forall} = \frac{h}{\forall} \frac{\partial \forall}{\partial h} u_h = \frac{h}{\pi r^2 h} (\pi r^2) u_h = u_h$$

The relative uncertainty in volume is then

$$u_\forall = \pm [(2 u_r)^2 + (u_h)^2]^{1/2} \tag{F.4}$$

Comment: The coefficient 2, in Eq. F.4, shows that the uncertainty in measuring cylinder radius has a larger effect than the uncertainty in measuring height. This is true because the radius is squared in the equation for volume.

APPLICATIONS TO DATA

Applications to data obtained from laboratory measurements are illustrated in the following examples.

EXAMPLE F.3 Uncertainty in Liquid Mass Flow Rate

The mass flow rate of water through a tube is to be determined by collecting water in a beaker. The mass flow rate is calculated from the net mass of water collected divided by the time interval,

$$\dot{m} = \frac{\Delta m}{\Delta t} \tag{F.5}$$

where $\Delta m = m_f - m_e$. Error estimates for the measured quantities are

Mass of full beaker, $m_f = 400 \pm 2$ g (20 to 1)
Mass of empty beaker, $m_e = 200 \pm 2$ g (20 to 1)
Collection time interval, $\Delta t = 10 \pm 0.2$ s (20 to 1)

The relative uncertainties in measured quantities are

$$u_{m_f} = \pm \frac{2 \text{ g}}{400 \text{ g}} = \pm 0.005$$

$$u_{m_e} = \pm \frac{2 \text{ g}}{200 \text{ g}} = \pm 0.01$$

$$u_{\Delta t} = \pm \frac{0.2 \text{ s}}{10 \text{ s}} = \pm 0.02$$

The relative uncertainty in the measured value of net mass is calculated from Eq. F.3 as

$$u_{\Delta m} = \pm \left[\left(\frac{m_f}{\Delta m} \frac{\partial \Delta m}{\partial m_f} u_{m_f} \right)^2 + \left(\frac{m_e}{\Delta m} \frac{\partial \Delta m}{\partial m_e} u_{m_e} \right)^2 \right]^{1/2}$$

$$= \pm \left\{ [(2)(1)(\pm 0.005)]^2 + [(1)(-1)(\pm 0.01)]^2 \right\}^{1/2}$$

$$u_{\Delta m} = \pm 0.0141$$

Because $\dot{m} = \dot{m}(\Delta m, \Delta t)$, we may write Eq. F.3 as

$$u_{\dot{m}} = \pm \left[\left(\frac{\Delta m}{\dot{m}} \frac{\partial \dot{m}}{\partial \Delta m} u_{\Delta m} \right)^2 + \left(\frac{\Delta t}{\dot{m}} \frac{\partial \dot{m}}{\partial \Delta t} u_{\Delta t} \right)^2 \right]^{1/2} \tag{F.6}$$

The required partial derivative terms are

$$\frac{\Delta m}{\dot{m}} \frac{\partial \dot{m}}{\partial \Delta m} = 1 \quad \text{and} \quad \frac{\Delta t}{\dot{m}} \frac{\partial \dot{m}}{\partial \Delta t} = -1$$

Substituting into Eq. F.6 gives

$$u_{\dot{m}} = \pm \left\{ [(1)(\pm 0.0141)]^2 + [(-1)(\pm 0.02)]^2 \right\}^{1/2}$$

$$u_{\dot{m}} = \pm 0.0245 \quad \text{or} \quad \pm 2.45 \text{ percent (20 to 1)}$$

Comment: The 2 percent uncertainty interval in time measurement makes the most important contribution to the uncertainty interval in the result.

F-5	SUMMARY

A statement of the probable uncertainty of data is an important part of reporting experimental results completely and clearly. The American Society of Mechanical Engineers requires that all manuscripts submitted for journal publication include an adequate statement of uncertainty of experimental data [5]. Estimating uncertainty in experimental results requires care, experience, and judgment, in common with many endeavors in engineering. We have emphasized the need to quantify the uncertainty of measurements, but space allows including only a few examples. Much more information is available in the references that follow (e.g., [4, 6, 7]). We urge you to consult them when designing experiments or analyzing data.

REFERENCES

1. Pugh, E. M., and G. H. Winslow, *The Analysis of Physical Measurements*. Reading, MA: Addison-Wesley, 1966.

2. Kline, S. J., and F. A. McClintock, "Describing Uncertainties in Single-Sample Experiments," *Mechanical Engineering*, 75, 1, January 1953, pp. 3–9.

3. Doebelin, E. O., *Measurement Systems*, 4th ed. New York: McGraw-Hill, 1990.

4. Young, H. D., *Statistical Treatment of Experimental Data*. New York: McGraw-Hill, 1962.

5. Rood, E. P., and D. P. Telionis, "JFE Policy on Reporting Uncertainties in Experimental Measurements and Results," *Transactions of ASME, Journal of Fluids Engineering, 113*, 3, September 1991, pp. 313–314.

6. Coleman, H. W., and W. G. Steele, *Experimentation and Uncertainty Analysis for Engineers*. New York: Wiley, 1989.

7. Holman, J. P., *Experimental Methods for Engineers*, 5th ed. New York: McGraw-Hill, 1989.

Appendix G

SI Units, Prefixes, and Conversion Factors

TABLE G.1 SI Units and Prefixes[a]

SI Units	Quantity	Unit	SI Symbol	Formula
SI base units:	Length	meter	m	—
	Mass	kilogram	kg	—
	Time	second	s	—
	Temperature	kelvin	K	—
SI supplementary unit:	Plane angle	radian	rad	—
SI derived units:	Energy	joule	J	$N \cdot m$
	Force	newton	N	$kg \cdot m/s^2$
	Power	watt	W	J/s
	Pressure	pascal	Pa	N/m^2
	Work	joule	J	$N \cdot m$

SI prefixes	Multiplication Factor	Prefix	SI Symbol
	$1\ 000\ 000\ 000\ 000 = 10^{12}$	tera	T
	$1\ 000\ 000\ 000 = 10^{9}$	giga	G
	$1\ 000\ 000 = 10^{6}$	mega	M
	$1\ 000 = 10^{3}$	kilo	k
	$0.01 = 10^{-2}$	centi[b]	c
	$0.001 = 10^{-3}$	milli	m
	$0.000\ 001 = 10^{-6}$	micro	μ
	$0.000\ 000\ 001 = 10^{-9}$	nano	n
	$0.000\ 000\ 000\ 001 = 10^{-12}$	pico	p

[a] Source: ASTM Standard for Metric Practice E 380–97, 1997.
[b] To be avoided where possible.

G-1 UNIT CONVERSIONS

The data needed to solve problems are not always available in consistent units. Thus it often is necessary to convert from one system of units to another.

In principle, all derived units can be expressed in terms of basic units. Then, only conversion factors for basic units would be required.

In practice, many engineering quantities are expressed in terms of defined units, for example, the horsepower, British thermal unit (Btu), quart, or nautical mile. Definitions for such quantities are necessary, and additional conversion factors are useful in calculations.

Basic SI units and necessary conversion factors, plus a few definitions and convenient conversion factors are given in Table G.2.

TABLE G.2 Conversion Factors and Definitions

Fundamental Dimension	English Unit	Exact SI Value	Approximate SI Value
Length	1 in.	0.0254 m	—
Mass	1 lbm	0.453 592 37 kg	0.454 kg
Temperature	1°F	5/9 K	—

Definitions:

Acceleration of gravity: $g = 9.8066$ m/s^2 ($= 32.174$ ft/s^2)

Energy: Btu (British thermal unit) $\equiv$ amount of energy required to raise the temperature of 1 lbm of water 1°F (1 Btu $= 778.2$ ft $\cdot$ lbf)

kilocalorie $\equiv$ amount of energy required to raise the temperature of 1 kg of water 1 K(1 kcal $= 4187$ J)

Length: 1 mile $= 5280$ ft; 1 nautical mile $= 6076.1$ ft $= 1852$ m (exact)

Power: 1 horsepower $\equiv 550$ ft $\cdot$ lbf/s

Pressure: 1 bar $\equiv 10^5$ Pa

Temperature: degree Fahrenheit, $T_F = \frac{9}{5} T_C + 32$ (where T_C is degrees Celsius)

degree Rankine, $T_R = T_F + 459.67$

Kelvin, $T_K = T_C + 273.15$ (exact)

Viscosity: 1 Poise $\equiv 0.1$ kg/(m $\cdot$ s)

1 Stoke $\equiv 0.0001$ m^2/s

Volume: 1 gal $\equiv 231$ in.^{3} (1 ft$^3 = 7.48$ gal)

Useful Conversion Factors:

1 lbf $= 4.448$ N

1 lbf/in.$^2 = 6895$ Pa

1 Btu $= 1055$ J

1 hp $= 746$ W $= 2545$ Btu/hr

1 kW $= 3413$ Btu/hr

1 quart $= 0.000946$ m$^3 = 0.946$ liter

1 kcal $= 3.968$ Btu

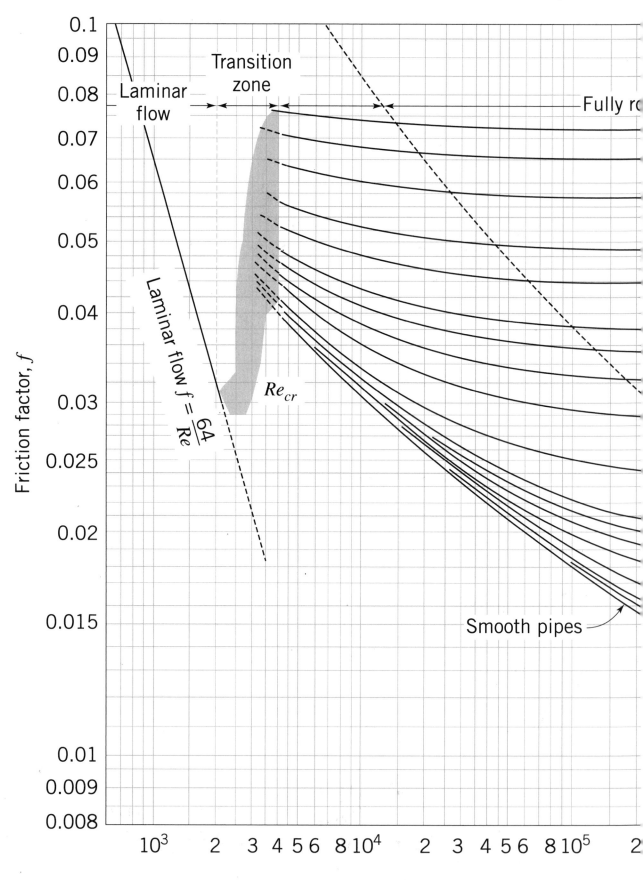